Contemporary

in B

Fifth Edition

Joseph R. DesJardins

College of St. Benedict

John J. McCall

St. Joseph's University

THOMSON
™
WADSWORTH

Australia

THOMSON

WADSWORTH

Publisher: *Holly J. Allen*
Philosophy Editor: *Steve Wainwright*
Assistant Editors: *Lee McCracken, Anna Lustig*
Editorial Assistant: *Barbara Hillaker*
Marketing Manager: *Worth Hawes*
Marketing Assistant: *Andrew Keay*
Advertising Project Managers: *Bryan Vann,
    Vicky Wan*
Composition Buyer: *Ben Schroeter*
Print/Media Buyer: *Lisa Claudeanos*

Permissions Editor: *Stephanie Lee*
Production Service: *Buuji, Inc.*
Copy Editor: *Kristina Rose McComas*
Cover Designer: *Don Kesner*
Cover Image: *Chad Baker and Ryan McVay /
PhotoDisc*
Cover Printer: *Coral Graphics*
Compositor: *Buuji, Inc.*
Text Printer: *Maple-Vail / NY*

Printed in the United States of America
1 2 3 4 5 6 7 08 07 06 05 04

For more information about our products,
contact us at:
**Thomson Learning Academic Resource Center
1-800-423-0563**

For permission to use material from this text,
contact us at:
Web: http://www.thomsonrights.com

Library of Congress Control Number: 2004102450

ISBN 0-534-58464-0

**Wadsworth/Thomson Learning
10 Davis Drive
Belmont, CA 94002-3098
USA**

Asia
Thomson Learning
5 Shenton Way #01-01
UIC Building
Singapore 068808

Australia/New Zealand
Thomson Learning
102 Dodds Street
Southbank, Victoria 3006
Australia

Canada
Nelson
1120 Birchmount Road
Toronto, Ontario M1K 5G4
Canada

Europe/Middle East/Africa
Thomson Learning
High Holborn House
50/51 Bedford Row
London WC1R 4LR
United Kingdom

Latin America
Thomson Learning
Seneca, 53
Colonia Polanco
11560 Mexico D.F.
Mexico

Spain/Portugal
Paraninfo
Calle Magallanes, 25
28015 Madrid, Spain

Brief Contents

❧

Contents

II   BUSINESS AND EMPLOYEES

5   EMPLOYEE RIGHTS: JOB SECURITY AND PARTICIPATION   113

6   EMPLOYEE RIGHTS: HEALTH, EQUALITY, PRIVACY   185

7   ETHICAL RESPONSIBILITIES IN BUSINESS: EMPLOYEES, MANAGERS, PROFESSIONALS   235

III   BUSINESS AND CONSUMERS

8   PRODUCT LIABILITY AND SAFETY   284

IV BUSINESS AND OTHER CONSTITUENCIES

Preface

When the previous edition of this textbook was published five years ago, Enron was best known to the general public as the corporate sponsor of a major league baseball stadium in Houston, Arthur Andersen was a "Big Five" accounting firm well-known for sponsoring conferences in business ethics, and a stock market boom fueled by the Internet made enormous CEO salaries seem almost reasonable. Today, Enron is a synonym for corporate corruption and greed, Arthur Andersen is out of business because of its own ethical failings, and exorbitant CEO salaries are universally vilified. The relevance and importance of business ethics has never been more obvious.

This edition has been updated with numerous new readings and cases addressing many of the events that have occurred in the past few years. New readings have been added on corporate governance, executive compensation, and the professional responsibility of accountants and auditors. New case and decision scenarios include Enron, Arthur Andersen, Martha Stewart, and market timing in the mutual fund industry.

But recent developments within business ethics have not been restricted to those brought about by corporate scandals. This edition also includes new readings and cases on meaningful work, consumerism, layoffs, sales and marketing, product safety, sustainable business, sweatshops, and global business.

Nevertheless, readers of the prior edition will recognize a familiar logical structure to this text. Thus, in Part I, we continue to introduce students to the conversation by beginning with the classic essay by Milton Friedman, "The Social Responsibility of Business Is to Increase Its Profits." Chapters 1 to 3 use this essay, and the ethical, social, and economic views it presupposes, to introduce students to the basics of philosophical ethics: utilitarianism, rights, duties, relativism, ethics and the law, and so forth. Chapter 4 examines in some depth alternative models of corporate social responsibility and corporate governance. The general conclusion from these chapters is that a philosophically adequate perspective must acknowledge that business has many ethical responsibilities beyond the narrow ones described by Friedman. To understand the full range and content of such responsibilities, we then examine business's ethical relationships with its major stakeholders: employees (Part II), consumers (Part III), and society at large (Part IV).

Likewise, this edition remains committed to the four original goals of the first edition. We seek to approach business ethics from a social and political perspective that considers the proper place of business within a society committed to democratic ideals. We also continue to bring special attention to the rights and responsibilities of employees. While many students who use this text will eventually hold managerial positions, they all, with few exceptions, will first and always be employees. Third, we seek a balance between philosophical analysis and accessibility to a wide range of student interest and abilities. We believe that this book will stimulate student interest both at first glance and after sustained study. Finally, we have presented readings and cases that reflect a wide range of disciplines and perspectives. Our readings come not only from philosophy and management, but also from law, economics, marketing, sociology, and industrial relations. Case and decision scenarios encourage students to apply the lessons from these diverse fields to practical real-world issues.

We would like to acknowledge the helpful suggestions of our reviewers: Richard Coughlan, University of Richmond; Marilyn Kaplan, University of Texas, Dallas; Michael R. Clifford, Mississippi State University; Mark A. Michael, Austin Peay State University; Daniel Primozic, Elmhurst College; Mark Bernstein, University of Texas, San Antonion; Scott Merlino, California State University, Sacramento; John W. Dienhart, Seattle University; and Robert C. Good, Rider University.

Once again, we thank everyone at Wadsworth for their support in shepherding this manuscript through the production process. We especially wish to thank Steve Wainwright, Lee McCracken, Sara Dovre Wudali, and Stephanie Lee for all their help. Finally, as always, we thank our families: Linda, Michael, and Matt in St. Cloud, and Kate and Alexa in Havertown.

1

꧁꧂

Business, Ethics, and the Free Market

INTRODUCTION

Since 2000, the year the previous edition of this textbook was published, the following companies have declared bankruptcy or gone out of business as a direct consequence of ethical corruption:

Enron—once one of the largest energy companies in the world

Arthur Andersen—formerly one of the "Big Five" accounting firms

WorldCom—the second-largest cable and long-distance provider

Adelphia Communications—the sixth-largest provider of cable services

Global Crossing—one of the world's largest providers of fiber-optic networks

In addition to many executives at each of these companies, the following senior executive officers of other major corporations have been charged by government investigators, in criminal or civil complaints, with fraud:

Al Dunlap—Sunbeam Corporation

Dennis Kozlowski—Tyco Corporation

Sam Waksal—ImClone Systems

Richard Scrushy—HealthSouth Corporation

Jeffrey Barbakow—Tenet Healthcare

Franklin Brown—Rite Aid

There are, of course, numerous institutions that are designed to prevent such abuse by providing oversight and regulation in financial markets. Boards of directors have legal and ethical obligations to oversee the activities of managers and ensure the best interests of the corporation are being served. Auditors and accountants have an obligation to conduct independent appraisals and testify to the integrity of corporate financial reports. Financial analysts have an obligation to provide truthful advice to investors. Government regulators and private oversight boards have an obligation to prevent fraud and conflicts of interest, and to promote responsible corporate governance.

Unfortunately, all of these watchdogs failed in their oversight function. In many of these cases, the very CEOs charged with corruption also held positions as chairmen of the board of directors. In such situations it would be extremely unlikely for the board to fulfill its oversight obligations. Accountants and auditors were involved in each of the scandals mentioned above, and in every case they, too, stand accused of fraud. Three of the leading worldwide financial institutions, J. P. Morgan, Citigroup, and Merrill Lynch paid more than $300 million in fines as a result of their participation in the Enron fraud. The Securities and Exchange Commission has charged other financial analysts and financial advisors at Credit Suisse First Boston, Merrill Lynch, Deutsche Bank Asset Management Division, and Citigroup Salomon Smith Barney with misleading investors by issuing fraudulent reports or by concealing conflicts of interest. Former judge William Webster resigned as chairman of the Public Company Accounting Oversight Board of the Securities and Exchange Commission when it was revealed that he had an undisclosed conflict of interest. In September of 2003, Richard Grasso resigned as chairman of the New York Stock Exchange under intense public pressure when it was revealed that he was paid $140 million the previous year.

Business is among the most powerful and influential social institutions in human history. The decisions made in business affect nearly every aspect of contemporary life. Almost half of our waking hours are spent in the workplace (at least for those of us fortunate enough to have full-time employment; for those who lack full-time work, *that* fact also is highly influenced by business decisions). What we eat, where we live, if and how we work, how we are governed, how we spend our leisure time, and how much access we have to education and health care are all strongly influenced by what happens in business.

It is crucial, therefore, that we think carefully about the ethical status of business. Businesses are not natural objects that humans have discovered; they are human institutions that humans have created. Therefore, we are responsible for the existence and structure of business institutions and must acknowledge that responsibility by monitoring the ethical dimensions of business activities.

What is the appropriate role of business in society? How should business institutions be structured to ensure that they are consistent with the fundamental values of a society? What responsibilities do businesses have to the society in which they operate? To their employees? To the consumers of the goods and services that they provide? Conversely, what responsibilities does a society have to business owners and managers? These questions make it easy to see why business ethics is relevant to every individual—as citizen, as employee, as consumer, as responsible business manager.

To understand more fully the relevance of ethics to business, it is worth considering the range of people harmed by these recent scandals. Most obviously, the individuals themselves and their families have been affected directly. In June 2003, Sam Waksal was the first of these executives to be sentenced to jail. He was sentenced to more than seven years in prison and had to pay over $4.3 million in fines and restitution. News reports at the time suggested that his decision to plead guilty was motivated by his desire to protect his family and friends from facing similar criminal charges. While some of the individuals involved in these cases may walk away with large amounts of money, most face years of legal and financial troubles, and social dishonor. Their families, in many cases innocent of any wrongdoing themselves, face similar burdens.

The employees of these firms have been harmed in many ways as well. Tens of thousands of innocent people lost their jobs because of these scandals. As a result, thousands of innocent families lost their income, health care insurance, and retirement funds. Consumers who relied on the services and products of these firms suffered as well. Tenet Healthcare settled criminal charges relating to unnecessary heart surgeries being performed at their facilities. Consumers in California suffered from electricity brownouts and blackouts that allegedly resulted from Enron's manipulation of energy trading.

Investors have suffered significantly from every one of these scandals. Quite literally, billions of dollars have been lost by investors due to the fraud and corruption within these companies. There is little doubt that these scandals undermined investor confidence in financial markets and that this contributed to a lengthening of the economic downturn. It is also fair to say that the general public has been harmed as well. Much of the public pressure on Richard Grasso came from the state treasurers of such states as New York and California, who did not want hundreds of millions of dollars in public funds jeopardized by negligent and imprudent regulators.

In light of these scandals, one would think that the case for the centrality of ethics to a business education would be made. It would be impossible even to begin talking about these cases without using the language, concepts, and categories of ethics. In this way, a course in business ethics would seem as central to a business education as courses in managerial accounting, marketing, human resource management, and all the other core disciplines of a business curriculum. Yet despite this, skepticism about the relevance of ethics to business remains. Many people simply think that ethics is irrelevant to business. To counter this common perception, this chapter will make the case for the need to study ethics in a business setting.

WHAT IS ETHICS?

Ethics is all about choices. What kind of person should I be? What should I do? How should I behave? What should I value? In what type of society ought we live? The Greek philosopher Socrates claimed that "the unexamined life is not worth living," and this statement captures the essence of an ethical life. Every single day each one of us faces innumerable ethical questions that boil down to perhaps the most fundamental question of all: How should I live my life? Answering these questions is unavoidable; we either go through life explicitly answering these questions, or we implicitly answer them by the choices we make each day.

In thinking about ethics it will be helpful to distinguish between two different senses of ethics. The word *ethics* itself is derived from the Greek word *ethos,* meaning "custom." In this sense, "business ethics" would refer to the actual customs, attitudes, values, and rules that operate within the business world. But from the earliest days of Greek philosophy, philosophers have not been satisfied with simply identifying what is customary with what is right. "Ethics" also refers to an intellectual and academic discipline, a subfield within philosophy, which studies and evaluates those customs, values, and rules by which people actually live. In this way, "business ethics" is understood as an academic discipline that evaluates the customary values and behavior of business. Thus, "ethics" in the first sense is the phenomenon that is studied by "ethics" in the second sense. "Ethics" in this first sense *describes* how people behave while "ethics" in the second sense is normative; it *prescribes* how we should behave. This textbook is a book about normative ethics.

It is fair to say that Western philosophy was born in Socrates' lifelong critical examination of the customary norms of Greek society. Philosophical ethics asks us to step back and abstract ourselves from the actual practices of society to analyze and evaluate those practices. Socrates described philosophy as the gadfly that buzzes around a noble, but sluggish, horse. The role of the gadfly (business ethics) is to prod the horse (business and society) out of complacency and keep it moving forward. Failing to do so is to live an unexamined life. The consequence of this is that one effectively sleepwalks through life, uncritically accepting the norms, values, and expectations of one's environment. This, Socrates tells us, is to live a life less than fully human and not worth living.

Returning to the skepticism about business ethics mentioned earlier, we see that it amounts to the claim that philosophical ethics are somehow irrelevant to the practice of business. In the remainder of this chapter, we examine two common versions of this skepticism. *Ethical relativism* holds that there are no objective or rational standards by which one can judge business. A second view, associated with defenders of free market economics, claims that business practices and customs already are ethical and therefore it is unnecessary to bring in external philosophical standards to judge the ethics of business.

ETHICAL RELATIVISM

Ethical relativists hold that all ethical beliefs and values are *relative* to one's own culture, religion, or feelings. "Ethics" truly is nothing more than "ethos" or custom. Relativists therefore deny that there are any objective or rational standards that can be applied across cultures or religions, or between individuals. The most common expression of relativism is found in the rhetorical question "Who's to say what is right or wrong?" Relativism poses a serious challenge because if it is true that there is no rational way to decide what is right or wrong, then business ethics, and indeed any philosophical ethics, is a waste of time. More importantly, without some rational standard that is independent of culture, religions, and individual beliefs, we are left with only power to settle conflicts. If there are no objective or rational standards by which we can judge if some customary norm is right or wrong, just or fair, then whoever has the ability and power to do so will establish those norms.

Fortunately, several considerations count strongly against the validity of ethical relativism. First, we should be careful to distinguish what people *believe* is right or wrong from what *is* right or wrong. It is true that beliefs about right and wrong, justice and fairness, differ among cultures, religions, and individuals. Some particular culture or religion might believe, for example, that women are inferior beings who deserve to be treated as slaves. But *believing* that this is right does not make it right.

What is sometimes called *cultural relativism* acknowledges the fact that cultures disagree about many beliefs and values. If this is all that ethical relativism involves, there would be little cause for worry. But ethical relativism is not just this descriptive claim; it is a normative viewpoint that claims there can be no objective or rational standards by which we can resolve disputes and disagreements.

The first consideration that counts against the plausibility of ethical relativism is simply to point out that the truth of cultural relativism—the fact that cultures disagree—is not evidence that objective agreement is impossible. After all, some cultures have believed that the earth is flat or at the center of the universe. But no matter how many people believe the earth is flat, it still remains round. If ethical relativism is to be defended, it must rely on something other than the fact that people disagree about what is right or wrong, just and fair, good or bad.

Second, we must be careful not to confuse tolerance and respect for diversity with relativism. Many of us believe that we should respect diverse cultures and tolerate a wide diversity within and among cultures. But, we must recognize that the very values cited in defending these conclusions—tolerance and respect—must be assumed to be ethically rational and objective. When one claims that diversity *ought* to be respected, one has made an ethical judgment. Either respect and tolerance are values that are rationally defensible, in which case we are justified in making those judgments, or respect and tolerance are themselves relative to one's own culture, in which case someone who disagrees has no reason to accept our prescriptions. The values of respect and tolerance are not reasons for accepting the legitimacy of ethical relativism.

This raises a third consideration. We need to be careful to distinguish disagreement about ethical principles from disagreement about particular judgments based on those principles. It may turn out that there is less disagreement about ethical principles than many relativists assume. The United Nations Universal Declaration of Human Rights, for example, was adopted without dissent. Every country in the world formally agrees to it. Of course, people do not always live up to their commitments, and there is wide disagreement over the application of general principles such as the right to life and liberty. Again, disagreement alone does not prove the ethical relativist conclusion. In fact, disagreement over the application of an agreed-upon principle calls for more, rather than less, ethical reasoning.

A fourth consideration reminds us not to ask too much of ethics. It is tempting to think that if ethical judgments cannot be proven beyond a doubt, and if one cannot persuade others to accept ethical conclusions, then they must be relative and unreasonable. But surely few, if any, of our rational beliefs can be proven beyond a doubt. Logicians would call this the fallacy of a false dilemma: either a judgment can be proven beyond a doubt or it is unreasonable. Ethics, like most other fields of inquiry, relies on a standard better understood as "rational justification" than as "certain proof." If we can give reasons to support our ethical views, if they can withstand criticism, if they are consistent with the facts, and if they are coherent with other deeply held values, then we can be rationally justified in holding them. If we hold ethics to a standard of certain proof—attainable in mathematics, perhaps, but in few other fields—then we will be unlikely to ever prove anything in ethics. However, if we use standards of rational justification—standards common in such diverse fields as medicine, history, and law—then we can be as justified in our ethical judgments as we are in medical, historical, and legal judgments.

Finally, we must recognize the costs involved in being a consistent ethical relativist. The relativist must claim that there is no reasonable and objective basis for establishing that freedom is better than slavery, democracy is better than totalitarianism, heroism is better than murder, and friendship is better than hatred. The relativist must claim that there is no rational ethical difference between a parent who loves and nurtures her child and the one who abuses and murders her child. Relativists deny objectivity in ethics because, after all, "Who is to say what's right or wrong?" and, as suggested by economist Milton Freidman in the essay that follows, "One man's good is another's evil." These examples suggest how dangerous such relativist conclusions can be.

Of course, one of the best ways to assess the objectivity of ethical reasoning is to participate in ethical reasoning. We turn now to the second source of skepticism about the relevance of ethics, the view that holds that business practices already are ethical and therefore it is unnecessary to bring in external philosophical standards to judge the ethics of business. We invite you to participate in some ethical reasoning to assess the validity of that position.

BUSINESS ETHICS:
THE "FREE MARKET" THEORY

The second source of skepticism about business ethics holds that philosophical business ethics is unnecessary because an adequate ethical code already governs normal business practice. That ethical view is implicit within the economic system of free market capitalism.

In much of Europe, Asia, and North America, but especially in the United States, there is a specific theory of business ethics that is implicit in the thinking of many people. What we will be calling the "free enterprise" or "free market" theory provides a systematic view of the proper role of business in society. For many people, especially for many business owners and managers as well as many economists, this theory functions as the "official" ethics of business. Like the moral customs and norms that Socrates discovered when he questioned the Athenian leaders, this theory can serve as our own starting point for philosophical analysis.

In general, the free market theory tells us that business managers have one overriding responsibility: to maximize the profits of business owners. This responsibility is constrained only by the responsibility to avoid fraud and coercion, and the obligation to obey the law. This theory also holds that government's responsibility is to protect the workings of the free market and otherwise remain out of economic matters. Markets should be "free" in the sense that individuals should be allowed to make choices free from outside interference, both from other individuals and from government regulation.

This free market perspective can be thought of as providing a normative ethics, offering analyses of and prescriptions for most issues of business ethics. We will see the free market perspective defended in most of the chapters of this book. While we believe that ultimately it is an unsatisfactory ethical philosophy, it remains an influential, popular, and highly regarded standpoint. Even if you do not agree with it, this perspective deserves your close consideration.

Fortunately, free market ethics has many articulate defenders. One such defender is the economist Milton Friedman, who sketches this view in the now classic article that follows. As you read through this article, begin your practice of philosophical ethics by asking the types of questions described in this introduction. Why is Friedman's view an ethical position? What values and norms does he appeal to? What, exactly, does he see as the proper role of business in society? How might Friedman respond to the skeptic who suggests that ethics is irrelevant to business managers and business owners? What responsibilities do business managers have? Consider what Friedman might say about the corporate scandals mentioned at the beginning of this chapter. What is the proper relationship between business and government? What reasons are offered to support this view? Are the reasons convincing?

READING 1.1 THE SOCIAL RESPONSIBILITY OF BUSINESS IS TO INCREASE ITS PROFITS

Milton Friedman

When I hear businessmen speak eloquently about the "social responsibilities of business in a free-enterprise system," I am reminded of the wonderful line about the Frenchman who discovered at the age of 70 that he had been speaking prose all his life. The businessmen believe that they are defending free enterprise when they declaim that business is not concerned "merely" with profit but also with promoting desirable "social" ends; that business has a "social conscience" and takes seriously its responsibilities for providing employment, eliminating discrimination, avoiding pollution and whatever else may be the catchwords of the contemporary crop of reformers. In fact they are—or would be if they or anyone else took them seriously—preaching pure and unadulterated socialism. Businessmen who talk this way are unwitting puppets of the intellectual forces that have been undermining the basis of a free society these past decades.

The discussions of the "social responsibilities of business" are notable for their analytical looseness and lack of rigor. What does it mean to say that "business" has responsibilities? Only people can have responsibilities. A corporation is an artificial person and in this sense may have artificial responsibilities, but "business" as a whole cannot be said to have responsibilities, even in this vague sense. The first step toward clarity in examining the doctrine of the social responsibility of business is to ask precisely what it implies for whom.

Presumably, the individuals who are to be responsible are businessmen, which means individual proprietors or corporate executives. Most of the discussion of social responsibility is directed at corporations, so in what follows I shall mostly neglect the individual proprietor and speak of corporate executives.

In a free-enterprise, private-property system a corporate executive is an employee of the owners of the business. He has direct responsibility to his employers. That responsibility is to conduct the business in accordance with their desires, which generally will be to make as much money as possible while conforming to the basic rules of the society, both those embodied in law and those embodied in ethical custom. Of course, in some cases his employers may have a different objective. A group of persons might establish a corporation for an eleemosynary purpose—for example, a hospital or a school. The manager of such a corporation will not have money profit as his objective but the rendering of certain services.

In either case, the key point is that, in his capacity as a corporate executive, the manager is the agent of the individuals who own the corporation or establish the eleemosynary institution, and his primary responsibility is to them.

Needless to say, this does not mean that it is easy to judge how well he is performing his task. But at least the criterion of performance is straightforward, and the persons among whom a voluntary contractual arrangement exists are clearly defined.

Of course, the corporate executive is also a person in his own right. As a person, he may have many other responsibilities that he recognizes or assumes voluntarily—to his family, his conscience, his feelings of charity, his church, his clubs, his city, his country. He may feel impelled by these responsibilities to devote part of his income to causes he regards as worthy, to refuse to work for particular corporations, and even to leave his job, for example, to join his country's armed forces. If we wish, we may refer to some of these responsibilities as "social responsibilities." But in these respects he is acting as a principal, not an agent; he is spending his own money or time or energy, not the money of his employers or the time or energy he has contracted to devote to their purposes. If these are "social responsibilities," they are the social responsibilities of individuals, not of business.

What does it mean to say that the corporate executive has a "social responsibility" in his capacity as businessman? If this statement is not pure rhetoric, it must mean that he is to act in some way that is not in the interest of his employers. For example, that he is to refrain from increasing the price of the product in order to contribute to the social objective of preventing inflation, even though a price increase would be in the best interests of the corporation. Or that he is to make expenditures on reducing pollution beyond the amount that is in the best interests of the corporation or that is required by law in order to contribute to the social objective of improving the environment. Or that, at the expense of corporate profits, he is to hire "hard-core" unemployed instead of better-qualified available workmen to contribute to the social objective of reducing poverty.

In each of these cases, the corporate executive would be spending someone else's money for a general social interest. Insofar as his actions in accord with his "social responsibility" reduce returns to stockholders, he is spending their money. Insofar as his actions raise the price to customers, he is spending the customers' money. Insofar as his actions lower the wages of some employees, he is spending their money.

The stockholders or the customers or the employees could separately spend their own money on the particular action if they wished to do so. The executive is exercising a distinct "social responsibility," rather than serving as an agent of the stockholders or the customers or the employees, only if he spends the money in a different way than they would have spent it.

But if he does this, he is in effect imposing taxes, on the one hand, and deciding how the tax proceeds shall be spent, on the other.

This process raises political questions on two levels: principle and consequences. On the level of political principle, the imposition of taxes and the expenditure of tax proceeds are governmental functions. We have established elaborate constitutional, parliamentary and judicial provisions to control these functions, to assure that taxes are imposed so far as possible in accordance with the preferences and desires of the public—after all, "taxation without representation" was one of the battle cries of the American Revolution. We have a system of checks and balances to separate the legislative function of imposing taxes and enacting expenditures from the executive function of collecting taxes and administering expenditure programs and from the judicial function of mediating disputes and interpreting the law.

Here the businessman—self-selected or appointed directly or indirectly by stockholders—is to be simultaneously legislator, executive and jurist. He is to decide whom to tax by how much and for what purpose, and he is to spend the proceeds—all this guided only by general exhortations from on high to restrain inflation, improve the environment, fight poverty and so on and on.

The whole justification for permitting the corporate executive to be selected by the stockholders is that the executive is an agent serving the interests of his principal. This justification disappears when the corporate executive imposes taxes and spends the proceeds for "social" purposes. He becomes in effect a public employee, a civil servant, even though he remains in name an employee of a private enterprise. On grounds of political principle, it is intolerable that such civil servants—insofar as their actions in the name of social responsibility are real and not just window dressing—should be selected as they are now. If they are to be civil servants, then they must be selected through a political process. If they are to impose taxes and make expenditures to foster "social" objectives, then political machinery must be set up to guide the assessment of taxes and to determine through a political process the objectives to be served.

This is the basic reason why the doctrine of "social responsibility" involves the acceptance of the socialist view that political mechanisms, not market mechanisms, are the appropriate way to determine the allocation of scarce resources to alternative uses.

On the grounds of consequences, can the corporate executive in fact discharge his alleged "social responsibilities"? On the one hand, suppose he could get away with spending the stockholders' or customers' or employees' money. How is he to know how to spend it? He is told that he must contribute to fighting inflation. How is he to know what action of his will contribute to that end? He is presumably an expert in running his company—in producing a product or selling it or financing it. But nothing about his selection makes him an expert on inflation. Will his holding down the price of his product reduce inflationary pressure? Or, by leaving more spending power in the hands of his customers, simply divert it elsewhere? Or, by forcing him to produce less because of the lower price, will it simply contribute to shortages? Even if he could answer these questions, how much cost is he justified in imposing on his stockholders, customers and employees for this social purpose? What is his appropriate share and the share of others?

And, whether he wants to or not, can he get away with spending his stockholders', customers' or employees' money? Will not the stockholders fire him? (Either the present ones or those who take over when his actions in the name of social responsibility have reduced the corporation's profits and the price of its stock.) His customers and his employees can desert him for other producers and employers less scrupulous in exercising their social responsibilities.

This facet of "social responsibility" doctrine is brought into sharp relief when the doctrine is used to justify wage restraint by trade unions. The conflict of interest is naked and clear when union officials are asked to subordinate the interest of their members to some more general social purpose. If the union officials try to enforce wage restraint, the consequence is likely to be wildcat strikes, rank-and-file revolts and the emergence of strong competitors for their jobs. We thus have the ironic phenomenon that union leaders—at least in the U.S.—have objected to Government interference with the market far more consistently and courageously than have business leaders.

The difficulty of exercising "social responsibility" illustrates, of course, the great virtue of private competitive enterprise—it forces people to be responsible for their own actions and makes it difficult for them to "exploit" other people for either selfish or unselfish purposes. They can do good—but only at their own expense.

Many a reader who has followed the argument this far may be tempted to remonstrate that it is all well and good to speak of government's having the responsibility to impose taxes and determine expenditures for such "social" purposes as controlling pollution or training the hardcore unemployed, but that the problems are too urgent to wait on the slow course of political processes, that the exercise of social responsibility by businessmen is a quicker and surer way to solve pressing current problems.

Aside from the question of fact—I share Adam Smith's skepticism about the benefits that can be expected from "those who affected to trade for the public good"—this argument must be rejected on grounds of principle. What it amounts to is an assertion that those who favor the taxes and expenditures in question have failed to persuade a majority of their fellow citizens to be of like mind and that they are seeking to attain by undemocratic procedures what they cannot attain by democratic procedures. In a free society, it is hard for "good" people to do "good," but that is a small price to pay for making it hard for "evil" people to do "evil," especially since one man's good is another's evil.

I have, for simplicity, concentrated on the special case of the corporate executive, except only for the brief digression on trade unions. But precisely the same argument applies to the newer phenomenon of calling upon stockholders to require corporations to exercise social responsibility (the recent G.M. crusade, for example). In most of these cases, what is in effect involved is some stockholders trying to get other stockholders (or customers or employees) to contribute against their will to "social" causes favored by the activists. Insofar as they succeed, they are again imposing taxes and spending the proceeds.

The situation of the individual proprietor is somewhat different. If he acts to reduce the returns of his enterprise in order to exercise his "social responsibility," he is spending his own money, not someone else's. If he wishes to spend his money on such purposes, that is his right, and I cannot see that there is any objection to his doing so. In the process, he, too, may impose costs on employees and customers. However, because he is far less likely than a large corporation or union to have monopolistic power, any such side effects will tend to be minor.

Of course, in practice the doctrine of social responsibility is frequently a cloak for actions that are justified on other grounds rather than a reason for those actions.

To illustrate, it may well be in the long-run interest of a corporation that is a major employer in a small community to devote resources to providing amenities to that community or to improving its government. That may make it easier to attract desirable employees, it may reduce the wage bill or lessen losses from pilferage and sabotage or have other worthwhile effects. Or it may be that, given the laws about the deductibility of corporate charitable contributions, the stockholders can contribute more to charities they favor by having the corporation make the gift than by doing it themselves, since they can in that way contribute an amount that would otherwise have been paid as corporate taxes.

In each of these—and many similar—cases, there is a strong temptation to rationalize these actions as an exercise of "social responsibility." In the present climate of opinion, with its widespread aversion to "capitalism," "profits," the "soulless corporation" and so on, this is one way for a corporation to generate goodwill as a by-product of expenditures that are entirely justified in its own self-interest.

It would be inconsistent of me to call on corporate executives to refrain from this hypocritical window-dressing because it harms the foundations of a free society. That would be to call on them to exercise a "social responsibility"! If our institutions, and the attitudes of the public make it in their self-interest to cloak their actions in this way, I cannot summon much indignation to denounce them. At the same time, I can express admiration for those individual proprietors or owners of closely held corporations or stockholders of more broadly held corporations who disdain such tactics as approaching fraud.

Whether blameworthy or not, the use of the cloak of social responsibility, and the nonsense spoken in its name by influential and prestigious businessmen, does clearly harm the foundations of a free society. I have been impressed time and again by the schizophrenic character of many businessmen. They are capable of being extremely far-sighted and clear-headed in matters that are internal to their businesses. They are incredibly short-sighted and muddle-headed in matters that are outside their businesses but affect the possible survival of business in general. This short-sightedness is strikingly exemplified in the calls from many businessmen for wage and price guidelines or controls or income policies. There is nothing that could do more in a brief period to destroy a market system and replace it by a centrally controlled system than effective governmental control of prices and wages.

The short-sightedness is also exemplified in speeches by businessmen on social responsibility. This may gain them kudos in the short run. But it helps to strengthen the already too prevalent view that the pursuit of profits is wicked and immoral and must be curbed and controlled by external forces. Once this view is adopted, the external forces that curb the market will not be the social consciences, however highly developed, of the pontificating executives; it will be the iron fist of Government bureaucrats. Here, as with price and wage controls, businessmen seem to me to reveal a suicidal impulse.

The political principle that underlies the market mechanism is unanimity. In an ideal free market resting on private property, no individual can coerce any other, all cooperation is voluntary, all parties to such cooperation benefit or they need not participate. There are no "social" values, no "social" responsibilities in any sense other than the shared values and responsibilities of individuals. Society is a collection of individuals and of the various groups they voluntarily form.

The political principle that underlies the political mechanism is conformity. The individual must serve a more general social interest—whether that be determined by a church or a dictator or a majority. The individual may have a vote and a say in what is to be done, but if he is overruled, he must conform. It is appropriate for some to require others to contribute to a general social purpose whether they wish to or not.

Unfortunately, unanimity is not always feasible. There are some respects in which conformity appears unavoidable, so I do not see how one can avoid the use of the political mechanism altogether.

But the doctrine of "social responsibility" taken seriously would extend the scope of the political mechanism to every human activity. It does not differ in philosophy from the most explicitly collectivist doctrine. It differs only by professing to believe that collectivist ends can be attained without collectivist means. That is why, in my book *Capitalism and Freedom,* I have called it a "fundamentally subversive doctrine" in a free society, and have said that in such a society, "there is one and only one social responsibility of business—to use its resources and engage in activities designed to increase its profits so long as it stays within the rules of the game, which is to say, engages in open and free competition without deception or fraud."

DOING BUSINESS ETHICS:
AN ANALYSIS OF FRIEDMAN

Before beginning the analysis of Friedman's essay, it would be useful to review the discussion of ethical relativism (pp. 4–6). Ethical discussions often deal with deeply held values and attitudes. They often challenge us to examine and perhaps even change some of the beliefs that we simultaneously take for granted and hold most dear. The standards of evidence and reasoning in ethics are not as obvious as they might be in such fields as science and math. For these reasons, we should go slowly as we begin our ethical analysis, examining Friedman's essay closely and carefully. We offer this analysis as a model for the type of analysis that you should do for each of the essays in this text. In what follows, we not only offer an analysis of Friedman, but we also hope to call your attention to the type of reasoning that will be helpful in what follows throughout this book.

Let us begin our practice of philosophical ethics by developing a clear understanding of Friedman's ethical views. Following common usage, we will refer to the views expressed in this essay as the "classical model of corporate social responsibility." It is a viewpoint that connects the responsibility of business management with the underlying economic theory of free market capitalism. We call this view "classical" in two senses: First, as previously mentioned, it is a view that has been presupposed by many people in Western culture; second, it is a view of business and industry that is derived from classical, free market economics.

The classical model offers recommendations and norms for the responsibilities of business managers. These responsibilities follow from the role of business in a free market economic system. This economic system itself is justified by appeal to certain ethical values. To understand these claims we now turn to a closer examination of Friedman's essay.

First, we should be clear that Friedman is advocating a position within normative ethics. When he recommends that business managers seek only to "increase profits" and "make as much money as possible," he is not suggesting that managers ignore ethical responsibilities and simply pursue their own greed and self-interest. Rather, he suggests that in pursuing maximum profits a business manager is fulfilling her responsibility to society and doing what is ethically correct.

Friedman also is doing more than descriptive ethics; he does much more than describe what, in fact, occurs in business. If Friedman's recommendations were followed, we would be required to change our business, social, and political institutions dramatically.

Finally, Friedman is not merely offering his *opinion* about what one should do in business. He presents numerous *reasons* to support these recommendations and, in this way, he is involved in doing *normative ethics*. Friedman does not simply accept what is customary in business practice. He steps back from what is actually occurring within business (the widespread assumption that business has a "social responsibility" to "promote desirable 'social' ends") and offers a reasoned critique of these practices. In his view, the doctrine of social responsibility violates important social norms and is therefore ethically irresponsible. Let us look more closely at these normative ethical claims.

Friedman begins by noting discussions of businesses' "social responsibilities" that suggest that business has responsibilities above and beyond profit. He then presents reasons to criticize this account of corporate social responsibility, and he presents reasons that support his own alternative theory. In arguing against the social responsibility thesis, Friedman suggests that to sacrifice profits for the sake of some "social objective" like "providing employment, eliminating discrimination, [and] avoiding pollution" is potentially to become "unwitting puppets of the intellectual forces that have been undermining the basis of a free society." This doctrine of social responsibility is called a "fundamentally subversive doctrine in a free society." Thus, Friedman rejects the business practice of pursuing social objectives because doing so violates certain fundamental norms of a free society.

In arguing to support his own alternative, Friedman appeals to the values of a "free-enterprise, private-property system" and concludes that in such a system a business manager's "primary" and "direct" responsibility is to act in accord with the desires and interests of the business owners. In all but the exceptional case, this means that the business manager's responsibility "will be to make as much money as possible while conforming to the basic rules of society, both those embodied in law and those embodied in ethical custom." To do otherwise, according to Friedman, is to usurp the role of duly elected government officials by imposing taxes on other individuals and by deciding how those taxes are to be spent.

Thus, we can see that the classical model of corporate social responsibility advances numerous normative ethical claims. It makes recommendations about how we as individuals *ought* to act within business ("act always so as to maximize profits") and about how we as citizens *ought* to arrange our social institutions ("business ought to be free from government interference in its pursuit of profits").

Friedman's Radical Position

In the analysis above, we can begin to see a wide gap between the actual society in which we live and the society envisioned by Friedman's normative ethics. In terms of requiring changes in customarily accepted behavior, Friedman's recommendations are quite radical. He offers a normative principle that will, on every occasion, determine our ethical responsibilities. He tells us that an ethical individual in business must always make the decision that will increase profits. He tells us that any government intervention in the market is ethically wrong. In other words, business managers need only look to their accountants, lawyers, and economists to determine their ethical responsibilities. The manager need not, and should not, be concerned with such issues as fairness, unemployment, or compassion for employees. Managers need only calculate costs and benefits and consult their lawyers before adopting whatever policy will maximize profits. So, too, with any other moral or public policy issue. Business managers can and should ignore all other ethical considerations for the sake of one overriding principle: Maximize profits.

This perspective is quite radical for a number of reasons. First, it conflicts with our ordinary understanding of ethical responsibilities. Ordinarily, it seems that our ethical responsibilities, on occasion at least, will require us to restrict our own behavior out of consideration for the well-being of others. Friedman tells us that, at least in our role as business managers, we can best fulfill our responsibilities to others by ignoring their interests and pursuing our own self-interest.★

This perspective is also radical in its political implications. Imagine a society in which government does not interfere with the economy except to prevent or rectify the harms done by fraud and coercion. Some government regulation of the

---

★Friedman's view is reminiscent of the conclusion of Adam Smith (1723–1790). In *The Wealth of Nations,* the earliest exposition of market economics, Smith claimed that widespread pursuit of individual self-interest within the structure of a free market would result, as if led by "an invisible hand," in the attainment of the greater overall good.

market could be accepted. The Securities and Exchange Commission, for example, might be justified as protection against security fraud or insider trading. Public utilities commissions might be required on local levels to set prices in ways that mimic the market in cases where natural monopolies exist. But there would be little, if any, role for such regulatory agencies as the Occupational Safety and Health Administration, the Environmental Protection Agency, the Consumer Products Safety Commission, the Food and Drug Administration, the Nuclear Regulatory Agency, or the Federal Deposit Insurance Commission. More dramatically, any taxation for reasons other than for policing the free market would be an unethical interference with the market. (Imagine the effect that this recommendation would have on the legal and accounting professions!) Such governmental departments and programs as Education, Health and Human Services, unemployment compensation, Social Security, or Medicare would all be unethical interferences with a free society. Finally, even government activities that seek to promote economic growth would be unethical. Aid to interstate commerce in such forms as highway, railroad, and airport subsidies; aid to specific industries like farming, oil, steel, automobiles; and government regulation of international trade through import quotas and tariffs would also be rejected if we adopted Friedman's normative ethics.

So far, we have not offered a criticism of Friedman's views. We have characterized Friedman's position as radical not because we disagree with him on the issues. Rather, we believe that each of these issues should be examined in turn on its merits. This is, after all, the only intellectually responsible approach, and it is the approach that a textbook especially needs to adopt. But part of the intellectual responsibility requires us to examine clearly the normative views of others. In doing ethics, we need to understand not only the specific claims of normative positions, but also the logical implications of these positions. The classical model of corporate social responsibility, as represented by Friedman's essay, asks us to change dramatically many of our standard ways of thinking and living. We should, therefore, expect good reasons offered to justify such fundamental changes.

Upon further examination, it might turn out that in any particular case Friedman's normative recommendation to maximize profits will be the reasonable one. It might turn out, for example, that regulating consumer product safety is best left to the workings of a competitive market. In challenging Friedman's views, we do not want to defend the equally radical position that in every case one must forsake profit in the pursuit of other moral responsibilities. Despite offering a critical evaluation of the classical model in this chapter, we will return to give a fair hearing to this perspective on many specific issues throughout the remainder of this text.

Free Society

Let us now examine the ethical reasoning that Friedman uses to defend his normative conclusions. He claims that a doctrine of social responsibility requiring business managers to sacrifice profits for other social objectives subverts our free society. The assumption here seems to be that a "free society" is identical to the type of society envisioned in Friedman's essay—that is, a society with totally free markets in which government's role is restricted to the prevention of coercion and fraud and where business is free to operate on a principle of self-interested pursuit of profit. Is this assumption valid?

The term *free society* has tremendous emotional appeal and a very positive connotation. An important rule to follow when we are reasoning about ethics is that we should be careful not to let appeals to emotion cloud our thinking or end the discussion. (Logicians call this *argumentum ad misocordium,* or "argument from emotion," and characterize such an appeal as a logical fallacy when it is used to persuade us to accept a conclusion.) Presumably "free society" refers to *democratic* political structures in which the ultimate authority for making political decisions rests in the hands of the voting population. It would be difficult to defend a society as free if it denied political participation to its citizens and gave authority only to some political elite.

But political thinkers for centuries have recognized that democratic structures alone do not guarantee freedom. Majorities can be just as tyrannical as minorities. For this reason, free societies also extend to their citizens a wide range of individual social and civil liberties. Among these liberties are freedom of speech, freedom of religion, freedom of the press, and the right to own and control private and productive property. As is the case in the United States and most contemporary democracies, these liberties are protected by constitutional restrictions on the freedom of the majority. The Bill of Rights to the U.S. Constitution, for example, limits the freedom of the majority when the First Amendment begins with "Congress shall make no laws which . . . ." Thus, we can see in the notion of a constitutional democracy that the concept of a free society is complex, typically involving trade-offs between many different forms of freedom.

Historically, the economic liberties and rights of individuals found expression in essentially *capitalist* or *free market* economic systems. In general, economic systems involve the social practices that determine how economic goods and services are *produced* and how they are *distributed.* Capitalism is an economic system in which the means of production are privately owned and in which economic distribution occurs through the workings of a free market.

Thus, capitalism is an *economic* system distinct from the *political* system of democracy. We could easily envision a society with widespread political freedoms without capitalist economic structures (the democratic socialist societies of many European countries, for example). We can also envision societies with capitalist economic structures (private individuals owning the means of production and unregulated markets to distribute these products) and few democratic and civil liberties. Historically, many dictatorships throughout Central and South America fit this model.

While these issues will be examined in more detail in Chapter Three, we can draw some lessons here. The crucial thing to note is that freedom is not an either/ or concept—either you have freedom, or you do not. Rather, there are many different freedoms, and a free society inevitably will involve trade-offs among these freedoms. Sometimes the freedom of the majority is limited by the freedom of the minority, as when, for example, mandatory prayer is prohibited in public schools even when the majority of citizens would want it. Sometimes my freedom to communicate privately with you comes into conflict with my employer's freedom to control and regulate the e-mail system at work. Sometimes economic freedoms are restricted by civil liberties, as when private business owners are prohibited from discriminating on the basis of race or sex in employment.

Furthermore, because democracy and capitalism are different concepts, it does not follow that a free society is threatened or subverted by restrictions upon the sort of capitalist economy that Friedman defends. Most of us would consider the United States a free society even though it falls far short of the laissez-faire capitalist society that Friedman envisions. When a business manager sacrifices profits for some social objective, she may well be restricting the freedom of stockholders to direct their property, but she may be doing it to increase the freedom of others to enjoy unpolluted air or a nondiscriminatory workplace. Friedman is simply wrong, then, when he claims that sacrificing profits for social objectives like "providing employment, eliminating discrimination, [and] avoiding pollution" undermines the basis of a free society.

The "Tax Argument"

Friedman's only other explicit argument is what we might call the "tax argument." Here he claims that business managers who act against the economic interests of the firm to achieve some social objective such as lowering unemployment are, in effect, imposing taxes on the owners, consumers, and/or employees in order to benefit society. Friedman tells us that imposing such taxes is wrong on two levels: principle and consequences. It is wrong in principle because it violates the political principle that taxes should not be imposed by private individuals. It is wrong at the level of consequences because business managers lack the expertise to solve social problems.

Before we begin a careful assessment of this argument, we should again take care when using emotionally charged language. Friedman speaks of "taxes" here, and many of us will have an automatic negative reaction to taxes. But we need to be careful that we not prejudge the question and accept Friedman's conclusion simply because he has chosen a rhetorically persuasive term. Again, this would be to fall victim of a logical fallacy. To avoid this temptation, we should translate Friedman's tax language into a more neutral discussion of costs. This should be unobjectionable, since the manager's decision doesn't really impose taxes in the traditional sense of government levies, but does add costs that otherwise would not exist. So hereafter we will speak of a manager's expenditures on social objectives that reduce profits as the imposition of costs on shareholders, employees, and consumers.

Now, why is it wrong for managers to impose costs on shareholders, employees, and consumers in the pursuit of some social objective? Friedman tells us that on the level of political principle such objectives and costs should be the product of joint decisions by the citizens; unilateral imposition of such costs is contrary to accepted and ethically justified democratic political principles. Additionally, even if such unilateral actions were not wrong on principle, the likely consequences of these private decisions would be harmful to society. Thus, Friedman has offered two moral reasons to support this normative claim.

Let us deal with the consequentialist branch of the argument first. Friedman claims that management lacks the expertise for making judgments about what acts would produce the greatest net benefit to society. His example is that of a manager who tries to reduce inflation. Ordinary managers have no procedure for making a careful estimate about the consequences of their pricing policy on inflationary trends in a society.

Perhaps this is an accurate description of management expertise on the complex economic problem of inflation. But Friedman has provided no reason for thinking that there cannot be other situations where a manager does have the expertise needed to address social problems. Suppose a manufacturing firm was discharging the by-products of its production process into a nearby river. Management of this firm should have exactly the expertise needed to determine if this by-product was harmful to local residents. (Indeed, if it was harmful and management claimed ignorance of that fact, the law would likely hold them negligent for not knowing!) Suppose that, knowing this, management could eliminate this toxic discharge with expenditures that would reduce profitability but not threaten the economic viability of the firm. Again, accomplishing corporate goals in an economically efficient manner is exactly the kind of expertise that is ordinarily required of management. Now, would voluntarily stopping the discharge, an action that Friedman would prohibit unless required by law, produce negative social consequences? Presumably it would not, especially if the discharge was harmful to the health of many people and the costs were relatively minor.

Thus, whether management assumption of responsibilities beyond the narrow range defined by Friedman would have unacceptable consequences appears to depend on the particular responsibility at issue. So we cannot assume that management lacks the expertise and ability for reasonable action on the basis of any social responsibility simply because it lacks the expertise or ability in one case. In some cases, management may have exactly the expertise necessary.

Friedman's consequentialist argument commits the fallacy of overgeneralizing from a small set of examples to a universal claim about all cases. This is another important lesson to learn about logic and reasoning. When attempting to support a conclusion by appeal to a specific example, we need to avoid reaching conclusions that go beyond the evidence. Examples, in science as well as in ethics, can highlight and illustrate, but they do not by themselves prove anything. This argument must be rejected as unconvincing.

Thus, Friedman's defense of his conclusion must rest with his argument from political principle. That argument demands that the imposition of costs in pursuit of social objectives must be the result of proper political decisions. The imposition of costs by private individuals is intolerable in principle, according to Friedman.

A word about costs can help begin our analysis of this argument. As any student of introductory economics who is familiar with the concept of opportunity costs will attest, cost is a relative thing. The full cost of any purchase, policy, or decision can be measured only in relation to the alternatives that one thereby forgoes. Thus, since resources are finite, to spend money on defense spending, for example, has a cost not only in terms of dollars but more precisely in terms of the inability to use those dollars for health care or education. Similarly, when a business executive spends money to modernize production facilities of a steel plant, that spending represents a cost to shareholders in that it precludes using those same dollars for greater dividends. Note that this expenditure is a cost to employees and consumers as well because it also precludes spending those dollars for higher salaries or lower product prices.

This reveals a characteristic mark of costs: What is a cost to one person or group is usually a benefit to another. Keeping a less profitable steel mill operating is a benefit to employees but a cost to shareholders and consumers if it means lower profits or higher prices. Costs and benefits can also be exchanged for a single individual. Increased wages can be an employee benefit won at the cost of decreased corporate pension contributions or of fewer health care benefits. The economic point should be clear. Since costs are always relative to alternatives forgone, every managerial decision will involve the imposition of costs. Friedman's economic system is no exception. In that system, when a manager acts to increase profits within the rules of the game, that action carries an implicit cost for others affected by corporate policy: consumers, employees, and society at large.

With this adjustment in language, let us restate Friedman's in-principle objection to the doctrine of social responsibility. Friedman tells us that the imposition of taxes is a governmental function. Thus, the imposition of taxes by business managers is "taxation without representation" and a violation of the separation of political powers. But, when we substitute the word "costs" for "taxes," we can see the absurdity of reaching a similar conclusion. Surely Friedman would not wish to say that we ought to establish "elaborate constitutional, parliamentary and judicial provisions . . . to assure that" *costs* "are imposed so far as possible in accordance with the preferences and desires of the public." Were that true, we would be left with the type of socialist economy that Friedman disparages.

As an economist, Friedman of course recognizes that the imposition of costs is unavoidable. Therefore, his point cannot be that it is wrong in principle to impose costs on others without their consent. Thus, to be fair and not reject his conclusion too quickly, we should look for another interpretation of his principle. But what might that be?

Perhaps Friedman is suggesting that it is wrong in principle for managers to impose costs on the basis of their own personal moral decisions. At this point in his essay he does say that "one man's good is another's evil," and this suggests that he is skeptical about the legitimacy of any individual's moral opinions. Unfortunately, if this is his view Friedman would be unable to sustain an in-principle rejection of the social responsibility thesis while remaining consistent with his own conclusions. (Logicians call this line of reasoning a *reductio ad absurdum*. If you can begin with someone's belief and show that it leads them to some absurdity—and holding two logically inconsistent beliefs is absurd—then one will have shown the original belief to be unreasonable.)

Remember that Friedman himself describes the only direct responsibility of managers as involving conformity to "the basic rules of society, both those embodied in law and those embodied in ethical custom." Surely there will be cases where conforming to these rules, both legal and ethical, will impose costs on shareholders. And just as surely, there will be times when what is required by these rules is unclear and the manager will need to exercise some discretion (and why else do we have managers except to make just these sorts of judgments?).Thus, on Friedman's own view, there can be times when a manager will, on the basis of his own personal value judgment, impose costs on shareholders for the sake of some ethical objective.

For example, Friedman would say that obtaining profits through fraudulent marketing is unethical. It is therefore ethical to impose costs on stockholders on the basis of this value. But not every case of fraud is clear and unambiguous. Suppose that a manager is considering a proposed advertising campaign for a sweepstakes contest that preys on the vulnerability of elderly people. The sweepstakes has been carefully crafted to ensure that it violates no law. Experience shows that these contests can be profitable. Yet the manager believes that this one is so deceptive that it really amounts to fraud. It would seem that in Friedman's view, the manager should exercise her personal judgment and avoid the fraudulent advertising, even at the risk of imposing significant costs upon stockholders.

Let us consider one final interpretation of Friedman's in-principle objection to the social responsibility thesis. Perhaps the key to understanding his view rests with the claim that "a corporate executive is an employee of the owners of the business." This suggests that what is wrong is imposing costs on *owners* in the pursuit of social objectives. But what would the political principle violated by such actions be? Supposedly it is that private owners have the right to control their property and when managers disregard the owner's desire to make as much money as possible, they violate this right.

Two serious challenges can be raised to this view. The first focuses on the nature of political and moral rights, and the second focuses on the nature of corporate ownership and control. We will examine these issues in more detail in Chapters Three and Four, but for now we can make a few brief observations.

First, even if imposing costs in the pursuit of social objectives does restrict the rights of private property owners, Friedman would need to say more to show that it is always wrong in principle to do this. As we saw earlier, free societies often require trade-offs among various and competing freedoms. This suggests a distinction between overriding people's rights (restricting freedom with a legitimate justification) and violating their rights (restricting freedom without justification). The existence of zoning laws, for example, attests to society's willingness to override the rights of private property owners in pursuit of such social objectives as the aesthetic integrity of a historical neighborhood, or for the sake of public safety. A zoning law restricting a certain neighborhood to single-family homes imposes significant costs on a property owner who seeks to build an apartment complex for college students. Yet few of us believe that such laws are "fundamentally subversive" to a free society. They may override the property owner's rights, but we don't say that they *violate* her rights.

Second, this interpretation really misrepresents the nature of corporate ownership and control. At least for large firms with publicly traded stocks, it is better to think of stockholders as "investors" than as "owners." While the right of ownership of personal property (your car, for example) implies a right to do with it what you want (within limits of course), the same cannot be said for owners of corporate stock. Here, ownership does not imply the right to control. That right is vested in corporate management. Ownership of stock, which rests more often with institutional investors like mutual funds, pension plans, and financial institutions than with private individuals, does imply certain rights. Investors can profit from this stock, sell it (usually), deed it to their children, give it away, and so on. But they cannot try to "micromanage" the daily operations of the firm. That responsibility rests with the management, who owes them only a competitive rate of return on their investment. If investors disagree with the decisions of management, they retain the freedom to sell their stock and seek a higher rate of return elsewhere.

Is Obedience to the Law Enough?

A final theme in Friedman's essay that deserves consideration is his suggestion that obedience to the law is the primary noneconomic obligation of business. This is a common view among many people both inside and outside of business. Over the last decade, many corporations have established ethics programs and hired ethics officers who are charged with managing corporate ethics programs. Much good work gets done by ethics officers, but it is fair to say that much of the work of this profession focuses on compliance issues. That is, in practice, much of corporate ethics is identified with obedience to the law. But is compliance with the law enough for ethical behavior? There are good reasons for thinking that it is not.

First, holding that obedience to the law is sufficient to fulfill one's ethical duties begs the question of whether or not the law itself is ethical. Dramatic examples from history, Nazi Germany, and apartheid South Africa being the most obvious, demonstrate that one's ethical responsibility may run counter to the law. You do not forgo your ethical responsibilities by a blind obedience to the law.

Second, societies that value individual freedom will be reluctant to legally require more than just a moral minimum. Such liberal societies will seek legally to prohibit the most serious ethical harms, but they will not legally require acts of charity, common decency, and personal integrity. The law can be an efficient mechanism for preventing serious harms, but it is not very good at promoting goods. Even if it were, the cost in human freedom of legally requiring such things as personal integrity would be too high. Imagine a society that legally required parents to love their children, or even a law prohibiting lying.

Third, on a more practical level, telling business that its ethical responsibilities end with obedience to the law is just inviting more legal regulation. It was the failure of personal ethics among such companies as Enron and WorldCom, after all, which led to the creation of the Sarbanes-Oxley Act and many other legal reforms. If business restricts its ethical responsibilities to obedience to the law, it should not be surprised to find a new wave of government regulations that require what were formerly voluntary actions.

Finally, the perspective that compliance is enough relies on a misleading understanding of law. To say that all a business needs to do is obey the law suggests that laws are clear-cut, unambiguous rules that can be easily applied. This rule model of law is very common but not very accurate. If the law was clear and unambiguous, there would not be much of a role for lawyers and courts.

An example may help here. At a recent training class for middle managers, corporate attorneys made a presentation on the responsibilities created by the Americans with Disabilities Act. This federal law requires that businesses must make a "reasonable accommodation" for employees with disabilities. One manager asked if asthma was considered a disability. The attorneys answered that it depends. Every law is written in general terms that need to be interpreted in light of specific facts. The legal answer "it depends" suggested that depending on the facts and on how different courts might interpret facts, one could not say in general if asthma was a disability. Given this ambiguity, any manager facing this question has a choice: make a reasonable accommodation to an employee with asthma, or not. That choice, given the ambiguity of law, is an ethical decision.

It is worth remembering that many of the people involved in the wave of recent corporate scandals were lawyers. In the Enron case, for example, corporate attorneys and accountants were encouraged to "push the envelope" of what was legal. Especially in civil law where much of the law is established by past precedent, there is always room for ambiguity in applying the law. After all, every new case is different in some way from the past. Further, in civil law there is a real sense that one has not done anything illegal unless and until a court decides that one has, and this means that if no one files a lawsuit to challenge some action, it was legal.

If a corporate manager is told, as Friedman suggests, that she has a social responsibility to maximize profits within the law, then responsible managers will consult their corporate attorneys and accountants to ask what the law allows. A competent attorney or accountant will advise on how far one can reasonably go before doing something that is obviously illegal. In this situation, it would seem a manager has a responsibility to "push the envelope" of legality in pursuit of profits. In Friedman's view, whatever *profitable action* that is not obviously illegal is socially responsible. Most of the cases of corporate scandal mentioned at the start of this chapter involved attorneys and accountants who advised their clients that what they were doing could be defended in court. The off-the-books partnerships that were at the heart of the collapse of Enron and Arthur Andersen were designed with the advice of attorneys who thought that, if challenged, they had at least a reasonable chance of winning in court. At this point, the decision to "push the envelope" becomes more a matter of risk assessment and cost-benefit analysis than a matter of ethics. In this model, there is a strong incentive to assess the likelihood of being challenged in court, the likelihood of losing the case, and the likelihood of settling for financial damages, and to compare those costs against the financial benefits of taking the action.

Because the law is ambiguous, because in many cases it simply is not clear what the law requires, business managers will often face decisions that rely on their ethical judgments. To suggest otherwise is simply to hold a false picture of corporate reality. Thus, the fundamental ethical questions will confront even the business person who is committed to obeying the law. What should I do? How should I live?

IN SUMMARY

Normative ethics involves stepping back from what is customarily accepted as proper behavior and asking questions about what *ought* to be proper. The views of Milton Friedman, identified as the classical model of corporate social responsibility, are an example of normative business ethics. Friedman offers numerous prescriptions for how one ought to behave in business and how business ought to be structured. He defends these prescriptions by appeal to certain ethical norms and values.

Our analysis of Friedman's practice of normative ethics must conclude that his supporting reasons are unconvincing. He relies on emotional appeals in several instances, he overgeneralizes from the evidence, he misunderstands or misrepresents the nature of a free society, and he even appears to be inconsistent with his own views.

But we should be careful not to make a logical mistake ourselves. Even if we conclude that Friedman's reasons are invalid, we are not justified in rejecting his overall conclusions and prescriptions. The classical model of corporate social responsibility is an important and influential normative theory. Just because one particular defense of it proves unconvincing does not mean that we are justified in rejecting the entire theory. After all, Friedman's essay was written for the popular press and perhaps was not intended to be a philosophically careful defense of this position. (Perhaps there is a lesson in here as well about how to read journalistic accounts of complex ethical issues!)

The views represented by Friedman's essay—the classical model of corporate social responsibility and the free market theory of economics on which it is based—continue to be influential positions throughout contemporary society. They have also received defenses that are much more philosophically sophisticated. In the next two chapters we will examine two of these philosophical defenses, each based in a major ethical theory. We will use our examination of these defenses to introduce the next level of ethics—philosophical ethics—and the two leading approaches to ethical theory—utilitarianism and individual rights.

In conclusion, we should step back from the content of this chapter to reflect on what we did, on the *activity* of ethical analysis. In one way, this chapter is an example of the kind of reasoning that philosophical ethics asks of us, and it provides an answer to the relativist and skeptic who thinks that ethics is all a matter of personal opinion. We did reason; we did make rational progress. We may not have proven anything absolutely, but we have advanced the debate. We encourage you to continue this activity throughout this text. We invite you to continue doing philosophy.

2

ॐ

Philosophical Ethics: Utilitarianism and the Free Market

INTRODUCTION

Chapter One described the role of philosophical ethics as a process of stepping back and abstracting ourselves from the actual values and practices of society to analyze and evaluate those values and practices. Ethical theories pursue this analysis in a systematic way, seeking to articulate and justify some general principles and values for living a good life. We cannot hope to cover the full range of ethical theories that have been developed throughout history in a business ethics textbook. Chapters Two and Three will provide a detailed introduction to two approaches to ethical theory—utilitarianism and a rights-based ethics—which are centrally important in the study of business. But before turning to a more detailed examination of how these approaches are relevant to business, it will be helpful to provide a more general introduction to philosophical ethics.

In examining Friedman's essay in Chapter One, we spoke of norms as the "oughts" and "shoulds" that guide behavior. We also pointed out that there are various norms that we use in guiding behavior: ethical, economic, financial, religious, political, legal, and even the norms of etiquette. How then do we distinguish ethical norms from other types of norms?

Consider economic or financial norms. Perhaps the most fundamental prescription in finance is "buy low and sell high." If we were to ask *why* buy low and sell high, the answer would be something like "because that will maximize your return on investment." Thus, the complete form of the financial prescription is "*if* you want a maximum return on your investment, *then* you ought to buy low and sell high." In logical terms, this is a hypothetical, or "if . . . then" statement. Likewise, other norms fit this hypothetical model. If you want to attain eternal salvation, then you ought to obey the teaching of your church. If you want to be considered polite, then you ought to follow the norms of etiquette. If you want to get reelected, then you ought to provide good constituent service.

Hypothetical norms depend upon other considerations for their force or legitimacy. The "if " in the hypothetical statement shows that I can be exempt from the norm by rejecting the hypothesis. The norms apply to me only if I care about or have an interest in maximizing return, eternal salvation, a reputation for politeness, or reelection.

Ethical norms, on the other hand, are seen as applying to all rational people regardless of their personal wants or interests. Ethical norms tell us how we, as rational human beings, ought to live our lives. Philosophers traditionally identified ethical norms as "universal," meaning that they apply to all people. (The great German philosopher, Immanuel Kant, called such ethical norms "categorical imperatives" to distinguish them from the hypothetical imperatives just mentioned.) An ethical theory attempts to provide a rational basis for making such universal judgments. Of course, an ethical relativist (as described in Chapter One) *denies* that such judgments are possible. Thus, ethical theories must also provide an answer to the relativist challenge that no norm can be applied to all people.

Besides this universal character, ethical norms are said to be impartial or fair. A norm that gives special privilege to my own interests is not an ethical norm; a norm that denies equal standing for the interests of others is not an ethical norm. Impartiality requires that the interests of all people involved be given equal consideration and equal weight. Ethics requires that everyone counts equally; no one counts for more.

We can say that an ethical theory provides a systematic explanation and justification for certain fundamental norms that apply to all people in an impartial manner. An ethical theory explains and defends universal principles that prescribe, in an impartial manner, how we ought to live our lives. We turn now to a brief overview of three such ethical theories.

ETHICAL THEORIES

Virtue Ethics: What Type of Person Should I Be?

When we think about ethics, especially within the context of a field such as business ethics, it is easy to concentrate on questions like "What should I do?" "How should I act?" After all, normative ethics is concerned with norms of ethical behavior. In doing normative ethics, we often seek a rule or a principle that will guide our behavior and answer these questions.

But there is another tradition within ethics that de-emphasizes the importance of rules and principles and instead focuses on the character of the person. "Virtue ethics," often associated with the ancient Greek philosopher Aristotle, asks not

"What should I do?" but rather "What type of person should I be?" In this way, the challenge of an ethical theory is not to defend some rules to guide our behavior and tell us what to do, but to describe and justify the characteristics of an ethically good person and a worthwhile human life. "Virtues" are the character traits that promote a meaningful and worthy human life; the "vices" are those character traits that undermine the ability of persons to live a good life.

Perhaps the central challenge of ethics is the problem of self-interest. Very often there seems to be a tension between doing the ethically right thing and pursuing our own self-interest. The problem of self-interest is, in part, the problem of motivating people to conform to principles that, because they are impartial, do not necessarily benefit themselves. Indeed, all of the corporate scandals in recent years are easily understood as occasions in which individuals pursued their own self-interest rather than doing the ethically responsible thing. Given this tension, much work in ethical theory involves attempts either to restrict self-interest with rules and laws or channel that self-interest in ethically beneficial ways. Thus, one might create a corporate code of ethics to prohibit conflicts of interest or structure salary packages in ways that provide incentives for ethical behavior.

Virtue ethics takes an altogether different approach to the challenge of self-interest. There are two basic responses to the tension between self-interest and ethical behavior. Either we accept the inevitability of self-interest and try to find ways to regulate it, or we look for ways to turn selfish interests into ethical interests. That is, two options are available if there is a tension between doing what is ethically responsible and doing what I want. We can try to prevent me from doing what I want, or we can find ways to encourage me to want to do what is ethically responsible. This latter approach is the one taken by the virtue ethics tradition that stretches back to Plato and Aristotle.

Consider the case of former Enron executives Kenneth Lay, Jeffrey Skilling, and Andrew Fastow. These men faced an ethical conflict: they could do the ethically responsible thing or they could commit fraud and walk away with tens of millions of dollars. Ethics seems to create a conflict between ethical responsibility and self-interest, and $10 million seems a very tempting option. But suppose that these men had more moderate wants; suppose they were satisfied with their salaries and were motivated to do good things. Would $10 million tempt someone who is content with life, has relatively modest desires, and has no interest in cheating others? A modest, honest, and unpretentious person does not struggle with a tension between selfishness and ethics; a good person wants to do what is ethical. In such a situation, the apparent tension between self-interest and ethics disappears. For a virtuous person, a person who is honest, moderate, and trustworthy, there is no conflict between what she wants to do and what is ethically right. For a person characterized by the vices of greed and arrogance, life is full of ethical conflicts.

Virtues are understood as character traits or dispositions. An honest person is not someone who wants to steal but decides not to; an honest person does not want to steal, is not predisposed to steal. We might say that it is not in the character of an honest person to steal. We also recognize that people sometimes act "out of character," as when an otherwise loyal friend betrays our trust. Thus, virtues are sometimes described as habits, and a virtuous person is someone who has developed the right type of personal habits.

The language of virtues and vices might seem foreign or old-fashioned to many of us, but with a little thought we can see that we experience a wide range of virtues and vices every day. Many of the recent scandals were described in the language of virtues and vices. We commonly speak of honest, courageous, loyal, trustworthy people. Individuals who blow the whistle on corruption are often described as having integrity and courage. Corrupt executives are described as dishonest, greedy, arrogant, envious, and self-centered. In these situations, we judge someone's ethics by describing their character.

In the Aristotelian tradition, virtues were understood as appropriate means between two extremes: the virtue of courage is a mean between the vices of cowardness and foolhardiness; the virtue of compassion is a mean between the vice of coldheartedness and the vice of a patronizing pity of others. The ethics of virtue also pays close attention to issues of education and psychology. Virtue ethics recognizes that individual wants and desires are not random occurrences. Richard Grasso did not simply wake up one morning to discover that he wanted $150 million. Our wants and desires emerge out of longer-standing personality traits, habits, and dispositions. Thus, virtue ethics asks us to think about how character traits and dispositions are formed. If we can avoid some ethical conflicts when individuals have the right sort of character and dispositions, then we should pay attention to how people develop character. Can someone be taught to be honest or loyal? How do people become trustworthy?

Virtue ethics will prove helpful for business ethics in several contexts. First, throughout the text the fundamental question of virtue ethics should never be far from your own consciousness: What type of person should I be? When faced with ethical issues, one might look for a rule to follow or calculate the consequences of available options. But one might also step back from the situation to reflect on one's own integrity and character. In this situation, asking not "What should I do?" but "Who am I?" might prove to be more helpful. Virtue ethics emphasizes the integrity and unity of one's character. It is not uncommon to find situations within business in which an individual is asked to step out of character and make a decision "as a manager" or "as an employee." Several readings and cases in this book provide clear examples in which employees are expected to ignore their own values and play the role of business person, manager, employer. It will be helpful in these cases to reflect on the virtues of personal integrity, trustworthiness, and reliability.

Virtue ethics' emphasis on the formation of habits and character traits can also provide insight into the social conditioning that occurs within a business context. In recent years, the topic of corporate culture has received much attention within management studies. It is not uncommon to find analyses of corporate corruption talking in terms of a culture of greed or an arrogant corporate culture. In describing exemplary corporate citizens, it is also not uncommon to find descriptions of a corporate culture that promotes integrity and honesty. In many ways, the corporate culture is nothing other than those social institutions that shape the habits, the virtues or vices, of the individuals who work within that corporate setting.

A corporate culture can be understood as those expectations and values that implicitly set the standard of behavior within a business. If, like Enron, the culture was one of aggression, arrogance, and greed, then all of the codes of ethics in the world (and Enron had a praiseworthy code of corporate ethics) will mean very little. Being sensitive to topics of virtues, vices, habits, and dispositions will help in the understanding of corporate culture.

Social conditioning of habits occurs not only as an employment issue within the corporation, it also occurs as an issue in marketing ethics. Topics such as impulse buying, branding, marketing to children, and even advertising in general raise issues of character formation and habits. Indeed, some critics would charge that our consumer culture is a culture in which the vices of greed and insatiable desires dominate the virtues of moderation, frugality, and thrift.

Finally, virtue ethics encourages us to think carefully about human happiness. A common view, especially common perhaps among economists, is that human beings are happy when they get what they desire. Thus, an economy in which consumer demand is efficiently met is an economy that promotes happiness. But if happiness is getting what we want and if our wants are insatiable, then we can never be happy. This point is especially important when thinking about an economic system in which growth in consumer satisfaction is both the goal and the necessary driving force in economic activity. As an alternative, virtue ethics suggests that with appropriate and modest desires, humans have a much better chance of being happy than if they have the ever-increasing desires of consumer culture.

An ethics of virtue does not claim to be a comprehensive ethical theory that successfully addresses every ethical situation. Virtue ethics is not as helpful in addressing issues of social ethics and public policy as it is in addressing issues of personal morality. But virtue ethics is a part of a comprehensive ethical theory, and it can be helpful in what follows.

Utilitarianism: Maximize the Overall Good

A second tradition within ethics, and one that is essential for the study of business ethics, is known as utilitarianism. This approach begins with what seems a common sense observation. When one is trying to decide how to act and what to do, it makes sense to look to the consequences of an action and decide accordingly. If my act produces more good consequences than bad, I should do it. Utilitarianism is an ethical theory that develops this insight and, roughly speaking, directs us to seek the "greatest good for the greatest number" or to "maximize the overall good." Utilitarianism is thus characterized as a *consequentialist* ethical theory, and this "greatest good" principle is the fundamental utilitarian social norm.

From this description we can say that utilitarianism adopts a means–ends form of reasoning. Acts are right if they are a means for attaining the ends of maximizing goodness. Consider the case of truth-telling. Utilitarians will value telling the truth because it will generally produce good consequences; for example, it engenders trust, it allows for accurate communication and understanding, and it earns one a good reputation. That is, truth-telling is not good in itself, but it is valued instrumentally as a means to good ends. It is useful (hence, the word "utility" as the basis of utilitarianism). For the utilitarian, no act is ever good in itself, at all times, and in all situations. Right or wrong always depends on the consequences.

Ultimately, this means—ends reasoning must stop somewhere. If the value of everything depends upon something else, then we would be involved in an infinite regress (the value of A depends on B, the value of B depends on C, the value of C depends on D . . .) and ultimately we would value nothing unconditionally. If all utilitarian reasoning was of this instrumental form, utilitarian ethics would remain hypothetical and contingent.

Consider the financial norms discussed previously: "Buy low and sell high." This, too, is a consequentialist norm; right and wrong financial decisions are judged by their consequences. But not every consequentialist norm qualifies as a utilitarian norm. To distinguish ethical norms from nonethical norms such as those used in finance, utilitarians do two things. First, they defend an account of the good that is valued for its own sake and, unlike financial norms, not solely for its utility in producing other goods. This intrinsic value is the utilitarians response to ethical relativism in that it provides an account of some good that is universally and objectively valid for all rational persons. Unlike the consequences produced by the norms of finance, religion, etiquette, or politics, the consequences of utilitarian ethics are taken to be objectively good for all people.

Second, utilitarianism stresses the overall good, the good for all involved. Other norms look at the consequences for only some subgroup. Ethical egoism, for example, would be a consequentialist theory that promotes the maximization of one's own good. But if there is some good that is objectively valuable and if some act produces more of this value than any alternative act, then we have an objective and impartial principle to follow. The "good" is objectively valid, the good of each person is treated as equally deserving, and attaining the optimal overall amount of good is a fair and impartial goal. No one could object to this goal except by claiming that an increase in his or her own good is more important than a greater overall increase in the good of others.

The classical statements of the utilitarian tradition are found in the writings of Jeremy Bentham (1748–1832) and John Stuart Mill (1806–1873). Through the writings of Adam Smith (1723–1790), utilitarian reasoning has been especially influential in economics. Later in this chapter we will examine a version of utilitarian thinking that has been used as a justification of the type of free market economics defended by Milton Friedman, and the model of corporate social responsibility that follows from it. Before turning to that defense, it will be helpful to examine some challenges that are often raised against utilitarian thinking. It will be useful to distinguish challenges that are raised within and among utilitarian thinkers from those that are raised from alternative ethical perspectives.

Two challenges arise from within the utilitarian tradition. We described utilitarian thinking previously in terms of means, which have instrumental value, and ends, which have intrinsic value. Not surprisingly, perhaps, utilitarians disagree about each aspect of their theory. Different utilitarians offer different versions of what is intrinsically good, and they disagree about the appropriate means for attaining the maximum amount of that good.

Different versions of utilitarian thinking defend different accounts of what is intrinsically good. Bentham, for example, argued that only pleasure was good in itself and only pain bad in itself. Mill defended a more qualitative understanding of happiness as the satisfaction of long-term interests. These disagreements also give rise to serious problems with measurement. Because utilitarianism requires us to calculate, measure, and compare consequences, it is important that the ends of utilitarianism be the sort of thing that can be measured, calculated, and compared. That is, the good of utilitarianism must, in some way, be quantifiable. Yet, as Mill argued, the human good must also account for a qualitative dimension that cannot be quantified. This debate will have implications within business ethics, for example, when we discuss such topics as employee or consumer health and safety, and environmental protection. Some goods that seem intrinsically valuable, such as health and safety, do not seem open to easy measurement; goods that do seem easily measured, such as costs and loss of earnings, do not seem to capture the intrinsic value of health and safety.

Another important aspect of these debates involves the degree to which an individual is free to choose his or her own good. Pleasure and happiness are attractive ends for utilitarianism because they allow a wide range of personal freedom of choice (what gives *you* pleasure or makes *you* happy may be different from what gives *me* pleasure or makes *me* happy). Yet, the more utilitarians allow individuals the freedom to pursue their own understanding of the good, the closer utilitarianism comes to ethical relativism, the view in which values are relative to each individual. On the other hand, the more utilitarianism specifies the content of human goodness, the less likely utilitarians will be able to defend the value of personal freedom. Individuals do not always want to do what someone else thinks is good for them. This debate will have clear implications for the ethical analysis of free markets.

Utilitarians also disagree about the appropriate means for attaining maximum good. As described previously, utilitarians judge actions in terms of their consequences, and because we can never be quite certain about the consequences of our acts, no act is ever good in itself, at all times, and in all situations. Nevertheless, utilitarianism must offer some advice on what to do in the present, and therefore utilitarians must make some judgments about the likely consequences of our acts. Two approaches to this dilemma will have implications for business ethics.

Since we are dealing with predictions about the future consequences of human action, one movement within utilitarian thinking argues that we should rely on the expertise of social scientists to shape and implement public policy. Policy experts trained in such fields as economics, law, medicine, environmental science, education, and political science are the people best able to predict consequences of public policy. Thus, if we want to know which environmental regulation is most likely to preserve a forest, we should turn to ecologists. If we wish to know the best tax policy to promote economic growth, we turn to economists. If we wish to know the best safety standard for automobile design, we turn to engineers. And so forth.

A second approach argues, in a way that echoes Adam Smith's faith in an invisible hand, that the greater overall good is best attained by leaving such decisions to the unintended results of a competitive, free, and open market. The inevitable result of efficient markets, according to this view, is the optimal satisfaction of consumer happiness. We will see versions of this approach at several points later in this text.

Finally, alternative ethical theories raise several major challenges against utilitarianism. These challenges go to the very heart of utilitarianism by rejecting consequentialism as an adequate basis of ethics.

Utilitarianism, remember, is concerned with maximizing the overall good. So, when a utilitarian decides how he should act, the only things that count in his calculation are the predicted consequences of the action. Whether a particular act is justified depends entirely on the results. Clearly, this purely consequentialist approach to moral decision making reduces to accepting that the end justifies the means. Many people find this aspect of utilitarianism troubling.

Another way to explain this point is to recognize that we sometimes describe good people as acting out of a duty or on principle. There seem to be many cases in which we have a duty or an obligation to do something *even if* doing otherwise produces better results in terms of collective happiness. (Philosophers sometimes refer to this approach to ethics as "deontological," derived from the Greek word for "duty," to distinguish it from consequentialist theories like utilitarianism.) Truth-telling, keeping one's promises, treating other people with respect, honoring friendships, maintaining loyalty to one's family or country are some simple examples of acting out of a duty or acting on principle. In contrast, utilitarians always calculate the effects of their acts before deciding what to do—seemingly just the opposite of acting from a duty or according to principle. Utilitarians will always reserve their final evaluation of such duties, as they will of such central human interests as respect, freedom, and life, until all resultant consequences have been calculated.

Perhaps the most troubling aspect of this means–ends problem arises when we recognize that utilitarianism is concerned not just with consequences, but with consequences for *aggregate* or *collective* welfare. That overriding concern for collective happiness runs counter to the moral sensibilities of many people. Most of us are committed to the belief that some individual interests should be protected from actions aimed at improving the common good, that the good of the many is not always sufficient justification for sacrificing the interests of the few. In other words, the dominant contemporary picture of morality holds that individuals have *rights* that should not be sacrificed merely for marginal increases in the collective welfare (or simply to satisfy the preferences of a majority). This alternative, rights-based picture of morality regards at least some aspects of individuals as off-limits to utilitarian maximizing calculations.

An admittedly extreme example can highlight this point. In theory, nothing prevents the utilitarian from endorsing slavery of a minority if it can be shown that this would result in a net increase in the overall good. If a small minority were enslaved, it might increase the aggregate happiness, perhaps because it would be the most efficient means to ensure completion of undesirable but socially necessary work. Most of us, of course, would reject such a policy as unfair or unjust. We believe instead that each person possesses a dignity that prohibits him or her from being used solely as a means to the ends of others. It would be unjust to enslave people even if doing so would make the rest of society happier.

We can summarize these challenges by sorting them into two groups: those that can arise from within utilitarian perspectives, and those that challenge the entire utilitarian enterprise. Even utilitarians acknowledge that they must provide a reasonable method for determining and measuring when that good has been maximized, and a defensible accounting of the nature of the good. Critics from outside of the utilitarian tradition point out that utilitarianism misses such important features of morality as acting on principle, acting from a sense of duty, and respecting individual dignity and rights. We will see versions of these challenges arise in this chapter as well as in many of the readings in this text.

Before turning to a more detailed examination of the utilitarian defense of the free market and the model of corporate social responsibility that follows from it, we will examine a third major approach to ethical theory.

Deontology: An Ethics of Rights and Duties

Like utilitarianism, the third ethical tradition we will consider starts with what seems to be a common sense observation: the ends don't always justify the means. While the utilitarian claims that right and wrong action are a matter of consequences, a deontological approach holds that some acts are right and wrong in principle, regardless of consequences. The word *deontology* is derived from the Greek words for the study *(logos)* of duty *(deon)*. Deontological ethics, in general, holds that while producing beneficial social consequences and minimizing harm are good things, they do not override ethical duties that we have. The ends of beneficial social consequences do not justify the means of failing to fulfill our duties.

But what duties do we have? What obligations do we have that are so important that we must fulfill them even if doing so results in unpleasant social consequences? Throughout this text, we will examine many situations in which individuals have duties that are role specific. That is, when one assumes the role of auditor or attorney or manager or member of the board of directors, one assumes certain duties that define the role of auditor, attorney, manager, or director. These role-specific duties are considered in some depth in Chapter Seven. But a general ethical theory must offer an account of duties that are not dependent on roles and therefore could be deserted by abandoning one's role. Fundamental ethical duties would be those that are universally and impartially binding on all people.

Different types of deontological ethics offer differing accounts of our basic ethical duties. Some within the deontological tradition argue that our most fundamental duties are to obey a natural law or obey the commands of God. But the foremost account of such universal ethical duties, and the version of deontological ethics that is most relevant for studying business ethics, appeals to the concept of individual rights. On this approach, our basic ethical duty is to respect the rights of others.

Chapter Three will examine this approach to ethics in more detail. In the following chapter, we will provide a more complete account of an ethics of rights and duties as an introduction to our examination of a rights-based defense of free market economics and the account of corporate social responsibility that flows from it. In the remainder of this chapter, we will turn to the utilitarian defense of that perspective.

UTILITARIAN DEFENSE
OF THE FREE MARKET

Given this overview of utilitarianism, we can now turn to the utilitarian defense of the free market economic system and the classical model of corporate social responsibility that follows from it. It is no overstatement to say that the utilitarian defense of the free market continues to have a profound influence on contemporary society and the modern business world.

Remember that the free market system was used to justify specific ethical recommendations. Individual business managers should seek to maximize profits because this is required of them by the free market economic system. For utilitarians in the classical economic tradition of Adam Smith, the free market system itself is ethically justified because it will maximize the overall good of society. Let us examine how this would work.

Consider a simple example. Alexa wants to sell her car, and two people, Michael and Matthew, want to buy it. This means that Alexa has decided that she would be better off with money than she presently is with the car. Michael and Matthew each have decided that they would be happier with a car than with the money they now have. Each individual is left to establish his or her own preferences. What happens if we leave these people alone to pursue these preferences? Presumably they would engage in the kind of bargaining that occurs in markets. Alexa offers her car for sale, and Michael and Matthew make bids for it. Initially, Michael offers $1000 and Matthew offers $1100. Alexa, looking to become as happy as possible, seeks to maximize her profits and asks for more. Michael and Matthew continue bidding, pushing the price higher and higher and therefore making Alexa happier and happier. Finally, one of the bidders drops out when he decides, completely on his own according to his preferences, that he prefers to keep his money rather than exchanging it for the car. The other bidder, say it is Michael, offers $2000 and gets the car. Again, this choice was freely made, so we must conclude that Michael is happier with the car than with his money (otherwise, why would he agree to the sale?). Assuming that Alexa also agrees to the sale, she, too, is as happy as she can be in that she has received what she most wants. Finally, assuming a competitive market (that is, assuming that there are other sellers competing with Alexa), Matthew will eventually get what he most wants, a car for under $2000.

By allowing rational, self-interested individuals to bargain for themselves, by giving them the freedom to decide what they most want and what they are willing to pay for, we have reached a point where we have optimally satisfied the wants of all parties. There is no way to improve the overall situation or to increase overall happiness. If any alternative exchange would benefit two parties, rational and self-interested people would have agreed to it. Anything we now do to increase Alexa's happiness—for example, by increasing the price she is paid—would decrease Michael's happiness, by requiring him to give up more for the car. Thus, we have reached a point of optimal happiness: No one's happiness can be increased without a loss of other happiness. (In technical terms used by economists, when we reach a point at which no one's situation can be improved without thereby inflicting an equal or greater loss on someone else, we have reached a point of economic efficiency, or *Pareto optimality.**) We have, in short, maximized the overall happiness.

According to utilitarian defenders of neoclassical economics, if we expand this example over an entire society, we can see that open and competitive markets produce the optimal outcome. With just a few structural requirements (that is, there is open and free competition; coercion and fraud are not allowed; individuals are rational and are pursuing their own self-interests), the workings of the market will guarantee maximizing the overall good. Eventually we will get to a point at which we can no longer improve anyone's situation without also harming someone else. If we provide the appropriate social structure (that is, a laissez-faire economy), the individual pursuit of self-interest will result, as if led by "an invisible hand," according to Smith, to the greatest overall good.

The ethical imperative for business managers follows from this as well. Managers ought to seek profit maximization because profits testify to the successful functioning of the market. When Alexa pursued maximum profits, she was ensuring that the person who most valued the car, that is, the person who was willing to pay most for it, would in fact get it. Michael was willing to pay more for the car than Matthew; therefore, pursuit of profits guarantees that goods get to those people who most want, or prefer, them. Alexa, of course, is happiest with maximized profits because now she will be able to satisfy more of her wants. If a manager could have increased profits and did not, that manager has prevented products from reaching people who value them more; in other words, that manager has prevented exchanges that would have increased the net overall benefits.

Thus, we have a fairly standard utilitarian justification for the classical model of corporate social responsibility and the free market economic system on which it is based. Like all utilitarian theories, this perspective offers both an account of the good and an explanation of the best means for maximizing that good. This justification adopts the version called *preference utilitarianism,* where happiness (the good) is identified with the satisfaction of individually chosen preferences. We have attained the maximum overall good when we have optimally satisfied the preferences expressed by individuals within the marketplace. The action of rationally self-interested individuals operating within the structures of a free and com-

---

*Pareto optimality refers to a particular interpretation of efficient distribution first articulated by the Italian social scientist, Vilfredo Pareto (1848–1923). A distribution is said to be Pareto Optimal if it is impossible to make anyone better off without making someone else worse off.

petitive market will prove to be the best means for attaining this goal. Thus, we can think of this defense in terms of means and ends: The free market is the best means to attaining the best end. To proceed with our ethical analysis, let us examine each of the above claims in turn.

AN ANALYSIS OF
THE UTILITARIAN DEFENSE

In our earlier discussion of utilitarianism, we introduced three general challenges to this ethical theory. First, we pointed out that utilitarians are challenged to defend their determination and measurement of consequences. How do we decide which means, among all those available, will attain the end, maximum happiness? We noted that even among utilitarians there is disagreement concerning the best means to the desired end. The second challenge concerned the nature of the good itself. Utilitarians must provide an account of the good that is rationally defensible as the ultimate ethical goal. Finally, the third challenge went to the heart of utilitarianism by claiming that a consequentialist ethics misses important ethical concerns of principles, duties, rights, and justice. We now will consider how these challenges reemerge for the utilitarian justification of the free market and the model of corporate social responsibility that follows from it.

Is the Free Market the Best Means?

The first set of challenges concerned our ability to determine the best means to the ethical end. Before deciding that a particular system is the best means to get us to our goals, we first need to know something about where we are going. Our simple example suggests that the utilitarian defense of the market is a version of preference utilitarianism. On this view, the human good is understood in terms of the satisfaction of those desires, or preferences, that individuals express in market transactions. In our example, Alexa, Michael, and Matthew all aimed to satisfy their desires, and they were allowed to rank–order their own desires as personal preferences. In fact, this is just the way that economists understand consumer demand and it is the ethical theory implicit in mainstream economic and managerial thinking. Thus, the goal of the free market is the optimal satisfaction of consumer demand or, perhaps in more common terms, attaining a high standard of living. For now let us assume the account of the good offered by this version of utilitarianism.

The utilitarian defense of free markets claims that this economic arrangement is the best means for attaining this ethical goal. The first question of our analysis, therefore, is: Is the free market the best means for attaining the end of maximally satisfying preferences or, in other words, attaining a high standard of living?

There are two general ways in which the free market could be an appropriate means to that end. On one hand, the market could be *necessary* to that end. That is, unless we adopt the market as our means, we will not be able to attain this end.

On the other hand, the free market could be a *sufficient* means to that end. In this sense, the market might not be necessary (we could get there in some other way), but it does guarantee that we will get there. Thus, we can evaluate the claim that the market is the best means by evaluating whether the market is either necessary or sufficient for that end.

Is the Market Necessary? Now, is a free market *necessary* for attaining such an end? On the surface, we know that some of the highest standards of living exist in Scandinavia, North America, Japan, and Western Europe. Measured in such terms as per capita income, life expectancy, education and literacy levels, infant mortality rates, health care, and civil liberties, countries in these regions boast very high standards of living. Yet no country in these regions could be classified as having a laissez-faire, free market economy. Within these regions, there is widespread government regulation of the market and centralized economic planning. It is very common to find business managers in these regions actively pursuing social objectives beyond profit maximization; and, in some cases, the entire economy is better characterized as socialist (that is, social ownership and control of the means of production) than as free market capitalist. It would appear, at least at first glance, that a free market economy is not necessary for attaining a high standard of living.

Of course, defenders of the market can claim that in all of these cases the standards of living would only improve by doing away with government regulation. But we need to be careful here. To say that the market is necessary is to make an in-principle claim: In all cases a freer economy would increase the overall good. But it is difficult to believe that this is true, especially in light of historical evidence. Critics of the market would argue that the overall quality of life in these regions increased only after these societies recognized failures within free markets and began regulating the economy.

But there is another problem with this claim. As we have seen, committed utilitarians always look to the consequences of actions to determine right from wrong action, and the consequences of our acts depend on a wide variety of occurrences "out there" in the world. Utilitarians always take a "let's see what happens" attitude; holding that a free market is always necessary to attain certain consequences seems too strong a position for a utilitarian, unless (and here's the potential trouble) *whatever* results from the workings of a free market is *defined as* ethically good. But if this is the view, then we have no independent ethical justification of the market, which is, after all, what we started out in search of. (If the consequences of the free market are *defined* as good, then to justify the market because it attains the good is to justify the market because it attains what it attains! Logicians identify the fallacy involved in such circular reasoning, where one assumes what needs to be proven, as *begging the question*.)

Consider the following example. In the United States the Federal Reserve Board sets monetary policy by establishing the interest rates at which banks are loaned money. The people who serve on this board are respected economists who, we can presume, share the utilitarian goal of maximizing happiness understood as maximally satisfying preferences. One very plausible way to interpret the workings of the Federal Reserve Board is to see it in utilitarian terms. If the economy is in a recession, then we are not maximizing consumer satisfaction. Thus, interest rates should be lowered to stimulate economic activity. The board then watches the consequences of its action: Too little growth, then perhaps rates should be lowered further; too much growth and a potential for inflation, then rates should be increased. Utilitarians look at any economic decision the way the Federal Reserve Board looks at monetary policy. Its instrumental value will always depend on the consequences that occur in the real world. Sometimes less government regulation increases the good; sometimes further regulation is needed. Since the right answer depends on the consequences and since the consequences will depend upon a variety of factors in each particular set of circumstances, seldom would utilitarians claim that any particular social, economic, or corporate policy is always necessary for maximizing the overall good.

Is the Market Sufficient? Nonetheless, perhaps a free market is *sufficient* for attaining this end. Perhaps a free market will get us there, even if other types of economic arrangements could do this as well. Is there any guarantee that a free market will maximize the overall good? A variety of phenomena that economists identify as *market failures* suggest that there are no such guarantees. Economists call these market "failures" precisely because they are instances in which the market fails to maximize the satisfaction of consumer preferences.

Let us return to the simple example that started this discussion to see how the market is thought to guarantee maximizing the good. The mechanism of the marketplace, the force that makes it work, is the pursuit of rational self-interest. The market promises the optimal satisfaction of preferences as long as all participants are allowed to, and in fact do, pursue their own rational self-interest. Alexa, Michael, and Matthew should calculate the expected benefits of alternative actions and then act in the way that will produce the highest net benefit to themselves. As Adam Smith suggested, when individuals "intend only their own gain," they will "be led by an invisible hand" to promote the good of society as a whole. But is it true that the whole of society benefits when each individual pursues only his or her own self-interest?

While a great deal of attention has been given to this question by philosophers and economists alike, no clear consensus has been reached. To understand certain problems associated with this claim, consider the well-known traffic phenomenon called "rubbernecking." Imagine yourself driving to work during morning rush hour. There has been a traffic accident across the roadway in the lanes coming out of the city. Being the rational, self-interested individual that classical economics takes you to be, you calculate the costs and benefits involved in slowing down for a look. On one hand, you don't want to be late for work, and slowing down will cost you a few seconds of time. On the other hand, you would gain something by learning about the accident; you would be satisfying your curiosity at the cost of only a few seconds. Calculating the net benefits, you ease off the accelerator and look across the road. Of course, every other rationally self-interested driver would make a similar calculation. This seems the reasonable choice for each individual. Unfortunately, the result of each individual pursuing their own self-interest and easing off the accelerator is a bumper-to-bumper traffic jam. The final overall result is that everyone is significantly late for work, much later than the mere seconds calculated by each individual.

Further, if any individual decides on her own to forgo a look and not slow down, she will still be caught in a traffic jam, but without the benefits that would have come from looking. Further still, if everyone agreed not to slow down, then it would be in your interest to slow down to look, thereby getting the benefits without the loss. In all possible scenarios, it seems to be in your own interest to slow down and look. But again, the same is true for each and every individual. The result is that the group is worse off, not better off, by the widespread pursuit of individual self-interest. The group would have been better off had everyone followed a strategy of cooperation and sacrificed the pursuit of individual self-interest.

Defenders of the free market will rightly point out that this single example does not capture the essence of a large-scale, free, and competitive market exchange. Nevertheless, rubbernecking and other so-called "prisoner dilemmas"* do give us some reason for thinking that, at certain levels in the day-to-day life of individuals at least, the pursuit of individual self-interest will not guarantee that the group as a whole will be best off. There seems reason to doubt Smith's "invisible hand."

Another reason to doubt the claim that a free market will attain the maximum overall good has to do with what economists call "externalities." Economists have long recognized that the price established in a market can fail to account for all of the costs involved. Certain costs may fall on someone other than the buyer or seller, with the result being an efficient exchange, in the sense that both buyer and seller are made better off, but it is an exchange that is not good for the entire society. Since the person who bears the cost is not a party to the exchange (the person is "external" to the transaction), he cannot influence the exchange and therefore the price does not accurately reflect the full costs.

Environmental pollution is often given as an example where such externalities occur. The cost (or "disutility") of a production process might include contaminating ground water with toxic discharges. Without government regulation to prevent this (which is the recommendation of free market defenders like Milton Friedman), the cost of this pollution is paid by neither the industry nor its customer. As a result, while both parties to the exchange are better off (through pro-

---

*A "prisoner's dilemma" refers to a thought experiment that demonstrates the pursuit of rational self-interest resulting in a situation in which each individual is made worse off than they would have been had they followed a strategy of cooperation. The classic formulation has two prisoners accused of a crime separately bargaining with a prosecutor who needs a confession to secure prosecution. If both confess, they both receive lengthy prison sentences, say 5 years. If neither confesses, they receive a minimum sentence of, say, 6 months. However, if one confesses and the other doesn't, the confessor goes free and the other receives a severe sentence, say 10 years. As a rationally self-interested individual, it is always most rational for me to confess. If my partner also confesses, then it is better that I confess as well. If she doesn't confess, it is also better for me to confess. But, since the same is true for my partner, as rational *individuals* we both confess and are sentenced to 5 years in prison. A more satisfactory solution is for us both not to confess, a possibility only if we cooperate and trust each other.

duction costs that do not reflect the costs of pollution), society as a whole is harmed by the uncompensated loss of clean water.

Likewise with the use of nonrenewable resources. The price of oil and gas for present-generation users does not reflect the opportunities for use of these resources that are forgone by future-generation users. (Remember from Chapter One that costs are defined in terms of "opportunities forgone.") There are significant costs to our present production of oil and gas that are not reflected in the present price. The parties to this exchange (the oil companies and all of us consumers) benefit, while those who are external to this transaction (future generations) must suffer the uncompensated loss of resources. Thus, whenever externalities exist, free market exchanges do not work to the greatest good for the greatest number.

The final challenge to the claim that the free market is the best means points out that the market is unlikely to lead to the maximization of happiness because not everyone's interests will be represented in the market. Specifically, in practice, individuals with less money will have less opportunity to participate in the market. With less opportunity, there is less likelihood that their preferences will be satisfied. So, too, with the preferences of future generations. Because they do not participate in market transactions, their happiness is not considered by this theory. Since utilitarianism is concerned to maximize the overall good, this is a significant shortcoming of the market version of utilitarianism.

Hence, so critics claim, unless markets are somehow adjusted to offset the advantages of wealth and to account for the interests of future people, there can be no guarantee that markets will maximize overall happiness. This point, of course, not only raises problems concerning the effectiveness of the market as a means but also raises serious problems about the fundamental fairness of the ends of the market as well.

The "Good" of Free Market Utilitarianism

A second general challenge to any version of utilitarianism concerns the nature of the good to be maximized. As we have seen, utilitarians often disagree about what this intrinsic good is. The version of utilitarianism assumed by defenders of the free market is what we previously called preference utilitarianism. In this version, the goal of any market exchange is the satisfaction of wants; individuals enter the market to try to get what they want. Because of scarcity and competition, we cannot always get all that we want. Thus, free individuals rank–order their wants and it is these rank-ordered wants that economists call preferences. In simple terms, no one would freely consent to a market exchange unless they preferred what they get from that exchange to what they give up for it. Because the end of any market transaction is the satisfaction of those consumer preferences that get expressed in the market, and because the goal of efficient markets is the optimal satisfaction of preferences, this theory is identified as preference utilitarianism.

The version of preference utilitarianism that underlies the free market denies that there are qualitative differences between preferences. (Remember Milton Friedman's essay, where he suggests that "one man's good is another's evil.") If some preferences are qualitatively more deserving than others, then there will be no guarantee that free exchanges within the marketplace will give these preferences the priority that they deserve. For example, some would argue that my preference for health care is ethically more important than your preference for a new car. But markets offer no way to regulate preference satisfaction other than through price and the law of supply and demand. Since you might be willing to pay more for a new car (especially if you are a high-paid attorney and I am a low-paid office worker) than I can pay for health care, market utilitarianism denies any qualitative difference between these preferences. Typically, economists will say that such preferences are equally deserving to the degree that they produce equal "utility."

Individuals rank-order their own wants by determining their preferences. When scarcity prevents competing preferences from all being satisfied (as when both Michael and Matthew preferred Alexa's car to their cash), price or "willingness to pay" determines which preference should get priority. Michael is willing to pay more for the car than Matthew, so selling the car to Michael will produce greater overall happiness (or "utility"), since he obviously values it more than Matthew. Likewise, since you might be willing to pay more for a new car than I will pay for health care, getting the car to you and denying me health care also produces greater overall happiness.

Let us begin the analysis of this view by asking why anyone would think that getting what you want, or satisfying preferences, is good in an ethical sense. Using terms introduced earlier in this chapter, we often say that things are either intrinsically good (good in themselves), or instrumentally good (good as a means to some other end). Is preference satisfaction intrinsically good? Recognizing that people prefer many different things, some of which are trivial, silly, crude, or even immoral and unjust, surely the satisfaction of preferences cannot be something that is good in itself. For example, preference utilitarianism would have us take the preferences of a Hitler into consideration as we calculate the overall consequences of social policy. We would just have to hope that these preferences get outnumbered by the preferences of Hitler's victims. Put another way, we would hope that the utility a Hitler derives from genocide is outweighed by the disutility of his victims. Critics charge that the preference for genocide can play no role in ethical decision making.

Perhaps, then, satisfying preferences is instrumentally good; perhaps by satisfying preferences we are producing some other good. Candidates for this further good typically include happiness, welfare, well-being or, in the words of economists, "utility." So, what evidence do we have that satisfying preferences will make people happy, or increase their welfare, well-being, or utility? Are you always happier, is your well-being always improved, when you get what you want?

One way to answer this question is simply to *define* the satisfaction of preferences as happiness, welfare, well-being, or utility. It would not be uncommon, for example, to find "utility" defined in this way within economic discussions. But note that this option is unavailable to utilitarian ethical theory. Defining the good in this way is to commit the logical fallacy of begging the question or circular reasoning mentioned earlier. We began with a challenge that asked why should we satisfy preferences. The suggested answer was that satisfying preferences leads to happiness (or well-being, welfare, utility). But if happiness is defined as preference satisfaction, then the purported answer is that we ought to satisfy preferences because doing so leads to the satisfaction of preferences.

The only option open to the defender of market utilitarianism is to offer an independent account of happiness and make the empirical claim that satisfying individual preferences will in fact produce greater happiness. But given any independent definition of happiness or well-being, it is not at all clear that satisfying preferences does lead to greater happiness. The smoker or alcoholic who wants another cigarette or drink will not be made happier, or his welfare will not be increased, by getting what he wants. In more general terms, there is ample evidence to suggest that some people are not made happier by increasingly getting more of what they want. What we want and, importantly, how much we want determines whether it will be an ethically good thing to get what we want. Sometimes the more we have the more we come to expect. The more we come to expect, the more we want and the more we want the less happy we are. Surely a more reasonable conclusion is that happiness is only contingently connected to the satisfaction of our preferences.

Let us recap this analysis. Defenders of market utilitarianism propose that the satisfaction of individual preferences is the proper understanding of what is ethically good. But preference satisfaction is either intrinsically good or instrumentally good. We have good reason to deny that it is intrinsically good (think of the preferences of a child molester, for example). However, there are also good reasons to deny that satisfying preferences does in fact produce happiness in an ethical sense. There are some clear cases in which people are not made happier when they get what they desire. The only other option is to define happiness in this way, but doing that commits the logical fallacy of begging the question, or assuming what needs to be proven.

The conclusion from this is not to assume that overall happiness is decreased when people get what they want or that human welfare is not improved by economic growth and a high standard of living. Certainly sometimes, perhaps even most times, it is. However, it does suggest that we need to look very carefully at the content of the preferences being satisfying or denied. We just shouldn't assume that ethical goals are identical to the goals of economic markets.

Means and Ends Challenges

In an earlier section we reviewed a set of challenges that go to the very heart of utilitarianism by rejecting consequentialism as an adequate basis for ethics. This perspective argues that good ends do not always justify the means. Ethics seems to demand that sometimes we act in certain ways—what we often call acting on principle or out of duty—even when this does not increase overall happiness. Similar challenges also arise for the free market version of utilitarianism.

We earlier suggested that a very troubling aspect of this means–ends problem concerned the utilitarian focus on the aggregate or collective good. In the view of critics this is troubling, since most of us believe that each and every individual possesses an inherent dignity and deserves to be treated as an individual and not simply as a means to the end of the happiness of others. To put it another way, we believe that individuals have rights that should not be violated merely to obtain a net increase in the overall aggregate happiness. Let us consider how this challenge reemerges for the preference utilitarianism that underlies the free market.

As described earlier in the chapter, markets make no in-principle distinction between consumer preferences. If consumers are willing to pay more for some property when used as a building lot than they will pay for it as park land, then the market will direct the landowner to sell the land to builders rather than preservationists. Markets make no judgments about the relative worthiness of the competing consumer preferences. Insofar as they produce equal happiness (as judged by what individuals are willing to pay), all preferences are equal.

The rights-based picture of morality rejects this assumption. Using the distinction between interests and desires outlined previously, this view of morality argues that individuals have certain interests that should not be sacrificed merely to increase the satisfaction of other people's desires. For example, my interests in life, health, and freedom ought not to be sacrificed simply to increase the total amount of consumer happiness in society. Treating these various goals as undifferentiated "preferences" obscures important differences between them. From this perspective, not all preferences are morally equal. Certain preferences do not deserve satisfaction (remember the preferences of a child molester); others, such as the preferences for life, liberty, and family, deserve special protection because they are so closely tied to the inherent value and dignity of the individual. If respect for the dignity of individuals means anything, it means that we cannot treat human beings merely as tools to produce a net increase in the overall total amount of social happiness.

The consequentialism that is an essential part of utilitarianism commits us to reserving ethical judgments until the consequences are known. In this sense, the ethical status of such things as genocide and slavery, for example, is an empirical matter. We don't know if they are unethical until we determine that, in fact, they produce less happiness (or good) than the alternative. Critics charge that this is absurd. Genocide and slavery are ethically wrong in principle; there are no circumstances under which they could be ethically justified. From this perspective, the fundamental norm of ethics is to treat individual people as ends in themselves, regardless of the consequences.

Of course, utilitarians are aware of this challenge and have developed responses to the charge that they allow the ends to justify the means and that they fail to recognize individual rights. Some utilitarians suggest that the focus of utilitarian evaluation be shifted from assessing the consequences of individual actions (the traditional version of utilitarianism, known as *act utilitarianism*). Instead, they suggest that utilitarians should assess the overall consequences of social *practices* or *rules* (a version known as *rule utilitarianism*). Rule utilitarians claim that if we choose practices and rules that maximize overall happiness and judge individual acts according to their conformity to the approved practice or rule, then utilitarianism will be able to accommodate both the rights and the duties referred to earlier.

Consider, they argue, that if we defend the practice of promise-keeping because of its social utility (and the disutility of not being able to depend on the promises of others), we can condemn individual actions that break promises and uphold a general obligation to abide by our commitments. Hence, it seems that rule utilitarianism can account for a class of duties that act utilitarianism cannot.

They also suggest imagining that we assess the social consequences of a rule requiring respect for property. Surely, rule utilitarians argue, that rule would produce better consequences for collective happiness than would an alternative that made people constantly worry about the security of their possessions. Of course, such a property-respecting rule is the practical equivalent of a *right* to property. The essence of the rule utilitarian argument, then, is that a concern for maximizing collective welfare requires that we encourage respect for individuals' rights. In this view, rights are valued not as ends in themselves, but as important or necessary means to ethical ends. Thus, rule utilitarians claim that their new version of utilitarianism can avoid the means–ends and rights criticisms leveled against more traditional versions of utilitarianism.

In spite of this clever utilitarian response, however, we believe that the means–ends and rights problems remain, even for rule utilitarianism. First, the general duties and obligations recognized by rule utilitarianism must allow for exceptions. To be consistent, rule utilitarians must determine what counts as an exception by determining whether, say, keeping or breaking a particular promise would maximize happiness. If happiness is marginally improved by allowing the exception to the rule in a particular case, then we would have no obligation to keep the promise in that case. However, since any given promise could conceivably be an exception, rule utilitarians will be forced to assess the consequences for each promise in order to determine if it is an exception to the general rule. The same will be true for other types of duties besides promise-keeping. So it appears that rule utilitarianism is no different than act utilitarianism because it too must assess the consequences of individual actions in order to determine what ought to be done.

Second, in any case, we need to question whether the purpose of a system of rights would adequately be captured under the rule-utilitarian account. It is very odd, in fact, paradoxical, to believe that we want to protect some interests of persons from being sacrificed for the common good merely because by doing so we are maximizing the very same common good. An alternative account of why we believe in individual rights would stress them as necessary for expressing a commitment to persons as having inherent value and dignity. Such an individual-centered, respect-based account of rights seems more natural than the argument that rights are a means of achieving the greatest collective welfare. In the end, then, our judgment remains that the rule-utilitarian response to the means–ends and rights problem is unconvincing.

IN SUMMARY

The ethical theory of utilitarianism advises us to calculate the consequences of our decisions and act in such a way that we maximize the overall welfare. Some utilitarian thinkers also maintain that a free market is the best economic and social arrangement for attaining this goal. However, significant challenges can be raised against this claim, both from within the utilitarian tradition and from alternative ethical perspectives.

Many utilitarians believe that a free market is neither a necessary nor sufficient means for attaining the maximum overall good. In more economic terms, many people now believe that a mixed economy, one that features both market mechanisms and government regulation and support, is more likely to produce a high standard of living. One important lesson from this is that utilitarians are committed neither to endorsing nor to rejecting market solutions for every issue. The question about what decision is most appropriate in a given case will depend on the specific consequences of that decision. What we have seen is that, even on utilitarian grounds, one cannot argue that market solutions are always the preferable alternative.

Challenges have also been raised against the ends of the market version of utilitarianism. Some utilitarians argue that preference satisfaction as it occurs within markets is not an appropriate ethical goal at all. Further difficulties arise for any attempt to measure the likely consequences of our actions. Finally, many people reject the utilitarian approach to ethics entirely. According to one alternative view, utilitarianism ignores important questions of ethical character and virtue. According to another alternative view, important human interests such as respect, freedom, and life (as well as our duty to honor these interests) should not be subject to utilitarian calculations. This approach to ethics holds that some human interests ought to receive special protection as individual rights. Even if free markets attained the maximum overall good, they would still be ethically flawed if they did not protect individual rights. In the next chapter, we examine this alternative, rights-based conception of ethics and critically examine how some versions of this approach have also been used to defend the workings of free markets.

3

Philosophical Ethics:
Rights and the Market

INTRODUCTION

The previous chapters show us the relevance of ethical theory for business decisions. As we saw in Chapter Two, common opinions about business often rest on hidden utilitarian foundations. Assessing the wisdom of these common opinions requires us to consider empirical claims about collective welfare effects of business policies. Assessing those common opinions also requires us to decide whether utilitarianism is an adequate account of morality. We saw that there are serious critical questions to be raised in both areas.

In this chapter, we continue to examine the relevance of philosophical ethics for business. Here, however, we look not at utilitarian underpinnings but rather at the role played by rights. Beliefs about rights exert an even more powerful influence on how we think about both ethics and business than does utilitarianism. Three contemporary business examples illustrate the importance of clear thinking about rights.

First, consider the recent financial and accounting scandals. Enron, WorldCom, and Tyco are all described as cases where management failed in its fiduciary duty to shareholders and where gatekeepers (accountants, financial analysts, investment bankers) failed in their duties to assure accurate information for the investing public. In the Enron case, for example, management frequently used legal off-the-books partnership arrangements to improve the appearance of corporate indebtedness. Some critics claim that this technique violated the rights of shareholders to accurate information about the corporation's long-term financial health.

However, investors could have discerned much about the true state of the company by a careful reading of the footnotes in the annual reports. Those notes revealed many of the aggressive accounting practices that ultimately led to the company's demise. In fact, some "massaging the numbers" is reported to be a widespread practice in corporate America. Enron is perhaps merely a more extreme example. Would the fact that the relevant information about the partnerships was included in footnotes to Enron's annual report be enough for us to say that management and accountants respected the rights of investors to information about the firm's condition? Or do investors have a right to more-overt disclosure than that? Careful analysis of the Enron case will force us to clarify just what rights to information shareholders have (and also whether common accounting practices in other companies are consistent with those rights).

As a second example, consider the debates over whether major pharmaceutical companies have a duty to provide low-cost anti-AIDS drugs to African communities ravaged by both poverty and epidemic levels of HIV infection. (Some estimates have rates of infection as high as 20% for some local populations.) Lobbyists for the major companies have sometimes fought the importation into Africa of pirated versions of their drugs produced in India (versions of the drugs that can cost $150 for a year's supply rather than the thousands of dollars per year charged for the drugs in the American market). The industry has argued that it needs to defend its intellectual property and patent rights on the drugs it has developed. The Indian manufacturers, of course, incur no research or development costs. This case forces us to clarify whether the rights of patent holders morally entitle them to gain income by blocking the distribution of cheaper, unlicensed copies of their drugs.

Finally, intellectual property rights also figure in a case that is closer to the daily lives of college students—access to free music downloads through file-sharing services such as Napster. Where many college students saw merely an opportunity to acquire free music, the recording industry and some recording artists saw a violation of their rights as copyright holders and creators of the music.

These examples should make clear the relevance of rights, and especially of property rights, to debates about corporate responsibility. Arriving at a reasoned judgment on any of these cases will require some careful thought about rights and their content. To help guide that thought process, we divide the remainder of this chapter into two main sections. The first provides a fairly complex theory of rights with special attention to the justification and limits of rights. The second section will apply that theory of rights to the question that is the focus of these first chapters: Should we accept a Friedman-like free market view of corporate responsibility?

RIGHTS THEORY

Rights and Respect

As we saw in the last chapter, talk of moral rights arises as we attempt to express a belief about the inherent value of individuals. Most of us believe strongly that persons ought to be treated with dignity and respect. However, adopting a utilitarian, interest-maximizing perspective prevents us from giving that belief practical significance. Utilitarianism requires that we be willing to sacrifice any interest of any person, even the most basic, on the altar of collective welfare. At its heart, utilitarianism requires us to see persons merely as tools for achieving aggregate interest satisfaction. Individual persons under utilitarianism seem to have little inherent value. Their significance is mainly as loci for the interests that are to be satisfied or frustrated in pursuit of the greatest common good.

In the 18th century, Immanuel Kant suggested that the problem with aggregating, consequentialist theories was that they treated persons merely as means and not as ends in themselves. More recently, John Rawls has argued that utilitarianism fails to take seriously the distinction between persons. Perhaps this anti-aggregate perspective is most forcefully maintained by traditional religious moralities that hold each person to be created in the image of God and, for that reason, to have intrinsic worth.

We cannot, then, claim to respect individuals if we are willing to do anything to them—for example, kill them, debase them, or enslave them—for the sake of some desired social goal. We can only give practical significance to the belief that persons deserve respect if we place some aspects of the person off-limits. This is a primary function of rights: to protect some areas of a person's life from utilitarian or majority rule deliberations, or merely from the harmful acts of other individuals. A right to life aims to protect the person's life from others; a right to free speech aims to protect a person's ability to express an opinion even if others disagree with it. In protecting interests from society or from other individuals, rights can be seen as entitlements or justified claims that impose obligations on others. In fact, there is a standard thesis about rights known as the "correlativity thesis." It maintains that all rights create obligations for some other party or parties. If I have a constitutional right to freedom from self-incrimination (as under U.S. law), I am entitled to refuse to testify at my own trial and the state is under an obligation not to punish me merely for that refusal. If I have a moral right to some property, such as my car, my claim to possess and use it places other individuals under an obligation not to deprive me of that car.

(Note that in talking about rights it is usually important to identify both what claims or entitlements a particular right justifies and which other person or persons are placed under an obligation by that right. It is also important that we distinguish between legal and moral rights. Legal rights are those granted by the principles and statutes of a legal system and they are often, but not always, enforced by courts. Moral rights, on the other hand, are derived from the principles of a moral system and are often enforced through subtler sanctions, such as social expressions of disapproval that can range in seriousness up to treating the rights-violator as a social outcast. Failure to distinguish between these types of rights can cause confusion, as for example when Alexa asserts that she has a (legal) right to park in an area on the street that has been shoveled clear of snow by a neighbor, while Matt claims that she has no (moral) right to occupy that space. The two may talk past each other if they do not understand that they are asserting rights of different kinds. In our discussions, we typically will be interested in identifying the relevant *moral* rights in a business ethics debate, though we will also sometimes try to specify the legal rights involved as well.)

So, rights give some real, practical significance to the intuition that persons deserve to be treated with dignity and respect. This, however, only scratches the surface of a theory of rights. A more developed theory must also address a number of other questions in detail: What is the basis of this belief in the dignity of persons? If rights protect interests, what interests of the person should be elevated to this protected status? For any given right, what is its limit or scope? For example, what specific entitlements are included in the right to property? What procedures, if any, are available when the rights of different persons conflict, as they inevitably will?

Here we will only outline answers to these questions. We cannot hope to provide a detailed and complete account of rights in the few pages available. And, in any case, the answers we provide will be controversial. Philosophers disagree widely about how to understand rights. Nonetheless, we believe that the picture of rights that follows best accounts for our deep commitment to rights and best explains how rights actually function in our shared moral experience. We will leave it to the reader to evaluate whether our confidence in the account is warranted or misplaced.

Dignity and Autonomy

What gives rise to the intuition that persons deserve respect? Two answers present themselves. The first is that the intuition is just a basic tenet of our morality, a commitment that depends on nothing and is explained by nothing further. This answer, though possible, is not terribly satisfying. Usually we prefer to be able to explain our central beliefs, although, of course, explanation cannot go on forever. Moreover, if the belief in the dignity of persons is itself basic, we will not be able to integrate that belief into an account of why particular interests ought to be protected as rights, of what specific actions the dignity of others requires from us.

In fact, a second answer is given by a historically important tradition running from the ancient Greeks through the medievals and up to contemporary moral theorists. That tradition finds the dignity of persons grounded in a peculiarly human attribute that philosophers have sometimes characterized as rationality, sometimes as free will. To unify these characterizations, we will identify this attribute as "autonomy." We define autonomy as the capacity to make reasoned, deliberative choices about how to act. This definition includes the human capacities of both reason and free will. It is interesting to note that explaining dignity by reference to autonomy parallels not only a long philosophical tradition but also many religious traditions that regard humans as created in the image of God. What could that mean other than having free will guided by reason?

If autonomy explains the belief in the dignity of persons, we have to ask what, in practical terms, it would mean to respect that autonomy. Certainly, it cannot mean allowing individuals complete control over their lives, absolute ability to act in any way they choose. That would be anarchy. More importantly, it would be impossible because allowing me to act as I want would inevitably prevent some others from doing what they wanted. This, then, is too strong an understanding of what is required by respect for autonomy.

Just as certainly, respect for a person's autonomy cannot mean allowing a person to have some merely formal choice available. This is too weak an understanding. It would mean that the behavior of a thief who sticks the barrel of a pistol in my ribs and says, "Your money or your life," is behavior that is compatible with respect for my autonomy. (He gave me a choice, didn't he?) What is needed is some understanding of respect for persons that steers between anarchy and the meaningless and merely formal existence of choice.

What Rights?

Since it is unreasonable to allow unlimited latitude of action and insufficient merely to provide formal choices, we have to articulate what constitutes respect for a person and her autonomy in some other way. A promising alternative is to sketch a zone of autonomy that would allow a person to exercise a real opportunity to control her life. We could sketch such a zone if we protected a set of important interests (life, for one instance). With these interests not in jeopardy from society or from others, a person could have a secure space within which she could deliberate and act. Of course, threats to these interests cannot be completely removed. But if threats from other persons or from humanly alterable conditions (such as treatable disease or abject poverty) can be minimized, capacities for choice would be substantially increased. This is true even if other persons occasionally violate the protection society tries to provide. Therefore, we can steer between anarchy and meaningless choice if we can identify a set of basic rights.

The crucial question then becomes, what interests ought to be protected? The interests must be important, not trivial. We could say that basic rights should be drawn from those interests whose enjoyment constitutes an adequate human life. To get any more specific than this will require some vision about the specific elements that constitute a decent human existence. Any attempt to completely describe "the human good" will be controversial, of course. But there are many elements of "the good" on which most will agree. Life is an undeniable element of human existence; protecting it would be a "no-brainer" selection. We might also say that a reasonable human life would require the minimal conditions of biological survival (food, clothing, shelter), or at the very least, the real opportunity to acquire them. In a less material vein, some will argue that other things are essential for a truly human life: freedom from threats of severe bodily harm by others; freedom to express one's opinions; the ability to collectively determine the conditions of a shared social system; freedom to associate with others of one's choosing; and freedom to exercise religious commitments. A number of these items are found in the U.S. Bill of Rights and/or the UN Declaration of Human Rights. (A fact that shows an overlap between moral and legal rights both in their content and their rationales. Though these are different categories of rights, it is not surprising that some strongly held moral intuitions about rights have found their way into legal systems.)

If interests such as these are protected—in other words, recognized as rights—persons would gain substantial control over their lives and be able to exercise their autonomy meaningfully. With no threat to my shelter or my physical security, I can more freely choose what to do. Alternatively, if I constantly must worry about my shelter or security, the courses of action open to me will be much more limited.

There is no denying that some of the items just identified as candidates for rights may be disputed, and the list is certainly incomplete. The point, here, is not to provide an exhaustive, uncontroversial catalog of basic rights. It is rather to indicate how one could argue for a right as basic by tying it to central human interests. Each of these interests is arguably constitutive of a decent human life, and violation of these interests cuts at the core of what it means to be a person. Consider the right to freedom of speech. If we regard persons as autonomous, as capable of deliberative choice about how to live their lives, we must regard the consideration of ideas as central to human life. Deliberation requires that people be able to express their ideas, opinions, and criticisms to each other. Hence, some level of free speech is required if we are to properly respect persons as capable of directing their own lives.

We leave you to articulate more carefully how the other items mentioned might be core human goods and how interference with those might involve disrespect for an individual as a person. We also leave it to you to add (or subtract) from the list. We do that with a caution, however. The idea is to articulate how dignity, autonomy, and respect might be integrated into a picture of morality that reserves a central place for individual rights. This notion of respect is not the same as respect for an individual because of his or her position (your "elders") or power (on some streets you can "dis" someone merely by making eye contact). Respect in this account is respect for a person's humanity.

You should note, too, that this account of rights thus far only addresses core or basic rights. We need to recognize that there are other, lower-level rights as well. How rights of different levels are related is the topic of a later section, "Basic and Derivative Rights: Resolving Conflicts."

The Scope of Rights

Identifying a list of core rights will raise further questions. Two are especially important, and the first is the topic of this section: What is the scope of each right? The second is the topic of the next section: What do we do when rights conflict?

When we speak of the scope of a right, we mean a specific list of the protections that it includes. Since these protections by definition impose obligations on others, defining the scope of a right will also require us to specify just which other persons are obligated because someone else holds a particular right. So "scope" refers to both the specific protections and the specific audience the protections are addressed to.

Since this is what the scope of a right involves, no general, easy answer applies to the question, what is the scope of each right? The particular protections and audiences will depend on the right at issue. Take my right to life as an example. Presumably it creates some obligation for *all* other people not to kill me. It also might obligate some smaller set of people to provide me with positive assistance if my life is in danger (if, for example, I am in an accident, need CPR, and there is an emergency medical technician present at the scene). Also, your presumptive obligation not to kill might not exist if I am threatening your life while committing a crime against your person or property. Hence, the scope of even a right to life will be difficult to identify in general terms. Additionally, the scope of a right will depend crucially on what other rights are in conflict and on how that conflict is to be adjudicated.

We caution, however, that the difficulty of detailing the scope of rights means neither that rights are empty of all content (as some critics have suggested) nor that any interpretation of the content of a right is as acceptable as any other. There will be clear cases where rights prohibit specific acts by others (your murdering me in retaliation for having to read this text) and clear cases where one's action falls outside of what one's rights entitle (falsely yelling fire in the proverbial crowded theater). Even in less immediately clear cases, there is the possibility that careful argument can provide a reasonable basis for concluding that something is either inside or outside the scope of a particular right. In fact, in the second half of this chapter we present such arguments for the rights to liberty and property. Following chapters present arguments concerning the scope of other rights, such as the right to privacy for employees.

Finally, before leaving the issue of scope, we must address a common distinction concerning the scope of rights. Sometimes rights are said to impose merely obligations to refrain from harming the interests of others. Rights of this sort are called "negative rights" and their correlative duties, "negative duties." Other times, rights are said to impose affirmative obligations to help secure another's interests. These rights are called "positive rights" and their correlative duties, "positive duties." One theory—too commonly held, from our perspective—suggests that all true rights are negative; that is, that rights never require us to give positive assistance to another. (This view is typically held by libertarians; it also has some affinity with Friedman's ideas about the limits of management responsibility.)

We believe that limiting all rights to negative rights is mistaken. First, as many have pointed out, the line between negative and positive rights is far from sharp. Even classic negative interpretations of rights, such as the right not to be killed by others, require enforcement, which in turn requires a significant institutional apparatus. For us to enforce the right not to be killed requires that we all make positive contributions (in the form of taxes, for example) to support institutions such as the courts and police. Thus, it is hard to even imagine a practical social circumstance where the rights of others merely oblige us not to harm them.

Second, if rights, at least core rights, are justified by the need to respect others, and if that respect requires that persons have a real opportunity to exercise their autonomy, then surely it seems contrary to the point of rights to allow an individual near us to starve when we have abundant food. If respect is defined in terms of conditions necessary for a decent human existence, then it is unlikely that rights are always negative and unlikely that rights never impose on us positive obligations to ensure that people have those conditions of a decent existence. Another's right to life may not require us to put our own life at risk, but surely it sometimes requires us to render positive assistance.

There is, however, a difficulty that we need to acknowledge with recognizing positive rights. Since rights impose correlative obligations on others, it is important to specify on just which others those obligations fall. With negative rights, that is easy. The obligation not to kill you falls equally on all of the rest of us. But when a person's positive right requires that others render assistance, it is sometimes hard to specify just which others have the duty to aid. If I enter my grandmother's house and at that very moment hear her fall in the bathtub, unconscious, with her head under water, it should be clear to all that I have the obligation to lift her out. But suppose a person is starving and that person's positive rights require that he be fed. Which of us has the obligation to supply the food? In institutional contexts, the questions become more complicated. If there are multiple institutions (governments, businesses, charitable organizations, and so on) that could render needed aid to a starving population, how do we determine which of them have duties to provide it?

Consider the previously mentioned debate on anti-AIDS drugs in Africa. The prices for the drugs developed by major manufacturers are higher than many African patients, or even African governments, can afford. In a case like this, who, if anyone, bears responsibility for assisting those suffering from epidemic levels of HIV infection? Should major Western pharmaceutical companies reduce their prices? Should African governments be responsible for paying for the treatment of their citizens? Should governments of developed nations subsidize AIDS drugs for Africans?

Philosophers, in considering questions like these, sometimes propose criteria for determining just when the duty to render assistance exists. For instance, some hold that a person (or institution) is obligated to assist (1) when there is a clear and important need, (2) when the person (or institution) can respond effectively to that need, (3) when there is no serious risk to oneself, and (4) when there is no guarantee that others will provide the needed assistance.*

A classic case from New York City in the 1960s illustrates both these criteria and the importance of recognizing positive rights. A woman named Kitty Genovese was stabbed to death outside her apartment building. The attack was loud and prolonged. Many people were in the building, with windows open, yet no one tried to assist. No one shouted out the window to frighten the attacker away; no one called the police. Clearly, in this instance, the witnesses to the attack who did nothing failed in their responsibilities. (A more lighthearted rendition of the moral duty to assist was the theme of the last episode of the popular *Seinfeld*

---

*See John Simon, Charles Powers, and Jon Gunneman, "The Responsibilities of Corporations and Their Owners," in *The Ethical Investor: Universities and Corporate Responsibility* (New Haven: Yale University Press, 1972).

television series. The self-centered characters not only failed to assist a victim of a robbery, but they laughingly mocked him.)

The Kitty Genovese case can help us identify both when a positive duty exists and the persons on whom that duty falls. So, while positive rights pose more difficulties than do negative rights in identifying our respective obligations, we can still have criteria for sensibly determining when and where positive rights obtain. The claim that all rights are negative is unduly restrictive. That claim ought to be rejected.

We turn next to the second question regarding core rights: What do we do when rights conflict?

Basic and Derivative Rights: Resolving Conflicts

The rights people claim often conflict. An employer's claimed right to select the best possible worker from a list of job applicants, perhaps by using undisclosed background checks, may conflict with a potential employee's claimed right to privacy. A student's right to share his digital music files may conflict with a record company's copyright claims.

Resolving such conflicts requires that we have some procedure for ranking rights by importance, because if all rights have exactly the same moral status, there is little hope of adjudicating conflicts. Conflicts will merely be cases of brute and irresolvable opposition. In that case, appeal to rights will be of little practical assistance in determining what we should do. Given the centrality of rights in modern moral discourse, moral debate would degenerate into a proliferation of "rights" simply to whatever people desire. (Some commentators believe that this is an accurate description of the state of morality in the late 20th century: selfishness masking itself as a serious moral claim.)

The first step, then, is to construct some schema that allows us to place right claims into a hierarchy and that provides a rational process for settling conflicts. Once again, we do not suggest that the analysis we provide is without controversy or that it will easily and mechanically resolve all conflict. We do, however, believe that something like it is the best available procedure.

Until now our focus has been on rights as the necessary antidote to the aggregating tendencies of utilitarianism and as a way of treating individuals with dignity and respect. A moment's reflection, however, reveals that not every right claimed in our culture is tied to respect for the person. Intuitively, the legal right to drive a car does not have the same status as the constitutional right to free speech. So, as a start in understanding how moral rights might be rank-ordered, let us first consider some relationships between legal rights.

Consider the following three legal rights: the right to free speech, the right to privacy, and the right to deduct from my taxable income the interest paid on my home mortgage. Each of these is an existing legal right, and each is recognized for different reasons. The differences in their underlying justifications will give the three rights different status or importance. We have already seen that the right to free speech can be directly tied to respect for the person since speech and the exchange of ideas is an integral part of what we take a person to be. In a political context, free speech also has great instrumental value in that civil liberties and democratic institutions are more secure when people have a right to express their grievances against the government. So, a right to speech free from government censorship, as enshrined in the First Amendment of the U.S. Constitution, has extremely strong foundations.

The right to a mortgage deduction, created by statute of the Congress, has much less significant foundations. That right was created to encourage home ownership and to stimulate the critical housing industry. Its primary purpose is to create economic benefits, such as greater employment, that can be shared throughout the society. While the benefits are real, the justification for the legal right is that it is one among a number of instruments for promoting the collective welfare. This right, then, is not tied to respect for the person but rather to a utilitarian calculation that it is beneficial policy.

The right to privacy also has instrumental value but of a different sort. It promotes individual autonomy by reducing the chance that a person can be controlled by blackmail or manipulation. It provides a sense of security by helping people consider particular relationships as more intimate than others because they can control what personal information is shared. Privacy thus has instrumental value, to be sure, but what it promotes is of greater moment than an incremental increase in collective welfare. We might reasonably see privacy as falling between the other two rights in its importance.

These examples show that legal rights can be hierarchically ordered according to their underlying justifications. Some rights are based directly on the need for respect, some are based only on their instrumental value, and some, such as free speech, are based on both of these foundations.

A similar analysis can be given for moral rights. In fact, the justifying reasons for speech and privacy rights are weighty enough from a moral perspective for those to be considered moral rights as well. In any case, the import of the preceding account of legal rights is that it suggests a method for ordering rights, whether they be legal or moral. We can categorize rights by looking to the values underlying them. The different types of justifying reasons (respect, utility, and so on) provide us with a rough schema that allows us to distinguish between what we will call "basic rights" and other nonbasic or "derivative rights." Basic rights are ones whose recognition is essential for individuals to be treated with dignity and respect. (Obviously, as was noted earlier, determining which rights are basic will require some vision of the elements that constitute an adequate human life.) Derivative rights depend for their importance on an instrumental contribution towards achieving some other good. Although derivative rights are not tied essentially to respect, they could nonetheless be very important in that the goods they help to secure may be of great significance. The right to privacy, as previously analyzed, is one example. Freedom of the press would be another derivative right of great importance, since it is instrumental in protecting other, more basic rights. However, at least some derivative rights are clearly less important because they are granted merely to promote social goals or policies that are believed to increase collective welfare.

Other derivative rights have their origins in the particular positions or relationships of an individual. For instance, presidents have the legal right to veto legislation. Parents have morally recognized rights to discipline their children. I have a moral right that my friend fulfills his promise to me.

This proposed method for categorizing rights by their foundational justifications provides a clue about how to resolve conflicts between right claims. If, after analyzing the relative justifications of two competing rights, we find that the rights are of different levels (basic vs. derivative; derivative but crucial vs. derivative and less compelling), the presumptive conclusion would be that the higher-level right takes precedence. This is, however, merely a presumptive conclusion. In the abstract, a right to free speech takes precedence over matters of mere convenience. But extending the right to free speech to cover a particular case might not promote the values underlying the right to free speech, and extending the right could cause great inconvenience. Consider if a right to free speech included a right to express political opinions by parading, unannounced, down the center lane of an urban expressway at rush hour. Obviously, restrictions on the time, place, and manner of speech might be justified in the name of convenience, especially when other effective avenues of expression are available. Thus, with conflicts between higher-order rights and lower-order rights, final conclusions about which right takes precedence must await more careful analysis of individual cases.

The need for such careful analysis is even more crucial when conflicting rights are of the same level or have the same foundations. When two claimed rights rest on the same moral grounds, a defense for the priority of one over the other must show that, in the given case, the justifying values are more centrally at stake in the one taking priority. To put this point another way, when two such rights conflict, we must decide which right to restrict by asking which restriction would least damage the values that underlie the conflicting rights.

Consider a business-related case. Owners of corporate property claim a right to control that property, including a right to control who has access to it. Employees claim a right not to be fired unjustly or arbitrarily. Both right claims can be supported by appeals to fairness, utility, and autonomy. (Detailed discussion of these justifications will come later in this chapter and in Chapter Five.) If employers' rights to control access include the right to hire and fire anyone for any reason (as had been the case in the United States until recently), then their rights would conflict with the rights claimed by employees. To resolve this conflict we have to ask which does greater damage to the values of fairness, autonomy, and utility: (1) allowing owners the right to fire at will and not allowing workers the right to be free from arbitrary dismissal or (2) restraining the ability to fire at will by granting the employees a right to be fired only for just cause? We leave the answer to that question open. (It is one major theme of Chapter Five.) What we emphasize is that resolving conflicts between rights of the same level requires us to look to the underlying foundations of the rights and to determine which right to limit by asking which limit least harms those values. (It would be interesting to apply these questions about relative impacts on fairness, autonomy, and utility to the previously discussed intellectual property cases of AIDs drugs and Napster file sharing.)

So while there are compelling reasons for introducing talk of rights into our moral discussions, introducing them into the debate does not make moral analysis any easier. Identifying which right claims are legitimate ones, defining the scope of particular rights, and resolving conflicts between rights are not simple tasks. Each requires that you carefully analyze the reasons justifying a right claim. In fact, if there is any single lesson that is most important in our discussion of rights, it is that we always need to clarify the foundations of right claims before there is any hope of progress in contemporary moral debate. Clarity about foundations will help us sort out those right claims that are frivolous and help us evaluate conflicts between those that are not.

A major note must be made about the procedure of ethical analysis we have proposed. The procedure is not algorithmic. Steps in the analysis will be open to debate and will involve value judgments about the relative importance of rights. What the process of analysis provides is a framework for reasonable debate between opposing points of view. Without such a framework, those who are most pessimistic about contemporary ethics are probably right: Ethical debate reduces merely to a conflict of wills. Under those circumstances, debate about issues in business ethics will not be reasonable deliberation but mere assertion of opinion. Careful analysis of moral concepts along the lines of our suggestions will help avoid that result. Now that we have the necessary analytical tools, we can finally return to a discussion of rights-based defenses of the free market view.

TWO RIGHTS ARGUMENTS
FOR THE FREE MARKET

It has been more than a few pages since we last addressed the free market view of business responsibility. It might be helpful at this point to review what that position involved. What we are dubbing the "free market view" is an extreme position that claims two things: (1) Management is responsible only for maximizing profits without using fraud or coercion, and (2) Government regulation of business is acceptable only when necessary to prevent fraud or coercion. We will not reiterate the reasons for calling this view extreme. We will, however, remind students that along a spectrum of positions about the degree to which markets may be properly constrained, the free market view as defined here is at one extreme. It accepts very few constraints, whether legal or moral, on the behavior of persons in the marketplace. We should also reiterate that our objections to the free market view do not mean that we reject the value of markets. In fact, we regard markets as valuable mechanisms for allocating and pricing goods. Rather, our objections to the extreme free market view of responsibility suggest that markets best serve the purposes of human societies when they are subject to some moral and legal limitations.

For the remainder of this chapter we will consider two common rights-based arguments for the free market approach to corporate responsibility. The first argues that the free market is required in order to respect individuals' rights to liberty. The second argues that the free market view is the only view compatible with recognition of a right to private property.

These two respective rights play a major role in contemporary Western morality, and they deserve careful attention. In the following pages we consider both of these arguments for the free market by applying some of the analytical tools we developed earlier. We suggest that both arguments fail because both inadequately understand the rights they appeal to. The presumptive conclusion we draw is that there are strong reasons for thinking that any morally defensible view of business responsibility must accept many more responsibilities than the free market position does. Just what those responsibilities are will be left for the issue-oriented debates of Chapters Five through Fourteen.

The Right to Liberty and the Market

One straightforward argument for the laissez-faire view starts with a right that is familiar in the rhetoric of our culture—a right to liberty. Traditionally, the right to liberty is understood to be a right to be free from human interference in one's pursuits. If we acknowledge such a right, it is easy to generate an argument for the free market: If individuals have a right to an absence of interference in their affairs, then they should be free to engage in any voluntary (in other words, noncoercive, nondeceptive) economic transactions they wish to enter. Similarly, government should respect liberty by regulating only to ensure that transactions are free and nondeceptive. Any interference with voluntary, nondeceptive transactions would violate the liberty of the transacting parties. According to this argument, a just society would be one where management was free to pursue profits and the government's role was limited to maintaining free and open competition.

Whether this argument succeeds will depend on whether we accept the general right to liberty with which it starts. Certainly, in our society there is a great attraction to the idea of a general right to noninterference. The free and independent individual is a character who plays a major role in our national mythology. But equally certain, any legitimate understanding of a right to liberty must admit that liberty cannot be absolute and unrestrained. This is for at least two reasons. First, an absolute right to liberty would result in social chaos. The conditions of any social life demand that sometimes people must be prevented from doing what they want.

Second, the concept of an absolute right to liberty is a practical impossibility. If I have an absolute right to be free in my pursuits and one of my pursuits is to steal your car, then you cannot have an absolute right to noninterference in your continued possession of the car.

In fact, interferences are an unavoidable and sometimes unobjectionable element of economic transactions. (I would always rather pay less for a product, and hence, I am often prevented from getting what I want. Is that a violation of my liberty?) Since interferences are unavoidable and sometimes unobjectionable, what we need is some approach to picking out those interferences that should be prohibited.

One traditional approach is to say that each of us ought to be able to do what we wish so long as we do not interfere with the liberty of others. This sounds nice but ultimately is of no help in specifically defining the limits of liberty because defining what my right to liberty includes will require that we already have an independent idea of what your right to liberty includes. The problem here is similar to the classic problem of defining a word by using that same word. So to say that my right to liberty allows me to do anything that does not violate the liberty of others is to say nothing in particular about what I am and am not allowed to do. We still need a principle that can tell us which interferences to prohibit and which to permit.

Another commonly used approach is to say that we will prohibit the greatest interferences. This will not help if "greatest" is understood in its usual quantitative sense. Quantitative judgments demand some unit of measurement. What is a unit of interference or of liberty? If we propose to measure liberty by the number of times a person is interfered with, we are likely to get counterintuitive results about which among a group of interferences is most objectionable. Which ban would cause the greatest number of interferences: a ban on Monday night football, Sunday beer sales, or Thursday religious services?

Any comparative evaluation of two interferences must look not to the quantity but to the quality of the interference. Making such a qualitative judgment requires that we look at the specific content of the interference and decide about the importance of what is being interfered with.★

Consider a number of examples to illustrate this point: Should we allow individual suburban homeowners the liberty of erecting ten-foot fences around their front lawns, or should we allow neighbors the liberty to set zoning ordinances requiring open vistas along streets? Should we allow private college fraternities and sororities the liberty to exclude minorities from membership, or should we allow every person, regardless of race and ethnicity, the liberty to apply for membership in any campus organization? Should we allow contemporary consumers the liberty of driving large and inefficient private autos, or should we allow future generations the liberty of access to more plentiful fossil fuels? Should we allow college students the liberty of unfettered file sharing or should we allow music and software companies the liberty of limiting access only to those who have paid for the music?

Obviously, any answer to these questions will result in a limit on someone's liberty. Limits on liberty are the unavoidable consequence of living with others. Also, no matter what side of these debates you come down on, it should be clear that the solution to the debate does not involve "measuring" liberty. Rather, our opinions on these issues are driven by beliefs about the qualitative importance of liberty in certain areas of life. Decisions about what interferences are legitimate, then, are decisions specifying areas of human conduct that ought to remain open to individual choice. In deciding to protect ourselves from interference in these areas, we will be forced to define what interests are most basic and central to

---

★For parallel views, see Ronald Dworkin, *Taking Rights Seriously* (Cambridge: Harvard University Press, 1977) as well as *A Matter of Principle* (Cambridge: Harvard University Press, 1985) and *Law's Empire* (Cambridge: Harvard University Press, 1986). See also Jefferie Murphy and Jules Coleman, *Philosophy of Law: An Introduction* (Boulder: Westview Press, 1990).

human life. As a consequence, it makes little sense to speak of a "general right to liberty." We must reject a view of liberty as one undifferentiated right and instead recognize that liberty is really a set of rights to specific liberties. (The Founding Fathers were more sophisticated than many contemporary Americans in that they recognized this point and, in the Bill of Rights, enumerated specific liberties that they believed were crucial.)

Accordingly, the argument for the laissez-faire theory of business responsibility that depends on a general right to liberty must be rejected as unsound. It rests on an untenable understanding of liberty. It is only when we see liberty as many separate rights that we can profitably discuss how and when freedom of choice can legitimately be limited. Any cogent liberty defense of the free market must depend, then, on the value of the specific economic liberties that the laissez-faire view proposes.

So, how central to human life is the good of unhindered, laissez-faire economic activity? Some have argued that production (economic activity) is a characteristic human activity and that it, therefore, ought to be protected. From this we might derive a universal right to employment (as does the UN Charter of Human Rights). Nevertheless, a laissez-faire right to be free from government regulation or broader management responsibilities does not seem to be required even if productive activity is central to human life. We could, of course, engage in productive activity without having an extensive laissez-faire economic liberty.

More importantly, allowing a right to such economic liberty would place other goods at the mercy of market bargaining power and, therefore, would effectively undermine the attempt to protect them from threat. Without coercing or defrauding, an ethnically biased White Anglo-Saxon Protestant (WASP) management might refuse to promote a Jew into a position of authority. A politically conservative management might dismiss an employee who spoke in favor of liberal causes. (In our current non-laissez-faire climate, the first action would be illegal under the Civil Rights Act. Interestingly, however, the second would not be a violation of the First Amendment right to freedom of speech. Federal courts have almost unanimously held that, since the constitutional prohibition pertains to acts by the government, private employers' retaliation for disfavored political speech is not unconstitutional.)

There is reason to believe, then, that threats to the effective enjoyment of important civil liberties can arise not just from government action. The laissez-faire system itself could threaten the effective exercise of these civil liberties since an extreme economic liberty makes it impossible to protect other liberties. (This point can be generalized to show that extreme liberty in one area can always make protecting liberty in other areas more difficult.)

Protecting basic liberties requires us to achieve a balance between free economic activity and legal or moral limits on corporate behavior. Thus, a real guarantee of important liberties demands broader government authority and management responsibility than the extreme free market view is willing to accept. The free market view is supported neither by an appeal to a general right to liberty nor by an argument that a specific laissez-faire economic liberty ought to be recognized as on a par with other basic liberty rights. A rights-based defense of the free market must look to other rights for support, then.

Private Property Rights and the Market

There is another argument in the arsenal of laissez-faire theorists, even if the liberty arguments fail to convince. Proponents of the extreme free market view of business responsibility and government regulation often claim that theirs is the only view compatible with a right to private property. The argument runs as follows: Property rights, if they mean anything, mean that the owner of property should be free to control that property. Ethical constraints and government regulation interfere with that control and are thus inconsistent with a belief in private property.

Stated so boldly, this argument is unlikely to convince anyone. We all, even laissez-faire theorists, recognize the need to limit the ability of property owners to determine what they will do with their property. (Laissez-faire theorists, by definition, will disapprove of any uses of property that are coercive or fraudulent.) The issue before us is what are the proper limits on the power of owners to control property? A particular instance is the emerging debate over federal environmental regulations such as the "wetlands" rules that limit private owners' rights to build on their land. Some claim that these regulations are illegitimate government "takings" of property because the rules limit the owner's ability to develop the property and because they reduce the market value of the land. Others find that the regulations are within the proper authority of government to protect the health and safety of citizens by ensuring clean water supplies.

Since the failings of the previous liberty arguments arose from a faulty understanding of the right to liberty, perhaps we ought to begin this analysis with some attention to the nature and justification of private property rights.

Traditionally, a "right to private property" has been understood as a shorthand expression for a set of more specific rights, all having to do with control over goods. Under this umbrella, a right to private property means a right to possess something, to use it, to benefit from it, to exclude others who have not paid from using or benefiting from it, to dispose or sell it, and so forth. Having a private property right to something means that an individual is entitled to exercise control over it in the ways specified and that others have obligations not to interfere with that control.

Most contemporary political theorists, even those of a socialist stripe, are willing to accept the legitimacy of some private property rights. Disagreements arise over what kinds of things can be privately owned (socialists reject private ownership of *productive* resources, though not necessarily the use of markets for allocating consumer goods; some religions reject private ownership of species and patents for genetically engineered "stock") and over the scope of the rights in the bundle. At issue between proponents and critics of laissez-faire is the scope of the rights to possess, use, exclude, dispose, and so on. Free market theorists understand private property rights as an entitlement to do anything with one's property except coerce or defraud. To see whether this is a viable understanding of property rights, we need to follow the method of analysis suggested above and identify the reasons offered to justify private property rights.

We obviously cannot catalog every possible justification of private property that might be offered. We will, however, briefly discuss what are probably the three most historically significant arguments for property. In fact, variations of these arguments can be found in Adam Smith and John Locke, the respective intellectual sources of our economic and political systems. The three arguments are based on utility, autonomy, and fairness.

1. *Utility.* This defense of property asserts that allowing people to privately own goods expands the economic product of the society and increases collective welfare. If we allow people to acquire goods through work or investment, that will provide the incentive needed for increasing levels of productivity and output. Alternatively, if we do not allow people to accumulate property, they will have little reason for working hard. (A major complaint about centralized socialist economies was that there was little economic incentive for workers or management to produce since rewards were not tied to levels of output.) Hence, a private property system will generate more jobs, more goods, and more wealth for the society to enjoy. Recognizing private property rights is a wise utilitarian policy.

2. *Autonomy.* Ever since the days of John Locke, private property has been seen as a way of preserving autonomy. On one hand, if the material conditions of our lives depend on the largesse of others, as the feudal serfs' lives depended on their lords, we are less able to exercise our autonomy. (Compare the job situation of most American workers!) On the other hand if individuals have the security provided by a base of material goods (land, money, housing), then they can be much more independent. In fact, the economic independence of the nobility and the emerging artisan class is seen as one major factor in the decline of monarchy and the development of democracy in Europe. Privately held goods are thus instrumental in promoting the ability of persons to speak and act independently.

3. *Fairness.* Locke also provided the germ of a fairness argument for private property. Locke explained that private rights to possess goods were created when an individual "mixed his labor with nature." He suggested that if I clear an unowned plot of land, till it, plant it, tend and harvest the crops, then it is only fair that I be given rights to the harvest I reap. (At least. One might also suggest that I also gain rights to the land since my labor made it into productive property.) We can imagine any number of contemporary variations of Locke's labor theory of property, for instance in the *intellectual* property of artists or software engineers, but the main point is constant: Private property rights are the fair return for one's productive labor.

The Laissez-Faire Conception of Property Given these historically powerful justifications of private property, we seem to be on firm ground in accepting the legitimacy of private property. Property rights are clearly in our derivative category inasmuch as they depend on their instrumental contributions to other values. Accepting private property as legitimate, however, still leaves plenty of questions about the scope of those rights. For instance, should the rights to possess, use, and exclude be so strong as to allow owners to do anything but coerce or defraud?

That question, we believe, is answered by the preceding justifications of property. And it is answered in the negative. The exercise of a right needs to be compatible with the underlying justifications of that right. If, for instance, we accept private property rights because they promote fairness, that very rationale will place limits on how the right may be exercised. The right holder ought not to be allowed to act unfairly under the guise of the right since that action would undermine the very justification for private property. We find that laissez-faire conceptions of property are not compatible with the three traditional rationales.

The best way to show this is to consider instances of the more specific rights that make up the bundle of rights that constitute the right to private property. Under the laissez-faire picture of property, owners should be able to dispose of their property so long as they do not coerce or defraud. Is it possible that this extensive disposal right could be net harmful to society (incompatible with utility)? Suppose I dispose of toxic materials, say old lead-containing batteries, on my farm. Suppose I revealed this fact to my neighbors and compensated them as they requested for any risk posed. Suppose also that I disclose the fact to buyers and lower my asking price when I sell the farm. I have not deceived nor coerced anyone, yet I have acted in a way that is arguably net harmful to overall social utility of current and future generations. If property rights are grounded on considerations of utility, the extreme laissez-faire conception of property is potentially incompatible with that justification.

The laissez-faire conception also has probable conflicts with the value of fairness in the scope that it admits for the right to exclude. A laissez-faire conception of corporate property would give owners and management a right to exclude employees from the workplace—in other words, fire them for any reason. If I, the employer, dismiss an employee, I am merely revoking the right of access that I temporarily granted to the employee. Since I can do this for any reason, I can do it for arbitrary and unfair reasons as well. Hence the laissez-faire conception runs counter to the fairness justification of property rights in that it permits those rights to be exercised unfairly.

Another example illustrates the point further. The laissez-faire view allows employers to pay the smallest wage that the market will bear. No minimum wage would be morally or legally required. However, we think it obvious that some wages that the market allows are not fair return for one's labors. Pennies a day paid to Pakistani child weavers for long hours and hard work is not a fair wage. Thus, the free market understanding of property has serious potential for undermining another foundational value of the right to private property.

Finally, the laissez-faire view also has strong potential for conflict with the last remaining justifying value—autonomy. We have already seen in the previous section how an extreme economic liberty can jeopardize the effective enjoyment of core civil liberties that are crucial to personal autonomy. Additionally, the laissez-faire conception would permit concentrated accumulations of wealth that might allow a moneyed elite inordinate influence over the political process, thus threatening the autonomy that comes with real political democracy. (The usual response to this concern is that competitive markets will prevent monopolistic or oligopolistic developments. We do not find this comforting on historical grounds; we also do not find it comforting because competitive games often tend to reward those with the largest initial stake.)

We conclude that the laissez-faire conception of property is inadequate because it has too great a potential for undermining the very values that make private property legitimate. Limiting owners' responsibility and government authority merely to prohibitions on fraud and coercion fails to ensure that private property systems achieve the goals of utility, autonomy, and fairness. Paying attention to these rationales for property rights reveals that acceptable approaches to property must recognize greater management responsibility and government authority.

The Alternative to Laissez-Faire Before we close this discussion, we feel some responsibility to more clearly outline the alternative to laissez-faire that is implied in the preceding chapters. This alternative theory cannot be applied easily or mechanically. In fact, what our alternative advises about practical moral problems of public policy or individual choice will often be open to debate. We consider that a virtue, however, since the problems of both the Friedman view and the belief in a general right to liberty derive from their very simple and mechanical resolutions of complex moral problems.

Our alternative begins with a commitment to human dignity expressed in a belief that individuals have rights that should not be sacrificed merely for increases in the general happiness. Those rights are best understood as socially sanctioned protections for basic or important human interests. The interests that are worthy of protection include but are not limited to the interest in liberty. Other interests, such as life, health, and privacy, are also important, since liberty is of little significance when these others are jeopardized. Thus, social and governmental institutions ought to be designed in ways that balance the importance of these interests and that treat the respective interests of each person fairly.

Achieving such a balance is not an easy task. It requires careful attention to the relationships between various rights. It requires us to determine the rationale for commonly claimed rights, such as property. It requires us to decide, when interests and rights conflict, which is based on the more central value and which should take precedence.

No simple answers can be given to these questions in advance. But any acceptable answers must admit that liberty and its underlying value of autonomy are values that apply in limited, albeit important realms of life. Controlling our lives cannot mean that we control *everything* about our lives.

As a consequence, we must recognize that there will be legitimate limits on business activity. This, however, is not to suggest the propriety of arbitrary interference with economic activity when more central goods are not at stake. It is still important to have autonomy in areas beyond that which would be guaranteed when basic interests are protected from threat. This more general absence of interference, however, must have a secondary moral importance that does not jeopard-ize the protections of more fundamental interests.

If we assume a moral perspective on social institutions, we should commit ourselves to institutions that by law or moral convention respect equally the fun-damental and common interests of each person, guaranteeing against other inter-ference as much as is compatible with a similar guarantee for all. As an example, the social institution of business should operate so that the interferences that jeop-ardize life and health are prohibited before interferences that threaten only the ability to enter specific economic transactions. What the other responsibilities of business are is up to you to decide.

IN SUMMARY

Retracing our steps a bit, we began in Chapter One with the free market view that business has no responsibility to society, consumers, or employees beyond the responsibility to avoid coercion and deception. That view also held that govern-ment's only proper role is to maintain free and open competition. Friedman's arti-cle provided arguments for that view. We saw, however, that his arguments were not cogent.

Consideration of other arguments for the free market view led us to two approaches to ethics that dominate the Western tradition: utilitarianism, in Chapter Two; and rights-based approaches in this chapter. Each of these is some-times used to defend the laissez-faire view. After analysis, we found the utilitarian defense of the free market wanting for two reasons. First, its empirical claim that laissez-faire policies will maximize happiness was suspect. Second, the utilitarian theory on which the defense was based is itself flawed because it is unable to accommodate a commitment to individual rights.

We also found that the two rights-based defenses of the free market were faulty. Both the liberty and property rights arguments depend on untenable con-ceptions of the rights at issue. Our presumptive conclusion is that the extreme laissez-faire view of corporate responsibility must be abandoned and that a more adequate conception of property and liberty rights allows for more frequent man-agement responsibility.

We hope that the introductory moral theory provided in this and the preced-ing chapters will provide some of the tools necessary for you to determine care-fully the obligations of business. We also hope that the specific discussions of utilitarianism, liberty, and property will alert you to how that theory is used in some of the issue-oriented debates of the later chapters. In the next chapter, we examine the nature of the corporation. There, we sketch a view of the corporation as an essentially social institution, discuss the content of corporate responsibilities, and review some of the governance mechanisms available for controlling corpo-rate action.

4

⚜

The Corporation as
a Social Institution

INTRODUCTION

Chapters One through Three explored some basic issues in social and political theory. The purpose of those chapters was to defeat an extreme view of corporate social responsibility. This chapter develops a view contrary to that extreme. It identifies the corporation as an essentially social institution. It focuses on the structure of the corporation, on possible categories of corporate obligation, and on how the perceived obligations of corporations have changed over the last century. Since we assume throughout that the corporation, in some sense, does have responsibilities, we must also address recent debates about whether the corporation is the type of entity that can possess obligations. Finally, this chapter describes approaches to corporate control—external, through government regulation, and internal, through alternative governance structures.

Any adequate understanding of the corporation must view it as an essentially social institution. Corporations exist only because individuals come together to carry out jointly the business of producing goods and services. The particular form of that joint activity in any society is determined by social norms. For instance, in contemporary American society, corporations are enterprises with explicit state charters, and they must function according to the positive laws of the society. At a deeper level, the particular form of the contemporary American corporation is the product of socially evolved conceptions of property rights. The powers those property rights confer and the limits on the exercise of those powers are defined by norms that develop over time through the pull and tug of forces within the society. Corporations exist in a particular historical form only because their society sanctions institutions with that form.

Corporations are also social institutions in another sense. The form they take helps determine the social relations and patterns of behavior for individuals. A given corporate structure will naturally lead to specifically defined duties and responsibilities for the people who inhabit that institution. The norms that define these duties, when internalized by corporate employees, will help shape the values and behavior of those employees. (These facts about how institutions influence the character of the human beings within them is one reason virtue ethics, mentioned in Chapter Two, is important for business ethics. We need to ask whether our business institutions promote the kinds of human character and virtues that are needed for a healthy, functional society.) Given all this, we reach the inescapable conclusion that the corporation is social by its very nature.

THE NATURE OF THE CORPORATION

The "American corporation" is an abstraction. Corporations have evolved many different organizational forms. However, we can understand the nature of the corporation better if we think about some generalities concerning the role, structure, and status of corporations.

The Role of the Corporation

The role of the corporation varies according to the perspective from which one views it. From the point of view of the investor, a corporation is a vehicle for potentially increased wealth. For an employee, the corporation is a place to exchange labor for an income with which to support oneself and one's family. Consumers see the corporation as a mechanism from which to acquire needed goods and services. From the perspective of society, however, the corporation is an institution that enables both human and material resources to be organized for the (one hopes) efficient production of the things the people of the society need to maintain a way of life.

The Structure of the Corporation

In our society, corporations are typically structured as follows. Institutions are created to attract investment from outside parties. These shareholders invest their funds to receive a profit, but they delegate the control of the operations to a team of managers who act as legal agents for them. This professional class of managers is expected to run the corporation efficiently and to produce a return for the investor-owners. (But see the article by Lynne Stout at the end of this chapter for a challenge to the idea that shareholders can reasonably be called "owners" in the usual sense.) Successfully achieving that management task requires the cooperation of a third group—the workers. Employees are hired on a fee-for-service basis to carry out the directions of management in the activities necessary for producing goods and services, which are in turn offered for sale to consumers in a market. Consumer purchases provide the finds necessary for satisfying the ongoing labor and material costs of production.

Most contemporary American corporations are operated by a group of managers headed by a board of directors. These managers must direct the corporation in a way that responds adequately to the respective demands of investors, workers, and consumers. Management must provide investors sufficient return so that the corporation can hold investors and attract new infusions of capital. But management must also adopt policies that guarantee a supply of productive workers and an adequate demand for the products or services produced. Corporate structure, then, reflects a complex web of interrelated activities and constituencies.

The Legal Status of the Corporation

In our society the corporation has a peculiar legal status. It is legally chartered and recognized as a person in the eyes of the law. That recognition, in part, allows the corporation standing to sue or to be sued in the courts. Also, as already noted, corporations differ from most property in that they are not directly controlled by their shareholders. Perhaps the most interesting feature of the corporation has to do with the liability of the shareholders. The law, perhaps originally as a means of encouraging investment and production, limits the risk for investors. Ordinarily, if you cause a compensable harm to someone with your property, you can be held liable for the full extent of the harm caused. This means that you are responsible for the costs to the victim even if those costs exceed the value of the property causing the harm. Thus, if my old VW (generously valued at $200) accidentally rolls out of my driveway and damages my neighbor's new Mercedes, I am liable for the thousands of dollars in repairs my car has made necessary. However, incorporated property has a much more limited liability. Shareholders in a corporation have a legal liability limited to the value of their investment, regardless of the amount of harm caused by their property. With this background about the peculiar institution that is the American corporation, we can move on to a brief discussion of issues surrounding the notion of "corporate responsibility."

CORPORATE RESPONSIBILITY

Stakeholder Theory

From the material in Chapters Two and Three we can see that the responsibilities of the corporation must extend beyond mere responsibility to shareholders. Even Milton Friedman acknowledges this. Moreover, any realistic view of the contemporary corporation will see that, at least politically, the management of a corporation must take account of interests in addition to those of its shareholder constituency. This recognition has led to an understanding of the corporation, an understanding that has grown in popularity among management theorists. This "Stakeholder Theory" distinguishes between a narrow concern for shareholder interests and a broader concern for all those who have a stake in corporate policy. This theory encourages management to expand its consideration to include a concern for consumers, employees, and members of the community at large.

Critics of stakeholder theory claim that it is normatively unjustified and that it cannot be operationalized in a way that would allow managers to apply it in concrete circumstances. First, what claim, they ask, do the various nonshareholder constituencies have on the corporation's assets? It would be one thing if the theory merely counseled consideration of these other constituencies as a strategy, as a means for maximizing shareholder wealth. But the theory's proponents usually see the mandate to consider the welfare of nonshareholders not merely as an instrument for achieving the good of the owners but as itself a basic moral goal. Critics challenge proponents of the theory to explain why nonshareholders are entitled to benefits from the corporation beyond those they can negotiate for themselves in the marketplace. Why, for instance, might community or employee interests justify keeping a plant open if shareholders would gain increased value from its closure? More generally, opponents of stakeholder theory find no clear moral grounds for identifying any particular people as possessing a right to reap non-negotiated, noncontractual benefits from the property of shareholders.

Second, critics of stakeholder theory ask how management should weigh the interests of its various constituencies in reaching a decision about how to act. They claim that the mandate to consider the conflicting interests of shareholders, employees, consumers, and others will present management with an impossible task. Under such a mandate, at best, managers will be left in a quandary with no clear guide about how to choose between these conflicting interests. At worst, the critics suggest, the stakeholder approach will exacerbate the problem of aligning the interests of management with those of the shareholders (a problem known as the "agency problem" and much discussed in the finance literature). An unscrupulous management will have a ready cover in stakeholder theory for self-enriching activity. When shareholders (or for that matter, even other stakeholders) complain about a management decision, management can always claim that it was attempting to satisfy some other stakeholder interest. The result is that there is no effective measure for whether management is doing its job. Better, the critics contend, to stick to a well-justified, well-understood, and well-governed approach that merely asks management to maximize shareholder wealth. At least that provides a clear yardstick for evaluating management performance.

Proponents of stakeholder theory have responded to each of these objections. They suggest, as we have in the earlier chapters, that there are ways of justifying moral rights for nonshareholders. The need to respect those rights, both positive and negative, can place limits on management's attempts maximize shareholder value. Additionally, all those whose efforts, contributions, and risks have, over time, benefited the corporation might arguably have some claims against it. (For instances of such arguments, see the references to "team production" in the Stout article at the end of this chapter. See also the comments on job security in the Introduction to Chapter Five.) Thus, the right to benefit from cooperative corporate activity might extend beyond shareholders to other contributors, such as employees and local communities.

Advocates of stakeholder theory also note that uncertainty and disagreement about the precise responsibilities of management are not unique to their theory. Proponents argue that unless we are willing to abandon altogether the idea that management has responsibilities to constituencies other than shareholders, it will always be difficult to operationalize those responsibilities in a mechanical way. Consider the difficulty even for Friedman in defining just when management acts are coercive or deceptive.

Some recent work by proponents of stakeholder theory openly admits that their theory is more a general framework for decision making than a technique that generates determinate advice about management decisions. They do not find that problematic, however. For, they argue, there will also inevitably be disagreement over how to maximize shareholder value under the shareholder primacy approach. The interests of different shareholder constituencies are different. For instance, are the financial interests of institutional investors always the same as those of individual shareholders? In fact, legal battles have been fought by opposing shareholders. (A classic battle was fought in the Delaware courts between shareholders who had different interests at stake in a plan by Marriott Corporation to spin off some of its business operations.) So, even the demand to maximize shareholder value cannot be fully "operationalized."

It is also possible to interpret the recent corporate scandals as the by-product of an overemphasis on share value. Evaluating (and compensating) management by short-term changes in share value can provide perverse incentives for management to manipulate quarterly sales and profit numbers, for example as "Chainsaw" Al Dunlop did when booking future sales as current quarter revenue or as Enron's management did when attempting to hide debt in off-the-books partnerships.

The article by Fuller and Jensen at the end of this chapter openly makes this argument. Jensen, interestingly, has been a leading proponent of the shareholder value maximization school. However, here he argues that management performance should not be measured by quarterly earnings but by long-term and sustained increases in share value. Proponents of stakeholder theory will point out that such a longer-term perspective removes even the appearance that the shareholder value approach provides a clear and useful metric for assessing management performance. With the long-term view of shareholder maximization, management can always claim that expenditures that reduce current earnings are a necessary investment in future growth.

(For more detail on these debates, see the readings by Evan and Freeman, Stout, McCall, and Fuller and Jensen at the end of this chapter.)

Finally, proponents of stakeholder theory have some support from various movements in management theory. It is now commonplace to hear management theorists advise that the best way to reap profits is by attending to the needs of employees, or to the needs of customers. The Total Quality Management (TQM) movement of the recent past, for example, emphasized that the way to ensure a profitable business is, paradoxically, to concentrate attention on the customer. If management sees its objective as providing goods and services that best satisfy the customer, the company will achieve financial rewards. Ironically, an overemphasis on shareholder wealth might produce less profit because it leads management myopically to undervalue the customer. This same point can be made with respect to recent work in the area of strategic human resources. A number of scholars in that area have begun to emphasize the crucial role of cooperative team production activity in sustaining a functional firm environment. Failure to attend to the needs and interests of workers can have a deleterious effect on output, as some firms have discovered when they have used layoffs as a first response to difficult times. (See the article by Pfeffer in Chapter Five for an example of this analysis.)

These ideas are similar to the "Hedonic Paradox" identified by Greek philosophers over two millennia ago. The person who always single-mindedly is concerned about his own happiness is not likely to achieve happiness; the person who takes the welfare of others to heart is. So, recent management theories provide additional support for the claim that management ought to focus on the interests of groups other than shareholders (although the thrust of stakeholder theory is normative—that management has a *moral* responsibility to other stakeholders—and these other management theories may make the focus on other constituencies not a moral but a merely instrumental one).

Chapters Five through Fourteen present discussions of specific responsibilities that corporations might have. We invite you to read the material of those chapters with these debates over stakeholder responsibilities in mind.

Social Contract Theory

Once we recognize how controversial proposed corporate responsibilities are, and once we notice how our expectations of corporations have changed over the years, we have to ask how corporate obligations are determined. The answer will depend in part on what human interests the society believes are important enough to protect as rights. In part, the answer will also depend on what the society believes about the factual consequences of certain corporate and institutional arrangements. Both of these beliefs are open to change and debate.

One instructive way of understanding this process is through Social Contract Theory. The notion of a social contract originated with political philosophers who hypothesized an implicit contract between the members of a society. Initially, this implicit contract was a device used to explain both the legitimacy of particular forms of government and the respective obligations of rulers and citizens. Recent applications of this theory to business can help explain how the perceived social obligations of business are determined and how they change over time. Consider how the social contract between American society and its corporations developed.

In the United States, the rise of the modern industrial corporation can be dated to the late 1800s. When those corporations were chartered, social expectations of them were centered on the expansion of production. As experience gradually accumulated regarding the social, economic, and political effect of the developing corporations, society perceived a need to alter the norms for corporate behavior. Corporate behavior that was once viewed as good for the society came to be viewed as having undesirable consequences as well. Since all contracts supposedly operate for the mutual benefit of the parties, changed perceptions of the consequences of corporate activity led to a change in the obligations of the implicit contract between the corporation and society. If we view the obligations of corporations as deriving from such an implicit contract, we can understand how those obligations are determined in the ongoing flux of social life.

Some of us might wonder about the fairness of this view of corporate responsibility. Ordinarily, unilaterally changing the terms of a preexisting contract to suit the interests of one of the parties is considered unacceptable. We should caution against too easy a charge of unfairness, however. The concept of fairness is, as we saw in Chapter Three, open to different interpretations. For instance, allowing one generation to bind another to harmful contract provisions would seem to violate a principle of fairness that holds that individuals should have a say in the policies that affect their lives.

Of course, social contract theory does not imply that the particular contractual understanding at any given time is a fully adequate one. Nor does it suggest that those understandings cannot be cynically manipulated by persons with special interest in the "contract." The model is meant only as a heuristic device for helping us understand how conceptions of corporate responsibility evolve in a given society and how they might evolve differently in different societies.

For instance, recent work by two prominent proponents of the social contract approach (Tom Donaldson and Tom Dunfee in their classic article "Integrative Social Contracts Theory") suggests an account both of universal moral norms and of variation in cultural understandings of corporate responsibility. Following the approach of political philosopher John Rawls, they imagine a hypothetical circumstance where rational and impartial contractors come together to agree on the basic terms of economic life. They argue that such contractors would settle on a set of principles for economic organization that allowed "moral free space" for different cultures to instantiate different specific norms for business behavior. Knowing that human societies exhibit wide variation along cultural, religious, and ideological lines, these hypothetical contractors would see the need for some freedom to respond to specific conditions and to express particular values. Thus, for example, one culture might find corporations responsible for housing and education of workers' families while another culture might leave those responsibilities to other institutions or to the marketplace. Or, gift giving between purchasers and distributors might be condoned as part of a cultural system in one society but condemned in another.

However, Donaldson's and Dunfee's version of the social contract also follows Rawls in that it sets limits on cultural variation. In particular, they argue that any culturally specific contract specifying economic duties and rights must allow individuals both the right of informed consent to the contract's terms and the right to exit from the contract. Hence, they would apparently reject as unjustified an economic system where individuals had no real choices about work or working conditions.

Perhaps more importantly, Donaldson and Dunfee limit the range of cultural variation by requiring that all local understandings be compatible with universal ethical principles that are fundamental to human existence, including basic human rights. (Thus they suggest that while gift giving may be culturally acceptable in some places, unconscionably sized gifts that warp the decisions of elected officials would be unacceptable violations of a right to political participation.) They believe that there is empirical evidence of convergence of beliefs across cultures and religions that can help to identify the content of these basic "hypernorms."

This approach to understanding the scope of business responsibilities, and their variation, gives appropriate attention to the impact of cultural context on moral analysis, and it is certainly useful in discussing issues in international business ethics. As we have argued in the comments on relativism, context matters; what is proper in one circumstance is not necessarily proper under differing circumstances. That is not relativism but mere common sense. No one believes that lies are always wrong. Certainly an elaborate system of lies to save people from the Holocaust (as depicted in the movie *Schindler's List*) is acceptable; ordinary lies for personal gain are typically not. We too would caution, however, that reasonable recognition of cultural variation needs to be limited by respect for basic rights. While the Donaldson and Dunfee approach gives us a heuristic for understanding both the origins of and variations in corporate responsibility, it leaves the most important work still to be done: specifying the content of the basic rights and identifying procedures for analyzing conflicting interpretations of those rights. Once again, we urge that as you read the material in the following chapters, you apply the method suggested in Chapter Three. That should aid in identifying which rights are basic and in resolving disputes about the proper scope of particular rights.

The Corporation as a Morally Responsible Agent

All along we have been assuming that corporations are the sorts of things that can possess responsibilities. That proposition has been challenged recently. Some commentators have held that corporations fail to satisfy ordinary, common-sense conditions necessary for having responsibilities.

The challenge to the idea of corporate responsibility comes from those who look to the paradigm case of an entity that can have moral responsibilities and can be held accountable: the human moral agent. Some of these theorists find that the characteristics that allow ascribing responsibility and accountability to human beings are not possessed by the corporation.

When we see a human being as responsible, we do so because we implicitly believe that he or she is capable of autonomous, rational decision making. Part of what is involved in such decision making is that the agent must understand the situation, intend to act on that understanding, and finally, act. Those who question ascribing responsibility and accountability to corporations find that it is only in an obscuringly metaphorical or anthropomorphic sense that we can speak of corporations in this way. For example, often corporate "acts" are the result of the combined actions of separate individuals within the corporation. It need not be the case that any single individual's intentional act brought about that corporate "act." Conversely, consider that corporate actions are not equivalent to the specific actions of individuals within the firm. As Manuel Velasquez points out, individuals do not merge with corporations; only other corporations can do that.

Opposing theorists contend that corporations can have responsibilities and be held accountable because there are senses in which corporations act rationally and with intention. For example, an expansion of production to meet increased consumer demand, though it may not be solely the product of one human individual's intentional decision, is surely a considered and rational action on the part of the business.

The position one takes in this somewhat metaphysical debate about conditions for responsibility can have potentially far-reaching practical consequences. For instance, if corporations cannot properly be held responsible, then who should bear the liability for harm caused by corporations? If corporations cannot act in a morally relevant way and if the policies of the corporation are not equivalent to the acts of individual members of the corporation, must corporately caused harm go unpunished and uncompensated? Or should we penalize each individual who had a part in the creation of the corporate "act"? Should the file clerk who simply stuffed an envelope be penalized for his part in a case of mail fraud? If corporations *are* morally responsible, is it just that we punish the corporation (through fines, perhaps) when doing so hurts ordinary shareholders or employees who had no part in the creation or execution of the harmful policies? (Interestingly, some of these same issues arise in considering the Nuremberg war crimes trials.)

Perhaps we can find a way around the problems posed by this debate if we hold that the notion of responsibility as applied to corporations differs from the application of that notion to human moral agents. For instance, as we will see in the discussion of product liability in Chapter Eight, there are defensible ways of talking about corporate liability that differ from our ordinary understanding of our personal liability for harm we cause. For instance, there are public policy reasons for holding corporations liable for injuries caused by their products even when the corporation could not have prevented those injuries. These same public policy considerations do not apply with equal force in the case of accidents caused by private individuals. Thus, we might be able to translate this talk of corporate responsibility and accountability into a language that allows us to speak about shaping the way our social institutions function. Public policy sanctions on corporations might be seen simply as the attempt to fashion a system of interrelated incentives for encouraging the desired institutional behavior. In creating a system of incentives (such as fines or exposure to economic liability), we would still need to be sensitive to the consequences of our incentives for the human individuals involved. For example, if corporate exposure to extreme degrees of liability for harms caused by products created shortages of necessary goods or unacceptably high levels of unemployment, we might abandon that as a mechanism for ensuring product safety. In addition, levying corporate fines that affect shareholders does not necessarily have to be seen as assigning to those investors moral blame for corporate policies. (Of course, identifiably criminal acts of individuals within the corporation can still be considered personally blameworthy.)

If we understand corporate responsibility in these terms, we might be able to discuss public policy toward corporations without committing ourselves either to a moral equating of corporations and human beings or to an abandoning of all reference to a corporation's responsibility for its policies.

CORPORATE GOVERNANCE AND CONTROL

However we settle this debate about corporate moral responsibility, it is clear that we all have social expectations about how corporations (or those within them) should behave. These expectations lead naturally to questions about corporate governance and control. More specifically, they raise three distinct but related questions: By what mechanisms should corporations be governed and controlled? Who should exercise that governance and control? What purposes are legitimate objectives in the control and governance of corporations?

Historically, our society has answered the first question by fashioning a complex mix of public and private mechanisms of control. As we will see, all of these mechanisms of control have been subjects of recent moral debates.

Some public control of corporations is achieved through direct governmental regulation. This direct government regulation has evolved in two broad stages over the past 100 years. In the United States, the initial forays into government control of industry began in the late 19th and early 20th centuries. The primary purpose of this early regulation was to protect businesses from the anticompetitive practices of other businesses. The early federal agencies created to regulate commerce, such as the Interstate Commerce Commission, were patently aimed at maintaining open, nonmonopolistic competition. This form of regulation supposedly provided indirect benefits to consumers, but the direct and principal beneficiary was the business community itself.

A second wave of direct regulatory public control includes contemporary regulation that intends to promote the welfare of consumers, employees, or members of the society at large. Much of this is a product of the past four decades. For instance, the Environmental Protection Agency (EPA) and the Occupational Safety and Health Administration (OSHA) were both created in 1970; the Consumer Product Safety Commission was created in 1972. This explosion of new regulatory bodies was a response to increased awareness of the external costs of business being shouldered by the public. These costs to health, safety, and the environment were the subject of ever more effective political complaint through the 1960s and 1970s.

Not surprisingly, the business community has little fondness for many of the actions of the new regulatory agencies of government. In the past decades, business has joined a debate about the acceptability of much government regulation. While defenders claim that the regulation generally serves to protect the public, critics have leveled a series of blasts at government involvement in corporate activity. Among the criticisms are the following: Regulatory agencies do not coordinate their directives and hence often work at cross purposes; many regulations are not effective at protecting the public (a charge often used against OSHA, as we will see in Chapter Six); the cost of complying with regulations outweighs the benefits the regulations provide; and regulation causes product shortages and unemployment. We invite you in the chapters that follow to consider these challenges to specific public policies involving government intervention in the marketplace.

In addition to these forms of direct regulation, there are mixed, public-private devices for corporate control. An example of this can be found in the manner through which the Securities and Exchange Commission regulates the disclosure of company financial information. The government has empowered other non-governmental industry bodies, such as the Financial Accounting Standards Board, to create standards, such as the well-known Generally Accepted Accounting Principles, that corporate auditors invoke when they certify company financial statements.

This cooperative public-private approach to corporate financial reporting has, of course, also been the subject of much recent debate since it is at the heart of the Enron, WorldCom, Tyco, and other financial scandals. There are some who claim that government, and the SEC in particular, has not done enough to assure that investors have access to accurate and fair representations of company financial health. Others lay fault at the feet of the accounting industry for aggressive lobbying in Congress that prevented the SEC from successfully mandating stricter governmental requirements on reporting. Cynics about the role of big accounting firms in this process will note that the continued reliance on increasingly complicated accounting rules has the inevitable result of increasing the demand for expensive accounting services while simultaneously decreasing potential legal liability (since the more complex the rules, the harder it will be to prove to a jury that the rules were broken).

More purely private mechanisms of control can be found in the systems of incentives created for management by the securities markets. Investors, particularly large, institutional investors, evaluate company performance and buy or sell stock accordingly. The resultant demand for a given company's stock will, in turn, determine the price of that stock. Management is thus under pressure to regulate its own actions to assure that they produce profitable and efficient enterprises. In theory, at least, a management that fails is in danger of losing its job.

In practice, however, shareholders, and the boards of directors that supposedly represent them, often face a difficult and expensive process if they wish to replace an entrenched management team. That reality has spawned a long literature on the "Agency Problem," or how to get management (the agents) to align its interests with those of the shareholders (the principals). The most recently favored answer to this problem has been to tie executive compensation to the performance of corporate stock. (This is why discussions of executive pay are often found under the heading of "corporate governance.") The idea is to make executives' compensation at least partly contingent upon stock prices and so create self-interested reasons for executives to improve share value. The typical compensation mechanism used to achieve this alignment has been the issuance of option rights to buy stock at a given price (often the stock price at the time of option issuance). If the stock rises, executives can purchase the stock at the old, lower price and increase their wealth; if the stock price falls, executives have lost value.

These private mechanisms of governance and control have also come under fire recently. Many charge that American management, in particular, has been so pressured by the need to show quarterly growth that they have neglected investment in the long-term health of the corporation. And there is certainly evidence that both the pressure to perform in the short term and the linking of compensation to changes in share value have created perverse incentives for duplicitous accounting maneuvers that ironically have damaged the interests of shareholders.

(Again, see the readings by Stout, by Fuller and Jensen, and by McCall at the end of this chapter for more on these debates.)

It is interesting to note that this last, private-sector approach to mechanisms of corporate control is an approach that contains implied answers to our second (Who should exercise control?) and third (For what purposes?) questions above. For the private-control approach presupposes a hierarchical model through which corporate activity is directed by an executive team headed by the CEO. It also presupposes that the executives ought to direct that activity in order to achieve maximal return for the shareholder-owner. These presuppositions reflect common beliefs about the rights of owners to reap the benefits of their property and about the need for central decision making if organizations are to function effectively (a corporate version of "Too many cooks spoil the broth"). Both of these presuppositions can be called into question.

There is another body of opinion that suggests that decision-making authority should be dispersed horizontally throughout the firm, for reasons of both ethics and efficiency. This participatory model of corporate governance derives from wholly different beliefs. Some proponents of greater employee participation in decision-making base their preference on productivity studies. There is evidence, for example, that employees who have a sense of participating in decision-making feel higher levels of satisfaction with their work lives and hence are more productive. Others argue that (1) property ownership cannot mean an absolute right to control and (2) the need to respect the autonomy of workers is sufficient to limit management-ownership authority. (The reading by Stout at the end of this chapter and the readings by Pfeffer and McCall in Chapter Five carry these arguments further.)

Development of the stakeholder theory has also provided some impetus for extending control to those affected by corporate policy. Such proposed extensions are defended on the ground that individuals can best judge their own interests and therefore ought to be allowed a voice of their own in corporate policies that might affect those interests. Similar arguments are found in recent political debates about plant closings; some argue that not only workers but also local communities should be allowed a say in such decisions. Throughout the remaining chapters, you will find frequent instances of these debates about who should exercise control over the corporation and about what goals that control should aim to achieve.

IN SUMMARY

Corporations as social institutions are chartered by society and owe responsibilities to society. Two current theories for helping to understand those responsibilities are Stakeholder Theory and Social Contract Theory. Stakeholder Theory suggests that when management acts, it needs to consider the interests of all constituencies—owners, employees, customers, and society at large. (See the Evan and Freeman reading at the end of this chapter for a classic statement of Stakeholder Theory.) Social Contract Theory attempts to explain why management must consider all those interests.

There is a recurrent philosophical debate about the locus of corporate responsibility: Can corporations themselves be considered morally responsible agents, or is this possible only for the human beings in them? Whatever answer to that question you decide on, the need to control corporate action is obvious. Government regulatory actions have evolved as a mechanism for corporate control.

This chapter has outlined some general views on these topics of responsibility and regulation. In the chapters that follow, you will be repeatedly asked to become more specific about just what responsibilities business has and just when government intervention in the marketplace is appropriate.

READING 4.1 A STAKEHOLDER THEORY OF THE MODERN CORPORATION: KANTIAN CAPITALISM

William M. Evan and R. Edward Freeman

INTRODUCTION

Corporations have ceased to be merely legal devices through which the private business transactions of individuals may be carried on. Though still much used for this purpose, the corporate form has acquired a larger significance. The corporation has, in fact, become both a method of property tenure and a means of organizing economic life. Grown to tremendous proportions, there may be said to have evolved a "corporate system"—which has attracted to itself a combination of attributes and powers, and has attained a degree of prominence entitling it to be dealt with as a major social institution.[1]

Despite these prophetic words of Berle and Means (1932), scholars and managers alike continue to hold sacred the view that managers bear a special relationship to the stockholders in the firm. Since stockholders own shares in the firm, they have certain rights and privileges, which must be granted to them by management, as well as by others. . . . Sanctions, in the form of "the law of corporations," and other protective mechanisms in the form of social custom, accepted management practice, myth, and ritual, are thought to reinforce the assumption of the primacy of the stockholder.

The purpose of this paper is to pose several challenges to this assumption, from within the framework of managerial capitalism, and to suggest the bare bones of an alternative theory, *a stakeholder theory of the modern corporation*. We do not seek the demise of the modern corporation, either intellectually or in fact. Rather, we seek its transformation. In the words of Neurath, we shall attempt to "rebuild the ship, plank by plank, while it remains afloat."[2]

Our thesis is that we can revitalize the concept of managerial capitalism by replacing the notion that managers have a duty to stockholders with the concept that managers bear a fiduciary relationship to stakeholders. Stakeholders are those groups who have a stake in or claim on the firm. Specifically we include suppliers, customers, employees, stockholders, and the local community, as well as management in its role as agent for these groups. We argue that the legal, economic, political, and moral challenges to the currently received theory of the firm, as a nexus of contracts among the owners of the factors of production and customers, require us to revise this concept along essentially Kantian lines. That is, each of these stakeholder groups has a right not to be treated as a means to some end, and therefore must participate in determining the future direction of the firm in which they have a stake. . . .[3]

The crux of our argument is that we must reconceptualize the firm around the following question: For whose benefit and at whose expense should the firm be managed? We shall set forth such a reconceptualization in the form of a *stakeholder theory of the firm*. We shall then critically examine the stakeholder view and its implications for the future of the capitalist system.

THE ATTACK ON MANAGERIAL CAPITALISM

The Legal Argument

The basic idea of managerial capitalism is that in return for controlling the firm, management vigorously pursues the interests of stockholders. Central to the managerial view of the firm is the idea that management can pursue market transactions with suppliers and customers in an unconstrained manner.[4]

The law of corporations gives a less clearcut answer to the question: In whose interest and for whose benefit should the modern corporation be governed? While it says that the corporations should be run primarily in the interests of the stockholders in the firm, it says further that the corporation exists "in contemplation of the law" and has personality as a "legal person," limited liability for its actions, and immortality, since its existence transcends that of its members.[5] Therefore, directors and other officers of the firm have a fiduciary obligation to stockholders in the sense that the "affairs of the corporation" must be conducted in the interest of the stockholders. And stockholders can theoretically bring suit against those directors and managers for doing otherwise. But since the corporation is a legal person, existing in contemplation of the law, managers of the corporation are constrained by law.

Until recently, this was no constraint at all. In this century, however, . . . the law has evolved to effectively constrain the pursuit of stockholder interests at the expense of other claimants on the firm. It has, in effect, required that the claims of customers, suppliers, local communities, and employees be taken into consideration, though in general they are subordinated to the claims of stockholders. . . .

For instance, the doctrine of "privity of contract," as articulated in *Winterbottom v. Wright* in 1842, has been eroded by recent developments in products liability law. Indeed, *Greenman v. Yuba Power* gives the manufacturer strict liability for damage caused by its products, even though the seller has exercised all possible care in the preparation and sale of the product and the consumer has not bought the product from nor entered into any contractual arrangement with the manufacturer. Caveat emptor has been replaced, in large part, with caveat venditor.[6] The Consumer Product Safety Commission has the power to enact product recalls, and in 1980 one U.S. automobile company recalled more cars than it built. . . . Some industries are required to provide information to customers about a product's ingredients, whether or not the customers want and are willing to pay for this information.[7]

In short, the supplier-firm-customer chain is far from that visualized by managerial capitalism. In their roles as customers and suppliers, firms have benefitted from these constraints, but they have been harmed to the degree to which the constraints have meant loss of profit. . . .

The same argument is applicable to management's dealings with employees. The National Labor Relations Act gave employees the right to unionize and to bargain in good faith. It set up the National Labor Relations Board to enforce these rights with management. The Equal Pay Act of 1963 and Title VII of the Civil Rights Act of 1964 constrain management from discrimination in hiring practices; these have been followed with the Age Discrimination in Employment Act of 1967.[8] The emergence of a body of administrative case law arising from labor-management disputes and the historic settling of discrimination claims with large employers such as AT&T have caused the emergence of a body of practice in the corporation that is consistent with the legal guarantee of the rights of the employees. . . . The law has protected the due process rights of those employees who enter into collective bargaining agreements with management. As of the present, however, only 30 percent of the labor force are participating in such agreements; this has prompted one labor law scholar to propose a statutory law prohibiting dismissals of the 70 percent of the work force not protected. . . .[9]

The law has also protected the interests of local communities. The Clean Air Act and Clean Water Act have constrained management from "spoiling the commons." In an historic case, *Marsh v. Alabama,* the Supreme Court ruled that a company-owned town was subject to the provisions of the U.S. Constitution, thereby guaranteeing the rights of local citizens and negating the "property rights" of the firm. Some states and municipalities have gone further and passed laws preventing firms from moving plants or limiting when and how plants can be closed. In sum, there is much current legal activity in this area to constrain management's pursuit of stockholders' interests at the expense of the local communities in which the firm operates. . . .

We have argued that the result of such changes in the legal system can be viewed as giving some rights to those groups that have a claim on the firm, for example, customers, suppliers, employees, local communities, stockholders, and management. It raises the question, at the core of a theory of the firm: In whose interest and for whose benefit should the firm be managed? The answer proposed by managerial capitalism is clearly "the stockholders," but we have argued that the law has been progressively circumscribing this answer.

The Economic Argument

In its pure ideological form managerial capitalism seeks to maximize the interests of stockholders. In its perennial criticism of government regulation, management espouses the "invisible hand" doctrine. It contends that it creates the greatest good for the greatest number, and therefore government need not intervene. However, we know that externalities, moral hazards, and monopoly power exist in fact, whether or not they exist in theory. Further, some of the legal apparatus mentioned above has evolved to deal with just these issues.

The problem of the "tragedy of the commons" or the free-rider problem pervades the concept of public goods such as water and air. No one has an incentive to incur the cost of clean-up or the cost of nonpollution, since the marginal gain of one firm's action is small. Every firm reasons this way, and the result is pollution of water and air. Since the industrial revolution, firms have sought to internalize the benefits and externalize the costs of their actions. The cost must be borne by all, through taxation and regulation; hence we have the emergence of the environmental regulations of the 1970s.

Similarly, moral hazards arise when the purchaser of a good or service can pass along the cost of that good. There is no incentive to economize, on the part of either the producer or the consumer, and there is excessive use of the resources involved. The institutionalized practice of third-party payment in health care is a prime example.

Finally, we see the avoidance of competitive behavior on the part of firms, each seeking to monopolize a small portion of the market and not compete with one another. In a number of industries, oligopolies have emerged, and while there is questionable evidence that oligopolies are not the most efficient corporate form in some industries, suffice it to say that the potential for abuse of market power has again led to regulation of managerial activity. In the classic case, AT&T, arguably one of the great technological and managerial achievements of the century, was broken up into eight separate companies to prevent its abuse of monopoly power.

Externalities, moral hazards, and monopoly power have led to more external control on managerial capitalism. There are de facto constraints, due to these economic facts of life, on the ability of management to act in the interests of stockholders. . . .

A STAKEHOLDER THEORY OF THE FIRM

Foundations of a Theory

Two themes are present throughout our argument. The first is concerned with the rights and duties of the owners (and their agents) of private property, and the effects of this property on the rights of others. The second theme is concerned with the consequences of managerial capitalism and the effects of the modern corporation on the welfare of others. These themes represent two branches of modern moral theory, Kantianism and consequentialism, and they are pitted together as the main tension in most existing moral theories. Our purpose here is not to argue that the stockholder theory of the firm seems to give precedence to one or the other interpretation, but that both are important in grounding a theory of the modern corporation. In other words, we need a theory that balances the rights of the claimants on the corporation with the consequences of the corporate form.

Those who question the legitimacy of the modern corporation altogether because of the evils of excessive corporate power usually believe that the corporation should have no right to decide how things are going to be for its constituents. While we believe that each person has the right to be treated not as a means to some corporate end but as an end in itself, we would not go so far as to say that the corporation has no rights whatsoever. Our more moderate stance is that if the modern corporation requires treating others as means to an end, then these others must agree on, and hence participate (or choose not to participate) in, the decisions to be used as such. Thus, property rights are legitimate but not absolute, particularly when they conflict with important rights of others. And any theory that is to be consistent with our considered judgment about rights must take such a balanced view. The right to property does not yield the right to treat others as means to an end, which is to say that property rights are not a license to ignore Kant's principle of respect for persons.

Those who question the legitimacy of the modern corporation altogether because of the resulting possibility of externalities or harm usually do not see that the corporation can be held accountable for its actions. We maintain that persons (even legal persons) are responsible for the consequences of their actions, regardless of how those actions are mediated, and must be able and willing to accept responsibility for them. Therefore, any theory that seeks to justify the corporate form must be based at least partially on the idea that the corporation and its managers as moral agents can be the cause of and can be held accountable for their actions.

In line with these two themes of rights and effects, . . . we suggest two principles that will serve as working rules, not absolutes, to guide us in addressing some of the foundational issues. We will not settle the thorny issues that these principles raise, but merely argue that any theory, including the stakeholder theory, must be consistent with these principles.

Principle of Corporate Rights (PCR) The corporation and its managers may not violate the legitimate rights of others to determine their own future.

Principle of Corporate Effects (PCE) The corporation and its managers are responsible for the effects of their actions on others.

The Stakeholder Concept

Corporations have stakeholders, that is, groups and individuals who benefit from or are harmed by, and whose rights are violated or respected by, corporate actions. The notion of stakeholder is built around the Principle of Corporate Rights (PCR) and the Principle of Corporate Effects (PCE). . . . The concept of stakeholders is a generalization of the notion of stockholders, who themselves have some special claim on the firm. Just as stockholders have a right to demand certain actions by management, so do other stakeholders have a right to make claims. The exact nature of these claims is a difficult question that we shall address, but the logic is identical to that of the stockholder theory. Stakes require action of a certain sort, and conflicting stakes require methods of resolution. . . .

Freeman and Reed (1983)[10] distinguish two senses of *stakeholder*. The "narrow definition" includes those groups who are vital to the survival and success of the corporation. The "wide definition" includes any group or individual who can affect or is affected by the corporation. While the wide definition is more in keeping with PCE and PCR, it raises too many difficult issues. We shall begin with a more modest aim: to articulate a stakeholder theory using the narrow definition.

Stakeholders in the Modern Corporation

Figure 1 depicts the stakeholders in a typical large corporation. The stakes of each are reciprocal, since each can affect the other in terms of harms and benefits as well as rights and duties. The stakes of each are not univocal and would vary by particular corporation. We merely set forth some general notions that seem to be common to many large firms.

Owners have financial stake in the corporation in the form of stocks, bonds, and so on, and they expect some kind of financial return from them. Either they have given money directly to the firm, or they have some historical claim made through a series of morally justified exchanges. The firm affects their livelihood or, if a substantial portion of their retirement income is in stocks or bonds, their ability to care for themselves when they can no longer work. Of course, the stakes of owners will differ by type of owner, preferences for money, moral preferences, and so on, as well as by type of firm. The owners of AT&T are quite different from the owners of Ford Motor Company, with stock of the former company being widely dispersed among 3 million stockholders and that of the latter being held by a small family group as well as by a large group of public stockholders.

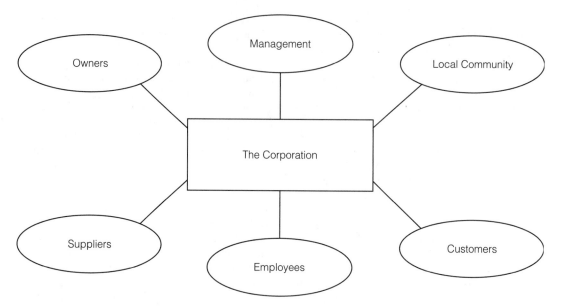

FIGURE 1. A Stakeholder Model of the Corporation

Employees have their jobs and usually their livelihood at stake; they often have specialized skills for which there is usually no perfectly elastic market. In return for their labor, they expect security, wages, benefits, and meaningful work. In return for their loyalty, the corporation is expected to provide for them and carry them through difficult times. Employees are expected to follow the instructions of management most of the time, to speak favorably about the company, and to be responsible citizens in the local communities in which the company operates. Where they are used as means to an end, they must participate in decisions affecting such use. The evidence that such policies and values as described here lead to productive company-employee relationships is compelling. It is equally compelling to realize that the opportunities for "bad faith" on the part of both management and employees are enormous. "Mock participation" in quality circles, singing the company song, and wearing the company uniform solely to please management all lead to distrust and unproductive work.

Suppliers, interpreted in a stakeholder sense, are vital to the success of the firm, for raw materials will determine the final product's quality and price. In turn the firm is a customer of the supplier and is therefore vital to the success and survival of the supplier. When the firm treats the supplier as a valued member of the stakeholder network, rather than simply as a source of materials, the supplier will respond when the firm is in need. Chrysler traditionally had very close ties to its suppliers, even to the extent that led some to suspect the transfer of illegal payments. And when Chrysler was on the brink of disaster, the suppliers responded with price cuts, accepting late payments, financing, and so on. Supplier and company can rise and fall together. Of course, again, the particular supplier relationships will depend on a number of variables such as the number of suppliers and whether the supplies are finished goods or raw materials.

Customers exchange resources for the products of the firm and in return receive the benefits of the products. Customers provide the lifeblood of the firm in the form of revenue. Given the level of reinvestment of earnings in large corporations, customers indirectly pay for the development of new products and services. Peters and Waterman (1982)[11] have argued that being close to the customer leads to success with other stakeholders and that a distinguishing characteristic of some companies that have performed well is their emphasis on the customer. By paying attention to customers' needs, management automatically addresses the needs of suppliers and owners. Moreover, it seems that the ethic of customer service carries over to the community. Almost without fail the "excellent companies" in Peters and Waterman's study have good reputations in the community. We would argue that Peters and Waterman have found multiple applications of Kant's dictum, "Treat persons as ends unto themselves," and it should come as no surprise that persons respond to such respectful treatment, be they customers, suppliers, owners, employees, or members of the local community. The real surprise is the novelty of the application of Kant's rule in a theory of good management practice.

The local community grants the firm the right to build facilities and, in turn, it benefits from the tax base and economic and social contributions of the firm. In return for the provision of local services, the firm is expected to be a good citizen, as is any person, either "natural or artificial." The firm cannot expose the community to unreasonable hazards in the form of pollution, toxic waste, and so on. If for some reason the firm must leave a community, it is expected to work with local leaders to make the transition as smoothly as possible. Of course, the firm does not have perfect knowledge, but when it discovers some danger or runs afoul of new competition, it is expected to inform the local community and to work with the community to overcome any problem. When the firm mismanages its relationship with the local community, it is in the same position as a citizen who commits a crime. It has violated the implicit social contract with the community and should expect to be distrusted and ostracized. It should not be surprised when punitive measures are invoked.

We have not included "competitors" as stakeholders in the narrow sense, since strictly speaking they are not necessary for the survival and success of the firm; the stakeholder theory works equally well in monopoly contexts. However, competitors and government would be the first to be included in an extension of this basic theory. It is simply not true that the interests of competitors in an industry are always in conflict. There is no reason why trade associations and other multiorganizational groups cannot band together to solve common problems that have little to do with how to restrain trade. Implementation of stakeholder management principles, in the long run, mitigates the need for industrial policy and an increasing role for government intervention and regulation.

The Role of Management

Management plays a special role, for it too has a stake in the modern corporation. On the one hand, management's stake is like that of employees, with some kind of explicit or implicit employment contract. But, on the other hand, management has a duty of safeguarding the welfare of the abstract entity that is the corporation. In short, management, especially top management, must look after the health of the corporation, and this involves balancing the multiple claims of conflicting stakeholders. Owners want higher financial returns, while customers want more money spent on research and development. Employees want higher wages and better benefits, while the local community wants better parks and day-care facilities.

The task of management in today's corporation is akin to that of King Solomon. The stakeholder theory does not give primacy to one stakeholder group over another, though there will surely be times when one group will benefit at the expense of others. In general, however, management must keep the relationships among stakeholders in balance. When these relationships become imbalanced, the survival of the firm is in jeopardy.

When wages are too high and product quality is too low, customers leave, suppliers suffer, and owners sell their stocks and bonds, depressing the stock price and making it difficult to raise new capital at favorable rates. Note, however, that the reason for paying returns to owners is not that they "own" the firm, but that their support is necessary for the survival of the firm, and that they have a legitimate claim on the firm. Similar reasoning applies in turn to each stakeholder group.

A stakeholder theory of the firm must redefine the purpose of the firm. The stockholder theory claims that the purpose of the firm is to maximize the welfare of the stockholders, perhaps subject to some moral or social constraints, either because such maximization leads to the greatest good or because of property rights. The purpose of the firm is quite different in our view. If a stakeholder theory is to be consistent with the principles of corporate effects and rights, then its purpose must take into account Kant's dictum of respect for persons. The very purpose of the firm is, in our view, to serve as a vehicle for coordinating stakeholder interests. It is through the firm that each stakeholder group makes itself better off through voluntary exchanges. The corporation serves at the pleasure of its stakeholders, and none may be used as a means to the ends of another without full rights of participation in that decision. We can crystallize the particular applications of PCR and PCE to the stakeholder theory in two further principles. These stakeholder management principles will serve as a foundation for articulating the theory. They are guiding ideals for the immortal corporation as it endures through generations of particular mortal stakeholders.

Stakeholder Management Principles

P1: The corporation should be managed for the benefit of its stakeholders: its customers, suppliers, owners, employees, and local communities. The rights of these groups must be ensured, and, further, the groups must participate, in some sense, in decisions that substantially affect their welfare.

P2: Management bears a fiduciary relationship to stakeholders and to the corporation as an abstract entity. It must act in the interests of the stakeholders as their agent, and it must act in the interests of the corporation to ensure the survival of the firm, safeguarding the long-term stakes of each group.

P1, which we might call The Principle of Corporate Legitimacy, redefines the purpose of the firm to be in line with the principles of corporate effects and rights. It implies the legitimacy of stakeholder claims on the firm. Any social contract that justifies the existence of the corporate form includes the notion that stakeholders are a party to that contract. Further, stakeholders have some inalienable rights to participate in decisions that substantially affect their welfare or involve their being used as a means to another's ends. We bring to bear our arguments for the incoherence of the stockholder view as justification for P1. If in fact there is no good reason for the stockholder theory, and if in fact there are harms, benefits, and rights of stakeholders involved in running the modern corporation, then we know of no other starting point for a theory of the corporation than P1.

P2, which we might call The Stakeholder Fiduciary Principle, explicitly defines the duty of management to recognize these claims. It will not always be possible to meet all claims of all stakeholders all the time, since some of these claims will conflict. Here P2 recognizes the duty of management to act in the long-term best interests of the corporation, conceived as a forum of stakeholder interaction, when the interests of the group outweigh the interests of the individual parties to the collective contract. The duty described in P2 is a fiduciary duty, yet it does not suffer from the difficulties surrounding the fiduciary duty to stockholders, for the conflicts involved there are precisely those that P2 makes it mandatory for management to resolve. Of course, P2 gives no instructions for a magical resolution of the conflicts that arise from prima facie obligations to multiple parties. An analysis of such rules for decision making is a subject to be addressed on another occasion, but P2 does give these conflicts a legitimacy that they do not enjoy in the stockholder theory. It gives management a clear and distinct directive to pay attention to stakeholder claims.

P1 and P2 recognize the eventual need for changes in the law of corporations and other governance mechanisms if the stakeholder theory is to be put into practice. P1 and P2, if implemented as a major innovation in the structure of the corporation, will make manifest the eventual legal institutionalization of sanctions. . . .

Structural Mechanisms

We propose several structural mechanisms to make a stakeholder management conception practicable. We shall offer a sketch of these here and say little by way of argument for them.

1. *The Stakeholder Board of Directors.* We propose that every corporation of a certain size yet to be determined, but surely all those that are publicly traded or are of the size of those publicly traded, form a Board of Directors comprised of representatives of five stakeholder groups, including employees, customers, suppliers, stockholders, and members of the local community, as well as a representative of the corporation, whom we might call a "metaphysical director" since he or she would be responsible for the metaphysical entity that is

"the corporation." Whether or not each representative has an equal voting right is a matter that can be decided by experimentation; issues of governance lend themselves naturally to both laboratory and organizational experiments.

These directors will be vested with the duty of care to manage the affairs of the corporation in concert with the interests of its stakeholders. Such a Board would ensure that the rights of each group would have a forum, and by involving a director for the corporation, would ensure that the corporation itself would not be unduly harmed for the benefit of a particular group. In addition, by vesting each director with the duty of care for all stakeholders, we ensure that positive resolutions of conflicts would occur.... The task of the metaphysical director, to be elected unanimously by the stakeholder representatives, is especially important. The fact that the director has no direct constituency would appear to enhance management control. However, nothing could be further from the truth. To represent the abstract entity that is the corporation would be a most demanding job. Our metaphysical director would be responsible for convincing both stakeholders and management that a certain course of action was in the interests of the long-term health of the corporation, especially when that action implies the sacrifice of the interests of all. The metaphysical director would be a key link between the stakeholder representatives and management, and would spearhead the drive to protect the norms of the interests of all stakeholders....

2. *Corporate Law.* The law of corporations needs to be redefined to recognize the legitimate purpose of the corporation as stated in P1. This has in fact developed in some areas of the law, such as products liability, where the claims of customers to safe products have emerged, and labor law, where the claims of employees have been safeguarded. Indeed, in such pioneering cases as *Marsh v. Alabama* the courts have come close to a stakeholder perspective. We envision that a body of case law will emerge to give meaning to "the proper claims of stakeholders," and in effect that the "wisdom of Solomon"

necessary to make the stakeholder theory work will emerge naturally through the joint action of the courts, stakeholders, and management.

While much of the above may seem utopian, there are some very practical transitional steps that could occur. Each large corporation could form a stakeholder advisory board, which would prepare a charter detailing how the organization is to treat the claims of each stakeholder. Initially this stakeholder advisory board would serve as an advisor to the current board of directors, and eventually it would replace that board. Simultaneously, a group of legal scholars and practitioners, such as the American Law Institute, could initiate discussion of the legal proposals and methods to change corporate charters, while business groups such as the Business Roundtable could examine the practical consequences of our proposals. Given the emergence of some consensus, we believe that a workable transition can be found....

NOTES

1. Cf. A. Berle and G. Means, *The Modern Corporation and Private Property* (New York: Commerce Clearing House, 1932), 1. For a reassessment of Berle and Means' argument after 50 years, see *Journal of Law and Economics* 26 (June 1983), especially G. Stigler and C. Friedland, "The Literature of Economics: The Case of Berle and Means," 237–68; D. North, "Comment on Stigler and Friedland," 269–72; and G. Means, "Corporate Power in the Marketplace," 467–85.

2. The metaphor of rebuilding the ship while afloat is attributed to [Otto] Neurath by W. Quine, *Word and Object* (Cambridge: Harvard University Press, 1960), and W. Quine and J. Ullian, *The Web of Belief* (New York: Random House, 1978). The point is that to keep the ship afloat during repairs we must replace a plank with one that will do a better job. Our argument is that Kantian capitalism can so replace the current version of managerial capitalism.

3. Kant's notion of respect for persons (i.e., that each person has a right not to be treated as a means to an end) can be found in (1) Kant, *Critique of Practical Reason* (1838 edition). See J. Rawls, *A Theory of Justice* (Cambridge: Harvard University Press, 1971) for an eloquent modern interpretation.

4. For an introduction to the law of corporations, see A. Conard, *Corporations in Perspective* (Mineola, NY: The

Foundation Press, 1976), especially section 19; and R. Hamilton, *Corporations* (St. Paul: West Publishing, 1981), Chapter 8.

5. For a modern statement of managerial capitalism, see the literature in managerial economics, for example R. Coase, "The Nature of the Firm," *Economica* 4 (1937): 386–405; M. Jensen and W. Meckling, "Theory of the Firm: Managerial Behavior, Agency Costs and Ownership Structure," *Journal of Financial Economics* 3 (1976): 305–60; and O. Williamson, *The Economics of Discretionary Behavior* (London: Kershaw Publishing, 1965).

6. See R. Charan and E. Freeman, "Planning for the Business Environment of the 1980s," *The Journal of Business Strategy* 1 (1980): 9–19, especially p. 15 for a brief account of the major developments in products liability law.

7. See S. Breyer, *Regulation and Its Reform* (Cambridge: Harvard University Press, 1983), 133, for an analysis of food additives.

8. See I. Millstein and S. Katsh, *The Limits of Corporate Power* (New York: Macmillan, 1981), Chapter 4.

9. Cf. C. Summers, "Protecting All Employees Against Unjust Dismissal," *Harvard Business Review* 58 (1980): 136, for a careful statement of the argument.

10. See E. Freeman and D. Reed, "Stockholders and Stakeholders: A New Perspective on Corporate Governance," in C. Huizinga, ed., *Corporate Governance: A Definitive Exploration of the Issues* (Los Angeles: UCLA Extension Press, 1983).

11. See T. Peters and R. Waterman, *In Search of Excellence* (New York: Harper and Row, 1982).

READING 4.2 BAD AND NOT-SO-BAD ARGUMENTS FOR SHAREHOLDER PRIMACY
Lynn A. Stout[*]

In 1932, the Harvard Law Review published a debate between two preeminent corporate scholars on the subject of the proper purpose of the public corporation. On one side stood the renowned Adolph A. Berle, coauthor of the classic *The Modern Corporation and Private Property*.[1] Berle argued for what is now called "shareholder primacy"—the view that the corporation exists only to make money for its shareholders.[2] According to Berle, "all powers granted to a corporation or to the management of a corporation, or to any group within the corporation . . . [are] at all times exercisable only for the ratable benefit of all the shareholders as their interest appears."[3]

On the other side of the debate stood esteemed professor Merrick Dodd of Harvard Law School. Dodd disagreed vehemently with Berle's shareholder primacy thesis. He argued for "a view of the business corporation as an economic institution which has a social service as well as a profit-making function."[4] Dodd claimed that the proper purpose of the corporation (and the proper goal of corporate managers) was not confined to making money for shareholders. It also included more secure jobs for employees, better quality products for consumers, and greater contributions to the welfare of the community as a whole.

As can be seen from Delaware Vice Chancellor Leo E. Strine's Essay [. . .], the debate over the social role of the corporation remains unresolved.[5] Does the firm exist only to increase shareholder wealth (a view that Strine dubs the "property" theory)? Or, should managers also seek to serve the interests of employees, creditors, customers, and the broader society (the "entity" view)?[6] After reading Strine's account of the current state of scholarly disagreement, and a similar account in another article he has coauthored, forthcoming in the *University of*

[*]Professor of Law, University of California at Los Angeles School of Law. The author would like to thank William Allen, Margaret Blair, Stephen Bainbridge, Allen Ferrell, Jeffrey Gordon, Ehud Kamar, William Klein, Mark Roe, Leo E. Strine, Jr., Eric Talley, and Jack Treynor for their insightful comments on earlier drafts of this Essay.

From Lynn A. Stout, "Bad And Not-So-Bad Arguments For Shareholder Primacy," 75 *Southern California Law Review,* pp. 1189–1209 (2002). Reprinted with permission of the *Southern California Law Review.* This paper may be downloaded without charge at The Social Science Research Network Electronic Paper Collection. http://papers.ssrn.com/abstract-331464

Chicago Law Review,[7] one might be tempted to throw up one's hands and conclude that academics have not lent much more insight into this question since the original Berle-Dodd debate.

In this essay, however, I would like to suggest that we have made at least some intellectual progress over the intervening decades on the question of the proper role of the corporation. In particular, we have learned that some of the most frequently raised arguments for shareholder primacy are, not to put too fine a point on it, bad arguments. By "bad" arguments, I do not mean arguments that are somehow morally offensive or normatively unattractive. Rather, I mean arguments that are, as a positive matter, inaccurate, incorrect, and unpersuasive to the careful and neutral observer.

I. THE SHAREHOLDER OWNERSHIP ARGUMENT FOR SHAREHOLDER PRIMACY

Consider first what is probably the most common, and the worst, of the standard arguments for shareholder primacy. This is the argument—really, the naked assertion—that the public corporation "belongs" to its shareholders.[8] This assertion is frequently employed by commentators in the popular media and business press to justify shareholder primacy. A classic example can be found in Milton Friedman's famed 1970 essay in the *New York Times,* in which he argued that, because the shareholders of the corporation are "the owners of the business," the only "social responsibility of business is to increase its profits."[9]

Milton Friedman is a Nobel Prize-winning economist, but he obviously is not a lawyer. A lawyer would know that the shareholders do not, in fact, own the corporation. Rather, they own a type of corporate security commonly called "stock." As owners of stock, shareholders' rights are quite limited. For example, stockholders do not have the right to exercise control over the corporation's assets. The corporation's board of director's holds that right.[10] Similarly, shareholders do not have any right to help themselves to the firm's earnings; the only time they can receive any payment directly from the corporation's coffers is when they receive

a dividend, which occurs only when the directors decide to declare one.[11] As a legal matter, shareholders accordingly enjoy neither direct control over the firm's assets nor direct access to them. Any influence they may have on the firm is indirect, through their influence on the board of directors. And (as Berle himself famously argued) in a public corporation with widely dispersed shareownership, shareholder influence over the board is often so diluted as to be negligible.[12] Thus, while it perhaps is excusable to loosely describe a closely held firm with a single controlling shareholder as "owned" by that shareholder, it is misleading to use the language of ownership to describe the relationship between a public firm and its shareholders.

From an intellectual perspective, matters have only gotten worse for the "ownership" argument in the years since Friedman published his essay. Three years after Friedman made his argument in the *New York Times,* Fischer Black and Myron Scholes published their famous paper on options pricing.[13] This work, which provides the foundation for modern options theory, demonstrates that it is not only misleading to say that dispersed shareholders "own" a public corporation, but that it is even questionable, from an economic perspective, to say that a single controlling shareholder "owns" a closely held firm after the firm has issued debt. Options theory teaches us that once a firm has issued debt (as almost all firms do), it makes just as much sense to say that the debtholders "own" the right to the corporation's cash flow but have sold a call option to the shareholder, as it does to say that the shareholder "owns" the right to the corporation's cash flow but has bought a put option from the debtholders.[14] Put differently, options theory demonstrates that bondholders and equity holders each share contingent control and bear residual risk in firms.

How, then, can one describe a publicly held corporation that has issued debt as being owned by its shareholders? The short answer is that one cannot—at least not if one is interested in accurately describing the legal and economic structure of the firm. From both a legal and an economic perspective, the claim that shareholders own the public corporation simply is empirically incorrect. The time has come to lead the "shareholder ownership" argument for shareholder primacy to the back of the barn, and to put it out of its misery.

II. THE RESIDUAL CLAIMANTS ARGUMENT FOR SHAREHOLDER PRIMACY

Thus, I would like to turn to what is arguably the second most frequently raised, and the second worst, of the standard arguments for shareholder primacy. This is the argument (again, one might say the naked assertion) that while shareholders may not be the owners of the corporation, they are at least its sole residual claimants.

A classic example of the use of this argument can be found in the influential work of Frank Easterbrook and Daniel Fischel of the "Chicago School" of law and economic analysis.[15] Adopting the notion that the corporation can be thought of as a nexus of contracts between and among the shareholders of the firm and other corporate participants, Easterbrook and Fischel argue that the contracts entered into by nonshareholder groups such as employees, managers, and creditors are explicit contracts that entitle them to fixed payments, such as salaries and interest payments.[16] In contrast, shareholders rely on an implicit contract that entitles them to whatever remains after the firm has met its explicit obligations and paid its fixed claims.[17] Thus, Easterbrook and Fischel describe shareholders as the sole "residual claimants" and sole "residual risk bearers" in public firms,[18] and argue that in accord with shareholders' implicit "contractual" rights, firms should be run with an eye toward maximizing shareholder wealth.[19]

The idea that shareholders are the sole residual claimants in firms has had a tremendous influence on contemporary scholarly thought regarding the advantages of shareholder primacy.[20] Nevertheless, there remains a fundamental flaw in the residual claimants argument. Like the ownership argument, the residual claimants argument for shareholder primacy is a naked assertion, and an empirically incorrect one at that.[21]

To understand this point, it is essential to recognize that the only time that corporate law comes close to treating shareholders like residual claimants is when the firm *is actually in bankruptcy.*[22] When the firm is not in bankruptcy, it is grossly misleading to suggest that the firm's shareholders are somehow entitled to—much less actually expect to receive—everything left over after the firm's explicit contrac-

tual obligations have been met. To the contrary, corporate law allows shareholders to receive payments from firms only when two conditions are met. First, the firm must be doing well enough financially (must have enough retained earnings or enough profits) to permit the directors to declare a dividend.[23] Second, the directors must actually decide to declare a dividend.[24]

Neither contingency can be met unless the directors want it to be met. "Retained earnings" and "profits" are accounting concepts over which directors have considerable control, because both depend not only on the firm's earnings, but also on its expenses. If a firm is doing well in the product market, its directors have the option of allowing reported profits to increase. But they also have the option of using some or all of the firm's new wealth to raise managers' salaries, start an on-site childcare center, improve customer service, beef up retirees' pensions, or make donations to charity. Thus, even when the firm is making money hand-over-fist, it remains for the directors to decide whether and to what extent that wealth will show up in the financial statements in a form that can be paid out to shareholders. Also, even when a firm's balance sheet or earnings statement permits a dividend, directors are not required to declare one, and often they do not. It is standard operating practice among many U.S. firms to pay either small dividends or no dividends to shareholders, while retaining the lion's share of earnings for future projects. If this practice boosts stock prices, shareholders ultimately enjoy an economic benefit. That benefit, however, is indirect, and dependent on the board of directors' decisions. If the board decides to run the firm with an eye primarily to serving the interests of its executives, employees, or customers—or if they simply run it into the ground—shareholders' rights to sell their shares on the open market are of little value.

Accordingly, as a legal matter, shareholders of a public corporation are entitled to receive nothing from the firm *unless and until the board of directors decides that they should receive it.* Moreover, shareholders who become dissatisfied with the manner in which the board treats them have only limited practical ability to change things. A proxy battle to remove the board would be both expensive and unlikely to succeed. Similarly, while disgruntled shareholders can always hope that a takeover bidder will appear on the horizon to rescue them, takeovers are also expensive and uncertain, and rescue may come too late, if at all.

Consequently, it is grossly inaccurate as a positive matter to describe the shareholders of a public corporation as the "sole residual claimants" of a firm while that firm is a going concern. To the contrary, shareholders are only one of several groups that can be described as "residual claimants" or "residual risk bearers," in the sense that they expect to enjoy benefits (and sometimes to endure burdens) beyond those provided in their explicit contracts. When the firm is doing well, for example, employees receive raises and enjoy greater job security, managers get use of a company jet, and bondholders enjoy increased protection from corporate insolvency. Conversely, these groups suffer along with shareholders when times are bad, as employees face "reductions in force," managers are told to fly coach, and debtholders face increased risk. Directors use their control over the firm to reward many groups with larger slices of the corporate pie when that pie is growing, and to spread the loss among many when the pie is shrinking. A corollary to this reality is that we cannot rely on the empirically false claim that shareholders are the "sole residual claimants" of firms in order to justify shareholder primacy.

Of course, one might still argue that if shareholders are not in fact the sole residual claimants of most modern firms, that they ought to be. In other words, one might argue that while shareholders do not actually enjoy all the firm's wealth after its fixed claims have been paid, this is the very problem to be remedied by the rule of shareholder primacy. This argument treats shareholders' supposed status as sole residual claimants as a normative desideratum rather than as a positive description of the state of the world.

At this point, however, the argument for shareholder primacy becomes a tautology: corporate law *ought* to incorporate shareholder primacy (or so the argument goes) because shareholders *ought* to be the firm's sole residual claimants. This approach simply begs the fundamental question: if shareholders are not, in fact, the sole residual claimants of the public firm, why should we want them to be?

This is the question that lies at the heart of the Berle-Dodd debate, and the answer to it is not obvious. Below, I explore what may be the only good argument (meaning the only empirically sound and

logically consistent argument) that can be advanced in favor of shareholder primacy. Yet to understand that argument, we must begin by considering an important argument *against* shareholder primacy. This is the argument based on the contracting problems associated with team production.[25]

III. THE TEAM PRODUCTION ARGUMENT AGAINST SHAREHOLDER PRIMACY

Team production analysis of the corporation begins by recognizing that corporate production often requires inputs from a number of different groups. Shareholders alone cannot make a firm—creditors, employees, managers, and even local governments often must make contributions in order for an enterprise to succeed. Why do these groups make such contributions?

To some extent, nonshareholder groups participate in and contribute to corporations because they expect to be compensated in accordance to their explicit contracts. For example, employees work, in part, because they are entitled to wages. Yet as labor economists have long argued, in a world of complexity and uncertainty, nonshareholder groups often rely on implicit contracts as well. Thus, for example, junior executives or employees might expect that if they do good work and remain loyal to the firm, and if the firm does well, they will receive not only the wages specified in their contracts but also, eventually, raises, job security, and the prospect of promotion.

Why is this expectation not reduced to writing, to a formal contract? In brief, because the resulting document would be inches thick and would raise more problems than it solved. For example, how is a court to decide how much, exactly, employees' salaries should be raised in light of the firm's profits, or to judge reliably the quality and importance of their relative contributions?[26] Instead, employees, managers, creditors, and even governments often prefer to contribute to firms on the basis of barebones formal contracts or no formal contract at all, relying on the understanding that they will be treated considerately and allowed to share some of the bounty if the firm does well. What's more, *it can be in the shareholders' interest to encourage such expecta-*

tions, because those expectations encourage managers to be loyal, employees to be committed, creditors to be patient, and governments to be supportive.

This observation offers important insights into the nature of the relationship between shareholder and nonshareholder participants in corporations. First, it suggests how it is possible to increase the value of shareholders' economic interest in the firm (shareholders' supposedly "residual claim") without increasing the economic value of the firm itself. Put differently, a board of directors focused solely on shareholder wealth can often make shareholders better off by simply taking wealth from other corporate constituencies.

This possibility is nicely illustrated by Strine's hypothetical. Consider the dilemma faced by James Trains' board of directors. It can maximize shareholder wealth by selling the firm to the highest bidder—a bidder that would pink-slip James Train's executives, fire its rank-and-file employees, and shut down its manufacturing plants (built and maintained with the help of tax breaks and financing from state and local governments). Alternatively, for a slightly lower price, the board can sell James Trains to a reputable firm that would both keep the plants operational and retain most of the firm's employees. One cannot help but suspect that much of the additional wealth that would go into the shareholders' pockets if the firm were sold to the first bidder would be counterbalanced by monetary losses (not to mention nonmonetary losses) to the James Trains managers, employees, and the local community. Indeed, the one-time gains to the James Trains shareholders can easily be outweighed by the losses to other groups.[27]

Strine's hypothetical consequently demonstrates how a rule of shareholder primacy that requires the James Trains directors to sell to the highest bidder can be inefficient ex post. This potential for inefficiency becomes even greater when we consider the ex ante effects of such a rule. If the employees and managers of James Trains really believed that the firm's directors not only could sell, but *were required to sell* the company to the highest bidder whenever the board received an offer of even a penny above market price, would the firm's executives have been as willing to commit their careers to James Trains? Would the rank-and-file have made the same effort to acquire firm-specific skills? Would state and local governments have been so willing to provide tax

breaks and financing? A priori, one cannot exclude the possibility (indeed, probability) that the answer to these questions is "no." In other words, as Margaret Blair and I have argued at length elsewhere, strict shareholder primacy of the sort described by Strine in his James Trains hypothetical may inefficiently discourage nonshareholder constituents from making the types of firm-specific investments that can be essential to a company's success.[28]

Once one takes account of the corporation's need for firm-specific investments by many groups, and of the difficulties of drafting complete contracts under conditions of complexity and uncertainty, one cannot avoid the conclusion that shareholder primacy easily can produce results that are inefficient from both ex post and ex ante perspectives. It also becomes clear that the ideal rule for corporate directors to follow is not to require them to focus solely on maximizing shareholders' current wealth. Rather, the ideal rule of corporate governance, at least from an efficiency perspective, is to require corporate directors to maximize the sum of *all* the risk-adjusted returns enjoyed by *all* of the groups that participate in firms.[29] These groups include not only shareholders, but also executives, employees, debtholders, and possibly even suppliers, consumers, and the broader community.

Because this ideal rule efficiently encourages firm-specific investment, it can be argued that it is consistent with shareholder primacy from an ex ante perspective. That is, it is in the best interests of shareholders as a class over the long run. But in the short run, it also allows directors discretion to refuse to maximize the wealth of the shareholders of a particular firm at a particular time in order to protect the extra-contractual expectations of essential nonshareholder groups. For example, it allows the James Trains directors to refuse to sell to the highest bidder. Thus, shareholders as a class may be served best not by shareholder primacy, but by what Stephen Bainbridge has called "director primacy."[30]

The superior efficiency, at least in theory, of a corporate governance rule that allows directors to take account of the interests of all of the corporations' constituents is increasingly acknowledged both in corporate scholarship[31] and in corporate case law.[32] Nevertheless, it remains common practice for even sophisticated commentators to assume that shareholder primacy is somehow preferable. Why?

IV. COUNTERBALANCING TEAM PRODUCTION CONCERNS: THE AGENCY COST ARGUMENT FOR SHAREHOLDER PRIMACY

So we come to the third, and arguably the best, of the standard arguments for shareholder primacy. This argument begins by acknowledging that, in theory, the ideal rule for corporate governance is a rule that grants directors discretion to balance the interests of all the firm's constituents. But we do not live in an ideal world. Corporate directors are only human. Accordingly, they are imperfect agents. They worry not only about the interests of the firms to which they owe fiduciary duties, but also about their own interests. As a result, they may sometimes allow self-interest to prevail over duty, and shirk or even steal from the firm. Economists frequently refer to this problem as the problem of "agency costs."[33]

Agency costs can be reduced when one can monitor and measure an agent's performance. This need to measure and monitor agent performance provides the foundation for the best of the standard arguments for shareholder primacy. If we ask directors to consider the interests of all the firm's constituents, we are asking them to maximize the joint welfare function of happy consumers, secure employees, self-actualized managers, and wealthier shareholders. How are we to tell when they are doing a good job? Although it may be simple enough, at least in theory, to determine how directors' decisions affect the market price of the firm's stock and even some of its bonds, measuring the value of employee security, manager self-actualization, and consumer satisfaction (to give only a few examples) is far more difficult.

In contrast, it is easy to measure stock price. As a result, a shareholder primacy rule leaves directors with far less leeway to claim that they are doing a good job for the firm when, in fact, they are doing well mostly for themselves. As Mark Roe has put it, shareholder wealth maximization may be the best rule of corporate governance because "a stakeholder measure of managerial accountability could leave managers so much discretion that managers could easily pursue their own agenda, one that might maximize neither shareholder, employee, consumer, nor national wealth, but only their own."[34]

So we have learned in the decades following the Berle-Dodd debate that the issue really boils down to this: which is worse? To require directors to maximize shareholder wealth, even in cases like Strine's James Trains, where shareholder wealth maximization is inefficient? Or to allow directors to look at the interests of nonshareholder "stakeholders," recognizing that they may use their enhanced discretion to serve themselves? Put differently, the best argument for shareholder primacy does not rest on its benefits for shareholders alone. Rather, it rests on the notion that shareholder primacy is a second-best solution that is good for all the stakeholders in the firm, because it limits what might otherwise be the runaway agency costs that might be incurred by all if directors were not held to a clear and easily observed metric of good corporate governance.

In this short essay, I do not attempt to address which of these two economic evils—increased agency costs from a rule of director primacy or the ex post and ex ante inefficiencies that flow from shareholder primacy—is worse. Instead, I point out that the question ultimately cannot be answered *except on the basis of empirical evidence*. Before we know whether social wealth is best promoted by a rule of shareholder primacy or a rule that allows directors discretion to consider other stakeholders, we must actually know the costs and the benefits that flow from each rule. We must somehow measure and weigh such matters as the importance of firm-specific human capital, the incompleteness of formal contracts, the value of a good corporate "reputation," and the risks of director self-interest. Put differently, the Berle-Dodd debate cannot be resolved by armchair theorizing.

V. SOME EMPIRICAL EVIDENCE: WHICH RULE DO LAWMAKERS, MANAGERS, AND SHAREHOLDERS ACTUALLY CHOOSE?

How, then, might it be resolved? Where can we search for empirical evidence on the question of whether shareholder primacy (the property model) or director primacy (the entity model) is the best approach to corporate governance?

For now, at least, I doubt that academics can provide a definitive answer. Whether the social losses from shareholder primacy outweigh the social losses from allowing greater director discretion is an extraordinarily complex question. Moreover, the answer is likely to vary from firm to firm and from one historical period to another. Case studies, and even large longitudinal studies, may be of limited value.

There is, however, another potential source of evidence to consider. This is the collective opinion of the business world itself—the opinion of the executives, directors, shareholders, and employees who actually participate in corporations, as well as the opinion of the judges and legislators who regulate them. These are the people in the trenches, the ones who experience business life as a day-to-day reality, or at least directly observe how America does business. They are also the people (as Strine reminds us) who are faced with the necessity of choosing between strategies and rules that favor shareholders, and strategies and rules that favor a broader range of corporate constituencies.[35] While academics debate the relative merits of the property and the entity theory, businesspeople must actually choose between them, and must live with the consequences if they do not choose wisely.

Which approach do they choose? If we focus only on rhetoric, the answer is not clear. At different times and at different places, lawmakers and business leaders can be found giving lip service to both shareholder primacy and the need to consider stakeholder interests.[36]

Thus, it may be more useful to focus on actual behavior—what economists call "revealed preferences"—to discern the business world's beliefs about the relative merits of shareholder versus director primacy. If one adopts this approach, an interesting pattern emerges. It appears that when forced to choose, managers and shareholders alike—as well as most judges and legislators—generally opt for rules that favor director primacy over rules that favor shareholder primacy. In other words, *the business world itself seems to favor the entity model.*

As an example of this behavioral pattern, let us consider first the choices of lawmakers and, in particular, the choices (as opposed to the rhetoric) of the Delaware judges whose decisions affect half of all publicly traded companies.[37] As Strine observes, Delaware case law generally follows the entity model.[38] For example, Delaware gives directors free rein to pursue strategies that reduce shareholder wealth while benefiting other constituencies.[39] Thus, directors can use earnings to raise employees' wages rather than to declare a dividend; they can "reprice" executive stock options even when share

prices are falling; they can retroactively increase retirees' pension benefits; and they can donate corporate funds to charity.[40]

Such discretion seems inconsistent (to put it mildly) with shareholder wealth maximization, at least if we are focusing on the wealth of the shareholders who own stock in that particular firm at that particular time. Nevertheless, corporate law in Delaware, like corporate law elsewhere, generally allows directors to redirect wealth from shareholders to other stakeholders. In the process, courts sometimes employ the language of shareholder primacy, suggesting that actions that appear to reduce current shareholder wealth might nevertheless offer some hope of a long-run shareholder benefit.[41] Such rhetoric may reflect what has been described as judicial "elision"—the tendency for courts to blur distinctions between contradictory ideas in order to decide cases while avoiding broad issues of public policy.[42] Alternatively, it may reflect an intuitive recognition of the team production problem and the possibility that allowing directors discretion to consider the interests of stakeholder groups can encourage firm-specific investment, and so be in the ex ante interests of shareholders as a class, even if not always in the ex post interests of the shareholders of a particular firm.[43] Whatever the explanation, the rhetoric does not change the reality. The courts have chosen between the property and the entity models of the public firm, and they have opted for the latter.

There is, of course, one notable exception to this rule—the case of *Revlon, Inc. v. MacAndrews & Forbes Holdings, Inc.*[44] (It is no coincidence that, in his hypothetical, Strine has chosen a situation similar to that in *Revlon* to illustrate the supposed clash between the property and the entity approaches in Delaware law.) In *Revlon*, the Delaware Supreme Court held that in an "end-game" situation where the directors of a publicly traded firm had decided to sell the firm to a company with a controlling shareholder—in brief, had decided to turn their publicly held company into a privately held one— the board had a duty to maximize shareholder wealth by getting the best possible price for the firm's shares.[45] *Revlon* thus defines the one context in which Delaware law mandates shareholder primacy.

This is a very limited context, however. Subsequent Delaware cases have dramatically reduced *Revlon's* significance by making clear that if the directors of the firm decide not to sell, or if they prefer a stock-for-stock exchange with another public firm, *Revlon* is irrelevant.[46] Accordingly, directors can avoid *Revlon* duties when they want to.[47] All this suggests that *Revlon* may prove to be an evolutionary dead end in corporate law, doctrinal deadwood that the courts have already pruned back and, eventually, may remove entirely.

The end result is that, if we judge their beliefs from their behavior, Delaware courts seem to have come down rather firmly on Dodd's side of the Berle-Dodd debate. This is even more true in the case of legislatures asked to address the merits of shareholder primacy. Although Delaware pruned back *Revlon* by case law rather than by statute, in the wake of *Revlon,* over thirty other states have passed "constituency" laws that expressly permit corporate directors to sacrifice shareholders' interests to serve other stakeholders.[48] As a group, lawmakers seem to have a rather strong revealed preference for the entity model.

Of course, one might argue that lawmakers' revealed preferences are suspect. For example, a shareholder primacy advocate might assert that even if Delaware judges are renowned for their sophistication and knowledge of corporate matters, they still fail to choose socially optimal corporate rules because they are subject to interest group pressures and other influences that lead them to favor unduly the interests of corporate managers or corporate lawyers (the so-called "race to the bottom" thesis).[49] Thus, in addition to considering the revealed preferences of lawmakers, it is perhaps more useful to consider the revealed preferences of corporate promoters and of *shareholders themselves.*

In assessing these preferences, it is important to distinguish between what the shareholders of a particular firm might favor ex post, and what shareholders as a class seem to prefer ex ante. In an ex post situation, such as Strine's James Trains hypothetical, one should not be surprised to hear at least some shareholders clamor for shareholder primacy. At this point in the game, many nonshareholder constituents—including, most obviously, the firm's employees and managers—have already made the firm-specific investments that promote efficient team production. Shareholders accordingly may be tempted to exploit those investments opportunistically and to line their own pockets at the expense

of other stakeholders.[50] Thus, once a firm is a going proposition, it is only to be expected that shareholders might sometimes adopt the position that maximizing shareholder wealth is the only proper goal of corporate governance.[51]

But a team production analysis of the corporation suggests that this sort of approach can be counterproductive if adopted by shareholders ex ante, when the corporation is being formed. When the corporate "contract" is first negotiated, equity investors may have a strong interest in inducing managers, employees, creditors, and even governments to commit resources to corporate production—resources that may be neither easy to recover once invested nor easy to protect by explicit contracts. One way to do this may be to place control of the firm not in the hands of the shareholders themselves, but in the hands of a board of directors that is charged with looking out for the interests of all the firm's stakeholders. Thus, director primacy may be a means for shareholders to benefit themselves by "tying their own hands" in a fashion that encourages firm-specific investments from other corporate stakeholders.[52]

If this analysis is correct, we can expect to see shareholders display a revealed preference for rules that promote director primacy at early stages of a firm's development. Indeed, there is considerable evidence to suggest they do. Recent studies have concluded that states that promote director primacy by providing incumbent boards of directors with relatively strong protections against hostile takeover bids, such as Delaware, are more successful both in attracting new incorporations and in retaining the incorporations of existing firms. In contrast, firms seem to avoid incorporating or reincorporating in states with a strong shareholder primacy bias, such as California.[53]

Similarly, another recent study has concluded that a majority of a sample of firms that have "gone public" in recent years amended their corporate charters before doing so in order to add additional antitakeover protections (for example, a classified board system).[54] This finding is almost impossible to reconcile with the claim that shareholder primacy is efficient. After all, if investors believed that the increase in agency costs associated with greater director protection from takeovers outweighed the benefits of such autonomy in terms of encouraging team production, they presumably would be less willing to buy the firm's shares. Knowing this, the firm's founders should be reluctant to adopt anti-takeover provisions. Put differently, at the IPO stage when the corporation's promoters are actually "negotiating" the corporate contract with outside investors, they should have a strong preference for efficient (wealth-maximizing) rules. It would seem that both shareholders and promoters prefer director primacy.

This conclusion is bolstered by a final and related observation: Delaware corporate law, like most corporate law, is an enabling system. This means that most of the rules provided by Delaware are default rules that corporate promoters are free to modify through charter and bylaw provisions. Thus, there is nothing to prevent a promoter who thinks that shareholders actually want shareholder primacy from providing in the firm's articles of incorporation that *Revlon* duties apply to all the board's decisions, not just to cash-out mergers. Put more bluntly, there is nothing to stop corporate promoters from expressly providing for shareholder wealth maximization as a corporate goal in the firm's charter.[55]

If shareholders really valued shareholder primacy rules, one would think at least a few promoters might have thought of inserting such provisions in the corporate charter at the IPO stage. However, I have never heard of, much less seen, such a charter provision. I suspect the reason may be that promoters and investors alike understand that if the firm did mandate shareholder primacy in its charter, it would find it far more difficult to attract qualified, motivated, and loyal employees, managers, and even creditors. Perhaps this suspicion is incorrect—perhaps firms that go public do not put shareholder primacy provisions into their charters simply because it has never occurred to anyone that there might be value in doing so. But if shareholder primacy is indeed clearly the optimal rule of corporate governance, as many academics believe, it seems curious that corporate participants, including shareholders themselves, have overlooked this possibility.

This is not to suggest that such observations alone provide proof that shareholder primacy is inefficient. More work remains to be done before one can reach a sound empirical conclusion about whether the agency costs associated with director primacy are greater or less than the cost of lost opportunities for team production that flow from a shareholder primacy regime. But at a minimum, the findings—that firms seem to prefer to incorporate in states with relatively strong antitakeover laws, that they often insert antitakeover provisions into their charters when going public, and that charter provisions mandating shareholder primacy are notably missing—ought to be enough to make careful and dispassionate observers suspicious. The claim that shareholder primacy is needed to control agency costs is clearly a better argument for the property model of the corporation than either the shareholder ownership argument or the residual claimants argument. Still, without some evidence that shareholders themselves desire shareholder primacy—not only ex post when they can extract wealth from other corporate stakeholders, but also ex ante when they need stakeholders cooperation and investment—it is perhaps a bit of a reach to describe the agency cost argument as a truly "good" argument for shareholder primacy. "Not-so-bad" may be a more precise description.

VI. CONCLUSION

Since the days of Berle and Dodd, scholars, commentators, lawmakers, and businesspeople have debated the purpose of the corporation. Does it exist only to create wealth for shareholders (the property model)? Or does good corporate governance demand that a firm's board of directors also consider the interests of other stakeholders, including managers, employees, creditors, and the broader society (the entity model)?

If the debate remains unresolved, at least there has been some progress in our understanding of it. In particular, we have learned that two of the most commonly advanced arguments for shareholder primacy—the argument that the shareholders "own" the firm and the argument that shareholders are the firm's sole residual claimants—are bad arguments, in the sense that they are built on empirical claims that are demonstrably false. There is a third argument for shareholder primacy that is much more reasonable. This is the argument that shareholder primacy is necessary to protect not just shareholders, but *all* the firm's stakeholders, by reducing the runaway agency costs that would be incurred if corporate directors were invited to consider the interests of both shareholders and other stakeholders as well. Put differently, shareholders and stakeholders alike are thought to be made better off by a rule that prevents directors from pursuing strategies that reduce share price whenever this can be rationalized as somehow serving the often-intangible interests of other constituencies.

There is one rather awkward and rather significant difficulty with this argument, however. Corporate law, in fact, *does* allow directors to pursue strategies that reduce share price whenever this can be rationalized as somehow serving the often-intangible interests of other constituencies. Put differently, outside the limited context of *Revlon,* corporate law follows the entity model. Moreover, both corporate managers and shareholders show little interest in departing from that model, even though the enabling nature of corporate law allows them to do so.

Berle himself eventually recognized this reality of modern business life.[56] More than two decades after he first crossed words with the Harvard professor, Berle published *The 20th Century Capitalist Revolution.*[57] In that book, Berle observed that corporate law had evolved in a direction that allowed directors almost total discretion over how to use corporate assets, including even giving them away to charity. He then offered his own view of the outcome of the Berle-Dodd debate:

> Twenty years ago, the writer had a controversy with the late Professor E. Merrick Dodd, of Harvard Law School, the writer holding that corporate powers were powers in trust for shareholders while Professor Dodd argued that these powers were held in trust for the entire community. The argument has been settled (at least for the time being) squarely in favor of Professor Dodd's contention.[58]

Half a century after Berle's concession, academics continue to argue the merits of the property versus the entity model of the firm. The business world continues to prefer the entity model of the firm.

NOTES

1. Adolph A. Berle & Gardiner C. Means, *The Modern Corporation and Private Property* (Harvest Books, 1968) (1932).

2. *See generally* D. Gordon Smith, *The Shareholder Primacy Norm,* 23 J. Corp. L. 277 (1998).

3. Adolph A. Berle, *Corporate Powers as Powers in Trust,* 44 Harv. L. Rev. 1049, 1049 (1931).

4. E. Merrick Dodd, *For Whom Are Corporate Managers Trustees?,* 45 Harv. L. Rev. 1145, 1148 (1932).

5. *See* Leo E. Strine, Jr., *The Social Responsibility of Boards of Directors and Stockholders in Change of Control Transactions: Is There Any "There" There?,* 75 S. Cal. L. Rev. 1169, 1170–73 (2002).

6. *See* William T. Allen, *Our Schizophrenic Conception of the Business Corporation,* 14 Cardozo L. Rev. 261, 264–66 (1992) (discussing property-entity debate).

7. William T. Allen, Jack B. Jacobs & Leo E. Strine, Jr., *The Great Takeover Debate: A Mediation on Bridging the Conceptual Divide,* U. Chi. L. Rev. (2002).

8. Although shareholder "ownership" language appears most often as a rhetorical device in the popular press, the assertion that shareholders own the firm also crops up even in contemporary corporate cases and commentary. *See, e.g.,* Malone v. Brincat, 722 A.2d 5, 10 (Del. 1998) ("The board of directors has the legal responsibility to manage the business of a corporation for the benefit of its shareholder owners."); Lewis D. Solomon, Donald E. Shwartz, Jeffrey D. Bauman, & Elliott J. Weiss, Corporations: Law and Policy, Cases and Materials 348 (4th ed. 1998) (observing that "shareholders are considered to be the corporation's ultimate owners").

9. Milton Friedman, *The Social Responsibility of Business Is to Increase Its Profits,* N.Y. Times Mag., Sept. 13, 1970, at 32–33, 122–26.

10. Del. Code Ann. tit. 8, §141(a) (2001).

11. *Id.* at §170(a).

12. Berle & Means, *supra* note 1, at 78–84. To some extent, the development of the hostile takeover has given public shareholders more power than they enjoyed in Berle's day because they can now sell *en masse* to a hostile bidder who can overcome the collective action problems faced by dispersed shareholders and can oust the board of directors. Given the expense and uncertainty associated with hostile takeover attempts, however, this remedy is likely to be effective only in extreme cases, leaving directors at most firms a great degree of leeway in pursuing goals other than shareholder wealth. *See infra* text accompanying notes 22–25.

13. Fischer Black & Myron Scholes, T*he Pricing of Options and Corporate Liabilities,* 81 J. Pol. Econ. 637, 637 (1973). Myron Scholes subsequently was awarded a Nobel Prize in Economics based on his work in this paper.

14. *See* Margaret M. Blair & Lynn A. Stout, *Director Accountability and the Mediating Role of the Corporate Board,*

79 Wash. U. L.Q. 403, 411–14 (2001) (describing implications of options theory for ownership arguments).

15. *See, e.g.,* Frank H. Easterbrook & Daniel R. Fischel, The Economic Structure of Corporate Law 36–39 (1991).

16. *Id.* at 36.

17. *Id.*

18. *Id.* at 36–37.

19. *Id.* at 36 ("For most firms the expectation is that the residual risk bearers have contracted for a promise to maximize long-run profits of the firm, which in turn maximizes the value of their stock.").

20. *See, e.g.,* Peter Coy, *High Turnover, High Risk,* Bus. Wk., Apr. 11, 2002, at 24 ("Professors teach that in exchange for supplying companies with capital, shareholders are entitled to receive all of a corporation's wealth in excess of what's paid out to contractual claimants—a group that includes customers, bondholders, and salaried employees.").

21. *See id.* (noting that "theory doesn't match reality").

22. There are reasons to doubt whether shareholders are treated as residual claimants even then. *See* Blair & Stout, *supra* note 14, at 417 n.29 (discussing shareholder rights in bankruptcy).

23. *See* Del. Code Ann. tit. 8, Sec. § 170(a) 2001 (describing circumstances under which directors of corporations may declare dividends).

24. *See id.*

25. *See generally* Margaret M. Blair & Lynn A. Stout, *A Team Production Theory of Corporate Law,* 85 Va. L. Rev. 247 (1999) (discussing team productions and its implications for corporate governance). *See also* Blair & Stout, *supra* note 14, at 418–22 (discussing team production problem).

26. To put the problem in economic terms, contracting is difficult whenever corporate production requires different parties to make contributions that become team specific (meaning that after the resources have been invested in team production, their value cannot be recovered easily except by waiting to share in the resulting profits) and whenever the output is nonseparable (meaning that it is impossible to determine exactly what portion of the output is attributable to which party's contribution). Consider the example of an entrepreneur and an investor who want to start a joint venture in which the investor provides financial capital and the entrepreneur contributes managerial skills. If the entrepreneur acquires knowledge, skills, and business contacts that are uniquely valuable to the joint venture, she will not be able to recover this investment in team-specific "human capital" by leaving and going to work for another employer. Similarly, after the investor's funds have been spent on salaries or specialized equipment, he cannot simply demand his money back. Thus both team members must wait until the venture turns a profit to recoup their investments. Furthermore, how are they to contract over how that profit will be shared? If they agree ex ante to share the wealth equally, this creates incentives for shirking. In the alternative, if they wait until the venture is a success to decide who gets what portion of the credit and the profits, they are likely to indulge in wasteful squabbling and "rent-seeking." *See* Blair & Stout, *supra* note 14, at 420 (discussing this contracting problem); Blair & Stout, *supra* note 25, at 418–22 (discussing same).

27. For example, suppose James Trains has encouraged its managers and employees to invest in firm-specific human capital through an informal understanding that so long as the firm is doing well, they will be paid a wage premium of ten percent over what they could expect to earn if forced to abandon their firm-specific investment by seeking employment elsewhere. Assume that the firm has annual sales of $120,000 and pays annual wages totaling $110,000, that wages are the firm's only expense, that annual profits accordingly are $10,000, and that these profits are paid out to shareholders in the form of dividends. If a takeover bidder were to purchase the firm and then renege on the implicit understanding that the firm's employees are to be paid for their firm-specific human capital (which is valueless elsewhere), such an acquirer would be able to reduce or even eliminate the wage premium, bringing annual wage expense down from $110,000 to as low as $100,000. The result would be to double the shareholders' total annual dividend payments from $10,000 to $20,000, and also to double the value of the shareholders stock. This 100% increase in value—much larger than the premium suggested by Strine in his hypothetical—reflects not real wealth gains, but a pure wealth transfer from employees to shareholders. If the shareholders were to sell for less than a 100% premium, the end result would be that their gains are outweighed by the employees' losses.

28. *See* Blair & Stout, *supra* note 25, at 305.

29. More particularly, from a purely ex post perspective, the most efficient rule would be to require directors to maximize aggregate social wealth, including the wealth of groups that do not make firm-specific investments. From an ex ante team production perspective, the most efficient rule would be the one that does the best job of encouraging efficient investment in team production despite incomplete contracts.

30. See Stephen P. Bainbridge, *Director Primacy: The Means and Ends of Corporate Governance,* Nw. U. L. Rev. (forthcoming 2003) (discussing how directors and not shareholders control firms). It should be noted that there are justifications for director primacy other than team production, including justifications that are consistent with share-

holder wealth maximization as the normative goal of corporate governance. For example, if the stock market does not always accurately price shares, giving directors discretion to turn down a premium offer may serve shareholders' long run interest when directors can recognize that an offering price is "too low" and shareholders cannot. *See id.* (discussing how director primacy allows directors to hire corporate factors of production in pursuit of goal of shareholder wealth maximization).

31. *See* Blair & Stout, *supra* note 25, at 253; G. Mitu Gulati, William A. Klein & Eric M. Zolt, *Connected Contracts,* 47 UCLA L. Rev. 887, 895 (2000); Frank Partnoy, *Adding Derivatives to the Corporate Law Mix,* 34 Ga. L. Rev. 599, 600, 612–16 (2000); Andrei Shleifer & Lawrence H. Summers, *Breach of Trust in Hostile Takeovers, in* Corporate Takeovers: Causes and Consequences 33, 37–41 (Alan J. Auerbach ed., 1988); Thomas A. Smith, *The Efficient Norm for Corporate Law: A Neotraditional Interpretation of Fiduciary Duty,* 98 Mich. L. Rev. 214, 218–20 (1999).

32. For a sophisticated and instructive example, see *Credit Lyonnais Bank Nederland, N.V. v. Pathe Communications Corp.,* 17 Del. J. Corp. L. 1099, 1155–56 (1991), concerning the economic efficiency of allowing directors to take account of debtholders' interests.

33. It should be noted that the observation that directors are imperfect agents incorporates both the possibility that directors can be imperfect agents for shareholders (the primary focus of those who adopt the property view of the firm) and the possibility that directors can be imperfect agents for the "firm," envisioned as an agglomeration of all the corporation's constituents (the entity view).

34. Mark J. Roe, *The Shareholder Wealth Maximization Norm and Industrial Organization,* 149 U. Pa. L. Rev. 2063, 2065 (2001).

35. *See* Strine, *supra* note 5, at 5.

36. *Compare* Dodge v. Ford Motor Co., 170 N.W. 668, 684 (Mich. 1919) (noting that "a business corporation is organized and carried on primarily for the good profit of the stockholders") and Richard Egan, *The Corporation's Responsibility to the Community,* NYSE Mag., Jan./Feb., 2002, at 40 (observing that "the company that serves its community best is the one that serves its shareholders first.") *with* Unocal Corp. v. Mesa Petroleum Co., 493 A.2d 946, 955 (Del. 1985) (stating that among the concerns directors may consider in managing the firm is "the impact on 'constituencies' other than shareholders (i.e., creditors, customers, employees, and perhaps even the community generally)") *and* Jorma Ollila, *The Business of Being Responsible,* NYSE Mag., Jan./Feb., 2002, at 34 ("Global issues of environment, health, diversity and human rights once at the periphery of management decisionmaking are fast becoming central. . . . The clear message from rising stakeholder expectations is that companies must contribute more.").

37. Guhan Subramanian, *The Influence of Antitakeover Statutes on Incorporation Choice: Evidence on the "Race" Debate and Antitakeover Overreaching,* 150 U. Pa. L. Rev. 1795, 1801 (2002).

38. Strine, *supra* note 5, at 1176 (stating that except when a publicly held firm is going to be merged with another private firm and acquire a controlling shareholder, "the entity model prevails"). *See also* Allen et al., *supra* note 7, at 21 ("Delaware law inclines toward the entity model.").

39. *See* Paramount Communications, Inc. v. Time Inc., 571 A.2d 1140, 1150 (Del. 1989) (finding that "a board of directors . . . is not under any per se duty to maximize shareholder value").

40. *See* Smith, *supra* note 2, at 279–80 (stating that "the shareholder primacy norm is nearly irrelevant to the ordinary business decisions of modern corporations. . . . Outside the takeover context . . . , application of the shareholder primacy norm . . . is muted by the business judgment rule").

41. *See* Shlensky v. Wrigley, 237 N.E.2d 776, 780 (Ill. App. Ct. 1968) (upholding directors' decisions that plaintiff alleged were harmful to shareholders, speculating that they might be in "long run" interests of firm); Revlon, Inc. v. MacAndrews & Forbes Holdings, Inc., 506 A.2d 173, 182 (Del. 1986) ("A board may have regard for various constituencies in discharging its responsibilities, provided there are rationally related benefits accruing to the stockholders.").

42. Allen, et al., *supra* note 7, at 6–7 (describing judicial elision between entity and property models of corporations).

43. *See supra* text accompanying notes 26–32 (discussing benefits of team production).

44. *Revlon,* 506 A.2d at 173.

45. *See Revlon,* 506 A.2d at 185.

46. *See, e.g.,* Paramount Communications, Inc. v. Time, Inc., 571 A.2d 1140, 1149–51 (Del. 1989).

47. For example, it is only because the James Train directors are considering a "cash out" merger that they have to worry about *Revlon* at all. Indeed, it is not uncontestably clear that *Revlon* would apply even in that situation. Recognizing as much, Strine has directed us to assume for the sake of the discussion that *Revlon* does apply. *See* Strine, *supra* note 5, at 5.

48. *See* Subramanian, *supra* note 37, at 30 tbl.4 (listing thirty-one states as having passed other-constituency statutes).

49. *See* Lucian Bebchuk, Alma Cohen & Allen Ferrell, *Does the Evidence Favor State Competition in Corporate Law,* Ca. L. Rev. (2002) (manuscript at 1–4, on file with author) (describing "race-to-the-bottom" thesis); Subramanian, *supra* note 37, at 8–10 (same).

50. *See supra* note 27 (providing example of this).

51. Similarly, it should not be surprising to find, as some studies have, that the adoption of antitakeover laws sometimes decreases the stock prices of firms incorporated in the state that adopts them. *See* Subramanian, *supra* note 37, at 31–33 (discussing studies of stock market reaction to antitakeover statutes). When a legislature imposes an antitakeover law on a corporation "mid-stream," it is changing the rules in the middle of the game. At that point, increasing director autonomy may not do much to encourage team production (for example, it may not do much to encourage human capital investment in firms where managers and employees made that decision years ago). Antitakeover laws may, however, work an immediate transfer of wealth from shareholders to other stakeholders, by providing the latter with even greater protection from shareholder demands than they expected to enjoy.

52. *See* Blair & Stout, *supra* note 25, at 273–87 (describing value of director primacy rules that allow board to serve as "mediating hierarch" of the firm).

53. *See, e.g.,* Lucian Bebchuk & Alma Cohen, Olin Center, Firms' Decisions Where to Incorporate 10–11 (Feb., 2002) (unpublished manuscript, on file with The

Southern California Law School); Bebchuk, Cohen & Ferrell, *supra* note 49, at 34–40; Subramanian, *supra* note 37, at 52–53.

54. *See* Robert Daines & Michael Klausner, *Do IPO Charters Maximize Firm Value? Antitakeover Protection in IPOs,* 17 J.L. Econ. & Org. 83, 95–97 (2001).

55. *See* Del. Code Ann. tit. 8, §102(b) (2001) (allowing firms to include in their charters "[a]ny provision for the management of the business," including "any provision creating, defining, limiting and regulating the powers of the corporation, the directors, and the stockholders").

56. Indeed, as Jack Treynor has pointed out, despite the impression given by his argument in the Harvard Law Review, Berle's contemporaneous writings with Gardiner Means gave a far more agnostic view of whether the shareholder primacy view could or should eventually prevail in the modern corporation. Jack L. Treynor, *Samizdat: The Value of Control,* Fin. Analysts J. 6 (July–Aug. 1993).

57. Adolphe A. Berle, The 20th Century Capitalist Revolution (1954).

58. *Id*. at 169.

READING 4.3 JUST SAY NO TO WALL STREET: PUTTING A STOP TO THE EARNINGS GAME

Joseph Fuller and Michael C. Jensen

"WE DO NOT WANT TO MAXIMIZE THE PRICE AT WHICH BERKSHIRE shares trade. We wish instead for them to trade in a narrow range centered at intrinsic business value . . . [We] are bothered as much by significant overvaluation as significant undervaluation."

　—Warren Buffett, Berkshire Hathaway Annual Report, 1988

First there were whispers and informal advisories to favored analysts of what to expect in coming earnings announcements. Then the conversations became more elaborate, engendering a twisted kind of logic. No longer were analysts trying to under-

stand and analyze a company so as to predict what it might earn; instead the discussion revolved around the analysts' forecasts themselves. Will expectations be met? What will management do to ensure that? Rather than the forecasts representing a financial byproduct of the firm's strategy, the forecasts came to drive those strategies. While the process was euphemistically referred to as "earnings guidance," it was, in fact, a high-stakes game with management seeking to hit the targets set by analysts—and being punished severely if they missed.

Last year, the Securities and Exchange Commission recognized that private conversations

From Joseph Fuller and Michael C. Jensen, "Just Say No to Wall Street: Putting A Stop to the Earnings Game," *Journal of Applied Corporate Finance,* vol. 14, no. 4, Winter 2002, pp. 41–46. Copyright ©2002, The Monitor Company and M. C. Jensen; reprinted with permission. Excerpts of this article were published in the *Wall Street Journal* "Manager's Journal" column under the title "Dare To Keep Your

Stock Price Low," December 31, 2001, and in the *Financial Times,* under the title "End the Myth-Making and Return to True Analysis," Jan 22, 2002. This paper can be downloaded without charge from the Social Science Research Network Electronic Library at: http://papers.ssrn.com/abstract=297156

between executives and analysts had become extensive, with analysts gaining access to critical data not otherwise broadly available to shareholders. The new regulations on fair disclosure addressed the mechanics of the conversation, but did little to change its underlying logic. The result has been blizzards of filings and dozens of press releases, and many more company-run conference calls. But such changes in the outward forms of corporate disclosure have done little if anything to deflect the underlying momentum of the earnings guidance game.

Nevertheless, there are some encouraging signs. In the past few months, a few courageous CEOs—notably, USA Networks' Barry Diller and Gillette's Jim Kilts—have attempted to put a halt to the earnings game by simply saying no. In a recent SEC filing, Diller balked at the sophisticated art form known as managing expectations, saying publicly what many have said privately for a long time: "The process has little to do with running a business and the numbers can become distractingly and dangerously detached from fundamentals."[1]

AN OVERVALUED STOCK DAMAGES A COMPANY

Witness the part that Wall Street's rising expectations played in the demise of once high flyers like Enron, Cisco, and Nortel. With analysts pushing these companies to reach for higher and higher growth targets, the managements of the companies responded with actions that have generated long-term damage. To resolve these problems, managers must abandon the notion that a higher stock price is *always* better and recognize that an overvalued stock can be as dangerous to a company as an undervalued stock. The proper management of investor expectations means being willing to take the necessary actions to eliminate such overvaluation when it occurs.

In his first meeting with analysts after taking over Gillette, James Kilts stood firm against the tide refusing to be forced into making predictions for his company. *The New York Times* reports that, in a June 2001 meeting with analysts, Kilts remained silent when Wall Street analysts repeatedly asked him for a more specific estimate of the company's performance: "Mr. Kilts stood on the stage, crossed his arms

and refused to give it."[2] By taking positions that we believe will benefit all the players in this game, Kilts and Diller have seized an important opportunity—even an obligation—to reshape and reframe the conversation for a new era.

Over the last decade companies have struggled more and more desperately to meet analysts' expectations. Caught up by a buoyant economy and the pace of value creation set by the market's best performers, analysts challenged the companies they covered to reach for unprecedented earnings growth. Executives often acquiesced to increasingly unrealistic projections and adopted them as a basis for setting goals for their organizations.

There were several reasons executives chose to play this game. Perhaps the most important was favorable market conditions in many industries, which enabled companies to exceed historical performance levels and, in the process, allowed executives and analysts alike to view unsustainable levels of growth as the norm. Adding to favorable conditions and exceptional corporate performance was a massive, broadbased shift in the philosophy of executive compensation. As stock options became an increasing part of executive compensation, and managers who made great fortunes on options became the stuff of legends, the preservation or enhancement of short-term stock prices became a personal (and damaging) priority for many a CEO and CFO. High share prices and earnings multiples stoked already amply endowed managerial egos, and management teams proved reluctant to undermine their own stature by surrendering hard-won records of quarter-over-quarter earnings growth. Moreover, overvalued equity "currency" encouraged managers to make acquisitions and other investments in the desperate hope of sustaining growth, continuing to meet expectations, and buying real assets at a discount with their overvalued stock.

Parallel developments in the world of the analysts completed a vicious circle. Once analysts were known to a handful of serious investors and coveted a spot on Institutional Investor's annual All-American team. In recent times, analysts became media darlings. An endless parade appeared on an increasing array of business programming. The views of celebrity analysts were accorded the same weight as the opinions of leading executives. Analysts Mary Meeker and Jack Grubman were quoted in the same breath and, more important, credited with the same insight as Cisco's CEO John Chambers and Qwest's Joe Nacchio. With the explosion in the markets came an explosion in analyst compensation, as leading analysts shared in the bonus pools of their investment banking divisions and thus had incentives to issue reports favorable to their banks' deals. Analysts with big followings, a reputation built on a handful of good "calls," and an ability to influence large investment banking deals sold by their firms commanded multimillion dollar salaries. In sum, analysts had strong incentives to demand high growth and steady and predictable earnings performance, both to justify sky-high valuations for the companies they followed and to avoid damage to their own reputations from missed predictions. In too many instances, too many executive teams and too many analysts engaged in the equivalent of liar's poker.[3]

Many will say, "So what? If overly aggressive analysts drove executives to create more shareholder value faster, what's the harm?" What they fail to recognize is that this vicious cycle can impose real, lasting costs on companies when analyst expectations become unhinged from what is possible for firms to accomplish. As the historic bankruptcy case of Enron suggests, when companies encourage excessive expectations or scramble too hard to meet unrealistic forecasts by analysts, they often take highly risky value-destroying bets. In addition, smoothing financial results to satisfy analysts' demands for quarter-to-quarter predictability frequently requires sacrificing the long-term future of the company. Because the inherent uncertainty in any business cannot be made to disappear, striving to achieve dependable period-to-period growth is a game that CEOs cannot win. Trying to mask the uncertainty inherent in every industry is like pushing on a balloon—smoothing out today's bumps means they will only pop up somewhere else tomorrow, often with catastrophic results.

More important, we have witnessed the consequences of executives' futile attempts to record growth rates that consistently and materially exceed growth in primary demand in their markets. Stated simply, companies participating in markets with 4% underlying growth in demand cannot register 15% growth in earnings quarter over quarter, year over year, indefinitely.

The technology and telecommunications sectors provide good examples of the effects of sustained pressure from analysts. In the last decade, analysts' expectations consistently and vastly exceeded what high-tech and telecom companies were capable of achieving. Managers collaborated in this fiction, either because they themselves had unrealistic expectations for their companies or, worse yet, because they used analysts' expectations to set internal corporate goals. The resulting destructive effects of overvaluation of corporate equity manifested itself in ill-advised actions aimed at fulfilling these unrealistic expectation—notably, value-destroying acquisitions and greenfield investments. When the fiction finally became obvious, the result was massive adjustments in earnings and growth projections and, consequently, in equity valuations. In many cases, the very survival of the affected companies came into question. Enron is perhaps the most dramatic example.

THE CASE OF ENRON

Enron was in many ways an extraordinary company. It boasted significant global assets, genuine achievements, dramatic innovations, and a promising long-run future. Taking advantage of a rapidly deregulating market and capitalizing on its deep knowledge of the industry, Enron had seized what was probably a once-in-a-corporate-lifetime opportunity to reinvent itself as a market maker in natural gas and energy.

Wall Street responded to this and other innovations by Enron with a series of positive reports and ever-higher valuations, eventually labeling Enron one of the best companies in the economy, even comparing it to Microsoft and GE.[4] However, the aggressive targets that Wall Street set for Enron's shares made the company a captive of its own success. To be sure, it was a game that Enron willingly played—but it's one the company clearly lost, with considerable consequences for not only the company's stockholders, but for its creditors, customers, employees and other major stakeholders.

To begin to see what went wrong, consider that Enron's peak valuation of $68 billion (in August 2001) effectively required the company to grow its free cash flow at 91% annually for the next six years, (and then to grow at the average rate for the economy)—a pace that required it to continuously come up with what were, in effect, one-time-only innovations. As if to confirm these expectations, one analyst blithely predicted that Enron would come to "dominate the wholesale energy market for electricity, natural gas, coal, energy derivatives, bandwidth, and energy services on three continents."[5] And Enron, to its own detriment, took up the challenge. In seeking to meet such expectations, it expanded into areas, including water, broadband, and even weather insurance, in which it had no specific assets, expertise, or experience.

Yet it didn't have to be this way. Had management not met Wall Street's predictions with its own hubris, the result could have been very different. As Gillette's Kilts is demonstrating, managers can refuse to collude with analysts' expectations when they don't fit with their strategies and the underlying realities of their markets. They can decline to bow to analysts' demand for highly predictable earnings.

If Enron's management had confronted the analysts with courage and conviction and resisted their relentless focus on outsized earnings growth, the company could have avoided questionable actions taken to please the analysts and markets. The result may well have been a lower-valued company, but a stable and profitable one with a promising future. And, as in other companies, these questionable actions went beyond the decisions to launch unwise investments and acquisitions, and included apparent manipulation of the information it provided to Wall Street. Some of these practices are currently being investigated by the SEC, including aggressive revenue recognition practices, off-balance-sheet financing that reduced Enron's apparent debt, and partnerships that allowed the company to show higher earnings.

When discovered, such practices—coupled with missed earnings expectations—first stirred Wall Street's concern and eventually caused the crisis of confidence that destroyed the company's most valuable asset—its ability to make markets in energy. As a result, by January of 2002, Enron's stock price had fallen by more than 99% from its peak just four months earlier. While the partnerships brought to the forefront issues of credibility for Enron and the integrity of their financial reporting, they also served to highlight the importance of Wall Street analysts and the nature of their relationship with the companies they cover.

THE CASE OF NORTEL NETWORKS

The story of Nortel is similar. Nortel's CEO, John Roth, launched a strategy in 1997 to transform the company from one dependent on its traditional strength in voice transmission into one focused on data networking. Nortel acquired 19 companies between 1997 and early 2001. And as its stock price soared (to reach a total capital value of $277 billion in July 2000), it came under pressure to do deals to satisfy the analysts' growth expectations. Ultimately, it paid over $32 billion—mostly in stock—for these companies. Most of those acquisitions have now been sold off for modest amounts or shut down and written off entirely.

The quest to transform Nortel clearly damaged this former mainstay of the telecommunication sector. With a year-end 2001 valuation of just $24 billion, the company's stock has fallen by more than 90% from its peak in September of 2000. In July 2001 it reported a record $19.4 billion second-quarter loss followed by a $3.6 billion loss in the third quarter. Its CEO resigned effective November 1, 2001 but remains as vice-chairman until the end of 2002. Employment has shrunk from 72,900 people when Roth took over (and from a high of 94,500) to a projected 45,000 by the end of this year. As of the end of 2001, Nortel's (adjusted) stock price was 44% lower than its level of $13.16 on Oct. 1, 1997 when Roth took over as CEO.[6] As these numbers make clear, the decline suffered by Nortel involved far more than the elimination of its overvaluation; it involved a significant destruction of value, mainly, again, through acquisitions and massive overinvestment. It is this kind of damage that can be stopped if managers can just say no to the pressure to fulfill unrealistic market expectations.

A number of factors encouraged Nortel's managers to collaborate in the fiction of a $270 billion valuation. One was the incentive to maintain the value of managerial and employee stock options. Another was the understandable reluctance of top management to admit they were not as good as analysts were projecting. And a third was management's unwillingness to give up the overvalued equity currency that gave them the leeway (and purchasing power) to make unwise, value-destroying investments. In sum, management's reluctance to bear the unpleasantness associated with correcting the market sooner led to far greater pain down the road.

This cycle is not without its costs for the financial community. Of course, many stockholders have incurred huge losses. Analysts, too, have taken their lumps. Their integrity has been called into question in congressional hearings. The press has pilloried many of the most prominent analysts, contrasting their earnings projections with actual results. Many unhappy clients have terminated long-standing relationships. One even went so far as to sue a prominent analyst in federal court.[7] And though that action proved unsuccessful, extensive coverage of the suit in the popular press reflects the depth of disillusionment. Where there is smoke from the public having been burned, political fire soon follows. If the SEC were willing to spend years and significant political capital pursuing restrictions on accounting firms providing consulting services to their statutory audit clients, it cannot be long before regulators become interested in the potential conflict of interest between the investment banking and the security analysis sides of investment banks.

RESTARTING THE CONVERSATION

Putting an end to this destructive cycle will require a new approach to disclosure based on a few simple rules of engagement.

- Managers must confront the capital markets with courage and conviction. They must not collude with analysts' expectations that don't fit with their strategies and the underlying characteristics of their markets. They must not bow to analysts' demands for highly predictable earnings. The art of analysis includes the capacity to understand phenomena like seasonality, cyclicality, and random events. Companies do not grow in a constant fashion with each quarter's results better than the last. In the long run, conforming to pressures to satisfy the market's desire for impossible predictability and unwise growth leads to the destruction of corporate value, shortened careers, humiliation, and damaged companies.

- Managers must be forthright and promise only those results they have a legitimate prospect of delivering, and they must be clear about the risks and uncertainties involved. They must dispel any air of unreality that settles over their stock and highlight what they cannot do as readily as they trumpet their prospects. While this can cause the stock price to fall, the associated pain is slight compared to colluding in myth-telling. This reflects more than the good conscience of a Boy Scout. It is, in fact, an act of self-preservation.

- Managers must recognize that an overvalued stock can be damaging to the long-run health of the company, particularly when it serves as a pretext for overpriced acquisitions. As the experience of companies like Nortel and Worldcom demonstrates, buying overpriced companies with overvalued stock not only fails to add value, but can end up demoralizing once successful organizations. While leveling with the markets can cause the stock price to fall to a sustainable level, the associated personal and organizational pain is slight compared to that arising from colluding in myth-telling.

- Managers must work to make their organizations far more transparent to investors and to the markets. USA Network's Diller, for example, has chosen to provide analysts with actual business budgets broken down by business segments. At the very least, companies should state their strategies clearly, identify associated value drivers and report auditable metrics on both. They should also address the "unexplained" part of their firm's share price—that part not directly linked to observable cash flows—through a coherent description of the growth opportunities they foresee *and be willing to tell the markets when they see their stock price as overvalued.*

- Similarly, to limit wishful thinking, managers must reconcile their own company's projections to those of the industry and their rivals' projections. Analysts develop models of an industry's growth. If the company's expectations lie outside what is widely viewed as the industry's growth rate, its managers must be able to explain how and why they will be able to outperform their market. Some executives will be concerned or complain that making this all clear to the analysts will reveal valuable information to their competitors. To this we have a simple response: *If your strategy is based on your competitor not knowing what you are doing, as opposed to not being able to do what you can do, you cannot be successful in the long run no matter who knows what.*

Finally, managers would be wise to remember that analysts are not always wrong. In fact, analysts have a vital monitoring role to play in a market economy. While recent history may have obscured that role, managers should not simply presume that analysts are wrong when disagreement occurs. It is worth noting that during the 1970s and 1980s managers regularly complained that analysts were undervaluing their companies. Yet, analysts were generally correct that managers of that era were not making effective use of corporate resources. They continued to invest in industries and activities with substantial excess capacity and consequent low returns, refused to downsize and distribute free cash flow to shareholders, and pursued inefficient value-destroying conglomerate mergers. In response to such value destruction, there emerged an active market for corporate control, as reflected in the wave of hostile acquisitions and LBOs, in which competing management teams took over and replaced the managers and directors of underperforming companies and created vast new value.

Contrasting the decades of the 1970s and 1980s with the recent era thus yields an important lesson: managers and analysts must pay close attention to each other's views. Both analysts and managers bring important information and important perspectives to the conversation and both sides benefit when each does their task well. Managers for their part must stop encouraging analysts to reach for ever-higher valuations and return to managing their companies. Analysts must stop making Nostradamus-like predictions and instead return to their true roots—the creation of original research and analysis. The Securities Industry Association issued an excellent statement entitled "Best Practices for Research" in 2001 that lays the foundations for resolving many of the conflicts of interest on the part of analysts. We look forward to its early and widespread implementation.[8]

Stock prices are not simply abstract numbers that exist apart from the reality of corporate enterprises. Gyrations initiated by Wall Street or managers have real effects on companies and society. The price that Wall Street puts on a company's securities and the trajectory of those prices affect the nature of the strategies firms adopt and, hence, their prospects for success. Stock prices also drive a company's cost of capital, its borrowing capacity, and its ability to make acquisitions. Ultimately, the viability of the companies themselves is at stake.

A dysfunctional conversation between Wall Street and Main Street is not the esoteric stuff of business school classroom discussions. It can rob investors of savings, cost employees their jobs, erode the nest eggs of retirees, and undermine the viability of suppliers and communities. Clearly, it is time to restart the conversation on a new, stable, and enduring footing.

NOTES

1. USA Networks. 2001. "USA Provides Internal Budget to Investment Community." *SEC Form* 425.1: October 24, 2001.

2. Barnes, Julian E. 2001. "Gillette's Chief Is Critical of the Company's Misstep." *New York Times,* June 7, 2001. http://college2.nytimes.com/guests/articles/2001/06/07/852365.xml

3. Evidence of the distortion of information provided to investors by companies, and of the collaboration of some financial intermediaries and analysts in this distortion, has grown considerably. For an excellent compilation and analysis of this evidence, see the paper by Gene D'Avolio, Efi Gildor, and Andrei Shleifer. 2001. "Technology, Information Production, and Market Efficiency." Harvard Institute of Economic Research Discussion Paper Number 1929, September 2001. Cambridge, MA. This paper can be downloaded without charge from the Social Science Research Network eLibrary at: http://papers.ssrn.com/abstract=286597 and at http://post.economics.harvard.edu/hier/2001papers/2001list.html

4. Fleischer, David N. 2001. "Enron Corp. Gas and Power Convergence." Conference Call Transcript, Goldman Sachs, July 12, 2001. New York.

5. Tirello, Edward J., Jr. 2000. "Enron Corporation: The Industry Standard for Excellence." Analyst Report, Deutsche Banc Alex. Brown., September 15, 2000. New York.

6. The breakeven share price for Nortel investors as of 12/31/2001 was $21.33 assuming a 12% cost of equity capital net of dividends. This implies the breakeven total value of Nortel at the end of 2001 was $68.5 billion. Thus investors lost a total of $44.5 billion as a result of the failed strategy.

7. Regan, Keith. 2001. "Lawsuit Against Noted Internet Analyst Tossed." *www.EcommerceTimes.com:* August 22, 2001, http://www.newsfactor.com/perl/story/13001 .html

8. Securities Industry Association. 2001. "Best Practices for Research." http://www.sia.com/publications/pdf/best .pdf

READING 4.4 ASSESSING EXECUTIVE COMPENSATION
John J. McCall

INTRODUCTION

Executive compensation is emerging as the main corporate governance issue in the United States. Corporate governance is a matter of assuring that firms are appropriately controlled and that the agents of corporate policies are accountable. In the United States, with its shareholder primacy norm, the end for which control and accountability are exercised is the financial benefit of the investor. In that environment, governance naturally raises the agency question: How might the interests of management be aligned to coincide with those of shareholders? The primary vehicle for achieving that alignment is the use of variable compensation that is tied to equity prices (often through the use of options to purchase stock at set prices). Hence executive compensation becomes a central issue of corporate governance.

However, even in environments where a stakeholder approach is dominant (in contrast to the U.S. shareholder primacy norm), the incentives created by executive compensation schemes will inevitably have an impact on the decisions that executives make. Executive compensation, then, is a matter of concern no matter what ends are imagined as appropriate goals of corporate governance.

The facts about U.S. executive compensation are these: The absolute value of executive pay has increased dramatically over the past decade. Much of that increase has been driven by large dollar amounts of pay in the form of stock options. While studies differ (due to different methodologies and/or different data sets), the patterns are clear. Executive pay increased between two and three times from the early 1990s until today. The ratio of executive pay to the typical blue-collar employee's pay also increased dramatically from a multiple of about 20 to, according to some estimates, a multiple of over 500. A large portion of this is due to option grants: Options as a percentage of executive pay increased from 27% to 60% through the 1990s.

It also appears that the U.S. model is gradually being exported, especially to the United Kingdom. The use of variable pay and stock options has grown rapidly (though from a low baseline) in Britain. Variable pay as a proportion of total executive compensation increased significantly between 1996 and 2001. Moreover, the disparity between CEO pay and manufacturing workers' pay has widened in Britain as well.

Many have begun to question the wisdom of both the large absolute amounts of CEO pay and the compensation strategies that have caused them. Salaries of $140 million and higher have shocked the conscience of a number of commentators. Some even find that high pay and stock option plans have a causal role in the recent financial and accounting scandals that have shaken U.S. equity markets. After all, when executive compensation is tied to share price, managers have incentives to "manage" sales and earnings reports with creative accounting.

Despite the increasing clamor about excessive CEO pay, any number of finance and legal theorists continue to defend the practice. Frequently, they point to strong correlations between the use of option grants and increases in share value. This suggests to the defenders that current compensation arrangements are consistent with good corporate governance and, indirectly, with social welfare (since rising equity prices are seen as an indicator of an efficient and healthy business climate).

This paper assesses executive pay from a moral perspective. It argues that defenses of high CEO pay that appeal to increased share value are unconvincing. First, share value arguments do not show that increased compensation is appropriate because they neither establish a baseline measure for acceptable compensation nor show that the increase in CEO income relative to increased share price is necessary and proportional. Second, share value arguments improperly presuppose that share value is a morally legitimate measure for the appropriateness of executive compensation.

The paper suggests that the assessment of CEO compensation is best done according to two traditional moral criteria: net social welfare and fairness/justice. On the criterion of net welfare, the consequences of such high CEO pay are arguably negative. Likely, if contingent, effects on employee morale, social cohesion, and even shareholder dilution suggest caution before accepting current compensation scales. Moreover, the size and nature of compensation packages create perverse incentives to focus on short term profit maximization, a focus that can have damaging long-term effects on social welfare, due, for instance, to insufficient investment.

On grounds of fairness/justice, high levels of executive compensation are troubling as well. While fairness is a notoriously vague concept, it can be operationalized through a focus on people's relative levels of contribution and risk in a cooperative enterprise. No rationale, however, suggests that the contributions made or risks assumed by executives are 500 times greater than those of ordinary employees. Accordingly, the paper concludes that the current levels of CEO pay ought to be reduced and the composition of such pay altered.

SIGNS OF CHANGE

It is not surprising that executive compensation has become one of the hottest topics in corporate governance. The recent scandals, combined with public disclosures of the exceedingly high levels of executive pay, naturally produce a rising volume of public outcry. When the public press discloses arrangements such as Dennis Koslowski's $71 million compensation, even while he was under the potential of indictment for using corporate funds for lavish personal expenses, ordinary wage earners begin to feel that something has gone amiss with the process of determining what CEOs are worth. It does not help when it is also disclosed that he refused to waive the $75,000 fee for attending board meetings, as is customary for many CEOs who sit on their company boards (Hunt 17; Millon 915).

When ordinary employees of struggling companies find out that their fired CEO has been given walk-away money of $3.3 million as well as loan forgiveness worth $4.2 million, as ex-Mattel CEO Jill Barad was (Bebchuck and Fried 11); or when they hear that their chief financial officer opposed accounting actions that would have saved the corporation substantial money but that would have reduced his own compensation, as Andrew Fastow did at Enron (Millon 914); or that the financial target for a $5 million performance bonus was lowered so that the CEO could achieve the goal, as Disney did for Michael Eisner (Useem 57)—they are likely to engage in quite a bit of critical griping around the proverbial water cooler. That critical response may eventually force reforms in some executive compensation packages.

More portentous in regard to reform, however, is that the investment community is showing signs of rebellion, now that it sees the failures of trying to link management and investor interests together through stock or option grants. The trader members of the New York Stock Exchange have even forced out their own chief officer over a $140 million compensation package that was negotiated without the knowledge of many (Hunt 17). Whether they found unsightly the appearance of paying so much to one whose role included regulatory responsibility over the market or whether they felt that the package was just too much money out of their own pockets is unclear. What is clear is that a number of large players in the market have begun to question the wisdom of both the amount and the composition of executive pay packages.

THE FACTS

The basic facts on executive compensation are these: In 2002, the median income of the Fortune 100 CEOs was $13.2 million and the average was $15.7 million (Useem 57). For companies with at least $500 million in sales, a Towers Perrin study found that U.S. CEOs earned an average of $1.93 million in 2001 (Towers Perrin). *Business Week* reported that average CEO compensation in the 256 large companies they surveyed was $7.4 million in 2002, while the median was $3.7 million. (The average number was down by 33% from $11 million in 2001, largely because the top earners were not able to reap the same level of rewards from exercising options in a declining stock market. With the rise in stock prices in 2003, we may or may not see a rising average again. The median number, however, was 5.9% higher than in 2001.) It is not only the CEOs who are handsomely paid. *Business Week* reported that the number-two executive in their survey was paid an average of $7.6 million in 1999 (Stabile 116n).

These figures reflect a meteoric rise in executive compensation over the past 15 or so years. That rapid increase has been largely fueled by the increase in the proportion of compensation derived from equity-based awards, especially in the form of options to buy company stock. In the ten years between 1990 and 2000, for instance, CEO compensation increased 571% (Stabile 116). From 1992 to 2000, stock options increased from 27% to 60% of total CEO compensation (Brown). If we take a longer-term look, we can see an even more dramatic rise in total compensation. In 1981, the average pay for the top ten CEOs was $3.5 million; in 2001, it was $155 million (Barlow).

By contrast, the average U.S. worker's pay has increased much less. In the decade of the 1990s, when there were gains in average salary adjusted for inflation for the first time in years, worker wages increased only 37% (compared to the 571% figure for executives) (Stabile 116). This radically different rate of growth in pay has created a widening gap between CEO pay and that of the average worker. In 1980, CEOs were paid about 40 times more than

the average worker (Hunt 17; Sklar). By 2000, the multiple was more than 500 (Barlow; Stabile 116 AFL/CIO). For another way of understanding this widening gap, consider that if the average production worker's pay had increased at the rate of increase for CEO pay, that average worker's pay would have been over $120,000 rather than the $24,600 that it was in 2000 (Stabile 116). It is also interesting to note that while the gap between CEO and average worker pay has widened considerably over the past 15 or so years, the gap between the pay of other management positions and average workers has not (Abowd and Kaplan 14; Towers Perrin).

U.S. CEOs also fare well in comparison to their international counterparts. The Towers Perrin survey of companies with $500 million in sales found U.S. CEOs earned $1.93 million in 2001, while German CEOs earned $454,900, Japanese CEOs earned $508,000 and U.K. CEOs earned 668,500 in U.S. dollar equivalents (Towers Perrin). U.S. compensation was more than three times the average of CEOs in all but 6 of the 21 other countries surveyed (Thomas 2003b, 17). Foreign CEOs also have much smaller multiples when compared to average worker pay, although that number has been rising in some countries (Sklar; Towers Perrin). Much of this international disparity is explained by the proportionally greater use of long-term incentive pay, particularly in the form of stock and stock options, in the U.S. (Thomas 2003b, 20). Variable pay has, however, been increasing as a percentage of total compensation in many other countries in the past few years, possibly foreshadowing an increasing future gap between CEO and average worker pay in those jurisdictions as well. In the U.K., for instance, long-term incentive pay for CEOs increased from about 25% of annual base salary in 1996 to about 45% in 2001 (Towers Perrin). At the same time, the spread between the pay of top executives and manufacturing employees was increased from about a multiple of 12 to about one of 25 (Abowd and Kaplan 27; Sklar; Towers Perrin).

For purposes of the subsequent discussion, it is important to note the component elements of executive compensation in the United States. Generally, executives receive quite a number of types of compensation in addition to annual salary. In fact, U.S. CEOs on average receive long-term incentive pay that is 161% of their annual base salary (Thomas 2003b, 18). Executives also get medical insurance, nonperformance- and performance-related bonuses, stock options, restricted stock grants (where full ownership of the equity vests over a specified time period), pension contributions, guaranteed separation payments, loans (often at below-market rates), the ability to defer compensation at guaranteed rates of return (and to shelter that compensation from taxes), life insurance contracts, and frequently other perquisites such as cars, club memberships, housing allowances, and so on. The actual mix of these elements will vary from executive to executive, as well as over time for any given CEO. (We shall see later how shifting between these compensation elements provides a mechanism for some boards to protect their executive's income in the face of cries for reform.)

DEFENDING HIGH CEO PAY

While many in the public regard these facts, just by themselves, as a clear and convincing demonstration that current U.S. levels of executive compensation are unjustifiable, there are others, including significant numbers in the business, legal, and academic communities, who believe that both the current absolute and relative levels of compensation are appropriate. Defense of the current patterns typically depends on data concerning the impacts on investor returns, on an assessment of relative risk and contribution, or on an economic analysis of incentive.

First, there are numerous studies purporting to show that rewarding executives with stock options has a positive effect on share value over time. In fact, some have suggested that executives in the 1970s and 1980s may have been underpaid because their compensation was too weakly tied to share value. In the 1990s, corporate America began to take more seriously the agency problem of assuring that executives' interests were properly aligned with the interests of investors. Many more corporations began to adopt compensation plans that used awards of options to purchase stock in the firm as way of addressing this perceived problem of corporate governance. The move to option-based compensation arrangements, many argue, helped increase share value, reward executives more appropriately, and bind together the interests of management and

investors. Hence, they conclude that it is not that executives are now overpaid; it is that they were previously well underpaid for their contribution to shareholder value (see Abowd and Kaplan; Guy; Jensen and Murphy; Nichols and Subramanian).

Second, some argue that American executives both undertake more complex tasks and are exposed to greater risks of job loss than their international counterparts. American firms are bigger, their financial and competitive environment more complex, and the CEO possess more discretion. U.S. CEOs experience a substantially greater turnover rate when compared to Europeans, and they have greater economic risk in that their fortunes are more closely tied to those of their firms (since so much compensation is in the form of stock or stock options) (Stabile 125–127; Thomas 2003b, 41–56).

Third, some claim that the need to provide performance incentives in an environment of ever-decreasing opportunities as one moves up the management ladder explains both the absolute and relative levels of executive compensation. In the pyramidal corporate hierarchy, there are fewer and fewer positions for advancement as one moves higher. In order to provide incentives to those on the lower rungs, the payoffs have to be increased at each level in order to induce individuals into a competition where their chances of success become successively smaller. (If the probability of the reward is reduced, incentives can be maintained by increasing the size of that less-likely reward.) Hence, a gap will emerge between pay at lower levels and the pay of higher-level executives. Moreover, as one moves higher, the measures of performance become more difficult, and performance is measured by the proxy of share value. So, it makes sense to provide high-level executives with performance incentives in the form of stock and options. This tournament competition analogy, some argue, gives an economic explanation and justification for current executive compensation arrangements (Stabile 123; Thomas 2003a, 448–450).

CHALLENGING HIGH EXECUTIVE PAY

While these three rationales for high executive pay are common, none of them is compelling. The risk and the tournament rationales have serious difficulties that will be examined in the following sections. The defects of the third rationale, the shareholder value assertion, will be addressed here.

Problems with the Shareholder Value Rationale

There are at least three distinct difficulties for those who attempt to justify current levels of executive pay by appeal to a relationship between high equity-based pay and increased shareholder value. First, even if it is the case that there is a positive correlation between incentive-based pay and stock price (as reported in Abowd and Kaplan 13; Thomas 2003a, 459; and Thomas 2003b, 463), there is no evidence that the relationship between executive compensation and shareholder gains exhibits the correct proportion. Since executive pay is a cost that shareholders ultimately foot, it is important to ask whether the executive's compensation is warranted based on his or her causal contributions to the increase in stock price. Just how much of that increase is due to executive performance? Further, just how much of that increase justifiably should be returned to executives as compensation for their contributions? Even given a correlation between pay and stock performance, might the pay be more than necessary to achieve the increase in equity price? Might comparable returns be achieved with less compensation? Partly because of the innumerable variables that determine a given company's stock price, there are no easy answers to these questions. Nonetheless, any attempt to justify a specific level of executive compensation based on the executive's contribution to the firm's performance must provide answers. In the absence of those answers, there is no basis for believing that the compensation is appropriate (Nichols and Subramanian 348).

Second, there is an important question to be raised about whether the executive pay increases of the past decade are due to improvements in firm-specific performance or merely to a general rise in the stock markets. If executive pay increases due to large awards of stock or options merely mirrors a bull-market period, executives may be garnering undeserved windfall profits. In fact, studies have found no significant link between a firm's performance relative to its peers and increased executive compensation (Abowd and Kaplan 11). Again, in the absence of evidence that management's performance improved firm value relative to a compar-

ison industry group, the increase in share value provides no compelling reason to justify high levels of executive compensation.

Third, and most importantly, even if current levels of executive compensation correlate with increases in share value, that alone is not sufficient justification of those pay levels. This is because the shareholder value rationale presupposes the controversial proposition that the role of the executive is to maximize returns to shareholders. While that has been the mantra of much finance and management literature for the past quarter century, there are serious moral questions to be raised about an exclusive focus on shareholder wealth. Typically, that exclusive focus has been defended on the basis of either net social welfare (utility) or shareholder ownership considerations. Both of these grounds have been subject to serious critical analysis. The following comments briefly rehearse some of those critical assessments.

There are reasons for believing that a management focus on shareholder value maximization will not increase overall social utility. This is especially the case when the metric for assessing management performance is short-term, even quarterly, earnings growth. While this is not the place to rehearse all those critical concerns, it is clear that a management that focuses on the short term may in fact harm the company's long-term interests. In fact, even Michael Jensen, a seminal figure in the rise to dominance of the shareholder value maximization rule, now stresses that this should be understood as a long-term goal (Fuller and Jensen). In any case, the belief that maximizing return to shareholders will produce, even in the long run, greater net utility is open to question.

While one might make an argument that under the conditions of an economist's ideal market, maximizing share value will also maximize social utility, in the real world it requires quite a bit of faith that the contingent outcomes of a single-minded focus on even longer-run share value will produce the highest levels of social utility. Even Adam Smith did not believe that unconstrained pursuit of profit would produce good results. His invisible hand operated in the context of a background set of shared moral responsibilities. So, some serious skepticism is in order here. That skepticism is reinforced, at least with respect to levels of executive pay, by the more detailed cost analysis that follows which itemizes some of the potential negative consequences of current approaches to executive compensation.

The presupposition that the role of management is to maximize share value is also driven by questionable assumptions concerning the rights of stockholders. The typical claim in this regard is that the executive is the agent of the shareholding principals and must therefore act to maximize the economic interests of those principals. This claim cannot be accepted in so blunt a form. While agents do have an obligation to further the interests of their principals, the agents cannot morally do so by any means. In particular, the actions of the agents must respect the legitimate rights of nonshareholding stakeholders as well. Those include employees, creditors, consumers, the public at large, and others. Clearly, it is possible that unbridled pursuit of share value could damage the legitimate rights of any of these other constituencies. Merely to show that a compensation practice increases share value, then, is not sufficient to justify that practice. It must also be shown that the practice increases share values in a way that respects the rights of others. Thus, even on the highly questionable assumptions (1) that current executive compensation practices increase share value, (2) that actual pay levels are proportionate to the increased stock price and (3) that compensation reflects relative firm performance and not a generally rising market, it is still not the case that we have a compelling rationale for current levels of executive compensation.

These brief comments about the insufficiency of the shareholder value rationale illustrate the need for a more thorough moral assessment of executive compensation. Two general approaches for conducting a moral assessment are an investigation into the aggregate social welfare consequences of a practice and an investigation into its justice or fairness. The remaining two sections of this paper will address executive compensation from these respective approaches.

SOCIAL WELFARE CONSEQUENCES

A complete social welfare cost/benefit analysis of executive compensation is not possible, in part given the number of variables that would need to be considered. However, the following facts are clear: The shareholder benefits of high levels of

executive compensation are speculative (especially given the dearth of evidence for relative performance increases with increases in pay). There are equally as many costs that have been alleged as the results of current executive compensation practices. These cost allegations are often supported by reasonable evidence. Moreover, these costs accrue to a variety of constituencies and, collectively, they make a strong, though not conclusive, aggregate welfare case against the current state of American executive pay.

The first constituency that suffers a loss under current practices is shareholders. When firms award equity stakes to executives, either through large option or restricted stock grants, shareholders suffer a dilution effect on their holdings. The new shares that are added to the pool of outstanding shares do not increase the firm value and hence, after an option or a stock award, each existing share is worth less than before. Estimates are that the dilution effect is substantial. In 2000, the average effect of CEO compensation on profits in a 1500-firm data set was 7.89% (Bebchuck and Fried 19). Another study found the mean dilution from equity compensation was 16.3%, a sizable impact on the value of investor shares (Commission on Public Trust 6).

Some might suggest that these costs to shareholders are offset by greater gains achieved through the incentive power of equity compensation. That is, when executives' pay is tied to corporate stock price, they will act as Adam Smith suggested: Though it is not their immediate intent, they will be led by an invisible hand to produce gains for others. The failure to establish any evidence of improved firm performance relative to the general market or to the industry based on higher pay incentives should raise skepticism about this story. More importantly, however, the story cannot be supported by the facts about option grants nor about the social processes involved in setting executive pay levels.

Even researchers who disagree about executive compensation seem to agree that current compensation arrangements are far from optimal. The use of options that are not counted as an expense on the company balance sheet (as they have not been in the past, though that may change in the fallout from the financial scandals) encourages a sub-optimal pay arrangement. Executives appear to place less value on the options (since they carry some bit of risk) than those options cost to shareholders through dilution. Shareholders, in turn, fail to appreciate the impact of the options on their own holdings because of the lack of any reported accounting of their costs (Murphy 859). So, the facts suggest that the use of option grants, which are largely responsible for the recent increases in executive pay, cannot clearly be said to provide a cost/beneficial return to shareholders.

What, then, produces these compensation practices? Executive compensation is set by the board of directors through its compensation committee. Frequently, members of the board are themselves executives and have been appointed through the influence of the company's CEO. Compensation committees often use consultants to determine what are appropriate pay levels. Again, the consultants are often recommended by the company's management team. Most firms would want to be sure that their CEO is paid above the median salary identified by the consultants. Hence, the natural tendency is for pay packages to experience a ratcheting-up effect (Useem; Stabile 132; Thomas 2003b, 31). In fact, there are established relationships between the pay of CEOs and the compensation received by outside directors from their own firms. The more a director makes in his or her own job, the higher the salary of the CEO on whose board that director sits (O'Reilly "CEO Pay"). All this suggests that CEO pay is a function not of some rational economic process that will guarantee optimal firm performance but rather is a function of CEO power in influencing the composition of the board of directors and of the social psychology of corporate environments (Bebchuck, Fried, and Walker; O'Reilly "CEO Pay"). How else can one explain why corporate executives often have their options repriced in order to make them still valuable after a stock price decline (Bebchuck, Fried, and Walker 822)? How else to explain the fact that option grants are often timed to occur just before a rise in earnings, a rise that executive management has substantial knowledge of and influence over (Millon 909)?

It is not only shareholders who suffer sub-optimal outcomes from current compensation practices. The firm and the economy as a whole may suffer because of the effects created by the size and structure of executive compensation packages. The tournament analogy used to provide an economic

rationale for high executive pay can itself reveal serious negative consequences. Tournament approaches, with their winner-take-all nature, create an environment of competition and mistrust between the executives who are vying for the prize. In an environment where cooperation and teamwork are essential for efficient internal functioning, tournaments may create resentment and dysfunction. In fact, sociologist Robert Jackall has powerfully described the internal workings of the "corporate ladder." It turns out that advancement in the tournament is determined as much by political maneuvering as by past productive performance (Jackall 39ff, 62ff, 192ff). These consequences of the internal corporate competition can be net damaging to morale and productivity.

The use of options as compensation also has serious potential for perverse incentives among CEOs. Options have value only when stock price rises. Since they are not, at the time of their granting, equity stakes, their use may produce asymmetric risks that encourage management to do all they can to increase share value without worrying equally that their strategy might have downside risk to those currently holding equity stakes in the firm (Thomas 2003a, 451).

The incentive to manage earnings in order to show short-term earnings growth is also a function of the increased use of equity compensation, whether in the form of options or in the form of restricted stock grants. Both typically provide return to the CEO over a relatively short term. (Given their influence over compensation decisions and given the average tenure of contemporary CEOs at large firms, executives would be averse to compensation packages that had longer terms before their value vested.) This creates an incentive to manage earnings, but that incentive for short-term earnings growth may lead to under investment in longer-term growth strategies, since such investments may require expenditures that reduce current profit growth. Enron was, of course, an extreme example of managing the numbers. But it is practice that is widespread when managers are judged on quarterly performance, and it is a practice that leads to sub-optimal investment in long-term productivity across the economy (Millon 893ff.).

Finally, the high levels of executive compensation can have debilitating effects on employee morale. Just as tournaments can create resentment among the losers, wide inequality in compensation leads to perceptions of unfairness on the part of other employees. These perceptions have proven impact on turnover of middle-level management, on the productivity of employees generally, on loyalty to the firm and on the effectiveness of work teams (Stabile 147ff; O'Reilly "Wage Imbalance"). These latter consequences are unlikely to be remedied by current proposals that merely shift executive pay between component elements, such as between options and restricted stock or cash bonuses. In fact, many recent changes in the composition of executive pay only further exacerbate the sense that executives are unfairly compensated and that they wield too much influence over their boards of directors. For instance, in a bear market where options have no value, a shift to cash bonuses or restricted stock (which will eventually have value no matter whether equity prices decline) raises even further questions about executives having undue influence over their own compensation (Useem 57).

THE RELATIVE FAIRNESS OF EXECUTIVE COMPENSATION

The immediately preceding identification of perceptions of unfairness, of course, does not establish actual unfairness. People notoriously identify as unfair things that they merely do not like. However, there are a number of considerations that can be advanced to support the stronger assertion of actual unfairness in the current American approach to executive compensation.

The fairness of a distribution is inevitably a relative matter. Distributional fairness necessarily involves assessment of the respective shares allocated to those participating in the cooperative enterprise that produced the goods to be distributed. There are two predominant elements that are used in assessing such relative fairness: contribution and risk. Both of these have been used to suggest that American executives are compensated fairly by their current high levels of pay. The suggestion is that American executives must deal with larger and more complex business environments at the same time that they are exposed to greater compensation risk (both from declining equity prices and from being dismissed) than are their international peers (Stabile 125, 137; Thomas 2003b, 38ff).

While it may be formally true that American executives are exposed to more compensation risk than most of their international counterparts, that formal risk may not be present in the reality of American corporate practices. Though American executives have a greater proportion of their pay in variable incentive arrangements, it is nonetheless the case that the formal risk is often mitigated by practices that work to guarantee sizeable compensation even in declining equity markets. Boards have often repriced options whose strike price was "underwater" because the market had declined. Instead of allowing its executives to lose the value of the option grant because the purchase price was greater than the current stock price, they have changed the exercise price to accord with current market price. Boards have also shifted compensation from equity to cash in declining equity markets. They have issued additional new options at the current price. They have moved from "underwater" options to restricted stock where substantial value is guaranteed, even if the executive may not sell the shares for a specified period. They have adjusted performance targets to allow executives to garner a bonus even though company performance fell short of the previously agreed bonus trigger (Bebchuck, Fried, and Walker 821ff; Useem 57). All of these practices not only suggest once more that executives wield substantial influence over their own pay but that they exercise that influence to hedge risk and guarantee current and future income. Further, while American executives are technically employed at will, able to be dismissed at a moment's notice, the ubiquity of "golden parachutes" for high-level executives reduces the risk disparity between themselves and their international counterparts.

As far as comparisons of risk with their own workers go, it is even less clear that American executives bear greater income risks. The vast majority of U.S. workers are also employed at will. They are less able, however, to guarantee substantial severance than their executive superiors. And when severance is awarded, it is typically much less of a cushion than that provided in executive severance packages. The risk of job loss through poor corporate performance, often the result of executive decisions, has increased for workers through the past decade as layoffs more frequently became permanent structural changes rather than cyclic responses to temporary downturns in demand (after which workers were recalled). And American workers are exposed to much more income risk than their European peers, who typically have much stronger job protection by statute and who have more effective guarantees of substantial severance when laid off (in addition to often having higher wage levels). Hence, the rising disparity between the pay of American executives and their workers does not seem to be explained by any differential in income risk, whether across economies or within the U.S. economy. Rather, the previously identified ability of executives to influence the size of their compensation package seems a much more likely explanation.

It is, of course, still possible that widening income disparities are a function not of risk differences but of contribution differences. Certainly, the complexity of corporate financial decisions has increased over the past decades. However, in order for this to explain the differences between American executives' pay and that of workers, it would have to be the case that executive pay is significantly sensitive not only to increased firm performance but also to decreased earnings. The previously cited mechanisms for hedging the risk of lowered income, thus, raise skeptical questions about the degree to which executive compensation is tied to contribution. While there has been some decline in average CEO pay as a result of the declining stock market (dropping 23% in 2002), that figure masks the reality. At the same time average pay dropped, median pay rose 14%, indicating that the declining average was the result of a significant fall in the earnings of a few extremely highly compensated executives (Useem 57). And this occurs in the bottom of a bear market when firms generally were experiencing financial difficulties. Again, the aforementioned aspects of the system for setting executive compensation help to explain these results. The ratcheting effect of the use of compensation consultants, the power to influence board composition and decisions, the social psychology of the relationships between CEO and directors, all account for what economists call wage "stickiness," the tendency of wages to respond well to the upside and respond less significantly to the downside.

In order for the widening disparity between executive wages and workers' wages to be justified by relative contribution, moreover, it must be the case that the respective contributions made by each party have changed significantly over the past few

decades. Is there a case to be made that worker contributions remained constant or declined while the contributions of executives increased during that period? Data about increases in working hours by the typical U.S. worker over the past two decades might lead to the opposite conclusion, as might the increasing complexity and cooperative work required for many lower-level jobs. Thus, even if executives must deal with more complex environments, that by itself cannot explain the rising inequality in wages between those executives and workers.

It would appear that on neither ground, risk nor contribution, can we find a rationale to justify the drastic widening of pay gap that has occurred over the past 20 years. Rather, the relative changes in risk and contribution appear more comparable than different for executives and employees alike. Instead of providing a rationale for the current state of affairs, fairness considerations suggest, just as do the collective welfare considerations of the previous section, that executive compensation has become morally distorted.

CONCLUSION

The considerations advanced here do not constitute a certain demonstration that American executive compensation is inappropriate. But very few conclusions can claim that sort of mathematical certainty. These considerations do, however, strongly suggest that current arrangements are unacceptable on moral grounds. Neither aggregate welfare considerations nor considerations of fairness support the current structure or level of executive compensation. Rather, those considerations give great weight to those who argue for reform and reduction of executive pay. Moreover, the typical economic rationales for current practices are incomplete and uncompelling. Not increased share value, not tournament accounts, not complexity, not risk is available to provide justification for executive pay practices that have become the norm in the United States and that may be spreading elsewhere.

If we look for explanations of the recent experience, we have to settle on CEO influence over the board and the dynamic created by interactions between a group of persons, all of whom typically hold high-level executive positions. The CEO of one company serves on the boards of other companies (and is usually handsomely rewarded, often in the range of tens or hundreds of thousands of dollars for board service). A star-system corporate culture that accepts a winner-take-all approach apparently has become entrenched, leading to both hubris and a sense of entitlement to extremely high compensation. While there have been some legislative reforms in corporate governance, for example the Sarbanes-Oxley Act, those do not appear to offer much possibility for significant change in the levels of compensation. It remains to be seen whether the past decades' cultural shift in America will be reversed by the response to the recent financial scandals and the disclosure of executive salary figures, or whether the American approach will increasingly become the international norm.

REFERENCES

Abowd, John, and David Kaplan. "Executive Compensation: Six Questions That Need Answering." *Journal of Economic Perspectives* 13:145 (April 1999).

AFL/CIO. "Executive Paywatch: 2002 Trends in Executive Pay." http://www.aflcio.org/corporate america/paywatch/pay

Barlow, Jim. "Top Executive Compensation Totally Out of Control." *The Houston Chronicle.* Business Section, page 1 (June 11, 2002).

Bebchuck, Lucian Ayre, and Jesse Fried. "Executive Compensation as an Agency Problem." Harvard Law School, John M. Olin Center For Law, Economics and Business Working Paper Number 421 (April 2003).

Bebchuck, Lucian Ayre, Jesse Fried, and David Walker. "Managerial Power and Rent Extraction in the Design of Executive Compensation." *University of Chicago Law Review* 69:751 (2003).

Brown, Jeff. "Personal Finance Column." *The Philadelphia Inquirer.* Business Section, page 1 (September 19, 2002).

Commission on Public Trust. The Conference Board. "Executive Compensation Isues: A Rationale." (September 17, 2002).

Fuller, Joseph, and Michael Jensen. "Just Say No to Wall Street." *Journal of Applied Corporate Finance.* 14:4 (Winter 2002).

Guy, Frederick. "CEO Pay, Shareholder Returns, and Accounting Profits." *International Journal of the Economics of Business* 7:3 (2000).

Hunt, Albert. "Greed, Grasso and a Gilded Age." *The Wall Street Journal.* A17 (September 18, 2003).

Jackall, Robert. *Moral Mazes.* Oxford University Press (Oxford, 1988).

Jensen, Michael, and Kevin Murphy. "Performance Pay and Top Management Incentives." *Journal of Political Economy* 98:225 (April, 1990).

McGeehan, Patrick. "Executive Pay: A Special Report." *The New York Times.* Section 3, page 4 (April 6, 2003).

Millon, David. "Why Is Corporate Management Obsessed with Quarterly Earnings and What Should Be Done About It?" *George Washington Law Review* 70:890 (December 2002).

Murphy, Kevin. "Explaining Executive Compensation: Managerial Power vs. the Perceived Cost of Stock Options." *University of Chicago Law Review* 69:847 (Summer 2002).

Nichols, Donald, and Chandra Subramanian. "Executive Compensation: Excessive or Equitable?" *Journal of Business Ethics* 29:4 (February 2001).

O'Reilly, Charles. (a) "CEO Pay and Compensation Boards." www.gsb.stanford.edu/news/research/ compensation_ceo.shtml

O'Reilly, Charles. (b) "Wage Imbalance Between CEO and Workers Sends a Bad Message." www.gsb .stanford.edu/news/research/compensation_wage .shtml

Stabile, Susan. "One for A, Two for B, And Four Hundred for C: The Widening Gap Between Executives and Rank and File Employees." *University of Michigan Journal of Law Reform* 36:115 (Fall 2002).

Sklar, Holly. "CEO Pay Still Outrageous." *The Ultimate Field Guide to the U.S. Economy.* www.fguide.org/ Buletin/ceopay.thm

Thomas, Randall S. (a) "Should Directors Reduce Executive Pay?" *Hastings Law Journal* 54:437 (January 2003).

Thomas, Randall S. (b) "Explaining the International CEO Pay Gap: Board Capture or Market Driven?" Vanderbilt University Law School: Law And Economics Working Paper Number 03–05 (February 2003).

Towers-Perrin. "Worldwide Total Remuneration Report." www.towersperrin.com/hrservices/webcache/towers/United_States/publications/Reports/2001_02_WorldwideRemun/WWTR_2001_English.pdf and http://www.towersperrin.com/hrservices/webcache/towers/United_States/ publications/Reports/2003_04 .WorldwideRemun/WWTR_2003_English.pdf

Useem, Jerry. "Have They No Shame?" *Fortune* 147: 57 (April 28, 2003).

5

❦

Employee Rights:
Job Security
and Participation

INTRODUCTION

Job security and a voice in workplace decisions. These are now central desires of workers, more central even than wages. The reasons for their importance to workers are clear. We spend untold hours at our workplaces. What happens at work impacts the character of our lives in fundamental ways. Often, our social lives center around those with whom we work. Whether we approach our lives with cheerfulness and optimism or with distress and irritability is often a function of what takes place at work. In fact, our very identity, in our own eyes and in the eyes of others, is largely determined by our jobs. (Consider how we typically answer questions about who we are.) No wonder, then, that the character of work is a matter of major moral concern. No wonder that workers want assurance that they can influence what happens at work and that they want assurance that they not be summarily separated from this fundamentally important part of their life.

Norman Bowie, in the first reading of this chapter, defends a view that workers are entitled to meaningful work. He develops a Kantian view in which "meaningful work" refers to work that respects the humanity and autonomy of employees by providing adequate wages, conditional job security, and a voice in decisions. Bowie finds that the contemporary American workplace frequently falls far short of what that ethical theory requires. (You should note the similarities between Bowie's Kantianism and the approach to rights taken in Chapter Three.) In the remainder of this chapter, we take a close look at two of the elements that

Bowie identifies as necessary for meaningful work—job security and participation in corporate decisions. The readings and cases of this chapter ask you to consider whether these are legitimate rights of employees and whether businesses must alter their practices in order to accommodate them.

JOB SECURITY:
DISMISSALS AND LAYOFFS

Job security, perhaps even more than wages and economic benefits, has become a primary concern of today's workers. For example, in these days of corporate downsizing, unions are often placing a greater emphasis on keeping jobs than on increasing members' wages. However, the employer's right to terminate employment, either through a group layoff or the dismissal of an individual, is an almost unquestioned assumption in the United States. The first set of readings in this chapter will examine the conflict between employer rights and employee interests in job security. It will consider whether any limits should be placed on the employer's ability to discharge workers. It will consider whether new (that is, new for the United States) employee rights that constrain management authority should be recognized. Since job security issues involve questions both of layoffs and individual dismissals, it is best if we analyze those topics separately.

Individual Dismissals

An understanding of the history of dismissal law in the United States will help us identify today's available policy options. Historically, employment law in the United States was governed by a doctrine known as Employment at Will. That doctrine held that when an explicit agreement of contractually binding terms of employment is absent, the employment relationship exists only so long as both parties will it to continue. That is, either party is free to end the relationship at his or her will. Moreover, the relationship may be terminated at any time and for any reason. One court even said that employment may be ended "for good cause, for no cause or even for cause morally wrong." The doctrine of employment at will (EAW) thus gives the employer absolute discretion to hire and fire.

(When the doctrine of EAW was the dominant legal rule, there were always employees who were not subject to it. Workers with explicit contracts, for example union members, typically have contractually guaranteed grievance procedures that specify how and when an employer may fire an individual worker. Additionally, government workers were not subject to EAW since the government is bound by constitutional constraints of due process. These are significant exceptions, but they still apply only to a distinct minority of American employees. Approximately 80 percent of the private sector labor force in the United States is governed by the modified EAW described here.)

Over time, this EAW doctrine has been challenged as providing insufficient protection to workers. Although it is true that employers and employees have equal formal rights under EAW (either may exit the relationship at any time), many commentators believe that employers have the greater power since most employees need their job more than the employer needs them. (Employers can find replacement workers more easily than employees can find replacement jobs under normal rates of unemployment.) In addition, some reasons for dismissing employees, for example, race, were found morally intolerable. As a result, the doctrine of EAW has been incrementally modified over recent decades in ways that limit the employers' discretionary authority.

Modifications to EAW The modifications to EAW have come primarily from two sources: legislative actions and precedents set by court decisions. Federal and state legislatures have enumerated exceptions to the employer's authority by prohibiting firings for, among other things, race or sex (the Civil Rights Act), requesting a safety inspection of the workplace (the Occupational Safety and Health Act), supporting unionization (the Wagner Act), and physical disability that is not related to reasonable job requirements (the Americans with Disabilities Act).

Courts have also carved out new legal exceptions to the employer's power to fire workers. Three exceptions are most significant. First, there is the "public policy exception" to EAW. Courts have sometimes found that the dismissal of an at-will employee, while not a violation of any explicit statute, nonetheless undermines the state's ability to pursue legitimate public policies and for that reason will not be accepted. An early case of this sort involved a food business employee who noticed that cans of food were regularly underweighted. Cans that should have contained 12 ounces were often fractionally less than that weight. The employee noted this in a complaint to his employer and was dismissed. (Apparently the underweighting was an intentional corporate policy.) Since he was an at-will employee, he could be dismissed for any or no reason; the firing was not technically illegal. However, the court held that permitting a dismissal in this case would undercut the state's ability to enforce its truth-in-labeling legislation and, hence, the firing was an unacceptable violation of public policy.

A second judicial exception to EAW is in cases where courts have found implicit contracts on the basis of representations that were made to employees either in their employee handbooks or through statements made in the hiring process. The Decision Scenario on unwritten contracts at the end of this chapter identifies some examples of this "implied contract exception." (You should note, however, that many firms now require employees to sign a statement that indicates that they have received and read their handbook. Most of these statements also contain a clause that indicates the employee understands that his employment is at will, regardless of any claims made in the handbook. Courts have upheld these waivers of implied contract rights in a number of cases. Thus, the implied contract exception to EAW may be a moot issue today.)

The third exception to EAW is the "implied covenant of good faith exception." Courts have fashioned this exception to EAW to prevent, for example, the discharge of employees days before they are due to receive annual bonuses for yearly sales performance.

The modified EAW that has evolved in the United States is perceived by many to have a number of serious problems. It is uncertain for both employers and employees. To be protected in their jobs, especially by the judicial exceptions to EAW, employees must file suit against their employers. Whether their particular jurisdiction will find an exception to EAW in their specific case is highly uncertain. The exceptions are defined rather vaguely. Similarly, employers suffer uncertainty in that they are never sure whether a discharge will be found to fall under some new exception. The employer's uncertainty is compounded when multimillion dollar damages are possible if a discharge is found unacceptable. (As an ironic result of this uncertainty, employers are becoming extremely cautious about dismissals. To block suits based on the Implied Contract exception, they are beginning to require signed disclaimers when they distribute employee manuals. They even sometimes fail to discharge unproductive workers for fear of large damage awards if the fired employee sues.)

Just Cause Policies Because they believe current legal policy fails to protect workers adequately or because they believe business is hamstrung by the threat of lawsuits, some commentators have begun to call for a different approach to employment law in the United States. They urge that the United States adopt a "just cause policy" modeled on those of most other industrialized nations. "Just cause policies" essentially require that any individual firing be done only for reasons judged to be legitimate. So, instead of identifying those reasons that are unacceptable and letting employers fire for any other reason (as the U.S. approach does), just cause policies further limit the power of employers by establishing a finite list of reasons that will justify a dismissal.

Typical just cause policies define acceptable reasons for dismissal loosely and let further definition come through decisions of arbitrators or labor courts. While acceptable reasons are not precisely defined by statute, common law develops a rather clear list of acceptable and unacceptable reasons for discharge of employees. Acceptable reasons will include theft, excessive absenteeism, intoxication on the job, substandard performance, and business downturns. Unacceptable reasons include political opinion, religion, race, personal bias of managers, and ethnicity. (It should be noted that the U.S. Constitution's guarantees of free speech and religion are constraints only on government actions. Courts have consistently held that private employers are not bound by the constitutional rights that citizens hold against their government.)

Just cause policies also usually include the following: specified minimum performance standards, a probationary period before employees are covered by just cause requirements, a requirement that employees be given notice of and reasons for intent to dismiss, a pretermination hearing to minimize the chance of unfair dismissal, an opportunity to appeal the employer's decision to an independent arbitrator, and some clearly defined remedy if the arbitrator finds the dismissal unjust. Remedies are usually limited to some multiple of wages plus back pay. Sometimes, though rarely, remedies will include reinstatement for dismissed employees.

One advantage of just cause policies for employers is that these remedies are known in advance and employers are not thrown into a litigation lottery where they might lose millions. (It was a consideration like this that led some Montana businesses to support the only just cause policy in the United States. See the Decision Scenario on Montana's just cause legislation at the end of this chapter.)

Just Cause versus EAW

Consequences Opponents of just cause policy argue that it is likely to be economically inefficient. Many believe that with increased job security comes decreased worker output. Opponents of just cause policy claim that when workers have no fear of losing their employment, they will be less motivated and less productive. Anecdotal evidence for this claim is often offered by reference to a caricature of government employees or tenured faculty who are unproductive and who have high job security. Opponents of just cause policy also point to the inefficiency created when management's time is taken up with the need to document performance problems and to appear at hearings. Finally, opponents claim that formal just cause policies are unnecessary, since an employer who fires productive workers without cause will be penalized by difficulty in recruiting new workers in the labor market. Workers, then, need no protections beyond what the market provides.

Proponents respond to these efficiency concerns in a number of ways. They challenge the notion that fear is an effective motivator. They claim, instead, that workers who fear arbitrary actions from management may make sure they comply with performance mandates, but they will be alienated, resentful, and unwilling to take risks. Workers with job security, proponents contend, will be more committed to the company and more likely to see their interests as tied to the long-term interests of the firm. (This particular debate mirrors past debates about worker motivation in management theory between followers of Frederick Taylor's "scientific management" and followers of Douglas McGregor's "Theory Y.") Moreover, they note that just cause policy is not equivalent to absolute job security. Workers may still be dismissed if their work is subpar.

Those defending just cause policies respond to the complaints about government employees by questioning whether, if the characterization is accurate, the poor performance is a consequence of job security alone or a conjunction of job security with work that is either alienating or that offers few incentives. They offer evidence of their own from studies showing that union plants are more productive and from facts about the productivity of European workers with just cause protections. From this anecdotal evidence, they argue that cases of lazy workers with job security need to be explained by something other than the job security alone. Perhaps the perceived lack of worker output is due, instead, to a failure of management to enforce productivity standards (possibly out of fear of lawsuits).

Those in favor of just cause also challenge the claims that it is a waste of management time and unnecessary for protecting workers. They argue that documenting employee performance can create a climate that leads to procedures for improving the productivity of current employees. And, they point out, if the market selected against unfair dismissals, we would not expect neutral parties (arbitrators and courts) to judge as without cause half (over 200,000 a year) of all contested firings.

Rights   The readings by Pat Werhane and Ian Maitland engage the debate over just cause and EAW, or the modified U.S. version of EAW. They give a clear picture of how different interpretations of rights produce different conclusions. (Note the use in these articles of the utilitarian and rights-based theories of Chapters Two and Three). Typically, those in favor of EAW argue that it is the approach most consistent with the rights to property and liberty. Maitland, for example, explicitly argues that mandatory due process rights will conflict with the rights of employees to freely contract for their preferred conditions of employment (an application of a liberty right). Others argue that owners, having the rights to control who gains access to their property and to exclusive benefit from their property, ought to be free to terminate any individual's employment at will. This is merely a corporate instance of the right that homeowners unquestionably have to permit or deny entry to an individual.

Werhane argues to the contrary, that due process rights are required by autonomy and fairness. She contends that employees are autonomous agents and not mere "human resources" (a common phrase that implicitly compares people with material resources of the productive process). Moreover, in contemporary times, the security of one's income functions to promote a person's autonomy in the way that ownership of land would have in an agrarian economy.

Werhane also argues that employees deserve a guarantee of fairness in dismissal proceedings as a matter of right. She contends that due process should be required of any institution that has the power to do serious and unfair damage to the welfare of individuals. As a result, she urges that we abandon the notion that civil rights only bind public institutions and not private corporations.

It should be noted that while the two authors present the debate as one about process, pure process is obviously not all that is at issue here. Requiring merely a formal procedure before dismissal would be little hindrance to an employer who wanted to dismiss a worker and little protection for the worker. If there were no limits on the reasons that can justify a dismissal, procedures would mean nothing. Real due process rights require as a corollary the existence of substantive standards identifying acceptable and unacceptable grounds for termination. So, while the articles employ the terminology of due process, the debate is really about whether dismissals should be governed by a just cause policy.

In assessing this debate, we suggest that you recall the comments on rights in Chapter Three. The debate here presents a conflict between property and liberty rights on the one hand and fairness and autonomy for employees on the other hand. From Chapter Three we know that property rights are derivative rights whose underlying values are fairness, autonomy, and utility. And we know that we need to justify liberty in specific areas (such as freedom of contract) by articulating why liberty in that area is important. These points would suggest that the conflict of claimed rights in this case is a conflict between rights that have the same status and the same foundational values. You need, then, to determine in which of the two competing rights are those underlying values most at stake in alternative employment termination policies. Your evaluation will tell you whether you ought to prefer an EAW or just cause approach.

Layoffs

Layoffs have dominated the economic news in the United States over the past decade. It seems that every week a major corporation announces a new round of "downsizing." The public emphasis on job loss may seem somewhat surprising if you look only at unemployment rates. Those rates have not been high by historic standards in the past few years, even during years of recession. However, in 2004 more unemployed workers are out of work for longer periods, and many who have found new jobs are working part time. The number of those underemployed and those so discouraged that they are no longer actively seeking work is almost equivalent to the number officially counted as unemployed. Moreover, the composition of the unemployed has changed dramatically over the last 15 or 20 years. Now, white-collar employees constitute a substantially higher percentage of the unemployed than they have in the past.

The rounds of layoffs stretching back into the 1990s may not be a temporary response to the business cycle but rather a permanent and structural decrease in corporate employment levels. Some commentators have attempted to reassure us that even though the United States has lost manufacturing jobs to low labor cost competitors, the future for employment is bright because of the growing service sector (which includes high-paying technology jobs). However, it now appears that the reality of a wired global trade network means that many of these technology jobs can also be performed elsewhere at lower costs. Moreover, they can have their work product transferred halfway around the world in an instant.

Other economic trends, too, create anxiety about employment security. In each of the past three recessions, job creation during recovery has been sluggish. These new features of contemporary downsizing help explain the increased media attention on layoffs. Corporate shedding of payroll is now threatening to middle-class suburbia. Political campaigns are now regularly making job losses and slow job creation major issues.

These economic conditions that lead to corporate downsizing affect most of the first-world industrial nations. Not all nations, however, approach the problems in the same way. In the United States, management has broad legal discretion to determine when and how employees will be laid off. Management may terminate employment for groups of employees for almost any reason. In the past, layoffs were often management's preferred response to temporary fluctuations in demand. Recent permanent layoffs have been done to achieve "international competitiveness" and to please the marketplace. And they have, in fact, usually improved investors' share values in the short term (which is often what large institutional investors are concerned about).

While management in the United States has a free hand in deciding *when* to downsize, one limit was placed on *how* American management may downsize by the Worker Adjustment and Retraining Act of 1988 (WARN). It demands that plants with more than 100 workers provide 60 days notice of impending layoffs if those layoffs will involve either 500 workers or more than one-third of the plant's workforce. These requirements were imposed by the federal Congress in an attempt to cushion the impact of mass layoffs on both individual employees and local communities. For example, while laid-off workers are eligible for unemployment, the time it takes them to find new, permanent work is substantially shortened when they are given advance notice. The drain on state-funded unemployment insurance coffers is thereby reduced as well.

A study of the effectiveness of the WARN Act by the nonpartisan Government Accounting Office (GAO) has raised doubts about how well the act has achieved its purposes, however. The GAO study noted that the 100 employee threshold effectively exempts 98% of American workplaces from the act. Moreover, the study found that two-thirds of the employers covered by the act failed to provide the required advance notice, most by failing to provide any notice at all. Workers whose employers violate the act may sue for lost wages, but the study also found that only 1 percent of the violations have been enforced in that way.

Layoff policies in other industrial nations are more limiting than those in the United States. This is particularly true of Europe. In Europe, both government and corporate policies have discouraged the use of layoffs as a short-term response to fluctuations in demand. Some European nations give public authorities the power to delay a layoff. France had a law, repealed in the 1980s, that required the approval of public authority for any mass layoff. Corporations themselves take steps to minimize layoffs caused by the business cycle. They often reduce the hours worked for each employee rather than terminate the employment of a few. Those employees experiencing such "short-time" work are eligible for prorated unemployment benefits, and they often retain their health care and other benefits. (Governments subsidize the cost of these benefits for employees.)

When permanent reductions of employment levels become unavoidable due to structural changes in the economy, reductions are first attempted through early retirement incentives and worker buyouts. When involuntary layoffs are needed, advance notice is required and severance pay is the norm. A study of layoffs in Germany found that median severance wages were the equivalent of 17 weeks of pay. In the privatizing of the British Steel Corporation by Margaret Thatcher's government, laid-off steel workers were given severance of 6 months of wages in many cases, and they were also eligible for a 52-week retraining program with 100 percent of previous pay and benefits.

Of course, it is the case that many companies in the United States provide generous notice and severance for their laid-off employees. Sunoco, for example, offered laid-off workers something on the order of two weeks of severance pay for every year of service, provided employees would sign a promise not to sue. Another recent survey found that somewhere between 10 percent and 25 percent of U.S. companies provide employees with severance pay in the event of a downsizing due to a merger.

Still, there are major differences between the typical patterns for layoffs in the United States and Western Europe. Those differences are a function of legally mandated employment policies, government fiscal choices, and corporate responses to government incentives. The differences affect both how readily layoffs are instituted and how they are accomplished. The differences also reflect radically different social understandings of how the pain of economic change, whether cyclical or structural, should be allocated. Clearly, the European model means that there will be more delay before a corporation can shift work to newer, more technologically advanced and efficient plants. It also means that investors, remaining workers, and citizens in general will experience a larger share of the costs of economic downturns. That cost shifting has been an accepted part of the implicit social compact between European workers, companies, and governments. In an age of increasing global competition for investment money, it remains to be seen whether Europe will move away from its historical compact. (A 1985 liberalization of German law allowed for more use of part-time and fixed-term contracts of employment. These contracts do not have the same notice and severance requirements that apply to full-time and permanent workers. Since the liberalization, a sizeable increase in these employment categories has occurred, though traditional employment arrangements continue to dominate.) It also remains to be seen whether the increasing anxiety about layoffs moves the United States closer to the European model or further in the direction of at-will downsizing policies.

Thus, just as the issue of individual dismissal involves questions of reasons (when to fire) and questions of process (how to fire), the issue of layoffs raises "when" and "how" questions as well. Morally, we need to ask what economic circumstances would justify terminating the employment of a group of workers and, when a termination is justified, what process ought to be followed. For instance, we need to ask whether temporary downturns in demand for a company's product justify a layoff in the same way that a permanent, structural change in demand does.

The debate over layoff policies once again forces us to consider arguments about both efficiency/utility and rights. Concerns about the efficiency of imposing layoff responsibilities on corporations often center on what Ian Maitland calls "Eurosclerosis," or what Ronald Reagan called "euro-malaise" when he commented on the 1988 WARN Act requiring advance notice of layoffs. The concern is that such responsibilities raise the cost of hiring an employee and, as a result, reduce the overall levels of employment in the nation. Europe, with its strong job security, has, of course, experienced decades of high unemployment.

Those more sympathetic to layoff responsibilities, however, note that job security provisions are only one variable affecting European economies, and it is dangerous to attribute unemployment effects to that single variable. They argue that rates of unemployment are more likely influenced by macroeconomic variables such as interest rates than by specific labor market regulations. In fact, one of the few empirical studies of the topic suggests that the effects are small and add primarily to the duration rather than to the rate of unemployment. Another comparative study suggested that economies that rely on layoffs in periods of economic downturns are likely to have longer and deeper recessions, presumably because layoffs reduce the willingness of consumers to spend the economy out of recession.

In addition, some will argue that strong commitment to job security can produce changes in employee attitudes that, in turn, increase productivity. Conversely, they argue that frequent layoffs (65 percent of firms that downsize do so repeatedly) severely damage morale and lower productivity, especially when the same amount of work is spread among fewer employees. The reading by Jeffrey Pfeffer provides a detailed example of this type of consequentialist argument. Further discussion of the efficiency of job security provisions can be found in the reading by Maitland.

At its deepest level, however, this debate about layoff responsibilities reflects disagreements about corporate property rights and the rights of employees. Opponents of employee job security provisions are often arguing that the benefits to shareholders should not be reduced to provide benefits for nonshareholders, namely employees or local communities. On the other hand, proponents of job security argue that corporate property ought to be treated differently from personal property. They argue that the specific rights associated with corporate property ought to be limited because of the major social impacts of mass layoffs and because of the contribution society has made to the value of shareholders' investments (for example, through support for necessary infrastructures such as highways, transportation systems, and public education).

For a more pragmatic perspective on these points, consider that while the long-term data on productivity and profitability is unclear, stock prices generally increase significantly once a company announces a downsizing. Layoffs, then, can be seen as one way of allocating costs and benefits among the various constituencies of a corporation. The question is what allocation best accords with the rights of the parties involved. Determining whether there ought to be moral limits on when and how employees are laid off will require you to identify the grounds of the claimed employee rights to continued employment in temporary economic downturns, to notice before dismissal, and to severance pay. Then, as before, you will need to compare those rights and their foundations against the traditional rights to property and freedom of contract that support broad management rights to downsize.

Consider, once more, that all these competing rights have common justifications in concerns for autonomy and fairness. Those opposing restrictions on employers' layoff powers will, as before, argue that employees were free to bargain for layoff protections. Hence, they will also claim that autonomy for employees is sufficiently guaranteed by the market.

Those in favor of employee rights, however, argue that market bargaining always presupposes a prior legal allocation of rights that the parties bring with them to the bargaining table. That allocation, they point out, will affect the parties' relative wealth and the outcome of the bargaining. William Joseph Singer claims that

> [t]he agreement between the parties is the result not of unconstrained choice, but of the relative power of the parties to withhold from the other party what it needs. Relative withholding power is determined, to a large extent, by the legal definition and allocation of property entitlements.

Moreover it is an odd fact of life that those with more power are able to get better terms and thus increase their power and wealth at the expense of others, which further enables them to get even better terms. ("The Reliance Interest in Property." *Stanford Law Review,* vol. 40, no. 611.)

Thus, proponents of employee rights argue that they are needed to assure effective choice and to correct market imbalances of power.

The opposing sides in this debate over job security also hold different views about what fairness requires. Those opposing moral or legal restrictions on layoff powers often argue that fairness demands merely a bargained day's wage for a day's work. They see no obligation for employers to continue the employment relationship into the indefinite future or to provide severance, especially if it will reduce return to shareholders. They note that shareholders bear the residual risk (that they will lose their investment if the firm goes under). Thus, fairness requires that the shareholders be the ones entitled to all the residual benefits.

Those who believe that there are moral grounds for severance or for limits on layoffs claim that employees bear risk as well. They believe that there is an implicit contract for longer-term employment. They support this idea in part by evidence that the increase in wages with seniority is not explicable by increased productivity of more senior employees. Some believe that the increasing wages that come with seniority are a device for binding the worker to the firm and buying loyalty through the promise of higher future wages. Thus, they argue, layoffs allow owners to reap the benefits of a committed workforce while failing to pay the promised costs for that benefit. This argument is a more general version of the "implied covenant of good faith" argument referred to above.

Another aspect of the debate arises from suggestions that we have recently evolved a new paradigm of employment. The suggestion is that under this new paradigm, instead of promising job or employment security (which many find anachronistic in today's labor market), firms merely assure that their workers have *employability* security. That is, firms and workers ought to act so as to assure that workers develop the skills necessary for landing a future job. The imagined bargain between workers and firms is not for security of employment with a particular firm but rather for the training needed for effective competition in the employment market.

Some are quite skeptical about this new employment paradigm. Some will question the new contract by asking whether firms are likely to invest in a skill development that makes a worker more marketable to other firms. Some even suggest that there is already a general market failure in the amount of training provided to workers because firms are afraid to invest in something that other firms may poach.

Assessing these competing analyses of contract and property rights, of autonomy and fairness obviously will require you to pursue the debate further than we have in this introduction. These preliminary points hope to indicate a direction for that further analysis by reinforcing the idea that adjudicating between competing rights requires careful investigation into the foundations of the claimed rights.

EMPLOYEE PARTICIPATION

In 1985 when the first edition of this text was published, employee participation in corporate decision making was a mere blip on the radar screen of America's corporate managers. Involving employees in decisions was sometimes advised by management theorists, but it was advice that was seldom heeded. In the intervening 20 years, the number of employee participation programs has expanded geometrically. One study, reported in December 1994 by the federal Commission on the Future of Worker-Management Relations (commonly known as the Dunlop Commission), estimated that perhaps up to 60 percent of American workplaces had some form of employee participation system. That same commission called for expansion of participation programs to cover more workers and more workplaces. The Dunlop Commission and many labor relations experts suggest that increasing the competitiveness of American industry will require abandoning the traditional adversarial approach to labor relations in favor of a more cooperative style of management. If that suggestion is heeded, as it appears increasingly to be, participation programs will proliferate even further through the workplace.

Varieties of Participation

While the increase in participatory programs is remarkable, it is still true that the vast majority of these programs are limited in both scope and authority. (In fact, American labor law has been interpreted to require limited scope for many programs. See Decision Scenario F, "Electromation," at the end of this chapter.) Most programs concern very well-defined issues, such as plant safety or product quality. Also, most function merely as advisory mechanisms with no real authority to make decisions on their own. This chapter considers whether employees should have a right to much stronger forms of participation than those now common in the United States.

Since employee participation programs vary so widely, it is necessary to have some idea of the range of possible approaches before engaging in arguments about the value of participation. The material in some of the decision scenarios will provide specific examples of possible programs. A more general description is provided by John McCall, who suggests that participation programs vary both by the amount of institutional authority they possess and by the kinds of issues that they address. You should try to understand these differences, since clarity about the variety of participative mechanisms is crucial for assessing the feasibility and justification of worker participation.

Participation and Rights

McCall argues that there are five strong ethical reasons that presumptively support a worker's right to participate. All these reasons derive from a need to protect centrally important human goods, such as autonomy and fairness. The arguments suggest that, in practice, protection for these goods is most effective when strong forms of employee participation are seen as important derivative rights. McCall also considers some traditional arguments against participation. Some of those opposing arguments derive from management or owner interests that are seen as conflicting with a right to participate in corporate decisions. For example, an owner's right to control his or her property appears to conflict with employees having strong participation rights that provide some control over corporate policies. McCall suggests, however, that these owner rights do not possess the moral weight necessary to override the presumptive support for participation.

Others claim that mandating participation for all workplaces as a matter of right is inconsistent with both employee's and employer's rights to freedom of association and freedom of contract. They argue that such rights are fundamental to our ideal of constitutional democracy. Why, they ask, should we mandate participation programs rather than let employees collectively bargain for them if they wish to have such programs in their workplace? Surely it is possible that some groups of employees would rather not have the responsibility of decision making thrust upon them. The contention, then, is that those who argue for workplace democracy have a flawed conception of democracy. In this chapter, we once more have a conflict of right claims that can be settled only if you pursue an investigation into the reasons behind the conflicting right claims. By appeal to what values are the rights to free association and employee participation justified? Which would advance those values more: limiting the freedom to negotiate terms of employment by mandating worker rights or denying workers a guaranteed right to participate? You need to pursue the same sort of analysis to resolve the conflict between owners' property rights and the claimed worker right to a voice in corporate decisions.

Participation and Firm Performance

Assessing the desirability of employee participation also requires that you address the practicality of allowing employees to participate in decision making. Consider the feasibility of participation by asking these questions: How does the economic performance of firms with strong forms of participation compare with the performance of firms without such programs? Are workers competent to make intelligent and informed decisions? Will ordinary workers have any desire for participation rights?

Some data does exist on these topics. A study of American workplaces by Joel Rogers of the University of Wisconsin and Richard Freeman of Harvard found a "participation gap" for workers. Of American workers surveyed, 63 percent report that they would like to have more influence in workplace decisions. The figure for manufacturing workers was 72 percent. Nonetheless, the question remains: Should participation programs force "empowerment" on workers who do not desire it?

Some concerns about the efficiency of participation reflect concerns about the attitude of employees. There are fears that if employees are involved in corporate decision making, they will sack the firm of its profits and underinvest in the capital plant in order to gain short-term wage or benefit increases. There are also fears that employees, while certainly competent to offer suggestions about their immediate work environment, are not competent to make decisions on complex financial matters. Proponents of employee participation regard this last concern as a red herring. Participation need not be equivalent to direct democracy where every worker votes on every issue. It can be instead analogous to representative democracy where employees select (or hire) a competent individual to represent their interests. After all, this is exactly what owners have done in allowing management to make decisions for them.

As for the more general efficiency concerns, the evidence on participatory workplaces is far from clear. It is true that sometimes workers would underinvest in the plant. (It is also true that management sometimes does this, too, as is evidenced by the instances where the focus on quarterly returns has led to a neglect of investment for longer-term profitability.) However, the tendency to underinvest is reduced to the degree that workers can be made to see that their interests coincide with the long-term health of the firm.

The evidence is mixed on the relationship between firm performance and employee participation taken by itself. But a number of commentators, including the Dunlop Commission and Laura D'Andrae Tyson (a member of the Clinton administration's team of economic advisors), have argued that participation is most likely to increase productivity when it offers workers a real say in the workplace and when it is combined with other human resources reforms that include a commitment to job security. In fact, that is a major theme of much contemporary research in industrial relations. Casey Ichniowski, echoing many (including Jeffrey Pfeffer, whose article appears in this chapter), finds that *sets* of human resource practices have greater impact than does the introduction of isolated participatory practices:

> The preponderance of the evidence suggests that . . . innovative employment practices tend to be complements, as is proposed in recent theoretical work on optimal incentive structures. That is, workers' performance is substantially better under incentive pay plans that are coupled with supporting innovative work practices—such as flexible job design, *employee participation* in problem solving teams, training to provide workers with multiple skills, extensive screening and communication, and *employment security*—than under more traditional work practices. ("The Effects of Human Resource Management Practices on Productivity." *The American Economic Review,* vol. 87, no. 3, italics added)

Evidence from some of the strongest forms of participation, worker cooperatives, is also mixed. Many newer cooperatives have resulted from worker buyouts of struggling firms. These firms often experience a dual problem of initial undercapitalization and poor competitive position. In other firms, the abrupt introduction of participatory management programs into conflicted workplaces has met with resistance and distrust from both workers and managers alike.

These problems are not insurmountable or unavoidable, however. Long-running lumber cooperatives in the Northwest have demonstrated financial success. In addition, more traditionally owned companies have reported profitable results from experiments in participation. As reported in the Dunlop Report, the Donnelly Mirrors Company has had a "Scanlon Plan" tying bonuses to company performance since the 1950s and has more recently introduced employee councils with wide authority. The reading by Joel Rogers and Wolfgang Streeck suggests a number of explanations for the observed positive impact of participation on some firms' performance. It would seem that firms with programs of participation experience the same financial and organizational difficulties that all firms do.

Participation and Organized Labor

Some have argued that workplace participation is unnecessary for protecting employee interests since employees can always form unions for that purpose. Others, however, challenge the belief that unions are effective at representing worker interests in the United States today. The proportion of nonagricultural private sector workers who are unionized is now about 11 percent. With that low rate of unionization unlikely to rise, many are uncomfortable with the notion that unions should be the primary vehicle for protecting worker interests. Even the economic benefit of union membership has not been great as of late. The 1980s saw a much more aggressive posture toward unions by American business.

Unions have often been forced by weak bargaining positions to make concessions or give-backs in contract negotiations. And, while the wages of union workers remain somewhat higher than those of nonunion workers, unions have not significantly increased labor's proportional share of the national income. As a result, some labor relations theorists, such as Paul Weiler of Harvard, have suggested that it is time for workers in individual enterprises to protect themselves through strong and independent in-house forms of employee participation.

Unions, in fact, have been historically ambivalent about workplace participation. Often they feared that it was a device for weakening work rules and squeezing more work from employees. Union activists have sometimes been cautious about participating in upper-level corporate decisions, worrying that it would threaten the union's adversarial position. Some feared, for example, that union representation on corporate boards would lead the union board members to identify with the perspective of management.

Middle management, of course, has also resisted stronger forms of employee participation. Those forms of participation that give employees some actual decision-making authority directly reduce both the power of and the need for middle-management positions. It is small wonder that some participation programs have met with outright hostility from line managers.

The debate over employee participation even reached the halls of the U.S. Congress. In the late 1990s, Republican leaders urged reform of the National Labor Relations Act. The NLRA, as interpreted by the Supreme Court in its *Electromation* decision, prohibits employers from playing certain roles in the formation and operation of employee-management committees that address "terms and conditions of employment" (matters such as wages and working conditions). The NLRA, in order to guarantee an independent labor voice and to avoid "company unions," prohibits employers from controlling such committees.

While some employers merely wink at the NLRA's interpretation and establish legally questionable labor-management teams anyway, others are concerned about possible suits being filed before the National Labor Relations Board. Hence, there has been a push for reform of the law in order to encourage more labor-management cooperation. Debate on these proposed reforms often centers on their impact on organized labor. Opponents argue that the reforms will further weaken the independent voice that workers have through labor unions. They also argue that sufficient scope exists within the current NLRA for labor-management cooperation, and they fear that some proposed reforms are merely a guise for greater management domination of the workforce. (Note the pre-NLRA history of "company unions" and employer-dominated committees that is described in the Rogers and Streeck article.) As a result of these concerns, even some who are in favor of reform of the NLRA urge that any reforms be accompanied by statutory protections that assure the independence of employee participation committees and/or encourage a more vital role for organized labor.

Regardless of any eventual reform of the NLRA, the respective labor and management fears about participation programs show us that any employee-involvement program must be carefully planned if it is to succeed. Both workers and managers need extensive preparation if participation programs are to decrease labor-management tensions and produce more cooperative and internationally competitive businesses.

CASE STUDY Employee Relations at EDS

Electronic Data Systems (EDS) provides business process and information technology outsourcing services to companies in over 60 countries. Its $21 billion in revenue in 2003 places it 80th among Fortune 500 firms in 2003. The Dallas-based firm employs upwards of 130,000 people in its worldwide operations, though that number is well down from its previous high. The company was created in 1996 as a spinoff from the industrial giant General Motors.

In 1998, EDS hired Dick Brown as CEO. Early in his tenure, Brown replaced much of the executive team and began a series of cost-cutting measures aimed at improving the company's financial position. EDS had suffered a series of disappointing earnings reports that were below expectations of Wall Street analysts. Among the cost-cutting measures were attempts to limit the severance costs associated with layoffs of employees. In October of 2001, EDS altered the severance packages it offered to its workers. It reduced the maximum severance pay award from 26 weeks, a relatively generous package in the U.S. context, to 4 weeks. At the time it made the change, EDS did not disclose layoff plans, but a company spokesperson indicated that EDS would continue to use a policy of eliminating from the payroll those people whose skills were dated and

replacing them with those whose skills enable the company to meet the ever-changing high-tech demands of its customers.

Within days, EDS began a new series of layoffs, most of them small enough that they did not require public announcements. Some dismissed workers attempted a class-action suit, alleging that the changed severance policy was not properly disclosed to employees before the rounds of layoffs began. Then, the following July 2, the company laid off another 2000 workers. Included in that number were 300 employees who EDS had acquired in the preceding year as part of a takeover of Sabre Corporation's travel reservations system. The previous Sabre employees were covered under a preexisting contract from their prior employer until July 1. That Sabre contract guaranteed workers a severance package of a month's salary with the possibility of up to another month of pay for each year of prior service. On July 2, their severance amounted to somewhere between two and four week's salary. The employees were told that their medical coverage would end at midnight of the day of their termination. Internal e-mail sent to management on June 28 reportedly directed that managers not hold any "separation meetings" to discuss the layoffs prior to their announcement on July 2. Moreover, previous layoff announcements came on Mondays; July 2 was a Tuesday. Both the workers who were laid off and the surviving employees were skeptical of the timing, despite company assertions that the timing was not targeted to coincide with the expiration of the Sabre employees' contract.

Over the succeeding year, employee morale at EDS appeared to suffer. Tech-savvy employees created Web sites and online message boards critical of the company and its CEO, Dick Brown. Rumors of impending layoffs also spread over these message boards. Employees criticized the performance ranking system instituted by Brown. Some believed it was used as a mechanism for selectively identifying employees for inclusion in subsequent layoffs.

In spite of his attempts to impress investors by slashing costs, Brown was unable to provide the type of returns Wall Street expected. The company fell short of earnings expectations and faced multiple SEC investigations surrounding its accounting practices. In particular, the SEC was interested in the events surrounding an earnings warning issued in September of 2002, when the company acknowledged that it would miss its target by almost 80 percent. That warning began a slide in share price of almost 50 percent over the next six months. On March 20, 2003, the EDS board removed Brown as CEO. His severance package was valued at $37 million. That package included over $12 million in cash, $5 million in stock, and, interestingly, over $19 million in retirement benefits that were actually not scheduled to vest until eight months later, at the end of 2003.

Brown was replaced by Michael Jordan, a former executive of CBS. Shortly after taking the helm at EDS, Jordan began a thorough review of the corporation's human resource practices. As a result of that review, the company increased the funds available for employee raises and bonuses. It also announced that the severance package would improve to a maximum of 20 week's pay and that terminated workers would receive 2 week's notice, as well as outplacement assistance and money to cover the cost of a month's medical insurance. These new policies were made retroactive to the day that Jordan took over; those laid off in July 2002 were unaffected, however. EDS's Human Resources VP appeared to have accepted the opinion of many consultants and academics when she asserted that the company's assets and intellectual capital are its workforce.

- What obligations does a company have to its workforce? Is severance in the event of a layoff among those obligations, or have workers been fairly compensated by wages already received for the work and time they have spent with a company?

- What is the most economically rational practice for a company facing the need for reduced labor? Should it attempt strategies that avoid layoffs? If it does cut payroll, how should it implement that reduction? Should workers always be given notice of the impending termination, or are there circumstances that make such notice economically problematic for the company? How will a company's handling of a workforce reduction impact the surviving employees?

- What evaluation do you make of the differences between the treatment of dismissed executives and the treatment of laid-off workers? On what basis could you defend the generous severance that most CEOs receive even after failing to meet the expectations of the company's board of directors?

This case was prepared from the following sources: "Electronic Data Systems Corp to Pay Less to Fired Workers," Jeff Bennett, *Detroit Free Press,* October 25, 2001; "Former Worker Sues Electronic Data Systems Over Change in Severance Policy," Clayton Harrison, *The Dallas Morning News,* December 12, 2001; "Former EDS Workers Protest Timing of Layoffs," Clayton Harrison, *The Dallas Morning News,* July 28, 2002; "EDS Tries to Reassure Workers," Clayton Harrison, *The Dallas Morning News,* October 16, 2002; "EDS Releases Details of Former Chairman and CEO Dick Brown's Severance," *PR Newswire,* March 21, 2003; "Former CEO Severance Plan to Cost EDS $37 Million," Roger Yu, *The Dallas Morning News,* March 22, 2003; "Electronic Data Systems Targets Morale with More Funding for Raises, Bonuses," Clayton Harrison, *The Dallas Morning News,* May 9, 2003; "EDS Accounting Charge Forces $2.2 Billion Charge," Liz Austin, *Philadelphia Inquirer,* October 28, 2003.

READING 5.1 MEANINGFUL WORK:
A KANTIAN APPROACH
Norman Bowie

For a Kantian, meaningful work is work that allows the worker to exercise her autonomy and independence, that enables the worker to develop her rational capacities, that provides a wage sufficient for physical welfare, that supports the moral development of the employee, and that is not paternalistic in the sense of interfering with the worker's conception of how she wishes to obtain happiness.

Although much of my argument will be based on the implications of Kant's moral theory when applied to the business world, Kant himself had a few explicit things to say about the nature of work.

KANT'S REFLECTIONS ON WORK

First, Kant argues that work is necessary for the development of selfhood.

> Life is the faculty of spontaneous activity, the awareness of all our human powers. Occupation gives us this awareness. . . . Without occupation man cannot live happily. If he earns his bread, he eats it with greater pleasure than if it is doled out to him. . . . Man feels more contented after heavy work than when he has done no work; for by work he has set his powers in motion.[1]

Somewhat surprisingly, perhaps, Kant endorses wealth and the pleasures it brings. Moreover, wealth contributes to self-respect because it provides independence. To work simply in order to make money is to display the vice of miserliness, a vice which is even worse than avarice. So long as work is required to make money so that one can provide for one's needs and pleasures and in so doing make oneself independent, work has value. Selected comments of Kant's will establish his view:

> A man whose possessions are sufficient for his needs is well-to-do. . . . All wealth is means . . . for satisfying the owner's wants, free purposes and inclinations. . . . By dependence on others man loses in worth, and so a man of independent means is an object of respect. . . . But the miser finds a direct pleasure in money itself, although money is nothing but a pure means. . . . The spendthrift is a lovable simpleton, the miser a detestable fool. The former has not destroyed his better self and might face the misfortune that awaits him with courage, but the latter is a man of poor character.[2]

This selection is from Kant's brief remarks, which amount to less than ten pages and represent student notes from his lectures on ethics in the 1770s before he had written his more famous and critical works on ethical theory. Nonetheless, they provide a starting point for a Kantian theory of meaningful work and for the obligations of a firm with respect to providing it.

So long as business firms provide jobs that provide sufficient wealth, they contribute to the independence and thus to the self-respect of persons. For a Kantian, the true contribution of capitalism would be that it provides jobs that help provide self-respect. The purchase of consumer goods in an affluent society often simply provides pleasure. Having a job provides the means for securing pleasure and the independence necessary for self-respect. If it is true that our current welfare programs make people dependent, Kant would consider them a great evil. And a capitalism that provides jobs that do not provide sufficient income for independence is also morally flawed. Kant would be as concerned as we are about the scope of corporate downsizing and the loss of jobs that do not provide a living wage.[3]

Kant evaluated thrift on moral rather than economic grounds. He said:

> Thrift is care and scruple in the spending of one's substance. It is no virtue; it requires neither skill nor talent. A spendthrift of good taste requires much more of these qualities than does he who merely saves; an arrant fool can save and put money aside; to spend one's money with refinement on pleasure needs knowledge and skill, but there is no cleverness in accumulating by thrift. The thrifty who acquire their wealth by saving, are as a rule small minded people.[4]

From Norman Bowie, *Business Ethics: A Kantian Perspective* (Blackwell Publishing, 1999), pp. 67–81. Reprinted by permission of Blackwell Publishing.

Alan Greenspan take note. It would be stretching the point to claim that Kant is a precursor of Keynes, but it is clear that wealth for Kant is something to be used to meet our material needs and that its moral value is in providing us with the independence needed to meet our material needs. In the *Metaphysical Principles of Virtue* Kant says: "Therefore become thrifty so you do not become destitute."[5] Somewhat surprisingly, Kant does not follow Luther and Protestant ethics here. Weber could not cite Kant in favor of his thesis. There is no intrinsic merit to saving itself. Savings are to be used to support one's autonomy in the material world. I say "surprisingly," because Kant's ethics was strongly influenced by German pietism, yet on this point is not consistent with it.

Although Kant's explicit remarks on work are rather limited, nonetheless I believe the following ideas concerning the obligation of the manager to employees have explicit warrant in the Kantian texts:

1. A corporation can be considered moral in the Kantian sense only if the humanity of employees is treated as an end and not as a means merely.

2. If a corporation is to treat the humanity of employees as an end and not as a means merely, then a corporation should honor the self-respect of the employees.

3. To honor the employees' self-respect, the employees must have a certain amount of independence as well as the ability to satisfy a certain amount of their desires. Thus, the corporation should allow a certain amount of independence and make it possible for employees to satisfy a certain amount of their desires.

4. In an economic system people achieve independence and satisfaction of their desires using their wages which they earn as employees.

5. Thus, a corporation should pay employees a living wage, that is, a wage sufficient to provide a certain amount of independence and some amount of satisfaction of desires.[6]

A few qualifications are required to the above argument. What if market conditions are such that a company cannot provide a living wage for certain jobs? Supply and demand for labor for certain tasks may be in equilibrium at a point below a living wage. Is a business firm morally required on Kantian grounds to pay the living wage even though doing so would make the firm uncompetitive and endanger its survival? No, for several reasons. First, I have not argued that meaningful work as it is spelled out here is an absolute requirement of Kantian morality. Rather, providing meaningful work is one possible and rather effective way for a firm to honor the requirement that it respect the humanity of its employees and the imperfect obligation of beneficence. However, if the labor market does not permit a firm to honor the obligation of beneficence in this way, it is not required to do so. Although I cannot argue for it here, I would maintain that in such situations there is an obligation on the part of the state that it pass minimum wage laws and that it serve as an employer of last resort.

Although this is as much as one can say about meaningful work given the Kantian text, I believe a Kantian can say more about the moral value of work than that it gives us independence and thus self-respect.[7] By combining Kant's explicit remarks on work with the rest of his ethical theory and with the insights of recent commentators on Kant, I believe a Kantian would endorse the following principles of meaningful work. These principles would be an effective way to honor the requirement that the humanity in employees be respected.

1. Meaningful work is work that is freely chosen and provides opportunities for the worker to exercise autonomy on the job.

2. The work relationship must support the autonomy and rationality of human beings. Work that unnecessarily deadens autonomy or that undermines rationality is immoral.[8]

3. Meaningful work is work that provides a salary sufficient for the worker to exercise her independence and provides for her physical well-being and the satisfaction of some of her desires.

4. Meaningful work is work that enables a person to develop her rational capacities.

5. Meaningful work is work that does not interfere with a person's moral development.

6. Meaningful work is work that is not paternalistic in the sense of interfering with the worker's conception of how she wishes to obtain happiness.

I remind the reader that these are normative conditions for meaningful work derived from Kantian moral philosophy. They need not be descriptive of how employees would define meaningful work, although as a matter of fact I believe the empirical evidence shows that there would be considerable overlap.

MEANINGFUL WORK AND CONTEMPORARY BUSINESS

Although a Kantian philosophy of the workplace is still the exception rather than the rule, some organizational theorists and individual companies are committed to providing more meaningful work to employees. Jeffrey Pfeffer has argued that firms can gain a competitive advantage if they focus on their employees. He identifies 16 practices for managing people successfully: (1) employment security; (2) selectivity in recruiting; (3) high wages; (4) incentive pay; (5) employee ownership; (6) information sharing; (7) participation and empowerment; (8) teams and job redesign; (9) training and skill development; (10) cross-utilization and cross-training; (11) symbolic egalitarianism; (12) wage compression; (13) promotion from within; (14) a long-term perspective; (15) the measurement of practices; (16) an overreaching philosophy.[9] What I wish to do is show how these human resource management practices are supportive of Kantian meaningful work. They are also consistent with earlier human resource theory. In 1981, William Ouchi published his famous book *Theory Z*, in which he argued for an organizational structure that departed radically from the traditional American hierarchical form of management in favor of a participative management style that more clearly resembled traditional Japanese management practices. Ouchi described 13 steps he thought were needed to go from the hierarchical form of management, which he called Theory A, to Theory Z. An examination of those steps would show a considerable overlap with Pfeffer.[10]

Moving from organizational studies to the shop floor one can look to the quality movement in the USA in the 1980s and 1990s for a defense of management practices that have much in common with our account of meaningful work. As Jeffrey Pfeffer himself has said:

The quality movement has legitimated management practices that have been around a long time but have not generated a lot of support, perhaps because of the language. "Worker empowerment," "employee participation" or "participative management," "employee voice," "equity and fairness," "due process," "high commitment work practices," and similar terms often used in describing the employment relation somehow seemed to smack of coddling the work force. . . . The language of quality and the political support behind the quality movement overcome some of these problems at least to some degree.[11]

A moral requirement that firms provide meaningful work would have been considered impossibly utopian until recently. However, if US firms must be concerned with the quality of their products in order to survive in international competition, then the provision of meaningful work becomes a prudential strategy as well as a moral one. Meaningful work provisions are not utopian; they can even provide a competitive advantage.

Out of the Crisis by the late W. Edwards Deming is often considered the Bible of the quality movement. Deming's recipe for quality focuses on 14 points. Although Deming is noted for bringing statistical analysis to the quality movement, an examination of his 14 points shows clearly that his main concern is with the management of employees. His management philosophy is one that a Kantian could endorse. His 14 points include a provision for training on the job, for eliminating fear as a motivator, for eliminating barriers that "rob the hourly employee of his pride of workmanship," and for instituting programs of self-improvement.[12]

The competitive necessity for quality products and the meaningful work provisions that are required by a concern with quality have been recognized by the United States government. In response to the perception that foreign manufacturers were producing goods of much higher quality than those in the USA, the government established the Baldridge Awards for quality. It is interesting to note how many of the good-practice criteria refer not to the product itself but rather to how employees are managed. Even more interesting is the fact that these good management practices embody Kantian language that respects employee autonomy and responsibility. Emphasis is placed on the following factors:

(a) management practices . . . such as teams or suggestion systems . . . the company uses to promote employee contributions . . . individually and in groups. (b) company actions to increase employee authority to act (empowerment), responsibility, and innovation . . . (c) key indicators . . . to evaluate the extent and effectiveness of involvement by all categories and types of employees . . . (d) trends and current levels of involvement by all categories of employees.[13]

Finally, let us consider some actual businesses that seem to endorse a Kantian notion of meaningful work. You do not find language in the business world that captures the pure Kantian spirit very often, but occasionally you do. In Pfeffer's terms few corporations have the appropriate overarching philosophy. Max DePree, CEO of Miller Furniture, captured the Kantian ideal when he described work as follows:

For many of us who work there exists an exasperating discontinuity between how we see ourselves as persons and how we see ourselves as workers. We need to eliminate the sense of discontinuity and to restore a sense of coherence in our lives. . . . Work should be and can be productive and rewarding, meaningful and maturing, enriching and fulfilling, healing and joyful. Work is one of the great privileges. Work can even be poetic.

What is it most of us really want from work? We would like to find the most effective, most productive, most rewarding way of working together. We would like to know that our work process uses all of the appropriate and pertinent resources: human, physical, and financial. We would like a work process and relationships that meet our personal needs for belonging, for contributing, for meaningful work, for the opportunity to make a commitment, for the opportunity to grow and be at least reasonably in control of our own destinies.[14]

Milliken and Company, a privately owned textile company with 14,000 employees, won the prestigious Baldridge Award in 1989. A booklet used in recruiting describes the company as follows:

In the process of arriving at new levels of quality, nothing supersedes the inner working of the human being. . . . There is emphasis on finding the best people for every career and on continuing education. . . . At Milliken, people are called Associates—not employees—implying the importance of each one as a contributor to our common objective. . . . All of this assumes a participatory management approach.[15]

But perhaps the statement of corporate philosophy that comes closest to the Kantian ideal is found in the way Hewlett-Packard expresses its philosophy toward its people. This passage is worth quoting at length:

Our People
Objective: To help HP people share in the company's success, which they make possible; to provide job security based on their performance, to recognize their individual achievements, and to insure the personal satisfaction that comes from a sense of accomplishment in their work. We are proud of the people we have in our organization, their performance, and their attitude toward their jobs and toward the company. The company has been built around the individual, the personal dignity of each, and the recognition of personal achievement. . . . The opportunity to share in the success of the company is evidenced by our above-average wage and salary level, our profit-sharing and stock purchase plans, and by other company benefits. In a growing company there are apt to be more opportunities for advancement than there are qualified people to fill them. This is true at Hewlett-Packard; opportunities are plentiful and it is up to the individual, through personal growth and development, to take advantage of them. We want people to enjoy their work at HP, and to be proud of their accomplishments. This means we must make sure that each person receives the recognition he or she needs and deserves. In the final analysis, people at all levels determine the character and strength of our company.[16]

Now that a general positive relationship between Pfeffer's research and other research in management theory has been established, let us return to Pfeffer's list to provide an explanation of those practices that might not be intuitively clear.

This will enable us to show how these items contribute to meaningful work as we have defined it. Cross-utilization and cross-training (Principle 10) is a technique that allows employees to do many different jobs. Symbolic egalitarianism (Principle 11) refers to the elimination of symbols of status from the workplace. Wage compression (Principle 12) refers to a policy that reduces large differences in pay between the top officials in the corporation and other employees, as well as differences between individuals at roughly the same functional level. If wage compression were adopted horizontally, the VP for Finance would not earn a premium over the VP for Personnel as is now the case in most US companies. Finally, overarching philosophy (Principle 14) refers to management's commitment that these employment practices are a basic corporate value.

Although some of the items on this list have received general management attention, most of the items involve a sharp departure from current business practice. A comprehensive implementation of all the items would be quite revolutionary. Certainly, a number of the practices are contrary to what is accepted as successful management practice.

Yet most of the items on this list offer a means for management to provide meaningful work for employees. They emphasize the importance of employee autonomy and independence. They emphasize the importance of a good wage. They are consistent with the development of our rational capacities and they do not interfere with an employee's moral development. They treat employees with respect. In the remainder of this chapter and in the next, many of these practices will be further elaborated and shown to be consistent with what a Kantian would expect of a moral firm. Using Pfeffer's list of good practices for the management of people, the abstract notion that meaningful work is work that supports the worker in leading a moral—and thus an autonomous—rational life can be given some content.

What is now required is to show how the specific items on Pfeffer's list are connected to the specific conditions of a Kantian notion of meaningful work. Meaningful work is work that provides an adequate wage. Principles 1, 3, and 12 are means for providing an adequate wage. Principle 3 (high wages) is obvious as a means to this goal. Job security (Principle 1) [challenges] the morality of downsizing. Much downsizing is wrong because it

violates the negative freedom of employees. In addition, economic security is often what employees want most as an element of positive liberty. Job security is essential because it is necessary for achieving the characteristics of meaningful work. Thus, Kantian morality requires it.

Despite the fact that many firms behave immorally here—and some like those managed by Al Dunlop flaunt their immoral behavior—other companies try to provide employment security. For many years IBM was the leader in this regard, but bad economic times in the 1990s led to the abandonment of IBM's policy. One company that still provides security for employees is—as one would expect from reading the previous quotation— Hewlett-Packard. William Ouchi describes Hewlett-Packard's policy as follows:

> Twice in recent times, Hewlett-Packard has adopted the nine-day fortnight along with a hiring freeze, a travel freeze, and the elimination of perquisites. Each time these steps kept employees on while other companies in the industry had layoffs. The result at Hewlett-Packard has been the lowest voluntary turnover rate, the most experienced workforce in the industry, and one of the highest rates of growth and profitability.[17]

Wage compression would partly address a developing social problem. Many people find that despite the fact that they have full-time jobs, they are poor. In the last decade there has been a steady increase in the ratio of the salaries of the top officials in a firm to wages paid to the least well compensated member of the firm. Moreover, the living standards of those at the bottom, often referred to as the working poor, have declined. Wage compression would be something of a corrective here. A situation where the rich get richer while the working poor fail to achieve an adequate standard of living is not acceptable to a Kantian.

Another important component of meaningful work is autonomy and independence. Principle 2, participation and empowerment, speaks directly to that issue.

Autonomy and independence are aided by the fact that more and more companies are adopting a policy of flex time. Flex time gives employees greater latitude over their work schedules. Baldridge Award winners Ritz Carlton and Granite Rock are noted for their flex time programs.

We have already seen that participation is a requirement in decisions regarding layoffs if the employment contract is not to be viewed as coercive. But participation is also required for positive freedom as well as for negative freedom. . . .

Another requirement of meaningful work is that the work contribute to the development of the employees' rational capacities. Principles 2 (selectivity in recruiting), 6 (information sharing), 8 (teams and job redesign), 9 (training and skill development), 10 (cross-utilization and cross-training), and 13 (promotion from within) are all a means to this goal. By selecting the right people in the first place, you do not get people who are overqualified for the job. Working on a job for which you are overqualified is usually boring and frustrating because it does not make best use of your rational capacities. All the other items on the list contribute to skill development, which is both valuable in itself (recall that one of Kant's imperfect duties is the duty to develop one's talents) and adapts one for changes in the workplace so that the employee can remain gainfully employed. For example, Pfeffer argues for the importance of cross-utilization. Routine assembly line work is often work that is dull, boring, and repetitive. By training a worker to do many different jobs a firm can eliminate or greatly mitigate the drudgery of assembly line manufacturing. Cross-utilization makes teamwork possible and vice versa. In fact many of these principles fit together to transform traditional manufacturing work into an approach more compatible with a Kantian theory of meaningful work.

One principle, Principle 11 (symbolic egalitarianism) is also necessary for self-respect and is a condition of fairness. It breaks down some of the class barriers that say not only is the work that I do different from yours, but it is more valuable than yours, and thus I am a more valuable person. The person who is doing what is perceived to be inferior work thus loses self-respect—and loses it unjustly. A business firm is a cooperative enterprise and thus every task is valuable to the enterprise. Market conditions, and other legitimate factors, may justify the fact that we pay one job category more than another, but these conditions do not justify inequality of respect.

This point has been recognized by many firms. You can see from the emphasis on teams that work, for many, is a social activity and the achievement of meaningful work requires the appropriate support of the organization. . . .

In summary, . . . we have tried to apply to the business context the message of the second formulation of the categorical imperative to treat the humanity in a person as an end in itself and never as a means merely. To do that a firm must treat all its corporate stakeholders in a noncoercive and nondeceptive manner. We have illustrated that principle with respect to management's obligations to employees. We have also shown how treating employees as ends in themselves, in contrast to merely using them, requires an obligation on the part of management to provide meaningful work. Finally, we have tried to develop a normative framework of meaningful work consistent with Kantianism and tried to show how good management practice can be supportive of this Kantian vision of meaningful work. Thus, Kant's ethics can inspire business firms to feats more noble than merely making money.

NOTES*

1. Immanuel Kant, *Lectures on Ethics* 1775 (New York: Harper Torchbooks, 1963), pp. 160–1.

2. Ibid., pp. 177, 181, 185.

3. Although admittedly Kant wants a job to provide more than a living wage. A living wage is a necessary but not sufficient condition for a "good" job.

4. Ibid., p. 184.

5. Immanuel Kant, *Metaphysical Principles of Virtue* 1797, in *Ethical Philosophy*, p. 99.

6. Again, I am indebted to Bryan Frances for the formalization of this summary. The argument has been reformulated after Robert Frederick pointed out the earlier version's inadequacies.

7. Although business ethicists have not emphasized meaningful work, some are giving it attention. Joanne Cuilla and Al Gini have both made important contributions. My own thinking on this topic has evolved from discussions with my graduate student Kathryn Brewer.

8. I am not claiming that the only way one can gain autonomy and independence is through work that provides wages sufficient for independence. One can gain self-respect by being a priest or by being an impoverished artist. One can also gain self-respect by identifying with a group or cause. However, if work in corporations is chosen and is to be morally justified, then something like the

---

*Notes have been renumbered.—ED.

arguments I have attributed to Kant are necessary. I am grateful to Tanya Kostova for raising this issue.

9. Pfeffer, *Competitive Advantage Through People,* chapter 2.

10. Ouchi's steps 2 and 3 involve developing a management philosophy. His steps 1, 7, 8, 11, and 12 all refer to the necessity for participation. Ouchi's step 8 refers to job security; his steps 5 and 10 address the need for training and skill development. Step 9 refers to a plan that enables the firm to retain and promote valued employees while at the same time permitting a more egalitarian pay structure. See William Ouchi, *Theory Z* (Reading, MA: Addison Wesley, 1981).

11. Pfeffer, *Competitive Advantage Through People,* pp. 215–16.

12. W. Edwards Deming, *Out of the Crisis* (Cambridge, MA: MIT Center for Advanced Engineering Study, 1982), pp. 23–4.

13. Quoted in Pfeffer, *Competitive Advantage Through People,* p. 209.

14. Max DePree, *Leadership Is An Art* (New York: Dell Publishing, 1989), pp. 23, 32.

15. Quoted in Pfeffer, *Competitive Advantage Through People,* p. 212.

16. Quoted in Ouchi, *Theory Z,* pp. 136–7.

17. Ibid., p. 118.

READING 5.2 THE RIGHT TO DUE PROCESS
Patricia H. Werhane

EMPLOYMENT AT WILL

The principle of Employment at Will, referred to in this essay's introduction, is an unwritten common-law idea that employers as owners have the absolute right to hire, promote, demote, and fire whom and when they please. The principle, hereafter abbreviated as EAW, was stated explicitly in 1887 in a document by H. G. Wood entitled *Master and Servant.* Wood said, "A general or indefinite hiring is *prima facie* a hiring at will."[1] But the principle behind EAW dates at least to the seventeenth century and perhaps was used as early as the Middle Ages. EAW has commonly been interpreted as the rule that all employers "may dismiss their employees at will . . . for good cause, for no cause, *or even for causes morally wrong,* without being thereby guilty of legal wrong."[2]

The principle of EAW is not self-evident and stands in need of defense. The most promising lines of defense involve appeals to the right to freedom, to the common notion that property is defined as private ownership (for example, of land, material possessions, or capital), to the supposed moral right to dispose freely of one's own property as one sees

fit, or to the utilitarian benefits of freely operating productive organizations. Let us briefly characterize the main elements of each defense.

The first justification for EAW in the workplace, at least in the private sector of the economy, involves both appeals to the right to freedom and considerations about the nature of places of employment in a free society. Places of employment are privately owned, voluntary organizations of all sizes, from small entrepreneurships to large corporations. As such, it is claimed, they are not subject to the same restrictions governing public and political institutions. And, as they are voluntary organizations, employees join freely and may quit at any time. Political procedures, needed to safeguard citizens against arbitrary exercise of power in society at large, do not apply to voluntary private institutions. Any restriction on the principle of EAW, those who argue in this way conclude, interferes with the rights of persons *and* organizations not to be coerced into activities that either are not of their own choosing or limit their freedom to contract.

The principle of EAW is also sometimes defended purely on the basis of property rights. The rights to freedom and to private ownership, we are assuming, are equally valid claims, and the latter right entitles owners, it is argued, to use and improve what they own, including all aspects of their businesses, as they wish. According to this

From Patricia H. Werhane, "Individual Rights in Business," in *Just Business: New Introductory Essays in Business Ethics,* ed. Tom Regan (New York: Random House, Inc., 1984), pp. 107–113, 124–126. Reprinted by permission of The McGraw-Hill Companies.

view, when an employee is working for another, this activity affects, positively or negatively, the employer's property and production. Because employers have property rights, and because these rights entitle them to control what happens to what they own, the employer has the right to dispose of the labor of employees whose work changes production. In dismissing or demoting employees, the employer is not denying *persons* political rights; rather, the employer is simply excluding their *labor* from the organization.

Finally, EAW is often defended on practical grounds. Viewed from a utilitarian perspective, hiring and firing "at will" is necessary in productive organizations if they are to achieve their goal of maximum efficiency and productivity. To interfere with this process, it is claimed, would defeat the purpose of free enterprise organizations. We shall consider each of these arguments more fully in the following section.

THE RIGHT TO DUE PROCESS IN THE WORKPLACE

Due process is a procedure by which one can appeal a decision or action in order to get a rational explanation of the decision and a disinterested, objective review of its propriety. In the workplace due process is, or should be, the right to grievance, arbitration, or some other fair procedure to evaluate hiring, firing, promotion, or demotion. For example, Geary and Alomar were fired without a hearing. Should they have been given some warning, a hearing by peers, a chance to appeal? The call to recognize the right to due process in the workplace extends the widely accepted view that every accused person, guilty or innocent, has a right to a fair hearing and an objective evaluation of his or her guilt or innocence. Those who deny due process in the workplace could argue (a) that this right does not extend to every sector of society, or (b) that rights of employers sometimes override those of employees and do so in this case. However we decide the merits of these arguments, the absence of due process in the workplace is not merely an oversight, as witness the principle of Employment at Will discussed in the last section. An employer, according to this principle, need not explain or defend its employee treatment in regard

to dismissal nor give a hearing to the employee before he or she is dismissed.

In order to support the validity of the claim to the right to due process in the workplace, we must examine the defenses of the principle of EAW given in the previous section. First, EAW was defended on the ground that every person has the right to own and accumulate private property and, relatedly, every person, and analogously every corporation, has the right to dispose of what they own as they see fit. To say that employers have the right to dispose of their property "at will" is a legitimate claim, which follows from the right to ownership. To say that employers have this same right to "dispose of," that is, to fire for *any* reason, their employees is quite another sort of claim. The right to private ownership gives one the right to dispose of *material possessions* as one pleases, but it in no sense implies that one has the right to dispose of *persons* as one pleases. Employees, although they work on, and labor to improve, the business of their employers, are not themselves property. They are autonomous persons. Their employers do not own them, just as the employers do not own members of their own families. So the right of an employer to hire or demote "at will' cannot be defended simply by appealing to employer ownership rights, because employees are not the property of employers.

A second attempted justification of EAW, we saw earlier, appeals to an employer's right to freedom. Voluntary private organizations in a free society rightly argue that they should be as free as possible from coercive and restrictive procedures. Due process might be thought of as such a procedure, since it requires checks for arbitrariness on the part of employers. However, one needs to evaluate the role of the employer and the coercive nature of "at will" employment in voluntary organizations more carefully before accepting a negative view of due process in the workplace.

Though private businesses are voluntary organizations which employees are free to leave at any time, employers are in a position of power relative to individual employees. This by itself is not a sufficient reason to restrict employer activities. But the possible abuse of this power *is* what is at issue when we question the principle of EAW. By means of his or her position, an employer can arbitrarily hire or fire an employee. The employee can, of course, quit arbitrarily too. But an "at will" employee is seldom in a position within the law to inflict harm on an employer. Legally sanctioned "at will" treatment by employers of employees, on the other hand, frequently harms employees, as the following observations confirm.

When one is demoted or fired, the reduction or loss of the job is only part of an employee's disadvantage. When one is demoted or fired, it is commonly taken for granted that one *deserved* this treatment, whether or not this is the case. Without an objective appraisal of their treatment, employees are virtually powerless to demonstrate that they were fired, demoted, and so forth, for no good reason. Moreover, fired or demoted employees generally have much more difficulty than other persons in getting new jobs or rising within the ranks of their own company. The absence of due process in the workplace places arbitrarily dismissed or demoted employees at an *undeserved* disadvantage among persons competing for a given job. Viewed in this light, the absence of due process is unfair because workers who do not deserve to be fired are treated the same as those who do, with the result that the opportunities for future employment for both are, other things being equal, equally diminished.

To put the point differently, a fired employee is harmed, at least *prima facie*. And this raises the question, Do employers exceed their right when they fire or demote someone arbitrarily? For it is not true that one has the right to do just anything, when one's activities harm those who have not done anything to deserve it. In order to justify the harm one does to another as a result of the exercise of one's freedom, one must be able to give good reasons. And good reasons are precisely what are lacking in cases where employers, by firing those in their employ, *prima facie* harm these people for "no cause, or even for causes morally wrong." It is difficult to see how a defense of EAW can elicit our rational assent, if it is based exclusively on an appeal to an employer's liberty rights, because the unrestrained exercise of such rights may cause undeserved harm to those employees who are the victims of its arbitrary use.

Worse, "at will" practices violate the very right the principle of EAW is based on. Part of the appeal of the principle of EAW is that it protects the employer's right not to be coerced. According to

the libertarian thinker Eric Mack, a coercive act is one that renders individual or institutional behavior involuntary.[3] Due process might be thought of as a coercive procedure because it *forces* employers to justify publicly their employment practices. But some of the employment practices sanctioned by EAW also are, or can be, coercive, according to Mack's definition. Persons who are fired without good reason *are involuntarily* placed in disadvantageous, undeserved positions by their employer. It is, therefore, difficult to defend "at will" employment practices on the basis of avoidance of coercion, since these practices themselves can be, and often are, coercive.

Defenders of EAW might make the following objection. EAW, they might claim, balances employee and employer rights because, just as the employer has the right to dispose of its business and production, so the employee has the right to accept or not to accept a job, or to quit or remain in a job once hired for it. Due process creates an imbalance of rights, this defense continues, because it restricts the freedom of the employer without restricting the freedom of the employee.

This objection lacks credibility. It supposes that the rights of employees and employers are equal when EAW prevails, but this is not the case. The principle of EAW works to the clear advantage of the owner or employer and to the clear disadvantage of the employee, because the employee's opportunity to change jobs is, other things being equal, significantly impaired when the employee is fired or demoted, while the employer's opportunity to hire is not similarly lessened. The employee's decreased opportunity to dispose of his or her labor, in other words, normally is *not* equal to the employer's decreased ability to carry on his business activities. So the operation of EAW, judged in terms of the comparative losses normally caused to employers and employees, does not treat the two, or their rights, equally.

"At will" treatment of employees is also advocated on the basis of maximizing efficiency. Unproductive or disruptive employees interfere with the business of the employer and hamper productivity. Employers must have the liberty to employ whom and when they wish. But without due process procedures in the workplace, what is to prevent an employer from making room for a grossly unqualified son-in-law by firing a good employee, for example, an action which is itself damaging to efficiency? And how inefficient *is* due process in the workplace really? Due process does not alter the employee-employer hierarchical arrangement in an organization. Due process does *not* infringe on an employer's *prima facie* right to dispose of its business or what happens in that business. The right to due process merely restricts the employer's alleged right to treat employees arbitrarily. Moreover, would not knowledge that employees are protected against arbitrary treatment go some way toward boosting employee morale? And will anyone seriously suggest that employee morale and employee efficiency are unrelated? In spite of the fears of some employers, due process does not require that employees never be dismissed on grounds of their inefficiency. Due process merely requires that employees have a hearing and an objective evaluation before being dismissed or demoted.

Finally, proponents of EAW will argue as follows. Ours is a free-market economy, they will say, and government should keep out of the economy. To heed the call for legally mandated due process in the workplace, which is what most critics of EAW seek, is to interfere with the free enterprise system. The government and the courts should leave employees and employers to work out matters on their own. Employees have the freedom to quit their jobs "at will." Therefore, the freedom of the employer to fire "at will" should be protected.

This is a peculiar defense. The plain fact is that employers, at least when they have the status of corporations, have not been reluctant to involve the government and the courts in the name of protecting *their* interests. The courts have recognized the right of corporations to due process while by and large upholding the principle of EAW for employees in the workplace. This at least appears to contravene the requirement of universality. . . . For if corporations have a moral right to be treated fairly, and this moral right grounds legal rights to due process for them, then one would naturally expect that employees would also have this moral right, and that the law should protect employees by requiring fair grievance procedures in the workplace, including, in particular, legal protection against arbitrary dismissals or demotions. Yet the sit-

uation is not as expected. *Employers* have a legally protected right to due process. Employees hired "at will" do *not*. The universality we expect and require in the case of moral rights is missing here.

The difference in the status of employers and employees under the law is defended by the courts by the claim that corporations, all of which have state charters, are "public entities" whose activities are "in the public interest." Employees, on the other hand, are not public entities, and, at least in private places of employment, the work they perform is, so the courts imply, *not* in the public interest. Now there are celebrated problems about conceiving of corporations as public entities, and one might want to contest this defense of EAW by challenging the obscurity of the difference on which it is based. The challenge we should press in this essay, however, is not that the distinction between what is and what is not a public entity is too obscure. It is that the distinction is not relevant. The *moral* importance of due process—of being guaranteed honest attempts at fair, impartial treatment—has nothing to do with who is or is not a public entity. Fundamentally, it has to do with the rights of the private citizen. The right to due process is the right to a fair hearing when the acts or accusations of others hold the promise of serious harm being done to a person who does not deserve it. To deny due process of employees in the workplace, given the *prima facie* harm that is caused by dismissal or demotion, and given that those who are harmed in these ways may not deserve it, is tantamount to claiming that *only some* persons have this right. Such a conclusion conflicts with the view, widely held in our society, that due process is a *moral* right, one that is possessed by *everyone* in *all* circumstances.

To make what is an obvious point, due process is an essential political right in any society that respects just treatment of every person. When people who do not deserve it are put at risk of being significantly harmed by the arbitrary decisions of others, the persons put at risk ought to be protected. Indeed, if those who make decisions are powerful, and those who are the recipients of these decisions are, by comparison, both weak and in danger of significant harm, then we must insist *all the more* on measures to protect the weak against the strong. Paradoxically, therefore, precisely in those cases where workers are individually weak—precisely, that is, in those areas where EAW prevails—is where it should not. Thus, the democratic political ideal of fairness is threatened if the principle of EAW is allowed.

There is, then, for the reasons given, a very strong presumptive case to be made against EAW and in favor of the right of employees to impartial grievance procedures in the workplace, independently of the presence of a contractual guarantee of such procedures. Let us give a summary statement of the right.

> Every person has a right to a public hearing, peer evaluation, outside arbitration or some other mutually agreed upon grievance procedure before being demoted, unwillingly transferred or fired.

The arguments given in favor of recognizing the right of employees to due process in the workplace were characterized as being strong presumptive arguments. It was not contended that the reasoning given "proves" this right conclusively. Rather, the arguments collectively provide a set of reasons that make it logical to recognize this right, while allowing that objections might be raised that show that there are better reasons against recognizing the right to due process in the workplace.

According to strong advocates of employee rights, the right to due process does not go far enough. It does not give an employee much in the way of *rights*. It simply precludes dismissal without a formal hearing. However, the worker's right to due process would, if appropriately institutionalized, make progress in the area of employee rights. This is because due process helps to prevent arbitrary treatment of persons in the workplace by making the cause and reason for the employee treatment public and by guaranteeing the opportunity to appeal. Respect for the rights of employees as persons will not be satisfied with anything less, even if it is true, as some contend, that genuine respect requires much more.

CONCLUSION: GUARANTEEING RIGHTS IN EMPLOYMENT

The widespread and persistent nonrecognition of employee rights in this country is inconsistent with the primary importance our nation places on the rights of the individual. This non-recognition remains one of the most questionable elements in the political and economic structure of our society. If the arguments in this essay are sound, standardly accepted individual rights need to be recognized and honored in the workplace. The rights to due process . . . are moral rights honored politically in public life. To deny them a place in the workplace is to assume that employer rights or economic interests always take precedence over the rights of employees. Neither assumption is tenable.

How does one institutionalize the recognition of rights in employment? In many European countries employee rights are recognized by law and enforced by the government. In West Germany, for example, after a trial period, employees acquire a right to their jobs. Persons may be dismissed for job-related negligence, absences, or disruptive and criminal activities, but the grounds for dismissal must be documented and hearings must be conducted before an employee can be fired. The United States is the only major industrial nation that offers little legal protection of the rights of workers to their jobs. It has been suggested that what is needed in this country is statutory protection for employees against unjust firing, an idea that embodies some of the principles of the German model. It has been further suggested that this statutory protection should include rights to expenses incurred in finding a new job, and rights to back pay for those unjustly dismissed.[4]

A second fruitful way to institutionalize recognition of employee rights is through written contracts between employers and employees, contracts that state the exchange agreement, the rights of each party, and the means for enforcing these rights (for example, arbitration, peer review, or outside negotiators). If properly done, such contracts could be relied upon to help give meaning to the sometimes loose talk about the moral rights of each party and would help settle, without the intervention of the courts, many disagreements about employee *and* employer rights.

A third, most propitious and less coercive way to institutionalize recognition of employee rights is simply for employers to do this voluntarily. This suggestion is not as preposterous as it may seem. Increasingly, employees are demanding rights in the workplace. Correspondingly, employers are beginning to recognize the expediency and, sometimes, the fairness of such employee demands. And the courts are beginning to take interest in employee rights. There is an obvious way for employers to avoid "coercive intervention" by government and the courts. This is for employers *voluntarily* to institute programs that respect and protect employee rights on their own.

There are many employee rights that remain to be considered in another essay. The rights to work safety, information, and participation in management decision-making, for example, are essential for employee autonomy and job development. And the question of meaningful work cannot be dismissed if employees are to be considered as autonomous individuals. . . . The continuation of a private free enterprise economy set within a democratic free community where individual rights are viewed as fundamental requires that employee rights be fully and fairly recognized *and* protected in the workplace.

NOTES*

1. H. G. Wood, *A Treatise on the Law of Master and Servant* (Albany, N.Y.: John D. Parsons, Jr., 1877), p. 134.

2. Lawrence E. Blades, "Employment at Will versus Individual Freedom: On Limiting the Abusive Exercise of Employer Power," *Columbia Law Review* 67 (1967), p. 1405, quoted from *Payne v. Western,* 81 Tenn. 507 (1884), *Hutton v. Watters,* 132 Tenn. 527, S.W. 134 (1915).

3. Eric Mack, "Natural and Contractual Rights," *Ethics* 87 (1977), pp. 153–59.

4. Clyde W. Summers, "Individual Protection Against Unfair Dismissal: Time for a Statute, "*Virginia Law Review* 62 (1976), pp. 481–532.

*Some notes have been deleted and the remaining ones renumbered.—ED.

READING 5.3 RIGHTS IN THE WORKPLACE: A NOZICKIAN ARGUMENT
Ian Maitland

ABSTRACT. There is a growing literature that attempts to define the substantive rights of employees in the workplace, a.k.a. the duties of employers toward their employees. Following Nozick, this article argues that—so long as there is a competitive labor market—to set up a class of moral rights in the workplace invades workers' rights to freely choose the terms and conditions of employment they judge best.

There is a growing literature that attempts to define the substantive rights of workers in the workplace, a.k.a. the duties of employers toward their workers. Thus it has been proposed that employers have (at least *prima facie*) duties to provide workers with meaningful/fulfilling/self-actualizing work, some degree of control over work conditions, advance notice of plant closures or layoffs, due process before dismissal, etc. (See, for example, Goldman, 1980; Schwartz, 1984; Donaldson, 1982; Werhane, 1985).

The argument of this paper is that in a competitive labor market these standards are superfluous and, indeed, may interfere with workers' rights to freely choose their terms of employment. Furthermore, these supposed moral rights in the workplace may come at the expense of non-consenting third parties—like other workers or consumers.

NOZICK ON MEANINGFUL WORK

Since my argument basically extends Nozick's (1974, pp. 246 ff) discussion of meaningful work, let us start with that. Assuming that workers wish to have meaningful work, how does and could capitalism respond? Nozick notes that if the productivity of workers *rises* when the work tasks are segmented so as to be more meaningful, then individual employers pursuing profits will reorganize the production process in such a way out of simple self-interest. Even if productivity were to remain the same, competition for labor will induce employers to reorganize work so as to make it more meaningful.

From *Journal of Business Ethics* 8 (1989): 951–954. © 1989 Kluwer Academic Publishers. Reprinted by permission of Kluwer Academic Publishers.

Accordingly, Nozick says, the only interesting case to consider is the one where meaningful work leads to reduced efficiency. Who will bear the cost of this lessened efficiency? One possibility is the employer. But the individual employer who unilaterally assumes this cost places himself at a competitive disadvantage and eventually—other things equal—will go out of business. On the other hand, if *all* employers recognize their workers' right to meaningful work (and if none cheats), then consumers will bear the cost of the industry's reduced efficiency. (Presumably, too, we would have to erect trade barriers to exclude the products of foreign producers who do not provide their workers with meaningful work, otherwise they would drive the domestic industry out of business.)

What about the workers? If they want meaningful work, they will presumably be willing to give up something (some wages) to work at meaningfully segmented jobs:

> They work for lower wages, but they view their total work package (lower wages plus the satisfactions of meaningful work) as more desirable than less meaningful work at higher wages. They make a trade-off. . . .

Nozick observes that many persons make just such trade-offs. Not everyone, he says, wants the same things or wants them as strongly. They choose their employment on the basis of the overall package of benefits it gives them.

THE MARKET FOR MEANINGFUL WORK

Provided that the firm's lessened efficiency is compensated for by lower wages, then the employer should be indifferent between the two packages (meaningful work at lower wages or less meaningful work at higher wages). Indeed, if workers prize meaningful work highly, then they might be prepared to accept *lower* wages than are necessary simply to offset the firm's lower productivity. In that case, entrepreneurial employers seeking higher profits should be expected to offer more meaningful work: they will, by definition, reduce labor costs by an amount greater than the output lost because of less efficient (but more meaningful) production methods. In the process, they will earn higher profits than other firms (Frank, 1985, pp. 164–5).

In other words, there is a market for meaningful work. The employer who can find the combination of pay and meaningful work that matches workers' desires most closely will obtain a competitive advantage. Thus Goldman (1980, p. 274) is wrong when he claims that "profit maximization may . . . call . . . for reducing work to a series of simple menial tasks." On the contrary, profit maximization creates pressures on employers to offer workers meaningful work up to the point where workers would prefer higher pay to further increments of meaningfulness. Goldman's claim holds only if we assume that workers place no value at all on the intrinsic rewards of their work.

To "legislate" moral rights in the workplace to a certain level of meaningfulness, then, would interfere with workers' rights to determine what package of benefits they want.

EXTENDING THE LOGIC (1): EMPLOYMENT AT WILL

In her discussion of employment at will (EAW), Werhane (1985, p. 91) says "[i]t is hard to imagine that rational people would agree in advance to being fired arbitrarily in an employment contract." According to her estimate, only 36% of the workforce is covered by laws or contracts which guarantee due process procedures with which to appeal dismissal. Werhane regards EAW as a denial of moral rights of employees in the workplace.

But, is it inconceivable that a rational worker would voluntarily accept employment under such conditions? Presumably, if the price is right, some workers will be willing to accept the greater insecurity of EAW. This may be particularly true, for example, of younger, footloose and fancy-free workers with marketable skills. It is also likely to be truer in a metropolitan area (with ample alternative employment opportunities) than a small town and when the economic outlook is good.

Likewise, some employers may value more highly the unrestricted freedom to hire and fire (smaller businesses, for example) and may be willing to pay higher wages for that flexibility. There may be other employers—larger ones in a position to absorb the administrative costs or ones with more stable businesses—who will find it advantageous to offer guarantees of due process in return for lower wages. Such guarantees are also more likely to be found where employees acquire firm-specific skills and so where continuity of employment is more important (Williamson, 1975).

According to this logic, wage rates should vary inversely with the extent of these guarantees, other things equal. In other words, workers purchase their greater security in the form of reduced wages. Or, put another way, some firms pay workers a premium to induce them to do without the guarantees.

If employers were generally to heed business ethicists and to institute workplace due process in cases of dismissals—and to take the increased costs or reduced efficiency out of workers' paychecks—then they would expose themselves to the pirating of their workers by other (less scrupulous?) employers who would give workers what they wanted instead of respecting their rights.

If, on the other hand, many of the workers not currently protected against unfair dismissal would in fact prefer guarantees of workplace due process—*and* would be willing to pay for it—then such guarantees would be an effective recruiting tool for an entrepreneurial employer. That is, employers are driven by their own self-interest to offer a package of benefits and rights that will attract and retain employees. If an employer earns a reputation for treating workers in a high-handed or inconsiderate way, then he (or she) will find it more difficult (or more expensive) to get new hires and will experience defections of workers to other employers.

In short, there is good reason for concluding that the prevalence of EAW does accurately reflect workers' preferences for wages over contractually guaranteed protections against unfair dismissal. (Of course, these preferences may derive, in part, from most workers' perception that their employers rarely abuse EAW anyway; if abuses were widespread, then you would expect the demand for contractual guarantees to increase.)

EXTENDING THE LOGIC (2): PLANT CLOSURE/LAYOFF NOTIFICATION

Another putative workplace right is notice of impending layoffs or plant closures. The basis for such a right is obvious and does not need to be rehearsed here. In 1988 Congress passed plant-closing notification provisions that mandate 60-days notice. Earlier drafts of the legislation had provided for 6 months' advance notification.

But the issue of interest here is employers' moral responsibilities in this matter. The basic argument is by now familiar: if employers have not universally provided guarantees of advance notice of layoffs, that reflects employers' and workers' choices. Some workers are willing to trade off job security for higher wages; some employers (e.g., in volatile businesses) prefer to pay higher wages in return for the flexibility to cut costs quickly. If employers have generally underestimated the latent demand of workers for greater security (say, as a result of the graying of the baby boomers), then that presents a profit opportunity for alert employers. At the same (or lower) cost to themselves, they should be able to put together an employment package that will attract new workers.

A morally binding workplace "right" to X days' notice of a layoff would preempt workers' and employers' freedom to arrive at an agreement that takes into account their own particular circumstances and preferences. In Nozick's aphorism, the "right" to advance notice may prohibit a capitalist act between consenting adults.

It would mean, for example, that workers and managers would be (morally) barred from agreeing to arrangements that might protect workers' jobs by enhancing a firm's chances of survival. This might be the case if, say, the confidence of creditors or investors would be strengthened by knowing that the firm would be free to close down its operations promptly if necessary.

Likewise, the increased expenses associated with a possible closure might deter firms from opening new plants in the first place—especially in marginal areas where jobs are most needed. In that case workers won't enjoy the rights due them in the workplace because there won't be any workplace. As McKenzie (1981, p. 122) has pointed out, "[r]estrictions on plant closings are restrictions on plant openings."

The effects of rights to notice of layoffs are not limited to the workers. If resources are diverted from viable segments of a (multiplant) firm in order to prolong the life of the plant beyond its useful economic life, then the solvency of the rest of the firm may be jeopardized (and so too the jobs of other workers).

If the obstacles to plant shutdowns are serious enough and if firms are prevented from moving to locations where costs are lower, then (as McKenzie, p. 120, points out) "Workers generally must pay higher prices for the goods they buy. Further, they will not then have the opportunity of having paying plants moving into their areas. . . ." And if such restrictions reduce the efficiency of the economy as a whole (by deterring investment, locking up resources in low-productivity, low-wage sectors of the economy), then all workers and consumers will be losers. Birch (1981, p. 7) has found that job creation is positively associated with plant closures: "The reality is that our most successful areas [at job creation] are those with the highest rates of innovation and failure, not the lowest." Europe has extensive laws and union agreements that make it prohibitively expensive to close plants, order layoffs or even fire malingerers and, not coincidentally, it has barely added a single job in the aggregate in the 1980's (as of 1987). Europe's persistent high unemployment is usually attributed to such "rigidities" in its labor market—what the London *Economist* picturesquely terms "Eurosclerosis."

It may be objected by some that workers' "rights claims cannot be overridden for the sake of economic or general welfare" (Werhane, 1985, p. 80; see also Goldman, p. 274). This is probably not the place to debate rights vs. utilities, but this discussion raises the question of whether workplace rights may sometimes violate the rights of third parties (other workers, consumers).

RESPECTING WORKERS' CHOICES

The argument of this paper has been that to set up a class of moral rights in the workplace may invade a worker's right to freely choose the terms and conditions that he (or she) judges are the best for him. The worker is stuck with these rights no matter whether he values them or not; they are inalienable in the sense that he may not trade them off for, say, higher wages. *We* might not be willing to make such a trade, but if we are to respect the worker's autonomy, then *his* preferences must be decisive.

Along the way the paper has tried to indicate how competition between employers in the labor market preserves the worker's freedom to choose the terms and conditions of his employment within constraints set by the economy. This competition means that employers' attempts to exploit workers (say, by denying them due process in the workplace without paying them the "market rate" for forgoing such protections) will be self-defeating because other would-be employers will find it profitable to bid workers away from them by offering more attractive terms. This point bears repeating because many of the accounts of rights in the workplace seem to assume pervasive market failure which leaves employers free to do pretty much what they want. Any persuasive account of such rights has to take into account the fact that employers' discretion to unilaterally determine terms and conditions of employment is drastically limited by the market.

REFERENCES

Birch, David: 1981, "Who creates jobs?," *Public Interest* (vol. 65), fall.

Donaldson, Thomas: 1982, *Corporations and Morality* (Prentice Hall, Englewood Cliffs, N.J.).

Frank, Robert: 1985, *Choosing the Right Pond* (Oxford University Press, New York).

Goldman, Alan: 1980, "Business ethics: profits, utilities, and moral rights," *Philosophy and Public Affairs* 9, no. 3.

McKenzie, Robert: 1981, "The case for plant closures," *Policy Review* 15, winter.

Nozick, Robert: 1974, *Anarchy, State and Utopia* (Basic Books, New York).

Schwartz, Adina: 1984, "Autonomy in the workplace," in Tom Regan, ed., *Just Business* (Random House, N.Y.).

Werhane, Patricia H.: 1985, *Persons, Rights and Corporations* (Prentice Hall, N.Y.).

Williamson, Oliver E.: 1975, *Markets and Hierarchies* (Free Press, N.Y.).

READING 5.4 PRACTICES OF SUCCESSFUL ORGANIZATIONS: EMPLOYMENT SECURITY
Jeffrey Pfeffer

I extract from various studies, related literature, and personal observation and experience a set of seven dimensions that seem to characterize most if not all of the systems producing profits through people.

1. Employment security.

2. Selective hiring of new personnel.

3. Self-managed teams and decentralization of decision making as the basic principles of organizational design.

4. Comparatively high compensation contingent on organizational performance.

5. Extensive training.

6. Reduced status distinctions and barriers, including dress, language, office arrangements, and wage differences across levels.

7. Extensive sharing of financial and performance information throughout the organization.

This list is somewhat shorter than my earlier list of sixteen practices describing "what effective firms do with people,"[1] for two reasons. First, this list focuses on basic dimensions, some of which, such as compensation and reduction of status differences, have multiple components that were previously listed separately. Second, some of the items on the previous list have more to do with the ability to implement high performance work practices—such as being able to take a long-term view and to realize the benefits of promoting from within—than with describing dimensions of the practices themselves. It is, however, still the case that several of the dimensions of high performance work arrangements listed, for instance employment security and high pay, appear to fly in the face of conventional wisdom. This chapter outlines these practices, provides examples to illustrate both their implementation and their impact, and explains their underlying logic. In subsequent chapters, I will take on the task of challenging prevailing conventional wisdom

about how to manage the employment relationship that is inconsistent with high commitment management practices.

EMPLOYMENT SECURITY

In an era of downsizing and rightsizing—or, as Donald Hastings, CEO of Lincoln Electric, called it in a speech to the Academy of Management in 1996,"dumbsizing"—how can I write about employment security as a critical element of high performance work arrangements? First, because it is simply empirically the case that most research on the effects of high performance management systems have incorporated employment security as one important dimension in their description of these systems. That is because "one of the most widely accepted propositions . . . is that innovations in work practices or other forms of worker-management cooperation or productivity improvement are not likely to be sustained over time when workers fear that by increasing productivity they will work themselves out of their jobs."[2]

This was recognized long ago by Lincoln Electric, the successful arc welding and electric motor manufacturer that has dominated its markets for decades. Years ago, it began offering guaranteed employment to workers after two (and now three) years on the job. It has not had a layoff since 1948. Nor is it the case that this is just because the company has never faced hard times. In the early 1980s, a recession and high interest rates caused Lincoln's domestic sales to fall about 40 percent over an eighteen-month period. Nevertheless, it did not resort to layoffs. One thing the company did to avoid laying off people was to redeploy them. Factory workers who had made Lincoln's products were put in the field with the task of selling them, in the process actually increasing Lincoln's market share and penetration. Over the years, Lincoln has enjoyed gains in productivity that are far above those for manufacturing as a whole, and its managers believe that the assurance workers have that innovations in methods will not cost them or their colleagues their jobs has significantly contributed to these excellent results. Similarly, when General Motors wanted to implement new work arrangements in its innovative Saturn plant in the 1990s, it guaranteed its people job security except in the most extreme circumstances. When New United Motors was formed to operate the Fremont automobile assembly plant, it offered its people job security. How else could it ask for flexibility and cooperation in becoming more efficient and productive?

Many additional benefits follow from employment assurances besides workers' free contribution of knowledge and their efforts to enhance productivity. One advantage to firms is the decreased likelihood that they will lay off employees during downturns. How is this a benefit to the firm? In the absence of some way of building commitment to retaining the work force—either through pledges about employment security or through employment obligations contractually negotiated with a union—firms may lay off employees too quickly and too readily at the first sign of financial difficulty. This constitutes a cost for firms that have done a good job selecting, training, and developing their work force: Layoffs put important strategic assets on the street for the competition to employ. When a colleague and I interviewed the Vice President for People at Southwest Airlines, she noted that the company had never had a layoff or furlough in an industry where such events were common. When we asked why, she replied, "Why would we want to put our best assets, our people, in the arms of the competition?" Seeing its people as strategic assets rather than as costs, Southwest has pursued a careful growth strategy that avoided overexpansion and subsequent cuts in personnel.

Employment security policies will also lead to more careful and leaner hiring, because the firm knows it cannot simply let people go quickly if it has overestimated its labor demand. Leaner staffing can actually make the work force more productive, with fewer people doing more work. The people are often happy to be more productive because they know they are helping to ensure a result that benefits them—having a long-term job and a career. Furthermore, employment security maintained over time helps to build trust between people and their employer, which can lead to more cooperation, forbearance in pressing for wage increases, and better

spirit in the company. Herb Kelleher, the CEO of Southwest, has written:

> Our most important tools for building employee partnership are job security and a stimulating work environment. . . . Certainly there were times when we could have made substantially more profits in the short term if we had furloughed people, but we didn't. We were looking at our employees' and our company's longer-term interests. . . . [A]s it turns out, providing job security imposes additional discipline, because if your goal is to avoid layoffs, then you hire very sparingly. So our commitment to job security has actually helped us keep our labor force smaller and more productive than our competitors'.[3]

For organizations without the strategic discipline or vision of Southwest, a guarantee of employment security can help the firm avoid making a costly decision to lay people off that has short-term benefits and long-term costs.

If you want to see just how costly such layoff decisions can be, consider Silicon Valley. Executives from the semiconductor and electronics industries often write newspaper and magazine articles and testify before Congress in favor of permitting immigration of skilled workers. These executives favor immigration because they manage companies that are frequently short of necessary talent. The executives complain about their difficulty in recruiting qualified personnel in their expanding industry.

What you don't see in their articles or testimony, but what you will find if you look at newspapers from a few years ago, is that many of these very same firms laid off engineers, technicians, and other skilled workers in some instances just two or three years—or even less—before subsequently complaining about labor scarcity. Think about it. My friends in the valley have perfected the art of buying high and selling low. When times are tough in the industry, common sense suggests that that is exactly the time to recruit and build your work force. Competition for talented staff will obviously be less, and salaries need not be bid up in attempts to lure people from their existing jobs. By hiring when times are poor and developing a set of policies, including assurances that people will be retained, a firm can become an employer of choice, and the organization will not have to enter the labor market at its very peak to acquire the neces-sary work force. Instead, many firms do exactly the opposite. They lay people off in cyclical downturns and then, when the entire industry is booming and staff is scarce, they engage in often fruitless bidding contests to rehire the skills that they not that long ago sent packing.

Employment security can confer yet another benefit, in that it encourages people to take a longer-term perspective on their jobs and organiza-tional performance. In a study of the financial per-formance of 192 banks, John Delery and Harold Doty observed a significant relationship between employment security and the bank's return on assets, an important measure of financial perfor-mance: "The greater the employment security given to loan officers, the greater the returns to banks."[4] Why might this be? In a bank that hires and lays off loan officers quickly to match economic fluctua-tions, the typical loan officer will worry only about booking loans—just what they have typically been rewarded for doing. With employment security and a longer-term perspective on the job, the bank offi-cer may be more inclined to worry as well about the repayment prospects of the loan and about building customer relationships by providing high levels of service. Although a specific loan officer's career may prosper by being a big loan producer and moving quickly from one bank to another, the bank's profitability and performance are undoubt-edly enhanced by having people who take both a longer-term and a more comprehensive view of their jobs and of the bank's financial performance. This is likely to occur, however, only with the prospect of long-term continuity in the employ-ment relationship.

The idea of employment security does not mean that the organization retains people who don't perform or work effectively with others—that is, performance does matter. Lincoln Electric has very high turnover for employees in their first few months on the job, as those who don't fit the Lincoln culture and work environment leave. Southwest will fire people who don't provide the level of customer service the firm is well-known for delivering and don't want to improve. Employment security means that employees are not quickly put on the street for things, such as economic down-turns or the strategic mistakes of senior manage-ment, over which they have no control. The policy

focuses on maintaining total employment, not on protecting individuals from the consequences of their individual behavior on the job.

The idea of providing employment security in today's competitive world seems somehow anachro-nistic or impossible and very much at variance with what most firms seem to be doing. But employ-ment security is fundamental to the implementation of most other high performance management practices, such as selective hiring, extensive training, information sharing, and delegation. Companies are unlikely to invest the resources in the careful screening and training of new people if those people are not expected to be with the firm long enough for it to recoup these investments. Similarly, delegation of operating authority and the sharing of sensitive performance and strategic information requires trust, and that trust is much more likely to emerge in a system of mutual, long-term commitments.

THE CONSEQUENCES OF DOWNSIZING

Few systematic studies have been made of the effects of a contingent work force on organizations, so the arguments about the potential problems must necessarily rely on logic, case examples, and the limited available data. The evidence on organiza-tional downsizing, however, is much more compre-hensive. The evidence indicates that downsizing is guaranteed to accomplish only one thing—it makes organizations smaller. But, downsizing is not a sure way of increasing the stock price over a medium- to long-term horizon, nor does it necessarily pro-vide higher profits or create organizational effi-ciency or productivity.

An article examining the stock prices of down-sizing firms showed that, two years after an initial increase, the stock prices of two-thirds of the com-panies lagged behind those of comparable firms by 5 to 45 percent; in more than half of the cases, stock prices lagged the general market by amounts rang-ing from 17 to 48 percent.[5] This result is not sur-prising in the context of other studies showing that downsizing does not necessarily increase productiv-ity or profits. One methodologically sophisticated study examined the approximately 140,000 manu-facturing plants that were in operation in both 1977 and 1987 using data from the Census of

Manufacturers. Thirty-two percent of these plants had increased both productivity and employment over the decade; 26 percent had increased productivity while reducing employment (downsizing); 14 percent had experienced both declining productivity and employment; and 29 percent had increased employment while productivity had declined.[6] More than one-third of the plants that had cut employment experienced a *decrease* in productivity, while 52 percent of the plants that grew employment over the period *increased* productivity.

Survey results generally reveal a similar pattern: Sometimes downsizing is successful, sometimes not, in about equal proportions. The American Management Association has been conducting regular surveys of downsizing to assess its extensiveness, its causes, and its effects. The 1994 survey results reported that "slightly more than half of the firms that have downsized since January 1989 report an increase in operating profits following the cuts, and just over one-third said that worker productivity improved," while 86 percent of the downsizing firms reported that employee morale declined.[7] If, in fact, downsizing does not solve basic issues of profitability and productivity, it follows that firms embarking on downsizing will be led to do it repeatedly. In fact, the 1994 AMA survey reported that "downsizing tends to be repetitive: on average, two-thirds of the firms that cut jobs in a given calendar year do so again the following year.[8] Other surveys reveal similar results. A 1991 survey by Wyatt of over 1,000 firms "suggested that most restructuring efforts fall far short of the object originally established for them."[9]

In some sense, the limited economic benefits to downsizing are not that surprising. Merely cutting staff, after all, will not necessarily fix problems with the organization's products or customer service, its process technology, the time needed to get products or services to market (cycle time), or even, as it turns out, its cost structure. Second, cutting staff is an activity that is readily copied, so as a source of competitive advantage over a long period of time, its efficacy is necessarily limited. And third, downsizing has a number of often unmeasured or unanticipated costs associated with it that also limit its economic benefits. A Louis Harris Survey of more than three hundred large companies in the United States reported that in 40 percent of the companies, downsizing resulted in undesirable consequences for

the organization.[10] Many of these undesirable consequences are both quite prevalent in downsizing firms and reasonably predictable—things such as lower morale and unanticipated severance costs. What the data also show is that companies often carry out downsizing in ways that lose the wrong people or wind up simply substituting temporary or contract employees, for permanent employees that have been laid off.

Moreover, when firms lay people off, they frequently lose an important reservoir of skill and wisdom.

> John Challenger, executive vice-president of Challenger, Gray & Christmas . . . thinks that shrinking companies are at risk of "corporate Alzheimer's." He argued that the success of a firm depends not only on its skills and knowledge but also on its collective business experiences, successes and failures, culture, and vision, and numerous other intangible qualities.[11]

Because downsizing has such limited positive effects, current rhetoric praises growth. But in this as in many other areas, the gap between what firms say and what they actually do is quite wide. Even as they talk about people as key strategic assets, firms jettison these assets with abandon.

AVOIDING DOWNSIZING

Some readers will say at this point that trying to offer a secure working environment and building long-term relationships with employees is fine for companies that are doing well and are growing consistently. But what happens in times of economic stress due to the economic fluctuations that affect even the best-managed companies? What should companies do about people who, because of changes in technology or market conditions, are simply no longer needed and too expensive to maintain in the firm? In response to these points, I would say first, that downsizing and layoffs are not inevitable and that organizations do have other choices. The automobile industry, for instance, is cyclical, and most firms lay off employees during economic downturns. Employment security, however, is one of the pillars of Japanese employment systems. Consequently, even in a social environment in which employment security is much less common, Japanese automobile manufacturers operating in the United States have adhered to their employment security practices, despite their cyclical industry and their use of fewer temporary workers than in Japan, which makes work force adjustment during downturns in demand more difficult. "None of the transplants have had any layoffs of core employees to date."[12]

Firms have a number of options for avoiding layoffs, even in the face of economic pressures. Firms that view their people as assets and manage in such a way as to achieve profits through people tend to use these options. The following are the most straightforward steps for avoiding downsizing or for mitigating its impact.

- Proportionally reducing work hours [to spread] the pain of reduced employment costs across the entire work force.

- Reducing wages for all employees (possibly weighted so that the highest paid take larger pay cuts) to reduce the wage bill.

- Taking work previously outsourced (such as maintenance or subcontracting) back into the organization.

- Building inventory while demand is slack.

- Freezing hiring to avoid making overstaffing worse.

- Having people do other things, such as deferred maintenance and repair, taking training courses, and similar activities for which they were too busy when business was better.

- Refraining from hiring to meet peak demand, which makes reductions in employment almost inevitable when demand decreases.

- Encouraging people to develop new products, services, or markets so that their skills can still be used by the firm.

- Putting production or staff people into sales to build demand.

Although none of these actions is particularly novel or even difficult, nevertheless, according to the American Management Association's 1994 Survey on Downsizing, little evidence shows that firms use these methods to try to avoid layoffs or to mitigate their consequences. Rather, "voluntary separation plans show a continuous upward trend. Policies intended to 'share the pain' are generally in decline."[13] This evidence speaks to how organizations actually view downsizing and their employees. Research evidence indicates that companies that implement at least some of these suggestions can minimize downsizing. One study of 152 organizations, for instance, found that when groups of employees were covered by variable compensation, so that pay adjusted according to organizational fortunes, employment levels were less variable.[14]

Organizations can do even more creative things if they are serious about either avoiding or minimizing layoffs. Have you ever seen larger organizations laying off people in one division or unit even as they were hiring in another? This has been common in some of the regional telephone operating companies and in many other organizations. It is disheartening to employees and costly to the organization, which faces recruiting expenses in one unit even as it confronts severance costs in another. In the early 1980s when Minnesota Mining and Manufacturing faced the prospect of layoffs, it implemented a policy called the Unassigned List. Under this policy, people whose positions are eliminated have six months to find another job within the company. During that period, workers receive their salaries and benefits and even any salary increases due them. During the first four months, employees are offered a generous severance package of one and one-half weeks' pay for each year of service, and older workers are eligible for a preretirement leave package that maintains benefits and accrues service credit toward retirement. The program has been quite successful in retaining talent in the organization and in ensuring that those who leave do so with a good feeling about the organization and its willingness to honor its commitments and value its employees.

> [O]f the approximately 200 people who went through the unassigned process during the first three quarters of 1994, only one or two of them made it to day 180 without finding work. On average, those who do find other positions within 3M, which is approximately 50% of the people who go through the process, do so within three and a half months.[15]

A similar approach is used by Hewlett-Packard, another firm that tries to provide some measure of employment security. When, for instance, the company exited the fabrication business at its Loveland,

Colorado, division, leaving four hundred surplus workers, it facilitated their move to other HP facilities; provided help to employees relocating to distant facilities, giving them priority in job assignments at other H-P locations; loaned employees to divisions with short-term hiring needs; and permitted employees to be reclassified to lower pay levels and other jobs. More than 50 percent of the employees were retained in the company.[16]

Companies facing only temporary slowdowns due to seasonal fluctuations in demand or a downturn in the economy have the option of "loaning" surplus workers to nearby firms, a tactic used by Brooks Beverage Management, Inc., a soft drink bottler.[17] A company might also develop projects internally that absorb surplus labor. At Harman International, with 8,000 employees worldwide in the business of manufacturing high-quality audio and video products, productivity improvements permitted employees to produce nearly three times the dollar value that they had only three years previously. The company's chairman, Sidney Harman, stated that "We have no greater responsibility to our employees and our shareholders than to free employees from the threat of job loss, simply because they respond to our urging for greater productivity."[18] The company developed a program, called Off-Line Enterprises, that involved creating "a job bank of projects that assembly workers, or employees supporting assembly operations, could be temporarily redeployed to work on until demand for their labor picked up again."[19] Among the things the company did was to train employees to become salespeople, build products customarily purchased from outside suppliers, provide service personnel usually obtained through outside suppliers, such as security guards, and convert waste byproducts into salable products.[20]

If companies are serious about seeing their people as assets and as the key to profits and, as a consequence, about avoiding layoffs, almost anything is possible. Consider the case of Pinnacle Brands Inc., one of the top five trading-card manufacturers—and the only one that survived the baseball strike that began in 1994 and extended into the following season. With no baseball being played, not many baseball cards were sold, and the company faced a loss of $40 million in trading card revenue. What the company did was to issue a challenge to its people—if they could find a way to replace the lost

revenue, they could keep their jobs.[21] People, working in teams that often crossed departmental boundaries, figured out ways to cut costs and came up with new product ideas that replaced lost revenue. Instead of laying off 190 people, the company wound up getting through the crisis without layoffs. Thus, the fundamental question confronting organizations facing economic stress is are they serious about treating their work force as assets rather than costs?

DOWNSIZING SENSIBLY

Even for firms that need to reduce the number of employees, downsizing can be accomplished while still treating people as important assets and maintaining morale and trust. By contrast, other ways of downsizing reduce morale, diminish trust, and signal that, whatever the rhetoric, management neither respects nor values its work force.

> At Tenneco, where 1,200 employees were laid off over a six-week period, many learned of their fates when confronted by armed guards carrying boxes for them to use in clearing out their desks. At Allied Bank of Texas, department heads called meetings and then read the names of those to be laid off in front of their coworkers.[22]

Contrast those incidents . . . with the following events at [the] New Zealand Post. When the Post became a state-owned enterprise on April 1, 1987, as part of the reform of the New Zealand economy, it was expected to operate as an efficient commercial enterprise. On that date, it got a new name, a new insignia, new employment contracts, new rules, and a new CEO. At that time, the organization had about 11,500 employees and was overstaffed. It had too many small facilities and did not contract out either enough or the right activities. Like many public organizations, it had been, to some extent, used as an employer of last resort as a way of coping with unemployment. Within a few years, its employment had fallen to about 8,500, a decrease of almost 30 percent, but the reductions were accomplished without leaving the organization weakened by a distrustful and unmotivated work force.

One of the things the organization did right was to do a large number, although not all, of the eventual layoffs almost immediately. As soon as he took over the organization, Harvey Parker, the managing director at the time, announced a 20 percent across the board budget cut and let the individual managers figure out how to make the cuts. This step got a lot of the pain out of the way as well as communicating that change was necessary. In contrast, New Zealand Telecom, created at the same time, waited some eighteen months before taking any initiatives to change the organization. The *Post* also shared a lot of budgetary and financial information with its people and established clear targets and goals, including an emphasis on customer service and productivity, that served to motivate the work force and to clarify what was needed and why.

Unfortunately, many organizations, such as IBM, Digital Equipment, and others engage in round after round of employee layoffs. Case study evidence shows that repeated waves of downsizing make the implementation of high commitment work practices almost impossible, although a one-time downsizing does not. Continuing rounds of layoffs create uncertainty that undermines the willingness of people to change because they view "it as increasing company profits as their plant went out of business."[23] One company that experienced technological change and that made inevitable reductions in the work force suffered as, "with repeated underestimates of the required work-force reductions, workers no longer believed the projections that were made or the promise that early retirements and annual turnover would be used instead of layoffs."[24] Without credibility or trust in management, implementing high involvement work practices becomes substantially more difficult.

The New Zealand Post endeavored to treat its people, including those being laid off, well. The organization worked hard during the restructuring to place employees elsewhere in the organization. When people could not be placed elsewhere, they received handsome redundancy packages, averaging $20,000. Because about 65 percent of the employees were female, in many instances earning a second income for the family, and many of the employees of both sexes were quite senior—as most employees had worked only for the Post for their entire working careers—the organization's demography made the redundancy packages reasonably attractive. The management told the truth about what they were doing and why, and the resulting credibility helped

tremendously. But the key was that the "people went with dignity."[25] The company let staff know as far in advance as possible about departures. Unlike at those companies that announce who is laid off and then escort them out the door with guards, the Post held parties for those leaving. The organization offered assistance to individuals looking for other jobs and preparing resumes. The Post allowed the work force to identify those who might be more willing to leave—in some instances, people who weren't targeted to be laid off offered to go in place of some who had. Finally, a number of the Post managers told me that because New Zealand had a safety net—a program of income maintenance—individuals did not fear the future as much as they might otherwise have.

Another example of an organization that handled the need for layoffs sensibly is Carlton & United Breweries, a large Australian brewer. When the company confronted the fact that some of its breweries were inefficient and possibly overstaffed, it considered simply announcing a reduction in the size of the work force. But the firm had embarked on a program of work redesign that was intended to implement high performance work practices. Its managers decided that an announcement of layoffs was inconsistent with the new culture of participation and empowerment they were trying to build and would probably have adverse effects on both motivation and trust. Yet, the business necessity for doing something was real and compelling. What the company did was to go to the union that represented most of the workers in the brewery and to lay out the financial situation, providing access to any books or records that the union leaders might want to see. The company and the employee organizations then reached joint decisions about how large a reduction in staff was necessary and other ways to address the business issues. In the end, fewer layoffs were required than the company had anticipated but, more importantly, the decisions on staffing levels were made in a way that was consistent with the high commitment culture that Carlton & United was attempting to build and reinforce.

Virtually all of the things I have described that either avoid layoffs or make them less traumatic cost resources, both of time and money. Generous severance is obviously more expensive than less generous payments and giving people assistance in finding other jobs and time to do so and to say goodbye also incurs costs. Carlton & United Breweries' consultation with its work force clearly delayed the speed of adjustment in the size of its work force. I asked Elmar Toime, the current chief executive of the New Zealand Post who had come to the firm in 1987 with Harvey Parker, why the organization was willing to incur these costs. He replied that they weren't really costs at all but instead an investment in building a relationship with the remaining work force that would permit the organization to prosper in what is, after all, a people-dependent, service business. His answer reflects a time horizon and perspective that is, unfortunately, all too rare. But it reflects an approach to management that is likely to be more successful.

> Memories of how victims of reductions are treated stick in the mind of surviving employees for a long time to come. If they observe that affected employees are treated poorly—given short notice, a piddling severance, and nothing in the way of personal or career counseling—then surviving employees are bound to fear that they are next in line for arbitrary and insensitive treatment.[26]

The following list summarizes the lessons from organizations that have shed people in ways that did not destroy their culture or the commitment and motivation of those who remained.

- Reduce staff levels promptly once the decision is made to do so.

- Reduce employment levels, to the extent possible, all at once rather than in repeated waves.

- Share economic and performance data on the reasons for the downsizing.

- Provide notice of the decision.

- Involve people in the decisions on how many staff to cut and who should leave.

- Provide people with fair severance and benefits.

- Let people leave with dignity, having ceremonies or social functions to let them say goodbye.

- Provide career transition assistance, such as outplacement, career and vocational interest assessments, and so forth.

THE VOLKSWAGEN EXPERIENCE

Volkswagen presents a useful example of how to handle work force reductions. In late 1993, the company was faced with stagnating sales, extremely low profit margins, and the need to dramatically increase productivity, quality, and customer responsiveness in order to be competitive. From a level of 103,000 employees in 1993, it projected a decrease to just 71,900 by the end of 1995, a reduction of some 31,000 people or 30 percent of its work force.[27] In fact, it took actions so that it decreased employment to 91,000 people by 1996. The company, moreover, remains committed to maintaining 58 percent of its jobs within Germany, a comparatively high-wage country. Volkswagen's efforts were part of a larger cultural change at the company that involved removing layers of management, instituting teamwork, and increasing the skill level of its work force. What I want to highlight here, however, is how the company handled the downsizing issue.

It is important to note that Volkswagen began this effort with some distinct advantages.

> In introducing variable forms of employment, Volkswagen was able to build on certain stable values: a level of wages virtually unrivaled in the region, a high level of social benefits, and finally a strong sense of security—as the jobs concerned had hitherto always carried life-long guarantees. . . . All these values have made Volkswagen such an attractive employer that applicants have often tended to put greater stress on working for the company than on the type of job concerned.[28]

Volkswagen proposed reducing the average working week from 36 to 28.8 hours, with a simultaneous reduction in earnings for the entire work force. But, monthly income was not reduced as much because redistribution of other income elements brought salaries back up to near their prereduction levels, although annual income fell, on average, about 12 percent. The annual income of Volkswagen employees was comprised of several elements: "monthly salary; a special one-off annual payment amounting to 96% of a twelfth of the gross annual salary earned during the previous year; holiday pay over and above the monthly salary . . . paid on two fixed dates; a Christmas bonus calculated according to the number of years' service in the company."[29] The company took some of the once-a-year payments and distributed them equally over the twelve months, brought some negotiated raises forward, and contributed an additional 2 percent of monthly income to achieve its goal of providing workers with the same monthly income they had previously received, thus allowing them to meet their ongoing financial obligations.

The company instituted two other programs to help manage the necessary reduction in work hours. One was a "block time" program, targeted at workers between 18 and 30 years of age. The program entails a period of limited duration unemployment, during which the employee undergoes training and skills acquisition. "This model converts the 'normal' double load of work and training into a combination which allows the employee scope to work and earn money as well as to upgrade his skills over the course of the year."[30]

The company also recognized that not everyone wants to work the same number of hours throughout their working life. So, it instituted a flexible working program that entails a phased increase or decrease in working time. This program "fits with the idea of Volkswagen being a 'family.' Older employees are able to gradually withdraw from work. . . . [T]he system allows for a working week which progressively increases for freshly qualified employees and . . . is gradually reduced for older employees."[31]

Volkswagen's experiment with the four-day, shortened work week made headlines when it was announced and was not greeted by universal approval from commentators in the business press or by other executives. The change did cut personnel costs by some 15 percent. More importantly, almost half of a sample of Volkswagen employees said they were "satisfied" or "very satisfied" with the new working arrangements, which only 16.6 percent were "dissatisfied" or "very dissatisfied." And, a survey of over 1,000 people in the country at large found that the Volkswagen model was evaluated positively by 51 percent of the respondents and negatively by only 29 percent.[32]

Volkswagen is an unusual company. It is headquartered in a country with a strong union movement and with mandated codetermination. It is a large employer in that country, and its actions, such as laying off people, have important consequences for governmental expenditures or unemployment benefits. Perhaps because of these factors, or because of the character of its leadership, Volkswagen has taken a different approach to the problem of excess employees.

Throughout the world, mass unemployment has become one of the most pressing problems of modern times. The automotive industry has been hit by a crisis of restructuring and excess capacity. It would have been easy enough for Volkswagen to follow the example of many other companies and simply shed jobs. But, as "Every Job has a Face," the company therefore decided . . . to break out of the vicious circle of mass unemployment. *It is all very well for market trends, technological progress, or productivity to define personnel requirements—but these factors alone should not be allowed to dictate the nature of the solution to the problem.*[33]

Meanwhile, Volkswagen's economic recovery has continued, and its profits have increased. Its program of cultural change might not have been possible or nearly as successful without its heroic efforts to maintain its commitment to its work force. But in any event, the company followed a course of action consistent with its values and its beliefs, and it did so thoughtfully and creatively.

CONCLUSION

The two decisions considered in this chapter—where to draw the organization's boundaries or how much temporary help and contract employment to use and what implicit or explicit agreement about employment continuity to offer employees—are two of the most basic, important, and fundamental choices organizations make. Much of what else managers do with respect to managing people will be dictated by these two choices. Given that fact, the evidence we have seen about the absence of planning, thought, and evaluation given these decisions is truly startling. Firms should draw at least this lesson from the material presented here: the economic and social importance of adopting a strategic, thoughtful, and comprehensive approach to evaluating these two basic questions of outsourcing and employment security.

Making smart decisions about these issues requires in the first place that managers take a longer term view of the consequences of staffing decisions. Downsizing may cut labor costs in the short run, but it can erode both employee and eventually customer loyalty in the long run. And, most basically, these decisions need to be evaluated! Outsourcing affects more than direct labor costs and should be assessed accordingly. Managers should ask not just what people cost but what they do and what value they create for the organization. Asking about productivity and other measures of effectiveness, assessing the reactions of managers and coworkers, and evaluating the impact on customer service, broadly defined, are crucial steps for ensuring that decisions about the use of contingent workers are truly thoughtful and sound.

As you can tell, my overall judgment is that organizations, particularly in the United States where they are free of virtually any regulations or constraints on their behavior, have moved too far in undermining employment security and using contingent labor. How can I talk about employment security in the current economic environment, given the prevalence of downsizing? First, it is an empirical fact that high commitment work systems frequently include some form of employment security. . . . Second, employment security relates logically to other elements of high performance work arrangements. Employees "are more willing to contribute to improvements in the work process when they need not fear losing their own or their co-worker's jobs. Employment security contributes to training as both employer and employee have greater incentives to invest in training when they expect their relationship will endure."[34] Third, the norm of reciprocity means that employees will not commit to a firm and its success unless the firm demonstrates a reciprocal commitment to its people.

Numerous examples besides those mentioned here might be used to show the connection between people and profits and the positive effects for firms that did not turn to downsizing at the first sign of economic distress and that handled work force redundancy with care and respect. Charles Schwab, for instance, the extremely successful discount stock brokerage firm, attempts to maintain employment during the periodic downturns in the securities industry. It does so because it does not want to lose its investment in training and loyalty in a work force that it believes provides the service edge that gives it an advantage over the competition.

It is not necessary, as some of my colleagues believe, to confront the competitive environment with a new social contract and a flexible work force. "Calling a layoff at the first sign of financial stress is a little like getting a paper cut and calling the paramedics."[35] The New Zealand Post is today one of the most efficient postal systems in the world, and it is probably the only one that has actually cut the price of a stamp. It is very profitable and earns an excellent return on its invested capital. Are these results a consequence of an approach to people that states "the Post's job is to equip people with the skills to be mobile but to give them a job that makes them want to stay"?[36] In a people-dependent, service business, such an approach to employment must certainly help. As Peter Hartz, the senior personnel executive at Volkswagen, reminds us, the competitive environment defines the requirements, but each company can define the solutions. In fact, the job of leadership is precisely the crafting of creative responses to competitive conditions that build competence, capability, and commitment in people and avoid destroying organizational memory, wisdom, and loyalty.

As we have seen in this chapter, little evidence exists to support the view that downsizing solves organizational profitability or productivity problems or that a contingent work force provides much competitive leverage. On the contrary, quite a bit of good empirical data opposes both these trends. Managers must decide whether they will be swept up in the fads and rhetoric of the moment or will recognize some basic principles of management and the data consistent with them. The great irony in all of this is that at a time when most employers offered reasonably stable and secure employment, any particular firm drew little advantage from doing so—it was just one of the many. But in today's world of downsizing, outsourcing, and separating human assets from the organization, firms can gain a tremendous advantage by being different: They will attract and retain a better work force and capitalize on the skills and knowledge developed by that work force.

NOTES*

1. See chapter 2 in Jeffrey Pfeffer, *Competitive Advantage Through People: Unleashing the Power of the Work Force* (Boston: Harvard Business School Press, 1994).

2. Richard M. Locke, "The Transformation of Industrial Relations? A Cross-National Review," in *The Comparative Political Economy of Industrial Relations,* eds. Kirsten S. Wever and Lowell Turner (Madison, WI: Industrial Relations Research Association, 1995), 18–19.

3. Herb Kelleher, "A Culture of Commitment," *Leader to Leader* 1 (Spring 1997): 23.

4. John E. Delery and D. Harold Doty, "Modes of Theorizing in Strategic Human Resource Management: Tests of Universalistic, Contingency, and Configurational Performance Predictions," *Academy of Management Journal* 39 (1996): 820.

5. J. R. Dorfman, "Stocks of Companies Announcing Layoffs Fire Up Investors, But Prices Often Wilt," *The Wall Street Journal,* 10 December 1991, C1, C2.

6. Martin Neil Baily, Eric J. Bartelsman, and John Haltiwanger, "Downsizing and Productivity Growth: Myth or Reality?" working paper 4741, National Bureau of Economic Research, Cambridge, MA, May 1994, 13.

7. American Management Association, *1994 AMA Survey on Downsizing: Summary of Key Findings* (New York: American Management Association, 1994), 4.

8. Ibid., 1.

9. Wayne F. Cascio, "Downsizing: What Do We Know? What Have We Learned?" *Academy of Management Executive* 7 (1993): 97.

10. Mitchell Lee Marks, "Restructuring and Downsizing," in *Building the Competitive Workforce: Investing in Human Capital for Corporate Success,* ed. Philip H. Mirvis (New York: John Wiley, 1993), 60–94.

11. "Fire and Forget?" *The Economist,* 20 April 1996, 51.

12. Frits K. Pil and John Paul MacDuffie, "Japanese and Local Influences on the Transfer of Work Practices at Japanese Transplants," in *Proceedings of the Forty-Eighth Meeting of the Industrial Relations Research Association,* ed. Paula B. Voos (Madison, WI: Industrial Relations Research Association, 1996), 282.

13. American Management Association, 3.

14. Barry Gerhart and Charlie O. Trevor, "Employment Variability Under Different Managerial Compensation Systems," *Academy of Management Journal* 39 (1996): 1692–1712.

15. Dawn Amfuso, "3M's Staffing Strategy Promotes Productivity and Pride," *Personnel Journal* 74 (February 1995): 31.

16. G. James Francis, John Mohr, and Kelley Andersen, "HR Balancing: Alternative Downsizing," *Personnel Journal* 71 (January 1992): 71–78.

17. Valerie Frazee, "Share Thy Neighbor's Workers," *Personnel Journal* 75 (June 1996): 81–84.

18. Valerie Frazee, "Insourcing Saves Jobs at Harman," *Personnel Journal* 75 (June 1996): 85–86.

19. Ibid., 86.

20. Ibid.

21. Gillian Flynn, "A Strike Puts Employees Up to Bat," *Personnel Journal* 75 (July 1996): 71.

22. Marks, 79.

23. Clair Brown, Michael Reich, and David Stern, "Becoming a High-Performance Work Organization: The Role of Security, Employee Involvement and Training," *The International Journal of Human Resource Management* 4(1993): 271.

24. Ibid.

25. Ron Christian, New Zealand Post, interview by author, Wellington, New Zealand, 2 April 1996.

26. Marks, 79–80.

27. Peter Hartz, *The Company that Breathes* (Berlin: Springer-Verlag, 1996), 20–21.

28. Ibid., 98.

29. Ibid., 107.

30. Ibid., 110–111.

31. Ibid., 112–113.

32. Ibid., 118–119.

33. Ibid., 96; emphasis added.

34. Brown, Reich, and Stern, 249–250.

35. Jennifer J. Laabs, "Share the Pain to Share the Gain," *Personnel Journal* 75 (June 1996): 91.

36. Elmar Toime, interview by author, Wellington, New Zealand, 2 April 1996.

---

*Some notes have been deleted and the remaining ones renumbered.—ED.

READING 5.5 AN ETHICAL BASIS FOR EMPLOYEE PARTICIPATION
John J. McCall

Until recently, worker participation in corporate decision-making was a topic largely ignored in American management training and practice. Even in recent years, the attention usually given to worker participation by management theory has been confined to small-scale experiments aimed at increasing labor productivity. Little, if any, attention has been given to the possibility that there is an ethical basis for extending a right to participation to all workers.

Numerous explanations for this lack of attention are possible. One is that management sees worker participation as a threat to its power and status. Another explanation may be found in a pervasive ideology underlying our patterns of industrial organization. The ruling theory of corporate property distinguishes sharply between the decision-making rights of ownership and its management representatives on the one hand, and employee duties of loyalty and obedience on the other. The justification for that distinction lies partly in a view of the rights of property owners to control their goods and partly in a perception that nonmanagement employees are technically unequipped to make intelligent policy decisions. The perceived threat to power and this dominant ideology of employment provide for strong resistance even to a discussion of broad worker participation in corporate decisions. But perhaps as strong a source of this resistance comes from a confusion about the possible meanings of and moral justifications for worker participation. The primary aim of this essay is to clarify those meanings and justifications. If the essay is successful, it might also suggest that these sources of resistance to participation should be abandoned.

What people refer to when they use the term *participation* varies widely. We can get a better grasp of that variation in meaning if we recognize that it is a function of variety in both the potential issues available for participatory decisions and the potential mechanisms for that decision-making. The potential issues for participation can be divided into three broad and not perfectly distinct categories.

First, employees could participate in decisions involving shop-floor operations. Characteristic shop-floor issues are the schedule of employee work hours, assembly line speed, and the distribution of work assignments. Second, employees could participate in decisions that have been the traditional prerogative of middle management. Issues here are hiring or discharge decisions, grievance procedures, evaluations of workers or supervisors, the distribution of merit wage increases, and so on. Finally, employees might participate in traditional board-level decisions about investment, product diversification, pricing or output levels, and the like. Simply put, employee participation might refer to participation in decision-making over issues that arise at any or all levels of corporate policy.

The mechanisms for participation vary as widely as do the potential issues. These participatory mechanisms vary both in terms of their location within or outside the corporation and in terms of the actual power they possess. For instance, some see employees participating in the shaping of corporate policy by individual acceptance or rejection of employment offers and by collective bargaining through union membership. These mechanisms are essentially external to the particular business institution. Internal mechanisms for participation in corporate policy-making include employee stock ownership plans, "quality circle" consulting groups, and bodies that extend employees partial or total effective control of the enterprise. Employee participation through stock ownership might exist either through union pension fund holdings or through individual employee profit sharing plans.

Internal participation can also exist in ways more directly related to the day-to-day functioning of the corporation. For example, quality circle participation is a recent adaptation of some Japanese approaches to the management of human resources. Employees in these quality circles are invited to participate in round-table discussions of corporate concerns such as improving productivity. It is important to note that these quality circle groups are advisory only; their function within the corporation is consultative and they have no actual authority to implement decisions.

Distinct from these advisory bodies are those mechanisms by which employees share in the actual power to make corporate policy. Among the mechanisms for such partial effective control are worker committees with authority to govern selected aspects of the work environment or worker representatives on the traditional organs of authority. An example of the former would be an employee-run grievance board; an example of the latter received significant notice in the United States when United Auto Workers' President Douglas Fraser assumed a seat on Chrysler's Board of Directors. Either of these mechanisms provides for only partial control, since one has a highly defined area of responsibility and the other provides employees with only one voice among many.

A final form of participation provides employees with full control of the operations of the corporation. Examples of this extensive participation are rare in North America, although some Midwest farm and Northwest lumber cooperatives are organized in this way.

Note that these varied mechanisms combine with the potential issues for participation in numerous ways. We might see union collective bargaining influence merit wage increases or working schedules; worker committee mechanisms of participation might deal with flexible work assignments or with evaluation of supervisors. This brief survey should indicate that discussions of employee participation must be pursued with care, since arguments criticizing or supporting participation might be sufficient grounds for drawing conclusions about one form of participation but not sufficient grounds for conclusions about other forms. That caution brings us to the second major aim of this essay—the clarification of moral arguments in favor of broad extensions of worker rights to participate in corporate decisions. Five justifications, or arguments, for participation will be sketched. Comments about the issues or mechanisms required by each justification will follow each argument sketch.

ARGUMENT 1

The first two ethical justifications for employee participation are applications of points developed in Part I of this text. The first takes its cue from the fundamental objective of any morality—the impartial promotion of human welfare. That requirement of impartiality can be understood as a requirement that we try to guarantee a fair hearing for the interests of every person in decisions concerning policies that centrally affect their lives. Certainly, many decisions at work can have a great impact on the lives of employees. For instance, an employee's privacy and health, both mental and physical, can easily be threatened in his or her working life. Morality, then, requires that there be some attempt to guarantee fair treatment for workers and their interests. We might attempt to institutionalize that guarantee through government regulation of business practices. However, regulation, while helpful to some degree, is often an insufficient guarantee of fair treatment. It is insufficient for the following reasons:

1. Regulation, when it does represent the interests of workers, often does so imprecisely because it is by nature indirect and paternalistic.

2. Business can frequently circumvent the intent of regulations by accepting fines for violations or by judicious use of regulatory appeal mechanisms.

3. Perhaps most importantly, corporate interests can emasculate the content of proposed legislation or regulation through powerful lobbying efforts.

So it seems that an effective guarantee that worker interests are represented fairly requires at least some mechanisms additional to regulation.

We might avoid many of the difficulties of legislation and regulation if workers were allowed to represent their interests more directly whenever crucial corporate decisions are made. Thus, a fair hearing for workers' interests might have a more effective institutional guarantee where workers have available some mechanisms for participation in those decisions. In practice, then, morality's demand for impartiality presumptively may require worker input in the shaping of corporate policies. (This requirement is presumptive since we have not yet investigated what countervailing moral arguments might be offered by opponents of participation.) We have already seen, though, that there are numerous issues and mechanisms for such participation. We need to decide what participatory mechanisms dealing with what issues could satisfy the requirement of fairness.

Clearly, if worker interests are to be guaranteed as much fair treatment as possible, the participatory mechanisms must have actual power to influence corporate decisions. For while workers might receive fair treatment even where they lack such power, possession of real power more effectively institutionalizes a *guarantee* of fairness. Thus, internal participatory mechanisms that serve in a purely advisory capacity (for example, quality circle groups) are obviously insufficient vehicles for meeting the fairness demands of morality.

Less obvious are the weaknesses of individual contract negotiations, union membership, and stock ownership as devices for guaranteeing fairness. None of these devices, in practice, can provide enough power to protect fair treatment for workers. Individual contract decisions often find the prospective employee in a very poor bargaining position. The amount of effective power possessed through union membership varies with the changing state of the economy and with changes in particular industrial technologies. In addition, the majority of workers are not unionized; the declining proportion of union membership in the total work force now stands at about 11 percent. Stock ownership plans provide employees very little leverage on corporate decisions because, commonly, only small percentages of stock are held by workers. Moreover, all three of these participation mechanisms most often have little direct power over the important operating decisions that affect worker interests. Those decisions are usually made and implemented for long periods before contract negotiations, union bargaining, or stockholder meetings could have any chance at altering corporate policy.

Thus, a serious moral concern for fairness, a concern central to any moral perspective, presumptively requires that mechanisms for employee participation provide workers with at least partial effective control of the enterprise. Since decisions that have important consequences for the welfare of workers are made at every level of the corporation, employees ought to participate on issues from the shop floor to the boardroom. Moreover, since a balanced and impartial consideration of all interests is more probable when opposing parties have roughly equal institutional power, employees deserve more than token representation in the firm's decision-making structure. Rather, they should possess an amount of authority that realistically enables them to resist policies that unfairly damage their interests. This first moral argument, then, provides strong presumptive support for the right of employees to codetermine corporate policy.

ARGUMENT 2

The second moral argument also derives from points that were made in Part I, and its conclusions are similar to those of the preceding argument. Any acceptable moral theory must recognize the inherent value and dignity of the human person. One traditional basis for that belief in the dignity of the person derives from the fact that persons are agents capable of free and rational deliberation. We move towards respect for the dignity of the person when we protect individuals from humanly alterable interferences that jeopardize important human goods and when we allow them, equally, as much freedom from other interferences as possible. Persons with this freedom from interference are able to direct the courses of their own lives without threat of external control or coercion. (Such a view of persons provides for the moral superiority of self-determining, democratic systems of government over oppressive or totalitarian regimes.)

This moral commitment to the dignity of persons as autonomous agents has significant implications for corporate organization. Most of our adult lives are spent at our places of employment. If we possess no real control over that portion of our lives because we are denied the power to participate in forming corporate policy, then at work we are not autonomous agents. Instead we are merely anonymous and replaceable elements in the production process, elements with a moral standing little different from that of the inanimate machinery we operate. This remains true of our lives *at* work even if we have the opportunity to change employers. (Many workers do not have even that opportunity, and if they did it would be of little consequence for this issue, since most workplaces are similarly organized.) The moral importance of autonomy in respecting the dignity of persons should make us critical of these traditional patterns of work and should move us in the direction of more employee participation. However, since autonomy is understood as an ability to control one's activities, the preferred mechanisms of participation should allow employees real control at work. Thus, a commitment to the autonomy and the dignity of persons, just as a commitment to fairness, appears to require that workers have the ability to codetermine any policy that directs important corporate activity.

ARGUMENT 3

These first two arguments for broad worker participation rights have ended in an explicit requirement that workers have real and actual power over corporate policy. The final three arguments focus not on actual power but on the worker's *perception* of his or her ability to influence policy. All of these last arguments concern the potential for negative consequences created when workers see themselves as having little control over their working lives.

The third argument warns that workers who believe themselves powerless will lose the important psychological good of self-respect.[1] Moral philosophers have contended that since all persons should be treated with dignity, all persons consequently deserve the conditions that generally contribute to a sense of their own dignity or self-worth. Psychologists tell us that a person's sense of self is to a large degree conditioned by the institutional relationships she has and the responses from others that she receives in those relationships. A person will have a stronger sense of her own worth and will develop a deeper sense of self-respect when her social interactions allow her to exercise her capacities in complex and interesting activities and when they reflect her status as an autonomous human being. Of course, in contemporary America the development of the division of labor and of hierarchical authority structures leaves little room for the recognition of the worker's autonomy or for the ordinary worker to exercise capacities in complex ways. The consequence of such work organization is the well-documented worker burnout and alienation; workers disassociate themselves from a major portion of their lives, often with the psychological consequence of a sense of their own unimportance. Contemporary American patterns of work, then, often fail to provide individuals with those conditions that foster a strong sense of self-respect; instead, they more often undermine self-respect. Numerous studies have indicated that a reversal of

these trends is possible when workers are provided greater opportunities for exercising judgment and for influencing workplace activities.

If we take seriously a demand for the universal provision of the conditions of self-respect, we ought to increase opportunities for satisfying work by allowing workers to participate in corporate policy decisions. It would seem, however, that this argument for worker participation need not conclude that workers be given actual power. All that the argument requires is that a worker's *sense* of self-respect be strengthened, and that is at least a possible consequence of participation in an advisory capacity. In fact, worker satisfaction has been shown to increase somewhat when employees are involved in Japanese-style quality circles that offer suggestions for improving production. Nor does it appear that the self-respect argument requires that workers be able to influence all aspects of corporate activity, since an increased sense of one's own significance could be had through participation only on immediate shop-floor issues.

However, we must be careful to estimate the long-range effects on worker alienation and self-respect of these less extensive forms of participation. Some evidence indicates that, over time, workers can grow more dissatisfied and alienated than ever if they perceive the participatory program as without real power or as simply a management attempt to manipulate workers for increased productivity.[2] We should consider, then, that a concern for long-run and substantial increases in self-respect might require workers to exercise some actual authority, more than a token amount, over the workplace.

ARGUMENT 4

The fourth argument supporting participation also takes its cue from the studies that show repetitive work without control over one's activities causes worker alienation. The specific consequence that this argument focuses on, however, is not a lessening of self-respect but a potential threat to the mental and physical health of workers. Certainly, everyone is now aware that alienated individuals suffer from more mental disturbances and more stress-related physical illnesses. Workers who are satisfied because they feel able to contribute to corporate policy are held to suffer from less alienation.

Since mental and physical health are undoubtedly very central human goods, there seems strong presumptive moral reason for minimizing any negative effects on them that institutional organizations might have. Since broader powers apparently help to minimize such effects, we again have an argument for an expansion of worker rights to participate in corporate decisions.

As with the self-respect argument, however, the issues and mechanisms of participation that this requires are unclear. It could be that negative health effects are minimized in the short run through advisory bodies of participation. On the other hand, minimizing threats to mental or physical well-being in the long run might require more actual authority. Which sorts of mechanisms help most is a question only further empirical research can answer. However, since we have already seen presumptive reasons for actual power to codetermine policy from the first two arguments and since that power can have positive effects on self-respect and health, we perhaps have reasons for preferring the stronger forms of participation if we are presented with a choice between alternatives.

ARGUMENT 5

The fifth argument for worker participation also derives from the purported negative consequences of hierarchical and authoritarian organizations of work. This argument, however, focuses on broader social consequences—the danger to our democratic political structures if workers are not allowed to participate in corporate decisions.[3]

Many political theorists are alarmed by contemporary voter apathy. They worry that with that apathy the political process will be democratic in name only, and that the actual business of government will be controlled by powerful and private economic interests. Reversing this trend that threatens democratic government demands that individual citizens become more involved in the political process. However, increased individual involvement is seen as unlikely unless citizens believe themselves to have political power. But an initial increased sense of one's own political power does not seem possible from involvement in the large macroscopic political institutions of contemporary government. Rather, involvement in smaller, more local and immediate social activities will nurture a sense of political efficacy. Since so much time and attention is devoted to one's work life, the place of employment appears a prime candidate for that training in democracy necessary for development of civic involvement. In fact, powerless and alienated workers can bring their sense of powerlessness home and offer their children lessons in the futility of involvement. Allowing those lessons to continue would only exacerbate the threat to vital democratic institutions. This fifth argument, then, sees participation at work as a necessary condition for the existence of a healthy and lasting system of democracy where citizens have the confidence to engage in self-determining political activities.

Again, since this argument focuses on the worker's perception of his or her own power, it provides presumptive support for those mechanisms that would increase both that sense of power and the tendency for political activity. Just what mechanisms these are can be open to argument. However, as before, if workers feel that their participatory mechanisms lack power, there is the danger that they will become even more cynical about their ability to influence political decisions. And since we have already seen arguments supporting participation with actual power to codetermine policy, there should be a presumption in favor of using mechanisms with real power.

SOURCES OF RESISTANCE

We have, then, five significant reasons for extending to workers a broad right to codetermine corporate policy. Now, in order to determine whether the presumption in favor of worker participation can be overridden, we need only to consider some of the common reasons for resisting this employee right to participate. Common sources of resistance to worker participation are that managers perceive it as a threat to their own status or power, that owners feel entitled to the sole control of their property, and that ordinary employees are believed incompetent to make corporate decisions. We shall consider briefly each of these sources of resistance in turn. Our evaluation of these claims will show them to be unacceptable sources of resistance when measured against the previously described ethical reasons in favor of broad participation.

First, in order for management's perception that participation threatens its power to count as an acceptable moral reason for resistance, management power must have some moral basis of its own. According to even traditional conservative theories of corporate property, management has no basic moral right of its own to control the corporation. Rather, management's authority stems from its position as an agent of the economic interests of shareholders, who are seen as the ultimate bearers of a right to use, control, or dispose of property. On the traditional theory, then, management can find a legitimate moral reason for resisting participation only if it can show that schemes of employee participation are real threats to the economic interests of shareholders. Presently, we shall refer to evidence that this case against participation cannot be supported by the available data. (Management, of course, might still resist even without a moral reason. However, such resistance can have no claim to our support; it is merely an obstacle to be overcome if there are moral reasons to support participation.)

Does participation damage the interests of ownership in a morally unacceptable way? To answer that question, we need to consider what interests ownership has and to what benefits property ownership should entitle one. In the process of confronting these issues, we will also see reasons for suspicion about claims that workers are not capable of participating in the intelligent setting of corporate policy.

In legally incorporated businesses, shareholders commonly have a monetary return on their investment as their principal desire.[4] Moreover, corporate property owners generally have surrendered their interest in day-to-day control of the corporation.[5] The usual owner interest, then, concerns the profitability of the business. Worker participation does not necessarily pose a serious threat to this interest in profit. Evidence shows that worker participation schemes often improve the economic condition of the business by increasing the interest, motivation, and productivity of employees.[6] In addition, corporations seeking qualified and motivated workers in the future might, out of self-interest, have to construct mechanisms for participation to satisfy the demands of a more slowly growing but more highly educated entry-level labor force.[7] Even when experiments at worker participation have not succeeded, the failures can often be explained by short-comings of the particular program that are not generic to all forms of participation. In fact, some of those with experience in constructing participatory work schemes believe that employees can be trained to operate most efficiently with expanded responsibilities.[8] When programs are designed carefully and when time is invested in training both former managers and employees, the competence of workers has not been seen as a crucial reason behind examples of participation's lack of success. Thus, in light of both the marked economic successes of broader worker participation programs and the apparent absence of any *generic* threats to profitability (such as employee incompetence), the economic interests of owners do not appear to provide a substantial basis for a justified resistance to an employee right to participate in corporate decision-making.

Some might object, however, on the basis that corporate property owners have other interests at stake. Many see a right to control one's goods as fundamental to the concept of property ownership, for example. Thus, they might claim that shareholders have, because of their property ownership, rights to retain control of the business enterprise even if they fail to exercise those rights on a day-to-day basis. This right to control one's property would effectively eliminate the possibility of an employee right to codetermine policy.

There are two reasons, however, to question whether a right to control property can provide a moral basis for denying workers a right to participate in corporate decisions. First, corporate property owners have been granted by society a limit on their legal liability for their property. If a legally incorporated business is sued, owners stand to lose only the value of their investment; an owner of an unincorporated business can lose personal property beyond the value of the business. Part of the motivation behind making this legal limit on liability available was that society would thereby encourage investment activity that would increase the welfare of its members.[9] It is not unreasonable to suggest that this justification for the special legal privilege requires that corporations concern themselves with the welfare of persons within the society in exchange for limited liability. Society, then, places limits on the extent to which owners can direct the uses of their corporate property. For example, society can require that corporations concern themselves with the environmental health effects of their waste disposal policies. Failure to require such concern is tantamount to allowing some to profit from harms to others while preventing those others from obtaining reasonable compensation for grievous harms. However, if the legal limitation on liability requires corporations to have some ethical concern for the welfare of others, it can also require corporations to protect the welfare of their employees. We have already seen, though, that morally serious goods are at stake when employees are unable to participate significantly in corporate decisions. Thus, if in exchange for limited liability the control of the corporation is to be limited by a concern for others, then the shareholders' interest in controlling corporate property could be limited to allow for an employee right to participate.

A second reason for rejecting the claim that an ownership right to control prohibits employee participation looks not on the legal privileges associated with corporate property but on the very concept of property itself. This argument makes points similar to ones made in the preceding paragraph, but the points apply to property whether it is incorporated or not. It is certainly true that property ownership is meaningless without some rights to control the goods owned. It is equally true, however, that no morally acceptable system of property rights can allow unlimited rights to control the goods owned. You, for example, are not allowed to do just anything you please with your car; you cannot have a right to drive it through my front porch. We accept similar restrictions on the control of business property; we prohibit people from selling untested and potentially dangerous drugs that they produce. The point of these examples is to illustrate that control of property, corporate or not, has to be limited by weighing the constraints on owners against the significance of the human goods that would be jeopardized in the absence of the constraints. Acceptable institutions of property rights, then, must mesh with a society's moral concern for protecting the fundamental human goods of all its members.

We have seen in the first part of this essay that there are significant reasons for thinking that important moral values are linked to a worker's ability to participate in corporate decision making. If control of property, personal or corporate, is to override these moral concerns, we need to be presented with an argument showing what more central goods would be jeopardized if employees were granted strong participation rights. The burden of proof, then, is on those who want to deny an employee right to codetermine corporate policy. They must show that an owner's interest in broad control of corporate policy can stand as an interest worthy of protection as a moral right even when such protection would threaten the dignity, fair treatment, self-respect, and health of workers, as well as the continued viability of a democratic polity with an actively self-determining citizenship.

SUMMARY

To summarize: We have seen that there are various understandings of worker participation. The difference between these various understandings is a function of the workplace issues addressed and the participatory mechanisms that address them. We have also seen sketches of five arguments that purport to show a moral presumption in favor of strong worker participation in the form of an ability to actually codetermine policy. We have seen, further, that some traditional sources of resistance to worker participation (a threat to management or owner prerogatives of control, a belief in the incompetence of workers, a fear that profits will suffer) are either not supported by the evidence or are incapable of sustaining a moral basis for rejecting participation. The provisional conclusion we should draw, then, is that our society ought to move vigorously in the direction of a broader authority for all workers in their places of employment.

NOTES

1. This argument has been made by Joe Grcic in "Rawls and Socialism," *Philosophy and Social Criticism* 8, no. 1 (1980), and in "Rawls' Difference Principle, Marx's Alienation and the Japanese Economy," a paper presented at the Ninth Plenary Session of Amintaphil, 1983. It is also suggested by John Cotter in "Ethics and Justice in the World of Work: Improving the Quality of Working Life," *Review of Social Economy* 40, no. 3 (1982).

2. Cf. Daniel Zwerdling, *Workplace Democracy* (New York: Harper and Row, 1980).

3. This argument is made forcefully by Carole Pateman, *Participation and Democratic Theory* (Cambridge: Cambridge University Press, 1970).

4. Of course, the matter is more complex than this simple statement indicates. Some investors might even have interests in losing money if they are attempting to avoid taxes. Others might want to guarantee that their company does not produce immoral goods (as some Dow Chemical investors claimed was the case with Dow's napalm production). Still, in most cases the primary motivation for investment is a monetary return.

5. It is, of course, not always true that shareholders surrender their interest in day-to-day control, since some corporations are headed by their principal stockholders.

6. Additional evidence is found in the experiences of the small but highly publicized experiments of Volvo and of Donnelly Mirrors, Inc. Interviews with heads of both Volvo and Donnelly can be found in *Harvard Business Review* 55, no. 4 (1977) and 55, no. 1 (1977), respectively. In West Germany, codetermination is mandated by law in some major industries that have been highly competitive with their American counterparts.

7. John Cotter, *op cit.* (note 1).

8. The Donnelly interview, *op cit.,* (note 6), and Nancy Foy and Herman Gadon, "Worker Participation: Contrasts in Three Countries," *Harvard Business Review* 54, no. 3 (1976).

9. Cf. W. Michael Hoffman and James Fisher, "Corporate Responsibility: Property and Liability," in *Ethical Theory and Business,* 1st ed., T. Beauchamp and N. Bowie, eds. (Englewood Cliffs, N.J.: Prentice-Hall, 1979), pp. 187–196.

READING 5.6 WORKPLACE REPRESENTATION OVERSEAS: THE WORKS COUNCILS STORY

Joel Rogers and Wolfgang Streeck

In the labor relations systems of most advanced countries, unions or other mechanisms of wage regulation and collective bargaining are supplemented by a "second channel" of industrial relations. This second channel consists of workplace-based institutions for worker representation and labor-management communication that have status and functions distinct from, though not necessarily in competition with, those of unions. Typically, second channel institutions benefit from statutory supports that define their rights and obligations and, not incidentally, extend their reach beyond the unionized sector.

The purpose of second channel institutions is to give workers a voice in the governance of the shop floor and the firm, and to facilitate communication and cooperation between management and labor on production-related matters, more or less free of direct distributive conflicts over wages. Where there are workplace-based unions, as in Japan, employees articulate their interests through the union, and second channel arrangements take the form of labor-management consultation committees. Where unions and collective bargaining are centralized at the national or sectoral level, outside the firm—as in the Netherlands and Germany—or where unions are weak and not widely present at the workplace—as in France and Spain—second channel functions are usually performed by what are known as *works councils.*[1]

Works councils are representative bodies elected by all workers at a particular workplace, regardless of union membership and inclusive of white-collar and many supervisory employees. They are typically statutorily "mandated" for a given class of firms, and they enjoy presumptions against their discontinuance once established.[2] The councils institutionalize rights of *collective* worker *participation,* including rights to information and consultation on the organization of production and, in some cases, formal *codetermination* in decision making.[3] Commonly, in addition to thus institutionalizing worker power-sharing in firm governance, works councils monitor and help enforce state regulation of the workplace in such areas as occupational safety and health.

The United States and United Kingdom are exceptions to this pattern of dual channels for worker representation. Apart from direct state regulation of the workplace, the formal labor relations systems in the United States and United Kingdom consist entirely of unions and collective bargaining. But while the United Kingdom still has a sizable union movement, unionism in the United States is in an advanced and possibly irreversible state of decline. Approaching the twenty-first century, the United States effectively stands alone among the developed nations, on the verge of having *no* effective system of worker representation and consultation.

There are reasons to be concerned about this. First, basic democratic ideals are compromised by the absence of collective representation for those workers who want it. Survey data indicate that some 30 to 40 million American workers without union representation desire such representation, and some 80 million workers, many of whom do not approve of unions, desire some independent collective voice in their workplace.[4] These numbers dwarf the 16 million or so members of organized labor and point to a large "representation gap" in the American workplace (Weiler, 1990; Freeman and Rogers, 1993). Second, there is good evidence that this gap harms the economy. Many studies show the critical role of effective labor relations in economic performance and the dependence of effective labor relations on worker representation.[5] Third, in many areas of public regulatory concern in the workplace—occupational safety and health, wages and hours, and work force training among them—an effective system of workplace representation appears vital to the achievement of social goals.

In this context, this chapter presents the findings of a nine-country comparative research project on works councils, the dominant second channel organization in the developed world. The discussion has two main parts. First, we provide an overview of councils, indicating their incidence and general powers, organizational character, and contributions to democracy, efficiency, and state regulation. Second, we review the experience of councils . . . in North America. A brief conclusion follows, summarizing the cross-national findings and pointing to a striking convergence among developed nations (the United States and United Kingdom excepted) in the importance they attach to their council systems.

WORKS COUNCILS: WHERE THEY ARE, HOW THEY WORK, WHAT THEY DO

Incidence and Powers

All Western European countries, except Ireland and the United Kingdom, have legislatively mandated works councils.[6] Some countries supplement these with mandatory health and safety councils; in others these functions are performed by the works councils themselves. Typically, national law requires elected works councils in establishments above a certain size; the law specifies the size and structure of the councils, rules for council elections, and other elements of procedure, and it provides enforcement mechanisms for agreements, conditions for works councilors to obtain paid time off for council activity, and sanctions against violations of specified rights.

The formal scope of issues addressed by councils varies inversely with the degree of extra firm wage setting. In Northern Europe, where unions are strong, negotiations are centralized, and legal extension of collective contracts is easy, the scope for council activity is often explicitly defined to exclude subjects dealt with by unions and employers' associations outside the individual firm. For example, the German Works Constitution Act forbids councils to bargain over basic wages and holds them legally responsible to uphold and supervise the implementation of any collective agreement applicable to their firm. Also, to emphasize the difference between unions and councils, the latter are typically placed under a legal obligation to seek cooperation with the employer. Thus Belgian law declares that works councils "exist to promote collaboration between employer and employee," and in France, where the Ministry of Labor extends collective contracts and where minimum wages are important, councils administer a firm's social funds but have little power in other areas. In contrast, where the external institutional structure is less elaborated, as in Spain, Greece, and Italy, council powers more closely resemble those of a local union. Spanish law, in fact, permits councils to bargain over wages and allows them to call strikes. In Italy, council functions are performed by union workplace organizations and their elected delegates, which for historical reasons often include workers not belonging to unions.

More important than the formal scope of permitted council activities is the *depth* of their power. The critical distinction is between councils that enjoy information and consultation rights only and those that also enjoy rights to codetermination in certain management decisions.

Information and consultation rights are universal and effectively define what is meant by a "mandated" council. Works councils laws invariably obligate employers to disclose to the council information about major new investment plans, acquisition and product market strategies, planned reorganization of production, use of technology, and so on. And council laws typically require employers to consult with the council on workplace and personnel issues, such as work reorganization, new technology acquisition, reductions or accretions to the work force, transfers of work, over-time, and health and safety. Typical of the information and consultation requirements are the provisions of the 1971 Dutch Works Council Act (Sections 31, 25):

Information: The employer must provide the council with all information which it may reasonably demand for accomplishing its task, more in particular, and at least once every year, with respect to the legal status of the firm, its financial and economic position, its long-term plans, and its social and personnel policies. . . .

Consultation: The employer must seek the council's advice with respect to decisions concerning a transfer of ownership of (parts of) the firm, merger, takeovers, plant or shop closure, major reduction, change or extension of activities, major changes in work organization, change in the location of production, the employment or lease of temporary staff, major investment, major capital loans, and assignments given to outside consultants or experts on any of the above issues. The council's advice is also needed on proposals concerning the dismissal and appointment of members of the executive board. The right of advice in matters of merger, takeovers and consultants does not apply when one of the firms involved is located outside the Netherlands.

Deeper rights to codetermination—requiring the employer to get works council approval for a decision to be "valid" or to withstand legal challenge—

complement the information and consultation rights in stronger union systems. The German case is exemplary. German works councils enjoy information rights on financial matters, and information and consultation rights on personnel planning and work reorganization. In addition, however, they have codetermination rights on such matters as principles of remuneration, introduction of new payment methods, fixing of job and bonus rates and performance-related pay, allocation of working hours, regulation of overtime and short-time working, leave arrangements, vacation plans, suggestion schemes, and the introduction and use of technical devices to monitor employees' performance (Section 87 of the Works Constitution Act). They also enjoy prescribed codetermination rights on individual staff movements, including hiring, evaluation, redeployment, and dismissal,[7] and the right to a "reconciliation of interests" between the council and the employer on a wide range of other matters bearing on the operation of the firm. The latter include those matters bearing on:

reduction of operations in or closure of the whole or important departments of the establishment; transfer of the whole or important parts of the establishment; important changes in the organization, purpose or plant of the establishment; introduction of entirely new work methods and production processes (Section 111).

In countries where councils have codetermination rights, the law provides mechanisms for resolving disputes without the use of economic force. Depending on the dispute and the country in question, such mechanisms include assignment of the dispute to a special joint grievance committee, to an outside arbitrator with binding powers, or to a labor court.

Organizational Character

If these are the formal attributes of councils, two aspects of their more substantive organizational character bear special note. The first is that councils are designed to guarantee some measure of *collective participation*. As *collective* institutions, they perform functions different from regimes in which workers express themselves as individuals. As *participatory* institutions, with obligatory status and real rights to information, consultation, and sometimes codetermination, councils are distinguished from new forms of work organization that are designed to increase, more or less contingently, the "involvement" of workers through decentralization and expansion of competence and responsibility in production tasks. While works councils may help managements implement work reorganization—or may demand such reorganization themselves—they are outside the managerial line of authority and not part of the functional organization of production. Their distinctive contribution to production decisions is based on a right to represent their constituents, not on job assignments or occupational competence. And while they make it easier for individual workers to speak up, as collective representatives they aggregate the views of workers, transforming individual views into some expression of what they take to be the interests of the work force as a whole.

As institutions of collective participation in the enterprise, works councils perform functions that unions and collective bargaining cannot easily perform, especially in the joint solution of problems and the resolution of conflicts in production. Where they are well developed, councils support collective bargaining by relieving it of tasks to which it is not well suited. By providing management and workers with a reliable channel for problem-oriented communication, they also help integrate workers into the firm. Councils are generally aided (except in Spain) in performing this intermediate role not only by statutory supports but also by their insulation from wage setting. With this crucial union function and source of conflict with management removed, they serve as instruments of negotiated exchange over such "qualitative," nonwage matters as work organization, technological change, personnel policy, and training—issues often best resolved at the level of the individual firm. They also serve as a mechanism, within the firm, for the enforcement of more encompassing social agreements. In centralized bargaining systems, works councils are commonly obliged not only to respect such general agreements but also to supervise their implementation at the workplace in ways appropriate to local conditions. More generally, they do the same for public labor regulation.

What is important to see, however—and this is the second key feature of councils' organizational

character—is that performance of this distinctive role requires that councils be "compromised." To be effective, they must be neither fish nor fowl—not merely disguised unions nor, surely, disguised management. They are mixed institutions, varying along a line of compromise between worker interests in institutionalized representation and collective voice, and employer interests in work force cooperation and communication to enhance economic performance. Depending on the distribution of power between capital and labor and national labor relations policies, the substance of that compromise differs across countries and over time. While French councils are presided over by the employer, German councils are worker-only bodies. For most of that postwar period, Dutch councils were employer-led, but legal changes in the 1970s reorganized them on the German model. German councils have the legal right to veto certain managerial decisions, while Italian councils do not. In the immediate postwar period, European councils were generally more consultative and employer-dominated, often to the extent of being rejected by unions as overly paternalistic, but in the 1960s and 1970s they become more representative, to the point that in Germany today, for example, they are often perceived as the "extended arm of the unions" at the workplace. In all cases, however, councils typically accommodate concerns and interests of both management and labor and serve to reconcile them, at least in part, in their daily operation.

Because of their mixed and compromised status, works councils have been alternately supported and rejected by both unions and managements in different countries and at different times. Employers have favored works councils to the extent that councils give them access to "reasonable" worker representatives who were not "outsiders"—that is, not full-time union officials—and in the hope that councils would foster worker loyalty to the firm by stressing their shared interest with the employer in the firm's success in the marketplace. But employers also worry that councils might interfere with the free exercise of managerial prerogative.

Unions have their own reasons for ambivalence. Certainly many unions have come to regard works councils as a chance for expanding collective worker representation beyond the limits of collective bargaining, through an institutionalized voice in managerial decisions. In Germany, unions accepted codetermination as an alternative to socialist demands for the nationalization of industry, as a way of sharing economic power between capital and labor. At the same time, however, unions are often suspicious that council participation will draw workers into responsibility for business decisions that workers have no capacity to affect; that employers will influence the selection of worker representatives; and that councils may turn into company unions that crowd out "real" unions, cutting the work force off from broader solidarities beyond company boundaries and identifying worker interests with those of the firm.[8]

Such concerns are ubiquitous and ongoing, even in mature council systems enjoying very broad union and managerial support. In substantial measure they are intrinsic to any functioning council system.

Contributions to Democracy, Efficiency, and Regulation

Workers and employers, then, seek different benefits from works councils. Workers are interested in representation and expanded democracy, while firms look for gains in efficiency and performance. Councils exist and function well to the extent that work forces are persuaded to contribute to efficiency in exchange for representation and managements are persuaded to accept worker voice as a condition of cooperation. Councils generate economic benefits by mobilizing for economic purposes what one may call the "productivity of democracy." Through its existence in the firm, a council legitimates a plurality of interests within the firm and gives workers a secure status as industrial citizens, with quasi-constitutional rights to participate in decision making at their place of employment that parallel the rights of citizens in political communities. Indeed in Germany the legislation that institutes works councils is called the Works *Constitution* Act.[9] Industrial citizenship of this kind can benefit democracy in society at large as well as within firms, and can improve national economic performance. It can also enlist industrial citizenship in the service of general public goals in workplace regulation.

Contributions to Democracy Political democracy and citizenship secure social integration by enabling people to hold authority accountable, to

question and influence decisions, and to redress outcomes regarded as illegitimate by the community at large. Democracy is based on the belief that social integration through citizenship is normatively and practically superior to monolithic unity imposed from above; that an accepted plurality of interests is more conducive to social cohesion and productive cooperation than an authoritatively enforced unity of purpose; and that, at least in the long run, constitutional recognition of different interests is the most effective way of reconciling such interests. The rationale for industrial democracy put forward by its defenders in the countries we have studied consists to a large part in the extension of this view from the polity at large to the firm.[10] The central claim is that not only is it normatively desirable for employees to have a say at their workplace but that a guaranteed voice for workers is also more effective than even enlightened managerial unilateralism in productively integrating capital and labor.

That councils are a substantive form of democratic participation is evident from workers' involvement in them. Regular works council elections give workers a chance to express their views on the representation provided to them by their unions. German works councils, for example, are elected every four years on a nationwide election day, with opposing slates of candidates in each workplace that has a council and turnout averaging 90 percent. During the election campaign, unions contend with opposition from competing unions and from nonunion groups, which often try to win votes by distancing themselves from unionism and emphasizing their closeness to the employer. For the largest German union confederation, the DGB (Deutscher Gewerkschaftsbund), the fact that the candidates of its affiliates regularly win about 80 percent of works council seats nationwide (more in most large firms) has been a source of strength, legitimacy, and pride. In countries with multiunionism, works council elections force unions to match their policies to the preferences of large numbers of workers, unionized or not, and to measure regularly and publicly their support against that of their competitors. In these ways, a council system promotes a certain accountability among unions themselves to those they purport to serve.[11]

Further benefits for democracy result from the difference a works council makes for the relationship between workers and their superiors. Works councils provide employees with a safe institution in which to raise concerns and complaints without fear of sanctions. Because they are in continuous discussions and negotiations with the employer, works council members can easily take up minor worker complaints with management and settle them without undue bureaucracy (William, 1988). By comparison, where people can express discontent with the exercise of authority only to those wielding that authority, they will usually remain silent—unless they can make themselves believe in the benevolence of those who they believe have violated their rights. Thus grievances will rarely be redressed, especially if they are more than trivial. The consequence can be a sense of powerlessness and inferiority on the part of workers that may disable their performance as workers and as citizens. Reciprocally, much benefit redounds, in public arenas as well as private ones, from permitting people to express discontent without fear.

Contributions to Efficiency   The economic contribution of works councils can be summarized in different ways. Concentrating on council functions themselves, we note their demonstrated ability to generate trust between employers and workers, to increase the flow of information within the firm, to aid in the diffusion and implementation of advanced production practices, and to force economic upgrading.

Trust.   Trust between management and workers is central for good economic performance under modern technological and market conditions. For firms to decentralize production decisions, managers must trust workers not to misuse their increased discretion. For workers to contribute to efficiency, they must trust management not to exclude them from the benefits of their effort. Generally trust is required to support cooperative exchange over longer periods, where outcomes and contingencies are not entirely predictable. Where deferral of rewards or long-term investments are important for competitiveness, lack of trust will make self-interested actors "cash in" too early, for fear of being victimized by opportunistic, short-termism on the part of others.

The availability of trust as a social resource depends on the extent to which actors can expect their counterparts not to defect from shared norms of reciprocity and "fairness," even when defection

might be attractive. The firmer such expectations are, the more trust is available to underwrite extended operating under some uncertainty. Most immediately, and particularly where (as between employers and employees) economic power is not equally shared, credible information that the other side has noneconomic as well as economic reasons not to defect—moral commitments or legal obligations that preclude opportunistic behavior—is an effective condition for the growth and consolidation of trusting relations.

Works councils provide such credible assurance and thereby assure a foundation for trusting relations. With strong works councils, employers cannot abolish worker participation unilaterally. Since they know this, they will consider it a waste of effort to try, and will direct their efforts to building constructive relations with the councils. Thus the operations of the councils themselves will not be shadowed by a history of employer resistance (as union relations typically are in the United States). On the side of workers, knowing that the employer cannot abolish the council and therefore will not try permits workers to be less defensive than they would be under less safe conditions. Finally, the permanence of the council structure permits both sides to extend their time horizons in mutual dealings through it. A council can extend "credit" to the employer over long periods. And because it does not have to ensure against aggressive short-termism from worker representatives uncertain of their long-term status, management is more inclined to assume the costs of building cooperative structures that precede payoffs to them.

In short, the formal institutionalization of worker participation rights—moving such rights outside the discretion of the parties involved, and especially that of the employer—can contribute to the growth of trust. While trust is an intangible resource that cannot itself be legislated, legislation can ensure against the self-interested short-term actions that destroy trust and can foreclose options whose mere exploration may undermine trust for a long time. This is what strong council legislation does.[12]

Information Flow.   Modern analyses of the firm recognize that in devising competitive strategies, managements face information problems that go beyond simple "black box" neoclassical models of the firm. These analyses stress the crucial role of different information held by different employees, as well as employees' strategic behavior in using that information. Recognizing that information exists at many levels of an organization leads to the understanding that, in many situations, it is inefficient for management to make key decisions without mobilizing information held by others and investigating the validity of divergent information in collective deliberation. Just as the center cannot efficiently run a centrally planned economy, neither can the center efficiently run a large modern enterprise.

The routes by which employee representation can improve enterprise efficiency through the flow of information have been modeled by Freeman and Lazear (1994). The authors stress the virtue of increasing information flows from management to labor which can lead to worker concessions in difficult economic times saving troubled enterprises; increasing information flows from workers to management outside the hierarchical chain; and providing a forum in which both sides can devise new solutions to problems. In this analysis, collective voice in the workplace has benefits for the enterprise beyond discouraging strikes due to unmet grievances (a major goal of the Wagner Act), saving the costs of turnover by reducing the number of workers who quit, or giving workers the compensation package they desire. It alters the way management and labor operate, creating a more cooperative and informed decision process. Because they are able to draw on formal entitlements to truthful information and are supported by obligations on the part of management to provide such information, irrespective of present inclinations and market constraints, works councils neutralize temptations for management to underinform or to inform only as suggested by short-term market pressures. They thereby increase employee confidence in the information they receive.

Employer obligations to consult with councils create in many situations an incentive for works councils to provide truthful information to management, in the hope of affecting managerial decisions. The more input work force representatives feel they can have in decisions, the more they will invest in mobilizing valid information, for example by researching the views of the work force at large. Workers, in turn, are more likely to give information and reveal their preferences to their elected representatives than to management. They may also speak to management more easily when they know

that their rights and interests to be protected by a strong works council.

Furthermore, consultation and codetermination rights vested in representative bodies create space for joint deliberation of decisions between management and worker representatives. Typically the exercise of consultation and codetermination rights delays decisions while at the same time improving their quality; this is the tenor of research findings on the impact of codetermination on German management. Works councils that provide managers with skillful interlocutors able to analyze proposals and projects in depth cause management to consider intended decisions more carefully and to mobilize extensive information for their justification. Codetermination, which gives works councils temporary veto power over decisions, may protect managements from narrow, short-term responses to market signals, helping them avoid costly mistakes arising from lack of reflection.

Diffusion of "Best Practice."   In successful works councils systems, councils serve liaison functions with the environment outside the firm, often helping the firm perceive and import good practice. In this way councils help diffuse innovations across firm boundaries. In dealing with technical change and its consequences for work organization, for example, councils in several countries may call in experts in ergonomics to advise them and the employer on state-of-the-art solutions.[13] Expert advice helps standardize conditions across firms and draws the attention of firms to advanced solutions that they might have found on their own only with delay and at high cost. In Germany, council members have rights to attend training courses, often organized by unions or employers' associations, on company time and at the employer's expense. These courses deal with questions of new technology, work organization, working time regimes, health and safety regulations, changes in labor law, and the like. Such courses spread information on high standard solutions to a large number of workplaces.

Industrial Upgrading.   Councils can pressure managers to consider productivity enhancement as opposed to other competitive strategies. Through their influence on firm decisions, they force managers to consider decisions in light of the interests of employees, to explore alternatives before presenting them for approval, and to learn about their interlocutors (the workers themselves) and the conditions under which they work. This creates a management style that looks closely for solutions compatible with employees' interests. Moreover, the sheer imposition of employees' demands, for example for further training, submits managers to certain productivity-enhancing constraints. Councils cannot bargain over wages, but they can effectively pressure management in ways that can push it toward high-wage strategies. These pressures, diffused throughout the economy, exert a cumulative force for restructuring along the path of upgrading labor.

Contributions to Regulatory Performance

Finally, works councils can make a major contribution as supplements to state inspectorates in government regulation. Every society regulates some market outcomes and some aspects of the exercise of hierarchical authority in organizations. However, regulation through general rules, created by legislation or otherwise, is typically beset with a twofold enforcement problem: a limited bureaucratic capacity to supervise the innumerable sites where regulated activity occurs, leading to a potential enforcement gap; and the inevitable rigidity of rules applying uniformly to a large number of diverse local conditions.

Works councils are often enlisted as on-site enforcement agents to supplement government inspectorates, and sometimes they make government inspection altogether dispensable. Together with the employer, councils may be given discretion to modify general rules in line with local conditions, increasing the "bite" of rules by making them more flexible. In this way works councils may reduce enforcement costs for the government and contribute to the effectiveness and sophistication of regulation. Rule-making agencies, in turn, can leave the details of regulatory enforcement to local interlocutors (providing, of course, that their interlocution is structured to "keep each other honest"). This option relieves pressure on the state either to write elaborate rules or to abandon regulatory projects simply because local conditions are too varied for uniform rules to apply. Rule makers may (and almost always do) still want to review the results, but on net they benefit from this debureaucratization of regulatory strategies.

The nearly universal European practice of using worker committees as deputy "inspectors" for health and safety regulation is one example of this phenomenon. The most developed example of

councils taking on broader regulatory functions, however, may again be found in Germany. German works councils are charged by law to monitor the employers' observance of pertinent labor regulations. In addition to health and safety regulations, these include legislation on employment protection and equal employment opportunities. Works councils that fail to comply with the law, or that allow an employer to circumvent it, may be taken to the Labor Court by individual employees or by the union, and councilors may be removed from office.

German works councils are also bound by any industrial agreement that unions and employers' associations may negotiate at the sectoral or the national level—which, given extension agreements, takes on at least the color of more general public regulation. They have the duty to ensure that employers do not pay wages below those set in the industrial agreement. Works councils also supervise employer compliance with statutory or collectively bargained worktime regulations, and they are typically charged with negotiating the details of their local implementation. Finally, works councils have the right and obligation to monitor employer compliance with Germany's public-private system of apprenticeship vocational training. They monitor implementation of the nationally standardized curricula for apprentice training at the workplace, and they are obligated to ensure that apprentices are not used unduly for production and that the skills they are taught are portable and not primarily workplace specific.

In all these areas the availability of competent enforcement agents—who have the interest and the powers to make regulation "work" in ways respectful of local variation—facilitates the achievement of public goals by facilitating cooperation both between labor and capital and between the private sector and the state. Employers would not have been willing to accept the German industrial agreements on work-time reduction in the 1980s, for example, had they not known that enforcement of those agreements through councils would allow flexible adjustment for local preferences and circumstances, and unions would not have been content with such enforcement had they not known that "flexibility" would not amount to subversion. Neither unions nor employers would support Germany's fabled apprenticeship-based vocational training system as strongly as they do without the same confidence in council flexibility and powers.

Nor could the state plausibly contemplate governing such a system—with two-thirds of each age cohort undergoing three-and-a-half years of apprenticeship in any one of about four hundred certified occupations—without the contribution of local enforcement agents who enjoy the confidence of private parties. And German industrial policy would not be nearly so extensive and sophisticated if the state could not look to councils as it regularly does, to provide information on emerging needs, worker perspectives, and the effectiveness of past use of government monies and other supports—information of a sort not necessarily provided by employers.[14]

U.S. Experience with Representation Committees

Although U.S. shop committees date back to the nineteenth century, the first great wave of employer representation plans in the United States came during World War I. Introduced to curb wartime strikes (they typically involved explicit renunciation of the strike weapon) and with an eye to inoculating the public against communist agitation, "works councils" or "shop committees" were promoted by various wartime authorities. From virtually zero in 1917, their number grew spectacularly. By 1919 the National Industrial Conference Board (NICB) reported 225 plans covering half a million employees, and by 1922 there were 725 plans operating throughout the country. Employers reported decreased threats of unionization, lower union turnout, and reduced grievances as benefits of the plans. However, with the exception of a small number of plans that provided more or less extensive participation rights, including representation in plant committees or on boards of directors and participation in profits and stock ownership or collective bargaining, most of these plans gave workers no real power in decision making.

While some large firms continued their company unions and welfare programs, these generally faded in the immediate postwar period. In the mid-1920s, however, the "American plan" open-shop drive to prevent unionization led many smaller firms to introduce representation plans. Between 1919 and 1928, total worker membership in employer-initiated representation schemes grew from 0.4 million to 1.5 million. Along with declining union membership during the 1920s, this shifted the relative strength of the two forms of representation. In 1919, plan membership had equaled only 10 percent of union membership; by 1928 the ratio was 45 percent (Millis and Montgomery, 1945, 837).

With the coming of the Depression, representation plans ebbed again: membership fell to 1.3 million over the years 1928 to 1932. But the National Industrial Recovery Act (NIRA) of 1933, which brought about a marked growth in trade union organization, also led to a resurgence in company unions. The NIRA forbade employers to force employees to join company unions but not to encourage the formation of such bodies (and such encouragement was often tantamount to force). Under increased threats of union organizing, the company union movement grew quickly. Data from NICB and the Bureau of Labor Statistics (BLS) indicate that by 1935 more than 3,100 companies, with 2.6 million employees, had some significant percentage of their employees covered by representation plans, two-thirds of which had been established after 1933 (Wilcock, 1957). The ratio of representation plan membership to trade union membership surged to 60 percent (Millis and Montgomery, 1945, 841). In some sectors coverage was even more widespread: for example, after passage of the National Recovery Act (NRA), most basic steel companies established employee representation plans, which then spread to 90 to 95 percent of the industry work force (Bernstein, 1970). This, however, was the highpoint for representation plans. In the late 1930s the massive organizing drives of the Congress of Industrial Organizations (CIO), aided by the prohibition of employer "encouragement" of worker representation in Section 8(2) of the National Labor Relations Act, killed most of them.

During World War II the government again promoted cooperative workplace relations, this time in the form of joint labor-management committees chiefly in union shops. These grew to cover some 7 million workers in the war years, but they faded thereafter (de Schweinitz, 1949). In the early postwar period, again chiefly in the organized portion of the work force, scattered efforts were made to formalize labor-management cooperation, including a variety of schemes aimed at increasing employee productivity through profit sharing and bonuses. Outside a few specific sites, however, these efforts never caught on in the union sector; economy wide their appeal was also limited (Derber, 1970, 478–482).[15] One survey found that no company with more than 1,000 employees and no establishment with more than 5,000 employees enjoyed an actively cooperative relationship with its union. With very rare exceptions, the "cooperative" strategy was limited to medium-size, closely held firms or to marginal companies; even there it essentially disappeared in the late 1950s (Harris, 1982, 1995).

As the prime case of employer-initiated works councils operating in a largely nonunion, decentralized labor market, the U.S. experience in the 1920s through the 1950s provides insight into the potential for councils in such a setting. It shows, first, that employer-initiated councils were neither a long-lived stable institution nor were extended to the majority of the work force. Even at its peak the council movement covered only a minority of workers, mostly in big firms, and the peak came under threat of outside unionization. Still, this minority exceeded at times the modest private-sector U.S. unionization rates of the early 1990s. Second, NICB reports and historical investigations of the operation of councils show considerable diversity (NICB, 1919 and 1922; Jacoby, 1989, Jacoby and Verma, 1992; Nelson, 1993). In many cases, company unions were the sham that unionists usually claimed them to be, but in some cases they offered significant and meaningful means of worker representation. According to the NICB, "successful" worker representation depended on management commitment—as evidenced in regular meetings, worker education, and, ideally, concrete payoffs to workers through, for example, the profit-sharing (collective dividend) system (NICB, 1922, Report 50). Not contemplating an extension of enforceable worker rights within the firm, the NICB concluded that "where management is not thoroughly sold to the idea . . . a Works Council should not be formed" (NICB, 1922, Report 50, 10).

Renewed interest in employee participation began in the early 1970s. Focused on "quality of work life" (QWL) programs, it was initially motivated by concerns about worker alienation (the "blue-collar blues"), which many viewed as being responsible for an increased militancy of assembly-line workers. The National Commission on Productivity and quality of Working Life and the Ford Foundation sponsored a number of QWL experiments in the early 1970s in both union and nonunion plants. The most widely known included those conducted at the Rushton Mining Company, and the General Motors (GM) Tarrytown plant, which prior to the QWL program had had one of the poorest labor relations and production records

of all GM plants but which, within a few years of QWL adoption, became one of the company's best performing assembly plants. Implementation of QWL programs was never widespread, however, and most experiments faded by the late 1970s when government funding stopped (Kochan, Katz, and Mower, 1984, 6–7). In the 1980s, worker involvement programs enjoyed a resurgence, so that in 1990 some 30,000 U.S. firms, including 80 percent of the top 1,000 firms, reported having some such program—an increase of 50 percent in the incidence of programs over 1987 (Katz, 1992). These programs had various names—QWL committees, quality circles, autonomous work teams, gainsharing and employee stock ownership plans (ESOPs)—and varied considerably in structure, representativeness, scope of issues, substantive decision making power, and links to other changes in work organization. Cutcher-Gershenfeld (1987) estimates that 10 to 15 percent of all American organizations had worker participation programs in the 1980s, covering about 20 percent of the work force. Cooke (1990) estimates that 40 to 50 percent of the unionized sector is involved with quality circles, QWL programs, or some form of employee involvement; of these, between one-third and two-thirds are jointly administered. About one-third of the unionized sector has committee-based participation, with health and safety being the most common focus.

Studies of these programs confirm the experience of the 1920s. The economic effects of worker involvement are most likely to be positive when workers have real power in decision making and receive concrete payoffs for cooperation (Blinder, 1990). The greatest gains from cooperation are seen in unionized settings, where worker power exists independent of management (Eaton and Voos, 1992; Kelley and Harrison, 1992). In nonunionized settings, where workers have no reserved rights, the performance and stability of the programs depends on management attitudes, which vary widely across firms and over time and which are subject to an important core ambivalence: even where managers recognize worker autonomy in their decision making as necessary to productivity gains, they are reluctant to relinquish control. Outside organized settings, much of the talk of worker "empowerment" is only that, involving a relatively trivial routinization of management access to employee opinion, rather than a substantive change.

CONCLUSIONS ABOUT WORKS COUNCILS

Our general discussion, and the review of specific country experiences, can be summarized in four simple claims.

First, works councils in general perform useful functions, at tolerable cost, and make an important net contribution to democracy and economic welfare. They facilitate representation and the achievement of public regulatory goals, and help underwrite a variety of desired economic practices. The latter include better intrafirm communication and the diffusion (across as well as within firms) of advanced practices with regard to training, technology, compensation, and other ingredients in industrial upgrading. Works councils are a means to greater social consensus and a greater capacity to respond to changed economic circumstances in broadly beneficial ways.

Second, there is striking convergence among developed nations, *with the sole exceptions of the United States and Great Britain,* that works councils or similar institutions, intermediate between managerial discretion and collective bargaining, are part of a well-functioning labor relations system. In most of Europe, the past decade witnessed both an expansion of the collective participation rights of workers and more extensive production-related communication and cooperation between managements and work forces. As union rejection of workplace participation as paternalistic and detrimental to worker solidarity has receded, so have management fears that collective participation will interfere with managerial prerogative. As a result, the consultative councils that were set up in all European countries to promote labor-management cooperation after World War II, and that later fell into disuse due to union opposition and lack of employer interest, came back in modified form in the 1970s and 1980s. They were enriched with participation rights to supplement their communication functions, and more closely linked to union movements—themselves exhibiting increased interest in and presence at the workplace.

Third, despite their usefulness and the support they eventually receive from labor and management, councils are as a rule initially resisted by managers, unions, or both. Their emergence and stable performance therefore normally require legal-institutional supports. In Sweden, exceptionally

strong unions live with, and indeed prefer, council-like structures based on collective bargaining or employer initiative, operating under no more than a general legal charter for industrial democracy. In Italy, unions and employers were able to agree on a largely voluntary council system, drawing for limited legal support on the statutory rights of union workplace organizations. But these are exceptions, reflecting the extraordinary strength and centralization of unions in Sweden, and union centralization and political multiunionism in Italy. Elsewhere, councils need specific juridicial guarantees of their powers.

Fourth, at least in Europe, the union-substitution effect of councils seems small. In France and, to an extent, Spain their introduction coincided with a sharp decline in unionism; the primary causes of this decline, however, appear not to have been the introduction of councils, but the inability of political unionism to adjust to the decline of communist parties. In the Netherlands, union decline in the 1980s is primarily attributed to fast economic and social-structural change. Elsewhere, in countries as diverse as Germany and Italy, councils have helped preserve or increase union strength, by safeguarding the presence of unions in the workplace and enabling unions to represent their members on "qualitative" nonwage matters. And in all European countries—except perhaps Spain, where the distinction between unions and councils is least developed—councils preserve some measure of worker influence in the governance of the workplace even as unions experience difficulty. Under more heavily decentralized and adversarial bargaining systems, like those of Canada and the United States, these results may not hold for general-purpose councils. The Canadian example of limited-purpose committees, however, appears to show little substitution even under "Wagner Act" conditions.

NOTES*

1. This chapter summarizes the results of a cross-national study of works councils (the Works Councils Project) that we directed as part of NBER's broader research project, *Working under Different Rules.* For purposes of the study, works councils were defined as any legally based and union-independent (not necessarily nonunion, let alone anti-union) institutions for the collective representation

*Some notes have been deleted and the remaining ones renumbered.—ED.

and participation of employees at the workplace. Countries surveyed included Canada, France, Germany, Italy, the Netherlands, Poland, Spain, Sweden, and the United States; in addition, one subproject investigated current efforts in the European Economic Community to institute "European Works Councils," while another sought to build a general model of works councils' economic effects. Research for the project was carried out in 1991 and 1992. The financial support of the NBER, the International Labor Organization in Geneva, the Washington bureau of the Friedrich-Ebert-Stiftung, the German Marshall Fund of the United States, the Hans-Böckler-Stiftung, and the Research Committee of the University of Wisconsin—Madison is gratefully acknowledged.

2. Even in systems classed as "mandate" systems, some expression of employee interest is typically required for their formation.

3. As used here, in reference to the structure of systems with works councils, "information" denotes rights to receive information and obligations to inform. "Consultation" involves obligations, usually for management, to inform before a decision is taken, to wait for a considered response or counter-proposal, and to take such a proposal into consideration when deciding the issue. Under joint decision making ("codetermination"), decisions can be made only if they are agreed to by both sides in advance.

4. This claim relies on various polls, including those reported in Gallup (1988), Fingerhut/Powers (1991), Quinn and Staines (1979), Louis Harris and Associates (1984), Davis and Smith (1991), and Farber and Kreuger (1993). See the review in Freeman and Rogers (1993).

5. See the review in Freeman and Rogers (1993).

6. In the case of Denmark and Italy, labor and management are permitted to establish such institutions at their discretion, with a strong presumption against their discontinuance once established.

7. In these areas, councils may refuse consent to an employer action:

   if there is factual reason to assume that the staff movement is likely to result in the dismissal of or other prejudice to employees of the establishment not warranted by operational or personal reasons; [or] if the employee concerned suffers prejudice through the staff movement although this is not warranted by operational or personal reasons (Section 99, Works Constitution Act).

8. Union fears of councils have been strong where unions or collective bargaining are not highly centralized, such as in the United States. Where all or most union functions are performed at the workplace, being crowded out by councils is more of a threat to unions than it is when they have a secure base outside the workplace, in strong territorial or sectoral organizations and in multiemployer

bargaining. Also, the dangers of worker identification with the market interests of their employers must appear greater where *bona fide* unionism itself is traditionally workplace-based, making it difficult even for unions to mobilize solidarities that transcend the limits of individual firms.

9. The legislation is also as rarely changed, and practically as difficult to change, as a constitution. For example, the Kohl government, which succeeded the Social-Liberal coalition in 1982, has let its predecessor's entire body of codetermination legislation stand.

10. For a review of the reasons that such an extension might be thought reasonable, see Freeman and Rogers (1993).

11. Some of course would argue that unions should only advance the interests of "vanguard" workers. That councils force unions to make wider policy appeals is one traditional reason radical and communist unions have often opposed them.

12. Typically, the German Works Constitution Act, while guaranteeing the existence of councils by "constitutionalizing" them, also obliges councils and employers to seek and maintain "trustful cooperation."

13. The German Works Constitution Act explicitly makes the state of ergonomic knowledge the criterion for what works councils may demand in job design and work organization.

14. Collusion between employer and works council against government agencies is possible and does occur. But this does not render obsolete the principle that partly opposed interests, if properly mobilized for the purpose, will often serve as checks and balances for each other enhancing the ability of the third-party state to "make them behave" and act as more perfect agents of the sovereign people.

15. Harris (1982, 138–139) also describes efforts at "progressive" firms—notably U.S. Rubber and General Electric—that were allied with the Committee for Economic Development and the National Planning Association, two industry associations that encouraged labor-management cooperation, to raise productivity through labor-management cooperation.

REFERENCES

Bernstein, Irving. 1970. *The Turbulent Years: A History of the American Worker,* 1933–1945. Boston: Houghton Mifflin.

Blinder, Alan S., ed. 1990. *Paying for Productivity: A Look at the Evidence.* Washington, D.C.: Brookings Institute.

Cutcher-Gershenfeld, Joel. 1987. "Collective Governance of Industrial Relations." *Proceedings of* the 40th Annual Meeting, Industrial Relations Research Association. Madison, Wis.: Industrial Relations Research Association. Pp. 533–543.

Cooke, William N. 1990. *Labor-Management Cooperation: New Partnerships or Going in Circles?* Kalamazoo, Mich.: Upjohn Institute for Employment Research.

Davis, James Allan, and Tom W. Smith. 1991. *General Social Surveys, 1972–1991,* Machine-readable data file. Chicago: National Opinion Research Center.

de Schweinitz, Dorothea. 1949. *Labor and Management in Common Enterprise.* Cambridge, Mass.: Harvard University Press.

Derber, Milton. 1970. *The American Idea of Industrial Democracy, 1865–1965.* Urbana: University of Illinois Press.

Eaton, Adrienne E., and Paula B. Voos. 1992. "Unions and Contemporary Innovations in Work Organization, Compensation, and Employee Participation." In L. Mishel and P. Voos, eds., *Unions and Economic Competitiveness.* Armonk, N.Y.: M. E. Sharpe. Pp. 173–215.

Farber, Henry, and Alan B. Krueger. 1993. "Union Membership in the United States: The Decline Continues." In M. Kleiner and B. Kaufman, eds., *Employee Representation: Alterna-tives and Future Directions.* Madison, Wis.: Industrial Relations Research Association.

Fingerhut/Powers. 1991. "National Labor Poll." Washington, D.C.: Fingerhut/Granados.

Freeman, Richard B., and Edward P. Lazear. 1994. "An Economic Analysis of Works Councils." In J. Rogers and W. Streeck, eds., *Works Councils: Consultation, Representation, Cooperation.* Chicago: University of Chicago Press for NBER. Forthcoming.

Freeman, Richard B., and Joel Rogers. 1993. "Who Speaks for Us? Employee Relations in a Non-Union Labor Market." In M. Kleiner and B. Kaufman, eds., *Employee Representation: Alternatives and Future Directions.* Madison, Wis.: Industrial Relations Research Association.

Gallup Organization (Gallup) 1988. "Public Knowledge and Opinion Concerning the Labor Movement." Princeton: Gallup Organization.

Harris, Howell John. 1982. *The Right to Manage: Industrial Relations Policies of American Business in the 1940s.* Madison, Wis.: University of Wisconsin Press.

Jacoby, Sanford M. 1989. "Reckoning with Company Unions: The Case of Thornton Products, 1934–1964." *Industrial and Labor Relations Review* 43, no. 1: 19–40.

Jacoby, Sanford M., and Anil Verma. 1992. "Enterprise Unions in the U.S." *Industrial Relations* 31, no. 1: 137–158

Katz, Diane. 1992. "Unions, Employers Watch Case on Labor Management Teams." *Detroit News,* September 1.

Kelley, Maryellen R., and Bennett Harrison. 1992. "Unions, Technology, and Labor Management Cooperation." In L. Mishel and P. Voos, eds., *Unions and Economic Competitiveness.* Armonk, N.Y.: M. E. Sharpe.

Kochan, Thomas A., Harry C. Katz, and Nancy R. Mower. 1984. *Worker Participation and American Unions: Threat or Opportunity?* Kalamazoo, Mich.: Upjohn Institute for Employment Research.

Louis Harris and Associates. 1984. *A Study on the Outlook for Trade Union Organizing.* New York: Louis Harris and Associates.

Millis, Harry, and Royal Montgomery. 1945. *Organized Labor.* New York: McGraw-Hill.

National Industrial Conference Board (NICB). 1919. *Works Councils in the United States.* Boston: NICB.

———. 1922. *Experience with Works Councils in the United States.* New York: Century.

Nelson, Daniel. 1993. "Employee Representation in Historical Perspective." In M. Kleiner and B. Kaufman, eds., *Employee Representation: Alternatives and Future Directions.* Madison, Wis.: Industrial Relations Research Association.

Quinn, Robert P., and Graham L. Staines. 1979. *The 1977 Quality of Employment Survey: Descriptive Statistics with Comparison Data from the 1969–70 and 1972–73 Surveys.* Ann Arbor, Mich.: Institute for Social Research.

Weiler, Paul C. 1990. *Governing the Workplace: The Future of Labor and Employment Law.* Cambridge, Mass.: Harvard University Press.

Wilcock, Richard C. 1957. "Industrial Management's Policies toward Unionism," In M. Derber and E. Young, eds., *Labor and the New Deal.* Madison, Wis.: University of Wisconsin Press. Pp. 275–315.

Williams, Karen. 1988. *Industrial Relations and the German Model.* Avebury, England: Aldershot.

Decision Scenario A
LEVI'S SHRINKS

Privately held Levi Strauss and Company has a reputation as one of the most socially responsible companies in the United States. *Money Magazine* named it the company with the best employee benefits in the United States. It was President Clinton's choice as the first recipient of the Ron Brown Award, honoring the company for its efforts to promote diversity. And it received high praise for its decision in the early 1990s to withdraw from China because it felt that it could not guarantee that its suppliers would abide by the company code of conduct. Levi's was worried that suppliers there engaged in widespread human rights abuses of employees, as well as in counterfeiting practices.

Moreover, after Coca-Cola, Levi's also has probably the second most-recognizable brand name in the worldwide retail business. Its jeans are an American icon around the globe, and they fetch premium prices, particularly outside the United States. However, none of this prevented the company from experiencing significant problems in the late 1990s marketplace.

Levi's sales fell 3 percent in 1997 and another 13 percent in 1998. Its share of the American denim market declined from 48 percent in 1990 to about 25 percent in 1998 at a time when the market was growing. Market analysts claim that Levi's has missed numerous sales trends in recent years and has lost connection with younger buyers' tastes. For instance, it missed out significantly on both the recent baggy and hip-hugger fashion trends in the youth market. Moreover, it alienated retailers when it limited products to larger stores and required strict pricing policies. Analysts also suggest Levi's labor costs are not in line with its competitors, many of whom produce offshore with lower-cost labor.

So, in 1999, for the second time in two years, Levi's announced a series of drastic employment cuts. In 1997, it closed 11 North American plants

and laid off about 7,000 workers, a third of its domestic employees. In that layoff, the company said that the North American employment reductions would allow the remaining plants to operate at fuller capacity and also allow Levi's to keep domestic production at its current level of 55 percent of total production. In 1999, it announced that it was laying off another third of its domestic workforce, this time around 6,000 jobs, and closing another 11 domestic production facilities. It also said that this time overall production would remain constant but that much of it would be shifted to independent suppliers in other countries. Management defended its production shift by noting that the use of contractors would allow quicker and less costly changes in its product mix, and would allow the company to get new products to customers more quickly.

These days, such waves of layoffs normally would be met with complaints from employees and with stiff criticism of the corporation by the popular press. Levi's, however, was spared that. In fact, both employee representatives and the press praised Levi's handling of the layoffs. The executive vice president of the union representing a number of the workers, Bruce Raynor, said after the 1997 announcement that he did not believe it was feasible for Levi's to expand domestic production since most of its competition abandoned the U.S. market for cheaper labor costs years ago. He also praised Levi's for constructing one of the most generous severance packages the industry had seen. The press, too, emphasized the size of the severance benefits instead of caustically painting the Levi's case as another where workers suffer for management missteps.

The packages in both layoffs were indeed generous, more than $245 million in the 1999 case. Workers were given eight months notice and were paid for the remainder of that time if the plant closed before eight months elapsed. They received up to three weeks' pay for each year of service; company-subsidized health care benefits for 18 months; a $6000 allowance for relocation, education, or childcare; outplacement services; and continued eligibility for an employee bonus of about one year's wages if the company met financial tar-

This case was prepared from the following sources: Mark Evans, "Levi Strauss China Move Questioned," *The Associated Press,* April 9, 1998; Suzette Hill, "Levi Strauss Shrinks to Fit U.S. Market," *Apparel Industry Magazine,* January, 1998; Greg Johnson, "Levi Strauss Is Trying to Give Its Product and Image a Better Fit," *Los Angeles Times,* November 6, 1997; Rebecca Quick, "Levi Strauss to Close Half Its Plants in North America," *The Wall Street Journal,* February 23, 1999; Stephanie Stoughton, "Jeans Market Now a Tight Fit for Levi's," *The Washington Post,* February 23, 1999; Frank Swoboda, "An American Emblem's Presence Fades," *The Washington Post,* February 23, 1999.

gets by the end of 2001. Communities where closed plants were located had $8 million in aid for economic development and community programs provided by Levi's.

The public expressions of good will toward the company were not unanimous, however. Protestors outside company headquarters in 1998 painted the company as hypocritical for its decision to resume doing business with suppliers in China as a part of its outsourcing strategy. Levi's claimed that it believed, five years after the initial withdrawal, that it could now find suppliers that would follow the company code of conduct prohibiting violations of human rights, child labor, and counterfeiting. Critics, however, charged that little had changed in China. They warned that subcontracting arrangements in China make it very difficult to know exactly where material is being produced, a fact athletic apparel makers discovered recently. Well-known Chinese dissident Henry Wu criticized the decision by noting the continued existence of forced labor and the absence of independent unions. He said that human rights conditions have not improved, only the business climate had. And

some protestors wondered about the morality of layoffs of long-term workers just when Levi's was expanding its use of independent Asian suppliers.

- Are there grounds for claiming that the displaced Levi's workers were entitled to the sizeable severance packages or was this an instance of corporate largesse that was "supererogatory," above and beyond the call of duty?

- Was Levi's relatively delayed decision (compared to its competitors) to shift production offshore a luxury afforded it only because the company is privately held and thus not as exposed to financial market pressures for short-term performance? What about the size of its severance offering? Are there moral limits on company options that are driven by the nature of ownership structure or by financing mechanisms?

- What obligations, if any, do firms have to current workers that might limit their ability to relocate production to cheaper foreign labor markets? Do American firms have obligations to American workers? On what basis do you support or reject such obligations?

Decision Scenario B
UNWRITTEN EMPLOYMENT CONTRACTS

Courts have cited three general exceptions to the doctrine of employment at will. The public policy exception restricts the right to fire when the dismissal would violate a specific law or a well-established principle of public policy. Examples of the public policy exception include an employee's refusal to commit perjury, a refusal to violate a professional code of ethics, and an employee's service on jury duty. The implied covenant of good faith exception restricts the right to fire when doing so is particularly arbitrary or unfair. An example was *Fortune v. National Cash Register*, in which a salesman was fired to avoid paying him a commission that he had earned but not yet received. A third category is based upon the existence of an expressed or implied contract between employer and employee. Since few employees have explicit, written contracts, courts have some latitude in determining the conditions of the implied contract.

Does an employee with a long history of successful service and promotions have an implied promise not to be fired at will? In *Pugh v. See's Candies*, the California Court of Appeals judged that a contractual promise not to terminate at will could be inferred from the employee's length of service, history of pay raises and promotions, and favorable reviews, as well as the employer's past policies and practices.

Employee handbooks and personnel manuals have also been interpreted as establishing a contractual relationship, although not by all courts. In *Gates v. Life of Montana Insurance Co.*, the Supreme Court of Montana decided that an employee handbook, which stated that employees were "subject to reprimand or dismissal with prior warning," had not established a contractual obligation. The court reasoned that because the handbook was distributed after Gates was hired, and because it was issued unilaterally by the employer, the requirement of prior notice was not a contractual right.

However, in *Toussaint v. Blue Cross & Blue Shield of Michigan,* a Michigan court reached the opposite decision. The Blue Cross personnel manual stated: "It is the policy of the company to treat employees leaving Blue Cross in a fair and consistent manner and to release employees for just cause only." The Michigan court decided that despite the absence of negotiation or explicit agreement, the manual did establish contractual rights. Since the handbook produced benefits to the employer, it should produce benefits to the employee as well.

A Nevada court, in *Southwest Gas Corp. v. Ahmad,* explicitly stated the reasoning involved in such cases. The court decided that the employer had violated an implied contract by ignoring an employee handbook statement that employees would be fired only for good cause and only after previous warnings had been issued. The court said:

The fact that the company issued such handbooks to its employees supports an inference that the handbook formed part of the employment contract of the parties . . . by continuing in employment after receiving the handbook, the employee supplied consideration for the promise of job security.

- Contracts usually require mutual consent of the contracting parties. How then can there be such a thing as an "implied contract" if both parties haven't agreed to it? Can there be a promise if only one side is aware of it?

- Suppose an employer unilaterally issued a handbook that *denied* any obligation of due process before dismissal. Should such a disclaimer be contractually valid?

- Would a newspaper job description that promised "career opportunities" constitute a promise not to terminate "at will"?

Decision Scenario C
MONTANA'S JUST CAUSE LEGISLATION

In 1987, Montana became the first and only state in the union to adopt a just cause employment termination law. It is interesting that the main support for the law came from business lobbies whose members felt threatened by the possibility of paying large damage awards in the litigation lottery. Just as interesting, organized labor reportedly was not a major player in the legislative activity leading up to the passage of the law.

The Wrongful Discharge from Employment Act requires that nonprobationary employees be dismissed only for "good cause"; that is, there must be "reasonable job-related grounds for dismissal based on a failure to satisfactorily perform job duties, disruption of the employer's operation, or other legitimate business reasons." This legislation also holds that violations of promises made in personnel hand-

books are violations of the act. The law, however, does not apply to those employees who are covered by collective bargaining agreements or who have written contracts of employment.

The act limits the ability of workers to sue for damages. It precludes suits for damages based on tort law or contract law (those areas of the law that have generated large damage awards for dismissed employees), and it limits punitive damages to those rare cases where dismissed employees can prove fraud or malice. Instead, it caps the maximum award level at four times annual wages and benefits minus any wages the employee earned (or could have earned with reasonable diligence) in the interim period. The act allows employees to pursue their cases in the court system, but it encourages the use of cheaper methods of binding arbitration. This is encouraged by a clause that holds that parties who refuse arbitration and then later lose in court must pay the other party's attorney fees. Employees who offer to accept arbitration and later win are to have their costs and fees paid by the employer.

This case was prepared from the following sources: the Montana Wrongful Discharge from Employment Act; Alan B. Krueger, "The Evolution of Unjust Dismissal Legislation in the United States," *Industrial and Labor Relations Review,* vol. 44 (1991): 644; Leonard Bierman, et al., "Montana's Wrongful Discharge from Employment Act," *Montana Law Review,* vol. 54 (1993): 367; Leonard Bierman and Stuart Youngblood, "Interpreting Montana's Pathbreaking Wrongful Discharge from Employment Act," *Montana Law Review,* vol. 53 (1992): 53.

A survey of members of the Montana Bar Association raises some questions about the effectiveness of the law. Most notably, 56.5 percent of respondents felt that the law does not offer adequate incentives for attorneys to take employees' cases. Half of those responding said they had personally declined cases, and their written comments indicated that the foremost reason was that the amount of compensation was not proportionate to the time and difficulty involved in dismissal cases. In addition, a number of attorneys thought that the law had changed employment practices for the worse. Some indicated that with the threat of large damage awards removed, some employers have become less concerned about wrongful discharge actions.

- Do you think that the reduction of damages by subtracting what a person earned or could have earned is appropriate? Why or why not?

- What changes would you have made in personnel practices if you were operating a business in Montana in 1987 when the law was passed?

- Does just cause legislation by itself provide workers increased protection against unfair dismissal, or does it provide protection only when management is committed to the idea?

- Do you believe that the attorneys' opinions show that a law passed primarily with business support will inevitably shortchange employees or that attorneys are interested only in large awards, or both?

Decision Scenario D
SATURN MOTORS: SHIFTING INTO REVERSE?

Saturn Motors was the poster child for U. S. labor-management cooperation in the 1990s. The product of an initiative by former General Motors Chairman Roger Smith (vilified in the comic documentary *Roger and Me*), the company was planned as an independent subsidiary of General Motors (GM). The company was to be a vertically integrated one, producing many of the parts and assembling the car in one large plant that was separate from and independent of the normal GM system. After GM decided in 1982 that it needed a new approach to compete with Japanese imports, a planning process was begun for "a new kind of car company," Saturn's successful advertising slogan. The

first vehicles were introduced onto the market in 1990 and the car has consistently had high owner satisfaction in the intervening years.

The innovative feature of Saturn Motors was its unusual partnership between GM and the United Auto Workers (UAW) union. The union and GM have had stormy relations over the years, but they decided to try a cooperative approach at Saturn's Greenfield production site in Spring Hill, Tennessee. They collaborated in the planning process and produced an agreement between the UAW and GM that guaranteed labor management cooperative structures unprecedented in the U.S. auto industry. The Saturn compact allows the UAW to share in decision making with management. Workers on the production floor are organized into teams of five to fifteen. The teams elect their own leaders, are self-managing, and have control over various items (including quality assurance, training, work scheduling, job assignments, and hiring issues). Teams are organized into modules that are co-managed by UAW and management partners. Decision making is supposed to be based on consensus. The UAW–management partnering extended beyond merely human resources and quality assurance into finance, product development, industrial engineering, and marketing.

This case was prepared from the following sources: Keith Bradsher, "Labor's Peace With GM Unraveling at Saturn," *The New York Times*, July 22, 1998; Del Jones, "Rubber Meets the Road for Saturn's Ballyhooed Contract," *USA Today*, August 10, 1998; Thomas Kochan and Paul Osterman, *The Mutual Gains Enterprise* (Boston, MA: Harvard, 1994); John Lippert, "UAW Fears Futility of Future Strikes If GM Realigns Manufacturing as Planned," *The Buffalo News*, July 3, 1998; David Phillips, "Saturn Needs Union to Help Cut Costs," *The Detroit News*, February 26, 1999; "Saturn Loses Two Leaders," *The Times Picayune*, February 28, 1999; Frank Swoboda, "Saturn Experiment in Jeopardy," *The Washington Post*, March 6, 1999; Saul Rubinstein, Michael Bennett, and Thomas Kochan, "The Saturn Partnership: Co-Management and the Re-invention of the Local Union," in B. Kaufmann and M. Kleiner, eds., *Employee Representation: Alternatives and Future Directions* (Madison, WI: Industrial Relations Research Association, 1993); Scott Reeves, "Changes at Saturn Mean the End of 'A Different Kind of Company,'" Associated Press, January 24, 2004.

A special feature of the contract was a risk/reward system that paid workers a salary that was lower than the industry standard annual wage. But annual take-home pay could be increased by bonuses that were tied to production, quality, and sales goals. With these bonuses, Saturn workers often received up to $4000 more than union workers under traditional contracts. Saturn also guaranteed job security for up to 80 percent of its workforce, barring severe economic declines. The union accepted responsibility for helping to make Saturn competitive in exchange for this guarantee. The Saturn arrangement also stressed training, reduced job classifications, and increased the flexibility with which workers could be deployed.

This unusual partnership that gave the union a substantial role in managing and planning seems to have worked well over the years. In fact, during the crippling strikes that affected the rest of GM's production in 1998, workers expressed their commitment to the Saturn approach and chose to continue production, even using foreign and nonunion parts for a time. The break with UAW solidarity was notable; the plant was the only one to continue operation. The employees also voted, two-to-one, in March of 1998 to continue the unusual contract arrangements.

But things began to sour at Saturn in mid-1998. In July of that year, 95 percent of Saturn workers voted to authorize a strike against GM. While the strike never came (such authorization votes are sometimes bargaining devices that signal deep dissatisfaction), the vote revealed a change in the attitude of the union partners. Explanations of the change center on two items: money and power.

Saturn sales were falling, as were small-car sales generally. In 1998, they were almost 7 percent below the previous years' sales; 1997 itself saw a drop of almost 10 percent. The company cut output to 240,000, down from a capacity of 315,000. As a result, workers' bonuses suffered to the point that in 1998 the annual salary and bonus was $4000 *less* than the wages of other UAW members under more standard contracts. Workers, and some analysts, blamed the decrease in sales and bonuses in part on GM's rejection of workers' suggestions that Saturn move into the Sport Utility Vehicle (SUV) market. SUVs have been the hottest market segment and are responsible for substantial profits for their manufacturers.

That leads to the other explanation of the union members' dissatisfaction. They complain that Saturn increasingly lost its autonomy by being folded into the GM management. They point to a decision, made in Detroit without worker input, to build a new mid-size Saturn in Wilmington, Delaware, a site with a traditional contract. Moreover, they worried that GM's overall strategy will inevitably lead both to the annihilation of Saturn as anything but a marketing image and to the emasculation of the UAW itself.

GM's plans call for integrating all car assembly operations by relying on the same car platforms for many models, Saturn included. They also call for standardization of parts for many models and for the use of nonunion parts suppliers. Saturn workers saw this as an abandonment of the autonomy of Saturn within the GM fold, since identical cars will be made at many sites. Union members worried that the strategy of standardization is merely a thinly veiled plan to make future strikes worthless as a bargaining threat. If a car's production can be shifted between plants worldwide and if supplies for that production come increasingly from nonunion sources, GM need not fear the economic consequences of a strike.

All these decisions by GM management have some Saturn workers and local union leadership feeling as if their strategic partnership over Saturn is dead. A growing feeling of mistrust was apparent in the union votes. Workers saw their local partnership being preempted by decisions in Detroit, decisions that not only renege on the labor-management cooperation process but that also cost Saturn workers money. As a result, in March of 1999, Saturn workers voted out the long-time union local leadership team, which was committed to the partnership concept (though disillusioned by GM's recent actions). They replaced it with a team of labor leaders promising a much more aggressive approach. The new team claimed it wanted to continue partnership, but it wanted more guaranteed money and more power on the floor. Observers worried that the combination of GM's central management strategy and the new local leadership desires to rewrite the contract may doom the Saturn experiment in labor management cooperation. In December 2003, the Saturn workers approved a new contract by a vote of 2953 to 317. The new contract gives the union members a $3000 bonus with a possibility of a 3 percent performance bonus in 2004, a 5 percent raise over two years, and a promise by General Motors to invest $90 million in Saturn production facilities. But the union also agreed to transition into the national UAW/GM contract. Observers believe that the union decision signals an end to the Saturn labor relations experiment. They suggest that the union acted because it felt that without the agreement, GM would close the Saturn lines and union members would lose their jobs.

■ What conditions seem necessary for a co-management arrangement, such as that planned for Saturn, to thrive over time?

■ GM faces cost problems, as does any manufacturer. It looks to streamline and standardize production as a cost-saving measure. The UAW, with reason, fears that is the first step toward eliminating unions. In this climate, could GM have handled Saturn, specifically, in a way that would have reassured the local union members and would have offered the national UAW an alternative other than hostility and resistance?

■ Do the problems with the Saturn experiment reveal that cooperative structures are inherently unstable? Is instability an unavoidable result of the conflicting interests of capital and labor? Can instability be reduced or removed by law or public policy?

Decision Scenario E
THE GERMAN MODEL OF EMPLOYEE PARTICIPATION

German law mandates worker participation in industrial decision making. Since the 1950s, workers in many industries were guaranteed one-third representation on the board of directors. In the coal and steel industries, workers were guaranteed equal representation on company boards. In 1976 a new law expanded the coal and steel industry policy of codetermination to all companies with over two thousand employees. Critics of this policy of placing worker representatives on company boards have worried that the workers will use their new powers to block management policies. However, studies of over 25 years of codetermination in coal and steel indicate that unanimous decisions of the directors were common and that in no case was a tie-breaking vote needed to end an impasse between employee and management representatives.

Although worker representation on boards is now mandated for most large companies in Germany, approximately half of all workers are employed in companies not covered by the 1976 law. For these workers, as well as for all other German workers, participation comes through works councils. These councils are composed of employees only and are mandated for all firms with more than five employees. Employee representatives on these councils are elected for three-year terms. Employers are required to pay costs associated with the operations of the councils. For example, worker representatives must be given release time for their obligations on the councils, and they must have paid leaves available for acquiring the education needed for their duties.

Works councils have broad authorities. They control the employee grievance process. They have the right to codetermine policies governing, among other things, work hours, wages, bonus plans, and safety regulations. They must be consulted about layoffs, plant closures or relocations, mergers, and new work methods. On these matters employers have the final decision, but the employer must codecide with works councils about any social plan for minimizing the effect of such decisions on workers. If the employer and works council cannot reach an agreement, the issue is subjected to binding arbitration. Works councils also are entitled to financial information about the firm.

This case was prepared from the following sources: John Simmons and William Mares, *Working Together* (NYU Press, 1985), 283; Paul Blumberg, *Industrial Democracy* (Schocken Books, 1969), 158–160; G. David Garson, "Models of Worker Self-Management: The West European Experience," in *Worker Self-Management in Industry*, edited by G. D. Garson (Praeger, 1977), 12; Alfred Daimant, "Democratizing the Workplace: The Myth and Reality of *Mitbestimmung* in the Federal Republic of Germany," in op. cit., 30–35; Frank Anton, *Worker Participation: Prescription for Industrial Change* (Detselig Enterprises Ltd., 1980), 31–37.

Again, American management has expressed fears about the likely results of sharing such powers with workers. But numerous commentators argue convincingly that the German system has produced greater labor peace and higher productivity. One report suggests that work stoppages in the United States are 17 times higher per 100,000 workers than in the Federal Republic of Germany. Even German management reports that the councils are an essential ingredient of their conception of effective management.

■ Are there conditions in the U.S. industrial relations tradition that would make a successful transplant of the German model impossible?

■ What explanations can we give of the failure of U.S. law to have requirements similar to those of Germany?

■ Why is there little evidence of significant differences between workers and management on German boards? Would the same experience be expected if American workers were given similar representation?

■ Would you expect a deterioration in employee discipline under the German model?

Decision Scenario F
ELECTROMATION: ILLEGAL EMPLOYEE PARTICIPATION

Electromation is a small nonunion manufacturer of electronic components used in cars and power tools. The company is located in Elkhart, Indiana. In 1989, it instituted an employee participation program, partly in response to employee complaints about new attendance and bonus policies. Separate committees were formed to offer proposals to management on policies for wage scales, absenteeism, bonus pay, and other issues. Management selected the employee members of the committees and also named one supervisor to each committee. The employee benefits manager was also named as an *ex officio* member of every committee. In committee discussions, some fledgling proposals were immediately rejected by the management members, and the teams then created alternate policy suggestions. Before any proposal could be acted on by management, however, a union organizing campaign began in the plant. Management informed workers that it could not interact with the committees until after the union election. In the union certification vote, employees voted against union representation by a vote of 95 to 82.

After the failed unionization campaign, a complaint was lodged with the National Labor Relations Board (NLRB) alleging that the employee participation committees were illegal under the National Labor Relations Act (NLRA), Section 8(a)(2) (also known as the Wagner

Act). When the Wagner Act was passed in 1935, one of its chief targets was the employer-sponsored labor groups that management used as a tactic to discourage employees from choosing representation by independent labor unions. Congress outlawed that tactic by banning "company dominated labor organizations." The act defined a labor organization as one that dealt with management and addressed conditions of work. The act proscribed company domination or interference with the formation or administration of any labor organization, and it also prohibited company financial or other support for a labor organization.

The NLRB found the Electromation committees to be illegal company-dominated labor organizations, and its judgment was affirmed by the United States Supreme Court in 1994. Both the NLRB and the Supreme Court held that the Electromation committees were labor organizations because they involved bilateral discussions of the conditions of work—that is, employee representatives made proposals about wages, benefits, smoking policies, grievance procedures, and the like that were to be accepted or rejected by management. The NLRB and the Court also held that Electromation dominated these labor organizations because it formed the committees, selected the membership and topics for the committees, set the agenda for meetings, gave management representatives implicit veto power over proposals, and paid for the employees' time, as well as for the supplies and space used by the committees. One NLRB member put it this way: "They gave the employees the illusion of a bargaining representative without the reality of one."

In this and subsequent decisions, the NLRB has made it clear that employee involvement committees such as those at Electromation will be found illegal unless and until Congress changes the Wagner Act's language. Through its decisions, the NLRB has also made clear the legality of employee committees that serve as mere "brainstorming" sessions that communicate employee opinions or other information to management. The Supreme Court has said that Section 8(a)(2) does not foreclose employee committees that do not function in a representative capacity and that focus solely on increasing company productivity, efficiency, and quality control (that is, do not deal with working conditions such as pay, grievances, hours of work, and so on). Additionally, in its later *DuPont* decision, the NLRB accepted a joint labor–management committee provided that "the committee were governed by majority decision-making, management representatives were in the minority, and the committee had the power to decide matters for itself, rather than simply make proposals to management."

Labor relations specialists are troubled by these decisions. They worry that the decisions allow only for either extreme: weak employee organizations that have very limited scope and no decision-making powers or strong, independent committees that have real authority to make and implement decisions. What appears to run afoul of the law are precisely the sorts of management-sponsored employee participation programs that management theorists have been urging as necessary for the competitiveness of American industry: programs that can discuss the sometimes interrelated issues of productivity and working conditions and that make proposals to management. A number of respected labor relations theorists have called for a revision of Section 8(a)(2) of the NLRA, as has the recent governmental Dunlop Commission. Union leaders, however, dissent from that call. They still are concerned that in a nation where employers are often hostile to unions, companies will use a change in the law to revert to the old tactics of in-house, company unions.

- If we allow employee participation in issues of working conditions, what features must the participation programs have to avoid becoming "company dominated unions"?

- Are participation programs helpful or harmful to the goals espoused by unions?

- Can we draw a sharp distinction between issues that relate to productivity and issues that relate to wages and other working conditions?

- Why do some believe that employee involvement is necessary for the competitiveness of American business?

Decision Scenario G

DONNELLY MIRRORS: FIFTY YEARS OF PARTICIPATION

Donnelly Mirrors, Inc., of Holland, Michigan, has been experimenting with worker participation for over five decades. In 1952, the company introduced a Scanlon gain-sharing plan. The plan at Donnelly involved teams of management and elected non-management employees that met to exchange information and suggest cost-saving ideas. Any savings from those ideas were shared among all the workers. The goal of Scanlon plans like the one at Donnelly is to improve productivity, but the plans achieve that goal by engendering a sense of ownership and team cooperation among employees.

Over the years, Donnelly Mirrors introduced a number of new elements to its participation scheme. When they realized that some cost-saving ideas were also job-elimination ideas, they also realized that there were disincentives for employees to offer some money-saving suggestions. So they guar-

This case was prepared from the following sources: *Harvard Business Review,* 55, no. 1 (1977): 118; the Dunlop Report; Alan Blinder, ed., *Paying for Productivity* (Washington, D.C.: The Brookings Institute, 1990); www.magna.com/magnaWeb .nsf/

anteed that a worker whose job was eliminated would receive 90 percent of his or her wage for twelve months.

The company also began to use the teamwork concept more broadly. It set up work teams at all levels throughout the company. The teams deal with all facets of the business. For any given level, the teams would be headed by a supervisor and would include representatives of the employees from that level. The team leaders are chosen by a selection group composed of employees from all levels of the firm. Each team leader is also a member of the team at the next highest level. The teams' overlapping membership is an attempt to ensure a free flow of communication both up and down the corporate structure. It also aims to develop feelings of trust and ownership among the employees. Donnelly must have had an intuitive sense of what works. More recent studies seem to confirm that gain-sharing plans are unlikely to succeed unless significant levels of trust and cooperation are present. After the introduction of this team organization, the company experienced a significant increase in productivity.

Donnelly Mirrors also created another committee that was independent of the work team structure. The committee is known as the Donnelly Committee. The committee has 15 members, including the company president, who sits *ex officio*. The other members are elected by the employees and come from all parts of the company. The Donnelly Committee governs issues related to working conditions, pay, grievances, and the like. A company spokesperson described the Donnelly Committee as a safety net on issues of fairness and a guarantee that all employees have a voice in personnel policies that affect them. Elected members serve a two-year term but are subject to recall by their constituencies if they vote in a manner the electors disapprove. Of interest, the committee takes no action unless there is unanimous agreement, so everyone knows how each member voted. The unanimity requirement, however, does not seem to prevent decisions from being made. Rather, it functions as a consensus builder.

The almost century-old Donnelly Corporation was acquired in October 2002 by a Canadian competitor, Magna International. The end of Donnelly's independence does not mean the end of its distinctive approach to labor relations, however. The new owners have long had a progressive employment system that sets aside 10 percent of pre-tax profits for employees and gives workers voice through fairness committees and an employee voting process. Time will tell whether the new Magna Donnelly can successfully merge the two workplace cultures, but the acquisition appears to be a good fit for both organizations.

- Donnelly and Magna were privately held businesses that were influenced by the values of their founders. Do you think that the Donnelly approach could work in a corporate culture that did not have that founder's influence?

- The team concept entails that workers spend a substantial amount of time in meetings. While that work time appears to produce productivity gains at Donnelly, do you believe that it would in all cases? What are the conditions that make productivity gains more probable? What conditions make them less probable?

- How significant in your mind was the presence of the separate Donnelly Committee in the effectiveness of the work team organizational structure?

6

꙳

Employee Rights: Health, Equality, and Privacy

INTRODUCTION

Chapter Five examined the nature and value of work and considered various procedural structures that might be implemented to insure that employees are treated fairly. In this chapter we look at other important goods—health and safety, equal opportunity, privacy—and consider the meaning and justification of employee rights to such goods.

Previous chapters introduced a distinction between legal and moral rights. As we turn to employment issues, it will be helpful to identify a third type of rights: *contractual rights.* As rights, all function to protect individual interests by entitling the rights holder to act in certain ways (for example, a right of freedom of religion) or possess something (for example, property). *Legal rights* are those entitlements that are granted by a legal system. *Moral rights* are those entitlements that derive from moral rules or principles. *Contractual rights,* as the name suggests, are those entitlements that are derived from a contract. Thus, we might say that an employee has a legal right to be paid a minimum wage, a contractual right to a certain number of paid holidays or a certain health care package, and moral rights to a safe and healthy workplace.

This chapter examines the moral entitlements, moral rights, that employees might deserve in the workplace. To understand how moral rights would function in the workplace, consider how contractual and legal rights function. To say that an employee has a contractual right to health care implies that this entitlement has been negotiated between employer and employee. Employees are entitled to this because employers have agreed to it as a condition of employment. But contractual rights, by their very nature, are always subject to the quirks of particular contracts. What is granted in a contract can be taken away in a contract. Legal rights do not function in this way. To have a legal right to a minimum wage is to say that this good has been removed from the normal bargaining that occurs between employers and employees. An employer cannot make acceptance of below-minimum wages a condition of the employment contract. Moral rights in the workplace function in a similar way. To say that an employee has a moral right to, for example, safe working conditions, is to claim that employers cannot negotiate safety as a condition of employment. Moral rights prevent employees from being placed in the fundamentally coercive position of having to choose between this good and their job.

But settling on an understanding of what employee rights are is not to establish that there are such moral rights in the workplace. This chapter will examine several potential moral rights in the workplace: rights to health and safety, rights to privacy, and rights to equal treatment and equal opportunity.

HEALTH AND SAFETY

In one sense, of course, everyone is in favor of a healthy and risk-free workplace. Nevertheless, significant controversy surrounds issues of workplace health and safety. For this reason it will prove helpful to consider the value of health and safety. First, if anything can be said to be *intrinsically* good, it would be health and safety. Except in the most extreme circumstances, life is better than death, health is better than illness, and bodily integrity is better than injury. Besides this intrinsic value, health and safety also have significant *instrumental* value. That is, they are very useful, if not necessary, for acquiring other things of value. However, unlike other instrumentally valuable things, like money, health and safety seem necessary for almost any other good that we seek. Whatever one desires, chances are that being healthy and safe will greatly improve one's chances for satisfying that desire.

But health and safety also function as ideals, seldom fully attainable (at least for any extended time) during our lives. It would be odd to claim that one is perfectly healthy, or completely safe. We seem to face risks to our health and safety at all times. When I kiss my child good night, I risk being infected with his flu. As I sit here typing at my word processor, I risk getting carpal tunnel syndrome from typing too much.

Many of the debates concerning workplace health and safety focus not on health and safety as such, but on reducing risks faced by workers. Risk can be understood as the probability of harm. Risk therefore can be measured and compared. Protecting worker health and safety, therefore, will involve questions of risk assessment and risk assumption: How high are the risks and how do they compare with alternatives? Who shall bear the risks and how much risk is acceptable? The first questions are technical and can be answered by scientists and engineers. The last questions are ethical and best not left to technicians.

But assessing risks also involves making judgments on the magnitude or seriousness of the harm involved. There is an important difference between a low probability of minor harm and a high probability of major harm. Again, scientists and engineers are capable of determining the probabilities of various harms, but judging whether or not these risks are worth taking and making judgments about the nature of the harms threatened are ethical questions also best not left to technicians.

These distinctions often get confused in debates about workplace health and safety. In many cases, highly technical and mathematical studies are done to evaluate workplace safety standards. In effect, these studies can measure the probability of various harms and compare those probabilities to other risks taken in other circumstances. For example, workers might be told that they stand a higher risk of being hit by a bus on their way to work than contracting cancer from airborne chemicals in the workplace. But we should always be careful to distinguish the factual questions from the normative ones. It may well be, as a matter of fact, more risky to drive on a busy highway than to inhale workplace carcinogens. But this fact alone does not answer the questions of whether employees *ought* to take such risks, of who should decide which risks are taken, of whether or not the benefits of these risks are worth it. Determining relative risks does not, in itself, decide the ethical questions.

While the value of health and safety is uncontroversial, there is also wide disagreement over the best means for pursuing these goals. One extreme would leave these decisions to the voluntary agreement reached through a bargaining process between employer and employee. In this view, acceptable risk is to be determined by individual employees bargaining with their employers. Those who place a high value on health and safety will demand a relatively safe workplace and presumably be willing to sacrifice wages and other benefits to get it. Others who are willing to take risks, would presumably bargain for higher wages as a trade-off for accepting greater workplace risk. In each case, all involved get what they most want and society maximizes happiness. Individual bargaining is the method favored by defenders of free market economics. Our first reading, by James Chelius, offers an account of occupational safety and health that is sympathetic to free market economics.

Government Regulation to Protect Health and Safety

Many observers deny that the individual bargaining approach associated with free market economics is an adequate means for protecting health and safety. Challenges to this approach echo many of the challenges raised to the utilitarian and liberty-based defense of the market.

First, critics object to treating health and safety as, in Chelius's words, an "economic commodity." This is to treat an intrinsic good of health and safety as a mere instrumental good that can be measured, compared, and traded off against other values. Second, critics also deny the claim that "work is simply one of the many activities which yields injuries." Unlike potentially dangerous activities such as mountain climbing or motorcycle racing, individuals seldom are free to choose whether or not to work. Typically, the less free individuals are to participate in some risky activity the more society regulates that activity. Driving an automobile was an activity relatively unregulated in the early days of driving that has become more regulated as driving has become more of a necessity of modern life. Further, the risks associated with work do not have the additional personal benefits that come from participation in other risky activities.

The individual bargaining approach also can ignore important social consequences. Minimal harms faced by individuals can, when generalized over a large population, create significant social harms. As an individual, I may choose to take a 1 in 100 chance of injury in the workplace, thinking that the odds are long that I will actually be injured. But if 100 people, or 1000 people, or 10,000 people make a similar choice, real injuries are certain to occur. Since we can know that injuries will occur, although we cannot know to whom, critics charge that social regulation aimed at limiting these injuries is justified.

Critics also point out that individual employees are seldom in a position to prevent many workplace harms. An individual employee may be able to prevent a workplace accident because he or she understands the risks involved in working with machinery. But few employees will understand the risks involved with, for example, inhaling airborne particles or exposure to workplace toxins, and therefore they will not be in a position to prevent workplace-related diseases. If employees do not understand workplace risks, bargaining between employees and employers will not attain an optimal level of workplace safety.

Finally, critics point out that the individual bargaining approach ultimately relies on prior experience to provide the information necessary for making efficient bargains. One learns that inhaling coal dust or benzene is dangerous after workers who have inhaled these toxins over time become ill and die from that exposure. What can be called the "first generation" challenge points out that efficient health and safety consequences are achieved through individual bargaining only by using the first generation of injured workers as a means to that end. This, critics charge, is unjust.

To avoid such problems, a system of government regulation to establish workplace health and safety standards has developed in recent decades. These standards, in effect, create the legal right to minimum health and safety in the workplace. Whereas the individual bargaining approach would treat health and safety as contractual rights established only through contractual agreements, health and safety regulation creates legal rights that trump individual agreements.

Cost-Benefit Analysis

Most of the ethical issues surrounding health and safety regulation concern the methods used to set standards. Beginning with the Reagan Administration in the 1980s, many have argued that economic criteria, and in particular cost-benefit analysis, ought to be used in setting health and safety standards. (A parallel argument has been developed concerning environmental standards and will be examined in Chapter Ten.) As described in the Chelius reading, this approach aims for an optimal balancing of economic costs and health and safety. According to this view, there is no such thing as a perfectly safe and risk-free workplace. Everything we do involves some risk and every choice we make involves trade-offs between risks and benefits. Thus, government regulation should use cost-benefit analysis to set standards at the point of equilibrium at which a decrease in risks is not worth the increase in costs.

Critics of using cost-benefit analysis point to a distinction between cost-benefit and cost-effective strategies. It is one thing to seek the most cost-effective means to an end; it is quite another to choose our ends based on costs. A cost-effective strategy would accept the ends of health and safety as given, then seek the least expensive means to achieve those ends. Cost-benefit analysis requires that the ends themselves be determined on economic grounds.

There are several ethical problems in using cost-benefit. First, it requires us to assign an economic value to health and safety. Similar to objections raised previously, critics charge that this is to treat something of intrinsic value as a mere instrumental value. Contrary to Chelius's claim, safety should not be treated as an economic commodity. To do so is to treat human beings merely as a means to an end.

A particularly offensive aspect of this approach is that proposals for it typically follow the model of costs developed by the insurance industry. The economic value of health and safety, as determined by the insurance industry in injury and death settlements, for example, is determined by calculating lost earnings. Thus, one life is "worth" the earning potential that was forgone after one has died. But this suggests that the value of the life of an investment banker is worth more than the life of a cook or janitor. (This objection was raised against proposed financial settlements with the families of the victims of the World Trade Center attack.) Such an approach seems to deny the equal and inherent dignity of each individual.

Finally, use of cost-benefit analysis takes decisions about public values and turns them into economic decisions that can be made by experts. The level of health and safety that is acceptable to society should, in this view, be a political decision made in a democratic way by citizens. There is a real risk that in using cost-benefit analysis the political process is disregarded and the decision is left in the hands of economists. Citizens are therefore treated as consumers, and health is treated as a commodity.

Health Insurance and Work

A relatively unique system of health insurance has evolved within the United States. Whereas in most Western industrial nations health insurance is seen as a public good to be supported by government, the United States relies on private employers to provide most of this country's health insurance. Thus, health insurance has evolved into a contractual right for millions of U.S. workers. But as suggested by our discussion of contractual rights, what is granted by a contract can be changed by a contract. While legal and moral rights in the workplace are one-directional in the sense that they protect employees from potential harms from employers, contractual rights, as do any conditions of a contract, exist to provide mutual benefits.

Two ethical issues involving employee health insurance are presented in this chapter. In the case study found later in this chapter, an employee with cancer and AIDS lost his insurance coverage when his employer changed insurance companies. The employer, Gus Mayer, made the change because the present insurance coverage no longer worked for the employer's benefit. Specifically, premiums for both employer and other employees had risen significantly when the insurance company learned of this employee's AIDS diagnosis. The employee filed a lawsuit charging that he was the victim of unjust discrimination on the basis of his illness.

A second ethical issue asks us to consider the purpose of health and life insurance. Corporate-owned life insurance (COLI) is insurance on employees that is paid for by employers, but it designates the employers themselves as beneficiaries. This insurance can occur in situations where the employees have no other employer-provided insurance and even in cases where the employees themselves do not even know about the policy. Sometimes called "dead peasants" insurance, such policies mean that an employer can benefit financially by the death of its employees. In *The Problem with "Dead Peasants" Insurance* (Reading 6.4), Earl Spurgin argues that there are serious ethical wrongs with this practice.

EQUAL TREATMENT IN THE WORKPLACE

The Gus Mayer discrimination case also raises questions concerning equal treatment of employees. Chapter Eleven will examine in some depth the issue of equal employment opportunities at the level of social policy and practice. In that chapter we examine the question of whether business has a responsibility to address the social problems of discrimination and inequality by instituting policies of affirmative action and preferential hiring. In this chapter we examine two issues of equal treatment faced by individual employees: sexual harassment and equal opportunity for disabled workers.

Sexual Harassment

The Civil Rights Act of 1964 was a landmark piece of legislation that prohibited all forms of employment discrimination on the basis of race, color, religion, national origin, and sex. This was the primary federal law that enforced equal treatment in the workplace. In part, this law states:

> It shall be an unlawful employment practice for an employer: (1) to fail or refuse to hire or to discharge any individual, or otherwise to discriminate against any individual with respect to compensation, terms, conditions or privileges of employment because of such individual's race, color, religion, sex, or national origin or (2) to limit, segregate, or classify his employees or applicants for employment in any way which would deprive or tend to deprive any individual of employment opportunities or otherwise adversely affect his status as an employee, because of such individual's race, color, religion, sex, or national origin.

It took almost a decade after the passage of this act for courts to begin recognizing sexual harassment as a form of employment discrimination. Beginning in the mid-1970s, federal courts acknowledged that sexual harassment was an illegal form of sexual discrimination. In 1980, the Equal Employment Opportunity Commission issued clear guidelines that defined illegal sexual harassment:

> Unwelcome sexual advances, requests for sexual favors, and other verbal or physical conduct of a sexual nature constitute sexual harassment when (1) submission to such conduct is made either explicitly or implicitly a term or condition of an individual's employment, (2) submission to or rejection of such conduct by an individual is used as a basis for employment decisions affecting such individual, or (3) such conduct has the purpose or effect of unreasonably interfering with an individual's work performance or creating an intimidating, hostile, or offensive work environment.

Based on the commission's ruling, two types of sexual harassment have been recognized: *quid pro quo* harassment and hostile work environment harassment. *Quid pro quo* (from the Latin for "this for that") harassment occurs when submission to sexual favors is made a condition for some job benefit. Such harassment can take the form of threats—"sleep with me or lose your promotion"—or sexual offers—"I can be a big help to your career if you'll go out with me." In both cases, a person exploits his or her position of authority in the workplace to obtain sexual favors from a coworker. In both cases, workers face unjust and discriminatory obstacles in the workplace. The second type of sexual harassment has its roots in the Civil Rights Act's prohibition against acts that would tend to deprive individuals employment opportunities or that adversely affect their work because of sex. Hostile work environment harassment occurs when the general sexual environment of a workplace is such that it interferes with a person's ability to do his or her job. Common examples would include repeated off-color jokes, lewd comments or suggestions, the display of sexually explicit or offensive material, touching, patting, or other physical contact. This conduct becomes sexual harassment when it is so distressing to a person that she or he finds it impossible to complete job duties.

In one sense, *quid pro quo* harassment raises familiar ethical and legal issues: Threats, intimidation, and coercion are common ethical and legal wrongs. In such cases, a worker would need only to prove that the wrongful behavior in fact occurred to prove the harassment claim. There are reasonably clear standards for what constitutes a threat or intimidating or coercive behavior. However, the issues are very different with hostile environment harassment. Here, one must show a continued pattern of activity and establish that this interfered with the person's ability to do his or her job. But, how do we decide what behavior is "offensive" enough to prevent people from doing their job? How do we distinguish between flirting and harassment, between an innocent comment and a lewd remark? It seems that what one person finds to be offensive, another takes to be a mild joke. Whether a workplace is a "hostile" environment would seem to depend on individual points of view. Doesn't "offensiveness" lie in the eye of the beholder? In cases where such disputes have arisen, courts have traditionally relied on what is called the "reasonable man" standard. (We see this standard come into play in discussion of deceptive advertising: What one person finds deceptive, another finds mere puffery. Courts decide if an ad is deceptive by asking if it would deceive a "reasonable man.") With sexual harassment, however, an interesting philosophical question is raised: Is what is "reasonable" for men the same as what is "reasonable" for women? Might the reasonable "man" standard be biased against women? Should harassment be judged by a reasonable man standard or a reasonable woman standard?

In the early 1990s, federal courts considered these questions, and in a 1991 case a Florida court concluded that the reasonable man standard was biased against women. Since this decision, courts have begun using a "reasonable woman" standard to interpret a hostile environment as one that a reasonable woman would find sufficiently offensive to prevent her from doing her job.

More recently another challenge to courts' interpretation of sexual harassment has been raised. Legal scholar Vicki Schultz (Reading 6.2) has argued that courts have been led astray, particularly in cases of hostile work environment, by adopting too narrow an understanding of sexual harassment. Whereas *quid pro quo* harassment typically involves sexual advances and threats, hostile work environments typically involve gender-based harassment and may or may not involve sexuality. Schultz cites many cases in which women have been subjected to harassment so severe as to deny them an equal opportunity to work. This should be a clear case of discrimination based on sex. However, in many cases the harassment does not involve sexuality, as much as it involves threats and intimidation based on gender. In the opinion of some male workers, women do not belong in certain jobs or certain positions of authority. Women who work such jobs can be subjected to vulgarity, threats, and intimidation. Schultz describes many cases in which courts have dismissed claims of sexual harassment because these vulgarities, threats, and intimidations have not been overtly sexual, even though they have been aimed exclusively at women. Schultz argues that courts and society need to reconceptualize sexual harassment as a form of gender, and not exclusively sexual, harassment.

Disabled Workers

In 1990, the U.S. Congress passed, and President Bush signed into law, the Americans with Disabilities Act (ADA). Among other things, this law extends to people with disabilities the same rights to equal employment opportunities that the Civil Rights Act of 1964 granted to women and minorities. This law prohibits discrimination against people with disabilities and requires business to make reasonable accommodations to both employees and applicants with disabilities. In essence, then, the law both grants equal treatment to people with disabilities and requires affirmative action to be taken to accommodate their special needs. If a disabled person is otherwise qualified for a job, business has a responsibility to provide that person with an equal and fair opportunity to get and keep that job.

This law defines a disabled person as "one who has a physical or mental impairment that substantially limits a major life activity, has a record of an impairment, or is regarded as having an impairment." The ADA gives examples of disabilities such as mental retardation, cancer, muscular dystrophy, AIDS, emotional illness, visual impairments, alcoholism (but not active alcohol abuse), and physical handicaps. Drug abuse, weight, homosexuality, and poverty are conditions explicitly excluded from this law. It is estimated that there are 43 million Americans who would be classified as disabled under these guidelines, 60 percent of whom are unemployed. This law and these figures suggest that the American workplace will be changing even more in future years.

But is the ADA a good law? Is it merely the latest in a long line of government entitlements that create a new class of disadvantaged citizens with new rights? Or does the ADA appropriately reflect a more general moral obligation to people who face undeserved disadvantages? Does society have a responsibility to provide disabled people with jobs, or would our social obligation be exhausted by welfare and charity? These questions are examined by philosopher Gregory Kavka in his essay "Disability and the Right to Work" (Reading 6.3). Kavka argues that disabled people have a strong right to employment that society in general and private employers in some cases have a duty to meet.

The ADA has been interpreted as defining a disabled person as someone who is regarded as having an impairment. This interpretation promises to raise some challenging future problems. Advances being made in genetic science and technology raise the probability that an employee's genetic background will soon enter into employment decisions. Human genetics allows for the identification of people who are genetically predisposed or susceptible to certain diseases and impairments. If this information becomes known to an employer and is the basis on which employment decisions are made, it would seem that such people are being regarded as impaired. Hence, genetic susceptibility to disease might make an employee protected by the ADA. But genetic screening also raises questions of privacy in the workplace. Do employers have a right to know such information about employees?

PRIVACY IN THE WORKPLACE

Nature and Value of Privacy

The legal right of privacy is a relatively recent development within the United States. The U.S. Supreme Court recognized a civil right to privacy only in 1965, in the case *Griswold v. Connecticut*. This case referred to a "zone of privacy" surrounding each individual. Following this case, the legal right of privacy is often understood as a right to "be let alone" within that zone of privacy. But persuasive objections have been raised against this interpretation of privacy. It is difficult to understand how a general claim to be let alone can be maintained as a civil right by anyone who wishes to participate in any social arrangement, particularly an essentially cooperative and social activity like work.

A more helpful understanding of privacy focuses not so much on being let alone as on the control of personal information. In this view, a right to privacy involves the right to control personal information. Philosopher George Brenkert has suggested that this right to privacy involves a three-place relation between a person (A), some information about that person (X), and another person (Z). The informational right of privacy is violated only when Z comes to know X, *and* no relation exists between A and Z that justifies Z coming to know X.

Thus, to understand privacy in the workplace we must consider the nature of the employer-employee relationship. What is this relationship and what information does it justify an employer coming to know about an employee? The reading by DesJardins and Duska examines these questions within the context of drug testing for employees.

Understanding what privacy is will not be sufficient for a complete evaluation of privacy in the workplace. Even if we could establish that employees do maintain a right of privacy in the workplace, we need to know something about the value of that right before deciding if employee privacy overrides the concerns of employers. Why should privacy be desirable? Is it so important that it should be protected by legal and ethical rights?

Let us begin by considering the value of informational privacy. What would be wrong, what values would be lost, if, for example, the content of your diary was published in the local newspaper? Why should we so value controlling our most personal thoughts and feelings?

One source of concern would be the embarrassment and anxiety we would no doubt feel if our most personal thoughts became public. But what explains this anxiety? Why don't we want others to know our most personal thoughts? Part of the reason may be a fear about what others might do with this information. We are made vulnerable by others knowing a great deal about us. Part also is the desire to maintain some basic core of personal integrity. To maintain a sense of personal identity—this is who I am—requires some boundary between self and others. Maintaining that boundary, whether by control of the personal information or by reserving certain decisions for the individual, is an important element of protecting the integrity of our own selves. Certainly it is part of what we mean by the ethical commitment to respect the dignity of individuals.

Another aspect of this concerns the relationships that we have with other people. Consider for a minute the differences between strangers, acquaintances, friends, "best" friends, family, lovers. Cannot these differences be explained in terms of the amount of information shared? Isn't the difference between an acquaintance and a friend due in large measure to the fact that friends know more about you? We confide in friends, we trust them, we let them see who we "really" are. Thus it seems our social identity—the roles we fill, the relationships that we have with others—also depends on privacy. When we compare this to the kinds of decisions that the Supreme Court has considered to involve privacy—decisions about family, children, sexuality, reproduction, abortion, even death—we can see that these all deeply affect our very identity as an individual. These decisions seem fundamental to establishing the persons that we are: parent, spouse, lover, even the person who is unwilling to exist dependent on a respirator.

Thus the value of privacy seems connected to respecting and protecting the integrity of individuals. Respecting others as individual persons seems to commit us to maintaining a boundary between the *personal* and the public. Privacy, whether it concerns certain basic decisions we make or controlling personal information, would appear to be a major element in the ethical responsibility to respect other persons. Thus, a reasonable case could be made that the *right* of privacy is derived from the more fundamental right to being treated with respect. A person whose privacy is violated is being treated with a lack of respect.

How others might use the personal information that they come to possess is the final consideration. We said earlier that a person who loses privacy often feels vulnerable. Typically, we have a reason for keeping personal information private. We are put into a fundamentally coercive position when someone possesses personal information about us, *and* they know that we had a reason not to divulge that information. Blackmail is perhaps the most dramatic example of a situation in which an individual can be coerced by a threat to disclose personal information.

With this examination of the nature and value of privacy in general, we turn next to the extent of privacy in the workplace. If we adopt Brenkert's understanding of informational privacy as our model, we can develop conclusions about workplace privacy by starting with an examination of the employer–employee relationship. Following the reasoning in earlier chapters, we can assume here that this relationship is a contractual relationship. In general, then, we can say that employee privacy is violated whenever personal information is collected or used by an employer for any purpose that is irrelevant to or in violation of the employment contract.

More specifically, there are three conditions of any valid contract: (a) It must arise out of the informed consent of both parties; (b) it must be free from fraud or coercion; and (c) it presupposes a legal system to be enforceable. Thus, we have a framework for determining the extent of employee privacy. Information that ensures that the contract is free from fraud (such as misinformation about past employment experience or educational background), that has been gathered with the informed consent of employees, or that is required by law would seem not to be rightfully private.

A helpful exercise is to apply this framework to information requested prior to employment. (For example, should a job applicant be required to supply his Social Security number?) Or apply this framework to the use to which employers can put personal information. (For example, can information gathered for health insurance purposes be used to deny jobs or dismiss employees?) Are all methods of gathering information (such as polygraph tests, drug tests, and electronic surveillance), even job-relevant information, equally valid?

Finally, there are a number of ethical reasons why an employee might wish to keep personal information from her employer. On one hand, of course, if an employee does have a legitimate ethical claim to a right of privacy, then the burden of proof rests on the employer to justify any infringement on this right. But as we've seen, employers can make the claim that they have a justification: Economic efficiency is served by this increase in employer knowledge. How might employees respond?

Two responses deserve note. First, as we've said, privacy is important for maintaining the boundaries that establish our personal identity. For many people it is important to maintain a distinction between work and home, between their life as an employee and their life outside of work. Very few people desire to be completely identified with their work. Most of us, whether we work at jobs we love or at jobs full of drudgery and toil, need to be able to "punch out" and leave work behind. There are good psychological as well as ethical reasons for being able to separate our role as employee from our roles as parent, spouse, citizen, neighbor, and so on. Privacy is a necessary part of maintaining this boundary.

Second, many employees have good reason to fear the uses to which personal information will be put by employers. Most obviously, the personal information that employers seek will be used to affect one's job status. Employers seek personal information about employees to improve managerial decisions. These personnel decisions ultimately rest on the ability to hire, fire, demote, and transfer employees. An employee's ability to protect his job can be a function of his ability to protect his privacy.

CASE STUDY: Health Insurance and Discrmination against the Sick

What responsibilities does an employer have for providing health insurance to its employees? Can an employer contract with a health insurance provider that will exclude coverage for some employees?

For more than ten years, David Anderson worked at Gus Mayer, a clothing store in Beaumont, Texas. Gus Mayer provided its employees with a health insurance plan for which the company and individual employees each paid 50 percent of the premiums. The insurance provider, Home Life Insurance, adjusted premiums twice each year to reflect present costs.

In 1988 Anderson was diagnosed with cancer. He had surgery and radiation treatment at that time. Home Life Insurance soon raised the company's premiums, in part to reflect the high costs of Anderson's treatments. In 1991, Anderson was diagnosed with Acquired Immunodeficiency Syndrome (AIDS). Fearful that he might be denied insurance coverage because of his AIDS status, Anderson began seeing a private doctor and paid for these visits out of his own pocket. In August 1991, his physician sent Home Life a bill for Anderson's medical treatment by mistake, thereby inadvertently informing Home Life of Anderson's AIDS status.

In September 1992, Home Life increased insurance premiums for Gus Mayer by 30 percent. Court records show that despite an overall rise in

health care costs, much of this increase was due to Anderson's health status. By 1992, Anderson's employer also knew of his AIDS status.

Other employees complained of the increased costs for their insurance, threatening to withdraw from the group health plan if lower premiums could not be found. As a result, Gus Mayer's management instructed its insurance agent to seek other coverage with new insurance carriers. Their agent soon contracted with a new insurance carrier, John Alden Life Insurance Company (JALIC).

Management soon instructed all employees to fill out application forms for this new insurance policy and assured employees that they would receive increased insurance coverage and lower premiums from this new company. Management had been informed that the new insurer had the flexibility to deny coverage to individual employees because of their prior medical history.

Predictably JALIC denied coverage to Anderson due to his prior cancer and AIDS status. Nevertheless, Gus Mayer decided to change insurance carriers and purchase the policy offered by JALIC. Management made no effort to find alternative group policies.

In testimony that a court described as "incredible," a representative of JALIC claimed that Anderson was denied coverage solely on the basis of his prior cancer. JALIC claimed that

Anderson's AIDS was never considered, but admitted that JALIC had never accepted an HIV-positive applicant. JALIC also admitted that it sometimes evaluated cancer patients on a case-by-case basis and acknowledged that at least one other Gus Mayer employee who had been accepted for coverage had been diagnosed with cancer.

Faced with the realization that his employer would no longer provide health insurance of any kind, Anderson filed a law suit alleging violation of the Americans with Disabilities Act, which prohibits discrimination against the disabled in all aspects of employment.

- Should insurance companies be allowed to deny coverage to individual members of an employee group as a means to reduce premiums to other members?

- Should an employer be free to seek the lowest-cost insurance coverage even if this means denying insurance to some employees?

- What responsibilities, if any, does an employer have to provide health insurance to employees?

- Courts have allowed discrimination on the basis of a disability if it has been shown to involve a bona fide occupational qualification. Is qualification for health insurance at rates acceptable to other employees a reasonable basis for determining employment qualifications?

READING 6.1 THE OCCUPATIONAL SAFETY AND HEALTH PROBLEM
James Chelius

THE NATURE OF THE PROBLEM

One of every ten workers in private industry each year suffers the effects of an accident or disease incurred while working.[1] Only one-third of these incidents involve lost worktime, but lost time totals over 31 million days per year in the United States.[2] Naturally, these accidents and diseases have aroused public concern.

Without slighting the seriousness of the work-injury problem, it is helpful to place it in perspective by considering other activities which give rise to similar harm. The National Safety Council estimates that many more deaths result from nonwork automobile accidents than from all work accidents. Accidents in the home and accidents in "public-place" activities, which include swimming and hunting, also produce more deaths than working.[3] Walter Oi has estimated that ". . . fully a third of all employed persons confront a risk of being injured on the job that is lower than the risk of living in general."[4] Thus, while work injuries are a serious concern, they do not represent a unique or isolated

phenomenon. Work is simply one of the many activities which yields injuries. Although there are certain aspects of work which make it different from other activities, there is much that is common to all injury-producing endeavors.

Safety as an Economic Commodity

Although work deaths and injuries are occurrences everyone would like to eliminate, unfortunately this is not possible. Many of these accidents and diseases cannot be prevented if we also want the desirable goods, services, and incomes which accompany them. All of life's activities entail the possibility of being injured or catching a disease but people do not choose just the least risky activities. Relatively hazardous activities such as working, driving, and consuming new products are freely chosen because people feel the benefits of participation outweigh the risks. Since there are benefits as well as risks to participation in all activities, the problem of risk control can be most usefully analyzed within the economist's framework of costs and benefits.

The moral anguish associated with accidents and disease notwithstanding, it must be understood that prevention is an economic commodity. Prevention can be "produced" only by the use of scarce resources which, if not allocated to preven-

From James Chelius, *Workplace Safety and Health* (Washington, D.C.: American Enterprise Institute, 1977).

tion, could serve other beneficial purposes. The resources used for prevention usually have an obvious economic character. For example, heavy-duty automobile bumpers, protective headgear, and safety experts use resources that could be devoted to other beneficial purposes than accident and disease prevention. Of all the resources available to us for accident prevention, the most expensive is abstaining from a risky activity. Each of us avoids many activities which could give us some form of satisfaction. However desirable the satisfaction, many of us feel that activities such as riding motorcycles or building skyscrapers are far too risky compared with the rewards of participation. The fact that there are many risky activities which we do not choose to avoid simply means that we savor the rewards of these activities more than we fear the risks.

Why Occupational Safety and Health Are Special

Although working is often no more dangerous than other activities, work risks receive attention disproportionate to their impact. To understand why, it is useful to consider how people decide whether to participate in a risky activity. This choice is often very difficult. However, people usually feel comfortable with these decisions, once made, because they did have a choice and were aware of the rewards and risks when they chose. The same decision process occurs in both work and nonwork settings, but there are substantial differences. In a nonwork situation the rewards of exposure to risk typically accrue directly to the participant. Furthermore, control over the decision is usually direct and immediate. In deciding whether to drive to the beach, an individual implicitly weighs the risks of driving against the pleasures of visiting the beach. If the anticipated pleasure outweighs the anticipated risks, the individual goes to the beach. If not he stays home.

A work situation with exactly the same risks and rewards may present a more difficult decision. Whereas the worker driving to the beach to deliver food supplies exposes himself directly to the same risks as the vacationer, the direct rewards of his drive accrue to the consumers of the food he delivers. If consumers desire the benefits created by having the food at the beach, they must pay the employee's company, and the company in turn rewards the employee. Therefore, even in an ideal situation where the company pays extra wages for

exposure to risk, the rewards for such risks are more indirect than in the typical nonwork situation.

In addition, the decisions controlling individual exposure to risks in the workplace frequently have a less immediate impact than nonwork decisions. An individual who considers going to the beach for his own recreation can quickly make a decision or change it if conditions change, whereas an individual in the work situation must negotiate with his employer for changes in the level of risk or benefits. An individual planning a family trip to the beach can change his mind if weather conditions change and he feels the drive is too risky. If a worker encounters such a change in driving conditions, however, he may not be able to alter his schedule to accommodate the increase in risk. A worker's recourse is to negotiate with his employer, individually or through his union, to lower the level of risk or to increase wages. If the situation is not corrected the individual may have to search for a new job. Certainly the process of bargaining with an employer or changing jobs is a more difficult and complicated method of responding to a change in the level of risk than is typical in a nonwork setting.

Another factor making work safety an object of special public attention is the availability of a relatively small group to serve as scapegoats. Employers serve this function admirably. They serve as an object of blame and scorn out of proportion to their responsibility for accidents and disease simply because there are fewer employers than employees. Just as "middlemen" are almost invariably blamed for food price increases, because there are fewer of them than there are farmers or retailers, so perhaps must employers serve as the objects to be blamed for occupational injuries. Since there is no readily available scapegoat for hunting or swimming accidents, we will probably always pay less attention to these sources of injuries than to injuries which arise from work. Thus, because the benefits of risk-taking on the job are indirect, because the immediate situation is often less controllable, and because there is a readily available group to blame, the risks of work have generated special concern. It is a difficult and sensitive issue which most people feel deserves extraordinary attention.

The Concept of Optimal Safety

Since both benefits and costs are associated with risky activities, it is desirable to balance them so as to achieve an ideal or optimal amount of risk. For each individual, this desired level of risk is one in which the value placed on benefits minus costs is at a maximum. In other words, the goal is the largest level of satisfaction net of all costs including risks. Since virtually all activities entail some degree of risk, it follows that we would not want to eliminate all risks, because this would entail avoiding all rewarding activities. What is needed is a compromising balance of prevention efforts, activity benefits, and activity risks. It is therefore desirable to have arrangements by which these trade-offs can be achieved in a manner satisfactory to the individuals who comprise our society.

The desirability of accepting some positive level of risk runs counter to many people's initial reaction to the subject. At first glance, accident and disease prevention are usually seen as an unmitigated benefit whose value is infinite. It therefore is seen as something that should not be constrained by the cost of the resources required for its accomplishment. Individuals who voice this opinion should ask themselves whether they act as if this were the value they placed on prevention. To do so, they would have to go through most of life's activities with prevention as their primary goal. Of course, very few (if any) people actually behave in this manner. However, one may place whatever value one wants on prevention. The goal, again, is to provide arrangements under which individuals may trade off risks and benefits in the manner that maximizes their personal satisfactions.

If all the costs and benefits of accidents and diseases accrued to the same person, determination of the appropriate exposure to risk would be relatively straightforward. A well-informed decision maker would participate in an activity if the value of expected benefits exceeded the value of expected costs. However, the costs and benefits of certain activities, such as work, generally accrue to different decision makers. For example, products go to customers while injuries go to workers. In these cases, it is necessary to devise mechanisms which allow the balancing of costs and benefits not directly and immediately borne by the individual participants. It follows from this that the ultimate goal of government intervention in safety and health affairs should be to facilitate the arrangements by which individuals and groups seek to achieve an optimal level of risk.

Many people of high purpose are offended by the expression of the occupational safety and health

problem in terms of costs and benefits. However, it must be remembered that this is not a normative structure imposed by economists but a formalization of the factors which concern individuals. To ignore the cost/benefit framework does not change the nature of the problem or the attributes of possible solutions. Such avoidance simply increases the likelihood that certain features of our desires or the constraints on our desires will be ignored. The use of cost/benefit labels merely categorizes and explicitly considers factors which might otherwise be ignored. Ignoring such factors does not cause them to go away, nor does it make difficult decisions easier.

We have defined the optimal level of risk as that at which the net value of benefits over costs is at a maximum for each individual. This goal is met by continuing to reduce the incidence of accidents and disease until the costs of achieving the reduction are equal to the extra benefits derived. After the equality of marginal benefits and costs has been achieved, further reduction in accidents and diseases will cost more than it is worth, which represents a net social loss. The difficulty of translating this abstract decision process into concrete identifiable terms should not deter us from recognizing the appropriateness of optimal risk as a public policy goal. To ignore this goal, because of its abstract character, can only lead to policy decisions that waste the limited resources at our disposal. While we cannot concretely and precisely define the "ideal" incidence of accidents and diseases, we must understand the nature of the trade-offs involved and make recognition of these realities an integral part of public policy.

THE ROLE OF PUBLIC POLICY

For a broad range of activities our society trusts private decision makers such as workers, consumers, unions, and firms to achieve through their interaction the desired amount of goods and services. The quantity of such varied "commodities" as travel, garbage, and books is largely determined by individuals deciding how much they care to produce and consume in view of how much is received or forgone in a trade. We rely on these decisions because, in making them, people at least implicitly balance the costs and benefits of production and consumption thus satisfying themselves while preserving freedom of choice for others. An important question to ask ourselves, therefore, is whether we can trust the decisions individuals make about the production and consumption of occupational safety and health.

Our society relies on private decisions for most commodities because the costs and benefits facing individuals are the same as the costs and benefits to society. In most cases, the optimal amount for society is simply the sum of the optimal amounts for each member of society. A problem arises, however, when the full value of either costs or benefits are not known or felt by the decision maker. If the cost which accrues to the decision maker is less than the true social cost of a product or activity, then the individual will consume or produce more than is appropriate from society's point of view since the individual is ignoring costs which others must bear. A classic example of this social cost problem is pollution. We know that, because the producers who pollute have not had to bear the total costs of polluting, their production exceeds optimal levels. Steel producers, for example, have not always borne their full costs, which include the aesthetic loss of clean waterways, ill health generated by polluted air, and extra cleaning bills for families living in the vicinity of the mills. From society's viewpoint these costs are as much a part of steel production as the costs of iron ore and coal for which steel companies pay. Because these pollution costs are not paid by steel companies, the cost of steel appears to be less than it truly is. Hence, the price of steel is less than it should be, and too much steel—and pollution—are produced.

Under certain conditions private market forces will eliminate the distortion caused by ignoring these social costs. If rights are well-defined, markets are competitive, decision makers are aware of all costs, and the costs of making and enforcing contracts are negligible, then there will be no distortions due to these social costs.[5] In the case of steel pollution, its effect on the company's neighbors would be borne by the steel producers if: (1) the neighbor was aware of the problem and its cost to him; and (2) the neighbor could bargain and enforce contracts with the steel company at negligible costs. Although few would contend that this is a likely situation, the point is important because the degree to which these conditions are met will determine the extent of the distortion in production due to the divergence between social and private costs.

In occupational safety and health, the issue is whether there are any differences in costs to decision makers and in social costs which will cause a nonoptimal amount of safety to be supplied in the absence of government regulation. A social cost problem might arise if the party bearing the costs of accident prevention is not the one who receives all the benefits of prevention. In many situations, the worker receives most of the benefits of accident prevention while both the worker and his employer have a substantial role in prevention. To the extent that the employer does not receive adequate benefits from safety measures, his prevention expenditures will not fully reflect the total benefits of prevention. This situation, of course, parallels the case where a steel firm does not bear the costs of pollution and hence produces a socially undesirable amount of pollution.

Just as economic theory predicts that the amount of pollution may be optimized even with differential private and social costs, it also predicts that the amount of safety and health may be optimized under analogous circumstances. If workers accurately perceive the risks of accidents and disease and if there are negligible costs of bargaining with employers, an optimal safety level can be achieved. Under such circumstances the cost of taking risks would be reflected in the wage structure. That is, in order to attract workers to risky work the employer would have to pay a wage premium. The extra wages reflecting compensation for danger are the mechanism by which the firm is made to carry the burden of not preventing accidents and disease. Insofar as the employer devotes resources to prevention, the wage premium needed to attract workers will decrease. Thus, true social costs are made to be the employer's private costs. By preventing accidents for employees, an employer receives a benefit for himself—a reduction in his wage bill. This arrangement, based on a private exchange between employers and employees, would yield the optimal amount of safety and health because the relevant decision makers feel the full burden and rewards of both costs and benefits.

Are workers and employers likely to be fully aware of injury and prevention costs? It is difficult to answer this question. Many observers feel that workers do not accurately perceive the risks and cost of injury. The typical worker is often viewed as having the philosophy, "It will never happen to me."

Although this view is intuitively no more appealing than the contrary view that the average worker is inappropriately fearful of his environment, neither view is based on compelling evidence.[6]

As to the ease of bargaining and enforcing contracts, it is again difficult to make a judgment. Certainly bargaining between parties with an ongoing contractual relationship, such as employers and employees, is cheaper and easier than bargaining between a steel factory manager and a neighboring home owner. Unfortunately there is no solid empirical evidence to guide us on these issues. Even if we had direct evidence there would be no reliable standard by which to judge it. For example, how much information is necessary before an accurate system of risk-compensating wage premiums will develop? At what point do bargaining and enforcement mechanisms become too costly to facilitate health and safety agreements? There are no *a priori* standards by which to judge these matters. The need for empirical evidence is obviously great; however, we do not have firm answers to any of these critical questions. Whether private individual and group exchange can optimize safety and health remains an unanswered question, although the longstanding assumption by public policy makers is that it cannot. It is this unsupported assumption that has led to the conclusion that the government has a positive role to play in this area.

Even if it were determined that the private interactions of employees and employers do not yield an optimal amount of safety, it does not necessarily follow that government could improve the situation. Theoretical or practical misfunctionings in private markets should not be compared with a theoretical ideal of perfect government intervention, that is, socially optimal production by government fiat. The relevant comparison is between the practical realities of the marketplace and the practical realities of government regulation.

WHO CAUSES ACCIDENTS?

One of the important factors that shapes policy is the actual source of industrial accidents. Who, or what, causes them? Various studies have found a startlingly wide range in the proportion of work accidents caused by employees (2 to 88 percent). Perhaps this is not so surprising given the lack of rigorous design in most of the studies.

The most thorough and credible analysis of accidents on the job appears to be a recent study sponsored by the state of Wisconsin.[7] The Wisconsin study found that approximately 45 percent of work injuries are due to careless behavior by workers, such as misuse of hand tools. An additional 30 percent are attributable to momentary physical hazards like open file drawers and wet floors. The remaining 25 percent of work injuries are caused by permanent physical factors like improperly guarded machines. The last category is the only one we might reasonably expect to reduce by the compulsory safety rules and inspection approach to regulation. Although there have been no formal studies, it would appear that the employee's role in disease prevention is not as critical as it is in accident prevention. The employee, of course, still has a role in disease prevention through careful use of the available prevention equipment, conscientious adherence to prescribed procedures, and monitoring of individual health.[8]

The employee's role in prevention is crucial because an effective policy must consider the underlying causes of accidents and diseases.[9] The current methods of regulation—both safety rules and workers' compensation—are geared toward the employer's role in prevention. Since many accidents and illnesses are not caused by the employer, the potential effectiveness of such regulation is limited. As an example of such policy ineffectiveness, consider the federal government's effort to make driving safer by mandating head rests on all new cars. There is no doubt that such head rests can help passengers avoid injuries from a crash. The National Safety Council, however, estimates that 80 percent of all drivers do not bother to adjust these head rests so that they will do any good. Similarly, in occupational safety regulation via controls on work environment, there will be little impact unless workers have incentives to act carefully.

Government officials have been reluctant to design public policies that recognize the employee's critical role in accident prevention. For example, in its concern about the impact of noise on workers' hearing, the government unhesitatingly requires expensive changes in the physical environment rather than less expensive worker-protection gear. A kind interpretation of the government's approach to prevention is the paternalistic one that workers must be protected from their own indiscretions. A cynic might argue that workers have far more votes than employers.

THE GOALS OF PUBLIC POLICY

Although we have concentrated on the role of public policy in achieving an optimal quantity of accident and disease prevention, workers' compensation has an additional goal. This goal is to alleviate a worker's financial hardship resulting from an injury.[10] This objective is usually labeled income maintenance or income security. Although income maintenance is viewed by many as the sole purpose of workers' compensation, this is not a compelling foundation for such a policy. It makes little sense to have a separate and rather complicated system that distinguishes work injuries from nonwork injuries and other sources of poverty unless the system also serves the goal of encouraging an appropriate amount of safety and health.

There is, unfortunately, a conflict between the efficient prevention and the income-maintenance objectives of workers' compensation. The conflict is best illustrated by considering two extremes—one in which the income-maintenance goal is completely ignored and one in which workers suffer absolutely no penalty from an injury.

If all forms of insurance against financial loss due to injury were prohibited, the incentive for employees to avoid accidents would certainly be maximized. Employees would take extraordinary measures to avoid uninsured losses caused by injury. Some observers feel that the potential physical suffering of an injury already provides a maximum safety incentive, but there can be little doubt that financial incentives are also important. For example, avoiding personal injuries is an important motive in home fire prevention. However, the importance of this incentive should not distract us from the role played by the financial protection of fire insurance. If insurance were not available, most of us would surely take additional measures to protect our homes with smoke detectors, electrical wiring checkups, and decreased use of fireplaces, candles, and matches. Similarly, in a work setting a complete lack of insurance protection would surely eliminate some horseplay and reckless driving and increase the use of safety equipment like hardhats, goggles, and gloves.

On the other hand, if there were 100 percent protection against all losses due to accidents, including full compensation for lost salary, pain, and loss of leisure, a worker would tend to be indifferent to accident prevention. This policy extreme would satisfy the income-maintenance goal, but it would have a most undesirable effect on safety since workers would lose nothing from injury.

Certainly a generous insurance plan will not cause many people to take risks that they think will cause death or serious injury. However, such financial protection might induce people to take risks that involve the possibility of minor injuries. Unfortunately, these minor risks sometimes turn out to have very serious consequences. A worker might for convenience remove the guard from a machine because he "knows" the only risk is a bruised hand. However, it is just such actions that too often result in severed hands rather than bruises.

The extremes of no income protection and complete income protection illustrate the conflict between the prevention and the income-maintenance objectives of workers' compensation. As income-maintenance benefits increase, the cost of an accident to an employee decreases. Accordingly, his incentive to avoid an accident also decreases. Conversely, while low income-maintenance benefits give employees added incentive to avoid accidents, they do not satisfy the demand for income maintenance or provide any additional prevention incentives for employers. As a practical matter, low income-maintenance benefits might not even yield the extra prevention incentives for employees, since other forms of income maintenance, such as welfare benefits financed by general tax revenues, would likely be used to prevent an injured worker from suffering the full financial consequences of an injury. Our society does have a general income-maintenance goal, and any specific regulatory effort that ignores this objective will in all probability be displaced or supplemented by other programs.

The achievement of adequate income maintenance does not, of course, mean that workers must have full protection against every financial consequence of an injury. Some current workers' compensation laws, and proposals for reforming these laws, appear not to recognize the nature of the conflict between income maintenance and injury prevention and opt for virtually unrestrained fulfillment of the income-maintenance goal. A continuing theme of this [article] is that while income maintenance and efficient prevention are both desirable goals, there unfortunately is a conflict between them. As a result, a compromise must be reached between them. It is a further theme of this analysis that the compromise embodied in the current system and suggested reforms overemphasizes income maintenance, while not being sufficiently sensitive to efficient accident and disease prevention.

NOTES

1. Throughout this [article], the term *injury* will be used to cover the result of both accidents and disease.

2. Data are from a news release by the U.S. Department of Labor, Bureau of Labor Statistics, *BLS Reports Results of Occupational Injuries and Illnesses for 1974* (Washington, D.C., 1975).

3. National Safety Council, *Accident Facts* (1975 ed.), 3.

4. Walter Oi, "An Essay on Workmen's Compensation and Industrial Safety," *Supplemental Studies for the National Commission on State Workmen's Compensation Laws,* vol. 1 (Washington, D.C., 1973), 72.

5. Ronald Coase, "The Problem of Social Cost," *Journal of Law and Economics,* vol. 3 (October 1960), 1–44.

6. Studies of the wage-premium issues include: R. Thaler and S. Rosen, "The Value of Saving a Life: Evidence from the Labor Market" (Paper presented at the National Bureau of Economic Research Conference, Washington,

D.C., November 30, 1973); R. Smith, "The Feasibility of an 'Injury Tax' Approach to Occupational Safety," *Law and Contemporary Problems* (Summer–Autumn 1974), 730–744; and J. Chelius, "The Control of Industrial Accidents: Economic Theory and Empirical Evidence," *Law and Contemporary Problems* (Summer–Autumn 1974), 700–729.

7. Wisconsin State Department of Labor, Industry, and Human Relations, *Inspection Effectiveness Report* (1971).

8. As an example of the worker's role in disease prevention, there is anecdotal evidence that textile workers are reluctant to wear available face masks, which offer some protection from lung diseases. This reluctance is apparently due to the discomfort associated with the masks.

9. Sam Peltzman, *Regulation of Automobile Safety* (Washington, D.C.: American Enterprise Institute, 1975), finds that the National Highway Safety Administration has been ineffective in reducing auto accidents for lack of recognition of their underlying causes.

10. Some literature on workers' compensation further differentiates the system's goals. For example, the National Commission on State Workmen's Compensation Laws distinguished between the provision of income and medical care to injured workers. The notion of "income maintenance" in this volume is intended to encompass all forms of benefits to injured workers. Similarly, a distinction is sometimes made between encouragement of safety and the allocation of injury costs to the productive process. Any system that achieves the goal of "efficient prevention" as described in this [article] would also allocate injury costs to the appropriate productive process.

READING 6.2 SEX IS THE LEAST OF IT: LET'S FOCUS HARASSMENT LAW ON WORK, NOT SEX
Vicki Schultz

The Clarence Thomas hearings, the Tailhook incident, the Gene McKinney trial, the Clinton scandals—if these events spring to mind when you hear the words "sexual harassment," you are not alone.

Vicki Schultz, a professor at Yale Law School, discusses these themes in more detail in "Reconceptualizing Sexual Harassment," in vol. 107, no. 6 of the *Yale Law Journal* (1998). Reprinted with permission from the May 25, 1998 issue of *The Nation.* For subscription information, call 1-800-333-8536. Portions of each week's Nation magazine can be accessed at http://www.thenation.com.

That such images of powerful men making sexual come-ons toward female subordinates should be the defining ones simply proves the power of the popular perception that harassment is first and foremost about sex. It's easy to see why: The media, the courts and some feminists have emphasized this to the exclusion of all else. But the real issue isn't sex, it's sexism on the job. The fact is, most harassment isn't about satisfying sexual desires. It's about protecting work—especially the most favored lines of work—as preserves of male competence and authority.

This term the Supreme Court heard three cases involving sex harassment in the workplace. Along with media coverage of current events, the Court's decisions will shape our understanding of this issue into the next century, for all these controversies raise the same fundamental question: Does sex harassment require a special body of law having to do with sexual relations, or should it be treated just like any other form of workplace discrimination?

If the Court decides that harassment is primarily a problem of sexual relations, it will be following the same misguided path some courts have taken since they first accepted that such behavior falls under the prohibitions of Title VII of the Civil Rights Act, the major federal statute forbidding sex discrimination in employment. Early decisions outlawed what is known as *quid pro quo* harassment—typically, a situation where a supervisor penalizes a subordinate who refuses to grant sexual favors. It was crucial for the courts to acknowledge that sexual advances and other interactions can be used in the service of discrimination. Yet their reasoning spelled trouble. The courts said harassment was sex bias because the advances were rooted in a sexual attraction that the harasser felt for a woman but would not have felt for another man. By locating the problem in the sexual character of the advances rather than in the workplace dynamics of which they were a part—for instance, the paternalistic prerogative of a male boss to punish an employee on the job for daring to step out of her "place" as a woman—the decisions threatened to equate sex harassment with sexual pursuits. From there it was a short step to the proposition that sex in the workplace, or at least sexual interactions between men and women in unequal jobs, is inherently suspect.

Yet the problem we should be addressing isn't sex, it's the sexist failure to take women seriously as workers. Sex harassment is a means for men to claim work as masculine turf. By driving women away or branding them inferior, men can insure the sex segregation of the work force. We know that women who work in jobs traditionally held by men are more likely than other women to experience hostility and harassment at work. Much of the harassment they experience isn't "sexual" in content or design. Even where sexually explicit harassment occurs, it is typically part of a broader pattern of

conduct intended to reinforce gender difference and to claim work as a domain of masculine mastery. As one experienced electrician put it in Molly Martin's *Hard-Hatted Women*, "[We] . . . face another pervasive and sinister kind of harassment which is gender-based, but may have nothing to do with sex. It is harassment aimed at us simply because we are women in a 'man's' job, and its function is to discourage us from staying in our trades."

This harassment can take a variety of forms, most of which involve undermining a woman on the job. In one case, male electricians stopped working rather than submit to the authority of a female subforeman. In another, Philadelphia policemen welcomed their new female colleagues by stealing their case files and lacing their uniforms with lime that burned their skin. Even more commonly, men withhold the training and assignments women need to learn to do the job well, or relegate them to menial duties that signal they are incompetent to perform the simplest tasks. Work sabotage is all too common.

Nor is this a purely blue-collar phenomenon. About one-third of female physicians recently surveyed said they had experienced sexual harassment, but almost half said they'd been subjected to harassment that had no sexual or physical component but was related simply to their being female in a traditionally male field. In one 1988 court case, a group of male surgical residents went so far as to falsify a patient's medical records to make it appear as though their female colleague had made an error.

Men do, of course, resort to sexualized forms of harassment. Sexual overtures may intimidate a woman or label her incompetent in settings where female sexuality is considered incompatible with professionalism. In one 1993 Supreme Court case, a company president suggested that a female manager must have had sex with a client to land an important account. Whether or not the harassment assumes a sexual form, however, what unites all these actions is that they create occupational environments that define womanhood as the opposite of what it takes to be a good worker.

From this starting point, it becomes clear that the popular view of harassment is both too narrow and too broad. Too narrow, because the focus on rooting out unwanted sexual activity has allowed us to feel good about protecting women from sexual abuse while leading us to overlook equally pernicious forms of gender-based mistreatment. Too broad, because the emphasis on sexual conduct has encouraged some companies to ban all forms of sexual interaction, even when these do not threaten women's equality on the job.

How has the law become too narrow? The picture of harassment-as-sex that developed out of the *quid pro quo* cases has overwhelmed the conception of the hostile work environment, leading most courts to exonerate seriously sexist misconduct if it does not resemble a sexual come-on. In *Turley v. Union Carbide Corp.,* a court dismissed the harassment claim of a woman whose foreman "pick[ed] on [her] all the time" and treated her worse than the men. Citing Catharine MacKinnon's definition of sexual harassment as "the unwanted imposition of sexual requirements in the context of a relationship of unequal power," the court concluded that the case did not involve actionable harassment because "the foreman did not demand sexual relations, he did not touch her or make sexual jokes."

By the same reasoning, in *Reynolds v. Atlantic City Convention Center,* the court ruled against a female electrical subforeman, Reynolds, whose men refused to work for her, made obscene gestures and stood around laughing while she unloaded heavy boxes. Not long before, the union's business agent had proclaimed, "[Now] is not the time, the place or the year, [nor] will it ever be the year for a woman foreman." When the Miss America pageant came to town, an exhibitor asked that Reynolds be removed from the floor—apparently, the incongruity between the beauty contestants and the tradeswoman was too much to take—and Reynolds's boss replaced and eventually fired her. Yet the court concluded that none of this amounted to a hostile work environment: The obscene gestures that the court considered "sexual" were too trivial, and the rest of the conduct wasn't sufficiently sexual to characterize as gender-based.

These are not isolated occurrences. I recently surveyed hundreds of Title VII hostile work environment cases and found that the courts' disregard of nonsexual forms of harassment is an overwhelming trend. This definitely works against women in male-dominated job settings, but it has also hurt women in traditionally female jobs, who share the experience of harassment that denigrates their competence or intelligence as workers. They are often subjected to sexist forms of authority, humiliation and abuse—objectified not only as sexual commodities but as creatures too stupid or worthless to deserve respect, fit only to be controlled by others ("stupid women who have kids," "too fat to clean rooms," "dumb females who [can't] read or write").

Just as our obsession with sexual misconduct obscures many debilitating forms of harassment facing women, it also leads us to overlook some pernicious harassment confronting men on the job. If the legal cases provide any indication, the most common form of harassment men experience is not, as the film *Disclosure* suggests, a proposition from a female boss. It is, instead, hostility from male coworkers seeking to denigrate or drive away men who threaten the work's masculine image. If a job is to confer manliness, it must be held by those who project the desired sense of manhood. It isn't only women who can detract from that image. In some work settings, men are threatened by the presence of any man perceived to be gay—for homosexuality is often seen as gender deviance—or any other man perceived to lack the manly competence considered suitable for those who hold the job. The case logs are filled with harassment against men who are not married, men who are not attractive to women, men who are seen as weak or slow, men who are openly supportive of women, men who wear earrings and even young men or boys. Some men have taunted and tormented, battered and beaten other men in the name of purging the brotherhood of wimps and fags—not suitable to stand alongside them as workers.

We have been slow to name this problem sex-based harassment because it doesn't fit our top-down, male-female, sexual come-on image of harassment. In *Goluszek v. Smith,* the court ruled against an electronic maintenance mechanic who was disparaged and driven out by his fellow workers. They mocked him for not having a wife, saying a man had to be married to be a machinist. They used gender-based images to assault his competence, saying that if he couldn't fix a machine they'd send in his "daddy"—the supervisor—to do it. They drove jeeps at him and threatened to knock him off his ladder, and when he filed a grievance, his supervisor wrote him up for carelessness and eventually fired him. Not only did the court dismiss Goluszek's claim, the judge simply couldn't conceive that what happened to him was sexual harassment." The 'sexual harassment' that is actionable under Title VII 'is the exploitation of a powerful position to impose sexual demands or pressures on an unwilling but less powerful person,'" the judge wrote. Perhaps lower courts will adopt a broader view now that the Supreme Court has ruled, in the recent *Oncale v. Sundowner Offshore Services* decision, that male-on-male harassment may be actionable even when it is not sexual in design.

Meanwhile, the traditional overemphasis on sex can lead to a repressive impulse to eliminate all hints of sexual expression from the workplace, however benign. Instead of envisioning harassment law as a tool to promote women's equality as workers, the popular understanding of harassment encourages courts and companies to "protect" women's sexual sensibilities. In *Fair v. Guiding Eyes for the Blind,* a heterosexual woman who was the associate director of a nonprofit organization claimed her gay male supervisor had created an offensive environment by making gossipy conversation and political remarks involving homosexuality. It is disturbing that current law inspired such a claim, even though the court correctly ruled that the supervisor's conduct was not sexual harassment.

Other men haven't fared so well. In *Pierce v. Commonwealth Life Insurance Co.,* a manager was disciplined for participating in an exchange of sexually explicit cards with a female office administrator. One of the cards Pierce had sent read, "Sex is a misdemeanor. De more I miss, de meanor I get." After thirty years with the company, he was summarily demoted and transferred to another office, with his pay slashed and his personal belongings dumped at a roadside Hardee's. True, Pierce was a manager and he was responsible for enforcing the company's harassment policy. Still, the reasoning that led to his ouster is unsound—and dangerous. According to his superiors, he might as well have been a "murderer, rapist or child molester; that wouldn't be any worse [than what he had done]." This sort of thing gives feminism a bad name. If companies want to fire men like Pierce, let them do it without the pretense of protecting women from sexual abuse.

Equally alarming are reports that, in the name of preventing sexual harassment, some companies are adopting policies that prohibit a man and woman from traveling or staying at the same hotel together on business, or prevent a male supervisor from giving a performance evaluation to a female underling behind closed doors without a lawyer present. One firm has declared that its construction workers can't even look at a woman for more than five seconds. With such work rules, who will want to hire women? How will women obtain the training they need if their male bosses and colleagues can't interact with them as equals?

It's a mistake to try to outlaw sexual interaction in the workplace. The old Taylorist project of purging organizations of all sexual and other emotional dynamics was deeply flawed. Sexuality is part of the human experience, and so long as organizations still employ people rather than robots, it will continue to flourish in one form or another. And sexuality is not simply a tool of gender domination; it is also a potential source of empowerment and even pleasure for women on the job. Indeed, some research suggests that where men and women work as equals in integrated settings, sex harassment isn't a problem. Sexual talk and joking continues, but it isn't experienced as harassment. It's not impossible to imagine sexual banter as a form of playfulness, even solidarity, in a work world that is increasingly competitive and stressful.

Once we realize that the problem isn't sex but sexism, we can re-establish our concept of harassment on firmer ground. Title VII was never meant to police sexuality. It was meant to provide people the chance to pursue their life's work on equal terms—free of pressure to conform to prescribed notions of how women and men are supposed to behave in their work roles. Properly conceived, quid pro quo harassment is a form of discrimination because it involves men exercising the power to punish women, as workers, who have the temerity to say no, as women. Firing women who won't have sex on the job is no different from firing black women who refuse to perform cleaning work, or female technicians who refuse to do clerical work, that isn't part of their job descriptions.

So, too, hostile-work-environment harassment isn't about sexual relations; it's about how work relations engender inequality. The legal concept was created in the context of early race discrimination cases, when judges recognized that Jim Crow systems could be kept alive not just through company acts (such as hiring and firing) but also through company atmospheres that made African-American workers feel different and inferior. That discriminatory environments are sometimes created by "sexual" conduct is not the point. Sex should be treated just like anything else in the workplace: Where it furthers sex discrimination, it should go. Where it doesn't, it's not the business of our civil rights laws.

It's too easy to allow corporate America to get away with banning sexual interaction without forcing it to attend to the larger structures of workplace

gender discrimination in which both sexual and not-so-sexual forms of harassment flourish. Let's revitalize our understanding of harassment to demand a world in which all women and even the least powerful men can work together as equals in whatever endeavors their hearts and minds desire.

READING 6.3 DISABILITY AND THE RIGHT TO WORK
Gregory S. Kavka

DEFINING THE PROBLEM

Do disabled people in advanced modern societies (like those of North America, Western Europe, and the Pacific Rim) have a right to work? Before we can begin to answer this question, we must be clearer about what it means. And this requires some preliminary comments on each of the question's key constituent terms. Of these, the notion of a disability (or handicap) is easiest to deal with, for we may adopt the broad definition contained in the Americans with Disabilities Act which says a disability is a physical or mental impairment that "substantially limits one or more of the major life activities of an individual." One could easily raise philosophical quibbles about this definition: the concepts of "substantial" limits and "major" life activities (even when the latter is illustrated by paradigm examples like walking and talking) are vague, and the inclusion of mental impairments along with these vague terms raises the possibility that too many of us would qualify under it as disabled (for example, the ordinary neurotic whose social life is substantially limited by irrational inhibitions). However, any concept of disability is going to admit of degrees and have vague borders: the vagueness will have to be resolved largely by implicit social conventions about what sort of impairments count as genuine handicaps. So, despite the potential problems with the Disabilities Act definition of disability, I will not pause over the task of improving it.

Characterizing the right to work, as I intend it, is a more complex matter. For present purposes, we may think of rights, in general, as potential claims by (or on behalf of) someone to some thing (an object or a liberty to act) against someone else. These rights are moral or legal, and *prima facie* or absolute, according to whether the underlying rules, principles, and standards which ground and justify the potential claims in question are themselves moral or legal, *prima facie* or absolute. (A *prima facie* right is overridable by competing considerations, while an absolute right is not. Among the rights thought to be absolute by some theorists are the right not to be tortured and the right not to be punished for a crime one did not commit.)

The right of handicapped people to work that I argue for is a moral right; it will be justified by appeals to moral considerations. However, since important moral rights concerning economic matters should be protected by and embodied in the law, my arguments will aim at showing that disabled people should be accorded a legal right to work. Disabled people's right to work is *prima facie*, not absolute: it can, in principle, be overridden by competing rights or other considerations (such as economic feasibility). But it is, I will contend, a *strong prima facie* right: the moral arguments in its favor are substantial enough it would take competing moral considerations of considerable weight to override it. In particular, I will argue that a small gain in social utility or economic efficiency is not enough to override this right.

If the disabled have a moral right to work, against whom is it a right? That is, who bears the moral obligation to offer them jobs or help them obtain employment? The most general answer is society as a whole. But the way this right must be vindicated in practice means that specific obligations generated by the right may fall especially upon governments, particular government officials, and certain private employers.

Why this is so becomes clear when we address the critical question of just what handicapped people's right to work is a right to. The "right to work," as I use the term, is the right to participate as an active member in the productive processes of one's society, insofar as such participation is reasonably feasible. A number of aspects of this characterization require comment.

Most importantly, the right to work is a right to *employment;* it is a right to *earn* income, not simply a right to receive a certain income stream or the resources necessary to attain a certain level of welfare. . . .

My "right to work" thesis makes the more controversial claim that disabled people in advanced societies have a right not only to receive a basic income, but to *earn* incomes at—or above—the basic maintenance level. I will argue for employment as a right, not a duty. I avoid the vexed question of whether disabled people should be forced to work for their basic support income if they do not want to do so. I focus on whether those disabled persons who want to work should be afforded special sorts of opportunities to do so.

What specific sorts of treatment or "special opportunities" are entailed by handicapped people's right to work? First, a right of nondiscrimination in employment and promotion—that people not be denied jobs on the basis of disabilities that are not relevant to their capacities to carry out the tasks associated with those jobs. Second, a right to compensatory training and education, funded by society, that will allow disabled people the opportunity to overcome their handicaps and make themselves qualified for desirable employment. Third, a right to reasonable investments by society and employers to make jobs accessible to otherwise qualified people with disabilities. Fourth, and most controversially, a right to minimal (or tie-breaking) "affirmative action" or "preferential treatment": being admitted, hired, or promoted when in competition with other equally qualified candidates. Spelled out in this way, the right of handicapped persons to work is seen to be, in its various elements, a right against society, government, and private employers.

In arguing for the disableds' right to work, in this sense, I limit my discussion in two ways to take account of problems of feasibility. I consider only the case of advanced modern societies; for in other societies, the economic resources needed to vindicate this right to any substantial degree are either not present or are very likely to be needed for even more urgent social tasks. And I acknowledge that employment of many people with severe handicaps may not be "reasonably feasible"—that is, it may be impossible or excessively costly. To take a recent example from the literature, I will not be arguing that we should hire blind persons to be school bus drivers. Nor do I think large costs should be sustained to retrain workers that become disabled very close to retirement age. But I will contend that applying a strict economic cost/benefit standard of hiring and training feasibility may be unfair to the disabled. . . .

EFFICIENCY, JUSTICE, AND THE RIGHT TO WORK

In presenting my arguments for a right to work of the disabled, it will be useful to have a foil. For this purpose, I choose a blunt form of objection to that right, derived from the notion that the economic rights of the disabled are strictly limited by considerations of economic efficiency that imply the desirability of a free market in labor in which employers are entitled to hire whomever they regard as best qualified for the jobs they offer. The objection runs as follows: "Society's obligations to the disabled extend no further than the previously assumed obligation to provide a basic welfare minimum. Because of their special medical and equipment needs, this may require a larger cash stipend to most disabled people than would be necessary to support able-bodied persons at the same basic welfare level. But society has a right to provide the necessary economic resources to the disabled in whatever way it deems to be most efficient. Perhaps for some classes of disabled persons, training and continued employment will allow them to achieve (or exceed) the basic welfare minimum at less net cost to society as a whole than receiving a public stipend. And perhaps private employers can profitably employ disabled workers by exploiting public sympathy for them and successfully charging higher prices for products they have produced. But if society (and private employers) find it cheaper just to pension off the handicapped, because it would cost more to provide handicapped people with special training and equipment, and to determine which handicapped people may be profitably employed, this is their prerogative. Disabled people therefore have no more right to work than anyone else does. If they can compete successfully for jobs, if private employers or government agencies want to hire them for specific jobs because of their qualifications, they will be hired. If not, they have a right to support payments, but no right to employment." For ease of reference, I will henceforth refer to the viewpoint expressed in this objection as the Crude Economic Efficiency Position, or CREEP.

What is wrong with CREEP? At least three things that I can think of: it employs an inappropriate notion of efficiency, it fails to attach sufficient importance to self-respect and the means to self-respect, and it ignores key issues involving distributive justice. . . .

Social Efficiency

CREEP says that the disabled have no right to work, and that society should see to their employment only to the extent that society (or individual employers) regard this as economically cost-effective. Though this line of argument seems to be based on a morally respectable *utilitarian* appeal to social efficiency, this is not really the case. First, CREEP is ambiguous between appealing to efficiency for society as a whole (including the handicapped) and appealing to efficiency for those who are offering aid to the handicapped (employers, the government, and taxpayers). The latter position is not a genuinely utilitarian one at all, and is supportable only if one believes that because the disabled are generally in a dependent role in these transactions, their interests are not to be counted (or counted equally) in determining which policies are most socially efficient overall. Second, the notion of "society" deciding the most efficient policies in these areas is ambiguous in a similar way: if efficiency decisions are left entirely to the discretion of particular employers, government bureaucrats, and managers, rather than being circumscribed politically, then the disabled (who currently occupy very few of these influential positions) will be effectively prevented from having their interests adequately represented where the relevant decisions are made. Third, by focusing on a narrow economic notion of

efficiency, rather than a broader utilitarian notion, CREEP ignores the importance of key noneconomic values, like self-respect, that may justify ascribing to disabled persons a right to work as well as a right to a basic welfare level. . . .

Distributive Justice and Self-Respect

Arguments purely in terms of economic efficiency or social utility, like CREEP, do not directly address questions of distribution. Once we turn to matters of distributive justice, the moral case for the disabled having a right to work is substantially strengthened.

The basic reason for this is that the handicapped typically are, in virtue of their condition, among the most disadvantaged members of advanced modern societies with respect to well-being and opportunities for well-being. By definition, a disability is a substantial impairment of a major life activity like seeing, hearing, walking, or talking. Two features of such impairments make them especially devastating to the welfare and life prospects of those who have them: their permanence and their pervasiveness.

People are often disabled temporarily, by disease or injury. But sick or injured people are not treated or regarded as a separate class of persons by society, and their work problems are dealt with by policies designed for "normal" workers—for example, sick leaves and short-term disability insurance. When people speak of the disabled or handicapped, however, they normally have in mind those who are in such a condition *permanently* (or at least for a period of years). It is the economic rights of such people—that is, those suffering long-term disablement—that is the subject of my discussion.

Significant permanent handicaps are usually pervasive, in the sense that their effects are not confined to a single sphere of the affected person's life, but tend to have damaging (or limiting) effects on all major spheres—family, personal, social, and recreational life, as well as economic and professional life. There are three closely related reasons for this. First, disabling impairments interfere with major activities that figure in all life spheres—seeing and talking, for example, are as much (or more) prerequisites of a normal social life as they are prerequisites of normal careers. Second, public and private environments, customs, and institutional structures are designed for people with normally functioning bodies and minds, and may create barriers to participation by the disabled. (Problems of physical access for people in wheelchairs is the most familiar example of this.) Third, and finally, all major spheres of life involve significant interaction with other people, who for a variety of psychological reasons may find it difficult to interact with disabled persons in normal ways, even when the disability in question is essentially irrelevant to the particular mode of interaction in question. In other words, the disabled tend to be stigmatized, as well as directly disadvantaged, in the interpersonal aspects of their activities. . . .

Special social provision for the welfare of the disabled thus follows from practically any account of social justice—Rawlsian, egalitarian, need-centered, or whatever—that pays attention to how social welfare or resources are distributed and correspondingly prescribes improving the lot of society's least advantaged members But how does a right to work rather than a right to disability pensions follow from such distributive considerations?

The key mediating concept here is self-respect. Suppose that we agree with Rawls that self-respect is a vital primary good, something of great importance that any rational person is presumed to want. Now given actual human psychology, self-respect, is—to a considerable degree—dependent upon other people's affirmation of one's own worth. And in modern advanced societies, employment, earnings, and professional success are, for better or worse, positively correlated with social assessments of an individual's value. Further, beyond the reactions of other people, work and career identifications form significant parts of some people's conceptions of themselves and their own worth; hence, these identifications may contribute directly to the creation and sustenance of self-respect, and their absence will frequently have the opposite effect.

To be sure, "economic" criteria are not the only standards of value used by oneself or others to assess one's worthiness. But, because of the *pervasiveness* of disability, as noted above, satisfaction of standards of value in other important spheres of life are also usually negatively affected by handicaps. Thus, on average, the handicapped are likely to be less convenient social companions, more limited in their sports and recreational activities, less able to fulfill nurturing and helping roles within the family, and so on. Thus, nonworkplace bases of self-respect will also be harder for the disabled to fulfill, making it even more important that the workplace bases of self-

respect be made available to them. (In addition, employment may foster success—and self-respect based on success—in the other spheres of life, as when one's social life is better because of friends one has made at work.)

In the end, then, the concept of self-respect plays a dual role in my refutation of CREEP. First, it serves as an example of an important aspect of utility that is overlooked in the narrow economic interpretations of CREEP. Once this narrowness is avoided, and the "indirect" utilitarian advantages of a social policy of training and employing the disabled are noted, it is evident that there are substantial utilitarian reasons in support of the disabled having a right to work. Second, the handicapped are disadvantaged in obtaining the bases of self-respect, a critically important good. And because of the way the psychology of self-respect interacts with the work ethic present in modern advanced societies, this disadvantage *cannot be rectified by transfer payments,* but (sometimes) can be rectified by training and employment opportunities. Hence, considerations of distributive justice, which prescribe easing the plight of society's less fortunate members, provide further support for ascribing to disabled people a right to work.

AFFIRMATIVE ACTION

A meaningful right to work for the disabled must entail an obligation of employers (and admissions officers) not to discriminate against handicapped people (that is, not to count their handicaps against them, except when those handicaps render them less able to perform the job in question). But should such a right also include an affirmative action requirement giving disabled persons some form of preference over others in hiring, promotion, and admissions decisions? In this section, I address this difficult question obliquely by considering which of the main arguments for and against affirmative action in the case of women and minorities also apply to the disabled. This will, I think, lead to the *conditional* conclusion that if affirmative action is justified for women and minorities, it is also justified for the handicapped.

There are, as I see it, three major groups of arguments in favor of affirmative action programs in general. First, there are *forward-looking utilitarian argu-*

ments, emphasizing various good effects of bringing more representatives of the disadvantaged group in question into responsible positions in society. These good effects include members of disadvantaged groups serving as effective role-models, bringing different and illuminating perspectives to their work, and being more likely to use their skills, expertise, and influence to help other members of the group (or disadvantaged people in general). Second, there are *error-correction* arguments. They emphasize that, because of past obstacles faced by disadvantaged candidates and current (conscious or unconscious) prejudices against them by most employers, employers' estimates of the qualifications of disadvantaged candidates are likely to systematically underrate their capabilities. Hence, requiring preference, in principle, for the disadvantaged is really an attempt to correct systematic errors in practice and enable the best qualified people to be hired more often. Third, there are various forms of arguments for *compensatory justice,* saying that members of disadvantaged groups should be given hiring preference to compensate for past hiring discrimination against them or members of their group, or other disadvantages they suffered at the hands of society.

Do these arguments for affirmative action apply as well to the disabled as they do to women and minorities? For the most part, it seems they do. Consider, first, forward-looking utilitarian considerations. Successful handicapped persons can serve as role models for the many people who are disabled, as well as for others who face serious obstacles of other sorts in life. Nor is there any reason to think they would bring a less distinct perspective to their jobs or be less inclined to help others in their situation than are women and minorities.

Application of the error-correction argument is less clear in the case of the disabled. Potential employers are perhaps even more likely to underestimate the relevant abilities of the disabled than to underestimate the abilities of women and minorities, simply because the issue of "potential special problems" is raised by the mere existence of their handicaps. On the other hand, some of the main obstacles that permanently disabled people faced in the past in obtaining their current skills and qualifications—namely, their disabilities—will remain with them through their period of employment and will continue to constitute barriers to peak perform-

ance. This is different from the case of a woman or minority group member whose main obstacle in the past may well have been lack of opportunity—an obstacle that will largely be removed simply by providing that opportunity. Further, some of the disabled obtained their main qualifications prior to the onset of their disability; hence their possession of them is no special sign of merit or determination. Different aspects of the error-correction argument, therefore, point in different directions on the question of whether this argument is stronger as regards the handicapped or minorities and women.

Compensatory-justice arguments are an odd lot, and are not easy to assess in the present context. Arguments for affirmative action as a form of group compensation are even less plausible for the disabled than for minority groups, because disabled people do not form an "identity-grounding" resource-sharing community in the way that specific racial or ethnic groups often do. But then, group-compensation arguments are widely regarded as philosophically problematic anyway.

When it comes to compensation for past disadvantages suffered by the very individuals to be helped by affirmative action programs, the handicapped are more deserving in some respects and less deserving in others. They are more deserving in the United States, at least, because they have not previously had legal protection against discrimination. This means that the current generation of handicapped people who might be advantaged by affirmative action programs contains many individuals who may have suffered unfair, but legal, discrimination. The disabled may also be viewed as more deserving of compensation because of the pervasiveness of their disadvantages, as noted [earlier].

The disabled may be less deserving of affirmative action, on the other hand, because their disadvantages are less purely the result of society's misconduct and more the result of simple bad luck. And despite earlier legal protection from discrimination, women and minorities have continued to face discrimination in practice that may equal what the disabled have faced. The force of this last consideration, in particular, depends upon complex empirical matters that I am in no position to sort out.

Turning to arguments *against* affirmative action, there are four main lines of argument to consider. First, any departures from a pure merit system of hiring will harm economic efficiency. Second, affirmative action programs tend to help the most advantaged members of disadvantaged groups—for example, the middle-class minority student who is well-educated enough to compete for law school admission. Third, such programs are counterproductive for the very disadvantaged groups they are designed to help, since they undermine confidence and stigmatize even the successful members of those groups as having needed preference to succeed. Fourth, and most important, such programs are unfair to more qualified candidates from groups not singled out for preference, since they are denied positions they would have otherwise obtained.

Do these same objections to affirmative action apply in the case of the disabled as well as women and minorities? The first clearly does, for I have interpreted the disabled's right to work as requiring efforts to employ them beyond the point of maximum economic efficiency. Further, the average "extra" costs of employment per worker may be higher in the case of the disabled than other disadvantaged groups because of the modifications in equipment and facilities that may be necessary to make certain jobs accessible to handicapped workers.

Nonetheless, the aggregate economic costs of the sort of affirmative action for the disabled which I espouse are kept within reasonable limits by three factors. The pool of work-age disabled people who want to work, and are able to do so at all, is likely to be relatively small (compared to the pool of employable women and minorities). And, as noted . . . below, I limit my advocacy to "tie-breaking" affirmative action for the disabled, which further restricts the effects of the policy. Finally, the argument for the right to work defended here advocates sacrificing *some* economic efficiency to provide job opportunities to the disabled, but it does not require sacrifices without limits. Its standard of "reasonable feasibility" implies that society's obligation to provide job opportunities for the handicapped lessens (and at some point disappears) as the marginal social cost of doing so increases.

The second objection, about *which* individuals in the disadvantaged group would benefit, seems less serious in the case of the disabled. For while it is likely to be the less disabled who would benefit most from preferential hiring, there need be no worry that these people have not been disadvan-

taged at all, as there might conceivably be in the case of middle-class minorities or women.

Objection three—about the counterproductive psychological and social effects on the members of the disadvantaged group of the affirmative action policy—appears to apply equally to the disabled and other disadvantaged groups. But it is an especially worrisome objection in the context of my argument, which defends opportunities for employment primarily as means for the disabled to achieve self-respect. Can self-respect be enhanced by receiving a job through government subsidies or affirmative action programs rather than open competition? Can self-respect be retained in a social environment in which others believe you were hired for reasons other than your qualifications? Can income received for work that is profit-making only with government subsidies said to be "earned" in a sense that will promote the sense of self-worth of the worker? If the answer to these questions is an unequivocal "no," then the right to work advocated in this paper would be essentially pointless.

I believe, however, that there are good reasons for answering these questions, as they apply to complex modern societies such as ours, in the affirmative. The first point to notice is that the relevant comparison in many cases will be between a member of a disadvantaged group having an "affirmative action" job rather than no job at all, or a good "affirmative action" job rather than a worse job. While the former alternatives may do less to promote self-respect than a good job otherwise obtained, they may do more to promote self-respect, and respect from others, than being unemployed or employed in a poor job. This is especially so if unemployment or menial employment—together with membership in a disadvantaged group—is regarded by society as characterizing "low worth" individuals.

Further, in a world of incomplete information and moral complexity, people judge their own—and others'—vocational worth by more than the criteria on the basis of which one was hired. Actual performance on the job is probably the most important measure of all, and hiring under affirmative action programs will give many members of disadvantaged groups opportunities to prove themselves at work that they would not otherwise have had. If, as the error-correction argument suggests, such people will—on average—perform better than their hirers initially expect, they will be able to earn the respect of themselves and others by their performance.

There is a down side to all this. Some highly qualified members of groups helped by affirmative action programs may have to deal with suspicions (on the part of themselves or others) that they have succeeded only because of their group membership. But their skills and performance should help them overcome these suspicions. And, given their *relatively* advantaged position, the burdens of this sort that they may bear would seem to be outweighed by the advantages provided to their less fortunate fellow group members.

The final objection to affirmative action, which is based on unfairness to the losing, but better qualified, candidates, clearly applies to affirmative action

programs for the disabled as well as for other groups. For if you are unemployed, or underemployed, it will hardly matter to your well-being whether the job opportunity you lost was to a disabled person or a member of a racial minority group. Further, the observations . . . about the significance of employment as a support of self-respect in advanced modern societies underscore the force of this objection to affirmative action.

This does not affect our main conclusion, however. For if we review the various lines of argument for and against affirmative action, it turns out that for *each* line of argument discussed, preferential hiring for the disabled fares *as well or better*, on balance, as preferential hiring for women and minorities. Thus, if the latter programs are justified, the former surely are. . . .

READING 6.4 THE PROBLEM WITH "DEAD PEASANTS" INSURANCE[1]
Earl W. Spurgin

Recent articles in *The Wall Street Journal* have raised ethical concerns about corporate-owned life insurance.[2] COLI, also known as "dead peasants" and "janitors" insurance, is insurance on the lives of rank-and-file employees, owned by corporations, with the corporations as beneficiaries. Although I share the view that COLI is ethically problematic, I will argue that the objections raised in those articles do not capture the real problem. Then, I will argue that the real problem is that COLI produces conflicts of interest for the corporations involved.

I. BACKGROUND

Prior to the 1980s, state laws granted corporations insurable interests in the lives of essential personnel. The justification for this is relatively clear. A corporation would suffer great hardships, perhaps even failure, should certain key personnel die. To offset

such hardships, a corporation should be allowed to insure the lives of those key personnel. Should one of them die, the insurance proceeds would provide helpful cash flow until the corporation can attract or develop other key personnel.

During the 1980s, however, many states redefined insurable interests so that corporations can insure the lives of rank-and-file employees.[3] Many corporations have jumped at the opportunity. Schultz and Francis list the following companies as owning COLI: American Electric Power, AT&T, Ball, Basset Furniture, Dow Chemical, Eaton, Nestle USA, Olin, Pitney Bowes, PPG Industries, Procter & Gamble, Trans World Entertainment, and Walt Disney.[4] They add, "Hundreds of banks have taken out insurance policies on employees. . . ."[5]

The justification for granting corporations insurable interests in rank-and-file employees is unclear. Corporations do not suffer great hardships if these employees die, so the justification provided for insurable interests in essential employees does not apply. Although they experience recruitment and training costs when employees die, such costs fall short of the hardships normally associated with

---

Reprinted by permission of the editor from "The Problem with 'Dead Peasants' Insurance," by Earl Spurgin, scheduled to be published in the *Business and Professional Ethics Journal* at the time of this printing.

insurable interests. This matter is even worse in Georgia. Schultz and Francis write of Georgia's laws, ". . . employers can even collect death benefits on the *children and spouses* of their employees."[6]

Spokespersons for corporations recognize the need to provide a justification for COLI. Often, this leads them to connect the proceeds of COLI to the employees themselves by claiming that the proceeds are used to fund employee benefits. Schultz and Francis write,

> A Pitney Bowes spokeswoman says the company instituted the program in 1994 to "offset the rising cost of employee benefits." . . . A spokeswoman for Procter & Gamble says the company uses the insurance "partially to finance retiree health benefits." Tom Ayres, spokesman for American Electric Power . . . says . . . the death benefits are "dedicated to retiree benefits" . . . .[7]

Albert J. Schiff, President of the Association for Advanced Life Underwriting, has joined corporate spokespersons in the attempt to defend COLI. In a self-admitted state of resentment and anger, he writes, "Mr. Francis and his colleague Ellen Schultz have devoted gallons of misleading ink—with numerous articles in the past year—attacking a very positive use of life insurance by businesses to finance employee benefits they could otherwise not afford."[8]

II. THE OBJECTIONS

Despite the attempts to justify COLI, these ethical concerns are raised, either directly or indirectly, in *The Wall Street Journal* articles:

1. COLI results in tax-free income for corporations.

2. Corporations often do not disclose COLI to employees.

3. Employees often do not consent to COLI.

4. Employees are being used as means to generate income.

Although these are important concerns, they do not capture the real problem with COLI.

The Tax-Free Income Objection

One might argue that COLI is unethical because it results in tax-free income for corporations. If one

lodges this objection, however, one must base the objection on one of the following views:

1. All forms of tax-free income for corporations are unethical.

2. Some forms of tax-free income for corporations are unethical.

Neither option results in an effective objection to COLI.

The first option requires adopting a rather strange view. Government often grants tax benefits to corporations that accord their activities with certain socially desirable goals such as protection of the environment, development of certain natural resources, limiting the use of certain natural resources, providing economic development in depressed areas, and providing job opportunities to underprivileged groups. Granting such tax breaks allows government to provide corporations with incentives to help bring about socially desirable outcomes. Adopting the first option, however, precludes this activity.[9]

One might be happy, of course, to do just that. A libertarian, for instance, might argue that government should not promote social outcomes. Nozick, perhaps the most well-known libertarian, writes,

> . . . no . . . distributional patterned principle of justice can be continuously realized without continuous interference with people's lives. . . . To maintain a pattern one must either continually interfere to stop people from transferring resources as they wish to, or continually (or periodically) interfere to take from some persons resources that others for some reason chose to transfer to them.[10]

From this idea that government cannot enforce distributional goals without violating the rights of individuals, one might construct an argument for the view that government should not promote social outcomes.

If one were to construct such a libertarian argument, however, it is still likely that one would accept the view that a corporation does no wrong by taking advantage of existing opportunities to generate tax-free income. Since libertarians generally see the income tax code itself as an unjust appropriation of people's wealth, they likely would view corporations that seek tax-free income as merely seeking ways to avoid unjust treatment.

Suppose, however, that one rejects libertarianism but still argues that government should not promote social outcomes. Even if the argument were sound, it would not demonstrate that corporations are unethical when they take advantage of the tax breaks provided by the system in which they operate. Rather, it would demonstrate that government is unethical in producing such a tax system.[11] To claim that corporations are unethical when they take advantage of tax breaks would be like claiming that a sports team is wrong to employ a particular tactic when the rules of the league allow it.[12] Instead, one should lobby league officials to change the rules. Likewise, if one objects to some aspect of the tax system, one should address the issue in the political arena.

Although the second option is a more plausible view, it is even more problematic as a basis for the tax-free income objection. If only some forms of tax-free income for corporations are unethical, then one must demonstrate why COLI is one of the unethical forms. This means that one must identify some feature of COLI other than the fact that it provides tax-free income that makes it unethical. When one does so, however, one acknowledges that it is not the tax-free income that makes COLI unethical. Instead, it is the feature one has identified.

The Disclosure Objection

Instead of focusing on the tax-free income generated by COLI, one might argue that COLI is unethical because employees often are not informed of the practice. Again, however, one must base the objection on one of the following views:

1. It is always unethical when corporations do not inform employees of their practices.

2. It is sometimes unethical when corporations do not inform employees of their practices.

Again, neither option results in an effective objection to COLI.

The first option requires one to adopt the view that every corporate decision should be disclosed to employees. Such a view is problematic for several reasons. First, corporate executives must make many decisions that require secrecy on their parts. If they informed all employees of pending mergers, buyouts, financing, new product developments, and the like, they would risk violating insider trading regulations. Second, even when law does not prohibit the sharing of information, it is reasonable for corporate executives to make decisions of which employees are unaware. The decision process would be too lengthy and burdensome if executives informed employees of every decision. Finally, in those cases where executives must engage in collective bargaining with unions, they would be at an extreme disadvantage if they were to disclose their plans to employees.

The second option fares no better. One would have to demonstrate why COLI is one of the cases where it is unethical for corporate executives to leave employees uninformed. Doing so would identify a different feature of COLI that renders it unethical. Moreover, once one identified that feature, it would not be overridden even if corporations disclosed COLI to employees. The mere act of informing another that you are doing something unethical does not render the act ethical. A rapist's action does not become ethical just because he informs his victim of his intentions. Likewise, if some feature of COLI renders it unethical, merely informing employees of the practice does not render it ethical.

The Consent Objection

One might argue, however, that consent, not notification, is at issue. COLI is unethical only when corporations do not obtain the legitimate consent of employees.[13] So, this objection advocates a reform of unethical instances of COLI rather than an abolition of the practice. In evaluating an instance of COLI, one must determine if the corporation has obtained consent and if that consent qualifies as legitimate. Suppose one discovered the following consent practice described by Schultz and Francis: ". . . companies in some cases give workers an incentive to agree . . . by promising them a $1,000 or $5,000 insurance benefit . . . without telling them that the insurance benefit the company receives is far larger."[14] One might conclude that this consent is illegitimate since a significant fact is withheld from employees. On the other hand, if one discovers that a corporation has obtained legitimate consent, then one would conclude that the instance of COLI is ethical.

Although the consent objection is more plausible than the notification objection, it encounters two difficulties. First, it rests on the problematic idea that employees are in a position to grant legitimate consent to corporations that overrides some other ethical consideration. To see why this is problematic, consider Locke's notion of tacit consent and Hume's argument against it.[15] Locke derives legitimate government authority from the consent of the governed. Along the way, he argues that one often gives one's consent to the government tacitly. He writes, ". . . every man, that hath any possessions, or enjoyment, of any part of the dominions of any government, doth hereby give his *tacit consent*. . . ."[16] For Locke, one gives tacit consent to a government by enjoying any of the benefits of that government including merely being within its territories. Hume rejects this view. He writes,

> . . . implied consent can only have place where a man imagines that the matter depends on his choice. . . . Can we seriously say that a poor peasant or artisan has a free choice to leave his country, when he knows no foreign language or manners, and lives from day to day by the small wages which he acquires?[17]

For Hume, since merely being within the territories of a government often is not truly a matter of choice, it cannot result in legitimate consent to government authority.

Tacit consent to government authority is not at issue here, but Hume's position provides some relevant insight. Often, employees feel that they have no choice but to agree to their employers' expectations. An unskilled employee may feel that rejecting the employer's request is tantamount to asking to be fired. This is because, in most cases, employers are in stronger positions than are employees.[18] This is especially true during tough economic periods with high unemployment. Even in good economic times, however, there could be so many corporations participating in the practice that many employees feel they must give their consent or not work. Thus, it is questionable whether employees' consent to COLI is legitimate.

Second, even if employees can grant legitimate consent to COLI, the issue of consent does not answer the ethical question with which we began. We came to the consent view because the mere notification view did not explain the feature of COLI that renders it unethical. The consent view, however, does not capture that feature either. It does

not identify the feature of COLI that renders it unethical unless employees consent to it.

The Employees as Means Objection

This objection could explain the feature of COLI that gives rise to the necessity of legitimate consent from employees. On Kantian grounds, one might argue that COLI, without employees' consent, treats employees as mere means to generate income rather than as [ends in themselves].[19]

Certainly, it is unethical to treat persons as mere means. Unfortunately, this still does not explain what makes COLI unethical. If one claims that it is because COLI treats employees as mere means, one must identify the feature of COLI that produces that result. Once one does that, however, one identifies a different feature of COLI that renders it unethical.

Of course, one might hold the view that all employment practices treat employees as mere means. On this view, COLI is unethical simply because it is an employment practice. This view, however, has three problems in the context of this paper.

First, the view is a fundamental rejection of capitalism. If all employment practices are unethical, capitalism itself is unjustified. I take it as a given, however, that capitalism is justified. Although I believe many capitalist practices, such as COLI, are unethical, I proceed under the assumption that the economic system itself is justified.

Second, it ignores empirical facts that indicate employees are often treated as [ends in themselves]. In many cases, they are well-paid, receive good fringe benefits, are treated with respect by their employers, and are provided with meaningful work. This is not always the case, but it is often enough that a Kantian indictment of all employment practices is unwarranted.

Finally, the view is problematic in theory. If all employment practices treat employees as mere means, then we act unethically any time we hire others to work for us. One who owns a house acts unethically when one employs others to work on the house or lawn. Likewise, one is unethical when one has someone else do one's dental work. If this view were correct, then the only way one could be ethical is by doing all one's work oneself.

If it is correct that not all employment practices treat employees as mere means, then one must identify a feature of COLI that results in treating employees as mere means. It might be tempting to point to the income-generating feature of COLI. That in itself, however, will not suffice. After all, the very point of hiring employees is to use them to generate income. Instead, one must point to something that is true of COLI that is not true of using employees to generate income generally. Once one does that, however, the emphasis on treating employees as mere means loses its significance. Instead, one need only look at that feature itself.

III. THE CONFLICTS OF INTEREST OBJECTION

The feature of COLI that separates it from most other employment practices and renders it unethical is that it produces conflicts of interest for the corporations involved. Whenever a competing interest calls into question one's ability to perform one's duties, one has a conflict of interest.[20] Such is the case for corporations that own COLI.

Consider insurance on the lives of essential personnel. Such insurance is important precisely because the personnel are crucial to the corporations. The corporations are better off if those personnel live than if they die. The insurance proceeds are intended to help corporations weather the storms caused by the loss of personnel that the corporations would be better off not losing. Consider a film studio that has signed Tom Cruise to star in a high-budget film. Since Cruise is a bankable star who is not easily replaced, the studio is better off if he lives than if he dies. Should Cruise die, the studio would suffer financial hardships. Should the studio purchase insurance on Cruise's life, no conflict of interest results.

COLI, however, produces a quite different picture. In cases of rank-and-file employees, corporations are better off if they die than if they live. Since such employees are easily replaced, corporations suffer no great hardships when such employees die. Unlike Cruise, the film studio can easily replace production assistants. Should it be in line to collect insurance proceeds, it is better off if they die. Likewise, CM Holdings could easily replace Felipe Tillman, a twenty-nine-year old music-store worker who died of AIDS in 1992, and National Convenience Stores could easily replace William

Smith, a twenty-year old convenience-store clerk who was murdered at work in 1991.[21] Moreover, the corporations were better off when they died. CM Holdings collected $339,302 and National Convenience Stores collected $250,000.[22]

This is different than the typical employment picture. Generally, corporations hire employees because they are the best available and are better off keeping those employees than incurring training costs to replace them. COLI proceeds, however, usually far exceed training costs. Tillman and Smith are cases in point.

The conflicts of interest that I am suggesting, however, are not yet complete. I have merely shown that corporations that own COLI are better off when particular rank-and-file employees die. Such is true of many people. An employee who has a personal hatred for a supervisor may be better off if that supervisor dies, but that does not mean the employee has a conflict of interest. A conflict of interest arises only if the employee's personal hatred calls into question the employee's ability to perform the duties associated with the job. If the employee is the supervisor's bodyguard, then the employee has a conflict of interest. Personal hatred could easily prevent one from making the life-saving judgments that a bodyguard must make.

Corporations have duties, both legal and ethical, to employees. COLI not only makes corporations better off when particular rank-and-file employees die, it calls into question corporations' abilities to perform those duties. I will demonstrate why through the duties to:

1. provide safe working conditions,
2. hire qualified employees, and
3. provide meaningful work.[23]

Duties to Provide Safe Working Conditions

Perhaps the most pertinent duties are those involving safety in the workplace.[24] The rights of corporations to collect proceeds on the deaths of their rank-in-file employees calls into question their abilities to be committed to safety. This is most obvious in cases of expensive equipment or procedures. Consider a convenience-store clerk. One of the greatest safety threats to a clerk is potential harm from robberies. New high-tech security equipment and procedures that could make a clerk's job safer, however, often are expensive. The proceeds of

COLI, on the other hand, are income. So, the right of the clerk's employer to collect on the clerk's death calls into question its ability to make good decisions regarding those security arrangements. A similar account can be constructed for virtually any employer.

Expensive equipment and procedures do not constitute the only relevant safety cases. Placements of employees are less obvious cases. Consider an aging assembly-line worker who has lost the coordination necessary to operate a particular station safely, but still possesses the abilities to operate other stations safely. COLI calls into question the employer's ability to make a good decision about that employee. COLI produces income, while moving the employee to another station produces expenses.

Duties to Hire Qualified Employees

COLI also calls into question corporations' abilities to fulfill their duties to hire qualified employees.[25] COLI provides corporations with incentives to search for employees who are likely to produce insurance proceeds rather than for those who are qualified to fill various employment positions. Instead of searching for employees who can ably fill a position, corporations have incentives to search for employees who are unhealthy, have risky lifestyles, or are likely to have accidents on the job that kill themselves or other employees.

Likewise, provided state law allows corporations to insure the lives of part-time employees, COLI provides corporations with incentives to hire part-time employees rather than full-time. Part-time employees are less expensive in terms of salaries and fringe benefits and provide more bodies to insure for potential COLI proceeds. Since part-time employees often are less qualified, the practice often runs afoul of the duty to hire qualified employees.

One might respond to the last point by claiming that often part-time employees are qualified people who, because of life circumstances such as parenthood or semi-retirement, prefer part-time work over full-time. By hiring such employees, corporations not only satisfy their duties to hire qualified employees, but, also, help to satisfy the needs of many people.

Although it is true that part-time positions often are filled by qualified employees who are happy to have the opportunities afforded them, this response is unsuccessful. COLI provides corporations with incentives to over-emphasize part-time work. Corporations that do so are unlikely to hire only those qualified people who are interested in part-time work because of life circumstances. There is a limited supply of such people, and, when that supply is depleted, corporations are likely to hire employees who either are unqualified or would prefer full-time work. Moreover, most people ultimately prefer full-time work for two reasons. First, part-time work often is less involved and diverse than is full-time work. Second, the rewards of part-time work, in terms of salaries and benefits, generally are much smaller.

Duties to Provide Meaningful Work

As the last point suggests, COLI also calls into question corporations' abilities to fulfill their duties to make employment meaningful. Although it is only a small part of an account of meaningful work, salaries and benefits constitute one salient feature.[26] Work often is not meaningful for employees who are underpaid or receive too few benefits. COLI, however, provides corporations with incentives to produce this problem by diverting funds from salaries and benefits to purchasing insurance on the lives of employees. The latter amounts to corporate investments rather than expenditures on employees.

As explained earlier, however, defenders of COLI dispute this point. They argue that COLI helps corporations fund employee benefits. As COLI proceeds increase profits, corporations have more funds to spend on employees.

This response, however, is unconvincing for two reasons. First, it is doubtful that COLI proceeds actually increase employee benefits. Although corporations may earmark those funds for employee benefits, it is likely that doing so merely allows them to use funds that would have supported employee benefits for other purposes. Those purposes may or may not be in the interests of rank-and-file employees. They may be used to fund executive parties and bonuses.

Second, even if it is true that COLI helps to fund employee benefits, it does so at the expense of another, perhaps even more important, salient feature of meaningful work. Generally, for work to be meaningful, employees must develop authentic relationships with at least some of their coworkers. Such relationships can develop only when employees believe that others genuinely care about their welfare. They do not develop when employees are pitted against one another. When COLI is used to fund employee benefits, however, it does just that.

Consider employees X and Y. X can develop an authentic relationship with Y only if X believes Y genuinely cares about X's welfare. This entails that Y has no interest in causing X harm or passively allowing harm to occur to X. If the employees' benefits are funded through COLI, however, Y has in an interest in X dying. So, Y has an interest in causing X harm or passively allowing harm to occur to X. Y's interest prevents X from developing an authentic relationship with Y. Such is true of employees generally when COLI is used to fund employee benefits. Thus, using COLI to fund employee benefits prevents corporations from providing meaningful work.

IV. CONCLUDING REMARKS

If what I have argued is correct, Schultz and Francis are right to question the ethical status of COLI. The considerations they raise, however, do not capture the real problem. The real problem lies in the conflicts of interest COLI produces by generating competing interests that call into question corporations' abilities to fulfill their duties to employees. Whereas corporations typically are better off if particular rank-and-file employees continue to live and work, corporations that own COLI are better off if those employees die. This is because COLI proceeds usually far exceed training costs.

Nevertheless, Schultz and Francis have done a tremendous service to the business ethics profession by bringing this practice to light. I hope they and other reporters will continue their efforts and bring other important ethical issues to our attention.

NOTES

1. I am indebted to Joseph D. Sweeney, a former student, for bringing this issue to my attention, and to Dr. Frank J. Navratil, Dean of John Carroll University's Boler School of Business, for encouraging me to write this paper.

2. See Francis (2002, 2003a, 2003b, 2003c and 2003d), Francis and Schultz (2002a, 2002b, and 2003), and Schultz and Francis (2002a, 2002b, 2002c) and [Wal-Mart] (2002). For a response from the president of the

Association for Advanced Life Underwriting, see Schiff (2003).

3. Some states, such as Texas, do not allow COLI. See Schultz and Francis (2002b, C1).

4. Schultz and Francis (2002a, A1).

5. Francis and Schultz (2002, A1).

6. Schultz and Francis (2002b, C1).

7. Schultz and Francis (2002a, A1-A8).

8. Schiff (2003, A19).

9. Even Milton Friedman seems to grant this role to government when he argues that business has no social responsibilities in any meaningful sense. See Friedman (1970).

10. Nozick (1974, 163).

11. This is not meant to imply that corporations do no wrong as long as they follow the law. Ethics and the law do not always coincide. For example, even though it would be legal, most would judge it unethical for an employer to dismiss an employee solely because the employee was late for work on the morning the employee's infant child was found dead in its crib.

12. This does not mean that I adopt the view implied by the game analogy argument. See Carr (1968). In fact, I have argued against that view elsewhere. See Spurgin (2000).

13. Some states, such as California, Michigan, Minnesota, New York, and Ohio require corporations to obtain prior consent from employees. See Schultz and Francis (2002b, C1).

14. Schultz and Francis (2002b, C1).

15. See Locke (1690; 1980, 63-65) and Hume 1748; 1948, 363-364). For examinations of tacit consent in contemporary philosophy literature, see Bennett (1979) and Simmons (1976).

16. Locke (1690; 1980, 64).

17. Hume (1748; 1948, 363).

18. Werhane (1998) makes this point against the doctrine of employment at will.

19. For his view that we should treat persons as [ends in themselves] and not merely as means, see Kant (1964, 95-98). For a Kantian approach to business ethics, see Bowie (1998a).

20. My purpose is not to provide an exhaustive definition of conflicts of interest, but, rather, to describe one common type. For more on the concept, see Boatright (1992 and 1993), Carson (1994), Davis (1982 and 1993), Luebke (1987), Margolis (1979), and Snead (1982).

21. Schultz and Francis (2002a, A8).

22. Schultz and Francis (2002a, A8).

23. This is not meant to imply that all business ethicists recognize these duties.

24. For examinations of this duty, see Faden and Beauchamp (1988), Machan (1987), Sass (1986), and Superson (1983). For related works on the doctrine of employment at will and employee rights, see DesJardins (1985), Hiley (1985), Maitland (1989), Sass (1985), and Werhane (1983 and 1988).

25. My position here is not intended to beg the question regarding the debate over affirmative action. Generally, those on both sides of that debate believe corporations should hire qualified employees and the crux of the debate lies in whether corporations should always hire the most qualified candidates. For more on that debate, see Beauchamp (1998), Beckwith (1999), Corlett (1993), Groarke (1990), Harwood (1990), Heilman (1997), Hook (1985), Levin (1981), Nagel (1993), Newton (1983 and 1991), Pojman (1992 and 1998), Purdy (1984 and 1994), Shaw (1988), and Valls (1999).

26. My purpose is not to provide an account of meaningful work, but, rather, to make use of two salient features. For more on the concept, see Arneson (1987), Attfield (1984), Bowie (1991 and 1998b), Gini (1992 and 1998), Schwartz (1982), and Walsh (1994).

REFERENCES

Arneson, R. J. 1987. "Meaningful Work and Market Socialism." *Ethics* 97: 517–545.

Attfield, R. 1984. "Work and the Human Essence." *Journal of Applied Philosophy* 1: 141–150.

Beauchamp, T. L. 1998. "In Defense of Affirmative Action." *Journal of Ethics* 2: 143–158.

Beckwith, F. J. 1999. "The 'No One Deserves His or Her Talents' Argument for Affirmative Action: A Critical Analysis." *Social Theory and Practice* 25: 53–60.

Bennett, J. G. 1979. "A Note on Locke's Theory of Tacit Consent." *Philosophical Review* 88: 224–234.

Boatright, J. R. 1992. "Conflict of Interest: An Agency Analysis." In N. E. Bowie and R. E. Freeman, eds., *Ethics and Agency Theory*, New York: Oxford University Press, 187–203.

———. 1993. "Conflict of Interest: A Response to Michael Davis." *Business & Professional Ethics Journal* 12: 43–46.

Bowie, N. E. 1991. "Challenging the Egoistic Paradigm." *Business Ethics Quarterly* 1: 1–21.

———. 1998a. "A Kantian Theory of Capitalism." *Business Ethics Quarterly*, The Ruffin Series No. 1: 37–60.

———. 1998b. "A Kantian Theory of Meaningful Work." *Journal of Business Ethics* 17: 1083–1092.

Carr, A. Z. 1968. "Is Business Bluffing Ethical?" *Harvard Business Review* 46: 143–153.

Carson, T. L. 1994. "Conflicts of Interest." *Journal of Business Ethics* 13: 387–404.

Corlett, J. A. 1993. "Racism and Affirmative Action." *Journal of Social Philosophy* 24: 163–175.

Davis, M. 1982. "Conflict of Interest." *Business & Professional Ethics Journal* 1: 17–28.

———. 1993. "Conflict of Interest Revisited." *Business & Professional Ethics Journal* 12: 21–41.

DesJardins, J. 1985. "Fairness and Employment-At-Will." *Journal of Social Philosophy* 16: 31–38.

Faden, R. R. and T. L. Beauchamp. 1988. "The Right to Risk Information and the Right to Refuse Health Hazards in the Workplace." In T. L. Beauchamp and N. E. Bowie, eds., *Ethical Theory and Business*, 3rd ed., Englewood Cliffs, NJ: Prentice Hall, 226–233.

Francis, T. 2002. "Court Finds 'Janitors Insurance' a Tax Sham at Camelot Music." *The Wall Street Journal* (August 23): C13.

———. 2003a. "Bill Seeks Disclosure on Insuring Employees." *The Wall Street Journal* (February 5): C3.

———. 2003b. "Workers' Lives: Best Tax Break?" *The Wall Street Journal* (February 19): C1, C9.

———. 2003c. "Proposal Aims to Cut Tax Breaks in Corporate-Owned Life Insurance." *The Wall Street Journal* (March 12): C9.

———. 2003d. "AEP Loses Appeal in 'Janitors' Case." *The Wall Street Journal* (April 29): A3.

———. 2003e. "COLI Revenue Declines Sharply At Large Insurers." *The Wall Street Journal* (September 3): B11.

Francis, T. and E. E. Schultz. 2002a. "Many Banks Boost Earnings With 'Janitors' Life Insurance." *The Wall Street Journal* (April 26): A1, A2.

———. 2002b. "Tax Advantages of Life Insurance Help Lift Income." *The Wall Street Journal* (December 30): A8.

———. 2003. "Dying to Donate: Charities Invest in Death Benefits." *The Wall Street Journal* (February 6): B1, B8.

Friedman, M. 1970. "The Social Responsibility of Business Is to Increase Its Profits." *The New York Times Magazine* (September 13): 32–33, 122–126.

Gini, A. 1992. "Meaningful Work and the Rights of the Worker: A Commentary on *Rerum Novarum* and *Laborem Exercens.*" *Thought* 67: 225–239.

———. 1998. "Work, Identity and Self: How We Are Formed by the Work We Do." *Journal of Business Ethics* 17: 707–714.

Groarke, L. 1990. "Affirmative Action as a Form of Restitution." *Journal of Business Ethics* 9: 207–213.

Harwood, S. 1990. "Affirmative Action is Justified: A Reply to Newton." *Contemporary Philosophy* 13: 14–17.

Heilman, M. E. 1997. "Sex Discrimination and the Affirmative Action Remedy: The Role of Sex Stereotypes." *Journal of Business Ethics* 16: 877–889.

Hiley, D. R. 1985. "Employee Rights and the Doctrine of At Will Employment." *Business & Professional Ethics Journal* 4: 1–10.

Hook, S. 1985. "Rationalizations for Reverse Discrimination." *New Perspectives* 17: 9–11.

Hume, D. 1748; 1948. "Of the Original Contract." In H. D. Aiken, ed., *Hume's Moral and Political Philosophy,* New York: Macmillan Publishing Company, 356–372.

Kant, I. 1964. *Groundwork of the Metaphysic of Morals.* H. J. Paton, tr. New York: Harper & Row.

Levin, M. E. 1981. "Is Racial Discrimination Special?" *Journal of Value Inquiry* 15: 225–234.

Locke, J. 1690; 1980. *Second Treatise of Government.* C. B. Macpherson, ed. Indianapolis: Hackett Publishing Company.

Luebke, N. R. 1987. "Conflict of Interest as a Moral Category." *Business & Professional Ethics Journal* 6: 66–81.

Machan, T. R. 1987. "Human Rights, Workers' Rights, and the 'Right' to Occupational Safety." In G. Ezorsky, ed., *Moral Rights in the Workplace,* Albany: State University of New York Press, 45–50.

Maitland, I. 1989. "Rights in the Workplace: A Nozickian Argument." *Journal of Business Ethics* 8: 951–954.

Margolis, J. 1979. "Conflicts of Interest and Conflicting Interests." In T. L. Beauchamp and N. E. Bowie, eds., *Ethical Theory and Business,* Englewood Cliffs, NJ: Prentice Hall, 361–372.

Nagel, T. 1993. "A Defense of Affirmative Action." In T. I. White, ed., *Business Ethics: A Philosophical Reader,* New York: Macmillan Publishing Company, 636–640.

Newton, L. H. 1983. "Affirmative Action as Unjustified." *Ethics* 83: 308–312.

———. 1991. "Corruption of Thought, Word and Deed: Reflections on Affirmative Action and Its Current Defenders." *Contemporary Philosophy* 14: 14–16.

Nozick, R. 1974. *Anarchy, State, and Utopia.* New York: Basic Books.

Pojman, L. P. 1992. "The Moral Status of Affirmative Action." *Public Affairs Quarterly* 6: 181–206.

———. 1998. "The Case Against Affirmative Action." *International Journal of Applied Philosophy* 12: 97–115.

Purdy, L. M. 1984. "In Defense of Hiring Apparently Less Qualified Women." *Journal of Social Philosophy* 15: 26–33.

———. 1994. "Why Do We Need Affirmative Action?" *Journal of Social Philosophy* 25: 133–143.

Sass, R. 1985. "Commentary on Hiley's 'Employee Rights and the Doctrine of At Will Employment.'" *Business & Professional Ethics Journal* 4: 11–16.

———. 1986. "The Workers' Right to Know, Participate and Refuse Hazardous Work: A Manifesto Right." *Journal of Business Ethics* 5: 129–136.

Schiff, A. J. 2003. "Letter to the Editor—You Continue to Attack Plans That Benefit Many." *The Wall Street Journal* (March 12): A19.

Schultz, E. E. and T. Francis. 2002a. "Worker Dies, Firm Profits—Why?" *The Wall Street Journal* (April 19): A1, A8.

———. 2002b. "Why Are Workers in Dark?" *The Wall Street Journal* (April 24): C1, C10.

———. 2002c. "How Corporations Built Finance Tool Out of Life Insurance." *The Wall Street Journal* (December 30): A1, A8.

Schwartz, A. 1982. "Meaningful Work." *Ethics* 92: 634–646.

Shaw, B. 1988. "Affirmative Action: An Ethical Evaluation." *Journal of Business Ethics* 7: 763–770.

Simmons, A. J. 1976. "Tacit Consent and Political Obligation." *Philosophy & Public Affairs* 5: 274–291.

Snead, W. 1982. "Commentary on Davis's 'Conflict of Interest.'" *Business & Professional Ethics Journal* 1: 29–32.

Spurgin, E. W. 2000. "What's So *Special* About a Special Ethics for Business?" *Journal of Business Ethics* 24: 273–281.

Superson, A. M. 1983. "The Employer-Employee Relationship and the Right to Know." *Business & Professional Ethics Journal* 3: 45–58.

Valls, A. 1999. "The Libertarian Case for Affirmative Action." *Social Theory and Practice* 25: 299–323.

[Wal-Mart]. 2002. "Wal-Mart Files Suit Over Losses Related to Insurance Plans." *The Wall Street Journal* (September 9): B2.

Walsh, A. J. 1994. "Meaningful Work as a Distributive Good." *Southern Journal of Philosophy* 32: 233–250.

Werhane, P. H. 1983. "Accountability and Employee Rights." *International Journal of Applied Philosophy* 1: 15–26.

———. 1988. "Employee and Employer Rights in an Institutional Context." In T. L. Beauchamp and N. E. Bowie, eds., *Ethical Theory and Business,* 3rd ed., Englewood Cliffs, NJ: Prentice Hall, 267–271.

READING 6.5 DRUG TESTING IN EMPLOYMENT
Joseph DesJardins and Ronald Duska

We take privacy to be an "employee right," by which we mean a presumptive moral entitlement to receive certain goods or be protected from certain harms in the workplace.[1] Such a right creates a *prima facie* obligation on the part of the employer to provide the relevant goods or, as in this case, refrain from the relevant harmful treatment. These rights prevent employees from being placed in the fundamentally coercive position where they must choose between their jobs and other basic human goods.

Further, we view the employer–employee relationship as essentially contractual. The employer–employee relationship is an economic one and, unlike relationships such as those between a government and its citizens or a parent and a child, exists primarily as a means for satisfying the economic interests of the contracting parties. The obligations that each party incurs are only those that it voluntarily takes on. Given such a contractual relationship, certain areas of the employee's life remain his or her own private concern, and no employer has a right to invade them. On these presumptions we maintain that certain information about an employee is rightfully private, in other words, that the employee has a right to privacy.

THE RIGHT TO PRIVACY

George Brenkert has described the right to privacy as involving a three-place relation between a person A, some information X, and another person Z. The right to privacy is violated only when Z deliberately comes to possess information X about A and no relationship between A and Z exists that would justify Z's coming to know X about A.[2] Thus, for example, the relationship one has with a mortgage company would justify that company's coming to know about one's salary, but the relationship one has with a neighbor does not justify the neighbor's coming to know that information.

Hence, an employee's right to privacy is violated whenever personal information is requested,

collected, or used by an employer in a way or for any purpose that is *irrelevant* to or *in violation* of the contractual relationship that exists between employer and employee.

Since drug testing is a means for obtaining information, the information sought must be relevant to the contract if the drug testing is not to violate privacy. Hence, we must first decide whether knowledge of drug use obtained by drug testing is job relevant. In cases in which the knowledge of drug use is *not* relevant, there appears to be no justification for subjecting employees to drug tests. In cases in which information of drug use is job relevant, we need to consider if, when, and under what conditions using a means such as drug testing to obtain that knowledge is justified.

IS KNOWLEDGE OF DRUG USE JOB-RELEVANT INFORMATION?

Two arguments are used to establish that knowledge of drug use is job-relevant information. The first argument claims that drug use adversely affects job performance, thereby leading to lower productivity, higher costs, and consequently lower profits. Drug testing is seen as a way of avoiding these adverse effects. According to some estimates $25 billion are lost each year in the United States through loss in productivity, theft, higher rates in health and liability insurance, and similar costs incurred because of drug use.[3] Since employers are contracting with an employee for the performance of specific tasks, employers seem to have a legitimate claim upon whatever personal information is relevant to an employee's ability to do the job.

The second argument claims that drug use has been and can be responsible for considerable harm to individual employees, to their fellow employees, and to the employer, and third parties, including consumers. In this case drug testing is defended because it is seen as a way of preventing possible harm. Further, since employers can be held liable for harms done to employees and customers, knowledge of employee drug use is needed so that

From *Business and Professional Ethics Journal* (1989). Reprinted by permission.

employers can protect themselves from risks related to such liability. But how good are these arguments?

THE FIRST ARGUMENT: JOB PERFORMANCE AND KNOWLEDGE OF DRUG USE

The first argument holds that drug use lowers productivity and that consequently, an awareness of drug use obtained through drug testing will allow an employer to maintain or increase productivity. It is generally assumed that the performance of people using certain drugs is detrimentally affected by such use, and any use of drugs that reduces productivity is consequently job relevant. If knowledge of such drug use allows the employer to eliminate production losses, such knowledge is job relevant.

On the surface this argument seems reasonable. Obviously some drug use, in lowering the level of performance, can decrease productivity. Since the employer is entitled to a certain level of performance and drug use adversely affects performance, knowledge of that use seems job relevant.

But this formulation of the argument leaves an important question unanswered. To what level of performance are employers entitled? Optimal performance, or some lower level? If some lower level, what? Employers have a valid claim upon some *certain level* of performance, such that a failure to perform at this level would give the employer a justification for disciplining, firing, or at least finding fault with the employee. But that does not necessarily mean that the employer has a right to a maximum or optimal level of performance, a level above and beyond a certain level of acceptability. It might be nice if the employee gives an employer a maximum effort or optimal performance, but that is above and beyond the call of the employee's duty and the employer can hardly claim a right at all times to the highest level of performance of which an employee is capable. . . .

If the person is producing what is expected, knowledge of drug use on the grounds of production is irrelevant since, by this hypothesis, the production is satisfactory. If, on the other hand, the performance suffers, then to the extent that it slips below the level justifiably expected, the employer has preliminary grounds for warning, disciplining,

or releasing the employee. But the justification for this action is the person's unsatisfactory performance, not the person's use of drugs. Accordingly, drug use information is either unnecessary or irrelevant and consequently there are not sufficient grounds to override the right of privacy. Thus, unless we can argue that an employer is entitled to optimal performance, the argument fails.

This counterargument should make it clear that the information that is job relevant, and consequently is not rightfully private, is information about an employee's level of performance and not information about the underlying causes of that level. The fallacy of the argument that promotes drug testing in the name of increased productivity is the assumption that each employee is obliged to perform at an optimal or at least quite high level. But this is required under few if any contracts. What is required contractually is meeting the normally expected levels of production or performing the tasks in the job description adequately (not optimally). If one can do that under the influence of drugs, then on the grounds of job performance at least, drug use is rightfully private. An employee who cannot perform the task adequately is not fulfilling the contract, and knowledge of the cause of the failure to perform is irrelevant on the contractual model.

Of course, if the employer suspects drug use or abuse as the cause of the unsatisfactory performance, then she might choose to help the person with counseling or rehabilitation. However, this does not seem to be something morally required of the employer. Rather, in the case of unsatisfactory performance, the employer has a *prima facie* justification for dismissing or disciplining the employee. . . .

THE SECOND ARGUMENT: HARM AND THE KNOWLEDGE OF DRUG USE TO PREVENT HARM

The performance argument is inadequate, but there is an argument that seems somewhat stronger. This is an argument that takes into account the fact that drug use often leads to harm. Using a variant of the Millian argument, which allows interference with a person's rights in order to prevent harm, we could argue that drug testing might be justified if such testing led to knowledge that would enable an employer to prevent harm.

Drug use certainly can lead to harming others. Consequently, if knowledge of such drug use can prevent harm, then knowing whether or not an employee uses drugs might be a legitimate concern of an employer in certain circumstances. This second argument claims that knowledge of the employee's drug use is job relevant because employees who are under the influence of drugs can pose a threat to the health and safety of themselves and others, and an employer who knows of that drug use and the harm it can cause has a responsibility to prevent it.

Employers have both a general duty to prevent harm and the specific responsibility for harms done by their employees. Such responsibilities are sufficient reason for an employer to claim that information about an employee's drug use is relevant if that knowledge can prevent harm by giving the employer grounds for dismissing the employee or not allowing him or her to perform potentially harmful tasks. Employers might even claim a right to reduce unreasonable risks, in this case the risks involving legal and economic liability for harms caused by employees under the influence of drugs, as further justification for knowing about employee drug use.

This second argument differs from the first, in which only a lowered job performance was relevant information. In this case, even to allow the performance is problematic, for the performance itself, more than being inadequate, can hurt people. We cannot be as sanguine about the prevention of harm as we can about inadequate production. Where drug use may cause serious harms, knowledge of that use becomes relevant if the knowledge of such use can lead to the prevention of harm and drug testing becomes justified as a means for obtaining that knowledge.

Jobs with Potential to Cause Harm

In the first place, it is not clear that every job has a potential to cause harm—at least, not a potential to cause harm sufficient to override a *prima facie* right to privacy. To say that employers can use drug testing where that can prevent harm is not to say that every employer has the right to know about the drug use of every employee. Not every job poses a

threat serious enough to justify an employer coming to know this information.

In deciding which jobs pose serious-enough threats, certain guidelines should be followed. First the potential for harm should be *clear* and *present*. Perhaps all jobs in some extended way pose potential threats to human well-being. We suppose an accountant's error could pose a threat of harm to someone somewhere. But some jobs—like those of airline pilots, school bus drivers, public transit drivers, and surgeons—are jobs in which unsatisfactory performance poses a clear and present danger to others. It would be much harder to make an argument that job performances by auditors, secretaries, executive vice-presidents for public relations, college teachers, professional athletes, and the like could cause harm if those performances were carried on under the influence of drugs. They would cause harm only in exceptional cases.[4]

Not Every Person Is to Be Tested

But, even if we can make a case that a particular job involves a clear and present danger for causing harm if performed under the influence of drugs, it is not appropriate to treat everyone holding such a job the same. Not every jobholder is equally threatening. There is less reason to investigate an airline pilot for drug use if that pilot has a twenty-year record of exceptional service than there is to investigate a pilot whose behavior has become erratic and unreliable recently, or one who reports to work smelling of alcohol and slurring his words. Presuming that every airline pilot is equally threatening is to deny individuals the respect that they deserve as autonomous, rational agents. It is to ignore their history and the significant differences between them. It is also probably inefficient and leads to the lowering of morale. It is the likelihood of causing harm, and not the fact of being an airline pilot per se, that is relevant in deciding which employees in critical jobs to test.

So, even if knowledge of drug use is justifiable to prevent harm, we must be careful to limit this justification to a range of jobs and people where the potential for harm is clear and present. The jobs must be jobs that clearly can cause harm, and the specific employee should not be someone who has a history of reliability. Finally, the drugs being tested should be those drugs that have genuine potential for harm if used in the jobs in question.

LIMITATIONS ON DRUG-TESTING POLICIES

Even when we identify those situations in which knowledge of drug use would be job relevant, we still need to examine whether some procedural limitations should not be placed upon the employer's testing for drugs. We have said when a real threat of harm exists and when evidence exists suggesting that a particular employee poses such a threat, an employer could be justified in knowing about drug use in order to prevent the potential harm. But we need to recognize that so long as the employer has the discretion for deciding when the potential for harm is clear and present, and for deciding which employees pose the threat of harm, the possibility of abuse is great. Thus, some policy limiting the employer's power is called for.

Just as criminal law imposes numerous restrictions protecting individual dignity and liberty on the state's pursuit of its goals, so we should expect that some restrictions be placed on employers to protect innocent employees from harm (including loss of job and damage to one's personal and professional reputation). Thus, some system of checks upon an employer's discretion in these matters seems advisable.

A drug-testing policy that requires all employees to submit to a drug test or to jeopardize their jobs would seem coercive and therefore unacceptable. Being placed in such a fundamentally coercive position of having to choose between one's job and one's privacy does not provide the conditions for a truly free consent. Policies that are unilaterally established by employers would likewise be unacceptable. Working with employees to develop company policy seems the only way to ensure that the policy will be fair to both parties. Prior notice of testing would also be required in order to give employees the option of freely refraining from drug use. Preventing drug use is morally preferable to punishing users after the fact, because this approach treats employees as capable of making rational and informed decisions.

Further procedural limitations seem advisable as well. Employees should be notified of the results of the test, they should be entitled to appeal the results (perhaps through further tests by an independent laboratory), and the information obtained through tests ought to be kept confidential. In summary, limitations upon employer discretion for administering drug tests can be derived from the nature of the employment contract and from the recognition that drug testing is justified by the desire to prevent harm, not the desire to punish wrongdoing.

THE ILLEGALITY CONTENTION

At this point critics might note that the behavior which testing would try to deter is, after all, illegal. Surely this excuses any responsible employer from being overprotective of an employee's rights. The fact that an employee is doing something illegal should give the employer a right to that information about his or her private life. Thus it is not simply that drug use might pose a threat of harm to others, but that it is an *illegal* activity that threatens others. But again, we would argue that illegal activity itself is irrelevant to job performance. At best, *conviction* records might be relevant, but since drug tests are administered by private employers we are not only ignoring the question of conviction, we are also ignoring the fact that the employee has not even been arrested for the alleged illegal activity.

Further, even if the due process protections and the establishment of guilt are acknowledged, it still does not follow that employers have a claim to know about all illegal activity on the part of their employees.

Consider the following example: Suppose you were hiring an auditor whose job required certifying the integrity of your firm's tax and financial records. Certainly, the personal integrity of this employee is vital to adequate job performance. Would we allow the employer to conduct, with or without the employee's consent, an audit of the employee's own personal tax return? Certainly if we discover that this person has cheated on a personal tax return we will have evidence of illegal activity that is relevant to this person's ability to do the job. Given one's own legal liability for filing falsified statements, the employee's illegal activity also poses a threat to others. But surely, allowing private individuals to audit an employee's tax returns is too intrusive a means for discovering information about that employee's integrity. The government certainly would never allow this violation of an employee's privacy. It ought not to allow drug testing on the same grounds. Why tax returns should be protected in ways that urine, for example, is not, raises interesting questions of fairness. Unfortunately, this question would take us beyond the scope of this paper.

VOLUNTARINESS

A final problem that we also leave undeveloped concerns the voluntariness of employee consent. For most employees, being given the choice between submitting to a drug test and risking one's job by refusing an employer's request is not much of a decision at all. We believe that such decisions are less than voluntary and thereby hold that employers cannot escape our criticisms simply by including with the employment contract a drug-testing clause.[5] Furthermore, there is reason to believe that those most in need of job security will be those most likely to be subjected to drug testing. Highly skilled, professional employees with high job mobility and security will be in a stronger position to resist such intrusions than will less skilled, easily replaced workers. This is why we should not anticipate surgeons and airline pilots being tested and should not be surprised when public transit and factory workers are. A serious question of fairness arises here as well.

Drug use and drug testing seem to be our most recent social "crisis." Politicians, the media, and employers expend a great deal of time and effort addressing this crisis. Yet, unquestionably, more lives, health, and money are lost each year to alcohol abuse than to marijuana, cocaine, and other controlled substances. We are well advised to be careful in considering issues that arise from such selective social concern. We will let other social commentators speculate on the reasons why drug use has received scrutiny while other white-collar crimes and alcohol abuse are ignored. Our only concern at this point is that such selective prosecution suggests an arbitrariness that should alert us to questions of fairness and justice.

In summary, then, we have seen that drug use is not always job relevant, and if drug use is not job relevant, information about it is certainly not job relevant. In the case of performance it may be a cause of some decreased performance, but it is the performance itself that is relevant to an employee's position, not what prohibits or enables that

employee to do the job. In the case of potential harm being done by an employee under the influence of drugs, the drug use seems job relevant, and in this case drug testing to prevent harm might be legitimate. But how this is practicable is another question. It would seem that standard motor dexterity or mental dexterity tests given immediately prior to job performance are more effective in preventing harm, unless one concludes that drug use invariably and necessarily leads to harm. One must trust the individuals in any system for that system to work. One cannot police everything. Random testing might enable an employer to find drug users and to weed out the few to forestall possible future harm, but are the harms prevented sufficient to override the rights of privacy of the people who are innocent and to overcome the possible abuses we have mentioned? It seems not.

Clearly, a better method is to develop safety checks immediately prior to the performance of a job. Have a surgeon or a pilot or a bus driver pass a few reasoning and motor-skill tests before work. The cause of the lack of a skill, which lack might lead to harm, is really a secondary issue.

NOTES

1. "A Defense of Employee Rights," Joseph DesJardins and John McCall, *Journal of Business Ethics* 4 (1985). We should emphasize that our concern is with the *moral* rights of privacy for employees and not with any specific or prospective *legal* rights. Readers interested in pursuing the legal aspects of employee drug testing should consult "Workplace Privacy Issues and Employer Screening Policies" by Richard Lehr and David Middlebrooks in *Employee Relations Law Journal* 11, no. 3, 407–421; and "Screening Workers for Drugs: A Legal and Ethical Framework," Mark Rothstein, in *Employee Relations Law Journal* 11, no. 3, 422–436.

2. "Privacy, Polygraphs, and Work," George Brenkert, *Journal of Business and Professional Ethics* 1, no. 1 (Fall 1981). For a more general discussion of privacy in the workplace see "Privacy in Employment" by Joseph DesJardins, in *Moral Rights in the Workplace*, edited by Gertrude Ezorsky (SUNY Press, 1987). A good resource for philosophical work on privacy can be found in "Recent Work on the Concept of Privacy" by W. A. Parent, in *American Philosophical Quarterly*, vol. 20 (Oct. 1983), 341–358.

3. *U.S. News and World Report,* 22 Aug. 1983; *Newsweek,* 6 May 1983.

4. Obviously we are speaking here of harms that go beyond the simple economic harm that results from unsatisfactory job performance. These economic harms are discussed in the first argument above. Further, we ignore such "harms" as providing bad role models for adolescents, harms often used to justify drug tests for professional athletes. We think it unreasonable to hold an individual responsible for the image he or she provides to others.

5. It might be argued that since we base our critique upon the contractual relationship between employers and employees, our entire position can be undermined by a clever employer who places within the contract a privacy waiver for drug tests. A full answer to this would require an account of the free and rational subject that the contract model presupposes. While acknowledging that we need such an account to prevent just any contract from being morally legitimate, we will have to leave this debate to another time. Interested readers might consult "The Moral Contract between Employers and Employees" by Norman Bowie in *The Work Ethic in Business,* edited by W. M. Hoffman and T. J. Wyly (Cambridge, MA: Oelgeschlager and Gunn, 1981), 195–202.

Decision Scenario A
AMERICAN CYANAMID AND JOHNSON CONTROLS

In the beginning of 1978, Glen Mercer, an officer of American Cyanamid Company's Willow Island plant in West Virginia, held meetings with groups of the plant's female employees. The subject of the meetings was the presence in the plant of numerous chemicals known to be hazardous to the health of fetuses. Mr. Mercer announced a new corporate policy that would exclude women of childbearing age from those areas of the plant where these chemicals were present. The exclusion would apply to every woman between the ages of 16 and 50 unless the woman presented documents proving that she had been sterilized. At the meetings the women were given information about the ease of sterilization procedures and about the local availability of those procedures.

Initially, the company's exclusionary policy was to apply to all but seven jobs in the plant. Mercer informed the approximately 30 women who would be subject to the policy that those who either were not sterilized or were not awarded the remaining nonhazardous jobs would be dismissed. After several months, American Cyanamid modified its policy so that it applied to only one department. Of the seven women in that department, five were sterilized and two were assigned to other jobs with reduced wages.

The final exclusionary policy applied to a department where there was environmental exposure to airborne lead. American Cyanamid claimed that it was unable to reduce the lead levels in the air to comply with Occupational Safety and Health Administration standards. OSHA believed that those standards were safe even for fetuses. When American Cyanamid failed to reduce lead levels, OSHA issued a citation and proposed a fine of $10,000 on the ground that the policy of sterilization or reassignment/termination was itself a hazard to the health of the women. On appeal, an administrative law judge exempted the plant from the OSHA standards on the ground that compliance was not "economically feasible."

The Oil, Chemical and Atomic Workers Union, which represented the female employees, brought two suits against the company. One alleged that the administrative law judge erred in determining that the exclusionary policy was not itself a health hazard prohibited by the intent of the Occupational Safety and Health Act of 1970 since, according to the union, sterilization is a serious harm. The other suit alleged that the exclusionary policy was a form of discrimination prohibited by the 1964 Civil Rights Act.

In the first case, Judge Robert Bork, then sitting on the District of Columbia Court of Appeals, wrote a decision upholding the original decision of the administrative law judge. Bork, in a characteristically clear and narrow decision, ruled that the precedent from previous court cases and legislative history of the OSHA act both indicate that the term *hazard* refers only to the physical or environmental conditions of the workplace. Thus, Cyanamid's exclusionary policy was not a hazard covered by the OSHA act.

The sex discrimination suit was settled out of court, and therefore no clear precedent emerged from this case. However, a few years later a similar case did make its way to the U.S. Supreme Court. In *Automobile Workers v. Johnson Controls,* the Court had to decide if policies that excluded women from certain jobs in order to protect their potential children constituted unfair and illegal discrimination.

Johnson Controls Inc. manufactures batteries, a major component of which is lead. Exposure to lead affects the reproductive abilities of both men and women, and poses additional health risks to all adults, children, and fetuses. Evidence suggests that a fetus is more vulnerable to harm than an adult.

Prior to the Civil Rights Act of 1964, Johnson Controls did not employ any women in jobs that involved exposure to lead. The company's first official policy regarding women in such positions strongly advised women capable of bearing children against taking these jobs. Women who applied for jobs involving exposure to lead were required to sign a statement informing them that "women exposed to lead have a higher rate of abortion . . . not as clear as the relationship between cigarette smoking and cancer . . . but medically speaking, it just makes good sense not to run that risk if you want children and do not want to expose the unborn child to risk, however small."

In 1982 Johnson Controls went further and excluded all women who were capable of bearing children from jobs involving lead exposure. This change resulted from the discovery that several employees who had recently become pregnant had tested for blood lead levels above the OSHA critical-level category. The new policy defined women capable of bearing children as "all women except those whose inability to bear children is medically documented."

In response to this policy, several employees filed suit, including a woman who chose to be sterilized rather than lose her job, a woman who was a single parent and who had been transferred to a lower-paying job, and a man who had been denied a leave of absence so that he could lower the level of lead in his system before he and his wife tried to become parents. This case was decided by the U.S. Supreme Court in 1991.

- Should employers be liable to health risks that the workplace poses to the unborn children of their employees? Why or why not?

- Typically it is cheaper to dismiss an employee who is susceptible to illness than it is to improve workplace conditions that might lessen health risks to employees. Should such economic considerations determine proper management decisions?

- Is the choice between sterilization and losing one's job a fully voluntary choice? Why or why not?

- If it turns out that women as opposed to men, or African-Americans as opposed to European-Americans, or Jews as opposed to non-Jews, are more susceptible to certain medical conditions, is it fair to make employment decisions on the basis of those medical conditions? Would such decisions be unjust discrimination? Would you reach the same conclusions about medical conditions not correlated with sex, race, or ethnic background?

Decision Scenario B
GENETIC SCREENING IN THE WORKPLACE

The Human Genome Project is a worldwide multi-billion-dollar project aimed at mapping and sequencing the entire human genome, the approximately one hundred thousand individual genes that form the molecular basis of human life. "Mapping" genes involves identifying and locating all the individual genes on a particular chromosome; "sequencing" involves identifying the particular sequence of DNA base pairs, thought to be perhaps three billion, that make up the human genome. Within the last decade thousands of genes have been located at specific sites on chromosomes, and dozens of major diseases have been linked to particular genes. Among those identified are genes linked to Huntington's chorea, cystic fibrosis, inherited forms of colon cancer and breast cancer, and Alzheimer's disease. Some evidence also suggests a genetic basis for heart disease, high blood pressure, diabetes, and arthritis. Claims have even been made that link genes to alcoholism, homosexuality, and criminality.

But the language of a genetic "link" or a genetic "basis" is ambiguous. In some cases, like sickle-cell anemia, Huntington's chorea, and Down syndrome, there is a direct causal connection between the presence of a particular gene and the resultant disease. The presence of a specific genetic structure causes the disease. But in other cases, like cancer and heart disease, the linkage is more a matter of a predisposition or a susceptibility than a cause. People with a specific genetic makeup are predisposed or susceptible to the disease, but many other factors like environment and diet also seem to be necessary. In still other cases where the gene is linked to complex phenomena like alcoholism, intelligence, schizophrenia, or homosexuality, the linkage amounts to little more than a statistical correlation: The presence of specific genes is statistically related to those phenomena.

The Human Genome Project has tremendous implications for medicine. It has already provided significant new knowledge for understanding and diagnosing disease. Unfortunately, therapy and treatment for these diseases often lag many years behind knowledge of their genetic basis. Nevertheless, significant therapeutic advances will certainly follow in coming years.

To some observers, the project raises serious ethical issues as well. Many fear that employers and insurance companies, in particular, would use genetic screening as a means for denying jobs and insurance. Even a small statistical correlation between a certain gene and cancer would provide a strong incentive for an insurance company to reduce its risks by denying insurance to carriers of this gene. Likewise, business can reduce its risk by not hiring people with a genetic susceptibility to disease, or whose genes suggest a predisposition to alcoholism, crime, or a psychological disorder.

Since most of the Human Genome Project is funded by the federal government, the Office of Technology Assessment (OTA) of the U.S. Congress was charged with examining some of these issues. The OTA's report, *Genetic Monitoring and Screening*

in the Workplace, found very few employers who were using genetic screening in the workplace. While only 12 of the 330 Fortune 500 companies surveyed reportedly used genetic monitoring or screening, half thought that genetic screening is acceptable and almost half report that the costs of insuring a job applicant would affect their decision to hire someone.

As the Human Genome Project progresses, new and less expensive techniques for genetic screening will no doubt be developed. This will provide employers and insurance companies with an added incentive to use these tools for screening employees. Since most people receive health insurance through work, both insurers and employers have incentives to work together to gather this information and reduce their risks.

One preliminary study found several cases in which individuals were denied jobs because of their genetic conditions.★ One case involved the brother of a person with Gaucher Disease (a disease affecting fat metabolism) who was denied a job after including this information on a job application. The brother was labeled a "carrier" and denied the job as a result. In another case, a woman was denied employment because she had Charcot-Marie-Tooth disease (a nonfatal, genetically based neuromuscular disease).

Several states have considered laws that would restrict the use of genetic information. The federal Americans with Disabilities Act (1990) prohibits employment discrimination on the basis of past and current disabilities. But the law says nothing about future disabilities or people with only a susceptibility to some disease. Insurance companies, of course, are free to treat people with preexisting conditions differently than those without. Additionally, there seems to be no legal protection for people identified as having predispositions to disease or behavioral traits such as alcoholism or crime.

The increasingly likely use of genetic screening in the workplace raises many ethical questions. In coming years, society must decide if employers have a legitimate claim to conduct genetic tests, to possess information about employees' genetic makeup, and to deny jobs or insurance to people on the basis of this information.

★Paul Billings et al., "Discrimination as a Consequence of Genetic Testing," *American Journal of Human Genetics* 50 (1992): 476–482.

Additionally, as in other privacy issues, we need to acknowledge the important role of consent. The most obvious way to justify diminishing privacy rights is to obtain the consent of the people affected. Society needs to decide if employees should be free to refuse genetic tests without fear of reprisal and if they should have the right to be informed of the results of any tests. In essence, we need to resolve the question of ownership. Does the information obtained by genetic tests belong to the employer or the employee? Even if the test results suggest a susceptibility to some risk, does it necessarily follow that employers should have the right to exclude others from taking that risk? Perhaps employees should have the freedom to take a job that, given their genetic makeup, increases health risks.

Finally, a number of concerns can be raised about the economics of the tests themselves. Employers will always want to reduce costs, and this will likely mean that the best available tests, as well as follow-up techniques to verify test results, will not always be used. The cost to follow up screening with genetic counseling and medical advice means that it will probably not be provided. Also, genetic tests will likely be used as screening devices rather than as monitoring tools because genetic screening is typically a one-time occurrence, whereas genetic monitoring is conducted on an ongoing basis to determine if the condition is worsening. Since monitoring is both more expensive and more likely to indicate that the workplace itself is contributing to the health risk, employers are more likely to rely on genetic screening to filter out "undesirable" employees.

- Should it be illegal to fire an employee whose illness causes a significant rise in insurance costs for other employees? Should it be illegal to fire an employee who is genetically susceptible to such conditions as heart disease or cancer?

- In order to verify the presence of a particular gene, it is standard scientific procedure to screen other family members. Should an employer be required to conduct such verification when they test employees? Should they be prohibited from conducting such verification?

- Who "owns" genetic information? Does the information gathered through genetic screening belong to the individual who was screened? The person who paid for the screening? The person who conducted the screening? Why does it matter?

- Are there limitations that should be placed upon the uses of information gathered through genetic screening? What might such limitations involve and how would you decide such questions?

Decision Scenario C
WHEN GENDER HARASSMENT IS NOT SEXUAL

On September 22, 1987, Margaret Reynolds was fired from her job as an electrician and "foreman" working at the Atlantic City Convention Center in New Jersey. She had worked as an electrician for over two years and she was a member of the local union, the International Brotherhood of Electrical Workers. Reynolds and another woman were among several electricians laid off during a slow work period. When many of the workers, all men, were rehired soon after, Reynolds sued the Convention Center and her union. She alleged that her dismissal was discriminatory and that the Convention Center was a hostile and offensive workplace that constituted sexual harassment.

The court record describes a workplace of constant vulgarity, verbal abuse, obscene gestures and language. Male coworkers would grab their crotch in Reynolds' presence, give her the "finger," and refer to her (and other women) by a vulgar term for female genitalia. The workplace was permeated by a culture of vulgarity, obscenity, and crude sexual language. The court record indicated that male coworkers resisted or refused to work for Reynolds, and some even threatened to quit rather than work for a woman "foreman." On one occasion, a convention hall exhibitor requested that Reynolds and another woman electrician be prohibited from working on the convention floor during the Miss

America pageant. Apparently, female electricians in the presence of a beauty contest was more than this exhibitor could handle.

At trial, the court had to decide if Reynolds had been discriminated against because of her sex, if any sexual harassment occurred and, if it did occur, did it rise to the level of creating a hostile work environment. The court ruled against Reynolds on all counts.

The court reasoned that while the workplace might be vulgar and obscene, relatively little of this was directed specifically at Reynolds. The entire workplace was vulgar and thus equally offensive (or not) to men or women. Thus, this case wasn't truly a matter of discrimination. Further, the vulgarity and obscenity that was directed at Reynolds, while perhaps antagonistic and hostile, was not explicitly "sexual." The fact that Reynolds and another woman used vulgar and obscene language themselves was considered a relevant factor in this case.

- Do you think that crude and vulgar language directed at female coworkers can make a workplace so hostile as to prevent women from an equal opportunity workplace?

- What is the difference between "sexual" harassment and harassment based on gender? Can men be harassed on the basis of sex?

- Should the law protect women from vulgarity and obscenity in the workplace? From discrimination? Under what conditions, if any, can vulgarity rise to the level of gender-based discrimination? Are some jobs likely to be so vulgar that women should not consider working at them?

Decision Scenario D

DISMISSAL FOR AN ABORTION?

Robin Flanigan was a 21-year-old unmarried hairdresser working at a salon in suburban Maryland in 1990 when she faced a decision that many young women confront: Should she choose to end her pregnancy through an abortion? According to Flanigan, she approached one of the salon owners, Patrice Davidson, for advice. Shortly thereafter Mrs. Davidson and her husband (the other salon owner) began, in the words of Flanigan, an "endless assault" to convince her not to go through with her decision to have an abortion. On December 11, 1990, Flanigan went through with her decision. On December 15 she was fired from her job. Flanigan filed a civil suit against the Davidsons, claiming that she was wrongfully fired for choosing to have an abortion.

In her suit, Flanigan alleged that the Davidsons aimed to "coerce and intimidate her into not having the abortion." Their activities included phone calls to her family, offers to help raise the child, let-ters, and, at one point, hanging pictures of aborted fetuses at her workplace. The Davidsons denied all of Flanigan's allegations. They claimed that she was fired for unsatisfactory work and that the timing of her dismissal was simply coincidental.

- Assume that the facts are as Flanigan claims. What, if anything, would be wrong with the Davidsons' activities? Assume that there was no campaign of harassment, but simply that the Davidsons fired Flanigan when they discovered that she had had an abortion. What, if anything, would be wrong with their action?

- Imagine a parallel case in which an employer encouraged an employee to have an abortion. Would the same issues be involved if the employee was fired for refusing?

- Shouldn't employers be allowed to make personnel decisions based upon their own judgments of moral character? Why or why not?

Decision Scenario E
IF YOU WORK HERE, DON'T SMOKE

In 1991, Ford Meter Box Co., a small manufacturing firm in Indiana, prohibited employees from smoking both on the job and away from work. Janice Bone worked for Ford Meter Box, and when a routine urinalysis detected nicotine in her system, she was fired for violating company policy. Bone sued, arguing that her off-work activities were private and should not be the basis for employment decisions.

Ford Meter is on a growing list of companies that are placing employment restrictions on smokers. The most obvious restriction is the prohibition of smoking on the job. A number of considerations have led companies to go further than this, leading to policies like Ford Meter's, which prohibits smoking altogether. Companies argue that increased health care and insurance costs associated with smoking justify these restrictions. Smokers use health care insurance more often, they have greater rates of absenteeism, and they tend to retire earlier than other workers due to health issues such as emphysema, lung cancer, and heart disease. In the opinion of many employers, these factors make smoking a job-relevant activity.

Some companies, like Texas Instruments and U-Haul, require smokers to pay higher rates—an insurance surcharge—for health insurance. In 1994 a Lockheed plant in Georgia joined companies like Turner Broadcasting in refusing to hire people who smoke. In defending their policy, a Lockheed spokesperson referred to an American Lung Association study that showed companies pay up to $5000 per year in additional health care costs for employees who smoke. The Lockheed policy applied only to new employees.

In response to Janice Bone's lawsuit, the state of Indiana passed a law protecting employees from dismissal because they smoke outside of the workplace. By 1993, 28 states had passed legislation protecting the rights of smokers.

- Is smoking an activity that is job relevant? Are all employee activities that can increase employer costs relevant for employment decisions?
- Ford Meter Box conducted routine urinalysis tests to check for traces of nicotine. Is this means of enforcing company policy reasonable?
- Should governments get involved in these issues, or should they be left to the individual bargaining between employers and employees?
- Ford Meter fired a present employee for smoking. Lockheed refused to hire smokers, but left alone present employees. Texas Instruments and U-Haul placed additional conditions on employees who smoke. Are all of these policies justified? Some of these policies? None of them?

Decision Scenario F
PREEMPLOYMENT PSYCHOLOGICAL TESTING

Target Stores, a division of Dayton Hudson Corporation, routinely used a psychological examination called "Psychscreen" as a preemployment test for all applicants for store security positions. Three applicants for such a position sued Target Stores, claiming that this test violated their privacy and should not be a condition of employment.

Psychscreen is a combination of two widely used psychological profile tests, the Minnesota Multiphasic Personality Inventory and the California Psychological Inventory. The test asks 704 true/false questions that are later evaluated by an independent consulting firm of psychologists. The test was used to ensure careful hiring of security guards, seeking to provide a profile of applicants' attitudes, personality, values, character, and emotional makeup. Target's own employees did not see answers given to these questions, but based their hiring decisions on the assessments provided by the outside consultants. While the scientific validity of these tests is open to debate, defenders claim that they are more objective and valid than the similar judgments that would be made intuitively during an interview.

The job applicants who filed suit, Sibi Soroka, William d'Arcangelo, and Sue Urry, found many of the questions intrusive. Questions included: "I feel very strongly attracted to members of my own sex. . . . I have never indulged in any unusual sex practices. . . . I feel sure that there is only one true religion. . . . I go to church almost every week. . . . I wish that I were not bothered by thoughts about sex. . . . I have had no difficulty starting or holding my urine. . . . I believe that my sins are unpardonable."

The state of California grants a specific constitutional right of privacy and has laws prohibiting preemployment questions concerning religious beliefs and sexual orientation. A trial court found in favor of Target, but a California Court of Appeal issued an injunction against the use of this test. Before the case returned to trial, Target settled out of court, agreeing to pay more than $2 million in class-action damages. Target discontinued the use of Psychscreen in 1991.

- Do you think that psychological testing violates an employee's privacy?

- Is personality a valid reason for refusing to hire someone? Is it a valid reason for firing someone? Which personality traits would justify refusal to hire someone as a store security officer?

- Would your views of these tests change if they were shown to be scientifically valid?

Decision Scenario G
E-MAIL PRIVACY

On February 1, 1995, Michael Smyth was fired from his job at the Pillsbury Co. in Pennsylvania for transmitting what the company judged to be "inappropriate and unprofessional comments" over the company e-mail system. Smyth sued Pillsbury on the grounds of a wrongful discharge, arguing that e-mail communications were private.

Like all businesses, Pillsbury owned the e-mail system and installed it as a means for improving corporate communication. In October 1994, Smyth used his home computer system to correspond with his supervisor at work. Referring to Pillsbury management, Smyth's e-mails contained apparent threats to "kill the backstabbing bastards" and referred to the company holiday party as the "Jim Jones Koolaid affair." Smyth denied that the threats were serious. The e-mails were saved on the company system and were later used as the basis for Smyth's dismissal.

Prior to this case, Pillsbury had assured its employees that all e-mail communications would remain confidential and privileged. It also had assured employees that e-mail communications would not be intercepted nor used by the company as grounds for termination or reprimand. Smyth claimed that he had relied on these assurances when he wrote the e-mail. Smyth also argued that this discharge violated his right of privacy.

Pennsylvania is an employment-at-will state in which an employer, in the words of the court, "may discharge an employee with or without cause unless restrained by some contract" and in which an employer's right to terminate an at-will employee is "virtually absolute." The Pennsylvania court ruled that, despite its assurances to the contrary, Pillsbury had no legal obligation to treat e-mail communication as confidential. Pennsylvania law recognizes that there can be some circumstances under which an invasion of privacy is so intrusive as to protect employees from dismissal. (Previous cases had related to urinalysis and personal property searches in which employees were required to disclose personal information under threat of dismissal.) However, in this case the court concluded that Smyth did not have a reasonable expectation of privacy. Because he voluntarily communicated with a supervisor using an e-mail system owned by his employer, Symth had no valid legal claims to privacy. The court concluded that the "company's interest in preventing inappropriate and unprofessional comments or even illegal activity over its e-mail system outweighs any privacy interest the employee may have in those comments."

- Do you agree with the court's decision in this case? Why or why not?

- The court ruled that Smyth did not have a reasonable expectation of privacy despite the fact that the company had assured him that e-mails would remain confidential. Where, then, do "expectations of privacy" arise, if not from company policy?

- How far do you think property rights extend in electronic communications? The company owned its own computers, but not the computer that Smyth used to communicate from home. The company owned, or had a license to use, the e-mail software and operating system. Does anyone "own" the e-mail message itself or does it belong to anyone who owns the computer system on which it is stored?

- Would it have made a difference if the e-mail did not contain threats, but rather tasteless or insulting comments? Would it make a difference if the comments were merely critical of management? Who gets to decide what are "inappropriate and unprofessional" comments?

7

ᛞᛞ

Ethical Responsibilities in Business: Employees, Managers, Professionals

INTRODUCTION

The previous two chapters have examined a broad range of employee rights. This present chapter will examine in more detail the nature and extent of ethical *responsibilities* within a business setting. A helpful way to understand responsibilities is to reflect back on our discussion of rights as the legitimate claims that people have on others. To ask "What are my responsibilities?" is to ask "What do I owe other people?" Thus, we should think about responsibilities in the workplace along two dimensions: *What* do I owe to *whom?* We cannot fully know "what" responsibilities we have without also answering the "who" question.

In the reading reprinted in Chapter One, economist Milton Friedman argued that business managers, as employees of the business owners, have a "direct" and "primary" responsibility to those owners. That responsibility, according to Friedman, is "to make as much money as possible" while conforming to law and ethical custom. Thus, in Friedman's view, once we understand that the primary responsibility of managers is *to* stockholders, we can see the nature of that responsibility is to make as much money as possible. A more general doctrine of corporate social responsibility is invalid, in Friedman's view, because it would require a business manager "to act in some way that is not in the interests of his employers." The stakeholder model, on the other hand, argues that business managers have ethical responsibilities to a wide range of other stakeholders.

Friedman's observation does contain an important insight. In many business situations, employees will face decisions in which their own interests conflict with the interests of the employer. Since employers often depend on employees to represent their interests, it is important to acknowledge the responsibility employees have to avoid such conflicts of interest. Employees ought not to pursue their own personal interests at the expense of their employers. However, Chapter One also argued that Friedman's point of view was too simplistic an understanding of managerial responsibilities. In part, this is because contemporary stock ownership is more complicated than Friedman's model suggests and that the duties owed to owners of stock are not as clear as Friedman imagines. Some stockholders seek short-term maximum profit, others seek long-term stable growth. Some are day-traders, some are long-term investors. Stockholder interests can vary significantly. But Friedman's view is also misleading because it fails to acknowledge the legitimate claims that many other stakeholders have on business managers and employees. The "interests" that conflict with a manager trying to make as much money as possible for stockholders might not be the personal interests of managers, but the ethically legitimate claims of employees, consumers, and society at large. In short, there may be many and diverse responsibilities that employees face within a business context.

Consider the case of David Duncan (which opens this chapter) as a test case of Friedman's viewpoint. Duncan was a partner at Arthur Andersen and thus was an employee of that business. But Arthur Andersen was hired by Enron's management, both to perform audits and to consult with Enron on its business. Duncan himself was also an accountant who had professional duties as an auditor. Where, exactly, are Duncan's "primary" responsibilities? Who, exactly, was his employer? Did he work for Arthur Andersen? For Enron's management? For Enron's stockholders? For whom should he "make as much money as possible"? Should any of those responsibilities trump the duties of a professional auditor? This chapter will examine such questions.

HONESTY, LOYALTY, AND TRUST

Honesty

Let us begin by examining some general ethical responsibilities relevant in the workplace. Few ethical values are as universally recognized as honesty. "Tell the truth," "don't lie" are responsibilities that most of us learn from our earliest years. But perhaps few rules are so often broken. "Stretching the truth," telling a "white lie," deceptive and misleading statements abound. No doubt, dishonesty can sometimes be justified, but this typically occurs when the truth might cause someone harm. Dishonesty is much more troubling, and typically unjustified, when it is done to benefit oneself at the expense of another. In such cases, we normally would hold that our responsibility to be honest overrides our self-interest.

Philosophically, we can identify three general justifications for a responsibility to be honest. Utilitarians typically see honesty as playing a crucial role in social life, particularly in enabling us to communicate with others. Dishonesty undermines the trust necessary for communicating with others; if you could not believe what others were saying to you, social intercourse would be difficult if not impossible. Rights theorists in the Kantian tradition argue that honesty is a fundamental principle of rational ethics. Dishonesty to further our own self-interests irrationally treats our own interests as superior to the equal interests of others. It violates the autonomy of others by, in the words of one commentator, "mugging their intellects." Other ethical theorists would focus on what dishonesty does to the person who lies. Dishonesty requires an individual to maintain two "personas": the one who maintains the outward appearance of honesty (dishonesty only works when others believe that you are honest), and the one who, underneath, knows and plans the deception. This "moral schizophrenia" can undermine personal integrity and self-respect.

It is also worth noting the important role that honesty plays in economic markets. Among the very few ethical limits that Milton Friedman (Reading 1.1) places on the pursuit of profits, for example, is the responsibility to avoid deception. Deception in economic transactions threatens the two fundamental ethical goals that justify markets in the first place: social utility and individual liberty. When I am deceived in an economic transaction I fail to improve my own position and, thus, the transaction was inefficient and did not improve social utility. Deception also unjustly interferes with my freedom of choice by manipulating me to do something that I would not have done had I not been deceived.

Nevertheless, the temptation to be dishonest is especially strong in business, where it can lead to great personal benefits. In a classic essay reprinted in this chapter, Albert Carr (Reading 7.1) argues that dishonesty is all part of the "rules of the game" and should not be thought of as unethical. Drawing on an analogy with bluffing in poker, Carr tells us that "falsehood ceases to be falsehood when it is understood on all sides that the truth is not expected to be spoken."

It might be easy to dismiss this perspective if we think only in terms of major cases of dishonesty such as cheating and fraud. But many business situations can involve a more subtle form of dishonesty that is sometimes referred to as "puffery" or "bluffing." If, for example, you are a college student about to initiate your first major job search, your résumé is likely to be quite modest. It would not be uncommon, or perhaps as Carr would say, unexpected, for a résumé to be "padded," or "puffed up" in such a way that the truth is stretched in a way favorable to the job applicant. In labor negotiations, it is not unusual for a union to overstate its willingness to go out on strike or for management to overstate its inability to meet the contract demands of employees. These examples suggest that there may be cases within business in which bluffing is like a game strategy, known and accepted by all participants. Such cases raise more interesting ethical questions than the more dramatic cases of cheating and fraud.

Loyalty

Some of the most well-known cases of corporate corruption in recent years have involved situations in which individual employees learn about unethical or illegal activities by their employer and thereby face a choice of blowing the whistle on their employer or remaining silent. Enron Vice President Sherron Watkins came to believe that Enron's accounting practices were ethically suspect. She then faced a choice between remaining a loyal employee and blowing the whistle by making such improprieties public. In each corporate scandal of recent years, countless individuals faced similar situations when they came to learn about illegal or unethical activities. They could remain a loyal team player and remain silent, or they could make public the illegal or unethical activities and blow the whistle on corruption.

Whistleblowing carries with it significant costs. In most cases, the whistleblower faces grave harms, ranging from lost jobs and careers, to lost friendships and resentment among co-workers. Whistleblowing also jeopardizes the well-being of the firm, disrupting its work and, in some cases, resulting in lost contracts and lost jobs. It also involves one or more individuals asserting that their judgments are superior to those made by other professionals and managers, sometimes without having the full information available to others. In the words of ethicist Sisela Bok, by blowing the whistle, "the whistleblower hopes to stop the game; but since he is neither referee nor coach, and since he blows the whistle on his own team, his act is seen as a violation of loyalty."

In our second reading in this chapter, Ron Duska argues that much of the debate about the ethics of whistleblowing assumes a misguided understanding of loyalty. For-profit businesses, according to Duska, are not the kinds of things to which we have a responsibility of loyalty. Since one cannot owe loyalty to one's corporate employer, the apparent conflict between responsibilities does not exist. In his view, whistleblowing not only is permissible, but is something we can expect from responsible individuals. Corporate loyalty cannot limit the moral autonomy and ethical responsibility of individuals.

Trust

In general, trust involves placing ourselves in a vulnerable position and relying on others not to exploit that vulnerability. I trust that drivers will stop as I enter a crosswalk, I trust that the food I eat is safe, I trust when I take my prescribed medicine that my doctor has accurately diagnosed my illness. In any social setting, individuals need to rely on others, need to trust others. In modern business, trust is a fundamental requirement. As a consumer, I trust the products that I purchase online will arrive and that my credit card information will be protected. As a business person, I trust that I will be paid for services performed and products delivered. I trust my loans will be repaid, my suppliers will deliver on time, my employees will perform their jobs, my competitors will not compete unfairly, my government will supply needed public services. As an employee, I trust that my employer's paycheck is good, that my medical insurance and retirement plan are secure, and that I will have a job next week. As an investor, I trust the advice of my financial advisor, who trusts the financial reports attested to by the auditor, who trusts the financial statements provided by management, who trusts the legal advice provided by the corporate attorney, who trusts the representations made by management and the research conducted by staff.

All of the corporate scandals in recent years involved violations of trust. Investors, employees, employers, suppliers, and consumers all suffered harms when the trust they placed in corporate management, in auditors, in lawyers, in financial advisors, and in banks was violated. The remaining readings in this chapter will examine the responsibility of trustworthiness that professionals have within business settings. Professionals such as auditors, attorneys, and financial advisors serve an important gatekeeper function in business, a function which requires many other people to place their trust in the honesty and integrity of these professionals. All too often, this trust has been misplaced.

PROFESSIONAL RESPONSIBILITIES
AND THE GATEKEEPER FUNCTION

As economists from Adam Smith on have recognized, certain conditions must be met in order for markets to function efficiently and fairly. They must be free from fraud and coercion, there must be competition and choices available, parties must have access to accurate information, and the transaction must be legal. Over time, a number of business professions have evolved in ways that ensure that these conditions will be met. Sometimes referred to as "gatekeepers," professional auditors, accountants, financial advisors, bankers, and lawyers play a role that helps secure the efficiency and fairness of business transactions within the economic system. All participants in the economic system depend on and must trust these people to fulfill their professional responsibility. As we have witnessed in recent years, when that trust is misplaced and professionals fail to live up to their professional responsibility, severe economic and ethical harms can occur.

In our next reading, law professor John Coffee argues that Enron's collapse is best understood as a systematic failure of a variety of professionals who serve as gatekeepers in economic markets. Not only auditors, but investment bankers, financial analysts, and attorneys have ethical and legal responsibilities to ensure the integrity of the economic system. Coffee offers several reasons that might explain the failure of gatekeepers to fulfill their responsibilities and prevent the massive fraud that was Enron.

Two final readings examine the issue of auditor independence and the ethical responsibilities that follow from the role that auditors and accountants play within an economic system. John Bogle, founder of the Vanguard Group of mutual funds, argues that the entire system of democratic capitalism depends on the integrity of financial markets, which in turn require complete, accurate, and honest financial information. The ethical and professional responsibility of auditors is to attest to the trustworthiness of financial information disclosed by every corporation. In Bogle's view, auditor independence is at the core of this responsibility. Unfortunately, this independence has been systematically eroded by a growing trend of accounting firms seeking to expand their business into areas of management consulting. One result is that "the great professions that have served our society so well are moving rapidly towards becoming businesses" and "when that line is crossed, we as society are the losers." Bogle's insights were written in October 2000, just one year before the collapse of Enron, a scandal that could have been prevented had Arthur Andersen's auditors maintained their independence and fulfilled their professional responsibilities. Brenda Shay Duska and Ronald Duska pick up the theme of auditor independence in their analysis of the ethical responsibilities of auditors.

CASE STUDY Accounting for Enron

Enron Corporation has come to symbolize the worst of recent corporate corruption scandals. Billions of dollars were lost by investors, and thousands of people lost their jobs and their retirement savings when the one-time seventh-largest United States corporation went bankrupt, the largest bankruptcy in history at the time, as a result of the fraud created by its highest-ranking executives. But the story of Enron is also the story of a failed watchdog system designed to prevent such fraud. Auditors, attorneys, and government officials who had responsibilities to protect investors and ensure the integrity of financial markets systematically failed to live up to their responsibilities.

Enron's collapse began in 2001 when some independent stock analysts and journalists publicly raised questions about the value of Enron's stock. At that time, Enron's stock was trading at more than $80 a share, and Enron's CEO Jeffrey Skilling was publicly claiming that it ought to be valued at well over $100 a share. During the summer of 2001, several Enron insiders, including Vice Chair Clifford Baxter, Treasurer Jeff McMahon, and Vice President Sherron Watkins, all expressed doubts internally about Enron's financial practices. During this same period, other Enron insiders, including CEO Skilling and Board Chair and former CEO Kenneth Lay, Enron's corporate counsel, and several board members were selling millions of shares of Enron stock.

In October 2001 when Arthur Andersen auditors finally reversed their previous decisions and restated Enron's financials, the collapse of Enron began in earnest. By December, when its stock was worth just pennies a share, Enron declared bankruptcy and dismissed over 4000 employees.

Enron's collapse was mirrored by the collapse of its auditing firm, Arthur Andersen. Once one of the "Big Five" accounting firms, Arthur Andersen was driven out of business by its role in the Enron scandal. On January 9, 2002, the United States Justice Department announced that it had begun a criminal investigation into Arthur Andersen's activities related to Enron. At the time, Arthur Andersen was already on probation by the SEC for its questionable accounting practices in previous scandals at Sunbeam Corporation and Waste Management. The next day, Andersen admitted that it had shredded thousands of documents related to its Enron audits. Five days later, Andersen fired David Duncan, an Andersen partner and head auditor for Enron. Soon after, the Justice Department indicted Arthur Andersen on charges of obstruction of justice. Finally, on June 15, 2002, Arthur Andersen was found guilty in a criminal trial of obstructing justice by shredding evidence relating to the Enron scandal and, as a result, the firm agreed to cease auditing public companies by August 31.

Records show that as early as May 1998, Andersen's auditors were expressing grave concerns about Enron's financial practices. On that date, in an e-mail to David Duncan, Benjamin Neuhausen, a member of Andersen's Professional Standards Group, expressed his thoughts on the Special Purpose Entities (SPEs) that were at the heart of the Enron scandal. "Setting aside the accounting, [sic] idea of a venture entity managed by CFO is terrible from a business point of view. Conflicts of interest galore. Why would any director in his or her right mind ever approve such a scheme?" Neuhausen then went on to highlight the many accounting problems with the SPEs being managed by Enron CFO Andrew Fastow. Duncan replied, "But first, on your point 1 (i.e. the whole thing is a bad idea), I really couldn't agree more." Nevertheless, the Andersen auditors continued to cooperate with Enron by attesting to the soundness of Enron's financial statements.

In February 2001, more than a dozen Andersen auditors once again met to discuss the financial status of Enron's SPEs. Evidence shows that Andersen's auditors had serious concerns about the validity of Enron's financial self-portrait. In light of these concerns, they considered dropping Enron as an audit client. Michael Jones, one of Andersen's Houston employees, summarized the meeting in an e-mail to David Duncan, who also participated. Jones' notes reveal "significant discussion was held regarding the related party transactions with LJM" (one of Enron's Special Purpose Entities). Apparently, several Andersen auditors thought that LJM costs should not be kept off of Enron's books. Jones goes on to say, "The discussion focused on Fastow's conflicts of interest in his capacity as CFO and the LJM manager, the amount of earnings that Fastow receives for his services and participation in LJM, the disclosures of the transaction in the financial footnotes, and Enron's BOD's [Board of Directors] views regarding the transactions." Enron's activities were described as "intelligent gambling," and Andersen's auditors acknowledged "Enron's reliance on its current credit rating to maintain itself," its "dependence" on a supporting audit to meet its financial objectives, and "the fact that Enron often is creating industries and markets and transactions for which there are no specific rules [and therefore] which requires significant judgment." Enron was also described as "aggressive" in the way it structured its financial statements.

But the risks of Enron were not the only issues discussed at that meeting. Andersen's auditors realized that Andersen was also doing significant consulting business with Enron, business that could be jeopardized by an unfavorable audit. "We discussed whether there would be a perceived independence issue solely considering our level of fees. We discussed that the concerns should not be on the magnitude of the fees but in the nature of the fees. We discussed that it would not be unforeseeable that fees could reach $100 million per year. Such amounts did not trouble the participants as long as the nature of the services was not an issue." In the end, Andersen decided that the risks were worth taking. "Ultimately the conclusion was reached to retain Enron as a client citing that it appeared that we had the appropriate people and processes in place to serve Enron and manage our risks."

Less than a year later, Enron's third-quarter financial report would reflect Andersen's new and different judgment concerning the SPEs. On October 16, Enron reported a quarterly loss of $618 million and announced that as a result of Andersen's auditing decisions, they would take a $1.2 billion reduction in shareholder equity. Within one week, the SEC announced that it had opened an investigation into Enron's accounting practices. By the end of October, Enron's stock was trading at just $10 per share, an almost a 90% drop in eight months.

It is fair to say that Andersen overestimated their ability to manage the risks of Enron. Several decisions made by Andersen's professional staff during October proved to be disastrous for the company. On October 12, as Andersen prepared for the public release of the new financial statements, Andersen attorney Nancy Temple advised head auditor David Duncan to get "in compliance" with Andersen's document retention policy. Because Andersen's document retention policy included directions to destroy documents that were no longer needed, Duncan interpreted that advice to mean that he should have Enron-related documents destroyed. Duncan then instructed Andersen employees to shred Enron documents. Duncan has acknowledged that he and others at Andersen were aware of a possible SEC investigation at the time.

Four days later, on October 16, Duncan shared a draft of a press release on Enron with Temple. In her role as Andersen attorney, Temple advised changing the press release to delete some language that might suggest that Andersen's audit was not in compliance with Generally Accepted Accounting Principles (GAAP), as well as certain references to discussions within Andersen's legal group concerning Enron. Temple concluded her e-mail by promising to "consult further within the legal group as to whether we should do anything more to protect ourselves from potential Section 10 issues" (Section 10 refers to SEC rules that require auditors to report illicit client activity). In early November, two weeks after they began shredding documents, Andersen received a federal subpoena for documents related to Enron. Only at this point did Temple advise Andersen to write a memo advising auditors at Andersen to "keep everything, do not destroy anything." By the end of November, the SEC investigation was officially expanded to include Arthur Andersen.

At one time, Sherron Watkins was an Arthur Andersen auditor who worked on the Enron account. In 1993, she left Andersen to join Enron, working for Andrew Fastow in Enron's finance, international, broadband, and finally, its corporate development division. Thus, for eight years she participated in a wide range of Enron's business activities. In August 2001, shortly after Jeffrey Skilling resigned as Enron's CEO, she wrote a memo to Kenneth Lay. Watkins became widely known as the Enron whistleblower as a result of this memo, despite the fact that she had not expressed concerns earlier and she did not share her concerns with anyone outside of the company. In part, her memo to Lay reads as follows:

Has Enron become a risky place to work? For those of us who didn't get rich over the last few years, can we afford to stay?

Skilling's abrupt departure will raise suspicions of accounting improprieties and valuation issues. Enron has been very aggressive in its accounting—most notably the Raptor transactions and the Condor vehicle. We do have valuation issues with our international assets and possibly some of our EES MTM positions.

The spotlight will be on us, the market just can't accept that Skilling is leaving his dream job. I think that the valuation issues can be fixed and reported with other good will write-downs to occur in 2002. How do we fix the Raptor and Condor deals? They unwind in 2002 and 2003, we will have to pony up Enron stock and that won't go unnoticed. . . .

It sure looks to the layman on the street that we are hiding losses in a related company and will compensate that company with Enron stock in the future. I am incredibly nervous that we will implode in a wave of accounting scandals. My 8 years of Enron work history will be worth nothing on my résumé, the business world will consider the past successes as nothing but an elaborate accounting hoax. Skilling is resigning now for "personal reasons" but I would think he wasn't having fun, looked down the road and knew this stuff was unfixable and would rather abandon ship now than resign in shame in 2 years. . . .

Is there a way our accounting gurus can unwind these deals now? I have thought and thought about a way to do this, but I keep bumping into one big problem—we booked the Condor and Raptor deals in 1999 and 2000, we enjoyed wonderfully high stock price, many executives sold stock, we then try and reverse or fix the deals in 2001, and it's a bit like robbing the bank in one year and trying to pay it back two years later. Nice try, but investors were hurt, they bought at $70 and $80 a share looking for $120 a share and now they're at $38 or worse. We are under too much scrutiny and there are probably one or two disgruntled "redeployed" employees who know enough about the "funny" accounting to get us in trouble. What do we do? I know this question

cannot be addressed in the all-employee meeting, but can you give some assurances that you and Causey will sit down and take a good hard objective look at what is going to happen to Condor and Raptor in 2002 and 2003? . . .

I realize that we have had a lot of smart people looking at this and a lot of accountants including AA & Co. have blessed the accounting treatment. None of that will protect Enron if these transactions are ever disclosed in the bright light of day. (Please review the late 90's problems of Waste Management where AA paid $130 million plus in litigation re questionable accounting practices.) . . .

I firmly believe that executive management of the company must have a clear and precise knowledge of these transactions and they must have the transactions reviewed by objective experts in the fields of securities law and accounting. I believe Ken Lay deserves the right to judge for himself what he believes the probabilities of discovery to be and the estimated damages to the company from those discoveries and decide one of two courses of action:

1. The probability of discovery is low enough and the estimated damage too great; therefore we find a way to quietly and quickly reverse, unwind, write down these positions/transactions.
2. The probability of discovery is too great, the estimated damages to the company too great; therefore, we must quantify, develop damage containment plans and disclose.

I firmly believe that the probability of discovery significantly increased with Skilling's shocking departure. Too many people are looking for a smoking gun. . . . There is a veil of secrecy around LJM and Raptor. Employees question our accounting propriety consistently and constantly. This alone is cause for concern. . . . I have heard one manager-level employee from the principal investments group say, "I know it would be devastating to all of us, but I wish we would get caught. We're such a crooked company." . . .*

Another group of Enron insiders who were in position and had a responsibility to protect investors from fraud was Enron's Board of Directors, and particularly the Board's audit committee. In

*From a report released by the U.S. House of Representatives Energy Committee, February 2002.

theory and in law, the board's primary responsibility is to represent the interests of shareholders. In practice, the board seemed less than vigilant in fulfilling these responsibilities. Enron's board approved of Andrew Fastow's violation of the corporate conflicts of interest prohibition when he negotiated contracts between Enron and the SPEs in which he was heavily invested and from which he profited tremendously. As Benjamin Neuhausen, one of Andersen's Enron accountants, claimed, the "idea of a venture entity managed by CFO is terrible from a business point of view. Conflicts of interest galore. Why would any director in his or her right mind ever approve such a scheme?"

The final line of defense against corporate fraud should be government officials and regulators. Arthur Levitt, chairman of the SEC throughout the 1990s, strongly criticized the dual auditing and consulting activities of the big accounting firms as involving conflicts of interest. Congress ignored his advice, apparently convinced by the lobbying efforts of the accounting profession to allow audit firms to continue working as consultants to the firms they audited.

The federal government was also actively dismantling a wide range of financial regulatory protections during the 1990s. During the first Bush Administration, the Federal government deregulated the energy industry, ostensibly to spur economic growth according to free market principles. One of the leading advocates for this deregulation was Wendy Gramm, who at the time

was chairwoman of the U.S. Commodity Futures Trading Commission. Gramm's husband is Phil Gramm, then U.S. Senator from Texas and a member of the Senate banking, finance, and budget committees that supported this deregulation. Senator Gramm had received over $100,000 in campaign contributions from Enron during his last two Senate campaigns. When Wendy Gramm left government in 1992, she joined Enron's Board of Directors as a member of their audit committee.

- What responsibilities did David Duncan owe to Arthur Andersen? To Enron's management? To Enron's stockholders? To the accounting profession?
- What are the ethical responsibilities of a corporate attorney, such as Nancy Temple, who works for an "aggressive" client wishing to push the envelope of legality?
- Under what conditions should an employee such as Sherron Watkins blow the whistle to outside authorities? To whom did she owe loyalty?
- To whom does the board of directors owe their primary responsibility? Can you think of any law or regulations that would help ensure that boards meet their primary responsibilities?
- What responsibilities do government regulators owe to business? To the market? To the general public?
- Are accounting and law professions or businesses? What is the difference?

READING 7.1 IS BUSINESS BLUFFING ETHICAL?

Albert Carr

A respected businessman with whom I discussed the theme of this article remarked with some heat, "You mean to say you're going to encourage men to bluff? Why, bluffing is nothing more than a form of lying! You're advising them to lie!"

I agreed that the basis of private morality is a respect for truth and that the closer a businessman comes to truth, the more he deserves respect. At the same time, I suggested that most bluffing in business

might be regarded simply as game strategy—much like bluffing in poker which does not reflect on the morality of the bluffer.

I quoted Henry Taylor, the British statesman who pointed out that "falsehood ceases to be falsehood when it is understood on all sides that the truth is not expected to be spoken"—an exact description of bluffing in poker, diplomacy, and business. I cited the analogy of the criminal court, where the criminal is not expected to tell the truth when he pleads "not guilty." Everyone from the judge down takes it for granted that the job of the defendant's attorney is to get his client off, not to reveal the truth; and this is considered ethical practice. I mentioned Representative Omar Burleson, the Democrat from Texas, who was quoted as saying, in regard to the ethics of Congress, "Ethics is a barrel of worms"—a pungent summing-up of the problem of deciding who is ethical in politics. I reminded my friend that millions of businessmen feel constrained every day to say *yes* to their bosses when they secretly believe *no* and that this is generally accepted as permissible strategy when the alternative might be the loss of a job. The essential point, I said, is that the ethics of business are game ethics, different from the ethics of religion.

He remained unconvinced. Referring to the company of which he is president, he declared: "Maybe that's good enough for some businessmen, but I can tell you that we pride ourselves on our ethics. In 30 years not one customer has ever questioned my word or asked to check our figures. We're loyal to our customers and fair to our suppliers. I regard my handshake on a deal as a contract. I've never entered into price-fixing schemes with my competitors. I've never allowed my salesmen to spread injurious rumors about other companies. Our union contract is the best in our industry. And, if I do say so myself, our ethical standards are of the highest!"

He really was saying, without saying it, that he was living up to the ethical standards of the business game—which are a far cry from those of private life. Like a gentlemanly poker player, he did not play in cahoots with others at the table, try to smear their reputations, or hold back chips he owed them.

But this same fine man, at the very time, was allowing one of his products to be advertised in a way that made it sound a great deal better than it actually was. Another item in his product line was notorious among dealers for its "built-in obsolescence." He was holding back from the market a much-improved product because he did not want it to interfere with sales of the inferior item it would have replaced. He had joined with certain of his competitors in hiring a lobbyist to push a state legislature, by methods that he preferred not to know too much about, into amending a bill then being enacted.

In his view these things had nothing to do with ethics; they were merely normal business practice. He himself undoubtedly avoided outright falsehood —never lied in so many words. But the entire organization that he ruled was deeply involved in numerous strategies of deception.

PRESSURE TO DECEIVE

Most executives from time to time are almost compelled, in the interests of their companies or themselves, to practice some form of deception when negotiating with customers, dealers, labor unions, government officials, or even other departments of their companies. By conscious misstatements, concealment of pertinent facts, or exaggeration—in short, by bluffing—they seek to persuade others to agree with them. I think it is fair to say that if the individual executive refuses to bluff from time to time—if he feels obligated to tell the truth, the whole truth, and nothing but the truth—he is ignoring opportunities permitted under the rules and is at a heavy disadvantage in his business dealings.

But here and there a businessman is unable to reconcile himself to the bluff in which he plays a part. His conscience, perhaps spurred by religious idealism, troubles him. He feels guilty; he may develop an ulcer or a nervous tic. Before any executive can make profitable use of the strategy of the bluff, he needs to make sure that in bluffing he will not lose self-respect or become emotionally disturbed. If he is to reconcile personal integrity and high standards of honesty with the practical requirements of business, he must feel that his bluffs are ethically justified. The justification rests on the fact that business, as practiced by individuals as well as by corporations, has the impersonal character of a game—a game that demands both special strategy and an understanding of its special ethics.

The game is played at all levels of corporate life, from the highest to the lowest. At the very instant that a man decides to enter business, he may be forced into a game situation, as is shown by the recent experience of a Cornell honor graduate who applied for a job with a large company:

This applicant was given a psychological test which included the statement, "Of the following magazines, check any that you have read either regularly or from time to time, and double-check those which interest you most. *Reader's Digest, Time, Fortune, Saturday Evening*

*Post, The New Republic, Life, Look, Ramparts,
Newsweek, Business Week, U.S. News & World
Report, The Nation, Playboy, Esquire, Harper's,
Sports Illustrated."*

His tastes in reading were broad, and at one
time or another he had read almost all of these
magazines. He was a subscriber to *The New
Republic,* an enthusiast for *Ramparts,* and an avid
student of the pictures in *Playboy.* He was not
sure whether his interest in *Playboy* would be
held against him, but he had a shrewd suspicion
that if he confessed to an interest in *Ramparts*
and *The New Republic,* he would be thought a
liberal, a radical, or at least an intellectual, and
his chances of getting the job, which he needed,
would greatly diminish. He therefore checked
five of the more conservative magazines.
Apparently it was a sound decision, for he got
the job.

He had made a game player's decision, consistent with business ethics.

A similar case is that of a magazine space salesman who, owing to a merger, suddenly found himself out of a job:

> This man was 58, and, in spite of a good record,
> his chance of getting a job elsewhere in a busi-
> ness where youth is favored in hiring practice
> was not good. He was a vigorous, healthy man,
> and only a considerable amount of gray in his
> hair suggested his age. Before beginning his job
> search he touched up his hair with a black dye
> to confine the gray to his temples. He knew
> that the truth about his age might well come
> out in time, but he calculated that he could deal
> with that situation when it arose. He and his
> wife decided that he could easily pass for 45,
> and he so stated his age on his résumé.

This was a lie; yet within the accepted rules of
the business game, no moral culpability attaches to it.

THE POKER ANALOGY

We can learn a good deal about the nature of business by comparing it with poker. While both have a
large element of chance, in the long run the winner
is the man who plays with steady skill. In both
games ultimate victory requires intimate knowledge
of the rules, insights into the psychology of the

other players, a bold front, a considerable amount of
self-discipline, and the ability to respond swiftly and
effectively to opportunities provided by chance.

No one expects poker to be played on the ethical principles preached in churches. In poker it is
right and proper to bluff a friend out of the rewards
of being dealt a good hand. A player feels no more
than a slight twinge of sympathy, if that, when—
with nothing better than a single ace in his hand—
he strips a heavy loser, who holds a pair, of the rest
of his chips. It was up to the other fellow to protect
himself. In the words of an excellent poker player,
former President Harry Truman, "If you can't stand
the heat, get out of the kitchen." If one shows
mercy to a loser in poker, it is a personal gesture,
divorced from the rules of the game.

Poker has its special ethics, and here I am not
referring to rules against cheating. The man who
keeps an ace up his sleeve or who marks the cards is
more than unethical; he is a crook, and can be punished as such—kicked out of the game or, in the
Old West, shot.

In contrast to the cheat, the unethical poker
player is one who, while abiding by the letter of the
rules, finds ways to put the other players at an unfair
disadvantage. Perhaps he unnerves them with loud
talk. Or he tries to get them drunk. Or he plays in
cahoots with someone else at the table. Ethical
poker players frown on such tactics.

Poker's own brand of ethics is different from the
ethical ideals of civilized human relationships. The
game calls for distrust of the other fellow. It ignores
the claim of friendship. Cunning deception and
concealment of one's strength and intentions, not
kindness and open-heartedness, are vital in poker.
No one thinks any worse of poker on that account.
And no one should think any worse of the game of
business because its standards of right and wrong
differ from the prevailing traditions of morality in
our society.

DISCARD THE GOLDEN RULE

This view of business is especially worrisome to
people without much business experience. A minister of my acquaintance once protested that business
cannot possibly function in our society unless it is
based on the Judeo-Christian system of ethics. He
told me:

I know some businessmen have supplied call girls to customers, but there are always a few rotten apples in every barrel. That doesn't mean the rest of the fruit isn't sound. Surely the vast majority of businessmen are ethical. I myself am acquainted with many who adhere to strict codes of ethics based fundamentally on religious teachings. They contribute to good causes. They participate in community activities. They cooperate with other companies to improve working conditions in their industries. Certainly they are not indifferent to ethics.

That most businessmen are not indifferent to ethics in their private lives, everyone will agree. My point is that in their office lives they cease to be private citizens; they become game players who must be guided by a somewhat different set of ethical standards.

The point was forcefully made to me by a Midwestern executive who has given a good deal of thought to the question:

So long as a businessman complies with the laws of the land and avoids telling malicious lies, he's ethical. If the law as written gives a man a wide-open chance to make a killing, he'd be a fool not to take advantage of it. If he doesn't, somebody else will. There's no obligation on him to stop and consider who is going to get hurt. If the law says he can do it, that's all the justification he needs. There's nothing unethical about that. It's just plain business sense.

This executive (call him Robbins) took the stand that even industrial espionage, which is frowned on by some businessmen, ought not to be considered unethical. He recalled a recent meeting of the National Industrial Conference Board where an authority on marketing made a speech in which he deplored the employment of spies by business organizations. More and more companies, he pointed out, find it cheaper to penetrate the secrets of competitors with concealed cameras and microphones or by bribing employees than to set up costly research and design departments of their own. A whole branch of the electronics industry has grown up with this trend, he continued, providing equipment to make industrial espionage easier.

Disturbing? The marketing expert found it so. But when it came to a remedy, he could only appeal to "respect for the golden rule." Robbins thought this a confession of defeat, believing that the golden rule, for all its value as an ideal for society, is simply not feasible as a guide for business. A good part of the time the businessman is trying to do unto others as he hopes others will *not* do unto him. Robbins continued:

Espionage of one kind or another has become so common in business that it's like taking a drink during Prohibition—it's not considered sinful. And we don't even have Prohibition where espionage is concerned; the law is very tolerant in this area. There's no more shame for a business that uses secret agents than there is for a nation. Bear in mind that there already is at least one large corporation—you can buy its stock over the counter—that makes millions by providing counterespionage service to industrial firms. Espionage in business is not an ethical problem; it's an established technique of business competition.

"WE DON'T MAKE THE LAWS"

Wherever we turn in business, we can perceive the sharp distinction between its ethical standards and those of the churches. Newspapers abound with sensational stories growing out of this distinction:

We read one day that Senator Philip A. Hart of Michigan has attacked food processors for deceptive packaging of numerous products.

The next day there is a Congressional to-do over Ralph Nader's book, *Unsafe at Any Speed,* which demonstrates that automobile companies for years have neglected the safety of car-owning families.

Then another Senator, Lee Metcalf of Montana, and journalist Vic Reinemer show in their book, *Overcharge,* the methods by which utility companies elude regulating government bodies to extract unduly large payments from users of electricity.

These are merely dramatic instances of a prevailing condition; there is hardly a major industry at which a similar attack could not be aimed. Critics of business regard such behavior as unethical, but the companies concerned know that they are merely playing the business game.

Among the most respected of our business institutions are the insurance companies. A group of insurance executives meeting recently in New England was startled when their guest speaker, social critic Daniel Patrick Moynihan, roundly berated them for "unethical" practices. They had been guilty, Moynihan alleged, of using outdated actuarial tables to obtain unfairly high premiums. They habitually delayed the hearing of lawsuits against them in order to tire out the plaintiffs and win cheap settlements. In their employment policies they used ingenious devices to discriminate [against] certain minority groups.

It was difficult for the audience to deny the validity of these charges. But these men were business game players. Their reaction to Moynihan's attack was much the same as that of the automobile manufacturers to Nader, of the utilities to Senator Metcalf, and of the food processors to Senator Hart. If the laws governing their businesses change, or if public opinion becomes clamorous, they will make the necessary adjustments. But morally they have in their view done nothing wrong. As long as they comply with the letter of the law, they are within their rights to operate their businesses as they see fit.

The small business is in the same position as the great corporation in this respect. For example:

> In 1967 a key manufacturer was accused of providing master keys for automobiles to mail-order customers, although it was obvious that some of the purchasers might be automobile thieves. His defense was plain and straightforward. If there was nothing in the law to prevent him from selling his keys to anyone who ordered them, it was not up to him to inquire as to his customers' motives. Why was it any worse, he insisted, for him to sell car keys by mail, than for mail-order houses to sell guns that might be used for murder? Until the law was changed, the key manufacturer could regard himself as being just as ethical as any other businessman by the rules of the business game.

Violations of the ethical ideals of society are common in business, but they are not necessarily violations of business principles. Each year the Federal Trade Commission orders hundreds of companies, many of them of the first magnitude, to "cease and desist" from practices which, judged by ordinary standards, are of questionable morality but which are stoutly defended by the companies concerned.

In one case, a firm manufacturing a well-known mouthwash was accused of using a cheap form of alcohol possibly deleterious to health. The company's chief executive, after testifying in Washington, made this comment privately:

> We broke no law. We're in a highly competitive industry. If we're going to stay in business, we have to look for profit wherever the law permits. We don't make the laws. We obey them. Then why do we have to put up with this "holier than thou" talk about ethics? It's sheer hypocrisy. We're not in business to promote ethics. Look at the cigarette companies, for God's sake! If the ethics aren't embodied in the laws by the men who made them, you can't expect businessmen to fill the lack. Why, a sudden submission to Christian ethics by businessmen would bring about the greatest economic upheaval in history!

It may be noted that the government failed to prove its case against him.

CAST ILLUSIONS ASIDE

Talking about ethics by businessmen is often a thin decorative coating over the hard realities of the game:

> Once I listened to a speech by a young executive who pointed to a new industry code as proof that his company and its competitors were deeply aware of their responsibilities to society. It was a code of ethics, he said. The industry was going to police itself, to dissuade constituent companies from wrongdoing. His eyes shone with conviction and enthusiasm.
>
> The same day there was a meeting in a hotel room where the industry's top executives met with the "czar" who was to administer the new code, a man of high repute. No one who

was present could doubt their common attitude. In their eyes the code was designed primarily to forestall a move by the federal government to impose stern restrictions on the industry. They felt that the code would hamper them a good deal less than new federal laws would. It was, in other words, conceived as a protection for the industry, not for the public.

The young executive accepted the surface explanation of the code; these leaders, all experienced game players, did not deceive themselves for a moment about its purpose.

The illusion that business can afford to be guided by ethics as conceived in private life is often fostered by speeches and articles containing such phrases as, "It pays to be ethical," or, "Sound ethics is good business." Actually this is not an ethical position at all; it is a self-serving calculation in disguise. The speaker is really saying that in the long run a company can make more money if it does not antagonize competitors, suppliers, employees, and customers by squeezing them too hard. He is saying that over-sharp policies reduce ultimate gains. That is true, but it has nothing to do with ethics. The underlying attitude is much like that in the familiar story of the shopkeeper who finds an extra $20 bill in the cash register, debates with himself the ethical problem—should he tell his partner?— and finally decides to share the money because the gesture will give him an edge over the s.o.b. the next time they quarrel.

I think it is fair to sum up the prevailing attitude of businessmen on ethics as follows:

We live in what is probably the most competitive of the world's civilized societies. Our customs encourage a high degree of aggression in the individual's striving for success. Business is our main idea of competition, and it has been ritualized into a game of strategy. The basic rules of the game have been set by the government, which attempts to detect and punish business frauds. But as long as a company does not transgress the rules of the game set by law, it has the legal right to shape its strategy without reference to anything but its profits. If it takes a long-term view of its profits, it will preserve amicable relations, so far as possible, with those with whom it deals. A wise businessman will not seek advantage to the point where he generates dangerous hostility among employees, competitors, customers, government, or the public at large. But decisions in this area are, in the final test, decisions of strategy, not of ethics.

THE INDIVIDUAL AND THE GAME

An individual within a company often finds it difficult to adjust to the requirements of the business game. He tries to preserve his private ethical standards in situations that call for game strategy. When he is obliged to carry out the company policies that challenge his conception of himself as an ethical man, he suffers.

It disturbs him when he is ordered, for instance, to deny a raise to a man who deserves it, to fire an employee of long standing, to prepare advertising that he believes to be misleading, to conceal facts that he feels customers are entitled to know, to cheapen the quality of materials used in the manufacture of an established product, to sell as a new product that he knows to be rebuilt, to exaggerate the curative powers of a medicinal preparation, or to coerce dealers.

There are some fortunate executives, who, by the nature of their work and circumstances, never have to face problems of this kind. But in one form or another the ethical dilemma is felt sooner or later by most businessmen. Possibly the dilemma is most painful not when the company forces the action on the executive but when he originates it himself— that is, when he has taken or is contemplating a step which is in his own interest but which runs counter to his early moral conditioning. To illustrate:

The manager of an export department, eager to show rising sales, is pressed by a big customer to provide invoices, which, while containing no overt falsehood that would violate a U.S. law, are so worded that the customer may be able to evade certain taxes in his homeland.

A company president finds that an aging executive, within a few years of retirement and his pension, is not as productive as formerly. Should he be kept on?

The produce manager of a supermarket debates with himself whether to get rid of a lot of half-rotten tomatoes by including one, with its good side exposed, in every tomato sixpack.

An accountant discovers that he has taken an improper deduction on his company's tax return and fears the consequences if he calls the matter to the president's attention, though he himself has done nothing illegal. Perhaps if he says nothing, no one will notice the error.

A chief executive officer is asked by his directors to comment on a rumor that he owns stock in another company with which he has placed large orders. He could deny it, for the stock is in the name of his son-in-law and he has earlier formally instructed his son-in-law to sell the holding.

Temptations of this kind constantly arise in business. If an executive allows himself to be torn between a decision based on business considerations and one based on his private ethical code, he exposes himself to a grave psychological strain.

This is not to say that sound business strategy necessarily runs counter to ethical ideals. They may frequently coincide; and when they do, everyone is gratified. But the major tests of every move in business, as in all games of strategy, are legality and profit. A man who intends to be a winner in the business game must have a game player's attitude.

The business strategist's decisions must be as impersonal as those of a surgeon performing an operation—concentrating on objective and technique, and subordinating personal feelings. If the chief executive admits that his son-in-law owns the stock, it is because he stands to lose more if the fact comes out later than if he states it boldly and at once. If the supermarket manager orders the rotten tomatoes to be discarded, he does so to avoid an increase in consumer complaints and a loss of good will. The company president decides not to fire the elderly executive in the belief that the negative reaction of other employees would in the long run cost the company more than it would lose in keeping him and paying his pension.

All sensible businessmen prefer to be truthful, but they seldom feel inclined to tell the *whole* truth. In the business game truth-telling usually has to be kept within narrow limits if trouble is to be avoided. The point was neatly made a long time ago (in 1888) by one of John D. Rockefeller's associates, Paul Babcock, to Standard Oil Company executives who were about to testify before a government investigating committee: "Parry every question with answers which, while perfectly truthful, are evasive of *bottom* facts." This was, is, and probably always will be regarded as wise and permissible business strategy.

FOR OFFICE USE ONLY

An executive's family life can easily be dislocated if he fails to make a sharp distinction between the ethical systems of the home and the office—or if his wife does not grasp that distinction. Many a businessman who has remarked to his wife "I had to let Jones go today" or "I had to admit to the boss that Jim has been goofing off lately," has been met with an indignant protest. "How could you do a thing like that? You know Jones is over 50 and will have a lot of trouble getting another job." Or, "You did that to Jim? With his wife ill and all the worry she's having with the kids?"

If the executive insists that he had no choice because the profits of the company and his own security were involved, he may see a certain cool and ominous reappraisal in his wife's eyes. Many wives are not prepared to accept the fact that business operates with a special code of ethics. An illuminating illustration of this comes from a Southern sales executive who related a conversation he had had with his wife at a time when a hotly contested political campaign was being waged in their state:

I made the mistake of telling her that I had had lunch with Colby, who gives me about half my business. Colby mentioned that his company had a stake in the election. Then he said, "By the way, I'm treasurer of the citizens' committee for Lang. I'm collecting contributions. Can I count on you for a hundred dollars?"

Well, there I was. I was opposed to Lang, but I knew Colby. If he withdrew his business I could be in a bad spot. So I just smiled and wrote out a check then and there. He thanked me, and we started to talk about his next order. Maybe he thought I shared his political views. I wasn't going to lose any sleep over it.

I should have had sense enough not to tell Mary about it. She hit the ceiling. She said she was disappointed in me. She said I hadn't acted like a man, that I should have stood up to Colby.

I said, "Look, it was an either-or situation. I had to do it or risk losing the business."

She came back at me with, "I don't believe it. You could have been honest with him. You could have said that you didn't feel you ought to contribute to a campaign for a man you weren't going to vote for. I'm sure he would have understood."

I said, "Mary, you're a wonderful woman, but you're way off the track. Do you know what would have happened if I had said that? Colby would have smiled and said, 'Oh, I didn't realize. Forget it.' But in his eyes from that moment I would be an oddball, maybe a bit of a radical. He would have listened to me talk about his order and would have promised to give it consideration. After that I wouldn't hear from him for a week. Then I would telephone and learn from his secretary that he wasn't yet ready to place the order. And in about a month I would hear through the grapevine that he was giving his business to another company. A month after that I'd be out of a job."

She was silent for a while. Then she said, "Tom, something is wrong with business when a man is forced to choose between his family's security and his moral obligation to himself. It's easy for me to say you should have stood up to him—but if you had, you might have felt you were betraying me and the kids. I'm sorry that you did it, Tom, but I can't blame you. Something is wrong with business!"

This wife saw the problem in terms of moral obligation as conceived in private life; her husband saw it as a matter of game strategy. As a player in a weak position, he felt that he could not afford to indulge an ethical sentiment that might have cost him his seat at the table.

PLAYING TO WIN

Some men might challenge the Colbys of business— might accept serious setbacks to their business careers rather than risk a feeling of moral cowardice. They merit our respect—but as private individuals, not businessmen. When the skillful player of the business game is compelled to submit to unfair pressure, he does not castigate himself for moral weakness. Instead, he strives to put himself into a strong position where he can defend himself against such pressures in the future without loss.

If a man plans to take a seat in the business game, he owes it to himself to master the principles by which the game is played, including its special ethical outlook. He can then hardly fail to recognize that an occasional bluff may well be justified in terms of the game's ethics and warranted in terms of economic necessity. Once he clears his mind on this point, he is in a good position to match his strategy against that of the other players. He can then determine objectively whether a bluff in a given situation has a good chance of succeeding and can decide when and how to bluff, without a feeling of ethical transgression.

To be a winner, a man must play to win. This does not mean that he must be ruthless, cruel, harsh, or treacherous. On the contrary, the better his reputation for integrity, honesty, and decency, the better his chances of victory will be in the long run. But from time to time every businessman, like every poker player, is offered a choice between certain loss or bluffing within the legal rules of the game. If he is not resigned to losing, if he wants to rise in his company and industry, then in such a crisis he will bluff—and bluff hard.

Every now and then one meets a successful businessman who has conveniently forgotten the small or large deceptions that he practiced on his way to fortune. "God gave me my money," old John D. Rockefeller once piously told a Sunday school class. It would be a rare tycoon in our time who would risk the horse laugh with which such a remark would be greeted.

In the last third of the twentieth century even children are aware that if a man has become prosperous in business, he has sometimes departed from the strict truth in order to overcome obstacles or has practiced the more subtle deceptions of the half-truth or the misleading omission. Whatever the form of the bluff, it is an integral part of the game, and the executive who does not master its techniques is not likely to accumulate much money or power.

READING 7.2 WHISTLEBLOWING AND EMPLOYEE LOYALTY
Ronald Duska

Three Mile Island. In early 1983, almost four years after the near meltdown at Unit 2, two officials in the Site Operations Office of General Public Utilities reported a reckless company effort to clean up the contaminated reactor. Under threat of physical retaliation from superiors, the GPU insiders released evidence alleging that the company had rushed the TMI cleanup without testing key maintenance systems. Since then, the Three Mile Island mop-up has been stalled pending a review of GPU's management.[1]

The releasing of evidence of the rushed cleanup at Three Mile Island is an example of whistleblowing. Norman Bowie defines whistleblowing as "the act by an employee of informing the public on the immoral or illegal behavior of an employer or supervisor."[2] Ever since Daniel Ellsberg's release of the Pentagon Papers, the question of whether an employee should blow the whistle on his company or organization has become a hotly contested issue. Was Ellsberg right? Is it right to report the shady or suspect practices of the organization one works for? Is one a stool pigeon or a dedicated citizen? Does a person have an obligation to the public which overrides his obligation to his employer or does he simply betray a loyalty and become a traitor if he reports his company?

There are proponents on both sides of the issue—those who praise whistleblowers as civic heroes and those who condemn them as "finks." Glen and Shearer who wrote about the whistleblowers at Three Mile Island say, "Without the *courageous* breed of assorted company insiders known as whistleblowers—workers who often risk their livelihoods to disclose information about construction and design flaws—the Nuclear Regulatory Commission itself would be nearly as idle as Three Mile Island. . . . That whistleblowers deserve both gratitude and protection is beyond disagreement."[3]

Still, while Glen and Shearer praise whistleblowers, others vociferously condemn them. For example, in a now-infamous quote, James Roche, the former president of General Motors said:

> Some critics are now busy eroding another support of free enterprise—the loyalty of a management team, with its unifying values and cooperative work. Some of the enemies of business now encourage an employee to be *disloyal* to the enterprise. They want to create suspicion and disharmony, and pry into the proprietary interests of the business. However this is labeled—industrial espionage, whistle blowing, or professional responsibility—it is another tactic for spreading disunity and creating conflict.[4]

From Roche's point of view, whistleblowing is not only not "courageous" and deserving of "gratitude and protection" as Glen and Shearer would have it, it is corrosive and not even permissible.

Discussions of whistleblowing generally revolve around four topics: (1) attempts to define whistleblowing more precisely; (2) debates about whether and when whistleblowing is permissible; (3) debates about whether and when one has an obligation to blow the whistle; and (4) appropriate mechanisms for institutionalizing whistleblowing.

In this paper I want to focus on the second problem, because I find it somewhat disconcerting that there is a problem at all. When I first looked into the ethics of whistleblowing it seemed to me that whistleblowing was a good thing, and yet I found in the literature claim after claim that it was in need of defense, that there was something wrong with it, namely that it was an act of disloyalty.

If whistleblowing was a disloyal act, it deserved disapproval, and ultimately any action of whistleblowing needed justification. This disturbed me. It was as if the act of a good Samaritan was being condemned as an act of interference, as if the prevention of a suicide needed to be justified. My moral position in favor of whistleblowing was being challenged. The tables were turned and the burden of proof had shifted. My position was the one in question. Suddenly instead of the company being the bad guy and the whistleblower the good guy, which is what I thought, the whistleblower was the bad guy. Why? Because he was disloyal. What I discovered was that in most of the literature it was taken as axiomatic that whistleblowing was an act of disloyalty. My moral intuitions told me that axiom was mistaken. Nevertheless, since it is accepted by a large segment of the ethical community it deserves investigation.

In his book *Business Ethics,* Norman Bowie, who presents what I think is one of the finest presentations of the ethics of whistleblowing, claims that "whistleblowing . . . violate[s] a *prima facie* duty of loyalty to one's employer." According to Bowie, there is a duty of loyalty which prohibits one from reporting his employer or company. Bowie, of course, recognizes that this is only a *prima facie* duty, i.e., one that can be overridden by a higher duty to the public good. Nevertheless, the axiom that whistleblowing is disloyal is Bowie's starting point. Bowie is not alone. Sisela Bok, another fine ethicist, sees whistleblowing as an instance of disloyalty.

> The whistleblower hopes to stop the game; but since he is neither referee nor coach, and since he blows the whistle on his own team, his act is seen as a *violation of loyalty* [italics mine]. In holding his position, he has assumed certain obligations to his colleagues and clients. He may even have subscribed to a loyalty oath or a promise of confidentiality. . . . Loyalty to colleagues and to clients comes to be pitted against loyalty to the public interest, to those who may be injured unless the revelation is made.[5]

Bowie and Bok end up defending whistleblowing in certain contexts, so I don't necessarily disagree with their conclusions. However, I fail to see how one has an obligation of loyalty to one's company, so I disagree with their perception of the problem, and their starting point. The difference in perception is important because those who think employees have an obligation of loyalty to a company fail to take into account a relevant moral difference between persons and corporations and between corporations and other kinds of groups where loyalty is appropriate. I want to argue that one does not have an obligation of loyalty to a company, even a *prima facie* one, because companies are not the kind of things which are proper objects of loyalty. I then want to show that to make them objects of loyalty gives them a moral status they do not deserve and in raising their status, one lowers the status of the individuals who work for the companies.

But why aren't corporations the kind of things which can be objects of loyalty? . . .

Loyalty is ordinarily construed as a state of being constant and faithful in a relation implying trust or confidence, as a wife to husband, friend to friend, parent to child, lord to vassal, etc. According to John Ladd "it is not founded on just *any* casual relationship, but on a specific kind of relationship or tie. The ties that bind the persons together provide the basis of loyalty."[6] But all sorts of ties bind people together to make groups. I am a member of a group of fans if I go to a ball game. I am a member of a group if I merely walk down the street. I am in a sense tied to them, but don't owe them loyalty. I don't owe loyalty to just anyone I encounter. Rather I owe loyalty to persons with whom I have special relationships. I owe it to my children, my spouse, my parents, my friends and certain groups, those groups which are formed for the mutual enrichment of the members. It is important to recognize that in any relationship which demands loyalty the relationship works both ways and involves mutual enrichment. Loyalty is incompatible with self-interest, because it is something that necessarily requires we go beyond self-interest. My loyalty to my friend, for example, requires I put aside my interests some of the time. It is because of this reciprocal requirement which demands surrendering self-interest that a corporation is not a proper object of loyalty.

A business or corporation does two things in the free enterprise system. It produces a good or service and makes a profit. The making of a profit, however, is the primary function of a business as a business. For if the production of the good or service was not profitable the business would be out of business. Since non-profitable goods or services are discontinued, the providing of a service or the making of a product is not done for its own sake, but from a business perspective is a means to an end, the making of profit. People bound together in a business are not bound together for mutual fulfillment and support, but to divide labor so the business makes a profit. Since profit is paramount if you do not produce in a company or if there are cheaper laborers around, a company feels justified in firing you for the sake of better production. Throughout history companies in a pinch feel no obligation of loyalty. Compare that to a family. While we can jokingly refer to a family as "somewhere they have to take you in no matter what," you cannot refer to a company in that way. "You can't buy loyalty" is true. Loyalty depends on ties that demand self-sacrifice with no expectation of reward, e.g., the ties of loyalty that bind a family together. Business functions on the basis of enlightened self-interest. I am devoted to a company not because it is like a parent to me. It is not, and attempts of some companies to create "one big happy family" ought to be looked on with suspicion. I am not "devoted" to it at all, or should not be. I *work* for it because it pays me. I am not in a family to get paid, but I am in a company to get paid.

Since loyalty is a kind of devotion, one can confuse devotion to one's job (or the ends of one's work) with devotion to a company.

I may have a job I find fulfilling, but that is accidental to my relation to the company. For example, I might go to work for a company as a carpenter and love the job and get satisfaction out of doing good work. But if the company can increase profit by cutting back to an adequate but inferior type of material or procedure, it can make it impossible for me to take pride in my work as a carpenter while making it possible for me to make more money. The company does not exist to subsidize my quality work as a carpenter. As a carpenter my goal may be good houses, but as an employee my goal is to contribute to making a profit. "That's just business!"

This fact that profit determines the quality of work allowed leads to a phenomenon called the commercialization of work. The primary end of an act of building is to make something, and to build well is to make it well. A carpenter is defined by the end of his work, but if the quality interferes with profit, the business side of the venture supercedes the artisan side. Thus profit forces a craftsman to suspend his devotion to his work and commercializes his venture. The more professions subject themselves to the forces of the marketplace, the more they get commercialized; e.g., research for the sake of a more profitable product rather than for the sake of knowledge jeopardizes the integrity of academic research facilities.

The cold hard truth is that the goal of profit is what gives birth to a company and forms that particular group. Money is what ties the group together. But in such a commercialized venture, with such a goal there is no loyalty, or at least none need be expected. An employer will release an employee and an employee will walk away from an

employer when it is profitable to do so. That's business. It is perfectly permissible. Contrast that with the ties between a lord and his vassal. A lord could not in good conscience wash his hands of his vassal, nor could a vassal in good conscience abandon his lord. What bound them was mutual enrichment, not profit.

Loyalty to a corporation, then, is not required. But even more it is probably misguided. There is nothing as pathetic as the story of the loyal employee who, having given above and beyond the call of duty, is let go in the restructuring of the company. He feels betrayed because he mistakenly viewed the company as an object of his loyalty. To get rid of such foolish romanticism and to come to grips with this hard but accurate assessment should ultimately benefit everyone.

One need hardly be an enemy of business to be suspicious of a demand of loyalty to something whose primary reason for existence is the making of profit. It is simply the case that I have no duty of loyalty to the business or organization. Rather I have a duty to return responsible work for fair wages. The commercialization of work dissolves the type of relationship that requires loyalty. It sets up merely contractual relationships. One sells one's labor but not one's self to a company or an institution.

To think we owe a company or corporation loyalty requires us to think of that company as a person or as a group with a goal of human enrichment. If we think of it in this way we can be loyal. But this is just the wrong way to think. A company is not a person. A company is an instrument, and an instrument with a specific purpose, the making of profit. To treat an instrument as an end in itself, like a person, may not be as bad as treating an end as an instrument, but it does give the instrument a moral status it does not deserve, and by elevating the instrument we lower the end. All things, instruments and ends, become alike.

To treat a company as a person is analogous to treating a machine as a person or treating a system as a person. The system, company, or instrument get as much respect and care as the persons for whom they were invented. If we remember that the primary purpose of business is to make profit, it can be seen clearly as merely an instrument. If so, it needs to be used and regulated accordingly, and I owe it no more loyalty than I owe a word processor.

Of course if everyone would view business as a commercial instrument, things might become more difficult for the smooth functioning of the organization, since businesses could not count on the "loyalty" of their employees. Business itself is well served, at least in the short run, if it can keep the notion of a duty to loyalty alive. It does this by comparing itself to a paradigm case of an organization one shows loyalty to, the team.

Remember that Roche refers to the "management team" and Bok sees the name "whistleblowing" coming from the instance of a referee blowing a whistle in the presence of a foul. What is perceived as bad about whistleblowing in business from this perspective is that one blows the whistle on one's own team, thereby violating team loyalty. If the company can get its employees to view it as a team they belong to, it is easier to demand loyalty. The rules governing teamwork and team loyalty will apply. One reason the appeal to a team and team loyalty works so well in business is that businesses are in competition with one another. If an executive could get his employees to be loyal, a loyalty without thought to himself or his fellow man, but to the will of the company, the manager would have the ideal kind of corporation from an organizational standpoint. As Paul R. Lawrence, the organizational theorist says, "Ideally, we would want one sentiment to be dominant in all employees from top to bottom, namely a complete loyalty to the organizational purpose."[7] Effective motivation turns business practices into a game and instills teamwork.

But businesses differ from teams in very important respects, which makes the analogy between business and a team dangerous. Loyalty to a team is loyalty within the context of sport, a competition. Teamwork and team loyalty require that in the circumscribed activity of the game I cooperate with my fellow players so that pulling all together, we can win. The object of (most) sports is victory. But the winning in sports is a social convention, divorced from the usual goings on of society. Such a winning is most times a harmless, morally neutral diversion.

But the fact that this victory in sports, within the rules enforced by a referee (whistleblower), is a socially developed convention taking place within a larger social context makes it quite different from competition in business, which, rather than being defined by a context, permeates the whole of society in its influence. Competition leads not only to

winners but to losers. One can lose at sport with precious few serious consequences. The consequences of losing at business are much more serious. Further, the losers in sport are there voluntarily, while the losers in business can be those who are not in the game voluntarily (we are all forced to participate) but are still affected by business decisions. People cannot choose to participate in business, since it permeates everyone's life.

The team model fits very well with the model of the free-market system because there competition is said to be the name of the game. Rival companies compete and their object is to win. To call a foul on one's own teammate is to jeopardize one's chances of winning and is viewed as disloyalty.

But isn't it time to stop viewing the corporate machinations as games? These games are not controlled and not over after a specific time. The activities of business affect the lives of everyone, not just the game players. The analogy of the corporation to a team and the consequent appeal to team loyalty, although understandable, is seriously misleading at least in the moral sphere, where competition is not the prevailing virtue.

If my analysis is correct, the issue of the permissibility of whistleblowing is not a real issue, since there is no obligation of loyalty to a company. Whistleblowing is not only permissible but expected when a company is harming society. The issue is not one of disloyalty to the company, but the question of whether the whistleblower has an obligation to society if blowing the whistle will bring him retaliation. I will not argue that issue, but merely suggest the lines I would pursue.

I tend to be a minimalist in ethics, and depend heavily on a distinction between obligations and acts of supererogation. We have, it seems to me, an obligation to avoid harming anyone, but not an obligation to do good. Doing good is above the call of duty. In between we may under certain conditions have an obligation to prevent harm. If whistleblowing can prevent harm, then it is required under certain conditions.

Simon, Powers and Gunnemann set forth four conditions:[8] need, proximity, capability, and last resort. Applying these, we get the following.

1. There must be a clear harm to society that can be avoided by whistleblowing. We don't blow the whistle over everything.

2. It is the "proximity" to the whistleblower that puts him in the position to report his company in the first place.

3. "Capability" means that he needs to have some chance of success. No one has an obligation to jeopardize himself to perform futile gestures. The whistleblower needs to have access to the press, be believable, etc.

4. "Last resort" means just that. If there are others more capable of reporting and more proximate, and if they will report, then one does not have the responsibility.

Before concluding, there is one aspect of the loyalty issue that ought to be disposed of. My position could be challenged in the case of organizations who are employers in non-profit areas, such as the government, educational institutions, etc. In this case my commercialization argument is irrelevant. However, I would maintain that any activity which merits the blowing of the whistle in the case of non-profit and service organizations is probably counter to the purpose of the institution in the first place. Thus, if there were loyalty required, in that case, whoever justifiably blew the whistle would be blowing it on a colleague who perverted the end or purpose of the organization. The loyalty to the group would remain intact. Ellsberg's whistleblowing on the government is a way of keeping the government faithful to its obligations. But that is another issue.

NOTES

1. Maxwell Glen and Cody Shearer, "Going after the Whistle-blowers," *The Philadelphia Inquirer*, Tuesday, Aug. 2, 1983, Op-ed Page, p. 11a.

2. Norman Bowie, *Business Ethics* (Englewood Cliffs, N.J.: Prentice-Hall, 1982), 140. For Bowie, this is just a preliminary definition. His fuller definition reads, "A whistle blower is an employee or officer of any institution, profit or non-profit, private or public, who believes either that he/she has been ordered to perform some act or he/she has obtained knowledge that the institution is engaged in activities which 1) are believed to cause unnecessary harm to third parties, 2) are in violation of human rights or 3) run counter to the defined purpose of the institution and who inform the public of this fact." Bowie then lists six conditions under which the act is justified. 142–143.

3. Glen and Shearer, "Going after the Whistleblowers," 11a.

4. James M. Roche, "The Competitive System, to Work, to Preserve, and to Protect," *Vital Speeches of the Day* (May 1971), 445. This is quoted in Bowie, 141 and also in Kenneth D. Walters, "Your Employee's Right to Blow the Whistle," *Harvard Business Review*, 53, no. 4.

5. Sisela Bok, "Whistleblowing and Professional Responsibilities," *New York University Education Quarterly*, vol. II, 4 (1980), 3.

6. John Ladd, "Loyalty," *The Encyclopedia of Philosophy*, vol. 5, 97.

7. Paul R. Lawrence, *The Changing of Organizational Behavior Patterns: A Case Study of Decentralization* as quoted in Kenneth D. Walters, op. cit. (Boston: Division of Research, Harvard Business School, 1958), 208.

8. John G. Simon, Charles W. Powers, and Jon P. Gunnemann, *The Ethical Investor: Universities and Corporate Responsibility* (New Haven: Yale University Press, 1972).

READING 7.3 UNDERSTANDING ENRON:
"IT'S ABOUT THE GATEKEEPERS, STUPID"

John C. Coffee, Jr.

What do we know after Enron's implosion that we did not know before it? The conventional wisdom is that the Enron debacle reveals basic weaknesses in our contemporary system of corporate governance. Perhaps, this is so, but where is the weakness located? Under what circumstances will critical systems fail? Major debacles of historical dimensions (and Enron is surely that) tend to produce an excess of explanations. In Enron's case, the firm's strange failure is becoming a virtual Rorschach test in which each commentator can see evidence confirming what he or she already believed.

Nonetheless, the problem with viewing Enron as an indication of any systematic governance failure is that its core facts are maddeningly unique. Most obviously, Enron's governance structure was *sui generis.* Other public corporations simply have not authorized their chief financial officer to run an independent entity that enters into billions of dollars of risky and volatile trading transactions with them; nor have they allowed their senior officers to profit from such self-dealing transactions without broad supervision or even comprehension of the profits involved. Nor have other corporations incorporated thousands of subsidiaries and employed them in a complex web of off-balance sheet partnerships.

In short, Enron was organizationally unique—a virtual hedge fund in the view of some, yet a firm that morphed almost overnight into its bizarre structure from origins as a stodgy gas pipeline company. The pace of this transition seemingly outdistanced the development of risk management systems and an institutional culture paralleling those of traditional financial firms. Precisely for this reason, the passive performance of Enron's board of directors cannot fairly be extrapolated and applied as an assessment of all boards generally. Boards of directors may or may not perform their duties adequately, but, standing alone, Enron proves little. In

this sense, Enron is an anecdote, an isolated data point that cannot yet fairly be deemed to amount to a trend.

Viewed from another perspective, however, Enron does furnish ample evidence of a systematic governance failure. Although other spectacular securities frauds have been discovered from time to time over recent decades, they have not generally disturbed the overall market. In contrast, Enron has clearly roiled the market and created a new investor demand for transparency. Behind this disruption lies the market's discovery that it cannot rely upon the professional gatekeepers—auditors, analysts, and others—whom the market has long trusted to filter, verify and assess complicated financial information. Properly understood, Enron is a demonstration of gatekeeper failure, and the question it most sharply poses is how this failure should be rectified.

Although the term "gatekeeper" is commonly used, here it requires special definition. Inherently, gatekeepers are reputational intermediaries who provide verification and certification services to investors. These services can consist of verifying a company's financial statements (as the independent auditor does), evaluating the creditworthiness of the company (as the debt rating agency does), assessing the company's business and financial prospects vis-à-vis its rivals (as the securities analyst does), or appraising the fairness of a specific transaction (as the investment banker does in delivering a fairness opinion). Attorneys can also be gatekeepers when they lend their professional reputations to a transaction, but, as later discussed, the more typical role of attorneys serving public corporations is that of the transaction engineer, rather than the reputational intermediary.

Characteristically, the professional gatekeeper essentially assesses or vouches for the corporate client's own statements about itself or a specific transaction. This duplication is necessary because the market recognizes that the gatekeeper has a lesser incentive to lie than does its client and thus regards the gatekeeper's assurance or evaluation as more credible. To be sure, the gatekeeper as watchdog is typically paid by the party that it is to watch,

From "Understanding Enron: It's About the Gatekeepers, Stupid" by John Coffee, Jr., published in *The Business Lawyer,* Volume 57, No. 4, August 2002. © 2002 by the American Bar Association. Reprinted by permission.

All notes in this reading have been deleted.

but its relative credibility stems from the fact that it is in effect pledging a reputational capital that it has built up over many years of performing similar services for numerous clients. In theory, such reputational capital would not be sacrificed for a single client and a modest fee. Here, as elsewhere, however, logic and experience can conflict. Despite the clear logic of the gatekeeper rationale, experience over the 1990s suggests that professional gatekeepers do acquiesce in managerial fraud, even though the apparent reputational losses seem to dwarf the gains to be made from the individual client.

Why has there been an apparent failure in the market for gatekeeping services? This brief comment offers some explanations, but also acknowledges that rival explanations lead to very different prescriptions. Thus, the starting point for responding to the Enron debacle begins with asking the right question. That question is not: why did some managements engage in fraud? But rather it is: why did the gatekeepers let them?

I. THE CHANGING STATUS OF THE GATEKEEPER

In theory, a gatekeeper has many clients, each of whom pay it a fee that is modest in proportion to the firm's overall revenues. Arthur Andersen had, for example, 2,300 audit clients. On this basis, the firm seemingly had little incentive to risk its considerable reputational capital for any one client. During the 1990s, many courts bought this logic hook, line and sinker. For example, in *DiLeo v. Ernst & Young,* Judge Easterbrook, writing for the Seventh Circuit, outlined precisely the foregoing theory:

> The complaint does not allege that [the auditor] had anything to gain from any fraud by [its client]. An accountant's greatest asset is its reputation for honesty, closely followed by its reputation for careful work. Fees for two years' audits could not approach the losses [that the auditor] would suffer from a perception that it would muffle a client's fraud . . . [The auditor's] partners shared none of the gain from any fraud and were exposed to a large fraction of the loss. It would have been irrational for any of them to have joined cause with [the client].

Of course, the modest fees in some of these cases (the audit fee was only $90,000 in *Robin v. Arthur Young & Co.*) were well less than the $100 million in prospective annual fees from Enron that Arthur Andersen & Co. explicitly foresaw. But does this difference really explain Arthur Andersen's downward spiral? After all, Arthur Andersen earned over $9 billion in revenues in 2001.

Once among the most respected of all professionals service firms (including law, accounting, and consulting firms), Andersen became involved in a series of now well-known securities frauds—e.g., Waste Management, Sunbeam, HBOC McKesson, The Baptist Foundation, and now Global Crossing—that culminated in its disastrous association with Enron. Little, however, suggests that Arthur Andersen was more reckless or less responsible than its peers. Instead, the evidence suggests that something led to a general erosion in the quality of financial reporting during the late 1990s. During this period, earnings restatements, long a proxy for fraud, suddenly soared. To cite only the simplest quantitative measure, the number of earnings restatements by publicly held corporations averaged 49 per year from 1990 to 1997, then increased to 91 in 1998, and finally skyrocketed to 150 and 156, respectively, in 1999 and 2000.

What caused this sudden spike in earning restatements? Because public corporations must fear stock price drops, securities class actions, and SEC investigations in the wake of earnings restatements, it is not plausible to read this sudden increase as the product of a new tolerance for, or indifference to, restatements. Even if some portion of the change might be attributed to a new SEC activism about "earnings management," which became an SEC priority in 1998, corporate issuers will not voluntarily expose themselves to enormous liability just to please the SEC. Moreover, not only did the number of earnings restatements increase over this period, but so also did the amounts involved. Earnings restatements thus seem an indication that earlier earnings management has gotten out of hand. Accordingly, the spike in earnings restatements in the late 1990s implies that the Big [Five] firms had earlier acquiesced in aggressive earnings management—and, in particular, premature revenue recognition—that no longer could be sustained.

This apparent pattern of increased deference by the gatekeeper to its client during the 1990s was not limited to the auditing profession. Securities analysts have probably encountered even greater recent public and Congressional skepticism about their objectivity. Again, much of the evidence is anecdotal, but striking. As late as October 2001, 16 out of the 17 securities analysts covering Enron maintained "buy" or "strong buy" recommendations on its stock right up until virtually the moment of its bankruptcy filing. The first brokerage firm to downgrade Enron to a "sell" rating in 2001 was Prudential Securities, which no longer engages in investment banking activities. Revealingly, Prudential is also believed to have the highest proportion of sell ratings among the stocks it evaluates.

Much like auditors, analysts are also "reputational intermediaries," whose desire to be perceived as credible and objective may often be subordinated to their desire to retain and please investment banking clients. One statistic inevitably comes up in any assessment of analyst objectivity: namely, the curious fact that the ratio of "buy" recommendations to "sell" recommendations has recently been as high as 100 to 1. In truth, this particular statistic may not be as compelling as it initially sounds because there are obvious reasons why "buy" recommendations will normally outnumber "sell" recommendations, even in the absence of conflicts of interest. Yet, a related statistic may be more revealing because it underscores the apparent transition that took place in the 1990s. According to a study by Thomson Financial, the ratio of "buy" to "sell" recommendations increased from 6 to 1 in 1991 to 100 to 1 by 2000. Again, it appears that something happened in the 1990s that compromised the independence and objectivity of the gatekeepers on whom our private system of corporate governance depends. Not surprisingly, it also appears that this loss of relative objectivity can harm investors.

II. EXPLAINING GATEKEEPER FAILURE

None of the watchdogs that should have detected Enron's collapse—auditors, analysts or debt rating agencies—did so before the penultimate moment. This is the true common denominator in the Enron debacle: the collective failure of the gatekeepers. Why did the watchdogs not bark in the night when it now appears in hindsight that a massive fraud took place? Here, two quite different, although

complementary, stories can be told. The first will be called the "general deterrence" story; and the second, the "bubble" story. The first is essentially economic in its premises; and the second, psychological.

a. The Deterrence Explanation: The Underdeterred Gatekeeper

The general deterrence story focuses on the decline in the expected liability costs arising out of acquiescence by auditors in aggressive accounting policies favored by managements. It postulates that, during the 1990s, the risk of auditor liability declined, while the benefits of acquiescence increased. Economics 101 teaches us that when the costs go down, while the benefits associated with any activity go up, the output of the activity will increase. Here, the activity that increased was auditor acquiescence.

Why did the legal risks go down during the 1990s? The obvious list of reasons would include:

1. the Supreme Court's *Lampf, Pleva* decision in 1991, which significantly shortened the statute of limitations applicable to securities fraud

2. the Supreme Court's *Central Bank of Denver* decision, which in 1994 eliminated private "aiding and abetting" liability in securities fraud cases

3. the Private Securities Litigation Reform Act of 1995 ("PSLRA"), which (a) raised the pleading standards for securities class actions to a level well above that applicable to fraud actions generally; (b) substituted proportionate liability for "joint and several" liability; (c) restricted the sweep of the RICO statute so that it could no longer convert securities fraud class actions for compensatory damages into actions for treble damages; and (d) adopted a very protective safe harbor for forward-looking information

4. the Securities Litigation Uniform Standards Act of 1998 ("SLUSA") which abolished state court class actions alleging securities fraud

Not only did the threat of private enforcement decline, but the prospect of public enforcement similarly subsided. In particular, there is reason to believe that, from some point in the 1980s until the late 1990s, the SEC shifted its enforcement focus away from actions against the Big Five accounting firms towards other priorities. In any event, the point here is not that any of these changes were necessarily unjustified or excessive, but rather that their collective impact was to appreciably reduce the risk of liability. Auditors were the special beneficiaries of many of these provisions. For example, the pleading rules and the new standard of proportionate liability protected them far more than it did most corporate defendants. Although auditors are still sued today, the settlement value of cases against auditors has gone way down.

Correspondingly, the benefits of acquiescence to auditors rose over this same period, as the Big Five learned during the 1990s how to cross-sell consulting services and to treat the auditing function principally as a portal of entry into a lucrative client. Prior to the mid-1990s, the provision of consulting services to audit clients was infrequent and insubstantial in the aggregate. Yet, according to one recent survey, the typical large public corporation now pays its auditor for consulting services three times what it pays the same auditor for auditing services. Not only did auditing firms see more profit potential in consulting than in auditing, but they began during the 1990s to compete based on a strategy of "low balling" under which auditing services were offered at rates that were marginal to arguably below cost. The rationale for such a strategy was that the auditing function was essentially a loss leader by which more lucrative services could be marketed.

Appealing as this argument may seem that the provision of consulting services eroded auditor independence, it is subject to at least one important rebuttal. Those who defend the propriety of consulting services by auditors respond that the growth of consulting services made little real difference, because the audit firm is already conflicted by the fact that the client pays its fees. More importantly, the audit partner of a major client (such as Enron) is particularly conflicted by the fact that such partner has virtually a "one-client" practice. Should the partner lose that client for any reason, the partner will likely need to find employment elsewhere. In short, both critics and defenders of the *status quo* tend to agree that the audit partner is already inevitably compromised by the desire to hold the client. From this premise, a prophylactic rule prohibiting the firm's involvement in consulting would seemingly achieve little.

While true in part, this analysis misses a key point: namely, how difficult it is for the client to fire the auditor in the real world. Because of this difficulty, the unintended consequence of combining consulting services with auditing services in one firm is that the union of the two enables the client to more effectively threaten the auditing firm in a "low visibility" way. To illustrate this point, let us suppose, for example, that a client becomes dissatisfied with an auditor who refuses to endorse the aggressive accounting policy favored by its management. Today, the client cannot easily fire the auditor. Firing the auditor is a costly step, inviting potential public embarrassment, public disclosure of the reasons for the auditor's dismissal or resignation, and potential SEC intervention. However, if the auditor also becomes a consultant to the client, the client can then easily terminate the auditor as a consultant (or reduce its use of the firm's consulting services) in retaliation for the auditor's intransigence. This low visibility response requires no disclosure, invites no SEC oversight, and yet disciplines the audit firm so that it would possibly be motivated to replace the intransigent audit partner. In effect, the client can both bribe (or coerce) the auditor in its core professional role by raising (or reducing) its use of consulting of services.

Of course, this argument that the client can discipline and threaten the auditor/consultant in ways that it could not discipline the simple auditor is based more on logic than actual case histories. But it does fit the available data. A recent study by academic accounting experts, based on proxy statements filed during the first half of 2001, finds that those firms that purchased more non-audit services from their auditor (as a percentage of the total fee paid to the audit firm) were more likely to fit the profile of a firm engaging in earnings management.

b. The Irrational Market Story

Alternatively, Enron's and Arthur Andersen's downfalls can be seen as consequences of a classic bubble that overtook the equity markets in the late 1990s and produced a market euphoria in which gatekeepers became temporarily irrelevant. Indeed, in an atmosphere of euphoria in which stock prices ascend endlessly and exponentially, gatekeepers are largely a nuisance to management, which does not need them to attract investors. Gatekeepers are necessary only when investors are cautious and skeptical, and in a market bubble, caution and skepticism are largely abandoned. Arguably, auditors were used in such an environment only because SEC rules mandated their use or because no individual firm wished to call attention to itself by becoming the first to dispense with them. In any event, if we assume that the auditor will be largely ignored by euphoric investors, the rational auditor's best competitive strategy (at least for the short term) was to become as acquiescent and low cost as possible.

For the securities analyst, a market bubble presented an even more serious problem: it is simply dangerous to be sane in an insane world. The securities analyst who prudently predicted reasonable growth and stock appreciation was quickly left in the dust by the investment guru who prophesied a new investment paradigm in which revenues and costs were less important than the number of "hits" on a website. Moreover, as the IPO market soared in the 1990s, securities analysts became celebrities and valuable assets to their firms; indeed, they became the principal means by which investment banks competed for IPO clients, as the underwriter with the "star" analyst could produce the biggest first day stock price spike. But as their salaries thus soared, analyst compensation came increasingly from the investment banking side of their firms. Hence, just as in the case of the auditor, the analyst's economic position became increasingly dependent on favoring the interests of persons outside their profession (i.e., consultants in the case of the auditor and investment bankers in the case of the analyst) who had little reason to respect or observe the standards or professional culture within the gatekeeper's profession.

The common denominator linking these examples is that, as auditors increasingly sought consulting income and as analysts increasingly competed to maximize investment banking revenues, the gatekeepers' need to preserve their reputational capital for the long run slackened. Arguably, it could become more profitable for firms to realize the value of their reputational capital by trading on it in the short-run than by preserving it forever. Indeed, if it were true that auditing became a loss leader in the 1990s, one cannot expect firms to expend resources or decline business opportunities in order to protect reputations that were only marginally profitable.

c. Towards Synthesis

These explanations still do not fully explain why reputational capital built up over decades might be sacrificed (or, more accurately, liquidated) once legal risks decline and/or a bubble develops. Here, additional factors need to be considered.

a. The Increased Incentive for Short Term Stock Price Maximization The pressure on gatekeepers to acquiesce in earnings management was not constant over time, but rather grew during the 1990s. In particular, during the 1990s, executive compensation shifted from being primarily cash based to being primarily equity based. The clearest measure of this change is the growth in stock options. Over the last decade, stock options rose from five percent of shares outstanding at major U.S. companies to fifteen percent—a three hundred percent increase. The value of these options rose by an even greater percentage and over a dramatically shorter period: from $50 billion in 1997 in the case of the 2,000 largest corporations to $162 billion in 2000—an over three hundred percent rise in three years. Stock options create an obvious and potentially perverse incentive to engage in short-run, rather than long-term, stock price maximization because executives can exercise their stock options and sell the underlying shares on the same day. In truth, this ability was, itself, the product of deregulatory reform in the early 1990s, which relaxed the rules under Section 16(b) of the Securities Exchange Act of 1934 to permit officers and directors to exercise stock options and sell the underlying shares without holding the shares for the previously required six month period. Thus, if executives inflate the stock price of their company through premature revenue recognition or other classic earnings management techniques, they could quickly bail out in the short term by exercising their options and selling, leaving shareholders to bear the cost of the stock decline when the inflated stock price could not be maintained over subsequent periods. Given these incentives, it becomes rational for corporate executives to use lucrative consulting contracts, or other positive and negative incentives, to induce gatekeepers to engage in conduct that made the executives very rich. The bottom line is then that the growth of stock options placed gatekeepers under greater pressure to acquiesce in short-term oriented financial and accounting strategies.

b. The Absence of Competition The Big Five obviously dominated a very concentrated market. Smaller competitors could not expect to develop the international scale or brand names that the Big Five possessed simply by quoting a cheaper price. More importantly, in a market this concentrated, implicit collusion develops easily. Each firm could develop and follow a common competitive strategy in parallel without fear of being undercut by a major competitor. Thus, if each of the Big Five were to prefer a strategy under which it acquiesced to clients at cost of an occasional litigation loss and some public humiliation, it could more easily observe this policy if it knew that it would not be attacked by a holier-than-thou rival stressing its greater reputation for integrity as a competitive strategy. This approach does not require formal collusion but only the expectation that one's competitors would also be willing to accept litigation losses and occasional public humiliation as a cost of doing business.

Put differently, either in a less concentrated market where several dozen firms competed or in a market with low barriers to entry, it would be predictable that some dissident firm would seek to market itself as distinctive for its integrity. But in a market of five firms (and only four for the future), this is less likely.

c. Observability That a fraud occurs is not necessarily the fault of auditors. If they can respond to any fraud by asserting that they were victimized by a dishonest management, auditors may be able to avoid the permanent loss of reputational capital—particularly so long as their few competitors have no desire to exploit their failures because they are more or less equally vulnerable. Put differently, a system of reputational intermediaries works only if fault can be reliably assigned.

d. Principal/Agent Problems Auditing firms have always known that an individual partner could be dominated by a large client and might defer excessively to such a client in a manner that could inflict liability on the firm. Thus, early on, they developed systems of internal monitoring that were

far more elaborate than anything that law firms have yet attempted. But within the auditing firm, this internal monitoring function is not all powerful. After all, it is not itself a profit center. With the addition of consulting services as a major profit center, a natural coalition developed between the individual audit partner and the consulting divisions; each had a common interest in checking and overruling the firm's internal audit division when the latter's prudential decisions would prove costly to them. Cementing this marriage was the use of incentive fees. If those providing software consulting services for an audit firm were willing to offer the principal audit partner for a client a fee of 1% (or so) of any contract sold to the partner's audit client, few others within the firm might see any reason to object. If software consulting contracts (hypothetically, for $50 million) were then sold to the client, the audit partner might now receive more compensation from incentive fees for cross-selling than from auditing and thus had greater reason to value the client's satisfaction above his interest in the firm's reputational capital. More importantly, the audit partner now also had an ally in the consultants' who similarly would want to keep their mutual client satisfied, and together they would form a coalition potentially able to override the protests of their firm's internal audit unit (if it felt that an overly aggressive policy was being followed). While case histories exactly matching this pattern cannot yet be identified, abundant evidence does exist for the thesis that incentive fees can bias audit decision-making. Interestingly, Enron itself presents a fact pattern in which the audit firm's on-the-scene quality control officer was overruled and replaced.

III. IMPLICATIONS

A. Models for Reform

Does it matter much which of the foregoing two stories—the deterrence story or the bubble story—is deemed more persuasive? Although they are complementary rather than contradictory, their relative plausibility matters greatly in terms of deciding what reform[s] are necessary or desirable. To the extent one accepts the deterrence story, we may need legal changes. In principle, these changes could either raise the costs or lower the benefits of acquiescence to auditors. To the extent one accepts the bubble story, the problem may be self-correcting. That is, once the bubble bursts, gatekeepers come back into fashion, as investors become skeptics who once again demand assurances that only credible reputational intermediaries can provide. To the extent, one takes the reverse position, regulatory action is needed.

This comment is not intended to resolve this debate, except in one small respect. Alan Greenspan has recently espoused the bubble story and expressed the view that the market will largely self-correct on its own. His arguments have some merit. Although reasonable people can certainly debate the degree to which markets can reform themselves and the reciprocal degree to which legal interventions are necessary, one special area stands out where regulatory interventions seem essential, because ultimately the market cannot easily self-correct within this area without external interventions. Enron has shown that we have a "rule-based" system of accounting that arguably only asks the gatekeeper to certify the issuer's compliance with an inventory of highly technical rules—without the auditor necessarily taking responsibility for the overall accuracy of the issuer's statement of its financial position. Understandably, the SEC has called for a shift to a "principles-based" system of accounting, and this shift cannot come simply through private action.

Even as a matter of theory, the gatekeeper's services have value only if the gatekeeper is certifying compliance with a meaningful substantive standard. Yet, it is seldom not within the power of the individual gatekeeper to determine that standard of measurement. In the case of auditors, organizational reform of the accounting firm thus will mean little without substantive reform of substantive accounting principles.

Again, reasonable persons can disagree as to the best means of improving the quality of the financial standards with which the auditor measures compliance. One means would be to require the auditor to certify not simply compliance with GAAP, but to read the auditor's certification that the issuer's financial statements "fairly present" its financial position to mean that these financial statements provide the necessary disclosures for understanding the issuer's overall financial position. This probably

was the law (and may still be). Interestingly, the SEC's staff has recently sought to resurrect the classic decision of Henry Friendly in *U.S. v. Simon* by arguing that compliance with GAAP was not itself the standard by which the auditor's performance was to be measured. The alternative route, which does not involve greater reliance on litigation, is to depend upon substantive regulation: here, this would require greater activism by the Financial Accounting Standards Board ("FASB"), which in the past has been constrained by industry and Congressional interference. Insulating the FASB and assuring its financial independence would thus be appropriate initial steps toward reform.

B. Lessons for Lawyers

What are the lessons for lawyers that emerge from this tour of the problems and failings of our allied professions? Arguably, just as analysts and auditors do, securities lawyers serve investors as the ultimate consumers of their services. Conceptually, however, differences exist because lawyers specialize in designing transactions to avoid regulatory, legal, and other costly hurdles, but seldom provide meaningful certifications to investors. Still, the same "commodification" of professional services that reshaped the accounting profession has also impacted the legal profession. Thus, there may be handwriting on the wall in fact that, as auditing firms evolved from offering a single professional service into a shopping center of professional services, they lost internal control. Bluntly, the same fate could face lawyers. Indeed, the audit firm always knew that the individual audit partner serving the large client could become conflicted (because the audit partner's job depended on satisfying its single client), but the audit firm also knew that it could monitor its individual audit partners to manage this conflict. For a long time, monitoring seemingly worked—at least passably well. More recently, incentive-based compensation has exacerbated the monitoring problem, and similarly the evolution of the auditing firm into a financial conglomerate has seriously compromised old systems of internal control.

Whatever the control problems within accounting firms, law firms have nothing even remotely approaching the substantial system of internal controls employed by audit firms (which still did not work for them). The contrast is striking. Both audit firms and broker-dealers have far more advanced systems of internal quality control than do law firms. For example, audit firms typically have an in-house "internal standards" or "quality assurance" division, and they rely on periodic "peer review" of their audits by similarly situated firms. Although peer review, at least as a formal system, may not work for law firms (because law is an adversarial profession and also one obsessed with protecting the attorney client privilege), this conclusion only raises the larger question: what will work?

In overview, law firms are today positioned on a learning curve that seems at least a decade behind auditing firms, as the law firms are moving, much later than auditing firms, from "ma and pa" single office firms to multi-branch organizations. Across the legal landscape, the combination of lateral recruitment of partners, based on revenues generated, plus the movement toward multi-branch law firms means that law firms as an organization are at least (and probably more) vulnerable to quality control problems as auditing firms. Yet, they lack the minimal institutional safeguards that the latter have long used (with only limited success) to protect quality control. Logically, law firms should perceive the need to institutionalize a greater quality control function. Realistically, however, law firms have not experienced the same pattern of devastating financial losses that, during the 1980s, threatened the very viability of auditing firms. Thus, as a practical matter, law firms will probably not respond before the first large financial disaster befalls a major law firm and motivates greater attention to internal control. Predictably but sadly, only then will "bottom line"-oriented law partners recognize that the "bottom line" includes liabilities as well as revenues.

CONCLUSION

This essay has sought to explain that Enron is more about gatekeeper failure than board failure. It has also sought to explain when gatekeepers (or "repu-

tational intermediaries") are likely to fail. Put simply, reputational capital is not an asset that professional services firms will inevitably hoard and protect. Logically, as legal exposure to liability declines and as benefits of acquiescence in the client's demands increase, gatekeeper failure should correspondingly increase—as it did in the 1990s. Market bubbles can also explain gatekeeper failure (and this perspective probably works better in the case of the securities analysts, who faced little liability in the past), because in an environment of euphoria investors do not rely on gatekeepers (and hence gatekeepers have less leverage with respect to their clients).

Popular commentary has instead used softer-edged concepts—such as "infectious greed" and a decline in morality—to explain the same phenomena. Yet, there is little evidence that "greed" has ever declined; nor is it clear that there are relevant policy options for addressing it. In contrast, focusing on gatekeepers tells us that there are special actors in a system of private corporate governance whose incentives must be regulated.

Reasonable persons can always disagree what reforms are desirable. But the starting point for an intelligent debate is the recognition that the two major, contemporary crises now facing the securities markets—i.e., the collapse of Enron and the growing controversy over securities analysts, which began with the New York Attorney General's investigation into Merrill Lynch—involve at bottom the same problem: both are crises motivated by the discovery by investors that reputational intermediaries upon whom they relied were conflicted and seemingly sold their interests short. Neither the law nor the market has yet solved either of these closely related problems.

READING 7.4 PUBLIC ACCOUNTING: PROFESSION OR BUSINESS?
John C. Bogle

In this debate on the future of the accounting profession, I'm going to focus largely on the issue of auditor independence. While I have no business degree nor attest certificate, I've pored over more than my share of corporate and mutual fund financial statements. And while I have never worked in a controllership or treasury function nor have I been trained as a security analyst, I have been both an eye-witness to, and active participant in, the sweep of financial history over the past fifty years and have accordingly garnered a considerable amount of study and experience in virtually all phases of American finance. Through this experience, I have developed a passionate concern about the well-being of our financial markets, and this evening I'd like to discuss my views with you. (I am, of course, speaking for myself and not for any of the organizations with which I am associated.)

The integrity of financial markets—markets that are active, liquid, and honest, with participants who are fully and fairly informed—is absolutely central to the sound functioning of any system of democratic capitalism worth its salt. It is only through such markets that literally trillions upon trillions of dollars—the well-spring of today's powerful American economy—could have been raised in the past decade that became capital for the plant and equipment of our Old Economy and the capital for the technology and innovation of our New Economy. Only the complete confidence of investors in the integrity of the financial information they received allowed these investment needs to be met at the lowest possible cost of capital.

Sound securities markets require sound financial information. It is as simple as that. Investors require—and have a right to require—complete information about each and every security, information that fairly and honestly represents every significant fact and figure that might be needed to evaluate the worth of a corporation. Not only is accuracy required but, more than that, a broad sweep of information that provides every appropri-

ate figure that a prudent, probing, sophisticated professional investor might require in the effort to decide whether a security should be purchased, held, or sold. Full disclosure. Fair disclosure. Complete disclosure. Those are the watchwords of the financial system that has contributed so much to our nation's growth, progress, and prosperity.

INDEPENDENCE

It is unarguable, I think, that the independent oversight of financial figures is central to that disclosure system. Indeed independence is at integrity's very core. And, for more than a century, the responsibility for the independent oversight of corporate financial statements has fallen to America's public accounting profession. It is the auditor's stamp on a financial statement that gives it its validity, its respect, and its acceptability by investors. And only if the auditor's work is comprehensive, skeptical, inquisitive, and rigorous, can we have confidence that financial statements speak the truth.

Our government, our regulators, our corporations, and our accountants have, over this long span, properly placed the auditor's independence from his client at the keystone of our financial reporting system. And auditor independence has come to mean an absence of any and all relationships that could seriously jeopardize—either in fact or in appearance—the validity of the audit, and, therefore, of the client's financial statements. The auditor, in short, is the guardian of financial integrity. On the need to maintain, above all, this principle of independence, I hear not a single voice of dissent—not from the corporations, not from the profession, not from the regulators, not from the bar, not from the brokers and bankers—the financial market intermediaries—and not from the institutional investors who, as trustees, hold and manage the securities portfolios of their clients. So far, so good.

But being for independence is a bit like being for God, for motherhood, and for the American way. For the relationship between auditor and client is complex—beginning with the fact that it is the client who pays the auditor for its services, creating

This essay was delivered at the New York University "Seymour Jones Distinguished Lecture" on Oct. 16, 2000. Reprinted with permission of The Vanguard Group and John C. Bogle.

an interdependency that is anything but independence. Long ago, we made a societal decision to accept that conflict because, simply put, we couldn't figure out any arrangement that was better. A system of mandatory audits by a Federal agency, for example, would probably have been intolerable even to those most disposed toward using government as the first line of attack in dealing with any other national issue.

So over the years we've developed a whole series of structures and safeguards to minimize the susceptibility of the audit firm to the dominion of the client, and put in place requirements designed to assure that the auditor remains free of entanglements that threaten his objectivity and independence. But as times have changed, these issues have become increasingly complex, and the entanglements have become more numerous. In 1997, in part as a response to these developments, Securities and Exchange Commission Chairman Arthur Levitt, in concert with the American Institute of Certified Public Accountants, established the Independence Standards Board (ISB), giving it the responsibility of establishing independence standards applicable to the audits of public entities, in order to serve the public interest and to protect and promote investors' confidence in the securities markets.

THE ISB

By agreement, the initial membership of the ISB consisted of four members from the accounting profession and four public members, one of whom would serve as Chairman. The same eight individuals who joined the Board in 1997 continue to serve today, and I have been privileged to serve as one of the public members. After nearly three years of meetings with my public colleagues, let me assure you that there can be no question of their staunch and complete independence, to say nothing of their integrity, their intelligence, and the dedication that they have brought to their task. *Business Week* recently stated that most of the Board members were "tied to" the profession, implying that one or more of the public members was less than independent. When I challenged its editors to specify the party or parties involved and describe any inappropriate bias, the inane allegation was promptly withdrawn. The independent members are independent.

While the four non-public members are of course members of the profession, I can tell you that in three years of working with them I have developed a high respect for the integrity, intelligence, and dedication they too have demonstrated. Of course their point of view is hardly independent of their professional interests, but it is a serious, respectable, thoughtful, informed viewpoint, one that has helped the public members better understand, not, I think, the principles involved, but the complex issues involved in implementation—in taking sound and fair actions that give force to the principles.

I came to the Board with but a single preconception: A growing concern that . . . many of the great professions that have served our society so well are moving rapidly toward becoming businesses, a trend that, if taken to the extreme, would undermine the sound and durable principles on which they were founded. In the dog-eat-dog, money-driven, competitive world in which we live today, I suppose it would be surprising were it not so. And surely many benefits have resulted: A greater appetite for enterprise growth, likely greater efficiency and organizational certainty, perhaps even greater creativity and innovation. Such benefits are not to be disdained. But those benefits can carry a societal cost—a diminution of traditional standards, a reduction in focus on clients, and, at least in some fields, an increase in costs. But the heart of the matter is that there is a difference, however difficult to measure, between a business and a profession. When that line is crossed, we as a society are the losers.

BUSINESS VS. PROFESSION

My concerns, as you might imagine, are not mere abstractions. As I observe the mutual fund industry, in which I've spent 50 years, I see it moving from a profession—investment management—to a business—product marketing. I see fewer mutual funds that focus on sound investment principles, and more funds—often higher-risk, aggressive funds—created to meet the demands of the marketplace for the transitory fads and fashions of the day—"hot new products," if you will. I see portfolio strategies based on short-term speculation rather than long-term investment, with an attendant quantum leap in portfolio turnover. And I see costs of management soaring primarily to fund massive advertising campaigns and only partly to enhance investment research and analysis. Fund expenses have risen almost in lock-step with assets, meaning that the lion's share of the truly staggering economies of scale inherent in managing money are being arrogated by the managers rather than flowed through to the shareholders. This diversion of investment returns means that the financial interests of the clients are being subordinated to the financial interests of their trustees, whose primary concern was once acting as good stewards for those who have entrusted them with their assets. It is not a big stretch to recognize a similar pattern—albeit in a very different way—in the medical profession, where the interests of the patient seem clearly to have been superseded by the interests of the caregivers—the insurance-industry/drug-producer/private-HMO complex.

I note the pervasiveness of the societal trend of professions to become businesses because it may help explain the similar trend in public accounting, though I would argue that the high standards of the attestation profession may, fortunately, have mitigated its full fruition. Nonetheless, over the years, attestation has come to account for only about one-third of the $26 billion of revenues of today's "Big Five" accounting firms, with tax services accounting for one-quarter. The remainder, not far from one-half of revenues, is derived from consulting, management, and advisory services. The potential problem that arises from this trend, obviously, is that the desire to garner or retain a highly lucrative consulting contract from an audit client could jeopardize the auditor's independence. Admittedly, I have seen no independent studies which have directly associated audit failures with related consulting contracts. On the other hand, those relationships, if they exist, would be difficult to discover, and in any event causality would be impossible to establish. But as I testified at the SEC's hearings on Auditor Independence Requirements in July: "Studies cannot always confirm what common sense makes clear."

THE SEC'S INDEPENDENCE PROPOSAL

The SEC's proposed Independence rule would, among other things, provide new—and often more appropriate—principles for determining whether an auditor is independent, largely tracking earlier standards established or being established by the ISB relating to investments in audit clients, family and employment relationships, and appraisal and valuation services. These enhanced and modernized standards seem to have generated little controversy, and I hold the view that the establishment and maintenance of such independence standards should remain the province of the ISB, and that the proposed rule-making in these areas is unnecessary.

The other principal rule amendment, however, has generated a firestorm of controversy. It identifies certain management and consulting services that, if provided to an audit client, would impair the auditor's independence. The services that the public accountant would be effectively barred from providing include those which involve either a mutual or conflicting interest with the client; the auditing of one's own work; functioning as management or an employee of the client; or acting as the client's advocate. Expressed as general principles, honestly, it is unimaginable to me that any reasonable person could disagree in the abstract that such roles would threaten—or, at the very least, be perceived to threaten—the auditor's independence.

It must also be clear that, whether or not the auditor has the backbone to maintain its independence under these circumstances, many management and consulting arrangements could easily be perceived as representing a new element in the relationship between auditor and corporation—a business relationship with a customer rather than a professional relationship with a client. Surely this issue goes to the very core of the central issue of philosophy that I expressed earlier: The movement of auditing from profession to business, with all the potential conflicts of interest that entails. So I come down with a firm endorsement of the substance of the proposed SEC rule, which would in effect bar such relationships.

Of course, I have read extensive material from the opponents of that rule making the opposite case. Some arguments seem entirely worthy of consideration, especially those relating to technical—but nonetheless real—issues that engender unnecessary constraints on an auditor's entering into any strategic alliances or joint ventures, or that relate to the complexity in clearly defining "material direct investment" or "affiliate of the audit client" and so on. Personally, I would hope and expect that this bevy of issues will be resolved by the profession and the Commission meeting and reasoning together.

But other opposition seemed to me to be rather knee-jerk and strident (rather like those debates I mentioned at the outset). No, I for one don't believe the SEC proposals represent "an unwarranted and intrusive regulation" of the accounting profession. And, no, I for one do not believe that the new rules "strait-jacket" the profession. And, yes, I do believe that the growing multiplicity of interrelationships between auditor and client is a serious threat to the concept of independence, the rock foundation of sound financial statements and fair financial markets alike. In this context, I was stunned to see this recent statement from one of the senior officers of the investment company industry group for one of the Big Five firms. "Fund companies have increasingly looked to . . . big accounting firms to help them with operational, regulatory, strategic and international decisions." If that isn't functioning as management, I'm not sure what would be.

THE FUTURE OF THE PROFESSION

While I am but a layman, I'd now like to comment on some issues that relate to the future of the profession. I begin by expressing not only my hope, but my expectation that public accounting will continue to operate successfully and in the public interest under the proposed SEC rules that prohibit the provision of most management and consulting services to clients. Doubtless, there are problems—serious problems—in determining the precise language and interpretation of the rules, but I'm enough of an optimist to believe that, in the environment of openness and good will on both sides, changes can be made without undermining the bedrock principle of the independence.

But there are other disturbing issues that affect the profession today, and I'd like to close by presenting just five of them. First is the question of basic accounting principles. Can the accounting principles that have served the Old Economy so well over so many years properly be applied to the New Economy? Is what is seen as a narrow accounting model applying to businesses with tangible capital equipment, hard assets, and even so-called "good will" applicable to businesses in which human capital is the principal asset, information is the stock in

trade, and "first mover" status is the driving force in valuation? Clearly, many, indeed most, New Economy companies are valued at staggering—even infinite—multiples of any earnings that GAAP could possibly uncover. Interestingly, however, during the past seven months, at least the Internet business-to-consumer companies have reconciled that gap, as it were, in favor of GAAP.

So while that seemingly omnipotent master, "the stock market," may be telling the profession that the 1930s-based model of reporting doesn't work any more, please don't write off too hastily the possibility that the model may be right and the market wrong. And don't forget that no matter what "the market" may say today, its level on future tomorrows well down the road will—not may—be determined by earnings and dividends. Nonetheless, a re-examination of today's of basic accounting principles should be a high priority. And let the chips fall where they may.

Second is the question of earnings management. I noted in a speech a year ago [that] we live in a world of managed earnings. While it is corporate executives who do the managing, they do so with at least the tacit approval of corporate directors and auditors, and with the enthusiastic endorsement of institutional investors with short-term time horizons, even speculators and arbitrageurs—a "happy conspiracy" as I called it then. Like it or not, corporate strategy and financial accounting alike focus on meeting the earnings expectations of "the Street" quarter after quarter. The desideratum is steady earnings growth—manage it to at least the 12% level if you can—and at all costs avoid falling short of the earnings expectations at which the corporation has hinted, or whispered, or "ballparked" before the year began. If all else fails, obscure the real results by merging, taking a big one-time write-off, and relying on pooling-of-interest accounting (although that procedure will soon become unavailable). All of this creative financial engineering apparently serves to inflate stock prices, [to] enrich corporate managers, and to deliver to institutional investors what they want.

But if the stock market is to be the arbiter of value, it will do its job best, in my judgment, if it sets its valuations based on accurate corporate financial reporting and a focus on the long-term prospects of the corporations it values. The market today seems to be focusing at least a bit more on those verities, but there is still much room for improvement. For while the accounting practices of America's corporations may well be the envy of the world, our nation's financial environment has become permeated with the concept of managed earnings. There is a "numbers game" going on, and pro forma operating profits permeate financial statements. Pro forma seems to mean, in an Alice-in-Wonderland world, whatever the Corporation chooses it to mean, excluding such charges as amortization of good will, taxes on option exercises, equity losses in investees, in-process R&D, for example, as these costs vanish in the struggle to meet earnings expectations. Since this game is played in press releases, it is not clear where the solution lies. But I hope that the accounting profession will get involved before the coin of the realm—earnings statements with integrity—is further debased. That corporate clients may not be enamored of having the issue of managed earnings raised is—or ought to be—irrelevant.

Third is the stock option issue. Financial statements place options in a sort of "no man's land" in which options are not treated as compensation. But, as Warren Buffett has long argued, if options are compensation, why aren't they charged to earnings? And if options aren't compensation, what are they? Surely the profession ought to play a more aggressive role in answering that question and taking a stand on proper stock option accounting. A recent study by a Wall Street firm listed four industry groups in which accounting for stock options would have reduced earnings by an average of 28% in 1997, 23% in 1998, and another 25% in 1999; 21 companies in which 1999 earnings would have been reduced from 50% to 700%(!); and 13 companies with 1999 pro forma (there's that word again) pre-tax stock option compensation ranging from $500 million to $1.1 billion. Quite important enough as an issue now, the question of accounting for stock options will rise to even greater importance as corporations whose stocks have faltered—even plummeted—in the recent market decline reprice their options. I hope that FASB interpretation 44 on repricing underwater options will help to deal with this issue.

ABUSIVE TAX SHELTERS

The case of overly aggressive and potentially illegal tax-shelters constitutes a fourth issue. Earlier this

year, Treasury Secretary Lawrence Summers excoriated the proliferation of "engineered transactions that are devoid of economic substance . . . with no goal other than to reduce a corporation's tax liabilities." The Secretary is right: Such transactions strike a blow at the integrity—here, an especially well-chosen word—of the tax system. And when companies demand—and receive—"black box" features in such transactions designed to make them impenetrable to all but those who designed them, something perilously close to fraud is going on. He challenges, I assume accurately, the professional conduct of the firms involved in the creation of abusive tax shelters and suggests sanctions on firms—here, the Treasury Secretary pointedly included public accountants—that issue opinions, limits on contingent fees, and excise taxes on such fee income.

It is not my place to evaluate the role of the accounting profession in these tax abuses. But it must be clear that any firm that helps develop such schemes or opines on their purported validity wins favor with the client involved, and runs a heavy risk of compromising its independence. Faustian bargains of that nature, to the extent they may exist, could even require the addition of tax services to the list of services that public accounting firms would be barred from offering to their clients. Surely, that's a high price for public accounting firms to pay.

The fifth and final issue I raise regarding independence of the future of the profession relates to the novel forms of firm structure and organizations that are now evolving. (The ISB published a Discussion Memorandum on this subject a year ago, and has received numerous comments, but has tabled the issue at the request of the SEC staff.) The traditional simple partnership model is being supplanted by alternative business structures. In one model, a group of smaller attest firms are consolidated through the sale of their non-audit practice to a third party (in a private or public offering) with the audit practice retained by the partners. An operational link remains between the two parties. In another—the "roll up" model—firms are united under a single umbrella through combination and then sale of their non-audit businesses to a third party or the public. Byzantine is the word that comes to mind as one looks [at] the organizational charts portraying these relationships. While "Byzantine" isn't necessarily bad, such dual employment surely raises important independence issues. And when CPA firms—whose integrity and independence are their stock in trade—are in fact principally investment advisory firms offering financial products sponsored by their parents, a whole other set of questions about the meaning of professional responsibility come to the fore.

How attest firms respond to these independence issues—and indeed whether they do—will shape the future of the profession. Most of them are clearly framed by the over-arching issue of the proper place to draw the line between business and profession. But perhaps my comments are just the ramblings of an aging Luddite who wants to bring back a proud age of tradition that will never return. In my own mutual fund industry, I know that the age of professional stewardship will return. While I do not understand the field of accounting nearly as well, I am confident that if financial market participants come to understand that the independent oversight of financial figures plays a critical role in our system of disclosure, that independence is at the core of integrity, and that the integrity of our financial markets is essential to their well-being, the age of professional accounting too will shake off today's challenges and return to its roots.

READING 7.5 AUDITING ETHICS
Ronald Duska and Brenda Shay Duska

In an article entitled, "Arthur Andersen's 'Double Duty' Work Raises Questions About Its Independence" *Wall Street Journal*, Jonathan Weil reported:

> In addition to acting as Enron Corp.'s outside auditor, Arthur Andersen LLP also performed internal auditing services for Enron, raising further questions about the Big Five accounting firm's independence and the degree to which it many have been auditing its own work.
>
> That Anderson performed "double duty" work for the Houston-based energy concern likely will trigger greater regulatory scrutiny of Andersen's role as Enron's independent auditor than would ordinarily be the case after an audit failure, accounting and securities-law specialists say. . . .
>
> Such arrangements have become more common over the past decade. In response, the Securities and Exchange Commission last year passed new rules, which take effect in August 2002, restricting the amount of internal audit work that outside auditors can perform for their clients, though not banning it outright. . . .

Andersen officials say their firm's independence wasn't impaired by the size of nature of the fees paid by Enron—$52 million last year. ($25 million for audit fees, $27 million for other services, including tax and consulting work.) An Enron spokesman said, "The company believed and continues to believe that Arthur Andersen's role as Enron's internal auditor would not compromise Andersen's role as independent auditor for Enron.". . .

Accounting firms say the double-duty arrangements let them become more familiar with client's control procedures and that such arrangements are ethically permissible, as long as outside auditors don't make management decisions in handling the internal audits. Under the new SEC rules taking effect next year, an outside auditor impairs its independence if it performs more than 40% of a client's internal-audit work. The SEC said the restriction wouldn't apply to clients with assets of $200 million or less. Previously, the SEC had imposed no such percentage limitation.[1]

The Enron/Arthur Andersen scenario reported above raises many ethical questions about what is appropriate behavior for auditors. We propose to examine them by taking a look at what the proper function of the auditor is and what sorts of things

From Ronald Duska and Brenda Shay Duska, *Accounting Ethics*, Chapter 7. Copyright © 2003. Reprinted with permission.

stand in the way of an auditor performing that function.

To increase profit, accounting firms add consulting services, quite often for the same companies that they are simultaneously auditing, thus creating at least apparent if not real conflicts of interest. This kind of practice has been going on for years, but until recently has remained under the radar. With the eruption of the Enron case, accounting firms have come under new scrutiny. The conflict of interest was writ[ten] large in stories like the following:

> Arthur Andersen LLP's role in Enron Corp.'s accounting problems is more proof of a need for tighter controls of the accounting industry, says former Securities and Exchange Commission Chairman Arthur Levitt . . . Arthur Andersen's Enron audit work is being scrutinized by the SEC, the Justice Department and six congressional committees.

> Mr. Levitt, despite his efforts, failed in late 2000 to enact rules banning auditors from acting as consultants for companies they audit. He argued that potential profits from consulting could create a conflict of interest that undermines auditors' independence. He also proposed that outside auditors be barred from working with company accountants on company financial reports. Otherwise, Big Five firms could be auditing their own work.

> Faced with opposition from three of the Big Five, including Andersen, the SEC eventually adopted new rules requiring corporate-board audit committees to monitor potential conflicts and banning auditors from providing some specific consulting activities, such as tax work. But the rules stop short of a total ban on auditors doing any consulting work for audit clients.

> Arthur Andersen collected $52 million in fees in 2000 from Enron: $25 million in audit fees and $27 million for other services, including consulting work.[2]

Human nature being what it is, it seems less likely that one will be able to keep a client on the consulting side if the client is given an unfavorable audit. The client might go shopping for an audit firm that would give a more lenient reading of the books. On the other hand, if the audit is inadequate and people suffer from mis-information that the accountants should have uncovered, the accounting firm might get sued, because auditors are expected to look out for the interests of the public before looking out for the best interest of the client. The fact that, as Steven Silber said, lawsuits happen to auditors with great frequency, only reinforces the point that the role the auditor in financial services is so critically important.[3]

Independence of management advisory services for auditors is required. Suppose an auditor questions a technique the consulting branch of his company employed. He might be asked to overlook it for any number of reasons. At any rate, to begin to worry about the interests of the firm being audited who is paying the accountant, more than the truth is to violate the duty of accountants to immediate third party users.[4]

Given the way financial markets and the economic system have developed, society has carved out a role for the independent auditor, which is absolutely essential for the effective functioning of the economic system. If accounting is the language of business, it is the auditor's job to see the language is used properly so that relevant material is communicated properly. That means that in the system the role of the independent auditor is "to see whether the company's estimates are based on formulas that seem reasonable in the light of whatever evidence is available and that choice formulas are applied consistently from year to year."[5]

Most times, when people talk about the ethics of public accounting, they are talking about the responsibilities of the independent auditor. Auditing the financial statements of publicly owned companies is certainly not the only role of an accountant, but an argument can be made that it is the, if not one of the, most important roles in the current economic system.

For years, independent auditing was the primary occupation of the large accounting firms. But that has changed. As we have been made aware of in the case of Arthur Anderson, which is by no means alone in this practice, large accounting firms in order to generate more income for the firm have taken on other tasks, particularly consulting. As one report says,

> In 1993, 31% of the industry's fees came from consulting. By 1999, that had jumped to 51%.

In 2002, for example PriceWaterhouse Coopers earned only 40% of its worldwide fees from auditing, 29% coming from management consulting and most of the rest from tax and corporate finance work . . . More telling, in a study of the first 563 companies to file financials after Feb. 5, 2001, . . . for every dollar of audit fees, clients paid their independent accountants $2.69 for non-audit consulting. . . . Marriott International Inc. . . . paid Andersen just over $1 million for its audit, but more than $30 million for information technology and other services. . . . It simply looks bad to have Andersen earning more on consulting to Enron than on auditing."[6]

However, even though the structure of the large accounting firms have changed, the need for the independent external auditor has grown while society's need to be able to trust the fidelity of the external corporate audit remains as strong as ever.

As John Bogel [founder of the Vanguard Group of mutual funds] notes, a free market economy needs to base transactions and decisions on truthful and accurate information. In market transactions the financial status of a company is vital information on which a choice to purchase is to be based. The role of the auditor is to attest to the fact that the financial picture of a company presented to whatever user needs to make a decision on the basis of that picture is as accurate as possible.

This function and responsibility is not new. It has only come to the glare of public publicity with the eruption of the Enron/Arthur Andersen debacle. The classic statement of this function and responsibility of the auditor is the opinion given by Justice Burger in the 1984 landmark Arthur Young case.[7]

Corporate financial statements are one of the primary sources of information available to guide the decisions of the investing public. In an effort to control the accuracy of the financial data available to investors in the securities markets, various provisions of the federal securities laws require publicly held companies to file their financial statements with the Securities and Exchange Commission. Commission regulations stipulate that these financial reports must be audited by an independent CPA in accordance with generally accepted auditing standards. *By examining the corporation's books and records, the independent auditor determines whether the financial reports of the corporation have been prepared in accordance with generally accepted accounting principles. The auditor then issues an opinion as to whether the financial statements, taken as a whole, fairly present the financial position and operations of the corporation for the relevant period.* (Italics added)

Burger puts the responsibility of the auditor clearly—to issue an opinion as to whether the financial statement *fairly* presents the financial position of the corporation. Performance of this role attesting that the financial positions and operations of the corporation are fairly presented requires that an auditor have as much integrity and honesty as possible. Further, to assure that an accurate picture has been presented it is essential that the integrity and honesty of the auditor not be imperiled by the presence of undue influence. To bolster integrity and honesty the auditor must have as much independence as possible. For the market to function efficiently those who need to make decisions about the company based on as true and accurate information as possible must be able to trust the accountants' pictures. But such trust is eroded if there is even an appearance of a conflict of interest.

TRUST

We can understand all this [if] we apply Immanuel Kant's first categorical imperative, the universalizability principle, "Act so you can will the maxim of your action to be a universal law." As we saw, the imperative demands that an action be capable of being universalized, i.e., we need to consider what would occur if everyone acted the same way for the same reason. Consider the reasons people have for not giving the most accurate picture of the financial status of a company that is possible. As we saw, one generally gives a false picture to get another party to act in a way other than they would act given full and truthful information. For example, a CFO misrepresents his company's profits to get a bank loan, thinking that if the bank had the true picture, no loan would be forthcoming. In the Enron case it was more complicated to buoy up the price of the stock, which was then used as collateral to float loans to cover (bad?) debts. What would happen if such behavior were universalized, i.e., if everybody misrepresented the financial health of their company when it was to their advantage to lie?

In such a situation two things would happen. First, trust in business dealings that required information about the financial picture would be eroded. This certainly happens, as Van Hovanesian relates. Chaos would ensue, because financial markets cannot operate without trust. Cooperation is essential, and trust is a precondition of cooperation. We engage in hundreds of transactions daily, which demand that we trust other people with our money and our lives. If misrepresentation were to become a universal practice, such trust and consequently such cooperation would be impossible.

Secondly, universalizing misrepresentation, besides leading to mistrust, chaos and consequently inefficiencies in the market, would make the act of misrepresentation impossible. When universalizing misrepresentation makes trust impossible, it simultaneously makes the very act of misrepresenting impossible, because misrepresentation can only occur if the person lied to trusts the person lying. Since prudent people don't trust known liars, if everyone lied, no one would trust another and it would be impossible to lie. So universalized lying makes lying impossible. Do we trust the defendant in a murder case to tell the truth? Do we trust young children who are concerned about being punished to tell the truth? Of course not. Once we recognize that certain people are unreliable or untrustworthy it becomes impossible for them to misrepresent things to us, because we don't believe a word they're saying. Hence the anomaly—if misrepresentation became universalized in certain situations, it would be impossible to misrepresent in those situations, since no one would trust what was being represented. This makes the universalizing of lying irrational or self-contradictory.

The contradiction here, according to Kant, is a will contradiction, and the irrationality lies in the fact that you are simultaneously willing the possibility of misrepresentation and the impossibility of misrepresentation, by willing out of existence the conditions (trust) necessary to perform the act you will to perform. Face it, people who lie, don't want lying universalized. Liars are free riders. Liars want an unfair advantage. They don't want others to lie— to act like the liars are acting. Liars want others to tell the truth and be trusting so that the liars can lie to those trusting people. Liars want the world to

work one way for them and differently for all others. In short, liars want a double standard. They want their cake and want to eat it too. But such a selfish self-serving attitude is the antithesis of the ethical. In this case auditing would become a useless function. As a matter of fact, in an issue of *Accounting Today*, Rick Teleberg thinks this has already happened: "CPA firms long ago became more like insurance companies—complete with their focus on assurances and risk-managed audits—than attesters." We won't risk telling the public what your financial state looks like; we'll just guarantee that your presentation won't be subject to charges of illegal behavior. They serve the client and not the public.

In this discussion we can see another important aspect of trust. Only a fool trusts someone who gives all the appearances of being a liar. Only a fool trusts someone who puts themselves in positions where they seem likely to have their integrity compromised. These are the reasons why people take precautions against getting involved with those who give even the appearance of being caught in a conflict of interest. Because trust is necessary, even the *appearance* of honesty and integrity of accountants becomes important. So the auditor must not only be trustworthy, he or she must also appear trustworthy, for the prudent manager as the prudent accountant has an obligation to be sufficiently skeptical in order to protect the legitimate claims of stakeholders. We will return to the arguments for avoiding even the appearance of independence later.

THE AUDITOR'S RESPONSIBILITY TO THE PUBLIC

This role and the consequent duty to attest to the fairness of the financial statements gives the accountant special responsibilities to the public. Possessing these responsibilities puts the accountant in a different relation to the client who hires him or her, than the relationships with clients found in the other professions. Justice Burger mentions this in his classic statement of auditor responsibility.

> The auditor, does not have the same relationship to his client that a private attorney who has a role as "... a confidential advisor and advocate, a loyal representative whose duty it is to present the client's case in the most favorable

possible light. An independent CPA performs a different role. *By certifying the public reports that collectively depict a corporation's financial status, the independent auditor assumes a public responsibility transcending any employment relationship with the client.* (Italics mine) The independent public accountant performing this special function owes ultimate allegiance to the corporation's creditors and stockholders, as well as to the investing public. This 'public watchdog' function demands that the accountant maintain total independence from the client at all times and requires complete fidelity to the public trust. To insulate from disclosure a CPA's interpretations of the client's financial statements would be to ignore the significance of the accountant's role as a disinterested analyst charged with public obligations."[8]

Given the conflict of interests between the public and clients, it is clear that auditors face conflicting loyalties. To whom are they primarily responsible, the public or the client who pays the bill? We have seen that accountants are professionals and consequently, should behave as professionals. Like most other professionals, they offer services to their clients. But the public accounting profession, because it includes operating as an independent auditor, has another function. The independent auditor acts not only as a recorder, but also as an evaluator of other accountant's records. The auditor has what Justice Burger calls "a public watch-dog [function]."

As we have seen, over time, the evaluation of another accountant's records has developed into a necessary component of capitalist societies, particularly that part of society that deals in money markets and offers publicly traded stocks and securities. In such a system, it is imperative for potential purchasers of financial products to have an accurate picture of the companies in which they wish to invest, to whom they are willing to loan money, or with whom they wish to merge. In such a system there needs to be a procedure for verifying the accuracy of the financial picture of companies. The role of verifier fell to the public accountant—the auditor.[9] Baker and Hayes reiterate the accountant's different kind of role.

Other professionals, such as physicians and lawyers, are expected to perform their services at the maximum possible level of professional competence for the benefit of their clients. Public accountants may at times be expected by their clients to perform their professional services in a manner that differs from the interests of third parties who are the beneficiaries of the contractual arrangements between the public accountant and their clients. This unusual arrangement poses an ethical dilemma for public accountants.[10]

In short, while auditors' clients are the ones who pay the fees for the auditor's services, the auditor's primary responsibility is to look out for the interest of a third party, the public, and not to look out primarily for the interests of the one who employs the accountant.

Since the auditor is charged with public obligations, he or she should be a disinterested analyst. The auditor's obligations are to certify that the public reports depicting a corporation's financial status *fairly* present the financial position and operations of the corporation for the relevant period. In short, the fiduciary responsibility of the auditor is to the public trust, and "independence" from the client is demanded for that trust to be honored. The importance of this can be seen in the interest which the Security and Exchange Commission puts on the independence factor.

In January of 2000, partners and employees at Pricewaterhouse-Coopers were found by the S.E.C. to have routinely violated rules forbidding their ownership of stock in companies they were auditing. The investigation found 8,064 violations at the firm, which then dismissed five partners. Pricewaterhouse said at the time that it did not believe that the integrity of any audit had been compromised by the violations.[11]

The fact that the auditor's role requires "transcending any employment relationship with the client" quite often creates dilemmas for the auditor. . . .

INDEPENDENCE

Thus far we have looked at the responsibilities of the auditor. But to meet those responsibilities it is imperative that the auditor maintains independence. Let's recall Justice Burger's statement.

The independent public accountant performing this special function owes ultimate allegiance to the corporation's creditors and stockholders, as well as to the investing public. *This 'public watchdog' function demands that the accountant maintain total independence from the client at all times and requires complete fidelity to the public trust.*

"Total independence" is the phrase that Burger uses. What does total independence require? Obviously an external auditor should be independent from the client. But must independence be total, as Justice Burger says? If so, what exactly does total independence require? What does "complete" fidelity to the public trust require? We need to examine whether total independence is a possibility or even a necessity. How much independence should an auditor maintain and how should the auditor determine that?

Let us suggest that what is usually meant by total independence is independence not only in fact, but also in appearance. As we have already noted, the AICPA code of ethics recognizes these two kinds of independence: independence in fact and independence in appearance. Independence in fact is applicable to all accountants, for if the function of the accountant is to render accurate pictures of the financial situation, then conflicts of interest that cause inaccurate pictures do a disservice to whomever is entitled to and in need of the accurate picture.

Whether independence in appearance need be applicable to all accountants or only to independent auditors is an open question. Some would claim[12] that independence in appearance is applicable only to independent auditors. Hence, it is clear that the appearance of independence is important for independent auditors, but whether it is necessary for all accountants is a discussion that can wait for a later time.

The most recent thinking about independence has been carried on by the Independence Standards Board which has recently published *A Statement of Independence Concepts: A Conceptual Framework for Auditor Independence*. The Independence Standards Board was established in 1997, by Securities and Exchange Commission Chairman Arthur Levitt in concert with the American Institute of Certified Public Accountants. "The ISB was given the responsibility of establishing independence standards applicable to the audits of public entities, in order to serve the public interest and to protect and promote investors' confidence in the securities markets." It recognizes that "The various securities laws enacted by Congress and administered by the SEC recognize that the integrity and credibility of the financial reporting process for public companies depends, in large part, on auditors remaining independent from their audit clients."[13]

As the home page of the Independence Standards Board (ISB) states, "The ISB was developed from discussions between the American Institute of Certified Public Accountants (AICPA), other representatives of the accounting profession, and the U.S. Securities and Exchange Commission (SEC).[14] However, indicative of the pressure being put on the AICPA by the large accounting firms, for whom independence might mean surrendering their lucrative consulting contracts with firms they audited, the ISB was dissolved in August of 2001. In the fall, of course, the [fallout] from the Enron/Andersen debacle occurred, and in the winter of 2002, the Big Five began separating their auditing and consulting functions. But enough of the history. We have learned that independence is necessary.

John Bogel gives us an eloquent account of why.

> Our government, our regulators, our corporations, and our accountants have, . . . properly placed the auditor's independence from his client at the keystone of our financial reporting system. And auditor independence has come to mean an absence of any and all relationships that could seriously jeopardize—either in fact or in appearance—the validity of the audit, and, therefore, of the client's financial statements. The auditor, in short, is the guardian of financial integrity. On the need to maintain, above all, this principle of independence, I hear not a single voice of dissent—not from the corporations, not from the profession, not from the regulators, not from the bar, not from the brokers and bankers—the financial market intermediaries—and not from the institutional investors who, as trustees, hold and manage the securities portfolios of their clients.[15]

But what did the proposed conceptual framework of the now-defunct ISB say about independence? The ISB board defined auditor independence as "freedom from those pressures and other factors that compromise or can reasonably be expected to compromise, an auditor's ability to make unbiased audit decisions." This of course does not mean freedom from all pressures, only those that are "so significant that they rise to a level where they compromise, or can reasonably be expected to compromise, the auditor's ability to make audit decisions without bias." By "reasonably be expected" the report has in mind the rationally based beliefs of well-informed investors and other users of financial information. For example if I stood to gain from a company to which I give a favorable attestation, because I am a shareholder in that company, or because the company is planning on hiring my firm to do extensive consulting work when it gets a loan from a bank which is contingent upon a favorable audit, the reasonable person would be somewhat skeptical of my ability to be unbiased in that case, not because I was a dishonorable person, but because human beings in general can be unduly influenced by such pressures.

But what sorts of pressures are there? To begin there are pressures that can come from relationships such as family, friends, acquaintances or business relationships. Standard setting bodies issue rules that limit certain activities and relationships which they believe represent "potential sources of bias for auditors generally." As we noted, some auditors might be able to remain unbiased in such situations, but the rules apply to them also because "it is reasonable to expect audit decisions to be biased in those circumstances." "Accordingly, non-compliance with those rules might not preclude a particular auditor from being objective, but it would preclude the auditor from claiming to be independent" at least in appearance if not in reality.

Finally not every situation can be identified or covered by a rule, so the absence of a rule covering a certain relationship does not mean the independence is not jeopardized by the relationship, if the audit decision could reasonably be expected to be compromised as a result of that relationship. "Compliance with the rules is a necessary, but not a sufficient, condition for independence. . . ."

To protect independence, the SEC released a Revision of the Commission's Auditor Independence Requirements, effective February 5, 2001. The revised rule identified certain non-audit services that impair auditor independence. It met with resistance from the accounting profession. But it was seen as necessary by Levitt of the SEC and those sympathetic with his position, a position that seemed prophetic in the light of subsequent events. As a matter of fact, since the Enron/Andersen debacle, Levitt has called for tighter controls.[16]

It is worth reviewing in some depth John C. Bogle's defense of the commission's recommendations. According to Bogle the independence requirements recommended by the commission ban "only those services which involve either a mutual or conflicting interest with the client; the auditing of one's own work; functioning as management or an employee of the client; or acting as the client's advocate."

Bogle rightly asserts that "it is unimaginable . . . that any reasonable person could disagree *in the abstract* that such roles would threaten—or, at the very least, be perceived to threaten—the auditor's independence.

> It must also be clear that, whether or not the auditor has the backbone to maintain its independence under these circumstances, many management and consulting arrangements could easily be perceived as representing a new element in the relationship between auditor and corporation—a *business* relationship with a *customer* rather than a professional relationship with a client. Surely this issue goes to the very core of the central issue of philosophy that I expressed earlier: The movement of auditing from profession to business, with all the potential conflicts of interest that entails. So I come down with a firm endorsement of the *substance* of the proposed SEC rule, which would in effect bar such relationships.

Bogle goes on to recognize that there is some merit to some of the objections raised to the commision's recommendations.

> Of course, I have read extensive material from the opponents of that rule making the opposite case. Some arguments seem entirely worthy of consideration, especially those relating to technical—but nonetheless real—issues that engender unnecessary constraints on an auditor's entering into *any* strategic alliances or joint ventures, or that relate to the complexity in clearly defining "material direct investment" or "affiliate of the audit client" and so on. Personally, I would hope and expect that this

bevy of issues will be resolved by the profession and the Commission meeting and reasoning together.

Still, there are objections he thinks are [knee-jerk], and without merit. Again, in the light of subsequent events like the Enron Andersen situation, Bogle's insights are remarkably astute.

But other opposition seemed to me to be rather knee-jerk and strident (rather like those debates I mentioned at the outset). No, I for one don't believe the SEC proposals represent "an unwarranted and intrusive regulation" of the accounting profession. And, no, I for one do not believe that the new rules "strait-jacket" the profession. And, yes, I do believe that the growing multiplicity of inter-relationships between auditor and client is a serious threat to the concept of independence, the rock foundation of sound financial statements and fair financial markets alike. In this context, I was stunned to see this recent statement from one of the senior officers of the investment company industry group for one of the Big Five firms. "Fund companies have increasingly looked to . . . big accounting firms to help them with operational, regulatory, strategic and international decisions." If that isn't functioning as management, I'm not sure what would be.[17]

In short, the threat to independence of the auditor was known well before the Enron/Andersen case and rather than being an isolated case it was simply the one that erupted with the most notoriety. In May of 2000, Gretchen Morgensen, in an article in *The New York Times,* caught the threats to independence. She stated that,

> The issue of auditor independence has grown thornier in recent years as accounting firms have remade themselves into full-service operations, in which auditing takes a back seat to more profitable consulting services. According to the S.E.C., auditing now represents 30 percent of accounting firms' revenue, down from 70 percent in 1977, while consulting and other advisory services represent more than half of revenue, up from 12 percent.[18]

The face of the accounting profession has changed. Whereas it was natural twenty-five years ago to think of an accountant as a CPA who did auditing, auditing is no longer the chief occupation of the accountant. Auditing is no longer the great moneymaker that it once was, forcing at least the Big Five firms to expend more and more energy on other moneymaking enterprises. But such enterprises, such as financial advising, tax accounting, and management consulting have the potential to create serious conflicts of interest or at the least the serious appearance of conflicts of interest.

> The potential for conflict is that an auditor, eager to get consulting fees from a corporate customer, would not be as aggressive on its audit as he might otherwise be. John H. Biggs, chairman of TIAA-CREF, the pension fund management group, said that his organization makes it a rule to hire separate firms for audits and for consulting services. "When you're paying the auditor $3 million to do an audit and paying them $17 million to do management consulting, it's way out of balance," he said.[19]

Thus, we can conclude that because of the financial pressures on accounting firms to gain revenue from other sources, there has been a move in the profession to be less stringent about the appearance of independence. But that did not sit well with Arthur Levitt, the head of the SEC, who in a speech at New York University on May 10, 2000, stated quite clearly that auditors must not only avoid conflicts of interest, but must avoid even the appearance of such conflicts that could be seen as sacrificing their independence. According to Levitt, "It is not enough that the accountant on an engagement act independently. . . For investors to have confidence in the quality of the audit, the public must perceive the accountant as independent."[20]

But even in the light of the Enron/Andersen debacle, is it all that clear that the *mere* appearance of independence is so important? After all couldn't one argue that even though it appears one has a conflict, they might have resolved it and/or avoided it. It is simply the case that people can set aside conflicts of interest and do the right thing.

Lynn Turner, former chief accountant at the SEC, weighed in with an extensive argument for the importance of appearing independent. He cited four different authors who emphasize the importance of the appearance of independence beginning with the Justice Berger's Supreme Court opinion that we have already mentioned.

The SEC requires the filing of audited financial statements to obviate the fear of loss from reliance on inaccurate information, thereby encouraging public investment in the Nation's industries. It is therefore not enough that financial statements *be* accurate; the public must also *perceive* them as being accurate. Public faith in the reliability of a corporation's financial statements depends on the public perception of the outside auditor as an independent professional. . . . If investors were to view the auditor as an advocate for the corporate client, the value of the audit function itself might well be lost.

The accounting profession has long embraced the need for auditors to not only be, but also to appear to be, independent. Statement on Auditing Standards No. 1 states,

"Public confidence would be impaired by evidence that independence was actually lacking, and it might also be impaired by the existence of circumstances which reasonable people might believe likely to influence independence . . . Independent auditors should not only be independent in fact, they should avoid situations that may lead outsiders to doubt their independence."

Witnesses at the Commission's hearings on the auditor independence rule strongly endorsed the need for auditors to maintain the appearance of independence from audit clients. Paul Volcker, former Chairman of the Federal Reserve Board, in response to a question about investors' perceptions of a conflict of interest when auditors provide non-audit services, said, "The perception is there because there is a real conflict of interest. You cannot avoid all conflicts of interest, but this is a clear, evident, growing conflict of interest. . . ."

John Whitehead, former co-chairman of Goldman Sachs and a member of numerous audit committees testified,

"Financial statements are at the very heart of our capital markets. They're the basis for analyzing investments. Investors have every right to be able to depend absolutely on the integrity of the financial statements that are available to

them, and if that integrity in any way falls under suspicion, then the capital markets will surely suffer if investors feel they cannot rely absolutely on the integrity of those financial statements."[21]

Thus, in summary, the reasons for avoiding even the appearance of having a conflict of interest, which might affect one's independence, are obvious. In order for people to make their best judgments they need faith in the representations upon which they make those judgments. And representations made by those who have or even appear to have conflicting interests do not inspire such faith. Reasonable people, taking a common sense approach to human behavior, would think that certain relationships would affect one's behavior. A skepticism that believes where there's smoke, there's fire, serves one well. It may be that where there appears to be a conflict, there is none, but there may also be self delusion, and where the appearance of conflict is the only thing to exist, such a situation presents a temptation, that while currently is being resisted, sooner or later will probably prevail.

People respond on the basis of what they think. If I think someone is angry, I will respond differently to him or her than if I think they are in pain. Similarly, if I trust someone, I will respond differently than if I suspect him or her. Contrast the perceptions we have of an independent prosecutor with those we have of one appointed by the justice department. Whom do we trust more? Compare the perceptions we have of a police department report clearing officers of illicit behavior with a report of an independent panel of judges clearing those same officers. The appearance of dependence will have major effects on the estimation of the worth of all sorts of financial entities.

To bolster the emphasis on independence, the SEC, with its revision of rule 2-01 and because of Arthur Levitt's speech, used pressures that the SEC could bring to bear to help provoke change in the profession. Mr. Levitt addressed the rapid growth in the past two decades in management consulting work to audit clients. In a section entitled "Serving Two Masters," Mr. Levitt described how this diversification could lead an auditor too close to its client's management. "In this dual role, the auditor . . . now both oversees and answers to management." After the Enron/Andersen failure, the accounting profes-

sion, the SEC and the government are all addressing
anew the issue of auditor independence.

NOTES

1. Jonathan Weil, "Arthur Andersen's 'Double Duty' Work
   Raises Questions About Its Independence," *Wall Street
   Journal,* December 14, 2001.

2. Michael Schroeder, "Former SEC Chairman Says Enron
   Case Shows Need for Tighter Accounting Curbs," *Wall
   Street Journal,* Jan. 11, 2002.

3. Steve Silber, as quoted in Karl Stark, "Lawsuit is Filed
   Against Auditors for Allegheny," *The Philadelphia Inquirer,*
   Section D, p. 1, Thursday, April 13, 2000.

4. William F. Hamilton and William D. Callahan, "The
   Accountant as a Public Professional," in Beauchamp and
   Bowie, 3rd edition, pp. 487ff.

5. *Encyclopedia Britannica,* "Accounting."

6. Nanette Byrnes et al., "Accounting in Crisis," *Business
   Week,* January 28, 2002, p.46.

7. 464 US 805, 1984.

8. As quoted in Abraham J. Briloff, "The 'Is' and the
   'Ought'," *Accounting Today,* Sept. 6–26, 1999, p. 6ff.

9. Interestingly enough, in Germany, where most capitaliza-
   tion is done through a bank and not through securities
   (of Buher and Hayes), the role of this public auditor (the
   WPK/WIRT shafts prefers) is not as essential. The verification function is handled by the bank.

10. C. Richard Baker and Rick Stephan Hayes, "Regulating
    the Public Accounting Profession: An International
    Perspective," from http://les.man.ac.uk/cpa96/papers
    .htm/baker2.htm, p. 9.

11. Gretchen Morgenson, "S.E.C. Seeks Increased Scrutiny
    and New Rules for Accountants," *The New York Times,*

May 11, 2000, Thursday, Late Edition, Section C
Business/Financial Desk; Page 1; Column 2.

12. Phillip G. Cottell, Jr. and Terry M. Perlin, *Accounting
    Ethics: A Practical Guide for Professionals* (Quorum Books,
    1990), p. 30ff.

13. John C. Bogle, "Public Accounting: Profession or
    Business," presentation at NYU, October 16, 2000.
    Available online at www.cpaindependence.org

14. Home Page of cpeindependence.org

15. John C. Bogle, "Public Accounting: Profession or
    Business?," NYU, October 16, 2000.

16. Mr. Levitt, who led a campaign to clean up accounting-
    industry conflicts of interest during his eight-year SEC
    tenure, said Arthur Andersen's disclosure Thursday that it
    destroyed documents related to its Enron accounting
    work adds urgency to the need for outside auditors to
    accept tough oversight through a new government-spon-
    sored self-regulatory organization. He has complained
    about the inadequacy of the American Institute of
    Certified Public Accountants, the primary accounting
    oversight organization. "It's time for the industry to dis-
    count the AICPA as an oversight mechanism and put in
    place something new," he said. *WSJ,* January 2002.

17. Bogel, *op. cit.*

18. Gretchen Morgenson, "S.E.C. Seeks Increased Scrutiny
    and New Rules for Accountants," *The New York Times,*
    May 11, 2000, Thursday, Late Edition, Section C
    Business/Financial Desk; Page 1; Column 2.

19. Morgenson, ibid.

20. Adrian Michaels, *Financial Times* (London), May 11, 2000,
    pg. 44.

21. Lynn E. Turner, "Current SEC Developments:
    Independence Matters," Chief Accountant, Office of the
    Chief Accountant, U.S. Securities & Exchange
    Commission, 28th Annual National Conference on
    Current SEC Developments, December 6, 2000.

Decision Scenario A
MARTHA STEWART, IMCLONE, AND INSIDER TRADING

ImClone Systems is a publicly traded company that
developed an anti-cancer drug called Erbitux in
partnership with Bristol-Myers Squibb Co. On
Monday, December 24, 2001, executives at Bristol-
Myers learned through their attorney that the Food

and Drug Administration (FDA) would officially
notify them on Friday, December 28 that the application for FDA approval of Erbitux had been
rejected. Since both ImClone and Bristol-Myers
had a legal right to the information about their

drug, there was nothing illegal about receiving this information, although early release by the FDA was unusual.

On Christmas Day, December 25, Harlan Waksal, then ImClone's Chief Operating Officer, was informed of this information and he, in turn, informed his brother, then CEO Sam Waksal, on December 26. Records show that Sam Waksal's family began to sell large blocks of ImClone's stock on December 27. Also on December 27, Waksal himself instructed his brokers to sell his ImClone stock, but they refused to do so because they judged that a violation of SEC regulations. By the time that the FDA announcement was made public after the stock market closed on Friday December 28, Waksal's family had sold $10 million worth of ImClone. When the market opened on Monday, December 31, the value of ImClone stock was in the $30 range, down from $60 the previous week.

Martha Stewart was a long-time close friend of Sam Waksal. On December 27, Stewart also sold all her ImClone stock, nearly 4,000 shares, at a price of $58 per share for a total of $228,000. Stewart, who began her career as a stockbroker and who, at the time, sat on the Board of Directors of the New York Stock Exchange, was the founder and former CEO of Martha Stewart Omnimedia Corporation. At the time of the sale of her ImClone stock, her personal fortune was estimated to be more than $1 billion.

The details of Stewart's sale of her ImClone stock are in dispute. According to Stewart, she had placed a standing "stop-loss" order with her Merrill Lynch stockbroker, Peter Bacanovic, to sell her shares of ImClone if the share price fell below $60. Bacanovic was both a friend and broker of Sam Waksal. Records show that on the morning of December 27, Bacanovic, who was out of the office on vacation, left a message with Stewart's assistant stating that he "thinks ImClone is going to start trading downward." Later, court records established that members of the Waksal family had contacted Bacanovic's assistant, Douglas Faneuil, and tried to sell almost 40,000 shares of ImClone, worth $2.5 million, earlier that day. Stewart, who was on an airplane traveling to Mexico at the time, called Bacanovic's office from an airport later in the day and spoke with Faneuil. Records show that within 10 minutes of that call, Faneuil executed an order to sell all of Stewart's ImClone shares. Phone records also show that minutes after speaking with Faneuil,

Stewart called Waksal and left a message asking what was going on with ImClone. The following day, a Connecticut doctor, Bart Pasternak, sold his 10,000 shares of ImClone. Pasternak's wife, Mariana, was traveling with Stewart to Mexico on December 27.

Stewart claims that she had a standing order to sell ImClone stock if the price dropped below $60. The price did drop below that level in heavy trading on December 27, not surprising perhaps given all the sales of the stock by members of the Waksal family. Stewart denies that Waksal had given her any information prior to her sale and claims that she was only selling because the falling price and heavy trading volume suggested trouble.

In June 2002, Bacanovic and Faneuil were placed on administrative leave by Merrill Lynch when inconsistencies in their accounts of the trading became known. In October, Faneuil pleaded guilty to charges that he had accepted payments to withhold information about the case, and was then fired by Merrill Lynch. Soon after, Bacanovic was fired for refusing to cooperate with investigators.

Two weeks after Faneuil pled guilty, Sam Waksal also pled guilty to charges of securities fraud. The following June, Waksal was sentenced to seven years in prison and fined $4 million. Two days later, on June 5, 2003, Martha Stewart and Peter Baconovic were indicted on charges of conspiracy to obstruct justice. On March 5, 2004, Stewart and Baconovic were both convicted on nine counts of obstruction of justice, charges that had less to do with their sale of ImClone stock than with lying to investigators after the fact.

- What, exactly, is wrong with insider trading? What did Sam Waksal do wrong? Who was hurt by his actions? Would the same ethical wrong have occurred if the news about ImClone was good and Waksal bought rather than sold his stock?

- Is there an ethical difference between "insider" information and "nonpublic" information? Did the Pasternaks do anything wrong if they sold their stock on the basis of information that Stewart shared with them? Would it matter if the information was simply that Stewart had sold her own shares in ImClone?

- Assume that Waksal did inform Stewart prior to her sale; what did she do wrong if she sold on the basis of this information? Who would have been hurt by this?

- Assume that Bacanovic learned, as Waksal's broker, that the Waksal family was selling their shares of ImClone. What responsibility would he have to his other client, Stewart, regarding this information? What, if anything, did Faneuil do wrong if he informed other clients of the Waksal family's activities in selling their stock?

Decision Scenario B
TIMING MUTUAL FUNDS

Beginning in the fall of 2003, a variety of federal and state authorities have charged many of the leading mutual fund companies and brokerage firms with improperly engaging in or aiding fraudulent trading schemes. Such mutual fund companies as Putnam, Janus, Bank of America, American Express, and Bank One, as well as such well-known brokerage firms as Charles Schwab, Morgan Stanley, and Prudential Securities, have been accused of giving favored clients unfair benefits in buying and selling mutual funds. Most of the allegations involve "market timing" or "late trading" schemes in which favored clients are allowed to buy and sell mutual fund stocks while the financial markets were closed to other buyers.

Mutual funds, as the name suggests, are investment instruments in which a large number of investors pool their money to purchase a wide variety of stocks and bonds. The economies of scale created by pooling resources allow the funds to purchase more stocks than an individual alone could afford. By spreading risk across a wide variety of investments and investors, mutual funds are generally considered safe and attractive investments. In fact, as many as 100 million Americans have almost $7 trillion invested in mutual funds, much of it in the form of individual retirement accounts.

While investors own the money in the mutual fund, the fund itself is owned by a separate company, owned by separate investors. A fund manager, who works for the fund owner, invests and manages the pool of money. For example, Putnam Investments is the fifth-largest mutual fund company in the United States and is a unit of the insurance company Marsh & McLennan. Thus, the shareholders of Marsh & McLennan own Putnam, which is managed by the fund managers to make a profit for those shareholders. Putnam Investments gets its money from individual investors, who

assume that fund managers will administer the fund to provide them with safe and profitable returns. Putnam Investments was one of the mutual funds charged by federal and state regulators with fraud for engaging in market timing.

Typically, the price of a mutual fund is set once a day, after the close of financial markets. The price is established by dividing the value of all the mutual fund's stocks by the number of individual investors. "Late trading" occurs when privileged clients are allowed to buy or sell mutual fund shares after the trading day has ended. If information concerning investments occurs after the trading ends, late trades allow these privileged clients to capitalize on that information by buying additional shares destined to increase in value on the basis of good news, or sell shares destined to decrease on the basis of bad news. All other shareholders must wait until the next day when the price of the shares available for them to purchase has already risen, or fallen, with the news. "Market timing" occurs when fund managers allow privileged clients to buy and sell large numbers of shares as close to the market close as possible, thereby improving their ability to predict future share price. Such trades are generally prohibited to all but these well-placed clients because such rapid buying and selling of large numbers of shares to capture small gains adds increased costs and risks to the fund. The privileged clients gain, while most other investors face lower profits and increased risks.

Potential conflicts of interest occur because the mutual fund companies and brokerage firms can make significant profits from frequent trades of large numbers of shares. Mutual fund companies profit from both the amount of money invested with them and by the number of trades executed. In short, large investors who engage in late trading or market timing can generate significant income for the mutual fund companies and brokerage houses. Large investors use this leverage to convince fund managers to allow for late trades and market timing. Thus, fund managers are faced with a decision that is in the interests of their firms yet that runs against the best interests of those people who have invested in their funds. The problem is compounded when individual fund managers themselves engage in market timing and late trading with their own personal money.

New York State Attorney General Elliot Spitzer is one of many government officials investigating these cases. In September 2003, Spitzer released to the public several documents discovered in his investigation of the Janus mutual funds. In one e-mail, a Janus official admitted that "our stated policy is that we do not tolerate timers. As such, we won't actively seek timers, but when pressed and when we believe allowing a limited and controlled amount of timing activity will be in Janus' best interests—increased profitability—we will make exceptions." In another document, a Janus official claimed that "I

have no interest in building a business around market timers, but at the same time I do not want to turn away $10–20 million."

- What are the responsibilities of mutual fund managers? How should conflicts of interest be decided?

- Late trades and market timing usually have only a small effect on the price of a mutual fund's share. Given the large number of individual investors in a mutual fund, it is unlikely that any individual suffered anything but minuscule financial losses. In what ways, and to what degree, has anyone been hurt by these practices?

- What, if anything, is ethically wrong with market timing and late trading?

- Should the regulation of financial markets be left to the workings of a competitive market, or is there a role for significant government regulation here?

Decision Scenario C
"SOFT MONEY" IN THE SECURITIES INDUSTRY

Kickbacks are illegal payments that occur when some portion of a payment is paid back, typically to an individual who made the original payment on behalf of some third party, as an incentive for the original payment. For example, a purchasing agent for a firm is responsible for making purchases for that firm at the best available price. An illegal kickback would occur if a purchasing agent enters into an agreement with a supplier by which part of the purchase price was "kicked back" to the purchasing agent. The fiduciary obligation that the purchasing agent owes to her firm is violated when she accepts personal benefits from the supplier, since those benefits by right belong to her firm.

In recent years a practice has evolved in the financial industry that, according to some critics, amounts to little more than institutionalized kickbacks. "Soft money" payments occur when financial advisors receive payments from a brokerage firm to pay for research and analyst services that, in theory, should be used to benefit the advisors' clients. Soft

money payments get abused when this money is used for the personal benefit of the financial advisors instead.

Consider how financial investments typically work. An investor gives money to a financial advisor to be invested on her behalf. This investment advisor then deals with a brokerage firm to carry out the specific investments that the advisor chooses and pays that brokerage firm commissions on these trades. In order to make responsible decisions, the financial advisor requires significant information, ranging from stock prices to corporate performance and financial records, and technical support such as computers and software. As it turns out, the brokerage firm is often exactly in the position to supply these services. Thus has developed the practice of soft money. In soft money transactions, the broker uses some of the money paid in commissions to pay for research and information services for the financial advisor. Typically, to do this they must charge higher commissions than they otherwise would to pay for this additional service. Encouraged by this practice, an entire research industry has developed, both within large brokerage houses and independently of them, to supply just these information and analyst services.

Soft money certainly can be a legitimate practice. Assuming the soft money is used for the benefit of the investor, and assuming the investor has understood and consented to paying higher costs for this added benefit, soft dollars appear to be an ethical and legitimate business practice. In 1975, the U.S. Congress legalized soft money payments by protecting financial advisors from charges of a conflict of interest as long as they disclose such payments to their clients. Problems arise when the money for research is used for the personal benefit of the advisor or the broker, or when investors are not informed of the practice.

On September 22, 1998, the Office of Compliance, Inspections and Examinations of the United States Securities and Exchange Commission released a major report on the practice of soft money payments. This report found that most products and services obtained by advisors fell within the legal definition of allowable research. However, they also reported that 35% of broker–dealers and 28% of advisors provided or received nonresearch products and services as part of their soft money payments. Examples included payments used for office rent and equipment, personal travel and automobile expenses, employee salaries, legal expenses, college tuition costs, and even membership at a private beach club. The report also concluded that while nearly all financial advisors complied with the requirement to disclose soft money payments to their clients, the disclosure did not appear to provide sufficient information to enable clients to understand the practice. Most disclosures occurred in generic language attached in small print to their investment agreements. In many cases disclosure of nonresearch payments was completely absent. Finally, the report noted some evidence that suggests that investors are paying higher commissions as a result of the practice. In some cases, as much as 63% of the commission charged by the broker was refunded in soft money. The SEC report estimated that almost $1 billion was paid in soft money during 1997.

- Exactly what, if anything, is wrong with the practice of soft money? Who benefits from the practice? Who is harmed? Other than the investor, the advisor, and the broker, can you think of other parties who are affected by this practice?

- How might a defender of the free market, such as Milton Friedman, evaluate this practice? If a financial advisor is self-employed, whose profit ought she maximize?

- Are abuses of this practice likely to be eliminated by government regulation? Should the practice be completely outlawed, or simply regulated?

- Can you specify where to draw the line between legitimate and illegitimate uses of soft money? What exactly is the difference between soft money and a kickback?

Decision Scenario D
BUY AMERICAN, OR ELSE!

During the 1980s the U.S. automobile industry suffered significant sales losses to foreign manufacturers. The once dominant "Big Three"—General Motors, Ford, and Chrysler—were losing the competition to Japanese and European firms. As a result, the Big Three were experiencing large financial losses, U.S. autoworkers were losing their jobs, and the American consumer, apparently, was benefiting from this competition by getting quality-built cars at reasonably low prices.

By the early 1990s a major public relations campaign began to encourage U.S. consumers to "Buy American." Supported by industry, labor, and many politicians, the "Buy American" movement promoted the purchase of American cars by appealing to patriotism, loyalty, and a responsibility to one's fellow Americans.

As part of a story on the "Buy American" movement, the CBS news program *60 Minutes* visited the Detroit auto show in January 1992. During this visit, two salesmen working at the General Motors Geo exhibit were questioned about the value of buying American products. One voiced strong support for the view that Americans should buy only American cars. The second, Matt Darcy, disagreed. While the cameras recorded his words, Darcy said, "If America makes a good product, buy it. If they don't, I buy what's good for my money. I don't have to spend money because it's American."

When Darcy returned to his job as a salesman at Gordon Chevrolet in Garden City, Michigan, after the show was aired, he was fired. Gordon Stewart, owner of Gordon Chevrolet, justified this dismissal on the grounds that Darcy's comments offended many customers who worked in the auto industry. Stewart was quoted as saying, "Truth is not the issue. You have to be careful."

Darcy's own parents were both assembly line workers for General Motors. Also, at the time of this issue, many so-called "American" cars were being manufactured at General Motors and Chrysler plants in Canada, while several Japanese manufacturers were producing "foreign" cars in the United States.

- Did Matt Darcy owe any loyalty to American workers, many of whom were his customers? Did he owe more loyalty to Americans who worked for American corporations, or to Americans who were employed by Japanese corporations? Did he owe any loyalty to General Motors, the corporation that employed his parents and, indirectly, created his own job?

- How might a defender of the free market such as Milton Friedman (Reading 1.1) respond to the "Buy American" movement? What is the socially responsible position in this case?

- Would it have been wrong for Darcy to lie in this case? Could there have been other things, short of an outright lie, that he could have said that would have pleased his employer? Would it have been ethical for him to do so?

- What might Albert Carr (Reading 7.1) say about this case? What might Ron Duska (Reading 7.2) say? Does it matter that U.S. automakers were manufacturing cars in Canada at the same time that they were encouraging U.S. citizens to "Buy American" in order to support "American" workers and "American" business?

8

Product Liability
and Safety

THE HISTORY OF PRODUCT LIABILITY

NEWS FLASH: Woman spills coffee and sues McDonald's for $2.8 million! That case, perhaps more than any other in the past decade, stimulated a growing national feeling that the court system has lost all connection to common sense. It has prompted calls for change in the way the law compensates people for injuries caused by products—product liability law.

Product liability law has for decades been under attack from business and the insurance industry. However, it is also now under a legislative assault. Democrats and Republicans alike are clamoring for reforms. Advocacy ads by groups with names like "Citizens for a Sound Economy" (along with competing ads by the Trial Lawyers Association) have flooded airwaves in states with swing-vote legislators. Sifting through all the arguments about reform is a daunting task. Before we try to assess the current debate, it is best to have an understanding of how the law on product liability has developed over the years.

The earliest approach to product liability in the law was a system known as *caveat emptor*, or "Let the buyer beware." It meant that a consumer injured by a defective product was unable to sue the manufacturer and recover damages. Gradually, individual states, which have primary jurisdiction over liability law, began to shift away from *caveat emptor* as the economy became less agricultural and more industrial. By the turn of the 20th century, the usual state law on product liability had become a conjunction of two doctrines: privity of contract and the negligence standard. The privity of contract doctrine allowed suits over product-related injuries only when the parties to the suit had a contractual relationship between them. In practice, this meant that consumers were typically unable to bring product liability suits against manufacturers, since most products purchased by the consumer were obtained from a retailer, not from the manufacturer. Since there was no direct economic transaction between consumer and manufacturer, the privity doctrine disallowed liability suits against the producers of defective products. Moreover, if a consumer was allowed to bring a suit against a seller, the consumer had to establish negligence in order to prevail. In the law, negligence generally is understood as a failure to exercise due care. If a product defect had its source in the manufacturing process, and if the defect was not easily apparent on visual inspection, then the retailer who sold the product would not be negligent in most cases.

In 1916, the New York Court of Appeals issued a ruling that, over time, came to be adopted as the law in most other states. In the case of *MacPherson v. Buick Motors,* the court held a manufacturer negligent and hence liable for failure to inspect the wooden spokes of its automobile wheels for defects. The case was one of the first to remove the privity doctrine's requirement of a direct contractual relationship between plaintiff and defendant. As a result of this decision, plaintiff consumers had merely to establish the following in order to sue and recover damages from a manufacturer of a defective product: (1) an injury occurred, (2) the product was defective, (3) the injury was the result of the product defect, (4) the product came from the defendant, and (5) the defendant was negligent in letting the defective product onto the market. Proving negligence was, however, often difficult. Negligence requires that the plaintiff establish facts about the defendant's state of mind or conduct. In many cases, the information required for proof is not available. The situation in the famous Ford Pinto case—where the plaintiffs secured internal Ford memoranda that indicated Ford executives knew about the risk of gas tank explosions yet calculated it was not cost-beneficial for Ford to correct the problem—is perhaps unusual in the degree of evidence available about the defendant's state of mind.

Another watershed case was decided in 1960. A New Jersey court, in the case of *Henningsen v. Bloomfield Motors,* decided that an injured consumer should be entitled to recover damages because the axle of the car she was riding in broke. The court held that the axle was defective and the product was not reasonably fit for its intended use. The court reasoned that consumers have a right to expect that a car, as a durable good, will not have such serious defects. The court's decision announced a new doctrine of liability law—the doctrine of implied warranty. It establishes that manufacturers implicitly warrant their products to be fit for intended use by the very act of offering them for sale. The crucial aspect of this case is that it removed the fifth item required for a successful product liability suit. Consumers under this theory would not have to establish negligence.

In 1963, a California court announced a similar decision in the case of *Greenman v. Yuba Power Products.* That case, decided on principles of tort law (the area of the law covering injuries between private parties), issued in the doctrine of strict liability. From the consumer plaintiff's position, it was practically equivalent to the implied warranty theory since both approaches removed the negligence requirement.

The strict liability approach has become the dominant approach to product liability in most states since that 1963 California decision. The shift in the law from negligence to strict liability is perhaps even greater than the shift away from the privity doctrine. Whereas the negligence standard focuses on the conduct and state of mind of the defendant, the strict liability standard concerns only the quality of the product. If the product is defective (usually defined as unreasonably dangerous), the manufacturer can be required to pay damages regardless of whether it was at fault. Essentially, with the adoption of the strict liability approach, product liability law has gone from a fault-finding exercise to a mechanism for compensating those injured by product defects.

This shift from a fault-based to a compensatory standard has been defended on two grounds. First, strict liability is seen as a mechanism for spreading the costs of accidental product defects. Under negligence, if a product is defective but the manufacturer is not negligent, the cost of the injury is located entirely on the injured party. (Defects can exist without negligence because, even with the strictest design and quality control standards, a defective product can slip through the net into the stream of commerce. The only way to guarantee zero defects is to cease all production.) With a strict liability standard, such a case would result in the manufacturer or, more likely, the manufacturer's insurance company, paying the injured consumer. The cost of that payment would eventually be turned back on other consumers of the injuring product.

The second traditional defense of strict liability is that it provides an incentive for manufacturers to make their products safer. If manufacturers know that they will be liable for any defect that causes injury, then they will take extra steps to ensure products are safe and defect free. (Some have claimed that strict liability will not increase safety since manufacturers are held liable for unforeseen product defects that they cannot prevent. This, of course, makes some sense. However, it seems to apply more to design defects than to defects that are the result of the manufacturing process. Some of those latter could still be eliminated if producers had financial incentives to exercise stricter quality controls.)

The law has obviously shifted away from protection for producers and more towards protection for consumers. Some have even suggested that we now have a legal system of "seller beware." While it is true that manufacturers are now more greatly exposed to financial liability for products that cause injury, it is not the case that manufacturers are without legal defenses or that we have reached a stage of absolute liability. First, plaintiffs in product liability cases must still establish that there was a defect. Second, even if that is established, there are many legal doctrines and tactics available for defendant manufacturers. Manufacturers can argue that the consumer misused the product (although the misuse cannot be one that was reasonably foreseeable, for that again makes the producer liable). They can prove that the consumer was contributorily negligent, for example by showing that the defect was obvious and that the consumer used the product anyway. They can argue that the product's inherent risks were patently known and that the consumer therefore voluntarily assumed the risk. (This has been quite a successful line of defense used by tobacco manufacturers. See Decision Scenario A, "Tobacco Companies Under Fire.") Producers can argue that the product contained a warning. Finally, they can claim that, although the product risk cannot be eliminated, the product provides great social utility. (Drugs are often placed in this last category.)

ASSESSING PRODUCT LIABILITY ALTERNATIVES

If we reflect on this brief historical sketch, we can imagine four broad policy alternatives for how to assign liability for defective products that cause injury. At one extreme, we could adopt a policy of *caveat emptor*. Under this policy, consumers would be unable to recover damages, and business would be totally insulated from liability suits.

Next, we can imagine a negligence approach similar to the one that predominated in the law between 1916 and 1963. Under this standard, consumers have increased opportunity to receive compensation relative to the first approach. Business, however, would be that much more exposed to financial liability for the consequences of its products.

Then, we can imagine the strict liability system of the recent past. Under this approach, a business would be held strictly liable for *any* injuries caused by a defective product. The costs of such injuries would initially be located on the business itself through its insurance premiums. Ultimately, those costs would be reflected in product prices.

Finally, we could imagine a hybrid policy that has been suggested as an alternative to the current approach. It would locate financial responsibility for injuries on the individual business when the defect was the result of negligence. However, if the defect were a pure accident, that is, not the result of corporate negligence, the consumer would still recover, but the monies would come from a general fund to which we all, as taxpayers, contribute. The idea of this hybrid is to retain the compassionate compensation for the injured found under strict liability but to lessen the financial burden on business.

As you read the cases and readings of this chapter, try to identify the advantages and disadvantages of each of these broad policies. For example, *caveat emptor* might provide for a greater variety and for cheaper products, since insurance for liability would not be a cost of doing business. It would also allow more consumer injuries to occur. Alternatively, strict liability with businesses purchasing private insurance to cover the costs of defect-related injuries would increase product costs. But it would also maximize the manufacturer's incentive to produce safe products, because the more numerous the injury-causing defects, the higher its insurance premiums will be. We encourage you to identify other benefits/costs of these four alternatives. Only after such an analysis can you arrive at an adequately informed decision about which alternative is the best public policy.

Before addressing specific legal reforms now under discussion, we should discuss a few criticisms that have been leveled against the current strict liability approach. Opponents of the current American system deride it as the most costly in the world. (Note the cost estimates in the first reading of the chapter.) They maintain that it harms American industry's competitiveness and costs the United States jobs. They argue that American business pays 10 to 50 times more for product liability insurance than does its international competition. Our largest trading partner, Canada, for instance, does not have the costs of a strict liability system. There, manufacturers are generally liable only for negligently caused product defects.

Opponents also charge the liability system as partly responsible for a decline in the willingness of Americans to accept responsibility for their actions. They point to a cultural climate where whatever bad happens to a person must be someone else's fault. Critics also claim that the system, with its potential for large awards, encourages fraudulent or frivolous suits that are filed as fishing expeditions by greedy lawyers and their clients. (In Philadelphia, known for its high number of insurance fraud cases, a woman filed a fraudulent suit against the public transit agency for injuries purportedly sustained in a train accident. Unfortunately for the woman, the "train accident" she saw reported on the news, and in which she claimed to be injured, was merely a report on an emergency preparedness drill!) As a result, the critics claim, we have experienced a flood of product liability lawsuits in recent years.

Those in favor of strict liability must admit that with every reduction in what a plaintiff must prove to win an award, more frivolous or fraudulent suits are possible. They also need to recognize a concern about the effect of the legal system on cultural attitudes. However, they argue that a return to negligence in order to avoid the economic costs of the current tort system would be a draconian overreaction that penalizes those who are the greatest victims, the seriously injured. And, they contend, strict liability has not created the difficulties alleged. They note that much of the litigation over the past 20 years is against a small number of defendants. If one removes the mass tort cases for damaging products, such as the Dalkon Shield (see Decision Scenario D on that case) or asbestos, the litigation flood slows remarkably. Proponents also point to reports that suggest the costs of the system are often overstated. A Rand study found that only 10 percent of those injured in product accidents ever bring suit.

Still, a problem must be recognized for small businesses that operate on narrow profit margins and yet have radically increasing insurance costs. There are questions, though, about whether the increase in insurance premiums is justified by the amount paid out in damage awards to victims. It is certainly true that many of the large jury verdicts that are reported in the news are subsequently reduced on appeal. The question, then, is whether the problems of the product liability system are severe enough to justify abandoning a strict liability approach in favor of one of the other alternatives. Some argue that any problems that exist can be addressed by marginal changes in the law. Others hold that adequate corrections demand a more wholesale change in liability rules.

Those in favor of more radical change often charge that the system of strict liability is unfair to business. They argue that business ought not be held responsible for accidents that are beyond its control. No matter how rigid the quality control standards of a business, a defective product might still slip through. As we have seen, that business will be financially liable for injuries that its product causes. Business lobbyists, however, point out that the business in that instance is not morally responsible for the injuries. Being forced to pay for negligence is one thing, they argue; being forced to pay for unforeseen, and perhaps unforeseeable, defects is quite another.

The reading by John McCall addresses this question of fairness. McCall suggests that many objections to the traditional defenses are ultimately questions about fairness. He argues that an adequate understanding of fairness will show that strict liability is compatible with fairness, and perhaps even required by it. He contends that when the traditional justifications of safety and cost sharing are conjoined with an adequate understanding of fairness, they are sufficient justification for adopting strict liability as our overall public policy. McCall notes, however, some problematic cases in which the legitimacy of the current standard may be called into question.

REFORMING PRODUCT LIABILITY LAW

Even some of those who are generally sympathetic to strict liability are now urging reform of liability law. Many, as noted in the reading from the Bush White House Council of Economic Advisors, regard the current system as imposing excessive costs on the society. One could imagine that such concerns might drive a move towards radical reform of the law. However, the recent reform proposals under consideration by both the House and Senate are more tinkering at the margins of the law rather than a wholesale reform of strict liability.

In the late 1990s, both the House and Senate passed bills changing liability law. Generally, those reform bills limited punitive damage awards to successful plaintiffs to the greater of $250,000 or three times the award for lost wages and medical expenses. They also capped pain and suffering awards at the same $250,000 figure. They sometimes required plaintiffs in federal liability cases to pay the defendant's legal fees if the plaintiff rejected a settlement offer and the jury award was less than that offer (a provision known as "loser pays"). Finally, they prohibited punitive damage awards in cases where a drug or medical device had FDA approval. However, the bills passed by the Congress were vetoed by President Clinton. More recent reform efforts in the federal Congress have stalled in the U.S. Senate. Advocates of reform have responded by attempting more piecemeal legislation that protects particular industries or businesses from liability lawsuits. In 2004 alone, Republicans in Congress were able to pass bills in the House of Representatives that would have prohibited liability judgments against the Texas manufacturer of a gasoline additive suspected of causing cancer, against gun manufacturers faced with suits alleging improper marketing that permitted criminals to acquire handguns (see both the reading by George Brenkert and Decision Scenario B on gun marketing), and against fast-food restaurants charged with responsibility for the increasing levels of obesity among Americans. As this text goes to press in the spring of 2004, none of these bills was able to garner a majority in both houses of Congress, however.

Reform advocates have had much more success at the state level. That is perhaps a more significant result given that most product liability law falls within state court jurisdictions. Caps on punitive damages and on awards for noneconomic damages (such as, for pain and suffering) have been passed by 24 states since the liability reform movement began in earnest in the mid 1980s (though some of those state laws have been struck down by state court decisions). States have also focused on specific areas of concern. Recently, medical malpractice rules have gained substantial attention. Spurred by stories of physicians facing doubled or even tripled premiums for liability insurance and by reports of physicians abandoning their practices in specialties such as obstetrics, legislatures have adopted special rules for medical liability lawsuits. Most frequently these include the now standard $250,000 limit on any pain and suffering compensation award.

There are serious questions, however, about whether these medical liability reforms will solve the identified problem. Some suspect that caps will do little to ease the insurance crisis. One Texas study noted, for instance, that noneconomic damages remained fairly constant during the period between 1988 and 2000. It found that the real increases in awards came in areas such as compensation for medical expenses and lost earnings. Insurance industry spokespeople, however, contended that a cap on pain and suffering awards would allow them to reduce liability insurance premiums for physicians by 12 percent.

More generally, those in favor of liability law reforms often claim that they are needed to restore fairness to the liability system and to remove innovation-stifling burdens on the competitiveness of American business. Critics of the reforms see proposals such as "loser pays" or the limits on plaintiff attorney legal fees as effectively removing access to the court system for many consumers. They also find the limits on punitive damages to be unnecessary and insufficient to deter wrongdoing by larger corporations. They note that punitive damage awards are a relatively small percentage of total awards. Critics of the recent reforms also contend that a limit of $250,000 on noneconomic damages will be insufficient to compensate the most seriously injured plaintiffs for their very real suffering.

It seems likely that federal and state legislatures will continue to attempt reforms in product liability law. We hope that the material in this chapter will allow you to assess both the current and future debates.

PRODUCT SAFETY REGULATION

If product liability law is about how and when to assess damages once a product injury has occurred, product safety regulation is about preventing accidents from happening in the first place. The current legal approach to product safety regulation is known as a standards enforcement approach. The government, through executive agencies such as the Consumer Product Safety Commission (CPSC) and the Food and Drug Administration, mandates that products meet certain safety standards if they are to be available for sale. The agencies have the authority to ban products from the market, to order recalls, and to impose fines for violations of mandated standards. (As with all administrative agencies' decisions, these actions of the CPSC and FDA are subject to appeal; the agencies are not the final authorities in these matters.)

This form of government regulation of consumer products has met with some resistance. One of the main complaints against safety standards is that those standards take too little notice of the costs that they impose on business and on society generally. Often, critics charge, business is made less efficient, products more costly, and jobs scarcer because of safety-oriented regulations. Obviously, we cannot eliminate product risks. What we must decide is when levels of risk are acceptable, which is a rough definition of "safety." Those critical of current safety regulation would have us answer this question by engaging in a formal cost-benefit analysis before promulgating any new safety standard. Many critics, for instance, suggest that our current regulations are often the result of public overestimation of the risks of harms. They believe that, as a society, we spend more trying to avoid minimal risks that gain public attention than we spend on more serious and more likely public health problems. In response to this perceived misallocation of national resources, reform legislation has been introduced into Congressional debate; it would require all federal agencies to conduct a complex review of regulatory costs and benefits that would then be subject to both corporate comment and judicial review. However, critics of the use of technical cost-benefit analysis in the context of safety regulation note that safety benefits are difficult to quantify in dollar terms. The standard methods used to assign dollar values to safety benefits have serious conceptual difficulties. For example, measuring the dollar value of safety by determining what consumers are willing to pay for safety in the market (a willingness-to-pay methodology) depends on assumptions that consumers have adequate information about the safety profile of the products they purchase. That assumption may not be accurate.

Another major criticism against safety regulation is that it expresses a paternalistic attitude towards consumers. Since the agencies set standards that all products in a given market must meet, the agencies also prevent consumers from choosing for themselves just what mix of safety features they are willing to pay for. Critics maintain that protecting consumers from their own choices is a paternalistic interference with consumer autonomy. Given the value placed on autonomy in Chapters Two and Three (and elsewhere throughout this text), that is a most serious charge. It is a charge made more serious since most protective legislation follows this same standards enforcement approach. (Consider the EPA, OSHA, and other agencies.) If the charge holds, and protective regulation is unjustifiably paternalistic, we would have an argument for dismantling much of the federal bureaucracy and for letting consumer demand determine safety levels through free-market bargaining.

A number of responses to this charge are possible. One could admit that regulation is paternalistic and claim that the paternalism is justified either because citizens are incapable of making intelligent choices (the justification for treating children paternalistically) or because the social benefits of paternalism are great enough to justify it. In our society, neither of these justifications is compatible with the deep-seated commitment to individual autonomy.

A second line of argument against the charge of paternalism is provided by those who contend that consumer choice in the marketplace is not really free. Proponents of regulatory standards who argue this way will claim that there are significant enough market imperfections that government intervention is needed in order to protect consumers. The pure market approach, they argue, places individual consumers in an unequal bargaining position that in fact jeopardizes their autonomy.

A third response would be to defend regulatory action as a way of protecting the rights of third parties. Laws requiring motorcyclists to wear safety helmets, for example, have been urged as a way of reducing the need for taxation to support the care of individuals who suffer severe brain damage in accidents. Similar arguments are obvious in the case of gun regulations.

A final line of response argues that safety regulation is not really paternalistic. It attempts to prove that it is economically rational for the consumer to autonomously surrender to the government his or her authority to choose. Such surrender is rational, they claim, when the costs of making the decision oneself are great. Note that this argument is not intended as a particular defense of every instance of government regulation.

Recently, one of the oldest federal consumer safety agencies, the FDA, came under fire in a different way. Critics of the agency charged that its drug and medical device approval process is still too slow, despite recent attempts to streamline the process and get life-saving medications onto the market more quickly. Previous House Speaker Newt Gingrich, in fact, called the FDA "America's leading job-killer." Critics have proposed both more streamlining of the approval process and a narrowing of the agency's charter. Now, the agency is responsible for assuring that drugs and medical devices are safe *and* efficacious. Reformers are suggesting that the agency limit its review to assuring safety and let consumers in the market determine if products are effective. That way, they argue, life-saving drugs and devices will be available sooner. Opponents of the reform worry that the narrowed charter will result in consumer purchases of useless products that will sometimes delay effective treatments. As you can see from this brief survey, the advisability and effectiveness of government safety regulation will continue to be subject to debate.

ETHICS AND THE MARKETING
OF DANGEROUS PRODUCTS

Whatever view you take on the issue of government regulatory action, there remains a further question for you to address. It is a question about what *ethical* standards should be used in assessing the marketing of dangerous products. We need to remember that it is possible for an act to be legal and yet not morally appropriate. It is possible, then, that the sale of some products would be legal but immoral. Some critics of the tobacco industry consider the sale of cigarettes to be an instance of this.

One reason for the difference between an action's legality and its moral acceptability is that the law is not always a desirable method for enforcing moral norms. For example, sometimes the law should not attempt to enforce a moral norm because that attempt will cause more moral problems than it solves, as some would say was the result of the Prohibition Era's attempt to enforce abstinence from alcohol. So, before we use law to enforce a moral norm, we need to ask whether the enforcement will be effective, whether it will lead to a decline in respect for law generally, and whether it will predictably cause other, significant harms.

This caution about using the law to enforce all of morality only makes more pressing the need to supplement your assessment of government safety regulation with a parallel moral assessment of the practice of marketing dangerous products. One possible moral assessment would be to argue that the autonomy of both consumer and seller generates a moral right to sell any product for which there is market demand.

This use of autonomy will not work, however. It merely is an application of the extreme *laissez faire* understanding of liberty that was discarded in Chapter Three. Autonomy does not mean having a right to do whatever one pleases. Rather, autonomy must be linked to areas of life that are of crucial importance for an adequate human existence. Buying or selling a particular product seems unlikely to qualify for that lofty status. There are intuitively reasonable cases where the sale of products is limited but where the extreme understanding of autonomy would object to those limits. The most addictive and dangerous of the currently illegal drugs are examples. Moreover, even if we acknowledge a right to sell any product that we wish to, that does not automatically mean that selling it is morally appropriate. Having a right to do something does not entail that you ought to do it, all things considered.

At the other extreme is a view holding that it is unethical to market any product that predictably causes harm or whose net social impact is negative. This, too, seems unacceptable. While the harmful consequences of products are a matter of serious concern, this method of assessment is merely the utilitarian approach that was challenged in Chapter Two. And, while the first approach gives too much weight to consumer and seller desires, this utilitarian approach appears to give too little weight to consumer sovereignty.

Another approach to the moral evaluation of the sale of harmful products would be to say that it is acceptable to sell products that are dangerous if consumers are adequately warned about those dangers. However, there is evidence that warnings are often not processed by consumers or are not forceful enough. Also, some question whether mere warnings are enough to morally justify marketing a dangerous product when the seller spends millions in advertising and public relations to counteract the effect of any warnings. Hence, some who accept the sale of harmful products argue that it is not morally appropriate to promote and advertise those products.

Others suggest that while it may be acceptable to sell potentially harmful products, with appropriate warnings, to wary adults, producers have a moral obligation to assure that those products are not sold in ways that provide easy access for minors.

We urge you to morally assess if, when, and how dangerous products should be sold. In developing such a position, you need to make specific reference to all the different products that people claim are dangerous. Should sales of tobacco, guns, alcohol, heroin, and crack cocaine all be assessed similarly? Or are there differences in the products that will justify reaching a different moral conclusion for each of these products? Whatever the law says, or whatever you believe the law *ought* to say, an ethical evaluation of their sale is still essential.

CASE STUDY Caution: McDonald's Coffee is HOT!— And Its Food Will Make You FAT!

Feeling the Heat

On February 27, 1992, 79-year-old Stella Liebeck was burned after spilling on her lap a cup of coffee that she had purchased at a McDonald's drive-through window. She brought suit against McDonald's and was awarded a jury verdict of $2.86 million—$160,000 in compensatory damages and $2.7 million in punitive damages. A judge reduced the punitive damage award to $480,000, or three times the amount of the award for the injury. McDonald's and Liebeck subsequently settled out of court for an undisclosed amount.

The initial jury award received quite a bit of media attention—most of it critical. And the award became a rallying cry for those interested in reform of the current product liability law. Advocacy ads excoriating the award as an example of the legal system gone haywire appeared on radio and television as the Congress was beginning debate on liability reform.

The legal case began when Ms. Liebeck requested $10,000 for medical expenses and an additional amount for pain and suffering. McDonald's refused a settlement. Liebeck's initial demand in court was for $300,000. The company argued, however, that the coffee was not unreasonably dangerous and that Liebeck was responsible for her own injuries. The jury obviously evaluated the case differently than did McDonald's or much of the media.

This case was prepared from information in the following sources: *Dateline NBC,* April 28, 1995; *Consumer Reports,* May, 1995, p. 312; *Jury Verdict Research, Liebeck v. McDonald's Restaurants,* Case # CV 932419; "Special Report: 'The first thing we do, let's kill all the lawyers,'" from the Consumer Freedom Foundation at www.consumerfreedom.com/headline_detail.cfm?HEADLINE_ID= 1500; "Whopper of a Lawsuit," Geraldine Sealey, July 26, 2002 at www.abc.com; *Pelman v McDonald's,* 237 F. Supp. 2d 512.

The jury's verdict was driven by a number of factors. McDonald's served its coffee at 185 degrees Fahrenheit, far higher than the temperature of typical home-brewed coffee. The jury found that coffee at that temperature was both undrinkable and more dangerous than a reasonable consumer would expect (part of the definition of a defective product). The coffee was hot enough to cause third degree burns over an extensive portion of Liebeck's thighs and buttocks. The injury required skin grafting and resulted in scarring.

Testimony at trial revealed that McDonald's had over 700 past burn claims lodged against it. The company claimed that it served the coffee at that temperature in response to consumer demand, but it had done no survey to assess the sales impact of coffee served at lower temperatures. As a result of past claims, McDonald's had put a warning on the cup and had designed a tighter-fitting lid. The latter, ironically, may have been a factor in Liebeck's injury; she held the cup between her legs in order to pry the lid off.

The jury found that Liebeck was 20 percent responsible for her own injury, but it also found McDonald's warning was not sufficiently noticeable to alert consumers to the danger. The punitive damage award of $2.7 million was, jurors later said, an attempt to send a message to fast-food chains. The amount was approximately two days of coffee sales for McDonald's. The judge reduced that punitive damage award. In doing so, however, he said that McDonald's action was "willful, wanton, reckless and callous."

Supersized Suits

Almost exactly 10 years after Ms. Liebeck's injury, Caesar Barber, a 5'10" 270 lb. man with a history of diabetes and heart attacks and also a habit of eating at McDonald's several times a week, filed a class-action lawsuit alleging that McDonald's was negligent in selling food laden in fat, cholesterol, salt, and sugar. His suit asked the court to hold McDonald's liable for its part in the epidemic of obesity now confronting the United States. Barber later admitted on a national television news show that he had failed to follow his doctor's advice by continuing to eat fast food even after his first heart attack.

Barber's lawyer withdrew the suit, but his explorations into liability lawsuits against the fast-food industry were not over. One month later, in August of 2002, he filed a class-action suit against McDonald's on behalf of two children and their parents, as well as unnamed others. The children were significantly overweight and as a result suffered from diabetes, high cholesterol, high blood pressure, and coronary heart disease. The suit, *Pelman v. McDonald's*, alleged that McDonald's was in substantial part responsible for the children's ills. Damages were sought based on claims that McDonald's had engaged in deceptive advertising and was negligent both in selling dangerous products and in failing to warn consumers. (In an earlier and unrelated deceptive advertising suit, McDonald's settled for $10 million with a group who claimed that they were misled by McDonald's advertising into believing that the chain's fries were vegetarian fare when, in fact, they were fried largely in beef lard.)

Obesity has become a major health problem in the United States. In March 2004, the Surgeon General released a report identifying obesity as the second-leading cause of preventable death in the United States, trailing only cigarette smoking. Each year, approximately 400,000 people in the United States die of obesity-related health problems. At the turn of the 21st century, obesity rates are nearly double what they were 20 years earlier, and the problem is especially troubling among the young. Today, at least 13 percent of children aged 6–11 and 14 percent of adolescents aged 12–19 are overweight or obese. In 1980, only 7 percent of children and 5 percent of adolescents fell into those categories. Obese persons face a 50 percent to 100 percent increased risk of premature death. Those deaths are complications of the heart disease, diabetes, hypertension, and cancer that accompany the extra weight.

A federal judge in New York initially dismissed the *Pelman* suit, but he did so "without prejudice," an indication that the plaintiffs were free to file an amended complaint. The judge took the unusual step of writing a lengthy opinion in which he provided clear instructions on how the suit might be amended to increase its chance of success. He even provided examples from past cases where similar allegations of deception and negligence were accepted by the courts.

On the charge of deceptive advertising, the judge found that the plaintiffs had not produced any specific advertisements as examples. Nor had the plaintiffs produced any evidence that there was a causal connection between McDonald's advertising and the health effects suffered. The judge required that any amended complaint address these failings. In fact, the judge gave a blueprint for refiling by noting past successful cases against McDonald's for deceptively advertising that "salt was down across the menu" and for emphasizing low cholesterol in some of its foods that were high in saturated fat. (While the foods themselves were low in cholesterol, they contained high levels of saturated fat, which produces increased blood cholesterol when processed by the body.) He indicated that the courts might look more favorably on the suit if it produced examples of such ads and provided evidence that the plaintiffs had relied on them.

On the negligence charges, the judge also found that the allegations were not substantiated. But he again noted how an amended complaint might succeed. He instructed the plaintiffs to provide a basis for assessing that McDonald's foods were more dangerous to health than a reasonable consumer would understand, perhaps by reference to the highly processed nature of the chain's products. He suggested that the plaintiff's attorneys pursue the charge that McDonald's foods were potentially not fit for their intended use by showing that advertising presented the foods as intended for daily consumption. And he invited the plaintiff's attorney to provide evidence that McDonald's was the proximate cause of the health problems. He recommended that the complaint include information about how frequently they ate at McDonald's and how it was unlikely that their health problems were the result of other causative factors. Finally, he indicated that an amended filing must show that McDonald's failed to warn consumers in an adequate way about unrecognized health dangers of its food.

The suit was refiled a few months after the initial dismissal. The judge this time dismissed the suit "with prejudice" because the amended complaint failed to include the arguments that he had suggested in the earlier opinion. He chastised the plaintiffs' attorneys and barred them from filing this same suit in the future.

Early in 2004, two related stories made the news. The U.S. House of Representatives passed a bill that would prohibit civil liability lawsuits against the fast-food industry. At press time for this text, however, the bill had not been adopted by the Senate. And McDonald's announced that it was discontinuing its famous promotional campaign that encouraged consumers to "supersize" by purchasing larger portions of fries and drinks for a few pennies extra.

- Punitive damage awards exist in order to deter future harmful actions. What level of award do you believe is necessary to achieve that deterrence effect? When would a cap on such awards undercut the purpose of the awards?
- How can a jury apportion responsibility for injury between plaintiff and defendant? What principles could be used to establish a respective percentage responsibility as was done in the Liebeck case?
- Was McDonald's action in the coffee case reckless as the judge claimed? Can a corporation legitimately block such a charge if it has evidence of customer preferences to explain its actions?

- Given the facts as presented, if you had been on the jury, would you have voted with all the other jurors to award Liebeck damages? Would you have awarded the same amount?
- What differences do you see in the coffee and obesity cases? Are those differences relevant enough to warrant different conclusions in the two cases?
- The judge in the *Pelman* case initially seemed willing to entertain the idea that a fast-food restaurant might be legally liable for obesity-related health problems suffered by customers. Is there basis for his apparent openness? Would it ever be reasonable to hold a corporation responsible for the effects of customers' food selections?
- What do you think of the wisdom of creating a permanent barrier to lawsuits against an industry or a company through targeted legislation?

READING 8.1 WHO PAYS FOR TORT LIABILITY CLAIMS? AN ECONOMIC ANALYSIS OF THE U.S. TORT LIABILITY SYSTEM

George W. Bush's White House Council of Economic Advisers

INTRODUCTION

With estimated annual direct costs of nearly $180 billion,[1] or 1.8 percent of GDP, the U.S. tort liability system is the most expensive in the world, more than double the average cost of other industrialized nations that have been studied.[2] This cost has grown steadily over time, up from only 1.3 percent of GDP in 1970, and only 0.6 percent in 1950. The current cost amounts to nearly $650 for every citizen of the United States, and is one reason that many commentators have called for reform of the tort liability system. The cost is especially troubling because only 20 percent of these dollars actually go to claimants for economic damages, such as lost wages or medical expenses.

Defenders of the status quo argue that the existing system protects consumers by making firms responsible for damages caused by their products and services.[3] Indeed, the underlying notion that firms are induced to recognize the full social cost of their products is one economic rationale for an *efficient* tort system.[4] That is, just as firms must pay compensation to employees and suppliers as part of the cost of producing output, ideally tort liability forces the firm to consider the potential for damage that the firm's products may cause. In this sense, it is analogous to "making polluters pay."

However, poorly designed policies can mistakenly make polluters pay too much and impose excessive costs on society through forgone production of public and private goods and services. Tort law alters firm behavior in a socially desirable manner if tort liability claims are optimal. If claims are excessive and fail to provide proper incentives, then these claims are a drain on resources that can deter the production of desired goods and services and reduce economic output. The United States bears the burden of an expensive and inefficient liability system through higher prices, lower wages, and

From "Who Pays for Tort Liability Claims? An Economic Analysis of the U.S. Tort Liability System," by the White House Council of Economic Advisers, April 2002; accessed via http://www.whitehouse.gov/cea/tortliabilitysystem_apr02.pdf.

decreased returns to investment, as well as lower levels of innovation.

The similarity between inefficient tort litigation and taxes suggests that the economic costs of the tort liability system may be better understood by pursuing the analogy between the expected costs arising from the tort system and taxes on firms. As with a tax, it is possible to examine the question of who bears the incidence of—that is, who pays for—excessive tort costs. An important lesson in the economics of taxation is that *people* pay taxes; firms are legal entities that can bear no real burden. Put differently, the burden of any tax depends not on who writes the check (the legal liability), which may be the firm, but rather on the market outcomes that shift the cost to workers, consumers or owners of capital.

WHAT ARE THE ROLE AND LIMITS OF LIABILITY LAWS IN A MARKET ECONOMY?

The production and sale of nearly every economic good or service entails a degree of risk, however small, that the product may cause unintended harm. Children can be injured playing with toys, patients may have adverse reactions to medications or medical procedures, and workers may fall off ladders or be injured by machinery. Because consumers often have less than perfect information about these risks and are generally unable to insure against them, the government plays a potentially important role in promoting health and safety.

Many policy tools are available to address such risks, including a reliance on market forces, contracts, direct regulation, social insurance, and the legal liability system. Each approach has its relative strengths and weaknesses, and reliance on any single one may not be desirable.[5] In the United States, the tort system of legal liability is sometimes viewed as contributing to overall social objectives by ensuring that firms consider more fully the health and safety aspects of their products.

A guiding insight is that competition in private markets for goods and services pushes firms to produce the kinds of goods that consumers prefer using the most efficient combination of labor, capital and other inputs. If consumers and firms are already faced with incentives to weigh the social costs and benefits of their respective consumption and production decisions, the burden of government policy is to preserve economic efficiency by avoiding intervention.

For some transactions, however, it may be infeasible to account fully for all of the relevant benefits and costs. A consumer purchasing a new car, for example, may have neither the technical expertise nor the information necessary to fully evaluate the risk of injury posed by a particular design feature. It could also be costly to obtain complete information on every key aspect. Alternatively, a patient purchasing a medical procedure, for example, may be unlikely to fully understand the complex risks, costs and benefits of that procedure relative to others. Such a patient must turn to a physician who serves as a "learned intermediary," though there remains the problem that the patient may also not be able to judge the skill of the physician from whom the procedure is "purchased." In such a case, the ability of the individual to pursue a liability lawsuit in the event of an improper treatment, for example, provides an additional incentive for the physician to follow good medical practice. Indeed, from a broad social perspective, this may be the least costly way to proceed—less costly than trying to educate every consumer fully. In a textbook example, recognition of the expected costs from the liability system causes the provider to undertake the extra effort or care that matches the customer's desire to avoid the risk of harm. This process is what economists refer to as "internalizing externalities." In other words, the liability system makes persons who injure others aware of their actions, and provides incentives for them to act appropriately.

Central to this view, however, is the notion that the exposure of firms to potential tort liability costs provides proper incentives. In the specific context of punitive damages, Professor W. Kip Viscusi of Harvard University makes the point that "the linchpin of any law and economics argument in favor of punitive damages is that these awards alter incentives."[6] In his research on corporate decisions regarding environmental and safety torts, Viscusi evaluates the effect of punitive damages "by examining the risk performance in the four states that do not permit punitive damages as compared with other states that do." He finds that "this detailed effort to detect a deterrent effect yielded no evidence of any safety incentive role. This lack of evidence is consistent with the proposition that puni-tive damages are random." If punitive damages are essentially random, then they will not provide proper incentives for risk mitigation. Instead, they will operate purely as a "tax" on firms—a cost with no corresponding benefit.

Some scholars disagree with Viscusi's conclu-sion. For example, Professor David Luban of Georgetown University argues that one should consider the "retributive aims of punishment" as well as the deterrent aims.[7] However, tort liability only achieves a goal of retribution if the economic burden of the punishment is borne by the responsi-ble party, which may not be the case if the costs are ultimately passed through to investors, workers or consumers, or if punitive damages are essentially random, as Viscusi argues. Professor Theodore Eisenberg of Cornell Law School and several coau-thors take an alternate view, claiming that tort lia-bility is largely predictable and is therefore capable of providing proper incentives to firms.[8] However, while both authors question Viscusi's findings, nei-ther provides direct empirical evidence to indicate that punitive damages actually have a deterrent effect. In fact, the empirical evidence that Eisenberg and co-authors do offer is consistent with the possi-bility that punitive damages are awarded on a ran-dom basis, as noted by Professor A. Mitchell Polinsky of Stanford University.[9]

Other research has examined the effect of expected tort liability costs on innovation and investments in safety. At lower levels of expected lia-bility costs, Viscusi and Professor Michael Moore of Duke University[10] find that firms have incentives to invest in product safety research in an effort to reduce liability costs while still bringing a particular product to market. At higher levels of expected lia-bility costs, however, firms will choose to forgo innovation or to withhold a product from the mar-ket, resulting in a net negative effect of expected liability costs on innovation. Based on their esti-mates, Viscusi and Moore identify many industry groups for which high liability costs exert a net negative effect on innovation.

Industry-specific studies by other authors have generally supported the results of Viscusi and Moore, documenting negative effects of liability on innovation in many areas, such as general aviation, chemicals, pharmaceuticals, and medical practice. The evidence of direct linkages between liability

and safety in industry-specific analyses has been weak. Other factors, such as regulation and the fear of bad publicity, may provide stronger incentives to improve safety features than does legal liability, though liability may play an indirect role by encouraging the spread of safety-related informa-tion and by bringing potential hazards to the atten-tion of regulators.[11]

Reconciling these alternative views is beyond the scope of this paper. Instead, recognizing the controversy that exists about the incentive effects of tort liability in general, and punitive damages in particular, this paper will consider several scenarios. For our most cautious estimates of the size of the "litigation tax," we make the very strong assump-tion that both economic (e.g., loss of wages, medical expenses) and non-economic (e.g., pain and suffer-ing, loss of consortium, punitive) damages are cur-rently set at an optimal level. We then consider an intermediate case that treats non-economic dam-ages as essentially random and therefore part of the litigation tax. Finally, we consider the case in which all of the costs of the U.S. tort system are treated as economically excessive, which would result if both economic and non-economic damages were largely random and failed to provide proper incentives.

WHAT ARE THE DIRECT COSTS OF THE U.S. TORT LIABILITY SYSTEM?

In the year 2000, according to a study by Tillinghast-Towers Perrin, the U.S. tort system cost $179 billion. This includes $128 billion of "insured" costs derived from financial data for the U.S. insur-ance industry. These data "are considered highly reliable in that they are subject to audit and reviewed by state regulatory agencies."[12] The costs include benefits paid to third parties or their attor-neys, claim handling, legal defense costs and insur-ance company administrative costs. Tillinghast estimates that $30 billion in costs is paid by firms that insure themselves. Finally, they estimate that an additional $21 billion is due to medical malpractice. We will make use of these Tillinghast estimates for illustrative purposes in this paper, although the main conceptual contribution of this paper—that exces-sive tort claims act as a tax paid by individuals— would hold with equal force with any alternative measure of direct costs.

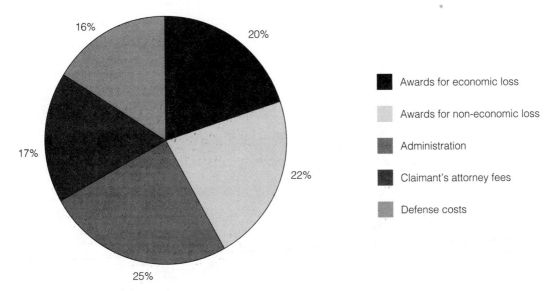

FIGURE 1. Distribution of Liability Costs

SOURCE: Tillinghast-Towers Perrin, "U.S. Tort Costs: 2000, Trends and Findings on the Costs of the U.S. Tort System," February 2002. Reprinted with permission.

The estimate of nearly $180 billion in direct costs of the U.S. tort system is likely to understate substantially the actual costs of the tort system for several reasons. First, the $180 billion estimate predates September 11. The terrorist attacks have increased the uncertainty surrounding legal liability claims. Insurance companies, uncertain how to assess new liability risks, are raising premiums and capping or denying coverage. As such, the cost of the tort system in the future will likely be even greater than the year 2000 estimates employed herein. Second, this estimate ignores the many economic distortions that arise as a result of individuals and firms trying to avoid lawsuits. These costs, which will be discussed in more detail below, can include distortions to labor markets (e.g., doctors deciding not to practice certain specialties or in particular communities for fear of being sued), the practice of "defensive medicine," or the decision by manufacturers to keep products off the market.[13] Third, this estimate also ignores the potential deleterious effect of excessive tort claims on innovation. In product areas where litigation is frequent and costly, the prospect of high liability claims may be enough to ward off any potential new entrants.

Lacking a more comprehensive estimate of total costs, however, we will use the $180 billion as an initial conservative estimate of total tort costs. An even more difficult issue is deciding how much of this $180 billion is economically "excessive." There is no easy or widely accepted empirical answer to this question. To the extent that awards are largely "random" and fail to provide incentives to firms, most, or even all, of the tort expenses are excessive. Alternatively, to the extent that damages awarded to claimants are a good proxy for the actual damages caused, the fraction of tort costs that go to claimants to compensate for damages, plus reasonable "transactions costs," could be loosely viewed as the "right" level, and costs above this amount as being excessive.

To pursue this line of reasoning, recall that more than half of the total annual cost of tort is due to administrative expenses and legal fees. As observed, "viewed as a mechanism for compensating victims for their economic losses, the tort system is extremely inefficient, returning only 20 cents of the tort cost dollar for that purpose."[14] This share of total tort costs that go to direct compensation for victims is lower than in the past. In the late 1980s and early 1990s, economic damages accounted for 22–25 percent of total tort system costs.[15]

As indicated in Figure 1, an additional 22 cents goes to claimants for non-economic damages, such

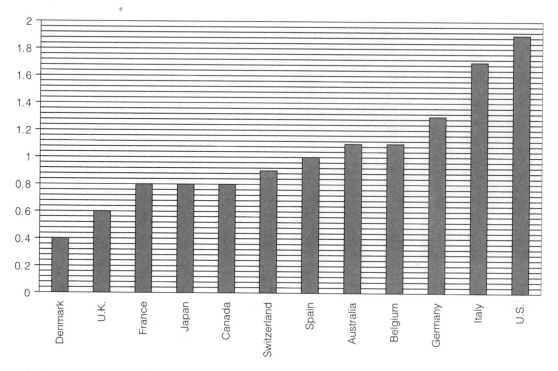

FIGURE 2. International Tort Costs as a Percentage of GDP, 1998

SOURCE: Tillinghast-Towers Perrin, "U.S. Tort Costs: 2000, Trends and Findings on the Costs of the U.S. Tort System," February 2002. Reprinted with permission.

as pain and suffering, loss of consortium and punitive damages. The remaining 58 percent of tort costs go to pay for administration, claimants' attorney fees, and defense costs. However, one should not necessarily view the entire 58 percent as "excessive," because some level of "transactions costs" is required in order to administer any system. As a guide for what is a reasonable level of costs, we use the experience of the Workers' Compensation system in the United States, which is designed to deliver compensation efficiently to workers who are injured on the job. Workers' compensation is a no-fault system, and thus litigation costs will be lower. According to the National Academy of Social Insurance, for every dollar paid to workers' compensation claimants, approximately 23 cents is paid in administrative costs.[16] Using this assumption that "fair" administrative costs should be roughly equal to 23 percent of damages paid to claimants, one can begin to estimate the "excessive" costs inherent in the U.S. tort system.

Even if we start with the extremely cautious assumption that both economic ($36 billion) and non-economic damages ($40 billion) are set at an economically efficient level, and that an additional 23 percent should be spent on administration, an efficient tort system would result in transfers of only $93 billion per year.[17] By this cautious calculation, the current U.S. tort system includes "excessive" tort costs of $87 billion per year.[18] Were one to adapt the assumption that non-economic damages are random, the "litigation tax" would rise to $136 billion per year, even after accounting for reasonable administrative expenses.[19] To the extent that the economic damages awarded by the tort system are not well targeted and therefore fail to provide proper incentives to firms, the entire $180 billion in direct costs is economically excessive.

Another useful perspective is provided by comparing the cost of tort liability in the United States to that of other developed countries. While it is difficult to make cross-national comparisons because of data limitations, estimates by Tillinghast–Towers Perrin suggest that the U.S. tort system is substantially more costly than that of other countries. As shown in Figure 2, U.S. tort costs in 1998 were 1.9 percent of GDP, approximately double the average cost of the other nations studied. Only Italy, with costs of 1.7 percent of GDP, rivaled the U.S. in total direct costs. Tort costs in Denmark, the United Kingdom, France, Japan, Canada and Switzerland are all estimated to be less than 1 percent of GDP.

HOW LARGE IS THE BURDEN OF THE LITIGATION TAX?

Regardless of which estimate of the direct cost presented [...] is closest to the truth, it is likely to substantially *underestimate* the total economic cost of the U.S. tort system. In the analysis of taxation, economists recognize that the total burden of a tax exceeds the revenue it collects. The excess burden or "deadweight loss" of taxation arises because taxes distort production and consumption decisions. In the current setting, an example of this phenomenon is that physicians may prescribe unnecessary precautionary treatments, often referred to as "defensive medicine," in order to avoid non-financial litigation penalties such as harm to their reputations and the time and stress associated with a malpractice suit.[20] Some socially desirable products and services are likely never produced due to excessive tort liability claims.

Anecdotal evidence suggests that some products that may have a net benefit to society as a whole are withheld from the marketplace due to excessive concerns of liability from the tort system. For example, concerns over liability have resulted in withdrawals of certain medicines, and halted the production of vaccines such as smallpox and DPT. In trying to gauge the size of these costs, the appropriate measure of loss is the difference between the value of the good that is not produced and the value of the next best alternative. Because only one of these goods is produced in the market, it is difficult to assess this loss. The net economic cost of these types of actions is difficult to quantify, and is not included in the $180 billion estimate.

Despite these difficulties, one can approximate the magnitude of the deadweight loss through the literature on taxation. Recent research by Professor Dale Jorgenson of Harvard University estimates that the marginal deadweight loss per dollar of revenue raised by the corporate income tax in the United States is 27.9 cents.[21] If all tort claims have a comparable deleterious effect on the economy, the deadweight loss resulting from the $180 billion in direct costs would be an *additional* $50 billion. Even using the most cautious estimate that excessive direct costs total $87 billion, an additional 27.9 percent deadweight loss would bring the total cost of the litigation tax to $111 billion. In the intermediate case with direct costs of $136 billion, the total economic burden would be $174 billion annually.

WHO PAYS FOR EXCESSIVE LIABILITY CLAIMS?

Who pays the litigation tax? While a tax may be collected from a firm, its burden must ultimately be borne by individuals through job loss or a reduction in wages (workers), an increase in consumer prices (consumers), a decline in property values (landowners), or a reduction in profits and thus share prices (owners of capital). Of course, these categories are not mutually exclusive. The same person could suffer from lower wages, face higher prices for products, and have lower returns on his pension assets.

Determining the true economic burden, or economic incidence, of a tax is a complex undertaking, as it requires that one consider how wages and prices have adjusted throughout the economy as a result of the tax. If wages fall as the result of a tax, economists say that the tax has been *shifted backward* onto labor. If prices rise, economists say that the tax has been *shifted forward* to consumers.[22] Alternatively, firm profitability could be reduced, in which case the tax burden is borne by participants in private pension plans and owners of stocks and mutual funds.

For example, in the United States, the Social Security system collects 12.4 percent of a worker's wages[23] to support retirement and disability benefit payments. Half of this, or 6.2 percent, is levied on the worker. The remaining 6.2 percent is levied on the employer. However, most of the employer-paid portion of the social security tax is shifted backward so that the employer portion of the payroll tax has the same effect on a worker as does the portion levied directly on the worker. Thus, even though employees *legally* bear only half of the payroll tax, they bear the full—or almost full—economic burden of the tax through lower wages.[24]

The *legal* incidence of the costs of the U.S. tort system falls on firms engaged in the production and sale of goods and services. Moreover, to the extent that the distribution of tort costs is largely random, tort costs only increase a firm's costs and decrease profits in a manner similar to the corporate income tax. Thus, to a first approximation, one can view the economic incidence of excessive tort costs as being similar to the corporate income tax in the United States.

The incidence of the corporate income tax is the subject of considerable debate among tax economists. Most economists believe that a substantial portion of the corporate tax is shifted to consumers through higher prices, or to workers if wages decline due to a decreased demand for the taxed good. The remainder falls on investors. Importantly, to the extent that it falls on capital, it is on owners of *all* capital, not just those firms most likely to fall subject to tort litigation. To see this, suppose that some industries or sectors are more likely to be subject to liability losses. If the high cost of liability makes investing in these sectors less attractive, capital will move out of the higher cost sector, driving down the rate of return to capital in other sectors. The lower return reflects the cost of the litigation tax. Thus part of the burden of these tort claims can be borne by all owners of capital not just those in the sector with higher tort claims.

Traditionally, three governmental agencies have engaged in the distributional analysis of tax policy: the Joint Committee on Taxation (JCT), the Office of Tax Analysis (OTA) at the Department of Treasury, and the Congressional Budget Office (CBO). During the 1980s and early 1990s, "JCT did not distribute corporate income tax changes at all, on the ground that the incidence of the tax was too uncertain."[25] Beginning in 1992, JCT allocated the corporate income tax to owners of capital generally, and for the past several years, the JCT has not conducted distributional analysis at all. OTA makes the assumption that the tax is borne by owners of capital. Traditionally, the CBO has used three different variations: 100 percent by capital, 100 percent by labor, and half by each. The inconsistent set of

assumptions and methodologies across agencies highlights the uncertainty about the economic incidence of the corporate income tax. In fact, a recent survey of economists who specialize in public finance found that virtually all of these economists believe that the burden of the corporate income tax is shared by both capital and labor generally, but "there is significant disagreement about the precise division."[26]

To the extent that capital markets are globally linked, allowing capital to flow freely across borders, the after-tax rate of return to capital must be equated across countries. One implication is that if tort liability raises the cost of capital in the United States, mobile capital will seek the relatively higher return available elsewhere, until rates of return are again equalized. The result is that the capital stock in the United States may be smaller with high tort costs than with low tort costs. A smaller capital stock means there is less capital per worker, thus lowering productivity and wages. In this way, the costs of tort may fall on the less mobile factors of production, namely labor. If global capital markets were fully integrated and capital freely mobile, then the entire burden of the costs of excessive tort in the United States could be shifted to labor through reduced real wages and consumers through higher prices.

The relative magnitude of the burden of excessive tort costs in the U.S. is quite substantial. For perspective, in the year 2000, total wage and salary disbursements to private industries (i.e., excluding government workers) totaled just over $4 trillion.[27] Taking the extremely conservative excessive cost estimate of $87 billion—an estimate that treats the current level of economic and non-economic damages as appropriate, allows for a reasonable administrative charge of 23 percent of the award, and ignores the deadweight burden—the litigation tax is equivalent to a 2.1 percent wage and salary tax shifted onto private sector workers. Alternatively, if this $87 billion were shifted forward to consumers through higher prices, this would be equivalent to a 1.3 percent tax on personal consumption.[28] If the excess burden were not passed through to labor or consumers, and instead was borne entirely by capital, then it would be equivalent to a tax on capital income of 3.1 percent.[29] It should be noted that nearly 80 million Americans own corporate stock,

Table 1 Size of the Tort Litigation Tax

Incidence Assumption	Equivalent Tax Base	Annual "Excessive" Tort Costs		
		$87 billion	$136 billion	$230 billion
Fully shifted forward through prices	Consumption Tax	1.3%	2.0%	3.4%
Fully shifted backward onto workers	Wage Tax	2.1%	3.3%	5.7%
Fully borne by investors	Capital Tax	3.1%	4.9%	8.2%
25% shifted through prices,	Consumption	0.3%	0.5%	0.8%
25% shifted through wages,	Wage	0.5%	0.8%	1.4%
50% borne by investors	Capital	1.6%	2.4%	4.1%

SOURCE: CEA calculations. The taxes are calculated by dividing the annual excessive tort costs by the appropriate base. The consumption base is total personal consumption expenditures which totaled $6,728 billion in the year 2000. The wage base is total wage and salary disbursements to private industries, which totaled $4,069 billion. The capital base is non-labor payments in national income, which totaled $2,789 in the year 2000.

either individually or through their pension funds.[30] In fact, over 20 percent of corporate stock in the U.S. is held by public and private pension funds—suggesting that if this litigation tax is not passed through to workers via wage reductions or price increases, workers are still harmed through reduced returns on their retirement saving.

Table 1 [...] illustrates the "tax equivalence" of tort litigation costs under various assumptions about the incidence of the tax, and the size of the excessive tort costs. As a lower bound on the size of the litigation tax, we treat all economic and non-economic damages as economically appropriate, allow for 23 percent administrative costs, and ignore the deadweight burden. This translates to a litigation tax of approximately $87 billion per year. For an intermediate estimate, we include non-economic damages in the excess cost of tort, following the work of Viscusi. This implies a litigation tax of $136 billion per year, ignoring the deadweight loss. For an upper-bound estimate, we treat *all* tort costs as economically excessive, and also include an estimated $50 billion in deadweight loss.

As illustrated in Table 1, under the assumption that the tax is fully shifted forward through prices, the annual excessive tort costs are equivalent to a tax on consumption ranging from 1.3 percent to 3.4 percent. Alternatively, if shifted backwards onto labor, the "litigation tax" is equivalent to a tax on wages from 2.1 percent to as high as 5.7 percent. If

the incidence of the tax falls on investors, it is equivalent to a tax on capital ranging from 3.1 percent to 8.2 percent. The final row of Table 1 illustrates the case in which the burden of the litigation tax is shared by consumers, workers and investors.[31]

Whether it falls entirely on labor, or whether some portion of it also falls on capital owners in the U.S., the cost to the U.S. economy is substantial. For example, in the year 2000, the intermediate cost estimate of $136 billion is more than the Federal government spent on all of the following programs *combined:* Education, training, and employment; general science; space and technology; conservation and land management; pollution control and abatement; disaster relief and insurance; community development; Federal law enforcement and administration of justice; and unemployment compensation.[32] Alternatively, $136 billion is two-thirds the amount of revenue collected from the corporate income tax[33] or nearly half (46 percent) of the amount spent on national defense.[34] Viewed differently, at more than 3 percent of wages per year, the cost of the litigation tax is also far more than enough money to solve Social Security's long-term financing crisis. To a family of average income, three percent of wages is also the cost of more than three months of groceries, six months of utility payments, or eight months of health care costs.[35] That is, $136 billion represents a large drain on the productive resources of the United States.

SUMMARY

The cost of the U.S. legal liability system has increased substantially over the past several decades. While economic theory suggests a potentially useful role for a tort system in providing proper incentives, excessive tort costs are akin to a tax on firms. Like any tax, this "litigation tax" imposes deadweight losses on the economy in the form of products and services that are never produced as a result of the fear of litigation. Both the direct and indirect costs of excessive tort must ultimately be borne by individuals in the economy through some combination of higher prices, lower wages, and reduced returns to investments.

NOTES

1. Direct costs include awards for economic and non-economic damages, administration, claimants' attorney fees and the costs of defense.

2. Tillinghast-Towers Perrin, "U.S. Tort Costs: 2000, Trends and Findings on the Costs of the U.S. Tort System," February 2002.

3. Throughout this paper, we use the term "firm" to refer to any producer of goods and services.

4. Another economic argument sometimes used to support tort liability is that the right to sue provides consumers with "insurance" in the event of an accident. For a discussion of the limitations of this view, see Paul Rubin, *Tort Reform by Contract,* Washington, D.C.: The AEI Press, 1993. For purposes of this paper, it should be noted that regardless of the rationale for the system, the cost is still borne by individual consumers, workers, or investors.

5. For broader discussion of the role of each of these approaches, see W. Kip Viscusi, "Toward a Diminished Role for Tort Liability: Social Insurance, Government Regulation, and Contemporary Risks to Health and Safety," *Yale Journal on Regulation,* Winter 1989.

6. W. Kip Viscusi, "Why There Is No Defense of Punitive Damages," *Georgetown Law Journal,* November 1998.

7. David Luban, "A Flawed Case Against Punitive Damages," *Georgetown Law Journal,* November 1998.

8. Theodore Eisenberg, John Goerdt, Brian Ostrom, David Rottman, and Martin Wells, "The Predictability of Punitive Damages," *The Journal of Legal Studies,* June 1997.

9. A. Mitchell Polinsky, "Are Punitive Damages Really Insignificant, Predictable, and Rational? A Comment on Eisenberg, et al.," *The Journal of Legal Studies,* June 1997.

10. W. Kip Viscusi and Michael Moore, "Product Liability, Research and Development, and Innovation," *Journal of Political Economy,* 1993.

11. Peter Huber and Robert Litan, eds., *The Liability Maze: The Impact of Liability Law on Safety and Innovation,* Washington, D.C.: The Brookings Institution, 1991.

12. Tillinghast-Towers Perrin, "U.S. Tort Costs: 2000, Trends and Findings on the Costs of the U.S. Tort System," February 2002, page 8.

13. Some anecdotal evidence of these costs can be found in Michael Freedman's "The Tort Mess," Forbes.com, May 13, 2002.

14. *Ibid,* page 12.

15. According to previous studies by Tillinghast-Towers Perrin published in 1995, 1992 and 1989.

16. National Academy of Social Insurance, "Workers' Compensation: Benefits, Coverage and Costs, 1999 New Estimates and 1996–1998 Revisions," May 2001.

17. (Economic damages ($36 b.) + Non-economic damages ($40 b.) × Administrative cost factor (1.23) = Non-excessive tort costs ($93 b.)

18. Total tort costs ($180 b.) − Non-excessive tort costs ($93 b.) = Excessive tort costs ($87 b.)

19. Total ($180 b.) − Economic($36 b.) × Admin cost factor (1.23) = Excessive tort costs ($136 b.)

20. Daniel Kessler and Mark McClellan, "Do Doctors Practice Defensive Medicine?" *The Quarterly Journal of Economics,* May 1996.

21. Dale Jorgenson and Kun-Young Yun, Investment, Volume 3, *Lifting the Burden: Tax Reform, the Cost of Capital, and U.S. Economic Growth,* 2001, Table 7.10, page 287.

22. Joseph E. Stiglitz, *Economics of the Public Sector,* Third Edition, New York: W. W. Norton, 2000, page 483.

23. Up to a maximum taxable amount of $84,900 in 2002.

24. Joseph E. Stiglitz, *Economics of the Public Sector,* Third Edition, New York: W. W. Norton, 2000, page 483.

25. Michael J. Graetz, "Distributional Tables, Tax Legislation, and the Illusion of Precision," in David F. Bradford, Ed., *Distributional Analysis of Tax Policy,* 1995, page 47.

26. Victor R. Fuchs, Alan B. Krueger, and James M. Poterba, "Why Do Economists Disagree about Policy? The Roles of Beliefs about Parameters and Values," National Bureau of Economic Research Working Paper No. 6151, August 1997, page 12.

27. *Economic Report of the President,* February 2002, Table B-29.

28. *Economic Report of the President,* February 2002, Table B-1.

29. According to unpublished data from the Productivity and Technology Division of the Bureau of Labor Statistics,

the capital (non-labor) share of nonfarm business output was $2,762 billion in 2001.

30. Investment Company Institute, *Equity Ownership in America*, 1999.

31. The assumed division is 25 percent through prices, 25 percent through wages, and 50 percent through reduced investment returns. This incidence assumption is based on one of the corporate tax incidence scenarios used by Joseph A. Pechman in *Who Paid the Taxes, 1966–85*, Washington, D.C., The Brookings Institution, 1985, p.35.

32. *Budget of the United States Government*, Fiscal Year 2003, Historical Tables, Table 3.2, pages 54–69.

33. *Ibid*, Table 2.1, page 30.

34. *Ibid*, Table 3.1, page 51.

35. Bureau of Labor Statistics, "Consumer Expenditures in 1999," May 2001.

READING 8.2 FAIRNESS, STRICT LIABILITY, AND PUBLIC POLICY

John J. McCall

The recent insurance crisis has intensified the public debate over product liability law. Business and insurance industry lobbyists have pressured for state and federal reform of the current strict liability standards. The main complaints about strict liability center on two claims: (1) the cost of a strict liability system is exorbitant and (2) holding business strictly liable for product-related injuries is unfair. This brief comment evaluates only the second of these claims.

The charge that strict liability is unfair to business gains credibility from an often unspoken underlying principle of fairness: Individuals should not be penalized (or, for that matter, advantaged) for things that are beyond their control and, hence, not their fault. This principle, or something like it, lies behind our intuition that the harms caused by severe mental incompetents do not deserve punishment. Something similar also explains the great attraction of John Rawls's recent theory of justice.

If we apply this principle to the case of product liability, it certainly appears unfair to adopt a strict liability approach when compensating for injuries due to defective products. For, according to strict liability, a business is held financially liable for harms caused by its products even when the defect is not the result of negligence. For example, if a defective product is released on the market despite a strict quality control inspection program, the business can still be held liable according to this standard.

Because no quality control system can prevent all defects, a company could escape financial jeopardy only by ceasing production. A corporation, then, can suffer serious economic damage under a strict liability standard for something that is not, in any morally significant sense, its fault.

We should look a bit closer, however, before concluding that strict liability is unfair. By definition, a strict liability standard applies to cases of accidental injury related to product defects. A consumer who is injured by a defective product is not at fault for the injury just as the business is not at fault. In an equally important way, then, the consumer is harmed by something beyond his or her control. (Ignore the complexities associated with contributory negligence on the part of the consumer since those complexities have no bearing on the general question of the fairness of any strict liability standard.)

If we accept the argument that strict liability is unfair to business, the paradoxical conclusion is that the alternative for cases of non-negligent defects is also unfair to the injured consumer. So, rather than drawing conclusions on the basis of the above fault/control principle about the fairness of strict liability, we instead should recognize that this principle is simply inapplicable when no one bears moral responsibility for the harm, that is, when the harm is purely accidental.

We need not abandon, however, any attempt to discuss the fairness of strict liability just because one common principle of fairness does not apply. We could, for instance, adapt another interpretation of fairness that is also associated with the work of John Rawls. Imagine a hypothetical choice of product liability policy under impartial and unbiased conditions. Suppose we ask an ordinary rational person to suspend her current views on product liability policy and to imagine two mutually exclusive alternative situations: one in which she is injured by a non-negligent-caused product defect and has no legal possibility of compensation; the other in which she is harmed by higher consumer prices or lower dividend return as a shareholder because the corporation must pay for strict liability product insurance. I suspect the first alternative is distasteful enough that the ordinary citizen would agree to accept the second alternative as a way of precluding the first.

If we develop this argument more completely by taking account of all associated costs, we may be able to construct a forceful argument for the conclusion that strict liability, far from being unfair, is actually *required* by fairness. Whatever we think of such an argument, the failure of the initial argument against strict liability is clear enough. At the very least, we ought to allow that a strict liability standard is, *prima facie, not unfair.*

If we do grant that strict liability is at least compatible with fairness, we still need to provide reasons for adopting it over other standards that may also be compatible with fairness. There are two such reasons frequently offered for a strict liability policy. First, proponents claim that a strict liability policy would reduce the number of product-related injuries. Because businesses would be exposed to greater financial jeopardy by a strict liability standard, they would have greater economic incentive to guarantee the safety of their products. The less cautious a company is, the more it can expect to have product liability judgments against it.

George Brenkert argues that this is not a sufficient reason for adopting a strict liability policy.[1] Brenkert suggests (a) that strict liability will not achieve any greater safety results than could be achieved through, say, legislated product safety standards; (b) some accidents are unpreventable; and (c) strict liability may be analogous to the unfair policy of imprisoning the wives (not husbands?) of criminals. Even though I agree that accident reduction is not, in itself, a sufficient justification for strict liability, I also believe that none of these objections is

compelling. For instance, lobbying and the appeals process may weaken congressional safety legislation so that fines become a less than effective deterrent. Moreover, even though some accidents will still occur under strict liability, this does not prove that strict liability will not eliminate other injuries when compared, say, with a negligence standard. Finally, the unfair imprisoning of wives who are not at fault is not analogous to compensation for a non-negligent, injury-causing product defect, which, for reasons stated above, is not unfair.

A second policy reason traditionally used in support of strict liability is that it distributes the cost of injuries in a way that minimizes their impact. It also distributes the costs to those who have benefitted from the availability of the injury-causing product. Ordinarily, the cost of product liability insurance is passed on in the form of higher product prices to those who demand the product. But even in cases in which an individual business in an elastic market has markedly higher insurance premiums, costs are still assigned to those who benefitted—the shareholders. (Why might one manufacturer have higher insurance premiums? Does this situation suggest a negligent failure to operate by the best available industry practice? One also wonders about entire industries with high insurance costs where the demand for the product is elastic. Does that indicate that the product is both dangerous and unnecessary?)

I would argue that the costs are more appropriately assigned to other consumers or to shareholders than to either the injured consumer or to society at large. Making the injured bear the full economic cost of the injury seems too harsh. Making society at large bear the cost through some form of socialized product liability insurance violates the principle of "user pays" and lessens the incentive to manufacture safe products. In ordinary circumstances, then, a strict liability standard is preferable to its alternatives.

A number of caveats for this conclusion are in order, however. First, if the social costs of a private insurance system under a strict liability policy were too great (for example, high unemployment, shortages of socially necessary products), perhaps some public subsidy for that insurance would be in order. I hesitate to acknowledge this qualification, though, because recent history indicates that such a policy exception could be manipulated by business and the insurance industry into a policy norm.

Second, cases arise in which the corporation that supplied the product no longer exists or the harms caused go beyond the available assets of the corporation and, hence, full recovery by the victim from the corporation is precluded. Perhaps in such cases public subsidy to complete the compensation of the victim is preferable to partial compensation. About whether the same subsidy should be available to the families of victims, I am less sure. About joint and several liability cases in which the harms are caused by more than one agent but some of the harm causers no longer exist and the remaining are liable for full compensation of the victim, I am also unsure. These cases indicate the difficulties in fashioning a fair, reasonable, and effective public policy on product liability. However, I hope to have suggested that any such policy ought to start from a strict liability basis.

NOTE

1. George Brenkert, "Strict Products Liability and Compensatory Justice" in *Business Ethics: Readings and Cases,* W. Michael Hoffman and Jennifer Mills Moore, eds. (McGraw-Hill, 1984).

READING 8.3 SOCIAL PRODUCTS LIABILITY: THE CASE OF THE FIREARMS MANUFACTURERS
George G. Brenkert

I. INTRODUCTION

One of the most important and challenging issues of business ethics—or indeed of ethics more generally—is that of "moral responsibility." And though this problem has been with us from the outset of reflection on ethics and business,[1] the following developments in the late twentieth century have exacerbated its difficulty: the increased mobility among people, the development of increasingly complex technologies with ever more significant consequences, the extension of the distance between people's actions and the effects of their actions, the extended distance between the manufacturers of products and the consequences of those products, the expanded possibilities for anonymous actions, and the collapse of many customary forms of restraints between both individuals and organizations. These developments have not only greatly increased the significance of the issue of moral responsibility, they have, at the same time, placed our standard notions of responsibility under considerable strain. The significance of this strain promises to become even greater during the 21st century. As a consequence, I believe, we are in the midst of rethinking and developing new and creative ways of extending our notion of responsibility. People and organizations are being held responsible in ways they were not held responsible in past years. New kinds of cases that attribute responsibility to individuals and organizations appear with increasing frequency.

This can be illustrated in a variety of ways. Companies marketing alcoholic drinks to inner-city blacks and tobacco companies targeting young, working-class women have been charged with violating their responsibilities to these individuals because of the special vulnerabilities they are said to have. Apparel manufacturers have been said to violate their responsibilities by using suppliers who underpay foreign labor to produce garments they market. Consumers are said to be irresponsible if they buy apparel manufactured in sweatshops. Manufacturers are said to be responsible to prevent the misuse of their products by children and adults in other lands. Power companies and manufacturing companies have been said to have responsibilities to reduce the emissions of their plants to help avoid global warming. The publisher of a book on how to commit a murder has been said to be liable in the

From "Social Products Liability: The Case of the Firearms Manufacturers" by George G. Brenkert, in *Business Ethics Quarterly,* Vol. 10, No. 1 (2000): 21–32. Reprinted by permission.

death of persons murdered by a hit man who followed the book's prescriptions. A television talk show has been found liable in the case of a man murdered by a talk show participant who felt that this man had humiliated him on the talk show. And gun manufacturers have been said to be partially responsible for the harm caused by the firearms they produce.

In this paper I want to explore, as one part of this important trend, a new form of responsibility that is, I believe, being developed in some of these cases. I call this "social products liability." I understand this to be an ethical, not a legal, doctrine. Still, its legal counterpart may be found, for example, in some of the lawsuits that have recently been brought against gun manufacturers. Nevertheless, my aim is to sketch a moral, not a legal, doctrine. As such, this paper does not pretend to resolve various legal issues, such as those concerning the liability of gun manufacturers in present lawsuits. Still, I believe that this new form of moral responsibility may be said to lie behind the legal claim that gun makers are partially liable for the harm caused by those who have illegally used the guns those manufacturers have produced. In the present article I can only briefly trace the outlines of such a moral account. I thereby leave the major effort to defend and expand on this view to future occasions.

II. SOCIAL PRODUCTS LIABILITY

The new form of responsibility I wish to sketch does not involve the question of whether a business is morally responsible for some harm caused by one of its products or activities over which it could directly or immediately exercise control. Nor is the defectiveness of the product in dispute. Rather the issue concerns a situation in which a manufacturer produces a non-defective product that is sold to one dealer, and then to some individual who may in turn sell it to another individual who injures or kills someone with it. May, for example, gun manufacturers be held (partially) morally responsible in such situations for the harms and costs involved when someone shoots another person in the course of a robbery, mugging, or argument? In the past, these intervening actors have absorbed such responsibility. Indeed, in the United States this was even true for defective products at the outset of this century. The

original manufacturer was able to hide behind those who distributed the product, even though the product was defective.[2] This is no longer the case. Instead, a doctrine of *strict products liability* was developed that allowed manufacturers to be held responsible when the product was defective, even though they had exercised due care in its production. Thus, when the product was not defective, but a person was injured, e.g., a drunk person drove into someone else and injured him or her, neither the dealer nor the manufacturer was held liable for the harms and costs involved.

The questions now being raised against gun manufacturers involve cases in which a non-defective product does what it is designed to do, but, because of the social circumstances in which it comes to be used, imposes significant harms through the actions of those who are using it in ways in which it was not supposed to be used. Gun manufacturers are said to be partially responsible for these harms because the ways in which they have marketed the guns permit, and perhaps encourage, the guns to fall more readily into the hands of those who would misuse them. This is the crux of what I am calling "social products liability." It stands in contrast to the doctrine of strict products liability.

This new view of responsibility involves, I suggest, four different conditions that are individually necessary and, jointly, sufficient for agents to be justifiably held responsible for the harms they cause. These four conditions may be referred to as: Harms and Costs, Contribution, Foresight, and Effective Alternatives. I can only very briefly survey here both the theoretical points and their applications to the firearm industry.

III. HARMS AND COSTS

There are three characteristics of the harms and costs that serve as the initial ground for attributing this extended sense of responsibility to a manufacturer. The first is simply the fact that their products are being used by some individuals to create considerable harm to other individuals (and sometimes themselves) and costs to society. These harms and costs are highly undesirable and disruptive both to the lives of the individuals affected and the healthy functioning of a society.

There are various ways, in the case of the manufacture of guns, that this harm can be portrayed.

One way is to note the number of deaths and injuries due to handguns. For example, it has been claimed that "in 1996, more than 34,000 people were killed nationwide with handguns, making handguns second only to motor vehicles as the most frequent cause of injury and/or death in the U.S. Of these firearm deaths, more than 14,300 were homicides, 18,100 were suicides. Of these, more than 1,100 deaths were from unintentional shootings."[3] By way of contrast, the number of accidental firearm deaths in 1995 was 1,400; that of poisonings was 10,600; 12,600 from falls; 4,500 from drownings; and 43,900 from motor vehicles. "In 1992, handguns were used in approximately 1 million violent crimes."[4] In addition, "approximately 99,000 individuals are treated annually in hospital emergency rooms for non-fatal firearm injuries, with about 20,000 of these victimized by unintentional shootings. Handguns cause most of these injuries."[5]

These figures say nothing of the personal and financial costs. Though the former would be difficult, if not impossible, to quantify, the latter have been quantified, though surely even this is only in a rough fashion. For example, "the Florida Department of Health has estimated the cost of medical, legal, administrative and productivity losses just for people under 25 years of age at more than $129 million. This estimate does not include the cost of gunshot wounds that do not end in death."[6] The costs of deaths and injuries for the entire United States have been estimated at about $20 billion every year.[7]

These figures, if accurate, are disturbing. They are way out of line with all other countries of the world. The individuals who have obtained and used these guns illegally have caused enormous harm. These figures are, however, unclear on a number of items. It is not terribly clear how many deaths and woundings are attributable to handguns as used by criminals. The most recent figures also indicate that there has been a decline in these deaths in most recent years.[8] Further, there are no figures that might represent costs saved through the presence of handguns, e.g., murders, muggings, robberies prevented by someone having a gun. Nevertheless, the figures from other countries suggest that there are other ways to prevent these criminal acts that do not involve the use of handguns. In addition, other numbers indicate that the number of times handguns have been used in self-defense are relatively low, though again any such numbers must be viewed very critically.

Secondly, it is important to note that such costs and harms do not derive from the fact that particular products of an otherwise acceptable product line are defective. Instead, they derive from the use of those products as they were designed. The lack of negligence in production of the product and the lack of physical defect in the product itself are features of social products liability that separate it from previous senses of moral liability or responsibility. Further, there appears to be few balancing goods or benefits that derive from the situations in which the harms and costs are produced. As such, it should be clear that the harms and costs noted here do not constitute a cost/benefit study of guns, or of guns being available, in some way, in a society. The preceding figures would be part of such a study, but do not themselves constitute such a study. Still, there is little doubt that real harm is being done. Further, it is of a nature and level that distinguishes the United States from other similar countries. For example, it is claimed that "more citizens die in handgun fire in just two days in the U.S. than in one year in Canada, Great Britain, Japan, Sweden and Australia combined."[9]

Third, these harms and costs are not always attributable to the use of specific weapons by particular individuals. That is, many times the exact weapon that was used to commit a crime is not identifiable. Even the person who used the gun to commit the harm may not be known. Rather, what is known is that certain manufacturers are selling guns that end up being used in a particular area. This does not allow those harmed, or the cities in which they reside, to bring a lawsuit against a particular manufacturer for the harm caused by a specific weapon. Instead, the charge is that weapons of certain (not wholly specifiable) kinds made by particular manufacturers are causing harm and costs in some region and to some people within that region. This is a unique and special feature of these harms and costs.

Now surely these claims, even if correct, do not imply that the manufacturers of handguns are (partially) responsible for those harms and costs. Thousands are also killed and injured by automobiles. Further, the general nature of the harm, without specification to particular weapons and/or manufacturers, singles out these charges of responsibility as unique and a considerable extension beyond ordinary forms of responsibility. Still, these figures do raise questions about the circumstances in which those causing the harm have obtained their guns. It is the latter that has led to charges of irresponsibility on the part of gun makers for their marketing practices.

IV. CONTRIBUTION

For social products liability to be attributed to a business, it must do something—other than simply produce the products harmfully used—that can be said to encourage, foster, or abet the process that leads to the harm and costs. There are two features that constitute this condition.

First, the products must be created and placed into the marketplace in ways that unreasonably increase the likelihood that their use will lead to the harms and costs they do. In the case of gun manufacturers, there are several interrelated aspects of their operations that have been said to contribute unreasonably to the increased likelihood of such harms. To begin with, the nature of guns is such that, any time they are used, they carry lethal force. Unlike automobiles, one cannot shoot a gun "slowly," though one may aim its lethal force in different directions. Instead, guns are more like highly lethal poisons and hand grenades. However, rather than designing guns to enhance the legitimate control of their lethal nature, it has been charged that the recent designs of handguns, with their short barrels, easy concealability and poor quality, are such that they are "particularly attractive for criminal use and virtually useless for the legitimate purposes of law enforcement, sport, and protection of persons, property and businesses."[10] Other designs involve special triggers and magazines that permit rapid firing of multiple bullets within a couple of seconds. In short, the design of the guns increases the chances that they will be used to cause harm (even extensive harm) in criminal ways. Of course some of these designs also permit women to carry a handgun for self-protection in their purse.[11] But they also mean that these guns can be carried by criminals more easily. In short, the designs of many of these guns have made them more deadly and dangerous than those produced decades ago.

Manufacturers are designing and producing guns with physical characteristics that encourage their use in the kinds of situations central to the harms and costs noted above. Their designs permit, if not encourage, their use in such situations.

At the same time, the advertising campaigns of gun manufacturers used to promote guns do so in ways that appeal to those with violent aims. R. G. Industries uses the slogan "As tough as your toughest customer" and emphasizes that the gun's finish provides "excellent resistance to fingerprints."[12] Similarly, the manufacturer S. W. Daniels Corp. marketed its 9-millimeter semi-automatic pistol as the weapon of "choice of the drug lords of the 80s."[13] Navagar advertised its TEC-DC9 as having a "special finish to increase bullet velocity." It is said to be a "radically new type of semiautomatic pistol designed to deliver high-volume firepower."

It is true that other manufacturers also play up the power or performance of their products in ways in which people may not use them, e.g., cars driving at very high rates of speed. They too sell the "sizzle" of their products. However, the analogy is questionable, in that the "sizzle" of guns, like that of poisons and hand grenades, is something directly connected with doing harm to other humans. Indeed, the more the performance of such products is enhanced, the greater, one would think, the likelihood that some oversight would be required of the way in which such products end up in the hands of their ultimate users. Especially, since unlike cars, high-powered guns will be used in their "high-powered" mode, as opposed to cars, which can be driven slowly.

Again, such marketing increases, rather than decreases, the likelihood that those who ought not to have access to guns, or who will use them in illegal ways, will seek them out. Advertising of this sort targets those who intend to use these guns in undesirable ways. Their advertising approves or validates the use of guns in undesirable manners that are also connected with the harms and costs described above.

Finally, and most importantly, gun makers market their guns to distributors who often do not in turn adequately or properly check those to whom they sell the guns. For example, the Chicago Police department sent two-person teams out to twelve gun stores ringing Chicago to investigate how they sold guns. Repeatedly, the stores sold guns to individuals without the proper identification, who indicated that they wanted to do harm to someone else, and who gave clear indications that they wished to resell the guns.[14] Gun makers also sell to those who resell the guns out of their cars, at car shows, and from their kitchens. Virtually all of the agreements between gun makers and dealers fail "to ban sales of guns at gun shows and to very small dealers with looser standards than the big retail operations."[15] Further, gun makers have resisted efforts to control or monitor the ways in which ultimate customers get their guns.

In short, gun makers make scant effort in their marketing to prevent guns from falling into the hands of those who should not have them. Though these guns may be used for desirable purposes, their use, at any time, is potentially deadly. In addition, assuming (for present purposes) that they do not have safety locks (and that this does not mean that they are defectively designed), they may potentially be used by anyone at any time without any training. They don't have to be re-registered each year or checked for safety. The eyesight or the skills of those using them are not monitored. Manufacturers don't oversee those to whom they sell the guns who sell to those who shouldn't have them. They sell to those who do not have restrictions placed on them by the state, thus multiplying guns reaching those who should not have them. These include felons, those without proper identification, those who are engaged in straw purchases, as well as those who seem to be angry and who want them to settle a score. In addition, they sell guns to markets that cannot plausibly themselves absorb those guns. In short, they sell to markets that are only intermediate to other more ultimate markets, the ones where the guns are actually used to cause harm and its associated costs.

The preceding points maintain that gun makers operate in such a way that, through the advertising and product design aspects of their marketing, they encourage the acquisition of their guns by members of society who are proscribed from having guns. Further, through their distribution practices they facilitate this. In short, their marketing practices foster the misuse of guns in the United States.

The second feature of the contribution condition is that it applies not simply to individual gun makers but to them collectively as well. It is the combined effect of their marketing practices

(design, advertising, and distribution) that promotes the harms noted above. Indeed, in some cases it is not known which guns are actually being used to harm this or that individual or to commit a particular crime. They might come from Navegar, Colt, Beretta, or some other manufacturer. What is known is that some gun was used. F n makers have not taken steps to alter the marketing practices noted [. . .] As such, the combined marketing contributions of these various manufacturers renders them both individually and collectively responsible for the harms their products cause.

Quite clearly, the preceding charges rest upon a number of factual claims. If the facts are mistaken, then the contribution condition against the gun makers would have to be modified or said to fail. The point here is not to ascertain the correctness of these factual claims. Rather it is to capture them as one part of the charge that, if correct, would substantiate the view that gun manufacturers have a responsibility for the harms and costs that their products cause. For it is with the assumption that these charges are correct that some (cities) have claimed that gun manufacturers bear a responsibility for the results of their marketing practices. Gun makers are said to have responsibilities to take special actions to curb some of the violence those using guns have engaged in.

V. FORESEEABILITY

The preceding two conditions, harm and contribution, do not, by themselves, allow for responsibility to be attributable to an agent. Some agent might be unable to anticipate or foresee where such harm might occur. Accordingly, another condition for such responsibility to be attributed to them is that they could foresee (not necessarily that they did foresee) the occurrence of the harm that their products produce and the way this harm is fostered by their own marketing. Foreseeability does not require that the agent planned or conspired in this train of events, although that is possible. It may also simply be that the agent's actions unwittingly were part of this train of events. Once this occurred, however, foreseeability may be attributed to the agent in other similar kinds of situations. This situation is further exacerbated when the agent does not, in a particular set of circumstances, take measures comparable to those taken by agents in other relevantly similar situations to protect downstream individuals from harm from their products.

Accordingly, it is claimed that gun manufacturers can foresee that their marketing practices contribute to the harms created by their products. The dealers who sell their guns permit persons to obtain them "who are not eligible to possess them or who do not wish to be identified as a purchaser on a firearm in official records, and who are likely to use the handguns that they obtain in the commission of crimes."[16] "If a buyer purchases five handguns of the same or similar make, the inference that the buyer intends to traffic the guns (or is a straw purchaser) outweighs any inference that the buyer intends to use the guns personally for legitimate reasons."[17] In effect, gun manufacturers initiate a process over which they exercise little or no control and yet which they should be able to foresee will lead to raised levels of harm by those who are able, inappropriately, to obtain the guns they purchase. "This failure to implement sufficient controls over the methods of firearm distribution has fueled the illegal market for handguns, which, in turn, has fueled crime."[18] Consequently, the manner in which gun manufacturers distribute handguns encourages a situation in which thousands of handguns come to be possessed and used illegally in the cities resulting in a higher level of crime, death, and injuries.[19]

However, gun makers have objected that they are not responsible. They invoke some version of what might be called "the veil of choice." This is the claim that those who buy the guns have a choice to make with regard to how they use the guns. This choice is all-important. And it shields or masks those who manufacture the guns from responsibility for what those individuals choose to do with them. The responsibility is theirs alone. Maybe this does not fully work with children. Their free choice is not yet fully developed. But with normal adults it is and we must, out of respect, treat them as adults. A veil of choice separates the two.

But does it? Suppose that John has good reason to know what the nature of Joe's choice will be. Whether Joe has a "free" choice or not, John has good reason to believe that he will use it to harm someone or to break the law. What then about John's responsibility? It is false that a "veil of choice" functions as an absolute barrier to John's complicity or responsibility. John does not acquire the full responsibility, but does acquire some of it. In short, the choice of others does not shield a manufacturer from responsibility when the manufacturer and distributor may and should know that their product will be used to harm and impose great costs on others.

However, the special nature of social products liability needs to be noted. For in this case the gun manufacturer does not know that some specific person will act in a particular harmful manner. Further, the manufacturer does not sell to the person doing the harm; even the retail gun dealer may not do this. Instead, the claim is that gun manufacturers should be able to foresee that making and marketing guns in the manner that they do will lead other, unspecified individuals to act in unspecified, but harmful and illegal manners. It is true, then, that gun makers cannot control the specific "outlaws" who illegally trafficked in guns or who misused them in crimes, once licensed dealers legally made the first sales of weapons. And as James P. Door, firearms industry lawyer, has noted, "[t]here has been no evidence that negligence by any manufacturer was the proximate cause of these shootings."[20] But it is false that they play no role and that the role they play is one that cannot be foreseen by them. In short, the contributory role they play is foreseeable.

VI. EFFECTIVE ALTERNATIVES

These preceding three conditions require a final condition to make an attribution of responsibility plausible. For agents to be held responsible according to social products liability, they must be able to do something else that will make a difference with regard to the occurrence of the harms and costs. Such alternatives may include altering the product or the service they provide, altering the way in which they offer or market it, or even (in extreme situations) simply stopping the production or marketing of that product.

There are two aspects to the claim that gun makers must also be able to take actions to reduce the harm their products are producing. First, there are actions gun makers could take that would reduce the harm and costs. These might include monitoring the actions of others or not selling to certain dealers. They could set certain standards that dealers of their guns would have to follow. They could even institute spot inspections of the operations of those dealers. In addition, they could stop or modify other actions they engage in that encourage people to act in potentially dangerous ways or to look with favor on the use of their guns in inappropriate ways. Even the design of guns themselves could be modified to make them less likely to kill high numbers of people. They might even support various gun laws that would take some of this moral burden off themselves.

On the contrary, present gun makers rarely make any effort to keep their guns from being sold at gun shows or by independent dealers who operate out of their homes or cars. Those kinds of sales are a major source of weapons to the illegal market.[21] For example, one distributor's accounts showed sales to 1,929 gun dealers in Florida alone even though fewer than 40 dealers operated full-scale retail outlets where regulations on waiting periods and background checks are observed more faithfully than by solo dealers.[22]

David Stewart has compared the distribution system in the handgun industry with those for other products that are potentially harmful. The manufacturers of herbicides and other farm chemicals, for example, strictly limit the number of dealers for their products so that sales personnel can be carefully trained and monitored to ensure that purchasers get full instructions on the appropriate use of the chemicals. "There is a very deliberate effort to prevent accidents or misuse of the products, Steward said, but he found no such effort in the gun industry."[23] Similarly, the paint industry tried to limit the sale of spray paint to juvenile graffiti.[24] On the other hand, gun makers have failed to exert their power to stem the flow of illegal guns to the black market.

Of course, some will argue that this will mean that some people will not be able to acquire the guns they have in the past. Of course this is true and is the very point at issue. However, this would not mean that people could not lawfully have guns. They might not have the same full range of guns. It would be a different range with guns that are not available today (with safety features). On the other hand, the burden of taking measures to stem this flow of illegal weapons is not an undue one for gun manufacturers. The main burden would be the loss of sales to those likely to use or possess a gun illegally.[25]

VII. CONCLUSION

The upshot of the preceding is that agents may be held responsible in far broader ways than in the past. Social products liability says that if you (together with others) make a product line that is used to cause significant harm to a no-table portion of society, you (and they) will be held collectively responsible for those harms, even if the product is not defectively manufactured or designed, when you have foreseeably contributed to this harm and avoided taking effective counter steps to prevent it. In short, products are not simply physical, but social, objects. The harm caused by some using them may come from a combination of their physical characteristics and the social circumstances in which they are made available to the public. This extended sense of responsibility applies to gun manufacturers.

Accordingly, gun manufacturers should do something about the harms and costs caused by the use of their products. They can no longer hide behind the sale. The "veil of choice" does not shield them from later sales and uses of their products. They participate in, and benefit from, this economic system. Their responsibility follows upon their partaking in this system and the responsibility of those in this system for the well-being of this system. Otherwise they are a form of free rider. In this sense, the present issue is also one of distributive justice, of the just sharing of benefits and burdens in an ongoing economic and social system. Gun makers are not sharing the burdens that are created by their products, though they are enjoying the benefits. If times were different, these claims would not be made. Instead, we see the effects of guns on society marketed in the ways described above. Gun manufacturers must recognize new responsibilities in light of this situation.[26]

NOTES

1. Cf. Cicero, "On Duties," in *Selected Works* (New York: Penguin Books, 1971).

2. Cf. MacPherson v. Buick Motor Co., 111 N.E. 1050 (N.Y. 1916).

3. "Complaint: Mayor Joseph P. Ganim and the City of Bridgeport v. Smith and Wesson, et al." Bridgeport, Connecticut. March 23, 1999, p. 11.

4. Mark D. Polston, "Civil Liability for High Risk Gun Sales: An Approach to Combat Gun Trafficking," *Seton Hall Legislative Journal* .19, no. 3 (1995).

5. Bridgeport v. Smith and Wesson, p. 11.

6. Cf. Penelas v. Arms Technology. The quoted text is from "Liability Suits Against Gun Manufacturers, Dealers and Owners," http://www.handguncontrol.org/legalaction dockets/

7. "The Economic Costs of Gun Violence," http://www.psr .org/econ.htm (April 2, 1999).

8. Beretta Defeats Handgun Control, Inc. in California Lawsuit," http://www.nrawinningteam.com/beretta.html (April 1, 1999).

9. "Embassies and Foreign Crime Reporting Agencies," *FBI Uniform Crime Reports* (1992); cf. "Handguns," http://www.ceasefire.org/html/handguns.html (April 2, 1999).

10. Kelley v. R. G. Industries, 497 A.2d 1143, 1154 (Md. 1985).

11. This assumes, of course, that carrying a handgun in one's purse does increase one's self-protection.

12. Cited in Dennis Henigan, "Victims' Litigation Targets Gun Violence," *Trial,* February, 1995. Cf. http://www .handguncontrol.org/legalaction/dockets/A3/a3vctmlg .htm (March 25, 1999).

13. Daniel Wise, "Claim Against Gun Industry on Trial in Federal Court," *New York Law Journal,* January 7, 1999, p. 1.

14. Cf. "Complaint: City of Chicago v. Beretta U.S.A. Corp., et al." Chicago, Illinois. November 12, 1998.

15. Vanessa O'Connell, "Jury in Suit That Blames Gun Makers for Shootings Doesn't Reach Verdict Yet," *Wall Street Journal,* February 5, 1999, p. B6.

16. Bridgeport v. Smith and Wesson, p. 25.

17. Ibid.

18. Ibid., p. 3.

19. Ibid., pp. 28f.

20. Cited in Joseph P. Fried, "9 Gun Makers Called Liable for Shootings," *The New York Times,* February 12, 1999, p. A1.

21. Roberto Suro, "Brooklyn Case is First to Put Firearms Industry Practices on Trial," *The Washington Post,* January 19, 1999, p. A2.

22. Ibid.

23. Ibid.

24. Ibid.

25. Bridgeport v. Smith and Wesson, p. 31.

Decision Scenario A
TOBACCO COMPANIES UNDER FIRE

On June 13, 1988, the tobacco industry suffered its first real loss in over three hundred product liability cases. In previous suits, the industry was able to emerge victorious. The industry usually carried the day through appeals to smokers' voluntary assumption of the risks of smoking, to the clear warnings present on the cigarette package since 1966, and to the "lack of conclusive scientific proof of a causal link between smoking and lung disease." In the case of Rose Cipollone, deceased, a Newark, New Jersey, jury found a single tobacco company partially responsible for injuries suffered by a consumer of its products. It awarded her husband $400,000 in damages.

The plaintiff's lawyer in the Cipollone case brought suit on a number of separate grounds. The Liggett Group, Inc., producers of the L&Ms and Chesterfields smoked by Mrs. Cipollone, was charged with failure to warn consumers prior to 1966 about the dangers of their product and with a breach of express warranty that the product was healthful. Those warranties were purportedly presented through ads associating cigarettes with health; some of those ads touted the brands as those most smoked by doctors. Liggett, together with two other tobacco companies, was also charged with conspiracy to conceal evidence about the health effects of smoking and with fraudulent misrepresentation.

The jury did not accept the charges of conspiracy or misrepresentation against any of the three

This case was prepared from the following sources: the Bureau of National Affairs *Product Liability Reporter* 16, no. 25 (June 17, 1988); *Cipollone v. Liggett,* 893 F. 2d 541 (1990); Sylvia Nasar, "Smokescreen: The Ifs and Buts of the Tobacco Settlement," the *New York Times,* November 29, 1998; the *New York Times,* February 18, 1995; "Effort to Revive Tobacco Bill Fails—Democrats Vow to Keep Measure Alive," the *Seattle Times,* June 18, 1998; John Schwartz, "Jury Awards Ex-Smoker $51.5 Million," the *Washington Post,* February 11, 1999.

companies. After the verdict, lawyers for the plaintiff argued that the jury's failure to return a guilty verdict on these charges should not be read as a rejection of the charge of conspiracy; they contended that the jury simply decided that prior to 1966, when warnings were first required on cigarettes by order of the surgeon general, no compensable conspiracy occurred. (The lawyer for the Cipollones was among the first to present documents obtained from tobacco industry files as evidence that the companies covered up data about the health effects of smoking.)

On the charge of failure to warn, the jury found Liggett guilty but responsible only for 20 percent of the subsequent harm to Mrs. Cipollone. The jury held that Mrs. Cipollone was 80 percent responsible for her own death. Because of a New Jersey law, no damages were assessed against the company on this verdict because Mrs. Cipollone was more than 50 percent responsible for her own condition.

On the final item, breach of express warranty, New Jersey allows damages on a proportional basis even when the victim is more than 50 percent responsible. The $400,000 award was compensation for Liggett's partial role in the harm caused to Mrs. Cipollone because of its breach of warranty.

The judgment of the jury was appealed, and in 1990 the Third Circuit Court of Appeals returned the case for retrial on a number of grounds. It held that the jury improperly considered Mrs. Cipollone's post-1965 behavior (after cigarette package warnings) in assessing her 80 percent responsible for her own injury. The Appeals Court also held that Liggett should have been permitted to argue that Mrs. Cipollone did not believe the advertising health claims. Court observers predicted that a retrial would still find Liggett guilty. However, the Cipollones' attorney gave up the case. He said that the litigation had already cost his small firm more than it could ever recoup and that his firm could no longer afford to press the case. It has not been retried.

The U.S. Surgeon General has declared that tobacco is an addictive drug. In 1994, David Kessler, then commissioner of the FDA, began investigating charges that the tobacco companies knew for years that nicotine was addictive and that they manipulated the levels of the drug to keep smokers hooked. As a result of this, and of other legal developments, numerous internal tobacco company documents have been released. As a result, plaintiffs have an increased likelihood of winning suits against tobacco companies.

In 1998, four states settled lawsuits out of court with the industry in their attempt to recoup state costs for treating smoking-related illness. After the tobacco companies successfully lobbied against a federal attempt at legislation, most other states settled similar potential suits for more than $200 billion. However, the damages from that suit are almost entirely financed by increased cigarette prices. One estimate was that the settlement would require raising prices by 35 cents per pack. Interestingly, the major manufacturers announced a 45-cents-per-pack increase the day after the settlement.

Individual suits may also benefit, however, from the information gained through the various legal actions. In February of 1999, a California jury awarded a man with inoperable lung cancer $51.5 million. $50 million of that amount was in punitive damages. The man began smoking before the surgeon general's warning appeared on cigarette packages. Even though the tobacco companies will appeal the verdict, the award may reinvigorate individual suits against the companies based on the newly released internal documents.

Ironically, the efforts by the industry to thwart the more expensive federal settlement may also encourage further suits. The federal legislation would have limited the industry's exposure to liability. The settlement with the states did not limit suits in that way. Thus, the door is again open for a flood of new claims. Fifteen class action suits on behalf of addicted smokers are underway. In addition, nearly 800 more individual suits are pending. The results of the California case and the documents revealed because of past legal actions may yet again expose the industry to substantial damage awards.

- Does heavy advertising of cigarettes have any bearing on the tobacco industry's defense that smokers have "voluntarily assumed a risk"? Would the age at which a person begins to smoke make any difference to your answer?

- What explains the relatively strict government regulation of alcohol consumption, given that the effects of tobacco are more harmful to the user? Is prohibition of any product legitimate?

- Are companies entitled to market any good for which there is demand, or do they have a responsibility to market only goods that have a net benefit to the consumer? Some authors point to psychic benefits associated with products, such as an enhanced self-image. Does this make tobacco a product that arguably produces net benefits?

- The tobacco industry pursues vigorous investigation into the background of plaintiffs who have brought suits. There are reports of unannounced visits late in the evening to take depositions from family members. The industry also steadfastly denied any link between tobacco and cancer. Is the industry justified in the activities it uses to defend itself?

Decision Scenario B
SELLING GUNS: NEGLIGENT MARKETING?

News of Nafis Jefferson's death on April 20, 1999, was dwarfed by the tragic shootings one day later at Columbine High School in Littleton, Colorado. His death, however, typifies the gun problems found in many large cities.

Nafis was shot to death on the streets of South Philadelphia. Neighborhood children were playing on Sigel Street that spring day when a five-year-old boy found a gun under an abandoned car, not an uncommon occurrence in drug-ravaged neighborhoods of the cities where dealers often stash drugs and guns in or under such cars. The child's older brother took the gun away, placed it on the car, and, as he had been taught, went to inform an adult. In the intervening moment, another child picked it up. The gun discharged, killing 7-year-old Nasif.

The gun was traced to a man who had a history of purchasing guns at rural gun shops and then selling them for a handsome profit to those not legally able to purchase them. Other guns he purchased have turned up in armed robberies and drug cases. So far, police have confiscated 12 of his guns from criminals in places ranging from New York to Philadelphia to Charlotte, North Carolina. This is a pattern that is seen repeatedly by police in major cities. Straw buyers purchase guns legally and then distribute them to others who would be barred

from purchases either because of age or because the background checks required by the Brady Handgun Control law would reveal them to have criminal records. Mayors of large cities charge that thousands of guns end up on their streets because of bulk purchases later resold by these traffickers. A Bureau of Alcohol, Tobacco, and Firearms study recently claimed that half of all guns seized from young criminals were purchased legally by straw buyers and then resold.

This situation has led a number of cities to file suits against the gun manufacturers, charging them with saturating the market with handguns, knowing that many will be illegally resold and end up in the hands of criminals on city streets. The suits allege that the gun makers negligently market their guns, knowing that the volume of sales is greater than the legal market can bear. In fact, in a complicated verdict, a jury in a private suit in New York City awarded one plaintiff damages on the grounds that his injuries were the result of three gun companies negligently failing to discourage sales of weapons that end up later being sold illegally.

Other suits allege that the companies are negligent for failing to develop technology that will decrease the chances that the gun can be fired by anyone other than its original purchaser. Trigger locks for handguns already exist. "Smart technology" is being developed by some manufacturers. Colt, with research funded by the Justice department, is working on a transmitter embedded in a ring that would only allow the ring wearer to fire the handgun. Other designs depend on handprints or hand density. The suits charge, though, that the companies have not moved quickly enough to pre-

This case was prepared from the following materials: Clea Benson, "Philadelphia Bill Promotes 'Smart' Guns," *The Philadelphia Inquirer,* April 30, 1999; Editorial, *The Philadelphia Inquirer,* February 23, 1999; Michael Matza, "Making Firearms Safer, Smarter," *The Philadelphia Inquirer,* April 21, 1999; Robert Moran, Craig McCoy, and Rita Giordano, "Tracing a Gun's Trail of Tears to Philadelphia," *The Philadelphia Inquirer,* April 21, 1999; Vanessa O'Connell, "Open Season," *The Sacramento Bee,* February 21, 1999; Ron Scherer, "Gunmakers in Legal Crosshairs," *The Christian Science Monitor,* February 16, 1999; Leslie Wayne, "In Difficult Times, a Gun Maker Tries to Counterattack," *The New York Times,* March 12, 1999.

vent the harms caused by unauthorized uses of their guns.

(In response to such suits, the gun industry is lobbying state legislatures to pass laws prohibiting cities from suing on these grounds. Georgia was the first state to pass such legislation. Texas joined it in June of 1999. At the urging of the gun lobby, other states, such as Pennsylvania, passed laws preempting municipal laws that limit sales or purchases of guns.)

Critics of the gun manufacturers allege that they should be held responsible for the harms caused by their products. Others find such claims of responsibility absurd and a dangerous "slippery slope." Why not, they suggest, hold auto manufacturers responsible for the deaths and injuries caused by people who drive recklessly or by drunk drivers? Holding the manufacturers responsible ignores the fact that the harms are caused by other people who irresponsibly misuse the manufacturer's products.

Critics of the industry are undeterred by this argument. They believe that it makes sense to sometimes hold firms responsible for the foreseeable, but unintended, harms caused by their products, even when those harms are caused by misuse. After all, they contend, failure to prevent foreseeable misuse is a traditional basis for product liability assignments. Moreover, they argue, the misuse, while not eliminable, is certainly reducible by actions that the manufacturers could take. They could monitor and control their distributors more vigilantly. They could design safer guns. They could avoid marketing guns in ways that highlight their attractiveness to criminals (by not emphasizing, as they sometimes have, the small, concealable size or fingerprint-resistant handles).

They also point to examples where other industries have taken steps to reduce the probability that their products will be used in harmful ways. Years ago, for example, sterno, the product used for keeping food warm in chafing dishes, was sold in liquid form. The manufacturer altered the formulation to a solid after it was found that alcoholics on skid rows were drinking the product for a cheap high. Medicine packaging was redesigned to prevent children from gaining access to a product that could cause them harm. When retailers in the Philadelphia area learned that aerosol products used for cleaning computer keyboards were being "huffed" by teenagers, they placed the products behind the counter and limited sales. The same has been done in coordinated efforts by manufacturers and retailers of spray paint in the attempt to limit disfiguring graffiti in urban areas. So, critics charge, it is possible for sellers to take steps to reduce the potential for harms caused by the marketing of their products. The critics suspect that the domestic gun industry, suffering from declining handgun sales, is simply not interested in anything that would further reduce its profits.

Gun manufacturers must not only assess their exposure to legal liability. They must also decide what moral responsibilities they have for their products and their marketing strategies. On the basis of their decisions, they have a number of options. They can take steps to limit illegal access to their own products (for example, by reviewing arrangements with sellers and distributors) while at the same time actively lobbying for stricter laws and increased enforcement across the industry. They could take no active role in urging stricter laws (such as the one-gun-a-month proposals) but tighten controls on the marketing and distribution of their own firms' products. They could continue supplying whatever market demand there is while leaving pro-gun lobbying to others like the NRA. Or they could continue business as they have and also play political hardball by urging passage of state and federal legislation limiting their liability and preventing cities from suing on grounds of negligent marketing. Activity in Congress indicates that they have at least pursued the last strategy. In the spring of 2004, legislation was debated that would have exempted gun manufacturers from liability suits. That legislation, however, was defeated after the manufacturers and the NRA withdrew their support when an amendment was attached extending a federal ban on the sale of certain assault weapons.

- Assuming that sometimes firms are responsible for foreseeable but unintended harms caused by their products (a principle of even the negligence standard of liability), under just what conditions does this responsibility exist? Just when do the intervening actions of another absolve the manufacturer of responsibility?

- Are there relevant differences among the following products that give rise to different levels of moral responsibility for harms caused by the products: guns, tobacco, automobiles, alcohol, and prescription medicines?

- What are your opinions of industry attempts to limit liability by lobbying for state legislative preempting of city law suits? Under what conditions would you find such political action legitimate or illegitimate? For what specific reasons?

- When ought manufacturers take steps to reduce access to their products by those who may misuse them?

Decision Scenario C

THE MICHIGAN TOY BOX COMPANY

The Michigan Toy Box Company of Detroit, Michigan, has established a reputation for producing durable, high-quality toy chests for children. Recently, however, they have discovered that the very durability of their toy chests can pose serious threats to the children who use them. The toy chests are constructed of prime hardwoods with a thickness of three quarters of an inch. The lids of these chests alone weigh eight pounds. Reports have returned to the company that nationally nearly one hundred children a year are either killed or seriously injured when a toy box lid falls on their heads or necks while they are reaching into the chest.

Consumer advocates have suggested a solution to the problem. It involves installing a friction hinge on the lid that prevents the lid from falling freely. The hinge functions by providing a resistance that causes the lid to close by dropping slowly. If all toy chests had such a safety device, consumer safety experts claim, the deaths and injuries suffered by children using toy chests would decline to almost zero. The recent nature of the safety problem and the slowness of government regulatory agencies concerned with safety, however, have prevented any mandatory safety standards for toy chests from being established as law. The Michigan Toy Box Company must decide whether to install the suggested safety device voluntarily.

The production costs associated with the addition of the safety hinge are clear. The cost per unit for the hinges is rather small, under $1.50. However, the company has determined that installation of the hinge will require an additional quarter-hour of labor time in the production of each chest. Salaries of workers at the plant are higher than national averages for unskilled laborers because of the com-

petition for labor in the Detroit area and because of the strength of unions in the local labor scene. The additional quarter-hour will cost the company $1.25 for each chest produced. Although the hinges would require no major retooling for the production line, the installation of the hinges will also entail capital and maintenance expenditures associated with the purchase of additional tools and the creation of a new work station in the assembly process. The company estimates that installation of the hinges will raise costs by about $5.00 per chest.

Although the company's reputation and sales are strong, there is increasing competition from other manufacturers because inflation has made the Michigan Toy Box product appear high-priced to parents of young children. The company doubts whether it could increase retail prices by $5.00 and retain an important segment of its consumer population. In fact, the relatively infrequent rate of injury associated with the toy chests makes it less than probable that marketing that emphasized the new safety feature could offset expected sales losses due to increased prices. The infrequent injury rate also makes less likely any major liability settlements against the company and in favor of families whose children were injured. (The expectation is that the courts will not find the product defective and that liability insurance will not increase because of large settlements.)

Management of the company decided for the interim to forgo installation of the hinges because of an impending recession that will dampen sales. They did not wish to exacerbate that decline in sales by installing the hinges, although the addition of the hinges would not have threatened the continued viability of the company.

The company's sales remained stable, though not as strong as expected, throughout the recession. The result was that the company had a backlogged stock of toy chests in its storage facilities. During the recession, however, consumer advocates succeeded in having mandatory safety standards requiring the hinges passed into law. To sell the boxes in the United States the company would have to remove them from storage, transport them to the factory, and install the hinges. The additional labor and transportation costs would add further to the list price of the chests. Rather than install the hinges, the company sold the chests to another company (which it has frequently supplied) in neighboring Windsor, Ontario. Canadian law does not require the safety hinge.

■ Was the company's financial judgment not to produce toy chests with safety hinges ethically acceptable? What about its decision to supply the stored chests to another legal jurisdiction to avoid installing the hinges on the chests in stock?

■ When should financial considerations be sufficient to override a concern for the safety of the product? Does the frequency of injury have any implications for an answer to the preceding question?

■ Would your judgment about the morality of the management decision have been any different were the injured from the adult consumer population? Does this indicate that standards of product safety should differ between types of products and types of consumers who use those products?

Decision Scenario D

A. H. ROBINS AND THE DALKON SHIELD

The A. H. Robins Company of Richmond, Virginia, marketed an intrauterine contraceptive device (IUD) known as the Dalkon Shield in the early 1970s. The company pursued an aggressive marketing program for the potentially profitable IUD despite early reports of medical complications in women who used the device. However, in 1974 the company stopped marketing the Dalkon Shield in the face of mounting suits against the company from women who were harmed by the product. The device, which was implanted in the uterus and could be removed by an attached string, caused serious infections, infertility, perforations of the uterine wall, and in some cases, damage to the stomach when it worked its way through the wall of the uterus and attached itself to the stomach.

Robins's response to product liability suits was as aggressive as its marketing program had been. It used its legal resources to delay litigation, and it subjected female plaintiffs to humiliating investiga-

tions of their sexual histories. Eventually, however, Robins began to lose in its courtroom battles. A Minnesota court ordered a search of company files and found evidence that the management of Robins marketed the Dalkon Shield with sketchy research and despite knowledge at an early stage that infectious bacteria could migrate up the attached string into the uterus. In these pretrial discovery proceedings, Robins claimed several significant documents had been lost; a company attorney later admitted to destroying documents.

After the company lost several large awards in product liability suits, it filed for bankruptcy under Chapter 11 of the U.S. bankruptcy code, arguing that its possible liability exposure was greater than the net assets of the company. The Chapter 11 filing froze all suits against the company until the court could determine the potential combined value of the liability suits that were either pending or expected.

Eventually, Robins's stock was priced in a way that made it an attractive takeover target. American Home Products, a New York–based company, reached an agreement to buy Robins. This agree-

This case was prepared from the following sources: *Product Safety and Liability Reporter*, vol. 16, nos. 4 and 29; *The Nation*, February 13, 1989; and *The MacNeil–Lehrer Report*.

ment, which was approved by the bankruptcy court, establishes a $2.5 billion trust fund for victims of the Dalkon Shield. Victims can collect by merely showing medical proof of injury; no lawyers or litigation will be required. Damage awards are predicted to be approximately $1,000 to $10,000 for the large majority of victims and $50,000 to $200,000 for those with the most serious injuries. The settlement also precludes further suits against Robins's officers and insulates them from punitive damage awards.

In addition, American Home Products will pay about $700 million to Robins's stockholders. Since Robins was about 40 percent family owned, much of that award will go to the Robins family and to E. Claiborne Robins Senior and Junior, who were executives of the company. These two Robins family officers must each pay $5 million into the trust fund. The settlement, however, will provide each of them many millions more than their respective contributions to the trust fund.

The Robins settlement has been criticized for inadequately compensating injured victims, for shielding the company's executives from personal liability, and for providing substantial profits to shareholders, especially members of the controlling family. The settlement's benefits for shareholders stand in marked contrast to the bankruptcy settlement in the case of Johns-Manville, the asbestos producer. In its bankruptcy settlement Johns-Manville was to pay 50% of its common stock and 20% of future profits to a trust fund for victims and their families.

- Should companies faced with potentially large damage awards follow Robins's example and pursue every legal mechanism within their power to avoid those awards?

- Should Chapter 11 settlements insulate corporate officers from personal liability for tortious actions performed in the exercise of their corporate authorities?

- What should be the priorities in a bankruptcy settlement that involves both traditional commercial debtors and persons injured by the company's products?

- If the bankruptcy or takeover settlement does not fully compensate consumers injured by a company's products, should the federal government subsidize such compensation?

Decision Scenario E
DIETHYLSTILBESTROL (DES)

Diethylstilbestrol (DES) is a synthetic estrogen hormone that was first produced by British medical researchers in the 1930s. The formula for the drug was not patented, so the drug was available for manufacture by any company. U.S. drug companies applied to the Food and Drug Administration (FDA) for permission to market the drug in the United States as a remedy for symptoms of menopause. FDA approval was granted in 1941 on the basis of clinical data developed by a joint project of a number of interested drug companies. Further FDA approval for the use of the drug in the prevention of miscarriages was granted in 1947.

Diethylstilbestrol was used throughout the 1950s and 1960s for the treatment of pregnancies that presented the danger of miscarriage. As many as 300 companies produced the drug during that period. The drugs produced by those companies were essentially identical in manufacture and medicinal action; the only differences between the drugs of different manufacturers were inessential differences in packaging. Therefore, DES is legally considered a "fungible" product.

In 1971 a statistical connection was found between the use of DES during pregnancy and the appearance of certain forms of vaginal cancer in the female children of women treated by the drug. It is now considered well established that DES caused those cancers, which developed after at least ten

---

This case was prepared from the decisions of the relevant state courts.

years had lapsed since the consumption of the drug. In 1972 the FDA prohibited all marketing of the drug for use during pregnancy.

Given both the long period before the appearance of the side effects and the unexpected place of occurrence (in the offspring rather than in the person treated), it seems that the difficulties with the drug were not forseen by the companies that marketed it, especially during the earlier 1950s period.

The two most common approaches to product liability law are the negligence and strict liability standards of liability. The negligence standard would normally allow a consumer injured by a product to recover damages from the company only on condition of proving that the injury resulted from the company's negligence. Under the strict liability standard, the consumer could recover damages without proving the company's negligence in cases of products that were nonetheless defective and unreasonably dangerous.

In the DES cases, the female victims of the drugs taken by their mothers could possibly have argued to the satisfaction of a jury that the companies were negligent for insufficiently testing the product or that the product was unreasonably dangerous. Under the standard requirements for bringing liability suits, however, the injured consumer must also establish that the defendant company was the source of the injuring product. In the DES cases, this requirement would effectively bar the victims from bringing suits successfully. Generally, the drug companies, the pharmacists who provided the prescriptions, and the women who took the drug could not establish which particular manufacturer was the source of the drugs any given woman had taken. Pharmacists, for example, often had supplies from different manufacturers that were used interchangeably. In addition, less than precise recordkeeping and the passage of time also made it nearly impossible to determine which manufacturer's drugs were the cause of specific cancers. Consequently, state courts, in whose jurisdiction product liability suits fall, had a dilemma. Fairness to the injured victims seemed to at least allow them the opportunity to make their case in court. Traditional standards of proof for causation in product liability cases, however, would lead to the summary dismissal of suits against the DES manufacturers. There are only two ways out of this

dilemma: Courts could pass a "hard-luck" judgment on the victims, or they could offer new theories of liability law that would allow some chance of recovery. Some states adopted the former approach, but some adopted the latter.

California, Wisconsin, and Michigan are three of the states in which proof of causation requirements were relaxed. A Michigan appellate court reversed the decision of a lower court and allowed a DES suit on the ground that the plaintiff had named all the known manufacturers that distributed DES in the area and at the time her mother had taken the drug. In the famous *Sindell* case, the California Supreme Court allowed a suit on the condition that the named defendants together constitute a "substantial" share of the market. If the drug companies lost the suit, they would be apportioned damages in direct proportion to their market share. The Wisconsin Supreme Court allowed an injured victim to sue just one company, even though she could not prove that company was the source of her mother's DES. The Wisconsin court required only that the plaintiff prove by a preponderance of the evidence that the defendant company marketed the type (according to characteristics such as pill or capsule form, shape, color) of DES taken by her mother.

On March 31, 1988, the California Supreme Court issued a decision that limits the scope of its previous *Sindell* market-share theory of liability. The court held that in cases involving drug manufacturers, consumers can sue only under a negligence standard of liability and not under a strict liability standard. In addition, the court held that damages for an injury in a market-share case can be assessed only in proportion to the defendant's share of the market. This means that unless the consumer sues all manufacturers who distributed the drug in the relevant area (an unlikely event, since many companies are no longer operating), the consumer can recover only partial costs of her injury.

The California Supreme Court reasoned that applying strict liability to drug companies, especially in a climate allowing market-share liability, might lead to company reluctance to develop and market new drugs that could provide great social benefits. In addition, the court was concerned that the needed drugs that do get produced might be prohibitively expensive if drug companies were subject to increasingly expensive product liability insurance. In essence, the California court declared that, as a class, prescription drugs fall into a category of products that are necessary yet unavoidably dangerous. The traditional approach to strict liability exempts such products, requiring instead that negligence be proved before damages are recovered.

Interestingly, the Wisconsin Supreme Court in its 1984 decision came to exactly the opposite conclusion after considering some of the same arguments. It reasoned that imposing strict liability on drug companies would still allow the production of socially beneficial drugs but would encourage their being produced with greater care. The Wisconsin court, then, explicitly refused to classify all prescription drugs as unavoidably dangerous. It left open the possibility that some drugs are unreasonably dangerous. The court preferred for public policy reasons

(encouraging adequate testing and safety) to judge harms caused by drugs on a case-by-case basis.

- What reasons can be found under product liability law for treating drugs and medical devices in a manner different from other consumer products?

- What principles could help us choose between the two following approaches to product liability: 1) telling the victims of DES that they cannot recover compensation because of traditional rules about proving causation or 2) abandoning traditional rules and creating new ones that permit compensation.

- If you believe that DES victims merit some compensation, which of the three states' (Michigan, Wisconsin or the early, California *Sindell*) approaches do you prefer? Why?

9

❧

Marketing Ethics: Advertising, Sales, and Consumerism

INTRODUCTION

A helpful starting point for thinking about the ethics of marketing is to consider a simple exchange between two individuals. You and I agree to exchange your money for my used car. You agree to give my son some money in exchange for his willingness to mow your lawn. An attorney agrees to represent a client in exchange for 20% of any settlement. The college bookstore buys back your used textbooks for cash. In each case, a free exchange between two parties is presumed to be ethically legitimate. From a utilitarian perspective, freely chosen exchanges are presumed to work to the mutual benefit of both parties and thereby will increase the overall good. From the Kantian perspective, such exchanges appear to respect the autonomous choices of free individuals.

However, there are three general situations in which the ethical presumption in favor of market exchanges is unwarranted. The exchange will not be mutually beneficial nor would it respect the autonomy of both parties if the parties involved do not fully understand its terms, or if it is not fully voluntary. Further, if other important ethical values are violated by the exchange, its legitimacy can be lost. These first two conditions are captured in the common ethical principle of *informed consent*. Parties to an exchange must freely consent to it, and they must be fully informed of its conditions. Utilitarians value informed consent because it would seem a good test for achieving mutual benefit; the fact that both parties fully understand the consequences and freely consent to it is the best way to determine that they will benefit by it. Kantians view informed consent as essentially synonymous with autonomous choice. Both traditions would also acknowledge that other ethical considerations might override the goods attained by free and voluntary exchanges.

These three factors provide a convenient framework for the ethical issues considered in this chapter. One of the prime ways in which an exchange can fail to meet the informed condition occurs when either party is the victim of deception or fraud. The first two readings in this chapter offer ethical analyses of deceptive advertising and sales practices. Market exchanges are also ethically suspect when the parties to the exchange have not given their full and voluntary consent to the exchange. The readings by Arrington, Brenkert, and Paine examine the issue of consumer autonomy and the practice of targeting potentially vulnerable consumer groups in marketing. The final reading by Juliet Shor addresses the harmful social effects of a type of consumerism encouraged by contemporary marketing.

DECEPTIVE ADVERTISING AND SALES

Much of the field of marketing, and especially the fields of advertising and sales, attempts to influence consumer behavior. In itself, attempted influence is not morally objectionable. We all attempt to influence the desires and actions of other people. Rational persuasion, for example, is a perfectly acceptable means of influence. Other attempts to influence, though, can be morally inappropriate. Our challenge is to find some consistent and principled way to distinguish ethically legitimate influences from those that are ethically illegitimate.

If rational persuasion is the most ethically legitimate means for attempting to influence the desires or actions of another, coercion or force sits at the opposite extreme. We find a number of categories of influence along the continuum between rational persuasion and coercion. Manipulation is one means of influence that is ethically problematic. Deception is another. Lying is yet another.

Unlike coercion or control, manipulation does not suggest having direct power over someone. Manipulation suggests more subtle, behind-the-scenes guidance. Manipulation involves influence without the person's explicit consent or conscious understanding. In this way, manipulation disregards the conscious choice of the other person and thereby seems a violation of his or her autonomy. There are many ways in which I can manipulate the desires and actions of another person. I might manipulate my students' behavior by hinting about an upcoming test or by reminding them of how much money their family is paying for college tuition. An attorney might manipulate a witness by asking leading or intimidating questions. A car salesman might manipulate a buyer by reminding her of the dangers women face if their car breaks down on a dark highway.

One effective way that I can manipulate another person is through deception, and the most direct form of deception is an outright lie. One is deceived when one is misled to believe something that is not true. Typically, the intention behind a deception is to get the deceived person to act upon the false belief. An obvious, but not the only, way to deceive someone is to tell an outright lie. Manipulation, deception, and lying all attempt to interfere with a person's autonomy. They try to prevent a person from making a fully informed and voluntary choice by having that person act on misleading or false beliefs.

These examples remind us that the more we know about another person, about their desires, motivations, and psychology, the better position we will be in to influence and manipulate his or her behavior. A good deal of marketing research is aimed at acquiring exactly such information about consumers. The more advertisers know about consumers, the better able they will be to influence their choices. But this applies both to the ethically legitimate influence of persuasion and the ethically illegitimate means of deception and lies. The more I know about your beliefs, fears, motivations, and desires, the better position I will be in to manipulate and deceive you. Critics charge that some marketing practices seek to identify and target consumers who would be especially vulnerable to deceptive and manipulative advertising and sales.

But consider the parallel between political campaigns and product marketing. Both seek to influence the desires and behaviors of other people. Both political polls and market research collect information to discover the beliefs, values, and motivations of voters and consumers, respectively. Both seek to use that information to influence behavior. "Vote for *my* candidate or buy *my* product." However, society gives political campaigns great freedom to influence voters. No matter how unhappy we might be with the quality of political campaigns, ultimately we trust the judgment of voters and accept their decisions as final and authoritative. Marketing defenders ask the same freedom and respect for commercial speech. Ultimately, we should trust the judgments of consumers and accept their purchasing choices as final. Advertising and marketing are no more guilty of deceptive and manipulative practices than political campaigns. The case study that opens this chapter pursues the parallels between commercial and political speech.

The first reading by John McCall explains in more detail the grounds for thinking that deception is wrong. It argues that, regardless of the effect, any attempt to deceive in advertising is presumptively immoral. The reading goes on to apply that analysis to a number of advertising techniques, and it concludes that advertisers and the public are insufficiently critical of contemporary advertising practices. The second reading by Thomas Carson extends the analysis of deceptive marketing practices by looking more specifically at deceptive sales practices. Carson argues that salespersons not only have duties to refrain from deception and lies, but also positive duties to warn about potential harms and to fully and honestly answer questions and disclose information.

NONDECEPTIVE MARKETING, AUTONOMY, AND CONSUMER VULNERABILITY

Debate on the other major issue of the chapter, the effect of nondeceptive ads on consumer autonomy, had its source in the classic John Kenneth Galbraith book, *The Affluent Society*. His argument may be stated as three simple propositions. First,

Galbraith claimed that advertising creates wants in the consumer. Second, he suggested that this shaping of consumer demand by marketers is a violation of the consumer's autonomy. Third, Galbraith contended that this want-creation by advertising encourages consumers to demand, and the economy to produce, less important goods instead of goods necessary for satisfying important needs. In a striking passage, Galbraith claimed that advertising causes an irrational economy that produces luxury autos but allows the pollution of the environment through which we drive. (We will not pursue a discussion of this final point in the text. We leave assessment of that to you.)

Attacks on Galbraith have continued for four decades. Those attacks have taken a number of forms, which we can separate into two categories. Empirical criticism of Galbraith claims that advertising is simply not all that effective at controlling consumer behavior. Studies of new product success rates have been used to indicate that advertisers are unable to guarantee success even for heavily advertised new products. This criticism has meager success itself because historical evidence consistently indicates that new products that are actively introduced into the marketplace have a success rate of about 60%. That figure is sufficiently ambiguous that it provides neither conclusive support nor conclusive refutation for Galbraith's contentions. Galbraith himself said that he did not believe that the power of advertisers was "plenary" (absolute). In addition, Galbraith may be interpreted as claiming not that advertisers have control over consumer *behavior* but that they have unacceptable influence on consumer *desire*. If Galbraith is interpreted this way, evidence about sales of new products (consumer behavior) would be irrelevant.

Another, more common, category of criticism of Galbraith focuses on purported conceptual errors in his argument. Critics have noted that advertising cannot create wants out of nothing. Rather, advertisers must appeal to some preexisting desire and then convince the consumer that their products are the means for best satisfying that original desire. Thus, deodorant ads may stimulate consumers to associate Arrid with their desire to be attractive to (or not to offend) the opposite sex. But this ad can be successful only if that desire to be attractive already exists. So, critics argue, ads merely persuade consumers to want products as vehicles for satisfying their already existing wants. This is still consistent with consumers remaining autonomous. The consumer is free, after all, to buy or not buy the product.

One possible response that those more sympathetic to Galbraith would make at this point would be in distinguishing two senses of autonomy. We can obviously speak of behavior as autonomous, as the preceding criticism of Galbraith does. But his defenders hold that it is also sensible to speak of desires as autonomous. Even when an ad does not compel behavior, it might still interfere with autonomy in the way it shapes our desires. As an example of this, consider the desire a person might acquire for a Coke after being subjected to a subliminal ad during a movie presentation. (A famous New Jersey case similar to this generated quite a bit of controversy a few decades back.) Even if the moviegoer decides not to act on the newly acquired desire, many of us have the vague feeling that the person's autonomy has been violated if he so much as desires the Coke. This feeling persists in the face of the recognition that the moviegoer freely chose not to buy a soft drink. We need some way of analyzing this feeling to assess its validity. One approach to that assessment involves getting some clarity about what it might mean to say a desire is autonomous.

One classic account of autonomous desire is the one provided by philosopher Gerald Dworkin. Dworkin contends that for a desire to be autonomous, it must have two elements something like the following: (1) It must be such that we do not try to renounce the desire and (2) it must be such that we are able effectively to step back and critically evaluate the desire. That is, we must not only accept the desire as our own but we must be able to do so on the basis of rational reflection.

Dworkin names these conditions the "authenticity condition" and the "independence condition." For him, autonomy demands that a person retain some independence. Desires obviously can be acquired both from a multitude of sources and through a multitude of influence mechanisms. As a result, Dworkin believes that independence can exist only if those acquired desires can be subjected to rational evaluation. Thus, Dworkin finds desires that are acquired based on deception are not autonomous, since they fail to satisfy the independence condition. He also suspects desires that are the product of other forms of manipulation.

This account of Dworkin's may provide some way of understanding that vague feeling about subliminally acquired desires. If we are unaware of how the desire came to be, we are less likely or able to critically evaluate it. When we know a desire has been acquired through some advertising pitch, on the other hand, we are more likely to take a critical and skeptical stance towards it. All of us have had the experience of catching ourselves being seduced by a particularly effective ad presentation.

Consider the alternative account of "autonomous desire" provided in the article by Robert Arrington (Reading 9.3). Arrington's analysis resembles the first part of Dworkin's. Arrington claims that his desire for A-1 Steak Sauce is autonomous so long as he does not kick himself for impulsively pouring the vile stuff over a choice steak. He does not find it necessary to include in his account a condition similar to Dworkin's second condition. As a consequence, Arrington's analysis would judge the moviegoer's desire for a Coke to be an autonomous one. Evaluating which of these competing accounts of "autonomous desire" is the more appropriate one will be a complex process of achieving some balance between the reasoned analyses themselves and our own considered intuitions about methods of influence.

Whichever perspective you adopt, it is clear that Galbraith is not correct if he intended to say that all advertisements individually threaten the consumer's autonomy. As Arrington points out, the question is *when* a particular nondeceptive ad crosses the line between acceptable persuasion and manipulation, between influence and undue influence. You should be careful in assessing Arrington's definitions of "control" and "manipulation" in reaching an answer to that question. Does he define them so strictly that anything, short of absolute domination, would be acceptable? For example, how would even deception satisfy Arrington's analysis of control and manipulation as requiring that the advertiser intend to assure *all* conditions necessary for getting a person to act in a desired way? Can there be unacceptable manipulation that falls short of full control?

Reading 9.4, by George Brenkert, questions whether some populations are more vulnerable to manipulation by advertising and whether advertisers bear a greater responsibility to assure that such populations are not harmed by marketing campaigns. Brenkert takes as the focus of his analysis complaints against brewer G. Heileman for its PowerMaster malt liquor advertising in inner city black neighborhoods. He rejects the idea that the black residents of those neighborhoods are generally and especially vulnerable on cognitive or motivational grounds. That, he claims, smacks of an unjustified moral paternalism. He does, however, see a vulnerability that is related to social conditions of poverty and racism, a vulnerability that is exploited not by Heileman individually but by alcohol advertising collectively (when, for instance, neighborhoods are saturated with billboards advertising alcohol). Brenkert sees the industry as collectively bearing some responsibility for the alcohol problems that disproportionally attend the inner city community. This is a case, he asserts, where it is not the individual ad that is the problem but rather the cumulative effect of exposure to the volume of alcohol advertising.

Brenkert's article raises a number of important questions for us to consider: Can advertisers as groups be responsible for harms when their ads are not individually harm causing? May some persons or populations be more vulnerable to advertising campaigns? Is there a sense in which specific populations, or the society as a whole, is less able to resist consumption of particular products, or consumption in general, because of the cumulative exposure to advertising?

The next article in the chapter, Reading 9.5 by Lynn Sharp Paine, continues the analysis of special vulnerability. It raises a question about the propriety of advertising to children. If advertising must respect the autonomy of consumers and if children are not yet capable of reasoned judgment, serious questions arise for children's advertising. Note that a common response to critics of children's ads is not available as a response to Paine's approach. Sometimes, people say that advertising to children is acceptable because parents can simply tell a child "No" when the child requests some advertised item. However, parental control of the purse strings is not a response if the original complaint is one about how the ads affect the desires and the mind of the child. This issue about desires cannot be addressed solely by noting that parents can refuse to satisfy those desires. Rather, this is an issue that forces you back to the relationship between desire and autonomy. It is an issue that once again forces you to decide what methods of influence are consistent with autonomy, fairness, and respect for the person.

MARKETING AND CONSUMERISM

Galbraith's third proposition, mentioned previously, was that marketing has helped create an irrational economy that produces an abundance of trivial luxury goods at the expense of necessary social goods. This claim reminds us that even informed and voluntary exchanges might have undesirable social costs. This challenge is still heard today, more than four decades after Galbraith's book was first published. In our final reading, economist Juliet Shor offers an analysis of why we consume as much as we do.

Consider a question that concerned earlier generations of economists. At first glance, one assumes that people work in order to earn money to buy what they need. However, satisfying needs became less of a challenge to most people as industrial economies grew and became more productive. Thus, logic might suggest that as people came to satisfy their needs, they would begin to work less in order to enjoy leisure activities. But, if people began to work less, the economy would slow down and head into a recession. Thus, economic growth and productivity seemed to contain within itself the seeds of its own destruction. This was a real challenge to economic theory.

But, of course, nothing at all like this occurred. As industrial economies became more productive, the amount of time spent working actually increased rather than decreased. The desire for luxury goods has kept many workers in industrialized countries working longer and longer hours. Critics charge that this consumerist culture, fueled by contemporary advertising and marketing, causes significant and widespread social harm.

Shor argues that while advertising and marketing do contribute to excessive consumption, various structural features of modern economies are equally responsible. These structural features include a "work and spend" cycle in which individuals are less than fully free to decrease the time and effort spent at work, an ecological bias in which ecological resources are treated as free goods, and the emergence of consumption as a form of social competition. In a world in which meeting basic human needs is only a dream for hundreds of millions of people and in which ecological systems are under real threat by economic exploitation, Shor suggests that there are pressing ethical reasons for asking "Why do we consume so much?"

CASE STUDY Nike: Advertising, Marketing, and Free Speech

In 1998, Marc Kasky, a California citizen, sued Nike, Inc. claiming that Nike had produced a series of false and misleading advertisements. California law allows individual citizens to file civil lawsuits on behalf of the general public, and Kasky did so, alleging that Nike's public statements defending itself against charges of unethical labor practices constituted unfair competition and false advertising. Nike denied that their statements were false or misleading but also claimed that because their statements were part of an important political debate, they were protected by the First Amendment. Kasky argued that Nike's campaign defending itself against charges of using child and sweatshop labor was little more than a marketing campaign aimed at convincing consumers to buy more Nike products.

While lower courts agreed with Nike, the California Supreme Court ruled that Nike's adver-

tising campaign was commercial speech and therefore was not due full First Amendment protection. After initially agreeing to consider the case, the United States Supreme Court dismissed the appeal in 2003 and thereby allowed the California State Supreme Court decision to stand. In September 2003, Nike and Kasky reached an out-of-court settlement in which Nike agreed to pay $1.5 million. The money was directed to The Fair Labor Association, a worker-advocacy group that promotes international standards for ethical working conditions. The money will help pay for inspections of factories that allegedly mistreat workers, the very type of conditions that critics claimed Nike tolerated in the factories of its suppliers.

Nike is the world's largest athletic shoe and apparel maker. In 1999, Nike held over 30% of the world's market share for athletic footwear, and, along with Adidas (15%) and Reebok (11%), controls more than half of the world market. U.S. sales of athletic footwear have grown from $5 billion in 1985 to over $13 billion in 2001. For the first time ever, Nike sales outside of the U.S. topped domestic sales in the 3rd quarter of 2003.

Nike began business in 1964 as Blue Ribbon Sports, an importer and marketer of low-priced Japanese sport shoes. As sales increased, they began to design their own line of shoes and subcontract the manufacturing of the shoes to Japanese firms, and eventually changed their name to Nike. Nike's website described their business philosophy decades later in the following words: "Our business model in 1964 is essentially the same as our model today: We grow by investing our money in design, development, marketing and sales and then contract with other companies to manufacture our products."

During the 1970s when economic conditions made Japanese products more expensive, Nike opened its own manufacturing facilities in the United States. By the mid-1980s, however, with U.S. manufacturing costs becoming more expensive, Nike closed its own U.S. facilities. Since that time, all of Nike's products have been manufactured by subcontractors. In 1982, 86% of their shoes were manufactured in Korea and Taiwan. Later, as costs in these countries rose, Nike sought suppliers in other Asian countries, particularly in Indonesia, China, and Vietnam. According to its 2001 Annual Report, Nike's products are manufactured in 700 factories, employing over 500,000 workers in 51 countries. In that same year, Nike directly employed slightly more than 22,000 people, almost all in the U.S. In terms of individual manufacturing facilities, the largest number of Nike subcontractors are in the U.S. (131), China (74), Thailand (62), Korea (49), Malaysia (42), Mexico (41), Taiwan (35), and Indonesia (30). In terms of footwear alone, 40% of Nike shoes were manufactured in China, 31% in Indonesia, and 13% each in Vietnam and Thailand.

Beginning in the 1980s but peaking in the late 1990s, Nike was subjected to intense international criticism for the working conditions in the factories where their products were manufactured. Critics charged that Nike relied on child labor and sweatshops in producing their shoes. They charged that workers in these factories were paid pennies a day; were subjected to cruel, unhealthy, and inhumane working conditions; were harassed and abused; and were prohibited from any union or collective bargaining activities.

To critics, Nike's entire business model was the epitome of all that was wrong with the modern global corporation. Nike was a multibillion dollar U.S. corporation that used slick marketing tools to create a consumer demand so strong that people would pay over $100 for a pair of shoes that cost only a few dollars to manufacture. The marketing campaign was ubiquitous; children throughout the world, many of whom were impoverished, eagerly sought out the Nike logo on expensive shoes and clothing. Workers who made the products were exploited by being paid only pennies a day in horrid working conditions. The corporate strategy seemed designed to continuously seek out the lowest-paying factories in the world's poorest countries. This strategy created a race to the bottom of labor standards as factories in impoverished countries competed to attract Nike's business. This global-sourcing model created large profits that then could be put back into design and marketing to create greater consumer demand. The corporation could deny culpability by describing itself as simply designing and marketing products manufactured by others. Its suppliers and their home countries, but not Nike itself, were responsible for the working conditions faced by the people, mostly women and children, who made the products.

Nike initially seemed content to ignore the critics and deflect any criticism by denying responsibility for the behavior of its suppliers. At one point, Nike's vice president for Asia claimed that Nike did not "know the first thing about manufacturing. We are marketers and designers." However, by 1998 this strategy changed. CEO Phil Knight, in a speech to the National Press Club in May 1998, complained that "the Nike product has become synonymous with slave wages, forced overtime, and arbitrary abuse." During the 1990s, Nike instituted a number of policies aimed at ending abuses. By most accounts, working conditions in factories that manufacture Nike products have improved.

As part of their response to such criticism, Nike engaged in a public relations campaign to defend itself and to publicize the new and improved policies. This campaign included paid advertising, press conferences, press releases, op-ed pieces, letters to the editors, and letters to major consumer groups such as universities and sports teams. As summarized by the California State Supreme Court, Nike's public statements claimed "that workers who made Nike products are protected from physical and sexual abuse, that they are paid in accordance with applicable local laws and regulations governing wages and hours, that they are paid on average double the applicable local minimum wage, that they receive a 'livable wage,' that they receive free meals and health care, and that their working conditions are in compliance with applicable local law and regulations governing occupational health and safety."

Nike's marketing strategy has always been distinctive in rejecting traditional informational advertising in favor of image ads and celebrity endorsements. The public relations campaign aimed at answering these criticisms was one of the few occasions that Nike made any factual claims about its products in paid advertisements. Unlike its regular marketing strategy, this campaign aimed to rationally persuade its audience of the correctness of the Nike position.

Nike's marketing strategy has typically aimed to have its products identified with great athletes rather than with any attempt to persuade consumers to purchase Nike products rather than those of their competitors. Instead, Nike has strived to get its "swoosh" logo known throughout the world. In 2003, for example, Nike reported that it was paying $1.4 billion a year in endorsement contracts. Among its celebrity endorsements, Nike pays Tiger Woods $100 million over five years, LeBron James $90 million over seven years, Michael Jordon $47 million over five years, and Kobe Bryant $40 million over five years. Manchester United, one of Europe's greatest soccer teams, has an endorsement contract worth almost $500 million. In releasing this data, a Nike spokesman assured investors that the company is confident that they will see an adequate return on this marketing investment. Nike's closest rival, Reebok, has endorsement deals valued at just $196 million annually.

Kasky argued that the claims made in this campaign were false or misleading and thus Nike violated California law prohibiting false and deceptive advertising. By misleading consumers, this campaign also gave Nike an unfair competitive advantage in the marketplace. Nike's campaign thereby violated California law prohibiting unfair competition.

U.S. law has traditionally made a distinction between political speech, which enjoys full First Amendment protection, and commercial speech, which receives less protection. But courts have struggled to make a clear and consistent distinction between political and commercial speech. Courts have argued, for example, that the economic motive behind commercial speech justifies reduced First Amendment protection. Yet newspapers and television, the media through which much political speech is transmitted, also have clear economic motivation yet enjoy full First Amendment protection. Other rationales for the different treatment

have included the claim that commercial speech is less likely than political speech to be deterred by regulation, that it is more easily verified as true, that commercial speech is more influential than political, and that government has a greater interest in regulating commerce. In each case, critics claim that the same could be said for political speech.

The California Supreme Court ruled that Nike's public relations campaign was a commercial enterprise aimed at a commercial audience making "representations of fact about its business operations for the purpose of promoting sales of its products." Thus, Nike's campaign was a form of advertising and therefore was subject to California advertising regulations.

Nike argued that, in fact, the entire campaign was not aimed at selling more shoes but was in response to political and social criticisms of its operations and therefore was part of a broader political debate about globalization and corporate social responsibility. They also claimed to be targeting not only their customers but the broader public who might have heard about the criticisms. Thus, their speech was political and deserved strong First Amendment protection. They also pointed out that their critics were clearly engaged in the type of political speech that is fully protected by the First Amendment. Fairness would seem to require that Nike be treated in the same manner. Nevertheless, when the U.S. Supreme Court refused to hear the appeal, Nike decided to settle the case.

- What do you think is the difference between political and commercial speech? Should the two types of speech be treated differently in law?
- What is the difference between advertising that provides information about products and marketing a product through celebrity endorsements? What is the goal of each? Is there an ethical difference between the two approaches?
- Critics charged that Nike's claim that it was not responsible for the treatment of employees of subcontractors because these workers were not Nike's employees was misleading and deceptive. Do you agree?
- Is it wrong for Nike to market its expensive shoes to young people in impoverished areas where even low-priced consumer goods are luxuries?
- Why do people pay so much money for name-brand athletic shoes? Do consumers make a fully informed and voluntary choice to buy such products?

READING 9.1 DECEPTIVE ADVERTISING
John J. McCall

MORAL PRESUMPTIONS AGAINST DECEPTION

Every society has rules against deception and lying. It is easy to understand this presumption against deception by imagining what a society would be like if its members could never expect that others were being honest and truthful. A group that so completely lacked trust would never be able to engage in the ongoing cooperative activities that are the hallmark of human social life. For one example that is relevant to this text, consider what business would be if there were not background expectations that others would abide by their prior agreements. No business could be done on credit; all transactions would have to be "cash on the barrel" exchanges. (To those who suggest that the law could be used to enforce the terms of an exchange on credit: Imagine what it would be like to assume that every transaction was likely to require instituting legal process.)

The conditions necessary for coordinated and cooperative social life, then, explain why all societies will have some presumptions against deception. The difficulty for applying this analysis to specific questions of advertising deception is that social life can obviously go on even where the presumption against deception is a very bounded presumption. That is, society can tolerate defined areas of deception as long as most of its members understand where the rules against deception operate and, more importantly, where they do not operate.[1]

This analysis of the reasons for a presumption against deception, therefore, does not allow us easily to conclude that any given act of deception is presumptively wrong. It might be that the specific deceptive act in question is one that takes place in an arena where the parties do not expect honesty and trustworthiness. In our culture, a very narrowly bounded exception to the presumption against deception exists in the game of poker. There, everyone expects the other players to misrepresent their current hands of cards. In a given culture, the same bounded exception to expectations of honesty might exist in the marketplace. (Though, of course, that culture's marketplace might never advance much beyond a bazaar. The evolution to more complex transactions seems to require a higher level of trust between parties, as do certain circumstances where the same individuals engage in repeated transactions over time.) In any case, the need for cooperation and trust does not entail a general presumption against deception *in advertising*. It only entails that societies have some rules against deception.

The morality of our culture, happily, also contains nonconsequentialist standards that can generate stronger and less bounded presumptions against deception. If . . . the ideas of individual rights and dignity rest in part on the autonomy of persons, then there are additional reasons to reject acts of lying and deception.[2]

Deception cuts at the core of another's autonomy because it is an attempt to short-circuit that person's ability to engage in free, reasoned choice. It is an attempt to manipulate another's decision by getting that person unknowingly to act on false beliefs. Even so conservative a picture of business responsibility as Milton Friedman's sees the relationship between deception and autonomy when it enjoins both coercion *and* deception. Thus, the contemporary moral commitment to individual rights and dignity allows us to derive a stronger and less bounded presumption against deception than we could if we depended only on the social necessity of some unspecified rule against deceit. We can argue now that any attempt to deceive is presumptively wrong because it attempts manipulatively to undermine the capacity for reasoned choice.

Of course, even this argument against deception will admit that there are instances of deception that can be justified. We cannot identify all possible exceptions to the rule against lying here, but we can identify three typical cases where lies and deception are acceptable. Perhaps the clearest case is the first one, where the deception is needed to save a life. No one, that is no one with moral sensitivity, seriously believes that Dutch villagers were acting wrongly when they deceived the Nazis about the presence of Jews among them. That elaborate deception was necessary to prevent an even greater wrong, an even greater violation of someone's autonomy.

Second, we generally accept harmless deceit where no unfair advantage is sought through the deception. "You look nice today!" when a person really doesn't may be a case in point. Such deception might merely be understood as appropriate sociability. (However, there are cases where falsely telling someone they look fine might be inappropriate— for example, when a person is on his way to a job interview and needs an honest opinion rather than reassurance. Telling when a lie is sociable and when it is inappropriate requires subtle skill and moral sensitivity.)

We also accept deception in the third case, where the parties involved *all* know that deception is likely. The poker game mentioned earlier is an example. So also is the labor negotiation where a party puts forward its "best offer." Even in these cases, however, the areas of permissible deception are narrowly defined. The poker player cannot legitimately deceive by slipping hidden cards into his hand; the negotiator cannot legitimately deceive by accepting a negotiated settlement and then later refusing to comply with the terms of the agreement.

Do these categories of exception have any implications for our topic of deceptive advertising? Can advertising be counted as an exception to the general rule against deception? Clearly, it cannot count as an instance of the first two types of acceptable deception. Typically, deceptive advertising is not required to save a life or to protect some equally important interest of another party from unjust harm. Nor is deceptive advertising usually a harmless act without any attempt to gain an unfair advantage. More typically, deception in advertising is calculated to create an unfair advantage for the advertiser both against the consumer targeted by the ad and against the business's competitors. It also intends some loss or harm to both of those parties. A consumer who buys one brand of product because she or he was deceived into thinking it a better value than a competitive product is harmed, as is the competitor.

It is frequently claimed, though, that deceptive advertising counts as an instance of the third category—that is, it is deception in a case where everyone expects (or ought to expect) deception to occur. The frequency of this opinion does not alter the fact that it is confused on both factual and conceptual grounds. There is ample evidence that consumers are in fact regularly tricked by deceptive advertising and marketing practices. (Why would those practices be used if those employing them did not believe they would be successful?) While this discussion is a discussion of the morality of deceptive advertising rather than one about government regulation of ads, a comment about the Federal Trade Commission is in order here. The FTC frequently concludes on the basis of market study that ads trick a significant number of consumers. Ivan Preston's [. . .] recent book, *The Tangled Web: Truth, Falsity and Advertising,* provides numerous examples where the FTC has found that 20–25% of the surveyed consumer population was misled by an intentionally deceptive advertising practice. So it seems as if the claim that consumers expect deception runs counter to the evidence from consumer research.

One possible, and I think very weak, retort to this is to point out that there is no logical inconsistency between saying that consumers expect deception and saying that they are simultaneously taken in by an act of deception. After all, some claim, in activities such as poker and labor negotiations the parties expect deception yet are sometimes successfully bluffed nonetheless. This is true enough. That mere logical possibility, however, is insufficient to convince me that consumers generally expect to be deceived. Here is where the second, conceptual confusion arises for those thinking that deceptive ads fall into the third exception category.

Consumers, having been burned once or twice by a particular deceptive practice, learn to be wary of falling for that practice again. Once you learned that "economy size" merely meant bigger but not cheaper per unit, you learned to compare unit prices for packages of different quantity. That alone, of course, suggests that you were not expecting that particular form of deception the first few times it happened to you.

Moreover, the attempt to assimilate deceptive advertising into the third category ignores the fact that for deception to be expected, it has to be expected in relatively well defined areas. It may be possible, after learning, to expect deception in the use of a word like *economy*. It is not possible, however, to expect deception to occur in all the places where advertisers might conceivably use it. Expecting deception to that degree is both conceptually and psychologically impossible. It's conceptually impossible because the available deceptive techniques are infinite in number and a consumer logically cannot expect all of them. In addition, a consumer who even attempted to guard against a significant number of those possible avenues of deception would soon experience overload and decision-making paralysis. Imagine pushing your cart down the supermarket aisle and looking out for the innumerable ways you might be deceived.

It seems clear, then, that deceptive marketing and advertising is not a case of deception everyone knows about and expects. The fact that many of us are cynical about advertising practices does not in the least diminish the conclusion that it is conceptually and factually confusing to place ads in the third exception category. Deceptive marketing and advertising practices should be subject to a strong presumption of immorality.

Another common retort to that conclusion is the view that the consumer has a responsibility to act warily and protect him- or herself against deception. A consumer foolish enough to be taken in by some intentionally deceptive scheme is at fault for failing to be adequately vigilant.

But even if we accept that consumers have responsibility and can be at fault for falling prey to the more obvious tricks of advertisers, the retort still misses the point. If the intent to deceive is present, as it is assumed by those who use this retort, and if advertisers trade upon the fact that some consumers will fail to process the deception, then the advertiser is still subject to the charge of moral impropriety. It is the mere intent to deceive that supports that moral judgment. If I walk onto a used car lot and the salesperson has illegally turned back the odometer so the car appears to have fewer miles than it actually does, I might be able to catch the deception. I might, for instance, take note of the excessive wear on the seats and note the discrepancy between that and the odometer's mileage. The fact that the attempted deception was unsuccessful does not diminish its immorality. And if I failed to detect the deception and bought the car, even if I bear some responsibility for believing the sales pitch, that personal responsibility does not amount to absolving

the car salesperson of ethical wrong. The consumer's behavior is simply not relevant one way or the other to the principle that intentional deception is immoral.[3]

DECEPTIVE ADVERTISEMENTS

This principle of assessment for the morality of advertising is not an easy one to apply, however. Any particular judgment will require speculation about the largely private mental states of the advertiser. We need to have some skepticism about our interpretation of a person's intentions. These mental states are not completely inaccessible, though, and there are reasonable presumptive judgments we can make about many advertisements just from their design and content. As a first step in evaluating whether ads are intentionally deceptive, we can categorize some techniques of deception and discuss some examples.

All ads attempt to communicate a message that intends to influence us. The vehicle of that communication can take a variety of forms. There is the linguistic element of the communication, of course—what is said, implied, and omitted. But of equal importance is the visual communication (at least for ads other than those on radio!). An anecdote from the political arena can help emphasize the importance of this category of communication. During Ronald Reagan's second presidential campaign, news reports were often critical of his policies. One such report had a visual of Reagan on the campaign trail. He was on a bandstand, surrounded by American flag bunting, cheerleaders, a pep band, and a cheering crowd. The news reader's voice-over was presenting a criticism of a Reagan policy. After the news spot aired, a Reagan press aide purportedly called the network to thank it for the helpful news story. He said that what the viewer would carry away was the positive image from the video footage, not the critical commentary. This point about the power of visual images can be even more true for commercials.

Examples where we can presume intended use of visuals to deceive are easy to find. Some classic ones are the following: (1) A shaving cream commercial that claimed the cream was so good at softening beards that it could even be used to shave sandpaper. The camera showed a razor apparently removing the grit from sandpaper that was sprayed with the foam. What was actually photographed was a piece of glass set against a tan background and sprinkled with loose sand. The razor had no blade. (2) A soup commercial touting its new chunky style loaded with vegetables. The picture showed a bowl with the vegetables mounded high above the broth. What was not disclosed was that the bowl had marbles in it to raise the vegetables for better display. (3) A car commercial that advertised the safety of the car, especially in rollovers, where the roofs of many vehicles collapse onto the passengers. The car was the only one in a group to withstand a "monster truck" rolling over it. The vehicle was not a stock model but was rather one with a specially reinforced roof.

In each of these examples, we can presume that the advertiser intended to deceive with the visuals because in each case the product was made to appear as something it was not. This is true regardless of whether the shaving cream was more effective than competitors at softening beards, whether the soup was indeed chunky, whether the car was safer than others in rollovers. It will not do, either, for the advertisers to defend themselves by saying that they merely intended to visualize a real product attribute, because that intended goal was achieved by a means that intentionally misrepresented the product in its visual display. Agents are, of course, responsible for the means they use as well as the ends they pursue.

More contemporary, and perhaps more controversial, examples of presumptive intent to deceive with visuals (and with language) have been proposed by students in business ethics classes. You should consider each of the following examples and decide whether it is reasonable to conclude that there was deceptive intent.

One example concerns a commercial for a child's action toy that is displayed against a background that makes the toy look larger, more realistic, and capable of more movements than it actually is.[4]

A second contemporary example is an ad for a brand of fat-free cookie. The ad shows a group of, shall we say, physically imposing women pursuing a cookie delivery man. The cookies are fat-free but they are definitely not low-calorie. Yet the visuals may be taken to suggest that the women are interested in the product for weight-loss reasons. It is

certainly true that the choice of women of this particular body type was a conscious decision by the ad team. (Note that most products try to associate themselves with more svelte body types.)

Another recent example might be frozen dinner packages with cover photos of a "serving suggestion." In reality, it would be difficult to make the contents of the package appear on the plate as does the food in the photo. All of these cases were proposed as cases where it is the advertiser's intentional decision to visually communicate messages that can be described as misleading. While those judgments are surely speculative to some degree, the conscious design of the ads makes it reasonable to question the intent of those creating them.

Similar questions can be raised about misleading intent based on the linguistic element of advertisements. Few ads these days make directly false statements. Ads can be designed, though, to deceive by ambiguity in their actual statements, by what advertisers hope the public, or some portion of it, will take as an implication of what was said, or by the intentional omission of pertinent information.

Food nutrition claims of the past decade have been notorious for misleading with carefully crafted use of language. (In fact, they have been so notorious that both the FDA and FTC have issued guidelines in the last two years to stop the use of deceptive nutrition claims on labels and in ads.) Some of the most notable of the claims surround the use of terms such as *fat-free, low-fat, lite/light, low-calorie*, and *cholesterol-free*. A manufacturer of potato chips, for example, has advertised its chips as cholesterol-free, which was technically true. However, the chips were high in fat and even in saturated fat (which the body processes into cholesterol). The claim was true, but we can surmise that the intent was to depend on a confusion in the consumer's mind about fats, cholesterol, and body chemistry. The ad clearly hoped some consumers would take away the message that the chips would not raise cholesterol. What else could the intent have been?

The plastics industry has been proposed as a more subtle example where we might reasonably conclude intent to deceive. The industry has, of course, come under criticism from environmentalists who are concerned that our "throw-away" society uses too much nonrenewable fossil fuel in its consumption of nonrecyclable plastic. Industry commercials defend plastic by praising its value for artificial limbs, automobile air bags, and the like. Some critics claim that the ads, like a shell game at a carnival, intend to deceive by obfuscating the issue and attempting to imply a generalized false conclusion that plastics are, in all their uses, essential.

Ads might intend to deceive even when they provide full and accurate information. Auto lease advertisements do disclose the terms of the lease that qualify the highly attractive monthly payment figures that dominate the ads. But those qualifying terms, when presented on television commercials, are displayed so quickly that even the speediest readers will be unable to process the information. Some say that the design of the ads suggests an intentional deception that depends on consumers being unable to assimilate the government-required disclosures.

Assessing intended deception is perhaps most difficult for ads that omit information. One might try to say that an ad is deceptive if an advertiser intentionally omits information that might lead the consumer to a different decision. The difficulty with this principle, however, is that it might require too much disclosure. Certainly, the principle would seem to require advertisers to disclose *all* the negative features of their products. It also seems to require disclosure of deficiencies of a product relative to competitor products. Not hiding major flaws is one thing; it is quite another to suggest that ads disclose everything that might be relevant to consumer judgment. Exactly where we should draw the line concerning what can knowingly be omitted without intending to mislead is a difficult question.

The difficulty of drawing that line should not obscure the obvious cases that intend to deceive by omission, however. Political campaign ads are perhaps the most corrupt example of misleading by omission. Often opponents will charge that "Senator Smith voted against funding for [choose a popular hot button issue]." While it is usually true that "Smith" did vote against a bill containing funding, what the ads fail to disclose is that the bill was a complex appropriation bill that dealt with a number of other appropriations as well. Political ads also fail to disclose instances where "Smith" supported the popular project. Despite the general difficulty in determining when omissions intend to deceive, then, there are cases where that intent is clearly present. Commercial examples of deceptive omission might be found in ads that omit reference to

hidden charges or costs, for instance, points paid on a mortgage, or that omit to say that a sale price applies only to a very small number of products.

The preceding examples are meant to illustrate some of the main ways in which ads can intend to deceive. Any controversy surrounding the examples should not cloud the main point: There are reasonable presumptive judgments of intended deception that we can make about ads based on the facts of their design, language, and context. Consumers have legitimate moral grounds for complaining about any ad where such reasonable presumption exists. More importantly, advertisers themselves have obligations to assess their own intentions self-critically. They should reject as inappropriate any technique whereby they hope to mislead by statement, implication, omission, or visual image. Intent is one main criterion by which ads should be evaluated. Both the public and advertisers need to apply that standard of evaluation more strictly. Currently advertisers too frequently engage in a corrupt cat-and-mouse game with consumers, and the public too frequently tolerates that corruption.

With that conclusion drawn, one final question needs to be posed. Are there cases where, lacking intent to deceive, advertisers nevertheless have a moral responsibility for consumers being misled? There are at least two kinds of case in which the answer to that question is yes. The first is one in which the false impression in the mind of the consumer was a reasonably forseeable result of an ad. Even if the advertiser did not intend that result, he or she can still be responsible for a negligent failure to exercise appropriate forethought in the design of the advertisement. Some examples of visual representations that aim to highlight the positive features of a product would be of this kind. If we refer to the classic cases of chunky soup or sturdy cars, even if the advertiser intended no deception, the false ideas carried away by consumers were predictable. Omissions that we cannot conclude are intentionally deceptive may often fall into this category. (So, even though it is hard to determine when omissions intend to deceive, we still have resources for concluding that advertisers sometimes bear responsibility for false impressions caused by omissions, intentional or not.)

The second kind of case is perhaps more common. On occasions where an ad intends no deception, it may be that consumers unpredictably misread the meaning of the ad. If an advertiser knows this has been the result and yet continues to use the same ad, there is reason for claiming the continued use of the ad is intentionally deceptive. For even if the ad in its debut did not intend to deceive, an advertiser who knowingly trades on a miscommunication knowingly allows a future false impression to be created. Thus, there are cases where, absent initial intent to deceive, the deceptive effect of an ad is nonetheless the ethical responsibility of the advertiser. Further discussion of deceptive effect (and the role it plays in government regulatory action) is left for later readings in this chapter.

NOTES

1. Some suggest that where no one expects honesty, there can be no deception. The reading by Albert Carr in Chapter 7 contains such a claim. Even if that were true, which it is not, it cannot apply to the point that societies can operate with bounded rules against deception. All that such bounded prohibition against deception requires is that most members understand where the rules operate, not that all members do. And, in any case, the claim is false. Even where the social rules against deception are

suspended, one person may still attempt to mislead another. The example of the poker game makes this point. Suspending the presumption against deception, then, means only that deception in that area is not considered wrong. It does not mean that deception is impossible.

2. Lying, by definition, is the intentional utterance of a falsehood with the intent to deceive another. As such, lying is a species of deception, and it is the element of *intended* deception that makes a lie presumptively wrong. Jokes or pieces of fiction, after all, are intentional falsehoods. They simply do not intend deception.

3. This analysis also points out the difference between standards of moral evaluation and standards for legal regulation of deceptive advertising. In regulatory matters it is of some importance whether the ad actually misleads the reasonable or only the ignorant consumer, that is, if the ad misleads many or only a very few. If it is few, and if the consequent harm to those few is also small, a government regulatory response may not be appropriate. However, regardless of the number or nature of those misled, if the ad intends to deceive some portion of the public, then there is a strong reason to say the behavior of the advertiser is immoral.

4. See the article by Lynn Sharp Paine later in this chapter for another criticism of advertising to children.

READING 9.2 DECEPTION AND WITHHOLDING INFORMATION IN SALES

Thomas Carson

INTRODUCTION

Approximately 10 percent of the U.S. work force is involved in sales. In addition, most members of our society occasionally sell major holdings such as used cars and real estate. The ethics of sales is an important, but neglected, topic in business ethics. Only a handful of papers, most of them quite short, have ever been written on this topic (no books have ever been written on the ethics of sales). David Holley's papers "A Moral Evaluation of Sales Practices" and

"Information Disclosure in Sales" are the only full-length papers ever written on this topic (they are the only full-length papers that state and defend a theory about the moral duties of salespeople).

Salespeople are often in a position to mislead customers and deceptive practices are common in many areas of sales. I argue that the likely harm to the buyer creates a strong presumption for thinking that deception in sales is morally wrong. Except in very unusual cases, deception in sales cannot be justified. I also argue that deception in sales is wrong because it violates the golden rule. . . .

I argue that salespeople have *prima facie* duties to do the following: (1) warn customers of potential hazards, (2) refrain from lying and deception,

From Thomas Carson, "Deception and Withholding Information in Sales," in Business Ethics Quarterly, Volume 11, Issue 2, pp. 275–306. © 2001 Business Ethics Quarterly. Reprinted by permission. All notes in this reading have been deleted.

(3) fully and honestly answer questions about what they are selling (insofar as their knowledge and time constraints permit), and (4) refrain from steering customers toward purchases they have reason to think will be harmful to the customers. I discuss several cases to illustrate and clarify my theory and offer a justification for the version of the golden rule to which I appeal. . . .

A Conceptual Roadmap

We need to distinguish between deception, lying, withholding information, and concealing information. Roughly, to deceive someone is to cause her to have false beliefs (or intentionally cause her to have false beliefs). Standard dictionary definitions of lying say that a lie is a false statement made with the intent to deceive others. The *Oxford English Dictionary* defines a lie as: "a false statement made with the intent to deceive." *Webster's International Dictionary of the English Language* (1929) gives the following definition of the verb "lie": "to utter a falsehood with the intent to deceive. Lying arguably requires the intent to deceive others, but lies that don't succeed in causing others to have false beliefs are not instances of deception. A further difference between lying and deception is that, while a lie must be a false statement, deception needn't involve false statements; true statements can be deceptive and some forms of deception don't involve making statements of any sort. Thus, many instances of deception do not constitute lying. Withholding information does not constitute deception. It is not a case of *causing* someone to have false beliefs; it is merely a case of failing to correct false beliefs or incomplete information. On the other hand, actively concealing information often constitutes deception. For example, if painting over the rust on a used car caused a potential buyer to believe falsely that the body of the car was in good condition, doing so would constitute deception.

The Common-Law Principle of *Caveat Emptor*

Traditionally, many salespeople have followed the principle of *caveat emptor* ("buyer beware"). According to the common-law principle of *caveat emptor*, sellers are not legally obligated to inform prospective buyers about the properties of the goods they sell. Under caveat emptor, sales and contracts to sell are legally enforceable even if the seller fails to inform the buyer of serious defects in the

goods that are sold. English common law sometimes called for the enforcement of sales in cases in which sellers made false or misleading statements about the goods they sold. Under *caveat emptor*, buyers themselves are responsible for determining the quality of the goods they purchase.

Currently, all U.S. states operate under the Uniform Commercial Code of 1968. Section 2-313 of the Code defines the notion of sellers' warranties. The Code provides that all factual affirmations or statements about the goods being sold are warranties. This means that sales are not valid or legally enforceable if the seller makes false statements about the features of the goods s/he is selling. The American legal system has developed the concept of an "implied" (as opposed to an express or explicit) warranty. Implied warranties are a significant limitation on the principle of *caveat emptor*. According to the Uniform Commercial Code, any transaction carries with it the following implied warranties: (1) that the seller owns the goods he is selling and (2) that the goods are "merchantable," i.e., suitable for the purposes for which they are sold. The implied warranty of merchantability does not apply to defects when the buyer inspects the goods and reasonable inspection ought to have revealed the defects. However, a buyer's failure to inspect doesn't negate implied warranties unless the buyer refuses the seller's demand that she inspect. Implied warranties may be expressly disclaimed by such statements as "all warranties express or implied are hereby disclaimed." Such disclaimers of warranty are often made by used car dealers. Many local ordinances require that people who sell real estate inform buyers about all known serious defects of the property they sell. These ordinances are also a significant limitation on the traditional principle of *caveat emptor*.

Many salespeople take the law to be an acceptable moral standard for their conduct and claim that they have no moral duty to provide buyers with information about the goods they sell, except for information that the law requires for an enforceable sale.

Who Is a Salesperson?

Car salespeople, realtors, sales representatives who sell supplies or equipment to businesses, and private individuals who sell their own cars or homes are paradigm cases of salespeople. A cashier in a store who rings up the bill and is not expected to advise customers in any way is not a salesperson. I will use the term "salesperson" fairly broadly to include people who "wait on customers in stores," e.g., clothing, hardware, and shoe stores. Roughly, a salesperson is anyone who sells things and whose position requires him to advise buyers on their purchases or supply them with information about what they are purchasing. People who assist customers on the floors of large warehouse stores are borderline cases for the concept of a salesperson.

It might be objected that the differences between different kinds of salespeople make it impossible to formulate a single theory about the moral duties of all salespeople. For example, the obligations of a realtor who spends many hours with a client and sells something of great importance and value are very different from those of a sales clerk in a store who spends a few minutes with a customer helping her buy an inexpensive birthday gift. However, . . . my theory can account for the fact that different kinds of salespeople have very different kinds of moral obligations.

DECEPTION IN SALES

Consider the following three cases of deception in sales:

Case 1: A customer in a shoe store asks to try on a particular kind of shoe. The salesperson falsely claims that the shoe is not in stock in her size. He does this in the hope of steering the customer to a higher priced shoe. If the customer is unwilling to purchase any of the other shoes, the salesperson plans to stage a "second look" for the model the customer initially asked for and produce the shoe in question. He will say that it is the only pair in stock in her size and that they are selling fast. In so doing, he hopes to create a sense of urgency on the part of the customer so that she will buy it from him now, rather than come back later when she will probably be served by a different salesperson.

Case 2: A salesperson feigns a friendly concern for a customer's interests. He expresses a desire to help the customer save money and says "I will try to help you find the product that is best suited for your needs. I don't want you to spend any more money than you need to. Take as much time as you need." The customer believes the salesperson, but she is deceived. In fact, the salesperson couldn't care less about customer s welfare. He only wants to sell the customer the highest priced item he can as quickly as he can. He does not like the customer, indeed, he is contemptuous of her. [This kind of deception is very common in sales. Often salespeople need to convince customers that they are acting for their benefit and gain their trust in order to be successful in selling to them.]

Case 3: A used car salesperson is trying to sell a car on which the odometer has been turned back. A prospective customer asks whether the odometer reading on the car is correct. The salesperson replies by saying that it is illegal to alter odometer readings.

[Cases] 1 and 2 are [examples] of lying. Case 3 does not constitute lying, since the salesman's statement is true.

There is a strong moral presumption against deception in sales because of the harm it is likely to cause potential buyers. Such deception is likely to harm buyers by causing them to have false beliefs about the nature of the products in question and thereby cause some consumers to make different purchasing decisions than they would have otherwise made. Suppose that in case #3 the salesperson's deceptive statements cause me to believe that the car's mileage is 50,000 when, in fact, it is 97,000. Acting on this belief, I purchase the car for a certain price. It is likely that I would have been unwilling to purchase the car for the same price if I had known the true mileage. I might not have been willing to buy the car at all in that case. The customer is likely to be harmed as a result of being deceived in case #2. If she believes the salesperson, then she will rely on the salesperson's judgment and is likely to be steered into purchasing something that is more expensive than she needs or something that is unsuitable for her interests. Her trust in the salesperson is likely to make her a less careful shopper than she ordinarily is.

In case #1, the customer will be harmed if she purchases the shoe the salesman tries to sell her—she preferred the less expensive shoe and would have purchased it if the salesman hadn't lied to her. Suppose that the customer decides not to buy the more expensive shoes. The salesman then takes a "second look" for the shoe she wanted and returns with it; he falsely claims that it is the last pair in stock in her size. She might still be harmed if she is pressured into making a purchase on the basis of this false information. It is possible that if she hadn't been misled in this way she would have left the store to think about the purchase and would have looked at the shoes in her closet, checked her bank balance, and then would have decided not to buy the shoes. This choice, made in a more leisurely way and made with more information, better reflects her true interests than the choice she actually made. (The customer's actual interests are determined by the purchasing decisions she would make if she were fully informed and fully rational.)

Customers are likely to be harmed when salespeople deceive them, but such deception doesn't necessarily harm the buyer. Deception might fail to alter someone's purchasing decisions. In the used car example, it might be the case that I will not purchase the car, whether or not I am deceived about the mileage. A person might even benefit as a result of being deceived by a salesperson. Consider the following variation on the used car example. The buyer wouldn't have purchased the car unless he had been misled about the mileage, but, despite the high mileage, it turns out to be a terrific car, much better for him than any car he would have purchased if he hadn't been deceived by the seller. In such cases we can't say that the deception is wrong on account of the actual harm it causes the buyer. But we can still say that deception is wrong because it *risks* harming the buyer (or is likely to harm the buyer). Such deception should be judged in terms of its *probable or likely consequences*. Here, I would appeal to the analogy between these cases and drunk driving. On most occasions, people who drive while intoxicated are not involved in accidents and don't harm anyone? In those cases, we can't say that drunk driving is wrong because of the actual harm it causes others. It is wrong to drive while intoxicated because it is wrong to (needlessly) subject others to the risk of harm. Sometimes we are justified in acting in ways that risk causing harm to others. Open heart surgery, generating electricity, and driving a car while sober all risk harming others. But, in these cases, the probable benefits exceed the probable harms (the extent of a probable harm is a function of the magnitude of the harm and the probability of its occurring) and the affected parties (or many of the affected parties), in some sense, consent to the risk. An adult person who drives a car or flies as a passenger in an airplane consents to the risks that these activities pose to him. (Consenting to something often legitimizes acts that would otherwise be morally wrong, e.g. physically taking your property with or without your consent, or performing elective surgery on you with or without your consent.) The probable harm of deception in sales exceeds the probable benefits . . . and the victims of deception in sales seldom consent to being deceived in this way. The probable harm of drunk driving greatly exceeds its benefits and few, if any, drivers consent to others driving while drunk.

Of course, there is no absolute moral prohibition against harming others (or risking harming others). One can be justified in harming someone else in self-defense. A judge can be justified in sending a violent criminal to a long term in prison, even though this would harm the criminal. However, harming others is *prima facie* wrong, or wrong, other things being equal. (To say that an act is one's *prima facie* duty is to say that it is one's actual duty, other things being equal; one's *prima facie* duty is one's actual duty in the absence of conflicting duties of greater or equal importance.) We need to have some kind of special justification in order for it to be right for us to harm others. In the case of the judge and the violent criminal, the presumption against harming others is overridden by the public's interest in being protected from the criminal and deterring other potential criminals.

The fact that deception in sales harms consumers (or is likely to harm them) gives us a presumption for thinking that it is wrong for salespeople to deceive customers. Are there any conceivable justifications for deception in sales that might override this presumption? What about the benefits to the salesperson? Can a salesperson justify deception on the grounds that it benefits her or those who are dependent on her? This is *possible*— we can always imagine cases in which the salesperson's family is in dire straits and the customer is very rich and unlikely to be harmed very much by the deception. But such cases are rare. In any given case, it is unlikely that the benefits derived by the seller outweigh the harms to others; deception not only harms the customer, it also harms competing sellers. We also need to factor in the indirect bad consequences of lying and deception. Lying and deception harm the social fabric and background of trust essential for a flourishing society and economy. The law alone cannot ensure the level of trust that people need in order to be willing and able to enter into mutually beneficial market transactions. No legal system can effectively police and deter rampant and universal dishonesty in the economic sphere. The enforcement mechanisms of the law can work only in a background in which most people are generally adhering to norms of honesty for moral reasons independently of the fear of getting caught. . . . Lying and deception also harm the salesperson's character by making her less honest. Economic necessity is very rarely a plausible justification for deceptive sales practices. A firm that needs to deceive the public about the nature of its goods or services in order to stay in business is of dubious value to society—the resources it utilizes could be put to better use in some other way. Similarly, if a salesperson needs to practice deception in order to get by, she should look for a different kind of job—her talents could probably be put to better use in some other line of work.

On the weak and scarcely debatable assumption that it is *prima facie* wrong to harm others or risk harm to others, we can show that there is a strong presumption for thinking that deception in sales is morally wrong. If lying and deception are *prima facie* wrong (apart from the harm they cause or risk causing), then there is an even stronger presumption against deception in sales. A modified version of Ross's theory, which includes the view that deceiving others is *prima facie* wrong, would give a somewhat stronger presumption against deception in sales than standard versions of act-utilitarianism. Act-utilitarianism and this modified Rossian theory yield different results in at least some cases of deception in sales. There are many controversies in ethical theory that bear on the issues of this paper. I cannot hope to resolve these controversies in the present paper. My claim here is that *any* plausible moral theory holds that harming others is *prima facie* wrong and that, therefore, given any plausible moral theory, there is a strong moral presumption against deception in sales.

We can also show that deception in sales is wrong because it violates the golden rule. All salespeople are themselves buyers and customers. As customers, they want to choose rationally on the basis of correct information; they don't want to act on the basis of false beliefs. Almost no one who is buying something is willing to be deceived by the salesperson. Salespeople who practice deception violate the golden rule; they act in ways that they are not willing to have others act. They are not willing to have other people make it a policy to deceive others whenever doing so promotes their own economic interests. This kind of golden rule argument against deception will be developed in much greater detail. . . .

TOWARD A MORE PLAUSIBLE THEORY ABOUT DECEPTION AND WITHHOLDING INFORMATION IN SALES

Salespeople have certain moral duties regarding the disclosure of information when dealing with *rational adult consumers*. I formulate and defend a provisional list of these duties below. These are *prima facie* duties that can conflict with other duties and are sometimes overridden by other duties. (A *prima facie* duty is one's actual duty, other things being equal. Alternatively, a *prima facie* duty is an actual duty in the absence of conflicting duties of greater or equal importance.) Salespeople have other duties to customers that don't concern the disclosure of information; my list does not purport to be a complete list of the moral duties of salespeople. The following are (prima facie) duties of salespeople concerning the disclosure of information:

1. Salespeople should provide buyers with safety warnings and precautions about the goods and services they sell. Sometimes it is enough for salespeople to call attention to written warnings and precautions that come with the goods and services in question. These warnings are unnecessary if the buyers already understand the dangers or precautions in question.

2. Sales people should refrain from lying and deception in their dealings with customers.

3. As much as their knowledge and time constraints permit, salespeople should fully answer customers questions about the products or services they are selling. They should answer questions forthrightly and not evade questions or withhold information that has been asked for

(even if this makes it less likely that they will make a successful sale). Salespeople are obligated to answer questions about the goods and services they, themselves, sell. However, they are not obligated to answer questions about competing goods and services or give information about other sellers. In such cases, the salesperson should refuse to answer the question, not evade it or pretend to answer it.

4. Salespeople should not try to "steer" customers toward purchases that they have reason to think will cause significant harm to customers (financial harm counts) or that customers will come to deeply regret. [Any means by which one tries to cause another to purchase a particular good or service counts as "steering" him toward purchasing it.]

[This] is a minimal list of the duties of salespeople concerning the disclosure of information. I am inclined to think that the following are also *prima facie* duties of salespeople concerning the disclosure of information, but I am much less confident that these principles can be justified:

5. Salespeople should not sell customers goods or services that they have reason to think will prove to be harmful to customers (financial harm counts) or that the customers will come to regret later, without giving the customers their reasons for thinking that this is the case. [This duty does not hold if the seller has good reasons to think that the customer already possesses the information in question. Ordinarily, salespeople are not obligated to warn customers about the dangers of such things as tobacco, alcohol, and fast cars.]

6. Salespeople should not sell items they know to be defective or of poor quality without alerting customers to this. [This duty does not hold if the buyer knows or can be reasonably expected to know about the poor quality of what he is buying.]

Connections between 2, 4, and 6

Lying and deception in sales are not confined to lying to or deceiving customers about the goods one sells. Many salespeople misrepresent their own motives to customers/clients (case 2 . . . is a good

example of this). Almost all salespeople invite the trust of customers/clients and claim, implicitly or explicitly, to be acting in their interests. Salespeople often ask customers to defer to their judgment about what is best for them. For most salespeople, gaining the trust of customers/clients is essential for success in sales. Many salespeople are *not* interested in helping customers in the way they represent themselves as being. A salesperson who misrepresents her motives and intentions to customers is guilty of violating [rule] 2 (or a least guilty of *attempting* to deceive customers/clients). This kind of simultaneous inviting and betrayal of trust is a kind of treachery. In ordinary cases, rules against lying and deception alone prohibit salespeople from steering customers toward goods or services they have reason to think will be bad for them. It is difficult to steer someone in this way without lying or deception. In order to do this, salespeople may need to deceive customers about the features of the items they sell or about the quality and availability of alternative goods and services. Salespeople are often asked to recommend what they think is best for the customer. To recommend something one knows to be unsuitable for the customer in response to such a request would be deceptive. In such a case, it would be a lie to assert that the item in question is, in one's opinion, the one that is best for the buyer. Similar remarks apply to selling defective goods. Often it is impossible to do this without lying to or deceiving customers. In practice, most violations of rules 4 and 6 are also violations of rule 2.

A JUSTIFICATION FOR MY THEORY

I have two different lines of argument for my theory. First, 1–4 yield intuitively plausible results in concrete cases and avoid *all* of the objections I raised against Holley and Ebejer and Morden. Second, I justify 1–4 by appeal to the golden rule and consistency requirements for moral judgments. Some readers may regard this second line of argument as redundant. However, I disagree. People don't always agree in their moral intuitions about moral issues in sales. Mere appeal to intuitions cannot settle these or any other controversial moral questions. The appeal to "our" moral intuitions doesn't give us any answer to skeptical challenges to morality or any answer to those who attempt to justify or rationalize ostensibly wrong acts that serve their own self-interests. These individuals—I'm thinking of people like Albert Carr—will simply report conflicting moral intuitions. Answering such individuals (and attempting to show why they are mistaken) is part of the task of business ethics. Work in business ethics cannot simply appeal to the moral intuitions or shared beliefs of the converted.

Taken together, 1–4 give us an intuitively plausible theory about the duties of salespeople regarding the disclosure of information. . . . But, 1–4 do not make unreasonable demands on salespeople. They don't require that salespeople provide information that they don't have or spend more time with customers than they can spend. Nor do they require salespeople to divulge information about the virtues of what competitors are selling or about what price competitors are charging. 1–4 do not prohibit selling things to people who have limited options, nor do they employ ambiguous concepts such as the concept of "expert knowledge. . . ."

In addition, my theory explains why different types of salespeople have different sorts of duties to their customers. For example, ordinarily, realtors have a duty to provide much more information to customers than sales clerks who sell inexpensive items in gift stores. My theory explains this difference in terms of the following: (1) the realtor's greater knowledge and expertise (the realtor is able to provide far more information than the sales clerk), (2) much greater amount of time the realtor can devote to the customer, (3) the greater importance of the purchase of a home than the purchase of small gift and the greater potential for harm or benefit to the buyer (this means that violations of moral obligations are a much more serious matter in the case of realtors), (4) the fact that home buyers generally *ask* realtors for a great deal more information than customers ask of sales clerks in gift stores, and (in some cases) (5) implicit or explicit claims by the relator to be acting on behalf of prospective home buyers (clerks in stores rarely make such claims).

An Objection Considered

On my view, salespeople are required to give safety warnings and answer customers' questions, but they are not obligated to ensure that customers are ade-

quately informed. Some customers aren't sufficiently well informed to know what questions they need to ask of salespeople. It might be objected that when dealing with such individuals salespeople are obligated to do more than follow 1–4. 1–4 imply that it is *prima facie* wrong to take advantage of customers' ignorance by deceiving them or steering them toward purchases that are likely to cause them significant harm. Suppose, however, that without being steered or deceived, an ill-informed customer who doesn't know what questions to ask is about to make a purchase that will harm him. What are the seller's obligations in such a case? Often salespeople don't know enough about the customer's state of knowledge or ignorance to know whether or not the customer is asking the right questions. (A customer who doesn't ask questions, might know so much that he doesn't need any further information, or he might be so ignorant that he doesn't know what questions to ask.) Suppose that the salesperson *knows* that the buyer is ignorant and unable to ask appropriate questions. (Such cases are, I think, unusual.) What are the seller's duties in such a case? My intuitions tell me that a salesperson has a *prima facie* duty to warn the customer about the harm he is likely to suffer. However, since others report very different moral intuitions about such cases, and because there is no reason to think that my moral intuitions are more reliable than theirs, the appeal to moral intuitions alone cannot settle this matter. The ultimate answer to the question about what sellers ought to do in cases of the sort at issue depends on the success or failure of other sorts of arguments for principle 5 or principles similar to 5. (5 implies that the seller is obligated to caution the buyer in this kind of case. For my own part, I think that it is unclear whether or not 5 can be justified . . ., so I take it to be an open question whether 5 is one of the *prima facie* duties of salespeople.

The view that 1–4, and 1–4 alone, are *prima facie* duties of salespeople conflicts with some peoples' moral intuitions in cases of the sort in question. But, *by itself*, this is not a decisive objection to the view in question. Salespeople typically work for themselves or their employers. Buyers understand this. In the case of major purchases such as automobiles and houses, buyers understand the importance of the purchase and the importance of making a rational informed decision. In cases in which buyers don't know enough to ask the right questions, it is common for them to seek help from friends or family members (or even bring them along when they talk to salespeople). It is reasonable for sellers to assume that uninformed customers have sought help or advice before making major purchases. Uninformed consumers do not fare as well in the market as informed consumers. Sellers are not obligated to act as agents for customers or to compensate for their ignorance.

The Golden Rule

The best-known version of the golden rule (at least in the West) is found in the New Testament. Jesus' version of the golden rule commands us to act toward others as we would be willing to have them act toward us. Jesus gives two statements of the golden rule in the New Testament (New Revised Standard Version): "Do to others as you would have them do to you" (Luke 6:3 1); "In everything do to others as you would have them do to you; for this is the law and the prophets" (Matthew 7:12). Jesus' version of the golden rule can be construed as a test of the moral rightness of actions that states a *necessary* condition for a right action. On this reading, the golden rule implies that an act is morally permissible only if the agent is willing to have others do the same act to him in similar circumstances (an act is morally wrong if the agent is unwilling to have others do the same act to him in similar circumstances). The golden rule can also be construed as a consistency principle (according to which those who violate the golden rule are guilty of inconsistency). I believe that the following version of the golden rule can be justified:

> GR. Consistency requires that if you think that it would be morally permissible for someone to do a certain act to another person, then you must consent to the idea of someone else doing the same act to you in relevantly similar circumstances.

This is consistent with, but not equivalent to, the version of the golden rule stated by Jesus.... I don't offer this as an interpretation of what Jesus and other religious teachers meant by the golden rule, nor I do I claim that this is the only version of the golden rule that can be justified. I claim only that this particular version of the golden rule *can* be justified and that it can be used to show that those

who reject 1–4 as *prima facie* duties for salespeople are inconsistent.

How the golden rule supports 1-4

Given this version of the golden rule, any rational and consistent moral judge who makes judgments about the moral obligations of salespeople must accept 1–4 as at least *prima facie* duties. Consider duty 1. All of us have reason to fear the hazards about us in the world and all of us depend on others to warn us of hazards. Few people would survive to adulthood were it not for the warnings of others about such things as oncoming cars, live electric wires, and approaching tornadoes. No one who values her own life can honestly say that she is willing to have others fail to warn her of dangers. 2. Like everyone else, a salesperson needs correct information in order to act effectively to achieve her goals and advance her interests. She is not willing to act on the basis of false beliefs. Consequently, she is not willing to have others deceive her or lie to her about matters relevant to her decisions in the marketplace. She is not willing to have members of other professions (such as law and medicine) make it a policy to deceive her or lie to her whenever they can gain financially from doing so. 3. Salespeople have questions about the goods and services they themselves buy. They can't say that they are willing to have others evade or refuse to answer those questions. We want our questions to be answered by salespeople or else we wouldn't ask them. We are not willing to have salespeople evade or refrain from answering our questions. [*Digression:* Principle 3 permits salespeople to refuse to answer questions that would force them to provide information about their competitors. Why should we say *this?* Why not say instead that salespeople are obligated to answer *all questions,* that customers ask? The answer is that we are not willing to do this if we imagine ourselves in the position of the salesperson's employer. A salesperson's actions affect *both* her customers and her employer. In applying the golden rule to this issue she can't simply ask what kind of information she would want were she in the customer's position.... 3 is a reasonable principle that takes into account the interests of customers, the salesperson, and her employer. 3 can probably be improved upon, but it is a decent first approximation. A reasonable person could endorse something like 3 as a policy for salespeople to follow. A disin-

terested person who was not trying to give preference to the interests of salespeople, employers, or
customers could endorse 3. We can and must recognize the legitimacy of employers' demands for loyalty. The role of being an advocate or agent for
someone who is selling things is legitimate within
certain bounds—almost all of us are willing to have
real estate agents work for us. A rational person
could consent to the idea that everyone follow
principles such as 3. *End of Digression.*] 4. All of us
are capable of being manipulated by others into
doing things that will harm us, especially in cases in
which others are more knowledgeable than we are.
No one can consent to the idea that other people
(or salespeople) should manipulate us into doing
things that significantly harm us whenever doing so
is to their own advantage. Salespeople who claim
that it would be permissible for them to make it a
policy to deceive customers, fail to warn them
about dangers, evade their questions, or manipulate
them into doing things that are harmful to them
whenever doing so is advantageous to them are
inconsistent because they are not willing to have
others do the same to them. They must allow that
1–4 are *prima facie* moral duties.

A Qualification

1–4 are only *prima facie* duties. The golden rule can
account for the cases in which 1–4 are overridden
by other more important duties. For example, we
would be willing to have other people violate 1–4 if
doing so were necessary in order to save the life of
an innocent person. In practice, I think that violating 1, 2, 3, or 4 is permissible only in very rare
cases. The financial interests of salespeople seldom
justify violations of 1, 2, 3, or 4. The fact that a
salesperson can make more money by violating 1, 2,
3, or 4 would not justify her in violating 1, 2, 3, or 4
unless she has very pressing financial obligations
that she cannot meet otherwise. Often salespeople
need to meet certain minimum sales quotas to avoid
being fired. Suppose that a salesperson needs to
make it a policy to violate 1–4 in order to meet her
sales quotas and keep her job. Would this justify her
in violating 1–4? Possibly. But, in order for this to
be the case, the following conditions would have to
be met: she has important moral obligations such as
feeding and housing her family that require her to
be employed (needing money to keep one's family
in an expensive house or take them to Disney

World doesn't justify violating 1–4) and (2) she
can't find another job that would enable her to
meet her obligations without violating 1–4 (or
other equally important duties). Those salespeople
who can't keep their jobs or make an adequate
income without violating 1–4 should seek other
lines of employment.

   1–4 are duties that salespeople have to customers. Many salespeople also have duties to their
employers. Salespeople who work for employers
arguably have a *prima facie* duty to serve the interests
of their employers. (I think that this duty is most
plausibly construed as an implied promise or contract.) However, this duty is not *prima facie* duty to
do anything whatever that promotes the interests of
the employer. Rather, it is a *prima facie* duty to promote the interests of the employer within the certain limits—respecting other moral and legal duties
(including 1–4). By the same token, one can't create
a *prima facie* duty to do something that is morally
wrong by promising to do it. Promising to murder
someone does not give one a *prima facie* duty to kill
that person. This has important implications for our
understanding of the duties of salespeople. Consider
a case in which a salesperson can make a sale (and
thereby promote the interests of her employer) if
she deceives her customers. We should *not* count
this as a case in which a salesperson has a conflict
between her duty not to deceive customers and her
duty to benefit her employer. The salesperson's
prima facie duty not to deceive customers does *not*
conflict with her duty to act for the benefit of her
employer (while respecting other moral and legal
duties). She has a duty to act for the benefit of her
employer only within the constraints of moral
and legal duties such as the duty not to deceive
customers. . . .

THE JUSTIFICATION OF 5–6

I would like to claim that 5–6 are also *prima facie*
duties of salespeople, but I am not sure that I can
give an adequate justification for this. I'm not sure
that 5–6 can be justified by appeal to the golden
rule. I take it to be an open question whether
informed consistent moral judges would take 5–6
to be *prima facie* duties for salespeople. Some of us
are unwilling to consent to the idea that salespeople
not follow 5–6. Others might consent to the idea

that salespeople not follow 5–6. For my own part, I am unwilling to consent to the idea that salespeople not follow 5–6. However, it would seem to be possible for a rational person consistently to endorse the idea that salespeople not follow 5–6. Suppose that someone endorses a kind of "rugged individualism." She believes that competent adults should be self-reliant and, as much as possible, make their own decisions without asking for the help and advice of others. Such a person could consent to the idea that sales people not adhere to 5–6. I do not subscribe to this view, but I am not sure that I can show that it is inconsistent or unreasonable. If fully rational and consistent people could disagree about whether are duties of salespeople, then it seems as if we might have to endorse some kind of qualified relativism about moral issues in sales.

I conjecture the following with regard to 5–6. If the golden rule is constrained by some kind of strong impartiality condition such as Rawls's veil of ignorance then the golden rule can justify 5–6. Rawls says that the principles of justice we endorse (for our society) must be principles we would endorse if we didn't know anything about our own personal circumstances or our place in society. Consider the following formulation of the golden rule, which incorporates this kind of impartiality requirement (I will call this the Rawlsian golden rule):

> If you are consistent and think that it would be morally permissible for someone (S) to do act A to another person S1, then it must be the case that you would, if you didn't know your own place in the situation, consent to the idea that people do A in relevantly similar circumstances. (Among other things, this would mean that, if you didn't know whether or not you were in the position of someone to whom A is done or someone who does A, you would consent to people doing A in relevantly similar circumstances.)

The benefit the public would gain if all salespeople followed 5–6 far exceeds any loss that this might cause salespeople. Thus, from a completely impartial point of view (in which we didn't know whether or not we were salespeople), we would not consent to have salespeople routinely violate 5–6 (we would want it to be the case that salespeople follow 5–6). The Rawlsian golden rule strongly supports 5–6, but I'm not sure that the Rawlsian version of the golden rule can be defended as a requirement of rationality for moral judgments.

Many questions in applied ethics turn on controversial issues in ethical theory. To the extent that those questions in ethical theory are open (and to extent that work in applied ethics does not attempt to settle them) those questions in applied ethics must also be regarded as open. None of the foregoing, however, should obscure the fact that *some* questions in ethical theory are not controversial. The other version of the golden rule stated above (GR) *can* be justified . . . and this gives us good reasons for thinking that 1–4 are *prima facie* duties. Similarly, it is not controversial that it is *prima facie* wrong to harm others and this also provides reasons for accepting 1, 2, and 4. Some conclusions can be justified with a high degree of confidence. We can be confident that 1–4 are *prima facie* duties of salespeople. I haven't given arguments that permit us to be as confident about 5–6 (but I would welcome such arguments).

CASE STUDY

Health Insurance

[True story.] In 1980, I received a 1-year Fellowship from The National Endowment for the Humanities. The fellowship paid for my salary, but not my fringe benefits. Someone in the benefits office of my university told me that I had the option of continuing my health insurance through the university, if I paid for the premiums out of my own pocket. I told the benefits person that this was a lousy deal and that I could do better by going to a private insurance company. I went to the office of Prudential Insurance agent Mr. A. O. "Ed" Mokarem. I told him that I was looking for a one-year medical insurance policy to cover me during the period of the fellowship and that I planned to resume my university policy when I returned to teaching. (The university provided this policy free of charge to all faculty who were teaching.) He showed me a comparable Prudential policy that cost about half as much as the university's policy. He explained the policy to me. I asked him to fill out the forms so that I could purchase the policy. He then told me that there was a potential problem that I should consider. He said roughly the following:

> You will want to return to your free university policy next year when you return to teaching.

The Prudential policy is a one-year terminal policy. If you develop any serious medical problems during the next year, Prudential will probably consider you "uninsurable" and will not be willing to sell you health insurance in the future. If you buy the Prudential policy, you may encounter the same problems with your university policy. Since you will be dropping this policy voluntarily, they will have the right to underwrite your application for re-enrollment. If you develop a serious health problem during the next year, their underwriting decision could be "Total Rejection," imposing some waivers and/or exclusions, or (at best) subjecting your coverage to the "preexisting conditions clause," which would not cover any preexisting conditions until you have been covered under the new policy at least a year.

If I left my current health insurance for a year, I risked developing a costly medical condition for which no one would be willing to insure me. That would have been a very foolish risk to take. So, I thanked him very much and, swallowing my pride, went back to renew my health insurance coverage through the university. I never bought any insurance from Mr. Mokarem and never had occasion to send him any business. I did not speak with him again until 1995 when I called him to check my recollection of the facts.

I have discussed this case with numerous classes through the years. It usually generates a lively discussion. Most of my students do not think that Mr. Mokarem was morally obligated to do what he did, but they don't think that what he did was wrong either—they regard his actions as supererogatory or above and beyond the call of duty. A number of my students proposed roughly the following argument:

> The potential buyer should have asked about (or known about) the possibility of being turned down for medical insurance on account of preexisting health problems. The buyer was foolish and imprudent not to have done so.

Therefore,

> In this case the insurance agent had no duty to inform the buyer of the potential harm the buyer might suffer, even though it is likely that the buyer would have been seriously harmed by his purchase. The fault or blame for this harm would lie with the buyer, not the agent.

This argument presupposes something like the following principle:

> If a person is about to harm himself through his own foolishness and rashness, others are not obligated to warn him about the harm he is likely to suffer.

On examination this principle is untenable. Surely we are obligated to warn other people about potential harms they might suffer, even if those harms are the result of their own folly. For example, suppose that a drunken man places coins on a subway track in order to flatten them out. He wanders out on to [the] track. He is careful to avoid oncoming trains but he is unaware of the fact that the third rail will electrocute him if he touches it. Surely onlookers would be obligated to warn him about the dangers posed by the third rail.

My View about This Case   On my theory, this is a difficult case to assess. If 1–4 are a salesperson's only duties concerning the disclosure of information, then Mr. Mokarem was not obligated to inform me as he did. (In this case the information in question was information about a competing product—the university's health insurance policy.) If 5 is a *prima facie* duty of salespeople, then (assuming that he had no conflicting moral duties of greater or equal importance) it was his duty, all things considered, to inform me as he did. Since I am uncertain that 5 can be justified, I'm not sure whether or not Mr. Mokarem was obligated to do what he did or whether his actions were supererogatory. This case illustrates part of what is at stake in the question of whether 5 is a *prima facie* duty of salespeople. . . .

A DEFENSE OF THE VERSION OF THE GOLDEN RULE EMPLOYED EARLIER

My argument for the version of the golden rule appealed to earlier is as follows:

1. Consistency requires that if you think that it would be morally permissible for someone to do a certain act to another person, then you must grant that it would be morally permissible for someone to do that same act to you in relevantly similar circumstances.

2. Consistency requires that if you think that it would be morally permissible for someone to

do a certain act to you in certain circumstances, then you must consent to him/her doing that act to you in those circumstances.

Therefore,

[GR. Consistency requires that if you think that it would be morally permissible for someone to do a certain act to another person, then you must consent to someone doing the same act to you in relevantly similar circumstances. [You are inconsistent if you think that it would be morally permissible for someone to do a certain act to another person, but do not consent to someone doing the same act to you in relevantly similar circumstances.]

This argument is valid (i.e., the conclusion follows from the premises) and both its premises are true. Both premises are consistency requirements. Premise 1 addresses questions about the consistency of a person's different moral beliefs. Premise 2 addresses questions about whether a person's moral beliefs are consistent with her attitudes and actions. Our attitudes and actions can be either consistent or inconsistent with the moral judgments we accept.

Premise 1

Premise 1 follows from, or is a narrower version of, the universalizability principle (UP). The UP can be stated as follows:

Consistency requires that, if one makes a moral judgment about a particular case, then one must make the same moral judgment about any similar case, unless there is a morally relevant difference between the cases.

The UP is much broader in scope than premise 1. Premise 1 is a principle of consistency for judgments about the moral permissibility of actions. The UP, by contrast, is a principle of consistency for *any kind of moral judgment,* including judgments about what things are good and bad.

Premise 2

How shall we understand what is meant by "consenting to" something? For our present purposes, we should not take consenting to something to be the same as desiring it or trying to bring it about. My thinking that it is morally permissible for you to beat me at chess does not commit me to desiring that you beat me, nor does it commit me to playing so as to allow you to beat me. Consenting to an action is more like not objecting to it, not criticizing, not resenting the other person for doing it. If I think that it is permissible for you to beat me at chess then I cannot object to your beating me. I am inconsistent if I object to your doing something that I take to be morally permissible. If I claim that it is permissible for someone to do something to another person, then, on pain of inconsistency, I cannot object if someone else does the same thing to me in relevantly similar circumstances. The gist of my application of the golden rule to sales is that since we do object to salespeople doing such things as lying to us, deceiving us, failing to answer our questions, we cannot consistently say that it is morally permissible for them to do these things. . . .

READING 9.3 ADVERTISING AND BEHAVIOR CONTROL
Robert L. Arrington

Consider the following advertisements:

1. "A woman in *Distinction Foundations* is so beautiful that all other women want to kill her."

From *Journal of Business Ethics* 1 (1982): 3–12. Copyright © 1982 by D. Reidel Publishing Co., Dordrecht, Holland. Reprinted by permission. All notes in this reading have been deleted.

2. Pongo Peach color for Revlon comes "from east of the sun . . . west of the moon where each tomorrow dawns." It is "succulent on your lips" and "sizzling on your finger tips (and on your toes goodness knows)." Let it be your "adventure in paradise."

3. "Musk by English Leather—The Civilized Way to Roar."

4. "Increase the value of your holdings. Old Charter Bourbon Whiskey—The Final Step Up."

5. Last Call Smirnoff Style: "They'd never really miss us, and it's kind of late already, and it's quite a long way, and I could build a fire, and you're looking very beautiful, and we could have another martini, and it's awfully nice just being home . . . you think?"

6. A Christmas Prayer. "Let us pray that the blessing of peace be ours—the peace to build and grow, to live in harmony and sympathy with others, and to plan for the future with confidence." New York Life Insurance Company.

These are instances of what is called puffery—the practice by a seller of making exaggerated, highly fanciful or suggestive claims about a product or service. Puffery, within ill-defined limits, is legal. It is considered a legitimate, necessary, and very successful tool of the advertising industry. Puffery is not just bragging; it is bragging carefully designed to achieve a very definite effect. Using the techniques of so-called motivational research, advertising firms first identify our often hidden needs (for security, conformity, oral stimulation) and our desires (for power, sexual dominance and dalliance, adventure) and then they design ads which respond to these needs and desires. By associating a product, for which we may have little or no direct need or desire, with symbols reflecting the fulfillment of these other, often subterranean interests, the advertisement can quickly generate large numbers of consumers eager to purchase the product advertised. What woman in the sexual race of life could resist a foundation which would turn other women envious to the point of homicide? Who can turn down an adventure in paradise, east of the sun where tomorrow dawns? Who doesn't want to be civilized and thoroughly libidinous at the same time? Be at the pinnacle of success—drink Old Charter. Or stay at home and dally a bit—with Smirnoff. And let us pray for a secure and predictable future, provided for by New York Life, God willing. It doesn't take very much motivational research to see the point of these sales pitches. Others are perhaps a little less obvious. The need to feel secure in one's home at night can be used to sell window air conditioners,

which drown out small noises and provide a friendly, dependable companion. The fact that baking a cake is symbolic of giving birth to a baby used to prompt advertisements for cake mixes which glamorized the "creative" housewife. And other strategies, for example involving cigar symbolism, are a bit too crude to mention, but are nevertheless very effective.

Don't such uses of puffery amount to manipulation, exploitation, or downright control? In his very popular book *The Hidden Persuaders,* Vance Packard points out that a number of people in the advertising world have frankly admitted as much:

As early as 1941 Dr. Dichter (an influential advertising consultant) was exhorting ad agencies to recognize themselves for what they actually were—"one of the most advanced laboratories in psychology." He said the successful ad agency "manipulates human motivations and desires and develops a need for goods with which the public has at one time been unfamiliar—perhaps even undesirous of purchasing." The following year *Advertising Agency* carried an ad man's statement that psychology not only holds promise for under-standing people but "ultimately for controlling their behavior."

Such statements lead Packard to remark: "With all this interest in manipulating the customer's subconscious, the old slogan 'let the buyer beware' began taking on a new and more profound meaning."

B. F. Skinner, the high priest of behaviorism, has expressed a similar assessment of advertising and related marketing techniques. Why, he asks, do we buy a certain kind of car?

Perhaps our favorite TV program is sponsored by the manufacturer of that car. Perhaps we have seen pictures of many beautiful or prestigeful persons driving it—in pleasant or glamorous places. Perhaps the car has been designed with respect to our motivational patterns: the device on the hood is a phallic symbol; or the horsepower has been stepped up to please our competitive spirit in enabling us to pass other cars swiftly (or, as the advertisements say, "safely"). The concept of freedom that has emerged as part of the cultural practice of our group makes little or no provision for recognizing or dealing with these kinds of control.

In purchasing a car we may think we are free, Skinner is claiming, when in fact our act is completely controlled by factors in our environment and in our history of reinforcement. Advertising is one such factor.

A look at some other advertising techniques may reinforce the suspicion that Madison Avenue controls us like so many puppets. T.V. watchers surely have noticed that some of the more repugnant ads are shown over and over again, *ad nauseum*. My favorite, or most hated, is the one about A-1 Steak Sauce which goes something like this: Now, ladies and gentlemen, what is hamburger? It has succeeded in destroying my taste for hamburger, but it has surely drilled the name of A-1 Sauce into my head. And that is the point of it. Its very repetitiousness has generated what ad theorists call *information*. In this case it is indirect information, information derived not from the content of what is said but from the fact that it is said so often and so vividly that it sticks in one's mind—i.e., the information yield has increased. And not only do I always remember A-1 Sauce when I go to the grocers, I tend to assume that any product advertised so often has to be good—and so I usually buy a bottle of the stuff.

Still another technique: On a recent show of the television program "Hard Choices" it was demonstrated how subliminal suggestion can be used to control customers. In a New Orleans department store, messages to the effect that shoplifting is wrong, illegal, and subject to punishment were blended into the Muzak background music and masked so as not to be consciously audible. The store reported a dramatic drop in shoplifting. The program host conjectured whether a logical extension of this technique would be to broadcast subliminal advertising messages to the effect that the store's $15.99 sweater special is the "bargain of a lifetime." Actually, this application of subliminal suggestion to advertising has already taken place. Years ago in New Jersey a cinema was reported to have flashed subthreshold ice cream ads onto the screen during regular showings of the film—and, yes, the concession stand did a landslide business.

Puffery, indirect information transfer, subliminal advertising—are these techniques of manipulation and control whose success shows that many of us have forfeited our autonomy and become a com-

munity, or herd, of packaged souls? The business world and the advertising industry certainly reject this interpretation of their efforts. *Business Week,* for example, dismissed the charge that the science of behavior, as utilized by advertising, is engaged in human engineering and manipulation. It editorialized to the effect that "it is hard to find anything very sinister about a science whose principle conclusion is that you get along with people by giving them what they want." The theme is familiar: businesses just give the consumer what he/she wants; if they didn't they wouldn't stay in business very long. Proof that the consumer wants the products advertised is given by the fact that he buys them, and indeed often returns to buy them again and again.

The techniques of advertising we are discussing have had their more intellectual defenders as well. For example, Theodore Levitt, Professor of Business Administration at the Harvard Business School, has defended the practice of puffery and the use of techniques depending on motivational research. What would be the consequences, he asks us, of deleting all exaggerated claims and fanciful associations from advertisements? We would be left with literal descriptions of the empirical characteristics of products and their functions. Cosmetics would be presented as facial and bodily lotions—and powders which produce certain odor and color changes; they would no longer offer hope or adventure. In addition to the fact that these products would not then sell as well, they would not, according to Levitt, please us as much either. For it is hope and adventure we want when we buy them. We want automobiles not just for transportation, but the feelings of power and status they give us. Quoting T. S. Eliot to the effect that "Human kind cannot bear very much reality," Levitt argues that advertising is an effort to "transcend nature in the raw," to "augment what nature has so crudely fashioned." He maintains that "everybody everywhere wants to modify, transform, embellish, enrich and reconstruct the world around him." Commerce takes the same liberty with reality as the artist and the priest—in all three instances the purpose is "to influence the audience by creating illusions, symbols, and implications that promise more than pure functionality." For example, "to amplify the temple in men's eyes, (men of cloth) have, very realistically, systematically sanctioned the embellishment of the houses of the gods with the same kind of luxurious design and expensive decoration that Detroit puts into a Cadillac." A poem, a temple, a Cadillac—they all elevate our spirits, offering imaginative promises and symbolic interpretations of our mundane activities. Seen in this light, Levitt claims, "Embellishment and distortion are among advertising's legitimate and socially desirable purposes." To reject these techniques of advertising would be "to deny man's honest needs and values."

Phillip Nelson, a Professor of Economics at SUNY-Binghamton, has developed an interesting defense of indirect information advertising. He argues that even when the message (the direct information) is not credible, the fact that the brand is advertised, and advertised frequently, is valuable indirect information for the consumer. The reason for this is that the brands advertised most are more likely to be better buys—losers won't be advertised a lot, for it simply wouldn't pay to do so. Thus even if the advertising claims made for a widely advertised product are empty, the consumer reaps the benefit of the indirect information which shows the product to be a good buy. Nelson goes so far as to say that advertising, seen as information and especially as indirect information, does not require an intelligent human response. If the indirect information has been received and has had its impact, the consumer will purchase the better buy even if his explicit reason for doing so is silly, e.g., he naively believes an endorsement of the product by a celebrity. Even though his behavior is overtly irrational, by acting on the indirect information he is nevertheless doing what he ought to do, i.e., getting his money's worth. "'Irrationality' is rational," Nelson writes, "if it is cost-free."

I don't know of any attempt to defend the use of subliminal suggestion in advertising, but I can imagine one form such an attempt might take. Advertising information, even if perceived below the level of conscious awareness, must appeal to some desire on the part of the audience if it is to trigger a purchasing response. Just as the admonition not to shoplift speaks directly to the superego, the sexual virtues of TR-7's, Pongo Peach, and Betty Crocker cake mix present themselves directly to the id, bypassing the pesky reality principle of the ego. With a little help from our advertising friends, we may remove a few of the discontents of civilization and perhaps even enter into the paradise of polymorphous perversity.

The defense of advertising which suggests that advertising simply is information which allows us to purchase what we want, has in turn been challenged. Does business, largely through its advertising efforts, really make available to the consumer what he/she desires and demands? John Kenneth Galbraith has denied that the matter is as straightforward as this. In his opinion the desires to which business is supposed to respond, far from being original to the consumer, are often themselves created by business. The producers make both the product and the desire for it, and the "central function" of advertising is "to create desires." Galbraith coins the term "The Dependence Effect" to designate the way wants depend on the same process by which they are satisfied.

David Braybrooke has argued in similar and related ways. Even though the consumer is, in a sense, the final authority concerning what he wants, he may come to see, according to Braybrooke, that he was mistaken in wanting what he did. The statement "I want x," he tells us, is not incorrigible but is "ripe for revision." If the consumer had more objective information than he is provided by product puffing, if his values had not been mixed up by motivational research strategies (e.g., the confusion of sexual and automotive values), and if he had an expanded set of choices instead of the limited set offered by profit-hungry corporations, then he might want something quite different from what he presently wants. This shows, Braybrooke thinks, the extent to which the consumer's wants are a function of advertising and not necessarily representative of his real or true wants.

The central issue which emerges between the above critics and defenders of advertising is this: do the advertising techniques we have discussed involve a violation of human autonomy and a manipulation and control of consumer behavior, *or* do they simply provide an efficient and cost-effective means of giving the consumer information on the basis of which he or she makes a free choice. Is advertising information, or creation of desire?

To answer this question we need a better conceptual grasp of what is involved in the notion of autonomy. This is a complex, multifaceted concept, and we need to approach it through the more determinate notions of (1) autonomous desire, (2) rational desire and choice, (3) free choice, and (4) control or manipulation. In what follows I shall offer some tentative and very incomplete analyses of these concepts and apply the results to the case of advertising.

(a) Autonomous Desire   Imagine that I am watching T.V. and see an ad for Grecian Formula 16. The thought occurs to me that if I purchase some and apply it to my beard, I will soon look younger—in fact I might even be myself again. Suddenly want to be myself! I want to be young again! So I rush out and buy a bottle. This is our question: was the desire to be younger manufactured by the commercial, or was it "original to me" and truly mine? Was it autonomous or not?

F. A. von Hayek has argued plausibly that we should not equate nonautonomous desires, desires which are not original to me or truly mine, with those which are culturally induced. If we did equate the two, he points out, then the desires for music, art, and knowledge could not properly be attributed to a person as original to him, for these are surely induced culturally. The only desires a person would really have as his own in this case would be the purely physical ones for food, shelter, sex, etc. But if we reject the equation of the nonautonomous and the culturally induced, as von Hayek would have us do, then the mere fact that my desire to be young again is caused by the T.V. commercial—surely an instrument of popular culture transmission—does not in and of itself show that this is not my own, autonomous desire. Moreover, even if I never before felt the need to look young, it doesn't follow that this new desire is any less mine. I haven't always liked 1969 Aloxe Corton Burgundy or the music of Satie, but when the desires for these things first hit me, they were truly mine.

This shows that there is something wrong in setting up the issue over advertising and behavior control as a question whether our desires are truly ours *or* are created in us by advertisements. Induced and autonomous desires do not separate into two mutually exclusive classes. To obtain a better understanding of autonomous and nonautonomous desires, let us consider some cases of a desire which a person does not *acknowledge* to be his own even though he *feels* it. The kleptomaniac has a desire to steal which in many instances he repudiates, seeking by treatment to rid himself of it. And if I were suddenly overtaken by a desire to attend an REO concert, I would immediately disown this desire,

claiming possession or momentary madness. These are examples of desires which one might have but with which one would not identify. They are experienced as foreign to one's character or personality. Often a person will have what Harry Frankfurt calls a second-order desire, that is to say, a desire *not* to have another desire. In such cases, the first-order desire is thought of as being nonautonomous, imposed on one. When on the contrary a person has a second-order desire to maintain and fulfill a first-order desire, then the first-order desire is truly his own, autonomous, original to him. So there is in fact a distinction between desires which are the agent's own and those which are not, but this is not the same as the distinction between desires which are innate to the agent and those which are externally induced.

If we apply the autonomous/nonautonomous distinction derived from Frankfurt to the desires brought about by advertising, does this show that advertising is responsible for creating desires which are not truly the agent's own? Not necessarily, and indeed not often. There may be some desires I feel which I have picked up from advertising and which I disown—for instance, my desire for A–1 Steak Sauce. If I act on these desires it can be said that I have been led by advertising to act in a way foreign to my nature. In these cases my autonomy has been violated. But most of the desires induced by advertising I fully accept, and hence most of these desires are autonomous. The most vivid demonstration of this is that I often return to purchase the same product over and over again, without regret or remorse. And when I don't, it is more likely that the desire has just faded than that I have repudiated it. Hence, while advertising may violate my autonomy by leading me to act on desires which are not truly mine, this seems to be the exceptional case.

Note that this conclusion applies equally well to the case of subliminal advertising. This may generate subconscious desires which lead to purchases, and the act of purchasing these goods may be inconsistent with other conscious desires I have, in which case I might repudiate my behavior and by implication the subconscious cause of it. But my subconscious desires may not be inconsistent in this way with my conscious ones; my id may be cooperative and benign rather than hostile and malign. Here again, then, advertising may or may not produce desires which are "not truly mine."

What are we to say in response to Braybrooke's argument that insofar as we might choose differently if advertisers gave us better information and more options, it follows that the desires we have are to be attributed more to advertising than to our own real inclinations? This claim seems empty. It amounts to saying that if the world we lived in, and we ourselves, were different, then we would want different things. This is surely true, but it is equally true of our desire for shelter as of our desire for Grecian Formula 16. If we lived in a tropical paradise we would not need or desire shelter. If we were immortal, we would not desire youth. What is true of all desires can hardly be used as a basis for criticizing some desires by claiming that they are nonautonomous.

(b) Rational Desire and Choice Braybrooke might be interpreted as claiming that the desires induced by advertising are often irrational ones in the sense that they are not expressed by an agent who is in full possession of the facts about the products advertised or about the alternative products which might be offered him. Following this line of thought, a possible criticism of advertising is that it leads us to act on irrational desires or to make irrational choices. It might be said that our autonomy has been violated by the fact that we are prevented from following our rational wills or that we have been denied the "positive freedom" to develop our true, rational selves. It might be claimed that the desires induced in us by advertising are false desires in that they do not reflect our essential, i.e., rational, essence.

The problem faced by this line of criticism is that of determining what is to count as rational desire or rational choice. If we require that the desire or choice be the product of an awareness of *all* the facts about the product, then surely every one of us is always moved by irrational desires and makes nothing but irrational choices. How could we know all the facts about a product? If it be required only that we possess all of the *available* knowledge about the product advertised, then we still have to face the problem that not all available knowledge is *relevant* to a rational choice. If I am purchasing a car, certain engineering features will be, and others won't be, relevant, *given what I want in a car.* My prior desires determine the relevance of information. Normally a rational desire or choice is

thought to be one based upon relevant information, and information is relevant if it shows how other, prior desires may be satisfied. It can plausibly be claimed that it is such prior desires that advertising agencies acknowledge, and that the agencies often provide the type of information that is relevant in light of these desires. To the extent that this is true, advertising does not inhibit our rational wills or our autonomy as rational creatures.

It may be urged that much of the puffery engaged in by advertising does not provide relevant information at all but rather makes claims which are not factually true. If someone buys Pongo Peach in anticipation of an adventure in paradise, or Old Charter in expectation of increasing the value of his holdings, then he/she is expecting purely imaginary benefits. In no literal sense will the one product provide adventure and the other increased capital. A purchasing decision based on anticipation of imaginary benefits is not, it might be said, a rational decision, and a desire for imaginary benefits is not a rational desire.

In rejoinder it needs to be pointed out that we often wish to purchase subjective effects which in being subjective are nevertheless real enough. The feeling of adventure or of enhanced social prestige and value are examples of subjective effects promised by advertising. Surely many (most?) advertisements directly promise subjective effects which their patrons actually desire (and obtain when they purchase the product), and thus the ads provide relevant information for rational choice. Moreover, advertisements often provide accurate indirect information on the basis of which a person who wants a certain subjective effect rationally chooses a product. The mechanism involved here is as follows.

To the extent that a consumer takes an advertised product to offer a subjective effect and the product does not, it is unlikely that it will be purchased again. If this happens in a number of cases, the product will be taken off the market. So here the market regulates itself, providing the mechanism whereby misleading advertisements are withdrawn and misled customers are no longer misled. At the same time, a successful bit of puffery, being one which leads to large and repeated sales, produces satisfied customers and more advertising of the product. The indirect information provided by such large-scale advertising efforts provides a measure of verification to the consumer who is looking for certain kinds of subjective effect. For example, if I want to feel well dressed and in fashion, and I consider buying an Izod Alligator shirt which is advertised in all of the magazines and newspapers, then the fact that other people buy it and that this leads to repeated advertisements shows me that the desired subjective effect is real enough and that I indeed will be well dressed and in fashion if I purchase the shirt. The indirect information may lead to a rational decision to purchase a product because the information testifies to the subjective effect that the product brings about.

Some philosophers will be unhappy with the conclusion of this section, largely because they have a concept of true, rational, or ideal desire which is not the same as the one used here. A Marxist, for instance, may urge that any desire felt by alienated man in a capitalistic society is foreign to his true nature. Or an existentialist may claim that the desires of inauthentic men are themselves inauthentic. Such concepts are based upon general theories of human nature which are unsubstantiated and perhaps incapable of substantiation. Moreover, each of these theories is committed to a concept of an ideal desire which is normatively debatable and which is distinct from the ordinary concept of a rational desire as one based upon relevant information. But it is in the terms of the ordinary concept that we express our concern that advertising may limit our autonomy in the sense of leading us to act on irrational desires, and if we operate with this concept we are driven again to the conclusion that advertising may lead, but probably most often does not lead, to an infringement of autonomy.

(c) Free Choice It might be said that some desires are so strong or so covert that a person cannot resist them, and that when he acts on such desires he is not acting freely or voluntarily but is rather the victim of irresistible impulse or an unconscious drive. Perhaps those who condemn advertising feel that it produces this kind of desire in us and consequently reduces our autonomy.

This raises a very difficult issue. How do we distinguish between an impulse we *do* not resist and one we *could* not resist, between freely giving in to a desire and succumbing to one? I have argued elsewhere that the way to get at this issue is in terms of the notion of acting for a reason. A person acts or chooses freely if he does so for a reason, that is, if he can adduce considerations which justify in his mind

the act in question. Many of our actions are in fact free because this condition frequently holds. Often, however, a person will act from habit, or whim, or impulse, and on these occasions he does not have a reason in mind. Nevertheless he often acts voluntarily in these instances, i.e., he could have acted otherwise. And this is because if there *had been* a reason for acting otherwise of which he was aware, he would in fact have done so. Thus acting from habit or impulse is not necessarily to act in an involuntary manner. If, however, a person is aware of a good reason to do x and still follows his impulse to do y, then he can be said to be impelled by irresistible impulse and hence to act involuntarily. Many kleptomaniacs can be said to act involuntarily, for in spite of their knowledge that they likely will be caught and their awareness that the goods they steal have little utilitarian value to them, they nevertheless steal. Here their "out of character" desires have the upper hand, and we have a case of compulsive behavior.

Applying these notions of voluntary and compulsive behavior to the case of behavior prompted by advertising, can we say that consumers influenced by advertising act compulsively? The unexciting answer is: sometimes they do, sometimes not. I may have an overwhelming, T.V. induced urge to own a Mazda Rx-7 and all the while realize that I can't afford one without severely reducing my family's caloric intake to a dangerous level. If, aware of this good reason not to purchase the car, I nevertheless do so, this shows that I have been the victim of T.V. compulsion. But if I have the urge, as I assure you I do, and don't act on it, or if in some other possible world I could afford an Rx-7, then I have not been the subject of undue influence by Mazda advertising. Some Mazda Rx-7 purchasers act compulsively; others do not. The Mazda advertising effort *in general* cannot be condemned, then, for impairing its customers' autonomy in the sense of limiting free or voluntary choice. Of course the question remains what should be done about the fact that advertising may and does *occasionally* limit free choice. We shall return to this question later.

In the case of subliminal advertising we may find an individual whose subconscious desires are activated by advertising into doing something his calculating, reasoning ego does not approve. This would be a case of compulsion. But most of us have a benevolent subconsciousness which does not overwhelm our ego and its reasons for action. And therefore most of us can respond to subliminal advertising without thereby risking our autonomy. To be sure, if some advertising firm developed a subliminal technique which drove all of us to purchase Lear jets, thereby reducing our caloric intake to the zero point, then we would have a case of advertising which could properly be censured for infringing our right to autonomy. We should acknowledge that this is possible, but at the same time we should recognize that it is not an inherent result of subliminal advertising.

(d) Control or Manipulation Briefly let us consider the matter of control and manipulation. Under what conditions do these activities occur? In a recent paper on "Forms and Limits of Control" I suggested the following criteria.

A person C controls the behavior of another person P if

1. C intends P to act in a certain way A;
2. C's intention is causally effective in bringing about A; and
3. C intends to ensure that all of the necessary conditions of A are satisfied.

These criteria may be elaborated as follows. To control another person it is not enough that one's actions produce certain behavior on the part of that person; additionally one must intend that this happen. Hence control is the intentional production of behavior. Moreover, it is not enough just to have the intention; the intention must give rise to the conditions which bring about the intended effect. Finally, the controller must intend to establish by his actions any otherwise unsatisfied necessary conditions for the production of the intended effect. The controller is not just influencing the outcome, not just having input; he is as it were guaranteeing that the sufficient conditions for the intended effect are satisfied.

Let us apply these criteria of control to the case of advertising and see what happens. Conditions (1) and (3) are crucial. Does the Mazda manufacturing company or its advertising agency intend that I buy an Rx-7? Do they intend that a certain number of people buy the car? *Prima facie* it seems more appropriate to say that they *hope* a certain number of people will buy it, and hoping and intending are not the same. But the difficult term here is "intend." Some philosophers have argued that to intend A it is necessary only to desire that A happen and to believe that it will. If this is correct, and if marketing

analysis gives the Mazda agency a reasonable belief that a certain segment of the population will buy its product, then, assuming on its part the desire that this happen, we have the conditions necessary for saying that the agency intends that a certain segment purchase the car. If I am a member of this segment of the population, would it then follow that the agency intends that I purchase an Rx-7? Or is control referentially opaque? Obviously we have some questions here which need further exploration.

Let us turn to the third condition of control, the requirement that the controller intend to activate or bring about any otherwise unsatisfied necessary conditions for the production of the intended effect. It is in terms of this condition that we are able to distinguish brainwashing from liberal education. The brainwasher arranges all of the necessary conditions for belief. On the other hand, teachers (at least those of liberal persuasion) seek only to influence their students—to provide them with information and enlightenment which they may absorb *if they wish*. We do not normally think of teachers as controlling their students, for the students' performances depend as well on their own interests and inclinations.

Now the advertiser—does he control, or merely influence, his audience? Does he intend to ensure that all of the necessary conditions for purchasing behavior are met, or does he offer information and symbols which are intended to have an effect only *if* the potential purchaser has certain desires? Undeniably advertising induces some desires, and it does this intentionally; but more often than not it intends to induce a desire for a particular object, *given* that the purchaser already has other desires. Given a desire for youth, or power, or adventure, or ravishing beauty, we are led to desire Grecian Formula 16, Mazda Rx-7's, Pongo Peach, and Distinctive Foundations. In this light, the advertiser is influencing us by appealing to independent desires we already have. He is not creating those basic desires. Hence it seems appropriate to deny that he intends to produce all of the necessary conditions for our purchases, and appropriate to deny that he controls us.

Let me summarize my argument. The critics of advertising see it as having a pernicious effect on the autonomy of consumers, as controlling their lives and manufacturing their very souls. The defense claims that advertising only offers information and in effect allows industry to provide consumers with what they want. After developing some of the philosophical dimensions of this dispute, I have come down tentatively in favor of the advertisers. Advertising may, but certainly does not always or even frequently, control behavior, produce compulsive behavior, or create wants which are not rational or are not truly those of the consumer. Admittedly it may in individual cases do all of these things, but it is innocent of the charge of intrinsically or necessarily doing them or even, I think, of

often doing so. This limited potentiality, to be sure, leads to the question whether advertising should be abolished or severely curtailed or regulated because of its potential to harm a few poor souls in the above ways. This is a very difficult question, and I do not pretend to have the answer. I only hope that the above discussion, in showing some of the kinds of harm that can be done by advertising and by indicating the likely limits of this harm, will put us in a better position to grapple with the question.

READING 9.4 MARKETING TO INNER-CITY BLACKS: POWERMASTER AND MORAL RESPONSIBILITY

George G. Brenkert

I. INTRODUCTION

The nature and extent of marketers' moral obligations is a matter of considerable debate. This is particularly the case when those who are targeted by marketers live in disadvantaged circumstances and suffer various problems disproportionately with other members of the same society. An interesting opportunity to explore this difficult area of marketing ethics is presented by Heileman Brewing Company's failed effort to market PowerMaster, a malt liquor, to inner-city blacks. The story of PowerMaster is relatively simple and short. Its ethical dimensions are much more complicated.

In the following, I wish to consider the moral aspects of this case within the context of a market society such as the U.S. which permits the forms of advertising it presently does. To do so, I first briefly evaluate three kinds of objections made to the marketing of PowerMaster. I contend that none of these objections taken by itself clearly justifies the criticism leveled at Heileman. Heileman might reasonably claim that it was fulfilling its economic, social and moral responsibilities in the same manner as were other brewers and marketers. Accordingly, I argue that only if we look to the collective effects of all marketers of malt liquor to the inner-city can

we identify morally defensible grounds for the complaints against marketing campaigns such as that of PowerMaster. The upshot of this argument is that marketers must recognize not only their individual moral responsibilities to those they target, but also a collective responsibility of all marketers for those market segments they jointly target. It is on this basis that Heileman's marketing of PowerMaster may be faulted. This result is noteworthy in that it introduces a new kind of moral consideration which has rarely been considered in discussions of corporate moral responsibilities.

II. HEILEMAN AND POWERMASTER

G. Heileman Brewing Co. is a Wisconsin brewer which produces a number of beers and malt liquors, including Colt Dry, Colt 45, and Mickey's. In the early 1990s, competition amongst such brewers was increasingly intense. In January 1991, Heileman was facing such economic difficulties that it filed for protection from creditors under Chapter 11 of the U.S. Bankruptcy Code (Horovitz, 1991b, D1). To improve its financial situation, Heileman sought to market, beginning in June 1991, a new malt liquor called "PowerMaster." At that time there was considerable growth in the "up-strength malt liquor category." In fact, "this higher-alcohol segment of the business [had] been growing at an explosive 25% to 30% a year" (Freedman, 1991a: B1). To

From *Business Ethics Quarterly*, Volume 8, Issue 1, pp. 1–18. Copyright © 1998. Reprinted by permission of the author.

All notes in this reading have been deleted.

attempt to capitalize on this market segment, Heileman produced PowerMaster, a malt liquor that contained 5.9% alcohol, 31% more alcohol than Heileman's top-selling Colt 45 (4.5% alcohol). Reportedly, when introduced, only one other malt liquor (St. Ides) offered such a powerful malt as PowerMaster (Freedman, 1991a: B1).

Further, since malt liquor had become "the drink of choice among many in the inner city," Heileman focused a significant amount of its marketing efforts on inner-city blacks. Heileman's ad campaign played to this group with posters and billboards using black male models. Advertisements assured consumers that PowerMaster was "Bold Not Harsh." Hugh Nelson, Heileman's marketing director, was reported to have claimed that "the company's research . . . shows that consumers will opt for PowerMaster not on basis of its alcohol content but because of its flavor. The higher alcohol content gives PowerMaster a 'bold not nasty' taste . . ." (Freedman, 1991a: B4).

In response, a wide variety of individuals and groups protested against Heileman's actions. Critics claimed that both advertisements and the name "PowerMaster" suggested the alcoholic strength of the drink and the "buzz" that those who consumed it could get. Surgeon General Antonia Novello criticized the PowerMaster marketing scheme as "insensitive" (Milloy, 1991: B3). Reports in *The Wall Street Journal* spoke of community activists and alcohol critics branding Heileman's marketing campaign as "socially irresponsible" (Freedman, 1991b: B1)."Twenty-one consumer and health groups, including the Center for Science in the Public Interest, also publicly called for Heileman to halt the marketing of PowerMaster and for BATF to limit the alcohol content of malt liquor" (Colford and Teinowitz, 1991: 29). A reporter for the *L. A. Times* wrote that "at issue is growing resentment by blacks and other minorities who feel that they are being unfairly targeted—if not exploited—by marketers of beer, liquor and tobacco products" (Horovitz, 1991: D6). Another reporter for the same paper claimed that "[a]nti-alcohol activists contend that alcoholic beverage manufacturers are taking advantage of minority groups and exacerbating inner-city problems by targeting them with high-powered blends" (Lacey, 1992:A32). And Reverend Calvin Butts of the Abyssinian Baptist Church in New York's Harlem

said that "this [Heileman] is obviously a company that has no sense of moral or social responsibility" (Freedman, 1991a: B1).

Though the Bureau of Alcohol, Tobacco and Firearms (BATF) initially approved the use of "PowerMaster" as the name for the new malt liquor, in light of the above protests it "reacted by enforcing a beer law that prohibits labels 'considered to be statements of alcoholic content'" (Milloy, 1991: B3). It insisted that the word "Power" be removed from the "PowerMaster" name (Freedman, 1991b: B1). As a consequence of the actions of the BATF and the preceding complaints, Heileman decided not to market PowerMaster.

III. THE OBJECTIONS

The PowerMaster marketing campaign evoked three distinct kinds of moral objections:

First, because its advertisements drew upon images and themes related to power and boldness, they were criticized as promoting satisfactions only artificially and distortedly associated with the real needs of those targeted. As such, the PowerMaster marketing campaign was charged with fostering a form of moral illusion.

Second, Heileman was said to lack concern for the harm likely to be caused by its product. Blacks suffer disproportionately from cirrhosis of the liver and other liver diseases brought on by alcohol. In addition, alcohol-related social problems such as violence and crime are also prominent in the inner-city. Accordingly, Heileman was attacked for its lack of moral sensitivity.

Third, Heileman was accused of taking unfair advantage of those in the inner-city whom they had targeted. Inner-city blacks were said to be especially vulnerable, due to their life circumstances, to advertisements and promotions formulated in terms of power, self-assertion and sexual success. Hence, to target them in the manner they did with a product such as PowerMaster was a form of exploitation. In short, questions of justice were raised.

It is important not only for corporations such as Heileman but also for others concerned with such marketing practices to determine whether these objections show that the PowerMaster marketing program was morally unjustified. The economic losses in failed marketing efforts such as Power-

Master are considerable. In addition, if the above objections are justified, the moral losses are also significant.

The first objection maintained that by emphasizing power Heileman was, in effect, offering a cruel substitute for a real lack in the lives of inner-city blacks. PowerMaster's slogan, "Bold not Harsh," was said to project an image of potency. "The brewers' shrewd marketing," one critic maintained, "has turned malt liquor into an element of machismo" (Lacey, 1992:A1). George Hacker, Director of the National Coalition to Prevent Impaired Driving, commented that "the real irony of marketing PowerMaster to inner-city blacks is that this population is among the most lacking in power in this society" (Freedman, 1991a, B1).

This kind of criticism has been made against many forms of advertising. The linking of one's product with power, fame, and success not to mention sex is nothing new in advertising. Most all those targeted by marketers lack (or at least want) those goods or values associated with the products being promoted. Further, other malt liquor marketing campaigns had referred to power. For example, another malt liquor, Olde English "800," claimed that "It's the Power." The Schlitz Red Bull was associated with the phrase "The Real Power" (Colford and Tenowitz, 1991:1). Nevertheless, they were not singled out for attack or boycott as PowerMaster was.

Accordingly, however objectionable it may be for marketers to link a product with something which its potential customers (significantly) lack and which the product can only symbolically or indirectly satisfy, this feature of the PowerMaster marketing campaign does not uniquely explain or justify the complaints that were raised against the marketing of PowerMaster. In short, this objection appears far too general in scope to justify the particular attention given PowerMaster. Heileman could not have reasonably concluded, on its basis, that it was being particularly morally irresponsible. It was simply doing what others had done and for which they had not been boycotted or against which such an outcry had not been raised. It is difficult to see how Heileman could have concluded that it was preparing a marketing program that would generate the social and moral protest it did, simply from an examination of its own plan or the similar individual marketing programs of other brewers.

The second objection was that the marketers of PowerMaster showed an especial lack of sensitivity in that a malt liquor with the potency of PowerMaster would likely cause additional harm to inner-city blacks. According to various reports, "alcoholism and other alcohol-related diseases extract a disproportionate toll on blacks. A 1978 study by the National Institute on Alcohol Abuse and Alcoholism found that black men between the ages of 25 and 44 are 10 times more likely than the general population to have cirrhosis of the liver" (*N.Y. Times,* 1991). *Fortune* reported that "The Department of Health and Human Services last spring released figures showing a decline in life expectancy for blacks for the fourth straight year—down to 69.2 years, vs. 75.6 years for whites. Although much of the drop is attributable to homicide and AIDS, blacks also suffer higher instances of . . . alcohol-related illnesses than whites" (*Fortune,* 1991: 100). Further, due to the combined use of alcohol and cigarettes, blacks suffer cancer of the esophagus at a disproportional rate than the rest of the population. Similarly, assuming that black women would drink PowerMaster, it is relevant that the impact of alcohol use in the inner-city is also manifested in an increased infant mortality rate and by [newborn] children with fetal alcohol syndrome (*The Workbook,* 1991:18). Finally, a malt liquor with a high percentage of alcohol was expected to have additional harmful effects on the level of social ills, such as violence, crime, and spousal abuse. As such, PowerMaster would be further destructive of the social fabric of the inner-city.

Under these circumstances, the second objection maintained, anyone who marketed a product which would further increase these harms was being morally obtuse to the problems inner-city blacks suffer. Accordingly, Heileman's PowerMaster marketing campaign was an instance of such moral insensitivity.

Nevertheless, this objection does not seem clearly applicable when pointed simply at PowerMaster. Surely inner-city blacks are adults and should be allowed, as such, to make their own choices, even if those choices harm themselves, so long as they are not deceived or coerced when making those choices and they do not harm others. Since neither deception nor coercion were involved in PowerMaster's marketing campaign, it is an unacceptable form of moral paternalism to deny them what they might otherwise wish to choose.

Further, those who raised the above complaints were not those who would have drunk Power-Master, but leaders of various associations both within and outside the inner-city concerned with alcohol abuse and consumption. This was not a consumer-led protest. Reports of the outcry over PowerMaster contain no objections from those whom Heileman had targeted. No evidence was presented that these individuals would have found PowerMaster unsatisfactory. Argument is needed, for example, that these individuals had (or should have had) overriding interests in healthy livers. Obviously there are many people (black as well as white) who claim that their interests are better fulfilled by drinking rather than abstinence.

Finally, argument is also needed to show that this increase in alcoholic content would have any significant effects on the targeted group. It might be that any noteworthy effects would be limited because the increased alcoholic content would prove undesirable to those targeted since they would become intoxicated too quickly. "Overly rapid intoxication undercuts sales volume and annoys consumers," *The Wall Street Journal* reported (Freedman, 1991a: B1). Supposedly this conse-quence led one malt brewer to lower the alcoholic content of its product (Freedman, 1991a: B1). Furthermore, malt liquor is hardly the strongest alcohol which blacks (or others) drink. Reportedly, "blacks buy more than half the cognac sold in the United States" (*The Workbook,* 1991: 18). Cheap forms of wine and hard liquor are readily available. Thus, it is far from obvious what significant effects PowerMaster alone would have in the inner-city.

One possible response to the preceding replies brings us to the third objection. This response is that, though inner-city blacks might not be deceived or coerced into drinking PowerMaster, they were particularly vulnerable to the marketing campaign which Heileman proposed. Because of this, Heileman's marketing campaign (wittingly or unwittingly) would take unfair advantage of inner-city blacks.

Little, if any attempt, has been made to defend or to explore this charge. I suggest that there are at least three ways in which inner-city blacks—or any-one else, for that matter—might be said to be spe-cially vulnerable.

A person would be cognitively vulnerable if he or she lacked certain levels of ability to cognitively process information or to be aware that certain information was being withheld or manipulated in deceptive ways. Thus, if people were not able to process information about the effects of malt liquor on themselves or on their society in ways in which others could, they would be cognitively vulnerable.

A person would be motivationally vulnerable if he or she could not resist ordinary temptations and/or enticements due to his or her own individ-ual characteristics. Thus, if people were unable, as normal individuals are, to resist various advertise-ments and marketing ploys, they would be motiva-tionally vulnerable.

And people would be socially vulnerable when their social situation renders them significantly less able than others to resist various enticements. For example, due to the poverty within which they live, they might have developed various needs or atti-tudes which rendered them less able to resist vari-ous marketing programs.

Nevertheless, none of these forms of vulnerabil-ity was explored or defended as the basis of the unfair advantage which the PowerMaster marketers were said to seek. And indeed it is difficult to see what account could be given which would explain how the use of the name "PowerMaster," and bill-boards with a black model, a bottle of PowerMaster and the slogan "Bold Not Harsh" would be enough to subvert the decision making or motivational capacities of inner-city blacks. To the extent that they are adults and not under the care or protection of other individuals or agencies due to the state of their cognitive or motivational abilities, there is a *prima facie* case that they are not so vulnerable. Accordingly, the vulnerability objection raises the legitimate concern that some form of unjustified moral paternalism lurks behind it.

In short, if we consider simply the individual marketing program of PowerMaster, it is difficult to see that the three preceding objections justified the outcry against Heileman. Heileman was seeking to satisfy its customers. As noted above, none of the reported complaints came from them. Heileman was also seeking to enhance its own bottom line. But in doing so it was not engaged in fraud, decep-tion or coercion. The marketing of PowerMaster was not like other morally objectionable individual marketing programs which have used factually deceptive advertisements (e.g., some past shaving commercials), taken advantage of the target group's special vulnerabilities (e.g., certain television advertisements to children who are cognitively vulnerable), or led to unusual harm for the group targeted (e.g., Nestlé's infant formula promotions to Third World Mothers). Black inner-city residents are not obviously cognitively vulnerable and are not, in the use of malt liquor, uniformly faced with a single significant problem such as Third World Mothers are (viz., the care of their infants). As such, it is mistaken to think that PowerMaster's marketing campaign was morally offensive or objectionable in ways in which other such campaigns have been. From this perspective, then, it appears that Heileman could be said to be fulfilling its individual corporate responsibilities.

IV. ASSOCIATED GROUPS AND COLLECTIVE RESPONSIBILITY

So long as we remain simply at the level of the individual marketing campaign of PowerMaster, it is doubtful that we can grasp the basis upon which the complaints against PowerMaster might be justified. To do so, we must look to the social level and the collection of marketing programs of which PowerMaster was simply one part. By pushing on the bounds within which other marketers had remained, PowerMaster was merely the spark which ignited a great deal of resentment which stemmed more generally from the group of malt liquor marketers coming into the inner-city from outside, aggressively marketing products which disproportionately harmed those in the inner-city (both those who consume the product and others), and creating marketing campaigns that took advantage of their vulnerabilities.

As such, this case might better be understood as one involving the collective responsibility of the group of marketers who target inner-city blacks rather than simply the individual responsibility of this or that marketer. By "collective responsibility" I refer to the responsibility which attaches to a group (or collective), rather than to the individual members of the group, even though it is only through the joint action (or inaction) of group members that a particular collective action or consequence

results. The objections of the critics could then more plausibly be recast in the form that the *collection* of the marketers' campaigns was consuming or wasting public health or welfare understood in a twofold sense: first, as the lack of illness, violence, and crime, and, second, as the presence of a sense of individual self that is based on the genuine gratification of real needs. When the individual marketers of a group (e.g., of brewers) engage in their own individual marketing campaigns they may not necessarily cause significant harms—or if they do create harm, the customers may have willingly accepted certain levels of individual risk of harm. However, their efforts may collectively result in significant harms not consciously assumed by anyone.

Similarly, though the individual marketing efforts may not be significant enough to expose the vulnerabilities of individuals composing their market segment, their marketing efforts may collectively create a climate within which the vulnerabilities of those targeted may play a role in the collective effect of those marketing campaigns. Thus, it is not the presence of this or that billboard from PowerMaster which may be objectionable so much as the large total number of billboards in the inner-city which advertise alcohol and to which PowerMaster contributed. For example, it has been reported that "in Baltimore, 76 percent of the billboards located in low-income neighborhoods advertise alcohol and cigarettes; in middle and upper-income neighborhoods it is 20 percent" (*The Workbook*, 1991: 18). This "saturation advertising" may have an effect different from the effect of any single advertisement. Similarly, it is not PowerMaster's presence on the market as such, which raises moral questions. Rather, it is that alcohol marketers particularly target a group which not only buys ". . . more than half the cognac sold in the United States and . . . consume[s] more than one-third of all malt liquor . . ." (*The Workbook*, 1991: 18), but also disproportionately suffers health problems associated with alcohol. The connection between the amount of alcohol consumed and the alcohol related health problems is hardly coincidental. Further, if the level of alcohol consumption is significantly related to conditions of poverty and racism, and the consequent vulnerabilities people living in these conditions may suffer, then targeting such individuals may also be an instance of attempting to take unfair advantage of them.

Now to make this case, it must be allowed that individual persons are not the only ones capable of being responsible for the effects of their actions. A variety of arguments have been given, for example, that corporations can be morally responsible for their actions. These arguments need not be recited here since even if they were successful, as I think some of them are, the marketers who target inner-city blacks do not themselves constitute a corporation. Hence, a different kind of argument is needed.

Can there be subjects of responsibility other than individuals and corporations? Virginia Held has argued that under certain conditions random collections of individuals can be held morally responsible. She has argued that when it would be obvious to the reasonable person what a random collection of individuals ought to do and when the expected outcome of such an action is clearly favorable, then that random collection can be held morally responsible (Held, 1970: 476).

However, again the marketers of malt liquor to inner city blacks do not seem to fit this argument since they are not simply a random collection of individuals. According to Held, a random collection of individuals ". . . is a set of persons distinguishable by some characteristics from the set of all persons, but lacking a decision method for taking action that is distinguishable from such decisions methods, if there are any, as are possessed by all persons" (Held, 1970: 471). The examples she gives, "passengers on a train" and "pedestrians on a sidewalk," fit this definition but are also compatible with a stronger definition of a group of individuals than the one she offers. For example, her definition would include collections of individuals with no temporal, spatial or teleological connection. Clearly marketers of malt liquor to inner-city blacks constitute a group or collection of individuals in a stronger sense than Held's random collection of individuals.

Consequently, I shall speak of a group such as the marketers who target inner-city blacks as an associated group. Such groups are not corporations. Nor are they simply random collections of individuals (in Held's sense). They are groups in a weaker sense than corporations, but a stronger sense than a random collections of individuals. I shall argue that such groups may also be the subject of moral responsibility. This view is based upon the following characteristics of such groups.

First, an associated group is constituted by agents, whether they be corporate or personal, who share certain characteristics related to a common set of activities in which they engage. Thus, the marketers who target inner-city blacks share the characteristic that they (and no one else) target this particular market segment with malt liquor. They engage in competition with each other to sell their malt liquor according to the rules of the (relatively) free market. Though they themselves do not occupy some single spatial location, the focus of their activities, the ends they seek, and their temporal relatedness (i.e., marketing to the inner-city in the same time period) are clearly sufficient to constitute them as a group.

Second, though such associated groups do not have a formal decision-making structure which unites them, Stanley Bates has reminded us that "there are other group decision methods, [that] . . . are not formal . . ." (Bates, 1971: 345). For example, the brewers presently at issue might engage in various forms of implicit bargaining. These informal and implicit group decision methods may involve unstructured discussions of topics of mutual interest, individual group member monitoring of the expectations and intuitions of other group members, and recognition of mutual understandings that may serve to coordinate the expectations of group members (cf. Schelling, 1963). Further, brewers in the United States have created The Beer Institute, which is their Washington-based trade group, one of whose main purposes is to protect "the market environment allowing for brewers to sell beer profitably, free from what the group views as unfair burdens imposed by government bodies." The Beer Institute provides its members with a forum within which they may meet annually, engage in workshops, discuss issues of mutual concern, agree on which issues will be lobbied before Congress on their behalf and may voluntarily adopt an advertising code to guide their activities. Such informal decision-making methods amongst these brewers and suppliers are means whereby group decisions can be made.

Third, members of associated groups can be said to have other morally relevant characteristics which foster a group "solidarity" and thereby also unify them as a group capable of moral responsibility (cf. Feinberg, 1974: 234). These characteristics take three different forms. (1) Members of the group share a community of interests. For example, they all wish to sell their products to inner-city blacks. They all seek to operate with minimal restrictions from the government on their marketing activities within the inner-city. They all are attempting to develop popular malt liquors. They all strive to keep the costs of their operations as low as possible. (2) Further, they are joined by bonds of sentiment linked with their valuing of independent action and successfully selling their products. Though they may try to outcompete each other, they may also respect their competitors when they perform well in the marketplace. (3) Finally, they can be said to share a common lot in that actions by one brewer that bring public condemnation upon that brewer may also extend public attention and condemnation to the other brewers as well—as happened in the PowerMaster case. Similarly, regulations imposed on one typically also affect the others. Thus, heavy regulation tends to reduce all their profits, whereas light regulation tends to have the opposite effect.

The unity or solidarity constituted by the preceding characteristics among the various marketers would be openly manifested, for example, if the government were to try to deny them all access to the inner-city market segment. In such a circumstance, they would openly resist, take the government to court, and protest with united voice against the injustice done to them, both individually and as a group. In this sense, there is (at the least) a latent sense of solidarity among such marketers (cf. May, 1987: 37). When they act, then each acts in solidarity with the others and each does those things which accord with the kinds of actions fellow group members are inclined to take. All this may occur without the need for votes being taken or explicit directions given among the various brewers (cf. May, 1987: 40).

Fourth, associated groups like inner-city marketers can investigate the harms or benefits that their products and marketing programs jointly do to those who are targeted. They can also study the overall effects of their own individual efforts. They could do so both as individual businesses and as a group. In the latter case, The Beer Institute might undertake such studies. Similarly, these marketers might jointly commission some other organization to study these effects. In short, they are capable both as individual businesses and as a group, of receiving

notice as to the effects of their individual and collective actions. In short, communication amongst the group members is possible.

Finally, associated groups can modify their activities. They are not simply inevitably or necessarily trapped into acting certain ways. For example, the inner-city malt liquor marketers might voluntarily reduce the number of billboards they use within the inner-city. They might not advertise in certain settings or in certain forms of media. They might not use certain appeals, e.g., touting the high alcoholic content of their products. As such, they could take actions to prevent the harms or injustices of which they are accused. At present brewers subscribe to an advertising code of ethics which The Beer Institute makes available and has recently updated. The Beer Institute might even lobby the government on behalf of this group for certain limitations on marketing programs so as to eliminate moral objections raised against such marketing programs.

The preceding indicates that this group can act: it has set up The Beer Institute; it may react with unanimity against new regulations; it may defend the actions of its members; it may investigate the effects its group members have on those market segments which they have targeted. It does not act as a group in marketing particular malt liquors. The law prevents such collective actions. However, marketing malt liquor to particular groups is an action which this group may approve or disapprove. The group lobbies Congress on behalf of its members' interests. The group has organized itself such that through development and support of The Beer Institute its interests are protected. There is no reason, then, that such a group may not also be morally responsible for the overall consequences of its members' marketing.

Does the preceding argument suggest that the group of marketers would run afoul of concerns about restraint of trade? The above argument need not imply that inner-city marketers are always a group capable of moral action and responsibility—only that under certain circumstances it could be. Hence, the above argument does not suggest that this group constitutes anything like a cartel. In addition, the above argument does not suggest that marketers agree on pricing formulas, on reserving certain distribution areas for this or that marketer, or similar actions which would constitute classic forms of restraint of trade. Further, the preceding argument leaves open what mechanisms might be legally used whereby these moral responsibilities are discharged. It might be that individual marketers voluntarily agree to such actions as they presently do with their advertising code. On the other hand, they might collectively appeal to the government to approve certain general conditions such that the playing field within which they compete would be altered to alleviate moral objections to their marketing campaigns, but would remain relatively level in comparison with their situations prior to the imposition of such conditions.

If the preceding is correct, then given the assumption that basic items of public welfare (e.g., health, safety, decision-making abilities, etc.) ought not to be harmed, two important conclusions follow regarding the marketing of malt liquor to inner-city blacks.

First, malt liquor marketers have a collective responsibility to monitor the effects of their activities and to ensure that they jointly do not unnecessarily cause harm to those they target or trade on their vulnerabilities. Assuming that malt liquor does harm inner-city blacks and that the marketing programs through which malt liquor is sold to this market segment play some significant causal role in creating this harm, then they have an obligation to alter their marketing to inner-city blacks in such a way that the vulnerabilities of inner-city blacks are not exploited and that unnecessary harm does not come to them.

Second, where the collective consequences of individual marketing efforts create the harms claimed for alcohol among inner-city blacks, and marketers as a group do not discharge the preceding collective responsibility, then there is a need for some agency outside those individual marketers to oversee or regulate their actions. Obviously, one form this may take is that of an industry or professional oversight committee; another form might be that of government intervention.

Two objections might be noted. It might be objected that the preceding line of argument faces the difficulty of determining the extent of harm which each marketer of malt liquor causes to the market segment targeted. Since this will be hard to determine, marketers of malt liquor may seek to escape the responsibility attributed to them. This difficulty, however, is no different in kind from other instances in which the actions of individual persons or businesses jointly produce a common problem. If the heavy trucks of several businesses regularly ply the city's streets contributing to the creation of potholes and broken asphalt, it will be difficult to determine the causal responsibility of each business. In all such instances there are difficult empirical and conceptual issues involved in establishing that harm has occurred, the levels at which it has occurred and the attendant moral responsibility. However, this is not to deny that such determinations can be made. I assume that similar determinations can be made in the present case.

Further, though it may be difficult to determine the harm which the marketing of a particular product may cause, it is less difficult—though by no means unproblematic—to determine the harm caused by the collection of marketing programs aimed at a particular market segment. Thus, though particular marketers may seek to escape individual responsibility for their actions, it will be much harder for them to escape their collective responsibilities. Still, we may anticipate that, in some cases, the results will be that an individual marketer has met his or her individual *and* collective responsibilities.

It might also be objected that this group cannot be responsible since it lacks control of its members. However, various forms of moral control are available to this group. They may try to persuade each other to change their course of action. And indeed, this occurred in the PowerMaster case: "Patrick Stokes, president of Anheuser-Busch Cos.' Anheuser-Busch Inc. unit and chairman of The Beer Institute, asked . . . Heileman's president, to reconsider the strategy for PowerMaster, which 'appears to be intentionally marketed to emphasize high alcohol content'" (Freedman, 1991b: B1). They might seek to expel a member from The Beer Institute and the benefits which such membership carries. Conceivably, they could turn to the public media to expose unethical practices on the part of that member. They might even, as with other groups within a nation state, seek outside help from the government. More positively, they could praise and hold up as models of marketing responsibility the marketing programs of certain group members.

Thus, this group can be said to be able to exercise moral influence and control over its members which is not dissimilar to that which is exercised by other similar groups and more generally within society as a whole.

V. COLLECTIVE RESPONSIBILITY AND SHARED RESPONSIBILITY

The nature of the collective responsibility discussed in the preceding section deserves further elaboration. Why, for example, should we not consider the responsibility attributed above to all marketers who target inner-city blacks as a form of shared (rather than collective) responsibility? By shared responsibility I understand that the responsibility for a certain event (or series of events) is shared or divided among a number of agents (personal or corporate). Shared or divided responsibility does not require that we are able to identify any group which could be said to be itself responsible for that (or those) event(s). As such, under shared responsibility each of those identified is, a least partially, responsible for the event(s). Shared responsibility, then, is a distributional concept. Each agent involved is assumed to have played some causal role in the occurrence of the event(s) in question. This does not mean that each agent had to have done exactly what the others did. One person might have knowingly and secretly loaded a truck with toxic chemicals, another might have driven the truck to an unauthorized and dangerous dump site, and a third pulled the lever to dump the chemicals. Each one did something different, yet they all played contributory causal roles in the immoral (and illegal) dumping of toxic chemicals. They share responsibility for this event and their responsibility exhausts the responsibility which may be attributed under these circumstances. Such shared responsibility differs from individual responsibility in that when a number of moral agents participate together in the production of some event (or series of events) it may not be possible to determine what the contribution of each agent was and hence to establish the nature or extent of their individual responsibility (cf. May, 1992: 39). Thus, if several corporations each make one of their marketing experts available to solve a problem confronting a regional council on tourism, it may not be possible to determine the exact contribution of each expert or each corporation to the resolution of this problem. Still, to the extent that each corporation (and each marketing expert) contributed and was a necessary part of the solution, they all share responsibility for the solution.

With collective responsibility, on the other hand, we must be able to identify some collective or group which itself has responsibility for the event (or series of events). Collective responsibility may or may not be distributional. Thus, some members of a group might be individually responsible as well as collectively responsible for what happens. In other instances, they may not be individually responsible, but only the group of which they are members be collectively responsible. For example, the members of some group might agree, by a divided vote, to undertake some project. Later, those who voted for the project may have died or left the group, while the negative voters (and others who have replaced the former members) remain. Still, that group remains responsible for (the completion of) the project, even though its individual members do not themselves have individual responsibilities for that project.

Now with regard to the group of marketers who target inner-city blacks, we have seen that we can refer to this as a group, which, though it does not have a formal decision-making structure, may still act. Its members have common interests; they communicate with each other regarding those interests; they share a solidarity which unites them in approving various things their fellow members do and defending those members when criticized. Further, within this group we may distinguish four situations concerning the marketing program of individual brewers: (1) It itself harms inner-city blacks; (2) It contributes to the harm of inner-city blacks; (3) It is indeterminate in its harm, or contributory harm, to inner-city blacks; and (4) It does not itself harm, or contribute to the harm of, inner-city blacks. In the first case, the marketer is individually responsible for such harm as is caused. In the second case, the marketer has shared responsibility with other marketers of this group. However, in the last two cases, though we may not speak of the individual or shared responsibility of the marketer, we may still speak of the collective responsibility of the group of marketers of which the last two are a part. We may also bring those in the first two cases under the same collective responsibility. The reason (in each of these cases) is that the group or collective of which they are members—whether they are individually responsible, share responsibility, or are responsible in neither of these cases—can collectively act, and could reduce such harms or evils by taking a stance against marketing practices which produce or foster them. For example, if Heileman dramatically revised its marketing campaign to inner-city blacks, but Pabst and Anheuser-Busch did not, then there might be little change in the results for inner-city blacks. Hence, it is only if the members of this group act in concert, as a group, that the objections raised against the marketing of malt liquors such as PowerMaster be responded to. This collective responsibility of the group of marketers will mean that individual marketers incur other individual responsibilities to act in certain ways as members of that group, e.g., to bring the harm created to the attention of other group members, to work within the group to develop ways to reduce or eliminate marketing practices which foster such harm, and to act in concert with other group members to reduce harm to targeted groups. Accordingly, it seems reasonable to attribute a collective responsibility to the group of these marketers, and not simply a shared responsibility.

It is also correct to say that the moral responsibility of the group of inner-city marketers does not replace or negate the individual responsibility of the members of this group. Still, the collective responsibility of this group does not simply reduce to the individual responsibility of its members in that, as argued above, an individual member of this group might fulfill his/her individual moral responsibilities and still the group not fulfill its collective responsibilities. Accordingly, marketers of alcohol to inner-city blacks may have individual, shared and collective responsibilities to which they must attend.

VI. IMPLICATIONS AND CONCLUSION

The implications of this social approach to the PowerMaster case are significant:

First, marketers cannot simply look at their own individual marketing campaigns to judge their moral level. Instead, they must also look at their campaign within the context of all the marketing campaigns which target the market segment at which they are aiming. This accords with Garrett

Hardin's suggestion that "the morality of an act is a function of the state of the system at the time it is performed" (Hardin, 1968: 1245; emphasis omitted). It is possible that marketers could fulfill their individual responsibilities but not their collective responsibilities.

Second, when the products targeted at particular market segments cause consumers to suffer disproportionately in comparison with other comparable market segments, marketers must determine the role which their products and marketing programs play in this situation. If they play a contributory role, they should (both individually and as a group) consider measures to reduce the harm produced. One means of doing this is to voluntarily restrict or modify their appeals to that market segment. In the present case, industry organizations such as The Beer Institute might play a leading role in identifying problems and recommending countermeasures. Otherwise when harm occurs disproportionately to a market segment, or members of that segment are especially vulnerable, outside oversight and regulation may be appropriate.

Third, marketers have a joint or collective responsibility to the entire market segment they target, not simply for the effects of their own products and marketing campaigns, but more generally for the effects of the combined marketing which is being done to that segment. The protests against PowerMaster are best understood against the background of this collective responsibility.

Thus, when we think of responsibility in the market we must look beyond simply the responsibility of individual agents (be they personal or corporate). We must look to the responsibility of groups of persons as well as groups of corporations. Such responsibility is not personal or individual, but collective. Examination of the case of PowerMaster helps us to see this.

Accordingly, the preceding analysis helps to explain both why PowerMaster was attacked as it was and also why it seemed simply to be doing what other marketers had previously done. Further, it helps us to understand the circumstances under which the above objections against marketing malt liquor to inner-city blacks might be justified. However, much more analysis of this form of collective harm and the vulnerability which is said to characterize inner-city blacks needs to be undertaken.

Finally, it should be emphasized that this paper advocates recognition of a new subject of moral responsibility in the market. Heretofore, moral responsibility has been attributed to individuals and corporations. Random collections of individuals have little applicability in business ethics. However the concept of associated groups and their collective responsibility has not been previously explored. It adds a new dimension to talk about responsibility within current discussions in business ethics.

BIBLIOGRAPHY

Bates, Stanley (1971), "The Responsibility of 'Random Collections'," *Ethics,* 81, 343–349.

Benn, Stanley, I. (1967), "Freedom and Persuasion," *The Australasian Journal of Philosophy,* 45, 259–275.

Brown, Jesse W. (1992), "Marketing Exploitation," *Business and Society Review,* Issue 83 (Fall), p. 17.

Colford, Steven W. and Teinowitz, Ira (1991), "Malt liquor 'power' failure," *Advertising Age,* July 1, pp. 1, 29.

Farhi, Paul (1991), "Surgeon General Hits New Malt Liquor's Name, Ads," *Washington Post,* June 26, pp. A1, A4.

Feinberg, Joel (1974), "Collective Responsibility," in *Doing & Deserving.* Princeton: Princeton University Press, pp. 222–251.

Fortune (1991), "Selling Sin to Blacks," October 21, p. 100.

Freedman, Alix (1991a), "Potent, New Heileman Malt Is Brewing Fierce Industry and Social Criticism," *Wall Street Journal,* June 17, pp. B1, B4.

———. (1991b), "Heileman, Under Pressure, Scuttles Power-Master Malt," *Wall Street Journal,* July 5, pp. B1, B3.

Hardin, Garrett (1968), "The Tragedy of the Commons," *Science,* 162, 1243–1248.

Held, Virginia (1970), "Can a Random Collection of Individuals Be Morally Responsible?", *The Journal of Philosophy,* 67, 471–481.

Horovitz, Bruce (1991) "Brewer Faces Boycott Over Marketing of Potent Malt Liquor," *L.A. Times,* June 25, pp. D1, D6.

Lacey, Marc (1992), "Marketing of Malt Liquor Fuels Debate," *L.A. Times,* December 15, pp. A32, A34.

May, Larry (1987), *The Morality of Groups.* Notre Dame: University of Notre Dame Press.

May, Larry (1992), *Sharing Responsibility.* Chicago: The University of Chicago Press.

Milloy, Courland (1991), "Race, Beer Don't Mix," *The Washington Post,* July 9, p. B3.

New York Times, The (1991), "The Threat of PowerMaster," July 1, p. A12.

Schelling, Thomas (1963), *The Strategy of Conflict.* New York: Oxford University Press.

Teinowitz, Ira and Colford, Steven W. (1991), "Targeting Woes in PowerMaster Wake," *Advertising Age,* July 8, 1991, p. 35.

"The Beer Institute," *Encyclopedia of Associations* (1995), Carolyn A. Fischer and Carol A. Schwartz (eds.), vol. 1. New York: Gale Research Inc.

Workbook, The (1991), "Marketing Booze to Blacks," Spring, 16, 18–19.

Zimmerman, Michael J. (1985), "Sharing Responsibility," *American Philosophical Quarterly,* 22, 115–122.

READING 9.5 CHILDREN AS CONSUMERS: AN ETHICAL EVALUATION OF CHILDREN'S TELEVISION ADVERTISING

Lynn Sharp Paine

Television sponsors and broadcasters began to identify children as a special target audience for commercial messages in the mid-1960s. Within only a few years, children's television advertising emerged as a controversial issue. Concerned parents began to

From *Business & Professional Ethics Journal,* vol. 3, no. 3/4 (1983): 119–125, 135–145. © Lynn Sharp Paine. Reprinted by permission of the author.

All notes in this reading have been deleted.

speak out and to urge the networks to adopt codes of ethics governing children's advertising. By 1970, the issue had attracted the attention of the Federal Trade Commission (FTC) and the Federal Communications Commission (FCC). The FCC received some 80,000 letters in support of a proposed rule "looking toward the elimination of sponsorship and commercial content in children's programming." Public attention to the controversy over children's television advertising peaked between 1978 and 1980, when the FTC, under its authority to regulate unfair and deceptive advertising, held public hearings on its proposal to ban televised advertising directed to or seen by large numbers of young children. More recently parents have complained to the FCC about so-called program-length commercials, children's programs designed around licensed characters.

As this brief chronology indicates, children's television advertising has had a history of arousing people's ethical sensibilities. In this paper I want to propose some explanations for why this is so and to argue that there are good ethical reasons that advertisers should refrain from directing commercials to young children. However, because so much of the public debate over children's advertising has focused on the FTC's actions rather than explicitly on the ethical aspects of children's advertising, a few preliminary remarks are called for.

First, it is important to bear in mind that the ethical propriety of directing television advertising to young children is distinct from its legality. Even if advertisers have a constitutional right to advertise lawful products to young children in a nondeceptive way, it is not necessarily the right thing to do. Our system of government guarantees us rights that it may be unethical to exercise on certain occasions. Terminology may make it easy to lose sight of the distinction between "having a right" and the "right thing to do," but the distinction is critical to constitutional governance. In this paper I will take no position on the scope of advertisers' First Amendment rights to freedom of speech. I am primarily interested in the moral status of advertising to young children.

A second preliminary point worth noting is that evaluating the ethical status of a practice, such as advertising to young children, is a different exercise from evaluating the propriety of governmental regulation of that practice. Even if a practice is unethical, there may be legal, social, economic, political, or administrative reasons that the government cannot or should not forbid or even regulate the practice. The public policy issues faced by the FTC or any other branch of government involved in regulating children's advertising are distinct from the ethical issues facing advertisers. The fact that it may be impossible or unwise for the government to restrict children's advertising does not shield advertisers from ethical responsibility for the practice.

Finally, I want to point out that public opinion regarding children's advertising is a measure neither of its ethical value nor of the propriety of the FTC's actions. Two critics of the FTC declared that it had attempted to impose its conception of what is good on an unwilling American public. There is reason to doubt the writers' assumption about the opinions of the American public regarding children's advertising, but the more critical point is the implication of their argument: that the FTC's actions would have been appropriate had there been a social consensus opposing child-oriented advertising. Majority opinion, however, is neither the final arbiter of justified public policy, nor the standard for assaying the ethical value of a practice like children's advertising. As pointed out earlier, constitutional limits may override majority opinion in the public policy arena. And although publicly expressed opinion may signal ethical concerns (as I suggested in mentioning the letters opposing commercial sponsorship of children's television received by the FCC), social consensus is not the test of ethical quality. We cannot simply say that children's advertising is ethically all right because many people do not object to it or because people's objections to it are relatively weak. An ethical evaluation requires that we probe our ethical principles and test their relation to children's advertising. Publicly expressed opposition may signal that such probing is necessary, but it does not establish an ethical judgment one way or the other.

. . . For purposes of this discussion, I will set aside the legal and public policy questions involved in government restrictions on children's advertising. Instead, as promised, I will explore the ethical issues raised by the practice of directing television advertising to young children. In the process of this investigation, I will necessarily turn my attention to the role of consumers in a free market economy, to the capacities of children as they relate to consumer activities, and to the relationships between adults and children within the family.

By *young children* I mean children who lack the conceptual abilities required for making consumer decisions, certainly children under eight. Many researchers have investigated the age at which children can comprehend the persuasive intent of advertising. Depending on the questions employed to test comprehension of persuasive intent, the critical age has been set as low as kindergarten age or as high as nine or ten. Even if this research were conclusive, however, it would not identify the age at which children become capable of making consumer decisions. Comprehending persuasive intent is intellectually less complex than consumer decisionmaking. Even if children appreciate the selling intent behind advertising, they may lack other conceptual abilities necessary for responsible consumer decisions. Child psychologists could perhaps identify the age at which these additional abilities develop. For purposes of this discussion, however, the precise age is not crucial. When I use the term *child* or *children* I am referring to "young children"— those who lack the requisite abilities.

Children's advertising is advertising targeted or directed to young children. Through children's advertising, advertisers attempt to persuade young children to want and, consequently, to request the advertised product. Although current voluntary guidelines for children's advertising prohibit advertisers from explicitly instructing children to request that their parents buy the advertised product, child-oriented advertising is designed to induce favorable attitudes that result in such requests. Frequently child-oriented ads utilize themes and techniques that appeal particularly to children: animation, clowns, magic, fantasy effects, superheroes, and special musical themes. They may also involve simply the presentation of products, such as cereals, sweets, and toys, that appeal to young children with announcements directed to them. The critical point in understanding child-directed advertising, however, is not simply the product, the particular themes and techniques employed, or the composition of the audience viewing the ad, but whether the advertiser intends to sell to or through children. Advertisers routinely segment their markets and target their advertising. The question at issue is whether children are appropriate targets.

Advertising directed to young children is a subcategory of advertising seen by them, since children who watch television obviously see a great deal of advertising that is not directed toward them—ads for adult consumer products, investment services, insurance, and so on. Occasionally children's products are advertised by means of commercials directed to adults. The toy manufacturer Fisher-Price, for example, at one time advertised its children's toys and games primarily by means of ads directed to mothers. Some ads are designed to appeal to the whole family. Insofar as these ads address young children they fall within the scope of my attention.

My interest in television advertising directed to young children, as distinct from magazine or radio advertising directed to them, is dictated by the nature of the medium. Television ads portray vivid and lively images that engage young children as the printed words and pictures of magazines, or even the spoken words of radio, could never do. Because of their immediacy television ads can attract the attention of young children who have not yet learned to read. Research has shown that young children develop affection for and even personal relationships with heavily promoted product characters appearing on television. At the same time, because of their immaturity, these children are unable to assess the status of these characters as fictional or real, let alone assess whatever minimal product information they may disclose. Technical limitations make magazine advertising and radio advertising inherently less likely to attract young children's attention. Consequently, they are less susceptible to ethical criticisms of the sort generated by television advertising.

CHILDREN AS CONSUMERS

The introduction of the practice of targeting children for televised commercial messages challenged existing mores. At the obvious level, the practice was novel. But at a deeper level, it called into question traditional assumptions about children and their proper role in the marketplace. The argument advanced on behalf of advertising to children by the Association of National Advertisers (ANA), the American Association of Advertising Agencies (AAAA), and the American Advertising Federation (AAF) reflects the rejection of some of these traditional assumptions:

> Perhaps the single most important benefit of advertising to children is that it provides information to the child himself, information which advertisers try to gear to the child's interests and on an appropriate level of understanding. This allows the child to learn what products are available, to know their differences, and to begin to make decisions about them based on his own personal wants and preferences. . . . Product diversity responds to these product preferences and ensures that it is the consumer himself who

dictates the ultimate success or failure of a given product offering.

The most significant aspect of this argument supporting children's advertising is its vision of children as autonomous consumers. Children are represented as a class of consumers possessing the relevant decision-making capacities and differing from adult consumers primarily in their product preferences. Children are interested in toys and candy, while adults are interested in laundry detergent and investment services. That children may require messages tailored to their level of understanding is acknowledged, but children's conceptual abilities are not regarded as having any other special significance. Advocates of children's advertising argue that it gives children "the same access to the marketplace which adults have, but keyed to their specific areas of interest."

When children are viewed in this way—as miniature adults with a distinctive set of product preferences—the problematic nature of advertising to them is not apparent. Indeed, it appears almost unfair not to provide children with televised information about products available to satisfy their special interests. Why should they be treated differently from any other class of consumers?

There are, however, significant differences between adults and young children that make it inappropriate to regard children as autonomous consumers. These differences, which go far beyond different product preferences, affect children's capacities to function as responsible consumers and suggest several arguments for regarding advertising to them as unethical. For purposes of this discussion, the most critical differences reflect children's understanding of self, time, and money.

Child-development literature generally acknowledges that the emergence of a sense of one's self as an independent human being is a central experience of childhood and adolescence. This vague notion, "having a sense of one's self as an independent human being," encompasses a broad range of capacities—from recognition of one's physical self as distinct from one's mother to acceptance of responsibility for one's actions and choices. Normally children acquire these capacities gradually in the course of maturation. While this mastery manifests itself as self-confidence and self-control in an ever-widening range of activities and relationships, it depends more fundamentally upon the emergence of an ability to see oneself as oneself. The reflexive nature of consciousness—the peculiar ability to monitor, study, assess, and reflect upon oneself and even upon one's reflections—underlies the ability to make rational choices. It permits people to reflect upon their desires, to evaluate them, and to have desires about what they shall desire. It permits them to see themselves as one among others and as engaging in relationships with others. Young children lack—or have only in nascent form—this ability to take a higher-order perspective on themselves and to see themselves as having desires or preferences they may wish to cultivate, suppress, or modify. They also lack the self-control that would make it possible to act on these higher-order desires if they had them.

Closely related to the sense of self, if not implicit in self-reflection, is the sense of time. Children's understanding of time—both as it relates to their own existence and to the events around them—is another area where their perspectives are special. Preschoolers are intrigued with "time" questions: "When is an hour up?" "Will you be alive when I grow up?" "When did the world begin and when will it end?" "Will I be alive for all the time after I die?" Young children's efforts to understand time are accompanied by a limited ability to project themselves into the future and to imagine themselves having different preferences in the future. It is generally true that children have extremely short time horizons. But children are also struggling with time in a more fundamental sense: they are testing conceptions of time as well as learning to gauge its passage by conventional markers. Young children's developing sense of time goes hand in hand with their developing sense of self. Their capacity for self-reflection, for evaluating their desires, and for making rational choices is intimately related to their understanding of their own continuity in time.

Young children are in many ways philosophers: they are exploring and questioning the very fundamentals of existence. Since they have not accepted many of the conventions and assumptions that guide ordinary commercial life, they frequently pose rather profound questions and make insightful observations. But although young children are very good at speculation, they are remarkably unskilled in the sorts of calculations required for making consumer judgments. In my experience, many young children are stymied by the fundamentals of arithmetic and do not understand ordinal relations among even relatively small amounts—let alone the more esoteric notions of selling in exchange for money. Research seems to support the observation that selling is a difficult concept for children. One study found that only 48 percent of six-and-a-half- to seven-and-a-half-year-olds could develop an understanding of the exocentric (as distinct from egocentric) verb *to sell*. A five-year-old may know from experience in making requests that a $5.00 trinket is too expensive, but when she concludes that $5.00 is also too much to pay for a piano, it is obvious that she knows neither the exchange value of $5.00, the worth of a piano, nor the meaning of *too expensive*.

What is the significance of the differences between adults and young children I have chosen to highlight—their differing conceptions of self, time, and money? In the argument for advertising quoted earlier, it was stated that advertising to children enables them "to learn what products are available, to know their differences, and to begin to make decisions about them based on [their] own personal wants and preferences." Ignore, for the moment, the fact that existing children's advertising, which concentrates so heavily on sugared foods and toys, does little either to let children know the range of products available or differences among them and assume that children's advertising could be more informative. Apart from this fact, the critical difficulty with the argument is that because of children's, shall we say, "naive" or "unconventional" conceptions of self, time, and money, they know very little about their own personal wants and preferences—how they are related or how quickly they will change—or about how their economic resources might be mobilized to satisfy those wants. They experience wants and preferences but do not seem to engage in critical reflection, which would lead them to assess, modify, or perhaps even curtail their felt desires for the sake of other more important or enduring desires they may have or may expect to have in the future. Young children also lack the conceptual wherewithal to engage in research or deliberative processes that would assist them in knowing which of the available consumer goods would most thoroughly satisfy their preferences, given their economic resources. The fact that children want so many of the products they see advertised is another indication that they do not

evaluate advertised products on the basis of their preferences and economic resources.

There is thus a serious question whether advertising really has or can have much at all to do with children's beginning "to make decisions about [products] based on [their] own personal wants and preferences" until they develop the conceptual maturity to understand their own wants and preferences and to assess the value of products available to satisfy them. If children's conceptions of self, time, and money are not suited to making consumer decisions, one must have reservations about ignoring this fact and treating them as if they were capable of making reasonable consumer judgments anyway. . . .

CHILDREN'S ADVERTISING AND BASIC ETHICAL PRINCIPLES

My evaluation of children's advertising has proceeded from the principle of consumer sovereignty, a principle of rather narrow application. Unlike more general ethical principles, like the principle of veracity, the principle of consumer sovereignty applies in the specialized area of business. Addressing the issue of children's advertising from the perspective of special business norms rather than more general ethical principles avoids the problem of deciding whether the specialized or more general principles should have priority in the moral reasoning of business people. Nevertheless, children's advertising could also be evaluated from the standpoint of the more general ethical principles requiring veracity and fairness and prohibiting harmful conduct.

Veracity

The principle of veracity, understood as devotion to truth, is much broader than a principle prohibiting deception. Deception, the primary basis of the FTC's complaint against children's advertising, is only one way of infringing the principle of veracity. Both critics and defenders of children's advertising agree that advertisers should not intentionally deceive children and that they should engage in research to determine whether children are misled by their ads. The central issue regarding veracity and children's advertising, however, does not relate to deception so much as to the strength of advertisers' devotion to truth. Advertisers generally do not make false statements intended to mislead children. Nevertheless, the particular nature of children's conceptual worlds makes it exceedingly likely that child-oriented advertising will generate false beliefs or highly improbable product expectations.

Research shows that young children have difficulty differentiating fantasy and reality and frequently place indiscriminate trust in commercial characters who present products to them. They also develop false beliefs about the selling characters in ads and in some cases have unreasonably optimistic beliefs about the satisfactions advertised products will bring them.

This research indicates that concern about the misleading nature of children's advertising is legitimate. Any parent knows—even one who has not examined the research—that young children are easily persuaded of the existence of fantasy characters. They develop (what seem to their parents) irrational fears and hopes from stories they hear and experiences they misinterpret. The stories and fantasies children see enacted in television commercials receive the same generous and idiosyncratic treatment as other information. Children's interpretations of advertising claims are as resistant to parental correction as their other fantasies are. One can only speculate on the nature and validity of the beliefs children adopt as a result of watching, for example, a cartoon depicting a pirate captain's magical discovery of breakfast cereal. Certainly, many ads are designed to create expectations that fun, friendship, and popularity will accompany possession of the advertised product. The likelihood that such expectations will be fulfilled is something young children cannot assess.

To the extent that children develop false beliefs and unreasonable expectations as a result of viewing commercials, moral reservations about children's advertising are justified. To the extent advertisers know that children develop false beliefs and unreasonable expectations, advertisers' devotion to truth and to responsible consumerism are suspect.

Fairness and Respect for Children

The fact that children's advertising benefits advertisers while at the same time nourishing false beliefs, unreasonable expectations, and irresponsible consumer desires among children calls into play principles of fairness and respect. Critics have said that

child-oriented advertising takes advantage of children's limited capacities and their suggestibility for the benefit of the advertisers. As expressed by Michael Pertschuk, former chairman of the FTC, advertisers "seize on the child's trust and exploit it as weakness for their gain." To employ as the unwitting means to the parent's pocketbook children who do not understand commercial exchange, who are unable to evaluate their own consumer preferences, and who consequently cannot make consumer decisions based on those preferences does indeed reflect a lack of respect for children. Such a practice fails to respect children's limitations as consumers, and instead capitalizes on them. In the language of Kant, advertisers are not treating children as "ends in themselves": they are treating children solely as instruments for their own gain.

In response to the charge of unfairness, supporters of children's advertising sometimes point out that the children are protected because their parents exercise control over the purse strings. This response demonstrates failure to appreciate the basis of the unfairness charge. It is not potential economic harm that concerns critics: it is the attitude toward children reflected in the use of children's advertising that is central. As explained earlier, the attitude is inappropriate or unfitting.

Another frequent response to the charge of unfairness is that children actually do understand advertising. A great deal of research has focused on whether children distinguish programs from commercials, whether they remember product identities, whether they distinguish program characters from commercial characters, and whether they recognize the persuasive intent of commercials. But even showing that children "understand" advertising in all these ways would not demonstrate that children have the consumer capacities that would make it fair to advertise to them. The critical questions are not whether children can distinguish commercial characters from program characters, or even whether they recognize persuasive intent, but whether they have the concepts of self, time, and money that would make it possible for them to make considered consumer decisions about the products they see advertised. Indeed, if children recognize that commercials are trying to sell things but lack the concepts to assess and deliberate about the products advertised, the charge that advertisers are "using" children or attempting to use them to sell their wares is strengthened. Intuitively, it seems that if children were sophisticated enough to realize that the goods advertised on television are for sale, they would be more likely than their younger counterparts to request the products.

Harm to Children

Another principle to which appeal has been made by critics of television advertising is the principle against causing harm. The harmful effects of children's advertising are thought to include the parent-child conflicts generated by parental refusals to buy requested products, the unhappiness and anger suffered by children whose parents deny their product requests, the unhappiness children suffer when advertising-induced expectations of product performance are disappointed, and unhappiness experienced by children exposed to commercials portraying life-styles more affluent than their own.

Replies to the charge that children's advertising is harmful to children have pinpointed weaknesses in the claim. One supporter of children's advertising says that the "harm" to children whose parents refuse their requests has not been adequately documented. Another, claiming that some experts believe conflicts over purchases are instructive in educating children to make choices, denies that parent-child conflict is harmful. As these replies suggest, demonstrating that children's advertising is harmful to children, as distinct from being misleading or unfair to them, involves much more than showing that it has the effects enumerated. Agreement about the application of the principle against causing harm depends on conceptual as well as factual agreement. A conception of harm must first be elaborated, and it must be shown to include these or other effects of advertising. It is not obvious, for example, that unhappiness resulting from exposure to more different life-styles is in the long run harmful.

Research indicates that children's advertising does contribute to the outcomes noted. Certainly, child-oriented television advertising is not the sole cause of these effects, but it does appear to increase their frequency and even perhaps their intensity. I believe that a conception of harm including some of these effects could be developed, but I will not attempt to do so here. I mention this argument rather to illustrate another general ethical principle on which an argument against children's advertising might be based. . . .

CONCLUSION

How might advertisers implement their responsibilities to promote consumer satisfaction and consumer responsibility and satisfy the principles of veracity, fairness, and nonmaleficence? There are degrees of compliance with these principles: some marketing strategies will do more than others to enhance consumer satisfaction, for example. One way compliance can be improved is by eliminating child-oriented television advertising for children's products and substituting advertising geared to mature consumers. Rather than employing the techniques found in advertising messages targeted to children under eleven, advertisers could include product information that would interest adult viewers and devise ways to let child viewers know that consumer decisions require responsible decision-making skills. If much of the information presented is incomprehensible to the five-year-olds in the audience, so much the better. When they reach the age at which they begin to understand consumer decision-making, they will perhaps have greater respect for the actual complexity of their responsibilities as consumers.

The problems of child-oriented advertising can best be dealt with if advertisers themselves recognize the inappropriateness of targeting children for commercial messages. I have tried to show why, within the context of a free market economy, the responsibilities of advertisers to promote consumer satisfaction and not to discourage responsible consumer decisions should lead advertisers away from child-oriented advertising. The problem of what types of ads are appropriate given these constraints provides a challenging design problem for the many creative people in the advertising industry. With appropriate inspiration and incentives, I do not doubt that they can meet the challenge.

Whether appropriate inspiration and incentives will be forthcoming is more doubtful. Children's advertising seems well entrenched and is backed by powerful economic forces, and it is clear that some advertisers do not recognize, or are unwilling to acknowledge, the ethical problems of child-focused advertising. The trend toward programming designed around selling characters is especially discouraging.

Even advertisers who recognize that eliminating child-oriented advertising will promote consumer satisfaction and consumer responsibility may be reluctant to reorient their advertising campaigns because of the costs and risks of doing so. Theoretically, only advertisers whose products would not withstand the scrutiny of adult consumers should lose sales from such a reorientation. It is clear that in the short run a general retreat from children's advertising would result in some lost revenues for makers, advertisers, and retail sellers of products that do not sell as well when advertised to adults. It is also possible that television networks, stations, and entrenched producers of children's shows would lose revenues and that children's programming might be jeopardized by the lack of advertisers' interest in commercial time during children's programs.

On the other hand, a shift away from children's advertising to adult advertising could result in even more pressure on existing adult commercial time slots, driving up their prices to a level adequate to subsidize children's programming without loss to the networks. And there are alternative means of financing children's television that could be explored. The extent to which lost revenues and diminished profits would result from recognizing the ethical ideals I have described is largely a question of the ability of all the beneficiaries of children's television advertising to respond creatively. The longer-term effect of relinquishing child-focused advertising would be to move manufacturers, advertisers, and retailers in the direction of products that would not depend for their success on the suggestibility and immaturity of children. In the longer run, the result would be greater market efficiency.

READING 9.6 WHY DO WE CONSUME SO MUCH?

Juliet B. Schor

"Why do we consume so much?" Observers of consumption have answered this question in many ways. Because it's our human nature. Because ads tell us to. Because we can't help ourselves. Because our economic system needs us to. Because we are trapped in a fruitless dynamic of desire, acquisition, and disappointment. Because he who dies with the most toys wins. Just because we can.

These answers are inadequate. But I believe we can find more satisfying ones by a critical application of both economic and sociological theory, which will not only help to explain why we consume the way we do, but also how we might start to live differently. But before proceeding I need to clarify two points. Whom do I mean by "we"? And what do I mean by "so much"?

The "we" is straightforward. I do not mean the "global" we. Indeed, the "global" we hardly consumes so much. Rather economic globalization, militarization, corruption, the monopolization of environmental resources, and the legacies of colonialism have meant that the global "South" doesn't consume enough—at least not in terms of basics such as food, clothing, shelter. In 1999, per capita GDP in the Less Developed Countries (or "global South") was $3,410 (measured as purchasing power parity). By contrast the Developed Countries ("global North") enjoyed average per capita GDP of $24,430, a gap of about eight times. One third of the population in the global South (1.2 billion) lives on less than $1 per day; 2.8 billion live on less than $2 per day. Together, this 4 billion comprises two-thirds of the world's population.

The "we" also does not cover everyone in the US. As you are all aware, despite this nation's enormous wealth, there continue to be significant numbers of people whose incomes are below poverty, and who lack access to basic consumption needs, such as adequate and nutritious food, decent shelter, reasonable transportation, health care, education, and other basic needs. Although poverty rates have declined, more than 30 million Americans have incomes below the poverty line, and probably twice that number do not have what most of would consider an adequate standard of living. Indeed, it is remarkable how little the long economic boom did to alleviate material deprivation. Thus, my "we" this evening stands for the majority of Americans—those whose basic needs are met, who have discretionary income, the large middle classes whose standard of living have risen so dramatically over this century.

And what about "so much?" By this phrase I intend to signal the material abundance of contemporary US consumption. Abundance in historical terms. In comparative terms. In ecological terms. And in absolute terms. Our lives are suffused with consuming—of material objects, experiences, services, media. There is increasingly little that we do which is not a consumption experience. Material abundance has only intensified in recent years, with the booming economy of the 1990s, and early 21st century. Indeed, it is hard to describe our current consumer patterns in terms other than excess. For example, the average US home has increased by more than 50% since the 1970s, rising more than 400 square feet, from 1,905 in 1987 to 2,322 in 1999 alone. (At the same time, there are an estimated 2 million homeless Americans, about 40% of whom are family groups.)

The number of vehicles per person has increased; as has the size and luxuriousness of those vehicles. The culture of excess has yielded $20,000 outdoor grills; $17,000 birthday parties for teen girls at FAO Schwarz; diamond studded bras from Victoria's Secret; a proliferation of Jaguars, Porsches and other luxury cars; status competitions in stone walls; professional quality appliances for people who are never home to cook; designer clothes for six year olds; and bed sheets costing a thousand dollars apiece. If these examples seem extreme, consider the more mundane example of clothes. Even ordinary ones. Clothing used to be costly, both because of materials and labor. Now, because of the combination of foreign sweatshops that don't even pay workers enough to eat, and artificially cheap materials, clothes are so plentiful that you can find them sold like beans or rice—by the pound. Charities are inundated with enormous amounts of superfluous clothing, for which there are no takers in our country. It's sent abroad in enormous quantities—sometimes to the detriment of local economies.

Americans spend more on cosmetics every year (in excess of $8 billion) than the extra expenditure needed to bring universal access to basic education for all children in the developing world. The US

and Europe together spend $17 billion a year on pet foods, more than the $13 billion increment it would cost to ensure basic health and nutrition around the world. And so on.

You can see from the direction of my examples that there is a sense in which I am also getting at the claim that "so much" is "too much." Indeed, that will be the core of my argument this evening. I mean this not merely in a semantic or an analytic sense, but in a critical one. For I believe that the culture of consumption excess which now pervades this country is wreaking havoc in many important ways. It is ecologically unsustainable, and those impacts are reaching crisis levels, with global warming, species depletion, deforestation, depletion of water supplies, and a variety of other pressing ecological effects. It has become socially unsustainable, as Americans work ever longer hours to support the dizzying rise in consumer norms which has characterized the last decade. It is financially unsustainable for many households, as consumption patterns are maintained by depleting savings and taking on debt. And finally, I believe that the culture of excess is partly responsible for a rising culture of social exclusion—two decades of increasing income and wealth inequality have yielded a society in which Americans are more likely to join gated communities, to tolerate poverty in their midst, to disavow responsibility for others and to abdicate a sense of community responsibility or common purpose. The events of September 11 have called attention to our growing callousness, and we are experiencing a surge of community feeling at the moment. But whether that remains durable, we will have to see.

These are strong claims. And they go very much against the conventional wisdom, both in economics, and throughout the culture more generally. What is that conventional wisdom? First, that consumption is good. That new and "improved" products really are improvements. That we consume because we love to. And that consuming has made our lives richer, fuller, more enjoyable, and better, in meaningful and important ways. Second, that more is always better. (After all, economics argues, if it weren't one could always ignore the extra consumption and be at least as well off as one was without it.) This superiority of more implies that sufficiency (or what some in the emergent simplicity movement like to call "enoughness") is never attained *in toto*. (We may easily reach satiation with particular commodities, but not for consumption as a whole.) And third, the conventional wisdom argues that the consumer market is best left relatively unattended by public policy, with the exception of some special cases (e.g., dangerous products). The consumer is sovereign and knows what he or she likes far better than the "government." Attempts to improve social welfare by steering consumption in particular directions will only backfire.

Now these are not conclusions that follow *logically* from economic theory. Rather, they represent the consensus view from the discipline, consumer economics and history as it has been practiced. As I shall argue shortly, I believe that much of this consensus is based on faulty assumptions about how and why we consume. Assumptions that, if altered, can lead to some very different conclusions.

On the other side, there is also a conventional wisdom among the critics of consumer culture. They begin with the view that while consumption may at one time have contributed significantly to human welfare, once basic needs have been satisfied, it is far less capable of doing so. New Coke is no better than Old Coke (and in some cases, such as this particular one, may even be worse). Besides, the critics say, we drink too much Coke anyway, and it's not good for us. Far better to drink water. So why are we paying scarce dollars for a can of sugar water that rots our teeth? Answers range from the observation that it's addictive, to the fact that it's everywhere (through monopolistic practices, such as exclusive contracts in schools.) And most importantly, in the critics' accounts, we're seduced into consuming by powerful advertising images, which equate the product with being cool, young, vital, sexy, or becoming an object of desire. The theme of many critiques of contemporary consumption is that consuming is a false god—our new religion—and that it takes us away from the true and durable satisfactions life has to offer. Consuming provides only temporary pleasures, is excessively hedonistic and seductive, and speaks not to the best in us, but often the worst. Most of these critiques center on the role of advertising, marketing, and the media, to account for how we get trapped into unsatisfying consumerist lifestyles.

I have sketched the two ends of the spectrum of belief about consumer society. While each contains important truths, I believe both are flawed. I accept the proposition that consuming is generally a "good" to the individual—the idea that people persistently act in ways which are so detrimental to their well-being is hard for an economist to swallow. (I say "generally" because there is plenty of empirical validation for cases in which consumption is out of control at the individual level.) But I agree with the critics that, as a society, we have too much of it. Instead of focusing on advertising and marketing, I argue that there are structural features in the operation of the economic system that have led us down a path of excessive consumerism.

What are those structural features and how do they operate?

THE CYCLE OF WORK AND SPEND

The first is what I have called "the cycle of work and spend." In the standard economic story, the level of consumption is set mainly by people's choices about how much to work, and therefore how much income to earn. (Unearned income is another matter, which I abstract from here.) The individual chooses between hours at work (which yield income) and leisure (a "good" in itself, but a costly one because it entails foregoing income). The income earned then determines the level of consumption. (*When* that income gets spent—now or later—has been a major preoccupation of economists but is not particularly relevant to my argument here.

Thus, individual workers/consumers choose the level of working hours and the quantity of consumption. In this story, there is no possibility of "too much" or too little" consumption. Those terms make no sense. Here, it is individuals' preferences that determine the quantity of consuming and free time. And whatever quantity is chosen must be optimal.

Now consider a situation in which individuals are not free to choose their hours of work, because employers set work norms and schedules, and those are tied to jobs. The individual has the ability to choose whether to work or not. But having taken a job, the hours are relatively inflexible. Furthermore, imagine that employers have a bias against allowing part-time or what I have called "short hour" jobs. Why is this? Because benefits are paid per person, not per hour; because employers prefer to hire fewer people; and because employees who work longer hours are more financially dependent on the firm. So the option of working less and earning less is not fully available. To see the point, consider that where employees do have the option to work short hours, they must pay large penalties—in the form of fewer or no benefits, and a significant reduction in upward career mobility.

There is also a dynamic aspect to this configuration: when productivity growth occurs, employers do not offer their employees the option of using it to reduce hours of work, but pass it on as income. And that turns into consumption. (There are a variety of technical and empirical aspects of this model which I gloss over here, such as the role of preferences, why innovative employers don't come along and offer short hours jobs, and indeed why there is an incomplete market to begin with.)

If there is not a freely functioning market in hours, and employers inhibit hours' reductions, then there is no sense in which one can describe the quantity of consumption as optimal. Rather, we get too much income and not enough leisure. It is not advertising, or marketing, or addictive commodities which create this "too much." It is the fact that more leisured, less consumerist lifestyles are structurally blocked—in the labor market. Having been offered only the long hours, high-income choice, it's hardly surprising that people choose to do lots of consuming. After working so hard, they feel deserving of their consumer comforts and luxuries. Indeed, consumption is the major form of reward for long hours and a harried pace of work. And consumer expenditures have become one means by which people with frenetic lives keep it all going— whether it's stress-busters like vacations, massages, or restaurant meals; the contracting out of household services; or the purchase of time-saving commodities. (Now why people don't work hard for a while, save up lots of money and leave the labor market is another question, which I will come to in a few minutes. And, as working hours have risen, there are plenty of people trying to do that.)

The too much work, not enough leisure story is more than theoretically possible. Average annual hours per capita have risen by 178 since 1973. Although some of the rise in hours of paid work has been accounted for by a shift from women's unpaid household production into employment, the picture from a household basis is unambiguous. The average household is devoting hundreds of addi-

tional hours to paid work in order to maintain its standard of living. According to the Council of Economic Advisers, between 1969 and 1999, annual hours of work for married couple households rose 18% (497 hours) and 28% in single-parent households (297 hours).

This has led to a widespread sense of time-squeeze. The fraction of Americans reporting that they "almost never" have time on their hands rose from 41% in 1982 to 56% in 1995.

In the National Survey of the Changing Workforce done by the Families and Work Institute, between a quarter and a third of all employees reported fairly serious and frequent problems of inadequate time for family, being in a bad mood or being too tired. A third of parents and a quarter of non-parents reported that "often or very often" "they do not have the energy to do things with their families or other important people in their lives."

The growth of work effort and time stress has resulted in increased desires for more time off the job. The National Survey of the Changing Workforce found that 63% of all employees said they worked more hours than they wished to, with median overwork at 11 hours per week. This represents a large increase to support my contention of a "cycle of work and spend."

THE ECOLOGICAL BIAS

The second structural feature that creates too much consumption is the overuse of "natural capital" (i.e., the ecological resources of the earth). This is a well-known argument within economics about particular kinds of pollution. If "air" is a free resource, corporations will pollute it "too much" because they do not have to pay for their pollution.

In practice, ecological resources are treated as externalities or free goods—after-thoughts in a world where production is created by capital and labor. The discipline of economics, and society more generally, has failed to consider the overall effects of treating natural capital so cavalierly. One result is that we consume too much, *in toto*. If we correctly accounted for the costs of ecological resources, or committed to using them sustainably (so that they would renew, rather than degrade over time), we would likely be producing less overall (and taking more leisure). Why? Because consumption would become more costly relative to free time.

What we consume would also shift, toward less ecologically damaging (and costly) products and services. Fewer SUVs and airplane trips. More organic farming. Fewer plastics and chemicals. Smaller but more durable wardrobes, cotton grown with fewer or no pesticides. (10% of the world's pesticide use is for cotton.) Less meat, more grain. Shade grown coffee. Solar and wind power. Instead of rising, as it has in the last decade, residential energy use would fall, as people economized on space and shifted toward energy-efficient practice. Ditto paper use, which incredibly enough given the introduction of computers, is rising in the United States.

IS THE ECOLOGICAL BIAS A SERIOUS ONE?

Ecological models suggest yes, that the rates at which resource use, pollution and ecological degradation are occurring far exceed the earth's absorption capacity. Meadows' and Meadows' W3 model, using reasonable assumptions for economic output, population and consumption, consistently produces its worst outcome of overshoot and collapse. One reason is that we have already undermined a significant amount of the earth's absorption capacity, so that some regenerative mechanisms are no longer able to reverse the overshoot. Downward spirals begin to dominate positive feedback loops. The model's effects can be seen in the concrete problems of:

Global warming. Warmer climate is associated with toxic algal blooms, increased flooding and droughts, thawing of the permafrost, increased weather uncertainty, deforestation through insect damage, and increased transmission of vector-borne infections. The United States, with 5% of the world's population, is responsible for 24% of global carbon dioxide emissions.

Species extinction. Among birds and mammals, species are now going extinct at rates that are estimated to be 100 to 1,000 times the natural rate of extinction. One in eight known plant species is threatened with extinction.

Ecosystem depletion. Since 1970, freshwater ecosystems have declined by 50%, marine ecosystems have declined by 30%, and world forests have declined by 10%. This rate of depletion is unprecedented in human history. Indeed, current rates of environmental resource use dwarf human usage in all of human history. (A comprehensive analysis of world ecosystem indicators by the World Resources Institute, the World Bank, the United Nations Development Programme, and the Limited Nations Environment Programme finds that in virtually all types of ecosystems around the world, quality is deteriorating.)

Water shortages. Approximately 1/3 of the world's population now lives in areas with moderate to heavy stress on water supplies, and if current trends continue, that number is expected to be 2/3 in 30 years. Already, 28% of the world's population lacks access to safe drinking water, and 5 million people die each year from inadequate access to water.

Deforestation and soil erosion. Some researchers believe that humans have now reduced the earth's original forest cover by up to 50%. The World Resources Institute estimates that we are losing 9 million hectares a year and rates of deforestation in tropical forests have accelerated, not declined in the 1990s, compared to the 1980s. It is now estimated that two-thirds of agricultural land has been degraded in the past 50 years, and 40% has been strongly or very strongly degraded.

The disequilibrium between pollution sources and sinks has been caused by the rapid increases in economic output over the last fifty years, made possible by advances in production technology. World industrial production has been accelerating at an exponential rate. Global consumption has tripled between 1980 and 1997. At the current rate of growth of the world economy, output doubles every 21 years. A mere one percent increase, to 4%, leads to doubling every 15 years. Yet, we are already well beyond a sustainable relationship with the earth. And when we consider the ongoing worldwide replication of US lifestyles, the prognosis is even grimmer. Ecological footprint analysis (which looks at the global impact of any given consumer lifestyle) suggests that for the rest of the world to live as Americans do, we will need four additional planets to provide the necessary

CONSUMPTION COMPETITIONS

I come now to my third argument, which is that we consume too much in part because consumption has become a social competition, something we engage in the esteem, recognition, status, and even envy it confers. We consume conspicuously, and excessively, because consumer lifestyles have become such an important part of how we are defined and how we fit into socially differentiated communities. Veblen made this point most famously a hundred years ago. His analysis was based mainly on the wealthy and the would-be wealthy, for whom attaining and displaying visible wealth had become the *sine qua non* of social standing. But the phenomenon is far broader today, with the large majority of the population participating. Today it is less insidious in some ways, because it's not only offensive (I get the big diamond because my best friend doesn't have one), but has become defensive. (I get the big diamond because my best friend does have one.)

In *The Overspent American,* I discussed the ways in which this process has changed. Fifty years ago it was a comparison among peers. "Keeping up with the Joneses"—the colloquial description of consumption competitions, occurred mainly within a neighborhood setting. Because neighborhoods are relatively homogeneous in terms of the social status and economic resources of their members, the folks keeping up with the Joneses tended to be their equals. They did aspire, but rarely more than to increase their consumer expenditures by 10–20%. Smiths wanted the Joneses Chevy and nifty fridge, not the Rockefellers' mansions and art collections.

That has changed. The "reference groups" (to use the sociological term) that Americans now use to calibrate their consumer aspirations have become more vertical and less horizontal (vertical in terms of economic and social standing). Now Rockefeller, rather Bill Gates, has become an important aspirational target for millions of Americans, especially young ones. And even more importantly, the upper twenty percent of the population (roughly those making $100,000 a year or more) have become an aspirational target throughout society. A decent or comfortable standard of living—once a widespread goal—is no longer enough. Now the dominant goal is for status products, and luxury. There is plenty of survey evidence, some of which I discussed in my book, which shows the increasing importance of earning a lot of money, earning

more than others, getting rich, and acquiring the trappings of upper middle class or truly wealthy lifestyles—second homes, swimming pools, foreign travel, expensive wardrobes, etc. Perhaps most telling is the fact that getting rich is now the number one aspiration of American youth, more important than being a famous athlete or celebrity, or being really smart.

How this happened is an interesting story, but I believe one of the major factors has been the decline of community and sociability, especially on a neighborhood level, and the growing importance of media, and especially television, in purveying "information" about consumption. We are now less likely to go into our neighbors' living room to see how they spend their money than we are to get into [Frasier's]. We find out about new consumer "trends" from movies and TV, print media both newspapers and magazines, and also the Internet. Our new "friends" are the ones we find on TV.

One consequence of this "up scaling of desire" is that consumer norms have risen faster and higher than in a world with more moderate consumer aspirations. This is partly because the target that everyone is chasing has become so prosperous—in addition to large increases in the *level* of income and wealth garnered by the top 2000, they have also increased their *share* dramatically. Between 1983 and 1998, the top 20% increased their share of income from 51.9% to 56.2%; their share of financial wealth rose from 81.3% to 83.4%. (So much for people's capitalism. The share of total financial wealth held by the top 1% stands at a stunning 47.3%, up from 42.9% in 1983. The bottom 60% holds no financial wealth at all, on average.) Unlike previous economic booms, this one did not yield a more equitable distribution of income and wealth.

The problem with consumption competition, such as the one we find ourselves in, is that they are difficult for individuals to resist. If everyone else is buying that SUV, we tend to want one too. And if we hold out for a while, avoiding the seductive message that the SUV will get us back to nature, and the simpler, slower, more meaningful life we crave (Never mind the hypocrisy there: it's more likely we'll be working longer to meet the car payments and ignoring the contribution the SUV makes to global warming.), [t]hen practical considerations start to weigh in. Everyone else has one, I'm no longer safe in a small vehicle. I can't see past all those behemoths; better elevate myself as well. Similarly with the up scaling to cell phones, or computers, or the kinds of lessons and cultural enhancements our children need to achieve in today's competitive world, or the kind of kitchen we have, and so on. We might all be happier driving slightly older cars, having fewer gizmos and gadgets, with a fashion style that didn't change quite so frequently, and maybe even with slightly smaller homes. In return we'd get with less debt and more financial security, more time outside of work, less anxiety about keeping up, and a healthier environment.

But in a consumption competition none of us can do it alone. Without a coordinating influence (be it the government, the church, the community, any social institution will do . . .) each of us is trapped in what I once called the upward creep of desire. (Except that in recent years it has turned into a gallop.) So collectively we are in what game theorists call a Prisoner's Dilemma, where we could all benefit from a slowing down. It's like a ballgame when people start standing to get a better view. The first few do succeed. (Those are the "early adopters" of new consumer trends, the Joneses we're all following.) But as everyone starts to stand, the quality of the view goes back to what it was, and everyone's legs get tired. Those who sit down on their own are drastically worse off. And the collective good can only be reached through the announcer's call: "Baseball fans, please sit down." I think that's where we've been in the last half-decade or so.

CONCLUSION

These then are my three arguments about why we consume too much: we are locked into a "cycle of work and spend," we have failed to value the earth's capital, and consuming has become a means to social esteem and belonging. In the process, we are undermining our quality of life. We fail to take enough leisure, and live excessively busy and stressful lives. We are poisoning the planet. And we find ourselves needing to earn too much money or going into debt, or getting stressed out by the rapid rise in consumer norms. Community, security, and the peace of mind that comes from having reached a state of sufficiency are increasingly elusive.

The standard economic analysis sees precious little of this. More is always better. Individuals will

act in their interest to avoid these traps. Collective action failures or externalities are rarely more than small problems. Similarly, the consumer critics have failed to understand the structural dynamics that make consuming a rational choice for the individual, even if it is [an] irrational one for society as a whole. They take an excessively dim view of people's abilities to act well for themselves. And they underestimate how important consumption can be in a society organized around it. But they are certainly right, that excessive consumption has become a serious problem—from the standpoint of our daily lives, our ethical obligations to others around the world, from the standpoint of the earth and its sacred bounty.

In recent years, increasing numbers of Americans have come to these and similar conclusions. They are individually escaping "the cycle of work and spend," by downshifting (working less and spending less). They are joining the emerging voluntary simplicity movement, living modestly, volunteering their time, spending their days doing the things they are passionate about. They are joining study groups in their workplace and churches. Some are even organizing an anti-consumerist movement, participating in Buy-Nothing Day (the Friday after Thanksgiving) or designing sub-vertising (anti-ads which turn the tools of advertising and marketing against itself). They are protesting corporate globalization of the economy. They are joining organic farms and drinking shade grown coffee. They are riding bicycles. And they are opposing the corporate co-optation of their lifestyles, as the Gap, Honda, Starbucks and Time-Warner try to make money selling "simplicity" as the latest hip consumer trend.

But they (we) need more Americans to join. The domination of the consumer culture remains impressive, and as patriotic appeals to consume have become common in the weeks since Sept. 11, we should resist the temptation to run to the mall. Instead, let us take this very painful but special time to step back and ask some fundamental questions. We do we consume so much? What are the effects of that consumption? And how can we create a community that respects the earth, respects each and every human being upon it, and truly meets human needs?

Decision Scenario A
MARKETING IN SCHOOL

Is there an age below which marketing commercial products ought not be targeted? Is every person, regardless of age, a potential consumer? Recent trends in education suggest that even preschoolers are treated as consumers by business and marketing agencies.

The market potential of young people is huge. According to one 2001 report, children's spending tripled in the 1990's. Children between the ages of 4 and 12 spent $2.2 billion in 1968, $4.2 billion in 1984, and $17.1 billion in 1994, and by 2002 their spending exceeded $40 billion. Estimates are that direct buying by children is expected to exceed $51.8 billion by 2006. This makes young people an attractive target for marketers, and where better to target marketing than in schools?

Commercials in schools occur in many forms. Products are directly advertised in a variety of formats and circumstances. Indirect advertising occurs with sponsorships of school activities and supplies. Many products are sold in and by schools, and many schools participate in a variety of marketing research studies. In every case, schools provide the occasion for students to learn about some commercial product.

Direct advertising in schools, something relatively unusual a few decades ago, is now very common. Perhaps the most well-known is Channel One, a for-profit media company that produces news programming shown daily in thousands of middle and high school classrooms. Daily 12-minute news programs contain 2 minutes of advertising. Thirty-second ads on Channel One reach 8 million students and can sell for as much as $195,000. Schools are full of many other advertisements. Book covers, often distributed for free by the schools, advertise potato chips and breakfast cereal. School Web sites and search engines contain advertisements and sponsor logos. Some school districts have sold ad space on school buses.

Indirect ads are equally widespread. Teaching materials at every educational level are produced by and advertise corporate sponsors. Corporate logos appear in books, on posters, in videos, and on student worksheets. Athletic fields, playgrounds, scoreboards, team uniforms and athletic shoes, school events, and even classrooms advertise corporate sponsors whose donations paid for them. Students and parents are given coupons for free and discounted products as "rewards" for reading programs. Of course, corporate ads and logos appear on student shirts, pants, shoes, and coats.

Many commercial products are directly sold in most schools as well. Vending machines advertise and sell fast food and soft drinks. Coke and Pepsi compete for the exclusive right to sell their products on many college and high school campuses. Lunch rooms and cafeterias may actually be fast-food franchise operations. Students themselves are even employed in sales of magazines and other products as part of many school fundraising programs.

Finally, schools are ideal locations for businesses and marketing firms to conduct research on products. Some schools will allow marketing firms to interview students directly or conduct focus group discussions in exchange for payments. More indirect marketing research occurs in the form of response cards found within teaching packets, evaluation forms that students, teachers, and parents use to assess teaching materials, as well as from Web site sign-ups and product registration forms.

Some observers do not see problems with marketing to children in general or at schools in particular. After all, parents and teachers have the responsibility to act as a filter to shield students from harmful ads or products. However, financial pressures on schools is one major explanation for why teachers and parents cannot shield students from advertising. Nationwide many school districts are underfunded, leaving teachers and administrators little choice but to seek commercial revenue sources. Faced with the option of no teaching supplies, or teaching packets supplied by and advertising Ford Motor Co. or the Care Bears, many teachers believe they have no choice but to deliver their students to marketers.

The school market has even extended to preschools. In 2003, some 4 million American children regularly attended a formal child care or preschool program, most of which are not part of the public education system. Such programs are fully funded by parents, most of whom need child care in order to be able to work. Thus, marketing now targets the youngest children at the very point at which they are forming many of the habits and basic desires that will shape their future personalities.

■ From the point of view of a parent, would you support marketing in your child's school? From the point of view of a teacher or school administrator, would you allow advertising in your classroom or school building?

■ Is there a difference between marketing soft drinks and fast food to school children and marketing public broadcasting material, such as Sesame Street characters and programs?

■ Are there some products that should not be sold or advertised in schools? How do you distinguish between good and bad children's products?

■ How do you respond to the claim that it is the responsibility of parents and teachers, and not advertisers, to protect children?

■ Are ads targeted at children fundamentally deceptive? Are children capable of distinguishing between true and deceptive ads?

■ Are indirect methods of marketing, such as product logos on teaching supplies, any different from product logos on clothing? What is the goal of indirect marketing?

Decision Scenario B
ADVERTISING'S IMAGE OF WOMEN

It has been estimated that U.S. children between the ages of two and five watch an average of 30 hours of television each week. At this rate, the average young person will watch some 350,000 television commercials by the end of high school. Given all forms of advertising (magazines, newspapers, packaging, radio, television) the average American will have seen some 50 million commercials by age 60. Thus advertising is inescapable in our culture, and its socializing impact cannot be ignored. Ads not only describe products but also present images, values, and goals; they portray certain concepts of normalcy and sexuality, and they promote certain types of self-images. Advertising not only aims to provide information to consumers but also aims to motivate them. What images of women does it present, and what motivations does it appeal to?

Many ads seek to motivate women by suggesting that they are inadequate without a particular product. Cosmetic ads purvey an ideal form of female beauty—a form that is unattainable. Women are portrayed as having no facial wrinkles, no lines, no blemishes—indeed, no pores. If you do not look like this, the ads suggest, you are not beautiful, and since no one (including the model) really looks like this, women need cosmetics to look beautiful. Beauty thus results from products and not from the woman herself. Advertising tells women that they should change their age (the "little-girl look"), weight, bust size, hair color, eye color, complexion—and even their smell. In many ads a woman's worth is measured not by her intelligence or her character or even her natural appearance. A woman's worth is measured by how closely she approaches an ideal created by an advertising agency.

Many ads also portray women as inferior to other women and to men. Women are seen as engaged in a constant competition with other women for the attention of men. When they are pictured with men, women are often shown as clinging to the male, as passive, as submissive. Men are seen in control, active, and dominant.

Besides feelings of inadequacy, many ads also use guilt to motivate women. The "housewife" is constantly being chided because the laundry is not as white nor does it smell as clean as the neighbor's. Her dishes have spots, her meals are unappealing, her floors and furniture have "wax buildup," and her clothes are out of style. Even when women are shown in the role of worker rather than home-maker, feelings of guilt and inadequacy are still rein-forced. The working woman is portrayed as a superwoman who harmonizes perfectly the roles of career woman, mother, wife, and homemaker. Despite all of these demands, the woman still looks like a model. In those few cases where the harmony breaks down, the woman is shown as being responsible for the breakdown or in need of drugs to cope with the stress. On the other hand, men are seldom seen as responsible for cooking, cleaning, and child care, or in need of drugs in order to cope.

- What kind of influence has advertising had on your own views of beauty, attractiveness, and sexuality?

- How does advertising influence our understanding of social role based on gender?

- To what degree have your family, friends, and classmates been socialized by advertising?

Decision Scenario C
ADVERTISING HEADACHES

The nonprescription pain reliever market in the United States has sales of over $2 billion annually. The market essentially involves just three drugs (all called analgesics): aspirin, acetaminophen, and ibuprofen. This market is dominated by four major pharmaceutical companies. Sterling Drug controls a major share of the aspirin market with its product Bayer Aspirin. Johnson & Johnson produces an acetaminophen (Tylenol) and an ibuprofen product (Mediprin). American Home Products makes an aspirin (Anacin), an acetaminophen (Anacin-3), and an ibuprofen (Advil). Bristol-Meyers also produces aspirin (Bufferin and Excedrin), an acetaminophen (Datril), and an ibuprofen (Nuprin).

Since there is no chemical and therefore no medicinal difference between brands of acetaminophen and ibuprofen, and no significant difference between aspirins (some differ by having caffeine added to the aspirin; others have a coating), these companies have two basic choices for succeeding in the marketplace: They can compete over price, or they can rely on advertising. Evidence suggests that all have followed the advertising route. The regulation history of advertising for these products shows that this route has been controversial.

As long ago as 1944 the Federal Trade Commission (FTC) investigated Anacin for the claim that its "combination of highly proven and active ingredients" were superior to and different from aspirin (no evidence exists to support that the caffeine in Anacin improves its analgesic effect). Through the 1960s television ads claimed that Anacin offered "fast, fast relief." Bufferin was "twice as fast as aspirin," St. Joseph's aspirin was "faster than other leading pain relief tablets," and

Bayer offered the "fastest relief of pain." Anacin also employed ads citing surveys that showed "three out of four doctors recommend the ingredients in Anacin" and calling Anacin's ingredients the "greatest pain fighter ever discovered." These ads did not disclose that this "ingredient" was plain aspirin.

The increasing popularity of acetaminophen throughout the 1970s brought with it similar advertising claims. "Last year hospitals dispensed ten times as much Tylenol as the next four brands combined" did not disclose that Johnson & Johnson supplied hospitals with Tylenol at costs well below what consumers pay. American Home Products sued Johnson & Johnson on the grounds that these ads implied that hospitals dispensed Tylenol because it was more effective than competing products. At the same time, American Home Products was advertising its acetaminophen, Anacin-3, by claiming that "hospitals recommend acetaminophen, the aspirin-free pain reliever in Anacin-3, more than any other pain reliever." The acetaminophen recommended by hospitals, of course, was Tylenol.

- If you applied both the "reasonable consumer" and the "ignorant consumer" standards, would these ads be deceptive? Are they unfair business practices?

- How might a defender of the free market like Milton Friedman analyze this scenario? Is this a case of market failure or the result of businesses ignoring market principles?

- Should there be more regulation of advertising of medicines? Would such regulation involve undue government paternalism?

Decision Scenario D
NEW, IMPROVED, . . . AND SMALLER

Consumer product companies often face a competitive marketplace where profit margins are slim and manufacturing cost increases frequent. Some companies have adopted a new technique called "downsizing" to respond to these pressures. They decrease product weight or quantity while holding package size and price constant. Consumer research suggests that consumers are less likely to process the label information that discloses the downsizing and the implicit price increase. Consumers, then, are less likely to respond as they would to a more obvious per package price increase. Downsizing can come in a variety of forms, some more creative than others. Perhaps the most common technique is to keep the exact same package but include less product. Some coffee manufacturers have a new twist on that strategy. They decreased the quantity of coffee in the can, but they claimed that a new "flaking" process allowed the consumer to get more brewed coffee per scoop. Other manufacturers reduce the package size and quantity, and lower the package price but increase the unit price. (New low price!) Another approach is to increase package size, quantity, and price but also increase unit price. (A variant of the old "economy size" package that had a higher unit price.)

This case was prepared from the following sources: Irwin Landau, "Why a Pound of Coffee Weighs 13 Ounces," *New York Times*, May 23, 1993 Section 3, p. 13; Steven Sakson (AP), "Will People Cough Up $50 for a $5 Drug?" *Philadelphia Inquirer*, October 14, 1994.

One drug manufacturer, barred from the continued use of an active ingredient in a prescription asthma drug, changed the formulation so that the new drug was similar in ingredients to an over-the-counter medication that cost one-tenth the price. Another drug company halved the quantity of active ingredients while doubling the suggested dosage for an over-the-counter cold medication.

Some report that a manufacturer of laundry detergent launched a new brand with very high initial levels of the active cleaning agent, the detergent's most costly ingredient. Then it gradually reduced the levels of the cleaning agent while carefully tracking consumer response. When noticeable decreases in cleaning effectiveness began to cause decreased sales, the manufacturer increased the proportion of the cleaning agent again.

- Are companies that downsize intentionally deceiving because they are relying on market research that shows consumers are less likely to notice such price increases?
- Are there ethically relevant differences between the preceding examples?
- What responsibility does the consumer have to protect him- or herself in the marketplace? What effect does that responsibility have on the obligations of manufacturers and advertisers? Are any of the techniques described ones that consumers cannot protect against?

Decision Scenario E
POLITICAL ADVOCACY MEETS HIGH-TECH AD AGENCIES

In its 1978 *Bellotti* decision, the United States Supreme Court struck down a Massachusetts statute that prohibited corporations from engaging in advocacy advertising on political issues. The Court, by a 5 to 4 majority, held that corporations are legal persons and, as such, are entitled to engage in debate over matters that come before the body politic. Of course, ads have often had political content to varying degrees. Even before the *Bellotti* decision, for example, oil companies were advertising devotion to national security in the expensive search for new and reliable sources of domestic crude oil. Congress was at the same time debating a windfall profits tax because oil companies were perceived to have profited handsomely from the effects of the Arab oil embargo. The *Bellotti* decision merely allowed more explicit expressions of political opinions.

Recently, corporate-sponsored political advocacy advertising has reached new levels of sophistication and directness. During the 1994 debate over health care reform in the United States, advertising expenditures by groups both opposing and supporting the Clinton plan topped $75 million. One ad, in particular, was seen as highly effective in generating opposition to the Clinton plan. The "Harry and Louise" ads featured a couple who expressed concern over the state of health care but who were fearful of the impact of Clinton's reform proposals. The Health Insurance Association of America, the sponsor of the ads, spent over $17 million trying to protect the private health insurance market from controls suggested in the Clinton reforms. The ads were widely regarded as one of the most successful tools used by those opposed to the reform proposal.

In 1995, advocacy ads urging reform of product liability law began to appear in media markets rep-

resented by legislators regarded as uncertain supporters of reform. They were paid for by a lobbying group, Citizens for a Sound Economy, that was funded by large corporate donations. Two important donors were CIGNA (an insurance company) and R. J. Reynolds (the tobacco giant). Both companies have huge stakes in the direction taken by product liability law.

The ads were created by the same team that produced the "Harry and Louise" spots. The agency produced a number of memorable liability reform ads. One features a volunteer emergency medical technician who plaintively wishes that the threat of lawsuits not be allowed to keep her from doing her job—saving lives. Another shows a team of Little Leaguers who disappear from the screen, representing the threat from lawsuits that, the commercial says, costs teams "more than bats, balls, and uniforms." When asked for statistics on that, a spokesperson for Little League Baseball, Inc., said, "It's not incumbent on us to provide those numbers." These advocacy ads, and those from the health care debate, are notable both because of their emotional impact and because they represent the newest chapter in corporate political advocacy, where corporations sponsor apparently independent advocacy lobbies. (One commentator, likening these lobbies to artificial grassroots movements, called them "Astroturf campaigns.")

The usually conservative Justice Rehnquist, now Chief Justice, in his dissent from the *Bellotti* decision suggested the following:

> A State grants a business corporation the blessings of potentially perpetual life and limited liability to enhance its efficiency as an economic entity. It might reasonably be concluded that those properties, so beneficial in the economic sphere, pose special dangers in the political sphere. . . . Indeed, the States might reasonably fear that the corporation would use its economic power to obtain further benefits than those already bestowed.

Despite Justice Rehnquist's reservations, corporate political advocacy activities appear to pass muster with the Supreme Court. They also appear

This case was prepared from the following sources: *First National Bank of Boston v. Bellotti* 435 U.S. 765; Elizabeth Kolbert, "Special Interests Special Weapon," *New York Times,* March 26, 1995; Katherine Seelye, "Agendas Clash in Bid to Alter Law on Product Liability," *New York Times,* March 8, 1995; Eric Schine and Catherine Young, "From the Folks Who Brought You Harry and Louise . . . ," *Business Week,* April 17, 1995; Cyndee Miller, "Ads Are Huge Weapon in the Battle Over Health Care Reform," *Marketing News,* September 12, 1994; Margaret Carlson, "Public Eye," *Time,* March 7, 1994.

to be a permanent and increasingly frequent part of political debate in the United States.

- Does the ability of a corporation to use its resources in advocacy ads threaten corporate domination of political debate?

- Does the fact that groups such as labor unions (the AFL–CIO spent $3 million on the health care debate) and the American Association for Retired Persons (AARP) also advertise guarantee a balanced debate on the public airwaves?

- Are advocacy ads effective at influencing opinion? Are they a good way to debate public policy issues? Do they contribute to informing the electorate?

- Even if you agree with Rehnquist's fears, what regulatory cures are there that would not be worse than the disease?

10

꙳

Business and the
Natural Environment

INTRODUCTION

Business interacts with the natural environment at many levels. Business is the primary social institution that extracts resources from the natural environment, processes them into form for human use, and disposes of the by-products back into the natural environment. According to some, business activities are the cause of, and therefore business is liable for, most environmental problems. Global warming, acid rain, water and air pollution, soil erosion, resource depletion, species extinction, and ecological destruction can all be attributed to the production, distribution, and disposal of commercial products.

But if business can be faulted for many environmental problems, business can also be cast in the role of problem solver. Clean, safe, and renewable energy sources, nonpolluting cars and trucks, mass transportation, eco-efficient design and technologies, recycling technologies, sustainable agriculture, forestry, and fisheries, all represent environmentally positive opportunities for business entrepreneurs. Business will always be the vehicle by which humans use natural resources. *That* we use natural resources in business is not the ethical issue; *what* we use and *how* we use it, is. Environmental issues create both barriers and opportunities to business. How should business in the 21st century address these barriers and opportunities?

BUSINESS, THE ENVIRONMENT, AND ECONOMICS

Many people believe that environmental problems are essentially economic problems. Environmentalists are, after all, concerned with the allocation of scarce resources, with risks and benefits, with the costs of clean-up, and with the production of a cleaner and healthier environment. These concepts—allocation of resources, risks and benefits, costs, production—are economic concepts and therefore, according to some observers, we should rely on economics for guidance. Not surprisingly, economists have addressed environmental issues in greater detail than have other social scientists. In this view, because environmental issues are economic issues and because what affects the economy also affects business, the business community has reason to be concerned with environmental issues.

Perhaps the most influential perspective on business's environmental responsibilities flows from the familiar free market approach to economics. Given the assumption that environmental problems are essentially economic ones, mainstream economic theory has much to say about environmental topics and much to recommend to business about its environmental responsibilities. The prescription that would follow from the free market perspective should be familiar by now. Just like the allocation and distribution of other goods that we have considered, such as employee health and safety and consumer safety, natural resources will be most efficiently handled by the workings of a free and competitive market.

This perspective is represented in our reading from William Baxter's classic book, *People or Penguins: The Case for Optimal Pollution* (Reading 10.1). Baxter argues that issues such as pollution, conservation, and preservation all involve the allocation of scarce resources. As such, we need to find ways to balance the competing views over the appropriate uses of these resources. This balance is exactly the equilibrium between competing preferences that is attained by an efficient market; hence, markets are the best means for attaining our environmental goals. Clean air and water, for example, are scarce resources that we must allocate. But just as it is possible not to have enough clean air or water, it is also possible to have too much. If the cost of cleaner air and water that we need for human health causes lost opportunities to do other things (for example, build a manufacturing plant that emits air pollutants), then we should find a lower level of cleanliness that allows us to do some of these other things. This "optimal level of pollution" is exactly what is achieved by efficient markets.

Two of the decision scenarios at the end of this chapter also raise issues of efficient allocation and distribution. The Pacific Lumber case asks whether a sustainable rate of timber harvest was the optimal use of those resources. Strong economic incentives suggest that it was not. The Mineral King Valley case also raises questions about the optimal use of wilderness areas. Given consumer willingness to pay more to visit expensive ski resorts than undeveloped wilderness areas, economics seems to suggest that the optimal use of such resources includes development.

Such views, of course, are consistent with the free market position on corporate social responsibility examined in Chapter One. Given these economic goals, the ethical responsibility of business is to seek profits within the law. This pursuit of profit will ensure that natural resources are allocated and distributed in the most efficient and optimal way. Thus, businesses have no particular environmental responsibility beyond their normal economic function of pursuing profit within the law.

There are a number of familiar challenges to this free market view. A variety of market failures, such as the externality of pollution, the lack of markets for such goods as endangered species and scenic vistas, the lack of tradable property rights for such things as oceans and the atmosphere, and the inability of future generations to represent their own interest in contemporary markets, raise insurmountable challenges for the pure free market view.

In response to such problems, some economists (often called "environmental economists") have developed models for reforming the market in ways that overcome these failures. Thus, some economists will seek to establish a "price" for such goods as endangered species, or have the interests of future generations "discounted" to capture their present value, or recommend creation of "pollution permits" that can be bought and sold on the open market. These reforms would mimic the workings of an efficient market and help us determine what the market would accomplish were it not for these market failures.

But even if an ideally efficient market for the natural environment were attainable (and few believe that this is possible), other ethical issues remain. Efficient markets, after all, aim for the utilitarian goal of optimizing overall beneficial consequences. In our second reading, Mark Sagoff argues that environmental issues revolve around matters of value, conviction, and belief, not matters of mere subjective preferences. As such, environmental issues properly belong in the domain of politics and public policy, not in the domain of economics.

The well-known Mineral King Valley case used as a decision scenario in this chapter provides an opportunity for evaluating these competing views. This case involved plans by the Disney Corporation to purchase public land and develop it into a ski resort. Defenders of this development argued that Disney's ability to earn greater profit from this land than could, say, the Sierra Club, proves that the public values ski resorts much more highly than it does undeveloped wilderness. Critics like Sagoff would argue that it is a mistake to try to place a price on undeveloped wilderness and perform a cost-benefit analysis to decide on the optimal use of such resources. The aesthetic and spiritual value of wilderness cannot be reduced to the subjective preferences of what people are willing to pay. Decades later, Disney was involved in a plan to develop a historical area near Manassas Civil War battlefield into a Civil War theme park. Critics would again argue that the symbolic and historical value of a Civil War battlefield would be lost among the clutter of a commercial development that would result from market decisions.

But what are the implications of this for business? Is it the responsibility of a business manager or owner to serve environmental goals if this means foregoing profit? In our third reading, Norman Bowie argues that business has no particular environmental responsibility. Bowie disagrees with the strict free market approach in that he defends strong moral limits on the pursuit of profit. Beyond the pursuit of profit within the law, Bowie argues that business has a duty to respect a wide array of human rights (see, for example, the essay by Bowie in Chapter Five). However, in Bowie's view, environmental considerations do not create any special ethical duties for business. The responsibility for deciding which and how natural resources can be used rests with all of us: as citizens to convince our government to enact environmental legislation, and as consumers to demand environmentally responsible products and services. Thus, the law and the market establish the limits of business's environmental responsibility. If the law does not require it, and if consumers are not demanding it, we cannot ask business to do it.

SUSTAINABLE DEVELOPMENT
AND BUSINESS

Economic growth is assumed to be of value by both the neoclassical economic model and, implicitly, by Bowie's modified version. Satisfying consumer demand is, given the minimal ethical constraints of law and moral rights, assumed to be an ethically good thing. However, a brief consideration of worldwide ecological, economic, ethical, and population realities suggests difficulties for this growth-based economic and business model.

Large percentages of the world's population lack adequate food, health care, shelter, clean water, and education. Meeting the simple needs of these hundreds of millions of people is an enormous economic challenge and ethical duty. Population growth, especially within the very poorest regions of the world, guarantees that these problems will only increase in the future. The ultimate source for all this needed economic activity, of course, is the productive capacity of the earth itself. Yet, we must recognize that the earth's ecosystem already is under great stress. Assuming that economic growth alone will meet these immense ethical and economic challenges without causing ecological collapse seems imprudent.

In response to such considerations, an alternative economic model emphasizes economic *development* rather than *growth*. Economic activity ought to improve the quality of human life, rather than simply trying to increase the size and amount of the economy. The concept of sustainable development cites "three pillars of sustainability." World economic activity must be *economically* sufficient for meeting the needs of a growing worldwide population, it must be *ethically* responsible in meeting those needs, and it must do so in an *ecologically* responsible manner.

In our fourth reading, Joseph DesJardins argues that both the free market and Bowie positions assume too passive a role for business managers and owners. Both assume that business can fulfill its ethical responsibility without initiating any action at all: business should *respond* to the market, *obey* the law, *violate no rights*. Environmental responsibilities that require that business actually *do* something is asking too much of business. "Ought implies can," argues Bowie, and if business cannot serve environmental ends without losing money, it ought not be required to do so. But, these views present us with a false dichotomy: Either pursue profits by satisfying consumer demand or serve environmentally beneficial goals. DesJardins argues that ethical and ecological factors demonstrate the inadequacy of the old business model of neoclassical economics. Instead, we need to create new business models inspired by sustainable economics, business models that encourage both profitability and environmental responsibility.

There are, of course, many ways to pursue profit and respond to the demands of the marketplace. Entrepreneurial businesses can find ways to succeed in the marketplace by creating products and services which support or, minimally, do not harm, the ecosystem. Our final two readings provide both frameworks for, and numerous examples of, environmentally sustainable business. Amory Lovins, Hunter Lovins, and Paul Hawken provide a framework for "natural capitalism," a model for operating productive, profitable, and ecologically stable business. William McDonough and Michael Braungart argue for a transformation of industry, the "next industrial revolution," based on nature-inspired design and production. Both readings emphasize a business model that mimics biological processes, that is hyperefficient in the use of energy and resources, provides services rather than products, and treats natural resources as capital rather than as income.

CASE STUDY Interface Corporation: Sustainable Business

The old cliché suggests that business ethics is, like jumbo shrimp and working vacations, an oxymoron. To that list, one might wish to add "industrial ecology." Yet if Interface Corporation, a Georgia-based carpeting manufacturer, has its way, industrial ecology will become the standard for 21st century manufacturing and the model for sustainable business.

The concept of industrial ecology requires that manufacturing processes be designed to mimic biological processes. Since 1994, Interface has worked to transform its business operations to become a leader in industrial ecology. In the words of their Mission Statement:

> Interface will become the first name in commercial and institutional interiors worldwide through its commitment to people, process, product, place and profits. We will strive to create an organization wherein all people are accorded unconditional respect and dignity; one that

allows each person to continuously learn and develop. We will focus on product (which includes service) through constant emphasis on process quality and engineering, which we will combine with careful attention to our customers' needs so as always to deliver superior value to our customers, thereby maximizing all stakeholders' satisfaction. We will honor the places where we do business by endeavoring to become the first name in industrial ecology, a corporation that cherishes nature and restores the environment. Interface will lead by example and validate by results, including profits, leaving the world a better place than when we began, and we will be restorative through the power of our influence in the world.

But it was not always this way.

Interface was founded in 1973 when Ray Anderson, current chairman of the board, recognized a growing market for flexible floor coverings for office environments. Interface soon began manufacturing and distributing modular carpet tiles, essentially carpeting that can easily be installed and replaced in modular sections.

Over the years, the company has grown to its current status as the world's leading producer of soft-surfaced modular floor coverings. Over time, Interface has grown by over 50 acquisitions. Today, Interface is a global company with sales offices in over 100 countries, with 26 factories, more than 7,000 employees, and annual sales in excess of $1.3 billion.

For more than two decades, Interface could rightly be described as a typical and responsible business. They were a good corporate citizen, treated their employees, customers, and suppliers well, and produced a quality product. Like most businesses, Interface believed that it was fulfilling its social responsibility simply by responding to consumer demand as reflected in the market and by obeying the law. It was, in short, doing all that society asked of it.

Carpet manufacturing, however, is not normally thought of as an environmentally commendable industry. Most carpeting is derived from petroleum, a nonrenewable resource. Petroleum-based products are synthesized with fiberglass and PVC, two known carcinogens, to create the fibers used to manufacture carpeting. The carpeting is dyed, and the waste produced from this process can contain various toxins and heavy metals. Carpet manufacturing factories are heavy industrial producers of CO_2 emissions. Used carpeting, especially nylon-based products, is not recycled and therefore usually ends up in landfills. One estimate holds that carpeting products add nearly 10 million pounds to American landfills each day.[1] Interface estimates that over 5 billion pounds of its own carpeting now exist in landfills. This carpet waste is toxic and non-biodegradable. Thus, for 25 years Interface was living up to normal standards of corporate social responsibility in a way that was environmentally dreadful.

The company's transformation from one that merely sold floor coverings while complying with social expectations to a leader in environmental responsibility was dramatic. Anderson states that "For the first twenty-one years of Interface's existence, I never gave one thought to what we took from or did to the Earth, except to be sure we obeyed all laws and regulations. Frankly, I didn't have a vision, except 'comply, comply, comply.' I had heard statesmen advocate 'sustainable development,' but I had no idea what it meant." The traditional standard of corporate social responsibility, a standard that asks business only to respond to consumer demand and obey the law, no longer seemed sufficient. Reflecting on this friction between ecological responsibility and compliance with the demands of the law and the marketplace, Anderson now believes that "In the future, people like me will go to jail."[2]

By all accounts, Interface's dramatic transformation has been spearheaded by the personal commitment of Ray Anderson. As Anderson recounts the story, his own conversion began with a book on sustainable business. In 1994, he was invited to deliver a keynote address at a conference of Interface managers. The conference was called to review Interface's environmental activities and Anderson realized that he had little to offer on this topic. In preparation for the address, Anderson read Paul Hawken's *Ecology of Commerce,* a book that provided a vision and rationale for sustainable business practices.[3] The resulting speech challenged Interface's employees to turn the company into a model of sustainable business.

Frameworks for Sustainable Business

"Sustainability" and "sustainable development" have perhaps become overused phrases in recent years. To some, sustainability is little more than environmental window dressing to rationalize the status quo. From this perspective, a sustainable business simply is one that can continue business as usual for the long-term. But this superficial understanding is not what Hawken, or Anderson, had in mind. Their concept of sustainable business can be traced to a U.N. report authored by then-Prime Minister Gro Bruntland of Norway in which sustainability was defined as the ability "to meet the needs of the present without compromising the ability of future generations to meet their own needs."

True sustainability requires radical changes in the status quo, and a recognition that compliance is not enough. To meet the needs (and not simply the desires) of the present without jeopardizing the morally equal needs of future generations requires action along three dimensions: economic, ecological, and social. These "three pillars of sustainability" require that business activities be economically, ecologically, and socially sustainable. As reflected in the Mission Statement quoted previously, Interface has committed itself to becoming sustainable on all three grounds.

The three general sustainability criteria can be applied more specifically to business. Some refer to similar criteria as the "triple bottom line" of sustainable business.[4] This "triple bottom line" holds that business must be judged by its performance on three bottom lines: financial, ecological, and ethical. In fact, this was the type of strategy being pursued by Paul Hawken in the book that so inspired Anderson. To be sustainable, business ought to be arranged in such a way that it adequately meets the economic expectations of society (for example, jobs, income, goods, and services) in an efficient and sustainable manner. But in meeting these responsibilities, business must also to be arranged in a way that supports, rather than degrades, the ability of the biosphere to sustain life, especially but not exclusively human life, over the long term. Business also ought to be arranged in ways that address minimum demands of social justice.

Some models exist for what such sustainable economic and business institutions might look like. *Natural Capitalism,* a more-recent book co-authored by Hawken, provides both a framework for, and numerous examples of, sustainable business practice.[5] Interface is prominently featured in this book as a model for sustainable business. *Natural Capitalism* offers four strategies for creating sustainable business: radical resource productivity (or eco-efficiency); biomimicry; service and flow economy; and investment in natural capital. These strategies can be thought of as reasonable means for attaining the three pillars/triple bottom line sustainability goals. *Natural Capitalism* argues that business can and must be made more efficient in use of natural resources and energy, suggesting that even a ten-fold increase in resource and energy efficiency is already attainable with present technologies. Biomimicry involves redesigning industrial systems to mimic biological processes, essentially enabling the constant reuse of materials and the elimination of waste. The service and flow economy would have business create value by providing services rather than by selling products. Instead of purchasing light bulbs, carpeting, copying machines, and air conditioners, the service economy has business renting or leasing illumination, floor-covering, copying, or climate control services. By investing in natural capital, business comes to recognize and value the significant benefits provided by living systems and natural resources. The ultimate capital on which all business relies is natural capital, not financial capital. Just as it would be a mistake to spend one's financial capital without reinvestment, so it is a mistake to spend one's natural capital without reinvesting.

Sustainable Practice at Interface

This sustainability model permeates all aspects of Interface's business. Their corporate vision statement commits itself:

> To be the first company that, by its deeds, shows the entire industrial world what sustainability is in all its dimensions: People, process, product, place and profits—by 2020—and in doing so we

will become restorative through the power of influence.

In its annual reports and on the company's Web site, Interface explains why this goal is so important:

> Here's the problem in a nutshell. Industrialism developed in a different world from the one we live in today: fewer people, less material well-being, plentiful natural resources. What emerged was a highly productive, take-make-waste system that assumed infinite resources and infinite sinks for industrial wastes. Industry moves, mines, extracts, shovels, burns, wastes, pumps and disposes of four million pounds of material in order to provide one average, middle-class American family their needs for a year. Today, the rate of material throughput is endangering our prosperity, not enhancing it. At Interface, we recognize that we are part of the problem. We are analyzing all of our material flows to begin to address the task at hand.
>
> What's the solution? We're not sure, but we have some ideas. We believe that there's a cure for resource waste that is profitable, creative and practical. We must create a company that addresses the needs of society and the environment by developing a system of industrial production that decreases our costs and dramatically reduces the burdens placed upon living systems. This also makes precious resources available for the billions of people who need more. What we call the next industrial revolution is a momentous shift in how we see the world, how we operate within it, what systems will prevail and which will not. At Interface, we are completely reimagining and redesigning everything we do, including the way we define our business. Our vision is to lead the way to the next industrial revolution by becoming the first sustainable corporation, and eventually a restorative enterprise. It's an extraordinarily ambitious endeavor; a mountain to climb that is higher than Everest.

To attain this goal, Interface has articulated seven steps along the way. Again from the company's own literature, these steps are:

1. **Eliminate Waste**—The first step to sustainability, QUEST is Interface's campaign to eliminate the concept of waste, not just incrementally reduce it.
2. **Benign Emissions**—We're focusing on the elimination of molecular waste emitted with negative or toxic impact into our natural systems.

3. **Renewable Energy**—We're reducing the energy used by our processes while replacing non-renewable sources with sustainable ones.
4. **Closing the Loop**—Our aim is to redesign our processes and products to create cyclical material flows.
5. **Resource Efficient Transportation**—We're exploring methods to reduce the transportation of molecules (products and people) in favor of moving information. This includes plant location, logistics, information technology, video-conferencing, e-mail, and telecommuting.
6. **Sensitivity Hookup**—The goal here is to create a community within and around Interface that understands the functioning of natural systems and our impact on them.
7. **Redesign Commerce**—We're redefining commerce to focus on the delivery of service and value instead of the delivery of material. We're also engaging external organizations to create policies and market incentives that encourage sustainable practices.

The relationships among these steps, and the synergies created by them, can be seen in what is perhaps the most significant transformation at Interface. Interface is making a transition from a company that manufactures and sells carpeting to a company that provides floor-covering services. This is very much the shift to the service and flow economy described in *Natural Capitalism.*

On a traditional business model, carpet is sold to consumers who, once they become dissatisfied with the color or style or once the carpeting becomes worn, are responsible for disposal of the carpet, typically sending the old carpeting to landfills. There is little incentive here for the manufacturer to produce long-lasting or easily recyclable carpeting. The old-time manufacturing strategy of planned obsolescence seems the rational corporate strategy in this situation. But once Interface shifted to leasing floor-covering services, incentives were created to produce long-lasting, easily replaceable and recyclable carpets. By selling carpeting services rather than the carpeting itself, Interface thereby accepts responsibility for the entire lifecycle of the product they market. Because they retain ownership and are responsible for maintenance, Interface strives to produce carpeting that can be easily replaced in sections rather than in its entirety, that is more durable, and that can eventually be remanufactured. Redesigning their carpets and shifting to a service lease has also improved production efficiencies and reduced material and energy costs signifi-

cantly. Consumers benefit by getting what they truly desire at lower costs and fewer burdens.

Thus, the shift to becoming a service provider addresses several of the seven goals outlined. By providing carpeting in modules and by being responsible for replacing worn sections, Interface has made great strides to eliminate waste. Strong incentives exist to create a fully closed loop process; carpeting that will be taken back is designed to be recycled and remanufactured. What was formerly waste now becomes resource, and any material that is destined for the landfill represents lost potential revenues. Because Interface's own employees will be recycling and remanufacturing its waste products, there is also a strong incentive to produce nontoxic and benign products. This shift truly does pioneer a new business model of delivering service and value rather than simply delivering the material of a planned obsolescence product model. Finally, a service lease creates an ongoing and stable relationship with customers, something that should benefit both the business and its customers.

In the decade that Interface has been moving towards a sustainable model, its economic outlook has been mixed. In the first four years, Interface's revenues doubled, its employment almost doubled, and its profits increased almost three-fold. The recession of the early 2000s resulted in a noticeable downturn in Interface's business. Nevertheless, the company is committed to a sustainable future. Ray Anderson's vision continues to inspire the company:

> We look forward to the day when our factories have no smokestacks and no effluents. If successful, we'll spend the rest of our days harvesting yesteryear's carpets, recycling old petro-chemicals into new materials, and converting sunlight into energy. There will be zero scrap going into landfills and zero emissions into the ecosystem. Literally, it is a company that will grow by cleaning up the world, not by polluting or degrading it.[6]

- Air conditioning, lighting, and computing are other goods besides carpeting that have been suggested as candidates for a service rather than product model of business. Can you think of others? What barriers exist to the transition to a service economy?
- The Interface Mission Statement speaks of a responsibility to stakeholders. Has Interface fulfilled its responsibility to its stockholders? How might Interface be judged by the Friedman prescription that business managers ought to make as much money as possible for stockholders?

- Can you think of any government policies that would help, or hinder, a business's transition towards sustainability?
- Has Interface gone above and beyond its social responsibility or has it acted in a way that all business should follow?
- Shouldn't normal market incentives already encourage a business to work toward greater efficiencies and less wastes? What might some barriers be to this?
- Do you agree with Anderson that in the future, executives like him will go to jail?

Notes

1. See P. Warshall, "The Tensile and the Tantric," *Whole Earth* 90: 4–7, Summer 1997, as quoted in *Natural Capitalism* by Paul Hawken, Amory Lovins, and Hunter Lovins (Boston: Little Brown, 1999), p. 77.

2. "In the Future, People Like Me Will Go to Jail," in *Fortune*, May 24, 1999, pp. 190–200. Other quotes from the Interface Mission Statement are from the company website, www.interfaceinc.com. Reprinted with permission. Further information for this case was taken from *Mid-Course Correction: Toward a Sustainable Enterprise: the Interface Model* by Ray Anderson (White River Junction, VT.: Chelsea Green Publishers, 1999), a public lecture and interview with Anderson at St. John's University, and *Natural Capitalism.*

3. *Ecology of Commerce*, by Paul Hawken (New York: Harper Business Books, 1994).

4. The "triple bottom line" was most notably introduced in John Elkington, *Cannibals with Forks: The Triple Bottom Line of 21st Century Business* (Gabriola Island, British Columbia: New Society Publishers, 1998).

5. *Natural Capitalism.*

6. *Interface Sustainability Report*, 1997, as quoted in *Natural Capitalism*, p. 168–169.

READING 10.1 PEOPLE OR PENGUINS: THE CASE FOR OPTIMAL POLLUTION

William F. Baxter

I start with the modest proposition that, in dealing with pollution, or indeed with any problem, it is helpful to know what one is attempting to accomplish. Agreement on how and whether to pursue a particular objective, such as pollution control, is not possible unless some more general objective has been identified and stated with reasonable precision. We talk loosely of having clean air and clean water, of preserving our wilderness areas, and so forth. But none of these is a sufficiently general objective: each is more accurately viewed as a means rather than as an end.

With regard to clean air, for example, one may ask, "how clean?" and "what does clean mean?" It is even reasonable to ask, "why clean air?" Each of these questions is an implicit demand that a more general community goal be stated—a goal sufficiently general in its scope and enjoying sufficiently general assent among the community of actors that such "why" questions no longer seem admissible with respect to that goal.

If, for example, one states as a goal the proposition that "every person should be free to do whatever he wishes in contexts where his actions do not interfere with the interests of other human beings," the speaker is unlikely to be met with a response of "why." The goal may be criticized as uncertain in its implications or difficult to implement, but it is so basic a tenet of our civilization—it reflects a cultural value so broadly shared, at least in the abstract—that the question "why" is seen as impertinent or imponderable or both.

I do not mean to suggest that everyone would agree with the "spheres of freedom" objective just stated. Still less do I mean to suggest that a society could subscribe to four or five such general objectives that would be adequate in their coverage to serve as testing criteria by which all other disagreements might be measured. One difficulty in the attempt to construct such a list is that each new goal added will conflict, in certain applications, with each prior goal listed; and thus each goal serves as a limited qualification on prior goals.

Without any expectation of obtaining unanimous consent to them, let me set forth four goals that I generally use as ultimate testing criteria in attempting to frame solutions to problems of human organization. My position regarding pollution stems from these four criteria. If the criteria appeal to you and any part of what appears hereafter does not, our disagreement will have a helpful focus: which of us is correct, analytically, in supposing that his position on pollution would better serve these general goals. If the criteria do not seem acceptable to you, then it is to be expected that our more particular judgments will differ, and the task will then be yours to identify the basic set of criteria upon which your particular judgments rest.

My criteria are as follows:

1. The spheres of freedom criterion stated above.

2. Waste is a bad thing. The dominant feature of human existence is scarcity—our available resources, our aggregate labors, and our skill in employing both have always been, and will continue for some time to be, inadequate to yield to every man all the tangible and intangible satisfactions he would like to have. Hence, none of those resources, or labors, or skills, should be wasted—that is, employed so as to yield less than they might yield in human satisfactions.

3. Every human being should be regarded as an end rather than as a means to be used for the betterment of another. Each should be afforded dignity and regarded as having an absolute claim to an evenhanded application of such rules as the community may adopt for its governance.

4. Both the incentive and the opportunity to improve his share of satisfactions should be preserved to every individual. Preservation of incentive is dictated by the "no-waste" criterion and enjoins against the continuous, totally egalitarian redistribution of satisfactions, or wealth; but subject to that constraint, everyone should receive, by continuous redistribution if necessary, some minimal share of aggregate wealth so as to avoid a level of privation from which the opportunity to improve his situation becomes illusory.

The relationship of these highly general goals to the more specific environmental issues at hand may not be readily apparent, and I am not yet ready to demonstrate their pervasive implications. But let me give one indication of their implications. Recently scientists have informed us that use of DDT in food production is causing damage to the penguin population. For the present purposes let us accept that assertion as an indisputable scientific fact. The scientific fact is often asserted as if the correct implication—that we must stop agricultural use of DDT—followed from the mere statement of the fact of penguin damage. But plainly it does not follow if my criteria are employed.

My criteria are oriented to people, not penguins. Damage to penguins, or sugar pines, or geological marvels is, without more, simply irrelevant. One must go further, by my criteria, and say: Penguins are important because people enjoy seeing them walk about rocks; and furthermore, the well-being of people would be less impaired by halting use of DDT than by giving up penguins. In short, my observations about environmental problems will be people-oriented, as are my criteria. I have no interest in preserving penguins for their own sake.

It may be said by way of objection to this position, that it is very selfish of people to act as if each person represented one unit of importance and nothing else was of any importance. It is undeniably selfish. Nevertheless I think it is the only tenable starting place for analysis for several reasons. First, no other position corresponds to the way most people really think and act—i.e., corresponds to reality.

Second, this attitude does not portend any massive destruction of nonhuman flora and fauna, for people depend on them in many obvious ways, and they will be preserved because and to the degree that humans do depend on them.

Third, what is good for humans is, in many respects, good for penguins and pine trees—clean air for example. So that humans are, in these respects, surrogates for plant and animal life.

Fourth, I do not know how we could administer any other system. Our decisions are either private or collective. Insofar as Mr. Jones is free to act privately, he may give such preferences as he wishes to other forms of life: he may feed birds in winter and do with less himself, and he may even decline to resist an advancing polar bear on the ground that the bear's appetite is more important than those portions of himself that the bear may choose to eat. In short my basic premise does not rule out private altruism to competing life-forms. It does rule out, however, Mr. Jones' inclination to feed Mr. Smith to the bear, however hungry the bear, however despicable Mr. Smith.

Insofar as we act collectively on the other hand, only humans can be afforded an opportunity to participate in the collective decisions. Penguins cannot vote now and are unlikely subjects for the franchise— pine trees more unlikely still. Again each individual is free to cast his vote so as to benefit sugar pines if that is his inclination. But many of the more extreme assertions that one hears from some conservationists amount to tacit assertions that they are specially appointed representatives of sugar pines, and hence that their preferences should be weighted more heavily than the preferences of other humans who do not enjoy equal rapport with "nature." The simplistic assertion that agricultural use of DDT must stop at once because it is harmful to penguins is of that type.

Fifth, if polar bears or pine trees or penguins, like men, are to be regarded as ends rather than means, if they are to count in our calculus of social organization, someone must tell me how much each one counts, and someone must tell me how these life-forms are to be permitted to express their preferences, for I do not know either answer. If the answer is that certain people are to hold their proxies, then I want to know how those proxy-holders are to be selected: self-appointment does not seem workable to me.

Sixth, and by way of summary of all the foregoing, let me point out that the set of environmental issues under discussion—although they raise very complex technical questions of how to achieve any objective—ultimately raise a normative question: what *ought* we to do. Questions of *ought* are unique to the human mind and world—they are meaningless as applied to a nonhuman situation.

I reject the proposition that we *ought* to respect the "balance of nature" or to "preserve the environment" unless the reason for doing so, express or implied, is the benefit of man.

I reject the idea that there is a "right" or "morally correct" state of nature to which we should return. The word "nature" has no normative connotation. Was it "right" or "wrong" for the earth's crust to heave in contortion and create mountains and seas? Was it "right" for the first amphibian to crawl up out of the primordial ooze? Was it "wrong" for plants to reproduce themselves and alter the atmospheric composition in favor of oxygen? For animals to alter the atmosphere in favor of carbon dioxide both by breathing oxygen and eating plants? No answers can be given to these questions because they are meaningless questions.

All this may seem obvious to the point of being tedious, but much of the present controversy over environment and pollution rests on tacit normative assumptions about just such nonnormative phenomena: that it is "wrong" to impair penguins with DDT, but not to slaughter cattle for prime rib roasts. That it is wrong to kill stands of sugar pines with industrial fumes, but not to cut sugar pines and build housing for the poor. Every man is entitled to his own preferred definition of Walden Pond, but there is no definition that has any moral superiority over another, except by reference to the selfish needs of the human race.

From the fact that there is no normative definition of the natural state, it follows that there is no normative definition of clean air or pure water—hence no definition of polluted air—or of pollution—except by reference to the needs of man. The "right" composition of the atmosphere is one which has some dust in it and some lead in it and some hydrogen sulfide in it—just those amounts that attend a sensibly organized society thoughtfully and knowledgeably pursuing the greatest possible satisfaction for its human members.

The first and most fundamental step toward solution of our environmental problems is a clear recognition that our objective is not pure air or water but rather some optimal state of pollution. That step immediately suggests the question: How do we define and attain the level of pollution that will yield the maximum possible amount of human satisfaction?

Low levels of pollution contribute to human satisfaction but so do food and shelter and education and music. To attain ever lower levels of pollution, we must pay the cost of having less of these other things. I contrast that view of the cost of pollution control with the more popular statement that pollution control will "cost" very large numbers of dollars. The popular statement is true in some senses, false in others; sorting out the true and false senses is of some importance. The first step in that sorting process is to achieve a clear understanding of the difference between dollars and resources. Resources are the wealth of our nation; dollars are merely claim checks upon those resources. Resources are of vital importance; dollars are comparatively trivial.

Four categories of resources are sufficient for our purposes: At any given time a nation, or a planet if you prefer, has a stock of labor, of technological skill, of capital goods, and of natural resources (such as mineral deposits, timber, water, land, etc.). These resources can be used in various combinations to yield goods and services of all kinds—in some limited quantity. The quantity will be larger if they are combined efficiently, smaller if combined inefficiently. But in either event the resource stock is limited, the goods and services that they can be made to yield are limited; even the most efficient use of them will yield less than our population, in the aggregate, would like to have.

If one considers building a new dam, it is appropriate to say that it will be costly in the sense that it will require x hours of labor, y tons of steel and concrete, and z amount of capital goods. If these resources are devoted to the dam, then they cannot be used to build hospitals, fishing rods, schools, or electric can openers. That is the meaningful sense in which the dam is costly.

Quite apart from the very important question of how wisely we can combine our resources to produce goods and services, is the very different question of how they get distributed—who gets how many goods? Dollars constitute the claim checks which are distributed among people and which control their share of national output. Dollars are nearly valueless pieces of paper except to the extent that they do represent claim checks to some fraction of the output of goods and services. Viewed as claim checks, all the dollars outstanding during any period of time are worth, in the aggregate, the goods and services that are available to be claimed with them during that period—neither more nor less.

It is far easier to increase the supply of dollars than to increase the production of goods and services— printing dollars is easy. But printing more dollars doesn't help because each dollar then simply becomes a claim to fewer goods, i.e., becomes worth less.

The point is this: many people fall into error upon hearing the statement that the decision to build a dam, or to clean up a river, will cost $X million. It is regrettably easy to say: "It's only money. This is a wealthy country, and we have lots of money." But you cannot build a dam or clean a river with $X million—unless you also have a match, you can't even make a fire. One builds a dam or cleans a river by diverting labor and steel and trucks and factories from making one kind of goods to making another. The cost in dollars is merely a shorthand way of describing the extent of the diversion necessary. If we build a dam for $X million, then we must recognize that we will have $X million less housing and food and medical care and electric can openers as a result.

Similarly, the costs of controlling pollution are best expressed in terms of the other goods we will have to give up to do the job. This is not to say the job should not be done. Badly as we need more housing, more medical care, and more can openers, and more symphony orchestras, we could do with somewhat less of them, in my judgment at least, in exchange for somewhat cleaner air and rivers. But that is the nature of the trade-off, and analysis of the problem is advanced if that unpleasant reality is kept in mind. Once the trade-off relationship is clearly perceived, it is possible to state in a very general way what the optimal level of pollution is. I would state it as follows:

People enjoy watching penguins. They enjoy relatively clean air and smog-free vistas. Their health is improved by relatively clean water and air. Each of these benefits is a type of good or service. As a society we would be well advised to give up one washing machine if the resources that would have gone into that washing machine can yield greater human satisfaction when diverted into pollution control. We should give up one hospital if the resources thereby freed would yield more human satisfaction when devoted to elimination of noise in our cities. And so on, trade-off by trade-off, we should divert our productive capacities from the production of existing goods and services to the production of a cleaner, quieter, more pastoral nation up to—and no further than—the point at which we value more highly the next washing machine or hospital that we would have to do without than we value the next unit of environmental improvement that the diverted resources would create.

Now this proposition seems to me unassailable but so general and abstract as to be unhelpful—at least unadministerable in the form stated. It assumes we can measure in some way the incremental units of human satisfaction yielded by very different types of goods. The proposition must remain a pious abstraction until I can explain how this measurement process can occur. In subsequent chapters I will attempt to show that we can do this—in some contexts with great precision and in other contexts only by rough approximation. But I insist that the proposition stated describes the result for which we should be striving—and again, that it is always useful to know what your target is even if your weapons are too crude to score a bull's eye.

READING 10.2 WHY POLITICAL QUESTIONS ARE NOT ALL ECONOMIC
Mark Sagoff

POLITICAL AND ECONOMIC DECISION MAKING

This essay concerns the economic decisions we make about the environment. It also concerns our political decisions about the environment. Some people have suggested that ideally these should be the same, that all environmental problems are problems in distribution. According to this view, there is an environmental problem only when some resource is not allocated in equitable and efficient ways.

This approach to environmental policy is pitched entirely at the level of the consumer. It is his or her values that count, and the measure of these values is the individual's willingness to pay. The problem of justice or fairness in society becomes, then, the problem of distributing goods and services so that more people get more of what they want to buy: a condo on the beach, a snowmobile for the mountains, a tank full of gas, a day of labor. The only values we have, according to this view, are those that a market can price.

How much do you value open space, a stand of trees, an "unspoiled" landscape? Fifty dollars? A hundred? A thousand? This is one way to measure value. You could compare the amount consumers would pay for a townhouse or coal or a landfill to the amount they would pay to preserve an area in its "natural" state. If users would pay more for the land with the house, the coal mine, or the landfill, than without—less construction and other costs of development—then the efficient thing to do is to improve the land and thus increase its value. That is why we have so many tract developments, pizza stands, and gas stations. How much did you spend last year to preserve open space? How much for pizza and gas? "In principle, the ultimate measure of environmental quality," as one basic text assures us, "is the value people place on these . . . services or their *willingness to pay.*"

Willingness to pay: what is wrong with that? The rub is this: not all of us think of ourselves simply as *consumers.* Many of us regard ourselves as *citizens* as well. We act as consumers to get what we want *for ourselves.* We act as citizens to achieve what we think is right or best *for the community.* The question arises, then, whether what we want for ourselves individually as consumers is consistent with the goals we would set for ourselves collectively as citizens. Would I vote for the sort of things I shop for? Are my preferences as a consumer consistent with my judgments as a citizen?

They are not. I am schizophrenic. Last year, I fixed a couple of tickets and was happy to do so since I saved $50. Yet, at election time, I helped to vote the corrupt judge out of office. I speed on the highway; yet I want the police to enforce laws against speeding. I used to buy mixers in returnable bottles—but who can bother to return them? I buy only disposables now, but to soothe my conscience, I urge my state senator to outlaw one-way containers. I love my car; I hate the bus. Yet I vote for candidates who promise to tax gasoline to pay for

From *Arizona Law Review* 23 (1981): 1283–1298. Copyright © 1981 by the Arizona Board of Regents. Reprinted by permission.

All notes in this reading have been deleted.

public transportation. And of course I applaud the Endangered Species Act, although I have no earthly use for the Colorado squawfish or the Indiana bat. I support almost any political cause that I think will defeat my consumer interests. This is because I have contempt for—although I act upon—those interests. I have an "Ecology Now" sticker on a car that leaks oil everywhere it's parked.

The distinction between consumer and citizen preferences has long vexed the theory of public finance. Should the public economy serve the same goals as the household economy? May it serve, instead, goals emerging from our association as citizens? The question asks if we may collectively strive for and achieve only those items we individually compete for and consume. Should we aspire, instead, to public goals we may legislate as a nation?

The problem, insofar as it concerns public finance, is stated as follows by R.A. Musgrave, who reports a conversation he had with Gerhard Colm:

> He [Colm] holds that the individual voter dealing with political issues has a frame of reference quite distinct from that which underlies his allocation of income as a consumer. In the latter situation the voter acts as a private individual determined by self-interest and deals with his personal wants; in the former, he acts as a political being guided by his image of a good society. The two, Colm holds, are different things.

Are these two different things? Stephen Marglin suggests that they are. He writes:

> The preferences that govern one's unilateral market actions no longer govern his actions when the form of reference is shifted from the market to the political arena. The Economic Man and the Citizen are for all intents and purposes two different individuals. It is not a question, therefore, of rejecting individual . . . preference maps; it is, rather, that market and political preference maps are inconsistent.

Marglin observes that if this were true, social choices optimal under one set of preferences would not be optimal under another. What, then, is the meaning of "optimality"? He notices that if we take a person's true preferences to be those expressed in the market, we may neglect or reject the preferences that person reveals in advocating a political cause or position. "One might argue on welfare grounds,"

Marglin speculates, "for authoritarian rejection of individuals' politically revealed preferences in favor of their market revealed preferences!"

COST-BENEFIT ANALYSIS VS. REGULATION

On February 19, 1981, President Reagan published Executive Order 12,291 requiring all administrative agencies and departments to support every new major regulation with a cost-benefit analysis establishing that the benefits of the regulation to society outweigh its costs. The order directs the Office of Management and Budget (OMB) to review every such regulation on the basis of the adequacy of the cost-benefit analysis supporting it. This is a departure from tradition. Historically, regulations have been reviewed not by OMB but by the courts on the basis of the relation of the regulation to authorizing legislation, not to cost-benefit analysis.

A month earlier, in January 1981, the Supreme Court heard lawyers for the American Textile Manufacturers Institute argue against a proposed Occupational Safety and Health Administration (OSHA) regulation which would have severely restricted the acceptable levels of cotton dust in textile plants. The lawyers for industry argued that the benefits of the regulation would not equal the costs. The lawyers for the government contended that the law required the tough standard. OSHA, acting consistently with Executive Order 12,291, asked the Court not to decide the cotton dust case in order to give the agency time to complete the cost-benefit analysis required by the textile industry. The Court declined to accept OSHA's request and handed down its opinion in *American Textile Manufacturers v. Donovan* on June 17, 1981.

The Supreme Court, in a 5–3 decision, found that the actions of regulatory agencies which conform to the OSHA law need not be supported by cost-benefit analysis. In addition, the Court asserted that Congress, in writing a statute, rather than the agencies in applying it, has the primary responsibility for balancing benefits and costs. The Court said:

> When Congress passed the Occupational Health and Safety Act in 1970, it chose to place preeminent value on assuring employees a safe and healthful working environment, limited

only by the feasibility of achieving such an environment. We must measure the validity of the Secretary's actions against the requirements of that Act.

The opinion upheld the finding of the District of Columbia Court of Appeals that "Congress itself struck the balance between costs and benefits in the mandate to the agency."

The Appeals Court opinion in *American Textile Manufacturers v. Donovan* supports the principle that legislatures are not necessarily bound to a particular conception of regulatory policy. Agencies that apply the law therefore may not need to justify on cost-benefit grounds the standards they set. These standards may conflict with the goal of efficiency and still express our political will as a nation. That is, they may reflect not the personal choices of self-interested individuals, but the collective judgments we make on historical, cultural, aesthetic, moral, and ideological grounds.

The appeal of the Reagan Administration to cost-benefit analysis, however, may arise more from political than economic considerations. The intention, seen in the most favorable light, may not be to replace political or ideological goals with economic ones, but to make economic goals more apparent in regulation. This is not to say that Congress should function to reveal a collective willingness-to-pay just as markets reveal an individual willingness-to-pay. It is to suggest that Congress should do more to balance economic with ideological, aesthetic, and moral goals. To think that environmental or worker safety policy can be based exclusively on aspiration for a "natural" and "safe" world is as foolish as to hold that environmental law can be reduced to cost-benefit accounting. The more we move to one extreme, . . . the more likely we are to hear from the other.

SUBSTITUTING EFFICIENCY FOR SAFETY

The labor unions won an important political victory when Congress passed the Occupational Safety and Health Act of 1970. That Act, among other things, severely restricts worker exposure to toxic substances. It instructs the Secretary of Labor to set "the standard which most adequately assures, to the extent feasible . . . that no employee will suffer material impairment of health or functional capac-

ity even if such employee has regular exposure to the hazard . . . for the period of his working life."

Pursuant to this law, the Secretary of Labor in 1977 reduced from ten to one part per million (ppm) the permissible ambient exposure level for benzene, a carcinogen for which no safe threshold is known. The American Petroleum Institute thereupon challenged the new standard in court. It argued, with much evidence in its favor, that the benefits (to workers) of the one ppm standard did not equal the costs (to industry). The standard therefore did not appear to be a rational response to a market failure in that it did not strike an efficient balance between the interests of workers in safety and the interests of industry and consumers in keeping prices down.

The Secretary of Labor defended the tough safety standard on the ground that the law demanded it. An efficient standard might have required safety until it cost industry more to prevent a risk than it cost workers to accept it. Had Congress adopted this vision of public policy—one which can be found in many economics texts—it would have treated workers not as ends-in-themselves but as means for the production of overall utility. This, as the Secretary saw it, was what Congress refused to do.

The United States Court of Appeals for the Fifth Circuit agreed with the American Petroleum Institute and invalidated the one ppm benzene standard. On July 2, 1980, the Supreme Court affirmed the decision in *American Petroleum Institute v. Marshal* and remanded the benzene standard back to OSHA for revision. The narrowly based Supreme Court decision was divided over the role economic considerations should play in judicial review. Justice Marshall, joined in dissent by three other justices, argued that the Court had undone on the basis of its own theory of regulatory policy an act of Congress inconsistent with that theory. He concluded that the plurality decision of the Court "requires the American worker to return to the political arena to win a victory that he won before in 1970."

The decision of the Supreme Court is important not because of its consequences, which are likely to be minimal, but because of the fascinating questions it raises. Shall the courts uphold only those political decisions that can be defended on economic grounds? Shall we allow democracy only to the extent that it can be construed either as a rational response to a market failure or as an attempt to redistribute wealth? Should the courts say that a regulation is not "feasible" or "reasonable"—terms that occur in the OSHA law—unless it is supported by a cost-benefit analysis?

The problem is this: An efficiency criterion, as it is used to evaluate public policy, assumes that the goals of our society are contained in the preferences individuals reveal or would reveal in markets. Such an approach may appear attractive, even just, because it treats everyone as equal, at least theoretically, by according to each person's preferences the same respect and concern. To treat a person with respect, however, is also to listen and to respond intelligently to his or her views and opinions. This is not the same thing as to ask how much he or she is willing to pay for them. The cost-benefit analyst does not ask economists how much they are willing to pay for what they believe, that is, that the workplace and the environment should be made efficient. Why, then, does the analyst ask workers, environmentalists, and others how much they are willing to pay for what they believe is right? Are economists the only ones who can back their ideas with reasons while the rest of us can only pay a price? The cost-benefit approach treats people as of equal worth because it treats them as of no worth, but only as places or channels at which willingness to pay is found.

LIBERTY: ANCIENT AND MODERN

When efficiency is the criterion of public safety and health, one tends to conceive of social relations on the model of a market, ignoring competing visions of what we as a society should be like. Yet it is obvious that there are competing conceptions of what we should be as a society. There are some who believe on principle that worker safety and environmental quality ought to be protected only insofar as the benefits of protection balance the costs. On the other hand, people argue—also on principle—that neither worker safety nor environmental quality should be treated merely as a commodity to be traded at the margin for other commodities, but rather each should be valued for its own sake. The conflict between these two principles is logical or moral, to be resolved by argument or debate. The

question whether cost-benefit analysis should play a decisive role in policy making is not to be decided by cost-benefit analysis. A contradiction between principles—between contending visions of the good society—cannot be settled by asking how much partisans are willing to pay for their beliefs.

The role of the *legislator,* the political role, may be more important to the individual than the role of *consumer.* The person, in other words, is not to be treated merely as a bundle of preferences to be juggled in cost-benefit analyses. The individual is to be respected as an advocate of ideas which are to be judged according to the reasons for them. If health and environmental statutes reflect a vision of society as something other than a market by requiring protections beyond what are efficient, then this may express not legislative ineptitude but legislative responsiveness to public values. To deny this vision because it is economically inefficient is simply to replace it with another vision. It is to insist that the ideas of the citizen be sacrificed to the psychology of the consumer.

We hear on all sides that government is routinized, mechanical, entrenched, and bureaucratized; the jargon alone is enough to dissuade the most mettlesome meddler. Who can make a difference? It is plain that for many of us the idea of a national political community has an abstract and suppositious quality. We have only our private conceptions of the good, if no way exists to arrive at a public one. This is only to note the continuation, in our time, of the trend Benjamin Constant described in the essay *De la liberté des anciens comparée à celle des modernes.* Constant observes that the modern world, as opposed to the ancient, emphasizes civil over political liberties, the rights of privacy and property over those of community and participation." Lost in the multitude," Constant writes, "'the individual rarely perceives the influence that he exercises," and, therefore, must be content with "the peaceful enjoyment of private independence." The individual asks only to be protected by laws common to all in his pursuit of his own self-interest. The citizen has been replaced by the consumer; the tradition of Rousseau has been supplanted by that of Locke and Mill.

Nowhere are the rights of the moderns, particularly the rights of privacy and property, less helpful than in the area of the natural environment. Here the values we wish to protect—cultural, historical, aesthetic, and moral—are public values. They depend not so much upon what each person wants individually as upon what he or she thinks is right for the community. We refuse to regard worker health and safety as commodities; we regulate hazards as a matter of right. Likewise, we refuse to treat environmental resources simply as public goods in the economist's sense. Instead, we prevent significant deterioration of air quality not only as a matter of individual self-interest but also as a matter of collective self-respect. How shall we balance efficiency against moral, cultural, and aesthetic values in policy for the workplace and the environment? No better way has been devised to do this than by legislative debate ending in a vote. This is very different from a cost-benefit analysis terminating in a bottom line.

VALUES ARE NOT SUBJECTIVE

It is the characteristic of cost-benefit analysis that it treats all value judgments other than those made on its behalf as nothing but statements of preference, attitude, or emotion, insofar as they are value judgments. The cost-benefit analyst regards as true the judgment that we should maximize efficiency or wealth. The analyst believes that this view can be backed by reasons, but does not regard it as a preference or want for which he or she must be willing to pay. The cost-benefit analyst tends to treat all other normative views and recommendations as if they were nothing but subjective reports of mental states. The analyst supposes in all such cases that "this is right" and "this is what we ought to do" are equivalent to "I want this" and "this is what I prefer." Value judgments are beyond criticism if, indeed, they are nothing but expressions of personal preference; they are incorrigible since every person is in the best position to know what he or she wants. All valuation, according to this approach, happens *in foro interno;* debate *in foro publico* has no point. With this approach, the reasons that people give for their views do not count; what does count is how much they are willing to pay to satisfy their wants. Those who are willing to pay the most, for all intents and purposes, have the right view; theirs is the more informed opinion, the better aesthetic judgment, and the deeper moral insight.

The assumption that valuation is subjective, that judgments of good and evil are nothing but expressions of desire and aversion, is not unique to economic theory. There are psychotherapists—Carl

Rogers is an example—who likewise deny the objectivity or cognitivity of valuation. For Rogers, there is only one criterion of worth: it lies in "the subjective world of the individual. Only he knows it fully." The therapist shows his or her client that a "value system is not necessarily something imposed from without, but is something experienced." Therapy succeeds when the client "perceives himself in such a way that no self-experience can be discriminated as more or less worthy of positive self-regard than any other. . . ." The client then "tends to place the basis of standards within himself, recognizing that the 'goodness' or 'badness' of any experience or perceptual object is not something inherent in that object, but is a value placed in it by himself."

Rogers points out that "some clients make strenuous efforts to have the therapist exercise the valuing function, so as to provide them with guides for action." The therapist, however, "consistently keeps the locus of evaluation with the client." As long as the therapist refuses to "exercise the valuing function" and as long as he or she practices an "unconditional positive regard" for all the affective states of the client, then the therapist remains neutral among the client's values or "sensory and visceral experiences." The role of the therapist is legitimate, Rogers suggests, because of this value neutrality. The therapist accepts all felt preferences as valid and imposes none on the client.

Economists likewise argue that their role as policy makers is legitimate because they are neutral among competing values in the client society. The political economist, according to James Buchanan, "is or should be ethically neutral: the indicated results are influenced by his own value scale only insofar as this reflects his membership in a larger group." The economist might be most confident of the impartiality of his or her policy recommendations if he or she could derive them formally or mathematically from individual preferences. If theoretical difficulties make such a social welfare function impossible, however, the next best thing, to preserve neutrality, is to let markets function to transform individual preference orderings into a collective ordering of social states. The analyst is able then to base policy on preferences that exist in society and are not necessarily his own.

Economists have used this impartial approach to offer solutions to many significant social problems, for example, the controversy over abortion. An economist argues that "there is an optimal number of abortions, just as there is an optimal level of pollution, or purity. . . . Those who oppose abortion could eliminate it entirely, if their intensity of feeling were so strong as to lead to payments that were greater at the margin than the price anyone would pay to have an abortion." Likewise, economists, in order to determine whether the war in Vietnam was justified, have estimated the willingness to pay of those who demonstrated against it. Following the same line of reasoning, it should be possible to decide whether creationism should be taught in the public schools, whether black and white people should be segregated, whether the death penalty should be enforced, and whether the square root of six is three. All of these questions arguably depend upon how much people are willing to pay for their subjective preferences or wants. This is the beauty of cost-benefit analysis: no matter how relevant or irrelevant, wise or stupid, informed or uninformed, responsible or silly, defensible or indefensible wants may be, the analyst is able to derive a policy from them—a policy which is legitimate because, in theory, it treats all of these preferences as equally valid and good.

PREFERENCE OR PRINCIPLE?

In contrast, consider a Kantian conception of value. The individual, for Kant, is a judge of values, not a mere haver of wants, and the individual judges not for himself or herself merely, but as a member of a relevant community or group. The central idea in a Kantian approach to ethics is that some values are more reasonable than others and therefore have a better claim upon the assent of members of the community as such. The world of obligation, like the world of mathematics or the world of empirical fact, is public not private, and objective standards of argument and criticism apply. Kant recognized that values, like beliefs, are subjective states of mind which have an objective content as well. Therefore, both values and beliefs are either correct or mistaken. A value judgment is like an empirical or theoretical judgment in that it claims to be *true* not merely to be *felt*.

We have, then, two approaches to public policy before us. The first, the approach associated with normative versions of welfare economics, asserts that the only policy recommendation that can or need be defended on objective grounds is efficiency or wealth maximization. The Kantian approach, on the other hand, assumes that many policy recommendations may be justified or refuted on objective grounds. It would concede that the approach of welfare economics applies adequately to some questions, for example, those which ordinary consumer markets typically settle. How many yo-yos should be produced as compared to how many frisbees? Shall pens have black ink or blue? Matters such as these are so trivial it is plain that markets should handle them. It does not follow, however, that we should adopt a market or quasi-market approach to every public question.

A market or quasi-market approach to arithmetic, for example, is plainly inadequate. No matter how much people are willing to pay, three will never be the square root of six. Similarly, segregation is a national curse and the fact that we are willing to pay for it does not make it better, but only us worse. The case for abortion must stand on the merits; it cannot be priced at the margin. Our failures to make the right decisions in these matters are failures in arithmetic, failures in wisdom, failures in taste, failures in morality—but not market failures. There are no relevant markets which have failed.

What separates these questions from those for which markets are appropriate is that they involve matters of knowledge, wisdom, morality, and taste that admit of better or worse, right or wrong, true or false, and not mere economic optimality. Surely environmental questions—the protection of wilderness, habitats, water, land, and air as well as policy toward environmental safety and health—involve moral and aesthetic principles and not just economic ones. This is consistent, of course, with cost-effectiveness and with a sensible recognition of economic constraints.

The neutrality of the economist is legitimate if private preferences or subjective wants are the only values in question. A person should be left free to choose the color of his or her necktie or necklace, but we cannot justify a theory of public policy or private therapy on that basis. If the patient seeks moral advice or tries to find reasons to justify a choice, the therapist, according to Rogers' model, would remind him or her to trust his visceral and sensory experiences. The result of this is to deny the individual status as a cognitive being capable of responding intelligently to reasons; it reduces him or her to a bundle of affective states. What Rogers' therapist does to the patient, the cost-benefit analyst does to society as a whole. The analyst is neutral among our "values"—having first imposed a theory of what value is. This is a theory that is impartial among values and for that reason fails to treat the persons who have them with respect or concern. It does not treat them even as persons but only as locations at which wants may be found. The neutrality of economics is not a basis for its legitimacy. We recognize it as an indifference toward value—an indifference so deep, so studied, and so assured that at first one hesitates to call it by its right name....

READING 10.3 MORALITY, MONEY, AND MOTOR CARS
Norman Bowie

Environmentalists frequently argue that business has special obligations to protect the environment. Although I agree with the environmentalists on this point, I do not agree with them as to where the obligations lie. Business does not have an obligation to protect the environment over and above what is required by law; however, it does have a moral obligation to avoid intervening in the political arena in order to defeat or weaken environmental legislation. In developing this thesis, several points are in order. First, many businesses have violated important moral obligations, and the violation has had a severe negative impact on the environment. For example, toxic waste haulers have illegally dumped hazardous material, and the environment has been harmed as a result. One might argue that those toxic waste haulers who have illegally dumped have violated a special obligation to the environment. Isn't it more accurate to say that these toxic waste haulers have violated their obligation to obey the law and that in this case the law that has been broken is one pertaining to the environment? Businesses have an obligation to obey the law—environmental laws and all others. Since there are many well-publicized cases of business having broken environmental laws, it is easy to think that business has violated some special obligations to the environment. In fact, what business has done is to disobey the law. Environmentalists do not need a special obligation to the environment to protect the environment against illegal business activity; they need only insist that business obey the laws.

Business has broken other obligations beside the obligation to obey the law and has harmed the environment as a result. Consider the grounding of the Exxon oil tanker *Valdez* in Alaska. That grounding was allegedly caused by the fact that an inadequately trained crewman was piloting the tanker while the captain was below deck and had been drinking. What needs to be determined is whether Exxon's policies and procedures were sufficiently lax so that it could be said Exxon was morally at fault. It might be that Exxon is legally responsible for the accident under the doctrine of respondent superior, but Exxon is not thereby morally responsible. Suppose, however, that Exxon's policies were so lax that the company could be characterized as morally negligent. In such a case, the company would violate its moral obligation to use due care and avoid negligence. Although its negligence was disastrous to the environment, Exxon would have violated no special obligation to the environment. It would have been morally negligent.

A similar analysis could be given to the environmentalists' charges that Exxon's cleanup procedures were inadequate. If the charge is true, either Exxon was morally at fault or not. If the procedures had not been implemented properly by Exxon employees, then Exxon is legally culpable, but not morally culpable. On the other hand, if Exxon lied to government officials by saying that its policies were in accord with regulations and/or were ready for emergencies of this type, then Exxon violated its moral obligation to tell the truth. Exxon's immoral conduct would have harmed the environment, but

From *Business, Ethics, and the Environment: The Public Policy Debate,* eds. W. Michael Hoffman, Robert Frederick, and Edward Petry, Jr. (New York: Quorum Books, 1990), 89–97. © 1990 by The Center for Business Ethics at Bentley College. Reprinted by permission of the author and the publisher.

it violated no special obligation to the environment. More important, none is needed. Environmentalists, like government officials, employees, and stockholders, expect that business firms and officials have moral obligations to obey the law, avoid negligent behavior, and tell the truth. In sum, although many business decisions have harmed the environment, these decisions violated no environmental moral obligations. If a corporation is negligent in providing for worker safety, we do not say the corporation violated a special obligation to employees; we say that it violated its obligation to avoid negligent behavior.

The crucial issues concerning business obligations to the environment focus on the excess use of natural resources (the dwindling supply of oil and gas, for instance) and the externalities of production (pollution, for instance). The critics of business want to claim that business has some special obligation to mitigate or solve these problems. I believe this claim is largely mistaken. If business does have a special obligation to help solve the environmental crisis, that obligation results from the special knowledge that business firms have. If they have greater expertise than other constituent groups in society, then it can be argued that, other things being equal, business's responsibilities to mitigate the environmental crisis are somewhat greater. Absent this condition, business's responsibility is no greater than and may be less than that of other social groups. What leads me to think that the critics of business are mistaken?

William Frankena distinguished obligations in an ascending order of the difficulty in carrying them out: avoiding harm, preventing harm, and doing good. The most stringent requirement, to avoid harm, insists no one has a right to render harm on another unless there is a compelling, overriding moral reason to do so. Some writers have referred to this obligation as the moral minimum. A corporation's behavior is consistent with the moral minimum if it causes no avoidable harm to others.

Preventing harm is a less stringent obligation, but sometimes the obligation to prevent harm may be nearly as strict as the obligation to avoid harm. Suppose you are the only person passing a 2-foot-deep [wading] pool where a young child is drowning. There is no one else in the vicinity. Don't you have a strong moral obligation to prevent the child's death? Our obligation to prevent harm is not

unlimited, however. Under what conditions must we be good samaritans? Some have argued that four conditions must exist before one is obligated to prevent harm: capability, need, proximity, and last resort. These conditions are all met with the case of the drowning child. There is obviously a need that you can meet since you are both in the vicinity and have the resources to prevent the drowning with little effort; you are also the last resort.

The least strict moral obligation is to do good—to make contributions to society or to help solve problems (inadequate primary schooling in the inner cities, for example). Although corporations may have some minimum obligation in this regard based on an argument from corporate citizenship, the obligations of the corporation to do good cannot be expanded without limit. An injunction to assist in solving societal problems makes impossible demands on a corporation because at the practical level, it ignores the impact that such activities have on profit.

It might seem that even if this descending order of strictness of obligations were accepted, obligations toward the environment would fall into the moral minimum category. After all, the depletion of natural resources and pollution surely harm the environment. If so, wouldn't the obligations business has to the environment be among the strictest obligations a business can have?

Suppose, however, that a businessperson argues that the phrase "avoid harm" usually applies to human beings. Polluting a lake is not like injuring a human with a faulty product. Those who coined the phrase *moral minimum* for use in the business context defined harm as "particularly including activities which violate or frustrate the enforcement of rules of domestic or institutional law intended to protect individuals against prevention of health, safety or basic freedom." Even if we do not insist that the violations be violations of a rule of law, polluting a lake would not count as a harm under this definition. The environmentalists would respond that it would. Polluting the lake may be injuring people who might swim in or eat fish from it. Certainly it would be depriving people of the freedom to enjoy the lake. Although the environmentalist is correct, especially if we grant the legitimacy of a human right to a clean environment, the success of this reply is not enough to establish the general argument.

Consider the harm that results from the production of automobiles. We know statistically that about 50,000 persons per year will die and that nearly 250,000 others will be seriously injured in automobile accidents in the United States alone. Such death and injury, which is harmful, is avoidable. If that is the case, doesn't the avoid-harm criterion require that the production of automobiles for profit cease? Not really. What such arguments point out is that some refinement of the moral minimum standard needs to take place. Take the automobile example. The automobile is itself a good-producing instrument. Because of the advantages of automobiles, society accepts the possible risks that go in using them. Society also accepts many other types of avoidable harm. We take certain risks—ride in planes, build bridges, and mine coal—to pursue advantageous goals. It seems that the high benefits of some activities justify the resulting harms. As long as the risks are known, it is not wrong that some avoidable harm be permitted so that other social and individual goals can be achieved. The avoidable-harm criterion needs some sharpening.

Using the automobile as a paradigm, let us consider the necessary refinements for the avoid-harm criterion. It is a fundamental principle of ethics that "ought" implies "can." That expression means that you can be held morally responsible only for events within your power. In the ought-implies-can principle, the overwhelming majority of highway deaths and injuries is not the responsibility of the automaker. Only those deaths and injuries attributable to unsafe automobile design can be attributed to the automaker. The ought-implies-can principle can also be used to absolve the auto companies of responsibility for death and injury from safety defects that the automakers could not reasonably know existed. The company could not be expected to do anything about them.

Does this mean that a company has an obligation to build a car as safe as it knows how? No. The standards for safety must leave the product's cost within the price range of the consumer ("ought implies can" again). Comments about engineering and equipment capability are obvious enough. But for a business, capability is also a function of profitability. A company that builds a maximally safe car at a cost that puts it at a competitive disadvantage and hence threatens its survival is building a safe car that lies beyond the capability of the company.

Critics of the automobile industry will express horror at these remarks, for by making capability a function of profitability, society will continue to have avoidable deaths and injuries; however, the situation is not as dire as the critics imagine. Certainly capability should not be sacrificed completely so that profits can be maximized. The decision to build products that are cheaper in cost but are not maximally safe is a social decision that has widespread support. The arguments occur over the line between safety and cost. What we have is a classical trade-off situation. What is desired is some appropriate mix between engineering safety and consumer demand. To say there must be some mix between engineering safety and consumer demand is not to justify all the decisions made by the automobile companies. Ford Motor Company made a morally incorrect choice in placing Pinto gas tanks where it did. Consumers were uninformed, the record of the Pinto in rear-end collisions was worse than that of competitors, and Ford fought government regulations.

Let us apply the analysis of the automobile industry to the issue before us. That analysis shows that an automobile company does not violate its obligation to avoid harm and hence is not in violation of the moral minimum if the trade-off between potential harm and the utility of the products rests on social consensus and competitive realities.

As long as business obeys the environmental laws and honors other standard moral obligations, most harm done to the environment by business has been accepted by society. Through their decisions in the marketplace, we can see that most consumers are unwilling to pay extra for products that are more environmentally friendly than less friendly competitive products. Nor is there much evidence that consumers are willing to conserve resources, recycle, or tax themselves for environmental causes.

Consider the following instances reported in the *Wall Street Journal*. The restaurant chain Wendy's tried to replace foam plates and cups with paper, but customers in the test markets balked. Procter and Gamble offered Downey fabric softener in concentrated form that requires less packaging than ready-to-use products; however the concentrate version is less convenient because it has to be mixed with water. Sales have been poor. Procter and Gamble manufactures Vizir and Lenor brands of detergents in concentrate form, which the customer mixes at home in reusable bottles. Europeans will take the trouble; Americans will not. Kodak tried to eliminate its yellow film boxes but met customer resistance. McDonald's has been testing mini-incinerators that convert trash into energy but often meets opposition from community groups that fear the incinerators will pollute the air. A McDonald's spokesperson points out that the emissions are mostly carbon dioxide and water vapor and are "less offensive than a barbecue." Exxon spent approximately $9,200,000 to "save" 230 otters ($40,000 for each otter). Otters in captivity cost $800. Fishermen in Alaska are permitted to shoot otters as pests. Given these facts, doesn't business have every right to assume that public tolerance for environmental damage is quite high, and hence current legal activities by corporations that harm the environment do not violate the avoid-harm criterion?

Recently environmentalists have pointed out the environmental damage caused by the widespread use of disposable diapers. Are Americans ready to give them up and go back to cloth diapers and the diaper pail? Most observers think not. Procter and Gamble is not violating the avoid-harm criterion by manufacturing Pampers. Moreover, if the public wants cloth diapers, business certainly will produce them. If environmentalists want business to produce products that are friendlier to the environment, they must convince Americans to purchase them. Business will respond to the market. It is the consuming public that has the obligation to make the trade-off between cost and environmental integrity.

Data and arguments of the sort described should give environmental critics of business pause. Nonetheless, these critics are not without counter-responses. For example, they might respond that public attitudes are changing. Indeed, they point out, during the Reagan deregulation era, the one area where the public supported government regulations was in the area of environmental law. In addition, *Fortune* predicts environmental integrity as the primary demand of society on business in the 1990s.

More important, they might argue that environmentally friendly products are at a disadvantage in the marketplace because they have public good characteristics. After all, the best situation for the individual is one where most other people use environmentally friendly products but he or she does not, hence reaping the benefit of lower cost and convenience. Since everyone reasons this way, the real demand for environmentally friendly products cannot be registered in the market. Everyone is understating the value of his or her preference for environmentally friendly products. Hence, companies cannot conclude from market behavior that the environmentally unfriendly products are preferred.

Suppose the environmental critics are right that the public goods characteristic of environmentally friendly products creates a market failure. Does that mean the companies are obligated to stop producing these environmentally unfriendly products? I think not, and I propose that we use the four conditions attached to the prevent-harm obligation to show why not. There is a need, and certainly corporations that cause environmental problems are in proximity. However, environmentally clean firms, if there are any, are not in proximity at all, and most business firms are not in proximity with respect to most environmental problems. In other words, the environmental critic must limit his or her argument to the environmental damage a business actually causes. The environmentalist might argue that Procter and Gamble ought to do something about Pampers; I do not see how an environmentalist can use the avoid-harm criterion to argue that Procter and Gamble should do something about acid rain. But even narrowing the obligation to damage actually caused will not be sufficient to establish an obligation to pull a product from the market because it damages the environment or even to go beyond what is legally required to protect the environment. Even for damage actually done, both the high cost of protecting the environment and the competitive pressures of business make further action to protect the environment beyond the capability of business. This conclusion would be more serious if business were the last resort, but it is not.

Traditionally it is the function of the government to correct for market failure. If the market cannot register the true desires of consumers, let them register their preferences in the political arena. Even fairly conservative economic thinkers allow government a legitimate role in correcting market failure. Perhaps the responsibility for energy conservation and pollution control belongs with the government.

Although I think consumers bear a far greater responsibility for preserving and protecting the environment than they have actually exercised, let us assume that the basic responsibility rests with the government. Does that let business off the hook? No. Most of business's unethical conduct regarding the environment occurs in the political arena.

Far too many corporations try to have their cake and eat it too. They argue that it is the job of government to correct for market failure and then use their influence and money to defeat or water down regulations designed to conserve and protect the environment. They argue that consumers should decide how much conservation and protection the environment should have, and then they try to interfere with the exercise of that choice in the political arena. Such behavior is inconsistent and ethically inappropriate. Business has an obligation to avoid intervention in the political process for the purpose of defeating and weakening environmental regulations. Moreover, this is a special obligation to the environment since business does not have a general obligation to avoid pursuing its own parochial interests in the political arena. Business need do nothing wrong when it seeks to influence tariffs, labor policy, or monetary policy. Business does do something wrong when it interferes with the passage of environmental legislation. Why?

First, such a noninterventionist policy is dictated by the logic of the business's argument to avoid a special obligation to protect the environment. Put more formally:

1. Business argues that it escapes special obligations to the environment because it is willing to respond to consumer preferences in this matter.

2. Because of externalities and public goods considerations, consumers cannot express their preferences in the market.

3. The only other viable forum for consumers to express their preferences is in the political arena.

4. Business intervention interferes with the expression of these preferences.

5. Since point 4 is inconsistent with point 1, business should not intervene in the political process.

The importance of this obligation in business is even more important when we see that environmental legislation has special disadvantages in the political arena. Public choice reminds us that the primary interest of politicians is being reelected. Government policy will be skewed in favor of poli-

cies that provide benefits to an influential minority as long as the greater costs are widely dispersed. Politicians will also favor projects where benefits are immediate and where costs can be postponed to the future. Such strategies increase the likelihood that a politician will be reelected.

What is frightening about the environmental crisis is that both the conservation of scarce resources and pollution abatement require policies that go contrary to a politician's self-interest. The costs of cleaning up the environment are immediate and huge, yet the benefits are relatively long range (many of them exceedingly long range). Moreover, a situation where the benefits are widely dispersed and the costs are large presents a twofold problem. The costs are large enough so that all voters will likely notice them and in certain cases are catastrophic for individuals (e.g., for those who lose their jobs in a plant shutdown).

Given these facts and the political realities they entail, business opposition to environmental legislation makes a very bad situation much worse. Even if consumers could be persuaded to take environmental issues more seriously, the externalities, opportunities to free ride, and public goods characteristics of the environment make it difficult for even enlightened consumers to express their true preference for the environment in the market. The fact that most environmental legislation trades immediate costs for future benefits makes it difficult for politicians concerned about reelection to support it. Hence it is also difficult for enlightened consumers to have their preferences for a better environment honored in the political arena. Since lack of business intervention seems necessary, and might even be sufficient, for adequate environmental legislation, it seems business has an obligation not to intervene. Nonintervention would prevent the harm of not having the true preferences of consumers for a clean environment revealed. Given business's commitment to satisfying preferences, opposition to having these preferences expressed seems inconsistent as well.

The extent of this obligation to avoid intervening in the political process needs considerable discussion by ethicists and other interested parties. Businesspeople will surely object that if they are not permitted to play a role, Congress and state legislators will make decisions that will put them at a severe competitive disadvantage. For example, if the United States develops stricter environmental controls than other countries do, foreign imports will have a competitive advantage over domestic products. Shouldn't business be permitted to point that out? Moreover, any legislation that places costs on one industry rather than another confers advantages on other industries. The cost to the electric utilities from regulations designed to reduce the pollution that causes acid rain will give advantages to natural gas and perhaps even solar energy. Shouldn't the electric utility industry be permitted to point that out?

These questions pose difficult questions, and my answer to them should be considered highly tentative. I believe the answer to the first question is "yes" and the answer to the second is "no." Business does have a right to insist that the regulations apply to all those in the industry. Anything else would seem to violate norms of fairness. Such issues of fairness do not arise in the second case. Since natural gas and solar do not contribute to acid rain and since the costs of acid rain cannot be fully captured in the market, government intervention through regulation is simply correcting a market failure. With respect to acid rain, the electric utilities do

have an advantage they do not deserve. Hence they have no right to try to protect it.

Legislative bodies and regulatory agencies need to expand their staffs to include technical experts, economists, and engineers so that the political process can be both neutral and highly informed about environmental matters. To gain the respect of business and the public, its performance needs to improve. Much more needs to be said to make any contention that business ought to stay out of the political debate theoretically and practically possible. Perhaps these suggestions point the way for future discussion.

Ironically business might best improve its situation in the political arena by taking on an additional obligation to the environment. Businesspersons often have more knowledge about environmental harms and the costs of cleaning them up. They may often have special knowledge about how to prevent environmental harm in the first place. Perhaps business has a special duty to educate the public and to promote environmentally responsible behavior.

READING 10.4 SUSTAINABLE BUSINESS: ENVIRONMENTAL RESPONSIBILITIES AND BUSINESS OPPORTUNITIES

Joseph R. DesJardins

It is fair to say that virtually all mainstream theories of corporate social responsibility (CSR) deny that business has any special environmental responsibilities. From the classical model of CSR associated with Milton Friedman and other defenders of the free market to the more recent stakeholder theory, environmental concerns function, at best, as side-constraints upon business managers. Business may have some negative duties associated with the environment, duties not to pollute and not to cause harm, but business certainly has no positive duty to conduct itself in ways that contribute to long-term ecological and environmental well-being. I would like to offer some reasons for thinking that this view asks too little of business. Expecting business to take a more active role in addressing environ-

mental and ecological concerns is, I believe, more reasonable than usually acknowledged.

MARKETS AND DUTIES

One can think of the competing models of CSR along a continuum of expanding ethical constraints upon a general goal of increasing profits by responding to consumer demand. At one extreme, we find the very narrow view of CSR associated with neoclassical economics. Business's social responsibility is to maximize profit by meeting consumer demand, and the only constraint is the duty to obey the law. At its most libertarian extreme, this view would also argue that the only appropriate laws are those that protect property and prohibit fraud and coercion. Theories of CSR become more moderate by expanding the range of constraints upon the pursuit of profit. Thus, one finds Norman Bowie, for example, arguing on Kantian grounds that beyond obedience to the law, business also has moral duties not to cause harm, even if not prohibited by law.[1] Various stakeholder theories essentially expand and develop this range of duties by identifying ethically legitimate stakeholders other than investors and by articulating the specific duties owed to them.

We can thus characterize these theories as variations on the theme of balancing utilitarian and deontological ethics. The pursuit of profit is the mechanism by which business is thought to serve the utilitarian goal of satisfying consumer demand and thereby maximizing the overall good. This utilitarian goal is itself to be constrained by the duties that one has to persons affected by these activities. Our duties to other people (and their rights) create side constraints or boundaries on business activity; as long as business does not overstep those boundaries, it is free to pursue profit. Depending on the theory of rights and duties that one adopts, those constraints range from the minimal duty of obeying the law to more extensive accounts of duties associated with the stakeholder theory.

What one will not find among these common views is an account of CSR that holds that business has positive duties either to *prevent* ecological harm or *to do* environmental good. Continuing the side constraint and boundary metaphor, one does not find ethical goals determining either the direction or the substance of business activity. In essence, these views adopt an ethically passive model of business management in which managers can fulfill their responsibilities by actively doing little or nothing at all. Business passively *responds to* the demands of the market. Business is passive in *not violating the law*. Business is passive when it *causes no harm*. According to these views, the social responsibility of business requires business *to do* virtually nothing at all.

This point, of course, reminds us that both utilitarian and the Kantian deontology are thorough-going *liberal* theories of ethics. Philosophical liberalism denies that ethics can require anyone actually to do good; that would be asking too much of free and autonomous individuals. Ethics does not provide the goals of our behaviour, only the limits. Liberty demands that we not coerce anyone to act in ways that they have not chosen, as long as their

choices cause no harm to other individuals. Negative, not positive, duties are obligatory for every individual. Besides, given the wide variety of competing conceptions of the good life, there is little chance that we can arrive at a defensible and commonly-accepted account of the good.

Thus, classical liberal theories tell us that doing good is supererogatory, an imperfect duty that we can encourage and praise but not require. Like charity, it is something that we hope for and encourage but not something that ethics obliges us to do. Unfortunately, many crucial environmental and ecological concerns are thought to fall within this sphere, particularly when the agent involved is business. Releasing toxic pollutants can be ethically prohibited, but preserving biological diversity, conserving natural resources, protecting wild and open spaces, reducing energy consumption, or designing fuel-efficient cars or sustainable production methods cannot. In fact, it is difficult to find many environmental concerns other than the ban on pollution that are thought to be part of business's social responsibility, and even that can be trumped when allowed by law. (CO_2 emissions being the obvious example—while they are known to cause harm, business is free to continue emitting copious amounts of this pollutant since it is all quite legal.)

The view I wish to put forth holds that business does have an ethical responsibility, even when not required by law and not demanded by consumers, to redesign its operations in a way that is ecologically and economically sustainable over the long-term. Environmental responsibilities should provide the direction in which business develops as well as the constraints within which it operates. My argument to support this conclusion falls into two parts: arguments against the ethical adequacy of the standard model and arguments in support of the alternative.

ARGUMENTS AGAINST THE STANDARD MODELS

Utilitarian Aspects

I shall begin by reviewing the arguments critical of these standard models. While there is little that is original here, it is worth bringing them together into one single section. We can begin with objections to the market-based, utilitarian aspects of the standard models.

First, let us mention the wide variety of market failures all too familiar within the economic literature. Quite simply, actual markets never attain the optimal welfare (or "efficiency" or "preference-satisfaction" or "overall happiness") goals of the ideal markets described in theoretical literature. If markets do not achieve the ends they are designed for, then no consequentialist justification of markets, as often claimed by their utilitarian defenders, can succeed. Externalities (such as pollution and harm to future generations), unpriced public goods (such as scenic vistas), unowned goods (such as ocean fisheries and endangered species), lack of competition (as with public utilities), and lack of information (as with the future effects of nuclear wastes) are just some of the barriers that prevent actual markets from achieving the objectives of the efficient market described in academic theories. Given these market failures, it is *prima facie* unreasonable to establish social policy on the basis of a model that we know does not work in practice.

There are two responses to this challenge. First, some argue that, despite its shortcomings, we must stay with market-based social policy because there are no reasonable or preferable alternatives. While inefficient actual markets are not ideal, they are better than the alternatives. Second, some argue that market failures can be repaired by well-crafted social policy. Indeed, the field of environmental economics is devoted to exactly this. Environmental economists seek to internalize the costs of pollution, establish shadow prices for unpriced goods, assign property rights to unowned goods, discount future costs, and, when necessary, even allow government regulation for uncompetitive markets. Thus, what is broken with actual markets can be fixed by well-intentioned theorists.

A version of this first response is raised by Norman Bowie in "Morality, Money, and Motor Cars." Bowie cites a standard ethical principle, "ought implies can," in making this point. This principle holds that one cannot be required ethically to do what one cannot, in fact, do. If one *ought,* then it must be the case that one *can.* But, argues Bowie, many alleged environmental duties, such as marketing a fuel-efficient car or withdrawing from the SUV market, would prove economically disastrous for automakers. If they did this, they would lose business and perhaps even go out of business. Since they *cannot* fulfill these duties with-

out jeopardizing their own survival, they *ought* not be expected to do so.

But, it is a mistake to interpret the "can" involved in the "ought implies can" principle as meaning that business cannot ethically be expected to do something that threatens profitability. This would mean that profitability trumps all ethical considerations, and this surely is a *reductio* of that interpretation. Ethical duties are not subservient to profitability, as ethical prohibitions of drugs, weapons, and child pornography show. The only reasonable interpretation of the "can" condition, is that there are no credible alternatives such that, even if one desired to do so, there is no option available that allows one to do one's duty. As I hope to show, I believe this is false when applied to ecologically and environmentally sound business practice. Thus, the first response is unpersuasive because there are alternatives to this model.

The second response echoes the claim of environmental economists who believe that policy experts (like themselves) can tinker with the failures of actual markets so that they will mimic the results of the efficient markets of economic theory. What I take to be the most convincing challenge to this response goes to the very heart of the alleged utilitarian justification of markets. Simply put, economic markets can find no justification in utilitarian ethics whatsoever. The results of efficient markets, even if they could be attained in practice, bear only a superficial resemblance to the consequentialist goals of utilitarianism.

Recognize that, ultimately and at best, markets can only attain the satisfaction of those preferences expressed by consumers in markets. The goal of any market exchange is the satisfaction of those desires expressed by the participants in that exchange. But why should the satisfaction of consumer preferences be taken as a goal of ethics? Why should one think that the world is, ethically, a better place when consumers get more of what they want?

The answer to these questions turns out to be an assumption, and it is this assumption that seems to make the connection between the results of markets and utilitarianism plausible. It is also an assumption that turns out to be false. This assumption is that consumer satisfaction, people getting what they want, can be identified with happiness. Thus, on this account, optimizing the satisfaction of consumer preferences is to optimize happiness.

But this identification is empirically false and conceptually confused. As an empirical claim, this can be shown false both at the level of individuals and at the level of societies. Individually, this claim would be that the more someone consumes, *of anything,* the happier he or she is. This, of course, is false, as any alcoholic, cigarette smoker, hospital patient, crime victim, or bankrupted consumer can testify. More generally, numerous empirical studies confirm that there is at best a mixed connection between consumption or economic growth and happiness. Individuals themselves often report that the more they buy and consume, the less happy they are. Conversely, many individuals report that they are happier leading a life of frugality and simplicity. As long as there are *some* people who are *less* happy when consuming *more,* identifying the economic goal of satisfying preferences with the utilitarian goal of happiness is a mistake.

As it turns out, economists are aware of these problems, and their reaction is to treat the identification of preference satisfaction and happiness not as an empirical claim, but as a conceptual one. That is, what they *mean* by happiness (or "welfare" or "well-being" or "utility" or whatever they think is increased by economic growth) is simply the satisfaction of those preferences expressed by consumers in the marketplace. But this collapses the ethical justification of markets into incoherence. The justification question begins with the query, "Why should, ethically, one accept the results of market transactions?" By *defining* consumer satisfaction with happiness, the answer turns out to be "Because markets will increase the amount of those things that markets produce." But, of course, the original ethical challenge remains, "Why should, ethically, one accept those results produced by markets?" The conceptual response is no response at all.

Thus, the utilitarian side of the standard models' justification for their views on the environmental responsibilities of business fails. It remains to be seen if the deontological aspect can salvage these views.

Deontological Aspects

The views that I am arguing against hold that business has only the negative environmental duty to cause no harm but no positive duty to do good. Traditionally, there are two general rationales offered in defense of this liberal conclusion: Positive duties would violate the respect owed to each individual as an autonomous agent, and there are no rationally defensible or widely acknowledged positive goods that can be binding on individuals. I contend that in the case of business's environmental responsibilities, neither of these two rationales is persuasive.

Let us consider the autonomy side first. Philosophical liberals argue that only negative duties prohibiting harm are compatible with the respect owed to an individual as a free and autonomous agent. Requiring an agent to perform positive acts of goodness is to treat that agent as a means to an end, to coerce that agent against her will, and to have one's ends chosen by another. Thus, the moral respect owed to individuals trumps the goods that can be attained through positive duties.

However, this is to forget the obvious: Business institutions are not moral agents who have an overriding right to be treated with the respect due to autonomous individuals. Business institutions are not autonomous individuals; they are precisely the type of thing Kant had in mind when he spoke of means, rather than ends. Thus, requiring business to serve human ends is to treat business exactly in accord with its nature as a human institution designed and created to serve human ends. Human beings, acting in concert through their social, political, and legal institutions, created the modern corporation and established its legal and ethical duties. My proposal is simply that those duties need to be rethought.

That leaves only the value-relativist claim standing opposed to my proposal. This response claims that we cannot expect business to be responsible for achieving social goods because society itself lacks any consensus on the nature of the good. In the terms of traditional liberalism, the right has priority over the good because of irreconcilable disagreements over the nature of the good. Who is to say what is, or is not, good?

The converse of this view, the priority of the good over the right, is highly contentious. Nevertheless, I would like to defend something very much like it. In this, of course, I am out of the mainstream in modern philosophy and especially out of the mainstream of business ethics. But what if we could offer a rationally defensible account of the good for business, one objectively better than the value-neutral model of business that emerges from neoclassical economics?

AN ALTERNATIVE MODEL OF CSR: SUSTAINABLE BUSINESS

The narrow views of CSR sketched in earlier sections implicitly rely on a distinction between actively causing harm and passively allowing it to happen. As we have seen, most liberal theories hold individuals responsible for harms that they cause but not for harms that they allow to happen. Thus, while I may have a strong duty not to cause the starvation of my neighbor (a perfect duty in Kantian terms), I have no duty (an imperfect duty in Kantian terms) to prevent that starvation. Doing good is praiseworthy but not obligatory. But this distinction has been challenged, persuasively, by many philosophers.[2] Only the most ethically callous person would insist that we have no moral duty to prevent serious harm if in doing so we face only minor inconveniences.

I would like to suggest that something like this faces contemporary business institutions. Significant harm can be prevented, at present and into the near future, if business institutions would remake themselves on a model of sustainability. I would further claim that this is possible without putting most businesses in any greater financial jeopardy than is already and normally faced under the present model. Risks exist, of course, but there is no reason to think they are any graver than the risks normally faced everyday by business entrepreneurs, managers, and business leaders.

Thus the view I wish to defend holds that business managers have an ethical responsibility for taking positive actions to create a more just and environmentally sustainable world. This is a view consistent with ordinary understanding of business management and leadership. Business managers, of course, take an active leadership role all the time. Managers have a great deal of discretion in choosing both the ends of their business and the means by which those ends might be attained. If managerial prerogative means anything, it means that society expects and demands managerial professionals to exercise their judgment in determining the proper course for business. If the concepts of business leadership or entrepreneurship mean anything at all, they mean that business managers are widely understood to be capable of, and responsible for, taking positive actions.

The harms to which I refer exist along two dimensions: ethical and ecological. First, hundreds of millions of people, most children and the overwhelming majority of them morally innocent in every way, lack the basic requirements of a decent human life. Lack of clean drinking water, nutritious food, health care, education, work, shelter, and clothing is a daily reality for hundreds of millions of people. Population growth, even at the most conservative rates, will only exacerbate these problems in the near future. Because population growth is the highest in those areas in which people are already most at risk due to the effects of poverty and oppression, these ethical challenges will only get worse in the future. To meet these needs, the world's economy must produce substantial amounts of food, clothing, shelter, health care, and jobs, and distribute these goods and services to those in need. Clearly then, significant worldwide economic activity must occur if these harms are to be addressed at all.

But these ethical goals and the economic activity to meet them must rely on the productive capacity of the earth's ecosystems. Two facts about that ecosystem are at the core of my argument. First, the economy is but a subsystem within earth's ecosystem, and therefore that ecosystem establishes the biophysical parameters of economic growth. Second, that very ecosystem is already under stress due to the economic activity of human beings. Unless a model of business can be created that allows significant economic activity without further depletion of the biosphere's ability to support both life and the very economic activity on which it depends, humans are facing global ecological, economic, and ethical tragedy.

Fortunately, such a model of business does exist. What has been called, alternatively, "sustainable business," "the next industrial revolution," or "natural capitalism" provides a model of business which can, in the words of the U.N. Commission on Sustainability, "meet the needs of the present without jeopardizing the ability of future generations to meet their own." It is a model of business that emerges out of a paradigm shift in economics. We must abandon the economic model that takes *growth* as the economic goal and replace it with one that targets economic *development*. Paraphrasing the economist Herman Daly, economic growth means the economy is only getting bigger; economic development means it is getting better. Where economic growth, within a finite biosphere is necessarily limited, economic development never is.[3]

What is the model of business that emerges from this new economics? First, we should recognize that there is not a single, unique way in which a sustainable business should be organized. Several models have been described in the literature, but we can abstract some common aspects of these various models.[4] The first aspect is a significant increase in economic efficiency brought about by design changes inspired by biological processes. This alternative business model should be based on a principle of biomimicry in which wastes of the production cycle are recycled back into a closed loop. "Waste equals food," in the words of McDonough and Braungart. Just as the detritus of decomposed material is turned back into fertile soil within biological systems, sustainable business must be designed so that its by-products are themselves the resources for new productivity.

A second feature of sustainable business shifts the goal of production from goods and products to services. Human beings *need* surprisingly very few *products:* food, water, and clean air are obvious examples, and so far at least, only the first two have become commodities. Human beings do need many *services:* education, health care, shelter, security. As consumers, we need very few of the products purchased in the marketplace. What we actually *want,* although we often do not fully understand ourselves, are *services.* As the popularity of auto leasing shows, consumers want convenient personal transportation, not ownership of a 2000-pound automobile. As the information technology industry is showing, consumers want easy access to software, Internet, and e-mail, not ownership of a soon-to-be-outdated piece of computer hardware or software written on three-and-one-half inch floppies. As Interface Corporation has shown, people want floor-covering services, not carpet ownership. This list goes on.

This focus on services rather than products has important implications for both business and consumers. By emphasizing services rather than products, business has strong financial incentives to create longer-lasting, more durable products that are easily recycled back into the product stream. Significant entrepreneurial opportunities exist here for creative business leaders to seize this initiative in creating a service economy. Significant economic opportunity also exists as one-time product purchasers become long-term service lessees. Consumers benefit if they are helped to escape what has been called a commodity fetish.

The final aspect of this alternative model requires business to invest in natural capital. For too long, business (and growth-based economics) has treated the productive capacity of the earth's biosphere as an unending revenue stream. Earth's productivity was something that could be spent without cost. Only in the last few decades have the true costs of spending down our natural capital been understood. The better metaphor is to think of the earth's productivity as capital, as something capable of generating revenue in the form of interest but not something that should be spent to the point where it is incapable of continuing to be a source of income. A prudent financial strategy is to spend interest but not capital. The earth has demonstrated a remarkable ability to produce life-sustaining necessities indefinitely, but only if we maintain sufficient savings in reserve to generate these necessities indefinitely.

One of the most interesting things about this alternative model of sustainable business is the huge potential it holds for entrepreneurial activity. Creative business leaders will find vast opportunities for new business ventures that transform business from the old industrial model to the new sustainable model. Thus, the fear that doing good is too much to ask of profit-seeking institutions is ill-founded. Sustainable business does not ask managers to forego profits (although it would require that profits from ecologically destructive activities be abandoned); it only requires that profits be obtained in ecologically sustainable ways.

The ecological guidelines for this new approach to business are, in their most general form, relatively straightforward. The entire economic production process takes resources from the biosphere, turns them into products and services, and generates by-products (or wastes) in the process. The ecological guidelines for sustainable business mirror the two sides of this production cycle. Resources going into the production process should be used only at the rate at which they can be replenished by the productive capacity of the biopshere. By-products and wastes of this production process should be generated no faster than the earth's capacity to absorb them.

More specifically, we can recognize that economic resources come in a variety of types. Some are nonrenewable, either in principle or in practice. Once a species becomes extinct, humans will never again have the ability to use it. Once oil or coal is burned, it is gone forever, in any practical sense of the word. Thus, use of nonrenewable resources ought, eventually, to be eliminated but should, in the meantime, be reduced to a minimum.

Other resources are renewable, some only within certain parameters, others practically without limit. Agriculture, fisheries, and forests are renewable, but only if we use them at moderate rates. Used wisely, the earth can produce biological resources at a sustainable rate indefinitely. Other resources—energy produced by the sun, hydrogen, wind, tides, and geothermal sources—are for all practical purposes infinite. An efficient, wise, and ethical sustainable business will use these infinitely available resources first, moderate its use of other renewables, and wean itself from reliance on nonrenewables.

Similar guidelines can be developed on the waste and by-product side of business. Waste is a bad thing, both economically and ecologically. Sustainable business must strive to eliminate all of the wastes created along each step of the production cycle. In general, all wastes are sent back into the earth's biosphere and, to be sustainable, must not be put there beyond the capacity of the biosphere to absorb them. For some by-products that will be easy. Much agricultural waste, for example, can be recycled back into the earth as mulch. For other by-products, the pollutants of much of the petrochemical or nuclear industry for example, that will be impossible. Such wastes will need to be eliminated. But, to emphasize, business wastes are not only an ecological harm, they are also an economic harm. As the word itself suggests, wastes are unused resources and any business that has a lot of waste is an inefficient and poorly-run business. Great economic opportunities exist for discovering ways to transform this waste into useful resources.

Perhaps the best test of the plausibility of this next industrial revolution is a test of vision. Try to envision two futures. One is a future in which business acts upon the principle of sustainable development, redesigning itself to meet the economic and social needs of the present without jeopardizing the ability of future people to meet their own needs. The second is one in which the present paradigm of growth and consumerism expands to the earth's entire population, at present slightly more than 6 billion people but in the near term even more. Envision a world in which the 1.3 billion people presently living in China used as many resources and created as many wastes as the 300 million people of the United States. One estimate has it that if China consumed oil at the rate of the United States, it would consume 80 million barrels of oil each day, more than the world's total production of 74 million barrels a day. If China consumed paper at the rate of the United States, it alone would use more paper each year than the entire world produces. If the Chinese economy ever reached the level of CO_2 emissions as the present U.S. economy, China alone would produce double the present worldwide CO_2 pollution.[5] Now imagine that same world in which the people of India, all 1 billion of them, join the economic party at the same rates. Add to that another billion people from Indonesia, Brazil, Russia, Pakistan, Bangladesh, and Nigeria. Which of these future worlds is likely to be economically and ecologically stable? Which of these future worlds is likely to be judged ethically better?

NOTES

1. See Norman Bowie, "Morality, Money, and Motor Cars," reprinted earlier in this chapter.

2. The distinction rests upon the view that there is an ethically significant difference between acting and refraining, a distinction that has been seriously challenged. See, for example, the well-known essay by James Rachels, "Active and Passive Euthanasia" in which Rachels argues against the moral significance of this distinction as it has been employed in the ethics of euthanasia. See "Active and Passive Euthanasia," New England Journal of Medicine, vol. 292, (Jan. 9, 1975) pp. 79–80.

3. See *Beyond Growth,* by Herman Daly (Beacon Press, Boston: 1997).

4. My own thinking on this has been particularly influenced by three approaches: Herman Daly's writing on

ecological economics and especially in *Beyond Growth;* Amory Lovin, Hunter Lovins, and Paul Hawken's *Natural Capitalism,* and William McDonough and Michael Braungart, in "The Next Industrial Revolution" and elsewhere.

5. These estimates are from Lester Brown, *Eco-Economy: Building an economy for the Earth* (W.W. Norton & Co., New York: 2001), Chapter One.

READING 10.5 A ROAD MAP FOR NATURAL CAPITALISM
Amory B. Lovins, L. Hunter Lovins, and Paul Hawken

On September 16, 1991, a small group of scientists was sealed inside Biosphere II, a glittering 3.2-acre glass and metal dome in Oracle, Arizona. Two years later, when the radical attempt to replicate the earth's main ecosystems in miniature ended, the engineered environment was dying. The gaunt researchers had survived only because fresh air had been pumped in. Despite $200 million worth of elaborate equipment, Biosphere II had failed to generate breathable air, drinkable water, and adequate food for just eight people. Yet Biosphere I, the planet we all inhabit, effortlessly performs those tasks every day for 6 billion of us.

Disturbingly, Biosphere I is now itself at risk. The earth's ability to sustain life, and therefore economic activity, is threatened by the way we extract, process, transport, and dispose of a vast flow of resources— some 220 billion tons a year, or more than 20 times the average American's body weight every day. With dangerously narrow focus, our industries look only at the exploitable resources of the earth's ecosystems—its oceans, forests, and plains—and not at the larger services that those systems provide for free. Resources and ecosystem services both come from the earth—even from the same biological systems— but they're two different things. Forests, for instance, not only produce the resource of wood fiber but also provide such ecosystem services as water storage, habitat, and regulation of the atmosphere and climate. Yet companies that earn income from harvesting the wood fiber resource often do so in ways that damage the forest's ability to carry out its other vital tasks.

Unfortunately, the cost of destroying ecosystem services becomes apparent only when the services start to break down. In China's Yangtze basin in 1998, for example, deforestation triggered flooding that killed 3,700 people, dislocated 223 million, and inundated 60 million acres of cropland. That $30 billion disaster forced a logging moratorium and a $12 billion crash program of reforestation.

The reason companies (and governments) are so prodigal with ecosystem services is that the value of those services doesn't appear on the business balance sheet. But that's a staggering omission. The economy, after all, is embedded in the environment. Recent calculations published in the journal *Nature* conservatively estimate the value of all the earth's ecosystem services to be at least $33 trillion a year. That's close to the gross world product, and it implies a capitalized book value on the order of half a quadrillion dollars. What's more, for most of these services, there is no known substitute at any price, and we can't live without them.

This article puts forward a new approach not only for protecting the biosphere but also for improving profits and competitiveness. Some very simple changes to the way we run our businesses, built on advanced techniques for making resources more productive, can yield startling benefits both for today's shareholders and for future generations.

This approach is called *natural capitalism* because it's what capitalism might become if its largest category of capital—the "natural capital" of ecosystem services—were properly valued. The journey to natural capitalism involves four major shifts in business practices, all vitally interlinked:

Dramatically increase the productivity of natural resources Reducing the wasteful and destructive flow of resources from depletion to pollution represents a major business opportunity. Through fundamental changes in both production design and technology, farsighted companies are developing ways to make natural resources—energy, minerals, water, forests—stretch 5, 10, even 100 times further than they do today. These major resource savings often yield higher profits than small resource savings do—or even saving no resources at all would—and not only pay for themselves over time but in many cases reduce initial capital investments.

Shift to biologically inspired production models Natural capitalism seeks not merely to reduce waste but to eliminate the very concept of waste. In closed-loop production systems, modeled on nature's designs, every output either is returned harmlessly to the ecosystem as a nutrient, like compost, or becomes an input for manufacturing another product. Such systems can often be designed to eliminate the use of toxic materials, which can hamper nature's ability to reprocess materials.

Move to a solutions-based business model The business model of traditional manufacturing rests on the sale of goods. In the new model, value is instead delivered as a flow of services—providing illumination, for example, rather than selling light bulbs. This model entails a new perception of value, a move from the acquisition of goods as a measure of affluence to one where well-being is measured by the continuous satisfaction of changing expectations for quality, utility, and performance. The new relationship aligns the interests of providers and customers in ways that reward them for implementing the first two innovations of natural capitalism—resource productivity and closed-loop manufacturing.

Reinvest in natural capital Ultimately, business must restore, sustain, and expand the planet's ecosystems so that they can produce their vital services and biological resources even more abundantly. Pressures to do so are mounting as human needs expand, the costs engendered by deteriorating ecosystems rise and the environmental awareness of consumers increases. Fortunately, these pressures all create business value.

Natural capitalism is not motivated by a current scarcity of natural resources. Indeed, although many biological resources, like fish, are becoming scarce, most mined resources, such as copper and oil, seem ever more abundant. Indices of average commodity prices are at 28-year lows, thanks partly to powerful extractive technologies, which are often subsidized and whose damage to natural capital remains unaccounted for. Yet even despite these artificially low prices, using resources manyfold more productively can now be so profitable that pioneering companies—large and small—have already embarked on the journey toward natural capitalism.[1]

Still the question arises—if large resource savings are available and profitable, why haven't they all been captured already? The answer is simple: scores of common practices in both the private and public sectors systematically reward companies for wasting natural resources and penalize them for boosting resource productivity. For example, most companies expense their consumption of raw materials through the income statement but pass resource-saving investment through the balance sheet. That distortion makes it more tax efficient to waste fuel than to invest in improving fuel efficiency. In short, even though the road seems clear, the compass that companies use to direct their journey is broken. Later we'll look in more detail at some of the obstacles to resource productivity—and some of the important business opportunities they reveal. But first, let's map the route toward natural capitalism.

DRAMATICALLY INCREASE THE PRODUCTIVITY OF NATURAL RESOURCES

In the first stage of a company's journey toward natural capitalism, it strives to wring out the waste of energy, water, minerals, and other resources throughout its production systems and other operations. There are two main ways companies can do this at a profit. First, they can adopt a fresh approach to design that considers industrial systems as a whole rather than part by part. Second, companies can replace old industrial technologies with new ones, particularly with those based on natural processes and materials.

Implementing Whole-System Design Inventor Edwin Land once remarked that "people who seem to have had a new idea have often simply stopped having an old idea." This is particularly true when designing for resource savings. The old idea is one of diminishing returns—the greater the resource saving, the higher the cost. But that old idea is giving way to the new idea that bigger savings can cost less—that saving a large fraction of resources can actually cost less than saving a small fraction of resources. This is the concept of expanding returns, and it governs much of the revolutionary thinking behind whole-system design. Lean manufacturing is an example of whole-system thinking that has helped many companies dramatically reduce such forms of waste as lead times, defect rates, and inventory. Applying whole-system thinking to the productivity of natural resources can achieve even more.

Consider Interface Corporation, a leading maker of materials for commercial interiors. In its new Shanghai carpet factory, a liquid had to be circulated through a standard pumping loop similar to those used in nearly all industries. A top European company designed the system to use pumps requiring a total of 95 horsepower. But before construction began, Interface's engineer, Jan Schilbam, realized that two embarrassingly simple design changes would cut that power requirement to only 7 horsepower—a 92% reduction. His redesigned system cost less to build, involved no new technology, and worked better in all respects.

What two design changes achieved this 12-fold saving in pumping power? First, Schilbam chose fatter-than-usual pipes, which create much less friction than thin pipes do and therefore need far less pumping energy. The original designer had chosen thin pipes because, according to the textbook method, the extra cost of fatter ones wouldn't be justified by the pumping energy that they would save. This standard design trade-off optimizes the pipes by themselves but "pessimizes" the larger system. Schilbam optimized the *whole* system by counting not only the higher capital cost of the fatter pipes but also the *lower* capital cost of the smaller pumping equipment that would be needed. The pumps, motors, motor controls, and electrical components could all be much smaller because there'd be less friction to overcome. Capital cost would fall far more for the smaller equipment than it would rise for the fatter pipe. Choosing big pipes and small pumps—rather than small pipes and big pumps—would therefore make the whole system cost less to build, even before counting its future energy savings.

Schilbam's second innovation was to reduce the friction even more by making the pipes short and straight rather than long and crooked. He did this by laying out the pipes first, *then* positioning the various tanks, boilers, and other equipment that they connected. Designers normally locate the production equipment in arbitrary positions and then have a pipe fitter connect everything. Awkward placement forces the pipes to make numerous bends that greatly increase friction. The pipe fitters don't mind: they're paid by the hour, they profit from the extra pipes and fittings, and they don't pay for the oversized pumps or inflated electric bills. In addition to reducing those four kinds of costs, Schilbam's short, straight pipes were easier to insulate, saving an extra 70 kilowatts of heat loss and repaying the insulation's cost in three months.

This small example has big implications for two reasons. First, pumping is the largest application of motors, and motors use three-quarters of all industrial electricity. Second, the lessons are very widely relevant. Interface's pumping loop shows how simple changes in design mentality can yield huge resource savings and returns on investment. This isn't rocket science; often it's just a rediscovery of good Victorian engineering principles that have been lost because of specialization.

Whole-system thinking can help managers find small changes that lead to big savings that are cheap, free, or even better than free (because they make the whole system cheaper to build). They can do this because often the right investment in one part of the system can produce multiple benefits throughout the system. For example, companies would gain 18 distinct economic benefits—of which direct energy savings is only one—if they switched from ordinary motors to premium-efficiency motors or from ordinary lighting ballasts (the transformer-like boxes that control fluorescent lamps) to electronic ballasts that automatically dim the lamps to match available daylight. If everyone in America integrated these and other selected technologies into all existing motor and lighting systems in an optimal way, the nation's $220-billion-a-year electric bill would be cut in half. The after-tax return on investing in these changes would in most cases exceed 100% per year.

The profits from saving electricity could be increased even further if companies also incorporated the best off-the-shelf improvements into their building structure and their office, heating, cooling, and other equipment. Overall, such changes could cut national electricity consumption by at least 75% and produce returns of around 100% a year on the investments made. More important, because workers would be more comfortable, better able to see, and less fatigued by noise, their productivity and the quality of their output would rise. Eight recent case studies of people working in well-designed, energy-efficient buildings measured labor productivity gains of 6% to 16%. Since a typical office pays about 100 times as much for people as it does for energy, this increased productivity in people is worth about 6 to 16 times as much as eliminating the entire energy bill.

Energy-saving, productivity-enhancing improvements can often be achieved at even lower cost by piggybacking them onto the periodic renovations that all buildings and factories need. A recent proposal for reallocating the normal 20-year renovation budget for a standard 200,000-square-foot glass-clad office tower near Chicago, Illinois, shows the potential of whole-system design. The proposal suggested replacing the aging glazing system with a new kind of window that lets in nearly six times more daylight than the old sun-blocking glass units. The new windows would reduce the flow of heat and noise four times better than traditional windows do. So even though the glass costs slightly more, the overall cost of the renovation would be reduced because the windows would let in cool, glare-free daylight that, when combined with more efficient lighting and office equipment, would reduce the need for air-conditioning by 75%. Installing a fourfold more efficient, but fourfold smaller, air-conditioning system would cost $200,000 less than giving the old system its normal 20-year renovation. The $200,000 saved would, in turn, pay for the extra cost of the new windows and other improvements. This whole-system approach to renovation would not only save 75% of the building's total energy use, it would also greatly improve the building's comfort and marketability. Yet it would cost essentially the same as the normal renovation. There are about 100,000 20-year-old glass office towers in the United States that are ripe for such improvement.

Major gains in resource productivity require that the right steps be taken in the right order. Small changes made at the downstream end of a process often create far larger savings further upstream. In almost any industry that uses a pump-

ing system, for example, saving one unit of liquid flow or friction in an exit pipe saves about ten units of fuel, cost, and pollution at the power station. Of course, the original reduction in flow itself can bring direct benefits, which are often the reason changes are made in the first place. In the 1980s, while California's industry grew 30%, for example, its water use was cut by 30%, largely to avoid increased wastewater fees. But the resulting reduction in pumping energy (and the roughly tenfold larger saving in power-plant fuel and pollution) delivered bonus savings that were at the time largely unanticipated.

To see how downstream cuts in resource consumption can create huge savings upstream, consider how reducing the use of wood fiber disproportionately reduces the pressure to cut down forests. In round numbers, half of all harvested wood fiber is used for such structural products as lumber; the other half is used for paper and cardboard. In both cases, the biggest leverage comes from reducing the amount of the retail product used. If it takes, for example, three pounds of harvested trees to produce one pound of product, then saving one pound of product will save three pounds of trees—plus all the environmental damage avoided by not having to cut them down in the first place.

The easiest savings come from not using paper that's unwanted or unneeded. In an experiment at its Swiss headquarters, for example, Dow Europe cut office paper flow by about 30% in six weeks simply by discouraging unneeded information. For instance, mailing lists were eliminated and senders of memos got back receipts indicating whether each recipient had wanted the information. Taking those and other small steps, Dow was also able to increase labor productivity by a similar proportion because people could focus on what they really needed to read. Similarly, Danish hearing-aid maker Oticon saved upwards of 30% of its paper as a by-product of redesigning its business processes to produce better decisions faster. Setting the default on office printers and copiers to double-sided mode reduced AT&T's paper costs by about 15%. Recently developed copiers and printers can even strip off old toner and printer ink, permitting each sheet to be reused about ten times.

Further savings can come from using thinner but stronger and more opaque paper, and from designing packaging more thoughtfully. In a 30-

month effort at reducing such waste, Johnson & Johnson saved 2,750 tons of packaging, 1,600 tons of paper, $2.8 million, and at least 330 acres of forest annually. The downstream savings in paper use are multiplied by the savings further upstream, as less need for paper products (or less need for fiber to make each product) translates into less raw paper, less raw paper means less pulp, and less pulp requires fewer trees to be harvested from the forest. Recycling paper and substituting alternative fibers such as wheat straw will save even more.

Comparable savings can be achieved for the wood fiber used in structural products. Pacific Gas and Electric, for example, sponsored an innovative design developed by Davis Energy Group that used engineered wood products to reduce the amount of wood needed in a stud wall for a typical tract house by more than 70%. These walls were stronger, cheaper, more stable, and insulated twice as well. Using them enabled the designers to eliminate heating and cooling equipment in a climate where temperatures range from freezing to 113°F. Eliminating the equipment made the whole house much less expensive both to build and to run while still maintaining high levels of comfort. Taken together, these and many other savings in the paper and construction industries could make our use of wood fiber so much more productive that, in principle, the entire world's present wood fiber needs could probably be met by an intensive tree farm about the size of Iowa.

Adopting Innovative Technologies Implementing whole-system design goes hand in hand with introducing alternative, environmentally friendly technologies. Many of these are already available and profitable but not widely known. Some, like the "designer catalysts" that are transforming the chemical industry, are already runaway successes. Others are still making their way to market, delayed by cultural rather than by economic or technical barriers.

The automobile industry is particularly ripe for technological change. After a century of development, motorcar technology is showing signs of age. Only 1% of the energy consumed by today's cars is actually used to move the driver: only 15% to 20% of the power generated by burning gasoline reaches the wheels (the rest is lost in the engine and drivetrain) and 95% of the resulting propulsion moves the car, not the driver. The industry's infrastructure is hugely expensive and inefficient. Its convergent products compete for narrow niches in saturated core markets at commodity-like prices. Auto making is capital intensive, and product cycles are long. It is profitable in good years but subject to large losses in bad years. Like the typewriter industry just before the advent of personal computers, it is vulnerable to displacement by something completely different.

Enter the Hypercar. Since 1993, when Rocky Mountain Institute placed this automotive concept in the public domain, several dozen current and potential auto manufacturers have committed billions of dollars to its development and commercialization. The Hypercar integrates the best existing technologies to reduce the consumption of fuel as much as 85% and the amount of materials used up to 90% by introducing four main innovations.

First, making the vehicle out of advanced polymer composites, chiefly carbon fiber, reduces its weight by two-thirds while maintaining crashworthiness. Second, aerodynamic design and better tires reduce air resistance by as much as 70% and rolling resistance by up to 50%. Together, these innovations save about two-thirds of the fuel. Third, 30% to 50% of the remaining fuel is saved by using a "hybrid-electric" drive. In such a system, the wheels are turned by electric motors whose power is made onboard by a small engine or turbine, or even more efficiently by a fuel cell. The fuel cell generates electricity directly by chemically combining stored hydrogen with oxygen, producing pure hot water as its only by-product. Interactions between the small, clean, efficient power source and the ultralight, low-drag auto body then further reduce the weight, cost, and complexity of both. Fourth, much of the traditional hardware—from transmissions and differentials to gauges and certain parts of the suspension— can be replaced by electronics controlled with highly integrated, customizable, and upgradable software.

These technologies make it feasible to manufacture pollution-free, high-performance cars, sport utilities, pickup trucks, and vans that get 80 to 200 miles per gallon (or its energy equivalent in other fuels). These improvements will not require any compromise in quality or utility. Fuel savings will not come from making the vehicles small, sluggish, unsafe, or unaffordable, nor will they depend on government fuel taxes, mandates, or subsidies. Rather, Hypercars will succeed for the same reason that people buy compact discs instead of phonograph records: the CD is a superior product that redefines market expectations. From the manufacturers' perspective, Hypercars will cut cycle times, capital needs, body part counts, and assembly effort and space by as much as tenfold. Early adopters will have a huge competitive advantage— which is why dozens of corporations, including most automakers, are now racing to bring Hyper-car-like products to market.[2]

In the long term, the Hypercar will transform industries other than automobiles. It will displace about an eighth of the steel market directly and most of the rest eventually, as carbon fiber becomes far cheaper. Hypercars and their cousins could ultimately save as much oil as OPEC now sells. Indeed, oil may well become uncompetitive as a fuel long before it becomes scarce and costly. Similar challenges face the coal and electricity industries because the development of the Hypercar is likely to accelerate greatly the commercialization of inexpensive hydrogen fuel cells. These fuel cells will help shift power production from centralized coal-fired and nuclear power stations to networks of decentralized, small-scale generators. In fact, fuel-cell-powered Hypercars could themselves be part of these networks. They'd be, in effect, 20-kilowatt power plants on wheels. Given that cars are left parked—that is, unused—more than 95% of the time, these Hypercars could be plugged into a grid and could then sell back enough electricity to repay as much as half the predicted cost of leasing them. A national Hypercar fleet could ultimately have five to ten times the generating capacity of the national electric grid.

As radical as it sounds, the Hypercar is not an isolated case. Similar ideas are emerging in such industries as chemicals, semiconductors, general manufacturing, transportation, water and wastewater treatment, agriculture, forestry, energy, real estate, and urban design. For example, the amount of carbon dioxide released for each microchip manufactured can be reduced almost 100-fold through improvements that are now profitable or soon will be.

Some of the most striking developments come from emulating nature's techniques. In her book, *Biomimicry,* Janine Benyus points out that spiders convert digested crickets and flies into silk that's as strong as Kevlar without the need for boiling sulfuric acid and high-temperature extruders. Using no furnaces, abalone can convert seawater into an inner shell twice as tough as our best ceramics. Trees turn sunlight, water, soil, and air into cellulose, a sugar stronger than nylon but one-fourth as dense. They then bind it into wood, a natural composite with a higher bending strength than concrete, aluminum alloy, or steel. We may never become as skillful as spiders, abalone, or trees, but smart designers are already realizing that nature's environmentally benign chemistry offers attractive alternatives to industrial brute force.

Whether through better design or through new technologies, reducing waste represents a vast business opportunity. The U.S. economy is not even 10% as energy efficient as the laws of physics allow. Just the energy thrown off as waste heat by U.S. power stations equals the total energy use of Japan. Materials efficiency is even worse: only about 1% of all the materials mobilized to serve America are actually made into products and still in use six months after sale. In every sector, there are opportunities for reducing the amount of resources that go into a production process, the steps required to run that process, and the amount of pollution generated and by-products discarded at the end. These all represent avoidable costs and hence profits to be won.

REDESIGN PRODUCTION ACCORDING TO BIOLOGICAL MODELS

In the second stage on the journey to natural capitalism, companies use closed-loop manufacturing to create new products and processes that can totally prevent waste. This plus more efficient production processes could cut companies' long-term materials requirements by more than 90% in most sectors.

The central principle of closed-loop manufacturing, as architect Paul Bierman-Lytle of the engineering firm CH2M Hill puts it, is "waste equals food." Every output of manufacturing should be either composted into natural nutrients or remanufactured into technical nutrients—that is, it should be returned to the ecosystem or recycled for further production. Closed-loop production systems are designed to eliminate any materials that incur disposal costs, especially toxic ones, because the alternative—isolating them to prevent harm to natural systems—tends to be costly and risky. Indeed, meeting EPA and OSHA standards by eliminating harmful materials often makes a manufacturing process cost less than the hazardous process it replaced. Motorola, for example, formerly used chlorofluoro-

carbons for cleaning printed circuit boards after sol-
dering. When CFCs were outlawed because they
destroy stratospheric ozone, Motorola at first
explored such alternatives as orange-peel terpenes.
But it turned out to be even cheaper—and to produce a better product—to redesign the whole sol-
dering process so that it needed no cleaning
operations or cleaning materials at all.

Closed-loop manufacturing is more than just a
theory. The U.S. remanufacturing industry in 1996
reported revenues of $53 billion—more than con-
sumer-durables manufacturing (appliances, furniture, audio, video, farm, and garden equipment).
Xerox, whose bottom line has swelled by $700 mil-
lion from remanufacturing, expects to save another
$1 billion just by remanufacturing its new, entirely
reusable or recyclable line of "green" photocopiers.
What's more, policy makers in some countries are
already taking steps to encourage industry to think
along these lines. German law, for example, makes
many manufacturers responsible for their products
forever, and Japan is following suit. Combining
closed-loop manufacturing with resource efficiency
is especially powerful. DuPont, for example, gets
much of its polyester industrial film back from customers after they use it and recycles it into new
film. DuPont also makes its polyester film ever
stronger and thinner so it uses less material and
costs less to make. Yet because the film performs
better, customers are willing to pay more for it. As
DuPont chairman Jack Krol noted in 1997,"Our
ability to continually improve the inherent properties [of our films] enables this process [of developing
more productive materials, at lower cost, and higher
profits] to go on indefinitely."

Interface is leading the way to this next frontier
of industrial ecology. While its competitors are
"down cycling" nylon-and-PVC-based carpet into
less valuable carpet backing, Interface has invented a
new floor-covering material called Solenium, which
can be completely remanufactured into identical
new product. This fundamental innovation emerged
from a clean-sheet redesign. Executives at Interface
didn't ask how they could sell more carpet of the
familiar kind; they asked how they could create a
dream product that would best meet their customers' needs while protecting and nourishing natural capital.

Solenium lasts four times longer and uses 40%
less material than ordinary carpets—an 86% reduc-

tion in materials intensity. What's more, Solenium is
free of chlorine and other toxic materials, is virtually stainproof, doesn't grow mildew, can easily be
cleaned with water, and offers aesthetic advantages
over traditional carpets. It's so superior in every
respect that Interface doesn't market it as an environmental product—just a better one.

Solenium is only one part of Interface's drive to
eliminate every form of waste. Chairman Ray C.
Anderson defines waste as "any measurable input
that does not produce customer value," and he considers all inputs to be waste until shown otherwise.
Between 1994 and 1998, this zero-waste approach
led to a systematic treasure hunt that helped to keep
resource inputs constant while revenues rose by
$200 million. Indeed, $67 million of the revenue
increase can be directly attributed to the company's
60% reduction in landfill waste.

Subsequently, president Charlie Eitel expanded
the definition of waste to include all fossil fuel
inputs, and now many customers are eager to buy
products from the company's recently opened solar-
powered carpet factory. Interface's green strategy
has not only won plaudits from environmentalists, it
has also proved a remarkably successful business
strategy. Between 1993 and 1998, revenue has more
than doubled, profits have more than tripled, and
the number of employees has increased by 73%.

CHANGE THE BUSINESS MODEL

In addition to its drive to eliminate waste, Interface
has made a fundamental shift in its business
model—the third stage on the journey toward natural capitalism. The company has realized that
clients want to walk on and look at carpets—but
not necessarily to own them. Traditionally, broad-
loom carpets in office buildings are replaced every
decade because some portions look worn out.
When that happens, companies suffer the disruption
of shutting down their offices and removing their
furniture. Billions of pounds of carpets are removed
each year and sent to landfills, where they will last
up to 20,000 years. To escape this unproductive and
wasteful cycle, Interface is transforming itself from a
company that sells and fits carpets into one that
provides floor-covering services.

Under its Evergreen Lease, Interface no longer
sells carpets but rather leases a floor-covering ser-

vice for a monthly fee and accepts responsibility for keeping the carpet fresh and clean. Monthly inspections detect and replace worn carpet tiles. Since at most 20% of an area typically shows at least 80% of the wear, replacing only the worn parts reduces the consumption of carpeting material by about 80%. It also minimizes the disruption that customers experience—worn tiles are seldom found under furniture. Finally, for the customer, leasing carpets can provide a tax advantage by turning a capital expenditure into a tax-deductible expense. The result: the customer gets cheaper and better services that cost the supplier far less to produce. Indeed, the energy saved from not producing a whole new carpet is in itself enough to produce all the carpeting that the new business model requires. Taken together, the 5-fold savings in carpeting material that Interface achieves through the Evergreen Lease and the 7-fold materials savings achieved through the use of Solenium deliver a stunning 35-fold reduction in the flow of materials needed to sustain a superior floor-covering service. Remanufacturing, and even making carpet initially from renewable materials, can then reduce the extraction of virgin resources essentially to the company's goal of zero.

Interface's shift to a service-leasing business reflects a fundamental change from the basic model of most manufacturing companies, which still look on their businesses as machines for producing and selling products. The more products sold, the better—at least for the company, if not always for the customer or the earth. But any model that wastes natural resources also wastes money. Ultimately, that model will be unable to compete with a service model that emphasizes solving problems and building long-term relationships with customers rather than making and selling products. The shift to what James Womack of the Lean Enterprise Institute calls a "solutions economy" will almost always improve customer value *and* providers' bottom lines because it aligns both parties' interests, offering rewards for doing more and better with less.

Interface is not alone. Elevator giant Schindler, for example, prefers leasing vertical transportation services to selling elevators because leasing lets it capture the savings from its elevators' lower energy and maintenance costs. Dow Chemical and Safety-Kleen prefer leasing dissolving services to selling solvents because they can reuse the same solvent scores of times, reducing costs. United Technologies'

Carrier division, the world's largest manufacturer of air conditioners, is shifting its mission from selling air conditioners to leasing comfort. Making its air conditioners more durable and efficient may compromise future equipment sales, but it provides what customers want and will pay for—better comfort at lower cost. But Carrier is going even further. It's starting to team up with other companies to make buildings more efficient so that they need less air-conditioning, or even none at all, to yield the same level of comfort. Carrier will get paid to provide the agreed-upon level of comfort, however that's delivered. Higher profits will come from providing better solutions rather than from selling more equipment. Since comfort with little or no air-conditioning (via better building design) works better and costs less than comfort with copious air-conditioning, Carrier is smart to capture this opportunity itself before its competitors do. As they say at 3M:"We'd rather eat our own lunch, thank you."

The shift to a service business model promises benefits not just to participating businesses but to the entire economy as well. Womack points out that by helping customers reduce their need for capital goods such as carpets or elevators, and by rewarding suppliers for extending and maximizing asset values rather than for churning them, adoption of the service model will reduce the volatility in the turnover of capital goods that lies at the heart of the business cycle. That would significantly reduce the overall volatility of the world's economy. At present, the producers of capital goods face feast or famine because the buying decisions of households and corporations are extremely sensitive to fluctuating income. But in a continuous-flow-of-services economy, those swings would be greatly reduced, bringing a welcome stability to businesses. Excess capacity—another form of waste and source of risk—need no longer be retained for meeting peak demand. The result of adopting the new model would be an economy in which we grow and get richer by using less and become stronger by being leaner and more stable.

REINVEST IN NATURAL CAPITAL

The foundation of textbook capitalism is the prudent reinvestment of earnings in productive capital. Natural capitalists who have dramatically raised their resource productivity, closed their loops, and shifted to a solutions-based business model have one key task remaining. They must reinvest in restoring, sustaining, and expanding the most important form of capital—their own natural habitat and biological resource base.

This was not always so important. Until recently, business could ignore damage to the ecosystem because it didn't affect production and didn't increase costs. But that situation is changing. In 1998 alone, violent weather displaced 300 million people and caused upwards of $90 billion worth of damage, representing more weather-related destruction than was reported through the entire decade of the 1980s. The increase in damage is strongly linked to deforestation and climate change, factors that accelerate the frequency and severity of natural disasters and are the consequences of inefficient industrialization. If the flow of services from industrial systems is to be sustained or increased in the future for a growing population, the vital flow of services from living systems will have to be maintained or increased as well. Without reinvestment in natural capital, shortages of ecosystem services are likely to become the limiting factor to prosperity in the next century. When a manufacturer realizes that a supplier of key components is overextended and running behind on deliveries, it takes immediate action lest its own production lines come to a halt. The ecosystem is a supplier of key components for the life of the planet, and it is now falling behind on its orders.

Failure to protect and reinvest in natural capital can also hit a company's revenues indirectly. Many companies are discovering that public perceptions of environmental responsibility, or its lack thereof, affect sales. MacMillan Bloedel, targeted by environmental activists as an emblematic clear-cutter and chlorine user, lost 5% of its sales almost overnight when dropped as a U.K. supplier by Scott Paper and Kimberly-Clark. Numerous case studies show that companies leading the way in implementing changes that help protect the environment tend to gain disproportionate advantage, while companies perceived as irresponsible lose their franchise, their legitimacy, and their shirts. Even businesses that claim to be committed to the concept of sustainable development but whose strategy is seen as mistaken, like Monsanto, are encountering stiffening public resistance to their products. Not surprisingly, University of Oregon business professor Michael

Russo, along with many other analysts, has found that a strong environmental rating is "a consistent predictor of profitability."

The pioneering corporations that have made reinvestments in natural capital are starting to see some interesting paybacks. The independent power producer AES, for example, has long pursued a policy of planting trees to offset the carbon emissions of its power plants. That ethical stance, once thought quixotic, now looks like a smart investment because a dozen brokers are now starting to create markets in carbon reduction. Similarly, certification by the Forest Stewardship Council of certain sustainably grown and harvested products has given Collins Pine the extra profit margins that enabled its U.S. manufacturing operations to survive brutal competition. Taking an even longer view, Swiss Re and other European reinsurers are seeking to cut their storm-damage losses by pressing for international public policy to protect the climate and by investing in climate-safe technologies that also promise good profits. Yet most companies still do not realize that a vibrant ecological web underpins their survival and their business success. Enriching natural capital is not just a public good—it is vital to every company's longevity.

It turns out that changing industrial processes so that they actually replenish and magnify the stock of natural capital can prove especially profitable because nature does the production; people need just step back and let life flourish. Industries that directly harvest living resources, such as forestry, farming, and fishing, offer the most suggestive examples. Here are three:

■   Allan Savory of the Center for Holistic Management in Albuquerque, New Mexico, has redesigned cattle ranching to raise the carrying capacity of rangelands, which have often been degraded not by overgrazing but by under-grazing and grazing the wrong way. Savory's solution is to keep the cattle moving from place to place, grazing intensively but briefly at each site, so that they mimic the dense but constantly moving herds of native grazing animals that coevolved with grasslands. Thousands of ranchers are estimated to be applying this approach, improving both their range and their profits. This "management-intensive rotational grazing" method, long standard in New Zealand, yields such clearly superior returns that over 15% of Wisconsin's dairy farms have adopted it in the past few years.

■ The California Rice Industry Association has discovered that letting nature's diversity flourish can be more profitable than forcing it to produce a single product. By flooding 150,000 to 200,000 acres of Sacramento valley rice fields—about 30% of California's rice-growing area—after harvest, farmers are able to create seasonal wetlands that support millions of wildfowl, replenish ground-water, improve fertility, and yield other valuable benefits. In addition, the farmers bale and sell the rice straw, whose high silica content—formerly an air-pollution hazard when the straw was burned—adds insect resistance and hence value as a construction material when it's resold instead.

■ John Todd of Living Technologies in Burlington, Vermont, has used biological Living Machines— linked tanks of bacteria, algae, plants, and other organisms—to turn sewage into clean water. That not only yields cleaner water at a reduced cost, with no toxicity or odor, but it also produces commercially valuable flowers and makes the plant compatible with its residential neighborhood. A similar plant at the Ethel M Chocolates factory in Las Vegas, Nevada, not only handles difficult industrial wastes effectively but is showcased in its public tours.

Although such practices are still evolving, the broad lessons they teach are clear. In almost all climates, soils, and societies, working with nature is more productive than working against it. Reinvesting in nature allows farmers, fishermen, and forest managers to match or exceed the high yields and profits sustained by traditional input-intensive, chemically driven practices. Although much of mainstream business is still headed the other way, the profitability of sustainable, nature-emulating practices is already being proven. In the future, many industries that don't now consider themselves dependent on a biological resource base will become more so as they shift their raw materials and production processes more to biological ones. There is evidence that many business leaders are starting to think this way. The consulting firm Arthur D. Little surveyed a group of North American and European business leaders and found that 83% of them already believe that they can derive "real business value [from implementing a] sustainable-development approach to strategy and operations."

A BROKEN COMPASS?

If the road ahead is this clear, why are so many companies straying or falling by the wayside? We believe the reason is that the instruments companies use to set their targets, measure their performance, and hand out rewards are faulty. In other words, the markets are full of distortions and perverse incentives. Of the more than 60 specific forms of misdirection that we have identified, the most obvious involve the ways companies allocate capital and the way governments set policy and impose taxes. Merely correcting these defective practices would uncover huge opportunities for profit.

Consider how companies make purchasing decisions. Decisions to buy small items are typically based on their initial cost rather than their full life-cycle cost, a practice that can add up to major wastage. Distribution transformers that supply electricity to buildings and factories, for example, are a minor item at just $320 apiece, and most companies try to save a quick buck by buying the lowest-price models. Yet nearly all the nation's electricity must flow through transformers, and using the cheaper but less efficient models wastes $1 billion a year. Such examples are legion. Equipping standard new office-lighting circuits with fatter wire that reduces electrical resistance could generate after-tax returns of 193% a year. Instead, wire as thin as the National Electrical Code permits is usually selected because it costs less up-front. But the code is meant only to prevent fires from overheated wiring, not to save money. Ironically, an electrician who chooses fatter wire—thereby reducing long-term electricity bills—doesn't get the job. After paying for the extra copper, he's no longer the low bidder.

Some companies do consider more than just the initial price in their purchasing decisions but still don't go far enough. Most of them use a crude payback estimate rather than more accurate metrics like discounted cash flow. A few years ago, the median simple payback these companies were demanding from energy efficiency was 1.9 years. That's equivalent to requiring an after-tax return of around 71% per year—about six times the marginal cost of capital.

Most companies also miss major opportunities by treating their facilities costs as an overhead to be minimized, typically by laying off engineers, rather than as profit center to be optimized—by using those engineers to save resources. Deficient measurement and accounting practices also prevent companies from allocating costs—and waste—with any accuracy. For example, only a few semiconductor plants worldwide regularly and accurately measure how much energy they're using to produce a unit of chilled water or clean air for their clean-room production facilities. That makes it hard for them to improve efficiency. In fact, in an effort to save time, semiconductor makers frequently build new plants as exact copies of previous ones—a design method nicknamed "infectious repetitis."

Many executives pay too little attention to saving resources because they are often a small percentage of total costs (energy costs run to about 2% in most industries). But those resource savings drop straight to the bottom line and so represent a far greater percentage of profits. Many executives also think they already "did" efficiency in the 1970s, when the oil shock forced them to rethink old habits. They're forgetting that with today's far better technologies, it's profitable to start all over again. Malden Mills, the Massachusetts maker of such products as Polartec, was already using "efficient" metal-halide lamps in the mid-1990s. But a recent warehouse retrofit reduced the energy used for lighting by another 93%, improved visibility, and paid for itself in 18 months.

The way people are rewarded often creates perverse incentives. Architects and engineers, for example, are traditionally compensated for what they spend, not for what they save. Even the striking economics of the retrofit design for the Chicago office tower described earlier wasn't incentive enough actually to implement it. The property was controlled by a leasing agent who earned a commission every time she leased space, so she didn't want to wait the few extra months needed to refit the building. Her decision to reject the efficiency-quadrupling renovation proved costly for both her and her client. The building was so uncomfortable and expensive to occupy that it didn't lease, so ultimately the owner had to unload it at a firesale price. Moreover, the new owner will for the next 20 years be deprived of the opportunity to save capital cost.

If corporate practices obscure the benefits of natural capitalism, government policy positively undermines it. In nearly every country on the planet, tax laws penalize what we want more of—jobs and income—while subsidizing what we want less of—resource depletion and pollution. In every state but Oregon, regulated utilities are rewarded for selling more energy, water, and other resources, and penalized for selling less, even if increased production would cost more than improved customer efficiency. In most of America's arid western states, use-it-or-lose-it water laws encourage inefficient water consumption. Additionally, in many towns, inefficient use of land is enforced through outdated regulations, such as guidelines for ultrawide suburban streets recommended by 1950s civil-defense planners to accommodate the heavy equipment needed to clear up rubble after a nuclear attack.

The costs of these perverse incentives are staggering: $300 billion in annual energy wasted in the United States, and $1 trillion already misallocated to unnecessary air-conditioning equipment and the power supplies to run it (about 40% of the nation's peak electric load). Across the entire economy, unneeded expenditures to subsidize, encourage, and try to remedy inefficiency and damage that should not have occurred in the first place probably account for most, if not all, of the GDP growth of the past two decades. Indeed, according to former World Bank economist Herman Daly and his colleague John Cobb (along with many other analysts), Americans are hardly better off than they were in 1980. But if the U.S. government and private industry could redirect the dollars currently earmarked for remedial costs toward reinvestment in natural and human capital, they could bring about a genuine improvement in the nation's welfare. Companies, too, are finding that wasting resources also means wasting money and people. These intertwined forms of waste have equally intertwined solutions. Firing the unproductive tons, gallons, and kilowatt-hours often makes it possible to keep the people, who will have more and better work to do.

RECOGNIZING THE SCARCITY SHIFT

In the end, the real trouble with our economic compass is that it points in exactly the wrong direction. Most businesses are behaving as if people were still scarce and nature still abundant—the conditions that helped to fuel the first Industrial Revolution. At that time, people were relatively scarce compared with the present-day population. The rapid mechanization of the textile industries caused explosive economic growth that created labor shortages in the factory and the field. The Industrial Revolution, responding to those shortages and mechanizing one industry after another, made people a hundred times more productive than they had ever been.

The logic of economizing on the scarcest resource, because it limits progress, remains correct. But the pattern of scarcity is shifting: now people aren't scarce but nature is. This shows up first in industries that depend directly on ecological health. Here, production is increasingly constrained by fish rather than by boats and nets, by forests rather than by chain saws, by fertile topsoil rather than by plows. Moreover, unlike the traditional factors of industrial production—capital and labor—the biological limiting factors cannot be substituted for one other. In the industrial system, we can easily exchange machinery for labor. But no technology or amount of money can substitute for a stable climate and a productive biosphere. Even proper pricing can't replace the priceless.

Natural capitalism addresses those problems by reintegrating ecological with economic goals. Because it is both necessary and profitable, it will subsume traditional industrialism within a new economy and a new paradigm of production, just as industrialism previously subsumed agrarianism. The companies that first make the changes we have described will have a competitive edge. Those that don't make that effort won't be a problem because ultimately they won't be around. In making that choice, as Henry Ford said, "Whether you believe you can, or whether you believe you can't, you're absolutely right."

NOTES

1. Our book, *Natural Capitalism,* provides hundreds of examples of how companies of almost every type and size, often through modest shifts in business logic and practice, have dramatically improved their bottom lines.

2. Nonproprietary details are posted at http://wwwhypercar .com.

3. Summarized in the report "Climate: Making Sense *and* Making Money" at http://www.rsni.org/catalog/climateh.

READING 10.6 THE NEXT INDUSTRIAL REVOLUTION
William McDonough and Michael Braungart

In the spring of 1912 one of the largest moving objects ever created by human beings left Southampton and began gliding toward New York. It was the epitome of its industrial age—a potent representation of technology, prosperity, luxury, and progress. It weighed 66,000 tons. Its steel hull stretched the length of four city blocks. Each of its steam engines was the size of a townhouse. And it was headed for a disastrous encounter with the natural world.

This vessel, of course, was the *Titanic*—a brute of a ship, seemingly impervious to the details of nature. In the minds of the captain, the crew, and many of the passengers, nothing could sink it. One might say that the infrastructure created by the Industrial Revolution of the nineteenth century resembles such a steamship. It is powered by fossil fuels, nuclear reactors, and chemicals. It is pouring waste into the water and smoke into the sky. It is attempting to work by its own rules, contrary to those of the natural world. And although it may seem invincible, its fundamental design flaws presage disaster. Yet many people still believe that with a few minor alterations, this infrastructure can take us safely and prosperously into the future.

During the Industrial Revolution resources seemed inexhaustible and nature was viewed as something to be tamed and civilized. Recently, however, some leading industrialists have begun to realize that traditional ways of doing things may not be sustainable over the long term. "What we thought was boundless has limits," Robert Shapiro, the chairman and chief executive officer of Monsanto, said in a 1997 interview, "and we're beginning to hit them."

The *1992 Earth Summit in Rio de Janeiro,* led by the Canadian businessman Maurice Strong, recognized those limits. Approximately 30,000 people from around the world, including more than a hundred world leaders and representatives of 167 countries, gathered in Rio de Janeiro to respond to troubling symptoms of environmental decline. Although there was sharp disappointment afterward that no binding agreement had been reached at the summit, many industrial participants touted a particular strategy: eco-efficiency. The machines of industry would be refitted with cleaner, faster, quieter engines. Prosperity would remain unobstructed, and economic and organizational structures would remain intact. The hope was that eco-efficiency would transform human industry from a system that takes, makes, and wastes into one that integrates economic, environmental, and ethical concerns. Eco-efficiency is now considered by industries across the globe to be the strategy of choice for change.

What is eco-efficiency? Primarily, the term means "doing more with less"—a precept that has its roots in early industrialization. Henry Ford was adamant about lean and clean operating policies; he saved his company money by recycling and reusing materials, reduced the use of natural resources, minimized packaging, and set new standards with his timesaving assembly line. Ford wrote in 1926, "You must get the most out of the power, out of the material, and out of the time"—a credo that could hang today on the wall of any eco-efficient factory. The linkage of efficiency with sustaining the environment was perhaps most famously articulated in *Our Common Future,* a report published in 1987 by the United Nations' World Commission on Environment and Development. *Our Common Future* warned that if pollution control were not intensified, property and ecosystems would be

threatened, and existence would become unpleasant and even harmful to human health in some cities. "Industries and industrial operations should be encouraged that are more efficient in terms of resource use, that generate less pollution and waste, that are based on the use of renewable rather than non-renewable resources, and that minimize irreversible adverse impacts on human health and the environment," the commission stated in its agenda for change.

The term "eco-efficiency" was promoted five years later, by the *Business Council (now the World Business Council) for Sustainable Development,* a group of forty-eight industrial sponsors including Dow, Du Pont, Con Agra, and Chevron, who brought a business perspective to the Earth Summit. The council presented its call for change in practical terms, focusing on what businesses had to gain from a new ecological awareness rather than on what the environment had to lose if industry continued in current patterns. In *Changing Course,* a report released just before the summit, the group's founder, Stephan Schmidheiny, stressed the importance of eco-efficiency for all companies that aimed to be competitive, sustainable, and successful over the long term. In 1996 Schmidheiny said, "I predict that within a decade it is going to be next to impossible for a business to be competitive without also being 'eco-efficient'—adding more value to a good or service while using fewer resources and releasing less pollution."

As Schmidheiny predicted, eco-efficiency has been working its way into industry with extraordinary success. The corporations committing themselves to it continue to increase in number, and include such big names as Monsanto, 3M, and Johnson & Johnson. Its famous three *R*s—reduce, reuse, recycle—are steadily gaining popularity in the home as well as the workplace. The trend stems in part from eco-efficiency's economic benefits, which can be considerable: 3M, for example, has saved more than $750 million through pollution-prevention projects, and other companies, too, claim to be realizing big savings. Naturally, reducing resource consumption, energy use, emissions, and wastes has implications for the environment as well. When one hears that Du Pont has cut its emissions of airborne cancer-causing chemicals by almost 75 percent since 1987, one can't help feeling more secure. This is another benefit of eco-efficiency: it diminishes guilt and fear. By subscribing to eco-efficiency, people and industries can be less "bad" and less fearful about the future. Or can they?

Eco-efficiency is an outwardly admirable and certainly well-intended concept, but, unfortunately, it is not a strategy for success over the long term, because it does not reach deep enough. It works within the same system that caused the problem in the first place, slowing it down with moral proscriptions and punitive demands. It presents little more than an illusion of change. Relying on eco-efficiency to save the environment will in fact achieve the opposite—it will let industry finish off everything quietly, persistently, and completely.

We are forwarding a reshaping of human industry—what we and the author *Paul Hawken* call the Next Industrial Revolution. Leaders of this movement include many people in diverse fields, among them commerce, politics, the humanities, science, engineering, and education. Especially notable are the businessman Ray Anderson; the philanthropist Teresa Heinz; the Chattanooga city councilman Dave Crockett; the physicist Amory Lovins; the environmental-studies professor David W. Orr; the environmentalists Sarah Severn, Dianne Dillon Ridgley, and Susan Lyons; the environmental product developer Heidi Holt; the ecological designer John Todd; and the writer Nancy Jack Todd. We are focused here on a new way of *designing industrial production*. As an architect and industrial designer and a chemist who have worked with both commercial and ecological systems, we see conflict between industry and the environment as a design problem—a very big design problem.

Any of the basic intentions behind the Industrial Revolution were good ones, which most of us would probably like to see carried out today: to bring more goods and services to larger numbers of people, to raise standards of living, and to give people more choice and opportunity, among others. But there were crucial omissions. Perpetuating the diversity and vitality of forests, rivers, oceans, air, soil, and animals was not part of the agenda.

If someone were to present the Industrial Revolution as a retroactive design assignment, it might sound like this: Design a system of production that

- puts billions of pounds of toxic material into the air, water, and soil every year

- measures prosperity by activity, not legacy

- requires thousands of complex regulations to keep people and natural systems from being poisoned too quickly

- produces materials so dangerous that they will require constant vigilance from future generations

- results in gigantic amounts of waste

- puts valuable materials in holes all over the planet, where they can never be retrieved

- erodes the diversity of biological species and cultural practices

Eco-efficiency instead

- releases *fewer* pounds of toxic material into the air, water, and soil every year

- measures prosperity by *less* activity

- *meets or exceeds* the stipulations of thousands of complex regulations that aim to keep people and natural systems from being poisoned too quickly

- produces *fewer* dangerous materials that will require constant vigilance from future generations

- results in *smaller* amounts of waste

- puts *fewer* valuable materials in holes all over the planet, where they can never be retrieved

- standardizes and homogenizes biological species and cultural practices

Plainly put, eco-efficiency aspires to make the old, destructive system less so. But its goals, however admirable, are fatally limited.

Reduction, reuse, and recycling slow down the rates of contamination and depletion but do not stop these processes. Much recycling, for instance, is what we call "downcycling," because it reduces the quality of a material over time. When plastic other than that found in such products as soda and water bottles is recycled, it is often mixed with different plastics to produce a hybrid of lower quality, which is then molded into something amorphous and cheap, such as park benches or speed bumps. The original high-quality material is not retrieved, and it eventually ends up in landfills or incinerators.

The well-intended, creative use of recycled materials for new products can be misguided. For example, people may feel that they are making an ecologically sound choice by buying and wearing clothing made of fibers from recycled plastic bottles. But the fibers from plastic bottles were not specifically designed to be next to human skin. Blindly adopting superficial "environmental" approaches without fully understanding their effects can be no better than doing nothing.

Recycling is more expensive for communities than it needs to be, partly because traditional recycling tries to force materials into more lifetimes than they were designed for—a complicated and messy conversion, and one that itself expends energy and resources. Very few objects of modern consumption were designed with recycling in mind. If the process is truly to save money and materials, products must be designed from the very beginning to be recycled or even "upcycled"—a term we use to describe the return to industrial systems of materials with improved, rather than degraded, quality.

The reduction of potentially harmful emissions and wastes is another goal of eco-efficiency. But current studies are beginning to raise concern that even tiny amounts of dangerous emissions can have disastrous effects on biological systems over time. This is a particular concern in the case of endocrine disrupters—industrial chemicals in a variety of modern plastics and consumer goods which appear to mimic hormones and connect with receptors in human beings and other organisms. Theo Colborn, Dianne Dumanoski, and John Peterson Myers, the authors of *Our Stolen Future* (1996), a groundbreaking study on certain synthetic chemicals and the environment, assert that "astoundingly small quantities of these hormonally active compounds can wreak all manner of biological havoc, particularly in those exposed in the womb."

On another front, new research on particulates—microscopic particles released during incineration and combustion processes, such as those in power plants and automobiles—shows that they can lodge in and damage the lungs, especially in children and the elderly. A 1995 Harvard study found that as many as 100,000 people die annually as a result of these tiny particles. Although regulations

for smaller particles are in place, implementation does not have to begin until 2005. Real change would be not regulating the release of particles but attempting to eliminate dangerous emissions altogether—by design.

APPLYING NATURE'S CYCLES TO INDUSTRY

"Produce more with less," "Minimize waste," "Reduce," and similar dictates advance the notion of a world of limits—one whose carrying capacity is strained by burgeoning populations and exploding production and consumption. Eco-efficiency tells us to restrict industry and curtail growth—to try to limit the creativity and productiveness of humankind. But the idea that the natural world is inevitably destroyed by human industry, or that excessive demand for goods and services causes environmental ills, is a simplification. Nature—highly industrious, astonishingly productive and creative, even "wasteful"—is not efficient but *effective*.

Consider the cherry tree. It makes thousands of blossoms just so that another tree might germinate, take root, and grow. Who would notice piles of cherry blossoms littering the ground in the spring and think, "How inefficient and wasteful"? The tree's abundance is useful and safe. After falling to the ground, the blossoms return to the soil and become nutrients for the surrounding environment. Every last particle contributes in some way to the health of a thriving ecosystem. "Waste equals food"—the first principle of the Next Industrial Revolution.

The cherry tree is just one example of nature's industry, which operates according to cycles of nutrients and metabolisms. This cyclical system is powered by the sun and constantly adapts to local circumstances. Waste that stays waste does not exist.

Human industry, on the other hand, is severely limited. It follows a one-way, linear, cradle-to-grave manufacturing line in which things are created and eventually discarded, usually in an incinerator or a landfill. Unlike the waste from nature's work, the waste from human industry is not "food" at all. In fact, it is often poison. Thus the two conflicting systems: a pile of cherry blossoms and a heap of toxic junk in a landfill.

But there is an alternative—one that will allow both business and nature to be fecund and productive. This alternative is what we call "eco-effectiveness." Our concept of eco-effectiveness leads to human industry that is regenerative rather than depletive. It involves the design of things that celebrate interdependence with other living systems. From an industrial-design perspective, it means products that work within cradle-to-cradle life cycles rather than cradle-to-grave ones.

WASTE EQUALS FOOD

Ancient nomadic cultures tended to leave organic wastes behind, restoring nutrients to the soil and the surrounding environment. Modern, settled societies simply want to get rid of waste as quickly as possible. The potential nutrients in organic waste are lost when they are disposed of in landfills, where they cannot be used to rebuild soil; depositing synthetic materials and chemicals in natural systems strains the environment. The ability of complex, interdependent natural ecosystems to absorb such foreign material is limited if not nonexistent. Nature cannot do anything with the stuff *by design:* many manufactured products are intended not to break down under natural conditions. If people are to prosper within the natural world, all the products and materials manufactured by industry must after each useful life provide nourishment for something new. Since many of the things people make are not natural, they are not safe "food" for biological systems. Products composed of materials that do not biodegrade should be designed as technical nutrients that continually circulate within closed-loop industrial cycles—the technical metabolism.

In order for these two metabolisms to remain healthy, great care must be taken to avoid cross-contamination. Things that go into the biological metabolism should not contain mutagens, carcinogens, heavy metals, endocrine disrupters, persistent toxic substances, or bio-accumulative substances. Things that go into the technical metabolism should be kept well apart from the biological metabolism.

If the things people make are to be safely channeled into one or the other of these metabolisms, then products can be considered to contain two kinds of materials: *biological nutrients* and *technical nutrients.*

Biological nutrients will be designed to return to the organic cycle—to be literally consumed by microorganisms and other creatures in the soil. Most packaging (which makes up about 50 percent by volume of the solid-waste stream) should be composed of biological nutrients—materials that can be tossed onto the ground or the compost heap to biodegrade. There is no need for shampoo bottles, toothpaste tubes, yogurt cartons, juice containers, and other packaging to last decades (or even centuries) longer than what came inside them.

Technical nutrients will be designed to go back into the technical cycle. Right now anyone can dump an old television into a trash can. But the average television is made of hundreds of chemicals, some of which are toxic. Others are valuable nutrients for industry, which are wasted when the television ends up in a landfill. The reuse of technical nutrients in closed-loop industrial cycles is distinct from traditional recycling, because it allows materials to retain their quality: high-quality plastic computer cases would continually circulate as high-quality computer cases, instead of being downcycled to make soundproof barriers or flowerpots.

Customers would buy the *service* of such products, and when they had finished with the products, or simply wanted to upgrade to a newer version, the manufacturer would take back the old ones, break them down, and use their complex materials in new products.

FIRST FRUITS: A BIOLOGICAL NUTRIENT

[A] few years ago we helped to conceive and create a compostable upholstery fabric—a biological nutrient. We were initially asked by Design Tex to create an aesthetically unique fabric that was also ecologically intelligent—although the client did not quite know at that point what this would mean. The challenge helped to clarify, both for us and for the company we were working with, the difference between superficial responses such as recycling and reduction and the more significant changes required by the Next Industrial Revolution.

For example, when the company first sought to meet our desire for an environmentally safe fabric, it presented what it thought was a wholesome option: cotton, which is natural, combined with PET (polyethylene terephthalate) fibers from recycled beverage bottles. Since the proposed hybrid could be described with two important eco-buzzwords, "natural" and "recycled," it appeared to be environmentally ideal. The materials were readily available, market-tested, durable, and cheap. But when the project team looked carefully at what the manifestations of such a hybrid might be in the long run, we discovered some disturbing facts. When a person sits in an office chair and shifts around, the fabric beneath him or her abrades; tiny particles of it are inhaled or swallowed by the user and other people nearby. PET was not designed to be inhaled. Furthermore, PET would prevent the proposed hybrid from going back into the soil safely, and the cotton would prevent it from re-entering an industrial cycle. The hybrid would still add junk to landfills, and it might also be dangerous.

The team decided to design a fabric so safe that one could literally eat it. The European textile mill chosen to produce the fabric was quite "clean" environmentally, and yet it had an interesting problem: although the mill's director had been diligent about reducing levels of dangerous emissions, government regulators had recently defined the trimmings of his fabric as hazardous waste. We sought a different end for our trimmings: mulch for the local garden club. When removed from the frame after the chair's useful life and tossed onto the ground to mingle with sun, water, and hungry microorganisms, both the fabric and its trimmings would decompose naturally.

The team decided on a mixture of safe, pesticide-free plant and animal fibers for the fabric (ramie and wool) and began working on perhaps the most difficult aspect: the finishes, dyes, and other processing chemicals. If the fabric was to go back into the soil safely, it had to be free of mutagens, carcinogens, heavy metals, endocrine disrupters, persistent toxic substances, and bio-accumulative substances. Sixty chemical companies were approached about joining the project, and all declined, uncomfortable with the idea of exposing their chemistry to the kind of scrutiny necessary. Finally one European company, Ciba-Geigy, agreed to join.

With that company's help the project team considered more than 8,000 chemicals used in the textile industry and eliminated 7,962. The fabric—in

fact, an entire line of fabrics—was created using only thirty-eight chemicals.

The director of the mill told a surprising story after the fabrics were in production. When regulators came by to test the effluent, they thought their instruments were broken. After testing the influent as well, they realized that the equipment was fine—the water coming out of the factory was as clean as the water going in. The manufacturing process itself was filtering the water. The new design not only bypassed the traditional three-R responses to environmental problems but also eliminated the need for regulation.

In our Next Industrial Revolution, regulations can be seen as signals of design failure. They burden industry, by involving government in commerce and by interfering with the marketplace. Manufacturers in countries that are less hindered by regulations . . . produce and sell things for less. If a factory is not emitting dangerous substances and needs no regulation, and can thus compete directly with unregulated factories in other countries, that is good news environmentally, ethically, and economically.

A TECHNICAL NUTRIENT

Someone who has finished with a traditional carpet must pay to have it removed. The energy, effort, and materials that went into it are lost to the manufacturer; the carpet becomes little more than a heap of potentially hazardous petrochemicals that must be toted to a landfill. Meanwhile, raw materials must continually be extracted to make new carpets.

The typical carpet consists of nylon embedded in fiberglass and PVC. After its useful life a manufacturer can only downcycle it—shave off some of the nylon for further use and melt the leftovers. The world's largest commercial carpet company, Interface, is adopting our technical-nutrient concept with a carpet designed for complete recycling. When a customer wants to replace it, the manufacturer simply takes back the technical nutrient—depending on the product, either part or all of the carpet—and returns a carpet in the customer's desired color, style, and texture. The carpet company continues to own the material but leases it and maintains it, providing customers with the *service* of the carpet. Eventually the carpet will wear out like any other, and the manufacturer will reuse its materials at their original level of quality or a higher one.

The advantages of such a system, widely applied to many industrial products, are twofold: no useless and potentially dangerous waste is generated, as it might still be in eco-efficient systems, and billions of dollars' worth of valuable materials are saved and retained by the manufacturer.

SELLING INTELLIGENCE, NOT POISON

Currently, chemical companies warn farmers to be careful with pesticides, and yet the companies benefit when more pesticides are sold. In other words, the companies are unintentionally invested in wastefulness and even in the mishandling of their products, which can result in contamination of the soil, water, and air. Imagine what would happen if a chemical company sold intelligence instead of pesticides—that is, if farmers or agro-businesses paid pesticide manufacturers to protect their crops against loss from pests instead of buying dangerous regulated chemicals to use at their own discretion. It would in effect be buying crop insurance. Farmers would be saying, "I'll pay you to deal with boll weevils, and you do it as intelligently as you can." At the same price per acre, everyone would still profit. The pesticide purveyor would be invested in *not* using pesticide, to avoid wasting materials. Furthermore, since the manufacturer would bear responsibility for the hazardous materials, it would have incentives to come up with less-dangerous ways to get rid of pests. Farmers are not interested in handling dangerous chemicals; they want to grow crops. Chemical companies do not want to contaminate soil, water, and air; they want to make money.

Consider the unintended design legacy of the average shoe. With each step of your shoe the sole releases tiny particles of potentially harmful substances that may contaminate and reduce the vitality of the soil. With the next rain these particles will wash into the plants and soil along the road, adding another burden to the environment.

Shoes could be redesigned so that the sole was a biological nutrient. When it broke down under a pounding foot and interacted with nature, it would nourish the biological metabolism instead of poisoning it. Other parts of the shoe might be designed as technical nutrients, to be returned to industrial cycles. Most shoes—in fact, most products of the current industrial system—are fairly primitive in their relationship to the natural world. With the scientific and technical tools currently available, this need not be the case.

RESPECT DIVERSITY AND USE THE SUN

The leading goal of design in this century has been to achieve universally applicable solutions. In the field of architecture the International Style is a good example. As a result of the widespread adoption of the International Style, architecture has become uniform in many settings. That is, an office building can look and work the same anywhere. Materials such as steel, cement, and glass can be transported all over the world, eliminating dependence on a region's particular energy and material flows. With more energy forced into the heating and cooling system, the same building can operate similarly in vastly different settings.

The second principle of the Next Industrial Revolution is "Respect diversity." Designs will respect the regional, cultural, and material uniqueness of a place. Wastes and emissions will regenerate rather than deplete, and design will be flexible, to allow for changes in the needs of people and communities. For example, office buildings will be convertible into apartments, instead of ending up as rubble in a construction landfill when the market changes.

The third principle of the Next Industrial Revolution is "Use solar energy." Human systems now rely on fossil fuels and petrochemicals, and on incineration processes that often have destructive side effects. Today even the most advanced building or factory in the world is still a kind of steamship, polluting, contaminating, and depleting the surrounding environment, and relying on scarce amounts of natural light and fresh air. People are essentially working in the dark, and they are often breathing unhealthful air. Imagine, instead, a building as a kind of tree. It would purify air, accrue solar income, produce more energy than it consumes, create shade and habitat, enrich soil, and change with the seasons. Oberlin College is currently working on a building that is a good start: it is designed to make more energy than it needs to operate and to purify its own wastewater.

EQUITY, ECONOMY, ECOLOGY

The Next Industrial Revolution incorporates positive intentions across a wide spectrum of human concerns. People within the sustainability movement have found that three categories are helpful in articulating these concerns: equity, economy, and ecology.

Equity refers to social justice. Does a design depreciate or enrich people and communities? Shoe companies have been blamed for exposing workers in factories overseas to chemicals in amounts that exceed safe limits. Eco-efficiency would [not just] reduce those amounts to meet certain efficiency . . . [or] reduce those amounts to meet certain standards; eco-effectiveness would not use a potentially dangerous chemical in the first place. What an advance for humankind it would be if no factory worker anywhere worked in dangerous or inhumane conditions.

Economy refers to market viability. Does a product reflect the needs of producers and consumers for affordable products? Safe, intelligent designs should be affordable by and accessible to a wide range of customers, and profitable to the company that makes them, because commerce is the engine of change.

Ecology, of course, refers to environmental intelligence. Is a material a biological nutrient or a technical nutrient? Does it meet nature's design criteria: Waste equals food, Respect diversity, and Use solar energy?

The Next Industrial Revolution can be framed as the following assignment: Design an industrial system for the next century that

- introduces no hazardous materials into the air, water, or soil

- measures prosperity by how much natural capital we can accrue in productive ways

- measures productivity by how many people are gainfully and meaningfully employed

- measures progress by how many buildings have no smokestacks or dangerous effluents

- does not require regulations whose purpose is to stop us from killing ourselves too quickly

- produces nothing that will require future generations to maintain vigilance

- celebrates the abundance of biological and cultural diversity and solar income

Albert Einstein wrote, "The world will not evolve past its current state of crisis by using the same thinking that created the situation." Many people believe that new industrial revolutions are already taking place, with the rise of cybertechnology, biotechnology, and nanotechnology. It is true that these are powerful tools for change. But they are only tools—hyperefficient engines for the steamship of the first Industrial Revolution. Similarly, eco-efficiency is a valuable and laudable tool, and a prelude to what should come next. But it, too, fails to move us beyond the first revolution. It is time for designs that are creative, abundant, prosperous, and intelligent from the start. The model for the Next Industrial Revolution may well have been right in front of us the whole time: a tree.

Decision Scenario A
GLOBAL WARMING

The 1990s were the warmest decade on record. Since scientific data was first available in the late 1800s, the ten warmest years on record were, in descending order, 1998, 2002, 2003, 2001, 1997, 1995, 1990, 1999, 1991, 2000. To some observers, this is evidence of global warming brought about by the greenhouse effect.

The greenhouse effect occurs when certain atmospheric gases trap the sun's heat within the atmosphere, causing temperatures to rise. These gases, primarily carbon dioxide, ozone, water vapor, methane, nitrous oxide, and chloroflourocarbons, allow solar energy into the earth's atmosphere and prevent the resultant heat from escaping back into space. Functioning much as glass panes function in a greenhouse, this greenhouse effect is the prevailing scientific explanation of the earth's temperature.

Scientific measurements suggest an increasing amount of greenhouse gases have been building up within the atmosphere in recent decades. An increase in carbon dioxide, due largely to human activity of burning fossil fuels, has been particularly apparent. While the long-range results of this buildup of greenhouse gases is unknown, many scientists argue that global warming and significant atmospheric changes may already be occurring.

- Two major industries, electric power generation and the automotive industry, account for a large portion of fossil fuel use worldwide. What responsibilities, if any, do these industries have to decrease the emission of greenhouse gases? What responsibilities, if any, do they have for development of alternative forms of energy and transportation?

- Industrialized countries are responsible for much of the past increase in atmospheric greenhouse gases. Developing countries, with growing economies and exploding populations, are likely to be responsible for the greatest future increase of greenhouse gases. What are the relative responsibilities of businesses in developed and developing economies?

- Global warming would be an example of what economists call an "externality." Who should bear the costs associated with products that contribute to global warming?

Decision Scenario B
BOOMER V. ATLANTIC CEMENT CO.

In 1962 the Atlantic Cement Company began operating a cement plant outside of Albany, New York. Over 300 residents of the area were employed at the plant, and by 1970 Atlantic had invested over $45 million in it. People living near the plant, including the Boomer family, filed suit against the company, claiming that the dust and vibrations caused by the plant were damaging both their health and property. These neighbors sought an injunction to require the plant to stop the dust and vibrations. Unfortunately, there was no technology that would allow the plant to continue operating without the dust and vibrations.

The courts decided that the Boomers and their neighbors were indeed suffering harms caused by the cement plant. It is normal in such cases for a court to issue an injunction. However, in this case the court reasoned that the costs that would be involved in closing down the plant far outweighed the costs of the harms being done to the neighbors. Accordingly, the court decided that Atlantic should pay the neighbors $185,000 for damages already done, and ongoing monthly payments to compensate them for the harms that they would continue to suffer. This amount, $535 per month, was calculated to be a fair market value for what they could receive if they were to rent their property. In calculating this amount, the court presumably figured that the neighbors would thus be free to leave the area and therefore the nuisance without suffering the economic loss of their property.

The case was appealed to New York State's highest court. This court agreed that the neighbors had established the existence of a nuisance and that it was normal in such cases to issue an injunction. The majority also agreed with the lower court that the disparity between the costs of closing the plant and the costs of the nuisances was too great to justify granting the injunction. However, instead of accepting the ongoing payment plan, this high court decided that Atlantic should pay only permanent damages for the total present and future economic loss to the neighbors' property.

In a dissenting opinion, one judge argued that the potential harms to the Boomers' health should have been factored into the calculation of costs involved. Further, he also argued that harms to the

general public were being ignored in these decisions. In effect, the court was allowing a company to harm its neighbors as long as it paid a fee to do so.

- Is this a case in which individual rights were overridden by utilitarian calculation of costs and benefits?

- Should the courts have treated this case as a simple dispute between private parties, or was there a larger public concern at stake?

- How much harm (economic and otherwise) would have to be done to the Boomers to justify closing the plant?

Decision Scenario C

THE DETROIT PROJECT

"The Detroit Project" is a self-described "grassroots campaign to prod Detroit automakers to build cars that will get Americans to work in the morning without sending us to war in the afternoon—cars that will end our dependence on foreign oil." Founded by author, columnist, and one-time candidate for California governor Arianna Huffington, the Detroit Project advocates for fuel-efficient cars and condemns automakers for manufacturing and promoting gas-guzzling SUVs.

The Detroit Project is best-known for producing television ads that mimic regular car commercials but criticize automakers, SUVs, and the consumers who buy them. The first two 30-second ads connected SUVs and low-mileage cars with support for terrorism. One ad parody, called "Talking Heads," features a series of faces looking into the camera with the following script:

> I helped hijack an airplane. I helped blow up a nightclub. So what if it gets 11 miles to the gallon? I gave money to a terrorist training camp in a foreign country. It makes me feel safe. I helped our enemies develop weapons of mass destruction. What if I need to go off-road? Everyone has one. I helped teach kids around the world to hate America. I like to sit up high. I sent our soldiers off to war. Everyone has one. My life, my SUV. I don't even know how many miles it gets to the gallon. What is your SUV

doing to our national security? Detroit, America needs hybrid cars now.

A second ad titled, simply, "George," connects a consumer filling up his SUV at the gas pump with terrorists. Its script simply states:

> This is George. This is the gas that George bought for his SUV. This is the oil company executive that sold the gas that George bought for his SUV. These are the countries where the executive bought the oil that made the gas that George bought for his SUV. And these are the terrorists who get money from those countries every time George fills up his SUV. Oil money supports some terrible things. What kind of mileage does your SUV get?

A third ad features what appears to be an SUV covered and disguised in the way that new car models often are. It chides automakers for not building a fuel efficient and environmentally friendly car:

> It is the first car built for the road and the world around it. It can take America to work in the morning without sending it to war in the afternoon. With a sophisticated braking system that stops our dependence on foreign oil, it gets 40 miles to every gallon with thousands of dollars saved at the pump. The only problem is Detroit won't build it."

- Before 1990, the SUV essentially did not exist. How do you think initial consumer demand for this product came about? How would the initial consumer demand for hybrid and fuel-cell automobiles come about? To what degree is marketing responsible for consumer demand?

- Is it fair to criticize automakers for selling SUVs?

- Is it fair to suggest that SUV owners and manufacturers are supporting terrorism?

- If the technology exists for more fuel-efficient cars and trucks, why are they not being built?

- Are there any government policies that subsidize SUVs? Should there be government policies to subsidize fuel-efficient cars?

Decision Scenario D
PACIFIC LUMBER

The 1980s witnessed a tremendous number of corporate takeovers financed largely by debt in the form of "junk bonds." Such "leveraged buy-outs" were driven by the possibility of enormous profits over short periods of time. Takeover specialists believed that they could either run the business more efficiently than present managers or, more commonly, that they could break up the existing company and sell it for large profits. "Junk bonds" refers to the risky loans that investors made to finance these takeovers. To balance the risk, these bonds promised high rates of return on investment. Since most of the purchase price for a takeover was financed by such high-interest loans, the new management (typically financial specialists with no experience in the particular industry involved) was under immediate pressure to generate substantial income to begin paying off the debt.

One such takeover target was Pacific Lumber Company, based in Humboldt County in northern California. Pacific Lumber was a publicly traded company run by the same family for almost one hundred years. The management philosophy of Pacific Lumber seemed to epitomize ethically responsible management. The company had a long record of satisfactorily meeting or exceeding the needs of many stakeholders: workers, shareholders, the local community, and the forests that it harvested. Pacific Lumber paid its employees well in good times, supported them financially in bad times, guaranteed jobs for family members, and generously supported scholarships for employee children and employee pension funds. Despite all of this, Pacific Lumber provided a steady profit picture and steady rate of return for investors and was debt-free. Throughout its history, the company harvested

little more than 2% of its trees annually, about equal to the annual growth rate of the trees. Unfortunately, perhaps Pacific Lumber managed its assets too responsibly.

Since the company was debt-free and possessed so many resources that it was not using to the maximum (for example, the other 98% of its forests), it made an inviting takeover target to outside financiers. In 1986, Charles Hurwitz and his company Maxxam, Inc., orchestrated a leveraged buyout of Pacific Lumber. Almost $800 million of the nearly $900 million purchase price was financed by high-interest junk bonds managed by Drexel Burnham Lambert, the home of the infamous junk-bond specialist and corporate raider Michael Milken.

The results of the takeover were predictable. The new owners increased the rate of timber harvest to help pay off their huge debt. Pacific Lumber was split into three separate concerns, and much of its debt was transferred to these new companies and refinanced with lower-interest loans, secured with the forest lands as collateral. Among these lands were thousands of acres of 100-year-old virgin redwood trees. The formerly overfunded pension plan was terminated. Some of this money was used to repay debt, and the rest was used to replace the pension fund with annuities purchased from an insurance company that Hurwitz owned. Employment in the area increased slightly as a result of the increased logging. From all appearances, the takeover was successful on economic grounds because virtually all resources were being used more efficiently after the takeover.

Hurwitz had been involved in numerous other controversial business deals. At one time he owned 24% of United Savings Association of Texas, a savings and loan company that was among the many that failed in recent years. This failure was traced to purchases of Drexel junk bonds that were also connected with Michael Milken. As a result of this collapse, taxpayers lost $1.6 billion and the Federal Deposit Insurance Corporation had a claim for over $500 million against United Savings' parent company, the United Financial Group. In light of this, some defenders of the old-growth forests now threatened by Pacific Lumber's increased logging have proposed a "debt-for-nature" swap. This proposal, supported by some in Congress and in the California state legislature, would forgive some of the debt owed to the government in exchange for thousands of acres of old-growth Pacific forests.

- Is the efficient and short-term use of resources always the ethically most responsible use? Were

Pacific Lumber's previous owners fulfilling their responsibility to shareholders when they did not maximize profits?

- Do 2000-year-old sequoia trees possess a value beyond the economic value that they could bring as timber? How would you explain and defend your answer?

- Assuming that increased harvesting of timber proves economically beneficial to an entire region, do people outside the region deserve "standing" in debates about resource use?

- Should the government pursue the debt-for-nature swap? Is the company holding nature hostage to pay for its own financial mismanagement?

Decision Scenario E
WALT DISNEY V. THE SIERRA CLUB

Mineral King Valley is an area of great natural beauty in the Sierra Nevada Mountains in California, adjacent to Sequoia National Park. It had been a part of that park since 1926 and had been left undeveloped as a wilderness area. Beginning in the late 1940s, the U.S. Forest Service began to consider plans for developing Mineral King as a recreational site. During the 1960s the Forest Service accepted bids from private developers, including Walt Disney Enterprises, to create a complex of motels, restaurants, swimming pools, ski slopes, and other facilities that would accommodate up to fourteen thousand visitors daily.

Representatives of the Sierra Club objected to the plans. They favored maintaining Mineral King as an undeveloped wilderness area. Failing in its earlier efforts to convince the Forest Service to stop development, the Sierra Club filed suit in federal court seeking an injunction to prevent the commercial development of Mineral King Valley.

This case raises many of the most significant ethical issues concerning business, economics, and the environment. Consider first the thinking of the Forest Service. As public servants in a democratic society, the Forest Service sought a decision that

would do the most good for society. But how to decide this? How does one measure what the public most wants when representatives of various public interests (the Sierra Club, Walt Disney) make conflicting demands? One very common answer, the answer suggested by market economics and the one presumably adopted by the Forest Service, is to determine what the public wants by looking to see what the public is willing to pay for. In effect, this is what the Forest Service did when it began accepting bids from private developers.

Walt Disney Enterprises was able to bid most for the right to develop this land because they believed (as did the financial institutions who would be loaning them the money) that they would be able to pay this price and still earn enough from this project to repay their loans and make a profit. They would be capable of doing all this, of course, because many people would be willing to pay large sums of money to visit a Disney ski resort high up in the picturesque Sierra Nevadas.

The Sierra Club was unable to compete with Disney in the bidding (they did not take part in the bidding but, presumably, could have). Although the Sierra Club does represent the interests of many citizens, apparently these people are unwilling to pay as much as Disney, either because they value wilderness less or because there are so few of them. Nor could the Sierra Club raise financing for their purchase as did Disney since there is little reason to believe that they could earn enough from their use of Mineral King to repay the loan. Again, the American people seem willing to pay significantly more for a ski resort than for the opportunity to explore an undeveloped mountain valley.

Over time, the demand for undeveloped wilderness areas will increase as they are turned into ski resorts to meet this demand. As the supply of wilderness areas decrease, the demand increases and the price that people are willing to pay rises. As the supply of ski resorts increases, the demand will decrease and the price will come down. Eventually, the market will reach a point of equilibrium between ski resorts and wilderness areas, and the American people will get exactly as much of each as they demand. Thus, in one view, the Forest Service fulfilled its responsibilities when it awarded Mineral King Valley to the highest bidder. In effect, the Forest Service let the American people decide for themselves what they most wanted to do with their own land.

A second major issue arising out of this case concerns legal "standing." "Standing to sue" is the first legal requirement that an individual must meet in order to be recognized by a court. Standing establishes the right of the individual to seek legal relief by demonstrating that this person has some actual interest at stake. In many environmental cases, standing can be established straightforwardly. A person who lives downstream from a factory that is discharging toxic wastes into a waterway can establish standing by showing that she is being harmed by that discharge. However, in cases involving conservation of natural resources, standing is less clear.

In the Mineral King Valley case, the Sierra Club had to establish two facts to demonstrate standing: (a) that some legally recognized injury would occur unless the injunction was issued; (b) that the Sierra Club would be the victim of that injury. In this case, the majority of the Supreme Court agreed that destruction of the aesthetic and ecological well-being of the valley was, like an economic harm, deserving of legal recognition as an "injury" requiring redress. Thus, the Court seemed to place aesthetic and ecological harms on a par with economic harms. However, the majority concluded that the Sierra Club failed to prove that its members were the victims of that harm.

In a dissenting opinion, Justice William O. Douglas argued that the legal concept of "standing" was too narrow. Douglas believed that the courts should allow natural objects themselves to have legal standing. On this view, the Sierra Club would be acting, not on behalf of its members, but on behalf of the valleys, meadows, rivers, trees, and even the clean air that would be harmed by development. In speaking of the valley, Douglas claimed that "those who hike it, fish it, hunt it, camp in it, frequent it, or visit it merely to sit in solitude and wonderment are legitimate spokesmen for it."

This case inspired law professor Christopher Stone to develop these ideas in his book *Should Trees Have Standing?* In this book, Stone offers a reasoned defense of the view that natural things such as trees, mountains, and ecosystems should be granted legal standing.

In light of increasing public pressure and increasing costs, Disney Enterprises withdrew their plan to develop Mineral King Valley.

- Did the Forest Service reasonably represent the interests of the American people by looking to the market to determine the appropriate use of Mineral King Valley?

- If aesthetic and ecological values are to be given standing, how are they to be measured or objectively determined?

- Should trees and other natural objects have legal standing? Should they have moral standing? If a corporation is a legal person, why not rivers?

- If Disney succeeded in developing Mineral King into a ski resort, would you be inclined to visit? If the property remained undeveloped, would you visit? Which would you be willing to pay more for? Is willingness to pay an accurate measure of your values?

- Why assume that environmental groups like the Sierra Club should represent the interests of natural objects? Might not a lumber company or a carpenters' union claim that their interest in managing the forests and harvesting trees should give them standing? Who speaks for the trees?

11

꘏

Affirmative Action
and Diversity

INTRODUCTION

Until the 1970s, white males made up most of the U.S. work force. By 1980, women made up 43 percent of the work force. African American males 10 percent and Hispanic males somewhat under 10 percent.★ Most recent growth in the U.S. work force has come from women, people of color, and new immigrants. By 2050, predictions are that the overall "minority" population will surpass the numbers of the nonHispanic white population. There can be no denial that the U.S. work force will continue to undergo significant change as the 21st century progresses. Workers today look differently, think differently, and have different interests than the workers of just 20 years ago. Workers of tomorrow will be an even more diverse lot than the workers of today.

Yet, when looking at positions of power, prestige, and wealth today, we continue to see a population that is overwhelmingly white and male. Many explanations are possible for this fact. The choices that women made concerning work and family, the social expectations placed on women, and the size of the nonwhite population can go a long way toward explaining the demographics of the work force of earlier decades. But these explanations only go so far. Unjust, although sometimes legally sanctioned, discrimination against women and African

---

★These statistics are from *Handbook of Labor Statistics,* Bulletin 2340 (Washington, D.C.: U.S. Dept. of Labor, Aug. 1989), and William Johnston and Arnold Packer, *Workforce 2000* (Indianapolis: Hudson Institute, 1987).

Americans explains much of their absence from the workplace. It must surely also explain their continued absence from positions of power, prestige, and wealth.

"Discrimination" has several meanings. In one sense it refers to attitudes of hatred of, superiority to, and prejudice against people who are seen as different. Thus, identifying someone as a sexist suggests that he dislikes women, believes that they are inferior to men, and so on. We might call this *attitudinal* discrimination. In another sense, discrimination refers to how people are treated, or how society is arranged. What we might call *behavioral* discrimination refers to the fact that people are treated as inferior because they are different. Thus, we might speak of sexist hiring policies that deny women equal treatment in job opportunities.

It is important to see that these two types of discrimination are independent. One could have sexist attitudes, but not allow these attitudes to affect one's behavior toward women. One could also be a part of a system that treats women as inferior without oneself having conscious sexist beliefs.

While ethics would condemn both versions of discrimination, public policy and the law are ill-suited to counter attitudinal discrimination. Even if it were possible to change people's attitudes and beliefs, this would be undesirable in a democratic society that values freedom of thought and expression. But public policy can, and should, address discrimination in how people are treated. Here, both justice and the law are committed to equal treatment.

PUBLIC POLICY
TO COUNTER DISCRIMINATION

We can see public policy aimed at countering discrimination as developing through three stages: equal treatment, affirmative action, and preferential treatment. As the first and perhaps most obvious step to counter discrimination, *equal treatment* policies guarantee legal access to social goods like jobs, promotions, and admissions to schools. Thus, it was in the name of equal treatment that the United States ended slavery and segregation, and granted women the right to vote. In effect, equal treatment amounts to a policy of passive nondiscrimination.

But typically the promise not to discriminate does little to change the imbalance in the workplace. People who have historically been disenfranchised might lack the experience, knowledge, or even the personal contacts that are often necessary in finding jobs. Both women and minorities might find the work environment unsupportive or even hostile once they get a job. We will reserve the term *affirmative action* for those programs that go beyond a passive acceptance of equal opportunity for all those who just happen to apply. Thus, affirmative action policies might actively recruit applicants from previously disadvantaged groups. Or they might establish programs or minority affairs offices to help support new hires. Such legal mandates as wheelchair accessible ramps and handicapped parking are affirmative action policies aimed at providing equal opportunity to the disabled. These programs and policies are affirmative action in the sense that they provide active, positive support for members of previously disadvantaged groups, and they do not provide the same support to others.

Preferential treatment policies, in contrast, extend to members of disadvantaged groups a different sort of consideration than that extended to others. Typically, preferential policies will actively prefer women or members of minority groups in hiring or promotion decisions.

In general, affirmative action policies do not raise serious ethical questions. Few object to a company policy aimed at recruiting women or African Americans, for example. The added "benefit" does not come at the expense of anyone else. When actual preference is given in hiring or promotion decisions, however, more significant ethical issues are raised. In particular, such issues are raised when an identifiable individual—the person who would have been hired or promoted were it not for the preference—is harmed by preferential decisions. Before considering the arguments for and against preferential treatment, it will be helpful to review different types of preferential treatment.

When a policy actually "prefers" members of disadvantaged groups over, typically, young white males, that policy effectively treats the characteristic of sex, race, or ethnic background as a qualification for the job. Thus, we can envision three types of preferential policies:

- Two equally qualified people apply for a job; person A is a member of a disadvantaged group and person B is not, so prefer A.

- Person A is a member of a disadvantaged group and is qualified for the job, so hire A (even if person B, who is not a member of that group, is more qualified).

- Person A is a member of a disadvantaged group, so hire A (regardless of other qualifications).

It is worth noting that the first policy is not significantly different from affirmative action. In the case of affirmative action, there is still some person, B, who is qualified and would have been hired had not the company actively gone out and recruited person A. But B has little room for complaint if person A is more qualified. This would typically be the goal under affirmative action policies. But suppose person A is not more qualified than B, but simply equally qualified. At this point the company has only three options: make the hiring decision on some random basis (flip a coin?); hire person B and help perpetuate discriminatory hiring practices (once again, the member of the disadvantaged group receives an undeserved disadvantage in the workplace); or hire person A and at least take one step towards ending discriminatory practices. Of course, person B is likely to complain at this point. But what legitimate claim can he make? He cannot claim some "right" to the job because any claim he can make can be made with equal strength by person A. At best he can claim that he was denied an equal opportunity to the job; the company should have flipped a coin. However, since A and B are otherwise equally qualified, and since A has, but B lacks, a characteristic that can be seen as relevant for helping the employer accomplish some goal (namely, being a woman, or being a member of another disadvantaged group), A can be judged as more qualified in virtue of this very characteristic. Thus, it can be argued that being a woman, or being an African American, in a society that has systematically denied benefits like jobs and income to women and African Americans, is an additional qualification for a position.

Of course, hiring decisions are seldom this clear. It is difficult to imagine a situation in which we would say that two people are exactly "equal" in qualifications. In actual cases the situation will more likely resemble mere affirmative action (if person A is more qualified than B), or the second or third type of preferential policy described earlier. Unfortunately, these two policies do raise serious ethical questions. If person B is more qualified than person A, yet A is hired instead of B, then it would appear that B is being denied something he otherwise would have deserved. Whether B did suffer some ethically relevant harm, and if so whether this harm was overridden by some greater good, is at the center of the ethical controversy over preferential treatment.

Arguments For and Against

The arguments for and against preferential treatment fall into four broad types: critical arguments based on considerations of justice, critical arguments based on utilitarian calculation, supporting arguments based on justice, or supporting arguments based on utilitarian calculations.

To many observers the crucial questions focus on considerations of justice. All agree that there are some utilitarian considerations against preferential treatment: Some efficiency may be lost when the most qualified is not hired, anger and resentment can be created among white males, self-doubt can be created among women and minorities. There are also utilitarian considerations in support of preferential policies: successful role models are provided for younger women and minorities, diverse work forces can bring new and beneficial perspectives to the firm, and so forth. However, if it turns out that preferential policies are unjust, then these beneficial consequences must yield to the demands of justice. If preferential policies turn out to be a requirement of justice, then likewise the detrimental consequences must yield.

Objections to preferential policies based on considerations of justice often claim that they violate the rights of those who are not preferred (typically, a young white male). Some argue that preferential treatment violates the right of equal treatment and amounts to nothing other than "reverse discrimination." Others argue that preferential policies violate the rights of the most qualified candidates by giving jobs and promotions based on something other than desert. This position argues that a just society is a meritocracy in which benefits are distributed according to merit and qualifications.

Justice arguments in support of preferential treatment are often grouped as either forward-looking justifications or backward-looking justifications. Forward-looking justifications claim that preferential policies are necessary to bring us to a just society, where income, jobs, power, and prestige are no longer unjustly distributed along racial or sexual lines. Backward-looking justifications see preferential treatment as needed to compensate victims of past injustice.

This compensatory argument is presented and critiqued in our first reading by Robert Fullinwider. Fullinwider claims that compensation fails to provide an ethical justification of preferential treatment because it violates the rights of white males. Fullinwider appeals to the right of equal consideration for his ultimate defense.

In our second reading Richard Wasserstrom offers a critique of the merit objection to preferential treatment. Wasserstrom claims that our society is not a meritocracy and that there are good reasons for not being one. He goes on to offer a forward-looking defense of preferential treatment.

HIRING FOR DIVERSITY

These arguments about the morality of affirmative action and preferential hiring have recently morphed into discussions about the importance of diversity for the 21st century workplace. While the issue of preference still energizes many in the public sphere and still dominates the national newscasts, less noticed have been the innumerable corporate initiatives meant to achieve diversity. The public debate on affirmative action has typically focused on the moral and legal rights of the parties involved: Do minorities have a right to preferential treatment based on the long history of discrimination? Are the rights of white males denied when schools or employers give preference to women and minorities? But these moral questions are not the forces driving current corporate attention to diversity. That is more a function of corporate attempts to assure a strong defense against discrimination lawsuits and, more importantly, to position the corporation in the intense competition for quality employees. Some law firms, for instance, have recognized the need to be more sensitive in their employment practices to the needs of women (though many female lawyers will attest that the changes are excruciatingly slow). Firms recognize this when they see competitors having difficulty attracting highly qualified law school graduates because they have acquired reputations as unfriendly places for women to work. When women comprise nearly half of all law school graduates, and some of the most qualified of those, law firms have a self-interested reason to respond to the shifting demands of a new work force. What is true of law firms in this regard is increasingly true of businesses in general. The changing demographics of the labor supply gradually are forcing employers to adjust their workplaces in hopes of appearing more congenial to women and minorities. These are not merely vague impressions. Academic studies are documenting the impact of perceived corporate diversity on the ability to recruit.

However, while the motivations for corporate diversity initiatives may be different from those that drove the earlier push for affirmative action, some of the same ethical questions are inescapable. That is because corporate diversity initiatives go well beyond training on how to behave in a more diverse environment. They include much more than directions about what language is appropriate for the workplace. Because the current composition of the work force at a company has an impact on whom it can successfully recruit, many corporate diversity initiatives include policies for assuring that hiring decisions produce a group of employees that will be an asset in recruiting and retaining talented women and minorities. Attention to demographic trends may mean that hiring decisions, at least in the medium and short run, will involve racial, ethnic, and gender considerations in addition to simple assessments of an individual's level of qualifications. Though the rationale is different, the ethical issues thus reappear. Is it acceptable to give preference to a woman or a minority even if the reason for doing so is not a broader concern for social equity but merely a concern for future corporate effectiveness? Is it the case that this rationale is acceptable while the older and broader social rationales for preferential hiring are suspect? If you believe so, you must articulate why that is the case. (Consider also the questions raised by Decision Scenario B: "Preferential Treatment for Men.")

The final reading of this chapter presents a vivid defense of diversity hiring. It is the *amicus curiae* (friend of the court) brief offered to the Supreme Court by General Motors in support of the University of Michigan's admissions policies. It may be surprising to see the extent to which a major American employer has adopted the rationale for a policy that awards preference based on race, gender, or ethnicity. What arguments might be used against this kind of rationale for private sector programs of preference? Do the traditional objections to preferential hiring (harmful social consequences and violations of other applicants' rights) have force here as well?

One thing is clear about affirmative action, preferential hiring, and diversity. They will continue to be the subject of intense and emotional debate in the coming years. The close votes of the Supreme Court and the strong sense of injustice expressed by both sides guarantee that the debates will continue. You should use the readings and cases of this chapter to help you move beyond the emotion of the debate to critical, reasoned judgments.

CASE STUDY The University of Michigan Cases

In July 2003, the United States Supreme Court issued its most significant affirmative action rulings in a decade. Although the cases dealt with a public sector educational institution, they almost certainly will have repercussions for private sector businesses. The cases involved two white female students who sued the University of Michigan, charging that admissions policies for two of its schools were both unconstitutional violations of the 14th Amendment's guarantee of equal protection of the law and illegal deviations from the Civil Rights Act's prohibition on racial discrimination in publicly funded programs.

Barbara Grutter had applied for admission into the highly selective University of Michigan Law School. Michigan received more than 3500 applications for seats in a class of 350 students. Grutter

was a Michigan resident who had a 3.8 undergraduate GPA and a 161 on the Law School Admissions Test (approximately an 80th percentile ranking). She was rejected. However, minority applicants whose numerical GPA/LSAT profiles were lower than Grutter's were admitted. The law school claimed it used an admissions policy that evaluated each application in light of a number of factors. Those included, beyond the GPA and LSAT score, letters of recommendation, a candidate's personal statement, and other information the candidate may provide. While it placed a substantial emphasis on the LSAT score, it admitted that it also used "soft variables," such as the enthusiasm of recommenders, the quality of the applicant's undergraduate school, the difficulty of the undergraduate course selection, and the applicant's ability to contribute to the social and intellectual aspects of the law school. It was this last item that was the center of Grutter's complaint, for the university openly admitted that it considered an applicant's race in its attempt to assure that the law school class contained a critical mass of minority students. The law school's assertion was that such a critical mass is an important element that contributes to the intellectual and legal development of its students.

In its past affirmative action decisions, the Court had established a precedent that any governmental use of race must be subject to "strict scrutiny." That standard required that if Michigan's law school admissions policy was to pass constitutional muster, it must serve a compelling state interest and must be narrowly tailored to satisfy that interest. The Court in the Grutter case accepted that the admissions goal of a diverse class with a critical mass of minority students did qualify as a compelling state interest. Past decisions (see the description of the *Croson* and *Adarand* cases in Decision Scenario D) had apparently limited governmental bodies to the goal of remedying the effects of past discrimination. However, in the Grutter decision, the Court asserted that compelling state interests are not limited to the backward-looking attempt to remedy past injustices. It accepted as constitutionally legitimate the more prospective goal of educating a class capable of working effectively in an increasingly diverse society. In doing so, it accepted the argument of U.S. military officers, General Motors Corporation, and others who filed *amicus curiae* (friend of the court) briefs urging the Court to acknowledge the necessity of leaders who have had educational experiences that prepare them for the challenges of leadership in contemporary America. It also affirmed the position of Justice Lewis Powell, who wrote in his widely cited opinion in the *Bakke* case 25 years earlier that the "nation's future depends on leaders trained through wide exposure to the ideas and mores of students as diverse as this Nation."

Though the Court accepted diversity as a compelling state interest, it still had to approve the law school's means for achieving that diversity. A majority of five justices were convinced by the law school's description of its admission practices. They accepted that the process was narrowly tailored to achieve its objectives in that it had considered race-neutral approaches (deciding on the basis of others' experience that such approaches would fail to produce sufficient diversity), that its policies were flexible and allowed consideration of each individual applicant, that it sometimes admitted nonminority candidates with grades and LSAT scores less than

some minorities who were rejected, and that it monitors its admissions experience in order to determine whether active measures are needed to assure a diverse class. Four justices, however, disagreed. They were unconvinced that the program was narrowly tailored, and they pointed to the fact that there was remarkable consistency over time in both the percentage of admitted and enrolled minority students. This, they suggested, indicated that the university's description of the process was merely a clever cover story for the use of an outright rigid quota system.

In the other Michigan case, Jennifer Gratz sued because she was denied admission into the undergraduate College of Literature, Science, and Arts. The undergraduate college used a different system of admission than did the law school. The undergraduate college relied on a point system where applicants could accumulate a maximum of 150 points. Applicants with more than 100 points were almost always admitted. Those between 90 and 99 were in an admit or postpone category; those between 75 and 89, in a delay category; those below 74 in a delay or reject category. Academic background accounted for up to 110 points while 40 points were assigned for nonacademic factors. For example, being a Michigan resident counted for 10 points, children of alumni received 4 points, notable personal achievement could count for 5 points, and 20 points were available for applicants who were members of an underrepresented minority group, had attended a predominantly minority high school, or were athletic recruits. Gratz complained that the award of 20 points for minority status was a violation of both the 14th Amendment and the Civil Rights Act.

The Court, having just approved the law school policy, could not reject the undergraduate college policy on grounds that diversity was not a compelling state interest. However, five justices did find that the undergraduate admissions policy failed the "narrowly tailored" test. They held that the award of 20 points virtually guaranteed the admission of minorities who had the minimal acceptable academic qualifications. It thus smacked of a constitutionally unacceptable quota that was unable to provide the kind of individualized assessment that had allowed the law school admissions process to survive the strict scrutiny review. The Court struck down the undergraduate admissions policy.

While these two cases do not immediately involve private-sector corporate affirmative action plans, they nonetheless contain significant implications for the business world. First, the standard of constitutional review is much stricter for governmental racial classification. The "strict scrutiny" discussed by the justices in these cases does not apply to the private sector. Hence, if the University of Michigan Law School admissions policy can satisfy the requirements of the law, then it is likely that businesses' diversity hiring will too. Second, and perhaps more significantly, the Court, in affirming a view that the law need not be color-blind in all its applications, recognized as compelling the business case for a diverse workforce. Its decisions, then, may have direct implications for the legality of private-sector affirmative action or diversity-hiring schemes. It should be noted, however, that these decisions carried by a slim 5 to 4 majority. Any change to the composition of the Court could mean that future cases will either limit the precedential value of these Michigan cases or will simply overturn them.

- The Court has now accepted that the use of a racial classification can satisfy a compelling state interest either because it is a remedy for the effects of past discrimination or because it is a mechanism to assure the diversity needed to achieve significant social objectives. From a moral perspective on equality, do you believe that using the race, ethnicity, or gender of a job applicant in a hiring decision is acceptable?

- What morally relevant differences, if any, are there between using race, gender, and ethnicity against minority and female job applicants and using those characteristics in their favor, for example, as is done in some preferential hiring programs?

- Do you believe that there is a morally significant difference between the undergraduate and the law school admissions policies? What is that relevant difference and why is it different?

This case was prepared from the following sources: *Grutter v. Bollinger*, Supreme Court of the United States, 2003 U.S. Lexis 4800; *Gratz v. Bollinger*, Supreme Court of the United States, 2003 U.S. Lexis 4801.

READING 11.1 PREFERENTIAL HIRING AND COMPENSATION
Robert K. Fullinwider

If a man shall steal an ox, or a sheep, and kill it, or sell it; he shall restore five oxen for an ox, and four sheep for a sheep.

Exodus 22

Persons have rights; but sometimes a right may justifiably be overridden. Can we concede to all job applicants a right to equal consideration, and yet support a policy of preferentially hiring female over white male applicants?

Judith Thomson, in her article "Preferential Hiring,"[1] appeals to the principle of compensation as a ground which justifies us in sometimes overriding a person's rights. She applies this principle to a case of preferential hiring of a woman in order to defend the claim that such preferential hiring is not unjust. Her defense rests upon the contention that a debt of compensation is owed to women, and that the existence of this debt provides us with a justification of preferential hiring of women in certain cases even though this involves setting aside or overriding certain rights of white male applicants.

Although she is correct in believing that the right to compensation sometimes allows us or requires us to override or limit other rights, I shall argue that Thomson has failed to show that the principle of compensation justifies preferential hiring in the case she constructs. Thus, by implication, I argue that she has failed to show that preferential hiring of women in such cases is not unjust. I proceed by setting out Thomson's argument, by identifying the crucial premise. I then show that Thomson fails to defend the premise, and that, given her statement of the principle of compensation, the premise is implausible.

THOMSON'S CASE

Thomson asks us to imagine the following case. Suppose for some academic job a white male applicant (WMA) and a female applicant (FA) are under final consideration.[2] Suppose further that we grant

From Robert K. Fullinwider, "Preferential Hiring and Compensation," *Social Theory and Practice*, vol. 3, no. 3 (Spring 1975): 307–320. Reprinted with the permission of the author and *Social Theory and Practice*.

that WMA and FA each have a *right to equal consideration* by the university's hiring officer. This means that each has a right to be evaluated for the job solely in terms of his or her possession of job related qualifications. Suppose, finally, that the hiring officer hires FA because she is a woman. How can the hiring officer's choice avoid being unjust?

Since being a woman is, by hypothesis, not a job related qualification in this instance, the hiring officer's act of choosing FA because she is a woman seems to violate WMA's right to equal consideration. The hiring officer's act would not be unjust only if in this situation there is some sufficient moral ground for setting aside or overriding WMA's right.

Consider, Thomson asks us, " . . . those debts which are incurred by one who wrongs another. *It is here that we find what seems to me the most powerful argument for the conclusion that preferential hiring of women is not unjust*" (emphasis added).[3] We are promised that the basis for justly overriding WMA's acknowledged right is to be found in the principle of compensation. But, at this crucial point in her paper, Thomson stops short of setting out the actual derivation of her conclusion from the application of the principle of compensation to her imagined case. The reader is left to construct the various steps in the argument. From remarks Thomson makes in dealing with some objections to preferential hiring, I offer the following as a fair construction of the argument she intends.

Women, as a group, are owed a debt of compensation. Historically women, because they were women, have been subject to extensive and damaging discrimination, socially approved and legally supported. The discriminatory practices have served to limit the opportunities for fulfillment open to women and have disadvantaged them in the competition for many social benefits. Since women have been the victims of injustice, they have a moral right to be compensated for the wrongs done to them.

The compensation is owed by the community. The community as a whole is responsible, since the discriminatory practices against women have not been limited to isolated, private actions. These practices have been widespread, and public as well as private. Nowhere does Thomson argue that the case for preferring FA over WMA lies in a debt to FA directly incurred by WMA. In fact, Thomson never

makes an effort to show any direct connection between FA and WMA. The moral relationship upon which Thomson's argument must rely exists between women and the community. The sacrifice on WMA's part is exacted from him by the community so it may pay its debt to women. This is a crucial feature of Thomson's case, and creates the need for the next premise: The right to compensation on the part of women justifies the community in overriding WMA's right to equal consideration. This premise is necessary to the argument. If the setting aside of WMA's right is to be justified by appeal to the principle of compensation, and the debt of compensation exists between the community and women, then something like the fourth premise is required to gain the application of the principle of compensation to WMA. This premise grounds the justness of WMA's sacrifice in the community's debt.

In short, Thomson's argument contains the following premises:

1. Women, as a group, are owed a debt of compensation.

2. The compensation is owed to women by the community.

3. The community exacts a sacrifice from WMA (i.e., sets aside his right to equal consideration) in order to pay its debt.[4]

4. The right to compensation on the part of women against the community justifies the community in setting aside WMA's right.

If we assume that the community may legitimately discharge its debt to women by making payments to *individual women,* then from premises 1–4 the conclusion may be drawn that WMA's right to equal consideration may be overridden in order to prefer FA, and, hence, that it is not unjust for the hiring officer to choose FA because she is a woman.

I shall not quarrel with the premises 1–3, nor with the assumption that *groups* can be wronged and have rights.[5] My quarrel here is with premise 4. I shall show that Thomson offers no support for 4, and that it does not involve a correct application of the principle of compensation as used by Thomson. I will examine the case for premise 4 [later]. In the next section I pause to look at Thomson's statement of the principle of compensation.

THE PRINCIPLE OF COMPENSATION

In the passage quoted earlier, Thomson speaks of those debts incurred by one who wrongs another. These are the debts of compensation. Using Thomson's own language, we may formulate the principle of compensation as the declaration that *he who wrongs another owes the other.*[6] The principle of compensation tells us that, for some person B, B's act of wronging some person A creates a special moral relationship between A and B. The relationship is a species of the relationship of *being indebted to.* In the case of compensation, the indebtedness arises as a result of wrongdoing, and involves the wrongdoer owing the wronged. To say that B owes something to A is to say that B's liberty of action with respect to what is owed is limited. B is under an obligation to yield to A what he owes him, and A has a right to it.[7] What B must yield will be a matter of the kind of wrong he has done A, and the optional means of compensation open to him. Thus, it is clearly the case that debts of compensation are grounds for limiting or overriding rights. But our being owed compensation by someone, though giving us some purchase on his liberty, does not give us carte blanche in limiting his rights. The debt is limited to what makes good our loss (restores our right), and is limited to us, his victims.

It might be that, for some reason, WMA directly owes FA compensation. If so, it would immediately follow that FA has a moral claim against WMA which limits WMA's liberty with respect to what he owes her. Furthermore, the nature of WMA's wrong may be such as to require a form of compensation interfering with the particular right we are focusing on—his right to equal consideration. Suppose the wrong done by WMA involved his depriving FA of fair opportunities for employment. Such a wrong may be the basis for requiring WMA, in compensation, to forego his right to equal consideration if he and FA were in direct competition for some job. This case would conform precisely to the model of Thomson's stated principle of compensation.

Thomson makes no effort to show that WMA has interfered with FA's chances of employment, or done her any other harm. She claims that it is "wrongheaded" to dwell upon the question of whether WMA has wronged FA or any other woman.[8] As we have already seen, Thomson maintains that the relevant moral relationship exists between *women* and the *community.* Consequently, the full weight of her argument rests on premise 4, and I now turn to it.

APPLYING THE PRINCIPLE OF COMPENSATION TO GROUPS

Thomson asserts that there is a relationship of indebtedness between the community and women. Yet it is the overriding of WMA's right which is purportedly justified by this fact. The sacrifice imposed upon WMA is not due to his directly owing FA. The community owes FA (as a woman), and exacts the sacrifice from WMA in order that *it* may pay its debt. This is supposed to be justified by premise 4.

May the community take *any* act it sees fit in order to pay its debts?[9] This question goes to the heart of Thomson's case: what support is there for her premise 4? What is the connection between the community's liability to women (or FA), and WMA's membership in the community? Can we find in the fact that the community owes something to women a moral justification for overriding WMA's right? In this section I explore two attempts to provide a positive answer to this last question. These are not Thomson's attempts; I consider her own words in the next section.

First, one might attempt to justify the imposition of a sacrifice on WMA by appeal to distributive liability. It might be urged that since the community owes FA, then every member of the community owes FA and thus WMA owes FA. This defense of premise 4 is unconvincing. While it is true that if the community owes FA then its members collectively owe FA, it does not follow that they distributively owe FA. It is not the case that, as a general rule, distributive liability holds between organized groups and their members.[10] What reason is there to suppose it does in this case?

Though this attempt to defend premise 4 is unsatisfactory, it is easy to see why it would be very appealing. Even though the indebtedness is established, in the first instance, between the community and FA, if distributive liability obtained we could derive a debt WMA owed to FA, a debt that arose as a result of the application of the principle of compensation to the community. In imposing a sacrifice on WMA, the community would be enforcing *his* (derived) obligation to FA.

Second, imagine a 36 hole, 2 round, golf tournament among FA, WMA, and a third party, sanctioned and governed by a tournament organizing committee. In previous years FA switched to a new model club, which improved her game. Before the match the third player surreptitiously substitutes for FA's clubs a set of the old type. This is discovered after 18 holes have been played. If we suppose that the match cannot be restarted or cancelled, then the committee is faced with the problem of compensating FA for the unfair disadvantage caused her by the substitution. By calculating her score averages over the years, the committee determines that the new clubs have yielded FA an average two-stroke improvement per 18 holes over the old clubs. The committee decides to compensate FA by penalizing the third player by two strokes in the final 18 holes.

But the committee must also penalize WMA two strokes. If FA has been put at a disadvantage by the wrongful substitution, she has been put at a disadvantage with respect to every player in the game. She is in competition with all the players; what the third player's substitution has done is to deprive her of a fair opportunity to defeat all the other players. That opportunity is not restored by penalizing the third player alone. If the committee is to rectify in mid-match the wrong done to FA, it must penalize WMA as well, though WMA had no part in the wrong done to FA.

Now, if it is right for the committee to choose this course of action, then this example seems promising for Thomson's argument. Perhaps in it can be found a basis for defending premise 4. This example seems appropriately similar to Thomson's case: in it an organization penalizes WMA to compensate FA, though WMA is innocent of any wrong against FA. If the two situations are sufficiently alike and in the golfing example it is not unjust for the committee to penalize WMA, then by parity of reasoning it would seem that the community is not injust in setting aside WMA's right.

Are the committee's action and the community's action to be seen in the same light? Does the committee's action involve setting aside any player's rights? The committee constantly monitors the game, and intervenes to balance off losses or gains due to infractions or violations. Unfair gains are nullified by penalties; unfair losses are offset by awards. In the end no player has a complaint because the interventions ensure that the outcome

has not been influenced by illegitimate moves or illegal actions. Whatever a player's position at the end of the game, it is solely the result of his own unhindered efforts. In penalizing WMA two strokes (along with the third player), the committee does him no injustice nor overrides any of his rights.

The community, or its government, is responsible for preserving fair employment practices for its members. It can penalize those who engage in unfair discrimination; it can vigorously enforce fair employment rules; and, if FA has suffered under unfair practices, it may consider some form of compensation for FA. However, compensating FA by imposing a burden on WMA, when he is not culpable, is *not* like penalizing WMA in the golf match. The loss imposed by the community upon WMA is not part of a game-like scheme, carefully regulated and continuously monitored by the community, wherein it intervenes continually to offset unfair losses and gains by distributing penalties and advantages, ensuring that over their lifetimes WMA's and FA's chances at employment have been truly equal. WMA's loss may endure; and there is no reason to believe that his employment position at the end of his career reflects only his unhindered effort. If the community exacts a sacrifice from WMA to pay FA, *it merely redistributes losses and gains without balancing them*.

Even though the golfing example looked promising as a source of clues for a defense of premise 4, on examination it seems not to offer any support for that premise. Indeed, in seeing how the golfing case is different from the hiring case, we may become even more dubious that Thomson's principle of compensation can justify the community in overriding WMA's right to equal consideration in the absence of his culpability.[11] Since Thomson never explicitly expresses premise 4 in her paper, she never directly addresses the problem of its defense. In the one place where she seems to take up the problem raised by premise 4, she says:

> Still, the community does impose a burden upon him (WMA): it is able to make amends for its wrongs only by taking something away from him, something which, after all, we are supposing he has a right to. And why should *he* pay the cost of the community's amends-making?

If there were some appropriate way in which the community could make amends to its . . . women, some way which did not require depriving anyone of anything he has a right to, then that would be the best course of action to take. Or if there were anyway some way in which the costs could be shared by everyone, and not imposed entirely on the young white male applicants, then that would be, if not the best, then anyway better than opting for a policy of preferential hiring. But in fact *the nature of the wrongs done is such as to make jobs the best and most suitable form of compensation (emphasis added)*.[12]

How does this provide an answer to our question? Is this passage to be read as suggesting, in support of premise 4, the principle that a group may override the rights of its (nonculpable) members in order to pay the "best" form of compensation?[13] If WMA's right to equal consideration stood in the way of the community's paying best compensation to FA, then this principle would entail premise 4. This principle, however, will not withstand scrutiny.

Consider an example: Suppose that you have stolen a rare and elaborately engraved hunting rifle from me. Before you can be made to return it, the gun is destroyed in a fire. By coincidence, however, your brother possesses one of the few other such rifles in existence; perhaps it is the only other model in existence apart from the one you stole from me and which was destroyed. From my point of view, having my gun back, or having one exactly like it, is the best form of compensation I can have from you. No other gun will be a suitable replacement, nor will money serve satisfactorily to compensate me for my loss. I prized the rifle for its rare and unique qualities, not for its monetary value. You can pay me the best form of compensation by giving me your brother's gun. However, this is clearly not a morally justifiable option. I have no moral title to your brother's gun, nor are you (solely in virtue of your debt to me) required or permitted to take your brother's gun to give to me. The gun is not yours to give; and nothing about the fact that you owe me justifies you in taking it.

In this example it is clear that establishing what is the best compensation (best makes up the wrongful loss) does not determine what is the morally appropriate form of compensation. Thus, as a defense of premise 4, telling us that preferential hiring is the best compensation begs the question.

The question of the best form of compensation may properly arise only after we have determined who owes whom, and what are the morally permissible means of payment open to the debtor. The question of the best form of compensation arises, in other words, only after we have settled the moral justifiability of exacting something from someone, and settled the issue of what it is that the debtor has that he can pay.

The case of preferential hiring seems to me more like the case of the stolen rifle than like the case of the golfing match. If WMA has a right to equal consideration, then he, not the community, owns the right. In abridging his right in order to pay FA, the community is paying in stolen coin, just as you would be were you to expropriate your brother's rifle to compensate me. The community is paying with something that does not belong to it. WMA has not been shown by Thomson to owe anybody anything. Nor has Thomson defended or made plausible premise 4, which on its face ill fits her own expression of the principle of compensation. If we reject the premise, then Thomson has not shown what she claimed—that it is not unjust to engage in preferential hiring of women. I fully agree with her that it would be appropriate, if not obligatory, for the community to adopt measures of compensation to women.[14] I cannot agree, on the basis of her argument, that it may do so by adopting a policy of preferential hiring.

BENEFIT AND INNOCENCE

Thomson seems vaguely to recognize that her case is unconvincing without a demonstration of culpability on the part of WMA. At the end of her paper, after having made her argument without assuming WMA's guilt, she assures us that after all WMA is not so innocent, and it is not unfitting that he should bear the sacrifice required in preferring FA.

> . . . it is not entirely inappropriate that those applicants (like WMA) should pay the cost. No doubt few, if any, have themselves, individually, done any wrongs to . . . women. But they have profited from the wrongs the community did. Many may actually have been direct beneficiaries of policies which excluded or downgraded . . . women—perhaps in school admissions, perhaps in access to financial aid, perhaps elsewhere; and even those who did not directly benefit in this way had, at any rate, the advantage in the competition which comes of confi-

dence in one's full membership, and of one's rights being recognized as a matter of course.[15]

Does this passage make a plausible case for WMA's diminished "innocence," and the appropriateness of imposing the costs of compensation on him? The principle implied in the passage is, "He who benefits from a wrong shall pay for the wrong." Perhaps Thomson confuses this principle with the principle of compensation itself ("He who wrongs another shall pay for the wrong"). At any rate, the principle, "He who benefits from a wrong shall pay for the wrong," is surely suspect as an acceptable moral principle.

Consider the following example. While I am away on vacation, my neighbor contracts with a construction company to repave his driveway. He instructs the workers to come to his address, where they will find a note describing the driveway to be repaired. An enemy of my neighbor, aware somehow of this arrangement, substitutes for my neighbor's instructions a note describing *my* driveway. The construction crew, having been paid in advance, shows up on the appointed day while my neighbor is at work, finds the letter, and faithfully following its instructions paves my driveway. In this example my neighbor has been wronged and damaged. He is out a sum of money, and his driveway is unimproved. I benefited from the wrong, for my driveway is considerably improved. Yet, am I morally required to compensate my neighbor for the wrong done him? Is it appropriate that the costs of compensating my neighbor fall on me? I cannot see why. My paying the neighbor the cost he incurred in hiring the construction company would be an act of supererogation on my part, not a discharge of an obligation to him. If I could afford it, it would be a decent thing to do; but it is not something I *owe* my neighbor. I am not less than innocent in this affair because I benefited from my neighbor's misfortune; and no one is justified in exacting compensation from me.

The very obvious feature of the situation just described which bears on the fittingness of compensation is the fact of *involuntariness*. Indeed I benefited from the wrong done my neighbor, but the benefit was involuntary and undesired. If I knowingly and voluntarily benefit from wrongs done to others, though I do not commit the wrongs myself, then perhaps it is true to say that I am less than innocent of these wrongs, and perhaps it is morally

fitting that I bear some of the costs of compensation. But it is not like this with involuntary benefits.

Though young white males like WMA have undeniably benefited in many ways from the sexist social arrangements under which they were reared, to a large extent, if not entirely, these benefits are involuntary. From an early age the male's training and education inculcate in him the attitudes and dispositions, the knowledge and skills, which give him an advantage over women in later life. Such benefits are unavoidable (by him) and ineradicable. Most especially is this true of "that advantage . . . which comes of confidence in one's full membership [in the community] and of one's rights being recognized as a matter of course."

The principle, "He who *willingly* benefits from wrong must pay for the wrong," may have merit as a moral principle. To show a person's uncoerced and knowledgeable complicity in wrongdoing is to show him less than innocent, even if his role amounts to no more than ready acceptance of the fruits of wrong. Thomson makes no effort to show such complicity on WMA's part. The principle that she relies upon, "He who benefits from a wrong must pay for the wrong," is without merit. So, too, is her belief that "it is not entirely inappropriate" that WMA (and those like him) should bear the burden of a program of compensation to women. What Thomson ignores is the moral implication of the fact that the benefits of sexism received by WMA may be involuntary and unavoidable. This implication cannot be blinked, and it ruins Thomson's final pitch to gain our approval of a program which violates the rights of some persons.[16]

NOTES

1. Judith Thomson, "Preferential Hiring," *Philosophy and Public Affairs,* 2 (Summer 1973): 364–84.

2. Thomson asks us to imagine two such applicants tied in their qualifications. Presumably, preferring a less qualified teacher would violate students' rights to the best available instruction. If the applicants are equally qualified, then the students' rights are satisfied whichever one is picked. In cases where third party rights are not involved, there would seem to be no need to include the tie stipulation, for if the principle of compensation is strong enough to justify preferring a woman over a man, it is strong enough whether the woman is equally qualified or not, so long as she is minimally qualified. (Imagine hiring a

librarian instead of a teacher.) Thus, I leave out the requirement that the applicants be tied in their qualifications. Nothing in my argument turns on whether the applicants are equally qualified. The reader may, if he wishes, mentally reinstate this feature of Thomson's example.

3. Thomson, 380.

4. The comments from which propositions 1–3 are distilled occur on pages 381–82.

5. For a discussion of these issues, see Robert Simon, "Preferential Hiring: A Reply to Judith Jarvis Thomson," *Philosophy and Public Affairs,* 3 (Spring 1974): 312–20.

6. There are broader notions of compensation, where it means making up for any deficiency or distortion, and where it means recompense for work. Neither of these notions plays a role in Thomson's argument.

7. On page 378, Thomson says: "Now it is, I think, widely believed that we may, without injustice, refuse to grant a man what he has a right to only if *either* someone else has a conflicting and more stringent right, *or* there is some very great benefit to be obtained by doing so—perhaps that a disaster of some kind is thereby averted . . . But in fact there are other ways in which a right may be overridden." The "other way" which Thomson mentions derives from the force of debts. A debt consists of rights and obligations, and the force of debts can perhaps be accounted for in terms of superior rights. Then, debts would not be a third ground, independent of the first listed by Thomson, for overriding a right.

8. Thomson, 380–81.

9. The U.S. Government owes Japanese companies compensation for losses they incurred when the President imposed an illegal import surtax. May the Government justly discharge its debt by taxing only Japanese-Americans in order to pay the Japanese companies?

10. See Joel Feinberg, "Collective Responsibility," *Journal of Philosophy,* 65 (7 November 1968); and Virginia Held, "Can a Random Collection of Individuals Be Morally Responsible?" *Journal of Philosophy,* 67 (13 July 1970).

11. George Sher, in "Justifying Reverse Discrimination in Employment," *Philosophy and Public Affairs,* 4 (Winter 1975), defends reverse discriminations to "neutralize competitive disadvantages caused by past privations" (165). He seems to view the matter along the lines of my golfing example. Thus, my comments here against the sufficiency of that model apply to Sher's argument. Also, see below . . . for arguments that bear on Sher's contention that the justification for discriminating against white male applicants is not that they are most responsible for injustice, but benefit the most from it.

12. Thompson, 383.

13. In the passage quoted, Thomson is attempting to morally justify the community's imposing a sacrifice on WMA. Thus, her reference to "best" compensation cannot be construed to mean "morally best," since morally best means morally justified. By best compensation Thomson means that compensation which will best make up the loss suffered by the victim. This is how I understand the idea of best compensation in the succeeding example and argument.

14. And there are many possible modes of compensation open to the community which are free from any moral taint. At the worst, monetary compensation is always an alternative. This may be second- or third-best compensation for the wrongs done, but when the best is not available, second-best has to do. For the loss of my gun, I am going to have to accept cash from you (assuming you have it), and use it to buy a less satisfactory substitute.

15. Thomson, 383–84.

16. But, if FA is not given preferential treatment in hiring (the best compensation), are *her* rights violated? In having a right to compensation, FA does not have a right to anything at all that will compensate her. She has a right to the best of the morally available options open to her debtor. Only if the community refuses to pay her this is her right violated. We have seen no reason to believe that setting aside the right of white male applicants to equal consideration is an option morally available to the community.

READING 11.2 A DEFENSE OF PROGRAMS OF PREFERENTIAL TREATMENT

Richard Wasserstrom

Many justifications of programs of preferential treatment depend upon the claim that in one respect or another such programs have good consequences or that they are effective means by which to bring about some desirable end, e.g., an integrated, equalitarian society. I mean by "programs of preferential treatment" to refer to programs such as those at issue in the *Bakke* case—programs which set aside a certain number of places (for example, in a law school) as to which members of minority groups (for example, persons who are nonwhite or female) who possess certain minimum qualifications (in terms of grades and test scores) may be preferred for admission to those places over some members of the majority group who possess higher qualifications (in terms of grades and test scores).

Many criticisms of programs of preferential treatment claim that such programs, even if effective, are unjustifiable because they are in some important sense unfair or unjust. In this paper I present a limited defense of such programs by showing that two of the chief arguments offered for the unfairness or injustice of these programs do not work in the way or to the degree supposed by critics of these programs.

The first argument is this. Opponents of preferential treatment programs sometimes assert that proponents of these programs are guilty of intellectual inconsistency, if not racism or sexism. For, as is now readily acknowledged, at times past employers, universities, and many other social institutions did have racial or sexual quotas (when they did not practice overt racial or sexual exclusion), and many of those who were most concerned to bring about the eradication of those racial quotas are now untroubled by the new programs which reinstitute them. And this, it is claimed, is inconsistent. If it was wrong to take race or sex into account when blacks and women were the objects of racial and sexual policies and practices of exclusion, then it is wrong

to take race or sex into account when the objects of the policies have their race or sex reversed. Simple considerations of intellectual consistency—of what it means to give racism or sexism as a reason for condemning these social policies and practices—require that what was a good reason then is still a good reason now.

The problem with this argument is that despite appearances, there is no inconsistency involved in holding both views. Even if contemporary preferential treatment programs which contain quotas are wrong, they are not wrong for the reasons that made quotas against blacks and women pernicious. The reason why is that the social realities do make an enormous difference. The fundamental evil of programs that discriminated against blacks or women was that these programs were a part of a larger social universe which systematically maintained a network of institutions which unjustifiably concentrated power, authority, and goods in the hands of white male individuals, and which systematically consigned blacks and women to subordinate positions in the society.

Whatever may be wrong with today's affirmative action programs and quota systems, it should be clear that the evil, if any, is just not the same. Racial and sexual minorities do not constitute the dominant social group. Nor is the conception of who is a fully developed member of the moral and social community one of an individual who is either female or black. Quotas which prefer women or blacks do not add to an already relatively overabundant supply of resources and opportunities at the disposal of members of these groups in the way in which the quotas of the past did maintain and augment the overabundant supply of resources and opportunities already available to white males.

The same point can be made in a somewhat different way. Sometimes people say that what was wrong, for example, with the system of racial discrimination in the South was that it took an irrelevant characteristic, namely race, and used it systematically to allocate social benefits and burdens of various sorts. The defect was the irrelevance of the characteristic used—race—for that meant that individuals ended up being treated in a manner that was arbitrary and capricious.

I do not think that was the central flaw at all. Take, for instance, the most hideous of the practices, human slavery. The primary thing that was wrong with the institution was not that the particular individuals who were assigned the place of slaves were assigned there arbitrarily because the assignment was made in virtue of an irrelevant characteristic, their race. Rather, it seems to me that the primary thing that was and is wrong with slavery is the practice itself—the fact of some individuals being able to own other individuals and all that goes with that practice. It would not matter by what criterion individuals were assigned; human slavery would still be wrong. And the same can be said for most if not all of the other discrete practices and institutions which comprised the system of racial discrimination even after human slavery was abolished. The practices were unjustifiable—they were oppressive—and they would have been so no matter how the assignment of victims had been made. What made it worse, still, was that the institutions and the supporting ideology all interlocked to create a system of human oppression whose effects on those living under it were as devastating as they were unjustifiable.

Again, if there is anything wrong with the programs of preferential treatment that have begun to flourish within the past ten years, it should be evident that the social realities in respect to the distribution of resources and opportunities make the difference. Apart from everything else, there is simply no way in which all of these programs taken together could plausibly be viewed as capable of relegating white males to the kind of genuinely oppressive status characteristically bestowed upon women and blacks by the dominant social institutions and ideology.

The second objection is that preferential treatment programs are wrong because they take race or sex into account rather than the only thing that does matter—that is, an individual's qualifications. What all such programs have in common and what makes them all objectionable, so this argument goes, is that they ignore the persons who are more qualified by bestowing a preference on those who are less qualified in virtue of their being either black or female.

There are, I think, a number of things wrong with this objection based on qualifications, and not the least of them is that we do not live in a society

in which there is even the serious pretense of a qualification requirement for many jobs of substantial power and authority. Would anyone claim, for example, that the persons who comprise the judiciary are there because they are the most qualified lawyers or the most qualified persons to be judges? Would anyone claim that Henry Ford II is the head of the Ford Motor Company because he is the most qualified person for the job? Part of what is wrong with even talking about qualifications and merit is that the argument derives some of its force from the erroneous notion that we would have a meritocracy were it not for programs of preferential treatment. In fact, the higher one goes in terms of prestige, power and the like, the less qualifications seem ever to be decisive. It is only for certain jobs and certain places that qualifications are used to do more than establish the possession of certain minimum competencies.

But difficulties such as these to one side, there are theoretical difficulties as well which cut much more deeply into the argument about qualifications. To begin with, it is important to see that there is a serious inconsistency present if the person who favors "pure qualifications" does so on the ground that the most qualified ought to be selected because this promotes maximum efficiency. Let us suppose that the argument is that if we have the most qualified performing the relevant tasks we will get those tasks done in the most economical and efficient manner. There is nothing wrong in principle with arguments based upon the good consequences that will flow from maintaining a social practice in a certain way. But it is inconsistent for the opponent of preferential treatment to attach much weight to qualifications on this ground, because it was an analogous appeal to the good consequences that the opponent of preferential treatment thought was wrong in the first place. That is to say, if the chief thing to be said in favor of strict qualifications and preferring the most qualified is that it is the most efficient way of getting things done, then we are right back to an assessment of the different consequences that will flow from different programs, and we are far removed from the considerations of justice or fairness that were thought to weigh so heavily against these programs.

It is important to note, too, that qualifications—at least in the educational context—are often not connected at all closely with any plausible conception of social effectiveness. To admit the most qualified students to law school, for example—given the way qualifications are now determined—is primarily to admit those who have the greatest chance of scoring the highest grades at law school. This says little about efficiency except perhaps that these students are the easiest for the faculty to teach. However, since we know so little about what constitutes being a good, or even successful lawyer, and even less about the correlation between being a very good law student and being a very good lawyer, we can hardly claim very confidently that the legal system will operate most effectively if we admit only the most qualified students to law school.

To be at all decisive, the argument for qualifications must be that those who are the most qualified deserve to receive the benefits (the job, the place in law school, etc.) because they are the most qualified. The introduction of the concept of desert now makes it an objection as to justice or fairness of the sort promised by the original criticism of the programs. But now the problem is that there is no reason to think that there is any strong sense of "desert" in which it is correct that the most qualified deserve anything.

Let us consider more closely one case, that of preferential treatment in respect to admission to college or graduate school. There is a logical gap in the inference from the claim that a person is most qualified to perform a task, e.g., to be a good student, to the conclusion that he or she deserves to be admitted as a student. Of course, those who deserve to be admitted should be admitted. But why do the most qualified deserve anything? There is simply no necessary connection between academic merit (in the sense of being the most qualified) and deserving to be a member of a student body. Suppose, for instance, that there is only one tennis court in the community. Is it clear that the two best tennis players ought to be the ones permitted to use it? Why not those who were there first? Or those who will enjoy playing the most? Or those who are the worst and, therefore, need the greatest opportunity to practice? Or those who have the chance to play least frequently?

We might, of course, have a rule that says that the best tennis players get to use the court before the others. Under such a rule the best players would deserve the court more than the poorer ones. But that is just to push the inquiry back one stage. Is

there any reason to think that we ought to have a rule giving good tennis players such a preference? Indeed, the arguments that might be given for or against such a rule are many and varied. And few if any of the arguments that might support the rule would depend upon a connection between ability and desert.

Someone might reply, however, that the most able students deserve to be admitted to the university because all of their earlier schooling was a kind of competition, with university admission being the prize awarded to the winners. They deserve to be admitted because that is what the rule of the competition provides. In addition, it might be argued, it would be unfair now to exclude them in favor of others, given the reasonable expectations they developed about the way which their industry and performance would be rewarded. Minority-admission programs, which inevitably prefer some who are less qualified over some who are more qualified, all possess this flaw.

There are several problems with this argument. The most substantial of them is that it is an empirically implausible picture of our social world. Most of what are regarded as the decisive characteristics for higher education have a great deal to do with things over which the individual has neither control nor responsibility: such things as home environment, socioeconomic class of parents, and, of course, the quality of the primary and secondary schools attended. Since individuals do not deserve having had any of these things vis-à-vis other individuals, they do not, for the most part, deserve their qualifications. And since they do not deserve their abilities they do not in any strong sense deserve to be admitted because of their abilities.

To be sure, if there has been a rule which connects, say, performance at high school with admission to college, then there is a weak sense in which those who do well at high school deserve, for that reason alone, to be admitted to college. In addition, if persons have built up or relied upon their reasonable expectations concerning performance and admission, they have a claim to be admitted on this ground as well. But it is certainly not obvious that these claims of desert are any stronger or more compelling than the competing claims based upon the needs or advantages to women or blacks from programs of preferential treatment. And as I have indicated, all rule-based claims of desert are very weak unless and until the rule which creates the claim is itself shown to be a justified one. Unless one has a strong preference for the status quo, and unless one can defend that preference, the practice within a system of allocating places in a certain way does not go very far at all in showing that that is the right or the just way to allocate those places in the future.

A proponent of programs of preferential treatment is not at all committed to the view that qualifications ought to be wholly irrelevant. He or she can agree that, given the existing structure of any institution, there is probably some minimal set of qualifications without which one cannot participate meaningfully within the institution. In addition, it can be granted that the qualifications of those involved will affect the way the institution works and the way it affects others in the society. And the consequences will vary depending upon the particular institution. But all of this only establishes that qualifications, in this sense, are relevant, not that they are decisive. This is wholly consistent with the claim that race or sex should today also be relevant when it comes to matters such as admission to college or law school. And that is all that any preferential treatment program—even one with the kind of quota used in the *Bakke* case—has ever tried to do.

I have not attempted to establish that programs of preferential treatment are right and desirable. There are empirical issues concerning the conse-

quences of these programs that I have not discussed, and certainly not settled. Nor, for that matter, have I considered the argument that justice may permit, if not require, these programs as a way to provide compensation or reparation for injuries suffered in the recent as well as distant past, or as a way to remove benefits that are undeservedly enjoyed by those of the dominant group. What I have tried to do is show that it is wrong to think that programs of preferential treatment are objectionable in the centrally important sense in which many past and present discriminatory features of our society have been and are racist and sexist. The social realities as to power and opportunity do make a fundamental difference. It is also wrong to think that programs of preferential treatment are in any strong sense either unjust or unprincipled. The case for programs of preferential treatment could, therefore, plausibly rest both on the view that such programs are not unfair to white males (except in the weak, rule-dependent sense described above) and on the view that it is unfair to continue the present set of unjust—often racist and sexist—institutions that comprise the social reality. And the case for these programs could rest as well on the proposition that, given the distribution of power and influence in the United States today, such programs may reasonably be viewed as potentially valuable, effective means by which to achieve admirable and significant social ideals of equality and integration.

READING 11.3 *AMICUS CURIAE** BRIEF
IN SUPPORT OF THE UNIVERSITY OF MICHIGAN

General Motors Corporation

SUMMARY OF ARGUMENT

General Motors files as *amicus curiae* in this case to explain that the nation's interest in safeguarding the freedom of academic institutions to select racially and ethnically diverse student bodies is indeed compelling: the future of American business and, in some measure, of the American economy depends upon it.

In General Motors' experience, only a well educated, diverse work force, comprising people who have learned to work productively and creatively with individuals from a multitude of races and ethnic, religious, and cultural backgrounds, can maintain America's competitiveness in the increasingly diverse and interconnected world economy. Diversity in academic institutions is essential to teaching students the human relations and analytic skills they need to succeed and lead in the work environments of the twenty-first century. These skills include the abilities to work well with colleagues and subordinates from diverse backgrounds; to view issues from multiple perspectives; and to anticipate and to respond with sensitivity to the cultural differences of highly diverse customers, colleagues, employees, and global business partners.

General Motors speaks from first-hand experience regarding the importance of such cross-cultural skills. As General Motors' global enterprises expand, it is increasingly critical that employees at every level of its operations utilize these skills in their daily tasks. General Motors now maintains major market presences in more than 200 different countries on six continents. General Motors' employees, customers, and business partners thus could scarcely be more racially, ethnically, and culturally diverse.

A ruling proscribing the consideration of race and ethnicity in admissions decisions likely would dramatically reduce diversity at our Nation's top institutions and thereby deprive the students who will become the corps of our Nation's business elite of the interracial and multicultural interactions in an academic setting that are so integral to their acquisition of cross-cultural skills. Such a ruling also likely would reduce racial and ethnic diversity in the pool of employment candidates from which the Nation's businesses can draw their future leaders, impeding businesses' own efforts to obtain the manifold benefits of diversity in the managerial levels of their work forces. Each of these results may diminish the ability of American businesses to utilize fully the opportunities of the global market.

ARGUMENT

The ability of American businesses to thrive in the twenty-first century will depend in large measure on our nation's responses to two inevitable forces: the increasingly global and interconnected nature of the world economy and the increasing diversity of our own population. The vast majority of businesses in the Fortune 500 currently maintain operations or do business in countries outside of the United States. Technological innovations, including the internet and other telecommunications tools, are creating a truly global, interlinked world economy. Global mergers and business expansion are continually increasing the diversity of American businesses' customer bases and business partners.

Nationally, our own population is also becoming increasingly diverse: by the year 2050, almost half of all Americans—47%—will be African American, Hispanic, Asian American, or Native American. After 2050, that "minority" population is projected rapidly to surpass the non-Hispanic white population in size

To succeed in this increasingly diverse environment, American businesses must select leaders who possess cross-cultural competence—the capacities to interact with and to understand the experiences of, and multiplicity of perspectives held by, persons of different races, ethnicities, and cultural histories. Numerous authorities concur that "crosscultural competence" is the most important new attribute

---

*Amicus Curiae: Friends of the Court, Supporting Either Petitioner or Respondant. Respondants: The University of Michigan. Petitioners: Barbara Grutter, Jennifer Gratz (opposing the University Admissions Policies). Footnotes omitted.

for future effective performance in a global market-place." [. . .] Thus, it is essential that the selective academic institutions that prepare students to enter the business and professional worlds adequately equip them with this skill.

Much research confirms what is intuitively obvious: students are likely to acquire greater cross-cultural competence in a multicultural and multi-racial academic environment, in which students and faculty of different cultures and races interact, than they are in a homogeneous one, in which cross-cultural communication is merely a theoretical construct.

The Court is presented with the question whether state universities have a compelling interest in ensuring that students receive these educational benefits. The answer to that question, originally provided by Justice Powell's opinion in *Regents of University of California v. Bakke,* 438 U.S. 265 (1978), and confirmed by the experience of the business community and academic institutions in the decades since Bakke was decided, is a resounding "yes," as the Sixth Circuit, sitting en banc, correctly concluded.

I. CONSIDERATION OF RACE AND ETHNICITY IN UNIVERSITY ADMISSIONS FURTHERS A COMPELLING INTEREST IN EDUCATING STUDENTS AND TRAINING THEM TO COMPETE IN THE GLOBAL MARKETPLACE

A. Institutions of Higher Education Have a Compelling Interest in Selecting Diverse Student Bodies

Justice Powell presciently declared in Bakke that "the 'nation's future depends upon leaders trained through wide exposure' to the ideas and mores of students as diverse as this Nation of many peoples." A majority of the Court held in Bakke that the University of California had "a substantial interest that legitimately may be served by a properly devised admissions program involving the competitive consideration of race and ethnic origin." In his opinion, Justice Powell explained that "attainment of a [racially and ethnically] diverse student body ★ ★ ★ clearly is a constitutionally permissible goal for an institution of higher education" because it augments the educational process in two ways.

First, racial and ethnic diversity in an academic institution teaches students skills that will improve their performance as leaders and professionals in a heterogeneous society. Immersion in a multiracial academic environment enhances students' knowledge of different cultures and their understanding of perspectives that are influenced by race. That augmented understanding in turn prepares students, upon graduation, to work cooperatively in multiracial environments and to serve multiracial clienteles. As Justice Powell observed, for example, racial diversity in a medical school "enrich[es] the training of its student body[,] ★ ★ ★ better equipping its graduates to render with understanding their vital service" to a "heterogeneous population."

Second, racial and ethnic diversity promotes "'speculation, experiment, and creation,'" thinking processes that are "essential to the quality of higher education." Differences among students allow them to "'stimulate one another to reexamine even their most deeply held assumptions about themselves and their world,'" teaching them to view issues from myriad perspectives.

The en banc Sixth Circuit concluded that Justice Powell's opinion in Bakke is controlling. Its decision that diversity is a compelling interest is supported by a mass of unrefuted evidence presented in the trial courts below, substantiating both of Justice Powell's statements regarding the ways in which racial and ethnic diversity enhance students' intellectual and social growth. Reviewing this evidence, Judge Duggan found that the University had presented "solid evidence regarding the educational benefits that flow from a racially and ethnically diverse student body" and, guided by Justice Powell's opinion, concluded that the University's interest in achieving these benefits is compelling.

Petitioners and their amici attack the Sixth Circuit's holding, arguing that the contention that racial diversity among students enhances educational diversity "reflect[s] ★ ★ ★ racial stereotyping about how people will (or should) think or behave on account of their skin color or ethnicity." But in *Metro Broadcasting, Inc. v. FCC,* 497 U.S. 547 (1990), the Court explicitly endorsed Justice Powell's view that racial diversity tends to promote a healthy and educational diversity of viewpoints. The Court explained: "the predictive judgment about the overall result of minority" representation "is not a rigid assumption about how minorit[ies] ★ ★ ★ will behave in every case but rather" merely recognizes "that greater admission of minorities would contribute, on average, 'to the robust exchange of ideas.'"

That conclusion is plainly correct. Although persons of a particular race or ethnicity of course do not necessarily share a common perspective, race and ethnicity are as likely as any other experience to influence an individual's own, unique perspective. Just as growing up in a particular region, living with a disability, or having particular professional experiences are likely to affect an individual's views, so too is one's experience of being a member of a racial minority in a society, like ours, in which, unfortunately, race still matters.

Numerous amici and Judge Boggs in his dissent all acknowledge that admitting students with diverse experiences is a valid academic goal because diverse experiences lead to divergent world views, which in turn enhance the quality of debate and promote learning among students. But they contend that pursuing "true experiential diversity" without direct reference to race would equally accomplish this goal. Petitioners and amici ignore, however, that the mere fact of being a member of a racial or ethnic minority in this society—standing alone—is itself an experience that creates unique perspectives. As Judge Clay explained in his concurrence, an individual can only experience racial or ethnic discrimination based on his or her race or ethnicity, and endeavoring to include in a law school class individuals who have actually experienced the kind of racial or ethnic discrimination being discussed in class requires consideration of race in admissions. Indeed, Judge Boggs acknowledged as much in his dissent. Thus, it is no answer, as Judge Boggs suggests, to favor in admissions students who attended "an under-funded public school, struggled with relative poverty, [or spent] a childhood ★ ★ ★ in urban rather than suburban areas"; these are insufficient proxies for the experience of being a member of a racial or ethnic minority in America, regardless of class or income.

Several amici contend that exposure to a broad reading list and to popular culture's purportedly "ubiquitous" message of tolerance are alternative means of achieving the educational effects of diversity. But it is self-evident that requiring students to read works authored by under-represented minorities, or having them watch a movie about "the black

experience"—without actually interacting with people of color—is grossly insufficient to expand the limited world views created by lifetimes spent in a largely segregated world. If the goal is to expand students' understanding of and ability to function in society as it now exists, actual interaction with peers of different races is far superior to merely reading or watching a movie about racial issues. For example, a student could too easily dismiss Martin Luther King's writings as reflecting a different, less-enlightened time; that same student would have a harder time dismissing the struggles of her classmates with race and identity issues on campus.

Importantly, it is not only in class discussions that these crucial interactions occur. As Justice Powell noted, quoting the comments of the then-president of Princeton University: "'[A] great deal of learning occurs informally ★ ★ ★ through interactions among students ★ ★ ★ of different races ★ ★ ★ who are able, directly or indirectly, to learn from their differences. ★ ★ ★ For many [students] ★ ★ ★, the unplanned casual encounters with roommates, fellow sufferers in organic chemistry class, student workers in the library, teammates on a basketball squad, or other participants in class affairs or student government can be subtle and yet powerful sources of improved understanding and personal growth.'"

Petitioners' suggestion that the Sixth Circuit's holding lacks support in this Court's precedents, save for Justice Powell's opinion in Bakke, also misses the mark. The Court often has recognized that racial and ethnic academic diversity promotes vital educational goals, and that achieving diversity through race-conscious decisionmaking accordingly is within the prerogative of state educational institutions. In *Swann v. Charlotte-Mecklenburg Board of Education,* 402 U.S. 1 (1971), for example, the Court observed that, even absent any constitutional violation, it would be "within the broad discretionary powers of [elementary and secondary] school authorities" to "conclude" as an "educational policy ★ ★ ★ that in order to prepare students to live in a pluralistic society each school should have a prescribed ratio of Negro to white students." Similarly, in *Washington v. Seattle School District No. 1,* 458 U.S. 457, 460, 472–474 (1982), the Court struck down a measure that would have restricted a school district's power to address defacto segregation for the purpose of augmenting education. In the course of its opinion, the Court noted that "it should be ★ ★ ★ clear that white as well as Negro children benefit from exposure to ethnic and racial diversity in the classroom." And it concluded that, "in the absence of a constitutional violation, the desirability and efficacy of school desegregation are matters to be resolved through the political process."

As shown [. . .], the experience of the business world confirms Justice Powell's and the Sixth Circuit's conclusion that state academic institutions have a compelling interest in using diversity to hone young minds and to "prepare ★ ★ ★ children [to act as] citizens" leaders, and professionals in our increasingly heterogeneous society.

B. Success in Today's Business World Demands Cross-Cultural Competence and the Ability to View Problems from Multiple Perspectives—Skills Best Learned in Diverse Academic Environments

The business world has learned that, just as Justice Powell observed, "the nation's future does indeed depend upon leaders trained" in diverse academic environments. The capacities to work easily with persons of other races and to view problems from multiple perspectives are essential skills in the business world of the twenty-first century. Indeed, the cross-cultural competence of a business' work force directly affects its bottom line. Academic institutions with diverse student bodies offer the best—and for many students, the only—opportunity to acquire these crucial skills.

1. To Achieve Excellence in the New, Diverse Global Economy, Employees of Any Race, Culture, or Ethnicity Must Possess Cross-Cultural Competence

Demographic changes in the racial and ethnic composition of business work forces, customer bases, and pools of potential business partners increasingly necessitate that entrants into the managerial levels of the business world come equipped with the abilities to work creatively with persons of any race, ethnicity, or culture and to understand views influenced by those traits. Such cross-cultural competence affects a business' performance of virtually all of major tasks: (a) identifying and satisfying the needs of diverse customers; (b) recruiting and retaining a diverse work force, and inspiring

that work force to work together to develop and implement innovative ideas; and (c) forming and fostering productive working relationships with business partners and subsidiaries around the globe.

Creating and Selling Products to a Diverse Population. Racial minorities in the United States presently wield an impressive $ 600 billion in annual purchasing power—a number that is increasing exponentially with expanding minority populations. Moreover, with the global expansion of many businesses and the advent of internet shopping, the customer bases of many businesses now include people from many races and diverse cultures around the world.

Having high-level employees who possess cross-cultural competence is essential for a business to profit from these vast market opportunities. It is undeniable that consumers' cultures can and often do influence their purchasing preferences. Businesses whose employees are able to identify and cater to these market preferences will prosper; those whose employees lack the sensitivity and domain knowledge to meet these diverse market demands will not.

To meet the challenge, businesses require managers and employees who understand that people from diverse backgrounds manifest diverse interests and who know how to translate that understanding into creative product development, community outreach, and marketing and advertising campaigns. Examples of such successful identification and satisfaction of the needs of culturally diverse populations abound.

Companies whose managers understand the importance of forging relationships with diverse communities similarly enhance their business opportunities. Author John Fernandez cites as one example General Motors' closure of a $ 1 billion automotive deal with China. The deal was aided by China's appreciation of the corporation's prior outreach efforts to Asian-American employees and the Asian-American community. Conversely, a business' lack of sensitivity to culturally based beliefs may disaffect an entire target market and result in decreased sales. Many of the best examples of this phenomenon have occurred in the global market, when American companies have failed to develop sufficient familiarity with the cultures of potential customers to avoid offending them.

Relationships in the Workplace. In the year 2000, more than one-third of all new labor force entrants in the United States were minorities. Over the next 50 years, that percentage is projected to exceed the percentage of Caucasian work force entrants. Businesses also employ citizens of other nations to staff their global manufacturing and production operations. General Motors, for example, employs citizens of 53 different countries, many of whom are non-Caucasians.

The capacity of many businesses to recruit and retain talented labor—a critical resource—therefore increasingly will depend upon the sensitivity of their managers to interracial and multicultural issues.

Indeed, companies that manage diversity well already are proving more successful in attracting and retaining top quality workers. The need to make work environments more hospitable to non-Caucasian workers is apparent: at present, minorities in general experience higher turnover rates and levels of job dissatisfaction.

Managers' and employees' cross-cultural competence augments not only recruiting and retention of employees, but also work force creativity and productivity. The best ideas and products are created by teams of people who can work together without prejudice or discomfort. The absence of such obstacles is of special import in the new work environments, of cutting-edge businesses, which stress teamwork and the free movement of ideas between people. General Motors, for example, strives for a "walls down" work environment to foster "idea flow"—an interactive process of creative brainstorming unhindered by titles and positions. Idea flow cannot be achieved across barriers of racial and cultural discomfort or among team members who are unable to accept diverse views.

A corporate management comprising individuals who have never before experienced the challenges of interracial and cross-cultural interactions that they will confront in the workplace poses great risks to efficiency and productivity. First, low-level unease between managers and employees of different races, ethnicities, and cultures may impede productivity and prevent the formation of the close working relationships that make a business "hum." Second, managers unskilled in considering diverse perspectives may fail to recognize excellent ideas when they come from unexpected sources. Third, a lack of exposure to persons of different races and

ethnicities may result in economically inefficient, and improper, hiring and promotion decisions, influenced by false stereotypes rather than an objective assessment of true merit. Such decisions not only destroy morale, but deprive the business of the benefit of excellent workers' untapped potential. In a worst-case scenario, insensitivity to issues of race or ethnicity could produce intense conflict or render a business vulnerable to costly and disruptive discrimination lawsuits.

In sum, the graduates whom businesses recruit from top academic institutions, such as the University of Michigan, to serve as managers and professionals will shape the corporate cultures and reputations for diversity of those businesses in the years to come. Graduates who lack sensitivity to perspectives influenced by race and ethnicity will be ill-equipped to meet the fundamental challenge of attracting, retaining, and managing the human capital that businesses need to survive.

Forming and Maintaining Relationships with Global Business Partners. Expanding global presences also mean that businesses increasingly transact with potential commercial partners from diverse races and cultures. General Motors, for example, has business partners and subsidiaries in many different countries and is constantly seeking to expand its operations and sales throughout the world. The company's global business objectives thus dictate that many of its managers and employees engage daily in transnational, cross-cultural, and interracial contacts. Such contacts occur at every level, from the business people to the engineers, who must work across national lines to develop and market the very best products.

Establishing trust across racial and cultural lines is a serious corporate challenge for all businesses that have international aspirations. Graduates from our Nation's elite academic institutions who have been immersed in cross-cultural learning environments will be better prepared to meet it.

2. Diversity in Academic Institutions Augments the Skills—Cross-Cultural Competence and Complex Thinking—That Students Need to Help Lead Our Country's Economic Future
Abundant research has verified Justice Powell's conclusion that racial and ethnic diversity in institutions of higher education assists

students in developing the skills that, as we have just explained, are so essential to their success in the business world: (1) understanding the views of persons from different cultures and (2) addressing issues from multiple perspectives.

Open-mindedness and complex thinking are skills best honed through exposure to multiple ideas and challenging debate in an educational environment. Academics attest, and researchers confirm, that racial and ethnic diversity enhances this process, elevating the level of discourse in institutions of higher education by exposing students to a broader range of perspectives. Students emerge from a diverse academic experience with greater tolerance and ability to interact with persons of other cultures, far less parochial views, and more highly developed cognitive abilities.

We do not undertake to catalogue the abundant research establishing the causal relationship between academic diversity and development of these cognitive and social skills—a task that other amici, representing numerous associations of university educators, have performed. We note only that Judge Duggan had ample basis for his conclusion that "solid evidence" establishes that "educational benefits ★ ★ ★ flow from a racially and ethnically diverse student body."

3. Institutions of Higher Learning Are Ideally Equipped to Provide the Exposure to Diversity, Development of Cross-Cultural Competence, and Critical Thinking Skills That Graduates Need to Thrive in the Business World Businesses depend upon institutions of higher learning to teach students the cross-cultural competence and cognitive skills they will need to perform at a high level in the business world. Higher education is the best, and for many students the only, opportunity to acquire these skills.

Selective academic institutions offer a large percentage of white students their first and last opportunity for significant contact with persons of other races and cultures prior to entering the working world. Despite our Nation's increasing racial diversity, historical patterns of de facto segregation in housing, and hence, also in primary and secondary education, persist. For many students, then, the college or university experience presents the first "opportunity to disrupt an insidious cycle of lifetime segregation."

It is also the best such opportunity. Of course, many businesses, including General Motors, can and do provide extensive diversity training to workers after their arrival in the work force. But these courses are designed to supplement, not substitute for, training and experiences most employees should have received earlier. Should the most selective institutions of higher education return to a state of de facto segregation—as research indicates most will do if the Court were to overrule Bakke and prohibit them from considering race in admissions decisions—businesses will be ill-equipped to bridge the gap.

A diminution of diversity in institutions of higher education would mean that a huge percentage of their graduates would arrive in the workplace having grown up in racially and ethnically homogeneous neighborhoods and attended racially and ethnically homogeneous schools: environments that empirical studies show breed prejudice and stereotypes. Having been "'surrounded only by the likes of themselves,'" such students are likely to hold highly parochial and limited perspectives. They may lack the openmindedness of students who have had more interactions with persons of other races.

It would be exceedingly difficult for businesses to play catch-up—to teach college graduates basic social and cognitive skills and values they should have acquired prior to entry into the workplace. First, businesses lack the pedagogical resources, including faculty, of academic institutions to provide the same training in these arenas. Businesses are primarily commercial, not educational, entities, incapable of replicating the safe academic environments that foster the robust exchange of ideas which discovers truth out of a multitude of tongues." Second, research suggests that interracial and cross-cultural contacts diminish prejudice and promote greater understanding primarily when they occur among individuals of equal status. Only schools, not businesses, offer a forum for cross-cultural contact among a society of equals, free of hierarchy. Finally, students tend to exhibit greater openness to such lessons at earlier stages of their development. "Students come to universities at a critical stage, ★ ★ ★ a time during which they define themselves in relation to others and experiment with different social roles."

Accordingly, universities, not businesses, "are [the] ideal institutions to foster" the skills and values necessary for participation in a heterogeneous society. . . . As two constitutional scholars recently observed: "If a far-flung democratic republic as diverse—and at times divided—as [modern] America is to survive and flourish, it must cultivate some common spaces where citizens from every corner of society can come together to learn how others live, how others think, how others feel. If not in public universities, where?"

In sum, institutions of higher learning have a compelling interest in selecting diverse student bodies: to enhance the educational experiences of students of all races and to equip them with the skills they need to thrive and lead our Nation as citizens and in the new global marketplace.

II. ELIMINATION OF AFFIRMATIVE ACTION IN EDUCATIONAL INSTITUTIONS LIKELY WOULD DEPRIVE BUSINESSES OF WELL-TRAINED MINORITY CANDIDATES WHO ARE ESSENTIAL TO OUR NATION'S ECONOMIC SUCCESS

Institutions of higher learning have a compelling interest in considering race and ethnicity in admission decisions, not only because diversity enhances the quality of education, but because diversity enhances the many enterprises students will undertake following graduation. Selective universities and colleges serve as training grounds for and gateways to the higher echelons of all realms of American society, including corporate America.

Businesses hire from selective academic institutions not only because they tend to select the students with greatest potential, but also because they tend to prepare their students well to perform in the top levels of the work force. Utilizing the highest quality faculty, most effective curricula, superior programs and facilities, and most powerful alumni and community contacts, these universities and colleges offer unparalleled training opportunities. The graduating classes of these institutions therefore, to some extent, define the pool from which future leaders and managers of the business world will emerge. Selective institutions of higher learning bear a special responsibility to make admissions

decisions that will not merely reward the past academic performance of individual students, but will enhance our Nation's economic future.

To accomplish that goal, academic institutions must be permitted to continue to consider, as one factor among many in their selection decisions, the race and ethnicity of applicants. Absent such consideration, the evidence suggests that the number of minorities admitted to and graduating from these selective institutions will plummet. Any reduction in diversity at these institutions accordingly would reduce the diversity of the pool of candidates from which businesses could select top corporate managers and professionals. That, in turn, threatens to deprive businesses of the manifold benefits of having a critical mass of people of color and persons of different ethnicities in their upper ranks and would strike a harmful blow to our Nation's economic well-being.

In this regard, it is notable that "higher education, by making up for educational inequities at early stages in life, can be the ramp up to a level playing field—with no further affirmative action—for the rest of one's future." Indeed as the United States recognizes, if undergraduate and graduate institutions are not open to all individuals and broadly inclusive to our diverse national community, then the top jobs ★ ★ ★ will be closed to some." If courts prohibit institutions of higher learning from performing this function, businesses will find it more difficult to hire superbly trained minority candidates.

There can be little doubt that racial and ethnic diversity in the senior leadership of the corporate world is crucial to our Nation's economic prospects. In a country in which minorities will soon dominate the labor force, commensurate diversity in the upper ranks of management is increasingly important. A stratified work force, in which whites dominate the highest levels of the managerial corps and minorities dominate the labor corps, may foment racial divisiveness. It also would be retrogressive, eliminating many of the productivity gains businesses have made through intensive efforts to eradicate discrimination and improve relations among workers of different races.

Instead of finding that the consideration of diversity leads to racial tension and stigmatization, as petitioner and amici argue, businesses have discovered just the opposite: valuing diversity has helped their bottom line. Abundant evidence suggests that heterogeneous work teams create better and more innovative products and idea than homogeneous teams. Homogeneity often causes teams to suffer from lock-step "group think." The most innovative companies therefore deliberately establish heterogeneous teams in order to create a marketplace of ideas, recognizing that a multiplicity of points of view need to be brought to bear on a problem.

In short, as GM President and CEO Jack Smith has said, "Having people of different ethnic, racial, and social backgrounds in our corporation has not slowed our pursuit of excellence—it has accelerated it." The chief executive officers of numerous Fortune 500 companies agree. As Robert J. Eaton, then-Chairman and CEO of Chrysler Corporation, explained, "workforce diversity is a competitive advantage. Our success as a global community is as dependent on utilizing the wealth of backgrounds, skills, and opinions that a diverse workforce offers, as it is on raw materials, technology and processes."

Empirical research buttresses the conclusion of these corporate executives and industry representatives that work force diversity is important to effective competition in today's market. The federal Glass Ceiling Commission, for instance, reported that "independent research has shown that companies that go the extra mile in hiring and promoting

minorities and women are more profitable." Other studies have reached similar conclusions.

General Motors strongly believes that the future of American businesses depends upon the availability of a diverse group of well-trained graduates. Only with the contributions of the best and brightest of every race, ethnicity, and culture can American businesses continue to create the world's most innovative products, manage the world's most productive work forces, and expand their operations across the globe. For the sake of the Nation's collective economic future, institutions of higher learning must be permitted to continue to achieve the diversity that enhances both the education of these individuals and the endeavors that they will undertake as graduates.

CONCLUSION

For the reasons stated, the Court should hold that the government has a compelling interest in achieving the educational benefits of diversity in higher education and that admissions parameters that are narrowly tailored to ensure a diverse, heterogeneous student body are permissible under the Constitution.

Decision Scenario A
UNITED STEELWORKERS OF AMERICA V. WEBER

For generations, blacks in America were denied jobs, were denied equal pay and promotions when they did get jobs, and were generally relegated to unskilled and semiskilled positions. Even many of these jobs were lost to increasing automation. Black unemployment was much higher than white and steadily worsening.

Congress passed the Civil Rights Act of 1964 to change all this. Title VII of that act reads, in part, that "It shall be an unlawful employment practice for any employer, labor organization, or joint labor-management committee controlling apprenticeship or other training or retraining, including on-the-job

training programs to discriminate against any individual because of his race. . . ." The legislative history of the act indicates that Congress believed that this would "open employment opportunities for Negroes in occupations which have been traditionally closed to them." But did the act prohibit any and all discrimination "because of . . . race," or only the insidious discrimination that historically had plagued blacks?

In 1974 United Steelworkers of America and Kaiser Aluminum entered into a collective-bargaining agreement that contained a plan "to eliminate conspicuous racial imbalances" in Kaiser's skilled craftwork positions. Future selection of trainees for these positions would be on the basis of seniority, except that 50% of the positions would be reserved for blacks until the percentages of blacks in these jobs approximated the percentage of blacks in the local labor force. At one Kaiser plant in Gramercy, Louisiana, for example, only 5 out of 273 (1.83%) skilled craftsworkers were black, despite the fact that 39% of the work force in the Gramercy area was black.

During the first year of the Kaiser–USWA plan, seven black and six white trainees were selected at the Gramercy plant. Several white workers who were denied admission to the training program had more seniority than the most senior black trainee. One of those rejected workers, Brian Weber, filed suit claiming that the Kaiser–USWA plan violated the section of Title VII quoted above. A district court and, later, a court of appeals decided in favor of Weber, concluding that the plan did violate Title VII's prohibition against discrimination "because of race." Upon appeal, the Supreme Court overruled these decisions and found in favor of the Kaiser–USWA plan.

The majority opinion reasoned that a literal interpretation of the law without examination of the legislative history was misplaced. They reasoned

that Congress sought to overcome the inequalities that resulted from past discrimination against blacks and that, therefore, a voluntary plan between employers and unions that had the same goals was consistent with the act. The minority opinion argued that the law explicitly prohibited any discrimination on the basis of race. In the words of Justice William Rehnquist, "Were Congress to act today specifically to prohibit the type of racial discrimination suffered by Weber, it would be hard pressed to draft language better tailored to the task than that found" in the section from Title VII quoted earlier.

- What, if anything, is the difference between the type of discrimination suffered by blacks for generations and that suffered by Weber?

- How might plans like Kaiser–USWA harm young white males? Is seniority a fair standard to use in determining qualifications? How would your views change if the Kaiser–USWA plan had been required by Congress rather than voluntarily established?

- To avoid such plans ultimately resulting in insidious discrimination against young white males, must they be ended somewhere? Where?

Decision Scenario B
PREFERENTIAL TREATMENT FOR MEN?

There are many factors that a college or university considers when evaluating applicants for admission. A number of factors testify to a student's past academic accomplishments. High school grades, quality of courses taken, and letters of recommendation are obvious examples. Other factors relate to the potential contribution that a student might make to the school. Extracurricular activities like school band or newspaper, athletic abilities, and even geographic origin might fit in this category. Still other factors consider responsibilities that the school might owe. Thus, children of alumni or faculty might be given preference, as might veterans or state citizens in a government-supported school, or members of a

religious community in a school with a religious affiliation. Finally, the school's own resources place limitations on the number of students who can be admitted to a particular major or college or assigned to on-campus living arrangements.

This variety of factors can lead to some interesting results. One student with relatively high SAT scores and high school grades might be denied admission, while another student with comparable or lower scores is admitted because his parents are alumni who contribute financially to the college. Or we might find that average SAT scores and grades for students admitted to the College of Liberal Arts are lower than those for students admitted to the Engineering College. Likewise, students who will commute to classes might face lower standards than those who require on-campus housing.

The dean of admissions for a college of business at a major university has discovered that women who are applying for admission have, on average, higher grades and College Board scores than men. This is not particularly unusual given differing social and cultural influences on male and female high school students. This dean calculates that if he decided solely on the basis of high school grades and College Board scores, the incoming freshman class would be 60% women and 40% men.

The dean has to consider several issues. The dormitory space on campus is equally divided between men and women, so a 60/40 split would create housing problems. The dean also believes that a 50/50 split of men/women is a preferable classroom environment and is preferable socially as well. He also believes that the different scores and grades are more a matter of social conditioning than they

are of innate differences. Evidence shows that males will do comparable work once admitted. Finally, the dean recognizes that both the business college and the workplace are traditionally male. He wonders whether job placement problems might arise if his college graduated a relatively large percentage of women.

The dean decides to admit an equal number of men and women, even if this requires, on average, slightly lower standards for men than women.

- Is this a case of preferential treatment? Is it unfair? What does the case say about merit? Would you have a different opinion if the roles were reversed?

- Schools often give preference to students with diverse geographical backgrounds. Can a similar argument be used for diversity of ethnic background?

- How well might this case parallel the job market situation?

Decision Scenario C
WOMEN WAGE EARNERS: LESS IS BEST?

Even when adjusted for such factors as education, experience, age, and type of job, statistics show that women continue to earn much less than men. Census data also show that women begin comparable jobs at lower salaries and that the gap between men and women increases as time goes on. It has been suggested that some women themselves, and not simply discrimination, have been responsible for differences in starting salaries. Many women may actually have lower expectations and consequently request lower salaries than men.

Place yourself in the role of personnel manager of a large accounting firm. You have interviewed a number of college seniors for several openings. In most ways the students are similar. They are seniors at the same business school, have taken the same courses, and have comparable grade point averages and experience. After conducting the interviews, you have settled upon six students to whom you intend to make offers; three are men and three are women.

You have a range from which you can offer starting salaries, with a difference of $5000 a year from the top to the bottom salaries. Since these candidates are all very well qualified and may have other offers, you want to offer a competitive salary. At the same time you need to keep your own company's costs to a minimum. At a final interview, you have asked each candidate about salary expectations and you have discovered that, in fact, the three women have lower salary expectations than the men. You have every reason to believe that you can hire the women at an average of $3000 a year less than the men, even though all six will be entering the same training program and will be doing the same jobs.

On one hand, you recognize that by starting at lower salaries the women will forever be at a disadvantage. Assuming comparable work and comparable evaluations, these employees will receive pay increases and bonuses that are a percentage of their base salary. Since they begin with a lower base, over time the women will fall farther and farther behind the men. From another perspective, to keep pace with the men's salary, these women will need to do superior work.

On the other hand, you do have a responsibility to your company to minimize costs. There is also some evidence that, at least in part, women have tended to leave your firm earlier and more often than men. Higher salaries for men, therefore, might be justified as an investment in the long run.

- Should you offer the women less? Should you advise them of what is happening?

- If the women were offered lower salaries, would this be a case of sexual discrimination? If so, who is responsible? If not, is there any ethical problem with unequal pay for equal work?

- What factors might contribute to the tendency for women to expect lower salaries? Are these factors ethically relevant?

Decision Scenario D

FEDERAL SET-ASIDES: FROM FULLILOVE TO ADARAND*

Federal government affirmative action policies cover more than individual hiring and promotion decisions. They can also involve rules for setting aside portions of federal contract money for minority-owned subcontractors. Municipal, state, and federal contract rules of the last few decades often required such affirmative action set-asides.

However, in its 1989 *Richmond v. Croson* decision, the United States Supreme Court ruled by a vote of 6–3 that cities and states may engage in racially conscious set-aside programs only if those programs 1) serve a compelling government interest and 2) are narrowly tailored to accomplish the purpose of remedying past discrimination. It ruled that the city of Richmond's 30% minority set-aside satisfied neither of these requirements. In the *Croson* case, five members of the court agreed that "while States may take remedial action when they possess evidence that their own spending practices are exacerbating a pattern of prior discrimination, they must identify that discrimination, public or private, with some specificity before they may use race-conscious relief." A sixth justice from the voting majority, Justice Scalia, rejected the idea that a state may use race-conscious remedies to address the effects of past discrimination.

The *Croson* court ruled that city or state racial classifications aimed at helping minorities were as constitutionally suspect as racial classifications aimed at discriminating against minorities. Since Richmond had not established proof of discrimination before establishing the program and since it had not proved that other, less extreme policies

could not accomplish its goals equally well, the Court found that the Richmond law violated white contractors' guarantee of equal protection of the law under the Fourteenth Amendment.

The Court, however, had previously ruled that a federal set-aside program *was* constitutionally permissible. In its 1980 decision in *Fullilove v. Klutznick,* the Court (by a vote of 6–3) accepted a congressionally mandated 10% set-aside of contract money for minority-owned business enterprises. The Court based its decision on a clause of the Reconstruction Era's Fourteenth Amendment, which gave Congress powers to ensure that racial discrimination would not continue. A plurality decision in *Fullilove* held that Congress has the "power under Section Five ... to enforce, by appropriate legislation, the equal protection guarantee ... Congress had abundant historical basis from which it could conclude that traditional procurement practices, when applied to minority businesses, could perpetuate the effects of prior discrimination, and that the prospective elimination of such barriers to minority firm access to public contracting opportunities was appropriate to ensure that those businesses were not denied equal opportunity to participate in federal grants...." It also held that Congress's use of racial and ethnic criteria as a condition of federal grants was a valid means to accomplish its constitutional objectives and that there was no requirement that Congress act in a wholly colorblind fashion. It said explicitly that when a program "narrowly tailored by Congress to achieve its objectives comes under judicial review, it should be upheld if the courts are satisfied that the legislative objectives and projected administration of the program give reasonable assurance that the program will function within constitutional limits." Apparently, in 1980, the Court felt that the federal set-aside met these conditions.

In 1995, however, another case, one involving a federal set-aside that provided financial incentives for contractors to hire "socially or economically disadvantaged" subcontractors, came before the Court. In *Adarand v. Pena,* the Court, by a vote of 5–4, reached a different conclusion. While it did not rule the federal set-aside was unconstitutional, the Court did send the case back to the lower court, which had accepted the program, for rehearing. The Supreme Court directed the lower court explicitly to decide whether the program served a "compelling interest" and was "narrowly tailored." The dissenting justices wondered about the majority's motivation in ordering a rehearing. In their eyes, the set-aside clearly satisfied the compelling interest/narrowly tailored test since the earlier set-aside from *Fullilove* passed that test and this more recent highway contract program made even less use of racial preferences.

As for the permissibility of racial classifications, two members of the *Adarand* majority joined in an opinion stating: "The unhappy persistence of both the practice and the lingering effects of racial discrimination against minority groups in this country is an unfortunate reality, and government is not disqualified from acting in response to it. . . . When race-based action is necessary to further a compelling interest, such action is within constitutional constraints if it satisfies the 'narrow tailoring' test. . . ." The four dissenting justices, of course, were willing to accept the program's race-conscious attempt to remedy past discrimination.

However, two other members of the majority, Justices Scalia and Thomas, rejected any use of race, holding that government must be totally colorblind. Thomas said that "government-sponsored racial discrimination based on benign prejudice is just as noxious as discrimination inspired by malicious prejudice."

The *Adarand* case bounced between the District, Appeals, and Supreme Courts for another eight years. It finally reached resolution in 2003 when the Supreme Court rejected a petition to hear arguments for overturning the last Court of Appeals decision. That Appeals Court decision held that the federal government had altered the rules for the minority set-aside so that the program was not now in conflict with the Constitution. Under "strict scrutiny" review, the court found that there was a compelling state interest in remedying the continuing effects of past discrimination and that the newly formed program was narrowly tailored to achieve its purpose. The set-aside passed the latter test for a number of reasons: First, the program was not a mandatory set-aside but rather an incentive system where contractors could receive financial benefits if they increased their hiring of minority-owned businesses as subcontractors. Moreover, the incentives that were provided for the hiring of disadvantaged subcontractors were capped at a small percentage of the overall contract amount. Thus, there would not be an incentive for the general contractor to award excessive numbers of subcontracts to minority enterprises and thereby effectively exclude white-owned subcontractors. Second, the federal rules encouraged contractors to use race-neutral means (such as assistance with overcoming financing obstacles faced by disadvantaged firms, providing technical assistance, and so on) to meet minority participation goals. Third, those participation goals were flexible, and the target goals for participation must be based on data about the percentages of potential minority subcontracting businesses in the immediate geographical area. Finally, the program required that businesses must provide a narrative statement about the disadvantages they have faced in order to be eligible for participation in the program. The Court reasoned that this requirement made sure that the program would not include businesses that were not disadvantaged nor exclude those that were.

While the Supreme Court let this Appeals Court decision stand, there were two justices (Scalia and Rhenquist) who took the unusual step of writing a dissent from the Courts refusal to hear further arguments. The debate over federal contract rules aimed at remedying the effects of past discrimination may thus be granted a continuance.

- Are contract set-asides different in any way from preferential treatment in individual hiring? What opportunities for abuse are there in each type of program?

- All Justices accept that race may be considered in directly remedying specific acts of discrimination.

They disagree, however, on whether race can be used in programs aimed at eradicating the effects of past discrimination. What are the practical effects of precluding race-conscious programs aimed at the effects of discrimination?

- Why would the Fourteenth Amendment have given Congress, and not the States, special powers to deal with discrimination?

Decision Scenario E
HIDE THE WEDDING RING

Equal employment opportunity has opened many doors for women. In recent decades women have entered the work force in increasing numbers and with increasing success. Unfortunately, many barriers remain.

While women are now legally free to make their own choices to pursue careers, many women still face social expectations (their own and others') that limit their choices. Traditional social roles still demand that women bear primary childcare responsibility as well as primary responsibility for maintaining the family's household. In the trite image portrayed by Madison Avenue, every working woman must be "supermom."

Of course, employers recognize the additional demands that women face. They also recognize that time and energy spent raising children and maintaining a household is time and energy not spent on the job. Employers are legally prohibited from holding women to unequal and unfair standards, but a combination of experience and prejudice can convince an employer that young married women make risky employees. This is perhaps especially true in entry-level management positions in which new hires are expected to devote significant amounts of time and energy climbing the competitive corporate ladder.

Business writer and consultant Felice Schwartz has studied the many demands placed on working women in the modern corporate world. She wrote an influential (and controversial) article for the *Harvard Business Review* in 1989 titled "Management Women and the New Facts of Life." Although she

did not use the phrase, this essay was seen (usually by critics) as calling for a "mommy track" for those women who did not wish to enter the "fast lane" of corporate management. Schwartz did argue that corporations would only benefit from removing barriers that working women faced when they tried to balance work and family. In a later book, Schwartz relates a story of how some young women cope with these barriers.

While visiting with some women MBA students at the Wharton School of Business (one of the very best business schools in the world), Schwartz was dismayed when she was told of a standard interviewing strategy. Some married women told her that they routinely removed their wedding rings when they went to a job interview. Over time it had become clear to women in the MBA program (remember, these women were among the finest business students in the world) that recruiters would not offer the best jobs to married women. The discrimination was no doubt subtle (since it is illegal), but it was real enough to give rise to this widespread defensive strategy. Apparently, recruiters believed that married women would not devote as much time and energy to their jobs as would unmarried women (to say nothing of men).

- Do you think that it is reasonable for women to remove their wedding rings when going to a job interview? Do you think that it is a good job-seeking strategy? Is it an honest one?

- Given that some employers likely do discriminate against married women, what is the best public policy approach to this problem? What is the best strategy for an individual job applicant?

- Do married men face similar barriers? Why or why not?

Portions of this case are based on material found in Felice Schwartz, *Breaking with Tradition: Women and Work, the New Facts of Life* (New York: Warner Books, 1992).

12

⁂

Ethics and Multinational Corporations

THE POWER OF MULTINATIONALS

Multinational corporations, by their nature, are largely independent of the social policies of the nation-states in which they operate. Although the national subsidiaries of multinationals must obey the regulations of the host country, the ability of multinationals to move resources on a global scale gives them great discretion about wages, workplace safety, taxes, environmental standards, and the costs of production generally. If a multinational believes that the legal or political climate of a given nation would allow more profit to be made elsewhere, the mobility of its capital allows it to shift operations more easily than would be possible for the ordinary company—although the multinational must consider such factors as the skill and educational level of local labor forces in such a relocation decision. Multinationals, then, have an ability to evade the very attempt to use public policy to control corporate behavior that has been the focus of many readings in this book.

The independence of multinationals also allows them greater influence on the creation of local and national policy. Those of us who have lived in major "rust-belt" metropolitan areas know how hard state and local governments try to attract and retain business operations. Even moderately sized local corporations can threaten relocation to a neighboring community. For fear of losing part of their tax base, local officials often make concessions on tax or regulatory policies in response to such threats. Multinationals, with their enormously greater capital, their mobility, their far-flung operations, and their lack of deeply ingrained community ties, have a magnified ability to influence public policy. This is especially true when subsidiaries operate in Third-World nations desperate for investment and employment.

Multinationals have been known to use this influence in ways that strain both legality and credulity. One of the most extreme examples is the case of International Telephone and Telegraph (ITT) in Chile. ITT had a profitable subsidiary telephone company in Chile. It feared reduced profits in the expected nationalization of that company by the government if a Marxist candidate for president, Salvadore Allende, were elected.

ITT attempted to block Allende's election through a series of maneuvers: ITT bankrolled Allende's opposition, including conservative newspapers. It lobbied Chilean legislators who would play a role in confirming the next president. It sought the support of the United States' Central Intelligence Agency in creating economic disruptions that would prevent Allende's ascent to the presidency. Even after Allende assumed office in 1970, ITT continued to undermine him through economic disruption by limiting credit, by political propaganda, and even through a boycott of Chile's important copper export trade.

Allende was eventually overthrown by a right-wing military group in 1973. The role of ITT in the overthrow is unclear, but the activities of the company provide a striking example of how multinationals can exert influence in the developing world. (Such influence is not complete, of course. Nations can attempt to limit it, for example, by placing restrictions on how much profit can be channeled offshore. These attempts are themselves subject to multinational lobbying, however.)

Since the public policy tools of nation-states are of diminished effectiveness in controlling multinationals, international business may be an area where the primary constraint on corporate behavior comes from the values and commitments of those who shape corporate policy. The opportunities for exercising those values are numerous in dealings with the developing world. As the Decision Scenarios in this chapter illustrate, specific issues of moral importance for corporate decisions include whether to trade with repressive governments, whether to market products that other nations have judged unacceptably dangerous, whether to influence the direction of local economies towards export trade, and so on. If you are interested in international business operations, try to apply the moral values expressed throughout this text in arriving at positions on these and other questions for multinational business.

THE ETHICAL RELATIVIST APPROACH

The attempt to apply these values in an international context raises the question of ethical relativism. Some people hold that moral values differ across cultures and that there is no objective way to discern whether one culture's set of values is better than another's. Some also claim that as a result of this, we cannot legitimately impose our values on those who disagree with us. A common example often offered to justify and illustrate these claims is the practice of bribery. Those who argue against the imposition of our values often point to the "fact" that bribery, as much as we condemn it, is simply a traditional way of doing business in other cultures.

A number of points need to be made in response to this reasoning. First, the social acceptance of bribery may not be as widespread as it seems. Witness the government-toppling scandals that have occurred when bribery and corruption were exposed in Japan and Italy, nations that were often offered as examples of countries where bribes are accepted practice. Perhaps the citizens of those nations are not as tolerant of bribery as we were led to believe. Perhaps the citizens see that bribes must cost someone money, probably themselves as consumers. Perhaps they see the unfairness inherent in widespread bribery when some competitors gain an undeserved advantage over others.

Second, there is a difference between bribery (an offer initiated by one party to entice another party to either violate his duties and/or extend special treatment) and extortion (the demand by another party to be paid for not disregarding another party's rights). Given this difference, bribing seems always problematic because the briber is the initiator of the harmful and unfair offer. Extortion makes the corporation seem more like a victim.

Finally, in any case, the 1977 Foreign Corrupt Practices Act settles much of the debate for United States-based multinationals and their affiliates. It makes it illegal to offer payment to foreign officials in order to obtain business or favorable treatment. (Excluded from the scope of the act, however, are payments necessary to get clerical workers to perform their duties. The act is also silent on payments to nongovernmental employees.)

Also in need of reconsideration is the more theoretical appeal to ethical relativism itself as a way of blocking the application of moral values to international business practices. We will refer you back to Chapter One for a more detailed discussion of some difficulties with relativism. Here we will only make a few brief points.

First, the claim that we cannot impose our values on others because values are relative has a name. It is known as *normative ethical relativism,* and it is widely regarded as an incoherent position. It claims, on the one hand, that it is objectively wrong for us to impose our values on those who disagree and, on the other hand, that no moral values are objective. If the latter is true, there can be no justification for believing the former. We might choose to be tolerant of some differences, but that choice is itself a moral choice. Tolerance cannot be argued as the correct approach once one adopts a relativist attitude.

Second, the fact that people disagree about particular moral matters does not establish that any moral opinion is as good as another. It may be that, in morality as in math, there are better and worse answers and procedures for arriving at them. The jump to relativism from the mere fact of disagreement is much too quick. Third, even if there is disagreement about specific moral issues, that disagreement may mask agreement about more fundamental moral principles. The disagreement about specifics may be due to differences in the relevant circumstances or in the estimation of the relevant facts.

Finally, as philosopher Richard DeGeorge has argued, even if there is fundamental disagreement about basic moral principles, a person who is willing to surrender his/her principles in the face of disagreement is a person who lacks integrity. Acting with integrity might mean that there are occasions when you have to forego doing business if the cost of that business is that you abandon your values. For example, if you really are committed to the ideal of equal moral rights for all persons, it will be impossible for you to pursue business as usual with enterprises that systematically discriminate or that use bonded labor. The only remaining choices in such circumstances are to "wash your hands" and terminate all transactions with the offending enterprise, or to continue business in a way that exerts a strong influence for change on that other enterprise. These were, incidentally, the choices pressed on American businesses in South Africa in the 1980s. Neither liberals nor conservatives were willing to accept business as usual with the apartheid regime in Pretoria. Liberals often urged full divestiture; conservatives, "constructive engagement" and adherence to the principles of equal employment suggested by the Rev. Leon Sullivan.

The consequence of having real moral commitments, then, is that there are choices that are foreclosed. Integrity makes the "easy" rationalization of the ethical relativist much less easy. (Consider, in addition, the self-interested reason for rejecting the radical relativist approach. There are costs to a business' identity, culture, and morale if its policies do not reflect consistency and commitment.)

THE NONRELATIVIST APPROACH

An alternative approach to international business ethics is taken by those who hold that not all moral values are relative. Instead, they would suggest that there are objective, universally valid norms that apply to all human action. This nonrelativist approach argues that while there can be international differences in business practices that are acceptable, there are also other practices that are unethical wherever they appear.

The difficulty of a nonrelativist approach is determining when moral beliefs are so significant that they ought to be maintained cross-culturally. Can there be any core moral beliefs that have universal authority? The reading by Tom Donaldson argues that there is a moral minimum that is required of all international businesses. He tries to identify the content of that minimum with some specificity, and he claims that there are at least ten fundamental international rights that multinationals must respect.

In another article (not reprinted here) Donaldson, with Tom Dunfee, argues that there are universal features, hypernorms, common to all social contracts. So while there is some "moral free space" within which cultures may legitimately institute different rules of behavior, there is also a discoverable set of norms that govern all cultures and economies. (You should refer back to Chapter Four for further information on this view as well as on the use of social contract theory in general.)

The next two readings, one by Ian Maitland and one by Denis Arnold and Norm Bowie, take up the topic of employment. Both readings express that there is a morally correct way to treat workers in developing nations but they disagree about what those moral requirements are. Maitland argues that many of the complaints against multinational employment practices in the developing world are mistaken. He suggests that student and labor activists, though perhaps well intentioned, are proposing employment rules that would harm the very workers they seek to protect. Arnold and Bowie, on the other hand, defend stricter moral limits on employment practices. They contend that the basic moral rights of workers are often violated in sweatshop factories. They also attempt a response to Maitland's charge that workers will suffer if stricter rules are imposed.

You should ask to what extent corporate moral obligations to employees might differ between nations. Is it acceptable for working conditions, for example, workplace safety standards, to vary between nations? Are there any universally valid minimum moral requirements for wages or for the age at which a child may work? Your answers to questions such as these, of course, require a consistent rationale. If you oppose racial discrimination in South Africa as morally objectionable but accept gender discrimination in Saudi Arabia, you must be able to identify morally relevant differences between the two.

The reading by George Brenkert shifts the focus from employment to marketing practices. Brenkert argues that marketers have a moral responsibility to consider the impact of their marketing on the cultural fabric of less-developed countries. He believes that marketing plays a partial role in the degradation of traditional cultural systems that historically have been a source of meaning and social identity for a people. Often, the introduction of Western consumer attitudes has created tensions within traditional socities when individuals forsake lifestyles that had existed for centuries. Brenkert's reading forces you to consider whether marketing's role in promoting a consumer value system has net harmful effects on economically less-developed countries. By extension, it should also force consideration of the general impact of marketing on systems of value and meaning even in the developed world.

Finally, most of the readings in the chapter discuss the negative duties of corporations not to cause unjustifiable harm. You should consider the question of whether there are ever any positive corporate duties to remedy the plight of impoverished peoples in underdeveloped nations. Donaldson, for example, argues that duties to assist the deprived do not generally fall upon for-profit corporations. Do you agree that corporations can never have a positive duty to assist, an *obligation* to act charitably towards the impoverished? How do you respond to the situation described in the Case Study on AIDS and Africa? In answering these questions, you should return to the discussions of positive and negative rights/duties in Chapter Three. Use those passages to help in your determination of whether there are ever any such corporate obligations, and if there are, specifically when and where they might arise.

The readings, case study, and decision scenarios of this chapter encourage you to develop reasoned and consistent views, based on clearly articulated moral principles, about what business practices are morally required in all contexts and about when business practices may legitimately differ across cultures. Sharpening your views on those questions in this international context will also force you to more clearly articulate the values that you believe ought to govern business practices on the home front.

CASE STUDY Africa, AIDS, and Drug Patents

The worldwide AIDS epidemic has hit hardest in sub-Saharan Africa. Almost one in five people in that region is infected by the HIV retrovirus. In some areas the figures are even more alarming. In Botswana and Swaziland, estimates are that nearly 40 percent of the population is infected. Southern Africa experiences 3 million new infections and 2.3 million AIDS deaths each year. The total numbers for the region are that nearly 27 million are infected; that represents 30 percent of those infected worldwide in a region that has only 2 percent of the world's population. Africa also has 11 million AIDS orphans, 80 percent of the world's total. Alarmingly, rates of infection are highest among women, especially young women. In addition to threatening to expand the number of orphans, the high rates of infection among women are likely to lead to increased numbers of children who acquire the infections from their mothers. Over the past 20 years, AIDS in sub-Saharan Africa has taken nearly 20 million lives.

The situation in Africa is a result of many factors. Unsafe sex and cultural factors leading to resistance to change are two of them. But so also are a dearth of organized prevention efforts and a paucity of anti-retroviral drugs that can slow the infection's progress and help prevent the virus' spread. The latter two factors are a by-product of the crushing poverty in the region. That lack of resources means that cash-strapped governments have little impact on the epidemic. It also means that most residents lack access to both anti-retroviral medicines and the medical infrastructure (clinics, education programs, health monitoring) that are essential for stemming the tide of the epidemic.

AIDS activists and health organizations argue that these conditions call for a major humanitarian effort on the part of pharmaceutical companies in the developed world. The activists allege, however, that what they have received from large Western drug companies is a stonewalling attempt to protect profits. They charge that

pharmaceutical companies have abused their market power at the expense of entire populations at risk from AIDS. In fact, in October of 2003, the South African Competition Commission, a body set up to investigate monopolistic practices, ruled that two European drug firms had engaged in anticompetitive practices that violate South African law. Specifically, the two firms, British drug giant GlaxoSmithKline (GSK) and the Swiss firm Boeringer Ingelheim, were found by the Commission to have engaged in acts of excessive pricing and exclusionary practices that have anticompetitive effects in the marketing of their AIDS drugs. GSK holds the patent on one of the most effective and widely used anti-retroviral drug cocktails, Combivir. Combivir allows patients to take both AZT and Lamivudine in a potent single pill form.

The drug firms denied the allegations. GSK pointed to the fact that it had reduced its prices by 40 percent in the developing world (though some claimed it was demanding that African countries purchase existing stock at the previous higher price). It noted that it had the lowest prices for anti-retrovirals in the South African private sector and that, just months earlier, the same Competition Commission had found GSK not guilty of a charge of excessive pricing on another of its antiviral medicines.

This specific debate between the drug companies and advocates for the AIDS patients is merely a recent instance of a long history of conflict. That conflict is centered around the World Trade Organization (WTO). In 1995, the WTO issued rules governing the protection of intellectual property rights. Western firms, especially drug and technology companies, had grown agitated over what they considered blatant pirating activity by companies in the developing world. Many of those companies would reverse-engineer Western products and then sell unlicensed or generic versions both in their home country and in other developing nations. The prices of these unlicensed generics drastically undercut the prices charged by the originating Western manufacturer. As a result of complaints about violations of intellectual property and patent rights, the WTO produced a set of rules entitled Trade-Related Aspects of Intellectual Property Rights (TRIPS). TRIPS attempted to standardize the variety of national patent and copyright laws in an effort to both improve the efficiency of international trade and guarantee some protection for the rights of patent holders (who could press for WTO trade sanctions against offending countries).

However, the TRIPS agreement did allow developing nations some time to achieve compliance, and it allowed a country to suspend the international patent rules in the case of a national emergency. South Africa passed legislation in 1998 that allowed drug patents to be suspended so that patent owners would be compelled to license the manufacture and sale of generic versions for a "reasonable fee." The law also approved the import of generic drugs manufactured in other countries. Both elements of the law are seen as essential by AIDS activists. The requirement to license generic versions pushes drug costs lower in a region where access to drugs is hampered by poverty. For instance, GSK's branded drugs are almost twice the price of the generics, and this is even after GSK lowered its prices dramatically. The ability to import generics is also seen as crucial, since most developing nations lack the manufacturing capacity to produce the anti-AIDS drugs. In South Africa, the major source of generic supply is the Indian firm, Cipla.

The South African law was vigorously resisted by Western pharmaceutical companies, as well as by the Bush administration. The U.S. government lobbied for changes in the WTO rules, in particular for a ban on export of generics from the country of manufacture. Four of the biggest (Bristol-Myers-Squibb, GSK, Merck and Hoffman-La Roche) brought suit. The companies argued that stricter respect for intellectual property rights is necessary in order to provide innovating manufacturers the incentives for future research and development. Without patent protection, companies will have little incentive to pursue breakthrough new therapies. They fear that their drugs will be copied and exported even to the developing world. They argue that, in the end, this would hurt all patients by reducing the number of new drugs.

Drug companies have also suggested that Africa's real problem is the absence of the medical infrastructure needed for the effective delivery of anti-retroviral drugs. These drugs must be used indefinitely. Moreover, patients must be constantly monitored for compliance, and they must be tested frequently to assure that the drugs are working. Most threatening, the companies warn, is the possibility that the quickly changing HIV virus will develop resistance to the only known therapies without strict compliance with the dosage regimen. Spread of such resistant strains of the virus could erase the progress against the disease that has been made in the past decade.

The activists and the African nations respond to these claims by admitting that infrastructure is a problem but so, too, are the availability and affordability of the drugs. They note that drug profits from Africa are a miniscule amount of the large margins enjoyed by major pharmaceutical companies and that, as a result, the claimed need for patent protection as an incentive to produce rings false. They point to WHO (World Health Organization) studies that indicate that those developing nations that have suspended patent protections have made more progress against the epidemic, though the progress is far from sufficient. As for the danger of developing resistant strains of HIV, they ask whether, in an age of global travel, the world is safer with an actually exploding infected population or with an attempt to prevent the potential emergence of new strains by delaying treatment for the developing world. They note that countries without past epidemics, including China, India, Vietnam, and Russia, are now experiencing rapidly increasing rates of infection that threaten to spread beyond their borders. One commentator, in a newsletter from drug maker Pfizer no less, suggested that the developing nations bear the costs of the international patent system through higher prices but are unable and unlikely to share the benefits of that system in the near or medium term.

Partly as a result of international public and political pressures, the drug companies dropped their suit against South Africa in late 2003. And Bristol-Myers-Squibb pledged $115 million to fund innovative initiatives aimed at improving the delivery and monitoring of AIDS medications. GSK agreed to provide licenses to generic manufacturers for a 5 percent royalty fee instead of the 30 percent it had charged previously. One hundred twenty major firms, including Chevron, Daimler-Chrysler, Heineken, and the Indian conglomerate Tata, have recently committed to spending millions to build clinics and to train healthcare workers to supplement African government programs. The Bush administration pledged $15 billion, including $3 billion for 2004 (although the administration budget request reduced that amount by a third and funding is perilous in an era of exploding U.S. government deficits). Interestingly, however, some of the same

Indian generic manufacturers who drew the ire of Western drug makers have resisted their own government's attempt to lower the cost of drugs. They are demanding tax concessions and sales assurances before they accept the government's proposals.

- What obligations do private sector firms have when confronted with devastating losses that they could mitigate? Is it possible to deflect the duty to assist those in need by placing the responsibility on local governments or on the governments of more affluent developed nations? When does a positive duty to assist those in need exist?
- Should the Indian firms mentioned in the last paragraph accede to their government's request for lower prices or do they have a moral right to demand financial assurances?
- How much of a threat to the patent system and to the possibility of future innovations is the suspension of drug patents by developing nations? How might one balance the legitimate

intellectual property rights of original manufacturers against the health needs of impoverished communities?

This case was prepared from the following sources: "High Stakes Game With the Lives of the Poorest," Johann Hari, *The Sunday Tribune*, September 7, 2003; "GSK Reneges on Lower AIDS Drug Prices," *PR Newswire*, September 15, 2003; "Nations That Have Suspended Patents for AIDS Drugs Show Some Success," Chris Tomlinson, *The Associated Press*, September 22, 2003; "AIDS Treatment for Africa," Richard Ingham, *Agence France Presse*, September 27, 2003; "Bush's AIDS Gift," Naomi Klein, *The Guardian*, October 13, 2003; "AIDS Healthcare Foundation Demands Immediate Action," *PR Newswire European*, October 17, 2003; "Foreign Firms Block Generic AIDS Drugs," Tamar Kahn, *Business Day South Africa*, October 17, 2003; "Pharmaceutical Companies Charging Unfair Prices," Sarah Boseley, *The Guardian*, October 17, 2003; "Bristol-Myers-Squibb Company Announces $30 Million," *PR Newswire*, November 24, 2003; "AIDS Epidemic Still Advancing," *Africa News*, November 25, 2003; "New Delhi Tries to Reach Deal with Drug Groups," Ray Marcelo, *The Financial Times*, December 3, 2003; "Seven Multinationals Contribute to Programmes to Fight Against AIDS," *AFX News Limited*, December 4, 2003; "Deal Paves the Way for Generic HIV Drugs," John Donnelly, *The Boston Globe*, December 11, 2003: "Agreement Expands Generic Drugs in South Africa," Michael Wines, *The New York Times*, December 11, 2003.

READING 12.1 RIGHTS IN THE GLOBAL MARKET
Thomas J. Donaldson

Rights we take for granted are sometimes trampled abroad. Child labor plagues Central America, and dozens of interviews with workers in Central America conducted in the fall of 1987 reveal that most respondents started working between the ages of 12 and 14.[1] In other countries the rights to minimal education, free speech, basic nutrition, and freedom from torture are little more than dreams. What obligations do multinational corporations have in such contexts? Are they obliged not only to honor but to encourage the protection of such rights? Consider the claim that persons everywhere have a right to adequate food. What are we to say when a multinational corporation, working in a country where malnutrition is rampant, buys a parcel of land and converts it from the production of a staple food source to one for cash export? If the land is purchased from a wealthy landowner and converted from growing black beans to coffee, has the company indirectly violated a right to adequate food if it turns out that the purchase lowers the food supply?

These questions exist in a class of questions concerned with establishing minimal conditions upon the behavior of multinational corporations. They are ones that have been largely neglected by academic researchers. Business academics have contributed significantly to understanding the problems of international business; they have offered a bounty of empirical analysis relevant to multinational corporations, and have conducted detailed inquiries into the structure of global markets and the strategies of multinational corporations.[2] Yet few of their efforts highlight the moral element. The notable exceptions are academics working out of the so-called social issues and business environment perspectives,[3] yet even here only a fraction of such normative work from academic business researchers has found application to multinational corporations, and when it has, the context has tended to be issue-specific, for example, Bhopal, or South African divestment.[4]

This paper will attempt to develop a list of fundamental human rights serviceable for international business. Ten specific rights are advanced to establish bottom-line moral considerations for multinational corporations. The paper concludes that corporations, individuals, and governments must respect these 10 rights, although it argues that the correlative duties that corporations must shoulder in honoring those rights are different from those of nation states and individuals. Much of the analysis is drawn from a more extensive treatment offered in my recent book, *The Ethics of International Business.*.[5]

RIGHTS ESTABLISH MINIMAL CORPORATE RESPONSIBILITIES

We should first distinguish those corporate responsibilities that hold as minimal conditions from those that exceed the minimum. "Minimal" duties for multinational corporations are similar to Kant's "perfect" duties; that is, they are mandatory and allow no discretion as to when or how they are performed. A "maximal" duty, on the other hand, is one whose fulfillment would be praiseworthy but not absolutely mandatory. Our concern, in turn, is with "minimal," rather than "maximal" duties. Our aim is to inquire, for example, whether a foreign corporation's minimal duties include refusing to hire children in a Honduran assembly plant, even if doing so harms the company's competitive position. It is not to establish guidelines for exemplary or "model" multinational behavior.

Our strategy will be to assume that most if not all minimal responsibilities can be framed through the language of rights, a language recognized for establishing minimal moral obligations. Rights may be seen to lie at the rock bottom of modern moral deliberation. Maurice Cranston writes that the litmus test for whether or not something is a right is whether it protects something of "paramount importance."[6] If I have a right not to be tortured, then in violating that right you threaten something of paramount value to me. It would be splendid if you did even more—if, for example, you treated me with love and charity; but *at a minimum* you must respect my rights.

The flip side of a right typically is a duty,[7] a fact that gives aptness to Joel Feinberg's well-known definition of a right as a "justified entitlement *to* something *from* someone."[8] It is the "from someone" part of the definition that reflects the assumption of a duty, for without a correlative duty that attaches to some moral agent or group of agents, a

right is weakened—if not beyond the status of a right entirely, then significantly. If we cannot say that a multinational corporation has a duty to keep the levels of arsenic low in the workplace, then the worker's right not to be poisoned means little.

Often, duties fall upon more than one class of moral agent. Consider, for example, the furor over the dumping of toxic waste in West Africa by multinational corporations. During 1988, virtually every country from Morocco to Zaire on Africa's west coast received offers from companies seeking cheap sites for dumping waste.[9] In the years prior, toxic waste dumping had become enormously expensive in the United States and Europe, in large part because of the costly safety measures mandated by U.S. and European governments. In February 1988 officials in Guinea Bissau, one of the world's poorest nations, agreed to bury 15 million tons of toxic wastes from European tanneries and pharmaceutical companies. The companies agreed to pay about $120 million, which is only slightly less than the country's entire gross national product. And in Nigeria, in 1987, five European ships unloaded toxic waste containing dangerous poisons such as polychlorinated biphenyls, or PCBs. Workers wearing thongs and shorts unloaded the barrels for $2.50 a day, and placed them in a dirt lot in a residential area in the town of Kiko.[10] They were not told about the contents of the barrels.[11] Who bears responsibility for protecting the workers' and inhabitants' rights to safety in such instances? It would be wrong to place it entirely upon a single group of agents such as the governments of West African nations. As it happens, the toxic waste dumped in Nigeria entered under an import permit for "non-explosive, non-radioactive and non-self-combusting chemicals." But the permit turned out to be a loophole; Nigeria had not meant to accept the waste and demanded its removal once word about its presence filtered into official channels. The example reveals the difficulty many developing countries have in generating the sophisticated language and regulatory procedures necessary to control high-technology hazards. It seems reasonable in such instances, then, to place the responsibility not upon a single class of agents but upon a broad collection of them, including governments, corporate executives, host country companies and officials, and international organizations. The responsibility for not violating the rights of people living in West Africa from the dangers of toxic waste then potentially falls upon every agent whose actions might harm, or contribute to harming, West African inhabitants. Nor is one agent's responsibility always mitigated when another "accepts" responsibility. To take a specific instance, corporate responsibility may not be eliminated if a West African government explicitly agrees to accept toxic waste. There is always the possibility—said to be a reality by some critics—that corrupt government officials will agree to accept and handle waste that threatens safety in order to fatten their own Swiss bank accounts.

Rights with international relevance should be viewed as occupying an intermediary zone between abstract moral principles such as liberty or fairness on the one hand, and national specifications of rights on the other.[12] International rights must be more specific than abstract principles if they are to facilitate practical implication, but be less specific than the entries on lists of rights whose duties fall on national governments if they are to preserve cosmopolitan relevance. One nation's particular social capacities or social traditions may favor the recognition of certain rights that are inappropriate to other nations. Citizens of a rich, technologically advanced nation, for example, but not of a poor, developing one, may be viewed as possessing a right to a certain technological level of health care. You, as a citizen of the United States, may have the right to kidney dialysis; but a citizen of Bangladesh may not.

As a first approximation, then, let us interpret a multinational's obligations by asking which international rights it should respect, where we understand *international rights* to be sort of moral precepts that lie in a zone between abstract moral principles and national rights specifications. Multinationals, we shall assume, should respect the international rights of those whom they affect, especially when those rights are of the most fundamental sort.

But whose list of international rights shall we choose? Libertarians tend to endorse well-pruned lists of liberty-centered rights, ones that look like the first 10 amendments to the U.S. Constitution (the Bill of Rights) without the subsequent constitutional amendments, while welfare liberals frequently endorse lush, well-tangled structures that include entitlements as well as freedoms. Who is to say that a given person's list, or a given country's list, for that matter, is preferable to another's?

One list receiving significant international attention, a list bearing the signatures of most of the world's nations, is the "Universal Declaration of Human Rights."[13] However, it and the subsequent "International Covenant on Social, Economic and Cultural Rights," have spawned controversy despite the fact that the Universal Declaration was endorsed by virtually all of the important post–World War II nations in 1948 as part of the affirmation of the U.N. Charter. What distinguishes these lists from their predecessors, and what serves also as the focus of controversy, is their inclusion of rights that have come to be called alternatively "social," "economic,"" positive," or "welfare" rights. Nuances separate these four concepts, but they need not detain us; all formulations share the feature of demanding more than forbearance from those upon whom the right's correlative duties fall. All four refer to rights that entail claims by rights holders to specific goods, where such goods must at least sometimes be provided by other persons (although sometimes by unspecified others). The goods at issue are typically such things as food, education, and shelter. For convenience, we shall use the term "welfare rights" to refer to all claims of this kind. Some international rights documents even specify *as* welfare rights claims to goods that are now regarded as standard benefits of the modern welfare state. For example, Articles 22 through 27 of the Universal Declaration assert rights to social security insurance, employment, protection against unemployment, health care, education, and limits on working hours.[14]

Many have balked when confronted with such lists, arguing that no one can have a right to a specific supply of an economic good. Can anyone be said to have a "right," for example, to 128 hours of sleep and leisure each week? And, in the same spirit, some international documents have simply refused to adopt the welfare-affirming blueprint established in the Universal Declaration.[15] The issue is critical for establishing the minimal responsibilities of multinational corporations, for it is only to the extent that, say, the right to adequate food exists, that multinationals can be chided for violating it.

Henry Shue advances a compelling notion of welfare rights—one with special relevance to our task—in his book, *Basic Rights.*[16] Shue's guiding concept of a "basic right" entails the existence of welfare rights. The essence of a basic right, says

Shue, is "something the deprivation of which is one standard threat to rights generally."[17] Basic rights include the right to subsistence, or "minimal economic security," to freedom of physical movement, security, and political participation. By way of explanation, the right to *subsistence* entails a claim to, e.g., "unpolluted air, unpolluted water, adequate food, adequate clothing, adequate shelter, and minimal preventative public health care."[18] The right to *freedom of physical movement* is a right to not have "arbitrary constraints upon parts of one's body, such as ropes, chains, . . . and the absence of arbitrary constraints upon the movement from place to place of one's whole body, such as . . . pass laws (as in South Africa)."[19] The right to *security* is a right not to be subjected to "murder, torture, mayhem, rape, or assault"; and the right to *political participation* is the right to have "genuine influence upon the fundamental choices among the societal institutions and the societal policies that control security and subsistence and, where the person is directly affected, genuine influence upon the operation of institutions and the implementation of policy."[20] The key to understanding a basic right for Shue is recognizing that it is a prerequisite for the enjoyment of other rights. Thus being secure from beatings is a prerequisite for the enjoyment of, e.g., the right to freedom of assembly, since one's freedom to hold political meetings is dependent upon one's freedom from the fear of beatings in the event one chooses to assemble. Shue insists correctly that benevolent despotism cannot ensure basic rights. One's rights are not protected even by the most enlightened despot in the absence of social institutions that guarantee that basic rights will be preserved in the event such benevolence turns to malevolence.[21] Illusions, as the saying goes, are not liberties.

Shue's analysis, moreover, provides a formidable argument on behalf of such rights. The argument is successful because it unpacks the sense in which it is contradictory to support any list of rights without at the same time supporting those specific rights upon whose preservation the list can be shown to depend. It is a strategy with direct application to the controversy between defenders and critics of welfare rights, for if Shue is correct, even a list of *non*-welfare rights ultimately depends upon certain basic rights, some of which are welfare rights. His argument utilizes the following, simple propositions:

1. Everyone has a right to something.

2. Some other things are necessary for enjoying the first thing as a right, whatever the first right is.

3. Therefore, everyone also has rights to the other things that are necessary for enjoying the first thing as a right.[22]

We shall grasp Shue's point even better by considering, on the one hand, a standard objection to welfare rights, and on the other, a response afforded by Shue's theory. Now many who criticize welfare rights utilize a traditional philosophical distinction between so-called negative and positive rights. A "positive" right is said to be one that requires persons to act positively to *do* something, and a "negative" right requires only that people not deprive directly. Hence, the right to liberty is said to be a negative right, whereas the right to enough food is said to be a positive one. With this distinction in hand, it is common to conclude that no one can be bound to improve the welfare of another (unless, say, that person has entered into an agreement to do so); rather, at most they can be bound to *refrain* from damaging the welfare of another.

Shue's argument, however, reveals the implausibility of the very distinction between negative and positive rights. Perhaps the most celebrated and best accepted example of a negative right is the right to freedom. Yet the meaningful preservation of freedom requires a variety of positive actions: for example, on the part of the government it requires the establishment and maintenance of a police force, courts, and the military, and on the part of the citizenry it requires ongoing cooperation and diligent (not merely passive) forbearance. And the protection of another so-called negative right, the right to physical security, necessitates "police forces; criminal rights; penitentiaries; schools for training police, lawyers, and guards; and taxes to support an enormous system for the prevention, detention, and punishment of violations of personal security."[23]

This is compelling. The maintenance and preservation of many non-welfare rights (where, again, such maintenance and preservation is the key to a right's status as "basic") requires the support of certain basic welfare rights. For example, certain liberties depend upon the enjoyment of subsistence, just as subsistence sometimes depends upon the enjoyment of some liberties. One's freedom to speak freely is meaningless if one is weakened by hunger to the point of silence.

THE PROBLEM WITH "BASIC" RIGHTS

But while establishing the legitimacy of some welfare rights, Shue's argument is nonetheless flawed.
To begin with, from the standpoint of moral logic,
his methodology appears to justify the more
important in terms of the less important. That is to
say, insofar as a basic right is defined as one whose
preservation is necessary for the preservation of all
rights generally, the determination of what counts
as "basic" will occur by a process that takes as fundamental all rights, including non-basic ones, and
then asks which among those rights are rights such
that their absence would constitute a threat to the
others. Not only does this fail to say anything
about the moral grounding or rights in general, it
also hinges the status of the basic rights on their
ability to support all rights, including non-basic
rights, and this appears to place the hierarchical
cart before the horse.[24] This problem enlarges
when we notice that many of the so-called non-
basic rights such as freedom of speech appear to be
of equal importance to some so-called basic rights.
One wonders why a few of the world's most
important rights, such as the rights to property, free
speech, religious freedom, and education, are
regarded as non-basic. One can see why, given
Shue's concept of a basic right, they are non-basic,
but then one wonders whether they might be basic
in an even more important sense.

Shue himself acknowledges that status as a basic
right does not guarantee that the right in question
is more important. At one point, while contrasting a
non-basic right, such as the right to education, to a
basic right, such as the right to security, he states, "I
do not mean by this to deny that the enjoyment of
the right to education is much greater and richer—
more distinctively human, perhaps—than merely
going through life without ever being assaulted."
But he next asserts the practical priority of basic
rights by saying, "I mean only that, if the choice
must be made, the prevention of assault ought to
supersede the provision of education."[25] So while
denying that basic rights are necessarily more
important than non-basic ones in all respects, he
grants that they are more important in the sense
that probably matters most: they are given priority
in decisions where a choice must be made between
defending one right and defending another. He
concludes, "therefore, if a right is basic, other, non-

basic rights may be sacrificed, if necessary, in order
to secure the basic right."[26]

But what Shue leaves obscure is the matter of
which rights *other* than basic rights are deserving of
emphasis. For Shue, every right must occupy one of
two positions on the rights hierarchy: it is either
basic or not. But if so, then how are individuals,
governments, and corporations to know which
rights should be honored in a crunch? Shue clearly
believes that individuals, governments, and corporations must honor *basic* rights, but how are the
remaining non-basic rights to be treated? What of
the right to freedom of speech, to property, or to a
minimal education? Are these rights *always* to be
given second-class status? And if they are to be
given priority in some instances, then why? Then
too, surely, Shue will agree that all *nation states* must
honor the right to freedom of speech, but is the
same true of all individuals and corporations? Does
it follow that corporations must tolerate all speech
affecting the workplace and never penalize offending workers, even when the speech is maliciously
motivated and severely damages profitability?
Similarly, are all states responsible for defending *all*
other non-basic rights?

FUNDAMENTAL INTERNATIONAL RIGHTS

Let us adopt another method of approach. Let us
attempt to determine which rights are most fundamental directly, i.e., by using criteria that ground
fundamental rights. In other words, instead of
employing an analytic argument that takes for
granted a body of rights and then analyzes the logic
of their interdependence (as Shue does), let us
employ a normative argument that looks to the
grounding of rights in general. Let us stipulate three
conditions that will be independently necessary and
jointly sufficient for considering a given prospective
as (a) a right and (b) a right of fundamental importance. Such a right we shall label a "fundamental
international right." These three conditions are that
(1) the right protects something of extreme importance, that (2) it is subject to significant, recurring
threats, and that (3) the obligations or burdens it
imposes are economically affordable and fair with
respect to the distribution of burdens generally.
These three conditions resemble, although they are

not identical to, three of the four conditions advanced by James Nickel, in his book, *Making Sense of Human Rights,*[27] for identifying rights imposing claims on nation-states. In the present context, however, they are advanced as having application to all three of the major classes of international actors, i.e., nation-states, individuals, and multinational corporations.

Consider each condition. The first recognizes that if claims are made to things that have little or only moderate importance, then even if those claims happen to be valid, they cannot aspire to the status of "rights." We are reminded of Maurice Cranston's "paramount importance" test cited earlier for bona fide rights. The second notes that rights also must be subject to what Shue calls "standard" threats or what Nickel has alternatively dubbed "recurrent" threats. A right must be subject to significant, recurring threats for the simple reason that the list of claims centering on interests of fundamental importance would otherwise expand indefinitely. And finally, as Nickel has shown convincingly, any right must satisfy what could be called an "affordability-fairness" criterion in that it must impose obligations or other burdens that are in Nickel's words "affordable in relation to resources, other obligations, and fairness in the distribution of burdens." Part of the justification for this condition is as simple as the time-honored dictum in moral philosophy that "ought implies can," or, in other words, that no person or entity can be held responsible for doing something if it is not in their power to do it. We need only add the reasonable proviso that sometimes a duty may be of a kind that is discouraged for moral reasons, i.e., either because it conflicts with another bona fide obligation or because it constitutes an unfairness in the distribution of burdens.

Next, consider the following list of fundamental international rights:

1. The right to freedom of physical movement

2. The right to ownership of property

3. The right to freedom from torture

4. The right to a fair trial

5. The right to non-discriminatory treatment (i.e., freedom from discrimination on the basis of such characteristics as race or sex)

6. The right to physical security

7. The right to freedom of speech and association

8. The right to minimal education

9. The right to political participation

10. The right to subsistence

This seems a minimal list. Some will wish to add entries such as the right to employment, to social security, or to a certain standard of living (say, as might be prescribed by Rawls's well-known "difference" principle). Disputes also may arise about the wording or overlapping features of some rights: for example, is not the right to freedom from torture included in the right to physical security, at least when the latter is properly interpreted? We shall not attempt to resolve such controversies here. Rather, the list as presented aims to suggest, albeit incompletely, a description of a *minimal* set of rights and to serve as a point of beginning and consensus for evaluating international conduct. If I am correct, many would wish to add entries, but few would wish to subtract them.

The list has been generated by application of the three conditions and the compatibility proviso. Readers may satisfy for themselves whether the ten entries fulfill these conditions; in doing so, however, they should remember that in constructing the list one looks for *only* those rights that can be honored in some form by *all* international agents, including nation-states, corporations, and individuals. Hence, to consider only the issue of affordability, each candidate for a right must be tested for "affordability" by way of the lowest common denominator—by way, for example, of the poorest nation-state. If, even after receiving its fair share of charitable aid from wealthier nations, that state cannot "afford" dialysis for all citizens who need it, then the right to receive dialysis from one's nation state will not be a fundamental international right, although dialysis may contribute a bona fide right for those living within a specific nation-state, such as Japan.

Although the hope for a definitive interpretation of the list of rights is an illusion, we can add specificity by clarifying the correlative duties entailed for different kinds of international actors. Because by definition the list contains items that all three major classes of international actors must respect, the next task is to spell out the correlative duties that fall upon our targeted group of international actors, namely, multinational corporations.

Doing so requires putting the third condition from Nickel's revised list to a second, and different, use. This "affordability-fairness" condition—which, again, concerns the affordability of respecting a right from the perspective of an agent's resources, other obligations, and overall fairness in the distribution of burdens—was used first as one of the criteria for generating the original list of fundamental rights. There it demanded satisfaction of an affordability-fairness threshold for each potential respecter of a right. For example, were the burdens imposed by a given right not fair (in relation to other bona fide obligations and burdens) or affordable for nation-states, individuals, and corporations, then presumably the prospective right would not qualify as a fundamental international right. In its second use, to which it is about to be put, the condition goes beyond the judgment *that* a certain affordability-fairness threshold has been crossed to the determination of *what* the proper duties are for multinational corporations in relation to a given right. In its second use, in other words, the condition's notions of fairness and affordability are invoked to help determine *which* obligations properly fall upon corporations, in contrast to individuals and nation-states. We shall use the condition to help determine the correlative duties that attach to multinational corporations in their honoring of fundamental international rights.

As we look over the list, it is noteworthy that except for a few isolated instances multinational corporations have probably succeeded in fulfilling their duty not to *actively deprive* persons of their enjoyment of the rights at issue. But correlative duties involve more than failing to actively deprive people of the enjoyment of their rights. Shue, for example, notes that three types of correlative duties are possible for any right, namely, duties to (1) avoid depriving, (2) help protect from deprivation, and (3) aid the deprived.[28]

While it is obvious that the honoring of rights clearly imposes duties of the first kind, i.e., to avoid depriving directly, it is less obvious, but frequently true, that honoring them involves acts or omissions that help prevent the deprivation of rights. If I receive a threat from Murder, Inc., and it looks like they mean business, my right to security is clearly at risk. If a third party has relevant information that if revealed to the police would help protect my right, it is no excuse for the third party to say that it is Murder, Inc., and not they (the third party), who wishes to kill me. Hence, honoring rights sometimes involves not only duties to *avoid depriving,* but to *help protect from deprivation* as well, and it is interesting that many critics of multinationals have faulted them not for the failure to avoid depriving but for failing to take reasonable protective steps.

Similarly, the duties associated with rights can often include duties from the third category, i.e., that of *aiding the deprived,* as when a government is bound to honor the right of its citizens to adequate nutrition by distributing food in the wake of a famine or natural disaster, or when the same government in the defense of political liberty is required to demand that an employer reinstate or compensate an employee fired for voting for a particular candidate in a government election.

Nonetheless, the honoring by multinational corporations of at least *some* of the ten fundamental rights requires the adoption of only the first class of correlative duties, i.e., the duty to avoid depriving. Correlative duties do not extend either to protecting from deprivation or aiding the deprived, because of the relevance of the "fairness-affordability" condition discussed before. This condition requires, again, that the obligations or burdens imposed by a right must be affordable in relation to resources, other obligations, and fairness in the distribution of burdens. (Certain puzzles affecting the affordability-fairness condition are discussed later in the context of the "drug lord" problem.)

Corporations cannot be held to the same standards of charity and love as individuals. Nor can corporations be held to the same standards to which we hold civil governments for enhancing social welfare—since frequently governments are dedicated to enhancing the welfare of, and actively preserving the liberties of, their citizens. The profit-making corporation, in contrast, is designed to achieve an economic mission and as a moral actor possesses an exceedingly narrow personality. It is an undemocratic institution, furthermore, which is ill-suited to the broader task of distributing society's goods in accordance with a conception of general welfare. The corporation is an economic animal; although one may deny that its sole responsibility is to make a profit for its investors, one will surely wish to define its responsibilities differently than for civil governments.

Let us employ a "minimal/maximal" distinction to draw the inference that duties of the third class, i.e., to aid the deprived, do not fall upon for-profit multinational corporations, except, of course, in instances where the corporations themselves have done the depriving. For example, although it would be strikingly generous for multinationals to sacrifice some of their profits to buy milk, grain, and shelter for persons in poor countries, assisting the poor is not one of the corporations' minimal moral requirements; such minimal obligations belong more properly to the peoples' respective governments or, perhaps, to better-off individuals. If corporations possess duties to aid those deprived of the benefits of rights (except, again, in instances where they have done the depriving), then they possess them as "maximal" not "minimal" duties, which means that a given corporation's failure to observe them does not deprive that corporation of its moral right to exist. Furthermore, since rights impose minimal, not maximal duties, it follows that whereas a corporation might have a maximal duty to aid the deprived in a given instance, their failure to honor that duty could not be claimed necessarily as a violation of someone's *rights*.

The same, however, is not true of the second class of duties, i.e., to protect from deprivation. These duties, like those in the third class, are also usually the province of government, but it sometimes happens that the rights to which they correlate are ones whose protection is a direct outcome of ordinary corporate activities. For example, the duties associated with protecting a worker from the physical threats of other workers may fall not only upon the local police but also to some extent upon the employer. These duties, in turn, are properly viewed as correlative duties of a person's right—in this instance, the worker's right—to personal security. This will become clearer in a moment when we discuss the correlative duties of specific rights.

The table of correlative duties (p. 486) reflects the application of the "affordability-fairness" condition to the earlier list of fundamental international rights, and indicates which rights do, and which do not, impose correlative duties upon multinational corporations of the three various kinds. A word of caution should be issued for interpreting the list: the first type of correlative obligation, i.e., of not depriving directly, is broader than might be supposed at first. It includes *cooperative* as well as exclu-

sively individual actions. Thus, if a company has personnel policies that inhibit freedom of movement, or if a multinational corporation operating in South Africa cooperates with the government's restrictions on pass laws, then those companies actively deprive persons of their right to freedom of movement, despite the fact that actions of other agents (in particular, of the South African government) may be essential in effecting the deprivation. Similarly, in an instance where a corporation cooperates with political groups in fighting land reforms designed to take land from a tiny aristocratic minority (a minority that, say, owns virtually all of a country's usable land) for redistribution to peasants, those corporations may well—at least under certain circumstances—violate the right to private property.

Still, the list asserts that at least six of the ten fundamental rights impose correlative duties of the second kind upon corporations, that is, to protect from deprivation.[29] What follows is a brief set of commentaries discussing sample applications of each of those six rights from the perspective of such correlative duties.

SAMPLE APPLICATIONS

Discrimination

The obligation to protect from deprivation a person's freedom from discrimination properly falls upon corporations as well as governments insofar as everyday corporate activities directly affect compliance with the right. Because employees and prospective employees possess the moral right not to be discriminated against on the basis of race, sex, caste, class, or family affiliation, it follows that multinational corporations have an obligation not only to refrain from discrimination but in some instances to protect the right to non-discriminatory treatment by establishing appropriate procedures. This may require, for example, offering notice to prospective employees of the company's policy of non-discriminatory hiring, or educating lower level managers about the need to reward or penalize on the basis of performance rather than irrelevant criteria.

Physical Security

The right to physical security similarly entails duties of protection: if a Japanese multinational corporation operating in Nigeria hires shop workers to run

Minimal Correlative Duties of Multinational Corporations

Fundamental Rights	To Avoid Depriving	To Help Protect from Deprivation	To Aid the Deprived
Freedom of physical movement	X		
Ownership of property	X		
Freedom from torture	X		
Fair trial	X		
Non-discriminatory treatment	X	X	
Physical security	X	X	
Freedom of speech and association	X	X	
Minimal education	X	X	
Political participation	X	X	
Subsistence	X	X	

metal lathes in an assembly factory but fails to provide them with protective goggles, then the corporation has failed to honor the workers' moral right to physical security (no matter what the local law might decree). Injuries from such a failure would be the moral responsibility of the Japanese multinational despite the fact that the company could not be said to have inflicted the injuries directly.

Free Speech and Association

In the same vein, the duty to protect the right of free speech and association from deprivation finds application in the ongoing corporate obligation not to bar the emergence of labor unions. Corporations are not obliged on the basis of human rights to encourage or welcome labor unions, but neither are they morally permitted to destroy them or prevent their emergence through coercive tactics; to do so would violate the workers' international right to association. Their duty to protect the right to association from deprivation, in turn, includes refraining from lobbying host governments for restrictions that would violate the right in question, and perhaps even to protesting host government measures that do violate it.[30]

Minimal Education

The correlative duty to protect the right of education may be illustrated through the very example used to open this paper: namely, the prevalence of child labor in developing countries. A multinational in Central America is not entitled to hire a 10-year-

old child for full-time work because, among other reasons, doing so blocks the child's ability to receive a minimally sufficient education. While what counts as a "minimally sufficient" education may be debated, and while it seems likely, moreover, that the specification of the right to a certain level of education will depend, at least in part, upon the level of economic resources available in a given country, it is reasonable to assume that any action by a corporation that has the effect of blocking the development of a child's ability to read or write will be proscribed on the basis of rights.

Political Participation

In some instances corporations have failed to honor the correlative duty of protecting the right to political participation from deprivation. The most blatant examples of direct deprivation are fortunately becoming so rare as to be non-existent, namely, cases in which companies directly aid in overthrowing democratic regimes, as when United Fruit helped overthrow a democratically elected regime in Honduras during the 1950s. But a few corporations have continued indirectly to threaten this right by failing to protect it from deprivation. A few have persisted, for example, in supporting military dictatorships in countries with growing democratic sentiment, and others have blatantly bribed publicly elected officials with large sums of money. Perhaps the most celebrated example of the latter occurred when the prime minister of Japan was bribed with $7 million by the Lockheed Corporation to secure a lucrative Tri-Star Jet contract. Here, the complaint from the perspective of this right is not against bribes or "sensitive payments" in general, but to bribes in contexts where they serve to undermine a democratic system in which publicly elected officials are in a position of public trust.

Even the buying and owning of major segments of a foreign country's land and industry has been criticized in this regard. As Brian Barry has remarked," the paranoia created in Britain and the United States by land purchases by foreigners (especially Arabs, it seems) should serve to make it understandable that the citizenry of a country might be unhappy with a state of affairs in which the most important natural resources are in foreign ownership."[31] At what point would Americans regard their democratic control threatened by foreign ownership of U.S. industry and resources? At 20 percent ownership? At 40 percent? At 60 percent? At 80 percent? The answer is debatable, yet there seems to be some point beyond which the right to national self-determination, and in turn national democratic control, is violated by foreign ownership of property.[32]

Subsistence

Corporations also have duties to protect the right to subsistence from deprivation. Consider the following scenario: a number of square miles of land in an underdeveloped country has been used for years to grow black beans. Further, the bulk of the land is owned, as it has been for centuries, by two wealthy landowners. Poorer members of the community work the land and receive a portion of the crop, a portion barely sufficient to satisfy nutritional needs. Next, imagine that a multinational corporation offers the two wealthy owners a handsome sum for the land, and does so because it plans to grow coffee for export. Now *if*—and this, admittedly, is a crucial "if"—the corporation has reason to *know* that a significant number of people in the community will suffer malnutrition as a result; that is, if the company has convincing reasons to believe that those persons will not be hired by the company, or that if forced to migrate to the city they will earn less than subsistence wages, i.e., inadequate to provide proper food and shelter, then the multinational may be said to have failed in its correlative duty to protect persons from the deprivation of the right to subsistence. This despite the fact that the corporation would never have stopped to take food from workers' mouths, and despite the fact that the malnourished will, in Coleridge's words, "die so slowly that none call it murder."

Disagreements: The Relevance of Facts and Culture

The commentaries above are obviously not intended to complete the project of specifying the correlative duties associated with fundamental international rights; only to begin it. Furthermore, here—as in the matter of specifying specific correlative duties generally—disagreements are inevitable. Take the land acquisition case above. One may claim that multinationals are never capable of knowing the consequences of land purchases with sufficient certainty to predict malnutrition or starvation. The issue obviously requires debate. Furthermore, one may wish to argue for the moral relevance of predictions about the actions of other agents. If the corporation in question refrains from buying land, won't another corporation rush in with the same negative consequences? And might not such a prediction mitigate the former corporation's responsibility in buying land in the first place? Here both facts and meta-moral principles must be debated.

The same point arises in the context of an even more controversial issue, one related also to the right of persons to subsistence. Critics have asserted that by promoting high technology agriculture in developing countries where wealthier farmers are preferred risks for loans to buy imported seeds and fertilizer, multinationals encourage the syndrome of land concentration and dependence upon imported food and fertilizer, leading to the situation where proceeds from cash crops buy luxuries for the rich and where poor farmers are forced to sell their small plots of land and move to the city. Whether such practices do violate rights will obviously be a subject of controversy. But what is central to the resolution of such a controversy is the *empirical* question of whether such practices *do* lead to starvation and malnourishment. That is to say, the problem may be positioned for solution, but it is certainly not solved, by establishing the right to subsistence and its correlative duties: facts remain crucial.

More generally, the solution to most difficult international problems requires a detailed understanding not only of moral precepts but of particular facts. The answer does not appear, as if by magic, simply by referencing the relevant rights and correlative duties, any more than the issue of whether welfare recipients in the United States should be required to work disappears by appealing to the state's correlative duty to aid the disadvantaged. Elsewhere I propose an "ethical algorithm" to aid multinational managers in making difficult trade-offs between home and host country values,[33] but while that algorithm augments the appeal to fundamental international rights established in this paper, neither it nor any other theory can draw moral conclusions when key facts are in dispute. Put simply, when facts are in irreconcilable dispute, so too will be the moral outcome.[34]

It may be that some of the above rights would not be embraced, or at least not embraced as formulated here, by cultures far different from ours. Would, for example, the Fulanis, a nomadic cattle culture in Nigeria, subscribe to this list with the same eagerness as the citizens of Brooklyn, New York? What list would they draw up if given the chance? And could we, or should we, try to convince them that our list is preferable? Would such a dialogue even make sense?[35]

I want to acknowledge that rights may vary in priority and style of expression from one culture to another. Yet in line with the conclusions of the earlier discussion of cultural relativism, I maintain that the list itself is applicable to all people even if they would fail to compose an identical list. Clearly the Fulanis do not have to accept the list of ten rights in question for it to constitute a valid means of judging the Fulani culture. If the Fulanis treat women unfairly and unequally, then at least one fundamental international right remains unfulfilled in their culture, and our discussion implies that their culture is poorer for that practice. Three of the rights are especially prone to varying cultural interpretation. These include that of non-discriminatory treatment (with special reference to women), to political participation, and to the ownership of property. The latter two raise tendentious political issues for cultures with traditions of communal property and non-democratic institutions. The list has no pretensions to solve these age-old political problems. While I may (as, in fact, I do) subscribe to a modified Lockean notion of property in which certain political systems incorporating social owner-

ship violate individual rights, the right to property advanced in our list need not be so narrowly interpreted as to rule out any instance of public ownership. For example, even primitive societies with communal property practices might be said to recognize a modified version of the right to property if those practices entail mutually agreed-upon, and fairly applied, rules of use, benefit, and liability. I am not prepared to say that each and every such instance violates the right to own property.

Even so, there will be a point beyond which the public ownership of property violates individual rights. State ownership of all land and movable property violates the individual's right to own property. Is the point passed when a country nationalizes its phone systems? Its oil industry? Is it passed when a primitive culture refuses to subordinate family to individual property? Although it is clear that such questions are of decisive significance, it is equally clear that establishing such a point is a task that cannot be undertaken satisfactorily here.

The same holds true for interpreting the right to political participation. I affirm the merits of a democratic electoral system in which representatives are chosen on the basis of one-person-one-vote; yet the list should not be interpreted to demand a photocopy of U.S. or English style democracy. For example, it is possible to imagine a small, primitive culture utilizing other fair means for reflecting participation in the political process—other than a representative electoral system—and thereby satisfying the right to political participation.

The Drug Lord Problem

One of the most difficult aspects of the rights list proposed concerns the affordability-fairness condition. We can see it more clearly by reflecting on what might be called the "drug lord" problem.[36] Imagine that an unfortunate country has a weak government and is run by various drug lords (not, it appears, a hypothetical case). These drug lords threaten the physical security of various citizens and torture others. The government—the country—cannot afford to mount the required police or military actions that would bring these drug lords into moral line. Or, perhaps, this could be done but only by imposing terrible burdens on certain segments of the society that would be unfair to others. Does it follow that members of that society do not have the fundamental international right not to be tortured and to physical security? Surely they do, even if the country cannot afford to guarantee them. But if that is the case, what about the affordability-fairness criterion?

Let us begin by noting that the "affordability" part of the affordability-fairness condition does imply some upper limit for the use of resources in the securing of a fundamental international right (such that, for example, dialysis cannot be a fundamental international right). With this established, the crucial question becomes *how* to draw the upper limit. The preceding argument commits us to draw that limit through at least two criteria: first, compatibility with other, already recognized, international rights, and second, the level of importance of the interest (moral or otherwise) being protected by the right (the first of the three conditions). As for the former, we remember that the affordability-fairness principle already entails a "moral compatibility" condition requiring that the duties imposed be compatible with other moral duties. Hence, a *prima facie* limit may be drawn on the certification of a prospective right corresponding to the point at which other bona fide international rights are violated. As for the latter, trade-offs among members of a class of prospective rights will be made by reference to the relative importance of the interest being protected by the right. The right not to be tortured protects a more fundamental interest than the right to an aesthetically pleasing environment.

This provides a two-tiered solution for the drug lord problem. At the first tier, we note that the right of people not to be tortured by the drug lords (despite the unaffordability of properly policing the drug lords) implies that people, and especially the drug lords, have a duty not to torture. Here the solution is simple. The argument of this chapter establishes a fundamental international right not to be tortured, and it is a right that binds all parties to the duty of forbearance in torturing others. For on the first pass of applying the affordability-fairness condition, that is, when we are considering simply the issue of which fundamental international rights exist, we are only concerned about affordability in relation to *any* of the three classes of correlative duties. That is, we look to determine only whether duties of *any* of the three classes of duties are fair and affordable. And with respect to the issue of affordability, clearly the drug lords along with every other moral agent can "afford" to refrain from

actively depriving persons of their right not to be tortured. That is, they can afford to refrain from torturing. It follows that people clearly have the fundamental international right not to be tortured, which imposes at least one class of duties upon all international actors, namely, those of forbearance.

At the second tier, on the other hand, we are concerned with the issue of whether the right not to be tortured includes a duty of the government to mount an effective prevention system against torture. Here the affordability-fairness criterion is used in a second pass, one that helps establish the specific kinds of correlative duties associated with the right not to be tortured. Here surely all nation states can "afford" to shoulder duties of the second and third categories, i.e., of helping prevent deprivation, and of aiding the deprived, although the specific extent of those duties may be further affected by considerations of fairness and affordability. For example, given an instance like the country described in the drug-lord problem, it clearly seems questionable that all countries could "afford" to *succeed* completely in preventing torture, and hence the duty to help prevent torture presupposed by a fundamental international right to freedom from torture probably cannot be construed to demand complete success. Nonetheless, a fairly high level of success in preventing torture is probably demanded by virtue of international rights, because, as I have argued elsewhere,[37] the ordinary protection of civil and political rights, such as the right not to be tortured, carries a negative rather than positive economic cost. That is, the economic cost of allowing the erosion of rights to physical security and fair trial—as an empirical matter of fact—tends to exceed the cost of maintaining the rights.

CONCLUSION

What the list of rights and corollary corporate duties establishes is that multinational corporations frequently do have obligations derived from rights where such obligations extend beyond abstaining from depriving directly, to protecting from deprivation. It implies, in other words, that the relevant factors for analyzing a difficult issue like that of hunger and high technology agriculture include not only the degree of factual correlation existing between multinational policy and hunger but also the recognition of the existence of a right to subsistence along with a specification of the corporate correlative duties entailed.

Hence the paper has argued that the ten rights identified earlier constitute minimal and bedrock moral considerations for multinational corporations operating abroad. While the list may be incomplete, the human claims it honors, and the interests those claims represent, are globally relevant. They are, in turn, immune from the Hobbesian or relativistically inspired challenges offered by skeptics. The existence of fundamental international rights implies that no corporation can wholly neglect considerations of racism, hunger, political oppression, or freedom through appeal to its "commercial" mission. These rights are, rather, moral considerations for every international moral agent, although, as we have seen, different moral agents possess different correlative obligations. The specification of the precise correlative duties associated with such rights for corporations is an on-going task that the paper has left incomplete. Yet the existence of the rights themselves, including the imposition of duties upon corporations to protect—as well as to refrain from directly violating—such rights, seems beyond reasonable doubt.

NOTES

Portions of this essay are contained in Thomas Donaldson, *The Ethics of International Business* (New York: Oxford University Press, 1990), and are reprinted here with permission.

1. James LeMoyne, "In Central America, the Workers Suffer Most," *New York Times,* October 26, 1987, p. 1.

2. Some work explores the issue of political risk (for example, Thomas Poynter, *Multinational Enterprises and Government Intervention* (New York: St. Martin's Press, 1985); Thomas Moran, ed., *Multinational Corporations; The Political Economy of Foreign Direct Investment* (Lexington, MA: Lexington Books, 1985); and J. N. Behrman, *Decision Criteria for Foreign Direct Investment in Latin America* (New York: Council of the Americas, 1974); while other work explores the nature of international corporate strategy (See W. J. Keegan, "Multinational Scanning: A Study of Information Sources Utilized by Headquarters Executives in Multinational Companies," *Administrative Science Quarterly* (1974): 411–21; and D. Cray, "Control and Coordination in Multinational Corporations," *Journal of International Business Studies* 15, no. 2 (1984): 85–98; and still other work explores multinational public policy issues (See Lee Preston, "The Evolution of Multinational Public Policy Toward Business: Codes of Conduct," in

Lee Preston, ed., *Research in Corporate Social Performance and Policy,* Vol. 10, Greenwich, CT: JAI Press, 1988).

3. This group has produced what is probably the best developed ethical literature from business schools. Their efforts evolve from the tradition of "business and society" research with roots in the sixties and early seventies. Contributors such as Buchholz, Cochran, Epstein, Frederick, Freeman, and Sethi have made significant advances, not only in developing descriptive studies with moral relevance, but in advancing normative hypotheses. See, for example, Rogene A. Buchholz, *Business Environment and Public Policy* (Englewood Cliffs, NJ: Prentice-Hall, 1982); Stephen L. Wartick and Philip L. Cochran, "The Evolution of the Corporate Social Performance Model," *Academy of Management Review* 10 (1985): 758–69; Edwin Epstein, "The Corporate Social Policy Process: Beyond Business Ethics, Corporate Social Responsibility, and Corporate Social Responsiveness," *California Management Review 29* (Spring 1987); William C. Frederick, "Toward CSR3: Why Ethical Analysis is Indispensable and Unavoidable in Corporate Affairs," *California Management Review* 28 (1986): 126–41; R. Edward Freeman, *Strategic Management: A Stakeholder Approach* (Boston: Pitman Press, 1984), and *Corporate Strategy and the Search for Ethics* (Englewood Cliffs, NJ: Prentice-Hall, 1988); and S. Prakash Sethi, "Corporate Law Violations and Executive Liability," in Lee Preston, ed., *Corporate Social Performance and Policy, Vol. 3* (Greenwich, CT: JAI Press, 1981), pp. 72–73, and S. Prakash Sethi et al., *Corporate Governance: Public Policy Social Responsibility Committee of Corporate Board* (Richardson, TX.: Center for Research in Business and Social Policy, 1979).

4. An exception is Duane Windsor's "Defining the Ethical Obligations of the Multinational Enterprise," in W. M. Hoffman et al., eds., *Ethics and the Multinational Corporation* (Washington, DC: University Press of America, 1986).

5. Thomas Donaldson, *The Ethics of International Business* (New York: Oxford University Press, 1990). See especially Chapter 6.

6. Maurice Cranston, *What Are Human Rights?* (New York: Tamlinger, 1973), p. 67.

7. H. J. McCloskey, for example, understands a right as a positive entitlement that need not specify who bears the responsibility for satisfying that entitlement. H. J. McCloskey, "Rights—Some Conceptual Issues," *Australasian Journal of Philosophy* 54 (1976): 99.

8. Joel Feinberg, "Duties, Rights, and Claims," *American Philosophical Quarterly* 3 (1966): 137–44. See also Feinberg, "The Nature and Value of Rights," *Journal of Value Inquiry* 4 (1970): 243–57.

9. James Brooke, "Waste Dumpers Turning to West Africa," *New York Times,* July 17, 1988, p. 1.

10. Ibid.

11. Nigeria and other countries have struck back, often by imposing strict rules against the acceptance of toxic waste. For example, in Nigeria officials now warn that anyone caught importing toxic waste will face the firing squad. Brooke, "Waste Dumpers Turning to West Africa," p. 7.

12. James W. Nickel, *Making Sense of Human Rights: Philosophical Reflections on the Universal Declaration of Human Rights* (Berkeley: University of California Press, 1987), pp. 107–8.

13. See Ian Brownlie, *Basic Documents on Human Rights* (Oxford: Oxford University Press, 1975).

14. For a contemporary analysis of the Universal Declaration of Human Rights and companion international documents, see James W. Nickel, *Making Sense of Human Rights: Philosophical Reflections on the Universal Declaration of Human Rights* (Berkeley: University of California Press, 1987).

15. For example, the "European Convention of Human Rights" omits mention of welfare rights, preferring instead to create an auxiliary document ("The European Social Charter of 1961") which references many of what earlier had been treated as rights as "goals."

16. Henry Shue, *Basic Rights* (Princeton, NJ: Princeton University Press, 1982).

17. Ibid., p. 34.

18. Ibid., p. 20–23.

19. Ibid., p. 78.

20. Ibid., p. 71.

21. Ibid., p. 76.

22. Ibid., p. 31.

23. Ibid., pp. 37–38.

24. I am indebted to Alan Gewirth who made this point in a conversation about Shue's theory of basic rights.

25. Shue, *Basic Rights*, p. 20.

26. Ibid., p. 19.

27. James Nickel, *Making Sense of Human Rights* (Berkeley: University of California Press, 1987), pp. 108–19. The phrasing of the third condition is derived almost directly from Nickel's condition that "the obligations or burdens imposed by the right must be affordable in relation to resources, other obligations, and fairness in the distribution of burdens."

28. Shue, *Basic Rights*, p. 57.

29. It is possible to understand even the remaining four rights as imposing correlative duties to protect from deprivation by imagining unusual or hypothetical scenarios. For example, if it happened that the secret police or a host country dictatorship regularly used corporate personnel files in their efforts to kidnap and torture suspected political opponents, then the corporation would be morally obligated to object to the practice, and to refuse to make their files available any longer. Here the corporation would have a correlative duty to protect from deprivation the right not to be tortured. The list of rights identified as imposing correlative duties of protection was limited to six, however, on the basis of the fact that their protection is directly related to activities frequently undertaken by corporations in the real world.

30. The twin phenomena of commercial concentration and the globalization of business, both associated with the rise of the multinational, have tended to weaken the bargaining power of organized labor. It is doubtful that labor is sharing as fully as it once did in the cyclical gains of industrial productivity. This gives special significance to the right in question.

31. Brian Barry, "'The Case for a New International Economic Order,'" in J. Roland Pennock and John W. Chapman, eds., *Ethics, Economics, and the Law: Nomos Vol. XXIV* (New York: New York University Press, 1982).

32. Companies are also charged with undermining local governments, and hence infringing on basic rights, by sophisticated tax evasion schemes. Especially when companies buy from their own subsidiaries, they can establish prices that have little connection to existing market values. This, in turn, means that profits can be shifted from high-tax to low-tax countries with the result that poor nations can be deprived of their rightful share.

33. See Donaldson, *The Ethics of International Business,* Chapter 5.

34. It is important to remember that it is "key" or "crucial" facts that are being discussed here. The ten fundamental international rights are not to be eroded in every instance by the old argument that "we don't have enough facts." Such a defense clearly has its limits, and these limits are overstepped by the demand that evidence be definitive in every sense. An excellent example of excess in this vein is that of cigarette companies denying that their products are dangerous because we do not yet understand the causal mechanism whereby cigarette smoking is correlated with cancer.

35. Both for raising these questions, and in helping me formulate answers, I am indebted to William Frederick.

36. I am indebted to George Brenkert for suggesting and formulating the "drug lord" problem.

37. Thomas Donaldson, "Trading Justice for Bread: A Reply to James W. Nickel," in Kenneth Kipnis and Diana T. Meyers, eds., *Economic Justice: Private Rights and Public Responsibilities* (Totowa, NJ: Rowman and Allenheld, 1985), pp. 226–29.

READING 12.2 THE GREAT NON-DEBATE OVER INTERNATIONAL SWEATSHOPS

Ian Maitland

In recent years, there has been a dramatic growth in the contracting out of production by companies in the industrialized countries to suppliers in developing countries. This globalization of production has led to an emerging international division of labor in footwear and apparel in which companies like Nike and Reebok concentrate on product design and marketing but rely on a network of contractors in Indonesia, China, Central America, etc., to build shoes or sew shirts according to exact specifications and deliver a high quality good according to precise delivery schedules. As Nike's vice president for Asia has put it, "We don't know the first thing about manufacturing. We are marketers and designers."

The contracting arrangements have drawn intense fire from critics—usually labor and human rights activists. These "critics" (as I will refer to them) have charged that the companies are (by proxy) exploiting workers in the plants (which I will call "international sweatshops") of their suppliers. Specifically the companies stand accused of chasing cheap labor around the globe, failing to pay their workers living wages, using child labor, turning a blind eye to abuses of human rights, being complicit with repressive regimes in denying workers the right to join unions and failing to enforce minimum labor standards in the workplace, and so on.

The campaign against international sweatshops has largely unfolded on television and, to a lesser extent, in the print media. What seems like no more than a handful of critics has mounted an aggressive, media-savvy campaign which has put the publicity-shy retail giants on the defensive. The critics have orchestrated a series of sensational "disclosures" on prime time television exposing the terrible pay and working conditions in factories making jeans for Levi's or sneakers for Nike or Pocahontas shirts for Disney. One of the principal scourges of the companies has been Charles Kernaghan who runs the National Labor Coalition (NLC), a labor human rights group involving 25 unions. It was Kernaghan

who, in 1996, broke the news before a Congressional committee that Kathie Lee Gifford's clothing line was being made by 13- and 14-year-olds working 20-hour days in factories in Honduras. Kernaghan also arranged for teenage workers from sweatshops in Central America to testify before Congressional committees about abusive labor practices. At one of these hearings, one of the workers held up a Liz Claiborne cotton sweater identical to ones she had sewn since she was a 13-year-old working 12 hours days. According to a news report, "[t]his image, accusations of oppressive conditions at the factory and the Claiborne logo played well on that evening's network news." The result has been a circus-like atmosphere—as in Roman circus where Christians were thrown to lions.

Kernaghan has shrewdly targeted the companies' carefully cultivated public images. He has explained: "Their image is everything. They live and die by their image. That gives you a certain power over them." As a result, he says, "these companies are sitting ducks. They have no leg to stand on. That's why it's possible for a tiny group like us to take on a giant like Wal-Mart. You can't defend paying someone 31 cents an hour in Honduras. . . .[1] Apparently most of the companies agree with Kernaghan. Not a single company has tried to mount a serious defense of its contracting practices. They have judged that they cannot win a war of sound bites with the critics. Instead of making a fight of it, the companies have sued for peace in order to protect their principal asset—their image.

Major U.S. retailers have responded by adopting codes of conduct on human and labor rights in their international operations. Levi-Strauss, Nike, Sears, JC Penney, Wal-Mart, Home Depot, and Philips Van-Heusen now have such codes. As Lance Compa notes, such codes are the result of a blend of humanitarian and pragmatic impulses: "Often the altruistic motive coincides with "bottom line" considerations related to brand name, company image, and other intangibles that make for core value to the firm."[2] Peter Jacobi, President of Global Sourcing for Levi-Strauss has advised: "If your company owns a popular brand, protect this priceless

From Ian Maitland, "The Great Non-Debate Over International Sweatshops," *British Academy of Management Annual Conference Proceedings,* September, 1997, pp. 240–265. Reprinted by permission of the author.

asset at all costs. Highly visible companies have any number of reasons to conduct their business not just responsibly but also in ways that cannot be portrayed as unfair, illegal, or unethical. This sets an extremely high standard since it must be applied to both company-owned businesses and contractors. . . .[3]And according to another Levi-Strauss spokesman, "In many respects, we're protecting our single largest asset: our brand image and corporate reputation. . . .[4] Nike recently published the results of a generally favorable review of its international operations conducted by former American U.N. Ambassador Andrew Young.

Recently a truce of sorts between the critics and the companies was announced on the White House lawn with President Clinton and Kathie Lee Gifford in attendance. A presidential task force, including representatives of labor unions, human rights groups and apparel companies like L.L. Bean and Nike, has come up with a set of voluntary standards which, it hopes, will be embraced by the entire industry. Companies that comply with the code will be entitled to use a "No Sweat" label.

OBJECTIVE OF THIS PAPER

In this confrontation between the companies and their critics, neither side seems to have judged it to be in its interest to seriously engage the issue at the heart of this controversy, namely: What are appropriate wages and labor standards in international sweatshops? As we have seen, the companies have treated the charges about sweatshops as a public relations problem to be managed so as to minimize harm to their public images. The critics have apparently judged that the best way to keep public indignation at boiling point is to oversimplify the issue and treat it as a morality play featuring heartless exploiters and victimized third world workers. The result has been a great non-debate over international sweatshops. Paradoxically, if peace breaks out between the two sides, the chances that the debate will be seriously joined may recede still further. Indeed, there exists a real risk (I will argue) that any such truce may be a collusive one that will come at the expense of the very third world workers it is supposed to help.

This paper takes up the issue of what are appropriate wages and labor standards in international sweatshops. Critics charge that the present arrangements are exploitative. I proceed by examining the specific charges of exploitation from the standpoints of both (a) their factual and (b) their ethical sufficiency. However, in the absence of my well-established consensus among business ethicists (or other thoughtful observers), I simultaneously use the investigation of sweatshops as a setting for trying to adjudicate between competing views about what those standards should be. My examination will pay particular attention to (but will not be limited to) labor conditions at the plants of Nike's suppliers in Indonesia. I have not personally visited any international sweatshops, and so my conclusions are based entirely on secondary analysis of the voluminous published record on the topic.

WHAT ARE ETHICALLY APPROPRIATE LABOR STANDARDS IN INTERNATIONAL SWEATSHOPS?

What are ethically acceptable or appropriate levels of wages and labor standards in international sweatshops? The following four possibilities just about run the gamut of standards or principles that have been seriously proposed to regulate such policies.

1. *Home-country standards:* It might be argued (and in rare cases has been) that international corporations have an ethical duty to pay the same wages and provide the same labor standards regardless of where they operate. However, the view that home-country standards should apply in host-countries is rejected by most business ethicists and (officially at least) by the critics of international sweatshops. Thus Thomas Donaldson argues that "[b]y arbitrarily establishing U.S. wage levels as the benchmark for fairness one eliminates the role of the international market in establishing salary levels, and this in turn eliminates the incentive U.S. corporations have to hire foreign workers."[5] Richard DeGeorge makes much the same argument: If there were a rule that said that "that American MNCs [multinational corporations] that wish to be ethical must pay the same wages abroad as they do at home, . . . [then] MNCs would have little incentive to move their manufacturing abroad; and if they

did move abroad they would disrupt the local labor market with artificially high wages that bore no relation to the local standard or cost of living.

2. *"Living wage" standard:* It has been proposed that an international corporation should, at a minimum, pay a "living wage." Thus DeGeorge says that corporations should pay a living wage, "even when this is not paid by local firms.[7] However, it is hard to pin down what this means operationally. According to DeGeorge, a living wage should "allow the worker to live in dignity as a human being." In order to respect the human rights of its workers, he says, a corporation must pay "at least subsistence wages and as much above that as workers and their dependents need to live with reasonable dignity, given the general state of development of the society."[8] As we shall see, the living wage standard has become a rallying cry of the critics of international sweatshops. Apparently, DeGeorge believes that it is preferable for a corporation to provide no job at all than to offer one that pays less than a living wage. . . .

3. *Classical liberal standard:* Finally, there is what I will call the classical liberal standard. According to this standard a practice (wage or labor practice) is ethically acceptable if it is freely chosen by informed workers. For example, in a recent report the World Bank invoked this standard in connection with workplace safety. It said: "The appropriate level is therefore that at which the costs are commensurate with the value that informed workers place on improved working conditions and reduced risk."[9] Most business ethicists reject this standard on the grounds that there is some sort of market failure or the "background conditions" are lacking for markets to work effectively. Thus for Donaldson full (or near-full) employment is a prerequisite if workers are to make sound choices regarding workplace safety: "The average level of unemployment in the developing countries today exceeds 40 percent, a figure that has frustrated the application of neoclassical economic principles to the international economy on a score of issues. With full employment, and all other things being equal, market forces will encourage workers to make trade-offs between job opportunities using

safety as a variable. But with massive unemployment, market forces in developing countries drive the unemployed to the jobs they are lucky enough to land, regardless of the safety."[10] Apparently there are other forces, like Islamic fundamentalism and the global debt "bomb," that rule out reliance on market solutions, but Donaldson does not explain their relevance.[11] DeGeorge, too, believes that the necessary conditions are lacking for market forces to operate benignly. Without what he calls "background institutions" to protect the workers and the resources of the developing country (e.g., enforceable minimum wages) and/or greater equality of bargaining power exploitation is the most likely result.[12] "If American MNCs pay workers very low wages . . . they clearly have the opportunity to make significant profits"[13] DeGeorge goes on to make the interesting observation that "competition has developed among multinationals themselves, so that the profit margin has been driven down" and developing countries "can play one company against another."[14] But apparently that is not enough to rehabilitate market forces in his eyes.

THE CASE AGAINST INTERNATIONAL SWEATSHOPS

To many of their critics, international sweatshops exemplify the way in which the greater openness of the world economy is hurting workers. . . . Globalization means a transition from (more or less) regulated domestic economies to an unregulated world economy. The superior mobility of capital, and the essentially fixed, immobile nature of world labor, means a fundamental shift in bargaining power in favor of large international corporations. Their global reach permits them to shift production almost costlessly from one location to another. As a consequence, instead of being able to exercise some degree of control over companies operating within their borders, governments are now locked in a bidding war with one another to attract and retain the business of large multinational companies.

The critics allege that international companies are using the threat of withdrawal or withholding of investment to pressure governments and workers to grant concessions. "Today [multinational companies] choose between workers in developing countries that compete against each other to depress wages to attract foreign investment." The result is a race for the bottom—a "destructive downward bidding spiral of the labor conditions and wages of workers throughout the world. . . .[15] . . . Thus, critics charge that in Indonesia wages are deliberately held below the poverty level or subsistence in order to make the country a desirable location. The results of this competitive dismantling of worker protections, living standards and worker rights are predictable: deteriorating work conditions, declining real incomes for workers, and a widening gap between rich and poor in developing countries. I turn next to the specific charges made by the critics of international sweatshops.

Unconscionable Wages

Critics charge that the companies, by their proxies, are paying "starvation wages" and "slave wages." They are far from clear about what wage level they consider to be appropriate. But they generally demand that companies pay a "living wage." Kernaghan has said that workers should be paid enough to support their families and they should get a "living wage" and "be treated like human beings."[16] According to Tim Smith, wage levels should be "fair, decent or a living wage for an employee and his or her family." He has said that wages in the maquiladoras of Mexico averaged $35 to $55 a week (in or near 1993) which he calls a "shockingly substandard wage," apparently on the grounds that it "clearly does not allow an employee to feed and care for a family adequately."[17] In 1992, Nike came in for harsh criticism when a magazine published the pay stub of a worker at one of its Indonesian suppliers. It showed that the worker was paid at the rage of $1.03 per day which was reportedly less than the Indonesian government's figure for "minimum physical need."[18]

Immiserization Thesis

Former Labor Secretary Robert Reich has proposed as a test of the fairness of development policies that "Low-wage workers should become better off, not worse off, as trade and investment boost national income." He has written that "[i]f a country pursues policies that . . . limit to a narrow elite the benefits of trade, the promise of open com-

merce is perverted and drained of its rationale."[19] A key claim of the activists is that companies actually impoverish or immiserize developing country workers. They experience an absolute decline in living standards. This thesis follows from the claim that the bidding war among developing countries is depressing wages. . . .

Widening Gap between Rich and Poor

A related charge is that international sweatshops are contributing to the increasing gap between rich and poor. Not only are the poor being absolutely impoverished, but trade is generating greater inequality within developing countries. Another test that Reich has proposed to establish the fairness of international trade is that "the gap between rich and poor should tend to narrow with development, not widen."[20] Critics charge that international sweatshops flunk that test. They say that the increasing GNPs of some developing countries simply mask a widening gap between rich and poor. "Across the world, both local and foreign elites are getting richer from the exploitation of the most vulnerable."[21] And, "The major adverse consequence of quickening global economic integration has been widening income disparity within almost all nations. . . .[22] There appears to be a tacit alliance 'between the elites of both first and third worlds to exploit the most vulnerable, to regiment and control and conscript them so that they can create the material conditions for the elites' extravagant lifestyles.

Collusion with Repressive Regimes

Critics charge that, in their zeal to make their countries safe for foreign investment, Third World regimes, notably China and Indonesia, have stepped up their repression. Not only have these countries failed to enforce even the minimal labor rules on the books, but they have also used their military and police to break strikes and repress independent unions. They have stifled political dissent, both to retain their hold on political power and to avoid any instability that might scare off foreign investors. Consequently, critics charge, companies like Nike are profiting from political repression. "As unions spread in [Korea and Taiwan], Nike shifted its suppliers primarily to Indonesia, China and Thailand, where they could depend on governments to suppress independent union-organizing efforts."[23]

EVALUATION OF THE CHARGES AGAINST INTERNATIONAL SWEATSHOPS

The critics' charges are undoubtedly accurate on a number of points: (1) There is no doubt that international companies are chasing cheap labor. (2) The wages paid by the international sweatshops are—by American standards—shockingly low. (3) Some developing country governments have tightly controlled or repressed organized labor in order to prevent it from disturbing the flow of foreign investment. Thus, in Indonesia, independent unions have been suppressed. (4) It is not unusual in developing countries for minimum wage levels to be lower than the official poverty level. (5) Developing country governments have winked at violations of minimum wage laws and labor rules. However, most jobs are in the informal sector and so largely outside the scope of government supervision. (6) Some suppliers have employed children or have subcontracted work to other producers who have done so. (7) Some developing country governments deny their people basic political rights. China is the obvious example; Indonesia's record is pretty horrible but had shown steady improvement until the last two years. But on many of the other counts, the critics' charges appear to be seriously inaccurate. And, even where the charges are accurate, it is not self-evident that the practices in question are improper or unethical, as we see next.

Wages and Conditions

Even the critics of international sweatshops do not dispute that the wages they pay are generally higher than—or at least equal to—comparable wages in the labor markets where they operate. According to the International Labor Organization (ILO), multinational companies often apply standards relating to wages, benefits, conditions of work, and occupational safety and health, which both exceed statutory requirements and those practiced by local firms."[24] The ILO also says that wages and working conditions in so-called Export Processing Zones (EPZs) are often equal to or higher than jobs outside. The World Bank says that the poorest workers in developing countries work in the informal sector where they often earn less than half what a formal sector employee earns. Moreover, "informal and rural workers often must work under more hazardous and insecure conditions than their formal sector counterparts.[25]

The same appears to hold true for the international sweatshops. In 1996, young women working in the plant of a Nike supplier in Serang, Indonesia were earning the Indonesian legal minimum wage of 5,200 rupiahs or about $2.28 each day. As a report in the *Washington Post* pointed out, just earning the minimum wage put these workers among higher-paid Indonesians: "In Indonesia, less than half the working population earns the minimum wage, since about half of all adults here are in farming, and the typical farmer would make only about 2,000 rupiahs each day."[26] The workers in the Serang plant reported that they save about three-quarters of their pay. A 17-year-old woman said: "I came here one year ago from central Java. I'm making more money than my father makes." This woman also said that she sent about 75 percent of her earnings back to her family on the farm.[27] Also in 1996, a Nike spokeswoman estimated that an entry-level factory worker in the plant of a Nike supplier made five times what a farmer makes.[28] Nike's chairman, Phil Knight, likes to teasingly remind critics that the average worker in one of Nike's Chinese factories is paid more than a professor at Beijing University.[29] There is also plentiful anecdotal evidence from non-Nike sources. A worker at the Taiwanese owned King Star Garment Assembly plant in Honduras told a reporter that he was earning seven times what he earned in the countryside.[30] In Bangladesh, the country's fledgling garment industry was paying women who had never worked before between $40 and $55 a month in 1991. That compared with a national per capita income of about $200 and the approximately $1 a day earned by many of these women's husbands as day laborers or rickshaw drivers.[31]

The same news reports also shed some light on the working conditions in sweatshops. According to the *Washington Post,* in 1994 the Indonesian office of the international accounting firm Ernst & Young surveyed Nike workers concerning worker pay, safety conditions and attitudes toward the job. The auditors pulled workers off the assembly line at random and asked them questions that the workers answered anonymously. The survey of 25 workers at Nike's Serang plant found that 23 thought the hours and overtime worked were fair, and two thought the overtime hours too high. None of the workers reported that they had been discriminated against

Thirteen said the working environment was the key reason they worked at the Serang plant while eight cited salary and benefits.[32] The *Post* report also noted that the Serang plant closes for about ten days each year for Muslim holidays. It quoted Nike officials and the plant's Taiwanese owners as saying that 94 percent of the workers had returned to the plant following the most recent break. . . .

There is also the mute testimony of the lines of job applicants outside the sweatshops in Guatemala and Honduras. According to Lucy Martinez-Mont, in Guatemala the sweatshops are conspicuous for the long lines of young people waiting to be interviewed for a job.[33] Outside the gates of the industrial park in Honduras that Rohter visited "anxious onlookers are always waiting, hoping for a chance at least to fill out a job application [for employment at one of the apparel plants]."[34]

The critics of sweatshops acknowledge that workers have voluntarily taken their jobs, consider themselves lucky to have them, and want to keep them. . . . But they go on to discount the workers' views as the product of confusion or ignorance, and/or they just argue that the workers' views are beside the point Thus, while "it is undoubtedly true" that Nike has given jobs to thousands of people who wouldn't be working otherwise, they say that "neatly skirts the fundamental human-rights issue raised by these production arrangements that are now spreading all across the world."[35] Similarly the NLC's Kernaghan says that "[w]hether workers think they are better off in the assembly plants than elsewhere is not the real issue."[36] Kernaghan, and Jeff Ballinger of the AFL-CIO, concede that the workers desperately need these jobs. But "[t]hey say they're not asking that U.S. companies stop operating in these countries. They're asking that workers be paid a living wage and treated like human beings."[37] Apparently these workers are victims of what Marx called false consciousness, or else they would grasp that they are being exploited. According to Barnet and Cavanagh, "For many workers . . . exploitation is not a concept easily comprehended because the alternative prospects for earning a living are so bleak."[38]

Immiserization and Inequality

The critics' claim that the countries that host international sweatshops are marked by growing poverty and inequality is flatly contradicted by the record. In fact, many of those countries have experienced sharp increases in living standards—for all strata of society. In trying to attract investment in simple manufacturing, Malaysia and Indonesia and, now, Vietnam and China, are retracing the industrialization path already successfully taken by East Asian countries like Taiwan, Korea, Singapore and Hong Kong. These four countries got their start by producing labor-intensive manufactured goods (often electrical and electronic components, shoes, and garments) for export markets. Over time they graduated to the export of higher value-added items that are skill-intensive and require a relatively developed industrial base.[39]

As is well known, these East Asian countries achieved growth rates exceeding eight percent for a quarter century. . . . The workers in these economies were not impoverished by growth. The benefits of growth were widely diffused: These economies achieved essentially full employment in the 1960s. Real wages rose by as much as a factor of four. Absolute poverty fell. And income inequality remained at low to moderate levels. It is true that in the initial stages the rapid growth generated only moderate increases in wages. But once essentially full employment was reached, and what economists call the Fei-Ranis turning point was reached, the increased demand for labor resulted in the bidding up of wages as firms competed for a scarce labor supply.

Interestingly, given its historic mission as a watchdog for international labor standards, the ILO has embraced this development model. It recently noted that the most successful developing economies, in terms of output and employment growth, have been "those who best exploited emerging opportunities in the global economy."[40] An "export-oriented policy is vital in countries that are starting on the industrialization path and have large surpluses of cheap labour." Countries which have succeeded in attracting foreign direct investment (FDI) have experienced rapid growth in manufacturing output and exports. The successful attraction of foreign investment in plant and equipment "can be a powerful spur to rapid industrialization and employment creation." "At low levels of industrialization, FDI in garments and shoes and some types of consumer electronics can be very useful for creating employment and opening the economy to international markets; there may be some entrepreneurial skills created in simple activities like garments (as has happened in Bangladesh). Moreover, in some cases, such as

Malaysia, the investors may strike deeper roots and invest in more capital-intensive technologies as wages rise.

According to the World Bank, the rapidly growing Asian economies (including Indonesia) "have also been unusually successful at sharing the fruits of their growth."[41] In fact, while inequality in the West has been growing, it has been shrinking in the Asian economies. They are the only economies in the world to have experienced high growth *and* declining inequality, and they also show shrinking gender gaps in education. . . .

Profiting from Repression?

What about the charge that international sweatshops are profiting from repression? It is undeniable that there is repression in many of the countries where sweatshops are located. But economic development appears to be relaxing that repression rather than strengthening its grip. The companies are supposed to benefit from government policies (e.g., repression of unions) that hold down labor costs. However, as we have seen, the wages paid by the international sweatshops already match or exceed the prevailing local wages. Not only that, but incomes in the East Asian economies, and in Indonesia, have risen rapidly. . . .

The critics, however, are right in saying that the Indonesian government has opposed independent unions in the sweatshops out of fear they would lead to higher wages and labor unrest. But the government's fear clearly is that unions might drive wages in the modern industrial sector *above* market-clearing levels—or, more exactly, further above market. It is ironic that critics like Barnet and Cavanagh would use the Marxian term "reserve army of the unemployed." According to Marx, capitalists deliberately maintain high levels of unemployment in order to control the working class. But the Indonesian government's policies (e.g., suppression of unions, resistance to a higher minimum wage and lax enforcement of labor rules) have been directed at achieving exactly the opposite result. The government appears to have calculated that high unemployment is a greater threat to its hold on power. I think we can safely take at face value its claims that its policies are genuinely intended to help the economy create jobs to absorb the massive numbers of unemployed and underemployed.[42]

LABOR STANDARDS IN INTERNATIONAL SWEATSHOPS: PAINFUL TRADE-OFFS

Who but the grinch could grudge paying a few additional pennies to some of the world's poorest workers? There is no doubt that the rhetorical force of the critics' case against international sweatshops rests on this apparently self-evident proposition. However, higher wages and improved labor standards are not free. After all, the critics themselves attack companies for chasing cheap labor. It follows that, if labor in developing countries is made more expensive (say, as the result of pressure by the critics), then those countries will receive less foreign investment, and fewer jobs will be created there. Imposing higher wages may deprive these countries of the one comparative advantage they enjoy, namely low-cost labor.

We have seen that workers in most "international sweatshops" are already relatively well paid. Workers in the urban, formal sectors of developing countries commonly earn more than twice what informal and rural workers get. Simply earning the minimum wage put the young women making Nike shoes in Serang in the top half of the income distribution in Indonesia. Accordingly, the critics are in effect calling for a *widening* of the economic disparity that already greatly favors sweatshop workers.

By itself that may or may not be ethically objectionable. But these higher wages come at the expense of the incomes and the job opportunities of much poorer workers. As economists explain, higher wages in the formal sector reduce employment there and (by increasing the supply of labor) depress incomes in the informal sector. The case against requiring above-market wages for international sweatshop workers is essentially the same as the case against other measures that artificially raise labor costs, like the minimum wage. In Jagdish Bhagwati's words: "Requiring a minimum wage in an overpopulated, developing country, as is done in a developed country, may actually be morally wicked. A minimum wage might help the unionized, industrial proletariat, while limiting the ability to save and invest rapidly which is necessary to draw more of the unemployed and nonunionized rural poor into gainful employment and income."[43] The World Bank makes the same point: "Minimum wages may help the most poverty-stricken workers in industrial countries, but they clearly do not in developing nations. . . . The workers whom minimum wage legislation tries to protect—urban formal workers—already earn much more than the less favored majority. . . . And inasmuch as minimum wage and other regulations discourage formal employment by increasing wage and nonwage costs, they hurt the poor who aspire to formal employment."[44]

The story is no different when it comes to labor standards other than wages. If standards are set too high they will hurt investment and employment The World Bank report points out that "[r]educing hazards in the workplace is costly, and typically the greater the reduction the more it costs. Moreover, the costs of compliance often fall largely on employees through lower wages or reduced employment. As a result, setting standards too high can actually lower workers' welfare. . . . "[45] Perversely, if the higher standards advocated by critics retard the growth of formal sector jobs, then that will trap more informal and rural workers in jobs which are far more hazardous and insecure than those of their formal sector counterparts.

The critics consistently advocate policies that will benefit better-off workers at the expense of worse-off ones. If it were within their power, it appears that they would reinvent the labor markets of much of Latin America. Alejandro Portes' description seems to be on the mark: "In Mexico, Brazil, Peru, and other Third World countries, [unlike East Asia], there are powerful independent unions representing the protected sector of the working class. Although there rhetoric is populist and even radical, the fact is that they tend to represent the better-paid and more stable fraction of the working class. Alongside, there toils a vast, unprotected proletariat, employed by informal enterprises and linked, in ways hidden from public view, with modern sector firms." . . .

Of course, it might be objected that trading off workers' rights for more jobs is unethical. But, so far as I can determine, the critics have not made this argument. Although they sometimes implicitly accept the existence of the trade-off (we saw that they attack Nike for chasing cheap labor), their public statements are silent on the lost or forgone jobs from higher wages and better labor standards. At other times, they imply or claim that improvements in workers' wages and conditions are essentially free. . . .

In summary, the result of the ostensibly humanitarian changes urged by critics are likely to be (1) reduced employment in the formal or modern sector of the economy, (2) lower incomes in the informal sector, (3) less investment and so slower economic growth, (4) reduced exports, (5) greater inequality and poverty.

CONCLUSION: THE CASE FOR NOT EXCEEDING MARKET STANDARDS

It is part of the job description of business ethicists to exhort companies to treat their workers better (otherwise what purpose do they serve?). So it will have come as no surprise that both the business ethicists whose views I summarized at the beginning of this paper—Thomas Donaldson and Richard DeGeorge—objected to letting the market alone determine wages and labor standards in multinational companies. Both of them proposed criteria for setting wages that might occasionally "improve" on the outcomes of the market.

Their reasons for rejecting market determination of wages were similar. They both cited conditions that allegedly prevent international markets from generating ethically acceptable results. Donaldson argued that neoclassical economic principles are not applicable to international business because of high unemployment rates in developing countries. And DeGeorge argued that, in an unregulated international market, the gross inequality of bargaining power between workers and companies would lead to exploitation.

But this paper has shown that attempts to improve on market outcomes may have unforeseen tragic consequences. We saw how raising the wages of workers in international sweatshops might wind up penalizing the most vulnerable workers (those in the informal sectors of developing countries) by depressing their wages and reducing their job opportunities in the formal sector. Donaldson and DeGeorge cited high unemployment and unequal bargaining power as conditions that made it necessary to bypass or override the market determination of wages. However, in both cases, bypassing the market in order to prevent exploitation may aggravate these conditions. As we have seen, above-market wages paid to sweatshop workers may discourage further investment and so perpetuate high unemployment In turn, the higher unemployment may weaken the bargaining power of workers vis-à-vis employers. Thus such market imperfections seem to call for more reliance on market forces rather than less. Likewise, the experience of the newly industrialized East Asian economies suggests that the best cure for the ills of sweatshops is more sweatshops. But most of the well-intentioned policies that improve on market outcomes are likely to have the opposite effect.

Where does this leave the international manager? If the preceding analysis is correct, then it follows that it is ethically acceptable to pay market wage rates in developing countries (and to provide employment conditions appropriate for the level of development). That holds true even if the wages pay less than so-called living wages or subsistence or even (conceivably) the local minimum wage. The appropriate test is not whether the wage reaches some predetermined standard but whether it is freely accepted by (reasonably) informed workers. The workers themselves are in the best position to judge whether the wages offered are superior to their next-best alternatives. (The same logic applies *mutatis mutandis* to workplace labor standards).

Indeed, not only is it ethically acceptable for a company to pay market wages, but it may be ethically unacceptable for it to pay wages that exceed market levels. That will be the case if the company's above-market wages set precedents for other international companies which raise labor costs to the point of discouraging foreign investment Furthermore, companies may have a social responsibility to transcend their own narrow preoccupation with protecting their brand image and to publicly defend a system which has greatly improved the lot of millions of workers in developing countries.

NOTES

1. Steven Greenhouse, "A Crusader Makes Celebrities Tremble." *New York Times* (June 18, 1996), p. B4.

2. Lance A. Compa and Tashia Hinchliffe Darricarrere, "Enforcement Through Corporate Codes of Conduct," in Compa and Stephen F. Diamond, *Human Rights, Labor Rights, and International Trade* (Philadelphia: University of Pennsylvania Press, 1996) p. 193.

3. Peter Jacobi in Martha Nichols, "Third-World Families at Work: Child Labor or Child Care." *Harvard Business Review* (Jan–Feb, 1993).

4. David Sampson in Robin Glivhan, "A Stain on Fashion; The Garment Industry Profits from Cheap Labor." *Washington Post* (September 12, 1995), p. B1.

5. Thomas Donaldson, *Ethics of International Business.* (New York: Oxford University Press, 1989), p. 98.

6. Richard DeGeorge, *Competing with Integrity in International Business* (New York: Oxford University Press, 1993) p. 79.

7. Ibid., pp. 356–7.

8. Ibid., p. 78.

9. World Bank, *World Development Report 1995, "Workers in an Integrating World Economy"* (Oxford University Press, 1995) p. 77.

10. Donaldson, Ethics of International Business, p.115.

11. *Ibid.*, p. 150.

12. DeGeorge, *Competing with Integrity*, p. 48.

13. *Ibid.*, p. 358.

14. *Ibid.*

15. Terry Collingsworth, J. William Goold, Pharis J. Harvey, "Time for a Global New Deal," *Foreign Affairs* (Jan–Feb, 1994), p. 8.

16. William B. Falk, "Dirty Little Secrets," *Newsday* (June 16, 1996).

17. Tim Smith, "The Power of Business for Human Rights." *Business & Society Review* (January 1994), p. 36.

18. Jeffrey Ballinger, "The New Free Trade Heel." *Harper's Magazine* (August, 1992), pp. 46–7. "As in many developing countries, Indonesia's minimum wage, . . . is less than poverty level." Nina Baker, "The Hidden Hands of Nike, *Oregonian* (August 9, 1992).

19. Robert B. Reich, "Escape from the Global Sweatshop; Capitalism's Stake in Uniting the Workers of the World." *Washington Post* (May 22, 1994). Reich's test is intended to apply in developing countries "where democratic institutions are weak or absent."

20. *Ibid.*

21. Kenneth P. Hutchinson, "Third World Growth." *Harvard Business Review* (Nov–Dec, 1994).

22. Robin Broad and John Cavanaugh, "Don't Neglect the Impoverished South." *Foreign Affairs* (December 22, 1995).

23. John Cavanagh & Robin Broad, "Global Reach; Workers Fight the Multinationals." *The Nation,* (March 18, 1996), p. 21. See also Bob Herbert, "Nike's Bad Neighborhood." *New York Times* (June 14, 1996).

24. International Labor Organization, *World Employment 1995* (Geneva: ILO, 1995) p. 73.

25. World Bank, *Workers in an Integrating World Economy*, p. 5.

26. Keith B. Richburg, Anne Swardson, "U.S. Industry Overseas: Sweatshop or Job Source?: Indonesians Praise Work at Nike Factory." *Washington Post* (July 28,1996).

27. Richburg and Swardson, "Sweatshop or Job Source?" The 17-year-old was interviewed in the presence of managers. For other reports that workers remit home large parts of their earnings see Seth Mydans, "Tangerang Journal; For Indonesian Workers at Nike Plant: Just Do It." *New York Times* (August 9, 1996), and Nina Baker, "The Hidden Hands of Nike."

28. Donna Gibbs, Nike spokeswoman on ABC's *World News Tonight,* June 6,1996.

29. Mark Clifford, "Trading in Social Issues; Labor Policy and International Trade Regulation," *World Press Review* (June 1994), p. 36.

30. Larry Rohter, "To U.S. Critics, a Sweatshop; for Hondurans, a Better Life." *New York Times* (July 18, 1996).

31. Marcus Brauchli, "Garment Industry Booms in Bangladesh." *Wall Street Journal* (August 6, 1991).

32. Richburg and Swardson, "Sweatshop or Job Source?"

33. Lucy Martinez-Mont, "Sweatshops Are Better Than No Shops." *Wall Street Journal* (June 25, 1996).

34. Rohter, "To U.S. Critics a Sweatshop."

35. Barnet & Cavanagh, *Global Dreams,* p. 326.

36. Rohter, "To U.S. Critics a Sweatshop."

37. William B. Falk, "Dirty Little Secrets," *Newsday* (June 16, 1996).

38. Barnet and Cavanagh, "Just Undo It: Nike's Exploited Workers." *New York Times* (February 13, 1994).

39. Sarosh Kuruvilla, "Linkages Between Industrialization Strategies and Industrial Relations/Human Resources Policies: Singapore, Malaysia, The Philippines, and India." *Industrial & Labor Relations Review* (July, 1996), p. 637.

40. The ILO's Constitution (of 1919) mentions that ". . . the failure of any nation to adopt humane conditions of labour is an obstacle in the way of other nations which desire to improve the conditions in their own countries." ILO, *World Employment 1995,* p. 74.

41. World Bank, *The East Asian Miracle* (New York: Oxford University Press, 1993)

42. Gideon Rachman, "Wealth in Its Grasp, a Survey of Indonesia." *Economist* (April 17, 1993), pp. 14–15.

43. Jagdish Bhagwati & Robert E. Hudec, eds. *Fair Trade and Harmonization* (Cambridge: MIT Press, 1996), vol. 1, p. 2.

44. World Bank, *Workers in an Integrating World Economy,* p. 75.

45. *Ibid.,* p. 77. As I have noted, the report proposes that the "appropriate level is therefore that at which the costs are commensurate with the value that informed workers place on improved working conditions and reduced risk. . . ." (p. 77).

READING 12.3 SWEATSHOPS AND RESPECT FOR PERSONS

Denis G. Arnold and Norman E. Bowie

From Denis G. Arnold and Norman E. Bowie, "Sweatshops and Respect For Persons," *Business Ethics Quarterly,* Vol. 13, No. 2 (2003): 221–242. © 2003 *Business Ethics Quarterly.* Reprinted by permission.

In recent years labor and human rights activists have been successful at raising public awareness regarding labor practices in both American and off-shore manufacturing facilities. Organizations such as Human Rights Watch, United Students Against Sweatshops, the National Labor Coalition, Sweatshop Watch, and the Interfaith Center on Corporate Responsibility have accused multinational enterprises (MNEs), such as Nike, Wal-Mart, and Disney. of the pernicious exploitation of workers. Recent violations of American and European labor laws have received considerable attention.[1]

However, it is the off-shore labor practices of North American and European based MNEs and their contractors that have been most controversial. This is partly due to the fact that many of the labor practices in question are legal outside North America and Europe, or are tolerated by corrupt or repressive political regimes. Unlike the recent immigrants who toil in the illegal sweatshops of North America and Europe, workers in developing nations typically have no recourse to the law or social service agencies. Activists have sought to enhance the welfare of these workers by pressuring MNEs to comply with labor laws, prohibit coercion, improve health and safety standards, and pay a living wage in their global sourcing operations. Meanwhile, prominent economists wage a campaign of their own in the opinion pages of leading newspapers, arguing that because workers for MNEs are often paid better when compared with local wages, they are fortunate to have such work. Furthermore, they argue that higher wages and improved working conditions will raise unemployment levels.

One test of a robust ethical theory is its ability to shed light on ethical problems. One of the standard criticisms of Immanuel Kant's ethical philosophy is that it is too abstract and formal to be of any use in practical decision making. We contend that this criticism is mistaken and that Kantian theory has much to say about the ethics of sweatshops.[2] We argue that Kant's conception of human dignity provides a clear basis for grounding the obligations of employers to employees. In particular, we argue that respecting the dignity of workers requires that MNEs and their contractors adhere to local labor laws, refrain from coercion, meet minimum safety standards, and provide a living wage for employees. We also respond to the objection that improving health and safety conditions and providing a living wage would cause greater harm than good.

I. RESPECT FOR PERSONS

Critics of sweatshops frequently ground their protests in appeals to human dignity and human rights. Arguably, Kantian ethics provides a philosophical basis for such moral pronouncements. The key principle here is Kant's second formulation of the categorical imperative: "Act so that you treat humanity, whether in your own person or in that of another, always as an end and never as a means only."[3] The popular expression of this principle is that morality requires that we respect people. One significant feature of the idea of respect for persons is that its derivation and application can be assessed independently of other elements of Kantian moral philosophy. Sympathetic readers need not embrace all aspects of Kant's system of ethics in order to grant the merit of Kant's arguments for the second formulation of the categorical imperative.[4] This is because Kant's defense of respect for persons is grounded in the uncontroversial claim that humans are capable of rational, self-governing activity. We believe that individuals with a wide range of theoretical commitments can and should recognize the force of Kant's arguments concerning respect for persons.

Kant did not simply assert that persons are entitled to respect, he provided an elaborate argument for that conclusion. Persons ought to be respected because persons have dignity. For Kant, an object that has dignity is beyond price. Employees have a dignity that machines and capital do not have. They have dignity because they are capable of moral activity. As free beings capable of self-governance they are responsible beings, since freedom and self-governance are the conditions for responsibility. Autonomous responsible beings are capable of making and following their own laws; they are not simply subject to the causal laws of nature. Anyone who recognizes that he or she is free should recognize that he or she is responsible (that he or she is a moral being). As Kant argues, the fact that one is a moral being entails that one possesses dignity.

> Morality is the condition under which alone a rational being can be an end in himself because only through it is it possible to be a lawgiving member in the realm of ends. Thus morality, and humanity insofar as it is capable of morality, alone have dignity.[5]

As a matter of consistency, a person who recognizes that he or she is a moral being should ascribe dignity to anyone who, like him or herself, is a moral being.

Although it is the capacity to behave morally that gives persons their dignity, freedom is required if a person is to act morally. For Kant, being free is more than freedom from causal necessity. This is negative freedom. Freedom in its fullest realization is the ability to guide one's actions from laws that are of one s own making. Freedom is not simply a spontaneous event. Free actions are caused, but they are caused by persons acting from laws they themselves have made. This is positive freedom. Onora O'Neill puts the point this way.

> Positive freedom is more than independence from alien causes. It would be absent in lawless or random changes, although these are negatively free, since they depend on no alien causes. Since will is a mode of causality it cannot, if free at all, be merely negatively free, so it must work by nonalien causality . . . it [free will] must be a capacity for self-determination or autonomy.[6]

When we act autonomously we have the capacity to act with dignity. We do so when we act on principles that are grounded in morality rather than in mere inclination. Reason requires that any moral principle that is freely derived must be rational in the sense that it is universal. To be universal in this sense means that the principle can be willed to be universally binding on all subjects in relevantly similar circumstances without contradiction. The fact that persons have this capability means that they possess dignity. And it is as a consequence of this dignity that a person "exacts respect for himself from all other rational beings in the world.[7] As such, one can and should "measure himself with every other being of this kind and value himself on a footing of equality with them."[8]

Respecting people requires honoring their humanity; which is to say it requires treating them as ends in themselves. In Kant's words,

> Humanity itself is a dignity; for a man cannot be used merely as a means by any man . . . but must always be used at the same time as an end. It is just in this that his dignity . . . consists, by which he raises himself above all other beings in the world that are not men and yet can be used, and so over all *things*.[9]

Thomas Hill Jr. has discussed the implication of Kant's arguments concerning human dignity at length.[10] Hill argues that treating persons as ends in themselves requires supporting and developing certain human capacities, including the capacity to act on reason; the capacity to act on the basis of prudence or efficiency; the capacity to set goals; the capacity to accept categorical imperatives; and the capacity to understand the world and reason abstractly.[11] Based on Kant's writings in the *Metaphysics of Morals,* we would make several additions to the list. There Kant argues that respecting people means that we cannot be indifferent to them. Indifference is a denial of respect.[12] He also argues that we have an obligation to be concerned with the physical welfare of people and their moral well-being. Adversity, pain, and want are temptations to vice and inhibit the ability of individuals to develop their rational and moral capacities.[13] It is these rational and moral capacities that distinguish people from mere animals. People who are not free to develop these capacities may end up leading lives that are closer to animals than to moral beings. Freedom from externally imposed adversity, pain, and want facilitate the cultivation of one's rational

capacities and virtuous character. Thus, treating people as ends in themselves means ensuring their physical well-being and supporting and developing their rational and moral capacities.

With respect to the task at hand, what does treating the humanity of persons as ends in themselves require in a business context—specifically in the context of global manufacturing facilities? In an earlier work Bowie has spelled out the implications of the Kantian view for businesses operating in developed countries.[14] Here we apply the same strategy in order to derive basic duties for MNEs operating in developing countries. Specifically, we derive duties that apply to MNEs that are utilizing the vast supplies of inexpensive labor currently available in developing economies. To fully respect a person one must actively treat his or her humanity as an end. This is an obligation that holds on every person *qua* person, whether in the personal realm or in the marketplace. As Kant writes, "Every man has a legitimate claim to respect from his fellow men and is *in turn* bound to respect every other."[15] There are, of course, limits to what managers of MNEs can accomplish. Nonetheless, we believe that the analysis we have provided entails that MNEs operating in developing nations have an obligation to respect the humanity of their employees. We discuss the implications of this conclusion below.

It is noteworthy that an application of the doctrine of respect for persons to the issue of the obligations of employers to employees in developing economies results in conclusions similar to the capabilities approach developed by Amartya Sen.[16] Over the last twenty years Sen has argued that development involves more than an increase in people's incomes and the GNP of the country. He argues that we should be concerned with certain basic human capabilities, the most important of which is freedom. Sen's perspective is similar in important respects to our own because both are concerned with providing work that enhances the positive freedom of the worker. The United Nations utilizes both the Kantian view and the capabilities view as a dual theoretical foundation for its defense of human rights. Among the rights identified by the UN are freedom from injustice and violations of the rule of law; freedom to decent work without exploitation; and the freedom to develop and realize one's human potential. It argues that all global actors, including MNEs, have a moral obligation to respect basic human rights.[17] This general approach to poverty and development has recently been embraced by the World Bank.[18] James Wolfensohn, President of The World Bank, writes:

> A better quality of life for the poor calls for higher incomes. This requires sound economic policies and institutions conducive to sustained growth. Achieving higher incomes and a better quality of life also calls for much more— improved and more equitable opportunities for education and jobs, better health and nutrition, a cleaner and more sustainable natural environment, an impartial judicial and legal system, greater civilian and political liberties, trustworthy and transparent institutions, and freedom of access to a rich and diverse cultural life . . . Poor women and men from around the world [note] emphatically the importance of dignity, respect, security, gender issues, a clean environment, health, and inclusion in addition to material well-being.[19]

Significantly, The World Bank has recognized "crucial gaps" in its efforts to encourage development and eliminate poverty through market liberalization. What has been missing is "adequate attention to the quality and sustainability of growth." The World Bank now explicitly acknowledges that all major stake holders have important roles to play in this process. "Functioning markets and liberalization are crucial" to poverty reduction. "But so is acknowledging the limits of the market and an essential role for governments *and other stakeholders* in the reform process."[20] MNEs have a significant interests in developing nations as sources of natural resources and inexpensive labor, and as emerging markets. As such, The World Bank properly recognizes MNEs as stakeholders with important moral obligations in the global reform process.

II. OUTSOURCING AND THE DUTIES OF MNEs

One significant feature of globalization that is of particular relevance to our analysis is the increase in outsourcing by MNEs. Prior to the 1970s most foreign production by MNEs was intended for local markets. In the 1970s new financial incentives led MNEs to begin outsourcing the production of goods for North American, European, and Japanese markets to manufacturing facilities in developing countries. Encouraged by international organizations such as The World Bank and the International Monetary Fund, developing nations established "free trade zones" to encourage foreign investment via tax incentives and a minimal regulatory environment. In the 1980s the availability of international financing allowed entrepreneurs to set up production facilities in developing economies in order to meet the growing demand by MNEs for offshore production.[21] Outsourcing production has many distinct advantages from the perspective of MNEs. These include the following:

> *Capacity.* Companies can expand their business more rapidly by focusing on marketing their products rather than investing in plant capacity, employees, and upgrading capital equipment. Companies can also accept special orders they would not be able to offer to large volume customers if their production capacity were fixed.
>
> *Specialization.* Companies can market products requiring specialized skills or equipment that the firm does not have in-house.
>
> *Reduced Production Costs.* In competitive industries where firms compete largely on the basis of price, outsourcing permits companies to reduce the size of their payroll and profit sharing obligations and shop around for lower and lower cost producers all across the globe.
>
> *Cycle Time.* Outsourcing gives companies the flexibility to turn products around quickly in order to meet consumer demand and also avoid inventory build-ups.
>
> *Flexibility.* The outsourcing model of production offers unique flexibility to firms that seek to cut costs in production or increase their capacity in that it offers opportunities to experiment with product lines and supplier relationships with minimal financial risk. The expense of developing new samples, for example, is borne by the factory that hopes to receive the order.[22]

Outsourcing has been especially popular in consumer products industries, and in particular in the apparel industry. Nike, for example, outsources all of its production.

Are MNEs responsible for the practices of their subcontractors and suppliers? We believe that they are. Michael Santoro has defended the view that MNEs have a moral duty to ensure that their business partners respect employees by ensuring that human rights are not violated in the workplace. Santoro argues as follows:

> [M]ultinational corporations are morally responsible for the way their suppliers and subcontractors treat their workers. The applicable moral standard is similar to the legal doctrine of *respondeat superior,* according to which a principal is "vicariously liable" or responsible for the acts of its agent conducted in the course of the agency relationship. The classic example of this is the responsibility of employers for the acts of employees. Moreover, ignorance is no excuse. Firms must do whatever is required to become aware of what conditions are like in the factories of their suppliers and subcontractors, and thereby be able to assure themselves and others that their business partners don't mistreat those workers to provide a cheaper source of supply.[23]

We concur with Santoro's judgment and offer the following two-fold justification for the view that MNEs have a duty to ensure that the dignity of workers is respected in the factories of subcontractors. First, an MNE, like any other organization, is composed of individual persons and, since persons are moral creatures, the actions of employees in an MNE are constrained by the categorical imperative. This means MNE managers have a duty to ensure that those with whom they conduct business are properly respected.[24] Second, as Kant acknowledges, individuals have unique duties as a result of their unique circumstances. One key feature in determining an individual's duties is the power they have to render assistance. For example, Kant famously argues that a wealthy person has a duty of charity that an impoverished person lacks. Corollary duties apply to organizations. Researchers have noted that the relationship of power between MNEs and their subcontractors and suppliers is significantly imbalanced in favor of MNEs:

> [A]s more and more developing countries have sought to establish export sectors, local manufacturers are locked in fierce competitive battles with one another. The resulting oversupply of export factories allows U.S. companies to move from one supplier to another in search of the lowest prices, quickest turnaround, highest quality and best delivery terms, weighted according to the priorities of the company. In this context, large U.S. manufacturer-merchandisers and retailers wield enormous power to dictate the price at which they will purchase goods.[25]

MNEs are well positioned to help ensure that the employees of its business partners are respected because of this imbalance of power. In addition, MNEs can draw upon substantial economic resources, management expertise, and technical knowledge to assist their business partners in creating a respectful work environment.

III. THE RULE OF LAW

Lawlessness contributes to poverty[26] and is deeply interconnected with human and labor rights violations. One important role that MNEs can play to help ensure that the dignity of workers is properly respected is encouraging respect for the rule of law. The United Nations has emphasized the importance of ensuring that citizens in all nations are not subject to violations of the rule of law.

> The rule of law means that a country's formal rules are made publicly known and enforced in a predictable way through transparent mechanisms. Two conditions are essential: the rules apply equally to all citizens, and the state is subject to the rules. How state institutions comply with the rule of law greatly affects the daily lives of poor people, who are very vulnerable to abuses of their rights.[27]

It is commonplace for employers in developing nations to violate worker rights in the interest of economic efficiency and with the support of state institutions. Violations of laws relating to wages and benefits, forced overtime, health and safety, child labor, sexual harassment, discrimination, and environmental protection are legion. Examples include the following:

1. Human Rights Watch reports that in Mexican maquiladoras, or export processing zones, U.S. companies such as Johnson Controls and Carlisle Plastics require female job applicants to submit to pregnancy screening; women are refused employment if they test positive.

Employment discrimination based on pregnancy is a violation of Mexican law.[28]

2. Guatemalan Ministry of the Economy study found that less than 30 percent of maquiladora factories that supply MNEs make the legally required payments for workers into the national social security system which gives workers access to health care. The report was not made public by the Ministry of the Economy due to its "startling" nature.[29]

3. An El Salvadoran Ministry of Labor study funded by the United States Agency for International Development found widespread violation of labor laws, including flagrant violation of the freedom to organize and unionize, in maquiladora factories that supply MNEs. The report was suppressed by the Ministry of Labor after factory owners complained.[30]

4. In North and Central Mexico widespread violation of Mexican environmental laws by MNEs and their contractors has been documented by both U.S. and Mexican nongovernmental organizations, and local Mexican governmental officials.[31]

5. In Haiti apparel manufacturers such as L.V. Myles Corporation, producing clothing under license with the Walt Disney Company in several contract factories, paid workers substantially less than the Haitian minimum wage. These clothes were sold in the U.S. at Wal-Mart, Sears, J.C. Penney and other retailers. This practice continued until the National Labor Committee documented and publicized this violation of Haitian law.[32]

Furthermore, in many nations in which MNEs operate those responsible for administering justice are violators of the law. Factory workers frequently have no legal recourse when their legal rights are violated.

The intentional violation of the legal rights of workers in the interest of economic efficiency is fundamentally incompatible with the duty of MNEs to respect workers. Indifference to the plight of workers whose legal rights are systematically violated is a denial of respect. At a minimum, MNEs have a duty to ensure that their offshore factories, and those of their suppliers and subcontractors, are in full compliance with local laws. Failure to honor

the dignity of workers by violating their legal rights—or tolerating the violation of those rights—is also hypocritical. In Kantian terms, it constitutes a pragmatic contradiction. A pragmatic contradiction occurs when one acts on a principle that promotes an action that would be inconsistent with one's purpose if everyone were to act upon that principle. In this case, the principle would be something like the following: "It is permissible to violate the legal rights of others when doing so is economically efficient." MNEs rely on the rule of law to ensure, among other things, that their contracts are fulfilled, their property is secure, and their copyrights are protected. When violations of the legal rights of MNEs take place, MNEs and business organizations protest vociferously. Thus, MNEs rely on the rule of law to ensure the protection of their own interests. Without the rule of law, MNEs would cease to exist. Therefore, it is inconsistent for an MNE to permit the violation of the legal rights of workers while at the same time it demands that its own rights be protected.

IV. COERCION

We have shown why it is reasonable to believe that all persons possess dignity and that this dignity must be respected. The obligation that we respect others requires that we not use people as a means only, but instead that we treat other people as capable of autonomous law guided action. The requirement not to use people can be met passively, by not treating them in certain ways. However, the requirement to treat them as ends-in-themselves entails positive obligations. We will explore these positive obligations as they relate to sweatshops in Section VI. In this section and the next we explore the requirement that we not use people as a means only. One common way of doing so recognized by Kant is coercion. Coercion violates a person's negative freedom. Coercion is prima facie wrong because it treats the subjects of coercion as mere tools, as objects lacking the rational capacity to choose for themselves how they shall act.

Are sweatshops in violation of the no coercion requirement? An answer to this question depends both on the definition of the concepts in question and on the facts of the particular case. Elsewhere Arnold has provided accounts of physical and psychological coercion.[33] Physical coercion occurs when one's bodily movements are physically forced. In cases where one person *(P)* physically coerces another person *(Q)*, *Q*'s body is used as an object or instrument for the purpose of fulfilling *P*'s desires. We assume that readers of this essay will agree that using physical coercion to keep people working in sweatshops against their will is disrespectful and morally wrong. While comparatively rare, physical coercion, or the threat of physical coercion, does take place. For example, at a shoe factory in Guangdong, China, it is reported that 2,700 workers were prevented from leaving the factory by 100 live-in security guards that patrolled the walled factory grounds.[34]

For psychological coercion to take place, three conditions most hold. First, the coercer must have a desire about the will of his or her victim. However, this is a desire of a particular kind because it can only be fulfilled through the will of another person. Second, the coercer must have an effective desire to compel his or her victim to act in a manner that makes efficacious the coercer's other regarding desire. The distinction between an other regarding desire and a coercive will is important because it provides a basis for delineating between cases of coercion and, for example, cases of rational persuasion. In both instances a person may have an other regarding desire, but in the case of coercion that desire will be supplemented by an effective first-order desire that seeks to enforce that desire on the person, and in cases of rational persuasion it will not. What is of most importance in such cases is that *P* intentionally attempts to compel *Q* to comply with an other regarding desire of *P*'s own. These are necessary, but not sufficient conditions of coercion. In order for coercion to take place, the coercer must be successful in getting his or her victim to conform to his or her other regarding desire. In all cases of coercion *P* attempts to violate the autonomy of *Q*. When *Q* successfully resists *P*'s attempted coercion, *Q* retains his or her autonomy. In such cases *P* retains a coercive will.

In typical cases, people work in sweatshops because they believe they can earn more money working there than they can in alternative employment, or they work in sweatshops because it is better than being unemployed. In many developing countries, people are moving to large cities from rural areas because agriculture in those areas can no longer support the population base. When people make a choice that seems highly undesirable

because there are no better alternatives available, are those people coerced? On the definition of coercion employed here, having to make a choice among undesirable options is not sufficient for coercion. We therefore assume that such persons are not coerced even though they have no better alternative than working in a sweatshop.

Nonetheless, the use of psychological coercion in sweatshops appears widespread. For example, coercion is frequently used by supervisors to improve worker productivity. Workers throughout the world report that they are forced to work long overtime hours or lose their jobs. In Bangladesh factory workers report that they are expected to work virtually every day of the year. Overtime pay, a legal requirement, is often not paid. Employees who refuse to comply are fired.[35] In El Salvador a government study of maquiladora factories found that

> in the majority of companies, it is an obligation of the personnel to work overtime under the threat of firing or some other kind of reprisal. This situation, in addition to threatening the health of the workers, causes family problems in that [the workers] are unable to properly fulfill obligations to their immediate family.
>
> On some occasions, because the work time is extended into the late hours of the night, the workers find themselves obligated to sleep in the factory facilities, which do not have conditions necessary for lodging of personnel.[36]

Bangladesh, El Salvador, and other developing economies lack the social welfare programs that workers in North America and Europe take for granted. If workers lose their jobs, they may end up without any source of income. Thus, workers are understandably fearful of being fired for noncompliance with demands to work long overtime hours. When a worker is threatened with being fired by a supervisor unless she agrees to work overtime, and when the supervisor's intention in making the threat is to ensure compliance, then the supervisors actions are properly understood as coercive. Similar threats are used to ensure that workers meet production quotas, even in the face of personal injury. For example, a 26-year-old worker who sews steering wheel covers at a Mexican maquila owned by Autotrim reports the following:

> We have to work quickly with our hands, and I am responsible for sewing 20 steering wheel

covers per shift. After having worked for nine years at the plant, I now suffer from an injury in my right hand. I start out the shift okay, but after about three hours of work, I feel a lot of sharp pains in my fingers. It gets so bad that I can't hold the steering wheel correctly. But still the supervisors keep pressuring me to reach 100 percent of my production. I can only reach about 70 percent of what they ask for. These pains began a year ago and I am not the only one who has suffered from them. There are over 200 of us who have hand injuries and some have lost movement in their hands and arms. The company has fired over 150 people in the last year for lack of production. Others have been pressured to quit. . . .[37]

We do not claim that production quotas are inherently coercive. Given a reasonable quota, employees can choose whether or not to work diligently to fill that quota. Employees who choose idleness over industriousness and are terminated as a result are not coerced. However, when a supervisor threatens workers who are ill or injured with termination unless they meet a production quota that either cannot physically be achieved by the employee, or can only be achieved at the cost of further injury to the employee, the threat is properly understood as coercive. In such cases the employee will inevitably feel compelled to meet the quota. Still other factory workers report being threatened with termination if they seek medical attention. For example, when a worker in El Salvador who was three months pregnant began hemorrhaging she was not allowed to leave the factory to receive medical attention. She subsequently miscarried while in the factory, completed her long work day, and took her fetus home for burial.[38] Other workers have died because they were not allowed to leave the factory to receive medical attention.[39] In cases where workers suffer miscarriages or death, rather than risk termination, we believe that it reasonable to conclude that the workers are coerced into remaining at work.

According to the analysis provided here, workers choose to work in sweatshops, because the alternatives available to them are worse. However, once they are employed, coercion is often used to ensure that they will work long overtime hours and meet production quotas. Respecting workers requires that they be free to decline overtime work without fear

of being fired. It also requires that if they are injured or ill—especially as a result of work related activities—they should be allowed to consult healthcare workers and be given work that does not exacerbate their illnesses or injuries. Using coercion as a means of compelling employees to work overtime, to meet production quotas despite injury, or to remain at work while in need of medical attention, is incompatible with respect for persons because the coercers treat their victims as mere tools. It is important to note that even if the victim of coercion successfully resisted in some way, the attempted coercion would remain morally objectionable. This is because the coercer acts as if it is permissible to use the employees as mere tools.

V. WORKING CONDITIONS

Critics of MNEs argue that many workers are vulnerable to workplace hazards such as repetitive motion injuries, exposure to toxic chemicals, exposure to airborne pollutants such as fabric particles, and malfunctioning machinery. One of the most common workplace hazards concerns fire safety. In factories throughout the world workers are locked in to keep them from leaving the factory. When fires break out workers are trapped. This is what happened in 1993 when a fire broke out at the Kader Industrial Toy Company in Thailand. More than 200 workers were killed and 469 injured. The factory had been producing toys for U.S. companies such as Hasbro, Toys "R" Us, J.C. Penney, and Fisher-Price.[40] In Bangladesh alone, there have been seventeen fires that have resulted in fatalities since 1995. A recent fire at Chowdhury Knitwears claimed 52 lives.[41]

Workers are also exposed to dangerous toxic chemicals and airborne pollutants. For example, a Nike commissioned Ernst & Young Environmental and Labor Practices Audit of the Tae Kwang Vina factory outside Ho Chi Minh City, Vietnam, was leaked to the press. Among the many unsafe conditions reported by Ernst & Young at this 10,000 person facility was exposure to toluene (a toxic chemical used as a solvent in paints, coatings, adhesives, and cleaning agents) at amounts 6 to 177 times that allowed by Vietnamese law.[42] The U.S. Environmental Protection Agency identifies the following acute effects of toluene exposure:

The central nervous system is the primary target organ for toluene toxicity in both humans and animals for acute (short-term) and chronic (long-term) exposures. CNS dysfunction (which is often reversible) and narcosis have been frequently observed in humans acutely exposed to low or moderate levels of toluene by inhalation; symptoms include fatigue, sleepiness, headaches, and nausea. CNS depression and death have occurred at higher levels of exposure. Cardiac arrhythmia has also been reported in humans acutely exposed to toluene[.][43]

In addition to toluene, workers at the Tae Kwang Vina factory were exposed to airborne fabric particles and chemical powders at dangerous levels. It is implausible to think that the (mainly) young women who work in the Tae Kwang Vina factory were informed about these health risks before they were hired. Ernst & Young reports that the employees received no training concerning the proper handling of chemicals after they were hired. Since that time Nike has overseen substantial health and safety improvements at the Tae Kwang Vina factory, and at the other Southeast Asian factories with which it contracts. Nonetheless, available evidence indicates that unsafe workplace conditions remain common among MNE factories.[44] Consider, for example, the report of Mexican maquila worker Omar Gil:

> Back in 1993 I got my first job in a maquiladora, at Delphi Auto Parts. They paid 360 pesos a week (about $40). There was a lot of pressure from the foreman on the assembly lines to work hard and produce, and a lot of accidents because of the bad design of the lines. The company didn't give us adequate protective equipment to deal with the chemicals—we didn't really have any idea of the dangers, or how we should protect ourselves. The Union did nothing to protect us.
>
> From Delphi I went to another company, National Auto parts. In that plant we made car radiators for Cadillacs and Camaros, and there was a lot of sickness and accidents there too. I worked in the area with the metal presses. There were not ventilators to take the fumes out of the plant, and they didn't give us any gloves. We had to handle the parts with our bare hands, and people got cut up a lot. I worked in an area

> with a lot of lead. If you worked with lead, you're supposed to have special clothing and your clothes should be washed separately. But the company didn't give us any of that. We had to work in our street clothes.
>
> For all of that they paid 400 pesos a week (about $43). We had no union, and there was the same pressure for production from the foreman and the group leaders as I saw at Delphi.
>
> Now I work at TRW, where I've been for about a month and a half. There's really no difference in the conditions in any of these plants—if anything, my situation now is even worse.[45]

If our analysis is correct, then those MNEs that tolerate such health and safety risks have a duty to improve those conditions. Lax health and safety standards violate the moral requirement that employers be concerned with the physical safety of their employees. A failure to implement appropriate safeguards means that employers are treating their employees as disposable tools rather than as beings with unique dignity.

We cannot provide industry specific health and safety guidelines in the space of this essay. However, we believe that the International Labour Organization's carefully worked out Conventions and Recommendations on safety and health provide an excellent template for minimum safety standards.[46] For example, the ILO provides specific recommendations regarding airborne pollutants in "Occupational Exposure to Airborne Substances Harmful to Health" (1980) and exposure to chemicals in "Safety in the Use of Chemicals at Work" (1993). Ethicists, business people, and labor leaders with widely divergent views on a number of issues can agree on a minimum set of health and safety standards that should be in place in factories in the developing world. We return to this issue in Section VII.

VI. WAGES

One of the most controversial issues concerning sweatshops is the demand that employers raise the wages of employees in order to provide a "living wage." Workers from all over the world complain about low wages. For example,

> [E]mployees of a maquiladora in Ciudad Acuna, Mexico, owned by the Aluminum Company of

America (Alcoa), calculated that to buy the most basic food items needed by a factory worker—items such a beans, tortilla, rice, potatoes, onions and cooking oil, and excluding such "luxuries" as milk, meat, vegetables and cereal—cost U.S. $26.87 per week. At the time, weekly wages at the plant ranged only from $21.44 to $24.60.[47]

While a living wage is difficult to define with precision, one useful approach is to use a method similar to that used by the U.S. government to define poverty. This method involves calculating the cost of a market basket of food needed to meet minimum dietary requirements and then adding the cost of other basic needs. The Council on Economic Priorities uses this approach to define a wage that meets basic needs in different countries. Their formula is as follows:

1. Establish the local cost of a basic food basket needed to provide 2,100 calories per person.

2. Determine the share of the local household income spent on food. Divide into 1 to get total budget multiplier.

3. Multiply that by food spending to get the total per person budget for living expenses.

4. Multiply by half the average number of household members in the area. (Use a higher share if there are many single-parent households.)

5. Add at least 10% for discretionary income.[48]

The United Nations Development Programme employs a similar method to distinguish between three different levels of poverty (see Table I).[49]

It is our contention that, at a minimum, respect for employees entails that MNEs and their suppliers have a moral obligation to ensure that employees do not live under conditions of overall poverty by providing adequate wages for a 48 hour work week to satisfy both basic food needs and basic non-food needs. Doing so helps to ensure the physical well-being and independence of employees, contributes to the development of their rational capacities, and provides them with opportunities for moral development. This in turn allows for the cultivation of self-esteem.[50] It is difficult to specify with precision the minimum number of hours per week that employees should work in order to receive a living wage. However, we believe that a 48 hour work

week is a reasonable compromise that allows employees sufficient time for the cultivation of their rational capacities while providing employers with sufficient productivity. In addition, MNEs and their suppliers have an obligation to pay appropriate host nation taxes and meet appropriate codes and regulations to ensure that they contribute in appropriate ways to the creation and maintenance of the goods, services, and infrastructure necessary for the fulfillment of human capabilities. Anything less than this means that MNEs, or their suppliers, are not respecting employees as ends in themselves.

VII. ECONOMIC CONSIDERATIONS

The failure of many MNEs to meet the standards required by the application of the doctrine of respect for persons has not gone unnoticed. Through consumer boycotts, letter writing campaigns, opinion columns, and shareholder resolutions, activists have been successful in persuading some MNEs to implement changes. For example, Nike recently created the position of Vice President for Corporate Social Responsibility, hired a public affairs specialist to fill the position, and began to aggressively respond to activist complaints. In a recent open letter to its critics Nike concedes that "Several years ago, in our earlier expansion into certain countries, we had lots to learn about manufacturing practices and how to improve them."[51] However, Nike reports that it has fully embraced the goals of higher wages, the elimination of child labor, and the creation of better working conditions. In short, Nike's response to its critics is " . . . guess what? You've already succeeded!"[52] Asked whether or not Nike would have made improvements without public pressure, a Nike official responded "Probably not as quickly, probably not to the degree."[53] Thus, ethical theory and a significant number of citizens of good will stand as one on this issue.

In a recent paper, Ian Maitland criticizes both the labor and human rights activists who have accused MNEs of unjust labor practices, as well as MNEs, such as Nike, that have responded by acquiescing to some of the activists demands.

In this confrontation between the companies and their critics, neither side seems to have judged it to be in its interest to seriously engage the issue at the heart of the controversy, namely: What are

Table 1

Types of Poverty	Deficiencies	Measures
Extreme Poverty (also known as Absolute Poverty)	Lack of income necessary to satisfy basic food needs	Minimum caloric intake and a food basket that meets that requirement
Overall Poverty (also known as Relative Poverty)	Lack of income necessary to satisfy basic non-food needs	Ability to secure shelter, energy, transportation, and basic health care, e.g.
Human Poverty	Lack of basic human capabilities	Access to goods, services, and infrastructure, e.g.

the appropriate wages and labor standards in international sweatshops?" . . . companies have treated the charges about sweatshops as a public relations problem to be managed so as to minimize harm to their public images. The critics have apparently judged that the best way to keep public indignation at boiling point is to oversimplify the issue and treat it as a morality play featuring heartless exploiters and victimized third world workers. The result has been the great non-debate over international sweatshops.[54]

Maitland hopes to do better. In addition to assessing the veracity of claims regarding worker exploitation, he sets out to determine "the ethically appropriate levels of wages and labor standards in international sweatshops."[55] He argues that philosophers, such as Thomas Donaldson and Richard DeGeorge, who object to letting market determinations alone set wage standards, are misguided on the grounds that "attempts to improve on market outcomes may have unforeseen tragic consequences."[56] Maitland's arguments regarding ethically appropriate levels of wages and labor standards may be summarized as follows:

1. Workers in the urban, formal sector of developing nations earn better wages than do workers in the rural, informal sector.

2. The imposition of wages or labor standards greater than that demanded by the market increases costs.

3. Increased costs result in layoffs and slow investment in the formal sector.

4. Formal sector layoffs result in a surplus supply of labor in the informal sector.

5. A surplus of informal sector workers depresses income in the informal sector.

Conclusion: Higher wages or labor standards increase poverty and limit economic growth in developing nations.

Appealing as it does to textbook economic theory, Maitland's conclusion retains an authoritative quality. Naive critics of MNEs fail to take into consideration rudimentary economic theory, and cynical corporate managers ignore these economic realities in order to preserve their brand images and corporate reputations. Maitland has done a valuable service by raising issues of central importance to the welfare of millions of powerless and impoverished people. However, is his conclusion correct? In the remaining portion of essay we argue that it is not.

First, despite Maitland's faith in the ability of international markets alone to generate ethically acceptable wage and labor standards for MNEs and their contractors, and despite his criticisms of Donaldson and DeGeorge's recommendations for improving market outcomes, Maitland does not himself defend an unrestricted market approach. It is not clear, however, that Maitland recognizes this fact. The most obvious evidence in support of this conclusion is his criticism of corporate managers who, he believes, merely seek to appease their critics. "Not a single company has tried to mount a serious defense of its contracting practices. They have judged that they cannot win a war of soundbites with the critics. Instead of making a fight of it, the companies have sued for peace in order to protect their principal asset—their image."[57] Thus, according to Maitland, corporate managers have made the strategic decision to respond to market forces—in this case consumers' preferences and other marketing considerations—in the manner they deem most consistent with profitability. Given Maitland's faith in the free market, one might expect him to criticize this strategy because it is inefficient.[58] However, Maitland does not pursue this approach. Instead, he argues that managers should not appease their critics—even if managers regard this as the strategy most consistent with profitability—because doing so will have undesirable economic and moral outcomes, namely, higher unemployment and slower economic growth. There is, then, a contradiction at the heart of Maitland's analysis. He argues in favor of improvements to current market outcomes, while at the same time he argues against attempts to improve on market outcomes on the grounds that doing so will result in undesirable moral consequences.[59]

Second, some of the most compelling evidence in support of the proposition that MNEs can improve workplace health and safety conditions while avoiding "tragic outcomes" comes from MNEs themselves. Companies such as Levis Strauss, Motorola, and Mattel have expended considerable resources to ensure that employees in their global sourcing operations work in healthy and safe environments. For example, Levis Strauss & Company stipulates that "We will only utilize business partners who provide workers with a safe and healthy environments."[60] Levis is known for acting in a manner consistent with this policy. Motorola explicitly endorses the idea of respect for persons in their Code of Business Conduct. The Code is built on two foundations:

> *Uncompromising integrity* means staying true to what we believe. We adhere to honesty, fairness and "doing the right thing" without compromise, even when circumstances make it difficult.
> *Constant respect for people* means we treat others with dignity, as we would like to be treated ourselves. Constant respect applies to every individual we interact with around the world.[61]

The physical instantiation of these principles can be seen at Motorola's factory in Tianjin, China:

> In the company cafeteria, workers queue up politely for a variety of free and nutritious meals. One area is set aside for a pregnancy well-care program. A booth is open at which

appointments can be made with the company medical staff. There is a bank branch dedicated to employee needs. It is a scene that one might expect in a Fortune 500 corporate campus in the United States. The overwhelming sense is of a pleasant, orderly place in which people are fulfilled in their work.[62]

Recently Mattel announced the creation of a global code of conduct for its production facilities and contract manufacturers. It has spent millions of dollars to upgrade its manufacturing facilities in order to improve worker safety and comfort. Furthermore, it has invited a team of academics lead by S. Prakash Sethi to monitor its progress in complying with its self-imposed standards and to make their findings public.[63] This is believed to be the first time that a major MNE has voluntarily submitted to external monitoring. The examples set by Levis, Motorola, and Mattel provide evidence that MNEs are capable of improving worker health and safety without causing further hardship in the communities in which they operate.

Finally, it is not clear that improving employee wages will inevitably lead to the "tragic consequences" that Maitland and others predict. The economic issues under consideration are complex and we cannot address them here in the detail they deserve. Nonetheless, several reasons are provided for thinking that Maitland's conclusion is incorrect. With regard to the lowest paid formal sector wage earners in developing countries, the assumption that productivity is independent of wage levels is dubious.

> As exceptionally low wages are raised, there may be increases in productivity either because of induced management improvements or because of greater labour efficiency due to a decrease in wasteful labour turnover and industrial disputes and to improvements in workers morale and nutrition resulting, in turn, in an increase in the workers willingness and capacity to work and a reduction in the incidence of debilitating diseases, time off due to illness and accidents caused by fatigue. If higher wages, at least over a certain range, are accompanied by certain improvements in labour productivity, it is conceivable that labour costs could decrease rather than increase and to such an extent that employment would not fall.[64]

Put simply, workers whose minimum daily caloric intakes are met, and who have basic non-food needs met, will have more energy and better attitudes at work; will be less likely to come to work ill; and will be absent with less frequency. Workers are thus likely to be more productive and loyal. Economists refer to a wage that if reduced would make the firm worse off because of a decrease in worker productivity as the efficiency wage. Empirical evidence supports the view that increased productivity resulting from better nutrition offsets the cost of higher wages.[65] Thus, if workers are being paid less than the efficiency wage in a particular market there are good economic reasons, in addition to moral reasons, for raising wages.

One might object that our analysis implies that MNE managers are unaware of the correlation between wages and productivity, and that such ignorance on the part of MNE managers is implausible. Our reply is two-fold. First, workers in developing nations *are* frequently paid less than the efficiency wage in those labor markets. Second, findings from an El Salvadoran Ministry of Labor study of maquiladora factories are instructive. Researchers found that "According to the production managers interviewed, some companies use North American and Asian efficiency and productivity levels as a parameter for establishing production goals, without considering the different nutritional conditions and technical capacity of our workers."[66] We believe that such erroneous assumptions may be widespread among MNE managers.

Part of Maitland's analysis rests on the assumption that increased labor costs will inevitably result in higher unemployment in competitive markets. Maitland is correct to identify this view as a common belief among many economists, especially as it relates to minimum wage legislation.[67] However, this view has been challenged in recent years. In their recent influential book-length study of the impact of minimum wage increases on employment, David Card and Alan Krueger argue that their reanalysis of the evidence from the Unites States, Canada, the United Kingdom, and Puerto Rico indicates that the existing data does not provide compelling evidence for the textbook view.[68] In addition, Card and Krueger analyzed new data for recent increases in the minimum wage in the U.S. Their analysis is complex, but the results of their analysis are straightforward. "In every case . . .

the estimated effect of the minimum wage was either zero or positive."[69] Increased labor costs appear to have been passed on to consumers in the form of higher prices without increasing unemployment. Again, this data undermines the textbook view regarding the impact of increases in the minimum wage. Economist Richard Freeman summarizes the impact of Card and Krueger's work as follows:

> [T]he Card-Krueger work is essentially correct: the minimum wage at levels observed in the United States has had little or no effect on employment. At the minimum, the book has changed the burden of proof in debates over the minimum, from those who stressed the potential distributional benefits of the minimum to those who stress the potential employment losses.[70]

After evaluating recent work on the impact of minimum wages, economists William Spriggs and John Schmitt reached a more determinate conclusion: "The overwhelming weight of recent evidence supports the view that low-wage workers will benefit overwhelmingly from a higher federal minimum."[71]

Two points concerning wages should be distinguished. First, conclusions concerning the impact of U.S. minimum wage legislation on unemployment cannot automatically be assumed to apply to developing nations. Careful study of the unique conditions of those labor markets is necessary before corollary claims can be assessed. Nonetheless, the textbook view rests significantly on studies concerning the U.S. labor market. As such, we believe that the burden of proof remains with those who maintain that increased labor costs must inevitably result in higher unemployment. Second, we wish to emphasize that we are not taking a position in this essay on increasing federally mandated minimum wages in developing nations. Rather, our contention is that it is economically feasible for MNEs to voluntarily raise wages in factories in developing economies without causing increases in unemployment. MNEs may choose to raise wages while maintaining existing employment levels. Increased labor costs that are not offset by greater productivity may be passed on to consumers, or, if necessary, absorbed through internal cost-cutting measures such as reductions in executive compensation.

VIII. CONCLUSION

As Kant argues, it is by acting in a manner consistent with human dignity that persons raise themselves above all things. Insofar as we recognize the dignity of humanity, we have an obligation to respect both ourselves and others.[72] We have argued that MNE managers who encourage or tolerate violations of the rule of law; use coercion; allow unsafe working conditions; and provide below subsistence wages, disavow their own dignity and that of their workers. In so doing, they disrespect themselves and their workers. Further, we have argued that this moral analysis is not undermined by economic considerations. Significantly, MNEs are in many ways more readily able to honor the humanity of workers. This is because MNEs typically have well defined internal decision structures that, unlike individual moral agents, are not susceptible to weakness of the will.[73] For this reason, MNE managers who recognize a duty to respect their employees, and those of their subcontractors, are well positioned to play a constructive role in ensuring that the dignity of humanity is respected.

NOTES

Earlier versions of this essay were presented to the Annual Meeting of the Society for Business Ethics, Washington D.C., August, 2001; and the American Philosophical Association 100th Anniversary Conference, "Morality in the 21st Century," Newark, Del., October, 2001. We are grateful to audience members for their comments on those occasions. Thanks also to George Brenkert, Heather Douglas, Laura Hartman, John McCall, Sara Arnold, and an anonymous reviewer for helpful comments on earlier drafts of this essay. Special thanks to Ian Maitland and Norris Peterson for detailed written comments; although we continue to disagree with them on some matters, their comments lead to several improvements in this essay.

1. See, for example, Susan Chandler, "Look Who's Sweating Now," *Business Week* October 16, 1995; Steven Greenhouse, "Sweatshop Raids Cast Doubt on an Effort By Garment Makers to Police the Factories," *New York Times,* July 18, 1997; and Gail Edmondson et al., "Workers in Bondage," *Business Week,* November 27. 2000.

2. For the purposes of this paper we define the term as any workplace in which workers are typically subject to two or more of the following conditions: income for a 48 hour work week less than the overall poverty rate for that country (see Table 1 [. . .]); systematic forced overtime; systematic health and safety risks that stem from negligence or the willful disregard of employee welfare; coercion; systematic deception that places workers at risk; and underpayment of earnings.

3. Immanuel Kant, *Foundations of the Metaphysics of Morals,* Lewis White Beck, trans. (New York: Macmillan, 1990), 46.

4. In making this claim we explicitly reject the conclusion reached by Andrew Wicks that one must either "fully embrace Kant's metaphysics" or "break from the abstract universalism of Kant." See Andrew Wicks, "How Kantian A Theory of Capitalism," *Business Ethics Quarterly,* The Ruffin Series: Special Issue 1 (1998): 65.

5. Kant, *Foundations of the Metaphysics of Morals,* 52.

6. Onora O'Neill, *Constructions of Reason* (Cambridge: Cambridge University Press, 1989), 53.

7. Immanuel Kant, *The Metaphysics of Morals,* Mary Gregor, trans., (Cambridge: Cambridge University Press, 1991), 230.

8. Ibid.

9. Ibid., 255.

10. Thomas Hill Jr., *Dignity and Practical Reason in Kant's Moral Theory* (Ithaca: Cornell University Press, 1992).

11. Ibid., 40–41.

12. Kant, *Metaphysics of Morals,* 245.

13. Ibid., 192–193 and 196–197.

14. Norman E. Bowie, *Business Ethics: A Kantian Perspective.* (Malden, Mass.: Blackwell, 1999). See 41–81 for further discussion of the second categorical imperative.

15. Kant, *Metaphysics of Morals,* 255.

16. His latest book is *Development as Freedom* (New York: Anchor Books, 1999). Martha Nussbaum has developed her own version of the capabilities approach, one that pays particular attention to the unique circumstances of women's lives. *Women and Human Development: The Capabilities Approach* (Cambridge: Cambridge University Press, 2000).

17. United Nations Development Programme, *Human Development Report 2000* (New York: Oxford University Press, 2000).

18. See, for example, Vinod Thomas et al., *The Quality of Growth* (Washington D.C.: The World Bank, 2000); Deepa Narayan et al., *Voices of the Poor: Crying Out for Change* (Washington D.C.: The World Bank, 2000); and Deepa Narayan et al., *Voices of the Poor: Can Anyone Hear Us?* (Washington D.C.: The World Bank, 2000).

19. Thomas et al., *The Quality of Growth,* xiv.

20. Ibid., xvii–xviii (italics added by authors).

21. Pamela Varley, ed., *The Sweatshop Quandary: Corporate Responsibility on the Global Frontier* (Washington D.C., Investor Responsibility Research Center, 1998), 185–186.

22. Ibid., 85.

23. Michael A. Santoro, *"Profits and Principles: Global Capitalism and Human Rights in China* (Ithaca: Cornell University Press, 2000), 161.

24. For a fuller discussion of this matter see Bowie, *Business Ethics: A Kantian Perspective,* esp. chap. 2.

25. Varley, ed., *The Sweatshop Quandary,* 95.

26. Better rule of law is associated with higher per capita income. See *World Development Report 2000/2001: Attacking Poverty,* (New York: Oxford University Press, 2000), 103.

27. Ibid., 102. See also the United National Development Programme's *Human Development Report 2000* (New York: Oxford University Press, 2000), esp. 37–38.

28. Human Rights Watch, "A Job or Your Rights: Continued Sex Discrimination in Mexico's Maquiladora Sector," volume 10, no. 1(B) December 1998. Available at http://www.hrw.org/reports981/women2/.

29. Varley, ed., *The Sweatshop Quandary,* 131.

30. Republic of El Salvador, Ministry of Labor, Monitoring and Labor Relations Analysis Unit, "Monitoring Report on Maquilas and Bonded Areas," (July 2000). Available at http://www.nlcnet.org/elsalvador/0401/translation.htm.

31. Edward J. Williams, "The Maquiladora Industry and Environmental Degradation in the United States-Mexican Borderlands," paper presented at the annual meeting of the Latin American Studies Association, Washington, D.C., September, 1995. Available at http://www.natlaw.com/pubs/williams.htm. See also, Joan Salvat, Stef Soetewey, and Peter Breuls, *Free Trade Slaves,* 58 min., (Princeton, N.J.: Films for the Humanities and Sciences, 1999), videocassette.

32. National Labor Committee, "The U.S. in Haiti: How To Get Rich on 11 Cents an Hour," 1995. Available at http://www.nlcnet.org/Haiti/0196/index.htm.

33. Denis G. Arnold, "Coercion and Moral Responsibility," *American Philosophical Quarterly* 38 (2001): 53–67. The view of psychological coercion employed here is a slightly revised version of the view defended in that essay. In particular, the condition that cases of psychological coercion always involve psychological compulsion has been replaced with the condition that cases of psychological coercion always involve the victim's compliance with the threat.

34. Varley, ed., *The Sweatshop Quandary,* 72.

35. Barry Bearak, "Lives Held Cheap In Bangladesh Sweatshops," *New York Times,* April 15, 2001.

36. Republic of El Salvador, Ministry of Labor, Monitoring and Labor Relations Analysis Unit, "Monitoring Report on Maquilas and Bonded Areas."

37. Varley, ed., *The Sweatshop Quandary,* 68.

38. Salvat et al., *Free Trade Slaves,* 58 min. (Princeton, N.J.: Films for the Humanities and Sciences, 1999), videocassette.

39. Ibid.

40. Varley, ed., *The Sweatshop Quandary,* 67.

41. Bearak, "Lives Held Cheap in Bangladesh Sweatshops."

42. "Ernst & Young Environmental and Labor Practice Audit of the Tae Kwang Vina Industrial Ltd. Co., Vietnam." Available at http://www.corpwatch.org/trac/nike/ernst/audit.html.

43. United States Environmental Protection Agency, Office of Air Quality, Planning, and Standards, "Toluene." Available at http://www.epa.gov/ttnuatw1/hlthef/toIuene.html.

44. See, for example, Varley, ed., *The Sweatshop Quandary,* esp. 59–398.

45. Campaign for Labor Rights, "The Story of a Maquiladora Worker: Interview with Omar Gil by David Bacon," September 6, 2000. Available at www.summersault.com/~agj/clr/alerts/thestoryofamaquiladoraeworker.html.

46. International Labour Organization, "SafeWork: ILO Standards on Safety and Health." Available at http://www.ilo.org/public/english/protection/safework/standard.htm.

47. After the complaint was raised in a shareholder meeting Alcoa raised the wages of the workers by 25%. Pamela Varley, ed., *Sweatshop Quandary,* 63.

48. Aaron Bernstein, "Sweatshop Reform: How to Solve the Standoff," *Business Week,* May 3, 1999.

49. *Poverty Report 2000: Overcoming Human Poverty* (New York: United Nations Development Programme, 2000).

50. Self-esteem is grounded in the conscious recognition of one's dignity as a rational being.

51. Nike, "An Open Letter Response to USAS Regarding Their National Protest of Nike Through August 16, 2000." Available at http://nikebiz.com/labor/usas_let.shtml.

52. Ibid.

53. Frank Denton, "Close Look at Factory for Nikes," *Wisconsin State Journal,* July 30, 2000.

54. Ian Maitland, "The Great Non-Debate Over International Sweatshops," reprinted in Tom L. Beauchamp and Norman E. Bowie, *Ethical Theory and Business,* 6th ed. (Englewood Cliffs: Prentice Hall, 2001), 595. First published in *British Academy of Management Conference Proceedings,* September 1997, 240–265.

55. Ibid.

56. Ibid., 603.

57. Ibid., 594.

58. Such an argument would likely maintain that corporate managers fail to recognize that a public relations strategy that includes higher wages and improved workplace standards is more costly than an alternative strategy that does

not. The details of such a strategy would then need to be worked out.

59. Maitland, "The Great Non-Debate Over International Sweatshops," 602.

60. Ibid., 539.

61. Motorola, "Code of Business Conduct." Available at http://www.motorola.com/code/code.html.

62. Santoro, *Profits and Principles,* 6.

63. S. Prakash Sethi, "Codes of Conduct for Multinational Corporations: An Idea Whose Time Has Come," *Business and Society Review* 104 (1999): 225–241.

64. Gerald Starr, *Minimum Wage Fixing* (Geneva: International Labour Organization, 1981), 157.

65. C. J. Bliss and N. H. Stern, "Productivity, Wages, and Nutrition, 2: Some Observations." *Journal of Development Economics* 5 (1978): 363–398. For theoretical discussion see C. J. Bliss and N. H. Stern, "Productivity, Wages, and Nutrition, 1: The Theory," *Journal of Development Economics* 5 (1978): 331–362.

66. Republic of El Salvador, Ministry of Labor, Monitoring and Labor Relations Analysis Unit, "Monitoring Report on Maquilas and Bonded Areas." Available at http://www.nlcnet.org/elsalvador/0401/translation.htm.

67. See, for example, the essays collected in *The Economics of Legal Minimum Wages,* Simon Rottenberg, ed. (Washington D.C.: The American Enterprise Institute, 1981).

68. See David Card and Alan B. Krueger, *Myth and Measurement: The New Economics of the Minimum Wage*

(Princeton: Princeton University Press, 1995). See also the special symposium on *Myth and Measurement in Industrial & Labor Relations Review* (July 1995) with contributions by Charles Brown, Richard Freeman, Daniel Hamermesh, Paul Osterman, and Finis Welch; David Neumark and William Wascher, "Minimum Wages and Employment: A Case Study of the Fast-Food Industry in New Jersey and Pennsylvania: Comment," *The American Economic Review* (December 2000): 1362–1396; and David Card and Alan B. Krueger, "Minimum Wages and Employment: A Case Study of the Fast-Food Industry in New Jersey and Pennsylvania: Reply," *The American Economic Review* (December 2000): 1397–1420. For a discussion of the living wage issue in the context of the U.S. economy see Robert Pollin and Stephanie Luce, *The Living Wage: Building a Fair Economy* (New York: The New Press, 1998).

69. Card and Krueger, *Myth and Measurement,* 389.

70. Richard B. Freeman, "In Honor of David Card: Winner of the John Bates Clark Medal," *Journal of Economic Perspectives* (Spring 1997): 173.

71. William Spriggs and John Schmitt, "The Minimum Wage: Blocking the Low-Wage Path," in *Reclaiming Prosperity: A Blueprint for Progressive Economic Reform,* Todd Schafer and Jeff Faux (Armonk, N.Y.: ME Sharpe, 1996), 170.

72. Kant *Foundations of the Metaphysics of Morals,* 255.

73. For a fuller defense of this position see Peter A. French, *Corporate Ethics* (Fort Worth, Tex.: Hartcourt Brace, 1995), 79–87.

READING 12.4 MARKETING, THE ETHICS OF CONSUMPTION, AND LESS-DEVELOPED COUNTRIES

George G. Brenkert

INTRODUCTION

Several centuries ago large numbers of western Europeans fanned out into the "new world" to serve as missionaries on behalf of the true way of life. They were to use subtle, as well as vicious, means to persuade, cajole, and coerce those they encountered to adopt the "true religion." To them, it was clear what their responsibilities were, viz., to convert the heathen to enlightened views and thereby to win salvation for them. They were little with the culture of these heathens, except insofar as it impeded their own efforts to bring them a superior culture.[1]

Centuries later large numbers of western Europeans and North Americans have also fanned out as modern missionaries, of a sort, on behalf of a

From George G. Brenkert, "Marketing, The Ethics of Consumption, and Less-Developed Countries," in *The Business of Consumption,* Laura Westra and Patricia Werhane, eds. (Lanham, MD: Rowman & Littlefield, 1998). Copyright 1998 by George Brenkert. Reprinted by permission of the author.

very different way of life. They too have sought to persuade, cajole, and even coerce people and societies in the less developed world to adopt their views on commerce and marketing, on economic development and the consumer society. Some of them, at least, also claim a sense of responsibility for bringing to the less developed world skills, techniques, and capital by which they might improve their lives and develop their societies.

However, the moral responsibilities of these modern missionaries are much less clear than at least some marketers think. In general, the moral responsibilities of marketers (and business) are discussed within the contexts of such issues as bribery, corruption, gift-giving, entertainment, market freedom, and international human rights. Only infrequently are the responsibilities of marketers to the cultures of the societies in which they operate noted. There are exceptions. For example, Laczniak and Murphy claim that "these influences [of international marketers] on local cultures, institutions, religions, and ways of life must . . . be carefully assessed."[2] And DeGeorge affirms as one of his ten moral guidelines that "to the extent that local culture does not violate ethical norms, multinationals should respect the local culture and work with and not against it."[3] However, though these authors recognize that marketers should be concerned about their effects on other cultures and that they respect those cultures, these claims, and their implications for the moral responsibilities of marketers remain largely unexplored.

This chapter ventures into this territory by exploring the responsibilities of marketers toward the peoples and cultures of less developed countries (LDCs) as they engage in activities that promote forms of economic development within those societies that alter their culture(s). In particular, I examine this issue with regard to the efforts of marketers to foster consumer societies in LDCs and thereby to promote a higher level and extent of consumption. The implications of my argument are not limited, it will be obvious, to the responsibilities of marketers to less-developed countries. Instead, they extend to the wider issues of the transfer of the marketing practices of one society to another society when the use of such practices is to promote consumer societies in the mode of their own society and culture.

MARKETING, CONSUMER SOCIETIES, AND THE ETHICS OF CONSUMPTION

To examine the moral responsibilities of marketers toward LDCs when their activities foster a consumer culture in those societies, I must first say something about the concepts of a consumer society and of contemporary western marketing.[4] By marketing I refer most frequently to advertising and other promotional components of marketing. However, other components of marketing such as product development, marketing research, and forms of distribution are also relevant to this discussion.[5] The concepts and techniques of these aspects of marketing variously involve a number of values and metaphysical assumptions that not all societies or cultures presently hold.[6] In short, promotion is not a neutral activity but comes value-laden and metaphysically charged.

Among the values that marketing assumes are the affirmative role of consumption rather than abstention in life; the link of consumption with happiness, acceptance, and status; the importance of individual freedom as the lack of restraint; and the needlessness of denial and the acceptability of "instant" gratification. Other values include self-interested behavior on behalf of individual wants and needs, the acquisitive nature of humans, the importance of promoting one's products to consumers, and the inappropriateness of blatant deception, fraud, or physical coercion in marketing relations. Finally, marketers are out to promote change. Growth is essential to their approach.[7] Accordingly, whether it is Calvin Klein ads using provocatively posed teenagers, Virginia Slims appeals to young women, or MasterCard efforts to encourage buying on credit, marketers have pressed upon social conventions and boundaries, customs, and traditions to expand the audience of those who might buy their products.

More metaphysically, marketing has tended to encourage the identification of people with what they possess. Marketers (and the consumer society they promote) view people as consumers. Thorelli, for example, comments that "all human beings are consumers."[8] Of course, in one sense this is correct. All humans do consume; they eat, drink, use clothing, and so forth. However, to be a consumer is different from being a person who consumes. To be a consumer is to be a person for whom one's identification is (more or less) closely bound up with what one owns or consumes within a certain set of values and assumptions (noted below). Some marketers put this very strongly. They argue that a person's sense of self comes from what that person possesses. Belk, for example, maintains that "we are what we have and . . . this may be the most basic and powerful fact of consumer behavior."[9] However, this is hardly a view that many cultures have countenanced. Indeed, in some societies, it is only through the renunciation of one's material possessions that one can become what one truly is. For example, Hinduism has traditionally distinguished four life stages (student, householder, anchorite, and *samnyasin*) that lead from one's youthful instruction by a guru to one's final attempt to seek spiritual liberation and release from worldly limitations. The standard representation of this final stage of human life is that of a person who turns into a "homeless beggar-mendicant, with no fixed place to lay one's head, no regular road, no goal, no belongings."[10] Only in this manner can one attain self-knowledge.

Consequently, comments such as those of Thorelli and Belk expose marketing's very modern, Western (if not American) concept of what it is to be a human, one in which one's identity or sense of oneself is bound up with one's consumption and possessions. They also reveal how action in accord with marketing's values and assumptions is, in effect, action that aims (wittingly or unwittingly) at creating a consumer society.

Finally, the preceding view of the self underlies not simply marketers' view of individuals but, according to Moravcsik, has also worked its way into some Western moral theories. Such theories might be taken to constitute the underlying "moral theory" of much of Western marketing. On such a view,

> life is just a stretch of time, to be filled with certain things and to be kept clean of others (the valuable and the immoral respectively). This view is in harmony with the consumer conception of the self (e.g., as a satisfaction-seeking mechanism) that reaches its climax with the development of industrial societies. The candidates for the "fillings" are the sorts of things that one can HAVE, POSSESS, or CONSUME

(pleasure, satisfaction, happiness, goods, etc.) rather than BE.[11]

Drawing upon the preceding brief discussion, we may characterize a consumer society in terms of what might be called its "ethics of consumption."[12]

a. Products are for individual satisfaction. They are to be acquired, exchanged, and disposed of to the extent they meet this criterion. More satisfaction is better than less satisfaction; present or "immediate" satisfaction is superior to delayed or future satisfaction.

b. There is a positive connection between consumerism and self-esteem.[13] Indeed, a person's identity tends to be bound up with the products he or she owns and uses. Thus, the consumption of goods and services is at least in part identified with human happiness and welfare.

c. Individuals have a right to choose freely among all the various products produced. Accordingly, the free market plays a central role in the ethics of consumption. This implies restricted government intervention.

d. Material success is emphasized as a dominant goal in a consumer society.[14]

e. Products are acquired by the exchange of money. Their price captures their interchangeability. Consumers need have little knowledge of how or where the objects they consume are produced.

f. The world is a collection of resources whose primary value lies in their use for consumption purposes according to the preceding precepts.

The connection between this ethics of consumption and modern, Western marketing should be clear.[15] Accordingly, the implications of applying Western marketing practices in LDCs are of considerable importance since they introduce not simply the resulting products, skills, knowledge and techniques, but also the preceding values, norms, and assumptions. They are the "hidden" dimensions of what LDCs accept. Thus, marketing in LDCs tends to portray an image of "the good life" as bound up with the consumption of products. This is not inconsequential since, as William Leach has commented," [w]hoever has the power to project a vision of the good life and make it prevail has the most decisive power of all."[16] Accordingly, assuming that marketers have, or seek to have, some influence in LDCs through the introduction of their marketing practices, an influence that may modify those societies and their cultures, what moral responsibilities do marketers have for the changes they might effect?[17]

THE CONTRADICTORY POSITIONS OF BUSINESS ETHICISTS

If we turn to contemporary philosophical business ethicists, very little, rather disappointingly, is said about the morality of economic development, their implications for the creation of consumer societies within LDCs, or, indeed, about the role of consumption in the good life.[18] Marketers are told to respect local cultures, at least insofar as they do not violate human rights.[19] What is meant by "respect of the culture" is left largely unexplored or unexamined. Indeed, there seems little awareness that marketers might be challenging the local culture through their very activities. Thus, though DeGeorge urges marketers to respect local cultures, he also maintains that Western business people do not have to give up their way of doing things.[20]

Philosophical business ethicists tend to be ethical universalists, though of a restricted sort.[21] They are prepared to apply various basic moral values, principles, or rights to all people. But they are also willing to leave some "moral space" for cultural variances that do not affect such basic norms. Thus, they have proposed two-dimensional analyses of the ethics of international business. One level is that of universal norms, rights, and values. The second level is the local moral space within which individual cultures might adopt moral measures for their own societies, which other societies might reject, for example, nepotism (the hiring of one's family members or friends into jobs, rather than impersonally and objectively considering only the person's job-related characteristics).[22]

We need, however, a three-dimensional analysis of international business ethics. This third dimension takes into account the effect of Western marketing and business activities on the culture of the society in which they take place. It focuses on how the activities of Western marketers might actually be challenging that moral space in more subtle ways than has caught the attention of philosophical business ethicists. This cultural setting plays an extremely important role in people's lives and is the context within which moral values and norms operate. To change this situation invariably ends up changing the local moral values and norms by which people live. Accordingly, philosophical business ethicists may be said to advocate contradictory policies. They urge that marketers should respect the local culture(s) of LDCs, but they also (unwittingly) permit them to engage in measures that undercut those cultures.

Philosophical business ethicists, however, are not the only ones who take contradictory positions. Though marketers have examined the effects of marketing on economic development, their concern has been primarily one of describing changes that are going on and advocating the use of marketing techniques to foster such economic development. When marketing business ethicists, in contrast to philosophical business ethicists, consider the effects of marketers on LDCs, they tend to be ethical relativists.[23] They advocate that marketers should behave in other countries as the people in those countries behave. But, once again, the very activities in which Western marketers engage are not neutral, value-free activities. Instead, they bring with them a train of assumptions and values that may undermine the values and assumptions of the cultures in which they carry on their activities. For example, they urge individual concern for one's needs and goals, but this may undercut the joint family system of other countries such as India in which "the needs and well-being of the individual is a responsibility of the system."[24] Likewise, Western organizational forms tend to be contractual, individualistic, and lacking the commitment between members and the system that has characterized organizations in LDCs. Furthermore, these Western organizational forms require personal characteristics of autonomy, self-assertion, and goal-centeredness, which contrast, for example, with "the psycho-cultural realities of Indian managers," which is to be "committed to systems and people rather than goals and tasks, [to] constructively channelise [their] dependence rather than be autonomous, and cope functionally with [their] ambivalence rather than polarize it."[25] Malhotra claims that the upshot of Indian managers working within such Western-style organizations has been an erosion of trust and alienation.[26] In short, the assumptions and values of Western marketing activities may conflict with various cultural and ethical values of LDCs apart from any of the standard questions of bribery, corruption, gifts, intellectual property and so on. Finally, other marketing activities bring with them a view of the good life and moral assumptions about the attainment of that good life that may be incompatible with various elements of the cultures of LDCs, for example, that looking to personal gain or satisfaction is acceptable, rather than the search for fulfillment without attachment to worldly goods that India's *Bhagavad Gita* urges.[27] Chakraborty, director of the Management Center for Human Values in Calcutta, claims that this latter view of human action is part of the Indian ethos. He refers to it as "a theory of work *(nishkam karma)* which requires work without concentration on reward."[28]

Thus, though marketing business ethicists hold that marketers should behave in other countries as do the people in those countries, the very marketing activities they advocate are often at odds with the cultural bases of the people in those countries. Accordingly, they too (at least unwittingly) take contradictory positions.

Part of the problem here is that marketing business ethicists tend to assume that they may distinguish two realms: the economic and the moral. Thus, they maintain, as noted above, that marketers ought to act in accord with the morals of the society in which they are active. Accordingly, marketers should be allowed to engage in gift giving, minor bribery, and the like as the local culture's morality prescribes. However, when it comes to economics, marketing business ethicists have thought that marketers can proceed apace because these activities do not raise moral issues. But this is an undefended and I suggest, an unwarranted separation. Moral values inhabit both realms.[29]

How, then, are we to get to the bottom of these problems and identify what (if any) moral responsibilities marketers have to the culture(s) of LDCs?

CRITICISMS OF MARKETING IN LDCS

Four points of clarification regarding the criticism of marketing efforts to promote economic development and consumer societies in LDCs will be helpful at the outset. First, it is clear that marketers have often provided positive benefits to LDCs: they have brought higher standards of quality for products

produced, reduced infant mortality rates, improved yields of crops, distributed those yields more efficiently, and so on. These beneficial results should not be denied. It is also obvious that, in general, people in LDCs both need and want greater goods and services than they presently have.[30] There is little to be said for a primitivist approach to LDCs that would defend realizing in such societies some past, idealized condition of "natural" humanity. We must also be wary of paternalistic efforts that have the effect of not sharing important material goods, services, and resources with people in LDCs because it would be "better" for them. In raising the question of the responsibilities of marketers to less-developed countries and their cultures, my point is not to deny the importance of increased consumption, and economic development for such countries, but to speak of the nature of that increased consumption, and thereby its relation to the cultures of LDCs.[31] Instead, my concern is with the *form* that development takes, and, in particular, the implications that arise for the culture(s) of LDCs when that development takes the form of a consumer culture.[32] In particular, my concern is that marketing to LDCs transforms their cultures, and that this transformation, when it takes the form of a Western-style consumer society, is morally questionable. It is here that I believe marketers must look more closely at their responsibilities.

Second, the objection against such marketing activities cannot simply be that they cause change or alteration in the unique cultures of LDCs. Cultures are dynamic features of a society. Some changes are desirable; others are not. In either case, change is inevitable. Marketers do not necessarily show disrespect for such cultures by participating in the changes they undergo. Further, marketers need not hold that all aspects of a culture are beyond moral criticism or may not be legitimate candidates for the changes they might bring. Though I cannot defend the view here, marketers may hold that there are certain international basic moral norms according to which cultures may be found morally lacking. For example, Donaldson has argued that such basic international moral norms include the rights to physical security, fair trial, subsistence, and minimal education.[33] Rather than delineating these norms, I focus on the situation of LDCs whose cultures accord with international basic moral norms, but which differ from Western consumer cultures.[34]

Third, I assume that the culture of a society is something that may be worthy of respect, for its own intrinsic value. The culture of each society represents the efforts of humans to create themselves as humans. As such, culture is the form in which the members of a society have given meaning and definition to their lives. Through one's culture one is provided with a sense of place, identity, connectedness, and tradition.[35] The disappearance or alteration, then, of a culture due to external forces is potentially an important loss for humanity. Whether or not it is a loss will depend upon the nature of the changes and how they are brought about. Further, it is through culture that the achievement of the self-creation of humans is transmitted to succeeding generations.[36] Thus, cultures also have instrumental value. Accordingly, the role that marketers play in cultural changes should be a matter of concern to everyone. And respect of the cultures of LDCs should be a matter of concern for marketers.

Finally, I assume that such respect includes (at least) the following four conditions:
(a) *Understanding.* Marketers understand the cultures with which they are dealing and which their activities may affect. One cannot respect someone or a culture if one is unaware of the basic values and assumptions of that person or culture.
(b) *Nondisruption.* Respect also requires that marketers do not undertake actions that would block or hinder culturally significant values or goals, as determined by that society. They do not seek to degrade or undercut these values and goals. (c) *Consideration.* Marketers give moral weight to the values of the culture in their own decisions. That is, the cultural values of an LDC are affirmatively included in marketing decisions. Conversely, marketers do not engage in actions that lead to modification of these values toward impossible or highly unrealistic ends without the culturally relevant determination of the culture's own members. (d) *Moral bounds.* Finally, for such respect to be compatible with morality it must occur within certain broad moral limits. Thus, for example, one does not show moral respect for a person or culture when one accedes to actions that violate basic international moral norms.

Our question, then, should focus on those marketing activities that may impinge upon and undercut the values of distinct cultures, for these affect the self-understanding and definition of people in the other society in ways that fail to show them respect. There are a number of objections that have been raised to the role that marketers have hitherto played.

At the outset, we may consider the criticism that marketing has brought about a homogenization of people and cultures. Marketing to LDCs is said to reduce their cultures and people to variations on a very few themes determined by profit-seeking corporations. The products and services they consume are transformed into nondistinct, abstracted goods. With this comes the homogenization of values across cultures. What defines a particular culture as unique is modified, molded, or made compatible with other cultures in a way that reduces them to a common denominator. Leach comments that "businesspeople and advertisers boast of their ability, through telecommunications, to 'homogenize' tastes throughout the world and to encourage everybody to desire the same goods and services."[37] And Korten charges that "[p]resent-day corporations have no reservations about reshaping the values of whole societies to create a homogenized culture of indulgence conducive to spurring consumption expenditures and advancing corporate political interests."[38]

The problem with such objections is that, through the generalized form they take, they fail to distinguish between different forms of homogenization, as well as blur a distinction between the moral and the aesthetic.[39] Surely not all homogenization between societies is undesirable. It depends upon the forms it takes. Thousands of years ago, common signals and ways of measuring weight between the traders of different societies was desirable, since it could prevent misunderstanding and violent conflict. More recently, it is plausible to think that common standards for steel girders, pipes, air traffic controls, and various commodities and services may be very desirable and leave the cultures of societies relatively untouched. Further, the prior differentiation of products such as radios, steel girders, and automobiles may not necessarily have meant those distinct products were of higher quality.

Instead, only that homogenization is morally undesirable that undercuts the cultural identification of LDCs, insofar as they accord with basic international moral norms. In short, the most interesting objection relates to the impact of marketing activities on the moral identity of cultures, rather than simply the homogenization (or differentiation) of products. It is here that a moral objection might be raised. There may also be other forms of homogenization (say, of products) that offend the aesthetic tastes of people and to which they object. These too should be considered by marketers. However, they raise a different question than the one presently under consideration.

One of the principal ways in which marketers may homogenize the cultural identity of LDCs is through fostering within them a consumer society, that is, a society in which an ethics of consumption prevails. When these cultures are altered such that people come to see themselves as consumers whose wants and needs require Western-style products and levels of consumption, the value of their own culture wanes. Thus, the real problem arises when marketers engage in marketing that fosters a consumer society, that is, forms and levels of consumption notsustainable (or even attainable) within those societies and not valued by their indigenous culture. For example, Western marketers have sought to alter the frugality of Indian customers by encouraging them to throw away used goods. They have met resistance in this.[40] Should they transform this aspect of Indian culture, given the scarcity of resources, their culture will be altered in ways that bring negative consequences of various sorts both for individuals and for society.

More generally, the relevant criticism is against that form of marketing that emphasizes the primary values of a consumer society, values that include efficiency, growth, and profit, to the exclusion of concern for those values and assumptions that uniquely define each society. This form of marketing ends up creating products and forms of consumption that import lifestyles to LDCs that level down morally important differences between societies and cultures. If one is concerned primarily about quantity of goods, low price, and economic efficiency, then one should be satisfied with these events. However, we should also be concerned that something important is being stripped away from society and its members. In effect, this approach to marketing does not take seriously the people or the cultures it modifies. Instead, it treats the cultures of such societies and individuals simply as means or vehicles, which may be used, or must be overcome, to promote the economic ends of marketers.

This criticism is similar to one that Rawls and others have made of utilitarianism. The criticism is that utilitarianism cares only about the maximization of utilities, while whose utilities are maximized is a matter of indifference. This, it has been said, denies, or at least neglects, the differences that make us who we are. Thus, Rawls and others have said that utilitarianism fails to take people seriously. Whether this criticism can be sustained against all forms of utilitarianism is not at issue here. What is at issue is that when marketers focus on the creation of more efficient channels of distribution, quantities of consumer goods, and so on (all of which are important) but neglect the effects of their activities in creating a consumer society and consequently the effect on the local culture, they become susceptible to the criticism that some have brought against utilitarianism.

A second important criticism of marketers when they foster a consumer society in LDCs is that they are promoting a form of society and a set of aspirations that people in LDCs will not be able to fulfill. "It is certain," G. A. Cohen has noted, "that we cannot achieve Western-style goods and services for humanity as a whole, nor even sustain them for as large a minority as has enjoyed them, by drawing on the fuels and materials that we have hitherto used to provide them."[41] If this is correct, then besides their products, services, values, and metaphysical assumptions, marketers are also fostering a set of frustrations. Such global marketing is "spreading global dreams of the good life based on spending and consuming, a window but not a door for the vast majority of people who lack money or credit to buy much of anything."[42] It is giving poor people dreams which cannot be fulfilled. It can create social tensions."[43]

The objection to this marketing implication stems from the respect owed the culture of other people and societies. Such respect would entail promoting forms of economic development within it that are attainable, as well as sustainable. The arguments concerning both notions are, of course, long and controversial. But if one seeks to promote a way of life or activity that the agent or society cannot achieve or live up to—and (perhaps) should not seek to live up to—then questions may justifiably be raised about the respect that one shows for that agent or society. Accordingly, reports that marketers view the frugality of the people in India as an important cultural hurdle to be overcome should be both striking and disturbing.[44] Whether it be razors, cigarette lighters, or old saris used as sanitary napkins, Jordan relates that Indians reuse, refill, and recycle. In a time when many are urging that greater measures be taken to promote sustainable business practices in all part of the world, marketing in India seeks to modify, or overturn, this facet of Indian culture. The preceding objection suggests that marketing that was properly attuned to the cultural values of Indians would seek to work with this cultural trait, rather than undermine it.

Third, some make even stronger charges against the impact of marketing on LDCs. Petras condemns the export of "cultural forms most conducive to depoliticizing and trivializing everyday existence. The images of individual mobility, the 'self-made persons', the emphasis on 'self-centered existence' (mass produced and distributed by the US mass media industry) now have become major instruments in dominating the third world."[45] Galbraith made a similar criticism regarding the influence of marketing on public and private values in developed nations years ago.[46] It is not surprising that this charge is now brought against Western marketing in the LDCs. Thus, the effort to expand personal consumption and greater economic productivity is an effort whose success has long been questioned in Western countries.[47] The point here is not to affirm or deny these contentions themselves, but to indicate that they too suggest that marketers have moral responsibilities to ascertain what the effects of their activities are on those distinctions crucial to social and cultural life. Since their activities may contribute to these effects, marketers cannot simply market their products without taking such considerations into account. Particularly crucial here is the focus of marketers on consumption activities, rather than on the importance of other values, such as work and the meaning of work in life. In contrast, "all religious traditions place primacy of importance on work over consumption. It is only the liberal tradition of the West that has reversed the ordering and given pride of place to consumption over work."[48]

Similarly, John Lachs speaks of a "Consumer's Fallacy," which is "the claim that we do not even begin to *live* until we have the right or approved kind of food bought in a good store, fashionable clothing, and a cave as good as our neighbor's. . . . We *live* when we have as many of these and other goods as our fortune will allow or our stratagems create."[49] At the basis of this fallacy "is the supposition that a man is what he has: that happiness is a

function of the goods we possess and the things we consume."[50] This supposition is, he insists, a fallacy as manifested by the unhappiness and dissatisfaction of the many who pursue it. Instead, he argues, "the cure for human dissatisfaction is not by concentrating on increasing our possessions, nor again by concentrating on combating the natural urge to have, but by relegating possession and consumption to their rightful and limited place in a comprehensive scheme of human values."[51] To the extent, then, that marketers promote consumer societies and "the Consumer's Fallacy" in LDCs they undercut important traditional cultural sources of meaningfulness, while offering forms of meaning in consumption that have proven to be of questionable value in the Western countries.

If the preceding objections are acceptable, it follows that marketers do indeed have moral responsibilities to market products to LDCs in a manner that is not only appropriate to their cultural, economic, and social situation, but which also meet other demands on behalf of the integrity of their culture(s). Accordingly, greater attention needs to be given to this responsibility than it has previously received.

IMPLICATIONS FOR MARKETERS

A number of implications appear to follow from the preceding. To begin with, many marketers have, quite understandably, attacked the inefficient distribution systems in LDCs. Kotler complains that such distribution is fragmented and inefficient, resulting in higher final prices to consumers.[52] Similarly, Zikmund and d'Amico note complaints that have been raised about the inefficiency in the channels of distribution even in non-Western, though developed, nations such as Japan. One of the reasons for this inefficiency, they note, is "tradition-bound commitments and long-standing relationships among distributors."[53] However, given the preceding considerations, marketers ought not simply look to criteria of efficiency. Longer channels of distribution may include other values that are important for the particular culture. For example, longer distribution channels may preserve other values such as customers being known by the businesses with which they deal. In addition to maintaining personal relationships, individuals may, in this way, gain better information about the products and services they purchase. Further, if we do not assume that traditions or customs have either no worth in themselves or have only negative value, then the fact that "tradition-bound commitments" give rise to inefficiencies does not imply that those commitments ought to be simply overturned to promote greater efficiency. On the other hand, shorter channels of distribution are not value-neutral either. They tend to require larger stores, which have other implications, for example, their customers must have means of transportation (often individual cars) and the stores require large parking lots, both of which can have negative environmental impacts. In short, respect for another culture entails recognizing that forms of production and distribution that marketers consider to be inefficient or to have less value than other forms of operation may fulfill important cultural values, goals, and assumptions. Changes in these practices must be considered within this cultural context.

Second, respect for the cultures of LDCs would mean not insisting on entry to their markets, or threatening to impose sanctions (or advocating that their government do so) if that society did not agree to permit such entry for reasons that pertained to protection of their own cultural values. Respect would also involve not standing in the way of those societies attempting to adopt measures that protect their culture, even if this had negative consequences for one's own marketing programs. Obviously this does not imply that one could not inform the government or its leaders that there were these negative impacts. But such information is one thing; threats and sanctions are another. The former is compatible with respect, the latter is not.

Suppose, however, that an LDC demanded access to the markets of the developed nation but did not permit return access. Suppose even further that access of the LDC's merchants did not negatively affect the developed country's culture, but the activities of marketers of the developed country might harm the culture of the LDC. Now, if a society's culture is something of intrinsic value and deserves protection and respect, then demands that a society open itself up to the marketing activities of developed nations cannot be viewed simply on the basis of higher levels of products, economic growth, and freedom as the lack of constraint. There is another variable that needs to be mixed into the equation and given weight in any final determinations. This cultural variable has a rightful place in the

ethical balance. It may also justifiedly require that marketing in a society may only be conducted in ways or forms that protect its local culture. On the other hand, if an LDC seeks to take part in a world economy then it also has responsibilities of seeking forms of economic interchange that not only protect its own culture but are also fair to all participants. The global market is not a one-way street.

Third, marketers require an account of the compatibility (or incompatibility) of their activities with the culture of the societies in which they are active. This involves identifying the essentials of that culture and attempting to anticipate the consequences their activities will have on them. In a discussion of marketing in India, Jordan has noted that "traditional family bonds inhibit Western marketers' access: Yuppies, deferring to their elders, don't make household-purchasing decisions."[54] The preceding discussion implies, at the least, that attempts to change purchasing decisions in India in ways that circumvent and destroy these traditional family bonds are matters for moral consideration by marketers. They are not matters of indifference to be determined simply on the basis of the efficiency or quantity of goods sold. The reasons may be both intrinsic (due to the inherent value of such relations) and extrinsic (due to the effects that their elimination might cause). For example, Chakraborty worries about the disintegrating effects of marketing on the Indian family and local communities. He observes that such effects

> will be especially detrimental in countries like India where the local community has often served as an informal social-welfare system. In the vacuum created by the disappearance of this system, due to the disintegration of the local community, people will inevitably turn to the state for the help they require. The demands which this will put on the state will in all likelihood be insupportable and will promote further political fractionalization and social turmoil.[55]

Thus, concern for the cultural implications of marketing activities may help to head off various problems that are otherwise avoidable. The cultures of LDCs are constituted by a web of values, norms, interrelationships, and patterns of dependencies that the introduction of marketing practices may disrupt without providing adequate replacements. Another example is that as a result of the imposition of the exchange centered marketing concept in LDCs . . . systems of need satisfaction which historically emerged in these societies, for example, reciprocity systems in the Urubamba Valley in Peru, and redistribution/shared labor systems in Anatolia, disappear from the scene. If recognized at all, they are treated as impediments for the development of market exchange systems, as primitive practices to be broken, rather than as alternative need satisfaction systems. Growth of market exchange, not satisfaction of human/social needs, becomes the foremost objective for scholars and policy makers who employ these approaches.[56]

It might be objected that this is just a failure of marketing's own precept, the marketing concept, which urges marketers to determine the needs and wants of the people and satisfy them. In this case, it might be said, marketers have not followed their own directives. However, though the marketing concept speaks of satisfying people's wants and needs, it advises such efforts because of their positive effect on profits. But this approach to people's wants and needs subordinates them to profit-making considerations. Consequently, marketers in LDCs have often allowed the determinations of profit to dominate other considerations regarding the local culture and the effects of their actions on that culture. Thus, marketing in these contexts has led to results such as those just noted. Accordingly, the introduction of modern marketing techniques and the creation, thereby, of a consumer culture has transformed some relations within LDCs with little consideration for collateral and background implications for people outside the market exchange system. Recognition of marketers' responsibility for the cultural effects of their actions would help avoid such consequences.

Fourth, how are marketers to know which aspects of a culture it might be acceptable to change and which not? There are two aspects of this question. Some of the preceding objections suggest that there are certain forms of marketing that are questionable in themselves because of their nature and implications. Thus, to instill an ethics of consumption that cannot be fulfilled in the same manner as presently in Western countries raises questions of justice and respect. This is particularly the case if Western countries are not prepared to alter their consumption patterns to accommodate greater con-

sumption levels of LDCs. There is hypocrisy in such behavior as well.

On the other hand, it is not simply up to marketers to make these decisions by themselves in other cases. It must be a "decision" of the society involved. Obviously, this is not a simple matter. This is where procedural matters enter in. The mere economic power that some marketers have, over and against local marketers and certain cultural forms of life, may tilt the balance against local values and assumptions. Dholakia notes, for example, that emphasis on the marketing of brand name products may homogenize consumer tastes by eliminating traditional products that may be more closely linked with the local or national culture:

> brand proliferation increases choice at the brand level but frequently reduces choice at the product/category level. While this creates larger markets and homogeneity in consumer tastes, it also reduces diversity. This is further exacerbated because the products/categories that are eliminated are frequently traditional, low capital and/or energy intensive and ecologically more compatible.[57]

However, more generally the problem of the commons arises here, since culture is not simply an individual, but a public or common, good. Perhaps this is why it has slipped through the fingers of philosophical and marketing ethicists. Popular demands in any number of different segments might not be terribly significant in themselves regarding the culture of the society. However, collectively they may have a significant effect. Similarly, the actions of this or that marketer may not in themselves be terribly significant, just as the pollution from any single manufacturing plant might not degrade the environment. However, once again, collectively their effects may be very significant. Accordingly, marketers ought not simply consider the individual effects of their actions as if they were unrelated to some larger set of consequences. They must also consider the role that their individual effects have within the collective consequences occasioned by all marketers.

It is at this point that marketers and public policy persons must work together.[58] In the past decade we have seen in Iran and, more recently, Turkey and India, cases in which those promoting Western-style consumer societies did not sufficiently take into account clashes of Western values and assumptions with the cultures of the society where they were introduced. It is not plausible to say that individual marketers are to blame for such societal and cultural upheavals. However, given the preceding arguments, it is also implausible to say that they do not share any of the responsibility. Surely Meffert is correct when he contends that "it cannot be recommended to uncritically transfer living and consumer styles from the industrial countries to the developing countries."[59] The responsibilities of marketers in this regard deserve greater attention. Laczniak and Murphy suggest that when a host community or culture brings pressures to bear upon a business organization that are opposed to the organization's core values, it should consider suspending its marketing activities in that society.[60] Conversely, they might also suggest that when the values an organization fosters, through its products and activities, are opposed to the core values of another culture, they should consider not doing business in that society, or modifying their products and activities to make them compatible with that culture.

CONCLUSION

Almost one hundred fifty years ago, that great critic of the capitalist system, Karl Marx, charged that

> [t]he bourgeoisie, by the rapid improvement of all instruments of production, by the immensely facilitated means of communication, draws all, even the most barbarian, nations into civilization. The cheap prices of its commodities are the heavy artillery with which it batters down all Chinese walls, with which it forces the barbarians' intensely obstinate hatred of foreigners to capitulate. It compels all nations, on pain of extinction, to adopt the bourgeois mode of production; it compels them to introduce what it calls civilization into their midst; i.e. to become bourgeois themselves. In one word, it creates a world after its own image.[61]

Though many of Marx's criticisms have been mistaken, in light of the globalization of the world economy, this one has proven to have considerable substance. However, whereas Marx appears to have shared Mill's views on customs and traditions and hoped that the extension of bourgeois forms of production would lead to a world society of abundant productivity, we should question the desirability of a world within which the cultures of different societies are homogenized into similar forms of an ethics of consumption.

Movement toward a global homogenized society characterized by the ethics of consumption is fostered, perhaps, by frequent and unreflective talk about the creation of "a global village" with a "borderless economy."[62] Since villages tend to have the same customs and values, we ought to consider whether such talk might not actually be threatening to the maintenance of distinct but morally valuable cultures around the world. Rarely when people use these phrases do they reflect on what the moral effects will be on the many distinct cultures presently existing.

In contrast, the argument of this essay has been that marketers in LDCs (or other countries for that matter) cannot approach their task as simply that of creating customers so as to foster higher levels of consumption without any regard for the implications of those higher levels of consumption on the society and culture within which those customers live. To do so is to reenact the role of European missionaries hundreds of years ago. The danger and the difficulty for marketers is that in marketing their goods to receptive people (due in part to their ads, promotions, etc.) they may be working to eliminate or modify something (viz., their culture) of importance and value, thereby creating problems and frustrations in the people of that society, while all the while seeming to be satisfying customer wants. D. H. Smith comments that "[w]ithout strong cultural identity, economic development can lead to simple consumerism."[63] By protecting the cultural identity of LDCs, marketers could help contribute to a solution of the above problems. This would still give those who market in these countries tremendous room to do business. But it would demand that they more closely consider their aims and responsibilities when they do business in less developed countries.

NOTES

I am indebted to Iain Clelland, Michael Davis, Richard DeGeorge, Donald Mayer, and Pat Werhane for helpful comments on earlier versions of this essay.

1. In the case of native North Americans, they were viewed by many as not having any culture at all. Cf. Michael K.

Green, "Images of Native Americans in Advertising: Some Moral Issues," *Journal of Business Ethics* 12 (1993), 155–62.

2. Gene R. Laczniak and Patrick E. Murphy, *Ethical Marketing Decisions: The Higher Road* (Upper Saddle, NJ: Prentice-Hall, 1993), 228. But according to what standards? If Korten is to be believed, then there are problems with "these influences" undercutting the culture, its members, etc. Cf. David Korten, *When Corporations Rule the World* (West Hartford: Kumarian, 1995).

3. Richard T. DeGeorge, *Competing with Integrity in International Business* (New York: Oxford University Press, 1993), 52.

4. I will speak of marketing only in the business context—not in the broader senses it has been given such as in "social marketing," where marketing techniques are used for purposes of advancing various social, educational, political, or religious purposes.

5. Fullerton's comment is relevant: "Operationally, Modern Western Marketing can be defined as the vigorous cultivation of existing markets and equally vigorous efforts to open up new ones through insistent promotion, frequent introduction of new products, careful study of market demand, and ongoing efforts to control and coordinate distribution channels. Existing channels may be bypassed in the quest for larger markets" (Robert A. Fullerton, "Modern Western Marketing as a Historical Phenomenon: Theory and Illustration," in *Historical Perspectives in Marketing,* ed[s]. Terence Nevett and Ronald A. Fullerton [Lexington: Lexington Books, 1988], 73–74). Accordingly, marketing is understood here in a broad sense. It would include, for example, decisions over whether to introduce products and techniques requiring high or low levels of technology.

6. Such marketing is clearly bound up with capitalism. Fullerton claims that "it is capitalism which provides the central value of Modern Western marketing" (Fullerton, *Historical Perspectives,* 74). To the extent, then, that capitalism reaches into less developed nations through marketing, this essay is also on capitalism and less-developed countries. However, the effects of capitalism in LDCs might be felt in other ways than through marketing, for example, through various financial and banking policies, theories of accounting, management, and so on. This essay does not consider these issues but, instead, focuses on ethical questions marketers face with regard to LDCs. Nevertheless, this essay has clear implications for these other areas of capitalism.

7. Fullerton, *Historical Perspectives,* 73.

8. Hans B. Thorelli, "Consumer Policy for the Third World," *Journal of Consumer Policy* 3 (1981): 201.

9. Russell W. Belk, "Possessions and the Extended Self," *Journal of Consumer Research* 15 (1988): 160.

10. Heinrich Zimmer, *Philosophies of India* (Cleveland: World Publishing Co., 1951), 159.

11. Julius M. E. Moravcsik, "On What We Aim At and How We Live," in *The Greeks and the Good Life,* ed. David J. Depew (Fullerton: California State University Press, 1980), 229.

12. It should be noted that this "ethics of consumption" is stated universally, i.e., without restriction to Western or American society. Such a universal statement is also a characteristic of this ethics. This is why it is taken to apply to all human societies.

13. Cf. Gregory P. Stone, "Comments on 'Careers and Consumer Behavior,'" in *Consumer Behavior* 2 (New York: New York University Press, 1995), 25.

14. Ernest Zahn, "The Consumer Society: Unstinted Praise and Growing Criticism," in *Human Behavior in Economic Affairs,* ed[s]. Burkhard Strumpel, James N. Morgan, and Ernest Zahn (San Francisco: Jossey-Bass Inc. 1972), 443.

15. Perhaps, for some, the ethnocentric nature of this consumer society is less clear due to the influence of logical positivism and neoclassical economic theory in marketing. These factors have isolated the treatment of the issues of consumption and development from social, moral, and historical contexts while seeking universally applicable laws. Cf. A. Fuat Firat, Erodoğan Kumcu, and Mehmet Karafakioğu, "The Interface between Marketing and Development: Problems and Prospects," in *Marketing and Development: Toward Broader Dimensions,* ed[s]. Erodoğan Kumcu and A. Fuat Firat (Greenwich, CT: JAI Press, 1988), 327–29.

16. William Leach, *Land of Desire: Merchants, Power and the Rise of a New American Culture* (New York: Pantheon Books, 1993), xiii.

17. I assume that marketers have had an influence in LDCs through the introduction of their marketing practices. If this is false, or if marketers cannot have any such influences, then discussion of their moral responsibilities for those influences is, obviously, unnecessary. It is not necessary for me to hold, however, that marketers create new basic wants or needs in people in LDCs. It is sufficient, for my present purposes, that they are able to create or foster desires in people for consumer goods that fulfill prior (basic) wants and needs but do so in ways that undercut the cultural identity those individuals share.

18. I distinguish here between philosophical business ethicists, such as DeGeorge, Donaldson, and Velasquez, and marketing business ethicists, such as Robin, Reidenbach, Laczniak, and Murphy. Though members of both groups may call themselves simply "business ethicists," their different backgrounds (philosophy or theology and marketing) tend to have a significant effect on their views of business ethics. Rather than simply refer to the former group as business ethicists, thereby denying that title to those in marketing who "do" business ethics, I prefer the present distinction.

19. This, of course, raises significant problems regarding women, children, and others. However, I do not discuss these problems.

20. DeGeorge, *Competing With Integrity*, 106.

21. Cf. Norman E. Bowie and Ronald F. Duska, *Business Ethics* (Englewood Cliffs, NJ: Prentice-Hall, Inc., 1990). Richard T. DeGeorge, *Competing with Integrity;* Thomas Donaldson, *The Ethics of International Business* (New York: Oxford University Press, 1989); Patricia H. Werhane, *Persons, Rights and Corporations* (Englewood Cliffs, NJ: Prentice-Hall, Inc., 1985).

22. Cf. Donaldson, *The Ethics of International Business.*

23. Cf. Donald P. Robin and R. Eric Reidenbach, "Searching for a Place to Stand: Toward a Workable Ethical Philosophy for Marketing," *Journal of Public Policy & Marketing* 12, no. 1 (1993): 97–105; Gene R. Laczniak and Patrick E. Murphy, "International Marketing Ethics," *Bridges* 2 (1990): 155–77.

24. Ashok Malhotra, "Value Erosion and Managerial Alienation in Indian Organisations," *Business India* (Jan. 14–27, 1985): 79.

25. Malhotra, "Value Erosion," 79.

26. Malhotra, "Value Erosion," 81.

27. P. L. Tandon, "The Propertyless Manager: Culture and Ethics in India," in *Corporate Ethics,* ed. T. A. Mathias (New Delhi: Allied Publishers, 1994), 4.

28. Darryl Reed, "Business Ethics in an Indian Setting," *Business Ethics: A European Review* 4, no. 4 (1995): 164.

29. This might be cited as an example of what has been called "the separation thesis." In fact, I suggest that there are two separation theses. One is the view that economics or business does not involve moral values or issues; it is morally neutral in itself. Ethics or morality is a separate area or field. The second separation thesis is that the morals of business differ from the morals of everyday life. The former thesis is what Ed Freeman has recently discussed. Cf. Edward R. Freeman, "The Politics of Stakeholder Theory: Some Future Directions," *Business Ethics Quarterly* 4, no. 4 (1994): 409–22. The latter is a view I have discussed. Cf. George G. Brenkert, "The Environment, the Moralist, the Corporation and Its Culture," *Business Ethics Quarterly* 5, no. 4 (1995): 675–98.

30. Still, we should remember that there are many very wealthy people in LDCs. Not everyone in an LDC requires greater goods and services.

31. From the fact that certain countries have been designated "less developed" it does not follow that their cultures are less developed as well.

32. The argument of this essay does not assume that there is a single, unified culture that all people, without exception, adhere to in each country. There may be subcultures

within any society. In addition, people within each country will variously adhere to different cultural strands within their country. Thus, for instance, there are clear cultural differences in India between Tamil Nadu and Uttar Pradesh. Still, there are similarities that unite these areas of India and distinguish them from New York and Georgia in the United States. Marketers, this chapter urges, must be sensitive to cultural differences on both levels.

33. Donaldson, *International Business,* 81.

34. Or at least we may assume that they correspond with these international basic norms approximately as well as do Western consumer societies. In short, I do not want to consider the case where marketers might have these kinds of justifications to bring change in the cultures of LDCs.

35. Cf. Michael K. Green, "Images of Native Americans in Advertising: Some Moral Issues," *Journal of Business Ethics* 12 (1993): 158.

36. Cf. Green, "Native Americans," 156.

37. Leach, *Land of Desire,* 384.

38. Korten, *Corporations Rule,* 150.

39. I do not claim that moral and aesthetic issues are wholly separable. Only that they are distinguishable.

40. I assume that such frugality among Indians is not simply their response to economic necessity. Scarcity may have played a role thousands of years ago in this value having a place within their cultural values. But it is also part of their culture, just as it used to be part of Western and American values. I assume, for example, that Benjamin Franklin advocated his prudent and frugal ways not simply because they were imposed by economic scarcity. Rather he viewed these as part of the construction of a moral person.

41. G. A. Cohen, *Self-Ownership, Freedom, and Equality* (Cambridge: Cambridge University Press, 1993), 9.

42. Richard J. Barnet and John Cavanagh, "The Sound of Money," *Sojourners* 23, no. 1 (1994): 14.

43. Barnet and Cavanagh, "Sound of Money," 14.

44. Miriam Jordan, "Marketing Gurus Say: In India, Think Cheap, Lose the Cold Cereal," *Wall Street Journal,* 11 Oct. 1996, 9 (A).

45. James Petras, "Cultural Imperialism in Late 20th Century," *Economics and Political Weekly,* 6 Aug. 1994: 2072.

46. John Kenneth Galbraith, *The Affluent Society,* 2d ed., rev. (Boston: Houghton Mifflin, 1969).

47. The implications of my argument for marketing within Western nations where a consumer society already exists are left unexplored in this essay. This is a topic for another work.

48. Raymond Benton Jr., "Work, Consumption, and the Joyless Consumer," in *Philosophical and Radical Thought in*

Marketing, ed. A Fuat Firat, Nikhilesh Dholakia, and Richard P. Bagozzis (Lexington, MA: Lexington Books, 1987), 241.

49. John Lachs, "To Have and To Be," *The Personalist* 45 (1964): 7.

50. Lachs, "To Have," 8.

51. Lachs, "To Have," 9.

52. Phillip Kotler, "The Potential Contributions of Marketing Thinking to Economic Development," *Research in Marketing,* Supplement 4, *Marketing and Development: Toward Broader Dimensions* (Greenwich, CT: JAI Press, 1988), 10.

53. William G. Zikmund and Michael d'Amico, *Effective Marketing: Creating and Keeping Customers* (Minneapolis: West Publishing Co., 1995), 314.

54. Jordan, "Marketing Gurus," 9 (A).

55. Reed, "Business Ethics," 165.

56. Firat et al., "Problems and Prospects," 331.

57. Ruby Roy Dholakia, "Consumer Issues in Development: Consumer Behavior in the Third World," in *The Role of Marketing in Development,* ed. Erodoğan Kumcu, A. Fuat Firat, Mehmet Karafakiolğu, Muhittin Karabulut and

Mehmet Oluc (Muncie, IN: Ball State University Publications, 1986), 18.

58. Cf. Ruby Roy Dholakia, Mohammed Sharif, and Labdhi Bhandari, "Consumption in the Third World: Challenges for Marketing and Development" in *Marketing and Development: Toward Broader Dimensions,* ed. Erodoğan Kuncu and A. Fuat Firat (Greenwich, CT: JAI Press, 1988).

59. Heribert Meffert, "Developing Countries: Role of Marketing," *Marketing and Management Digest* 9, no. 6 (1976): 49.

60. Gene R. Laczniak and Patrick E. Murphy, *Ethical Marketing Decisions: The Higher Road* (Upper Saddle River, NJ: Prentice-Hall, Inc., 1993), 166.

61. Karl Marx, "Manifesto of the Communist Party," in *The Marx-Engels Reader,* ed. Robert C. Tucker (New York: W. W. Norton, 1972), 339.

62. Cf. Akio Morita, "Toward a New World Economic Order," *Atlantic Monthly* (June 1993): 92.

63. Dean Howard Smith, "The Issue of Compatibility between Cultural Integrity and Economic Development among Native American Tribes," *American Indian Culture and Research Journal* 18, no. 2 (1994): 199.

Decision Scenario A
INDONESIAN CORRUPTION AND MULTINATIONALS

The economies of the Pacific Rim were growing quickly in the early 1990s. Indonesia, in particular, looked to be a potentially profitable investment opportunity for foreign firms. Its economy was growing 7% a year and was predicted to grow even more as development accelerated. It had natural resources aplenty, low labor costs, and a large potential market. Growth possibilities made its energy sector ripe for foreign investment. The national

energy company, PNL, was unable to meet the growing demand for electricity and was inefficient in the delivery of the energy that it could produce. The opportunity for large and profitable ventures lured many multinationals into the nation.

Indonesia, however, presented some difficulties. One was known from the start. The country was ruled by a powerful figure, President Suharto. His family and close associates controlled or had significant holdings in most Indonesian industries. Moreover, Indonesian law required that foreign enterprises have an Indonesian partner. The possibilities for exposure to corruption and questionable practices were obvious, especially when most large energy projects were not competitively bid. Other problems, however, were less apparent in the early '90s. The political instability that would topple Suharto's government in 1998 was not as easily foreseen. And, even if they saw the economic risk in

This case was prepared from the following materials: Evelyn Iritani, "The Ties That Bind," *Los Angeles Times,* June 6, 1998; "Indonesia Sharply Increases Energy Costs," the *New York Times,* May 5, 1998; Melinda Morris, "CalEnergy Denies Ties to Suharto Family," *Omaha World Herald,* December 24, 1998; "Indonesia Gambles With Electricity Tariff Rise," *Power Economics,* June 30, 1998; Alex Spillius, "Suharto's British Links Scrutinised," the *Daily Telegraph,* May 28, 1998; Andrew Taylor and Sander Thoenes, "Moody's Downgrades Big Power Schemes," the *Financial Times,* September 30, 1998; Sander Thoenes, "Indonesia Reviews Power Deals," the *Financial Times,* June 9, 1998; Peter Waldman and Jay Solomon, "How U.S. Companies and Suharto's Circle Electrified Indonesia," the *Wall Street Journal,* December 23, 1998.

developing economies, many multinationals failed to anticipate the extent of the economic collapse that would rock Southeast Asia at the end of the decade.

Gaining access to the potentially profitable Indonesian energy sector inevitably meant dealing with Suharto's associates as partners. U.S. companies that had ties included: Mission Energy and General Electric in the Paiton I coal-fired electricity plant, Unocal in the Salak geothermal plant, CalEnergy in a number of geothermal projects, Enron Corporation in the Pasuruan gas-powered plant and Duke Energy in the Cilicap plant. These are some of the largest U.S. energy firms. British firms, too, had ties. In the energy sector, chief among them was Power-Gen's involvement with the Paiton II plant in conjunction with Germany's giant Seimans. Critics charge that in many cases, the Indonesian partners were provided substantial ownership in the projects for little actual investment. Some were, according to the charges, given stakes in exchange for their "expertise," which often meant access to the ruling family. Others, including Hashim Djojohadikusomo, a brother-in-law of Suharto's daughter, were paid inflated prices for coal from the mining enterprises they control, according to the critics and some current government officials. They charge that the coal costs, some 30–40% higher than average, were not justified by the coal's low sulfur content, as Hashim claims. In addition, Hashim and his partners received a 15% stake without investing cash in the Paiton I project. The shares were paid for by a loan that the Indonesian partners were to repay from the project's profits. The American partners assert that such arrangements are legal under the Foreign Corrupt Practices Act, which prohibits paying foreign officials for favorable treatment. The act does not explicitly prohibit the arrangements described, particularly when there is an arguable business contribution by the local partner.

These arrangements in the Paiton I plant were not unusual. The British PowerGen's Paiton II had Suharto's second son, Bambang Trihatmodjo, as its partner. In fact, some foreign firms' spokespersons openly admit that doing business in Indonesia meant having a relationship with the ruling family. Some former Indonesian energy officials, however, dispute that. One said not all foreign firms paid off Suharto family members or cronies. For instance,

one American firm is reported to have pulled out of an arrangement because Suharto's daughter refused to sign anticorruption documents.

Criticism is also directed at the international projects because it is claimed that, collectively, they have resulted in a predictable over-supply of power and a substantial foreign debt. The World Bank, for example, warned in 1993 about potential oversupply. They also claim that the expense of the projects has lead Indonesia to have some of the highest energy rates in the region. Moreover, some have questioned whether influence with Suharto caused the Indonesian government to accept higher contract rates for electricity than it otherwise would have. The initial negotiations over the Paiton I rates started with the consortium requesting 10.3 cents per kilowatt-hour and the government offering 5.3. After intercessions with Suharto by Hashim, the government accepted a rate of 8.3 cents. Deutsche Bank estimates that the cost of the noncompetitively bid power in Indonesia is 30% higher than the world average.

Two events conspired to exacerbate the Indonesians' problems of high cost and oversupply, as well as to create serious financial consequences for the foreign investors. The speculative bubble in the Southeast Asian economies burst in the late '90s, causing a serious devaluation of the Indonesian currency, the rupiah. Because the contracts required Indonesia to pay for the foreign generated power in dollars while the locals paid for their power consumption in rupiahs, the Indonesian power company, PNL, was unable to discharge its debt to the foreign-owned firms. With the economy in tatters, the foreign firms demanding payment, and the World Bank insisting on governmental austerity before it would grant emergency assistance, the Suharto government decided to raise electric energy prices 60% over six months. What had been a growing student movement in opposition to official corruption exploded into general unrest with the word of the price increases.

The riots that ensued toppled the Suharto government. The successor government, to appease the calls for anticorruption initiatives, has begun to review the arrangements made with foreign firms in the energy sector. The PNL is resisting full payment for the electricity delivered and the government has threatened the cancellation of expensive contracts. The U.S. and British firms, with the backing of their governments, are pressing for the contracts to be honored.

- What responsibilities do multinationals have for estimating the impact of their investments on the welfare of the local population? Should they question whether the local population can afford the projects, even if the companies stand to make a profit from them? Does the responsibility change when one partner is involved only initially and plans to sell its stake soon after? Does the presence of local government representatives in the start-up negotiations remove any multinational responsibility to assess the impact on the host populations?

- Should investors insist on full payment from foreign nations in economic crisis? What role should the U.S. government play in pressing for payment?

- What role should the U.S. government play in brokering deals for U.S. multinationals? The Clinton administration pushed hard for U.S. firms to be accepted as partners in Indonesia. Does it have a responsibility to be concerned about the impact of the projects on the local population as a whole?

- What steps should have been taken to avoid corruption among the Indonesian partners? Is the Foreign Corrupt Practices Act sufficient to avoid corruption, given the legality of the arrangements described in the case?

Decision Scenario B

BRAZIL: ECONOMIC DEVELOPMENT VERSUS ENVIRONMENTAL PROTECTION

Beginning in the early 1960s, Brazil's military government embarked upon a program of tremendous economic development. At least in theory, the goal of this program was to improve the quality of life for the citizens of this poor agrarian country. Almost 40 years later Brazil is one of the world's leading debtor nations; its citizens suffer from one of the world's lowest standards of living; it is the scene of some of the world's worst environmental destruction. These facts are closely connected.

The story of Brazil's "development" is a familiar one: A third world country begins an aggressive plan to build factories, dams, highways, hydroelectric projects, and other necessities of a modern industrialized society. International banks and foreign lending institutions are anxious to finance these projects with large loans. But the environmental and cultural impact of these development projects is devastating.

In Brazil, millions of acres of tropical rain forests were destroyed, often by massive burnings during the dry seasons, but also by the harvesting of trees for lumber and fuel. Millions of people were forcibly relocated by these projects; millions more emigrated to the frontier in search of work, land, and wealth. Native tribes, some of whom had never before been in contact with the outside world, found their lands taken from them.

In the early 1970s drought and crop failures combined with a worldwide economic recession, bringing Brazil to the brink of economic collapse. To prevent this from happening, Brazil needed to raise large amounts of foreign money simply to pay the interest on the development loans from a decade earlier. A new, aggressive economic development program was launched, not to provide food and jobs for Brazilians but to raise cash. This difference is important, for an emphasis on internal economic development was supplanted by an emphasis on growing cash crops and producing goods for export.

This time development of the rain forests was explicitly targeted, and the environmental costs were willingly paid. At a 1972 United Nations conference on the environment, Brazil asserted its right to pay whatever environmental costs were necessary to achieve a level of economic development that is taken for granted in the industrialized world. Brazil accused the industrialized nations of hypocrisy in demanding that less developed countries refrain from the same kind of environmental exploitation that had fostered their own economic development.

Destruction of a tropical rain forest has frightening environmental effects. These forests are home to a large percentage of all biological species. Some scientists have estimated that 1.2 million species of plants and animals, nearly 25 percent of all species existing in the mid-1980s, will vanish by the end of the century as rain forests are decimated. The fertility of forest soil is surprisingly delicate. As trees are burned, their ashes provide nutrients for farming, but only for a few years. When the soil's few nutrients are exhausted, farmers move on to burn new forest areas, leaving behind infertile land. Water pollution and many diseases like malaria and dysentery follow to plague areas where forests have been burned. Finally, rain forests serve a crucial role in the ecological cycle of carbon.

Scientists have come to recognize that large amounts of carbon dioxide, in the atmosphere can produce a "greenhouse effect," with changes in climate associated with a global warming trend. In their normal growth cycle, plants absorb carbon dioxide from the atmosphere, releasing some of it slowly as they naturally die and decompose. Mass burnings of forests not only prevent these plants from removing

carbon dioxide, but significantly add to the amount present in the atmosphere because of the fast release. Deforestation is believed to account for almost half the carbon dioxide released into the atmosphere, and Brazil itself is responsible for 20 percent of that.

In recent years Brazil's civilian government has taken steps to control the destruction of these rain forests. The World Bank and other creditors have promised to work with the Brazilians to ensure that economic development does not entail environmental destruction. Nevertheless, Brazil continues to face major problems in paying its debts, going so far as to suspend interest payments in 1987. As this is written, it is difficult to see how Brazil can attain both environmental and economic health.

- International financial institutions like the World Bank have dual functions: the *banking* function of making loans and investments, and the *development* function of using these loans to further economic development. To what degree have these functions been compatible in Brazil?

- What responsibilities does the United States government have in this case?

- How would you respond to a Brazilian who claimed that environmental concerns are a luxury that only the economically developed countries can enjoy?

Decision Scenario C
"WHEN IN ROME": INTERNATIONAL AFFIRMATIVE ACTION

In recent decades a number of questions have been raised concerning the conduct of U.S. business in foreign countries. American business executives have often been faced with a dilemma. When local customs and ethics conflict with one's own values, should an individual adapt to the local customs or insist on the enforcement of American values in a foreign land? The most publicized examples of this dilemma involve the payment of "gratuities" to foreign officials. In some countries, these payments are standard business practice and are considered to be little more than a thank-you. Americans would call such payments bribes or extortion and judge them to be seriously unethical.

Similar problems arise when foreign firms invest in the United States. To some foreign business

executives, American ethics and social practices seem unfair or unreasonable. The hiring practices of some Japanese automobile firms operating in the United States are a case in point. There is some evidence to suggest that some Japanese auto manufacturers systematically exclude African Americans and other minorities when hiring.

Two issues are involved in this case; they must be kept distinct. First, discrimination on the basis of race is illegal within the United States. No one would suggest that the Japanese firms be allowed to violate the law. In a 1988 case, the Equal Employment Opportunity Commission announced that Honda of America had agreed to pay 370 African Americans and women some $6 million in back pay to resolve a discrimination complaint. There seems a clear ethical consensus: Violators of the law deserve punishment. Nevertheless, a number of more subtle issues remain. Before deciding on a plant location, some Japanese executives have been known to study the ethnic, religious, and racial makeup of the local community. Evidence shows that many Japanese firms choose to locate in rural, nonunion areas with a relatively small African American population.

A second issue concerns various customs and business practices that go beyond what is legally required. The United States auto industry has always employed a large number of African Americans. At one point 17 percent of all auto workers were African American, compared to an 11 percent African American population in the overall U.S. labor force. Typically unionized, these jobs provided many African Americans with decent pay and security at a time when they generally were suffering from widespread economic discrimination. The U.S. auto industry and its unions have always considered this factor one of their social responsibilities.

As U.S. auto manufacturers have lost their former market dominance, and as the Great Lakes region has suffered deindustrialization, many unionized African Americans living in the Midwest have been hard hit economically. The "Big Three" U.S. automakers and the United Auto Workers have made an effort to offset these problems by seeking to employ many of these displaced workers at new plants and other locations. Japanese automakers

seem to have no inclination to follow a similar pattern of recruiting displaced former auto workers.

One final point that deserves mention: Many local and state governments have developed plans for tax abatements and other economic incentives to attract Japanese investment in their community. In effect, these local communities compete in a bidding war to subsidize plant location.

- In deciding claims of racial discrimination, the Equal Employment Opportunity Commission will typically compare the racial composition of the local community with that of the work force. How might this fact influence a decision to locate a plant in an area with little or no African American population?

- Should a foreign firm conform to the social practices of U.S. firms when doing business in the United States? Should such practices be considered the price of doing business here? Would the competitive advantage gained by ignoring these practices be fair?

- What responsibilities do local communities have when developing an economic incentive package to attract foreign investment? If a city with a large African American population is at a competitive disadvantage when seeking foreign investment, are federal responsibilities created? What might they be?

Decision Scenario D

CHILD AND BONDED LABOR: BUSINESS RESPONSIBILITY FOR SUPPLIER PRACTICES

The global economy has changed the relationship between manufacturers and workers. In the past, it was more likely that a manufacturer and its workers resided within the same national borders. Now, it is common for component parts to be made elsewhere and assembled in the manufacturer's plant. It is also common for entire products to be made else-

where and to simply carry the manufacturer's label. These developments raise serious issues about workplace standards and about a manufacturer's responsibility for the practices of its suppliers. An actual story illustrates the difficulty.

Twelve-year-old Iqbal Masih gained international renown when he led a Pakistani children's movement to abolish the practice of bonded labor. For his campaign, Reebok gave him a $15,000 Youth in Action award. The bonded labor practice he campaigned against is a system where workers typically receive less than subsistence wages. To survive, workers take salary advances from their

This case was prepared from the following sources: Farhan Bokhari, "Death Spotlights Plight of Child Laborers," the *Christian Science Monitor*, May 1, 1995; *New York Times*, April 19, 1995; "Eye to Eye with Connie Chung," April 6, 1995; ABC World News Tonight, September 21, 1994; *United States Department of State 1993 Human Rights Report: Pakistani Human Rights Practices; The MacNeil–Lehrer Newshour*, August 17, 1995.

employers. This starts a cycle where workers work only to pay off those advances and where they find their debt escalating. It is, in essence, a form of slavery where people are forced to work without receiving wages.

When Iqbal was four, his family sold him into bonded labor in order to get money and food. He worked in a carpet factory where he was physically shackled to a loom. He earned one rupee (the equivalent of 3¢) while working fifteen hours a day. When he escaped from his employer, he owed 13,000 rupees in future work.

In Pakistan, it is estimated that 25 percent of the children between five and fifteen work in similar conditions in carpet weaving factories, brick kilns, and soccer ball workshops. Up to one third of the total labor force is composed of child labor. Pakistani law prohibits bonded labor, and it limits the workday for children to six hours of work. However, those laws are not frequently enforced.

Although some businesses that receive goods produced by child labor claim that it is an age-old practice of family work, the facts tell a different story. In villages, where crushing poverty is common and education unavailable, families often sell their children to factory owners to obtain money for the remaining family. Children, in reality, are not working in family businesses; they are serving as slave labor for owners of village workshops. The products of these village shops are then passed on to larger factories that have supply contracts with international firms.

In fact, some of the factories identified as receiving goods from workshops using children were supplying soccer balls to multinational sports equipment giants Adidas and, yes, even Reebok. Spokespersons expressed surprise that suppliers handled goods made with child labor. The reality of the countryside, though, is that there is great difficulty in preventing remote village workshops from using children. CBS's newsmagazine "Eye to Eye" even discovered one workshop that was supplying instruments for UNICEF, "the UN agency committed to abolishing child labor," as the network described.

Lest anyone think that such labor abuses are present only in the developing world, we should note that in August 1995 the United States Department of Labor raided a California garment-sewing sweatshop that used illegal Thai workers. Some of the workers were imported into the country under the guise of tourists; their airfare was paid for by their employers. The workers were paid less than $1.60 per hour, were detained in a guarded compound behind barbed wire, and were required to buy provisions from a "company store." The sweatshop owners deceived the retailers and manufacturers with whom they had contracts by also operating a legitimate garment-sewing plant through which they passed the goods made at the sweatshop. Montgomery Ward, Sears, Neiman Marcus, and The Gap were among the retailers and manufacturers whose labels were discovered at the sweatshop. Labor Department officials believe that this operation is not an isolated case.

- What responsibilities do multinational firms have for the practices employed by their suppliers? How far down the chain of supply do those responsibilities extend?

- What specific actions could Reebok or UNICEF have taken to prevent, or at least make less likely, the use of child labor in their products?

- How would you define a fair wage in a country that suffers levels of poverty unimaginable to most Americans? What factors would you use to determine a wage's fairness: market forces of supply and demand; profit margins of factory owners and/or multinationals; income needed for subsistence?

- What responsibility do consumers have for perpetuating the use of such practices as child labor, bonded labor, and prison labor (as in China)?

Decision Scenario E
DRUG SAFETY AND THE THIRD WORLD

The vast populations in the developing world represent a significant market for pharmaceutical manufacturers. Some critics have charged that the potential profits to be reaped there have led multinational drug firms to disregard the safety of third world citizens. Two drugs have been the focus of particular complaints over the years.

Dipyrone is an analgesic (pain reliever) and antipyretic (fever reducer) that was sold widely throughout the world from the 1950s to the 1980s. By the late 1970s, however, it was disappearing from the market in industrialized nations. Medical authorities in many nations suspected that the drug caused agranulocytosis, a serious blood disorder marked by a sharp decrease in white blood cells and, therefore, in the body's ability to fight infection. Patients developing the disease have a high probability of death unless they receive prompt and modern medical treatment.

Medical authorities in the United States, Great Britain, and the European continent also found that dipyrone presented an unacceptable risk given that alternative treatments were available—namely aspirin, acetaminophen, and ibuprofen. Though the incidence of agranulocytosis in persons taking dipyrone was not firmly established, many still felt that the small but uncertain risk was too great. That judgment was made despite recognition that all the other products had risks as well. Aspirin can cause a serious disease, Reyes syndrome, if it is given to children. It and ibuprofen can cause stomach problems if taken in excess. Excess dosage of acetaminophen can cause liver damage. Nonetheless, dipyrone was judged to have an unacceptable risk/benefit profile. By the late 1970s in the United States, it was used only for terminal cancer patients.

In the third world, however, multinationals continued through the 1980s to distribute the drug as a common remedy for pain and fever. In many cases,

there were no warnings provided to the physicians, pharmacists, or patients on the label, package insert, or privately published physicians' reference books. Hoechst, a main supplier of the drug, claimed that given the risks and side effects of the other analgesics, it was as safe as aspirin.

In response to consumer pressures in the mid-1980s, many multinationals began to include warnings on the product label and package inserts, though the drug is still promoted widely. The private publishers of the physicians' references resisted changes but are now bowing to manufacturer demands for editorial approval of drug descriptions.

A second drug, depoprovera, also caused controversy for its use in the developing world. It is an injectable hormone that provides effective birth control for up to 13 weeks. For years, the United States' FDA refused approval of the drug because there were concerns that it caused cancer in laboratory animals. Critics of its distribution in the third world charged that drug firms were exposing women to unacceptable cancer risks. However, some physicians in the third world argued that in their environment, death in childbirth was a greater risk than cancer and that depoprovera provided more effective birth control than condoms or the pill, which were often improperly used. The FDA recently approved the drug for use in the United States.

- A judgment of safety is a judgment that a level of risk is acceptable. Is it possible that the same drug is safe in one country but not in another? What differences could lead to that conclusion?

- Should drugs contain the same listing of indications and contraindications, the same warnings of side effects no matter where they are marketed?

- Dipyrone continues to be marketed in the third world as a remedy for minor pain. Should drug companies cease that marketing? Does the list of available alternatives and their respective risks mean that dipyrone is an unnecessary and unacceptably harmful drug?

This case was prepared from the following sources: *For Export Only: Pharmaceuticals,* A Richter Productions Video, 1981; Milton Silverman et al., *Bad Medicine: The Prescription Drug Industry in the Third World* (Palo Alto, Calif.: Stanford University Press, 1992); John Quelch and Craig Smith, "Pharmaceutical Marketing Practices in the Third World," *Journal of Business Research,* vol. 23, 1991.

Index